LITIGATION LIBRARY

CIVIL LITIGATION

AUSTRALIA
Law Book Co.
Sydney

CANADA and USA
Carswell
Toronto

HONG KONG
Sweet & Maxwell Asia

NEW ZEALAND
Brookers
Auckland

SINGAPORE and MALAYSIA
Sweet & Maxwell Asia
Singapore and Kuala Lumpur

PLEASE DONATE YOUR OLD EDITION OF THIS BOOK TO THE ILBF

If you still have the old edition of this book, why not donate it to the International Law Book Facility (ILBF)? This title is particularly needed by law schools, law societies, pro bono groups and other institutions and individuals in Africa, Asia and the Caribbean.

The ILBF is a new charity. It aims to provide key legal texts to worthy recipients in developing jurisdictions. It is headed by a Board and Operating Committee consisting of solicitors, barristers and legal librarians, as well as by officers of Book Aid International, The Law Society, The Bar Council, The International Bar Association, Sweet & Maxwell and LexisNexis Butterworths. The Chairman of the Board is Lord Justice Thomas of the Court of Appeal.

Your help is needed both in donating old editions and donating funds to cover the costs of shipment. To make a donation, please send cheques payable to 'ILBF' to the ILBF at the following address. To donate your old edition of this book, simply send it DX or post, to DX 149121 Canary Wharf 3 (10 Upper Bank St, London E14 5JJ).

LITIGATION LIBRARY

CIVIL LITIGATION
Thirteenth Edition

By

John O'Hare, LL.B.

*(Leicester), Barrister,
Costs Judge,
Master of the Supreme Court Costs Office*

Kevin Browne, LL.B.

*(Newcastle), Solicitor
Associate Professor at the College of Law, London
Associate Director of Design of the Civil Litigation Legal
Practice Course at the College of Law, London*

LONDON
SWEET & MAXWELL
2007

First published in 1980. This
edition is edited by John O'Hare
and Kevin Browne

Published in 2007 by
Sweet & Maxwell Limited of
100 Avenue Road, Swiss Cottage, London NW3 3PF
(*www.sweetandmaxwell.co.uk*)
Typeset by J&L Composition, Filey, North Yorkshire
Printed and bound in Great Britain by
TJ International Ltd, Padstow, Cornwall

No natural forests were destroyed to make this product;
only farmed timber was used and replanted

A CIP catalogue record for this book
is available from the British Library

ISBN 9780421957008

All rights reserved. UK statutory material in this
publication is acknowledged as Crown copyright.

No part of this publication may be reproduced or
transmitted in any form or by any means, or stored in any
retrieval system of any nature without prior written
permission, except for permitted fair dealing under the
Copyright, Designs and Patents Act 1988, or in accordance
with the terms of a licence issued by the Copyright Licensing
Agency in respect of photocopying and/or reprographic
reproduction. Application for permission for other use of
copyright material including permission to reproduce
extracts in other published works shall be made to the
publishers. Full acknowledgment of author, publisher and
source must be given.

©
Sweet & Maxwell
2007

Preface

This book has now reached its thirteenth edition. Fortunately, like the claimant in *Doherty v Reynolds* [2004] IEHC 25, whose hospital operation took place at thirteen hundred hours on Friday 13, the authors are not superstitious!

2007 has seen criminal judges retain their popular media image as being rather aloof from the so-called "real" world. Hence, whilst all of them may now know who the Beatles were, it has been reported that some of them are still clueless about the Internet. Civil judges appear to move more easily with the times. Notable comments included those made by His Honour Judge Seymour Q.C. in *SES Contracting Limited v UK Coal Plc* [2007] EWHC 161 ("the punk in *Dirty Harry* responding positively to Clint Eastwood's question whether he felt lucky") and Mummery L.J. in *The Bolton Pharmaceutical Co. 100 Ltd v Doncaster Pharmaceuticals Group Ltd* [2006] EWCA Civ 661 ("rubbishy defences" and "the cocky claimant").

Moreover, from 2008, civil judges will sit without wigs, wing collars and bands but no decision has yet been made as to the sort of robe they will wear. The Circuit Bench will continue to wear the same gown. All other judges will wear a new, simple gown which is in the course of design and most likely will be based upon the European judicial gown. Different ranks of judges will sport different coloured sashes; gold for the Court of Appeal, redc for the High Court and green for District Judges. Circuit judges already wear a purple sash. Our fear is that this might lead to more dressing up rather than less!

We like to think that in updating the text we are never panicked by the ever changing nature of civil procedure. A quick check of the Ministry of Justice's website (out with the old Department for Constitutional Affairs) confirms that since 1999 there have been 44 updates to the Civil Procedure Rules. Some changes are still at the consultation stage (notably proposals to reform case track limits and the claims process for personal injury claims and proposed amendments to Pt 6 on the rules of service of proceedings). Other changes are awaiting enactment (see, for example, The Tribunals, Courts and Enforcement Bill). Whilst the new Supreme Court for the United Kingdom has found a home at Middlesex Guildhall in Parliament Square, Westminster, its doors are not likely to be opened until late 2009. The following year, 2010, should hopefully see completion of the new business court in London, making it the biggest dedicated commercial court in the world.

One major change already in force concerns a substantially revised Pt 36 which no longer requires a defendant to make a payment into court. See our rewritten Ch.29.

In updating this book the authors are anxious to acknowledge and pay tribute to those closest to us who permit us to spend so many hours in darkened rooms muttering into a Dictaphone or bashing away at the keyboard. John acknowledges with gratitude the help he received from Alison, Alexander and Joanne. Kevin wishes to thank his family, friends and colleagues for all their support and encouragement and dedicates this edition to the memory of his mother, Mary.

We have endeavoured to state the law as at July 1, 2007.

John O'Hare
Kevin Browne

Contents

	page
Preface	v
Table of Cases	xxxi
Table of Statutes	xci
Table of Statutory Instruments	xcvii
Table of Civil Procedure Rules	xcix
Table of Practice Directions and Protocol	cxiii

Chapter 1: Civil Litigation in Outline
para.

THE CIVIL COURTS	1.001
The High Court	1.001
The county courts	1.002
Jurisdiction of the High Court and county courts	1.003
The Court of Appeal	1.004
THE CIVIL PROCEDURE RULES	1.005
THE OVERRIDING OBJECTIVE	1.006
A new procedural code	1.007
Speed, economy and proportionality	1.008
Ensuring parties are on an equal footing	1.009
Use by court when exercising powers and interpreting the rules	1.010
Parties must help the court further the overriding objective	1.011
Court to actively manage cases	1.011A
PRACTICE DIRECTIONS	1.012
THE CASE MANAGEMENT TRACKS	1.013
COURT FEES	1.014
EFFECT OF NON-COMPLIANCE	1.015
COMPUTATION OF TIME	1.016
DEFINITION OF "THE COURT"	1.017
RIGHTS OF AUDIENCE	1.018
Other persons authorised by statute or statutory instrument	1.019
Litigants in person	1.020
Persons authorised by the court	1.021
THE COURT FILE	1.022
HUMAN RIGHTS ACT 1998	1.023
Jurisdiction and procedure in HRA cases	1.024

Chapter 2: Funding Civil Litigation

Funding Civil Litigation 2.001
SOLICITORS CODE OF CONDUCT 2.002
   Information about the firm 2.003
   Costs information at the outset 2.004
   Information about the case 2.005
   Information about funding methods 2.006
   Updating costs information 2.007
LEGAL EXPENSES INSURANCE 2.008
   Before the event insurance 2.008
   After the event insurance 2.009
BASIC CHARGING AGREEMENT 2.010
   How much is payable 2.010
   Factors determining reasonableness of bills 2.011
   When is money payable? 2.012
REFERRALS BY CLAIMS MANAGEMENT COMPANIES 2.013
CONDITIONAL FEE AGREEMENTS 2.014
   CFA without success fee 2.015
   CFA with success fee 2.016
   Collective Conditional Fee Agreement 2.017
BARRISTERS' FEES 2.018
COSTS INCURRED BY LITIGANTS IN PERSON 2.019
COSTS FUNDED BY THE LEGAL SERVICES COMMISSION 2.020
   Costs 2.021
COSTS FUNDED BY NON-PARTIES 2.022
PROVIDING INFORMATION ON FUNDING TO OPPONENTS 2.023
   Notices of funding 2.023
   Notices under the Legal Aid Regulations 2.024

Chapter 3: Interest

CLAIMS FOR INTEREST 3.001
   Interest payable as of right 3.001
   Interest payable in the court's discretion 3.002
   Stating interest 3.003
   Default judgments 3.004
   Personal injuries claims 3.005
   Statutory interest on commercial contracts 3.006
   Interest where part of the claim is paid before judgment 3.007
   Claim for a debt: interest where whole Debt is paid before judgment .. 3.008
INTEREST ON JUDGMENT 3.009

Chapter 4: Personal Injury Damages

SPECIAL DAMAGES 4.002
   Loss of earnings to trial 4.002
   Contractual sick pay 4.003

State benefits	4.004
Non-listed benefits	4.005
Medical expenses	4.006
Services rendered by third persons	4.007
Agreeing special damages	4.008
GENERAL DAMAGES	4.009
Pain and suffering	4.009
Loss of amenities	4.010
Loss of future	4.011
Loss of earnings and loss of marriage prospects	4.012
Loss of earnings and loss of life expectancy	4.013
Loss of earning capacity	4.014
Provisional damages	4.015
Periodical payments	4.016
Structured settlements (PD 40)	4.017
Fatal Accident Act cases	4.018
INTEREST ON DAMAGES	4.019
Guidelines as to the calculation of interest	4.020
Explanation of the guidelines	4.021
Special reasons for not awarding interest	4.022
ADVISING ON QUANTUM	4.023

Chapter 5: Limitation of Actions

INTRODUCTION	5.001
ORDINARY TIME LIMITS	5.002
Actions founded on simple contract or on tort (ss.2 and 5)	5.002
Defamation cases (s.4A)	5.003
Limitation in respect of certain loans (s.6)	5.004
Actions on a speciality (s.8)	5.005
Claims for contribution (s.10)	5.006
Personal injury litigation (s.11)	5.007
Fatal Accidents Acts claims (s.12)	5.008
New claims in pending actions (s.35)	5.009
Mortgage actions (s.20)	5.010
EXTENTSION OR EXCLUSION OF ORDINARY TIME LIMITS	5.011
Disability (ss.28 and 28A)	5.012
SUPERVENING BANKRUPTCY OR LIQUIDATION OF THE DEFENDANT	5.013
Debts: acknowledgment or part payment (s.29(5))	5.014
Fraud, concealment or mistake (s.32)	5.015
Defamation cases (s.32A)	5.016
Consumer Protection Act 1987	5.017
Personal injury and death claims (s.33)	5.018
Sections 33 and "second action cases"	5.019
FOREIGN LIMITATION PERIODS	5.020

Chapter 6: The Preliminary Stages of Litigation

THE FIRST INTERVIEW 6.001
   Identify the client's agenda 6.002
   Identify the correct parties 6.003
   Take the clients statement 6.004
   Give general advice on the law 6.005
   Emphasise the overriding objective 6.006
   Answer the client's questions 6.007
FIRST STEPS IN THE PREPARATION OF EVIDENCE 6.008
   The client's statement 6.008
   Preparing for disclosure 6.009
   Obtaining official records 6.010
   Inspecting and photographing property etc. 6.011
   Interviewing witnesses 6.012
   Pre-action protocols 6.013
   The standard letter of claim 6.014
   Timetable for acknowledgment and response by defendant 6.015
   The defendants response letter 6.016
   Disclosure of documents 6.017
   Experts 6.018
   Negotiations and Alternative Dispute Resolutions (ADR) 6.019
   Costs 6.020
   Letters if claim in a debt action 6.021
NEGOTIATIONS WITH A VIEW TO SETTLEMENT 6.022
   Compromise 6.023
   Without prejudice 6.024
   Part 36 offers 6.025
   Pre-action negotiations as to costs 6.026
MOTOR INSURERS 6.027
   The claimant's policy 6.027
   The defendant's policy 6.028
THE MOTOR INSURER'S BUREAU (MIB) 6.029
   MIB (Compensation of Victims of Uninsured Drivers) Agreement 6.030
   MIB (Compensation of Victims of Untraced Drivers) Agreement 6.031
THE CRIMINAL INJURIES COMPENSATION AUTHORITY
(CICA) 6.032

Chapter 7: Parties to Actions

TITLE TO THE ACTION 7.002
TYPE OF LITIGANTS 7.003
   Adult individuals 7.004
   Children (Pt 21) 7.005
   Patients (Pt 21) 7.006
   Companies and other corporate Bodies 7.007
   Partnerships (CPR, r.2.7A, PD 7 and PD 73) 7.008

Limited liability partnerships 7.009
Estates of deceased persons (Pt 19) 7.010
Vexatious litigants (PD 3 and SCA 1981 s.42(1A)) 7.011
CLAIMS INVOLVING MULTIPLE PARTIES AND/OR CAUSES OF
  ACTION (R.7.3) 7.012
THE ADDITION AND SUBSTITUTION OF PARTIES (PT 19) 7.013
  Case where the limitation period has not expired (r.19.2) 7.014
  Cases where the relevant limitation period has expired (r.19.5) 7.015
CONSOLIDATION (R.3.1(2)(G) and (H)) 7.016
INTERVENERS 7.017
REPRESENTATIVE PROCEEDINGS (PT 19, S.II) 7.018
REPRESENTATION OF INTERESTED PERSONS WHO CANNOT
  BE ASCERTAINED, ETC. (R.19.7) 7.019
GROUP LITIGATION ORDERS (PT 19, S.II) 7.020
DERIVATIVE CLAIMS (R.19.9) 7.021
MICELLANEOUS ACTIONS 7.022
WHOM TO SUE? 7.023
THE SOLICITOR'S ROLE GENERALLY 7.024

Chapter 8: Service of Documents

THE GENERAL RULE—SERVE ON SOLICITORS WHERE
  POSSIBLE 8.001
METHODS OF SERVICE 8.002
  Personal service (r.6.4) 8.002
  Postal service (r.6.2(1)(b)) 8.003
  Leaving the document at "the place of service" (rr.6.2(1)(c)
    and 6.5(4)(b)) 8.004
  Document exchange (DX) (PD 6, para.2.1) 8.005
  Facsmile (Fax) (PD 6, para.3.1) 8.006
  Email and similar electronic means of service (PD 6, para.3.1) 8.007
WHO IS TO SERVE (R.6.3) 8.008
  Address for service (r.6.5) 8.009
SERVICE ON COMPANIES 8.010
SERVICE OF DOCUMENTS ON CHILDREN AND PATIENTS 8.011
SERVICE OF DOCUMENTS ON MEMBERS OF THE FORCES 8.012
DEEMED SERVICE (R.6.7) 8.013
SERVICE BY AN ALTERNATIVE METHOD (R.6.8) 8.014
ORDER TO DISPENSE WITH SERVICE (R.6.9) 8.015
SPECIAL PROVISIONS ABOUT SERVICE OF THE CLAIM FORM ... 8.016
  Service by a contractually agreed method (r.6.15) 8.016
  Ad hoc agreements for service 8.017
  Service on an agent of a principal who is overseas (r.6.16) 8.018
CERTIFICATES OF SERVICE (R.6.10) 8.019

Chapter 9: From Issue to Allocation

INTRODUCTION	9.001
HIGH COURT OR COUNTY COURT?	9.002
WHICH COURT OFFICE?	9.003
WHEN ARE PROCEEDINGS COMMENCED? (R.7.2)	9.004
SERVICE OF CLAIM FORM	9.005
Time for service	9.005
Application for extension of time for service	9.006
DEFENDANT'S RIGHT TO CALL FOR SERVICE	9.007
PARTICULARS OF CLAIM (R.7.4)	9.008
When must particulars be served? (r.7.4)	9.009
What if particulars are served late?	9.010
What if particulars are never served	9.011
DOCUMENTS TO BE SERVED ON THE DEFENDANT	9.012
Acknowledgment of service (Pt 10)	9.013
Consequences of failing to acknowledge	9.014
Amending or withdrawing an acknowledgment	9.015
Admissions	9.016
Defence	9.017
What if the defence is never served	9.017
DOCUMENTS SERVED AFTER THE DEFENCE	9.018
Counterclaim	9.018
Reply to Defence and Defence to Counterclaim	9.019
FIXED DATE CLAIMS	9.020
PRODUCTION CENTRE CASES (R.7.10 AND PD 7C)	9.021
MONEY CLAIM ONLINE ("MCOL")	9.022
TRANSFER OF PROCEEDINGS (PT 30)	9.023
Automatic transfer (r.26.2)	9.024
Application for a transfer	9.025
The transfer criteria under r.30.3	9.026
ALLOCATION TO A PARTICULAR TRACK	9.027
Completing the allocation questionnaire Form N150	9.028
Time for filing questionnaires	9.029
Identifying the "normal track"	9.030
The small claims track	9.031
The fast track	9.032
The multi-track	9.033
Assessing the financial value	9.034
Exaggerated claims	9.035
RULE 26.8(1) ALLOCATION FACTORS	9.036
Allocation hearings (r.26.5(4))	9.037
Allocation to a different track by consent (r.26.7(3))	9.038
Different claims and different tracks?	9.039
Notice of allocation (r.26.9)	9.040
Appeals and re-allocation	9.041

Chapter 10: Part 8 Claims

INTRODUCTION	10.001
THE PART 8 CLAIMS FORM (R.8.2)	10.002
ACKNOWLEDGMENT OF SERVICE (R.8.3)	10.003
FILING EVIDENCE (RR.8.5 AND 8.6)	10.004
CASE MANAGEMENT	10.005

Chapter 11: Cases with a Foreign Element

THE COUNTRIES OF THE EU AND THE EUROPEAN FREE TRADE ASSOCIATION (EFTA)	11.002
Scope of the Regulation	11.003
The "first seised" rule	11.004
Contracting States: the domicile rule	11.005
Exclusive jurisdiction	11.006
Some of the special jurisdiction rules	11.007
NON-CJJA 1982 CASES	11.008
Applying for permission to serve	11.009
CHALLENGING THE COURT'S JURISDICTION (R.11)	11.010
Time for service of claim form (r.7.7(3))	11.011
METHODS OF SERVICE	11.012
THE PERIOD FOR RESPONDING TO A CLAIM FORM	11.013
COUNTERCLAIMS AND ADDITIONAL CLAIMS	11.014
FORUM NON CONVENIENS	11.015
ANTI-SUIT INJUNCTIONS	11.016
CLAIM FOR A NEGATIVE DECLARATION	11.017

Chapter 12: Drafting Statements of Case

INTRODUCTION	12.001
THE FUNCTION OF STATEMENTS OF CASE	12.002
GENERAL FORMALITIES	12.003
Statements of truth	12.004
FORMAT OF A STATEMENT OF CASE	12.005
PRINCIPALS OF DRAFTING STATEMENTS OF CASE	12.006
Sufficient facts should be stated concisely, yet precisely	12.006
Reference may be made to a point of law (PD 16, para.13.3(1))	12.007
The name of an intended witness may be stated (PD 16, para.13.3(2))	12.007A
Documentary evidence may be attached (PD 16, para.13.3(3))	12.008
DRAFTING A CLAIM	12.009
The claim form	12.009
The statement of value	12.010
The particulars of claim	12.011
A concise statement of the facts on which the claimant relies	12.012
Claims for interest	12.013
Claims for aggravated or exemplary damages	12.014

Claims for provisional damages 12.015
Claims for wrongful interference with goods 12.016
Defamation claims 12.017
Matters Required by PD 16 .... 12.018
Injunction or declaration (para.7.1) 12.019
Recovery of goods (para.7.3) 12.020
Written agreement (para.7.3) 12.021
Oral agreement (para.7.4) 12.021
Agreement by conduct (para.7.5) 12.022
High Court consumer credit agreement cases (para.7.6) 12.023
Civil Evidence Act 1968, ss.11 and 12 statements (para.8.1) 12.024
Clinical negligence (para.9.3) 12.025
Competition Act 1998 (para.14) 12.026
Human Rights (para.15.1) 12.027
Miscellaneous matters 12.028
PERSONAL INJURY CLAIMS 12.029
INCONSISTENT STATEMENTS OF CASES (PD 16, PARA.9.2) 12.030
ANTICIPATING A PARTICULAR DEFENCE 12.031
TEMPLATES FOR CLAIMS 12.032
DRAFTING A DEFENCE 12.033
Sample defences 12.034
Tender before claim (r.37.3) 12.035
Defences under the Limitation Act (PD 16, para.13.1) 12.036
Defence of set-off (r.16.6) 12.037
Contributory negligence 12.038
Specific proceedings 12.039
DRAFTING A COUNTERCLAIM 12.040
FORMS OF ADMISSION, DEFENCE AND COUNTERCLAIM 12.041
DRAFTING A REPLY AND/OR DEFENCE TO
    COUNTERCLAIM 12.042
FURTHER STATEMENTS OF CASE? 12.043
SUGGESTED DOCUMENTS 12.044
PARTICULARS OF CLAIM 12.046
PARTICULARS 12.047
DEFENCE 12.048
PARTICULARS 12.049
AMENDING STATEMENTS OF CASE 12.050
Amendments before service (r.17.1(1)) 12.051
Amending after service (r.17.1(2)) 12.052
Amendments after the expiry of the limitation period 12.053
Making an application for permission 12.054
Consequential amendments 12.055
Cost of amendments 12.056
Practice on amending 12.057

Chapter 13: Interim Applications

TYPES OF APPLICATION	13.001
APPLICATIONS NOTICES	13.002
DOCUMENTS IN SUPPORT OF AN APPLICATION	13.003
APPLICATIONS WITHOUT NOTICE	13.004
Serving orders made without noise	13.005
APPLICANTS WITH NOTICE	13.006
Hearing the application	13.007
Application with notice but without a hearing	13.008
COSTS IN INTERIM APPLICATIONS	13.009
Summary assessment	13.010
Detailed assessment	13.011

Chapter 14: Drafting Applications, Witness Statements and Affidavits

DRAFTING APPLICATION NOTICES	14.001
USE OF A WITNESS STATEMENT AND AFFIDAVITS	14.002
WITNESS STATEMENTS AND AFFIDAVITS:	
GENERAL FORMALITIES	14.003
SOLICITOR'S DUTIES	14.004
DRAFTING EVIDENCE FOR USE AT AN INTERIM HEARING	14.005
DRAFTING WITNESS STATEMENTS FOR USE AT TRIAL	14.006
Identify all the issues upon which the party	
Needs to adduce evidence	14.007
For each witness prepare a statement in	
The proper form	14.008
Send a draft statement to the witness for checking	14.009
Additional formalities if the witness is being called to give oral	
hearsay	14.010
Review the evidence	14.011
THE FINAL VERSION	14.012

Chapter 15: Default Judgment

THE GENERAL PICTURE	15.001
What is a defence?	15.002
Filing an acknowledgment of service or defence late	15.003
CLAIMS IN WHICH DEFAULT JUDGMENT IS NOT AVAILABLE	
(RR.12.2 AND 12.3(3) AND PD 12, PARAS 1.2 AND 1.3)	15.004
DEFAULT JUDGMENT ON REQUEST (R.12.4)	15.005
Claim for a specified amount of money (r.12.5(1))	15.006
Claim for an unspecified amount of money	15.007
Claim for delivery of goods or payment of their value	15.008
Request in claim against two or more defendants (r.12.8(1))	15.008
DEFAULT JUDGMENT ON APPLICATION	15.009
Application for default judgment against two or more Defendants	
(r.12.8(2))	15.010

SETTING ASIDE A DEFAULT JUDGMENT 15.011
   Where the court must set aside a default judgment 15.012
   Is there "a real prospect of successfully defending the claim"? 15.013
   Is there some other good reason to set aside 15.014
   Conditions the court may impose 15.015
   Practice on application 15.016
VARYING A DEFAULT JUDGMENT 15.017
DEFAULT JUDGMENT AND ADDITIONAL CLAIMS 15.018

Chapter 16: Admissions and Requests for Time to Pay

WHAT IS AN ADMISSION 16.001
JUDGMENT ON A WRITTEN ADMISSION 16.002
ADMISSIONS IN FORM N9A OR N9C 16.003
   Admission of whole of claim for a specified amount of money
     (r.14.4) 16.004
   Admissions of part of claim for a specified amount of money
     (r.14.5) 16.005
   Defendant's offer to satisfy a claim for unspecified amount of
     money (r.14.7) 16.006
DEFENDANTS REQUEST FOR TIME TO PAY (R.14.9) 16.007
   Determination of rate of payment (rr.14.10 to 14.12) 16.008
AMENDING OR WITHDRAWING AN ADMISSION 16.009
STAY OF PROCEEDINGS AFTER SIX MONTHS' INACTIVITY
   (R.15.11) 16.010

Chapter 17: Disposal Hearings

RELEVANT ORDERS 17.002
JUDGMENT OBTAINED BEFORE ALLOCATION 17.003
   Allocation 17.004
   Disposal hearing 17.005
   Other directions 17.006
JUDGMENT OBTAINED AFTER ALLOCATION 17.007

Chapter 18: Counterclaims and Additional Claims (Pt 20)

COUNTERCLAIM BY A DEFENDANT AGAINST A CLAIMANT
   (R.20.4) 18.002
COUNTERCLAIM BY A DEFENDANT AGAINST SOMEONE
   OTHER THAN A CLAIMANT (R.20.5) 18.003
CO-DEFENDANT'S CONTRIBUTION AND INDEMNITY
   CLAIMS AGAINST EACH OTHER (R.20.6) 18.004
CLAIMS BY A DEFENDANT AGAINST A NON-PARTY 18.005
CLAIMS BY A THIRD PARTY AGAINST A FOURTH PARTY,
   ETC 18.006

APPLYING FOR PERMISSION TO ISSUE AN ADDITIONAL
  CLAIM 18.007
SERVICE OF AN ADDITIONAL CLAIM FORM (RR.20.8
  AND 20.12) 18.008
CONSEQUENCES OF A NON-PARTY FAILING TO
  ACKNOWLEDGE AND/OR DEFEND (R.20.11) 18.009
CASE MANAGEMENT OF ADDITIONAL CLAIMS 18.010
ADDITIONAL CLAIMS AND COSTS 18.011

Chapter 19: Summary Judgment

SCOPE AND EFFECT OF CPR, PT 24 .... 19.001
  Exceptions to Pt 24 .... 19.002
  Summary judgment in cases with a right to jury trial 19.003
  Overlap with r.3.4 .... 19.004
  Summary judgment not summary trial 19.005
THE "NO REAL PROSPECTS" TEST 19.006
  Some other compelling reason for a trial 19.007
  Effect of a set-off 19.008
  No set-off in cheque actions 19.009
WHEN TO APPLY 19.010
  Application by claimant 19.010
  Application by defendant 19.011
HOW TO APPLY 19.012
EVIDENCE IN RESPONSE AND FURTHER EVIDENCE
  IN REPLY 19.013
ORDERS MADE IN SUMMARY JUDGMENT APPLICATIONS ... 19.014
  Granting summary judgment 19.014
  Refusing summary judgment 19.015
  Consequential orders 19.016

Chapter 20: The Small Claims Track (Pt 27)

TYPE OF CASES 20.001
RETAINING SOLICITORS TO CONDUCT SMALL CLAIMS 20.002
ALLOCATION 20.003
  Allocation with directions (Form N157) 20.004
  Allocation followed by a preliminary hearing (Form N158) 20.005
  Allocation followed by a "paper disposal" (Form N159) 20.006
  Allocation by consent (Form N160) 20.007
EXPERT EVIDENCE (R.27.5) 20.008
THE HEARING OF A SMALL TRACK CLAIM 20.009
COSTS 20.010
  Routine award of costs 20.010
  Costs where party has behaved unreasonably 20.011
  Cases allocated to the small claims track by consent 20.012

CONTENTS

SUMMARY JUDGMENT (PT 24) 20.013
APPEAL 20.014

Chapter 21: The Fast Track (Pt 28)

TYPICAL CASES 21.001
HOW FAST IS "FAST?" 21.002
THE NEED FOR CASE PLAN 21.003
DIRECTIONS ON ALLOCATIONS (R.28.2) 21.004
   Disclosure 21.005
   Exchange of witness statements 21.006
   Exchange of experts' reports 21.007
   Trial date 21.008
   Implication for the parties 21.009
   Failure to comply with directions 21.010
   Adjourning the trial 21.011
PRE-TRIAL CHECKLIST 21.012

Chapter 22: The Multi-Track (Pt 29)

TYPICAL CASES 22.001
CASE MANAGEMENT AT THE OUTSET 22.002
   The need for a case plan 22.002
   Issue identification 22.003
   Case management conference 22.004
   Disclosure 22.005
   Experts 22.006
   Trial date 22.007
   Conducting a case management conference 22.008
   Directions on allocation 22.009
   Suggested directions 22.010
   Variation of directions 22.011
   Failure to comply with directions 22.012
   Adjourning the trial 22.013
   Case management in the Royal Courts of Justice 22.014
CASE MANAGEMENT PRE-TRIAL 22.015
   The pre-trial checklist 22.015
   Pre-trial review 22.016
INFORMATION TECHNOLOGY (IT) 22.017
TRIAL 22.018

Chapter 23: Experts

INTRODUCTION 23.001
PRE-ACTION MATTERS 23.002
RESTRICTIONS ON EXPERT EVIDENCE IN COURT
   PROCEEDINGS 23.003

Expert evidence must be reasonably required	23.004
Case management of issues and evidence	23.005
Single jointly appointed expert	23.006
EXPERT EVIDENCE OBTAINED BY EACH PARTY	23.007
Conditional permission and refusal of permission	23.008
Expert's duties and format of report (PD35, paras 1 and 2) (PIE para.4)	23.009
When is an "expert" not an expert?	23.010
Legal profession privilege and the instructions to an expert	23.011
Directions sought by an expert(r.35.14)	23.012
The provision of information (r.35.9)	23.013
How many experts?	23.014
Impartiality and proportionality	23.015
When will change occur?	23.016
Sequential exchange	23.017
Discussions between experts (r.3512)	23.018
Disclosed reports as evidence (r.35.12)	23.019
Written questions to expert (r.36.6)	23.020
Inspection of documents in an expert's report	23.021
Expert evidence in low-velocity collision claims	23.022
Evidence of expert opinion or fact?	23.023

Chapter 24: Cases Not Governed By Standard Track Allocation

JUDICIAL REVIEW (PT54)	24.001
INTERPLEADER PROCEEDINGS	24.004
ACTIONS FOR THE RECOVERY OF LAND	24.005
Mortgage possession proceedings	24.006
Interim possession orders	24.007
Other possession proceedings	24.008
Other landlord and tenant matters	24.009
Probate and inheritance claims (Pt 57)	24.010
Technology and Construction Court (CCT) (Pt 60)	24.011
The Commercial Court (Pt 58)	24.012
Mercantile Courts (Pt 59)	24.013
Admiralty claims (Pt 61)	24.014
Arbiration claims (Pt 62)	24.015
Patents and other intellectual property claims (Pt 63)	24.016
Estates, Trusts and charities (Pt 64)	24.016
Proceedings relating to anti-social behaviour and harassment (Pt 65)	24.017
Crown Proceedings (Pt 66)	24.018
Proceedings relating to solicitors (Pt 67)	24.019
Reference to the European Court (Pt68)	24.020

Chapter 25: Interim Payments

THE OBJECT OF THE RULES	25.001
CONDITIONS TO BE SATISFIED	25.002
Admission of liability: ground (a)	25.003
Judgment for a sum to be assessed: ground (b)	25.004
At trial the claimant will obtain judgment for a substantial sum again the respondent: ground (c)	25.005
Claim for occupation and use of land: ground (d)	25.006
At trial the claimant will obtain judgment for a substantial sum against one or more of the defendant: ground (e)	25.007
VOLUNTARY PAYMENTS	25.008
APPLICATION FOR INTERIM PAYMENTS	25.009
Making the application	25.009
Opposing the application	25.010
The order for an interim payment	25.011
FURTHER CONDUCT OF THE ACTION	25.012

Chapter 26: Security For Costs

INTRODUCTION	26.001
APPLICATION AGAINST CLAIMANTS AND APPELLANTS	26.002
How to apply	26.003
DEFENCE APPLICATIONS AGAINST SOMEONE OTHER THAN THE CLAIMANT	26.004
SECURITY FOR COSTS ORDERS UNDER R.3.1	26.005
SECURITY FOR COSTS UNDER CPR 24	26.006

Chapter 27: Interim Injunctions

INTRODUCTION	27.001
UNDERTAKING AS TO DAMAGES (PD 25, PARA.5.1A)	27.002
GENERAL PRINCIPLES UPON WHICH GRANTED: *AMERICAN CYANAMID V ETHICON*	27.003
Whether there is a serious issue to be tried	27.004
Which way the balance of convenience lies	27.005
EXCEPTIONS TO AMERICAN CYANAMID	27.006
Where the injunction will finally dispose of the action	27.007
Where the injunction will restrict freedom of expression	27.008
Interim mandatory injunctions	27.009
Where the defendant has no arguable defence	27.010
Defamation and malicious falsehood	27.011
PROCEDURE ON APPLICATIONS	27.012
Applications without notice	27.012
Applications made on notice	27.013
Non-disclosure of all material facts	27.014
Serving the injunction	27.014A
FREEZING INJUNCTIONS (R.25.1(F))	27.015

Importance of freezing injunction	27.016
Applying for a freezing injunction	27.017
Applying for a freezing injunction in aid of foreign proceedings	27.018
Terms of a freezing injunction	27.019
Serving freezing injunctions	27.020
Applications to discharge or vary the order	27.021
Rights of third parties in the property attached	27.022
SEARCH ORDERS (R.25.1(h))	27.023
How to apply	27.024
Form of order	27.025
DISCLOSURE OF INFORMATION BY THE DEFENDANT	27.026
Privilege against self-incrimination	27.027
Enfacing orders for disclosure	27.028
EFFECT OF A R.3.7 STRIKE OUT (R.25.11)	27.029
INTERIM RECEIVERSHIP ORDERS	27.030
INTERIM ORDERS RELATING TO RELEVANT PROPERTY	27.031

Chapter 28: Change of Solicitors

CHANGE OF SOLICITORS	28.001

Chapter 29: Part 36 offers to settle

THE RATIONALE OF PT 36	29.001
What has happened to payments into court?	29.002
Pt 36 and the small claims track	29.003
MAKING OFFERS TO SETTLE	29.004
When to offer	29.004
What to offer	29.005
Form and content of offers	29.006
Defence offers to pay money	29.007
Defence offers affected by the Social Security (Recovery of Benefits) Act 1997	29.008
Offers solely in relation to liability	29.009
Offers to settle which are outside Pt 36	29.010
Withdrawing or altering a Pt 26 offer	29.011
ACCEPTING OFFERS TO SETTLE	29.012
Clarification of offers to settle	29.012
When and how to accept	29.013
The effect of acceptance	29.014
Stay of all relevant proceedings	29.015
Provision for the costs of proceedings	29.016
Implementation of the terms agreed	29.018
Further consequences	29.019
WHERE OFFERS TO SETTLE ARE NOT ACCEPTED	29.020
The rule of secrecy	29.020
Orders for costs following judgement	29.021

Where claimant made an offer which was not beaten 29.022
Enhanced interest and costs 29.023
Where defendant made an offer which was not beaten 29.024

Chapter 30: Disclosure and Inspection

INTRODUCTION 30.001
THE MEANING OF DISCLOSURE (R.31.2) 30.002
STANDARD DISCLOSURE 30.003
WHAT IS A "DOCUMENT"? (R.31.4) 30.004
DOCUMENTS UNDER A PARTY'S "CONTROL" (R.31.8) 30.005
THE SOLICITOR'S ROLE IN DISCLOSURE 30.005A
SEARCHING FOR STANDARD DISCLOSURE DOCUMENTS
  (R.31.7) 30.006
LIMITED OR EXTENDED DISCLOSURE? 30.007
DRAFTING A STANDARD DISCLOSURE LIST OF
  DOCUMENTS 30.008
A CONTINUING DUTY (R.31.33 AND PD 31, PARA.3.3) 30.009
PRIVILEGE FROM DISCLOSURE (R.31.19(1)) 30.010
INSPECTION 30.011
LIMITING INSPECTION ("THE DISPROPORTIONATE GROUND)
  (R.31.3(2)) 30.012
PRIVILEGE FROM INSPECTION 30.013
  Legal professional privilege 30.013
  Privilege against self-incrimination 30.014
  Challenging a claim to privilege 30.015
DISCLOSURE IN STATES (R.31.13) 30.016
INSPECTION OF DOCUMENTS REFERRED TO IN
  STATEMTENTS OF CASE, ETC (R.31.14) 30.017
INSPECTION ON TERMS 30.018
INADVERTENT INSPECTION 30.019
SUBSEQUENT USE OF DISCLOSED DOCUMENTS 30.020
SPECIFIC DISCLOSURE (R.31.12 AND PD 31, PARA.5) 30.021
FAILURE TO DISCLOSE OR ALLOW INSPECTION (R.31.21) 30.022
DISCLOSURE AGAINST A NON-PARTY (R.31.17) 30.023
PRE-ACTION DISCLOSURE (R.31.16) 30.024
THE RULE IN NORWICH PHARMACAL 30.025

Chapter 31: Evidence

KEY QUESTIONS 31.001
THE LEGAL BURDEN 31.002
THE EVIDENTIAL BURDEN 31.003
THE STANDARD OF PROOF 31.004
EXCHANGE OF WITNESS STATEMENTS 31.005
  Supplemental witness statements 31.006
  Serving witness statements late 31.007

Witness summaries 31.008
Objections to contents 31.009
Use at trial 31.010
OPINION EVIDENCE 31.011
HEARSAY EVIDENCE 31.012
   What is it in practice? 31.013
   Formalities 31.014
   Calling the maker of a hearsay statement (r.33.4) ... 31.015
   Attacking the credibility of hearsay evidence (r.33.5) .. 31.016
   Weight and credibility of hearsay evidence 31.017
   Evidence sworn out of court and video conferencing .. 31.018
   Previous statements of witnesses 31.019
DOCUMENTARY EVIDENCE 31.020
REAL EVIDENCE 31.021
PLANS, PHOTOGRAPHS, MODELS, ETC 31.022
SIMILAR FACT EVIDENCE 31.023
RECONSTRUCTION EVIDENCE 31.024
ADVICE ON EVIDENCE 31.025

Chapter 32: Fact Management

FURTHER INFORMATION (Pt 18) 32.001
WHEN TO ASK 32.002
HOW TO ASK 32.003
WHAT NOT TO ASK 32.004
RESPONDING TO A REQUEST 32.005
APPLYING FOR AN ORDER 32.006
NOTICES TO ADMIT (R.32.18) 32.007
   When to serve 32.008

Chapter 33: Judicial Case Management

COURT'S POWER TO MAKE AN ORDER OF ITS OWN
   INITIATIVE 33.001
   Extending or shortening time for compliance 33.002
STAY OF PROCEEDINGS (R.3.1 (2)(F)) 33.003
   Stay pending appeal in another decision 33.003A
   Stay pending arbitration 33.004
   Other grounds for a stay 33.005
SPLIT TRIAL AND PRELIMINARY ISSUES 33.006
CONDITIONAL ORDERS (R.3.1(3)) 33.007
STRIKING OUT A STATEMENT OF CASE (R.3.4) 33.008
   Court acting of its own initiative 33.009
   Consequences of strike out 33.010
SANCTIONS AND RELIEF FROM SANCTIONS
   (RR.3.7, 3.8 AND 3.9) 33.011

CONTROLLING EVIDENCE 33.012
CONTROLLING COSTS 33.013

Chapter 34: Termination of an Action by Consent

REACHING A BINDING SETTLEMENT OUTSIDE COURT
   PROCEEDINGS 34.001
     Negotiations 34.001
     Alternative dispute resolution (ADR) 34.002
UNDERTAKINGS 34.003
COURT APPROVAL OF SETTLEMENT 34.004
CONSENT ORDERS AND JUDGEMENTS 34.005
     "Tomlin Orders" 34.006
BY CONSENT IT IS ORDERED 34.007
IN THE EVENT OF DEFAULT BY THE DEFENDANT 34.008

Chapter 35: Discontinuance

INTRODUCTION 35.001
DISCONTINUANCE BY NOTICE (R.38.3) 35.002
     Where other parties' consent is needed 35.003
     Where permission of the courts is needed 35.004
     Setting aside notice of discontinuance (r.38.4) 35.005
     Liability for costs (r.38.6) 35.006
SUBSEQUENT PROCEEDINGS (R.38.7) 35.007

Chapter 36: Preparations for Trial

COMPLETING THE PRE-TRIAL CHECKLIST 36.001
     Directions on listing 36.002
PRE-TRIAL REVIEW 36.002A
ORGANISING WITNESSES 36.003
     Witness summons (r.34.3) 36.003
     Unavailable witnesses 36.004
     Getting everybody to court 36.005
THE TRIAL BUNDLE 36.006
     Core bundles 36.007
     Skeleton arguments 36.007
     Reading lists and time estimates 36.008
     CHOICE OF ADVOCATES 36.009
     Drafting the brief for trial 36.010
     Delivering a brief to counsel 36.011
RECUSAL OF JUDGE 36.012

Chapter 37: Trial

SITTING BEHIND COUNSEL 37.001
WITNESSES 37.002

PROCEDURE AT TRIAL	37.003
Small claims track and Pt 8 claims	37.003
Fast track and multi-track	37.004
Submission of no case to answer	37.005
Order of witnesses	37.006
Failure to attend trial (r.39.3)	37.007
THE ART OF ADVOCACY	37.008
Preparation	37.009
Opening and closing statements	37.010
Examination-in-chief	37.011
Cross-examination	37.012
Re-examination	37.014
THE ROLE OF THE TRIAL JUDGE	37.015
JUDGEMENT	37.016

Chapter 38: Costs Payable by One Party to Another

DEFINTION OF COSTS	38.001
What does an order for costs cover?	38.002
Costs usually refers to legal costs	38.003
Litigants in person	38.004
In-house solicitors	38.005
Expenses and witness allowances	38.006
Additional liability	38.007
DISCRETIONARY NATURE OF COSTS	38.008
METHODS OF ASSESSMENT	38.009
Fixed costs on early judgements	38.010
Fixed costs in fast track trial	38.011
Fixed costs in some RTA claims which settle pre-issue	38.012
Fixed success fees in some RTA claims and employers' liability claims	38.013
Summary assessment	38.014
Detailed assessment	38.015
BASIS OF ASSESSMENT	38.016
Proportionality	38.017
Conduct of the parties	38.018
THE INDEMNITY PRINCIPLE	38.019
Small claims	38.021
Statutory restrictions	38.022
ADDRESSING THE REASONABLENESS OF SUCCESS FEES	38.023
Risk element: assessment by solicitor	38.024
Risk element: assessment by the court	38.025
Decisions on the amount of success fee	38.026
The fee deferment element	38.027
Assessing the reasonableness of insurance cover costs	38.028
Factors for the court	38.029
Decisions on ATE premiums	38.030

DETAILED ASSESSMENT PROCEEDINGS 38.031
Earliest time for detailed assessment 38.031
Form of bill 38.032
Notice of commencement 38.033
Latest time for commencement 38.034
Points of dispute: general practice 38.035
Points of dispute challenging success fees 38.036
Default costs certificates 38.037
Request for a hearing 38.038
Interim costs certificates 38.039
Conduct of the hearing 38.040
Production of documents at the hearing 38.040
Costs of detailed assessment proceedings 38.041
Final costs certificates 38.042
Agreed costs certificates 38.043
Appeals 38.044
Costs payable by one party to another 38.045

Chapter 39: Costs: Special Cases

COSTS ONLY PROCEEDINGS 39.001
WASTED COSTS ORDERS 39.002
APPLICATIONS UNDER S.70 OF THE SOLICITORS ACT 1974 ... 39.003
Awarding costs in proceedings under Solicitors Act 1974, s.70 ..... 39.004
OTHER METHODS OF CHALLENGING SOLICITORS' BILLS ... 39.005
Non-contentious business; remuneration certificates 39.005
Contentious business agreements 39.006
Non-contentious business agreements 39.007
COSTS FUNDED BY THE LSC 39.008
The winner's bill 39.009
The loser's bill 39.010
Enhancements 39.011
Reduction 39.012
LSC-funded client's involvement in assessment Proceedings 39.013
ORDERS FOR COSTS AGAINST LSC-FUNDED CLIENTS
   AND/OR THE LSC 39.014
COSTS ORDERS IN FAVOUR OF OR AGAINST NON-PARTIES ... 39.015
COSTS WHERE A GROUP LITIGATION ORDER HAS
   BEEN MADE 39.016
PROTECTIVE COSTS ORDERS 39.017
PROSPECTIVE COSTS ORDERS 39.018
ASSESSMENT OF COSTS PAYABLE PURSUANT TO A
   CONTRACT 39.019

Chapter 40: Enforcement of Money Judgements

INTRODUCTION	40.001
HIGH COURT ENFORCEMENT OF COUNTY COURT JUDGEMENTS	40.002
INFORMATION HEARING (PT 71)	40.003
WRIT OF FIERI FACIAS (HIGH COURT); WARRANT OF EXECUTION (COUNTY COURT)	40.004
THIRD PARTY DEBT PROCEEDINGS (PT 72)	40.005
ATTACHMENT OF EARNINGS	40.006
CHARGING ORDER ON LAND (PT 73)	40.008
Jurisdiction of the High Court and county court	40.009
Changing order procedure	40.010
CHARGING ORDER ON SECURITIES (PT 73)	40.011
EQUITABLE EXECUTION: APPOINTMENT OF A RECEIVER (PT 69)	40.012
CHARGING ORDER ON DEBTOR'S INTEREST IN PARTNERSHIP PROPERTY	40.013
SEQUESTRATION	40.014
JUDGEMENT SUMMONS	40.015
BANKRUPTCY AND WINDING UP OF COMPANIES	40.015A
ENFORCEMENT OF FOREIGN JUDGEMENTS (PT 74)	40.016
ENFORCEMENT OUTSIDE ENGLAND AND WALES	40.018
ADVISING THE JUDGEMENT DEBTOR	40.019

Chapter 41: Enforcement of Other Judgements

RECOVERY OF LAND	41.001
Recovery of goods	41.002
Injunctions	41.003
Specific performance	41.004

Chapter 42: Insolvency

INTRODUCTION	42.001
What is insolvency?	42.002
Insolvency law as an aid to debtors	42.003
STATUTORY DEMANDS	42.004
Service and proof of service	42.004A
Responses to a statutory demand	42.005
Challenge made by an individual	42.006
Challenge made by a company	42.007
Complying with a statutory demand	42.008
No response to a statutory demand	42.009
Demand first or sue to judgement first?	42.010
PERSONAL INSOLVENCY: BANKRUPTCY	42.011
Grounds for a creditor's petition	42.011
Presentation of bankruptcy petition	42.012

The debtor's responses 42.013
Hearing of bankruptcy petition 42.014
Effects of bankruptcy on enforcement procedures in other actions .. 42.015
Procedure following the bankruptcy order 42.016
CORPORATE INSOLVENCY: WINDING UP 42.017
Grounds for a creditor's petition 42.017
Presentations of winding-up petition 42.018
Certificate of compliance 42.019
Hearing of winding-up petition 42.020
Effect of a winding-up order 42.021
Specialist topics in insolvency law and practice 42.022
Corporate insolvency: winding up proceedings 42.023

Chapter 43: Applications to Set Aside or Vary Orders

ORDERS MADE IN THE ABSENCE OF ONE PARTY 43.002
ORDERS DIRECTLY AFFECTING NON-PARTIES 43.003
ORDERS WORKING OUT, SUPPLEMENTING OR ENFORCING
  ORDERS PREVIOUSLY MADE 43.004
COURT'S POWER UNDER CPR 3.1(7) 43.005
RELIEF FROM SANCTIONS 43.006
CORRECTING ACCIDENTAL SLIPS OR OMISSIONS IN
  JUDGEMENTS AND ORDERS 43.007
OTHER AMENDMENTS TO JUDGEMENTS AND ORDERS
  MADE BEFORE SEALING 43.008
Re-opening of final appeals (R.52.7) 43.009

Chapter 44: Appeals Up To the Court of Appeal

ROUTES OF APPEAL 44.001
Final decisions in multi-track cases and specialist proceedings 44.002
Leapfrog appeals 44.003
Orders from which no appeal lies 44.004
PERMISSION TO APPEAL 44.005
Seeking permission 44.006
Second appeals 44.007
The rule in *Lane v Esdaile* 44.008
THE APPELLANT'S NOTICE 44.009
Time for filing and service 44.009
Form and content of appellant's notice 44.010
Documents to accompany the appellant's notice 44.011
PROCEDURE WHERE PERMISSION IS NOT REQUIRED OR IS
  OBTAINED 44.012
First steps by the respondent 44.013
Form and content of a respondent's notice 44.014
Skeleton arguments 44.015
Applications ancillary to appeals 44.016

Hearing of the appeal	44.017
Summary assessment of appeal costs	44.018
PROCEDURE IN THE COURT OF APPEAL	44.019
Who may exercise the powers of the Court of Appeal	44.019
The Civil Appeals Office	44.020
The Civil Appeals List	44.021
Hearing the appeal	44.022
Judicial review appeals	44.023

Chapter 45: Appeals to the House of Lords

INTRODUCTION	45.001
PETITION FOR LEAVE TO APPEAL	45.002
PETITION OF APPEAL OR CROSS-APPEAL	45.003
Statement of facts and issues	45.004
Appendix	45.005
Time estimates	45.006
Appellants' and respondents' cases	45.007
The hearing of the appeal	45.008

	page
Index	693

TABLE OF CASES

7E Communications Ltd v Vertex Antennentechnik Gm bH [2007] EWCA Civ 140; [2007] I.L.Pr. 18; *The Times*, March 19, 2007, CA (Civ Div) 44.003
A v B Hospitals NHS Trust [2006] EWHC 2833; (2006) L.T.L. 17 November, Q.B.D. (Admin) 4.016
    A v B Plc; sub nom. B and C v A; A v B (A Firm) [2002] EWCA Civ 337; [2003] Q.B. 195; [2002] 3 W.L.R. 542; [2002] 2 All E.R. 545; [2002] E.M.L.R. 21; [2002] 1 F.L.R. 1021; [2002] 2 F.C.R. 158; [2002] H.R.L.R. 25; [2002] U.K.H.R.R. 457; 12 B.H.R.C. 466; [2002] Fam. Law 415; (2002) 99(17) L.S.G. 36; (2002) 152 N.L.J. 434; (2002) 146 S.J.L.B. 77; *The Times*, March 13, 2002; *The Independent*, March 19, 2002; *The Daily Telegraph*, March 11, 2002, CA(Civ Div) 27.008, 27.011
A v C (No.2) [1981] Q.B. 961; [1981] 2 W.L.R. 634; [1981] 2 All E.R. 126; [1981] 1 Lloyd's Rep. 559, Q.B.D. (Comm) 27.021
A v Hoare; H v Suffolk CC; X v Wandsworth LBC [2006] EWCA Civ 395; [2006] 1 W.L.R. 2320; [2006] 2 F.L.R. 727; [2006] 3 F.C.R. 673; [2006] Fam. Law 533; (2006) 103(18) L.S.G. 29; (2006) 150 S.J.L.B. 536; *The Times*, April 28, 2006; *The Independent*, April 28, 2006, CA (Civ Div) 5.007
A v X (Disclosure: Non-Party Medical Records) [2004] EWHC 447; (2004) L.T.L. April, Q.B.D. 3.023
AB v Leeds Teaching Hospitals NHS Trust [2003] EWHC 1034; [2003] 3 Costs L.R. 405; [2003] Lloyd's Rep. Med. 355, Q.B.D. 33.013
A (Children) (Conjoined Twins: Medical Treatment) (No.1), Re; sub nom. A (Children) (Conjoined Twins: Surgical Separation), Re [2001] Fam. 147; [2001] 2 W.L.R. 480; [2000] 4 All E.R. 961; [2001] 1 F.L.R. 1; [2000] 3 F.C.R. 577; [2000] H.R.L.R. 721; [2001] U.K.H.R.R. 1; 9 B.H.R.C. 261; [2000] Lloyd's Rep. Med. 425; (2001) 57 B.M.L.R. 1; [2001] Crim. L.R. 400; [2001] Fam. Law 18; (2000) 150 N.L.J. 1453; *The Times*, October 10, 2000; *The Independent*, October 3, 2000, CA (Civ Div) 7.005
AEI Rediffusion Music Ltd v Phonographic Performance Ltd (Costs); sub nom. Phonographic Performance Ltd v AEI Rediffusion Music Ltd (Costs) [1999] 1 W.L.R. 1507; [1999] 2 All E.R. 299; [1999] C.P.L.R. 551; [1999] E.M.L.R. 335; [1999] R.P.C. 599; (1999) 22(5) I.P.D. 22046; (1999) 96(12) L.S.G. 33; (1999) 143 S.J.L.B. 97; *The Times*, March 3, 1999; *The Independent*, February 24, 1999, CA (Civ Div) 38.008
A Ltd v B Ltd [1996] 1 W.L.R. 665, Ch D 26.003
AWG Group Ltd (formerly Anglian Water Plc) v Morrison; sub nom. Morrison v AWG Group Ltd (formerly Anglian Water Plc) [2006] EWCA Civ 6; [2006] 1 W.L.R. 1163; [2006] 1 All E.R. 967; *The Independent*, January 25, 2006, CA (Civ Div) 36.012
AXA Equity & Law Life Assurance Society Plc v National Westminster Bank Plc [1998] C.L.C. 1177, CA (Civ Div); affirming [1998] P.N.L.R. 433, Ch D .. 30.023
AXA Equity & Law Life Assurance Society Plc (No.2), Re; Axa Sun Life Plc (No.2), Re [2001] 1 All E.R. (Comm) 1010; [2001] 2 B.C.L.C. 447; (2001) 98(10) L.S.G. 43; (2001) 145 S.J.L.B. 51; *The Times*, January 31, 2001, Ch D 39.017
Aaron v Shelton [2004] EWHC 1162; [2004] 3 All E.R. 561; [2004] 3 Costs L.R. 488; (2004) 154 N.L.J. 853, Q.B.D. 38.018

TABLE OF CASES

Abbey National Plc v Frost [1999] 1 W.L.R. 1080; [1999] 2 All E.R. 206; [1999] Lloyd's Rep. P.N. 301; [1999] E.G. 16 (C.S.); [1999] N.P.C. 13; *The Times*, February 5, 1999; *The Independent*, February 10, 1999, CA (Civ Div) 8.014
Accident Group Test Cases, 2003, SCCO transcript 38.030
Adams v Bracknell Forest BC; sub nom. Bracknell Forest BC v Adams [2004] UKHL 29; [2005] 1 A.C. 76; [2004] 3 W.L.R. 89; [2004] 3 All E.R. 897; [2004] E.L.R. 459; [2005] P.I.Q.R. P2; (2004) 101(26) L.S.G. 28; (2004) 148 S.J.L.B. 761; *The Times*, June 24, 2004, HL 5.007
Adams v Cape Industries Plc [1990] Ch.433; [1990] 2 W.L.R. 657; [1991] 1 All E.R. 929; [1990] B.C.C. 786; [1990] B.C.L.C. 479, CA (Civ Div) 8.010
Adelson v Associated Newspapers Ltd [2007] EWHC 997 (QB); *The Times*, May 10, 2007, Q.B.D. 12.053
Aectra Refining & Marketing Inc v Exmar NV; The New Vanguard and The Pacifica [1994] 1 W.L.R. 1634; [1995] 1 All E.R. 641; [1995] 1 Lloyd's Rep. 191; *The Times*, August 15, 1994; *The Independent*, August 22, 1994, CA (Civ Div) 12.037
Aegis Group Plc v Inland Revenue Commissioners [2005] EWHC 1468; [2006] S.T.C. 23; [2005] S.T.I. 989; (2005) L.T.L., May 13, Ch D 24.003
Aer Lingus Plc v Gildacroft Ltd [2006] EWCA Civ 4; [2006] 1 W.L.R. 1173; [2006] 2 All E.R. 290; [2006] C.P. Rep. 21; [2006] P.I.Q.R. P16; (2006) 103(6) L.S.G. 32; (2006) 156 N.L.J. 147; (2006) 150 S.J.L.B. 129; [2006] N.P.C. 4; *The Times*, January 23, 2006; *The Independent*, January 19, 2006, CA (Civ Div) 5.006
Aerospace Publishing Ltd v Thames Water Utilities Ltd [2007] EWCA Civ 3; [2007] Bus. L.R. 726; 110 Con. L.R. 1; (2007) 104(4) L.S.G. 32; (2007) 151 S.J.L.B. 123; [2007] N.P.C. 5; *The Times*, January 22, 2007, CA (Civ Div) 44.011
Afzal v Ford Motor Co. Ltd; Caldwell v Wiggins Teape Fine Papers Ltd; Green v British Gas (North Eastern) Plc; Willingham v Kimberly-Clark Ltd; Featherstone v Ideal Standard Ltd; Joyce v Ford Motor Co. Ltd; Kavanagh v Ideal Standard Ltd; Sokhal v Ford Motor Co. Ltd [1994] 4 All E.R. 720; [1994] P.I.Q.R. P418; (1994) 144 N.L.J. 935; *The Times*, July 6, 1994; *The Independent*, June 16, 1994, CA (Civ Div) 9.036
Agassi v Robinson (Inspector of Taxes) (Costs); sub nom. Agassi v Robinson (Inspector of Taxes) (No.2) [2005] EWCA Civ 1507; [2006] 1 W.L.R. 2126; [2006] 1 All E.R. 900; [2006] S.T.C. 580; [2006] 2 Costs L.R. 283; [2006] B.T.C. 3; [2005] S.T.I. 1994; (2005) 155 N.L.J. 1885; (2006) 150 S.J.L.B. 28; [2005] N.P.C. 140; *The Times*, December 22, 2005; *The Independent*, December 7, 2005, CA (Civ Div) 38.003, 38.004, 38.006
Ahmed v Jaura. *See* Jaura v Ahmed
Airbus Industrie GIE v Patel [1999] 1 A.C. 119; [1998] 2 W.L.R. 686; [1998] 2 All E.R. 257; [1998] 1 Lloyd's Rep. 631; [1998] C.L.C. 702; [1999] I.L.Pr. 238; (1998) 95(18) L.S.G. 32; (1998) 148 N.L.J. 551; (1998) 142 S.J.L.B. 139; *The Times*, April 6, 1998, HL 11.016
Aird v Prime Meridian Ltd [2006] EWCA Civ 1866; [2007] B.L.R. 105; (2007) 104(2) L.S.G. 31; (2007) 151 S.J.L.B. 60; *The Times*, February 14, 2007, CA (Civ Div) 23.018
Akram v Adam [2004] EWCA Civ 1601; [2005] 1 W.L.R. 2762; [2005] 1 All E.R. 741; [2005] C.P. Rep. 14; [2005] H.L.R. 14; [2005] L. & T.R. 9; [2004] 50 E.G. 84 (C.S.); (2005) 102(5) L.S.G. 28; (2004) 148 S.J.L.B. 1433; [2004] N.P.C. 182; [2005] 1 P. & C.R. DG13; *The Times*, December 29, 2004, CA (Civ Div) 8.013, 15.014

Albon (t/a N A Carriage Co.) v Naza Motor Trading SDN BHD [2007] EWHC 327
(Ch); [2007] 1 All E.R. (Comm) 813; (2007) L.T.L., April 11, Ch D 1.009, 8.014
Albon (t/a NA Carriage Co.) v Naza Motor Trading SDN BHD [2007] EWHC 665
(Ch); (2007) L.T.L., April 11, Ch D 33.008
Aldi Stores Ltd v WSP Group Plc [2007] EWHC 55; [2007] B.L.R. 113; (2007)
L.T.L., February 8, Q.B.D. (TCC) 33.008
Alex Lawrie Factors Ltd v Morgan [2001] C.P. Rep. 2; The Times, August 18, 1999,
CA (Civ Div) 14.008
Alexander v Arts Council of Wales [2001] EWCA Civ 514; [2001] 1 W.L.R. 1840;
[2001] 4 All E.R. 205; [2001] E.M.L.R. 27; (2001) 98(22) L.S.G. 35; (2001)
145 S.J.L.B. 123; The Times, April 27, 2001; The Independent, April 27,
2001, CA (Civ Div) 19.003, 19.005
Al-Fayed v Commissioner of Police of the Metropolis (No.1) [2002] EWCA Civ
780; (2002) 99(30) L.S.G. 39; (2002) 146 S.J.L.B. 153; The Times, June 17,
2002, CA (Civ Div) 30.019
Alfred Crompton Amusement Machines Ltd v Customs and Excise
Commissioners (No.2) [1974] A.C. 405; [1973] 3 W.L.R. 268; [1972] 1
W.L.R. 833; [1973] 2 All E.R. 1169; (1973) 117 S.J. 602, HL 30.013
Ali v Hudson (t/a Hudson Freeman Berg) [2003] EWCA Civ 1793; [2004] C.P. Rep.
15, CA (Civ Div) 19.015, 26.005
Ali v Lane [2006] EWCA Civ 1532; [2007] 1 P. & C.R. 26; [2006] 48 E.G. 231
(C.S.); [2006] N.P.C. 124; The Times, December 4, 2006, CA (Civ Div) ... 1.008
Ali v Naseem, The Times, October 3, 2003, Ch D 27.028
Ali Finance Ltd v Havelet Leasing Ltd. See Arbuthnot Leasing International Ltd
v Havelet Leasing Ltd (No.1)
Ali Reza-Delta Transport Co. Ltd v United Arab Shipping Co. SAG (Costs) [2003]
EWCA Civ 811; [2004] 1 W.L.R. 168; [2003] 3 All E.R. 1297; [2003] 2 All
E.R. (Comm) 276; [2003] 2 Lloyd's Rep. 455; [2003] C.P. Rep. 57; [2004] 1
Costs L.R. 18; (2003) 100(34) L.S.G. 29; (2003) 147 S.J.L.B. 753; The Times,
July 4, 2003; The Independent, June 20, 2003, CA (Civ Div) 29.005
Allen v Jambo Holdings Ltd [1980] 1 W.L.R. 1252; [1980] 2 All E.R. 502; (1980)
124 S.J. 742, CA (Civ Div) 27.021
Alliance and Leicester Plc v Pellys (1999) L.T.L., June 9 .... 12.053
Allied Arab Bank v Hajjar [1989] Fam. Law 68; The Times, January 20, 1988, CA
(Civ Div); affirming [1988] Q.B. 787; [1988] 2 W.L.R. 942; [1987] 3 All E.R.
739; [1987] 1 F.T.L.R. 455; (1988) 132 S.J. 659, Q.B.D. (Comm) 7.019, 27.028
Amedeo Hotels Ltd Partnership v Zaman [2007] EWHC 295 (Comm); (2007)
L.T.L., April 2, Q.B.D. (Comm) 27.018
American Cyanamid Co. (No.1) v Ethicon Ltd [1975] A.C. 396; [1975] 2 W.L.R.
316; [1975] 1 All E.R. 504; [1975] F.S.R. 101; [1975] R.P.C. 513; (1975) 119
S.J. 136, HL 27.001, 27.003, 27.004, 27.005,
27.006, 27.010, 27.017, 27.030
Amoco (UK) Exploration Co. v British American Offshore Ltd (2000) L.T.L.,
December 13, Q.B.D. (Comm) 35.006
Anderton v Clwyd CC; sub nom. Bryant v Pech; Home Office v Dorgan;
Cummins v Shell International Trading & Shipping Ltd; Bryant v Mike
Beer Transport Ltd; Dorgan v Home Office; Chambers v Southern
Domestic Electrical Services Ltd; Cummins v Shell International Manning
Services Ltd [2002] EWCA Civ 933; [2002] 1 W.L.R. 3174; [2002] 3 All E.R.
813; [2002] C.P. Rep. 71; (2002) 99(35) L.S.G. 38; (2002) 152 N.L.J. 1125;
(2002) 146 S.J.L.B. 177; The Times, July 16, 2002; The Independent, July 11,
2002, CA (Civ Div) 8.013, 9.006, 11.009

TABLE OF CASES

Andrews v Hopkinson [1957] 1 Q.B. 229; [1956] 3 W.L.R. 732; [1956] 3 All E.R.
    422; (1956) 100 S.J. 768, Assizes (Leeds) 18.007
Andrews v Initial Cleaning Services Ltd [2000] I.C.R. 166; (1999) 96(33) L.S.G. 31;
    The Times, August 18, 1999, CA (Civ Div) 18.004
Angel Airlines v Dean & Dean Solicitors [2006] EWCA Civ 1505; The Times,
    November 28, 2006, CA (Civ Div) 44.006
Anglian Windows Ltd v GMB [2007] EWHC 917 (QB) (2007) L.T.L., May 8,
    Q.B.D. 27.006
Anglo Eastern Trust Ltd v Kermanshahchi (No.2); Alliance v Kermanshahchi
    [2002] EWCA Civ 198; [2002] C.P. Rep. 36; [2002] C.P.L.R. 281; (2002) 146
    S.J.L.B. 76, CA (Civ Div) 19.014
Anton Piller KG v Manufacturing Processes Ltd [1976] Ch. 55; [1976] 2 W.L.R.
    162; [1976] 1 All E.R. 779; [1976] F.S.R. 129; [1976] R.P.C. 719; (1975) 120
    S.J. 63; The Times, December 9, 1975, CA (Civ Div) 27.024
Apex Frozen Foods Ltd (In Liquidation) v Ali [2007] EWHC 469 (Ch); (2007)
    L.T.L., April 11, Ch D 27.002
Apple Corp Ltd v Apple Computer Inc (1991) Law Society's Gazette, May 22 ... 30.020
Arab Monetary Fund v Hashim (No.8) (1994) 6 Admin. L.R. 348; The Times, May
    4, 1993; The Independent, April 30, 1993, CA (Civ Div); affirming [1989] 1
    W.L.R. 565; [1989] 3 All E.R. 466; (1989) 133 S.J. 749; The Times, January
    16, 1989, Ch D 30.018
Araghchinchi v Araghchinchi [1997] 2 F.L.R. 142; [1997] 3 F.C.R. 567; [1997] Fam.
    Law 656, CA (Civ Div) 27.017
Arbuthnot Leasing International Ltd v Havelet Leasing Ltd (No.1); sub nom. ALI
    Finance Ltd v Havelet Leasing Ltd [1992] 1 W.L.R. 455; [1991] 1 All E.R.
    591; [1990] B.C.C. 627; [1990] B.C.L.C. 802, Ch D 27.021
Arkin v Borchard Lines Ltd (Costs Order) [2005] EWCA Civ 655; [2005] 1 W.L.R.
    3055; [2005] 3 All E.R. 613; [2005] 2 Lloyd's Rep. 187; [2005] C.P. Rep. 39;
    [2005] 4 Costs L.R. 643; (2005) 155 N.L.J. 902; The Times, June 3, 2005;
    The Independent, June 7, 2005, CA (Civ Div) 33.013, 39.015
Armstrong v First York Ltd [2005] EWCA Civ 277; [2005] 1 W.L.R. 2751; [2005] C.P.
    Rep. 25; [2005] R.T.R. 19; The Times, January 19, 2005, CA (Civ Div) ... 23.001
Arnup v MW White Ltd [2007] EWHC 601 (QB); [2007] Pens. L.R. 135; (2007)
    L.T.L. April 16, Q.B.D. 4.018
Ash v Buxted Poultry Ltd, The Times, November 29, 1989, Q.B.D. 31.021
Ashmore v Corp of Lloyd's [1992] 1 W.L.R. 446; [1992] 2 All E.R. 486; [1992] 2
    Lloyd's Rep. 1; (1992) 136 S.J.L.B. 113; The Times, April 3, 1992; The
    Independent, April 3, 1992; The Financial Times, April 7, 1992, HL 37.009
Ashworth Hospital Authority v MGN Ltd; sub nom. Ashworth Security Hospital
    v MGN Ltd [2002] UKHL 29; [2002] 1 W.L.R. 2033; [2002] 4 All E.R. 193;
    [2002] C.P.L.R. 712; [2002] E.M.L.R. 36; [2002] H.R.L.R. 41; [2002]
    U.K.H.R.R. 1263; 12 B.H.R.C. 443; [2003] F.S.R. 17; (2002) 67 B.M.L.R.
    175; (2002) 99(30) L.S.G. 37; (2002) 146 S.J.L.B. 168; The Times, July 1,
    2002; The Independent, July 3, 2002, HL 30.025
Aspinall v Sterling Mansell [1981] 3 All E.R. 866, Q.B.D. 6.018
Assi v Dina Foods Ltd [2005] EWHC 1099; (2005) L.T.L. May, 20, Q.B.D. 14.007
Assicurazioni Generali SpA v Arab Insurance Group (BSC) [2002] EWCA Civ 1642;
    [2003] 1 W.L.R. 577; [2003] 1 All E.R. (Comm) 140; [2003] 2 C.L.C. 242;
    [2003] Lloyd's Rep. I.R. 131; (2003) 100(3) L.S.G. 34; The Times, November
    29, 2002, CA (Civ Div) 44.017
Astro Exito Navegacion SA v Southland Enterprise Co.; The Messiniaki Tolmi
    (No.2) [1983] 2 A.C. 787; [1983] 3 W.L.R. 130; [1983] 2 All E.R. 725; [1983]
    Com. L.R. 217; (1983) 80 L.S.G. 3083; (1983) 127 S.J. 461, HL 7.017

TABLE OF CASES

Atack v Lee; Ellerton v Harris [2004] EWCA Civ 1712; [2005] 1 W.L.R. 2643; [2005] 2 Costs L.R. 308; [2006] R.T.R. 11; [2005] P.I.Q.R. Q6; (2005) 155 N.L.J. 24; (2005) 149 S.J.L.B. 60; *The Times*, December 28, 2004, CA (Civ Div) 38.024, 39.026

Atlas Maritime Co. SA v Avalon Maritime Ltd; The Coral Rose (No.3) [1991] 1 W.L.R. 917; [1991] 4 All E.R. 783; [1991] 2 Lloyd's Rep. 374; (1991) 135 S.J.L.B. 59; *The Times*, June 24, 1991; *The Financial Times*, July 2, 1991, CA (Civ Div) 27.014, 27.019, 27.021

Atos Consulting Ltd v Avis Plc [2007] EWHC 323 (TCC), Q.B.D. (TCC) 30.015

Attorney General v BBC [2007] EWCA Civ 280; (2007) 104(13) L.S.G. 25; (2007) L.T.L., March 12, CA (Civ Div) 13.007

Attorney General of Zambia v Meer Care & Desai (A Firm); sub nom. Zambia v Meer Care & Desai (A Firm) [2006] EWCA Civ 390; [2006] 1 C.L.C. 436; (2006) L.T.L., March 7, CA (Civ Div) 33.005

Aujla v Sanghera [2004] EWCA Civ 121; [2004] C.P. Rep. 31; (2004) 148 S.J.L.B. 147; (2004) L.T.L., January 23, CA (Civ Div) 44.009

Austin-Fell v Austin-Fell [1990] Fam. 172; [1990] 3 W.L.R. 33; [1990] 2 All E.R. 455; [1989] 2 F.L.R. 497; [1990] F.C.R. 743; [1989] Fam. Law 437; (1989) 139 N.L.J. 1113, Fam Div 40.010

Avinue Ltd v Sunrule Ltd; sub nom. Sunrule Ltd v Avinue Ltd [2003] EWCA Civ 1942; [2004] 1 W.L.R. 634; [2004] C.P. Rep. 19; (2004) 101(2) L.S.G. 30; *The Times*, December 5, 2003, CA (Civ Div) 1.020, 20.009

B v B (Injunction: Restraint on Leaving Jurisdiction); sub nom. B v B (Passport Surrender: Jurisdiction) [1998] 1 W.L.R. 329; [1997] 3 All E.R. 258; [1997] 2 F.L.R. 148; [1997] 3 F.C.R. 262; [1997] Fam. Law 538; (1997) 94(14) L.S.G. 25; (1997) 141 S.J.L.B. 93; *The Times*, April 1, 1997, Fam Div 27.028

B v B (Passport Surrender: Jurisdiction). *See* B v B (Injunction: Restraint on Leaving Jurisdiction)

BBC Worldwide Ltd v Bee Load Ltd (t/a Archangel Ltd) [2007] EWHC 134, Q.B.D. (Comm) 19.001

BICC Plc v Burndy Corp [1985] Ch. 232; [1985] 2 W.L.R. 132; [1985] 1 All E.R. 417; [1985] R.P.C. 273; (1984) 81 L.S.G. 3011; (1984) 128 S.J. 750, CA (Civ Div) 12.037

BJ Crabtree (Insulation) v GPT Communications Systems, 59 B.L.R. 43, CA (Civ Div) 26.002

BRB v Franklin [1993] Law Society's Gazette, June 23 .... 4.003

BTC v Gourley. *See* British Transport Commission v Gourley

Babbings v Kirklees MBC [2004] EWCA Civ 1431; (2004) 101(45) L.S.G. 32; *The Times*, November 4, 2004, CA (Civ Div) 44.020

Baigent v Random House Group Ltd; sub nom. Lawyer, The [2006] EWHC 1131; (2006) 150 S.J.L.B. 603; *The Times*, May 24, 2006, Ch D 37.016

Bailey v Warren [2006] EWCA Civ 51; [2006] C.P. Rep. 26; [2006] W.T.L.R. 753; *The Times*, February 20, 2006, CA (Civ Div) 34.004

Baldock v Addison [1995] 1 W.L.R. 158; [1995] 3 All E.R. 437; [1994] F.S.R. 665; (1995) 92(3) L.S.G. 38; *The Times*, July 7, 1994, Ch D 30.016

Banham Marshalls Services Unlimited v Lincolnshire CC [2007] EWHC 402, Q.B.D. 3.006

Bank fur Gemeinwirtschaft AG v City of London Garages Ltd [1971] 1 W.L.R. 149; [1971] 1 All E.R. 541; (1970) 114 S.J. 970, CA (Civ Div) 19.007

xxxv

TABLE OF CASES

Bank Mellat v Kazmi [1989] Q.B. 541; [1989] 2 W.L.R. 613; [1989] 1 All E.R. 925; (1989) 133 S.J. 185, CA (Civ Div) 27.020
Bank of Ireland Home Mortgages Ltd v Bissett (1999) C.L. 409, CC (Northampton) 24.006
Bank of Ireland v Robertson (2003) L.T.L., February 21, Ch D 44.017
Bansal v Cheema [2001] C.P. Rep. 6; (2001) L.T.L., September 13, CA (Civ Div) ... 33.011
Barclays Bank Plc v Ellis [2001] C.P. Rep. 50; *The Times*, October 24, 2000, CA (Civ Div) 37.007
Barclays Bank Plc v O'Brien [1994] 1 A.C. 180; [1993] 3 W.L.R. 786; [1993] 4 All E.R. 417; [1994] 1 F.L.R. 1; [1994] 1 F.C.R. 357; (1994) 26 H.L.R. 75; (1994) 13 Tr. L.R. 165; [1994] C.C.L.R. 94; [1994] Fam. Law 78; [1993] E.G. 169 (C.S.); (1993) 143 N.L.J. 1511; (1993) 137 S.J.L.B. 240; [1993] N.P.C. 135; *The Times*, October 22, 1993; *The Independent*, October 22, 1993, HL ... 14.008
Barings Plc, Re. *See* Secretary of State for Trade and Industry v Baker (No.2)
Barnes v St Helens MBC; sub nom. St Helens MBC v Barnes [2006] EWCA Civ 1372; [2007] 1 W.L.R. 879; [2007] C.P. Rep. 7; [2007] P.I.Q.R. P10; *The Times*, November 17, 2006; *The Independent*, October 27, 2006, CA (Civ Div) 5.001, 9.005
Barnet LBC v Hurst [2002] EWCA Civ 1009; [2003] 1 W.L.R. 722; [2002] 4 All E.R. 457; [2002] C.P. Rep. 74; [2003] H.L.R. 19; (2002) 99(36) L.S.G. 39; (2002) 152 N.L.J. 1275; (2002) 146 S.J.L.B. 198; [2002] N.P.C. 99; *The Times*, August 12, 2002, CA (Civ Div) 44.001
Baron v Lovell [1999] C.P.L.R. 630; [2000] P.I.Q.R. P20; *The Times*, September 14, 1999, CA (Civ Div) 14.007, 23.008, 36.002
Barry v Ablerex Construction (Midlands) Ltd [2001] EWCA Civ 433; (2001) 98(22) L.S.G. 35, CA (Civ Div); reversing [2000] P.I.Q.R. Q263; *The Times*, March 30, 2000, Q.B.D. 4.020
Bates v Microstar Ltd (2000) L.T.L., July 4, CA (Civ Div) 19.005
Bath and North East Somerset DC v Mowlem Plc [2004] EWCA Civ 115; [2004] B.L.R. 153; 100 Con. L.R. 1; (2004) 148 S.J.L.B. 265, CA (Civ Div) 27.005
Bayer AG v Harris Pharmaceuticals Ltd [1991] F.S.R. 170, Ch D 30.011
Bayer AG v Winter (No.1) [1986] 1 W.L.R. 497; [1986] 1 All E.R. 733; [1986] F.S.R. 323; (1986) 83 L.S.G. 974; (1985) 136 N.L.J. 187; (1985) 130 S.J. 246, CA (Civ Div) 27.028
Beahan v Stoneham (2001) L.T.L., May 16 .... 3.002
Beaverbrook Newspapers Ltd v Keys [1978] I.C.R. 582; [1978] I.R.L.R. 34, CA (Civ Div) 27.005
Beck v Ministry of Defence [2003] EWCA Civ 1043; [2005] 1 W.L.R. 2206; [2003] C.P. Rep. 62; [2004] P.I.Q.R. P1; (2003) 100(31) L.S.G. 31; *The Times*, July 21, 2003, CA (Civ Div) 23.008
Belgolaise SA v Rupchandani; sub nom. Belgolaise SA v Purchandani [1999] Lloyd's Rep. Bank. 116; (1998) 95(37) L.S.G. 36; (1998) 142 S.J.L.B. 252; *The Times*, July 30, 1998, Q.B.D. (Comm) 27.028
Bell v Tuohy; sub nom. Tuohy v Bell [2002] EWCA Civ 423; [2002] 1 W.L.R. 2703; [2002] 3 All E.R. 975; [2002] C.P. Rep. 46; [2003] B.P.I.R. 749; (2002) 152 N.L.J. 587; (2002) 146 S.J.L.B. 109; [2002] N.P.C. 50; *The Independent*, May 27, 2002, CA 41.001, 41.003
Bell Electric Ltd v Aweco Appliance Systems GmbH & Co. KG (Application to Stay Appeal) [2002] EWCA Civ 1501; [2003] 1 All E.R. 344; [2003] C.P. Rep. 18; *The Times*, November 20, 2002, CA (Civ Div) 44.016

Benham Ltd v Kythira Investments Ltd; sub nom. Benhams Investments Ltd (t/a Benham & Reeves) v Kythira Investments Ltd [2003] EWCA Civ 1794; [2004] C.P. Rep. 17; (2004) 154 N.L.J. 21, CA (Civ Div) 19.005, 31.004, 37.005
Bentley v Jones Harris & Co. [2001] EWCA Civ 1724; (2001) L.T.L., November 2, CA (Civ Div) 33.001
Bermuda International Securities Ltd v KPMG [2001] EWCA Civ 269; [2001] C.P. Rep. 73; [2001] C.P.L.R. 252; [2001] Lloyd's Rep. P.N. 392; (2001) 98(15) L.S.G. 33; (2001) 145 S.J.L.B. 70; *The Times*, March 14, 2001, CA (Civ Div) 30.024
Best v Charter Medical of England Ltd [2001] EWCA Civ 1588; [2002] E.M.L.R. 18; (2001) 98(47) L.S.G. 27; *The Times*, November 19, 2001, CA (Civ Div) ... 32.004
Bhamjee v Forsdick [2003] EWCA Civ 1113; [2004] 1 W.L.R. 88; [2003] C.P. Rep. 67; [2003] B.P.I.R. 1252; (2003) 100(36) L.S.G. 41; *The Times*, July 31, 2003; *The Independent*, July 29, 2003, CA (Civ Div) 7.011
Biguzzi v Rank Leisure Plc [1999] 1 W.L.R. 1926; [1999] 4 All E.R. 934; [2000] C.P. Rep. 6; [1999] C.P.L.R. 675; [2000] 1 Costs L.R. 67; *The Times*, October 5, 1999; *The Independent*, October 13, 1999, CA (Civ Div) ... 1.016, 33.008, 33.011
Binks v Securicor Omega Express Ltd [2003] EWCA Civ 993; [2003] 1 W.L.R. 2557; [2004] C.P. Rep. 4; [2004] P.I.Q.R. P13; (2003) 147 S.J.L.B. 991; *The Times*, August 27, 2003, CA (Civ Div) 12.030
Birchall, Re; sub nom. Wilson v Birchall (1880–81) L.R. 16 Ch. D. 41, CA 7.005
Birkett v Hayes [1982] 1 W.L.R. 816; [1982] 2 All E.R. 70; (1982) 126 S.J. 399, CA (Civ Div) 4.020
Birkett v James [1978] A.C. 297; [1977] 3 W.L.R. 38; [1977] 2 All E.R. 801; (1977) 121 S.J. 444, HL 45.001
Black v Davies [2005] EWCA Civ 531, CA (Civ Div) 3.002
Black v Pastouna; sub nom. Pastouna v Black [2005] EWCA Civ 1389; [2006] C.P. Rep. 11; (2005) 155 N.L.J. 1847; *The Independent*, December 2, 2005, CA (Civ Div) 13.007, 44.016
Black v Sumitomo Corp [2001] EWCA Civ 1819; [2002] 1 W.L.R. 1562; [2003] 3 All E.R. 643; [2002] 1 Lloyd's Rep. 693; [2002] C.P.L.R. 148; *The Times*, January 25, 2002; *The Independent*, December 13, 2001, CA (Civ Div) 30.024
Black & Decker Inc v Flymo Ltd [1991] 1 W.L.R. 753; [1991] 3 All E.R. 158; [1991] F.S.R. 93; *The Times*, November 21, 1990, Ch D 30.018
Blackham v Entrepose UK [2004] EWCA Civ 1109; [2005] C.P. Rep. 7; [2005] 1 Costs L.R. 68; (2004) 101(35) L.S.G. 33; (2004) 148 S.J.L.B. 945; *The Times*, September 28, 2004, CA (Civ Div) 29.022
Blenheim Leisure (Restaurants) Ltd (No.1), Re [2000] B.C.C. 554; (1999) 96(33) L.S.G. 29; [1999] N.P.C. 105; *The Times*, August 13, 1999; *The Independent*, November 8, 1999, CA (Civ Div) 7.014
Bloomsbury Publishing Group Plc v News Group Newspapers Ltd (Continuation of Injunction); sub nom. Bloomsbury Publishing Group Ltd v Newsgroup Newspapers Ltd (Continuation of Injunction) [2003] EWHC 1205; [2003] 1 W.L.R. 1633; [2003] 3 All E.R. 736; [2003] C.P. Rep. 55; [2003] F.S.R. 45; (2003) 100(29) L.S.G. 35; (2003) 153 N.L.J. 882; *The Times*, June 5, 2003, Ch D 7.023, 8.014
Blundell v Rimmer [1971] 1 W.L.R. 123; [1971] 1 All E.R. 1072; [1971] 1 Lloyd's Rep. 110; (1970) 115 S.J. 15; *The Times*, December 4, 1970, Q.B.D. 16.001
Board v Thomas Hedley & Co. [1951] 2 All E.R. 431; [1951] 2 T.L.R. 779; [1951] W.N. 422; (1951) 95 S.J. 546, CA 30.003
Bolton Metropolitan District Council v Secretary of State for the Environment [1995] 1 W.L.R. 1176 .... 45.007

Bolton Pharmaceutical Co. 100 Ltd v Doncaster Pharmaceuticals Group Ltd; sub
nom. Doncaster Pharmaceuticals Group Ltd v Bolton Pharmaceutical Co.
100 Ltd; Bolton Pharmaceutical Co. 100 Ltd v Swinghope Ltd [2006]
EWCA Civ 661; [2006] E.T.M.R. 65; [2007] F.S.R. 3; (2006) L.T.L., May 26,
CA (Civ Div) 19.005
Boot v Boot [1996] 2 F.C.R. 713; (1997) 73 P. & C.R. 137; [1996] C.C.L.R. 68;
(1996) 72 P. & C.R. D30; *The Times,* May 9, 1996, CA (Civ Div) 5.004
Booth v Britannia Hotels Ltd [2002] EWCA Civ 579; [2003] 1 Costs L.R. 43, CA
(Civ Div) 9.035, 38.018
Boss Group Ltd v Boss France SA [1997] 1 W.L.R. 351; [1996] 4 All E.R. 970;
[1996] L.R.L.R. 403; [1996] C.L.C. 1419; [1996] I.L.Pr. 544; (1996) 146
N.L.J. 918; *The Times,* April 15, 1996, CA (Civ Div) 11.004, 11.017
Bovey's Case (1684) Vent 217 .... 12.031
Bovis Lend Lease Ltd (formerly Bovis Construction Ltd) v Braehead Glasgow Ltd
(formerly Braehead Park Retail Ltd) 71 Con. L.R. 208, Q.B.D. (TCC) 25.005
Boxhall v Waltham Forest LBC (2001) L.T.L., January 5 .... 24.003
Bracknell Forest BC v N, *The Times,* November 6, 2006, CA (Civ Div) 44.016
Bradburn v Great Western Railway Co. (1874–75) L.R. 10 Ex. 1; [1874–80] All
E.R. 195, Ex Ct 4.005
Bradford & Bingley Plc v Rashid [2006] UKHL 37; [2006] 1 W.L.R. 2066; [2006] 4
All E.R. 705; [2006] 2 All E.R. (Comm) 951; [2006] 29 E.G. 132 (C.S.);
(2006) 103(30) L.S.G. 30; (2006) 156 N.L.J. 1172; (2006) 150 S.J.L.B. 983;
The Times, July 14, 2006, HL 5.014, 6.024
Brayson v Wilmot-Breedon, unreported, November 1, 1976, Crown Ct
(Birmingham) 4.002
Breeze v Ahmad [2005] EWCA Civ 223; [2005] C.P. Rep. 29; (2005) L.T.L., March 8,
CA (Civ Div) 44.017
Breeze (Disclosure) v John Stacey & Sons Ltd; sub nom. Breeze v John Stacy &
Sons Ltd [2000] C.P. Rep. 77; (1999) 96(28) L.S.G. 27; *The Times,* July 8,
1999; *The Independent,* July 19, 1999, CA (Civ Div) 30.019
Bridgeman v McAlpine-Brown (2000) L.T.L., January 19 .... 33.008
Bristol & West Building Society v Marks & Spencer Plc [1991] 2 E.G.L.R. 57;
[1991] 41 E.G. 139 .... 27.004
Bristol & West Plc v Bartlett; Paragon Finance Plc v Banks; Halifax Plc v Grant
[2002] EWCA Civ 1181; [2003] 1 W.L.R. 284; [2002] 4 All E.R. 544; [2002]
2 All E.R. (Comm) 1105; [2003] H.L.R. 22; [2003] 1 E.G.L.R. 85; [2003] 01
E.G. 69; [2002] 33 E.G. 97 (C.S.); (2002) 99(38) L.S.G. 34; [2002] N.P.C. 109;
The Times, September 9, 2002; *The Independent,* October 9, 2002, CA (Civ
Div) 5.010
Bristol & West Building Society v Ellis (1997) 29 H.L.R. 282; [1996] 1 All E.R. 21;
(1997) 73 P. & C.R. 158; [1996] E.G. 74 (C.S.); [1996] N.P.C. 63; (1996) 72
P. & C.R. D41; *The Times,* May 2, 1996, CA (Civ Div) 24.006
Bristol City Council v Hassan; Bristol City Council v Glastonbury [2006] EWCA
Civ 656; [2006] 1 W.L.R. 2582; [2006] 4 All E.R. 420; [2006] C.P. Rep. 37;
[2006] H.L.R. 31; [2006] L. & T.R. 17; [2006] 22 E.G. 176 (C.S.); (2006)
103(23) L.S.G. 33; [2006] N.P.C. 61; [2006] 2 P. & C.R. DG20; *The Times,*
July 17, 2006, CA (Civ Div) 24.005
British & Commonwealth Holdings Plc v Quadrex Holdings Inc (No.1) [1989] Q.B.
842; [1989] 3 W.L.R. 723; [1989] 3 All E.R. 492; (1989) 86(23) L.S.G. 42;
(1989) 133 S.J. 694; *The Times,* March 13, 1989; *The Independent,* March 7,
1989; *The Independent,* February 27, 1989, CA (Civ Div) 25.001, 25.005

British Broadcasting Corp v Her Majesty's Attorney General. *See* Attorney General v BBC
British Transport Commission v Gourley [1956] A.C. 185; [1956] 2 W.L.R. 41; [1955] 3 All E.R. 796; [1955] 2 Lloyd's Rep. 475; 49 R. & I.T. 11; (1955) 34 A.T.C. 305; [1955] T.R. 303; (1956) 100 S.J. 12, HL 4.002
Brown v Bennett (Exchange of Skeleton Arguments), *The Times,* June 13, 2000, Ch D 36.007
Brown v Bennett (Witness Summons), *The Times,* November 2, 2000, Ch D 36.003
Brown v KMR Services Ltd (formerly HG Poland (Agencies) Ltd); Sword Daniels v Pitel [1995] 4 All E.R. 598; [1995] 2 Lloyd's Rep. 513; [1995] C.L.C. 1418; [1995] 4 Re. L.R. 241; *The Times,* July 26, 1995; *The Independent,* September 13, 1995; Lloyd's List, October 3, 1995, CA (Civ Div) 3.002
Buchanan-Michaelson v Rubinstein [1965] 1 W.L.R. 390; [1965] 1 All E.R. 599; (1965) 109 S.J. 111, CA 30.016
Buckland v Palmer [1984] 1 W.L.R. 1109; [1984] 3 All E.R. 554; [1985] R.T.R. 5; (1984) 81 L.S.G. 2300; (1984) 128 S.J. 565, CA (Civ Div) 6.027
Buckland v Watts [1970] 1 Q.B. 27; [1969] 3 W.L.R. 92; [1969] 2 All E.R. 985; (1969) 113 S.J. 384; *The Times,* July 2, 1969, CA (Civ Div) 38.003, 38.006
Burchell v Bullard [2005] EWCA Civ 358 (2005); L.T.L., April 8 .... 18.011, 34.002, 38.008, 38.018
Burns v Shuttlehurst Ltd; sub nom. Burns v General Accident Fire and Life Assurance Corp Plc [1999] 1 W.L.R. 1449; [1999] 2 All E.R. 27; [1999] P.I.Q.R. P229; (1999) 96(6) L.S.G. 35; *The Times,* January 12, 1999, CA (Civ Div) .. 30.024
Burrows v Vauxhall Motors Ltd [1998] P.I.Q.R. P48 .... 39.002
Burton v Kingsley [2005] EWHC 1034; [2006] P.I.Q.R. P2, Q.B.D. 38.026
Busch v Stevens [1963] 1 Q.B. 1; [1962] 2 W.L.R. 511; [1962] 1 All E.R. 412; (1962) 106 S.J. 153, Q.B.D. 12.031
Butterworth v Kingsway Motors Ltd [1954] 1 W.L.R. 1286; [1954] 2 All E.R. 694; (1954) 98 S.J. 717, Assizes (Liverpool) 18.006

C v Mirror Group Newspapers; sub nom. Clare v Mirror Group Newspapers (1986) Ltd [1997] 1 W.L.R. 131; [1996] 4 All E.R. 511; [1996] E.M.L.R. 518; [1996] 2 F.L.R. 532; [1997] 1 F.C.R. 556; [1996] Fam. Law 671; (1996) 146 N.L.J. 1093; *The Times,* July 15, 1996; *The Independent,* July 19, 1996, CA (Civ Div) 5.016
CBS United Kingdom Ltd v Lambert [1983] Ch. 37; [1982] 3 W.L.R. 746; [1982] 3 All E.R. 237; [1983] F.S.R. 127; (1983) 80 L.S.G. 36; (1982) 126 S.J. 691, CA (Civ Div) 27.024
CEL Group Ltd v Nedlloyd Lines UK Ltd [2003] EWCA Civ 1716; [2004] 1 All E.R. (Comm) 689; [2004] 1 Lloyd's Rep. 381; (2003) 147 S.J.L.B. 1399; *The Independent,* December 5, 2003, CA (Civ Div) 29.023
C Inc Plc v L [2001] 2 All E.R. (Comm) 446; [2001] 2 Lloyd's Rep. 459; [2001] C.L.C. 1054; (2001) 151 N.L.J. 535; *The Times,* May 4, 2001, Q.B.D. (Comm) 27.017
C Plc v P; sub nom. W v P [2007] EWCA Civ 493; (2007) L.T.L., May 23; *The Times,* May 28, 2007, CA (Civ Div) 27.027
C Shippam Ltd v Princes-Buitoni Ltd [1983] F.S.R. 427; (1983) C.L.Y. 3027, Ch D 30.016
Calderbank v Calderbank [1976] Fam. 93; [1975] 3 W.L.R. 586; [1975] 3 All E.R. 333; (1975) 5 Fam. Law 190; (1975) 119 S.J. 490, CA (Civ Div) 29.002

TABLE OF CASES

Calenti v North Middlesex NHS Trust (2001) L.T.L., April 10 .... 23.008
Callery v Gray (No.1); sub nom. Callery v Gray (No.2); Callery v Gray (Nos.1 and
    2); Russell v Pal Pak Corrugated Ltd (No.1) [2002] UKHL 28; [2002] 1
    W.L.R. 2000; [2002] 3 All E.R. 417; [2002] 2 Costs L.R. 205; [2003] R.T.R.
    4; [2003] Lloyd's Rep. I.R. 203; [2002] P.I.Q.R. P32; (2002) 152 N.L.J. 1031;
    The Times, July 2, 2002; *The Independent,* July 2, 2002; *The Daily
    Telegraph,* July 11, 2002, HL 38.026, 45.001
Callery v Gray (No.2); Russell v Pal Pak Corrugated Ltd (No.2) [2001] EWCA Civ
    1246; [2001] 1 W.L.R. 2142; [2001] 4 All E.R. 1; [2001] C.P.L.R. 501; [2001]
    2 Costs L.R. 205; [2002] R.T.R. 11; [2001] Lloyd's Rep. I.R. 765; (2001)
    98(35) L.S.G. 33; (2001) 145 S.J.L.B. 204; *The Times,* October 24, 2001, CA
    (Civ Div) 38.030
Cambridge Nutrition Ltd v BBC [1990] 3 All E.R. 523; *The Times,* December 5,
    1987, CA (Civ Div) 27.001
Camdex International Ltd v Bank of Zambia (No.2) [1997] 1 W.L.R. 632;
    [1997] 1 All E.R. 728; [1996] 5 Bank. L.R. 336; [1996] C.L.C. 1945, CA
    (Civ Div) 27.016
Campbell v Mylchreest [1998] EWCA Civ 60; [1999] P.I.Q.R. Q17; (1998) L.T.L.,
    January 26, CA (Civ Div) 25.001, 25.004,
                                                                      25.009
Campbell v Thompson [1953] 1 Q.B. 445; [1953] 2 W.L.R. 656; [1953] 1 All E.R.
    831; (1953) 97 S.J. 229, Q.B.D. 7.018
Canada Trust Co. v Stolzenberg (No.2) [2002] 1 A.C. 1; [2000] 3 W.L.R. 1376, HL;
    affirming [1998] 1 W.L.R. 547; [1998] 1 All E.R. 318; [1998] C.L.C. 23;
    [1998] I.L.Pr. 290; *The Times,* November 10, 1997, CA (Civ Div) 27.028
Capital Trust Investments Ltd v Radio Design TJ AB; sub nom. Capital Trusts
    Investments Ltd v Radio Design TJ AB [2002] EWCA Civ 135; [2002] 2
    All E.R. 159; [2002] 1 All E.R. (Comm) 514; [2002] C.L.C. 787; *The
    Independent,* February 21, 2002, CA (Civ Div) 33.004
Carlson v Townsend [2001] EWCA Civ 511; [2001] 1 W.L.R. 2415; [2001] 3 All E.R.
    663; [2001] C.P. Rep. 86; [2001] C.P.L.R. 405; [2001] P.I.Q.R. P24; (2001) 62
    B.M.L.R. 50; *The Daily Telegraph,* April 24, 2001, CA (Civ Div) 23.002
Carnduff v Inspector Rook (2001) L.T.L. May 11 .... 30.010
Carnegie v Giessen [2005] EWCA Civ 191; [2005] 1 W.L.R. 2510; [2005] C.P. Rep.
    24; [2005] 1 C.L.C. 259; (2005) 102(18) L.S.G. 23; *The Times,* March 14,
    2005; *The Independent,* March 18, 2005, CA (Civ Div) 40.010
Carruthers v MP Fireworks Ltd (2007) L.T.L., February 6, CC (Bristol) 23.008
Carter Commercial Developments v Bedford BC [2001] EWHC Admin 669; [2001]
    34 E.G. 99 (C.S.), Q.B.D. (Admin) 33.008
Cases of Taffs Well Ltd, Re [1992] Ch. 179; [1991] 3 W.L.R. 731; [1991] B.C.C.
    582; [1992] B.C.L.C. 11, Ch D (Companies Ct) 5.013
Casey v Cartwright [2006] EWCA Civ 1280; [2007] 2 All E.R. 78; [2007] C.P. Rep.
    3; [2007] R.T.R. 18; [2007] P.I.Q.R. P6; (2006) 103(40) L.S.G. 34; (2006) 150
    S.J.L.B. 1331; *The Times,* October 10, 2006; *The Independent,* October 11,
    2006, CA (Civ Div) 23.022
Castanho v Brown & Root (UK) Ltd [1981] A.C. 557; [1980] 3 W.L.R. 991, HL;
    affirming [1980] 1 W.L.R. 833; [1980] 3 All E.R. 72; [1980] 2 Lloyd's Rep.
    423; (1980) 124 S.J. 375, CA (Civ Div) 35.005
Catlin v Cyprus Finance Corp (London) Ltd [1983] Q.B. 759; [1983] 2 W.L.R. 566;
    [1983] 1 All E.R. 809; (1983) 80 L.S.G. 153; (1982) 126 S.J. 744; *The Times,*
    October 27, 1982, Q.B.D. 7.013

Cave v Robinson Jarvis & Rolf; sub nom. Robinson Jarvis & Rolf v Cave; Cave v
Robinson Jarvis & Rolfe [2002] UKHL 18; [2003] 1 A.C. 384; [2002] 2
W.L.R. 1107; [2002] 2 All E.R. 641; [2003] 1 C.L.C. 101; 81 Con. L.R. 25;
[2002] P.N.L.R. 25; [2002] 19 E.G. 146 (C.S.); (2002) 99(20) L.S.G. 32; (2002)
152 N.L.J. 671; (2002) 146 S.J.L.B. 109; *The Times,* May 7, 2002; *The
Independent,* April 30, 2002, HL 5.015
Cayne v Global Natural Resources Plc [1984] 1 All E.R. 225, CA (Civ Div) 27.005
Cebora SNC v SIP (Industrial Products) [1976] 1 Lloyd's Rep. 271, CA (Civ Div) .. 18.009
Ceredigion CC v Jones; sub nom. R. (on the application of Jones) v Ceredigion
CC (No.2); R. (on the application of Jones) v Ceredigion CC [2007] UKHL
24; (2007) 104(23) L.S.G. 32; (2007) 157 N.L.J. 778; (2007) 151 S.J.L.B. 706;
[2007] 1 W.L.R. 1400; *The Times,* May 24, 2007, HL 44.003
Chan U Seek v Alvis Vehicles Ltd; sub nom. Guardian Newspapers Ltd (Court
Record: Disclosure), Re [2004] EWHC 3092; [2005] 1 W.L.R. 2965; [2005] 3
All E.R. 155; [2005] E.M.L.R. 19; *The Times,* December 14, 2004, Ch D ... 1.022
Chantrey Vellacott v Convergence Group Plc; sub nom. Convergence Group Plc v
Chantrey Vellacott (A Firm) [2005] EWCA Civ 290; *The Times,* April 25,
2005, CA (Civ Div) 44.007
Chapple v Williams [1999] C.P.L.R. 731; (1999) L.T.L. December 8, CA (Civ
Div) 33.007, 33.011
Charles v NTL Group Ltd [2002] EWCA Civ 2004; [2003] C.P. Rep. 44; *The
Independent,* February 10, 2003, CA (Civ Div) 29.024
Charles Church Developments Ltd v Stent Foundations Ltd [2006] EWHC 3158
(TCC); [2007] 1 W.L.R. 1203; [2007] B.L.R. 81; [2007] T.C.L.R. 2; [2007]
C.I.L.L. 2408; *The Times,* January 4, 2007, Q.B.D. (TCC) 12.053
Cheltenham & Gloucester Building Society v Norgan [1996] 1 W.L.R. 343; [1996]
1 All E.R. 449; [1996] 2 F.L.R. 257; [1996] 3 F.C.R. 621; (1996) 28 H.L.R.
443; (1996) 72 P. & C.R. 46; [1996] Fam. Law 610; [1995] E.G. 198 (C.S.);
(1996) 93(2) L.S.G. 29; (1995) 145 N.L.J. 1849; (1996) 140 S.J.L.B. 11; [1995]
N.P.C. 192; (1996) 71 P. & C.R. D25; *The Times,* December 8, 1995; *The
Independent,* December 14, 1995, CA (Civ Div) 24.006
Cheltenham & Gloucester Plc v Krausz [1997] 1 W.L.R. 1558; [1997] 1 All E.R. 21;
(1997) 29 H.L.R. 597; (1996) 93(43) L.S.G. 26; (1996) 146 N.L.J. 1813;
(1996) 140 S.J.L.B. 260; [1996] N.P.C. 144; (1997) 73 P. & C.R. D16; *The
Times,* November 20, 1996, CA (Civ Div) 24.006
Cherney v Deripaska [2007] EWHC 965 (Comm); (2007) L.T.L., May 10, Q.B.D.
(Comm) 8.009
Childs v Vernon [2007] EWCA Civ 305; (2007) L.T.L, March 16, CA (Civ Div) ... 23.006
Choudhury v Hussain (1989) 139 N.L.J. 1416; *The Times,* October 10, 1989, CA
(Civ Div) 7.018
Church of Scientology of California v Department of Health and Social
Security [1979] 1 W.L.R. 723; [1979] 3 All E.R. 97; (1979) 123 S.J. 304, CA
(Civ Div) 30.018
Cie Financiére et Commerciale du Pacifique v Peruvian Guano Co. (1882–83) L.R.
11 Q.B.D. 55, CA 30.007
Citro (Domenico) (A Bankrupt), Re; Citro (Carmine) (A Bankrupt), Re [1991] Ch.
142; [1990] 3 W.L.R. 880; [1990] 3 All E.R. 952; [1991] 1 F.L.R. 71; [1990] E.G.
78 (C.S.); (1990) 154 N.L.J. 1073; (1990) 134 S.J. 806, CA (Civ Div) 40.010
Claims Direct Test Cases, Re [2003] EWCA Civ 136; [2003] 4 All E.R. 508; [2003]
2 All E.R. (Comm) 788; [2003] 2 Costs L.R. 254; [2003] Lloyd's Rep. I.R.
677; [2003] P.I.Q.R. P31; (2003) 100(13) L.S.G. 26; (2003) 147 S.J.L.B. 236;
The Times, February 18, 2003, CA (Civ Div) 38.030

Clark v Ardington Electrical Services (Appeal against Order for Disclosure) [2001]
EWCA Civ 585; (2001) L.T.L. April 4, CA (Civ Div) 30.023
Clark v University of Lincolnshire and Humberside [2000] 1 W.L.R. 1988; [2000]
3 All E.R. 752; [2000] Ed. C.R. 553; [2000] E.L.R. 345; [2000] C.O.D. 293;
(2000) 150 N.L.J. 616; (2000) 144 S.J.L.B. 220; *The Times*, May 3, 2000; *The
Independent*, May 3, 2000, CA (Civ Div) 24.001
Clark (Inspector of Taxes) v Perks (Permission to Appeal); sub nom. Perks
(Inspector of Taxes) v Clark; Perks (Inspector of Taxes) v Macleod; Guild
v Newrick; McNicholas Construction Co. Ltd v Customs and Excise
Commissioners; Jenkins v BP Oil UK Ltd [2001] 1 W.L.R. 17; [2000] 4 All
E.R. 1; [2000] S.T.C. 1080; [2000] B.T.C. 282; [2000] B.V.C. 365; [2000]
S.T.I. 1676; (2000) 150 N.L.J. 1376, CA (Civ Div) 44.001, 44.003, 44.008
Clarke v Marlborough Fine Art (London) Ltd (Amendments) [2002] 1 W.L.R.
1731; [2002] C.P. Rep. 17; (2002) 99(3) L.S.G. 26; (2001) 145 S.J.L.B. 278;
The Times, December 4, 2001, Ch D 12.004, 12.030
Clarkson v Gilbert (Rights of Audience) [2000] C.P. Rep. 58; [2000] 2 F.L.R. 839;
[2000] 3 F.C.R. 10; [2000] Fam. Law 808; *The Times*, July 4, 2000; *The
Independent*, July 17, 2000, CA (Civ Div) 1.021
Clayhope Properties Ltd v Evans [1986] 1 W.L.R. 1223; [1986] 2 All E.R. 795;
(1986) 18 H.L.R. 361; (1986) 52 P. & C.R. 149; [1986] 2 E.G.L.R. 34; (1986)
279 E.G. 855; (1986) 83 L.S.G. 2001; (1986) 130 S.J. 483, CA (Civ Div) ...27.030
Claymore Services Ltd v Nautilus Properties Ltd [2007] EWHC 805 (TCC), Q.B.D.
(TCC) 3.002
Clenshaw v Tanner [2002] EWHC 1848; (2002) L.T.L. September 24, CA (Civ Div) ...4.005
Cleveland Bridge UK Ltd v Multiplex Constructions (UK) Ltd [2005] EWHC
2101; (2005) L.T.L., October 24, Q.B.D. (TCC) 1.022
Coad v Cornwall and Isles of Scilly HA [1997] 1 W.L.R. 189; [1997] P.I.Q.R. P92;
[1997] 8 Med. L.R. 154; (1997) 33 B.M.L.R. 168; (1996) 93(27) L.S.G. 28;
(1996) 140 S.J.L.B. 168; *The Times*, July 30, 1996, CA (Civ Div) 5.018
Coal Mining Contractors v Davies; sub nom. Davies v Department of Trade and
Industry [2006] EWCA Civ 1360; [2007] 1 All E.R. 518; (2006) 150 S.J.L.B.
1428; [2007] P.I.Q.R. P13, CA (Civ Div) 7.014
Coca-Cola Co. v Gilbey; Schweppes Ltd v Gilbey [1995] 4 All E.R. 711; (1995) 145
N.L.J. 1688; *The Times*, November 28, 1995; *The Independent*, October 10,
1995, Ch D 27.027
Coca-Cola Financial Corp v Finsat International Ltd; The Ira [1998] Q.B. 43;
[1996] 3 W.L.R. 849; [1996] 2 Lloyd's Rep. 274; [1996] 2 B.C.L.C. 626;
[1996] C.L.C. 1564; *The Times*, May 1, 1996; Lloyd's List, June 5, 1996, CA
(Civ Div) 12.037
Cole v British Telecommunications Plc [2000] EWCA Civ 208; [2000] 2 Costs L.R.
310; *The Independent*, October 2, 2000, CA (Civ Div) 38.020
Coll v Tattum (2002) 99(3) L.S.G. 26; *The Times*, December 3, 2001, Ch D 15.003
Colledge v Bass Mitchells & Butlers Ltd [1988] 1 All E.R. 536; [1988] I.C.R. 125;
[1988] I.R.L.R. 63, CA (Civ Div) 4.005
Collier v Williams; Marshall v Maggs; Leeson v Marsden; Glass v Surrendran
[2006] EWCA Civ 20; [2006] 1 W.L.R. 1945; [2007] 1 All E.R. 991; [2006]
C.P. Rep. 22; [2006] P.I.Q.R. P18; (2006) 103(7) L.S.G. 23; (2006) 150 S.J.L.B.
128; *The Times*, February 3, 2006, CA (Civ Div) 8.001, 8.009, 9.006,
13.004, 13.005, 43.005
Color Drack GmbH v Lexx International Vertriebs GmbH (Case C-386/05),
[2007] W.L.R. (D) 117; [2007] All E.R. (D) 51 (May), ECJ 11.007

TABLE OF CASES

Columbia Pictures Industries v Robinson [1987] Ch. 38; [1986] 3 W.L.R. 542; [1986] 3 All E.R. 338; [1986] F.S.R. 367; (1986) 83 L.S.G. 3424; (1986) 130 S.J. 766, Ch D 27.014
Commissioners of Customs & Excise v Barclays Bank Plc. *See* Customs and Excise Commissioners v Barclays Bank Plc
Compagnie Noga d'Importation et d'Exportation SA v Abacha (No.5); Compagnie Noga d'Importation et d'Exportation SA v Australia and New Zealand Banking Group; Compagnie Noga d'Importation et d'Exportation SA v Ani [2004] EWHC 2601, Q.B.D. (Comm) 26.004
Company (No.008790 of 1990), Re [1992] B.C.C. 11; [1991] B.C.L.C. 561, Ch D . . 42.003
Company (No.012209 of 1991), Re [1992] 1 W.L.R. 351; [1992] 2 All E.R. 797, Ch D 42.006, 42.007
Company (No.006798 of 1995), Re [1996] 1 W.L.R. 491; [1996] 2 All E.R. 417; [1996] B.C.C. 395; [1996] 2 B.C.L.C. 48; 49 Con. L.R. 39, Ch D 42.007
Connaught Restaurants Ltd v Indoor Leisure Ltd [1994] 1 W.L.R. 501; [1994] 4 All E.R. 834; [1993] 46 E.G. 184; [1993] E.G. 143 (C.S.); (1993) 143 N.L.J. 1188; [1993] N.P.C. 118; *The Times*, July 27, 1993, CA (Civ Div) 12.037
Connelly v RTZ Corp Plc (No.2) [1998] A.C. 854; [1997] 3 W.L.R. 373; [1997] 4 All E.R. 335; [1997] C.L.C. 1357; [1997] I.L.Pr. 805; [1998] Env. L.R. 318; (1997) 94(32) L.S.G. 28; (1997) 147 N.L.J. 1346; (1997) 141 S.J.L.B. 199; *The Times*, August 4, 1997, HL 11.015
Contract Facilities Ltd v Rees Estate (Application to Strike Out) [2003] EWCA Civ 1105; (2003) 147 S.J.L.B. 933; (2003) L.T.L., July 24, CA (Civ Div) 44.016
Contractreal Ltd v Davies [2001] EWCA Civ 928; (2001) L.T.L., May 17, CA (Civ Div) 13.010
Cooke v United Bristol Healthcare NHS Trust; Sheppard v Stibbe; Page v Lee [2003] EWCA Civ 1370; [2004] 1 W.L.R. 251; [2004] 1 All E.R. 797; [2004] P.I.Q.R. Q2; [2004] Lloyd's Rep. Med. 63; (2004) 78 B.M.L.R. 1; (2003) 100(43) L.S.G. 32; *The Times*, October 24, 2003, CA (Civ Div) 4.011
Cookson v Knowles [1979] A.C. 556; [1978] 2 W.L.R. 978; [1978] 2 All E.R. 604; [1978] 2 Lloyd's Rep. 315; (1978) 122 S.J. 386, HL 4.020
Cooper v Firth Brown, Ltd [1963] 1 W.L.R. 418; [1963] 2 All E.R. 31; (1963) 107 S.J. 295, Assizes (Sheffield) 4.002
Corporacion Nacional del Cobre de Chile v Metallgesellschaft AG Ltd; sub nom. Corporacion Nacional del Cobre de Chile v Metallgesellschaft Ltd AG [1999] C.P.L.R. 309; *The Times*, January 6, 1999, Ch D 32.002
Corus UK Ltd v Erewash BC [2006] EWCA Civ 1175; [2006] C.P. Rep. 41; [2007] 1 P. & C.R. 22; (2006) L.T.L., June 22, CA (Civ Div) 10.002
Cosgrove v Pattison [2001] C.P. Rep. 68; [2001] C.P.L.R. 177; (2001) L.T.L., February 7; *The Times*, February 13, 2001, Ch D 23.006
Coulter v Chief Constable of Dorset [2004] EWCA Civ 1259; [2005] 1 W.L.R. 130; [2005] B.P.I.R. 62; (2004) 101(40) L.S.G. 28; (2004) 148 S.J.L.B. 1213; *The Times*, October 22, 2004, CA (Civ Div) 42.006
Coulthard v Disco Mix Club Ltd [2000] 1 W.L.R. 707 .... 5.002
Couwenbergh v Valkova [2004] EWCA Civ 676; [2004] C.P. Rep. 38; [2004] W.T.L.R. 937; (2004) 148 S.J.L.B. 694; (2004) L.T.L., May 28, CA (Civ Div) . . 43.009
Cowl v Plymouth CC. *See* R. (on the application of Cowl) v Plymouth City Council
Cox v Hockenhull [2000] 1 W.L.R. 750; [1999] 3 All E.R. 582; [1999] R.T.R. 399; [2000] P.I.Q.R. Q230; (1999) 96(26) L.S.G. 27; (1999) 143 S.J.L.B. 188; *The Times*, June 17, 1999, CA (Civ Div) 4.018

xliii

TABLE OF CASES

Cranfield v Bridgegrove Ltd; Claussen v Yeates; McManus v Sharif; Murphy v
Staples UK Ltd; Smith v Hughes [2003] EWCA Civ 656; [2003] 1 W.L.R.
2441; [2003] 3 All E.R. 129; [2003] C.P. Rep. 54; [2003] 21 E.G. 191 (C.S.);
(2003) 147 S.J.L.B. 599; [2003] N.P.C. 66; The Times, May 16, 2003, CA (Civ
Div) 8.009, 8.011, 8.013, 8.015,
8.017, 9.005, 9.006, 11.009
Cream Holdings Ltd v Banerjee [2004] UKHL 44; [2005] 1 A.C. 253; [2004]
3 W.L.R. 918; [2004] 4 All E.R. 617; [2005] E.M.L.R. 1; [2004] H.R.L.R. 39;
[2004] U.K.H.R.R. 1071; 17 B.H.R.C. 464; (2005) 28(2) I.P.D. 28001; (2004)
101(42) L.S.G. 29; (2004) 154 N.L.J. 1589; (2004) 148 S.J.L.B. 1215; The
Times, October 15, 2004, HL 27.008
Crest Homes Plc v Marks [1987] A.C. 829; [1987] 3 W.L.R. 293; [1987] 2 All E.R.
1074; [1988] R.P.C. 21; (1987) 84 L.S.G. 2362; (1987) 137 N.L.J. 662; (1987)
131 S.J. 1003, HL 30.020
Cretanor Maritime Co. Ltd v Irish Marine Management Ltd; The Cretan
Harmony [1978] 1 W.L.R. 966; [1978] 3 All E.R. 164; [1978] 1 Lloyd's Rep.
425; (1978) 122 S.J. 298, CA (Civ Div) 27.022
Crofton v National Health Service Litigation Authority [2007] EWCA Civ 71;
[2007] 1 W.L.R. 923; (2007) 10 C.C.L. Rep. 123; [2007] LS Law Medical 254;
(2007) 104(8) L.S.G. 36; (2007) 151 S.J.L.B. 262; The Times, February 15,
2007, CA (Civ Div) 4.006
Crosbie v Munroe [2003] EWCA Civ 350; [2003] 1 W.L.R. 2033; [2003] 2 All E.R.
856; [2003] C.P. Rep. 43; [2003] 3 Costs L.R. 377; [2003] R.T.R. 33; (2003)
100(20) L.S.G. 27; (2003) 147 S.J.L.B. 356; The Times, March 25, 2003; The
Independent, March 26, 2003, CA (Civ Div) 38.041
Crouch v King's Healthcare NHS Trust; Murry v Blackburn, Hyndburn and
Ribble Valley Healthcare NHS Trust [2004] EWCA Civ 1332; [2005] 1
W.L.R. 2015; [2005] 1 All E.R. 207; [2005] C.P. Rep. 10; [2005] 2 Costs L.R.
200; [2005] P.I.Q.R. Q4; [2005] Lloyd's Rep. Med. 50; (2005) 83 B.M.L.R.
47; (2004) 101(44) L.S.G. 29; (2004) 154 N.L.J. 1616; (2004) 148 S.J.L.B.
1245; The Times, November 9, 2004, CA (Civ Div) 29.002
Crystal Decisions (UK) Ltd v Vedatech [2006] EWHC 3500, Ch D 13.010
Cullen v London Fire & Civil Defence Authority (1999) L.T.L. August 8 ...... 33.006
Customs and Excise Commissioners v Anchor Foods Ltd (No.2) [1999] 1 W.L.R.
1139; [1999] 3 All E.R. 268; [2000] C.P. Rep. 19; (1999) 96(12) L.S.G. 34;
(1999) 143 S.J.L.B. 96; The Times, April 1, 1999; The Independent, March 8,
1999, Ch D 27.002, 27.017
Customs and Excise Commissioners v Barclays Bank Plc [2006] UKHL 28; [2006]
3 W.L.R. 1; [2006] 4 All E.R. 256; [2006] 2 All E.R. (Comm) 831; [2006] 2
Lloyd's Rep. 327; [2006] 1 C.L.C. 1096; (2006) 103(27) L.S.G. 33; (2006) 156
N.L.J. 1060; (2006) 150 S.J.L.B. 859; [2007] 1 A.C. 181; The Times, June 22,
2006, HL 27.020
Cutts v Head [1984] Ch. 290; [1984] 2 W.L.R. 349; [1984] 1 All E.R. 597; (1984) 81
L.S.G. 509; (1984) 128 S.J. 117; The Times, December 14, 1983, CA
(Civ Div) 29.002
Cyril Leonard & Co. v Simo Securities Trust Ltd [1972] 1 W.L.R. 80; [1971] 3 All
E.R. 1318; (1971) 115 S.J. 911, CA (Civ Div) 32.001

D (A Child) v Walker; sub nom. Walker v D (A Child) [2000] 1 W.L.R. 1382;
[2000] C.P.L.R. 462; [2001] H.R.L.R. 1; [2000] U.K.H.R.R. 648; [2000]
P.I.Q.R. P193; (2000) 97(22) L.S.G. 44; The Times, May 17, 2000; The
Independent, June 12, 2000, CA (Civ Div) 23.006

D (A Child) (Representation: McKenzie friend), Re [2005] EWCA Civ 347; (2005)
    L.T.L. March 15 .... 1.021
DB Deniz Nakliyati TAS v Yugopetrol [1992] 1 W.L.R. 437; [1992] 1 All E.R. 205;
    The Independent, February 15, 1991; The Daily Telegraph, March 7, 1991,
    CA (Civ Div) 27.021
DHL Air Ltd v Wells [2003] EWCA Civ 1743; The Times, November 14, 2003, CA
    (Civ Div) 33.006
DN v Greenwich LBC [2004] EWCA Civ 1659; [2005] 1 F.C.R. 112; [2005]
    B.L.G.R. 597; [2005] E.L.R. 133; (2005) 149 S.J.L.B. 25; The Times,
    December 23, 2004, CA (Civ Div) 23.009, 23.015
DPR Futures Ltd, Re [1989] 1 W.L.R. 778; (1989) 5 B.C.C. 603; [1989] B.C.L.C.
    634; (1989) 133 S.J. 977, Ch D (Companies Ct) 27.013
Dadourian Group International Inc v Simms [2006] EWCA Civ 399; [2006]
    1 W.L.R. 2499; [2006] 3 All E.R. 48; [2006] 1 All E.R. (Comm) 709; [2006]
    2 Lloyd's Rep. 354; [2006] C.P. Rep. 31; [2006] 1 C.L.C. 744; The Times,
    May 23, 2006; The Independent, April 26, 2006, CA (Civ Div) 27.020
Daiches v Bluelake Investments Ltd (1985) 17 H.L.R. 543; (1986) 51 P. & C.R. 51;
    [1985] 2 E.G.L.R. 67; (1985) 275 E.G. 462; (1985) 82 L.S.G. 3258, Ch D ... 27.030
Davies v Inman [1999] P.I.Q.R. Q26, CA (Civ Div) 4.022
Davies (Joy Rosalie) v Eli Lilly & Co. (No.1) [1987] 1 W.L.R. 428; [1987] 1 All E.R. 801;
    [1987] E.C.C. 340; (1987) 84 L.S.G. 826; (1987) 131 S.J. 360, CA (Civ Div) .. 30.001
Davy v Garrett (1877–78) L.R. 7 Ch. D. 473, CA 12.028
Davy v Spelthorne BC [1984] A.C. 262; [1983] 3 W.L.R. 742; [1983] 3 All E.R. 278;
    82 L.G.R. 193; (1984) 47 P. & C.R. 310; [1984] J.P.L. 269; (1983) 133 N.L.J.
    1015; (1983) 127 S.J. 733, HL 24.001
Dawodu v American Express Bank [2001] B.P.I.R. 983, Ch D 42.014
De Beer v Kanaar & Co. (No.1) [2001] EWCA Civ 1318; [2003] 1 W.L.R. 38;
    [2002] 3 All E.R. 1020; [2001] C.P. Rep. 118; [2002] C.L.C. 114; [2002]
    I.L.Pr. 24, CA (Civ Div) 26.002
De Bry v Fitzgerald [1990] 1 W.L.R. 552; [1990] 1 All E.R. 560; [1990] 1 C.M.L.R.
    781; [1991] I.L.Pr. 64; The Independent, November 14, 1988, CA (Civ Div) ..26.002
De Franco v Commissioner of Police of the Metropolis, The Times, May 8, 1987,
    CA (Civ Div) 7.014
Dean v Dean [1987] 1 F.L.R. 517; [1987] 1 F.C.R. 96; [1987] Fam. Law 200; (1987)
    151 J.P.N. 254, CA (Civ Div) 41.003
Debtor (No.1 of 1987), Re [1989] 1 W.L.R. 271; [1989] 2 All E.R. 46; (1989) 86(16)
    L.S.G. 35; (1989) 133 S.J. 290, CA (Civ Div) 42.003, 42.006
Debtor (No.310 of 1988), Re [1989] 1 W.L.R. 452; [1989] 2 All E.R. 42; (1989) 133
    S.J. 848, Ch D 42.006
Debtor (No.2389 of 1989), Re [1991] Ch. 326; [1991] 2 W.L.R. 578; [1990] 3 All
    E.R. 984, Ch D 42.008
Debtor (No.88 of 1991), Re [1993] Ch. 286; [1992] 2 W.L.R. 1026; [1992] 4 All
    E.R. 301; (1992) 142 N.L.J. 1039; (1992) 136 S.J.L.B. 206; The Times, July 10,
    1992; The Independent, July 10, 1992, Ch D 42.006
Debtor (No.490/SD/1991), Re [1992] 1 W.L.R. 507; [1992] 2 All E.R. 664; [1993]
    B.C.L.C. 164; The Times, April 9, 1992; The Independent, April 6, 1992,
    Ch D 42.006
Debtor (Nos.49 and 50 of 1992), Re [1995] Ch. 66; [1994] 3 W.L.R. 847, CA
    (Civ Div) 42.006
Debtor (No.50A-SD-1995), Re; sub nom. Jelly v All Type Roofing Co. [1997] Ch.
    310; [1997] 2 W.L.R. 57; [1997] 2 All E.R. 789; [1997] B.C.C. 465; [1997]
    1 B.C.L.C. 280; [1996] B.P.I.R. 565, Ch D 40.004, 42.006

Debtor (No.87 of 1999), Re; sub nom. Debtor v Johnston [2000] B.P.I.R. 589; (2000) 97(7) L.S.G. 40; *The Times*, February 14, 2000, Ch D 18.007
Deeley v McCarthy and Leeds AHA (Teaching) [1977] C.L.Y. 764 .... 4.009
Deeny v Gooda Walker Ltd (No.4) [1996] L.R.L.R. 168; [1995] S.T.C. 696; *The Times*, June 29, 1995; Lloyd's List, September 28, 1995, Q.B.D. 3.002
Del Grosso v Payne & Payne (A Firm) [2007] EWCA Civ 340; (2007) 151 S.J.L.B. 336, CA (Civ Div) 12.053
Den Norske Bank ASA v Antonatos [1999] Q.B. 271; [1998] 3 W.L.R. 711; [1998] 3 All E.R. 74; [1998] Lloyd's Rep. Bank. 253, CA (Civ Div) 27.027
Department of Economic Policy and Development of the City of Moscow v Bankers Trust Co; sub nom. Department of Economics, Policy and Development of the City of Moscow v Bankers Trust Co; Moscow City Council v Banker; Trust Co. [2004] EWCA Civ 314; [2005] Q.B. 207; [2004] 3 W.L.R. 533; [2004] 4 All E.R. 746; [2004] 2 All E.R. (Comm) 193; [2004] 2 Lloyd's Rep. 179; [2004] 1 C.L.C. 1099; [2004] B.L.R. 229; (2004) 148 S.J.L.B. 389, CA (Civ Div) 13.007
Derby & Co. Ltd v Weldon (No.1) [1990] Ch. 48; [1989] 2 W.L.R. 276; [1989] 1 All E.R. 469; [1989] 1 Lloyd's Rep. 122; [1989] E.C.C. 283; (1988) 138 N.L.J. Rep. 236; (1989) 133 S.J. 83; *The Times*, August 2, 1988, CA (Civ Div) ... 27.017
Derby & Co. Ltd v Weldon (No.6) [1990] 1 W.L.R. 1139; [1990] 3 All E.R. 263; [1991] I.L.Pr. 24; (1990) 140 N.L.J. 1001; (1990) 134 S.J. 1041; *The Times*, May 14, 1990; *The Independent*, June 1, 1990; *The Financial Times*, May 16, 1990, CA (Civ Div) 27.030
Derby & Co. Ltd v Weldon (No.9), *The Times*, November 9, 1990, CA (Civ Div); affirming [1991] 1 W.L.R. 652; [1991] 2 All E.R. 901, Ch D 30.004, 30.018
Derby & Co. Ltd v Weldon (Nos.3 and No.4) [1990] Ch. 65; [1989] 2 W.L.R. 412; [1989] 1 All E.R. 1002; [1989] E.C.C. 322; (1989) 139 N.L.J. 11; (1989) 133 S.J. 83; *The Times*, December 26, 1988; *The Independent*, December 20, 1988, CA (Civ Div) 27.030
Derby & Co. v Larsson [1976] 1 W.L.R. 202; [1976] 1 All E.R. 401; (1976) 120 S.J. 117, HL 11.014
Det Danske Hedelskabet v KDM International Plc [1994] 2 Lloyd's Rep. 534, Q.B.D. (Comm) 32.004
Deutsche Ruckversicherung AG v Walbrook Insurance Co. Ltd. *See* Group Josi Re Co. SA v Walbrook Insurance Co. Ltd
Devine v Franklin (Costs) [2002] EWHC 1846, Q.B.D. 9.035
Dews v National Coal Board [1988] A.C. 1; [1987] 3 W.L.R. 38, HL; affirming [1987] Q.B. 81; [1986] 3 W.L.R. 227; [1986] 2 All E.R. 769; (1986) 83 L.S.G. 2084; (1986) 130 S.J. 553, CA (Civ Div) 4.002
Dexter v Courtaulds [1984] 1 W.L.R. 372; [1984] 1 All E.R. 70; (1984) 81 L.S.G. 510; (1984) 128 S.J. 81, CA (Civ Div) 4.020, 4.021
Dian AO v Davis Frankel & Mead (A Firm) [2004] EWHC 2662; [2005] 1 W.L.R. 2951; [2005] 1 All E.R. 1074; [2005] 1 All E.R. (Comm) 482; [2005] C.P. Rep. 18, Q.B.D. (Comm) 1.022
Dietz v Lennig Chemicals Ltd [1969] 1 A.C. 170; [1967] 3 W.L.R. 165; [1967] 2 All E.R. 282; (1967) 111 S.J. 354, HL 7.005
Director General of Fair Trading v Proprietary Association of Great Britain; sub nom. Medicaments and Related Classes of Goods (No.2), Re [2001] 1 W.L.R. 700; [2001] U.K.C.L.R. 550; [2001] I.C.R. 564; [2001] H.R.L.R. 17; [2001] U.K.H.R.R. 429; (2001) 3 L.G.L.R. 32; (2001) 98(7) L.S.G. 40; (2001) 151 N.L.J. 17; (2001) 145 S.J.L.B. 29; *The Times*, February 2, 2001; *The Independent*, January 12, 2001, CA (Civ Div) 36.012

Distributori Automatici Italia SpA v Holford General Trading Co. Ltd [1985]
1 W.L.R. 1066; [1985] 3 All E.R. 750; (1985) 82 L.S.G. 3454; (1985) 129 S.J.
685, Q.B.D. 27.024
Dobbie v Medway HA [1994] 1 W.L.R. 1234; [1994] 4 All E.R. 450; [1994] P.I.Q.R.
P353; [1994] 5 Med. L.R. 160; (1994) 144 N.L.J. 828; *The Times,* May 18,
1994; *The Independent,* June 6, 1994, CA (Civ Div) 5.018
Dolling-Baker v Merrett [1990] 1 W.L.R. 1205; [1991] 2 All E.R. 890; (1990) 134
S.J. 806, CA (Civ Div) 30.012
Dolman v Rowe [2005] EWCA Civ 715 .... 25.001
Donsland Ltd v Van Hoogstraten; sub nom. Healys v Van Hoogstraten [2002]
EWCA Civ 253; [2002] P.N.L.R. 26; [2002] W.T.L.R. 497, CA (Civ Div) ... 7.024
Douglas v Hello! Ltd (No.3) [2003] EWHC 55; [2003] 1 All E.R. 1087 (Note);
[2003] E.M.L.R. 29; (2003) 100(11) L.S.G. 34; (2003) 153 N.L.J. 175; *The
Times,* January 30, 2003, Ch D 30.005
Douglas v Hello! Ltd (No.5) [2003] EWCA Civ 332; [2003] C.P. Rep. 42; [2003]
E.M.L.R. 30; (2003) 147 S.J.L.B. 297, CA (Civ Div) 31.015
Dove v Banhams Patent Locks Ltd [1983] 1 W.L.R. 1436; [1983] 2 All E.R. 833;
(1983) 133 N.L.J. 538; (1983) 127 S.J. 748, Q.B.D. 5.002
Dover DC v Sherred (1997) 29 H.L.R. 864; [1997] N.P.C. 13; *The Times,* February
11, 1997, CA (Civ Div) 23.001
DPP v Kilbourne; sub nom. R. v Kilbourne (John) [1973] A.C. 729; [1973] 2
W.L.R. 254; [1973] 1 All E.R. 440; (1973) 57 Cr. App. R. 381; [1973] Crim.
L.R. 235; (1973) 117 S.J. 144, HL 31.023
DPP v P [2007] EWHC 1144; [2007] All E.R. (D) 246 (Apr), Q.B.D. (Admin) ... 37.016
DPP v Turner; sub nom. R. v Turner (John Eric) [1974] A.C. 357; [1973] 3 W.L.R.
352; [1973] 3 All E.R. 124; (1973) 57 Cr. App. R. 932; [1974] Crim. L.R. 186;
(1973) 117 S.J. 664, HL 4.018
Drinkall v Whitwood [2003] EWCA Civ 1547; [2004] 1 W.L.R. 462; [2004] 4 All
E.R. 378; (2003) 100(47) L.S.G. 21; (2003) 147 S.J.L.B. 1308; *The Times,*
November 13, 2003, CA (Civ Div) 7.005
Drury v BBC [2007] All E.R. (D) 205 (May) 36.012
Dubai Aluminium Co. Ltd v Al-Alawi [1999] 1 W.L.R. 1964; [1999] 1 All E.R. 703;
[1999] 1 All E.R. (Comm.) 1; [1999] 1 Lloyd's Rep. 478; *The Times,* January
6, 1999; *The Independent,* December 21, 1998, Q.B.D. (Comm) 30.013
Dubai Bank Ltd v Galadari (No.2), *The Times,* October 11, 1989, Ch D 27.002
Dubai Bank Ltd v Galadari (No.3) [1990] 1 W.L.R. 731; [1990] 2 All E.R. 738;
(1990) 134 S.J. 986; *The Times,* January 4, 1990, CA (Civ Div) 30.017
Dubai Bank Ltd v Galadari (No.7) [1992] 1 W.L.R. 106; [1992] 1 All E.R. 658;
(1992) 89(7) L.S.G. 31, Ch D 30.013
Duer v Frazer [2001] 1 W.L.R. 919; [2001] 1 All E.R. 249, Q.B.D. 40.004
Dun & Bradstreet Ltd v Typesetting Facilities Ltd [1992] F.S.R. 320; (1992) C.L.Y.
579, Ch D 30.016
Dunn International Ltd v CDE, 57 Con. L.R. 11; (1998) C.L.Y. 819, Q.B.D. (OR) ... 31.017
Dunning v United Liverpool Hospital's Board of Governors [1973] 1 W.L.R. 586;
[1973] 2 All E.R. 454; (1973) 117 S.J. 167, CA (Civ Div) 30.024
Dyson Appliances Ltd v Hoover Ltd (Costs); sub nom. Dyson Ltd v Hoover Ltd
[2002] EWHC 2229; [2003] F.S.R. 21; (2002) 25(12) I.P.D. 25087; (2002)
99(45) L.S.G. 34; *The Times,* November 6, 2002, Ch D (Patents Ct) 29.017
Dyson Appliances Ltd v Hoover Ltd (Costs: Interim Payment); sub nom. Dyson
Ltd v Hoover Ltd (Costs: Interim Payment) [2003] EWHC 624; [2004] 1
W.L.R. 1264; [2003] 2 All E.R. 1042; [2003] C.P. Rep. 45; (2003) 100(15)
L.S.G. 25; *The Times,* March 18, 2003, Ch D (Patents Ct) 38.016, 38.039

Dziennik v CTO Gesellschaft fur Containertransport MBH and Co; sub nom.
    CTO Gesellschaft fur Containertransport MBH and Co. v Dziennik [2006]
    EWCA Civ 1456; (2006) L.T.L., November 13, CA (Civ Div) 12.038

ED&F Man Liquid Products Ltd v Patel [2003] EWCA Civ 472; [2003] C.P. Rep.
    51; [2003] C.P.L.R. 384; (2003) 100(24) L.S.G. 37; (2003) 147 S.J.L.B. 416;
    The Times, April 18, 2003, CA (Civ Div) 15.013, 19.006
EDO MBM Technology Ltd v Campaign to Smash EDO [2005] EWHC 837,
    Q.B.D. 7.018
EI Du Pont de Nemours & Co. v ST Dupont. *See* ST Dupont v EI du Pont de
    Nemours & Co
EMI Records Ltd v Modern Music Karl-Ulrich Walterbach GmbH [1992] Q.B.
    115; [1991] 3 W.L.R. 663; [1992] 1 All E.R. 616; [1992] I.L.Pr. 30; (1991) 135
    S.J. 180; *The Times*, May 27, 1991, Q.B.D. 27.020
ES v Chesterfield and North Derbyshire Royal Hospital NHS Trust; sub nom. S v
    A Health Authority [2003] EWCA Civ 1284; [2004] C.P. Rep. 9; [2004]
    Lloyd's Rep. Med. 90; (2003) 100(38) L.S.G. 34, CA (Civ Div) 23.015
Eagle v Chambers (No.2) [2004] EWCA Civ 1033; [2004] 1 W.L.R. 3081; [2005]
    1 All E.R. 136; [2005] P.I.Q.R. Q2; [2004] Lloyd's Rep. Med. 413; (2005) 82
    B.M.L.R. 22; (2004) 154 N.L.J. 1451; (2004) 148 S.J.L.B. 972; *The Times*,
    August 30, 2004, CA (Civ Div) 4.004, 4.020
Eastwood (Deceased), Re; sub nom. Lloyds Bank Ltd v Eastwood [1975]
    Ch. 112; [1974] 3 W.L.R. 454; [1974] 3 All E.R. 603; (1974) 118 S.J. 533, CA
    (Civ Div) 38.005, 38.020
Ebert v Birch; Ebert v Venvil [2000] Ch. 484; [1999] 3 W.L.R. 670; [2000] B.P.I.R.
    14; (1999) 96(19) L.S.G. 28; (1999) 149 N.L.J. 608; (1999) 143 S.J.L.B. 130;
    [1999] N.P.C. 46; *The Times*, April 28, 1999; *The Independent*, April 28,
    1999, CA (Civ Div) 33.008
Ebert v Official Receiver (No.2) [2001] EWCA Civ 340; [2002] 1 W.L.R. 320;
    [2001] 3 All E.R. 942; [2002] B.P.I.R. 80; [2001] A.C.D. 66; *The
    Independent*, March 21, 2001, CA (Civ Div) 7.011
Ebert v Venvil. *See* Ebert v Birch
Economic Department of the City of Moscow v Bankers Trust Company. *See*
    Department of Economic Policy and Development of the City of Moscow
    v Bankers Trust Co.
Edo Technology Ltd v Hills [2006] EWHC 589; *The Times*, May 24, 2006 ..... 12.052
Electricity Supply Nominees Ltd v Farrell [1997] 1 W.L.R. 1149; [1997] 2 All E.R.
    498; [1998] 1 Costs L.R. 49; *The Times*, March 10, 1997; *The Independent*,
    March 10, 1997, CA (Civ Div) 43.004
Eller v Grovecrest Investments Ltd [1995] Q.B. 272; [1995] 2 W.L.R. 278; [1994]
    4 All E.R. 845; (1995) 70 P. & C.R. 350; [1994] 27 E.G. 139; [1994] E.G. 28
    (C.S.); (1994) 144 N.L.J. 390; [1994] N.P.C. 21, CA (Civ Div) 12.037
Elmes v Hygrade Food Products Plc [2001] EWCA Civ 121; [2001] C.P. Rep. 71,
    CA (Civ Div) 8.014
Emanuel v Emanuel [1982] 1 W.L.R. 669; [1982] 2 All E.R. 342; (1982) 12 Fam.
    Law 62, Fam Div 27.024
Enfield LBC v Mahoney [1983] 1 W.L.R. 749; [1983] 2 All E.R. 901; (1983) 127 S.J.
    392, CA (Civ Div) 41.003

English v Emery Reimbold & Strick Ltd; DJ&C Withers (Farms) Ltd v Ambic
  Equipment Ltd; Verrechia (t/a Freightmaster Commercials) v Commissioner
  of Police of the Metropolis [2002] EWCA Civ 605; [2002] 1 W.L.R. 2409;
  [2002] 3 All E.R. 385; [2002] C.P.L.R. 520; [2003] I.R.L.R. 710; [2002]
  U.K.H.R.R. 957; (2002) 99(22) L.S.G. 34; (2002) 152 N.L.J. 758; (2002) 146
  S.J.L.B. 123; *The Times*, May 10, 2002; *The Independent*, May 7, 2002, CA
  (Civ Div) 44.011
Ernst & Young v Butte Mining Plc [1996] 1 W.L.R. 1605; [1996] 2 All E.R. 623;
  (1996) 146 N.L.J. 553; *The Times*, March 22, 1996, Ch D 35.005
Ernst & Young v Butte Mining Plc (No.2); sub nom. Butte Mining Plc v Ernst &
  Young (No.2) [1997] 1 W.L.R. 1485; [1997] 2 All E.R. 471; [1997] 1 Lloyd's
  Rep. 313, Ch D 18.010
Esso Petroleum Co. Ltd v Milton [1997] 1 W.L.R. 938; [1997] 1 W.L.R. 1060;
  [1997] 2 All E.R. 593; [1997] C.L.C. 634; (1997) 16 Tr. L.R. 250; *The Times*,
  February 13, 1997; *The Independent*, February 19, 1997, CA (Civ Div) ... 19.009
Estate Acquisition & Development Ltd v Wiltshire [2006] EWCA Civ 533; [2006]
  C.P. Rep. 32; *The Times*, June 12, 2006, CA (Civ Div) 43.002
Estmanco (Kilner House) Ltd v Greater London Council [1982] 1 W.L.R. 2; [1982]
  1 All E.R. 437; 80 L.G.R. 464; (1981) 125 S.J. 790, Q.B.D. 7.021
Evans v Clayhope Properties Ltd [1988] 1 W.L.R. 358; [1988] 1 All E.R. 444, CA
  (Civ Div); affirming [1987] 1 W.L.R. 225; [1987] 2 All E.R. 40; (1987) 3
  B.C.C. 553; [1987] B.C.L.C. 418; (1987) 19 H.L.R. 117; [1987] 1 E.G.L.R.
  67; (1987) 282 E.G. 862; (1987) 84 L.S.G. 340; (1987) 131 S.J. 74; *The Times*,
  November 10, 1986, Ch D 27.030
Evans v James. *See* James v Evans
Evans v Tarmac Central Ltd [2005] EWCA Civ 1820, (2005) L.T.L., December 12,
  CA (Civ Div) 4.014
Everton v WPBSA Promotions Ltd, December 13, 2001, Q.B.D. 35.006
Ewing v Office of the Deputy Prime Minister. *See* R. (on the application of
  Ewing) v Office of the Deputy Prime Minister
Excelsior Commercial & Industrial Holdings Ltd v Salisbury Hamer Aspden &
  Johnson (Costs); sub nom. Excelsior Commercial & Industrial Holdings Ltd
  v Salisbury Hammer Aspden & Johnson [2002] EWCA Civ 879; [2002] C.P.
  Rep. 67; [2002] C.P.L.R. 693; *The Independent*, June 18, 2002, CA (Civ Div) . . 38.016
Ezekiel v Orakpo [1997] 1 W.L.R. 340; [1996] N.P.C. 108; *The Times*, September
  16, 1996, CA (Civ Div) 40.008

FKI Engineering Ltd v Dewind Holdings Ltd [2007] EWHC 72 (Comm); [2007]
  I.L.Pr. 17; (2007) L.T.L., January 25, Q.B.D. (Comm) 11.006
Factortame Ltd v Secretary of State for the Environment, Transport and the
  Regions (Costs) (No.1); sub nom. R. v Secretary of State for Transport Ex
  p. Factortame Ltd (Costs: Part 36 Payments) [2002] EWCA Civ 22; [2002] 1
  W.L.R. 2438; [2002] 2 All E.R. 838; [2002] C.P.L.R. 385; (2002) 152 N.L.J.
  171, CA (Civ Div) 29.012, 29.017, 29.024
Factortame Ltd v Secretary of State for the Environment, Transport and the
  Regions (Costs) (No.2); sub nom. R. (on the application of Factortame Ltd) v
  Secretary of State for Transport, Local Government and the Regions (Costs:
  Champertous Agreement) [2002] EWCA Civ 932; [2003] Q.B. 381; [2002] 3
  W.L.R. 1104; [2002] 4 All E.R. 97; [2003] B.L.R. 1; [2002] 3 Costs L.R. 467;
  (2002) 99(35) L.S.G. 34; (2002) 152 N.L.J. 1313; (2002) 146 S.J.L.B. 178; *The
  Times*, July 9, 2002; *The Independent*, July 10, 2002; *The Daily Telegraph*,
  July 11, 2002, CA (Civ Div) 23.015

xlix

Fairmays (formerly Palmer Cowen) (A Firm) v Palmer [2006] EWHC 96; (2006)
150 S.J.L.B. 223; (2006) L.T.L., January 31, Ch D 8.009
Federal Bank of the Middle East v Hadkinson (Stay of Action); Hadkinson v Saab
(No.1) [2000] 1 W.L.R. 1695; [2000] 2 All E.R. 395; [2000] C.P.L.R. 295;
[2000] B.P.I.R. 597; (2000) 97(12) L.S.G. 42; (2000) 150 N.L.J. 393; (2000)
144 S.J.L.B. 128; *The Times,* March 16, 2000; *The Independent,* March 14,
2000, CA (Civ Div) 27.017
Femis-Bank (Anguilla) Ltd v Lazer; Singh (Dinesh Kumar) v Lazer [1991] Ch. 391;
[1991] 3 W.L.R. 80; [1991] 2 All E.R. 865; *The Times,* February 11, 1991,
Ch D 27.011
Field v Leeds City Council [1999] C.P.L.R. 833; [2001] C.P.L.R. 129; (2000) 32
H.L.R. 618; [2000] 1 E.G.L.R. 54; [2000] 17 E.G. 165; *The Times,* January
18, 2000; *The Independent,* December 16, 1999, CA (Civ Div) 23.015
Fielding & Platt Ltd v Selim Najjar [1969] 1 W.L.R. 357; [1969] 2 All E.R. 150;
(1969) 113 S.J. 160, CA (Civ Div) 18.009
Fifield v Denton Hall Legal Services [2006] EWCA Civ 169; [2006] Lloyd's Rep.
Med. 251; *The Times,* March 22, 2006, CA (Civ Div) 12.039, 31.039
Films Rover International Ltd v Cannon Film Sales Ltd [1987] 1 W.L.R. 670;
[1986] 3 All E.R. 772, Ch D 27.009
Financial Services Compensation Scheme Ltd v Larnell (Insurances) Ltd (In
Liquidation); sub nom. Financial Services Compensation Scheme v Larnell
Insurance [2005] EWCA Civ 1408; [2006] Q.B. 808; [2006] 2 W.L.R. 751;
[2006] C.P. Rep. 14; [2006] B.C.C. 690; [2006] B.P.I.R. 1370; [2006] Lloyd's
Rep. I.R. 448; [2006] P.N.L.R. 13, CA (Civ Div) 5.013
First Discount Ltd v Guinness [2007] EWCA Civ 378; (2007) L.T.L., May 1, CA
(Civ Div) 43.009
First Express Ltd, Re [1991] B.C.C. 782; *The Times,* October 10, 1991, Ch D
(Companies Ct) 27.012
Firstdale Ltd v Quinton [2004] 1 All E.R. 639 .... 8.001
Fitter v Veal (1701) 12 Mod. 542 .... 4.015
Flaviis v Pauley [2002] EWHC 2886, Q.B.D. 16.009
Flightline Ltd v Edwards; sub nom. Edwards v Flightline Ltd; Swissair
Schweizerische Luftverkehr AG, Re [2003] EWCA Civ 63; [2003] 1 W.L.R.
1200; [2003] 3 All E.R. 1200; [2003] B.C.C. 361; [2003] 1 B.C.L.C. 427;
[2003] B.P.I.R. 549; (2003) 100(13) L.S.G. 28; (2003) 147 S.J.L.B. 178; *The
Times,* February 13, 2003; *The Independent,* February 21, 2003, CA (Civ
Div) 27.019
Flora v Wakom (Heathrow) Ltd (formerly Abela Airline Catering Ltd) [2006]
EWCA Civ 1103; [2007] 1 W.L.R. 482; [2006] 4 All E.R. 982; [2007] P.I.Q.R.
Q2; [2007] LS Law Medical 62; (2006) 156 N.L.J. 1289, CA (Civ Div) 4.016
Flynn v Scougall [2004] EWCA Civ 873; [2004] 1 W.L.R. 3069; [2004] 3 All E.R.
609; [2004] C.P. Rep. 37; [2005] 1 Costs L.R. 38; (2004) 148 S.J.L.B. 880; *The
Times,* July 21, 2004; *The Independent,* July 16, 2004, CA (Civ Div) 29.011
Foenander v Bond Lewis & Co. [2001] EWCA Civ 759; [2002] 1 W.L.R. 525;
[2001] 2 All E.R. 1019; [2001] C.P. Rep. 94; [2001] C.P.L.R. 333; (2001) 151
N.L.J. 890; *The Times,* June 18, 2001; *The Independent,* June 8, 2001, CA
(Civ Div) 44.008
Folks v Faizey [2006] EWCA Civ 381; [2006] C.P. Rep. 30; *The Independent,* April
12, 2006, CA (Civ Div) 7.006
Ford v GKR Construction Ltd [2000] 1 W.L.R. 1397; [2000] 1 All E.R. 802; [1999]
C.P.L.R. 788; *The Times,* November 4, 1999, CA (Civ Div) 29.001, 29.024

l

Forrester v British Railways Board, *The Times,* April 8, 1996, CA (Civ Div) 30.006
Forum (Holdings) Ltd v Brook Street Computers Ltd [1998] Masons C.L.R. 256,
    CA (Civ Div) 30.021
Foster v Zott GMBH & Co. (2000) L.T.L., May 24, CA (Civ Div) 5.007, 44.002
Fourie v Le Roux; sub nom. Herlan Edmunds Engineering (Pty) Ltd, Re [2007]
    UKHL 1; [2007] Bus. L.R. 925; [2007] 1 W.L.R. 320; [2007] 1 All E.R. 1087;
    [2007] 1 All E.R. (Comm) 571; [2007] B.P.I.R. 24; (2007) 157 N.L.J. 178; *The
    Times,* January 25, 2007, HL 1.022, 27.017
Francom v Williams (1999) C.L. May 43, CC (Birkenhead) 6.018
Francome v Mirror Group Newspapers Ltd [1984] 1 W.L.R. 892; [1984] 2 All E.R.
    408; (1984) 81 L.S.G. 2225; (1984) 128 S.J. 484, CA (Civ Div) 27.005
Fraser v Oystertec Plc (Proposed Amendments) [2004] EWHC 2225; [2005]
    B.P.I.R. 389; [2004] All E.R. (D) 253 (Nov), Ch D 40.005
Friends Provident Life Office v Hillier Parker May & Rowden [1997] Q.B. 85;
    [1996] 2 W.L.R. 123; [1995] 4 All E.R. 260; [1995] C.L.C. 592; (1996) 71 P.
    & C.R. 286; [1995] E.G. 64 (C.S.); [1995] N.P.C. 63; *The Times,* April 15,
    1995, CA (Civ Div) 18.005
Fulham Leisure Holdings Ltd v Nicholson Graham & Jones [2006] EWHC 2017;
    [2006] 4 All E.R. 1397 (Note); [2007] P.N.L.R. 5, Ch D 31.004, 31.024
Fuller v Strum [2001] EWCA Civ 1879; [2002] 1 W.L.R. 1097; [2002] 2 All E.R. 87;
    [2002] 1 F.C.R. 608; [2002] W.T.L.R. 199; (2001–02) 4 I.T.E.L.R. 454; (2002)
    99(7) L.S.G. 35; (2002) 146 S.J.L.B. 21; *The Times,* January 22, 2002; *The
    Independent,* January 28, 2002, CA (Civ Div) 23.001, 23.006

GE Capital Corporate Finance Group v Bankers Trust Co. [1995] 1 W.L.R. 172;
    [1995] 2 All E.R. 993; (1994) 91(37) L.S.G. 50; (1994) 138 S.J.L.B. 178;
    The Times, August 3, 1994; *The Independent,* September 2, 1994, CA
    (Civ Div) 30.008
GKR Karate (UK) Ltd v Yorkshire Post Newspapers Ltd (No.1) [2000] 1 W.L.R.
    2571; [2000] 2 All E.R. 931; [2000] C.P. Rep. 47; [2000] E.M.L.R. 396; (2000)
    97(4) L.S.G. 32; (2000) 144 S.J.L.B. 50; *The Times,* February 9, 2000; *The
    Independent,* February 21, 2000, CA (Civ Div) 33.006, 33.012
Gaca v Pirelli General Plc; sub nom. Pirelli General Plc v Gaca [2004] EWCA Civ
    373; [2004] 1 W.L.R. 2683; [2004] 3 All E.R. 348; [2004] P.I.Q.R. Q5; (2004)
    101(17) L.S.G. 30; (2004) 148 S.J.L.B. 416; *The Times,* April 2, 2004; *The
    Independent,* March 30, 2004, CA (Civ Div) 4.005
Galaxia Maritima SA v Mineral Importexport; The Eleftherios [1982] 1 W.L.R.
    539; [1982] 1 All E.R. 796; [1982] 1 Lloyd's Rep. 351; [1982] Com. L.R. 38;
    (1982) 126 S.J. 115, CA (Civ Div) 27.022
Gall v Chief Constable of the West Midlands [2006] EWCA Civ 2638, (2006)
    L.T.L., November 1, Q.B.D. 33.011
Gallaher International Ltd v Tlais Enterprises Ltd; Gallaher International Ltd v
    Ptolemeos Tlais [2007] EWHC 464 (Comm); (2007) L.T.L., April 19, Q.B.D.
    (Comm) 23.015
Gandolfo v Gandolfo (Standard Chartered Bank, Garnishee) [1981] Q.B. 359;
    [1980] 2 W.L.R. 680; [1980] 1 All E.R. 833; (1979) 10 Fam. Law 152; (1980)
    124 S.J. 239, CA (Civ Div) 41.003
Garden Cottage Foods Ltd v Milk Marketing Board [1984] A.C. 130; [1983]
    3 W.L.R. 143; [1983] 2 All E.R. 770; [1983] Com. L.R. 198; [1983] 3 C.M.L.R.
    43; [1984] F.S.R. 23; (1983) 127 S.J. 460, HL 27.005, 45.001

li

Garratt v Saxby [2004] EWCA Civ 341; [2004] 1 W.L.R. 2152; [2004] C.P. Rep. 32; (2004) 101(11) L.S.G. 35; (2004) 148 S.J.L.B. 237, CA (Civ Div) ... 29.020, 44.011
Gaskins v British Aluminium Co. Ltd [1976] Q.B. 524; [1976] 2 W.L.R. 6; [1976] 1 All E.R. 208; (1975) 119 S.J. 848; *The Times*, November 7, 1975, CA (Civ Div) 29.020
Gaydamak v UBS Bahamas Ltd [2006] UKPC 8; [2006] 1 W.L.R. 1097; *The Times*, March 7, 2006, PC (Bah) 43.002
General Mediterranean Holdings SA v Patel [2000] 1 W.L.R. 272; [1999] 3 All E.R. 673; [1999] C.P.L.R. 425; [1999] 2 Costs L.R. 10; [2000] H.R.L.R. 54; [2000] U.K.H.R.R. 273; [1999] Lloyd's Rep. P.N. 919; [1999] P.N.L.R. 852; (1999) 149 N.L.J. 1145; [1999] N.P.C. 98; *The Times*, August 12, 1999, Q.B.D. (Comm) 30.015
Giambrone v JMC Holidays Ltd (formerly t/a Sunworld Holidays Ltd) (Costs) [2002] EWHC 2932; [2003] 1 All E.R. 982; [2003] 2 Costs L.R. 189; (2003) 153 N.L.J. 58, Q.B.D. 38.017, 38.039
Gilham v Browning [1998] 1 W.L.R. 682; [1998] 2 All E.R. 68; (1998) 142 S.J.L.B. 99; *The Times*, February 26, 1998, CA (Civ Div) 35.005
Gillies v Secretary of State for Work and Pensions; sub nom. Secretary of State for Work and Pensions v Gillies [2006] UKHL 2; [2006] 1 W.L.R. 781; [2006] 1 All E.R. 731; 2006 S.C. (H.L.) 71; 2006 S.L.T. 77; 2006 S.C.L.R. 276; [2006] I.C.R. 267; (2006) 9 C.C.L. Rep. 404; (2006) 103(9) L.S.G. 33; (2006) 150 S.J.L.B. 127; 2006 G.W.D. 3-66; *The Times*, January 30, 2006, HL 36.012
Glass v Surrendran. *See* Collier v Williams
Gloag & Son Ltd v Welsh Distillers Ltd (1999) L.T.L., June 11 .... 28.001
Global Multimedia International Ltd v Ara Media Services [Global Multimedia International Ltd v ARA Media Services [2006] EWHC 3612; *The Times*, August 1, 2006, Ch D, *The Times*, August 1, 2006 .... 12.007
Godwin v Swindon BC [2001] EWCA Civ 1478; [2002] 1 W.L.R. 997; [2001] 4 All E.R. 641; [2002] C.P. Rep. 13; *The Independent*, October 19, 2001, CA (Civ Div) 1.012
Gomba Holdings (UK) Ltd v Minories Finance Ltd (No.2) [1993] Ch. 171; [1992] 3 W.L.R. 723; [1992] 4 All E.R. 588; [1992] B.C.C. 877; (1992) 136 S.J.L.B. 54; [1992] N.P.C. 12, CA (Civ Div) 24.006
Goode v Martin [2001] EWCA Civ 1899; [2002] 1 W.L.R. 1828; [2002] 1 All E.R. 620; [2002] C.P. Rep. 16; [2002] C.P.L.R. 74; [2002] C.L.C. 420; [2002] P.I.Q.R. P24; (2002) 152 N.L.J. 109; *The Times*, January 24, 2002; *The Independent*, January 16, 2002, CA (Civ Div) 12.030, 12.053
Goodridge v Chief Constable of Hampshire [1999] 1 W.L.R. 1558; [1999] 1 All E.R. 896, Q.B.D. 30.010, 30.015
Gordano Building Contractors v Burgess [1988] 1 W.L.R. 890; (1988) 85(30) L.S.G. 36; (1988) 138 N.L.J. Rep. 127; (1988) 132 S.J. 1091, CA (Civ Div) 26.003
Gotha City v Sotheby's (No.2); Germany v Sotheby's (No.2), *The Times*, October 8, 1998, Q.B.D. 5.020
Graham v Chorley BC [2006] EWCA Civ 92; [2006] C.P. Rep. 24; [2006] P.I.Q.R. P24; *The Times*, March 20, 2006; *The Independent*, February 23, 2006, CA (Civ Div) 37.005, 44.002
Graham v Dodds [1983] 1 W.L.R. 808; [1983] 2 All E.R. 953; (1983) 147 J.P. 746, HL (NI) 8.014
Grant v Southwestern and County Properties Ltd [1975] Ch. 185; [1974] 3 W.L.R. 221; [1974] 2 All E.R. 465; (1974) 118 S.J. 548, Ch D 30.004 30.011
Gray v Going Places Leisure Travel Ltd [2005] EWCA Civ 189; [2005] C.P. Rep. 21; [2005] 3 Costs L.R. 405; [2005] P.N.L.R. 26, CA (Civ Div) 39.002

Green v Hancocks (A firm) [2001] Lloyd's Rep. P.N. 212; (2000) L.T.L. December
    15, CA (Civ Div) 1.017
Greene v Associated Newspapers Ltd; sub nom. Green v Associated Newspapers
    Ltd [2004] EWCA Civ 1462; [2005] Q.B. 972; [2005] 3 W.L.R. 281; [2005] 1
    All E.R. 30; [2005] E.M.L.R. 10; (2004) 101(45) L.S.G. 31; (2004) 148
    S.J.L.B. 1318; *The Times*, November 10, 2004; *The Independent*, November
    9, 2004, CA (Civ Div) 27.011
Gregory v Turner; R. (on the application of Morris) v North Somerset Council
    [2003] EWCA Civ 183; [2003] 1 W.L.R. 1149; [2003] 2 All E.R. 1114; [2003]
    C.P. Rep. 40; [2003] 3 E.G.L.R. 129; *The Times*, February 21, 2003; *The
    Independent*, February 27, 2003, CA (Civ Div) 1.020, 7.004
Gregson v Channel Four Television Corp (Amendment of Party Name); sub nom.
    Gregson v Channel Four Television Co. Ltd [2000] C.P. Rep. 60; *The Times*,
    August 11, 2000; *The Independent*, October 2, 2000, CA (Civ Div) 12.053
Gregson v Channel Four Television Corp, *The Times*, August 19, 2000 .... 8.003
Grepe v Loam; sub nom. Bulteel v Grepe (1888) L.R. 37 Ch. D. 168, CA 7.011
Group Josi Re Co. SA v Walbrook Insurance Co. Ltd; sub nom. Group Josi Re
    (formerly Group Josi Reassurance SA) v Walbrook Insurance Co. Ltd;
    Deutsche Ruckversicherung AG v Walbrook Insurance Co. Ltd [1996] 1
    W.L.R. 1152; [1996] 1 All E.R. 791, CA (Civ Div); affirming [1995] 1 W.L.R.
    1017; [1994] 4 All E.R. 181; [1995] 1 Lloyd's Rep. 153; [1994] C.L.C. 415;
    (1994) 91(25) L.S.G. 30; (1994) 138 S.J.L.B. 111; *The Times*, May 6, 1994,
    Q.B.D. (Comm) 14.005
Groupama Insurance Co. Ltd v Overseas Partners Re Ltd (Costs); sub nom.
    Groupama Insurance Co. Ltd v Aon Ltd (Costs) [2003] EWCA Civ 1846;
    [2004] 1 All E.R. (Comm) 893; [2004] C.P. Rep. 18; [2004] 1 C.L.C. 779;
    (2004) 148 S.J.L.B. 28, CA (Civ Div) 38.018
Grovit v Doctor [1997] 1 W.L.R. 640; [1997] 2 All E.R. 417; [1997] C.L.C. 1038;
    (1997) 94(20) L.S.G. 37; (1997) 147 N.L.J. 633; (1997) 141 S.J.L.B. 107; *The
    Times*, April 25, 1997; *The Independent*, May 1, 1997, HL 33.008
Guardian Media Group Plc v Associated Newspapers Ltd (2000) L.T.L. January
    20, CA 27.005
Guardians of Tendring Union v Dowton [1891] 3 Ch. 265, CA; reversing (1890)
    L.R. 45 Ch. D. 583, Ch D 7.018
Guinle v Kirreh; Kinstreet Ltd v Balmargo Corp Ltd; Interfisa Management Inc v
    Hamam [2000] C.P. Rep. 62; (1999) L.T.L., December 3, Ch D 26.003
Gulf Azov Shipping Co. Ltd v Chief Idisi (No.2); United Kingdom Mutual
    Steamship Assurance Association (Bermuda) Ltd v Lonestar Drilling
    Nigeria Ltd; Gulf Azov Shipping Co. Ltd v Lonestar Drilling Nigeria Ltd;
    United Kingdom Mutual Steamship Assurance Association (Bermuda) Ltd
    v Lonestar Overseas Ltd [2001] EWCA Civ 505; [2001] 2 All E.R. (Comm)
    673; [2001] 1 Lloyd's Rep. 727, CA (Civ Div) 41.003
Gulf Interstate Oil Co. v ANT Trade & Transport Ltd of Malta; The Giovanna
    [1999] 1 All E.R. (Comm.) 97; [1999] 1 Lloyd's Rep. 867; [1999] C.L.C. 554;
    The Independent, January 11, 1999, Q.B.D. (Comm) 27.017
Gulf Oil (Great Britain) Ltd v Page [1987] Ch. 327; [1987] 3 W.L.R. 166; [1987]
    3 All E.R. 14; (1987) 84 L.S.G. 1968; (1987) 137 N.L.J. 408; (1987) 131 S.J.
    695, CA (Civ Div) 27.011
Gundry v Sainsbury [1910] 1 K.B. 645; [1997] Costs L.R. (Core Vol.) 1, CA 38.020
Gurney Consulting Engineers v Gleeds Health & Safety Ltd [2006] EWHC 43;
    The Times, April 24, 2006, Q.B.D. (TCC) 23.019

Gurtner v Circuit [1968] 2 Q.B. 587; [1968] 2 W.L.R. 668; [1968] 1 All E.R. 328; [1968] 1 Lloyd's Rep. 171; (1968) 112 S.J. 73; (1968) 112 S.J. 63, CA (Civ Div) 8.014

H v A, *The Times,* July 13, 1983, CA (Civ Div) 29.020
H v Lambeth, Southwark and Lewisham HA [2001] EWCA Civ 1455; [2001] C.P. Rep. 117; [2002] P.I.Q.R. P14; [2002] Lloyd's Rep. Med. 8; *The Times,* October 8, 2001, CA (Civ Div) 23.018
H v N & T. *See* H v Northampton CC
H v Northampton CC [2004] EWCA Civ 526; [2005] P.I.Q.R. P7; (2004) 101(21) L.S.G. 36; (2004) 148 S.J.L.B. 540, CA (Civ Div) 5.007
HFC Bank Plc v HSBC Bank Plc (formerly Midland Bank Plc) [2000] C.P.L.R. 197; (2000) 97(19) L.S.G. 43; (2000) 144 S.J.L.B. 182; (2000) L.T.L., April 3; *The Times,* April 26, 2000; *The Independent,* April 3, 2000, CA (Civ Div) 37.016
H (Minors) (Sexual Abuse: Standard of Proof), Re; sub nom. H and R (Child Sexual Abuse: Standard of Proof), Re; H (Minors) (Child Abuse: Threshold Conditions), Re [1996] A.C. 563; [1996] 2 W.L.R. 8; [1996] 1 All E.R. 1; [1996] 1 F.L.R. 80; [1996] 1 F.C.R. 509; [1996] Fam. Law 74; (1995) 145 N.L.J. 1887; (1996) 140 S.J.L.B. 24; *The Times,* December 15, 1995; *The Independent,* January 17, 1996, HL 31.004
HSS Hire Services Group Plc v BMB Builders Merchants Ltd (Costs) [2005] EWCA Civ 626; [2005] 1 W.L.R. 3158; [2005] 3 All E.R. 486; [2006] 2 Costs L.R. 213; *The Times,* May 31, 2005, CA (Civ Div) 29.020
H West & Son Ltd v Shephard; sub nom. Shepherd v H West & Son Ltd [1964] A.C. 326; [1963] 2 W.L.R. 1359; [1963] 2 All E.R. 625; (1963) 107 S.J. 454, HL 4.010
Habib Bank Ltd v Ahmed; sub nom. Ahmed v Habib Bank Ltd [2001] EWCA Civ 1270; [2002] 1 Lloyd's Rep. 444, CA (Civ Div); reversing (2000) 97(43) L.S.G. 37; (2000) 144 S.J.L.B. 275; *The Times,* November 2, 2000, Q.B.D. 40.015
Habib Bank Ltd v Jaffer (Gulzar Haider); Habib Bank Ltd v Jaffer (Haider Ladhu) [2000] C.P.L.R. 438; (2000) 97(17) L.S.G. 34; (2000) 144 S.J.L.B. 187; *The Times,* April 5, 2000, CA (Civ Div) 33.008
Hadmor Productions v Hamilton [1983] 1 A.C. 191; [1982] 2 W.L.R. 322; [1982] 1 All E.R. 1042; [1982] I.C.R. 114; [1982] I.R.L.R. 102; (1982) 126 S.J. 134, HL 27.006
Halki Shipping Corp v Sopex Oils Ltd; The Halki [1998] 1 W.L.R. 726; [1998] 2 All E.R. 23; [1998] 1 Lloyd's Rep. 465; [1998] C.L.C. 583; (1998) 142 S.J.L.B. 44; [1998] N.P.C. 4; *The Times,* January 19, 1998; *The Independent,* January 12, 1998, CA (Civ Div) 33.004
Halloran v Delaney [2002] EWCA Civ 1258; [2003] 1 W.L.R. 28; [2003] 1 All E.R. 775; [2002] 3 Costs L.R. 503; [2003] R.T.R. 9; [2003] P.I.Q.R. P5; (2002) 152 N.L.J. 1386; (2002) 146 S.J.L.B. 205, CA (Civ Div) 38.026
Halsey v Milton Keynes General NHS Trust; Steel v Joy [2004] EWCA Civ 576; [2004] 1 W.L.R. 3002; [2004] 4 All E.R. 920; [2004] C.P. Rep. 34; [2004] 3 Costs L.R. 393; (2005) 81 B.M.L.R. 108; (2004) 101(22) L.S.G. 31; (2004) 154 N.L.J. 769; (2004) 148 S.J.L.B. 629; *The Times,* May 27, 2004; *The Independent,* May 21, 2004, CA (Civ Div) 9.028, 34.002, 38.018
Hamilton v Hertfordshire CC [2003] EWHC 3018; [2004] C.P. Rep. 22; [2004] P.I.Q.R. P23, Q.B.D. 16.009
Hanak v Green [1958] 2 Q.B. 9; [1958] 2 W.L.R. 755; [1958] 2 All E.R. 141; 1 B.L.R. 1; (1958) 102 S.J. 329, CA 12.037

Hannigan v Hannigan (2000) L.T.L., May 18 .... 33.008
Hannigan v Hannigan (2000) I.L.R., July 3 .... 12.052
Hannigan v Hannigan [2000] 2 F.C.R. 650; [2006] W.T.L.R. 597; *The Independent*,
   July 3, 2000; *The Independent*, May 23, 2000, CA (Civ Div) 1.011
Hansom v F Rex Makin & Co; sub nom. Hansom v Makin [2003] EWCA Civ
   1801; (2004) 148 S.J.L.B. 57, CA (Civ Div) 33.011
Haq v Singh [2001] EWCA Civ 957; [2001] 1 W.L.R. 1594; [2001] C.P. Rep. 95;
   [2001] B.P.I.R. 1002; *The Times*, July 10, 2001, CA (Civ Div) 12.053
Hardwick v Hudson [1999] 1 W.L.R. 1770; [1999] 3 All E.R. 426; [1999] P.I.Q.R.
   Q202; [1999] Lloyd's Rep. Med. 208; (1999) 96(22) L.S.G. 34; (1999) 149
   N.L.J. 806; *The Times*, May 20, 1999; *The Independent*, May 27, 1999, CA
   (Civ Div) 4.007
Harlow & Milner Ltd v Teasdale [2006] EWHC 1708 (TCC); [2006] B.L.R. 359,
   Q.B.D. (TCC) 40.008
Harman v Glencross [1986] Fam. 81; [1986] 2 W.L.R. 637; [1986] 1 All E.R. 545;
   [1986] 2 F.L.R. 241; [1986] Fam. Law 215; (1986) 83 L.S.G. 870; (1986) 136
   N.L.J. 69; (1986) 130 S.J. 224, CA (Civ Div) 40.010
Harmon CFEM Facades (UK) Ltd v Corporate Officer of the House of Commons
   [2000] EWHC Technology 84; 67 Con. L.R. 1; (2000) 2 L.G.L.R. 372,
   Q.B.D. (TCC) 25.001, 25.004, 25.005
Harrington v Link Motor Policies at Lloyd's; sub nom. Harrington v Pinkey
   [1989] 2 Lloyd's Rep. 310; [1989] R.T.R. 345; *The Times*, May 12, 1989, CA
   (Civ Div) 6.028
Harris v Empress Motors Ltd; Cole v Crown Poultry Packers Ltd [1984] 1 W.L.R.
   212; [1983] 3 All E.R. 561; (1983) 80 L.S.G. 2362; (1983) 127 S.J. 647; *The
   Times*, July 18, 1983, CA (Civ Div) 4.013
Harrison and Harrison v Bloom Camillin (A firm) (1999) L.T.L., March 30 .... 31.008
Harrison and Harrison v Bloom Camillin (A firm) (1999) L.T.L., May 14 ..... 36.003
Harrison v Bloom Camillin (2000) L.T.L., February 4 .... 9.035
Harrison v Bottenheim [1878] 26 W.R. 362 .... 19.007
Harrison v Tew [1990] 2 A.C. 523; [1990] 2 W.L.R. 210; [1990] 1 All E.R. 321;
   (1990) 87(8) L.S.G. 44; (1990) 134 S.J. 374, HL 39.003
Hart Investments Ltd v Fidler [2006] EWHC 2857 (TCC); [2007] B.L.R. 30; [2007]
   T.C.L.R. 1; 109 Con. L.R. 67; [2006] C.I.L.L. 2397; (2007) L.T.L., January
   18, Q.B.D. (TCC) 8.006
Hart v Emelkirk Ltd; Howroyd v Emelkirk Ltd [1983] 1 W.L.R. 1289; [1983] 3 All
   E.R. 15; (1983) 9 H.L.R. 114; (1983) 267 E.G. 946; (1983) 127 S.J. 156,
   Ch D 27.030
Hartley v Birmingham City Council [1992] 1 W.L.R. 968; [1992] 2 All E.R. 213;
   The Independent, August 16, 1991, CA (Civ Div) 5.018
Hartley v Sandholme Iron Co. Ltd [1975] Q.B. 600; [1974] 3 W.L.R. 445; [1974] 3 All
   E.R. 475; [1974] S.T.C. 434; 17 K.I.R. 205; (1974) 118 S.J. 702, Q.B.D 4.002
Hashtroodi v Hancock [2004] EWCA Civ 652; [2004] 1 W.L.R. 3206; [2004] 3 All
   E.R. 530; [2005] C.P. Rep. 17; *The Times*, June 4, 2004; *The Independent*,
   June 16, 2004, CA (Civ Div) 9.006
Haward v Fawcetts (A Firm) [2006] UKHL 9; [2006] 1 W.L.R. 682; [2006] 3 All
   E.R. 497; [2006] P.N.L.R. 25; [2006] 10 E.G. 154 (C.S.); [2006] N.P.C. 25;
   The Times, March 3, 2006, HL 5.007, 5.008
Haycocks v Neville [2007] EWCA Civ 78, CA (Civ Div) 1.008
Hayes v Transco Plc [2003] EWCA Civ 1261; (2003) 147 S.J.L.B. 1089, CA (Civ
   Div) 33.012

Helitune Ltd v Stewart Hughes Ltd [1994] F.S.R. 422; (1995) C.L.Y. 4156, Ch D .. 30.018
Hellenic Industrial Development Bank SA v Atkin; The Julia [2002] EWHC 1405;
    [2003] Lloyd's Rep. I.R. 365, Q.B.D. (Comm) 3.002
Henderson v Merrett Syndicates Ltd (No.1); sub nom. Gooda Walker Ltd v
    Deeny; McLarnon Deeney v Gooda Walker Ltd; Arbuthnott v Fagan;
    Hallam-Eames v Merrett Syndicates Ltd; Hughes v Merrett Syndicates Ltd;
    Feltrim Underwriting Agencies Ltd v Arbuthnott; Deeny v Gooda Walker
    Ltd (Duty of Care) [1995] 2 A.C. 145; [1994] 3 W.L.R. 761; [1994] 3 All E.R.
    506; [1994] 2 Lloyd's Rep. 468; [1994] C.L.C. 918; (1994) 144 N.L.J. 1204;
    The Times, July 26, 1994; The Independent, August 3, 1994, HL 5.008
Heppenstall v Jackson [1939] 1 K.B. 585, CA 40.005
Hertsmere Primary Care Trust v Rabindra-Anandh [2005] EWHC 320; [2005]
    3 All E.R. 274; [2005] C.P. Rep. 41; The Times, April 25, 2005,
    Ch D 1.011, 29.010
Heyward v Plymouth Hospital NHS Trust [2005] EWCA Civ 939; [2006] C.P.
    Rep. 3; The Times, August 1, 2005; The Independent, June 29, 2005, CA
    (Civ Div) 13.007
Hicks v Chief Constable of South Yorkshire Police; sub nom. Hicks v Wright;
    Wafer v Wright [1992] 2 All E.R. 65; [1992] P.I.Q.R. P433; The Times,
    March 9, 1992; The Independent, March 11, 1992; The Guardian, March
    11, 1992, HL 4.013
Hill v Bailey [2003] EWHC 2835; [2004] 1 All E.R. 1210; [2004] C.P. Rep. 24;
    [2004] 1 Costs L.R. 135; (2004) 101(2) L.S.G. 28; The Times, January 5,
    2004, Ch D 39.014
Hill v Hart-Davies; sub nom. Hill v Hart-Davis (1884) L.R. 26 Ch. D. 470, CA 30.008
Hirschorn v Evans; sub nom. Hirschorn v Barclays Bank Ltd [1938] 2 K.B. 801,
    CA 40.005
Hodgson v Imperial Tobacco Ltd (No.1) [1998] 1 W.L.R. 1056; [1998] 2 All E.R.
    673; [1998] 1 Costs L.R. 14; [1999] P.I.Q.R. Q1; (1998) 41 B.M.L.R. 1;
    (1998) 95(15) L.S.G. 31; (1998) 148 N.L.J. 241; (1998) 142 S.J.L.B. 93; The
    Times, February 13, 1998; The Independent, February 17, 1998, CA
    (Civ Div) 1.017, 39.05
Hoffmann (F) La Roche & Co. AG v Secretary of State for Trade and Industry
    [1975] A.C. 295; [1974] 3 W.L.R. 104; [1974] 2 All E.R. 1128; [1975] 3 All
    E.R. 945; (1973) 117 S.J. 713; (1974) 118 S.J. 500, HL 27.002
Hollins v Russell; Tichband v Hurdman; Dunn v Ward; Pratt v Bull; Worth
    v McKenna; Sharratt v London Central Bus Co. Ltd (No.3) [2003] EWCA
    Civ 718; [2003] 1 W.L.R. 2487; [2003] 4 All E.R. 590; [2003] 3 Costs
    L.R. 423; (2003) 100(28) L.S.G. 30; (2003) 153 N.L.J. 920; (2003) 147 S.J.L.B.
    662; The Times, June 10, 2003; The Independent, June 3, 2003, CA (Civ
    Div) 38.021, 38.040, 39.006
Homebase Ltd v LSS Services Ltd [2004] EWHC 3182, Ch D 19.014
Honey v Newman (1997) C.L.Y. 634, CC (Birkenhead) 32.002
Hooper v Biddle & Co. [2006] EWHC 2995, (2006) L.T.L., October 11, Ch D 9.035
Horne (A Bankrupt), Re; sub nom. Dacorum BC v Horne; Horne v Dacorum BC
    [2000] 4 All E.R. 550; [2000] B.P.I.R. 1047; The Times, June 14, 2000; The
    Independent, June 7, 2000, CA (Civ Div) 42.003
Horton v Sadler [2006] UKHL 27; [2007] 1 A.C. 307; [2006] 2 W.L.R. 1346; [2006]
    3 All E.R. 1177; [2006] R.T.R. 27; [2006] P.I.Q.R. P30; (2006) 91 B.M.L.R.
    60; (2006) 103(26) L.S.G. 27; (2006) 156 N.L.J. 1024; (2006) 150 S.J.L.B. 808;
    The Times, June 19, 2006, HL 5.019

House of Spring Gardens Ltd v Waite (No.2) [1991] 1 Q.B. 241; [1990] 3 W.L.R.
347; [1990] 2 All E.R. 990, CA (Civ Div) 27.028
Housecroft v Burnett [1986] 1 All E.R. 332; (1985) 135 N.L.J. 728, CA
(Civ Div) 4.012
Howe v David Brown Tractors (Retail) Ltd [1991] 4 All E.R. 30, CA (Civ Div) ... 5.007
Howells v Dominion Insurance Co. Ltd (2005) L.T.L. April 4 .... 7.018
Howglen Ltd (Application for Disclosure), Re [2001] 1 All E.R. 376; [2001] B.C.C.
245; [2001] 2 B.C.L.C. 695; *The Times*, April 21, 2000, Ch D 30.023
Hubbard v Lambeth Southwark & Lewisham HA. *See* H v Lambeth, Southwark
and Lewisham HA
Huck v Robson [2002] EWCA Civ 398; [2003] 1 W.L.R. 1340; [2002] 3 All E.R.
263; [2002] C.P. Rep. 38; [2002] C.P.L.R. 345; [2003] 1 Costs L.R. 19; [2002]
P.I.Q.R. P31, CA (Civ Div) 29.009, 29.022
Hughes v McKeown [1985] 1 W.L.R. 963; [1985] 3 All E.R. 284; (1985) 82 L.S.G.
3447; (1985) 135 N.L.J. 383; (1985) 129 S.J. 543, Q.B.D. 4.012
Hunt v Severs; sub nom. Severs v Hunt [1994] 2 A.C. 350; [1994] 2 W.L.R. 602;
[1994] 2 All E.R. 385; [1994] 2 Lloyd's Rep. 129; [1994] P.I.Q.R. Q60; (1994)
144 N.L.J. 603; (1994) 138 S.J.L.B. 104; *The Times*, May 2, 1994; *The
Independent*, May 5, 1994, HL 4.007
Huntingdon Life Sciences Group Plc v Stop Huntingdon Animal Cruelty (SHAC)
[2007] EWHC 522, (2007) L.T.L. April 19, Q.B.D. 7.018
Hurst v Barnet LBC. *See* Barnet LBC v Hurst
Hurstwood Developments Ltd v Motor & General & Andersley & Co. Insurance
Services Ltd; sub nom. Hurstwood Developments Ltd v Motor & General
& Aldersley & Co. Insurance Services Ltd [2001] EWCA Civ 1785; [2002]
Lloyd's Rep. I.R. 185; [2002] Lloyd's Rep. P.N. 195; [2002] P.N.L.R. 10, CA
(Civ Div) 18.005
Hussain v Hussain [1986] Fam. 134; [1986] 2 W.L.R. 801; [1986] 1 All E.R. 961;
[1986] 2 F.L.R. 271; [1986] Fam. Law 269; (1986) 83 L.S.G. 1314; (1986) 136
N.L.J. 358; (1986) 130 S.J. 341, CA (Civ Div) 27.014, 34.003
Hytec Information Systems Ltd v Coventry City Council [1997] 1 W.L.R.
1666; (1997) 13 Const. L.J. 344; *The Times*, December 31, 1996, CA
(Civ Div) 33.007

IM Properties Plc v Cape & Dalgleish [1999] Q.B. 297; [1998] 3 W.L.R. 457; [1998]
3 All E.R. 203; (1998) 95(31) L.S.G. 34; (1998) 95(24) L.S.G. 34; (1998)
148 N.L.J. 906; (1998) 142 S.J.L.B. 174; *The Times*, May 28, 1998, CA
(Civ Div) 3.007
Independiente Ltd v Music Trading On-Line (HK) Ltd [2007] EWCA Civ 111;
(2007) 151 S.J.L.B. 159; (2007) L.T.L., January 26, CA (Civ Div) 34.004
Industrie Chimiche Italia Centrale v Alexander G Tsavliris & Sons Maritime Co;
The Choko Star; Industrie Chimiche Italia Centrale v Pancristo Shipping
Co. SA; Industrie Chimiche Italia Centrale v Bula Shipping Corp [1996] 1
W.L.R. 774; [1996] 1 All E.R. 114; [1995] 2 Lloyd's Rep. 608; [1995] C.L.C.
1461; *The Times*, August 8, 1995; *The Independent*, September 4, 1995,
Q.B.D. (Comm) 7.015
International Credit & Investment Co. (Overseas) Ltd v Adham (Appointment of
Receiver) [1998] B.C.C. 134, Ch D 27.030
Interoute Telecommunications (UK) Ltd v Fashion Gossip Ltd, *The Times*,
November 10, 1999, Ch D 27.020

TABLE OF CASES

Investment Invoice Financing Ltd v Limehouse Board Mills Ltd; sub nom. Investment Invoice Financial Ltd v Limehouse Board Mills Ltd [2006] EWCA Civ 9; [2006] 1 W.L.R. 985; [2006] 4 Costs L.R. 632; (2006) 150 S.J.L.B. 161; *The Times,* January 23, 2006, CA (Civ Div) 33.005
Iraqi Ministry of Defence v Arcepey Shipping Co. SA [1981] Q.B. 65; [1980] 2 W.L.R. 488; [1980] 1 All E.R. 480; [1980] 1 Lloyd's Rep. 632; (1980) 124 S.J. 148, Q.B.D. (Comm) 27.021
Irtelli v Squatriti [1993] Q.B. 83; [1992] 3 W.L.R. 218; [1992] 3 All E.R. 294; (1992) 136 S.J.L.B. 100; *The Times,* March 2, 1992, CA (Civ Div) 41.003
Irvine v Commissioner of Police of the Metropolis (Costs) [2005] EWCA Civ 129; [2005] C.P. Rep. 19; [2005] 3 Costs L.R. 380; (2005) 149 S.J.L.B. 182, CA (Civ Div) 38.008
Islam v Meah [2005] EWCA Civ 1485, CA (Civ Div) 1.009
Islington LBC v Uckac [2006] EWCA Civ 340; [2006] 1 W.L.R. 1303; [2006] 1 F.C.R. 668; [2006] H.L.R. 35; [2006] L. & T.R. 10; [2006] N.P.C. 39; *The Times,* April 19, 2006; *The Independent,* April 7, 2006, CA (Civ Div) 12.054

JFS (UK) Ltd v Dŵr Cymru Cyf [1999] 1 W.L.R. 231; [1999] B.L.R. 17; (1999) 1 T.C.L.R. 187; (1998) 95(39) L.S.G. 40; (1998) 142 S.J.L.B. 256; *The Times,* October 10, 1998, CA (Civ Div) 18.002
JP Morgan Chase Bank v Springwell Navigation Corp [2005] EWCA Civ 1602; (2005) L.T.L., December 20, CA (Civ Div) 31.023, 33.012
JP Morgan Chase Bank v Springwell Navigation Corp (Application to Strike Out) [2006] EWHC 2755 (Comm); [2007] 1 All E.R. (Comm) 549; (2006) L.T.L, December 4, Q.B.D. (Comm) 23.005
J Sainsbury Plc v Broadway Malyan, 61 Con. L.R. 31; [1999] P.N.L.R. 286, Q.B.D. (OR) 18.005
Jackson v Marley Davenport Ltd [2004] EWCA Civ 1225; [2004] 1 W.L.R. 2926; [2005] C.P. Rep. 8; [2005] B.L.R. 13; [2005] P.I.Q.R. P10; [2005] 1 E.G.L.R. 103; (2004) 101(38) L.S.G. 29; (2004) 148 S.J.L.B. 1121; *The Times,* October 7, 2004, CA (Civ Div) 23.011
Jafari-Fini v Skillglass Ltd [2005] EWCA Civ 356; [2005] B.C.C. 842, CA (Civ Div) . .7.021
Jaggard v Sawyer [1995] 1 W.L.R. 269; [1995] 2 All E.R. 189; [1995] 1 E.G.L.R. 146; [1995] 13 E.G. 132; [1994] E.G. 139 (C.S.); [1994] N.P.C. 116; *The Independent,* August 22, 1994, CA (Civ Div) 27.001
James v Baily Gibson & Co. [2002] EWCA Civ 1690; [2003] C.P. Rep. 24; (2002) 99(46) L.S.G. 33(2002) L.T.L., October 30, CA (Civ Div) 33.003
James v Evans; sub nom. Evans v James (Administratrix of Hopkin's Estate) [1999] EWCA Civ 1759; [2001] C.P. Rep. 36; [2003] C.P.L.R. 163; [2000] 3 E.G.L.R. 1; [2000] 42 E.G. 173; [2000] E.G. 95 (C.S.); [2000] N.P.C. 85; (2000) 80 P. & C.R. D39; *The Times,* August 2, 2000, CA (Civ Div) 19.005
James E McCabe Ltd v Scottish Courage Ltd [2006] EWHC 538, (2006) L.T.L., April 5, Q.B.D. (Comm) 19.011
Jameson v Central Electricity Generating Board (No.1) [2000] 1 A.C. 455; [1999] 2 W.L.R. 141; [1999] 1 All E.R. 193; [1999] 1 Lloyd's Rep. 573; [1999] P.I.Q.R. Q81; (1999) 96(5) L.S.G. 37; (1999) 143 S.J.L.B. 29; *The Times,* December 17, 1998, HL 4.018
Jani-King (GB) Ltd v Prodger [2007] EWHC 712, (2007) L.T.L., April 10, Q.B.D. 33.007

Jaura v Ahmed [2002] EWCA Civ 210; *The Times,* March 18, 2002, CA (Civ Div) 3.002
Jefford v Gee [1970] 2 Q.B. 130; [1970] 2 W.L.R. 702; [1970] 1 All E.R. 1202; [1970] 1 Lloyd's Rep. 107; (1970) 114 S.J. 206, CA (Civ Div) 4.020
Jet West v Haddican [1992] 1 W.L.R. 487; [1992] 2 All E.R. 545, CA (Civ Div) 27.016, 29.019
Jeyapragash v Secretary of State for the Home Department; sub nom. R. (on the application of Jeyapragash) v Immigration Appeal Tribunal [2004] EWCA Civ 1260; [2005] 1 All E.R. 412; *The Times,* October 12, 2004; *The Independent,* October 27, 2004, CA (Civ Div) 44.013
John v Rees; Martin v Davis; Rees v John [1970] Ch. 345; [1969] 2 W.L.R. 1294; [1969] 2 All E.R. 274; (1969) 113 S.J. 487, Ch D 7.018
Johnson v Gore Wood & Co. (No.1); sub nom. Johnson v Gore Woods & Co. [2002] 2 A.C. 1; [2001] 2 W.L.R. 72; [2001] 1 All E.R. 481; [2001] C.P.L.R. 49; [2001] B.C.C. 820; [2001] 1 B.C.L.C. 313; [2001] P.N.L.R. 18; (2001) 98(1) L.S.G. 24; (2001) 98(8) L.S.G. 46; (2000) 150 N.L.J. 1889; (2001) 145 S.J.L.B. 29; *The Times,* December 22, 2000; *The Independent,* February 7, 2001, HL 33.008
Johnson v Gore Wood & Co. (No.3) [2004] EWCA Civ 14; [2004] C.P. Rep. 27; (2004) 148 S.J.L.B. 148; *The Times,* February 17, 2004; *The Independent,* February 5, 2004, CA (Civ Div) 29.024
Johnson v Warren (2007) L.T.L., May 2, CA (Civ Div) 4.014
Jones v Arthur (1840) 8 Dowl 442 .... 12.035
Jones v Caradon Catnic Ltd [2005] EWCA Civ 1821; [2006] 3 Costs L.R. 427, CA (Civ Div) 38.023
Jones v Greavison (1998) C.L.Y. 327, CC (Dudley) 30.021
Jones v National Coal Board [1957] 2 Q.B. 55; [1957] 2 W.L.R. 760; [1957] 2 All E.R. 155; (1957) 101 S.J. 319, CA 37.015
Jones v Sherwood Computer Services Plc [1992] 1 W.L.R. 277; [1992] 2 All E.R. 170; [1989] E.G. 172 (C.S.); *The Times,* December 14, 1989, CA (Civ Div) 23.006
Jones v Swift Structures (1995) C.L.Y. 4160, CC (Romford) 32.002
Jones v Warwick University; sub nom. Jones v University of Warwick [2003] EWCA Civ 151; [2003] 1 W.L.R. 954; [2003] 3 All E.R. 760; [2003] C.P. Rep. 36; [2003] P.I.Q.R. P23; (2003) 72 B.M.L.R. 119; (2003) 100(11) L.S.G. 32; (2003) 153 N.L.J. 231; (2003) 147 S.J.L.B. 179; *The Times,* February 7, 2003; *The Independent,* February 11, 2003, CA (Civ Div) 31.020
Joseph v Joseph (2003) L.T.L., February 27 .... 33.008

KR v Bryn Alyn Community (Holdings) Ltd (In Liquidation); sub nom. Various Claimants v BACHL; Various Claimants v Bryn Alyn Community (Holdings) Ltd (In Liquidation) [2003] EWCA Civ 85; [2003] Q.B. 1441; [2003] 3 W.L.R. 107; [2004] 2 All E.R. 716; [2003] 1 F.L.R. 1203; [2003] 1 F.C.R. 385; [2003] Lloyd's Rep. Med. 175; [2003] Fam. Law 482; *The Times,* February 17, 2003, CA (Civ Div) 5.018
KR v Bryn Alyn Community (Holdings) Ltd (In Liquidation) (Permission to Amend); sub nom. R v Bryn Alyn Community (Holdings) Ltd (Permission to Amend); Rowlands v Bryn Alyn Community (Holdings) Ltd (In Liquidation) [2003] EWCA Civ 383; [2003] C.P. Rep. 49; [2003] P.I.Q.R. P30; (2003) 147 S.J.L.B. 387; [2003] N.P.C. 40, CA (Civ Div) 29.023

TABLE OF CASES

Kamal v Redcliffe Close (Old Brompton Road) Management Ltd (2005) L.T.L., January 21, Ch D 15.016

Kamali v City & Country Properties Ltd; sub nom. City & Country Properties Ltd v Kamali [2006] EWCA Civ 1879; [2007] 1 W.L.R. 1219; (2007) L.T.L., January 31, CA (Civ Div) 8.009

Kapur v JW Francis & Co. (No.1), *The Times*, March 4, 1998, CA (Civ Div) . . . 30.016

Kastor Navigation Co. Ltd v AGF MAT; The Kastor Too; sub nom. Kastor Navigation Co. Ltd v Axa Global Risks (UK) Ltd (The Kastor Too) [2004] EWCA Civ 277; [2005] 2 All E.R. (Comm) 720; [2004] 2 Lloyd's Rep. 119; [2004] 2 C.L.C. 68; [2004] 4 Costs L.R. 569; [2004] Lloyd's Rep. I.R. 481; *The Times*, April 29, 2004, CA (Civ Div) 29.001, 29.023

Kaye v Robertson [1991] F.S.R. 62; *The Times*, March 21, 1990; *The Independent*, March 22, 1990; *The Guardian*, March 22, 1990, CA (Civ Div) 27.011

Keen Phillips (A Firm) v Field [2006] EWCA Civ 1524; [2007] C.P. Rep. 8; [2007] 1 W.L.R. 686; *The Times*, December 7, 2006, CA (Civ Div) 33.011

Kelly v Commissioner of Police of the Metropolis, *The Times*, August 20, 1997, CA (Civ Div) 30.010

Kelly v Dawes, *The Times*, September 27, 1990, Q.B.D. 4.017

Kemper Reinsurance Co. v Minister of Finance [2000] 1 A.C. 1; [1998] 3 W.L.R. 630; (1998) 142 S.J.L.B. 175; *The Times*, May 18, 1998, PC (Ber) 24.001

Kenneth Allison Ltd (In Liquidation) v AE Limehouse & Co. [1992] 2 A.C. 105; [1991] 3 W.L.R. 671; [1991] 4 All E.R. 500; (1991) 141 N.L.J. 1448; (1991) 135 S.J.L.B. 172; *The Times*, October 18, 1991; *The Independent*, October 18, 1991; *The Financial Times*, October 20, 1991, HL 8.017

Kent (Chapper's Executrix) v M&L Management & Legal Ltd [2005] EWHC 2546, Ch D` 7.015

Kew v Bettamix Ltd (formerly Tarmac Roadstone Southern Ltd) [2006] EWCA Civ 1535; (2006) 103(46) L.S.G. 30; (2006) 150 S.J.L.B. 1534; [2007] P.I.Q.R. P16; *The Times*, December 4, 2006, CA (Civ Div) 5.007, 5.018

Khetani v Kanbi [2006] EWCA Civ 1621; (2006) 150 S.J.L.B. 1603, CA (Civ Div) . . .44.017

Khiaban v Beard; sub nom. Khaiban v Beard [2003] EWCA Civ 358; [2003] 1 W.L.R. 1626; [2003] 3 All E.R. 362; [2003] C.P. Rep. 60; [2003] R.T.R. 28; (2003) 100(19) L.S.G. 31; *The Times*, April 17, 2003, CA (Civ Div) . .9.036, 20.001

Kiam v MGN Ltd [2002] EWCA Civ 43; [2003] Q.B. 281; [2002] 3 W.L.R. 1036; [2002] 2 All E.R. 219; [2002] E.M.L.R. 25; (2002) 99(11) L.S.G. 35; *The Times*, February 11, 2002, CA (Civ Div) 38.016

King v Boston (1789) 7 East 481 .... 12.037

King v Telegraph Group Ltd [2004] EWCA Civ 613; [2005] 1 W.L.R. 2282; [2004] C.P. Rep. 35; [2004] 3 Costs L.R. 449; [2004] E.M.L.R. 23; (2004) 101(25) L.S.G. 27; (2004) 154 N.L.J. 823; (2004) 148 S.J.L.B. 664; *The Times*, May 21, 2004, CA (Civ Div) 33.013, 44.017

King v Weston-Howell [1989] 1 W.L.R. 579; [1989] 2 All E.R. 375; (1989) 139 N.L.J. 399; (1989) 133 S.J. 750, CA (Civ Div) 29.024

Kirklees MBC v Wickes Building Supplies Ltd; Mendip DC v B&Q Plc [1993] A.C. 227; [1992] 3 W.L.R. 170; [1992] 3 All E.R. 717; [1992] 2 C.M.L.R. 765; 90 L.G.R. 391; (1992) 142 N.L.J. 967; [1992] N.P.C. 86; *The Times*, June 29, 1992; *The Independent*, June 26, 1992; *The Financial Times*, July 3, 1992; *The Guardian*, July 1, 1992, HL 27.002

Kirkman v Euro Exide Corp (CMP Batteries Ltd) [2007] EWCA Civ 66; (2007) 104(6) L.S.G. 31; (2007) 151 S.J.L.B. 164; *The Times*, February 6, 2007, CA (Civ Div) 1.009, 23.014, 23.023, 31.011

Kirkup v British Rail Engineering Ltd; Priestly v British Rail Engineering Ltd;
　　Painter v British Rail Engineering Ltd [1983] 1 W.L.R. 1165; [1983] 3 All
　　E.R. 147; *The Times*, October 8, 1982, CA (Civ Div) 23.017
Knauf UK GmbH v British Gypsum Ltd (No.1) [2001] EWCA Civ 1570; [2002]
　　1 W.L.R. 907; [2002] 2 All E.R. 525; [2001] 2 All E.R. (Comm) 960; [2002]
　　1 Lloyd's Rep. 199; [2002] C.L.C. 239; [2002] I.L.Pr. 30; (2001) 145 S.J.L.B.
　　259; *The Times*, November 15, 2001; *The Independent*, November 7, 2001,
　　CA (Civ Div) 8.014
Knight v Sage Group Plc (1999) L.T.L., April 28, CA (Civ Div) 23.006
Kuddus v Chief Constable of Leicestershire [2001] UKHL 29; [2002] 2 A.C. 122;
　　[2001] 2 W.L.R. 1789; [2001] 3 All E.R. 193; (2001) 3 L.G.L.R. 45; (2001)
　　98(28) L.S.G. 43; (2001) 151 N.L.J. 936; (2001) 145 S.J.L.B. 166; *The Times*,
　　June 13, 2001; *The Independent*, June 12, 2001; *The Daily Telegraph*, June
　　12, 2001, HL 12.014
Kuenyehia v International Hospitals Group Ltd [2006] EWCA Civ 21; [2006] C.P.
　　Rep. 34; (2006) L.T.L., December 15; *The Times*, February 17, 2006, CA
　　(Civ Div) 8.015
Kufaan Publishing Ltd v Al-Warrak Publishing Ltd; Kufaan Publishing Ltd v
　　Al-Warrak Bookshop Ltd; Kufaan Publishing Ltd v Shubber, March 1,
　　2000, CA (Civ Div) 26.003
Kuwait Airways Corp v Iraqi Airways Co. [2005] EWCA Civ 943 .... 44.005
Kuwait Airways Corp v Iraqi Airways Co. (No.6) [2005] EWCA Civ 286; *The
　　Times*, April 25, 2005 .... 30.013
Kyle Bay Ltd t/a Astons Nightclub v Underwriters Subscribing under Policy
　　No.019057/08/01 [2007] EWCA Civ 57, (2007) L.T.L., February 7 .... 34.005

L v L [2007] EWHC 140, Q.B.D. 27.023
LA Gear Inc v Hi-Tec Sports Plc [1992] F.S.R. 121; *The Times*, December 20, 1991,
　　CA (Civ Div) 27.001
La Caisse Regional Du CreditAgricole Nord de France v Ashdown [2007] EWHC
　　528 (QB); [2007] I.L.Pr. 23; (2007) L.T.L., March 21, Q.B.D. 40.017
La Chemise Lacoste SA v Sketchers USA Ltd [2006] EWHC 3642, (2006) L.T.L.,
　　May 24, Ch D 12.056
Ladd v Marshall [1954] 1 W.L.R. 1489; [1954] 3 All E.R. 745; (1954) 98 S.J.
　　870, CA 44.017
Lahey v Pirelli Tyres Ltd [2007] EWCA Civ 91; (2007) 104(9) L.S.G. 30; (2007) 157
　　N.L.J. 294; [2007] 1 W.L.R. 998; *The Times*, February 19, 2007, CA
　　(Civ Div) 38.018
Lakah Group v Al Jazeera Satellite Channel (Permission to Appeal) [2003] EWCA
　　Civ 1781; [2004] B.C.C. 703, CA (Civ Div) 8.010
Lamont v Burton [2007] EWCA Civ 429; (2007) 104(21) L.S.G. 26; (2007)
　　157 N.L.J. 706; (2007) 151 S.J.L.B. 670; *The Times*, June 7, 2007, CA
　　(Civ Div) 38.013, 38.021
Lane v Esdaile; sub nom. Esdaile v Payne [1891] A.C. 210, HL 44.004, 44.008
Lansing Linde Ltd v Kerr [1991] 1 W.L.R. 251; [1991] 1 All E.R. 418; [1991] I.C.R.
　　428; [1991] I.R.L.R. 80; (1990) 140 N.L.J. 1458; *The Independent*, October
　　11, 1990, CA (Civ Div) 27.007
Latimer Management Consultants Ltd v Ellingham Investments Ltd [2006]
　　EWHC 3662 (Ch), Ch D 43.005

TABLE OF CASES

Law Society v Sephton & Co. [2006] UKHL 22; [2006] 2 A.C. 543; [2006] 2 W.L.R. 1091; [2006] 3 All E.R. 401; [2006] P.N.L.R. 31; (2006) 156 N.L.J. 844; (2006) 150 S.J.L.B. 669; [2006] N.P.C. 56; *The Times,* May 11, 2006, HL 5.002

Lawal v Northern Spirit Ltd [2003] UKHL 35; [2004] 1 All E.R. 187; [2003] I.C.R. 856; [2003] I.R.L.R. 538; [2003] H.R.L.R. 29; [2003] U.K.H.R.R. 1024; (2003) 100(28) L.S.G. 30; (2003) 153 N.L.J. 1005; (2003) 147 S.J.L.B. 783; *The Times,* June 27, 2003, HL 36.012

Lawrence David Ltd v Ashton [1991] 1 All E.R. 385; [1989] I.C.R. 123; [1989] I.R.L.R. 22; [1989] 1 F.S.R. 87; (1988) 85(42) L.S.G. 48; *The Independent,* July 25, 1988, CA (Civ Div) 27.007

Lawrence v Chief Constable of Staffordshire, *The Times,* July 25, 2000 .... 4.020

Leeson v Marsden. *See* Collier v Williams

Leigh v Michelin Tyre Plc [2003] EWCA Civ 1766; [2004] 1 W.L.R. 846; [2004] 2 All E.R. 175; [2004] C.P. Rep. 20; [2004] 1 Costs L.R. 148; *The Times,* December 16, 2003; *The Independent,* December 18, 2003, CA (Civ Div) 33.013

Lewis v Eliades (No.4); sub nom. Karis v Lewis [2005] EWCA Civ 1637; [2006] 2 P. & C.R. DG2, CA (Civ Div); reversing in part [2005] EWHC 488; [2005] All E.R. (D) 345 (Apr), Ch D 40.010

Liff v Peasley [1980] 1 W.L.R. 781; [1980] 1 All E.R. 623; (1980) 124 S.J. 360, CA (Civ Div) 7.015

Lilly ICOS Ltd v Pfizer Ltd (No.2); sub nom. Lilly ICOS LLC v Pfizer Ltd (No.2); Lily ICOS Ltd v Pfizer Ltd (No.2) [2002] EWCA Civ 2; [2002] 1 W.L.R. 2253; [2002] 1 All E.R. 842; [2002] F.S.R. 54; (2002) 25(3) I.P.D. 25016; (2002) 99(10) L.S.G. 33; (2002) 146 S.J.L.B. 29; *The Times,* January 28, 2002, CA (Civ Div) 30.020

Lim Poh Choo v Camden and Islington AHA [1980] A.C. 174; [1979] 3 W.L.R. 44; [1979] 2 All E.R. 910; (1979) 123 S.J. 457, HL 4.006

Lindsay v Wood [2006] EWHC 2895; *The Times,* December 8, 2006, Q.B.D. 7.006

Littaur v Steggles Palmer [1986] 1 W.L.R. 287; [1986] 1 All E.R. 780; (1986) 83 L.S.G. 1138; (1985) 130 S.J. 225, CA (Civ Div) 39.008

Liverpool Roman Catholic Archdiocesan Trustees Inc v Goldberg (No.2) [2001] Lloyd's Rep. P.N. 518; (2001) 98(17) L.S.G. 38; *The Times,* March 9, 2001, Ch D 23.015

Lloyds Bank Plc v Byrne [1993] 1 F.L.R. 369; [1993] 2 F.C.R. 41; (1991) 23 H.L.R. 472; [1991] E.G. 57 (C.S.); *The Independent,* June 3, 1991, CA (Civ Div) 40.010

Lloyds Bank Plc v Rogers (No.2) [1999] 3 E.G.L.R. 83; [1999] 38 E.G. 187; [1999] E.G. 106 (C.S.); (1999) 96(30) L.S.G. 30, CA (Civ Div) 12.053

Lloyds Investment (Scandinavia) v Ager-Hanssen [2003] EWHC 1740 (Ch), Ch D 43.005

Locabail (UK) Ltd v Bayfield Properties Ltd (Leave to Appeal); Locabail (UK) Ltd v Waldorf Investment Corp (Leave to Appeal); Timmins v Gormley; Williams v Inspector of Taxes; R. v Bristol Betting and Gaming Licensing Committee Ex p. O'Callaghan [2000] Q.B. 451; [2000] 2 W.L.R. 870; [2000] 1 All E.R. 65; [2000] I.R.L.R. 96; [2000] H.R.L.R. 290; [2000] U.K.H.R.R. 300; 7 B.H.R.C. 583; (1999) 149 N.L.J. 1793; [1999] N.P.C. 143; *The Times,* November 19, 1999; *The Independent,* November 23, 1999, CA (Civ Div) 36.012

Lock International Plc v Beswick [1989] 1 W.L.R. 1268; [1989] 3 All E.R. 373; [1989] I.R.L.R. 481; (1989) 86(39) L.S.G. 36; (1989) 139 N.L.J. 644; (1989) S.J. 1297, Ch D 27.014

Lockley v National Blood Transfusion Service [1992] 1 W.L.R. 492; [1992] 2 All E.R. 589; [1992] 3 Med. L.R. 173; *The Times*, November 11, 1991; *The Independent*, November 4, 1991, CA (Civ Div) 2.021
Lonrho Ltd v Shell Petroleum Co. Ltd (No.1) [1980] 1 W.L.R. 627; (1980) 124 S.J. 412, HL 45.001
L'Oreal SA v Bellure NV [2006] EWHC 1503, Ch D 14.002
Lownds v Home Office; sub nom. Home Office v Lownds; Lownds v Secretary of State for the Home Department [2002] EWCA Civ 365; [2002] 1 W.L.R. 2450; [2002] 4 All E.R. 775; [2002] C.P. Rep. 43; [2002] C.P.L.R. 328; [2002] 2 Costs L.R. 279; (2002) 99(19) L.S.G. 28; (2002) 146 S.J.L.B. 86; *The Times*, April 5, 2002, CA (Civ Div) 38.017, 38.040
Lowsley v Forbes (t/a LE Design Services) [1999] 1 A.C. 329; [1998] 3 W.L.R. 501; [1998] 3 All E.R. 897; [1998] 2 Lloyd's Rep. 577; (1998) 95(35) L.S.G. 37; (1998) 148 N.L.J. 1268; (1998) 142 S.J.L.B. 247; *The Times*, August 24, 1998, HL 40.004, 40.008
Lucas v Barking, Havering and Redbridge Hospitals NHS Trust [2003] EWCA Civ 1102; [2004] 1 W.L.R. 220; [2003] 4 All E.R. 720; [2003] C.P. Rep. 65; [2003] Lloyd's Rep. Med. 577; (2004) 77 B.M.L.R. 13; (2003) 100(37) L.S.G. 34; (2003) 153 N.L.J. 1204; *The Times*, August 28, 2003, CA (Civ Div) .. 23.011, 30.017
Lunn Poly Ltd v Liverpool & Lancashire Properties Ltd [2006] EWCA Civ 430; [2007] L. & T.R. 6; [2006] 2 E.G.L.R. 29; [2006] 25 E.G. 210; [2006] 12 E.G. 222 (C.S.); *The Times*, April 18, 2006, CA (Civ Div) 27.002
Lunnun v Singh (Hajar); Lunnun v Singh (Hari); Lunnun v Singh (Bhadur); Lunnun v Singh (Sher) [1999] C.P.L.R. 587; (1999) 96(31) L.S.G. 36; [1999] N.P.C. 83; *The Times*, July 19, 1999; *The Independent*, July 26, 1999, CA (Civ Div) .. 17.005

M v Plymouth HA [1993] P.I.Q.R. P223; (1994) C.L.Y. 3668; *The Times*, November 26, 1992, Q.B.D. 30.024
MV Yorke Motors v Edwards [1982] 1 W.L.R. 444; [1982] 1 All E.R. 1204; (1982) 126 S.J. 245, HL 19.014, 33.007
Mabey and Johnson Ltd v Danos [2007] EWHC 1094; (2007) L.T.L., May 14, Ch D 33.004
McCoubrey v Ministry of Defence [2007] EWCA Civ 17; [2007] LS Law Medical 150; (2007) 151 S.J.L.B. 159; *The Times*, January 26, 2007, CA (Civ Div) 5.007
McDonald v Horn [1995] 1 All E.R. 961; [1995] I.C.R. 685; [1994] Pens. L.R. 155; (1994) 144 N.L.J. 1515; *The Times*, August 10, 1994; *The Independent*, August 8, 1994, CA (Civ Div) 39.017
MacDonald v Taree Holdings Ltd [2001] C.P.L.R. 439; [2001] 1 Costs L.R. 147; (2001) 98(6) L.S.G. 45; *The Times*, December 28, 2000, Ch D 13.010
McGhie v British Telecommunications Plc [2005] EWCA Civ 48; (2005) 149 S.J.L.B. 114, CA (Civ Div) 5.018
McIntyre v Harland & Wolff Plc; sub nom. Harland & Wolff Plc v McIntyre [2006] EWCA Civ 287; [2006] 1 W.L.R. 2577; [2007] 2 All E.R. 24; [2006] I.C.R. 1222; [2006] P.I.Q.R. Q8; (2006) 103(15) L.S.G. 23, CA (Civ Div) ... 4.018
McIvor v Southern Health Board [1978] 1 W.L.R. 757 .... 30.018
McLeod v Butterwick; sub nom. Khazanchi v Faircharm Investments Ltd [1998] 1 W.L.R. 1603; [1998] 2 All E.R. 901; (1999) 77 P. & C.R. 29; [1998] 3 E.G.L.R. 147; [1999] R.V.R. 190; [1998] E.G. 46 (C.S.); (1998) 95(17) L.S.G. 31; (1998) 148 N.L.J. 479; (1998) 142 S.J.L.B. 142; [1998] N.P.C. 47; (1998) 76 P. & C.R. D8; *The Times*, March 25, 1998, CA (Civ Div) 40.004

TABLE OF CASES

McLoughlin v Grovers; sub nom. McLoughlin v Jones; McCloughlin v Grovers [2001] EWCA Civ 1743; [2002] Q.B. 1312; [2002] 2 W.L.R. 1279; [2002] P.I.Q.R. P20; [2002] P.N.L.R. 21, CA (Civ Div) 33.006
McPhilemy v The Times Newspapers Ltd (Costs) [2001] EWCA Civ 933; [2002] 1 W.L.R. 934; [2001] 4 All E.R. 861; [2002] C.P. Rep. 9; [2001] 2 Costs L.R. 295; [2001] E.M.L.R. 35; *The Times,* July 3, 2001, CA (Civ Div) 29.023
McPhilemy v The Times Newspapers Ltd (No.2). *See* McPhilemy v The Times Newspapers Ltd (Costs)
McPhilemy v The Times Newspapers Ltd [2000] 1 W.L.R. 1732; [2000] C.P. Rep. 53; [2000] C.P.L.R. 335; [2000] E.M.L.R. 575; *The Times,* June 7, 2000, CA (Civ Div) 31.010
Maes Finance Ltd v AL Phillips & Co, *The Times,* March 25, 1997, Ch D 17.005
Maguire v Molin [2002] EWCA Civ 1083; [2003] 1 W.L.R. 644; [2002] 4 All E.R. 325; [2002] C.P. Rep. 75; [2002] C.P.L.R. 791; [2003] P.I.Q.R. P8; (2002) 99(39) L.S.G. 40; *The Times,* August 12, 2002; *The Independent,* October 28, 2002, CA (Civ Div) 9.034, 9.41
Malkinson v Trim [2002] EWCA Civ 1273; [2003] 1 W.L.R. 463; [2003] 2 All E.R. 356; [2003] C.P. Rep. 11; [2003] C.P.L.R. 99; [2002] 3 Costs L.R. 515; (2002) 99(40) L.S.G. 33; (2002) 152 N.L.J. 1484; (2002) 146 S.J.L.B. 207; [2002] N.P.C. 116; *The Times,* October 11, 2002, CA (Civ Div) 38.004
Maltez v Lewis (2000) 16 Const. L.J. 65; (1999) 96(21) L.S.G. 39; *The Times,* May 4, 1999; *The Independent,* June 21, 1999, Ch D 1.009, 30.011
Manatee Towing Co. Ltd v Oceanbulk Maritime SA (The Bay Ridge) (Discovery); Oceanbulk Maritime SA v Manatee Towing Co. Ltd (Discovery); Manatee Towing Co. Ltd v McQuilling Brokerage Partners Inc (Discovery) [1999] 1 Lloyd's Rep. 876; [1999] C.L.C. 1197; (1999) 143 S.J.L.B. 111; *The Times,* May 11, 1999; *The Independent,* March 15, 1999, Q.B.D. (Comm) 30.003
Manning v Stylianou [2006] EWCA Civ 1655, CA (Civ Div) 44.017
Mareva Compania Naviera SA v International Bulk Carriers SA; The Mareva [1980] 1 All E.R. 213; [1975] 2 Lloyd's Rep. 509; [1980] 2 M.L.J. 71; (1981) 145 J.P.N. 204; (1981) 131 N.L.J. 517; (1981) 131 N.L.J. 770; (1975) 119 S.J. 660; *The Times,* July 1, 1975, CA (Civ Div) 27.015
Markem Corp v Zipher Ltd; Markem Technologies Ltd v Buckby [2005] EWCA Civ 267; [2005] R.P.C. 31; (2005) 28(6) I.P.D. 28042, CA (Civ Div) 31.004
Maronier v Larmer [2002] EWCA Civ 774; [2003] Q.B. 620; [2002] 3 W.L.R. 1060; [2003] 3 All E.R. 848; [2003] 1 All E.R. (Comm) 225; [2002] C.L.C. 1281; [2002] I.L.Pr. 39; (2002) 99(28) L.S.G. 30; (2002) 146 S.J.L.B. 161; *The Times,* June 13, 2002; *The Independent,* June 21, 2002, CA (Civ Div) 40.017
Marshall Rankine v Maggs. *See* Collier v Williams
Marshall v Allotts (A Firm) [2004] EWHC 1964; [2005] P.N.L.R. 11, DR (Leeds) ..30.024
Martin v Holland & Barrett [2002] 3 Costs L.R. 530, Q.B.D. 36.011
Masquerade Music Ltd v Springsteen; sub nom. Springsteen v Masquerade Music Ltd; Springsteen v Flute International Ltd [2001] EWCA Civ 563; [2001] C.P. Rep. 85; [2001] C.P.L.R. 369; [2001] E.M.L.R. 25; (2001) L.T.L., April 10; *The Independent,* April 24, 2001; *The Daily Telegraph,* April 17, 2001, CA (Civ Div) 31.020
Masri v Consolidated Contractors International (UK) Ltd; sub nom. Masri v Consolidated Contractors Group SAL [2005] EWCA Civ 1436; [2006] 1 W.L.R. 830; [2006] 1 All E.R. (Comm) 465; [2006] 1 Lloyd's Rep. 391; [2006] C.P. Rep. 10; [2005] 2 C.L.C. 704; [2006] I.L.Pr. 24; (2005) 102(43) L.S.G. 28; *The Times,* October 27, 2005, CA (Civ Div) 11.005

TABLE OF CASES

Mass Energy Ltd v Birmingham City Council [1994] Env. L.R. 298, CA (Civ Div) .. 24.002
Masterman-Lister v Brutton & Co. (Costs); Joseph v Jewell [2003] EWCA Civ 70;
 (2002) L.T.L., December 19, CA (Civ Div) 7.006
Matadeen v Caribbean Insurance Co. Ltd [2002] UKPC 69; [2003] 1 W.L.R. 670;
 The Times, January 20, 2003, PC (Trin) 5.005
Matthews v Metal Improvements Co. Inc [2007] EWCA Civ 215; (2007) 151
 S.J.L.B. 396, CA (Civ Div) 29.017
Matthews v Tarmac Bricks & Tiles Ltd [1999] C.P.L.R. 463; (2000) 54 B.M.L.R.
 139; (1999) 96(28) L.S.G. 26; (1999) 143 S.J.L.B. 196; The Times, July 1,
 1999, CA (Civ Div) 36.004
May v Woollcombe Beer & Watts [1999] P.N.L.R. 283; [1998] 3 E.G.L.R. 94;
 [1998] 51 E.G. 88, Q.B.D. (Merc) 23.004
McPhilemy v The Times Newspapers Ltd (Re-Amendment: Justification) [1999] 3
 All E.R. 775; [1999] C.P.L.R. 533; [1999] E.M.L.R. 751; The Times, May 26,
 1999; The Independent, June 9, 1999, CA (Civ Div) 12.002, 12.006,
  12.052, 33.012
Meadow v General Medical Council; sub nom. General Medical Council v
 Meadow [2006] EWCA Civ 1390; [2007] 2 W.L.R. 286; [2007] 1 All E.R. 1;
 [2007] I.C.R. 701; [2006] 3 F.C.R. 447; [2007] LS Law Medical 1; (2006) 92
 B.M.L.R. 51; [2007] Fam. Law 214; [2006] 44 E.G. 196 (C.S.); (2006) 103(43)
 L.S.G. 28; (2006) 156 N.L.J. 1686; The Times, October 31, 2006; The
 Independent, October 31, 2006, CA (Civ Div) 23.010
Mealey Horgan Plc v Horgan, The Times, July 6, 1999, Q.B.D. 14.012, 31.007, 33.002
Mealing McLeod v Common Professional Examination Board (Assessment of
 Costs) [2000] 2 Costs L.R. 223, Q.B.D. 38.006
Medcalf v Mardell (Wasted Costs Order); sub nom. Medcalf v Weatherill [2002]
 UKHL 27; [2003] 1 A.C. 120; [2002] 3 W.L.R. 172; [2002] 3 All E.R. 721;
 [2002] C.P. Rep. 70; [2002] C.P.L.R. 647; [2002] 3 Costs L.R. 428; [2002]
 P.N.L.R. 43; (2002) 99(31) L.S.G. 34; (2002) 152 N.L.J. 1032; (2002) 146
 S.J.L.B. 175; [2002] N.P.C. 89; The Times, June 28, 2002, HL 12.028, 39.002
Mehmet v Perry [1977] 2 All E.R. 529, DC 4.018
Memory Corp Plc v Sidhu (No.1); sub nom. Sidhu v Memory Corp Plc (No.1)
 [2000] 1 W.L.R. 1443; [2000] C.P.L.R. 171; [2000] F.S.R. 921; The Times,
 February 15, 2000, CA (Civ Div) 27.013, 27.014
Mercer v Chief Constable of Lancashire; Holder v Chief Constable of Lancashire
 [1991] 1 W.L.R. 367; [1991] 2 All E.R. 504; The Times, February 22, 1991;
 The Independent, March 6, 1991, CA (Civ Div) 31.005
Merchantbridge & Co. Ltd v Safron General Partner I Ltd [2006] EWCA Civ 158;
 (2006) L.T.L., February 14, CA (Civ Div) 19.005
Meretz Investments NV v First Penthouse Ltd [2003] EWHC 2324; (2003) L.T.L.,
 October 16, Ch D 30.024
Merial Ltd v Sankyo Co. Ltd [2004] EWHC 3077; (2004) L.T.L., December 16,
 Ch D (Patents Ct) 6.020
Mersey Docks Property Holdings Ltd v Kilgour [2004] EWHC 1638; [2004]
 B.L.R. 412, Q.B.D. (TCC) 8.009
Messer Griesheim GmbH v Goyal MG Gases PVT Ltd; sub nom. Air Liquide
 Deutschland GmbH v Goyal MG Gases PVT Ltd [2006] EWHC 79; [2006]
 1 C.L.C. 283; The Times, February 14, 2006, Q.B.D. (Comm) 15.014
Microsoft Corp v Plato Technology Ltd [1999] Masons C.L.R. 370; (1999) 22(11)
 I.P.D. 22108, CA (Civ Div); affirming [1999] F.S.R. 834; [1999] Masons
 C.L.R. 87; (1999) 22(5) I.P.D. 22047(1999) L.T.L., March 11; The
 Independent, April 19, 1999, Ch D 30.025

lxv

TABLE OF CASES

Midland Bank Plc v Pike [1988] 2 All E.R. 434, Ch D 40.010
Miles v Bull (No.1) [1969] 1 Q.B. 258; [1968] 3 W.L.R. 1090; [1968] 3 All E.R. 632;
   (1969) 20 P. & C.R. 42; (1968) 112 S.J. 747; (1968) 112 S.J. 723, Q.B.D. ... 19.007
Miles Platts Ltd v Townroe Ltd; sub nom. Miles Platt Ltd v Townroe Ltd [2003]
   EWCA Civ 145; [2003] 1 All E.R. (Comm) 561; [2003] 2 C.L.C. 589; [2003]
   I.L.Pr. 47; (2003) L.T.L., February, CA (Civ Div) 11.004
Miller v Allied Sainif (UK) Ltd, The Times, October 31, 2000, Ch D 28.001
Miller v Garton Shires (A Firm) (formerly Gartons) [2006] EWCA Civ 1386;
   [2007] R.T.R. 24; [2007] P.N.L.R. 11; [2007] C.P. Rep. 9; (2006) L.T.L.,
   October 31, CA (Civ Div) 19.005, 44.007
Miller v Hales (Costs) [2006] EWHC 1717, Q.B.D. 36.011
Miller v Sweden (App. No.55853/00) (2006) 42 E.H.R.R. 51, ECHR 7.011
Ministry of Defence and Support of the Armed Forces for Iran v Faz Aviation
   (formerly FN Aviation Ltd) [2007] EWHC 1042 (Comm); (2007) L.T.L.
   May 16, Q.B.D. (Comm) 11.005
Mir v Mir; sub nom. M v M (Sequestration: Sale of Property) [1992] Fam. 79;
   [1992] 2 W.L.R. 225; [1992] 1 All E.R. 765; [1992] 1 F.L.R. 624; [1992] 1
   F.C.R. 227; [1992] Fam. Law 378; (1992) 89(4) L.S.G. 33; (1992) 136 S.J.L.B.
   10, Fam Div 40.014
Mitchell v James (Costs) [2002] EWCA Civ 997; [2004] 1 W.L.R. 158; [2003] 2 All
   E.R. 1064; [2002] C.P. Rep. 72; [2002] C.P.L.R. 764; (2002) 99(36) L.S.G. 38;
   (2002) 146 S.J.L.B. 202; The Times, July 20, 2002; The Independent, July 18,
   2002, CA (Civ Div) 29.005, 29.022
Mitsui & Co. Ltd v Nexen Petroleum UK Ltd [2005] EWHC 625; [2005] 3 All E.R.
   511; The Times, May 18, 2005, Ch D 30.025
Mlauzi v Secretary of State for the Home Department [2005] EWCA Civ 128; The
   Times, February 15, 2005, CA (Civ Div) 44.013
Moat Housing Group-South Ltd v Harris (Application for Stay of Execution)
   [2004] EWCA Civ 1852; The Times, January 13, 2005, CA (Civ Div) 44.010
Moeliker v A Reyrolle & Co. Ltd [1977] 1 W.L.R. 132; [1976] I.C.R. 253, CA
   (Civ Div) 4.014
Mondel v Steel (1841) 8 M. & W. 858 .... 12.037
Monk v Redwing Aircraft Co. Ltd [1942] 1 K.B. 182; [1942] 1 All E.R. 133, CA 32.002
Monsanto Technology LLC v Cargill International SA [2006] EWHC 2864; (2006)
   L.T.L., November 13, Ch D 19.005
Montgomery v Foy Morgan & Co. [1895] 2 Q.B. 321, CA 18.003
Montlake v Lambert Smith Hampton Group Ltd (Costs) [2004] EWHC 1503;
   [2004] 4 Costs L.R. 650; [2004] N.P.C. 112, Q.B.D. (Comm) 29.023
Moon v Atherton [1972] 2 Q.B. 435; [1972] 3 W.L.R. 57; [1972] 3 All E.R. 145;
   (1972) 116 S.J. 374, CA (Civ Div) 7.018
Moons Motors v Kiuan Wou [1952] 2 Lloyd's Rep. 80, CA 43.008
Morgan & Son v Martin Johnson & Co. [1949] 1 K.B. 107; [1948] 2 All E.R. 196;
   64 T.L.R. 381; [1948] L.J.R. 1530; (1948) 92 S.J. 391, CA 12.037
Morgan Est (Scotland) Ltd v Hanson Concrete Products Ltd [2005] EWCA Civ
   134; [2005] 1 W.L.R. 2557; [2005] 3 All E.R. 135; [2005] C.P. Rep. 23; [2005]
   B.L.R. 218; (2005) 102(17) L.S.G. 32; The Times, February 28, 2005, CA
   (Civ Div) 7.015, 12.053
Morris v Bank of America National Trust (Appeal against Striking Out) [2000]
   1 All E.R. 954; [2000] B.C.C. 1076; [2001] 1 B.C.L.C. 771; [2000] B.P.I.R.
   83; (2000) 97(3) L.S.G. 37; (2000) 144 S.J.L.B. 48; The Times, January 25,
   2000, CA (Civ Div) 12.005

Morris v Bank of India [2004] EWCA Civ 1286, CA (Civ Div) 44.006
Morris v London Iron & Steel Co. [1988] Q.B. 493; [1987] 3 W.L.R. 836; [1987]
   2 All E.R. 496; [1987] I.C.R. 855; [1987] I.R.L.R. 182; (1987) 131 S.J. 1040,
   CA (Civ Div) 31.004
Morris v Wentworth-Stanley; sub nom. Morris v Molesworth [1999] Q.B. 1004;
   [1999] 2 W.L.R. 470; [1999] 1 F.L.R. 83; (1998) 95(39) L.S.G. 34; (1998)
   148 N.L.J. 1551; (1998) 142 S.J.L.B. 258; *The Times,* October 2, 1998, CA
   (Civ Div) 6.003
Mortgage Corp Plc v Sandoes [1997] P.N.L.R. 263; (1997) 94(3) L.S.G. 28;
   [1996] T.L.R. 751; (1997) 141 S.J.L.B. 30; *The Times,* December 27, 1996,
   CA (Civ Div) 33.002
Mortimer v Bailey [2004] EWCA Civ 1514; [2005] B.L.R. 85; [2005] 2 P. & C.R. 9;
   [2005] 1 E.G.L.R. 75; [2005] 02 E.G. 102; [2004] N.P.C. 162, CA (Civ Div) .. 27.001
Moses-Taiga v Taiga [2004] EWCA Civ 1399, CA (Civ Div) 44.066
Motor and General Insurance Co. v Pavey [1994] 1 W.L.R. 462; [1994] 1 Lloyd's
   Rep. 607, PC (Trin) 6.028
Motorola Credit Corp v Uzan (No.6) [2003] EWCA Civ 752; [2004] 1 W.L.R. 113;
   [2003] C.P. Rep. 56; [2003] 2 C.L.C. 1026; (2003) 100(32) L.S.G. 34; (2003)
   147 S.J.L.B. 752; *The Times,* June 19, 2003; *The Independent,* July 23, 2003,
   CA (Civ Div) 27.018, 27.020, 27.026
Moy v Pettman Smith (A Firm) [2005] UKHL 7; [2005] 1 W.L.R. 581; [2005] 1 All
   E.R. 903; [2005] Lloyd's Rep. Med. 293; [2005] P.N.L.R. 24; (2005) 102(11)
   L.S.G. 31; (2005) 155 N.L.J. 218; (2005) 149 S.J.L.B. 180; [2005] N.P.C. 15;
   The Times, February 4, 2005, HL 33.008
Multigroup Bulgaria Holding AD v Oxford Analytica Ltd (1999) L.T.L.,
   August 17 .... 30.021
Multiplex Construction (UK) Ltd v Honeywell Control Systems Ltd [2007]
   EWHC 236 (TCC); [2007] B.L.R. 167; [2007] Bus. L.R. D13; (2007) L.T.L.,
   March 27, Q.B.D. (TCC) 44.006
Murphy v Murphy; sub nom. Murphy's Settlements, Re [1999] 1 W.L.R. 282;
   [1998] 3 All E.R. 1; [1998] N.P.C. 62; *The Times,* May 2, 1998; *The
   Independent,* April 27, 1998, Ch D 30.025
Mutch v Allen [2001] EWCA Civ 76; [2001] C.P. Rep. 77; [2001] C.P.L.R. 200;
   [2001] P.I.Q.R. P26; *The Independent,* March 5, 2001; (2001) L.T.L.,
   January 22, CA (Civ Div) 23.020
Myers v Design Inc (International) Ltd [2003] EWHC 103; [2003] 1 W.L.R. 1642;
   [2003] 1 All E.R. 1168, Ch D 27.031
Myers v Dortex International Ltd [2000] Lloyd's Rep. I.R. 529; *The Times,* March
   18, 1999, CA (Civ Div) 7.014
Myers v Elman; sub nom. Myers v Rothfield [1940] A.C. 282, HL 30.005

NWL Ltd v Woods (The Nawala) (No.2); NWL Ltd v Nelson and Laughton
   [1979] 1 W.L.R. 1294; [1979] 3 All E.R. 614; [1980] 1 Lloyd's Rep. 1; [1979]
   I.C.R. 867; [1979] I.R.L.R. 478; (1979) 123 S.J. 751, HL ... 27.005, 27.006, 27.007
Nanglegan v Royal Free Hampstead NHS Trust [2001] EWCA Civ 127; [2002]
   1 W.L.R. 1043; [2001] 3 All E.R. 793; [2001] C.P. Rep. 65; [2001] C.P.L.R.
   225; *The Times,* February 14, 2001, CA (Civ Div) 8.001, 11.009
Naskaris v ANS Plc [2002] EWHC 1782, Ch D 35.006
Nasser v United Bank of Kuwait (Security for Costs) [2001] EWCA Civ 556; [2002]
   1 W.L.R. 1868; [2002] 1 All E.R. 401; [2001] C.P. Rep. 105, CA (Civ Div) ...26.002

TABLE OF CASES

National Justice Compania Naviera SA v Prudential Assurance Co. Ltd; The Ikarian Reefer (No.2); sub nom. Comninos v Prudential Assurance Co. Ltd [2000] 1 W.L.R. 603; [2000] 1 All E.R. 37; [1999] 2 All E.R. (Comm) 673; [2000] 1 Lloyd's Rep. 129; [2000] C.P. Rep. 13; [2000] C.L.C. 22; [2000] 1 Costs L.R. 37; [2000] I.L.Pr. 490; [2000] Lloyd's Rep. I.R. 230; (1999) 96(41) L.S.G. 35; (1999) 96(42) L.S.G. 40; (1999) 149 N.L.J. 1561; (1999) 143 S.J.L.B. 255; *The Times,* October 15, 1999; *The Independent,* October 20, 1999; *The Independent,* November 22, 1999, CA (Civ Div) 11.011

National Westminster Bank Ltd v Stockman; sub nom. National Westminster Bank Ltd v Stockton [1981] 1 W.L.R. 67; [1981] 1 All E.R. 800; (1980) 124 S.J. 810; *The Times,* August 19, 1980, Q.B.D. 40.010

National Westminster Bank Plc v Bowles (2005) L.T.L., February 23 .... 15.012

National Westminster Bank Plc v Rabobank Nederland (Application to Strike Out) [2006] EWHC 2959 (Comm); [2007] 1 All E.R. (Comm) 975; (2006) L.T.L., December 1, Q.B.D. (Comm) 33.001

National & Provincial Building Society v Lloyd [1996] 1 All E.R. 630; (1996) 28 H.L.R. 459; [1995] N.P.C. 193; *The Times,* January 24, 1996; *The Independent,* January 5, 1996, CA (Civ Div) 24.006

Nawaz v Crowe Insurance Group [2003] EWCA Civ 316; [2003] C.P. Rep. 41; [2003] R.T.R. 29; [2003] Lloyd's Rep. I.R. 471; [2003] P.I.Q.R. P27; *The Times,* March 11, 2003; *The Independent,* March 7, 2003, CA (Civ Div) ... 6.028

Naylor v Preston AHA; Foster v Merton and Sutton HA; Thomas v North West Surrey HA; Ikumelo v Newham HA [1987] 1 W.L.R. 958; [1987] 2 All E.R. 353; (1987) 84 L.S.G. 1494; (1987) 137 N.L.J. 474; (1987) 131 S.J. 596, CA (Civ Div) 23.007

Neck v Taylor [1893] 1 Q.B. 560, CA 26.002

Nedlloyd BV v Arab Metals Co. *See* P&O Nedlloyd BV v Arab Metals Co

Nelson v Clearsprings (Management) Ltd [2006] EWCA Civ 1252; [2007] 1 W.L.R. 962; [2007] 2 All E.R. 407; [2007] C.P. Rep. 2; [2007] H.L.R. 14; (2006) 103(39) L.S.G. 32; (2006) 156 N.L.J. 1525; (2006) 150 S.J.L.B. 1250; [2006] N.P.C. 103; *The Times,* October 5, 2006, CA (Civ Div) 15.014

Nelson v Nelson [1997] 1 W.L.R. 233; [1997] 1 All E.R. 970; [1997] B.P.I.R. 702; [1997] P.N.L.R. 413; (1997) 94(2) L.S.G. 26; (1997) 147 N.L.J. 126; (1997) 141 S.J.L.B. 30; *The Times,* January 8, 1997, CA (Civ Div) 7.024

Nelson v Rye [1996] 1 W.L.R. 1378; [1996] 2 All E.R. 186; [1996] E.M.L.R. 37; [1996] F.S.R. 313; *The Times,* December 5, 1995, Ch D 5.008

Nesbitt v Holt [2007] EWCA Civ 249; (2007) 151 S.J.L.B. 430, CA (Civ Div) ... 33.008

Nesheim v Kosa [2006] EWHC 2710 (Ch); [2007] W.T.L.R. 149; (2006) L.T.L., October, Ch D 11.011

Newman (t/a Mantella Publishing) v Modern Bookbinders Ltd [2000] 1 W.L.R. 2559; [2000] 2 All E.R. 814; *The Independent,* February 3, 2000, CA (Civ Div) 24.004, 40.004

Nikitin v Richards Butler LLP; Skarga v Richards Butler LLP [2007] EWHC 173; (2007) L.T.L., February 19, Q.B.D. 30.025

Ninemia Maritime Corp v Trave Schiffahrts GmbH & Co. KG; The Niedersachsen [1983] 1 W.L.R. 1412; [1984] 1 All E.R. 398; [1983] 2 Lloyd's Rep. 600; (1984) 81 L.S.G. 198, CA (Civ Div) 27.017, 27.021

Nixon v F Morris Contracting Ltd (1999) L.T.L., August 31 .... 33.003

Nizami v Butt; sub nom. Butt v Nizami; Butt v Kamuluden; Kamaluden v Butt [2006] EWHC 159; [2006] 1 W.L.R. 3307; [2006] 2 All E.R. 140; [2006] 3 Costs L.R. 483; [2006] R.T.R. 25; (2006) 103(9) L.S.G. 30; (2006) 156 N.L.J. 272, Q.B.D. 38.021

Nolan v Devonport [2006] EWHC 2025, DR (Leeds) 1.011
Nomura International Plc v Granada Group Ltd [2007] EWHC 642, (2007) L.T.L.,
   March 30, Q.B.D. (Comm) 12.009, 33.008
Norman v Ali (Limitation Period); Aziz v Norman [2000] R.T.R. 107; [2000]
   Lloyd's Rep. I.R. 395; [2000] P.I.Q.R. P72; (2000) 97(2) L.S.G. 30; (2000) 144
   S.J.L.B. 18; *The Times*, February 25, 2000; *The Independent*, February 7,
   2000, CA (Civ Div) 5.007
Northstar Systems Ltd v Fielding. *See* Ultraframe (UK) Ltd v Fielding (Costs)
Norwich Pharmacal Co. v Customs and Excise Commissioners; sub nom.
   Morton-Norwich Products Inc v Customs and Excise Commissioners
   [1974] A.C. 133; [1973] 3 W.L.R. 164; [1973] 2 All E.R. 943; [1973] F.S.R.
   365; [1974] R.P.C. 101; (1973) 117 S.J. 567, HL 30.003, 30.025
Nottingham Building Society v Eurodynamics Systems Plc [1995] F.S.R. 605, CA
   (Civ Div); affirming [1993] F.S.R. 468, Ch D 27.009

O'Brien v Seagrave [2007] EWHC 788; *The Times*, May 2, 2007, Ch D 24.010
O'Brien v Chief Constable of South Wales [2005] UKHL 26; [2005] 2 A.C. 534;
   [2005] 2 W.L.R. 1038; [2005] 2 All E.R. 931; *The Times*, April 29, 2005; *The
   Independent*, May 4, 2005, HL 31.023
Ocean Software v Kay [1992] Q.B. 583; [1992] 2 W.L.R. 633; [1992] 2 All E.R. 673;
   (1992) 89(11) L.S.G. 33; (1992) 136 S.J.L.B. 62; *The Times*, January 29,
   1992, CA (Civ Div) 27.021
Official Custodian for Charities v Mackey [1985] Ch. 168; [1984] 3 W.L.R. 915;
   [1984] 3 All E.R. 689; (1985) 49 P. & C.R. 242; (1984) 81 L.S.G. 3425; (1984)
   128 S.J. 751, Ch D 27.010
Olafsson v Gissurarson (No.2) [2006] EWHC 3214; [2007] 1 Lloyd's Rep. 188;
   (2007) L.T.L., January 4, Q.B.D. 8.015
Olatawura v Abiloye [2002] EWCA Civ 998; [2003] 1 W.L.R. 275; [2002] 4 All E.R.
   903; [2002] C.P. Rep. 73; [2002] C.P.L.R. 778; (2002) 99(36) L.S.G. 39; (2002)
   152 N.L.J. 1204; (2002) 146 S.J.L.B. 197; *The Times*, July 24, 2002; *The
   Independent*, October 14, 2002, CA (Civ Div) 15.016, 19.014, 26.006
O'Neill v O'Brien; O'Neill v Motor Insurers Bureau [1997] P.I.Q.R. P223; *The
   Times*, March 21, 1997, CA (Civ Div) 6.028
O'Reilly v Mackman; Millbanks v Secretary of State for the Home Department;
   Derbyshire v Mackman; Dougan; Mackman; Millbanks v Home Office
   [1983] 2 A.C. 237; [1982] 3 W.L.R. 1096; [1982] 3 All E.R. 1124; (1982) 126
   S.J. 820, HL 24.001
O'Rourke v Darbishire; sub nom. Whitworth, Re [1920] A.C. 581, HL 30.013
Owners of the Sardinia Sulcis v Owners of the Al Tawwab [1991] 1 Lloyd's Rep.
   201; *The Times*, November 21, 1990; *The Independent*, December 3, 1990;
   The Financial Times, November 13, 1990, CA (Civ Div) 7.015
Owusu v Jackson; Owusu v Mammee Bay Club Ltd; Owusu v Enchanted Garden
   Resorts & Spa Ltd; Owusu v Town & Country Resorts Ltd [2002] EWCA
   Civ 877; [2003] 1 C.L.C. 246; [2002] I.L.Pr. 45; [2003] P.I.Q.R. P13; (2002)
   L.T.L., June 19, CA (Civ Div) 11.004, 37.016
Oxford University v Webb [2006] EWHC 2490, Q.B.D. 7.018
Oyston v Blaker [1996] 1 W.L.R. 1326; [1996] 2 All E.R. 106; [1996] E.M.L.R. 125;
   The Times, November 15, 1995, CA (Civ Div) 5.016

TABLE OF CASES

P v T Ltd; sub nom. A v B Ltd [1997] 1 W.L.R. 1309; [1997] 4 All E.R. 200; [1997]
　　I.C.R. 887; [1997] I.R.L.R. 405; *The Times,* May 7, 1997, Ch D 30.025
P&O Developments Ltd v Guy's & St Thomas NHS Trust; Guy's & St Thomas
　　NHS Trust v P&O Developments Ltd [1999] B.L.R. 3; 62 Con. L.R. 38;
　　(1999) 15 Const. L.J. 374, Q.B.D. (TCC) 18.003
P&O Nedlloyd BV v Arab Metals Co; The UB Tiger; sub nom. P&O Nedlloyd
　　BV v Arab Metals Co. (No.2) [2006] EWCA Civ 1717; [2006] 2 C.L.C. 985;
　　The Times, January 15, 2007, CA (Civ Div) 5.002
Painting v Oxford University [2005] EWCA Civ 161; [2005] 3 Costs L.R. 394;
　　[2005] P.I.Q.R. Q5; (2005) 102(14) L.S.G. 26; (2005) 149 S.J.L.B. 183; *The
　　Times,* February 15, 2005, CA (Civ Div) 9.035
Palk v Mortgage Services Funding Plc [1993] Ch. 330; [1993] 2 W.L.R. 415; [1993]
　　2 All E.R. 481; (1993) 25 H.L.R. 56; (1993) 65 P. & C.R. 207; [1992] N.P.C.
　　114; *The Times,* August 7, 1992; *The Independent,* August 25, 1992;
　　The Guardian, August 19, 1992, CA (Civ Div) 24.006
Paragon Finance Plc v DB Thakerar & Co; Paragon Finance Plc v Thimbleby &
　　Co. [1999] 1 All E.R. 400; (1998) 95(35) L.S.G. 36; (1998) 142 S.J.L.B. 243;
　　The Times, August 7, 1998, CA (Civ Div) 12.053
Parker v Camden LBC; Newman v Camden LBC [1986] Ch. 162; [1985] 3 W.L.R.
　　47; [1985] 2 All E.R. 141; (1985) 17 H.L.R. 380; 84 L.G.R. 16; (1985) 129 S.J.
　　417, CA (Civ Div) 27.030
Parker v CS Structured Credit Fund Ltd [2003] EWHC 391; [2003] 1 W.L.R. 1680;
　　(2003) 100(15) L.S.G. 26; *The Times,* March 10, 2003, Ch D 27.026
Parker v Snyder [2003] EWCA Civ 488; (2003) L.T.L., April 1, CA (Civ Div) ... 19.007
Parkin v Brew (1999) C.L. May 38, Q.B.D. 32.006
Parnass/Pelly Ltd v Hodges [1982] F.S.R. 329, Ch D 27.007
Parry v Cleaver [1970] A.C. 1; [1969] 2 W.L.R. 821; [1969] 1 All E.R. 555; [1969]
　　1 Lloyd's Rep. 183; 6 K.I.R. 265; (1969) 113 S.J. 147, HL 4.005
Pars Technology Ltd v City Link Transport Holdings Ltd (1999) L.T.L., July 7 .... 6.024
Partco Group Ltd v Wragg; sub nom. Wragg v Partco Group Ltd [2002] EWCA
　　Civ 594; [2002] 2 Lloyd's Rep. 343; [2004] B.C.C. 782; [2002] 2 B.C.L.C.
　　323; (2002) 99(23) L.S.G. 27; (2002) 146 S.J.L.B. 124; *The Times,* May 10,
　　2002, CA (Civ Div) 33.008
Patel v Singh (2002) L.T.L., December 13 .... 40.004
Patel v WH Smith (Eziot) Ltd [1987] 1 W.L.R. 853; [1987] 2 All E.R. 569; (1987)
　　84 L.S.G. 2049; (1987) 131 S.J. 888, CA (Civ Div) 27.010
Patel (A Debtor), Re; sub nom. Debtor v Dallomo [1986] 1 W.L.R. 221; [1986]
　　1 All E.R. 522; (1986) 83 L.S.G. 520; (1986) 136 N.L.J. 68; (1986) 130 S.J. 70,
　　DC 42.008
Patel (Jitendra) v Patel (Dilesh) [2000] Q.B. 551; [1999] 3 W.L.R. 322; [1999] 1 All
　　E.R. (Comm.) 923; [1999] B.L.R. 227; 65 Con. L.R. 140; (1999) 15 Const.
　　L.J. 484; (1999) 143 S.J.L.B. 134; *The Times,* April 9, 1999, CA (Civ Div) ... 33.004
Payabi v Armstel Shipping Corp; The Jay Bola; Baker Rasti Lari v Armstel
　　Shipping Corp; The Jay Bola [1992] Q.B. 907; [1992] 2 W.L.R. 898; [1992]
　　3 All E.R. 329; [1992] 2 Lloyd's Rep. 62; (1992) 136 S.J.L.B. 52; *The Times,*
　　February 26, 1992, Q.B.D. (Comm) 12.053
Pearce v Ove Arup Partnership (2001) L.T.L., November 8 .... 23.010
Pearless de Rougemont & Co. v Pilbrow [1999] 3 All E.R. 355; [1999] 2 Costs L.R.
　　109; [1999] 2 F.L.R. 139; (1999) 149 N.L.J. 441; (1999) 143 S.J.L.B. 114;
　　The Times, March 25, 1999; *The Independent,* May 10, 1999, CA (Civ
　　Div) 2.003, 6.001

Peco Arts Inc v Hazlitt Gallery Ltd [1983] 1 W.L.R. 1315; [1983] 3 All E.R. 193; (1984) 81 L.S.G. 203; (1983) 127 S.J. 806, Q.B.D. 5.015
Peet v Mid Kent Area Healthcare NHS Trust; sub nom. MP v Mid Kent Healthcare NHS Trust; P (A Child) v Mid Kent NHS Healthcare Trust (Practice Note) [2001] EWCA Civ 1703; [2002] 1 W.L.R. 210; [2002] 3 All E.R. 688; [2002] C.P.L.R. 27; [2002] Lloyd's Rep. Med. 33; (2002) 65 B.M.L.R. 43; (2001) 98(48) L.S.G. 29; (2001) 145 S.J.L.B. 261; The Times, November 19, 2001; The Daily Telegraph, November 13, 2001, CA (Civ Div) 23.006
Pelling v Bow County Court [2005] EWCA Civ 384; (2005) L.T.L., February 25, CA (Civ Div) 40.003
Perotti v Collyer-Bristow (A Firm) (Vexatious Litigant: Directions) [2004] EWCA Civ 639; [2004] 4 All E.R. 53, CA (Civ Div) 44.010
Perry v Phoenix Assurance Plc [1988] 1 W.L.R. 940; [1988] 3 All E.R. 60; (1988) 56 P. & C.R. 163; (1988) 85(33) L.S.G. 42, Ch D 40.010
Pesskin v Mishcon de Reya (A Firm) [2003] EWHC 1745, Ch D 31.024
Petereit v Babcock International Holdings Ltd [1990] 1 W.L.R. 350; [1990] 2 All E.R. 135; [1992] I.L.Pr. 331; (1990) 87(10) L.S.G. 36, Q.B.D. 40.017
Petrotrade Inc v Texaco Ltd [2002] 1 W.L.R. 947 (Note); [2001] 4 All E.R. 853; [2001] C.P. Rep. 29; [2000] C.L.C. 1341; [2002] 1 Costs L.R. 60; The Times, June 14, 2000; The Independent, July 10, 2000, CA (Civ Div) 29.001, 29.023
Phillips v Associated Newspapers Ltd; sub nom. Phillipps v Associated Newspapers Ltd [2004] EWHC 190; [2004] 1 W.L.R. 2106; [2004] 2 All E.R. 455; [2004] E.M.L.R. 12; (2004) 154 N.L.J. 249, Q.B.D. 29.019
Phillips v Avena [2005] EWHC 3333; The Times, November 22, 2005, Ch D 19.012
Phillips v Symes (A Bankrupt) (Expert Witnesses: Costs) [2004] EWHC 2330; [2005] 1 W.L.R. 2043; [2005] 4 All E.R. 519; [2005] 2 All E.R. (Comm) 538; [2005] C.P. Rep. 12; [2005] 2 Costs L.R. 224; (2005) 83 B.M.L.R. 115; (2004) 101(44) L.S.G. 29; (2004) 154 N.L.J. 1615; The Times, November 5, 2004, Ch D 23.010
Phipps v Brooks Dry Cleaning Services Ltd [1996] P.I.Q.R. Q100; (1996) 93(29) L.S.G. 29; (1996) 140 S.J.L.B. 173; The Times, July 18, 1996, CA (Civ Div) ...4.013
Phoenix Finance Ltd v Federation International de l'Automobile (Costs) [2002] EWHC 1242; [2003] C.P. Rep. 1; (2002) 99(26) L.S.G. 36; (2002) 146 S.J.L.B. 145; The Times, June 27, 2002, Ch D 6.020
Pickett v British Rail Engineering Ltd; sub nom. Ralph Henry Pickett (Deceased), Re [1980] A.C. 136; [1978] 3 W.L.R. 955; [1979] 1 All E.R. 774; [1979] 1 Lloyd's Rep. 519; (1978) 122 S.J. 778, HL 4.013
Piglowska v Piglowski [1999] 1 W.L.R. 1360; [1999] 3 All E.R. 632; [1999] 2 F.L.R. 763; [1999] 2 F.C.R. 481; [1999] Fam. Law 617; (1999) 96(27) L.S.G. 34; (1999) 143 S.J.L.B. 190; The Times, June 25, 1999, HL 44.007
Pirelli General Plc v Gaca. See Gaca v Pirelli General Plc
Pirie v Ayling, 2003, SCCO transcript 38.030
Polanski v Condc Nast Publications Ltd [2005] UKHL 10; [2005] 1 W.L.R. 637; [2005] 1 All E.R. 945; [2005] C.P. Rep. 22; [2005] E.M.L.R. 14; [2005] H.R.L.R. 11; [2005] U.K.H.R.R. 277; (2005) 102(10) L.S.G. 29; (2005) 155 N.L.J. 245; The Times, February 11, 2005; The Independent, February 16, 2005, HL ... 31.018
Porter v Magill; sub nom. Magill v Weeks; Magill v Porter; Weeks v Magill; Hartley v Magill; England v Magill; Phillips v Magill [2001] UKHL 67; [2002] 2 A.C. 357; [2002] 2 W.L.R. 37; [2002] 1 All E.R. 465; [2002] H.R.L.R. 16; [2002] H.L.R. 16; [2002] B.L.G.R. 51; (2001) 151 N.L.J. 1886; [2001] N.P.C. 184; The Times, December 14, 2001; The Independent, February 4, 2002; The Daily Telegraph, December 20, 2001, HL 36.012

lxxi

Post Office Counters Ltd v Mahida [2003] EWCA Civ 1583; *The Times,* October 31, 2003, CA (Civ Div) 31.020, 33.012
Post Office v Norwich Union Fire Insurance Society Ltd [1967] 2 Q.B. 363; [1967] 2 W.L.R. 709; [1967] 1 All E.R. 577; [1967] 1 Lloyd's Rep. 216; (1967) 111 S.J. 71, CA (Civ Div) 7.023
Powell v Pallisters of Hereford Ltd (2002) L.T.L., July 1 .... 18.007
Prekookeanska Plovidba v LNT Lines SrL [1989] 1 W.L.R. 753; [1988] 3 All E.R. 897; (1988) 85(33) L.S.G. 42; (1988) 138 N.L.J. Rep. 196; (1988) 132 S.J. 1215, Q.B.D. 27.021
Prescott v Bulldog Tools [1981] 3 All E.R. 869, Q.B.D. 6.018
Prescott v Dunwoody Sports Marketing [2007] EWCA Civ 461; (2007) L.T.L., May 17; *The Times,* May 25, 2007, CA (Civ Div) 7.013
President of India v La Pintada Compania Navigacion SA (The La Pintada) [1985] A.C. 104; [1984] 3 W.L.R. 10; [1984] 2 All E.R. 773; [1984] 2 Lloyd's Rep. 9; [1984] C.I.L.L. 110; (1984) 81 L.S.G. 1999; (1984) 128 S.J. 414, HL 3.008
Prest v Rich & Co. Investment AG [2006] EWHC 927, Q.B.D. (Comm) 30.005
Primus Telecommunications Netherlands BV v Pan European Ltd [2005] EWCA Civ 273; (2005) L.T.L., February 23, CA (Civ Div) 33.011
Project Development Co. Ltd SA v KMK Securities Ltd [1982] 1 W.L.R. 1470; [1983] 1 All E.R. 465; [1982] Com. L.R. 255; (1982) 126 S.J. 837, Q.B.D. 27.022
Prokop v Department of Health and Social Security [1985] C.L.Y. 1037, CA (Civ Div) 4.021
Prudential Assurance Co. Ltd v McBains Cooper [2000] 1 W.L.R. 2000; [2001] 3 All E.R. 1014; [2001] C.P. Rep. 19; [2000] C.P.L.R. 475; (2000) 97(24) L.S.G. 40; (2000) 150 N.L.J. 832; *The Times,* June 2, 2000, CA (Civ Div) 37.016
Punjab National Bank v Jain [2004] EWCA Civ 589; [2004] All E.R. (D) 01 (May), CA (Civ Div) 30.008
Purfleet Farms Ltd v Secretary of State for Transport, Local Government and the Regions; sub nom. Purfleet Farms Ltd v Secretary of State for the Environment, Transport and the Regions [2002] EWCA Civ 1430; [2003] 1 P. & C.R. 20; [2003] 1 E.G.L.R. 9; [2003] 02 E.G. 105; [2002] R.V.R. 368; [2002] 43 E.G. 204 (C.S.); (2002) 99(42) L.S.G. 40; (2002) 146 S.J.L.B. 234; [2002] N.P.C. 125; *The Times,* November 7, 2002; *The Independent,* November 1, 2002, CA (Civ Div) 38.018

QPS Consultants Ltd v Kruger Tissue (Manufacturing) Ltd [1999] C.P.L.R. 710; [1999] B.L.R. 366, CA (Civ Div) 12.006

R. v Bow County Court Ex p. Pelling (No.1) [1999] 1 W.L.R. 1807; [1999] 4 All E.R. 751; [1999] 2 F.L.R. 1126; [1999] 3 F.C.R. 97; [1999] Fam. Law 698; (1999) 96(32) L.S.G. 33; (1999) 149 N.L.J. 1369; *The Times,* August 18, 1999; *The Independent,* October 1, 1999, CA (Civ Div) 1.020
R. v Bow Street Metropolitan Stipendiary Magistrate Ex p. Pinochet Ugarte (No.2); sub nom. Pinochet Ugarte (No.2), Re; R. v Evans Ex p. Pinochet Ugarte (No.2); R. v Bartle Ex p. Pinochet Ugarte (No.2) [2000] 1 A.C. 119; [1999] 2 W.L.R. 272; [1999] 1 All E.R. 577; 6 B.H.R.C. 1; (1999) 11 Admin. L.R. 57; (1999) 96(6) L.S.G. 33; (1999) 149 N.L.J. 88; *The Times,* January 18, 1999; *The Independent,* January 19, 1999, HL 43.009

R. v Bow Street Metropolitan Stipendiary Magistrate Ex p. Pinochet Ugarte
(No.3) [2000] 1 A.C. 147; [1999] 2 W.L.R. 827; [1999] 2 All E.R. 97; 6
B.H.R.C. 24; (1999) 96(17) L.S.G. 24; (1999) 149 N.L.J. 497; *The Times,*
March 25, 1999, HL 24.003
R. v Bryn Alyn Community (Holdings) Ltd. *See* KR v Bryn Alyn Community
(Holdings) Ltd (In Liquidation) (Permission to Amend)
R. v Customs & Excise Commissioners Ex p. British Sky Broadcasting Group Plc
(2000) L.T.L., July 14 .... 24.001
R. v Glennie. *See* R. v Miller (Raymond Karl)
R. v Gough (Robert) [1993] A.C. 646; [1993] 2 W.L.R. 883; [1993] 2 All E.R. 724;
(1993) 97 Cr. App. R. 188; (1993) 157 J.P. 612; [1993] Crim. L.R. 886; (1993)
157 J.P.N. 394; (1993) 143 N.L.J. 775; (1993) 137 S.J.L.B. 168; *The Times,*
May 24, 1993; *The Independent,* May 26, 1993; *The Guardian,* May 22,
1993, HL 36.012
R. v Hammersmith & Fulham LBC Ex p. Burkett. *See* R. (on the application of
Burkett) v Hammersmith and Fulham LBC (No.1)
R. v Hayes (Geoffrey) [1977] 1 W.L.R. 234; [1977] 2 All E.R. 288; (1977) 64 Cr.
App. R. 194, CA (Crim Div) 37.004
R. v Inland Revenue Commissioners Ex p. National Federation of Self Employed
and Small Businesses Ltd; sub nom. Inland Revenue Commissioners v
National Federation of Self Employed and Small Businesses Ltd [1982]
A.C. 617; [1981] 2 W.L.R. 722; [1981] 2 All E.R. 93; [1981] S.T.C. 260; 55
T.C. 133; (1981) 125 S.J. 325, HL 24.002
R. v Legal Aid Board Ex p. Kaim Todner; sub nom. R. v Legal Aid Board Ex p.
T (A Firm of Solicitors) [1999] Q.B. 966; [1998] 3 W.L.R. 925; [1998] 3 All
E.R. 541; (1998) 95(26) L.S.G. 31; (1998) 148 N.L.J. 941; (1998) 142 S.J.L.B.
189; *The Times,* June 15, 1998; *The Independent,* June 12, 1998, CA
(Civ Div) 1.017
R. v Legal Aid Board No.15 Area Office (Liverpool) Ex p. Eccleston; sub nom. R.
v Legal Aid Board (Merseyside) Area Office Ex p. Eccleston [1998] 1 W.L.R.
1279; [1999] P.I.Q.R. P38; [1998] C.O.D. 482; (1998) 95(20) L.S.G. 35; (1998)
142 S.J.L.B. 155; *The Times,* May 6, 1998; *The Independent,* May 4, 1998,
Q.B.D. 38.003
R. v Lichfield DC Ex p. Lichfield Securities Ltd. *See* R. (on the application of
Lichfield Securities Ltd) v Lichfield DC
R. v Miller (Raymond Karl); R. v Glennie (Alastair Kincaid) [1983] 1 W.L.R.
1056; [1983] 3 All E.R. 186; (1984) 78 Cr. App. R. 71; [1983] Crim. L.R.
615; (1983) 133 N.L.J. 745; (1983) 127 S.J. 580; *The Times,* June 1, 1983,
Q.B.D. 2.022, 38.020
R. v Ministry of Agriculture, Fisheries and Food Ex p. Monsanto Plc
(No.2) [1999] Q.B. 1161; [1999] 2 W.L.R. 599; [1998] 4 All E.R. 321; [1999]
F.S.R. 223; *The Times,* October 10, 1998; *The Independent,* October 7,
1998, DC 24.003
R. v Sandwell MBC Ex p. Wilkinson (1999) 31 H.L.R. 22; [1998] C.O.D. 477,
Q.B.D. 24.002
R. v Secretary of State for Home Department Ex p. Harris (2002) L.T.L.,
February 1 .... 24.003
R. v Secretary of State for Scotland; sub nom. AHLR, Petitioner [1999] 2 A.C.
512; [1999] 2 W.L.R. 28; [1999] 1 All E.R. 481; 1999 S.C. (H.L.) 17; 1999
S.L.T. 279; 1999 S.C.L.R. 74; (1999) 96(4) L.S.G. 37; 1998 G.W.D. 40–2075;
The Times, December 7, 1998; *The Independent,* December 8, 1998, HL . . .24.001

TABLE OF CASES

R. v Secretary of State for the Home Department Ex p. Salem [1999] 1 A.C. 450; [1999] 2 W.L.R. 483; [1999] 2 All E.R. 42; (1999) 11 Admin. L.R. 194; [1999] C.O.D. 486; (1999) 96(9) L.S.G. 32; (1999) 143 S.J.L.B. 59; *The Times,* February 12, 1999, HL 44.004

R. v Secretary of State for Trade and Industry Ex p. Eastaway. *See* R. (on the application of Eastaway) v Secretary of State for Trade and Industry

R. v Secretary of State for Transport Ex p. Factortame Ltd (No.2) [1991] 1 A.C. 603; [1990] 3 W.L.R. 818; [1991] 1 All E.R. 70; [1991] 1 Lloyd's Rep. 10; [1990] 3 C.M.L.R. 375; (1991) 3 Admin. L.R. 333; (1990) 140 N.L.J. 1457; (1990) 134 S.J. 1189, HL 27.004, 27.005

R. v Southwark London BC, Ex p. Kuzeva. *See* R. (on the application of Kuzeva) v Southwark LBC (Costs)

R. v The Advertising Standards Authority Ltd Ex p. Rath. *See* R. (on the application of Matthias Rath BV) v Advertising Standards Authority Ltd

R. (on the application of B) v Lambeth LBC; sub nom. R (B by her litigation friend MB) v Lambeth LBC [2006] EWHC 639 (Admin); (2006) 9 C.C.L. Rep. 239; [2007] Fam. Law 118, Q.B.D. (Admin) 24.003

R. (on the application of Bhamjee) v First Secretary of State [2005] EWHC 350 .... 7.011

R. (on the application of Burkett) v Hammersmith and Fulham LBC (Costs) [2004] EWCA Civ 1342; [2005] C.P. Rep. 11; [2005] 1 Costs L.R. 104; [2005] J.P.L. 525; [2005] A.C.D. 73; (2004) 101(42) L.S.G. 30; (2004) 148 S.J.L.B. 1245; *The Times,* October 20, 2004, CA (Civ Div) 2.021

R. (on the application of Burkett) v Hammersmith and Fulham LBC (No.1); sub nom. Burkett, Re; R. v Hammersmith and Fulham LBC Ex p. Burkett [2002] UKHL 23; [2002] 1 W.L.R. 1593; [2002] 3 All E.R. 97; [2002] C.P. Rep. 66; [2003] Env. L.R. 6; [2003] 1 P. & C.R. 3; [2002] 2 P.L.R. 90; [2002] J.P.L. 1346; [2002] A.C.D. 81; [2002] 22 E.G. 136 (C.S.); (2002) 99(27) L.S.G. 34; (2002) 152 N.L.J. 847; (2002) 146 S.J.L.B. 137; [2002] N.P.C. 75; *The Times,* May 24, 2002; *The Independent,* May 28, 2002, HL 24.002, 44.023

R. (on the application of Corner House Research) v Secretary of State for Trade and Industry [2005] EWCA Civ 192; [2005] 1 W.L.R. 2600; [2005] 4 All E.R. 1; [2005] C.P. Rep. 28; [2005] 3 Costs L.R. 455; [2005] A.C.D. 100; (2005) 102(17) L.S.G. 31; (2005) 149 S.J.L.B. 297; *The Times,* March 7, 2005; *The Independent,* March 4, 2005, CA (Civ Div) 33.013, 39.017

R. (on the application of Cowl) v Plymouth City Council; sub nom. Cowl v Plymouth City Council; Cowl (Practice Note), Re [2001] EWCA Civ 1935; [2002] 1 W.L.R. 803; [2002] C.P. Rep. 18; (2002) 5 C.C.L. Rep. 42; [2002] A.C.D. 11; [2002] Fam. Law 265; (2002) 99(8) L.S.G. 35; (2002) 146 S.J.L.B. 27; *The Times,* January 8, 2002, CA (Civ Div) 24.002

R. (on the application of Eastaway) v Secretary of State for Trade and Industry; sub nom. R. v Secretary of State for Trade and Industry Ex p. Eastaway [2000] 1 W.L.R. 2222; [2001] 1 All E.R. 27; [2001] C.P. Rep. 67; [2001] A.C.D. 17; (2000) 97(46) L.S.G. 40; (2000) 144 S.J.L.B. 282; *The Times,* November 8, 2000; *The Independent,* December 18, 2000, HL 24.003, 44.023

R. (on the application of England) v Tower Hamlets LBC (Permission to Appeal) [2006] EWCA Civ 1742, CA (Civ Div) 39.017

R. (on the application of Ewing) v Department for Constitutional Affairs [2006]
EWHC 504; [2006] 2 All E.R. 993, Q.B.D. (Admin) 7.011
R. (on the application of Ewing) v Office of the Deputy Prime Minister; sub nom.
Ewing v Office of the Deputy Prime Minister [2005] EWCA Civ 1583;
[2006] 1 W.L.R. 1260; [2005] N.P.C. 146; *The Independent,* January 20,
2006, CA (Civ Div) 24.002
R. (on the application of Gunn) v Secretary of State for the Home Department
(Recovery of Costs); sub nom. R. v Secretary of State for the Home
Department Ex p. Gunn; R. (on the application of Kelly) v Secretary of
State for the Home Department; R. (on the application of Khan (Zahid)) v
Secretary of State for the Home Department [2001] EWCA Civ 891; [2001]
1 W.L.R. 1634; [2001] 3 All E.R. 481; [2001] C.P. Rep. 107; [2001] 2 Costs
L.R. 263; (2001) 98(27) L.S.G. 38; (2001) 151 N.L.J. 936; (2001) 145 S.J.L.B.
160; *The Times,* June 20, 2001; *The Independent,* June 19, 2001; *The Daily
Telegraph,* June 26, 2001, CA (Civ Div) 39.014
R. (on the application of Johnson (Deceased)) v Secretary of State for Health
[2006] EWHC 288, Q.B.D. (Admin) 7.015
R. (on the application of Jones) v Ceredigion CC. *See* Ceredigion CC v Jones
R. (on the application of Kumar) v Secretary of State for Constitutional Affairs
[2006] EWCA Civ 990; [2007] 1 W.L.R. 536; [2006] C.P. Rep. 43; (2006) 150
S.J.L.B. 982; *The Independent,* July 18, 2006, CA (Civ Div) 7.011
R. (on the application of Kuzeva) v Southwark LBC (Costs); sub nom. R. (on the
application of Kuzjeva) v Southwark LBC (Costs) [2002] EWCA Civ 781;
(2002) L.T.L. May 30, CA (Civ Div) 24.003
R. (on the application of Lichfield Securities Ltd) v Lichfield DC; sub nom. R. v
Lichfield DC Ex p. Lichfield Securities Ltd [2001] EWCA Civ 304; (2001) 3
L.G.L.R. 35; [2001] 3 P.L.R. 33; [2001] P.L.C.R. 32; [2001] J.P.L. 1434
(Note); [2001] 11 E.G. 171 (C.S.); (2001) 98(17) L.S.G. 37; (2001) 145
S.J.L.B. 78; *The Times,* March 30, 2001, CA (Civ Div) 24.003
R. (on the application of Matthias Rath BV) v Advertising Standards Authority
Ltd; sub nom. R. v Advertising Standards Authority Ltd Ex p. Matthias
Rath BV [2001] E.M.L.R. 22; [2001] H.R.L.R. 22; *The Times,* January 10,
2001, Q.B.D. (Admin) 24.002
R. (on the application of MB by her litigation friend) v Lambeth LBC. *See* R. (on
the application of B) v Lambeth LBC
R. (on the application of Mount Cook Land Ltd) v Westminster City Council;
sub nom. Mount Cook Land Ltd v Westminster City Council [2003] EWCA
Civ 1346; [2004] C.P. Rep. 12; [2004] 2 Costs L.R. 211; [2004] 2 P. & C.R.
22; [2004] 1 P.L.R. 29; [2004] J.P.L. 470; [2003] 43 E.G. 137 (C.S.); (2003)
147 S.J.L.B. 1272; [2003] N.P.C. 117; *The Times,* October 16, 2003, CA
(Civ Div) 1.012, 24.002
R. (on the application of Payne) v Caerphilly CBC (Costs); sub nom. Payne v
Caerphilly CBC (Costs) [2004] EWCA Civ 433; (2004) 148 S.J.L.B. 384, CA
(Civ Div) 24.002
R. (on the application of Quark Fishing Ltd) v Secretary of State for Foreign and
Commonwealth Affairs (No.1); sub nom. Secretary of State for Foreign and
Commonwealth Affairs v Quark Fishing Ltd [2002] EWCA Civ 1409;
(2002) L.T.L., October 30, CA (Civ Div) 24.002

lxxv

R. (on the application of Wilkinson) v Broadmoor Hospital; sub nom. R. (on the application of Wilkinson) v Broadmoor Special Hospital Authority; R. (on the application of Wilkinson) v Responsible Medical Officer Broadmoor Hospital [2001] EWCA Civ 1545; [2002] 1 W.L.R. 419; [2002] U.K.H.R.R. 390; (2002) 5 C.C.L. Rep. 121; [2002] Lloyd's Rep. Med. 41; (2002) 65 B.M.L.R. 15; [2002] A.C.D. 47; (2001) 98(44) L.S.G. 36; (2001) 145 S.J.L.B. 247; *The Times*, November 2, 2001; *The Independent*, December 10, 2001; *The Daily Telegraph*, October 30, 2001, CA (Civ Div) 24.003
RBG Resources Plc v Rastogi [2002] L.T.L., May 31 .... 27.019
RH Tomlinssons (Trowbridge) Ltd v Secretary of State for the Environment, Transport and the Regions [2000] B.C.C. 576; [1999] 2 B.C.L.C. 760; [1999] N.P.C. 110; *The Times*, August 31, 1999, CA (Civ Div) 1.020
RHM Foods Ltd v Bovril Ltd [1982] 1 W.L.R. 661; [1982] 1 All E.R. 673; [1983] R.P.C. 275, CA (Civ Div) 30.016
R&H Green & Silley Weir Ltd v British Railways Board [1985] 1 W.L.R. 570; [1985] 1 All E.R. 237, Ch D 5.009
R+V Versicherung AG v Risk Insurance and Reinsurance Solutions SA [2007] EWHC 79; *The Times*, February 26, 2007, Q.B.D. (Comm) 43.007
Radu (Prince) of Hohenzollern v Houston [2006] EWCA Civ 1575; (2006) 156 N.L.J. 1847; (2006) 150 S.J.L.B. 1567; [2007] C.P. Rep. 11; *The Times*, January 1, 2007, CA (Civ Div) 26.003, 33.007
Rafidain Bank v Agom Universal Sugar Trading Co. [1987] 1 W.L.R. 1606; [1987] 3 All E.R. 859; (1987) 84 L.S.G. 3658; (1987) 131 S.J. 1591; *The Times*, December 23, 1986, CA (Civ Div) 30.017
Rahman v Sterling Credit Ltd; sub nom. Sterling Credit Ltd v Rahman [2001] 1 W.L.R. 496; (2001) 33 H.L.R. 63; (2000) 97(32) L.S.G. 37; (2000) 144 S.J.L.B. 243; [2000] N.P.C. 84; (2001) 81 P. & C.R. DG4; *The Times*, October 17, 2000, CA (Civ Div) 18.007
Raja v Van Hoogstraten (2002) L.T.L., October 11 .... 41.003
Rall v Hume [2001] EWCA Civ 146; [2001] 3 All E.R. 248; [2001] C.P. Rep. 58; [2001] C.P.L.R. 239; (2001) 98(10) L.S.G. 44; (2001) 145 S.J.L.B. 54; *The Times*, March 14, 2001; *The Independent*, March 19, 2001, CA (Civ Div) 30.004, 31.020
Rayment v Ministry of Defence (1999) 47 B.M.L.R. 92; *The Times*, July 6, 1998, Q.B.D. 23.017
Read v Edmed [2004] EWHC 3274; [2006] 2 Costs L.R. 201; [2005] P.I.Q.R. P16; *The Times*, December 13, 2004, Q.B.D. 29.009
Reed Executive Plc v Reed Business Information Ltd (Costs: Alternative Dispute Resolution) [2004] EWCA Civ 887; [2004] 1 W.L.R. 3026; [2004] 4 All E.R. 942; [2005] C.P. Rep. 4; [2004] 4 Costs L.R. 662; [2005] F.S.R. 3; (2004) 27(7) I.P.D. 27067; (2004) 148 S.J.L.B. 881; *The Times*, July 16, 2004, CA (Civ Div) 6.025
Regan v Paul Properties Ltd [2006] EWCA Civ 1391; [2007] Ch. 135; [2006] 3 W.L.R. 1131; [2007] B.L.R. 56; [2006] 46 E.G. 210; [2007] C.I.L.L. 2411; [2006] 44 E.G. 197 (C.S.); (2006) 103(43) L.S.G. 27, CA (Civ Div) 27.005
Regan v Williamson [1976] 1 W.L.R. 305; [1976] 2 All E.R. 241; (1976) 120 S.J. 217, Q.B.D. 4.018
Reichhold Norway ASA v Goldman Sachs International [2000] 1 W.L.R. 173; [2000] 2 All E.R. 679; [1999] 2 All E.R. (Comm) 174; [1999] 2 Lloyd's Rep. 567; [2000] C.L.C. 11; *The Times*, July 20, 1999, CA (Civ Div) 33.004
Reid v Secretary of State for Scotland. *See* R v Secretary of State for Scotland

Remmington v Scoles [1897] 2 Ch. 1, CA 12.030
Renworth Ltd v Stephansen [1996] 3 All E.R. 244; *The Times,* January 16, 1996;
    The Independent, January 10, 1996, CA (Civ Div) 30.014
Restick v Crickmore; Nisbet v Granada Entertainment; Reed v Department of
    Employment; Warren v Hinchcliffe [1994] 1 W.L.R. 420; [1994] 2 All E.R.
    112; (1993) 143 N.L.J. 1712; (1994) 138 S.J.L.B. 4; [1993] N.P.C. 155; *The
    Times,* December 3, 1993, CA (Civ Div) 9.025
Richards & Wallington (Plant Hire) Ltd (1984) Costs L.R. (Core) 79 .... 38.004
Richardson, Re [1933] W.N. 90 .... 12.037
Richardson, Re; Richardson v Nicholson [1933] W.N. 90 .... 18.007
Richmond upon Thames LBC v Secretary of State for Transport [2006] EWCA
    Civ 193; (2006) L.T.L., March 2, CA (Civ Div) 44.009
Rickards v Rickards [1990] Fam. 194; [1989] 3 W.L.R. 748; [1989] 3 All E.R. 193;
    [1990] 1 F.L.R. 125; [1990] F.C.R. 409; (1990) 154 J.P.N. 346; (1989) 86(41)
    L.S.G. 39; (1989) 139 N.L.J. 899, CA (Civ Div) 44.008
Ridehalgh v Horsefield [1994] Ch.205 .... 39.002
Riniker v University College London (Practice Note) [2001] 1 W.L.R. 13 ...... 44.018
River Thames Society v First Secretary of State [2006] EWHC 2829, (2006) L.T.L.
    September 22 .... 7.013
Roadrunner Properties Ltd v Dean [2004] EWCA Civ 376; (2004) 11 E.G. 140 ... 43.007
Robert v Momentum Services Ltd [2003] EWCA Civ 299; [2003] 1 W.L.R. 1577;
    [2003] 2 All E.R. 74; [2003] C.P. Rep. 38; (2003) 100(14) L.S.G. 29; *The
    Times,* February 13, 2003, CA (Civ Div) 9.010, 33.002
Roberts Petroleum Ltd v Bernard Kenny Ltd [1983] A.C. 192 .... 40.005
Roberts v Johnstone [1988] 3 W.L.R. 1247 .... 4.006
Robin Ellis Ltd v Malwright (1999) C.L. June 23.018
Robinson v Bird; sub nom. Robinson v Fernsby; Scott-Kilvert's Estate, Re [2003]
    EWCA Civ 1820; [2004] W.T.L.R. 257; (2004) 101(7) L.S.G. 36; (2004) 148
    S.J.L.B. 59; *The Times,* January 20, 2004, CA (Civ Div) 43.008
Rocco Giuseppe & Figli v Tradax Export SA [1984] 1 W.L.R. 742; [1983] 3 All
    E.R. 598; [1983] 2 Lloyd's Rep. 434; (1984) 81 L.S.G. 1518; (1983) 133 N.L.J.
    868; (1984) 128 S.J. 243, Q.B.D. (Comm) 3.009
Roche v Sherrington [1982] 1 W.L.R. 599; [1982] 2 All E.R. 426; (1982) 126 S.J.
    312, Ch D 7.013
Rockwell Machine Tool Co. Ltd v EP Barrus (Concessionaires) Ltd (Practice
    Note) [1968] 1 W.L.R. 693; [1968] 2 All E.R. 98 (Note); (1968) 112 S.J. 380,
    Ch D 30.005
Rofe v Kevorkian [1936] 2 All E.R. 1334; 80 S.J. 719, CA 32.004
Rogers v Merthyr Tydfil CBC [2006] EWCA Civ 1134; [2007] 1 All E.R. 354;
    [2006] Lloyd's Rep. I.R. 759; (2006) 150 S.J.L.B. 1053; [2007] 1 W.L.R. 808,
    CA (Civ Div) 2.009, 2.023, 38.028, 38.030
Rollinson v Kimberly-Clark Ltd; sub nom. Rollinson v Kimberley Clark Ltd
    [2000] C.P. Rep. 85; [1999] C.P.L.R. 581; *The Times,* June 22, 1999; *The
    Independent,* July 5, 1999, CA (Civ Div) 36.004
Rose v Lynx Express Ltd [2004] EWCA Civ 447; [2004] B.C.C. 714; [2004]
    1 B.C.L.C. 455; (2004) 101(17) L.S.G. 31; (2004) 148 S.J.L.B. 477; *The
    Times,* April 22, 2004, CA (Civ Div) 30.024
Rose (Fanny), Re; sub nom. Rose v Laskington Ltd [1990] 1 Q.B. 562; [1989]
    3 W.L.R. 873; [1989] 3 All E.R. 306; (1989) 5 B.C.C. 758; (1989) 86(39)
    L.S.G. 36; (1989) 139 N.L.J. 973; (1989) 133 S.J. 1033, DC 40.014
Roshdi v Thames Trains Ltd [2002] EWCA Civ 284, CA (Civ Div) 28.001

TABLE OF CASES

Ross v Owners of the Bowbelle; East Coast Aggregates Ltd v Para-Pagan; Ross v Owners of the Marchioness [1997] 1 W.L.R. 1159; [1997] 2 Lloyd's Rep. 191; [1998] 1 Costs L.R. 32; *The Times*, April 8, 1997, CA (Civ Div) 38.041

Rourke v Barton, *The Times*, June 23, 1982, Q.B.D. 4.009

Rover Ltd v Cannon Film Sales Ltd. *See* Films Rover International Ltd v Cannon Film Sales Ltd

Rowland v Bock [2002] EWHC 692; [2002] 4 All E.R. 370; *The Daily Telegraph*, May 13, 2002, Q.B.D. 31.018

Royal Brompton Hospital NHS Trust v Hammond (No.3) [2002] UKHL 14; [2002] 1 W.L.R. 1397; [2002] 2 All E.R. 801; [2002] 1 All E.R. (Comm) 897; [2003] 1 C.L.C. 11; [2002] B.L.R. 255; [2002] T.C.L.R. 14; 81 Con. L.R. 1; [2002] P.N.L.R. 37; *The Times*, April 26, 2002, HL 18.007

Royal Brompton Hospital NHS Trust v Hammond (No.5) [2001] EWCA Civ 550; [2001] B.L.R. 297; [2001] Lloyd's Rep. P.N. 526; (2001) 98(23) L.S.G. 39; (2001) 145 S.J.L.B. 118; *The Times*, May 11, 2001, CA (Civ Div) 15.013

Rush & Tompkins Ltd v Greater London Council [1989] A.C. 1280; [1988] 3 W.L.R. 939; [1988] 3 All E.R. 737; 43 B.L.R. 1; 22 Con. L.R. 114; [1988] E.G. 145 (C.S.); (1988) 138 N.L.J. Rep. 315; (1988) 132 S.J. 1592, HL 30.008

S v Chesterfield & North Derbyshire Royal Hospital NHS Trust [2003] EWCA Civ 1284; (2004) Lloyd's Rep.Med 90 .... 23.014

SCF Finance Co. Ltd v Masri (No.1); sub nom. Masri v SCF Finance Co. Ltd (No.1) [1985] 1 W.L.R. 876; [1985] 2 All E.R. 747; [1985] 2 Lloyd's Rep. 206; (1985) 82 L.S.G. 2015; (1985) 129 S.J. 450, CA (Civ Div) 27.017

SEB Trygg Holding AB v Manches; sub nom. AMB Generali Holding AG v SEB Trygg Liv Holding AB; AMB Generali Holding AG v Manches [2005] EWCA Civ 1237; [2006] 1 W.L.R. 2276; [2006] 1 All E.R. 437; [2006] 2 All E.R. (Comm) 38; [2006] 1 Lloyd's Rep. 318; [2006] 1 C.L.C. 849; (2005) 102(45) L.S.G. 28; (2005) 155 N.L.J. 1781; *The Times*, December 1, 2005, CA (Civ Div) 7.024

SES Contracting Ltd v UK Coal Plc [2007] EWHC 161; (2007) L.T.L., April 16, Q.B.D. 30.024

ST Dupont v EI du Pont de Nemours & Co; sub nom. EI Du Pont de Nemours & Co. v ST Dupont; DU PONT Trade Mark [2003] EWCA Civ 1368; [2006] 1 W.L.R. 2793; [2006] C.P. Rep. 25; [2004] F.S.R. 15; (2004) 27(2) I.P.D. 27009; (2003) 147 S.J.L.B. 1207, CA (Civ Div) 44.017

Saab v Saudi American Bank [1999] 1 W.L.R. 1861; [1999] 4 All E.R. 321; [1999] 2 All E.R. (Comm) 353; [2000] B.C.C. 466; [1999] 2 B.C.L.C. 462; [1999] I.L.Pr. 798; (1999) 96(31) L.S.G. 42; (1999) 143 S.J.L.B. 211; *The Times*, July 29, 1999, CA (Civ Div) 8.010

Safeway Stores Plc v Tate [2001] Q.B. 1120; [2001] 2 W.L.R. 1377; [2001] 4 All E.R. 193; [2001] C.P. Rep. 56; [2001] E.M.L.R. 13; (2001) 98(8) L.S.G. 45; (2001) 145 S.J.L.B. 16; *The Times*, January 25, 2001; *The Independent*, February 12, 2001, CA (Civ Div) 19.003

Saluja v Gill (t/a P Gill Estate Agents Property Services) [2002] EWHC 1435, Ch D 44.017

Sandry v Jones, *The Times*, August 3, 2000, CA (Civ Div) 17.005

Sansom v Metcalfe Hambleton and Co. (1995) Law Society's Gazette, February 4 ...23.001

Sardinia Sulcis, The. *See* Owners of the Sardinia Sulcis v Owners of the Al Tawwab

Sarwar v Alam; sub nom. Sawar v Alam [2001] EWCA Civ 1401; [2002] 1 W.L.R.
125; [2001] 4 All E.R. 541; [2002] 1 Costs L.R. 37; [2002] R.T.R. 12; [2002]
Lloyd's Rep. I.R. 126; [2002] P.I.Q.R. P15; (2001) 151 N.L.J. 1492; *The
Times,* October 11, 2001; *The Daily Telegraph,* September 25, 2001, CA
(Civ Div) 6.001
Saunders (A Bankrupt), Re; sub nom. Bristol and West Building Society v
Saunders; Bearman (A Bankrupt), Re [1997] Ch. 60; [1996] 3 W.L.R. 473;
[1997] 3 All E.R. 992; [1997] B.C.C. 83; [1996] B.P.I.R. 355, Ch D 42.015
Sayers v Clarke Walker (Permission to Appeal: Extension of Time Limits) [2002]
EWCA Civ 645; [2002] 1 W.L.R. 3095; [2002] 3 All E.R. 490; [2002] C.P.
Rep. 61; *The Times,* June 3, 2002; *The Independent,* May 22, 2002, CA (Civ
Div) 33.002, 33.011, 44.009
Scribes West Ltd v Relsa Anstalt (No.2); sub nom. Scribes West Ltd v Anstalt
(No.2) [2004] EWCA Civ 965; [2005] 1 W.L.R. 1839; [2004] 4 All E.R. 653;
[2005] C.P. Rep. 5, CA (Civ Div) 44.002
Sebuliba v Dagenham Motors [2002] EWHC 2701; (2002) L.T.L., November 12,
Ch D 42.016
Secretary of State for Trade and Industry v Baker (No.2); sub nom. Barings Plc
(No.2), Re [1998] Ch. 356; [1998] 2 W.L.R. 667; [1998] 1 All E.R. 673;
[1998] B.C.C. 888; [1998] 1 B.C.L.C. 16; *The Times,* October 23, 1997; *The
Independent,* October 7, 1997, Ch D (Companies Ct) 30.013, 30.024
Secretary of State for Trade and Industry v Pollock (1998) C.L.Y. 681 .... 33.005
Securum Finance Ltd v Ashton (No.1); sub nom. Ashton v Securum Finance Ltd
[2001] Ch. 291; [2000] 3 W.L.R. 1400; (2000) 97(27) L.S.G. 38; *The Times,*
July 5, 2000; *The Independent,* June 30, 2000, CA (Civ Div) 33.008
Seechurn v Ace Insurance SA NV; sub nom. Ace Insurance SA NV v Seechurn
[2002] EWCA Civ 67; [2002] 2 Lloyd's Rep. 390; [2002] Lloyd's Rep. I.R.
489, CA (Civ Div) 5.001
Selvanayagam v University of the West Indies [1983] 1 W.L.R. 585; [1983] 1 All
E.R. 824, PC (Trin) 12.044
Seray-Wurie v Hackney LBC (Jurisdiction: Reopening of Appeal) [2002] EWCA
Civ 909; [2003] 1 W.L.R. 257; [2002] 3 All E.R. 448; [2002] C.P. Rep. 68;
[2002] A.C.D. 87; (2002) 99(33) L.S.G. 21; (2002) 146 S.J.L.B. 183; *The
Times,* July 4, 2002, CA (Civ Div) 43.009
Series 5 Software Ltd v Clarke [1996] 1 All E.R. 853; [1996] C.L.C. 631; [1996]
F.S.R. 273; (1996) 19(3) I.P.D. 19024; *The Times,* January 19, 1996, Ch D ... 27.005
Sharma v Sood [2006] EWCA Civ 1480; (2006) L.T.L., October 13, CA (Civ
Div) 33.012
Sharman v Sheppard [1989] C.L.Y. 1190, CC (Bromley) 4.020, 4.021
Shearson Lehman Brothers Inc v MacLaine Watson & Co. Ltd (Damages: Interim
Payments) [1987] 1 W.L.R. 480; [1987] 2 All E.R. 181; [1987] 2 F.T.L.R 464;
(1987) 84(0) L.S.G. 1058; 131 S.J. 475, CA (Civ Div) 25.003
Sheldon v RHM Outhwaite (Underwriting Agencies) Ltd [1996] A.C. 102; [1995]
2 W.L.R. 570; [1995] 2 All E.R. 558; [1995] 2 Lloyd's Rep. 197; [1995] C.L.C.
655; [1995] 4 Re. L.R. 168; (1995) 92(22) L.S.G. 41; (1995) 145 N.L.J. 687;
(1995) 139 S.J.L.B. 119; *The Times,* May 5, 1995; *The Independent,* May 9,
1995; Lloyd's List, May 24, 1995, HL 5.015
Shelfer v City of London Electric Lighting Co. (No.1); Meux's Brewery Co. v City
of London Electric Lighting Co. [1895] 1 Ch. 287, CA 27.005
Shell UK Ltd v Enterprise Oil Plc [1999] 2 All E.R. (Comm) 87; [1999] 2 Lloyd's
Rep. 456; *The Times,* June 17, 1999, Ch D 23.006

TABLE OF CASES

Shevill v Presse Alliance SA [1996] A.C. 959; [1996] 3 W.L.R. 420; [1996] 3 All E.R. 929; [1996] I.L.Pr. 798; [1996] E.M.L.R. 533; (1996) 93(38) L.S.G. 42; (1996) 140 S.J.L.B. 208; *The Times,* July 26, 1996, HL 11.007
Shire v Secretary of State for Work and Pensions [2003] EWCA Civ 1465; [2004] C.P. Rep. 11; (2003) 100(42) L.S.G. 32; *The Times,* October 30, 2003, CA (Civ Div) 44.010
Sim v Rotherham MBC; Townend v Doncaster MBC; Barnfield v Solihull MBC; Rathbone v Croydon LBC [1987] Ch. 216; [1986] 3 W.L.R. 851; [1986] 3 All E.R. 387; [1986] I.C.R. 897; [1986] I.R.L.R. 391; 85 L.G.R. 128; (1986) 83 L.S.G. 3746; (1986) 130 S.J. 839, Ch D 12.037
Simaan General Contracting Co. v Pilkington Glass Ltd [1987] 1 W.L.R. 516; [1987] 1 All E.R. 345; (1987) 3 Const. L.J. 300; (1987) 84(0) L.S.G. 819; (1986) 136 N.L.J. 824; 131 S.J. 297, Q.B.D. (OR) 26.002
Simba-Tola v Elizabeth Fry Hostel [2001] EWCA Civ 1371; (2001) L.T.L., July 30, CA (Civ Div) 30.018
Simmons v Liberal Opinion Ltd; sub nom. Dunn, Re [1911] 1 K.B. 966, CA 7.024
Sinclair Investment Holdings SA v Cushnie [2006] EWHC 219; (2006) L.T.L., February 6, Ch D 19.014
Sinclair v British Telecommunications Plc [2001] 1 W.L.R. 38; [2000] 2 All E.R. 461; [2001] 1 Costs L.R. 40; *The Independent,* March 13, 2000, CA (Civ Div) 35.007
Sisu Capital Fund Ltd v Tucker (Costs); Sisu Capital Fund Ltd v Wallace [2005] EWHC 2321; [2006] 1 All E.R. 167; [2006] B.C.C. 463; [2006] 2 Costs L.R. 262; [2006] B.P.I.R. 154; [2006] F.S.R. 21; (2005) 155 N.L.J. 1686; *The Times,* November 4, 2005, Ch D (Companies Ct) 38.003
Slazengers Ltd v Seaspeed Ferries International Ltd; The Seaspeed Dora [1988] 1 W.L.R. 221; [1987] 3 All E.R. 967; [1988] 1 Lloyd's Rep. 36, CA (Civ Div) 26.002
Smith v Hampshire CC [2007] EWCA Civ 246; (2007) 151 S.J.L.B. 433, CA (Civ Div) 5.018
Smith v Ian Simpson & Co. [2001] Ch. 239; [2000] 3 W.L.R. 495; [2000] 3 All E.R. 434; [2000] B.P.I.R. 667; (2000) 150 N.L.J. 582; *The Times,* April 24, 2000; *The Independent,* April 18, 2000, CA (Civ Div) 42.023
Smith v Kvaerner Cementation Foundations Ltd [2006] EWCA Civ 242; [2007] 1 W.L.R. 370; [2006] 3 All E.R. 593; [2006] C.P. Rep. 36; [2006] B.L.R. 244; [2006] A.C.D. 51; (2006) 103(14) L.S.G. 33; (2006) 156 N.L.J. 721; [2006] N.P.C. 35; *The Times,* April 11, 2006, CA (Civ Div) 36.012, 44.009
Smith v Manchester Corp (1974) 17 K.I.R. 1 .... 4.014
Smith v Probyn (2000) 97(12) L.S.G. 44; (2000) 144 S.J.L.B. 134; *The Times,* March 29, 2000, Q.B.D. 8.001
SmithKline Beecham Biologicals SA v Connaught Laboratories Inc (Disclosure of Documents) [1999] 4 All E.R. 498; [1999] C.P.L.R. 505; [2000] F.S.R. 1; (2000) 51 B.M.L.R. 91; (1999) 22(10) I.P.D. 22092; *The Times,* July 13, 1999; *The Independent,* July 15, 1999, CA (Civ Div) 30.020
SmithKline Beecham Plc v Apotex Europe Ltd [2003] EWCA Civ 137; [2003] F.S.R. 31; (2003) 26(4) I.P.D. 26020, CA (Civ Div) 27.005
SmithKline Beecham Plc v Apotex Europe Ltd [2006] EWCA Civ 658; [2006] 3 W.L.R. 1146; [2006] 4 All E.R. 1078; [2006] C.P. Rep. 39; [2007] F.S.R. 6; (2006) 29(10) I.P.D. 29072; (2006) 103(23) L.S.G. 32; (2006) 156 N.L.J. 952; [2007] Ch. 71; *The Times,* June 9, 2006, CA (Civ Div) 27.002

SmithKline Beecham Plc v Generics (UK) Ltd; BASF AG v SmithKline Beecham
  Plc [2003] EWCA Civ 1109; [2004] 1 W.L.R. 1479; [2003] 4 All E.R. 1302;
  [2003] C.P. Rep. 66; [2004] F.S.R. 8; (2003) 26(11) I.P.D. 26071; (2003)
  100(34) L.S.G. 31; *The Times*, August 25, 2003, CA (Civ Div) 30.020
Smyth v Behbehani [1999] I.L.Pr. 584; *The Times*, April 9, 1999, CA (Civ Div) ... 11.017
Snookes v Jani-King (GB) Ltd; Little v Jani-King (GB) Ltd [2006] EWHC 289;
  [2006] I.L.Pr. 19, Q.B.D. 9.004
Société Commerciale de Réassurance v Eras International Ltd (formerly Eras
  (UK)); sub nom. Eras EIL Actions, Re [1992] 2 All E.R. 82 (Note); [1992] 1
  Lloyd's Rep. 570; *The Times*, November 28, 1991; *The Independent*, January
  27, 1992; *The Financial Times*, November 29, 1991, CA (Civ Div) 5.008
Societé Nationale Industrielle Aerospatiale (SNIA) v Lee Kui Jak [1987] A.C.
  871; [1987] 3 W.L.R. 59; [1987] 3 All E.R. 510; (1987) 84 L.S.G. 2048, PC
  (Bru) 11.016
Society of Lloyd's v Jaffray (1999) C.L. June 33.005
Society of Lloyd's v Jaffray (Witness Statements), *The Times*, August 3, 2000,
  Q.B.D. 31.009
Soinco SACI v Novokuznetsk Aluminium Plant (Appointment Of Receiver) [1998]
  Q.B. 406; [1998] 2 W.L.R. 334; [1997] 3 All E.R. 523; [1997] 2 Lloyd's Rep.
  330, Q.B.D. (Comm) 40.012
Sollitt v DJ Broady Ltd [2000] C.P.L.R. 259, CA (Civ Div) 16.009
South Cambridgeshire DC v Persons Unknown [2004] EWCA Civ 1280; [2004]
  4 P.L.R. 88; [2005] J.P.L. 680; (2004) 148 S.J.L.B. 1121; [2004] N.P.C. 138;
  The Times, November 11, 2004, CA (Civ Div) 7.023, 8.014
South Coast Shipping Co. Ltd v Havant BC [2002] 3 All E.R. 779; [2002] 1 Costs
  L.R. 98; (2002) 152 N.L.J. 59, Ch D 38.040
Southern & District Finance Plc v Turner [2003] EWCA Civ 1574; (2003) 147
  S.J.L.B. 1362; (2003) L.T.L., November 7, CA (Civ Div) 44.016
Southwark LBC v Kofi-Adu [2006] EWCA Civ 281; [2006] H.L.R. 33; [2006]
  N.P.C. 36; *The Times*, June 1, 2006, CA (Civ Div) 37.015
Southwark LBC v Nejad [1999] 1 Costs L.R. 62; *The Times*, January 28, 1999; *The
  Independent*, February 1, 1999, CA (Civ Div) 33.002
Southwark LBC v St Brice. *See* St Brice v Southwark LBC
Spelling Goldberg Productions Inc v BPC Publishing Ltd (Application for
  Intervention) [1981] R.P.C. 280, CA (Civ Div) 7.017
Spiliada Maritime Corp v Cansulex Ltd; The Spiliada [1987] A.C. 460; [1986]
  3 W.L.R. 972; [1986] 3 All E.R. 843; [1987] 1 Lloyd's Rep. 1; [1987]
  E.C.C. 168; [1987] 1 F.T.L.R. 103; (1987) 84 L.S.G. 113; (1986) 136
  N.L.J. 1137; (1986) 130 S.J. 925; *The Financial Times*, November 25,
  1986, HL 11.008, 11.015
Spiller v Brown (1999) L.T.L., July 20, CA (Civ Div) 12.038
Spillman v Bradfield Riding Centre [2007] EWHC 89, Q.B.D. 25.001
Spittle v Bunney [1988] 1 W.L.R. 847; [1988] 3 All E.R. 1031; [1988] Fam. Law 433;
  (1988) 138 N.L.J. Rep. 56; (1988) 132 S.J. 754, CA (Civ Div) 4.018
Springsteen v Flute International Ltd. *See* Masquerade Music Ltd v Springsteen
St Albans Court Ltd v Daldorch Estates Ltd, *The Times*, May 24, 1999, Ch D ...31.006,
  33.012
St Brice v Southwark LBC; sub nom. Southwark LBC v St Brice [2001] EWCA Civ
  1138; [2002] 1 W.L.R. 1537; [2002] H.L.R. 26; [2002] B.L.G.R. 117; [2002]
  1 P. & C.R. 27; [2002] L. & T.R. 11; (2001) 98(35) L.S.G. 34; (2001) 145
  S.J.L.B. 214; [2001] N.P.C. 120; *The Times*, August 6, 2001; *The
  Independent*, November 12, 2001, CA (Civ Div) 41.001

TABLE OF CASES

St Helens Metropolitan BC v Barnes. *See* Barnes v St Helens MBC
Staines v Walsh (2003) L.T.L., June 10, Ch D 27.019
Stallwood v David [2006] EWHC 2600; [2007] 1 All E.R. 206; [2007] R.T.R. 11;
　The Times, December 27, 2006, Q.B.D. 23.018
Stanton v Callaghan [2000] Q.B. 75; [1999] 2 W.L.R. 745; [1998] 4 All E.R. 961;
　[1999] C.P.L.R. 31; [1999] B.L.R. 172; (1999) 1 T.C.L.R. 50; 62 Con. L.R. 1;
　[1999] P.N.L.R. 116; [1998] 3 E.G.L.R. 165; (1999) 15 Const. L.J. 50; [1998]
　E.G. 115 (C.S.); (1998) 95(28) L.S.G. 32; (1998) 95(33) L.S.G. 33; (1998) 148
　N.L.J. 1355; (1998) 142 S.J.L.B. 220; [1998] N.P.C. 113; *The Times*, July 25,
　1998; *The Independent*, July 16, 1998, CA (Civ Div) 23.018
Starr v National Coal Board [1977] 1 W.L.R. 63; [1977] 1 All E.R. 243; (1976) 120
　S.J. 720, CA (Civ Div) 6.018
Steedman v BBC [2001] EWCA Civ 1534; [2002] E.M.L.R. 17; (2001) 98(47) L.S.G.
　27; (2001) 145 S.J.L.B. 260; *The Times*, December 13, 2001, CA (Civ Div) 5.016
Steele v Moule (1999) C.L. May 23, CC (Bedford) 30.007, 30.018
Stephens v Cannon [2005] EWCA Civ 222; [2005] C.P. Rep. 31; [2006] R.V.R. 126;
　The Times, May 3, 2005, CA (Civ Div) 31.004
Sterling Credit Ltd v Rahman. *See* Rahman v Sterling Credit Ltd
Stevens v Gullis 124672 [2000] 1 All E.R. 527; [2001] C.P. Rep. 3; [1999] B.L.R.
　394; (2000) 2 T.C.L.R. 385; 73 Con. L.R. 42; [2000] P.N.L.R. 229; [1999] 3
　E.G.L.R. 71; [1999] 44 E.G. 143; (2000) 16 Const. L.J. 68; *The Times*,
　October 6, 1999; *The Independent*, October 14, 1999, CA (Civ Div) 23.010
Stewart v Engel (Permission to Amend) [2000] 1 W.L.R. 2268; [2000] 3 All E.R.
　518; [2001] C.P. Rep. 9; [2001] E.C.D.R. 25; *The Times*, May 26, 2000; *The
　Independent*, June 26, 2000, CA (Civ Div) 43.008
Stocker v Planet Building Society (1879) 27 W.R. 877 .... 27.010
Stocznia Gdanska SA v Latreefers Inc; sub nom. Latreefers Inc, Re; Stocznia
　Gdanska SA v Latvian Shipping Co. (Abuse of Process) [2000] EWCA Civ
　36; [2000] C.P.L.R. 65; [2001] B.C.C. 174; [2001] 2 B.C.L.C. 116; [2001]
　C.L.C. 1267; *The Times*, March 15, 2000; *The Independent*, February 15,
　2000, CA (Civ Div) 26.004
Stocznia Gdanska SA v Latvian Shipping Co. (2001) L.T.L., February 12 ...... 30.010
Stringman v McArdle [1994] 1 W.L.R. 1653; [1994] P.I.Q.R. P230; [1994] J.P.I.L.
　69; *The Times*, November 19, 1993; *The Independent*, December 6, 1993,
　CA (Civ Div) 25.009
Stroh v Haringey LBC (1999) L.T.L., July 13, CA (Civ Div) 31.007, 33.002
Stroude v Beazer Homes Ltd [2005] EWCA Civ 265; [2005] N.P.C. 45; *The Times*,
　April 28, 2005, CA (Civ Div) 31.009
Stubbings v Webb [1993] A.C. 498; [1993] 2 W.L.R. 120; [1993] 1 All E.R. 322;
　[1993] 1 F.L.R. 714; [1993] P.I.Q.R. P86; [1993] Fam. Law 342; (1993) 137
　S.J.L.B. 32; *The Times*, December 17, 1992; *The Independent*, January 19,
　1993, HL 5.007
Sumitomo Corp v Credit Lyonnais Rouse Ltd [2001] EWCA Civ 1152; [2002]
　1 W.L.R. 479; [2002] 4 All E.R. 68; [2001] 2 Lloyd's Rep. 517; [2002] C.P.
　Rep. 3; [2001] C.P.L.R. 462; (2001) 98(34) L.S.G. 41; (2001) 145 S.J.L.B. 208;
　(2001) L.T.L., July 20; *The Times*, August 15, 2001; *The Independent*,
　October 18, 2001, CA (Civ Div) 30.011, 30.013
Surrey Oaklands NHS Trust v Hurley (1999) L.T.L., June 25 .... 33.005
Swain v Hillman [2001] 1 All E.R. 91; [2001] C.P. Rep. 16; [1999] C.P.L.R. 779;
　[2000] P.I.Q.R. P51; *The Times*, November 4, 1999; *The Independent*,
　November 10, 1999, CA (Civ Div) 19.001, 19.005

Symphony Group Plc v Hodgson [1994] Q.B. 179; [1993] 3 W.L.R. 830; [1993] 4 All E.R. 143; (1993) 143 N.L.J. 725; (1993) 137 S.J.L.B. 134; *The Times,* May 4, 1993; *The Independent,* May 14, 1993, CA (Civ Div) 39.015

TSB Private Bank International SA v Chabra [1992] 1 W.L.R. 231; [1992] 2 All E.R. 245, Ch D 7.014, 27.017
TSN Kunstoff Recycling Gmbh v Jurgens (2001) L.T.L., February 22 .... 40.017
T (formerly H) v Nugent Care Society (formerly Catholic Social Services) [2004] EWCA Civ 51; [2004] 1 W.L.R. 1129; [2004] 3 All E.R. 671; (2004) 101(6) L.S.G. 33; (2004) 148 S.J.L.B. 114; *The Times,* January 28, 2004; *The Independent,* January 22, 2004, CA (Civ Div) 7.020
Taiga v Taiga. *See* Moses-Taiga v Taiga
Tajik Aluminium Plant v Hydro Aluminium AS [2005] EWCA Civ 1218; [2006] 1 W.L.R. 767; [2005] 4 All E.R. 1232; [2006] 2 All E.R. (Comm) 295; [2006] 1 Lloyd's Rep. 155; [2006] C.P. Rep. 7; [2005] 2 C.L.C. 604; *The Independent,* October 28, 2005, CA (Civ Div) 36.003
Tanfern Ltd v Cameron-MacDonald [2000] 1 W.L.R. 1311; [2000] 2 All E.R. 801; [2001] C.P. Rep. 8; [2000] 2 Costs L.R. 260; (2000) 97(24) L.S.G. 41; *The Times,* May 17, 2000; *The Independent,* May 16, 2000, CA (Civ Div) 44.001
Tasyurdu v Immigration Appeal Tribunal; sub nom. Tasyurdu v Secretary of State for the Home Department [2003] EWCA Civ 447; [2003] C.P. Rep. 61; [2003] C.P.L.R. 343; (2003) 147 S.J.L.B. 508; *The Times,* April 16, 2003, CA (Civ Div) 44.017
Tavoulareas v Tsavliris [2006] EWCA Civ 1772; [2006] 2 C.L.C. 1034; [2007] C.P. Rep. 16; *The Times,* January 5, 2007, CA (Civ Div) 40.016
Taylor's, Re [1972] 2 Q.B. 369; [1972] 2 W.L.R. 1337; [1972] 2 All E.R. 873; (1972) 116 S.J. 314, CA (Civ Div) 7.005
Taylor v Anderson [2002] EWCA Civ 1680; [2003] R.T.R. 21; (2003) 100(1) L.S.G. 25; *The Times,* November 22, 2002, CA (Civ Div) 33.008
Taylor v Lawrence (Appeal: Jurisdiction to Reopen) [2002] EWCA Civ 90; [2003] Q.B. 528; [2002] 3 W.L.R. 640; [2002] 2 All E.R. 353; [2002] C.P. Rep. 29; (2002) 99(12) L.S.G. 35; (2002) 152 N.L.J. 221; (2002) 146 S.J.L.B. 50; *The Times,* February 8, 2002; *The Independent,* February 14, 2002; *The Daily Telegraph,* February 14, 2002, CA (Civ Div) 36.012, 43.009
Taylor v Midland Bank Trust Co. Ltd (1999) L.T.L., August 21 .... 33.008
Taylor v Nugent Care Society. *See* T (formerly H) v Nugent Care Society (formerly Catholic Social Services)
Teltscher Brothers Ltd v London & India Dock Investments Ltd [1989] 1 W.L.R. 770; [1989] 2 E.G.L.R. 261; (1989) 133 S.J. 660, Ch D 12.053
Thames Trains Ltd v Adams [2006] EWHC 3291; (2007) L.T.L., January 3, Q.B.D. 34.001
Thane Investments Ltd v Tomlinson (No.1) [2003] EWCA Civ 1272, CA (Civ Div); reversing, *The Times,* December 10, 2002, Ch D 27.020
Thistle Hotels Ltd (formerly Thistle Hotels Plc) v Gamma Four Ltd; sub nom. Thistle Hotels Ltd v Orb Estates Plc [2004] EWHC 322; [2004] 2 B.C.L.C. 174, Ch D 26.002
Thomas v Home Office [2006] EWCA Civ 1355; [2007] 1 W.L.R. 230; [2007] C.P. Rep. 6; [2007] P.I.Q.R. P9; (2006) 103(42) L.S.G. 35, CA (Civ Div) 1.016
Thompstone v Tameside & Glossop Acute Services NHS Trust; sub nom. Thompstone (A Child), Re [2006] EWHC 2904 (QB); [2007] LS Law Medical 71; (2006) L.T.L., November 23, Q.B.D. 4.016

TABLE OF CASES

Three Rivers DC v Bank of England (Application for Judgment in Private)
  [2005] EWCA Civ 933; [2005] C.P. Rep. 47; (2005) L.T.L., August 18, CA
  (Civ Div) 13.007
Three Rivers DC v Bank of England (No.1) [1996] Q.B. 292; [1995] 3 W.L.R. 650;
  [1995] 4 All E.R. 312; [1995] C.L.C. 99; *The Times*, December 6, 1994; *The
  Independent*, December 13, 2000, CA (Civ Div) 7.015
Three Rivers DC v Bank of England (No.3) (Summary Judgment) [2001] UKHL
  16; [2003] 2 A.C. 1; [2001] 2 All E.R. 513; [2001] Lloyd's Rep. Bank. 125;
  (2001) 3 L.G.L.R. 36; *The Times*, March 23, 2001, HL 19.005, 19.006,
  15.013, 15.014, 33.008
Three Rivers DC v Bank of England (Disclosure) (No.1); sub nom. Three Rivers
  DC v HM Treasury; Three Rivers DC v Bank of England (No.5); Three
  Rivers DC v Bank of England (No.4) [2002] EWCA Civ 1182; [2003] 1
  W.L.R. 210; [2002] 4 All E.R. 881; [2003] C.P. Rep. 9; [2003] C.P.L.R. 181;
  (2002) 99(39) L.S.G. 40; *The Times*, October 4, 2002; *The Independent*,
  November 11, 2002, CA (Civ Div) 30.023, 30.024
Three Rivers DC v Bank of England (Disclosure) (No.4) [2004] UKHL 48; [2005]
  1 A.C. 610; [2004] 3 W.L.R. 1274; [2005] 4 All E.R. 948; (2004) 101(46)
  L.S.G. 34; (2004) 154 N.L.J. 1727; (2004) 148 S.J.L.B. 1369; *The Times*,
  November 12, 2004; *The Independent*, November 16, 2004, HL 30.013
Three Rivers DC v Bank of England (Indemnity Costs) [2006] EWHC 816; [2006]
  5 Costs L.R. 714; (2006) L.T.L., April 24, Q.B.D. (Comm) 35.006
Three Rivers DC v Bank of England (Restriction on Cross Examination)
  [2005] EWCA Civ 889; [2005] C.P. Rep. 46; (2005) L.T.L, August 23, CA
  (Civ Div) 33.021
Three Rivers DC v HM Treasury. See Three Rivers DC v Bank of England
  (Disclosure) (No.1)
Tilling v Whiteman [1980] A.C. 1; [1979] 2 W.L.R. 401; [1979] 1 All E.R. 737;
  (1979) 38 P. & C.R. 341; (1979) 250 E.G. 51; [1979] J.P.L. 834; (1979) 123 S.J.
  202, HL 33.006
Tinsley v Sarkar; sub nom. Tinsley v Sarker [2004] EWCA Civ 1098; (2004) L.T.L.,
  July 23, CA (Civ Div) 25.001, 25.009
Tito v Waddell (No.2); Tito v Attorney General [1977] Ch. 106; [1977] 3 W.L.R.
  972; [1977] 2 W.L.R. 496; [1977] 3 All E.R. 129 (Note), Ch D 12.043
Tolley v Morris [1979] 1 W.L.R. 592; [1979] 2 All E.R. 561; (1979) 123 S.J. 353,
  HL 5.012
Total E&P Soudan SA v Edmonds [2007] EWCA Civ 50; (2007) 104(9) L.S.G. 30;
  (2007) 151 S.J.L.B. 195; (2007) L.T.L., January 31, CA (Civ Div) 30.024
Totalise Plc v Motley Fool Ltd [2001] EWCA Civ 1897; [2002] 1 W.L.R. 1233;
  [2003] 2 All E.R. 872; [2002] C.P. Rep. 22; [2002] E.M.L.R. 20; [2002] F.S.R.
  50; [2002] Masons C.L.R. 3; (2002) 99(9) L.S.G. 28; (2002) 146 S.J.L.B. 35;
  The Times, January 10, 2002, CA (Civ Div) 30.025
Toth v Jarman [2006] EWCA Civ 1028; [2006] 4 All E.R. 1276 (Note); [2006] C.P.
  Rep. 44; [2006] Lloyd's Rep. Med. 397; (2006) 91 B.M.L.R. 121; *The Times*,
  August 17, 2006, CA (Civ Div) 23.015
Totty v Snowden; Hewitt v Wirral and West Cheshire Community NHS Trust
  [2001] EWCA Civ 1415; [2002] 1 W.L.R. 1384; [2001] 4 All E.R. 577; [2002]
  C.P. Rep. 4; [2002] P.I.Q.R. P17; (2001) 98(38) L.S.G. 37; (2001) 151 N.L.J.
  1492; *The Times*, August 10, 2001; *The Independent*, October 10, 2001, CA
  (Civ Div) 9.010

Tradigrain SA v Intertek Testing Services (ITS) Canada Ltd [2007] EWCA Civ
   154; [2007] 1 C.L.C. 188; [2007] Bus. L.R. D32; *The Times*, March 20, 2007,
   CA (Civ Div) 44.006
Trinity Insurance Co. Ltd, Re [1990] B.C.C. 235, Ch D (Companies Ct) 42.007
Trustees of Dennis Rye Pension Fund v Sheffield City Council [1998] 1 W.L.R.
   840; [1997] 4 All E.R. 747; (1998) 30 H.L.R. 645; (1998) 10 Admin. L.R. 112;
   (1998) 162 J.P.N. 145; *The Times*, August 20, 1997, CA (Civ Div) 24.001
Trustor AB v Barclays Bank Plc (2000) 97(44) L.S.G. 45; *The Times*, November 22,
   2000, Ch D 11.007
Trustor AB v Smallbone (No.1) [2000] 1 All E.R. 811, Ch D 1.017
Turner v Fenton [1982] 1 W.L.R. 52; [1981] 1 All E.R. 8, Ch D 6.024
Turner v Grovit (C-159/02); sub nom. Turner, Re (C-159/02) [2005] 1 A.C. 101;
   [2004] 3 W.L.R. 1193; [2004] All E.R. (EC) 485; [2004] 2 All E.R. (Comm)
   381; [2004] 2 Lloyd's Rep. 169; [2004] E.C.R. I-3565; [2004] 1 C.L.C. 864;
   [2004] I.L.Pr. 25; [2005] I.C.R. 23; [2004] I.R.L.R. 899; *The Times*, April 29,
   2004, ECJ 11.016
Turner v Royal Bank of Scotland PLL (2000) L.T.L., June 30 .... 42.006, 42.013
Tweed v Parades Commission for Northern Ireland [2006] UKHL 53; [2007]
   2 W.L.R. 1; [2007] 2 All E.R. 273; [2007] H.R.L.R. 11; [2007] U.K.H.R.R.
   456; (2007) 151 S.J.L.B. 24; *The Times*, December 15, 2006, HL (NI) 24.003

U (A Child) v Liverpool City Council; sub nom. KU (A Child) v Liverpool City
   Council [2005] EWCA Civ 475; [2005] 1 W.L.R. 2657; [2005] 4 Costs L.R.
   600; *The Times*, May 16, 2005, CA (Civ Div) 38.024, 38.026
U (A Child) (Serious Injury: Standard of Proof) (Permission to Reopen Appeal),
   Re; sub nom. U (Re-Opening of Appeal), Re [2005] EWCA Civ 52; [2005] 1
   W.L.R. 2398; [2005] 3 All E.R. 550; [2005] 2 F.L.R. 444; [2005] 1 F.C.R. 583;
   [2005] Fam. Law 449; (2005) 102(16) L.S.G. 30; (2005) 155 N.L.J. 325; (2005)
   149 S.J.L.B. 266; *The Times*, March 31, 2005, CA (Civ Div) 43.009
Uddin (A Child), Re. *See* U (A Child) (Serious Injury: Standard of Proof)
   (Permission to Reopen Appeal), Re
Ultraframe (UK) Ltd v Fielding (Costs); sub nom. Ultraframe (UK) Ltd v Fielding
   (No.2); Northstar Systems Ltd v Fielding (Costs) [2006] EWCA Civ 1660;
   [2007] 2 All E.R. 983; [2007] C.P. Rep. 12; *The Times*, January 8, 2007, CA
   (Civ Div) 37.016, 38.018
Unilever Plc v Chefaro Proprietaries Ltd (Application for Expedited Appeal);
   Chiron Corp v Organon Teknika Ltd (Application for Expedited Appeal);
   Henderson v Merrett Syndicates Ltd (Application for Expedited Appeal);
   Brown v KMR Services Ltd (Application for Expedited Appeal) [1995] 1
   W.L.R. 243; [1995] 1 All E.R. 587; (1994) 144 N.L.J. 1660; *The Times*,
   November 28, 1994; *The Independent*, November 24, 1994, CA (Civ Div) .. 44.021
Unilever Plc v Procter & Gamble Co. [2000] 1 W.L.R. 2436; [2001] 1 All E.R. 783;
   [2000] F.S.R. 344; (2000) 23(1) I.P.D. 23001; (1999) 96(44) L.S.G. 40; (1999)
   143 S.J.L.B. 268; *The Times*, November 4, 1999; *The Independent*,
   November 5, 1999, CA (Civ Div) 6.024
Union Transport v Continental Lines SA; sub nom. Cross AM Lines [1992]
   1 W.L.R. 15; [1992] 1 All E.R. 161; [1992] 1 Lloyd's Rep. 229; [1992] I.L.Pr.
   385; (1992) 89(2) L.S.G. 30; (1992) 136 S.J.L.B. 18; *The Times*, December 16,
   1991; *The Independent*, January 10, 1992; *The Financial Times*, December
   17, 1991, HL 11.007

TABLE OF CASES

United Carriers Ltd v Heritage Food Group (UK) Ltd [1996] 1 W.L.R. 371; [1995] 4 All E.R. 95; [1995] 2 Lloyd's Rep. 269; [1995] C.L.C. 364; (1995) 139 S.J.L.B. 83; *The Times*, March 8, 1995, Q.B.D. 12.037

Uphill v BRB (Residuary) Ltd [2005] EWCA Civ 60; [2005] 1 W.L.R. 2070; [2005] 3 All E.R. 264; [2005] C.P. Rep. 20; (2005) 102(15) L.S.G. 35; (2005) 149 S.J.L.B. 181; *The Times*, February 8, 2005; *The Independent*, February 17, 2005, CA (Civ Div) 44.007

VSEL Ltd v Cape Contracts Plc; sub nom. Vickers Shipbuilding & Engineering Ltd v Cape Contracts Plc [1998] P.I.Q.R. P207; (1998) C.L.Y. 338, Q.B.D. ... 30.008

Van Uden Maritime BV (t/a Van Uden Africa Line) v Kommanditgesellschaft in Firma Deco-Line (C-391/95) [1999] Q.B. 1225; [1999] 2 W.L.R. 1181; [1999] All E.R. (E.C.) 258; [1999] 1 All E.R. (Comm.) 385; [1998] E.C.R. I-7091; [1999] I.L.Pr. 73; *The Times*, December 1, 1998, ECJ 11.004

Various Ledward Claimants v Kent and Medway HA [2003] EWHC 2551; [2004] 1 Costs L.R. 101, Q.B.D. 33.013

Vasiliou v Hajigeorgiou; sub nom. Hajigeorgiou v Vasiliou [2005] EWCA Civ 236; [2005] 1 W.L.R. 2195; [2005] 3 All E.R. 17; [2005] C.P. Rep. 27; (2005) 102(18) L.S.G. 22; [2005] N.P.C. 39; *The Times*, March 22, 2005, CA (Civ Div) 23.008

Vedatech Corp v Seagate Software Information (No.2) [2002] EWCA Civ 54 ... 26.003

Vehicle and General Insurance Co. Ltd (In liquidation) v H&W Christie Ltd [1976] 1 All E.R. 747, Q.B.D. 6.026

Vellacott v Convergence Group Plc. *See* Chantrey Vellacott v Convergence Group Plc

Ventouris v Mountain; The Italia Express (No.1) [1991] 1 W.L.R. 607; [1991] 3 All E.R. 472; [1991] 1 Lloyd's Rep. 441; (1991) 141 N.L.J. 237; *The Times*, February 18, 1991; *The Financial Times*, February 15, 1991, CA (Civ Div); reversing [1990] 1 W.L.R. 1370; [1990] 3 All E.R. 157; [1990] 2 Lloyd's Rep. 154; (1990) 87(35) L.S.G. 40; (1990) 140 N.L.J. 666; *The Times*, March 17, 1990; *The Financial Times*, March 6, 1990, Q.B.D. (Comm) 7.018, 30.013, 30.018

Venture Finance Plc v Mead [2005] EWCA Civ 325; [2005] All E.R. (D) 376 (Mar); [2006] 3 Costs L.R. 389, CA (Civ Div) 43.008

Vernon v Bosley (No.2) [1999] Q.B. 18; [1997] 3 W.L.R. 683; [1997] 1 All E.R. 614; [1997] R.T.R. 275; [1998] 1 F.L.R. 304; [1997] P.I.Q.R. P326; (1997) 35 B.M.L.R. 174; [1997] Fam. Law 476; (1997) 94(4) L.S.G. 26; (1997) 147 N.L.J. 89; (1997) 141 S.J.L.B. 27; *The Times*, December 19, 1996; *The Independent*, January 21, 1997, CA (Civ Div) 30.009

Vickers Shipbuilding & Engineering Ltd v Cape Contracts Plc. *See* VSEL Ltd v Cape Contracts Plc

Vinos v Marks & Spencer Plc [2001] 3 All E.R. 784; [2001] C.P. Rep. 12; [2000] C.P.L.R. 570; *The Independent*, July 17, 2000, CA (Civ Div) 9.005

Virk v Gan Life Holdings Plc [2000] Lloyd's Rep. I.R. 159; (2000) 52 B.M.L.R. 207, CA (Civ Div) 7.015

Voaden v Champion; The Baltic Surveyor and the Timbuktu [2002] EWCA Civ 89; [2002] 1 Lloyd's Rep. 623; [2002] C.L.C. 666, CA (Civ Div); reversing in part [2001] 1 Lloyd's Rep. 739, Q.B.D. 23.006

Voice & Script International Ltd v Alghafar [2003] EWCA Civ 736; [2003] C.P. Rep. 53, CA (Civ Div) 9.035, 20.013, 44.007

WPP Holdings Italy Srl v Benatti; sub nom. Benatti v WPP Holdings Italy Srl
[2007] EWCA Civ 263; (2007) 104(15) L.S.G. 21; [2007] 1 C.L.C. 324; *The
Times,* April 16, 2007, CA (Civ Div) 11.004
Wade v Turfrey (2007) L.T.L., March 22, Q.B.D. 25.009
Wake v Wylie; sub nom. Wylie v Wake; Wake v Page [2001] R.T.R. 20; [2001]
P.I.Q.R. P13; *The Times,* February 9, 2001, CA (Civ Div) 6.028
Walker & Knight v Donne Mileham & Haddock (A firm), *The Times,* November
9, 1976, CA (Civ Div) 18.005
Walker v Daniels. *See* D (A Child) v Walker
Walker v Turpin [1994] 1 W.L.R. 196; [1993] 4 All E.R. 865; *The Times,* November
2, 1993, CA (Civ Div) 29.012
Walker v Walker; sub nom. Walker Wingsail Systems Plc, Re [2005] EWCA Civ
247; [2006] 1 W.L.R. 2194; [2005] 1 All E.R. 272; [2005] C.P. Rep. 33; [2005]
3 Costs L.R. 363; [2005] B.P.I.R. 454; *The Times,* March 3, 2005, CA
(Civ Div) 35.006
Walker v Wilsher (1889) L.R. 23 Q.B.D. 335, CA 29.002
Walkley v Precision Forgings Ltd [1979] 1 W.L.R. 606; [1979] 2 All E.R. 548; (1979)
123 S.J. 548, HL 5.019
Wallis v Valentine [2002] EWCA Civ 1034; [2003] E.M.L.R. 8; (2002) 99(37) L.S.G.
39; *The Times,* August 9, 2002, CA (Civ Div) 33.008
Walsh v Misseldine [2000] C.P. Rep. 74; [2000] C.P.L.R. 201; (2000) L.T.L., March
1, CA (Civ Div) 33.008
Walton v Egan [1982] Q.B. 1232; [1982] 3 W.L.R. 352; [1982] 3 All E.R. 849; (1982)
126 S.J. 345, Q.B.D. 39.006, 39.007
Wandsworth LBC v Winder (No.1) [1985] A.C. 461; [1984] 3 W.L.R. 1254; [1984]
3 All E.R. 976; (1985) 17 H.L.R. 196; 83 L.G.R. 143; (1985) 82 L.S.G. 201;
(1985) 135 N.L.J. 381; (1984) 128 S.J. 838, HL 24.001
Warriner v Warriner [2002] EWCA Civ 81; [2002] 1 W.L.R. 1703; [2003] 3 All E.R.
447; [2002] P.I.Q.R. Q7; [2002] Lloyd's Rep. Med. 220; (2002) 99(14) L.S.G.
25; *The Times,* March 28, 2002, CA (Civ Div) 4.011
Wates Construction Ltd v HGP Greentree Allchurch Evans Ltd [2005] EWHC
2174; (2005) L.T.L., November 4; [2006] B.L.R. 45; 105 Con. L.R. 47,
Q.B.D. (TCC) 35.006
Watts v Morrow [1991] 1 W.L.R. 1421; [1991] 4 All E.R. 937; 54 B.L.R. 86; 26
Con. L.R. 98; (1991) 23 H.L.R. 608; [1991] 2 E.G.L.R. 152; [1991] 43 E.G.
121; (1992) 8 Const. L.J. 73; [1991] E.G. 88 (C.S.); (1992) 89(14) L.S.G. 33;
(1991) 141 N.L.J. 1331; [1991] N.P.C. 98; *The Independent,* August 20, 1991;
The Guardian, September 4, 1991, CA (Civ Div) 3.002
Wauchope v Mordecai [1970] 1 W.L.R. 317; [1970] 1 All E.R. 417; (1969) 113 S.J.
941, CA (Civ Div) 12.024
Waugh v HB Clifford & Sons Ltd [1982] Ch. 374; [1982] 2 W.L.R. 679; [1982]
1 All E.R. 1095, CA (Civ Div) 6.023
Wealands v CLC Contractors Ltd; sub nom. Wealand v CLC Contractors Ltd
[2000] 1 All E.R. (Comm) 30; [1999] 2 Lloyd's Rep. 739; [1999] C.L.C. 1821;
[1999] B.L.R. 401; (2000) 2 T.C.L.R. 367; 74 Con. L.R. 1; *The Times,*
November 16, 1999; *The Times,* October 5, 1999, CA (Civ Div); affirming
[1998] C.L.C. 808, Q.B.D. (Comm) 33.004
Weet v Packer (1999) L.T.L. December 1 .... 24.011
Welsh v Parnianzadeh (t/a Southern Fried Chicken); sub nom. Welsh v
Parianzadeh [2004] EWCA Civ 1832; [2004] All E.R. (D) 170 (Dec), CA
(Civ Div) 33.011

lxxxvii

West Bromwich Building Society v Wilkinson; sub nom. Wilkinson v West
 Bromwich Building Society [2005] UKHL 44; [2005] 1 W.L.R. 2303; [2005]
 4 All E.R. 97; [2005] 27 E.G. 221 (C.S.); (2005) 102(28) L.S.G. 32; [2005] 2
 P. & C.R. DG20; The Times, July 4, 2005; The Independent, July 7, 2005,
 HL 5.010
West End Hotels Syndicate v Bayer (1912) 29 T.L.R. 92 .... 7.024
West Tankers Inc v RAS Riunione Adriatica di Sicurta SpA; The Front Comor
 [2007] UKHL 4; [2007] 1 All E.R. (Comm) 794; [2007] 1 Lloyd's Rep. 391;
 [2007] I.L.Pr. 20; (2007) 104(10) L.S.G. 30, HL 11.016
Westminster City Council v Porter (Third Party Disclosure: Costs Basis) [2003]
 EWHC 2373; [2005] 2 Costs L.R. 186, Ch D 27.022
Weston v Gribben [2006] EWCA Civ 1425; (2006) 103(44) L.S.G. 27; (2006) 150
 S.J.L.B. 1463; [2007] C.P. Rep. 10; The Independent, November 8, 2006, CA
 (Civ Div) 12.053
White v Brunton [1984] Q.B. 570; [1984] 3 W.L.R. 105; [1984] 2 All E.R. 606;
 (1984) 81 L.S.G. 1685; (1984) 128 S.J. 434, CA (Civ Div) 7.012, 44.008
Whitehouse v Jordan [1981] 1 W.L.R. 246; [1981] 1 All E.R. 267; (1981) 125 S.J.
 167, HL 23.001
Wilkinson v Kitzinger; sub nom. X v Y (Overseas Same-Sex Relationship) [2006]
 EWHC 2022 (Fam); [2007] 1 F.L.R. 295; [2007] 1 F.C.R. 183; [2006]
 H.R.L.R. 36; [2007] U.K.H.R.R. 164; [2006] Fam. Law 1030; (2006) 103(33)
 L.S.G. 25; The Times, August 21, 2006, Fam Div 39.017
Williams v Alpha Mechanical Handling and National Power (1996) C.L.Y. 994 . . 31.005
Williams v Devon CC [2003] EWCA Civ 365; [2003] C.P. Rep. 47; [2003] P.I.Q.R.
 Q4; The Times, March 26, 2003, CA (Civ Div) 29.008
Williams v Fanshaw Porter & Hazelhurst [2004] EWCA Civ 157; [2004] 1 W.L.R.
 3185; [2004] 2 All E.R. 616; [2004] Lloyd's Rep. I.R. 800; [2004] P.N.L.R. 29;
 (2004) 101(12) L.S.G. 36; The Times, February 27, 2004, CA (Civ Div) 5.015
Willis v Nicolson [2007] EWCA Civ 199; (2007) 104(13) L.S.G. 26; (2007) 151
 S.J.L.B. 394; (2007) L.T.L., March 13, CA (Civ Div) 33.013
Willson v Ministry of Defence; sub nom. Wilson v Ministry of Defence [1991]
 1 All E.R. 638; [1991] I.C.R. 595, Q.B.D. 4.015
Wilson, Re. See Wilson v Colchester Justices
Wilson v Colchester Justices; sub nom. R. v Colchester Justices Ex p. Wilson
 [1985] A.C. 750; [1985] 2 All E.R. 97; (1985) 81 Cr. App. R. 158; (1985) 149
 J.P. 337; [1985] Crim. L.R. 512; (1985) 82 L.S.G. 1857; (1985) 129 S.J. 245;
 The Times, March 29, 1985, HL 45.001
Wise v Kaye [1962] 1 Q.B. 638; [1962] 2 W.L.R. 96; [1962] 1 All E.R. 257; (1962)
 106 S.J. 14, CA 4.009
Wisely v John Fulton (Plumbers) Ltd; Wadey v Surrey CC [2000] 1 W.L.R. 820;
 [2000] 2 All E.R. 545; 2000 S.C. (H.L.) 95; 2000 S.L.T. 494; 2000 S.C.L.R.
 693; [2000] P.I.Q.R. Q306; (2000) 97(22) L.S.G. 43; (2000) 144 S.J.L.B. 197;
 2000 G.W.D. 13–487; The Times, April 7, 2000, HL 4.022
Wiszniewski v Central Manchester HA; sub nom. Wisniewski v Central
 Manchester HA [1998] P.I.Q.R. P324; [1998] Lloyd's Rep. Med. 223, CA
 (Civ Div) 31.004
Wood v Collins [2006] EWCA Civ 743; The Times, June 26, 2006, CA (Civ Div) ... 44.005
Woodhouse v Consignia Plc; Steliou v Compton [2002] EWCA Civ 275; [2002]
 1 W.L.R. 2558; [2002] 2 All E.R. 737; [2002] C.P. Rep. 42; (2002) 99(16)
 L.S.G. 38; (2002) 152 N.L.J. 517; (2002) 146 S.J.L.B. 76; The Times, April 5,
 2002; The Independent, March 13, 2002, CA (Civ Div) 33.011, 43.005

Woods v Martins Bank [1959] 1 Q.B. 55; [1958] 1 W.L.R. 1018; [1958] 3 All E.R. 166; (1958) 102 S.J. 655, Assizes (Leeds) 30.005
Woodworth v Conroy; Conroy v Woodworth [1976] Q.B. 884; [1976] 2 W.L.R. 338; [1976] 1 All E.R. 107; (1975) 119 S.J. 810; *The Times*, November 12, 1975, CA (Civ Div) 30.018
Woolley v Essex CC [2006] EWCA Civ 753; (2006) 150 S.J.L.B. 671; (2006) L.T.L., May 17, CA (Civ Div)
Wright v British Railways Board [1983] 2 A.C. 773; [1983] 3 W.L.R. 211; [1983] 2 All E.R. 698, HL 4.020, 4.021
Wrightson, Re; sub nom. Wrightson v Cooke [1908] 1 Ch. 789, Ch D 12.028

Yasuda Fire & Marine Insurance Co. of Europe Ltd v Orion Marine Insurance Underwriting Agency Ltd [1995] Q.B. 174; [1995] 2 W.L.R. 49; [1995] 3 All E.R. 211; [1995] 1 Lloyd's Rep. 525; [1994] C.L.C. 1212; [1995] 4 Re. L.R. 217; *The Times*, October 27, 1994, Q.B.D. (Comm) 30.005
Yell Ltd v Garton [2004] EWCA Civ 87; [2004] C.P. Rep. 29; (2004) 148 S.J.L.B. 180; *The Times*, February 26, 2004; *The Independent*, February 11, 2004, CA (Civ Div) 44.017
Yonge v Toynbee [1910] 1 K.B. 215, CA 7.024
Yorke v Katra [2003] EWCA Civ 867; (2003) L.T.L., June 9, CA (Civ Div) 23.006
Yousif v Salama [1980] 1 W.L.R. 1540; [1980] 3 All E.R. 405; [1980] F.S.R. 444; (1980) 124 S.J. 480, CA (Civ Div) 27.024
Yuill v Yuill [1945] P. 15, CA 37.015

Zambia v Meer Care & Desai. *See* Attorney General of Zambia v Meer Care & Desai (A Firm)
Zockoll Group Ltd v Mercury Communications Ltd (No.1) [1998] F.S.R. 354, CA (Civ Div) 27.009
ZYX Music GmbH v King [1997] 2 All E.R. 129; [1997] E.C.C. 477, CA (Civ Div); affirming [1995] 3 All E.R. 1; [1996] E.C.C. 314; [1995] E.M.L.R. 281; [1995] F.S.R. 566, Ch D 14.004

TABLE OF STATUTES

1838	Judgments Act (1 & 2 Vict. c.110) 40.002	1947	Crown Proceedings Act (10 & 11 Geo. 6 c.44) 24.018
	s.17 .... 3.009	1948	Law Reform (Personal Injuries) Act (11 & 12 Geo. 6 c.41)
1873	Supreme Court of Judicature Act (36 & 37 Vict. c.66) 12.037, 24.011		s.2(4) 4.006
		1954	Landlord and Tenant Act (2 & 3 Eliz. 2 c.56) 24.009
1875	Judicature Act (38 & 39 Vict. c.77) 12.037, 24.011		s.23(3) 7.014
1882	Bills of Exchange Act (45 & 46 Vict. c.61) 3.001		s.24 .... 9.005
			s.29(2) 9.005
1890	Partnership Act (53 & 54 Vict. c.39)	1958	Variation of Trusts Act (6 & 7 Eliz. 2 c.53) 24–016
	s.23 .... 7.008, 40.013	1960	Administration of Justice Act (8 & 9 Eliz. 2 c.65)
1891	Slander of Women Act (54 & 55 Vict. c.51) 38.022		s.12 .... 1.017
		1962	Civil Aviation (Euro-control) Act (10 & 11 Eliz. 2. c.8) 11.007, 11.008
1920	Administration of Justice Act (10 & 11 Geo. 5 c.81) ..40.016		
1925	Law of Property Act (15 & 16 Geo. 5 c.20)	1967	Criminal Law Act (c.58)
			s.13 .... 2.022
	s.91 .... 24.006		s.14 .... 2.022
1927	Landlord and Tenant Act (17 & 18 Geo. 5 c.36) 24.009	1967	Leasehold Reform Act (c.88) 24.009
1930	Third Parties (Rights against Insurers) Act (20 & 21 Geo. 5 c.25) ...5.013, 6.028, 7.023, 30.024	1968	Theft Act (c.60)
			s.31 .... 27.027
		1968	Civil Evidence Act (c.68) ..12.024
			s.11 .... 12.024, 31.002
	s.2 .... 30.024		s.12 .... 12.024, 31.002
1932	Chancel Repairs Act (22 & 23 Geo. 5 c.20) 24.009	1969	Administration of Justice Act (c.58)
1933	Foreign Judgments (Reciprocal Enforcement) Act (23 & 24 Geo. 5 c.13) 40.016		s.12 .... 44.003
			s.12(5) 44.004
			s.13 .... 44.003
		1970	Administration of Justice Act (c.31) 24.006
1934	Administration of Justice (Appeals) Act (24 & 25 Geo. 5 c.40) 45.001		s.36 .... 24.006
		1971	Attachment of Earnings Act (c.32) 40.006
1934	Law Reform (Miscellaneous Provisions) Act (24 & 25 Geo. 5 c.41) ... 4.013, 5.017, 29.013		s.7 .... 40.007
			s.8(2)(b) 40.004
			s.23 .... 41.003
1938	Leasehold Property (Repairs) Act (1 & 2 Geo. 6 c.34) 24.009	1971	Armed Forces Act (c.33) 40.006
		1972	Civil Evidence Act (c.30)
1939	Limitation Act (2 & 3 Geo. 6 c.21) 7.015		s.3 .... 23.001
			s.3(2) 31.011

xci

1974	Consumer Credit Act (c.39) 3.001, 9.020, 13.007, 15.004, 15.005, 19.015, 40.002	1977	Patents Act (c.37) 24.016
			s.70 .... 24.016
		1977	Rent Act (c.42)
			s.141 .... 38.022
	s.8 .... 24.006	1978	Interpretation Act (c.30)
	s.113 .... 24.006		s.7 .... 8.010
	s.129 .... 24.006	1978	State Immunity Act (c.33) ..15.009
	ss.137–140A 3.001	1978	Civil Liability (Contribution) Act (c.47) 18.004
	s.139 .... 18.007		s.1 ..... 5.006, 18.005, 18.007
	s.141 .... 9.020, 12.023		s.6 .... 18.005, 18.007
1974	Solicitors' Act (c.47)		s.7(3) 18.004
	Pt III 24.019, 36.003	1979	Charging Orders Act (c.53)
	s.57 .... 39.005, 39.007		s.1 .... 40.009
	s.57(5) 39.006, 39.007		s.2 .... 40.011
	s.57(7) 39.006, 39.007		s.2(2) 40.011
	s.59 .... 39.005, 39.006	1979	Sale of Goods Act (c.54)
	s.60(1) 39.006		s.53 .... 12.037
	s.61(1) 39.006	1980	Limitation Act (c.58) 5.001, 5.011, 5.013, 7.015, 9.004, 40.004
	s.61(4B) 39.006, 39.007		
	s.61(5) 39.006		
	s.61(6)(b) 39.006		s.2 ...... 5.001, 5.007, 12.036
	s.61(1)(c) 39.006		s.4A 5.016
	s.62 .... 39.006		s.5 ...... 5.001, 5.009, 12.036
	s.63 .... 39.006		s.6 .... 5.004
	s.65(2) 2.012		s.8 .... 5.005
	s.67 .... 39.004		s.9 .... 5.005
	s.69 .... 39.003, 39.006, 39.007		s.10 .... 5.006
	s.70 ... 24.006, 39.003, 39.004, 39.005, 39.006, 39.007		s.11 ...... 5.007, 5.008, 5.016, 5.017, 5.018, 7.015
	s.70(5) 39.004		s.11A 5.017
	s.70(6) 39.004		s.12 ......5.008, 5.016, 5.017, 5.018, 7.015
	s.70(7) 39.004		
	s.70(9) 39.004		s.12(1) 5.008
	s.70(10) 39.004		s.13 .... 5.008
	s.71 .... 24.006, 39.019		s.14 ...... 5.007, 5.008, 5.018
	s.74(3) 2.011		s.14A 5.008, 5.012, 5.013, 5.015, 5.016
	s.87 .... 2.010		
	Sch.1 .... 24.019		s.14B 5.002, 5.008, 5.012, 5.013
1975	Litigants in Person (Costs and Expenses) Act (c.47) 38.004, 38.020		
			s.14B(2) 5.008
			s.19 .... 5.005
1975	Inheritance (Provision for Family and Dependants) Act (c.63) 7.010, 10.002, 13.007, 24.010		s.20 .... 5.005, 5.010
			s.20(5) 5.010
			s.24 .... 42.018
1976	Fatal Accidents Act (c.30) ..4.013, 4.015, 4.018, 5.017, 25.009, 29.013		s.28 .... 5.011, 5.017
			s.28(7) 5.017
			s.28A 5.011, 5.012
	s.4 .... 4.018		s.29(5) 5.013
1977	Torts (Interference with Goods) Act (c.32)		s.29(7) 5.014
			s.30 .... 5.014
	s.4 .... 17.031		

	s.31 .... 5.014		s.1(3) 40.017
	s.32 .... 5.015		s.4(2) 40.017
	s.32(2) 5.015		s.7 .... 40.017
	s.32(3) 5.015		s.16 .... 11.002
	s.32(4) 5.015		s.25 .... 27.018, 27.020
	s.32(5) 5.015		s.41 .... 11.005
	s.32A 5.003, 5.016		s.42 .... 11.005
	s.33 .....5.007, 5.008, 5.017,		Sch.1
	5.018, 5.019		art.2 .... 11.005
	s.33(3) 5.018		art.3 .... 11.005
	s.33(3)(a) 5.018		art.5(1) 11.007
	s.35 .... 5.009, 12.053		art.5(3) 11.007
	s.35(3) 18.002		art.22 .... 11.006
	s.35(6) 12.053		para.38 .... 40.017
	s.36 .... 5.002		Sch.6
1981	Contempt of Court Act (c.49)		para.6 .... 40.017
	s.14 .... 41.003		para.8 .... 40.017
1981	Supreme Court Act (c.54)		para.9 .... 40.017
	s.18(1)(b) 44.008		Sch.7
	s.19 .... 1.003		para.6 .... 40.017
	s.30 .... 24.001		para.7 .... 40.017
	s.31(2) 24.001		para.8 .... 40.017
	s.31(4) 24.001	1982	Administration of Justice Act
	s.32A 4.015, 12.015		(c.53)
	s.33 .... 30.024		s.5 .... 4.005
	s.34 .... 30.003, 30.023	1983	Mental Health Act (c.20)
	s.35 .... 12.013		Pt VII 7.006, 8.011
	s.35A 3.002, 3.004, 3.007,		s.94(2) 7.006
	3.009, 12.013, 16.004	1983	County Courts (Penalties for
	s.35A(2) 3.005		Contempt) Act (c.45)
	s.35A(3) 3.008		s.1 .... 41.003
	s.37 .... 27.015, 27.030	1984	Foreign Limitation Periods Act
	s.39 .... 41.004		(c.16) 5.020
	s.40 .... 40.005	1984	County Courts Act (c.28)
	s.40(6) 40.005		s.14 .... 41.003
	s.40A 40.005		s.15(1) 1.003
	s.42 .... 7.011, 13.002		s.15(2) 1.003
	s.42(1A) 7.010		s.23 .... 1.003
	s.51(6) 39.002		s.23(c) 40.010
	s.51(7) **39.002**		s.32 .... 24.010
	s.54(5) 44.022		s.38 ....24.001, 24.004, 40.014,
	s.58(2) 44.019		41.003, 41.004
	s.61 .... 1.001		s.40(1) 9.025
	s.69 .... 19.003		s.40(2) 9.025
	s.72 .... 27.027		s.42 .... 40.009
	s.128 .... 2.010, 24.010		s.42(5) 40.002, 40.009
1982	Civil Jurisdiction and Judgments		s.51 .... 4.015, 12.015
	Act (c.27) ...11.001, 11.002,		s.52 .... 30.024
	11.007, 11.008, 11.014,		s.53 .... 30.003, 30.023
	11.015, 11.016, 11.017,		s.66 .... 19.003
	40.016, 40.017		s.69 ..... 3.002, 3.004, 12.013,
			12.047, 16.004

1984	County Courts Act—*cont'd*	1986	Financial Services Act
	s.69(2) 3.005		(c.60) 30.023
	s.69(3) 3.008	1987	Landlord and Tenant Act
	s.74 .... 3.009		(c.31) 24.009
	s.79 .... 44.004	1987	Banking Act (c.37) 42.018
	s.89 .... 40.004	1987	Consumer Protection Act
	s.92 .... 40.004		(c.43) 5.017, 7.023
	s.108 .... 40.005		Pt 1 .... 5.017
	s.109 .... 40.005		Sch.1 .... 5.017
	s.110 .... 41.003	1988	Legal Aid Act (c.34) 2.020
	s.118 .... 41.003	1988	Housing Act (c.50) 24.008,
	s.124 .... 40.004		24.017
1985	Companies Act (c.6) 8.010	1988	Road Traffic Act (c.52)
	s.651 .... 42.002		Pt VI 6.028
	s.694A 8.010		s.3 .... 12.024
	s.695 .... 8.010		s.145 .... 6.028
	s.725 .... 8.010		s.151 .... 6.028
	s.726 .... 26.002, 26.003		s.151(2)(b) 6.028
	s.726(1) 13.007		s.152 .... 6.028
1985	Administration of Justice Act	1989	Law of Property (Miscellaneous
	(c.61)		Provisions) Act (c.34)
	s.48 .... 24.016		s.2 .... 29.018
1985	Housing Act (c.68) 24.017	1989	Children Act (c.41)
	s.21 .... 27.030		s.25 .... 44.005
	s.110 .... 38.022		s.96 .... 37.004
1985	Landlord and Tenant Act	1990	Town and Country Planning Act
	(c.70) 24.009		(c.8)
1986	Latent Damage Act (c.37)		s.287(4) 10.002
	s.3 .... 5.008	1990	Courts and Legal Services Act
1986	Insolvency Act (c.45) 42.001		(c.41)
	s.117 .... 48.018		s.27 .... 1.018, 1.019,
	s.122 .... 42.017		1.021, 7.004
	s.123 .... 42.004, 42.017		s.27(2A) 1.018
	s.123(1)(a) 42.003		s.27(9) 1.019
	s.125 .... 42.003, 42.020		s.58 .... 2.014
	s.129 .... 42.021		s.61 .... 2.018
	s.130 .... 42.021	1990	Environmental Protection Act
	s.252 .... 42.013		(c.43)
	s.254 .... 42.013		s.82 .... 2.014, 2.016
	s.267(4) 42.004	1991	Civil Jurisdiction and Judgments
	s.268 .... 42.011		(c.12) 11.001, 11.002,
	s.271(3) 42.008		40.017
	s.276 .... 42.011	1992	Access to Neighbouring Land Act
	s.278 .... 42.015		(c.23) 24.009
	s.285 .... 42.015	1992	Trade Union and Labour
	s.307 .... 42.016		Relations (Consolidation)
	s.346 .... 42.015		Act (c.42)
1986	Company Directors		s.221(1) 27.012
	Disqualification Act	1993	Charities Act (c.10)
	(c.46) 42.023		s.33(5) 24.016

	s.33(8) 24.016		s.3(6) 41.003
1993	Leasehold Reform, Housing and Urban Development Act (c.28) 24.009	1998	Late Payment of Commercial Debts (Interest) Act (c.20) 3.006, 3.008, 3.009, 12.013
1995	Civil Evidence Act (c.38) .. 31.018, 36.006		s.3 .... 3.006
	s.1(2)(a) 31.012		s.4 .... 3.066
	s.2 .... 31.014, 31.017		s.5 .... 3.006
	s.2(4) 31.014		s.5A 3.006
	s.4 .... 31.017	1998	Crime and Disorder Act (c.37) 24.017
	s.4(2) 31.017	1998	Competition Act (c.41) ... 12.026
	s.6 .... 31.019		s.58 .... 12.026
	s.6(2) 31.019	1998	Human Act (c.42) .. 1.003, 1.023, 1.024, 7.011, 12.010, 12.027, 12.053, 24.003, 26.002, 44.014
1996	Arbitration Act (c.23) 4.015, 33.013		
	s.9 .... 24.015, 33.004		s.2 .... 1.024, 36.007
	s.70(6) 26.002		s.3 .... 1.023, 1.024
	s.93 .... 34.002		s.4 .... 1.023, 7.013, 9.026, 12.027
1996	Defamation Act (c.31) 5.003, 19.003		s.6 .... 1.023
1996	Trusts of Land and Appointment of Trustees Act (c.47)		s.7 .... 1.023
	s.14 .... 40.010		s.8 .... 1.023
1996	Damages Act (c.48)		s.9 .... 1.023
	s.1 .... 4.011		s.9(3) 12.027
	s.1(2) 4.011		s.10 .... 1.023
	s.2 .... 4.016, 4.017		s.12 .... 27.008
	s.2(9) 4.016		s.12(2) 27.012
	s.2A 4.016		s.12(3) **27.008**
	s.2B 4.016	1999	Access to Justice Act (c.22) 2.020, 39.008
	s.3 .... 4.015		s.10(7) 2.020
	s.6 .... 4.016		s.11 ..... 2.021, 38.022, 39.014
1996	Housing Act (c.52) 24.017		s.11(1) 39.014
1997	Civil Procedure Act (c.12) ..1.005, 19.003		s.54(4) 44.008
	s.1(3) 1.005		ss.55–57 .... 44.001
	s.2(7) 1.005		s.55 .... 44.007
	s.5 .... 1.012		s.57 .... 44.003
	s.7 .... 27.023, 27.026	1999	Contracts (Rights of Third Parties) Act (c.31) 7.023
1997	Social Security (Recovery of Benefits) Act (c.27) .. 9.002, 29.008		s.1 .... 7.023
	s.15 .... 29.008		s.2 .... 7.023
	Sch.2 .... 4.004		s.3 .... 7.023
	column 1 .... 25.011		s.4 .... 7.023
	column 2 .... 25.011		s.6 .... 7.023
1997	Protection from Harassment Act (c.40) 13.007, 41.003		s.7(1) 7.023
	s.3 .... 24.017, 41.003	2000	Limited Liability Partnerships Act (c.12) 7.009

2000	Insolvency Act (c.39) 42.023	2006	Compensation Act (c.29) .. 2.013, 12.007
2003	Anti-social Behaviour Act (c.38)		s.1 .... 12.007
	s.91(3) 24.017		s.2 .... 16.001
2003	Courts Act (c.39)		
	s.100 .... 4.016		

TABLE OF STATUTORY INSTRUMENTS

1965	Rules of the Supreme Court (SI 1965/1776)		1990	Insurance Companies (Legal Expenses Insurance) Regulations (SI 1990/1159)
	Ord.14 .... 42.007			reg.6 .... 2.008
1986	Insolvency Rules (SI 1986/1925) 42.001		1991	High Court and County Courts Jurisdiction Order (SI 1991/724)
	r.4.7 .... 42.018			art.2 .... 1.003
	r.4.8 .... 42.018			art.2(1)(p) 40.010
	r.4.11 .... 42.018			art.8 .... 40.002
	r.4.12 .... 42.004, 42.018		1991	County Courts (Interest on Judgment Debts) Order (SI 1991/1184) 40.007
	r.6.1(5) 42.006			
	r.6.4 .... 42.006			
	r.6.4(3) 42.006			art.4(2) 40.008
	r.6.5 .... 42.006			art.4(3) 40.007, 40.019
	r.6.5(4) 42.006		1991	Family Proceedings Rules (SI 1991/1247)
	r.6.5(5) 42.006			
	r.6.5(6) 42.006			r.4.10(9) 7.005
	r.6.9(4A) 42.012		1994	Legal Aid in Civil Proceedings (Remuneration) Regulations (SI 1994/339) 39.012
	r.6.11 .... 42.003			
	r.6.12 .... 42.012			
	r.6.14 .... 42.012		1994	Insolvent Partnerships Order (SI 1994/2421) 42.002
	r.6.21 .... 42.013			
	r.6.25(3) 42.009		1994	Solicitors (Non-Contentious Business) Remuneration Order (SI 1994/2616) ..2.011, 3.001, 39.005
	r.6.30 .... 42.013			
	r.6.31 .... 42.013			
	r.6.32 .... 42.013			
	r.6.34 .... 42.014			art.9 .... 39.007
	r.6.40 .... 42.006		1997	Social Security (Recovery of Benefits) Regulations (SI 1997/2205) 25.011
	r.13.13 .... 42.018			
1986	Insolvency Fees Order (SI 1986/2030)			
	art.9 .... 42.012		1998	Late Payment of Commercial Debts (Rate of Interest) Order (SI 1998/2480) ..40.002
1987	Non-Contentious Probate Rules (SI 1987/2024) 24.010			
1989	Civil Legal Aid (General) Regulations (SI 1989/339) 39.008		1998	Late Payment of Commercial Debts (Interest) (Legal Aid Exceptions) Order (SI 1998/2482) 3.006
	reg.50 .... 2.024			
	reg.59 .... 36.011		1999	High Court and County Courts Jurisdiction (Amendment) Order (SI 1999/724) ..40.002
	reg.64 .... 39.008			
	reg.105 .... 39.008			
	reg.106A 39.008		1999	Family Proceedings (Miscellaneous Amendments) Rules (SI 1999/1012) 1.005
	reg.107 .... 39.008			
	reg.107A 39.008			
	reg.107B 38.020			
	reg.111 .... 39.008			

1999	Insolvency Proceedings (Amendment) (No.2) Rules (SI 1999/1022) 1.005	2000	Community Legal Service (Cost Protection) Regulations (SI 2000/824) . . 39.014, 39.015
1999	Lay Representatives (Rights of Audience) Order (SI 1999/1225) 1.019		reg.5 . . . . 39.014
		2000	Access to Justice Act 1999 (Destination of Appeals) Order (SI 2000/1071) . . 44.001
1999	Court of Protection (Amendment) Rules (SI 1999/2504) 1.005		art.5 . . . . 44.001
		2000	Collective Conditional Fee Agreements Regulations (2000/2988) 38.036
2000	Community Legal Service (Costs) Regulations (SI 2000/441)		
	reg.4 . . . . 28.001	2000	Collective Conditional Fee Agreements Regulations (SI 2000/2988) 38.036
	reg.20(3) 25.011		
2000	Access to Justice Act 1999 (Commencement No.3, Transitional Provisions and Savings) Order (SI 2000/774)	2005	Damages (Variation of Periodical Payments) Order (SI 2005/841) 4.016
		2005	Conditional Fee Agreements (Revocation) Regulations (SI 2005/2305) . . 2.015, 38.036
	para.8.3 . . . . 39.014		

TABLE OF CIVIL PROCEDURE RULES

1998 Civil Procedure Rules
(SI 1998/3132) . .1.005, 1.009,
1.011, 1.012, 1.013, 1.022,
6.024, 7.015, 7.020, 8.002,
8.010, 8.014, 10.014, 12.053,
13.009, 15.003, 15.014,
16.009, 18.003, 20.001,
22.016, 23.006, 24.001,
24.003, 29.003, 29.012,
29.018, 30.017, 30.023,
31.012, 31.018, 37.015,
38.008, 38.017, 38.024,
38.026, 38.032, 39.002,
39.004, 39.019, 44.017
Pt 1 . . . . .1.006, 18.007,
19.001, 23.010
r.1.1 . . . . **1.006**, 14.006, 37.015
r.1.1(2) 9.006, 9.026,
21.002, 43.005
r.1.1(2)(a) 23.013
r.1.1(2)(b) 7.016
r.1.1(2)(c) 25.001, 25.005
r.1.1(2)(d) 7.016, 25.005
r.1.1(2)(e) 7.016, 25.011
r.1.2 . . . . **1.006**, 1.010,
19.014, 24.006
r.1.2(d) 18.003
r.1.3 . . . . . **1.006**, 1.011, 29.010
r.1.4 . . . . **1.006**
r.1.4(1) 19.001
r.1.4(2) . . . 1.011, 9.026, 19.001
r.1.4(2)(a) 1.011, 13.008
r.1.4(2)(c) 22.003
r.1.4(2)(e) 6.019
r.1.4(2)(f) 19.001
r.1.4(2)(i) 1.011
r.2.1 . . . . 1.005
r.2.3 . . . . 7.011, 9.013
r.2.3(1) 9.002, 9.015,
11.001, 12.001
r.2.3(3) 1.017
r.2.5 . . . . 1.017
r.2.7 . . . . 9.023
r.2.8 . . . . 8.013
r.2.8(2) 1.016
r.2.8(3) 1.016

r.2.8(4) 1.016
r.2.8(5) 1.016
r.2.11 . . . . 1.016, 9.010, 10.003,
21.009, 22.011, 33.002
PD 2 . . . . 13.002
para.2 . . . . 19.012
para.2.3(c) 40.012
para.4.1 . . . . 24.004
para.11.1 . . . . 24.004
PD 2B . . 14.001, 27.021, 41.003
para.7 . . . . 27.028
para.15 . . . . 1.024
Pt 3 . . . . 17.003, 43.006
r.3.1 . . . . 9.005, 9.010,
26.001, 26.005
r.3.1(2)(a) 10.002, 13.010,
33.002, 38.014, 43.002
r.3.1(2)(b) 28.001
r.3.1(2)(e) 7.012
r.3.1(2)(g) 7.015
r.3.1(2)(h) 7.015
r.3.1(2)(i) 33.006
r.3.1(2)(k) 23.001
r.3.1(2)(l) 33.006
r.3.1(2)(m) 7.015
r.3.1(3) 15.015, **26.005**,
32.007, 43.006
r.3.1(5) **26.005**, 43.006
r.3.1(6) 19.014, **26.005**
r.3.1(6A) **26.005**
r.3.1(7) 43.005
r.3.2 . . . . 16.008
r.3.3 . . . 13.005, 33.001, 43.002
r.3.3(5) 13.005
r.3.3(5)(b) 43.002
r.3.4 . . . 10.005, 15.012, 19.004,
33.002, 33.008, 43.006
r.3.4(2) 15.002, 33.008
r.3.4(2)(a) 33.009
r.3.4(2)(b) 33.009
r.3.4(2)(c) 1.015, 9.011
r.3.4(3) 33.008
r.3.4(4) 33.005
r.3.5 . . . . 33.010
r.3.6 . . . . 33.010
r.3.7 . . . 27.029, 33.011, 43.006

r.3.8	33.011	r.6.15(2)	8.016
r.3.8(3)	33.002	r.6.16	8.017, 8.018
r.3.9	9.010, 10.003, 33.002, 33.010, 33.011, 43.006, 44.009	r.6.19(1)	11.007
		r.6.19(3)	11.007
		r.6.20	11.008, 11.009, 11.015
r.3.10	1.015, 11.007, 11.009, 15.014, 25.010	r.6.20(4)	27.018
		r.6.21	11.009
PD 3	7.010	r.6.24	11.012
para.1.9	33.007	PD 6	8.001
PD 3.4		para.2.1	8.003
para.1.4	33.008	paras 3.1–3.4	8.006
para.1.5	33.008	para.3.1	8.006, 7.007
para.1.6	33.008	para.3.2	7.007
para.2	33.009	para.3.3	8.006
para.3	33.009	para.4.1	8.002
PD 3C	7.011	para.4.2	8.002
r.4.5(3)	38.017	para.5	8.012
PD 4, table 3	24.004	para.6.2	8.002
r.5.2(2)	1.022	para.7	8.009
r.5.4B	1.022	para.8.1	8.008
r.5.4C	1.022	PD 6B	11.013
PD 5, para.4.A1	1.022	paras 1.1–.3C	11.007
Pt 6	8.001, 9.013, 11.014	Pt 7	1.024, 9.022, 10.001, 10.002, 10.003, 12.010, 16.003, 18.005, 24.003, 24.005, 24.010, 24.012, 24.013, 24.016, 39.001, 39.003
r.6.1	8.017		
r.6.2(1)(b)	8.003		
r.6.2(1)(c)	8.003		
r.6.2(2)	8.010		
r.6.3	8.008		
r.6.3(2)	8.008	r.7.1	9.002
r.6.4	1.020, 8.002	r.7.2	9.004
r.6.4(2)	8.001	r.7.2A	7.008
r.6.4(4)	8.002	r.7.3	7.011, 7.012
r.6.4(5)	8.002	r.7.4	9.008, 9.009
r.6.5	8.009	r.7.4(1)	9.009
r.6.5(4)	8.009	r.7.4(2)	9.009
r.6.5(4)(b)	8.003	r.7.4(2)(b)	9.011
r.6.5(5)	8.002	r.7.5	9.005, 9.006
r.6.5(6)	8.002, 8.009, 28.001	r.7.6	9.005, 9.006, 10.002
r.6.5(8)	24.018	r.7.6(2)	9.006
r.6.6	8.011	r.7.6(3)	9.006
r.6.7	8.013	r.7.6(3)(b)	9.006
r.6.7(1)	8.013	r.7.6(3)(c)	9.006
r.6.7(3)	8.013	r.7.7	9.007
r.6.8	8.014, 11.009	r.7.7(3)	11.011
r.6.8(1)	8.014	r.7.9	1.013
r.6.9	8.015, 11.009	PD 7.9	1.003, 9.020
r.6.10	8.019	r.7.10	9.021
r.6.11	8.008	r.7.11	1.024
r.6.13	8.017	r.7.12	9.022
r.6.14(2)(a)	8.019	PD 7	7.008, 7.012
r.6.15	8.016	para.2.1	9.002

para.2.2 . . . . 9.002	Pt 12 . . . . 15.017, 15.018,
para.2.4 . . . . 9.002	16.003, 17.003
para.4.1(1) 7.023	r.12.2 . . . . 15.004
para.4.2 . . . . 7.002	r.12.3(1) 15.001
para.5.1 . . . . 5.001, 9.004	r.12.3(2) 15.001
para.5.5 . . . . 7.010	r.12.3(2)(b) 15.018
para.5A.3 . . . . 7.008	r.12.3(3) 15.004, 19.011
para.5B.2 . . . . 7.008	r.12.4 . . . . 15.005, 19.010
para.8.1 . . . . 9.006	r.12.4(2) 19.010
para.8.2 . . . . 9.006	r.12.4(4) 24.018
PD 7A, para.3.9 . . . . 9.031	r.12.5(1) 15.006
PD 7C 9.021	r.12.5(2) 15.007, 15.017
PD 7E 9.022	r.12.6 . . . . 15.006
Pt 8 . . . . . 1.024, 9.001, 10.001,	r.12.7 . . 15.006, 15.007, 15.008
10.002, 10.003, 10.004,	r.12.8(1) 15.008
10.005, 12.001, 12.010,	r.12.8(2) 15.010
15.004, 19.010, 22.001,	r.12.10 . . . . 15.009
24.001, 24.004, 24.010,	PD 12
24.012, 24.015, 24.016,	para.1.1 . . . . 15.002
33.008, 34.004, 37.003,	para.1.2 . . . . 15.004
39.001, 39.003, 40.013,	para.1.3 . . . . 15.004
40.017, 41.003, 44.002	Pt 13 . . . . 15.011, 15.014,
r.8.1(2)(a) 10.001	34.005, 43.002
r.8.2 . . . . 10.002, 24.001	r.13.2 . . . . 15.012, 15.015
r.8.2A 10.001	r.13.3 . . 15.012, 15.015, 15.017
r.8.3 . . . . 10.003	r.13.3(1) 15.013
r.8.4 . . . . 10.003, 41.003	r.13.3(1)(a) 15.013, 15.015
r.8.5 . . . . 10.004, 10.005	r.13.3(1)(b) 15.014
r.8.6 . . . . 10.004	r.13.3(2) 15.012
r.8.8(1) 10.003	r.13.4 . . . . 9.024, 15.016
r.8.9(c) 1.013, 44.002	r.13.6 . . . . 15.016
PD 8 . . . . 40.010	Pt 14 . . . . 9.024, 16.003, 17.003
s.A 39.003	r.14.1(5) 16.009
s.B 24.004, 39.003	r.14.1A 16.001, 16.009
para.3.4 . . . . 10.005	r.14.2 . . . . 15.003
para.4.2 . . . . 10.002	r.14.2(3) 16.003, 16.010
para.5.3 . . . . 10.003	r.14.3 . . . . 16.002
para.7.2 . . . . 10.002	r.14.4 . . . . 15.004, 16.001,
para.7.4 . . . . 10.004	16.003, 16.004,
para.7.5(2) 10.004	16.007, 16.008
PD 8B	r.14.5 . . 16.001, 16.003, 16.005
s.A 24.004	r.14.6 . . . . 16.001, 16.005
s.B 24.008, 40.010	r.14.7 . . . . 15.004, 16.001,
para.B.1(2) 24.008	16.003, 16.006
r.9.1(2) 9.011	r.14.7(9) 38.021
Pt 10 . . . . 9.013, 9.013, 24.005	r.14.9 . . . . 16.007
r.10.3 . . . . 19.010	r.14.10 . . . . 16.008
PD 10, para.5.4 . . . . 9.015	r.14.11 . . . . 16.008
Pt 11 . . . . 11.010	r.14.12 . . . . 16.008
r.11(1) 11.010	r.14.13 . . . . 13.007
r.11(2) 9.013	r.14.14 . . . . 16.004

PD 14
para.1.1 . . . . 16.001
para.2.2 . . . . 16.007
para.5.1 . . . . 16.008
para.6.1 . . . . 16.008
para.7.2 . . . . 16.009
r.15.2 . . . . 24.005
r.15.4 . . . 9.013, 19.010, 24.005
r.15.4(1) 9.017
r.15.5 . . . . 9.017
r.15.6 . . . . 9.017, 12.051
r.15.8 . . . . 9.019
r.15.8(b) 12.051
r.15.9 . . . . 12.043
r.15.10 . . . . 9.027
r.15.11 . . . . 9.011, 9.017,
  15.003, 16.010
PD 15
para.3.2 . . . . 9.019
para.3.2A 9.019
Pt 16 . . . . 12.001
r.16.2 . . . . 12.009
r.16.2(1A) 24.018
r.16.2(1)(cc) 12.009
r.16.2(5) 12.009
r.16.3 . . . . 9.002
r.16.3(7) 12.010
r.16.4 . . . . 12.011, 12.013
r.16.5 . . . . 12.033
r.16.5(3) 12.033
r.16.5(4) 12.033
r.16.5(6) 12.033
r.16.6 . . . . 12.037, 19.008
r.16.7 . . . . 12.042
PD 16 . . . . 12.018, 12.029,
  12.039
para.2.5 . . . . 12.009
para.2.6 . . . . 7.004
para.3.1 . . . . 9.008, 12.011
para.4.4 . . . . 12.014
para.7.1 . . . . 12.018
para.7.2 . . . . 12.020
para.7.3 . . . . 12.021
para.7.4 . . . . 12.021
para.7.5 . . . . 12.021
para.7.6 . . . . 12.023
para.8.1 . . . . 12.024
para.82 . . . . 12.028
para.9.2 . . . . 12.030
para.9.3 . . . . 12.025
para.10.1 . . . . 3.003

para.10.7 . . . . 12.003
para.13.1 . . . . . 12.007, 12.036
para.13.3(1) 12.007
para.13.3(2) 12.007A
para.13.3(3) 12.008
para.14 . . . . 12.026
para.15 . . . . 1.024
para.15.1 . . . . 12.027
para.16.1 . . . . . 44.010, 44.014
Pt 17 . . . . 12.050
r.17.1(1) 12.051, 12.057
r.17.1(2) 12051
r.17.1(2)(a) 12.052, 12.057
r.17.1(2)(b) 12.052
r.17.2 . . . . 12.051
r.17.4 . . . . 12.053, 18.002
r.17.4(2) 12.053
PD 17 . . . . 12.050
para.1.4 . . . . 12.057
Pt 18 . . . . 12.001, 20.001,
  30.007, 32.001, 32.003,
  32.004, 32.006
r.18.1 . . . . 32.001
PD 18
para.1.1 . . . . 32.003
para.1.2 . . . . 32.003
para.1.3 . . . . 32.002
para.1.6 . . . . 32.003
Pt 19 . . . . 7.009, 7.013, 18.003,
  18.007, 39.016
r.19.2 . . . . 7.013
r.19.2(2) 7.015
r.19.2(2)(b) 7.017
r.19.4A 7.013
r.19.5 . . . . 7.014, 12.053
r.19.5(3) 7.015
r.19.5(4) 7.015
r.19.5A(1) 12.016
r.19.6 . . . . 7.018
r.19.6(4)(b) 7.018
r.19.7 . . . . 7.019
r.19.7(1) 7.019
r.19.7(5) 7.019
r.19.7A 7.010
r.19.8 . . . . 7.010
r.19.8(3) 7.010
r.19.9 . . . . 7.021
r.19.9(7) 39.017
r.19.11 . . . . 7.020
PD 19, para.6 . . . . 1.024
PD 19B 7.020, 39.016

Pt 20 .... 5.009, 10.003, 12.01, 18.001, 18.007, 23.010, 25.001, 26.002, 26.004	
r.20.3 .. 11.014, 19.011, 35.001	
r.20.3(2)(b) 12.040	
r.20(3)(3) 15.018	
r.20.4 .... 18.002	
r.20.5 .... 18.003	
r.20.5(1) 18.003	
r.20.6 .... 18.004	
r.20.8 .... 18.008	
r.20.9 .... 18.007	
r.20.9(2) 18.007	
r.20.11 .... 15.018, 18.009	
r.20.12 .... 18.008	
PD 20	
para.5.3 .... 18.010	
para.7.4 .... 18.006	
para.7.10 .... 18.006	
para.7.11 .... 18.006	
Pt 21 .... 7.005, 7.006	
r.21.6 .... 15.009	
r.21.7(1) 7.005	
r.21.10 .... 10.001, 16.003, 25.008, 29.013	
r.21.11 .... 15.011, 29.002	
PD 21	
para.6.2 .... 34.004	
para.6.3 .... 34.004	
para.8 .... 25.011	
Pt 22 .... 1.020	
r.22.1(2) 12.056	
r.22.1(8) 12.004	
r.22.2 .... 12.004	
PD 22	
para.2.3 .... 12.003	
para.3.1 .... 13.003	
para.3.5 .... 12.004	
para.3.6(2) 12.004	
para.3.7 .... 12.004	
para.3.8 .... 12.004	
para.3.11 .... 12.004	
para.3A 14.003	
para.4.3 .... 12.004	
Pt 23 .. 13.001, 26.003, 39.002, 40.014, 40.017, 41.001, 41.003, 41.004, 43.007	
r.23.1 .... 13.002	
r.23.2(3) 13.003	
r.23.2(4) 13.003, 35.007	
r.23.2(5) 13.003	
r.23.3 .... 13.002	
r.23.4 .... 13.006, 27.029	
r.23.5 .... 11.010, 13.003	
r.23.6 .... 13.003	
r.23.7 .... 19.012	
r.23.7(1) 13.006	
r.23.7(2) 13.006	
r.23.7(4) 13.004	
r.23.8 .... 13.008	
r.23.8(c) 13.004	
r.23.9 .... 13.005	
r.23.9(3) 13.005	
r.23.10 .... 9.006, 13.004, 13.005, 43.002	
r.23.10(2) 43.002	
r.23.11 .... 43.002	
r.23.12(b) 7.011	
PD 23 .... 13.007	
para.1 .... 13.003	
para.2.1 .... 13.002	
paras 2.2–2.4 .... 13.008	
para.2.6 .... 13.003	
para.2.8 .... 1.011, 13.007	
para.2.9 .... 13.007	
para.2.10 .... 13.004	
para.3 .... **13.004**	
para.4.2 .... 13.004	
para.5 .... 35.007	
para.5.3 .... 23.020	
para.6 .... 13.007	
para.6.2 .... 13.007	
para.9.2 .... 13.006	
para.9.3 .... 19.012	
paras 9.4–9.6 .... 13.006	
para.9.6 ...... 13.003, 19.012	
para.10 .... 13.008	
para.11.2 ...... 1.016, 43.002	
para.12.1 .... 13.003	
Pt 24 .... 15.012, 15.013, 17.003, 19.001, 19.002, 19.004, 19.005, 19.011, 19.012, 20.013, 24.001, 26.006, 32.002, 33.002, 33.008, 42.007, 43.005	
r.24.2 .. 15.013, 19.001, 19.003, 19.007, 26.006, 33.001, 33.002	
r.24.3(2) 19.002	
r.24.4 .... 19.010	
r.24.4(1) 15.014, 19.010	
r.24.4(2) 19.010	

TABLE OF CIVIL PROCEDURE RULES

r.24.4(3) 19.012
r.24.5 . . . . 19.013
r.24.5(1) 19.012
r.24.6 . . . . 19.015
PD 24
para.1.2(2) 19.001
para.2 . . . . 14.005
para.2(2) 19.012
para.2(3) 19.012
para.2(4) 19.012
para.2(6) 19.010
para.3 . . . . 19.012
para.4 . . . . 19.014
para.7 . . . . 19.010
para.8 . . . . 19.014
para.10 . . . . 19.015
Pt 25 . . . . 20.001, 25.001
r.25.1 . . . . 27.031
r.25.1(h) 27.023
r.25.1(f) 27.015
r.25.1(g) 27.026
r.25.1(1)(l) 27.031
r.25.3(1) 27.012
r.25.3(3) 27.012
r.25.4(1)(b) 11.012
r.25.6 . . . . 25.011
r.25.6(2) 25.011
rr.25.6–25.9 . . . . 25.001
r.25.7 . . . . 25.001
r.25.7(1)(a) 38.021
r.25.7(4) 25.001
r.25.7(5) 25.001, 25.005
r.25.11 . . . . 27.029
r.25.11(2) 27.029
r.25.12 . . . . 26.001
r.25.13 . . . . 26.001, 26.002
r.25.13(1)(b)(ii) 26.002
r.25.14 . . . . 26.001, 26.004, 35.007
r.25.15 . . . . 20.014, 26.001, 44.014
PD 25 . . . . 27.014, 27.019
para.1.1 . . . . . . 27.017, 27.024
para.2.2 . . . . 27.013
para.3.1 . . . . 13.003
para.3.3 . . . . 27.012
para.4 . . . . 27.012
para.4.3 . . . . 13.002
para.4.3(3) 13.004, 27.012
para.4.5 . . . . 27.012
para.5.1A 27.002

para.5.2 . . . . 43.005
para.5.3 . . . . 27.012
paras 7.2–7.5 . . . . 27.025
PD 25B
para.1.2 . . . . 25.008
para.2.1 . . . . 25.009
para.2.1(2) 25.009
para.4.1 . . . . 25.011
r.26.2 . . . . 9.024
r.26.3(6) . . . 9.019, 9.019, 9.029
r.26.3(6A) 9.029
r.26.4(2) 9.028
r.26.4(4) 9.028
r.26.5(3) 9.027, 9.035
r.26.5(4) 9.037
r.26.5(5) 9.029
r.26.6 . . . . 9.030
r.26.6(1) 9.031
r.26.7 . . . . 20.001
r.26.7(3) 9.038
r.26.8 . . . . 9.002, 24.005
r.26.8(1) 9.036
r.26.8(1)(h) 9.035
r.26.8(2) 9.035, 38.021
r.26.9 . . . . 9.040
PD 26
para.2.2(2) 9.028
para.2.3 . . . . 9.028
para.3.1 . . . . 9.028
para.4.1 . . . . 9.027
para.4.2 . . . . 9.027
para.5 . . . . 19.012
para.5.3 . . . . . . 19.010, 19.011
para.6.1 . . . . 9.037
para.6.5 . . . . 9.037
para.7 . . . . 38.021
para.7.3(2) 9.035
para.7.4 . . . . 9.034
para.7.5 . . . . 9.036
para.7.7 . . . . 9.036
para.8.1 . . . . 9.031, 20.001
para.8.1(c) 24.008
para.8.1(2) 9.038
para.9.1 . . . . 9.032
para.9.1(3)(c) 9.032
para.11.1 . . . . 9.041
para.12 . . . . . . 17.001, 17.002, 19.015
para.12.1 . . . . 17.002
para.12.1(4) 17.002
para.12.3 . . . . 17.004

para.12.10 . . . . 17.007	Pt 30 . . . . 9.023
Pt 27 . . . . 20.001	r.30.2 . . . . 9.024
r.27.2(3) 20.001	r.30.3 . . . . 9.025
r.27.5 . . . . 20.008	r.30.3(g) 1.024
r.27.6 . . . . 20.005	r.30.6 . . . . 9.023
r.27.6(1)(b) 20.005	PD 30
r.27.6(1)(c) 20.005	para.2 . . . . 9.026
r.27.11(3) 20.009	para.7 . . . . 9.026
r.27.14 . . . . 13.009, 17.004,	Pt 31 . . . . 20.001, 31.020,
20.010, 20.012, 38.021	36.003, 36.006
r.27.14(2) 20.014, **38.021**	r.31.1(2) 33.012
r.27.14(2)(d) 20.011	r.31.2 . . . . 30.002
r.27.14(3) **38.021**	r.31.3(2) 30.012
r.27.14(4) 38.021	r.31.4 . . . . 30.004
r.27.14(5) 9.038, 38.021	r.31.5 . . . . 30.003
PD 27	r.31.5(1) 22.005
para.3 . . . . 1.019, 20.009	r.31.5(2) 22.005
para.3.1 . . . . 38.21	r.31.6 . . 30.003, 30.007, 30.008
para.4.3 . . . . . . 20.009, 37.003	r.31.6(b) 30.006
Appendix A 20.004	r.31.6(c) 30.006
Pt 28 . . . . 21.009	r.31.7 . . . . 30.006, 30.007
r.28.2 . . . . 21.004	r.31.8 . . . . 30.005
r.28.3(2) 21.005	r.31.12 . . . . 22.005, 30.021
r.28.4 . . . . 33.002	r.31.12(2) 22.005, 30.007
PD 28 . . . . 9.028	r.31.14 . . . . 30.017
para.3.6(4)(b) 21.005	r.31.14(2) 23.021
para.5.2 . . . . 21.010	r.31.15 . . . . 30.11
para.5.4(6) 21.011	r.31.16 . . . 11.012, 30.024, 30.25
para.6.1(4) 21.012	r.31.17 . . . . 30.023
Appendix 21.004	r.31.18 . . . . 30.025
r.29.2(2) 22.007	r.31.19(1) 30.010
r.29.3(2) 22.008, 22.016	r.31.21 . . . . 30.022
r.29.5 . . . . 33.002	r.31.22 . . . . 30.020
r.29.8 . . . . 36.002	r.31.33 . . . . 30.009
r.29.9 . . . . 36.002	PD 31 . . . . 30.003
PD 29	para.2 . . . . 30.006
para.2 . . . . 9.026	para.3.2 . . . . 30.008
para.2.2 . . . . 22.014	para.3.3 . . . . 30.009
para.2.6 . . . . 9.028, 22.014	para.4.2(2) 30.008
para.3.2 . . . . 22.001	para.4.7 . . . . 30.008
para.3.5 . . . . 1.011	para.5 . . . . 30.021
para.4.3 . . . . 22.003	para.7 . . . . 23.021
para.4.6 . . . . 22.009	Pt 32 . . . . 20.001
para.4.7 . . . . 22.009	r.32.1(2) 31.014
para.4.10(9) . . . 22.004, 34.002	r.32.2 . . . . 36.006
para.5.2(2) 22.008	r.32.3 . . . . 31.018
para.5.7 . . . . 22.004	r.32.2(1)(a) 31.005
para.5.8(1) 22.009	r.32.5(3) 31.010
para.7.2 . . . . 22.012	r.32.5(5) 31.010
para.7.4(6) 22.013	r.32.6 . . . . 10.002, 13.003
para.8.1(5) 22.015	r.32.9 . . . . 31.008

r.32.11 . . . . 31.010	r.35.10(3) 23.011
r.32.12 . . . . 14.002	r.35.10(4) 23.011, 30.017
r.32.14 . . . . 12.004	r.35.12 . . . . 23.018, 23.019
r.32.15 . . . . 13.003	r.35.13 . . . . 23.007
r.32.18 . . . . 32.007	r.35.14 . . . . 23.012
r.32.19 . . . . 31.020	r.35.15 . . . . 38.044
PD 32	PD 35 . . . . 23.001, 23.010
para.7 . . . . 14.003	para.1 . . . . 23.009, 23.010
para.9.1 . . . . 14.002	para.1.2 . . . . 23.010
para.17.1 . . . . 14.003	para.1.4 . . . . 23.009
para.18.1 . . . . 14.008	para.2 . . . . 23.009
para.19.1 . . . . 12.005	para.2.1(3) 23.011
para.19.2 . . . . 14.008	para.3 . . . . 23.013
para.20.2 . . . . 14.003	para.4 . . . . 23.011
para.21 . . . . 14.003	para.6 . . . . 23.006
para.25.2 . . . . 14.003	Pt 36 . . . . . 1.011, 4.015, 6.025,
para.27 . . . . 12.004	6.026, 7.005, 9.035,
para.29 . . . . 13.007	12.006, 16.006, 16.009,
Annex 3 . . . . . . 13.007, 31.018	18.002, 18.004, 20.001,
Pt 33 . . . . 20.001	25.012, 29.001, 29.002,
r.33.1(a) 31.012	29.003, 29.005, 29.006,
r.33.2 . . . . 22.010	29.007, 29.008, 29.009,
r.33.2(1)(a) 31.014	29.010, 29.011, 29.012,
r.33.2(2) 31.014	29.013, 29.015, 29.016,
r.33.2(3) 31.014	29.017, 29.018, 29.019,
r.33.3 . . . . 13.003, 31.014	29.020, 29.021, 29.022,
r.33.4 . . . . 31.014	29.023, 29.024, 30.016,
r.33.5 . . . . 31.016	32.002, 33.003, 36.003,
r.33.6 . . . . 31.022, 36.006	38.008, 38.041, 39.002,
Pt 34 . . . . 31.018	39.004, 44.011
r.34.2(5) 36.003	r.36.1(2) 29.010
r.34.3 . . . . 36.003	r.36.2 . . . . 29.006, 29.010
r.34.3(4) 36.003	r.36.2(2)(c) 29.006
r.34.8 . . . . 36.003	r.36.2(2)(e) 29.006
r.34.13 . . . . 36.003	r.36.2(5) 29.009
Pt 35 . . 20.001, 20.008, 23.006,	r.36.3(1)(c) 29.006
23.009, 23.010, 23.015	r.36.3(2) 29.004
r.35.1 . . . . 23.004	r.36.3(3) 29.007
r.35.2 . . . . 23.015	r.36.3(4) 29.023
r.35.3 . . . . 23.001, 23.011	r.36.3(5) 29.011
r.35.4(1) 23.005	r.36.3(6) 29.011
r.35.4(4) 23.005	r.36.3(7) 29.011
r.35.5(1) 23.005	r.36.4 . . . . 29.007
r.35.5(2) 21.007	r.36.4(1) 29.010, 29.012
r.35.6 . . . . 23.020	s.36.4(2) 29.007, 29.010
r.35.6(2)(c) 23.020	r.36.5 . . . . 29.006
r.35.7(1) 23.006	r.36.5(2) 29.010
r.35.8 . . . . 23.006	r.36.5(7) 29.019
r.35.8(3)(b) 23.006	r.36.6 . . . . 29.006
r.35.9 . . . . 23.013	r.36.6(2) 29.010
r.35.10 . . . . 23.021	r.36.6(5) 29.019

r.36.7	29.006	r.39.3(5)	37.007, 43.002
r.36.8	29.012	r.39.6	1.020, 1.021
r.36.9	29.006, 29.016	PD 39	
r.36.9(2)	29.013	paras 1.1–1.10	1.017
r.36.9(3)	29.013	para.1.5	1.017, **13.007**
r.36.9(5)	29.013	para.1.5(2)	24.008
r.36.10	29.006, 29.010, 29.017	para.1.5(8)	26.003
r.36.11	29.010, 29.015, 29.016	para.1.9	13.007
		para.1.10	1.017, 13.007
r.36.11(6)	29.007, 29.018	para.3.1	36.006
r.36.11(7)	29.007, 29.018	para.3.6	36.007
r.36.11(8)	29.018	para.6.1	1.017
r.36.12(2)	29.013	para.8	1.024
r.36.12(3)	29.015	para.8.1	36.007
r.36.12(4)	29.015	r.40.2(2)	43.008
r.36.13	29.001, 38.041	r.40.3	13.005
r.36.13(1)	29.020	r.40.3(1)	1.022
r.36.13(2)	29.020	r.40.3(3)	1.022
r.36.14	29.010, 29.023	r.40.4	13.005
r.36.14(2)	29.024	r.40.4(1)	1.022
r.36.14(3)	3.002, 29.023	r.40.6	34.005, 38.043
r.36.14(4)	29.001, 29.023, 29.024	r.40.7	43.008
		r.40.8	3.009
r.36.14(5)	3.002	r.40.9	43.003
r.36.14(6)	29.011	r.40.11	38.010
r.36.15	29.002, 29.008	r.40.11(a)	15.017
r.36.15(7)	29.008	r.40.12	43.007, 43.008
r.36.15(8)	29.008	r.40.12(1)	43.007
r.36.15(9)	29.008	r.40.14	15.008
r.36.21	38.016, 38.032, 39.004	PD 40	4.016
		para.8.1	24.006
PD 36	29.013	PD 40B	
para.2.2	29.011	para.3.2	34.005
para.3.2	29.013	para.3.5	34.006
r.37.3	12.035, 29.002	para.4	43.007
r.37.4	29.002	para.9.1	41.003
PD 37	29.002	para.13.1	45.001
Pt 38	35.001	PD 40E	37.016
r.38.2(2)(b)	25.012	Pt 41	4.015, 4.016
r.38.3	35.001	r.41.2	29.019
r.38.3(3)	35.003	r.41.3	4.015
r.38.4	35.005	r.41.3A	29.013
r.38.6	35.006	r.41.8	29.019
r.38.7	35.007	PD 41	4.015
r.38.8	35.006	para.4.1	4.016
Pt 39	20.001	para.5.1	4.015
r.39.2	1.017, 13.007	PD 41B	4.016
r.39.2(2)	13.007	r.42.1	28.001
r.39.2(3)	1.017, 13.007	r.42.2	28.001
r.39.3	37.006, 43.002	r.42.3	28.001
		PD 42, para.2.2	28.001

r.43.2 . . . . 38.007, 38.21	rr.45.7–45.14 . . . . 38.012
r.43.2(1) **38.001**, 38.004, 38.006	r.45.13 . . . . 38.012
r.43.3 . . . . 13.010	r.45.14 . . . . 38.012
r.43.4 . . . . 13.011	r.45.15(1) 2.023
PD 43, para.6.4 . . . . 9.028	Pt 46 . . . . 38.011
Pts 44–48 . . . . 38.001	r.46.2 . . . . 24.005, 38.011
r.44.2 . . . . 13.009	r.46.3 . . . . 38.011
r.44.3 . . . . 24.003, 29.010, 38.008, 38.018	r.46.4 . . . . 38.011
r.44.3(1)(c) 13.010	Pt 47 . . . . . . 13.011, 38.015
r.44.3(4) 9.035, 38.008	r.47.1 . . . . 13.011, 38.031
r.44.3(5) 9.035, 38.008	r.47.2 . . . . 38.034
r.44.3(5)(a) 38.018	r.47.7 . . . . 38.034
r.44.3(5)(a)(i) 38.018	r.47.8(1) 38.034
r.44.3(6) 38.008, 38.019	r.47.8(3) 38.034
r.44.3(6)(g) 3.009	r.47.10 . . . . 38.043
r.44.3(7) 38.008	r.47.12 . . . . 38.037, 43.002
r.44.3(8) 17.005, 38.015, 38.039	r.47.12(3) 38.037
r.44.3A 2.016, 2.023, 13.010, 38.007, 38.014	r.47.12(4) 38.037
r.44.3B . . 2.023, 38.007, 38.014	r.47.14 . . . . 38.038, 38.040
r.44.3B(1)(a) 38.027	r.47.15 . . . . 38.015, 38.039
r.44.4 . . . . 38.016	r.47.16 . . . . 38.041
r.44.4(4) 27.022, 38.016	r.47.18 . . . . 38.034, 38.041
r.44.5 . . . 2.011, 38.016, 38.018	r.47.19 . . . . 38.040, 38.041, 38.041
r.44.7 . . . . 1.012	rr.47.20–47.23 . . . . 38.044
r.44.8 . . . . 13.010, 38.014, 38.015, 38.037, 38.041	PD 47
r.44.9 . . . . 38.21	para.1.1 . . . . 38.031
r.44.11 . . . . 38.21	para.2.18 . . . . 38.043
r.44.12 . . . . 29.016	r.48.1 . . . . 39.015
r.44.12A 6.026, 10.001, 10.003, 10.005, 38.012, 39.001, 39.019	r.48.1(2) 30.023, 30.024
r.44.13(1) 13.009, 14.001, 38.002	r.48.2 . . . . 39.015
r.44.13(1A) 13.009	r.48.3 . . . . 39.019
r.44.13(1B) 13.009	r.48.3(2) 39.019
r.44.14 . . . . 37.016, 38.041	r.48.3(8) 13.011
r.44.15 . . . . 2.023	r.48.6 . . . . 1.020, 2.019. 38.001, 38.004
Pt 45 . . . . 38.010, 38.021	r.48.6(5) 38.006
s.III 38.013, 38.024	r.48.6A 39.016
s.IV 38.013	r.48.7(2) 39.002
s.V 38.013	r.48.7(6) 39.002
r.45.1(1) 38.010	r.48.7(7) 39.002
r.45.3(1) 16.004	r.48.8 . . . . 39.003, 39.019
r.45.3(3) 16.005	r.48.8(1A) 2.011
r.45.7(2)(b) 38.012	r.48.10 . . . . 39.003
r.45.7(4)(a) 38.012	PD 48, para.52.5 . . . . . . 38.004
	Pt 50 . . . . 1.005, 24.004
	Pt 51 . . . . 1.005
	Pt 52 . . . 20.014, 24.003, 38.044
	r.52.3(4) 44.006
	r.52.3(4A) 44.006
	r.52.3(6) 20.014, 44.005

r.52.3(7) 20.014	para.15.4 . . . . 44.023
r.52.4 . . . . 43.008, 44.009	para.15.11A(2) 44.013
r.52.5 . . . . 44.013	Pt 53 . . . . 12.017, 19.003
r.52.6 . . . . 44.009, 44.016	r.53.3 . . . . 32.004
r.52.7 . . . . 43.008, 44.010	PD 53 . . . . 12.017
r.52.8 . . . . 44.016	para.6.1 . . . . 29.019
r.52.9 . . . . 44.007	Pt 54 . . . 1.024, 24.001, 24.002,
r.52.10 . . . . 44.017	24.003, 33.008
r.52.10(5) 7.011	r.54.1(2)(a) 24.001
r.52.11 . . . . 38.044, 44.017	r.54.5 . . . . 24.001
r.52.11(3) 44.017	r.54.14 . . . . 24.002, 24.003
r.52.11(4) 44.017	PD 54
r.52.11(5) 44.017	para.4.1 . . . . 24.001
r.52.12 . . . . 29.020, 44.011	para.5.6 . . . . 24.002
r.52.13 . . . . 44.007	para.5.7 . . . . 24.002
r.52.14 . . . . 44.003	para.8.4 . . . . 24.002
r.52.15 . . . . 44.023	para.12.1 . . . . 24.002
r.52.16 . . . . 44.019	Pt 55 . . . . 9.022, 24.005, 24.007
PD 52 . . . . 43.009	Pt II 24.008
para.2A 44.001	r.55.1 . . . . 24.005
para.2A.3 . . . . 44.002	r.55.3 . . . . 1.002, 9.002
para.3.2 . . . . 44.010	r.55.4 . . . . 9.020
para.4.3A 44.006	r.55.5 . . . . 9.020, 24.005
para.4.5 . . . . 44.005	r.55.9 . . . . 20.001, 20.012,
para.4.15 . . . . 44.013	24.005, 38.021
para.4.16 . . . . 44.013	r.55.12 . . . . 24.008
paras 4.18–4.21 . . . . 44.005	PD 55 . . . . 24.005
para.4.23 . . . . 44.013	para.1.3 . . . . 9.002
para.5.2 . . . . . . 44.009, 44.010	para.1.4 . . . . 9.002
para.5.3 . . . . 44.010	para.10 . . . . 24.005
para.5.6 . . . . 44.011	PD 55B 9.022
para.5.6A 44.011	Pt 56
para.5.8A 44.011	s.I 24.009
para.5.9(1) 44.015	s.II 24.009
para.5.9(3) 44.015	r.56.3 . . . . 9.005
para.5.10 . . . . 44.015	Pt 57 . . . . 24.010
para.5.11 . . . . 44.015	s.I 24.010
para.5.12 . . . . 44.011	s.II 24.010
para.5.19 . . . . 44.009	s.III 24.010
para.5.22 . . . . 44.013	s.IV 24.010
para.6.3A 44.011	r.57.16(1) 24.010
para.7.3A 44.014	Pt 58 . . . . 24.012
para.7.6 . . . . 44.015	r.58.1(2) 24.012
para.7.7A 44.015	r.58.8 . . . . 24.012
para.7.10 . . . . 44.013	Pt 59 . . . . 24.013
para.9.1 . . . . 44.017	r.59.1 . . . . 24.013
paras 12.1–13.5 . . . . 44.016	PD 59
para.14 . . . . 44.018	Annex A 24.013
para.15.1A 44.020	Annex B 24.013
para.15.1B 44.020	Annex C 24.013
para.15.3 . . . . 44.023	Pt 60 . . . . 24.011

PD 60	24.011	s.III	7.008, 40.013
Appendix A	24–011	para.1.2	40.010
Appendix B	24–011	Pt 74	40.016
Appendix C	24–011	Pt II	40.018
para.3.3	24.011	Pt IV	40.017
para.3.4	24.011	r.74.5	40.017
Pt 61	24.014	r.74.8	40.017
Pt 62	24.015	r.74.15	40.017
s.I	24.015	r.74.16	40.017
s.II	24.015	Sch.1, RSC	1.005, 7.022, 10.001
s.III	24.015	Ord.17	24.004
r.62.4	24.015	r.1	1.005
Pt 63	24.016	Ord.45	
s.I	24.016	r.1	40.004
s.II	24.016	r.3	41.001
Pt 64	7.023, 24.016, 39.019	r.4	41.002
s.I	24.016	r.7	27.014
s.II	24.016	r.7(6)	27.014
r.64.6	24.016	r.8	41.003
PD 64	39.019	r.11	40.019
para.6	39.019	Ord.46	
PD 64B, para.4.2	1.01	r.2	40.004
Pt 65	24.017	r.5	40.014
Pt 66	24.018	r.6	40.004
r.66.4	24.018	Ord.47	
r.66.6	24.018	r.1	40.019, 42.012
r.66.7	24.018	r.3	40.004
PD 66	24.018	Ord.52	41.003
Pt 67	24.019	Ord.113	41.001
r.67.3	39.003	Sch.2, CCR	1.005, 7.022, 10.001
Pt 68	24.020	Ord.22, r.10	15.017, 40.019
Pt 69	40.012	Ord.24	
Pt 71	40.003	Pt II	24.007
r.71.4	40.003	r.10(2)	24.007
r.71.8(3)	40.003	r.12(4)	24.007
PD 71		r.13	24.007
Appendix A	40.003	Ord.25	
Appendix B	40.003	r.1	1.005
Pt 72	40.005	r.11	40.006
r.72.7	40.005	r.13	40.002
PD 72		Ord.26	
para.1.2	40.005	r.1	40.004
para.1.3	40.005	r.1(5)	40.004
para.5	40.005	r.5	40.004
Pt 73	40.004, 40.008, 40.011	r.16	41.002
Pt II	40.011	r.17	41.001
Pt III	40.010	Ord.27	40.006
r.73.10	40.010		
PD 73	7.008		

r.9	10.007	r.1A	41.003
rr.18–22	40.019	r.3	41.003
Ord.28	40.015	Ord.33	24.004
Ord.29	41.003	Ord.39	40.019
r.1	27.014	Ord.49, r.6	24.008
r.1(6)	27.014	Ord.54	7.022

TABLE OF PRACTICE DIRECTIONS AND PROTOCOL

CPR Practice Direction-Committal
    Proceedings 41.003
    para.2.5(4) 41.003
    para.10 . . . . 41.003
House of Lords Practice Direction,
    2007 . . . . 45.001
    Direction 4.25 . . . . 45.002
    Direction 5.1 . . . . 45.002
    Direction 8.1 . . . . 45.001
    Direction 10 . . . . 45.003
    Direction 11.1 . . . . 45.004
    Direction 12.1 . . . . 45.005
    Direction 15 . . . . 45.007
    Direction 15.8 . . . . 45.007
    Direction 16 . . . . 45.007
    Direction 17 . . . . 45.007
    Direction 19.1 . . . . 45.008
    Direction 22.1 . . 45.001, 45.008
    Direction 43 . . . . 45.001
    Appendix B 45.007
    Appendix C 45.001
Practice Direction about Costs . . . 2.023,
    13.010, 38.21, 38.032,
    38.041, 39.014
    s.6 . . . . 33.013
    s.20 . . . . 38.036
    ss.21–23 . . . . 39.014
    para.2.2 . . . . 38.007
    para.4.1(6) 39.014
    para.4A.1 . . . . 2.023
    para.6.2 . . . . 38.007
    para.6.5A 33.013
    para.6.6 . . . . 38.014
    para.7.2 . . . . 13.009
    para.8.5 . . . . 13.009
    para.8.7 . . . . 13.011
    para.10.1 . . . . 2.023
    para.11.5 . . . . 38.017
    para.11.7 . . . . 38.023
    para.11.8 . . . . **38.025**
    para.11.9 . . . . 38.017
    para.11.10 . . . . 38.029
    para.12.3 . . . . . 13.011, 38.015
    para.13.2 . . . . . 13.010, 38.014
    para.13.13(a) 13.010
    para.13.4 . . . . 13.010
    para.13.5 . . . . 13.010
    para.13.5(3) 13.010
    para.13.5(4) 13.010
    para.13.5(5) 38.014
    para.13.6 . . . . 13.010
    para.13.9 . . . . 13.010
    para.14.1 . . . . 13.010
    para.14.3 . . . . 13.010
    para.14.4 . . . . 13.010
    para.15.1(3) 38.21
    paras 17.1–17.11 . . . . . . 39.001
    para.17.9 . . . . 39.001
    para.19.1 . . . . 2.023
    para.19.1(1) 2.023
    para.19.2(5) 2.023
    para.19.4 . . . . 2.023
    para.21.5 . . . . 2.021
    paras 21.12–21.14 . . . . . 2.021,
    39.014
    para.22.3 . . . . 2.021
    para.23.3 . . . . . 39.002, 39.014
    para.23.14 . . . . 39.014
    para.25.1 . . . . 38.037
    para.30.1 . . . . 38.040
    para.31.1 . . . . 38.038
    para.31.1A 38.038
    para.32.11 . . . . 38.032
    para.33.1 . . . . 38.034
    para.33.3 . . . . 38.034
    para.35.4 . . . . 38.035
    para.35.6 . . . . 38.035
    para.36.1 . . . . 38.043
    para.36.2 . . . . 38.043
    para.37.5 . . . . 38.037
    paras 38.1–38.4 . . . . 38.037
    para.38.1 . . . . 38.037
    para.40.2 . . . . 38.038
    para.40.2(c) 39.009
    para.40.2(d) 38.035
    para.40.5 . . . . 38.038

Practice Direction about Costs—cont'd
    para.40.6 . . . . 38.038
    para.40.9 . . . . 38.039
    para.40.10 . . . . . 38.038, 38.040
    para.40.11 . . . . 38.040
    para.40.12 . . . . 38.040
    para.40.14 . . . . 38.040
    para.41.1 . . . . 38.039
    para.42.11 . . . . 38.041
    para.45.2 . . . . 38.014
    para.48.3 . . . . 38.044
    para.48.3(3) 38.044
    paras 50.1–50.4 . . . . 39.019
    para.53.4 . . . . 39.002
    para.53.6 . . . . 39.002
    para.56.1 . . . . 39.019
    para.56.5 . . . . 39.019
Practice Direction Insolvency
    Proceedings 42.001
    para.11 . . . . 42.003
    para.11.4 . . . . 42.012
    para.12.3 . . . . 42.006
    para.12.4 . . . . 42.006
    para.12.5 . . . . 42.006
    para.15 . . . . 42.012
    para.15.9 . . . . 42.014
    para.16A 42.016
    para.16.3 . . . . . 42.006, 42.013
Practice Directions—Protocols
    para.1.4 . . . . 6.013
    para.2.3(4) 6.013
    para.4.2 . . . . 6.013
    para.4.3 . . . . 6.014
    para.4.4 . . . . 6.014
    para.4.6 . . . . 6.016
Practice Direction (CA: Citation of
    Authorities) [2001] 1 W.L.R.
    1001; [2001] 2 All E.R. 510;
    [2001] 1 Lloyd's Rep. 725;
    [2001] C.P.L.R. 301; [2001]
    1 F.C.R. 764; (2001) 145
    S.J.L.B. 132; *Times,* May
    1, 2001, CA (Civ
    Div) 36.007, 44.020
Practice Direction (Royal Courts of
    Justice: Reading List: Time
    Estimates) [2000] 1 W.L.R.
    208; [2000] 1 All E.R. 640;
    Times, February 1, 2000,
    Ch D 36.008

Practice Statement (Ch D: Trust
    Proceedings: Prospective
    Costs Orders); sub nom.
    Practice Statement (Ch D:
    Applications to the Court in
    Relation to the
    Administration of a Trust:
    Prospective Costs Orders);
    Practice Direction (Ch D:
    Trust Proceedings:
    Prospective Costs Orders)
    [2001] 1 W.L.R. 1082; [2001]
    3 All E.R. 574; [2001]
    W.T.L.R. 949, Ch D . . 39.018
Pre-Action Protocol for Defamation
    para.3.6 . . . . 6.020
    paras 3.7–3.9 . . . . 6.019
Pre-Action Protocol for Disease and
    Illness Claims
    para.10.3 . . . . 6.017
Pre-Action Protocol for Judicial Review
    para.6 . . . . 24.002
Pre-Action Protocol for Personal Injury
    Claims 6.017
    para.2.10 . . . . 6.017
    para.2.11 . . . . 23.022
    para.2.12 . . . . 6.016
    paras 2.16–2.19 . . . . 6.19
    para.3.13 . . . . 6.017
Pre-Action Protocol for the Construction
    and Engineering Disputes
    para.5 . . . . 6.19
Pre-Action Protocol for the Resolution of
    Clinical Disputes
    paras 5.1–5.4 . . . . 6.019
Pre-action Protocol Practice Direction
    para.4A.1 . . . . 6.020
Protocol for the Instruction of Experts in
    Civil Cases 23.001
    para.4 . . . . 23.008
    para.4.7 . . . . 23.010
    para.11 . . . . 23.021
    para.13.5 . . . . 23.009
    para.13.15 . . . . 23.011
    para.14.1 . . . . 23.016
    para.15.2 . . . . 23.011
    para.15.4 . . . . 23.018
    para.15.5 . . . . 23.018
    para.16.1 . . . . 23.020
    para.17.7 . . . . 23.006

CHAPTER 1

Civil Litigation in Outline

THE CIVIL COURTS

The High Court

The High Court is one of three constituent courts going to make up the Supreme Court of England and Wales (the other two courts are the Crown Court and the Court of Appeal). The High Court itself comprises three divisions:

(1) the Chancery Division (which includes the Companies court and the Patents Court);
(2) the Queen's Bench Division (which includes the Admiralty Court and the Commercial Court); and
(3) the Family Division.

1.001

Business is allocated between the divisions as prescribed principally by the SCA 1981, s.61, for which see the *White Book*, para.9A–296 (for further details about the *White Book*, see para.1.005). Despite this allocation of business, all three Divisions have equal jurisdiction. Each has wide powers to transfer any case to any other Division or indeed to retain a case, even though it was started in the wrong Division.

In London, the High Court is based at the Royal Courts of Justice. Cases may be commenced there or at any of its district registries, the 130 or so provincial offices of the High Court throughout England and Wales.

The county courts

There are just under 220 county courts throughout England and Wales. This system was created in 1846 to provide a cheap and simple system for the recovery of small debts which were disproportionately expensive or uneconomic to recover in the then Court of Queen's Bench. Over the years the financial jurisdiction of the county courts has been steadily increased culminating in the High Court and County Courts Jurisdiction Order 1991 (see para.1.003). In times past there were also territorial limits on the jurisdiction of each county court.

1.002

Under current law these territorial limits have largely been swept away save in particular types of case, for example, proceedings for possession of land (CPR, r.55.3—see para.24.005)) and some consumer credit claims (Practice Direction supplementing CPR, r.7.9: see para.9.020).

Jurisdiction of the High Court and county courts

1.003 The jurisdiction of the High Court is described in the SCA 1981, s.19 (*White Book*, para.9A–56). It is virtually unlimited. However, claims for money must now be commenced in the county court unless they exceed £15,000. Claims which include claims for damages for personal injuries must be commenced in the county courts, unless the total sum claimed is £50,000 or more. See further Ch.9.

The county courts have unlimited jurisdiction in most contract and tort cases (CCA 1984, s.15(1)). However, there are exceptions, notably proceedings for libel and slander unless commenced in a county court by consent or transferred to a county court from the High Court (CCA 1984, s.15(2)). The equity jurisdiction of county courts has largely remained at the £30,000 level set in 1981 (CCA 1984, s.23; *White Book*, para.9A–525 and the County Courts Jurisdiction Order 1981). To determine the jurisdiction of the county court under a variety of statutes it is necessary to have regard to Art.2 of the High Court and County Courts Jurisdiction Order 1991 (*White Book*, para.9B–138). As to jurisdictional points concerning the Human Rights Act 1998, see para.1.024, below.

The Court of Appeal

1.004 The Court of Appeal comprises two divisions, civil and criminal. The civil division can hear appeals from almost any decision made in the High Court or county courts. However, most appeals from the lesser judicial officers of the High Court or county court lie, in the first instance, to the senior judicial officers of those courts and second appeals to the Court of Appeal are rare. This is more fully explained in Ch.44.

THE CIVIL PROCEDURE RULES

1.005 The primary sources of civil procedural law are the Civil Procedures Rules ("CPR") which are a form of delegated legislation made under the CPA 1997 (*White Book*, para.9A–826). The full text of these rules and commentaries upon them are set out in various practitioners' books most notably the *White Book Service* 2007, a two-volume work commonly referred to as the *White Book*.

The CPR comprise one unified body of rules which apply to all cases in the county courts, High Court and Court of Appeal except the proceedings listed in the table in r.2.1. Even in the excepted proceedings, the CPR may be applied to them by another enactment, for example, Insolvency Proceedings (Amendment) (No.2) Rules (SI 1999/1022), the Family Proceedings (Miscellaneous Amendments) Rules 1999 (SI 1999/1012) and the Court of Protection (Amendment) Rules 1999 (SI 1999/2504). For cases commenced under the previous sets of rules, transitional provisions are set out in CPR, Pt 51.

The CPR are intended to ensure that "the civil justice system is accessible, fair and efficient" (CPA 1997, s.1(3)) and the rule committee which made them was required to "try to make rules which are both simple and simply expressed" (CPA 1997, s.2(7)). The work involved in this civil justice revolution is not yet complete. New rules have not yet been drafted for a few areas of procedural law. For them, the previous rules of court have been re-enacted, slightly modified, and scheduled to CPR, Pt 50. Schedule 1 sets out old Rules of the Supreme Court (RSC). Schedule 2 sets out old County Court Rules (CCR). In Vol.1 of the *White Book*, the CPR are listed numerically (e.g. para.2.1 sets out r.2.1 and para.2.1.1 indicates the first paragraph of commentary to that rule). At the end of the CPR the schedules of Pt 50 are set out, first the RSC (sc 17.1 indicates RSC, Ord.17, r.1) and then the CCR are set out (para.cc25.1 indicates CCR, Ord.25, r.1).

The high degree of success achieved by the rule committee in making the current rules simple and simply expressed will be appreciated by everyone who is familiar with the previous sets of rules. Unlike them, the current rules do not seek to provide a solution for every possible problem. Instead they make general provisions applicable to the widest possible range of cases. In this way the rules provide clear and understandable guidance which will assist the court and the parties towards the just resolution of cases. The lack of detail in these rules is supplied in three ways all described below: the overriding objective, judicial case management and the practice directions.

THE OVERRIDING OBJECTIVE

The overriding objective is set out in Pt 1 of the rules. Although a brief summary of it is attempted below its overriding importance is such that the full text of the rules must first be considered. 1.006

The overriding objective

1.1 (1) These rules are a new procedural code with the overriding objective of enabling the court to deal with cases justly.

    (a) ensuring that the parties are on an equal footing;
    (b) saving expense;
    (c) dealing with the case in ways which are proportionate—

        (i) to the amount of money involved;
        (ii) to the importance of the case;
        (iii) to the complexity of the issue; and

                (iv) to the financial position of each party;
        (d) ensuring that it is dealt with expeditiously and fairly; and
        (e) allotting to it an appropriate share of the court's resources, while taking into account the need to allot resources to other cases.

Application by the court of the overriding objective

1.2 The court must seek to give effect to the overriding objective when it—

        (a) exercises any power given to it by the rules; or
        (b) interprets any rule.

Duty of the parties

1.3 The parties are required to help the court to further the overriding objective.

Court's duty to manage cases

1.4 (1) The court must further the overriding objective by actively managing cases.

    (2) Active case management includes:
        (a) encouraging the parties to cooperate with each other in the conduct of the proceedings;
        (b) identifying the issues at an early stage;
        (c) deciding promptly which issues need full investigation and trial and accordingly disposing summarily of the others;
        (d) deciding the order in which issues are to be resolved;
        (e) encouraging the parties to use an alternative dispute resolution procedure if the court considers that appropriate and facilitating the use of such procedure;
        (f) helping the parties to settle the whole or part of the case;
        (g) fixing timetables or otherwise controlling the progress of the case;
        (h) considering whether the likely benefits of taking a particular step justify the cost of taking it;
        (i) dealing with as many aspects of the case as it can on the same occasion;
        (j) dealing with a case without the parties needing to attend at court;
        (k) making use of technology; and
        (l) giving directions to ensure that the trial of a case proceedings quickly and efficiently.

A new procedural code

1.007 No one would seek to argue that the objective of dealing with cases justly is in itself new. However, there is a widely held belief that the old procedural code sometimes restricted the court's ability to achieve this objective. By setting out a new procedural code the court is now freed from the dead weight of old case law which was built upon the old rules. Procedural problems and uncertainties in cases should be resolved by reference to the rules and cases thereon. Previous case law is not definitive and is only of value where it appears to illustrate the overriding objective.

Speed, economy and proportionality

The court and the parties should strive to avoid those tactics which bedevilled the old rules which caused delays and disproportionate expense: wasting time and effort on side issues by striving to deliver a knock-out blow pre-trial. 1.008

Boundary disputes are a common problem area. In *Ali v Lane* [2006] EWCA Civ 1532, *The Times*, December 4, 2006, Carnwath L.J. stated:

> "It was disturbing that neither of the experienced leading counsel before us was able to give a clear indication of the practical significance of the strip to their respective clients, nor to inform the court what if any attempts have been made at mediation. It is sadly a commonplace that boundary disputes can be fought with a passion which seems out of all proportion to the importance of what is involved in practical terms. In such cases, professional advisors should regard themselves as under a duty to ensure that their clients are aware of the potentially catastrophic consequences of litigation of this kind and of the possibilities of alternative dispute procedures." See also *Haycocks v Neville* [2007] EWCA Civ 78.

Ensuring parties are on an equal footing

Parties may be on unequal footings as to financial resources and as to information resources. As to financial inequality, the court will not allow a financially stronger party to intimidate a weaker party by escalating costs. In *Maltez v Lewis*, *The Times*, May 4, 1999, Neuberger J. gave guidance as to two further topics concerning this principle. First, where one side has a disproportionately deeper pocket than the other, the court may place upon him the burden of preparing trial bundles. However, secondly, the court will not use the equal footing principle to invade the fundamental right of every citizen to be represented by the legal advisers of their choice. Thus, a claimant who cannot afford to instruct leading counsel cannot obtain an order debarring the defendant from instructing leading counsel. The financially weaker party's protection here lies in the fact that the cost of unreasonably expensive representation will not be recoverable from him. In *Islam v Meah* [2005] EWCA Civ 1485 the claimant was the 28 year old son of the defendant. He alleged that he had been subject to false imprisonment in his father's house. Whilst the claimant was representing himself in the proceedings, the court observed that he was clearly a 1.009

man of some intellectual ability with a good grasp of English who had had the advantage of a university education. In contrast, the defendant was 64 years of age of Bengali origin and of modest education. He could not speak, read or write English other than at a very basic level and had a very limited understanding of the legal system. In those circumstances the court put back the trial date by several months so the defendant could pursue an application he had made for the public funding required to enable him to obtain legal representation.

In *Albon v Naza Motor Trading SDN BHD* (No.2) [2007] EWHC 327 the court was prepared to allow service of the claim form (see Ch.8) by a method not permitted by the CPR as that advanced the overriding objective.

> "This is a very important case for Mr Albon: the sums at stake (as well as the costs) are critical to his financial survival. The order saved further expense and time, promoted the objective of dealing with the case justly and was necessary to protect Mr Albon whose financial position fighting an immensely wealthy opponent called for such protection" (*per* Lightman J.).

Inequality of information may put a defendant at a disadvantage to a claimant who has fully prepared his case before giving notice of it to the defendant. The pre-action protocols (see para.6.013) are intended to remedy this inequality. Where they do not apply or have not been complied with, the court will grant any extensions of time to the defendant which are necessary to redress the inequality.

The courts should not rigidly apply this aspirational objective that the parties to litigation should operate under equality of arms.

> "This objective has been interpreted to mean that it is desirable for each party to have permission to deploy similar resources. Each party will, in general, be limited to instructing the same number of experts; the number will depend upon what is proportionate, bearing in mind the importance and complexities of the issues in the case. However, the desirability for equality of arms was not intended to result in an absolute rule that, in every case, the parties must be limited to calling the same number of experts"

(*per* Smith L.J. in *Kirkman v Euro Exide Corp (CMP Batteries) Ltd* [2007] EWCA Civ 66, *The Times*, February 6, 2007. The topic of experts is dealt with in Ch.23).

Use by court when exercising powers and interpreting the rules

1.010 Under many rules the court has a discretion whether or not to permit or require some step and also has the power to impose sanctions on recalcitrant parties. Rule 1.2 requires the court to apply the overriding objective when determining whether and how to exercise such discretions and powers. It also requires the court to use the overriding objective as the touchstone by reference to which the rules are to be interpreted.

Parties must help the court further the overriding objective

Rule 1.3 requires the parties to assist the court to achieve its objective of dealing with cases justly. Assistance involves co-operating with other parties in the conduct of the proceedings (see r.1.4(2)(a)), striving to combine all applications to court so as to minimise the number of hearings necessary (see r.1.4(2)(i), Pt 23 PD, para.2.8 and Pt 29, PD, para.3.5) and, of course, complying with any orders and directions made by the court fully and timeously. The courts will not tolerate an aggressive and competitive style of litigation which relies upon continuous hostility, stonewalling tactics and multiple applications to court pre-trial. Indeed; 1.011

> "it is not enough for a party to sit back and to await further directions of the court, albeit that the court is under a duty to manage the application. If there is delay, Part 1.3 makes it clear that the parties do have a duty to prompt the court"

(*per* Judge Grenfield in *Nolan v Devonport* [2006] EWHC 2025).

Examples

In *Hannigan v Hannigan* [2000] 2 F.C.R. 650, the Court of Appeal was faced with a claim that had been started on the wrong form and included several errors in other documentation. The defendants sought to strike out the claim (see para.33.008). The court refused, Brooke L.J. stating that "the interests of the administration of justice would have been much better served if the defendants' solicitors had simply pointed out all the mistakes that had been made" and "the overriding objective is not furthered by arid squabbles about technicalities".

In *Hertsmere Primary Trust v The Estate of Rabindra-Anandh* [2005] EWHC 320; *The Times*, April 25, 2005, the claimants wrote a settlement proposal letter to the defendant purportedly under Pt 36 (see Ch.29) but the letter failed to comply with certain formalities. The defendant was aware of the defects but did not provide any details until it sought to rely on those at trial. The defendant submitted that it was perfectly proper to withhold the information and to take advantage of the non-compliance at a later date. The court held that pursuant to r.1.3 the defendant was duty bound to co-operate with the claimants and this duty obliged it to provide the details. The defendant would not be entitled to reap any benefit from its breach of this duty.

Court to actively manage cases

Of the many cultural changes made by the CPR judicial case management is the most important. Previously, civil litigation was said to be "in the hands of the parties". Time proved again and again that such hands made heavy and expensive work. The CPR seek to avoid the evils which bedevilled cases under the old rules by handing over control of cases to the court. Cases, once started, will be conducted at the speed and on the dates which the court thinks appropriate. The court will identify the issues to be resolved and will fix the order in which it will resolve them. Case management by the court does not, of course, exclude case management by the parties. Indeed, "encouraging the parties to co-operate with each other in the conduct of the proceedings" is placed first in the list of examples of judicial case management given in r.1.4(2).

The most obvious demonstration of case management in the rules is the procedure by which most cases are allocated to one of three case management tracks. This is considered more fully later in this Chapter and in Ch.9.

PRACTICE DIRECTIONS

1.012   In the High Court, practice directions are issued by the Heads of Divisions in the exercise of inherent power. In the county courts practice directions are valid only if made or approved by the Lord Chancellor (see generally CPA 1997, s.5 and the *White Book* commentary thereto, para.9A–839 onwards).

Nearly every Civil Procedure Rule has its own practice direction. Practice directions provide the details necessary to put into practice the general principles of the rules. Dividing up the details and the principles between the practice directions and the rules was a deliberate policy adopted by the rule committee. In some rules, especially the costs rules, this policy is explicit. See, for example, r.44.7 (procedures for assessing costs) which states "the costs practice directions sets out the factors which will affect the court's decision under this rule". This policy of separation reduces complexity in the rules themselves and so makes them easier to understand. Armed with an understanding of the rules the reader finds it much easier to grapple with the details set out in the practice directions.

To the extent that there is any conflict between a rule and its practice direction, the Court Of Appeal has repeatedly made it plain that, in such circumstances, it is the rule that must apply. The practice directions have been described as "at best a weak aid to the interpretation of the rules themselves" (by May L.J. in *Godwin v Swindon BC* [2004] 4 All E.R. 641) which should "yield to the CPR where there is a clear conflict between them" (*per* Auld L.J. in *R. (Mount Cook Land Ltd) v Westminster City Council* [2003] ECWA Civ 1346, *The Times*, October 16, 2003).

THE CASE MANAGEMENT TRACKS

1.013   The CPR set out three case management tracks: the small claims track, the fast track and the multi-track. Most cases will be allocated to one of these tracks if and when the defendant files a defence. Exceptions are made for certain specialist proceedings (see Ch.24) certain claims for the return of goods (see r.7.9) and cases in which the alternative procedure for claims has been used (which are treated as allocated to the multi-track (see Ch.10 and r.8.9(c)).

The small claims track is a normal track for cases which have a financial value of £5,000 or less. There are some exceptions including, notably, personal injury claims below £5,000 in which the claim for compensation for pain, suffering and loss of amenity exceeds £1,000. Cases on this track will normally be disposed of at a single hearing or by means of a paper adjudication. Costs spent on legal representation in the conduct of cases on this track will not normally be recoverable (see para.20.010).

The fast track is the normal track for other cases with a financial value which does not exceed £15,000, if in the opinion of a court, they can be tried in one day or less and, usually, without the need for any oral expert evidence. These cases will normally be tried within 30 weeks of the date of allocation, the court giving directions on allocation as to disclosure of documents, witness statements and expert evidence. In these cases there will be few if any court hearings before the trial (see further Ch.21).

The multi-track is the track appropriate for cases with a financial value exceeding £15,000 and cases with a lower financial value which because of their complexity or likely trial length, are unsuitable for the other two tracks. At the time of allocation to the multi-track the court will give timetable directions including, if possible, the fixing of the trial date or trial period and/or will fix the date of a case management conference and/or a pre-trial review (see further Ch.22).

COURT FEES

In certain circumstances parties may gain exemption from the obligation to pay court fees on grounds of poverty (see further *White Book*, paras 10–6 and 10–18). Subject to that, prescribed fees are payable at the following stages of most proceedings: issue of claim form, return of allocation questionnaire and return of pre-trial. Fees are also payable on applications to the court and on the filing of a request for a detailed assessment of costs. Provided one has the current Fees Order available (see *White Book*, para.10–1 onwards) it is not necessary to memorise them and, in view of the frequent changes made it is not worth trying to do so. The brief moment it takes to check the fee is well spent. It causes a considerable amount of inconvenience and delay if the wrong fee is sent through the post and the court has to write back with a refund or asking for the balance.

1.014

EFFECT OF NON-COMPLIANCE

Failure to comply with a rule or practice direction does not invalidate any step taken in the proceedings unless the court so orders (r.3.10). The non-compliance is an error of procedure as to which the court has a discretion. It may remedy it

1.015

and may do so on terms including terms as to costs. Alternatively, it may make a dispensing order waiving the error or if appropriate make an order striking out the statement of case of the party at fault (r.3.4(c) as to which see further Ch.33). Striking out will not be appropriate save in the most exceptional cases (*Biguzzi v Rank Leisure Plc* [1999] 1 W.L.R. 1926). The court will not insist upon compliance with the rules and practice directions merely for the sake of it. Therefore, if the error of procedure causes no prejudice to the other side the court is likely to dismiss with costs any application by the other party complaining about it. In addition to the question of prejudice, the court may also have regard to other factors including the gravity of the error and the conduct of the parties and their advisers (see further Ch.33).

COMPUTATION OF TIME

1.016 Where a rule, practice direction or order of the court fixes a time period expressed as a number of days, the period of time is to be treated as specifying so many "clear days", i.e. days excluding the day from and/or to which the period is measured (see r.2.8(2) and (3) which include examples).

Two provisions concern computation of time with regard to days when the court office is closed:

(1) in computing time periods of five days or less, Saturdays, Sundays, Bank Holidays, Christmas Day and Good Friday are not counted (r.2.8(4));
(2) where a time period for doing an act at the court office ends on a day on which the office is closed "that act shall be in time if done on the next day on which the court office is open" (r.2.8(5)).

Rule 2.11 states that, "Unless these Rules or a practice direction provide otherwise or the court orders otherwise, the time specified by a rule or by the court for a person to do any act may be varied by the written agreement of the parties." So what constitutes a written agreement? In *Thomas v Home Office* [2006] EWCA Civ 1355, the Court of Appeal held that a written agreement to extend time does not have to be in a single document but may consist of an exchange of letters or emails. An oral agreement that is then confirmed in writing by both sides is also a written agreement. However, an oral agreement between two solicitors that is subsequently recorded in a letter sent by one solicitor to the other, but not answered by the other, does not constitute a written agreement. Further, it is not enough for solicitors to make an attendance note of an oral agreement, unless those notes are subsequently exchanged.

In any proceedings the court may, on such terms as it thinks just, make an order extending or shortening any time period fixed by any rule, practice direction or court order. An application for such an order will often be suitable for consideration without a hearing, the court sending to the parties an order dismissing the application or allowing it wholly or partly and in all cases specifying the parties' rights to apply to the court to have that order set aside, varied or stayed (Pt 23, PD, para.11.2 and see further Ch.13). The court's approach to applications to extend or shorten time periods is considered in detail at para.33.002.

DEFINITION OF "THE COURT"

In most cases a reference in the rules or practice directions to "the court" means the particular county court, District Registry or the Royal Courts of Justice in which the relevant proceedings are being taken (r.2.3(3)). At that place, formal and administrative acts are usually performed by court clerks, subject to the payment of any fee prescribed (r.2.5). 1.017

The court's judicial function may be exercised, in the High Court, by a High Court judge and, in the county court, by a circuit judge. Unless a rule or practice direction otherwise states, it may also be exercised by one of the lesser judicial officers of the court. In the High Court the lesser judicial officers are, in London masters and in District Registries, district judges. Masters and district judges are persons appointed by the Lord Chancellor from barristers and solicitors of at least seven years' standing. In the county court the lesser judicial officers are district judges, whose qualification for appointment are the same as that of their High Court equivalents. Indeed, outside London, all county court district judges are also appointed district judges of the High Court.

The main business of masters and district judges is the management of cases pre-trial and, in the county courts, the trial of all cases on the small claims track and many cases on the fast track. The main business of High Court judges and circuit judges when sitting in the civil courts is the trial of cases on the multi-track or fast track and the hearing of appeals from lesser judicial officers.

The general rule is that all hearings in the civil courts are in public (see generally r.39.2). However, this rule does not require the court to make special arrangements for accommodating members of the public who wish to attend and, in practice, most hearings before masters and district judges (other than trials on the fast track) take place in the master or district judge's private room. Members of the public and members of the press rarely seek admission. They have no right to admission if their admission is impractical. However, the court may, if appropriate, adjourn the proceedings to a larger room or court to make their admission practicable (Pt 39, PD, para.1.10).

Any hearing, including a trial, may be held in private if the court so decides having regard to any representations made on the subject (see generally Pt 39, PD, paras 1.1–1.10). If the court does so decide, members of the public who are not parties to the proceedings will not be admitted unless the court permits. Part 39, PD, para.1.5 gives a list of hearings which, unless the court otherwise orders, will be listed at hearings in private. Most cases on the list concern information relating to personal financial matters. This in fact is only part of one of several factors which justify the conduct of hearings in private. A long list of such factors is set out in r.39.2(3): see para.13.003, below.

At any hearing, whether in a court or in a private room, the judgment given will be recorded unless the court directs otherwise. Oral evidence will normally be recorded also (Pt 39, PD, para.6.1).

Once a judgment is given, is there any restriction on its publication and, if not, can the parties require anonymity in any report? In the case of proceedings conducted in private, s.12 of the Administration of Justice Act 1960 restricts publication in certain specified cases and where the court (having the power to do so) expressly prohibits publication. That provision apart, the general principle, fortified of course by ECHR, Art.6(1), is that justice should be conducted and reported openly and publicly (*Hodgson v Imperial Tobacco Ltd* [1998] 1 W.L.R. 1056; *R. v Legal Aid Board Ex p. Kaim Todner (a firm)* [1999] Q.B. 966). In *Trustor A B v Smallbone* [2000] 1 All E.R. 811 the court refused to impose restrictions on reporting which were said to be necessary to protect a litigant from investigation by Swedish investigating authorities. In *Green v Hancocks (a firm)* (2000) L.T.L. December 15, the Court of Appeal refused the second defendant's request for anonymity in the reporting of proceedings in a professional negligence claim against lawyers.

RIGHTS OF AUDIENCE

1.018　Most of the law as to rights of audience can be found in s.27 of the Courts and Legal Services Act 1990. There are four classes of person who have, or who may be given, rights of audience:

(i) professional advocates duly authorised by the General Council of the Bar, the Law Society or other bodies designated by Statutory Instrument;
(ii) other persons authorised by statute or statutory instrument;
(iii) litigants in person;
(iv) persons authorised by a court in relation to proceedings before the court.

Barristers, solicitors and other professional advocates

Barristers have full rights of audience in all cases and in all courts. Solicitors have full rights of audience in all cases and in all courts except in public hearings before a High Court judge or a Court of Appeal judge unless, in respect of a particular solicitor, the Law Society has granted that solicitor a higher courts qualification. Fellows of the Chartered Institute of Patent Agents, the Institute of Legal Executives and the Association of Law Costs Draftsmen may also acquire rights of audience granted to them by their professional bodies. In these cases the rights are restricted to particular types of proceedings (see further *White Book*, para.7C–222).

Section 27(2A) of the Courts and Legal Services Act 1990 provides that every person who exercises a right of audience granted by an authorised body has a duty to the court to act with independence in the interest of justice and to comply with that body's rules of conduct. It would be difficult if not impossible for an authorised advocate to act with independence in the interest of justice if appearing for his or her spouse or close relative. In such a case the advocate should not exercise a right of audience as a professional but should seek the court's permission (see para.1.021).

It is possible for a member of the public to instruct a barrister direct rather than through a solicitor. However, as the Bar Council stresses, the essential function of a barrister is that of an advocate and adviser, whose role is not to conduct litigation or to take general responsibility for their clients' affairs. A barrister receiving instructions direct from the public must comply with the Code of Conduct, Public Access Rules. For further details see *www.barcouncil.org.uk*.

Other persons authorised by statute or statutory instrument

Section 27 of the Courts and Legal Services Act 1990 gives rights of audience to solicitors' clerks and corresponding employees of other qualified litigators in proceedings being heard in private; the rights do not apply to "reserved family proceedings" (as to which see s.27(9)). Officers acting for local authorities in possession claims, and similar claims, have rights of audience in the county court, whether the court is sitting in public or in private, insofar as the proceedings in the action are heard by a district judge (County Courts Act 1984, s.60).   1.019

The Lay Representatives (Rights of Audience) Order 1999 authorises any person to exercise rights of audience in proceedings allocated to the small claims track provided that the litigant represented also attends the hearing (see *White Book*, para.9A–612 and 27PD.3).

Litigants in person

Litigants in person are best treated as having rights of audience in all cases in all courts. The rights must be exercised in person, not by another person acting under a power of attorney (*Gregory v Turner* [2003] 1 W.L.R. 1149, CA). A litigant who is a company has no visible person. Can a company act or take any other step "in person"? Rule 6.4 defines "personal service" on a company (see para.8.002). Under the current rules, companies are not now required to act by a solicitor when starting proceedings or defending them (*R H Tomlinson (Trowbridge) Ltd v Secretary of State for the Environment*, The Times, August 31, 1999, CA). Many documents in proceedings have to contain a "statement of truth". The practice direction to Pt 22 makes provision for the signing of statements of truth on behalf of companies. Finally, r.48.6 permits companies to recover costs they incur as litigants in person. However, despite all this, it seems that companies, by their officers or employees or otherwise, have no personal rights of audience. Rule 39.6 permits the representation of a company "at trial" by an employee, but this is not as of right; the rule states the court must give   1.020

permission. But the rule does not apply to claims on the small claims track when a lay representative who is not an officer or employee of the company may be allowed to act for a company: see *Avinue Ltd v Sunrule Ltd* [2003] EWCA Civ 1942; [2004] 1 W.L.R. 634. Representation of companies is considered further in para.1.021, below.

When acting in person, a litigant is entitled to bring to the court a friend to take notes, quietly make suggestions and give advice. Such persons are often called *McKenzie* friends, a title which derives from an old case of that name. Current law on this topic is set out in the Court of Appeal decision in *R. v Bow County Court*, Ex p. Pelling [1999] 1 W.L.R. 1807. In public hearings, a litigant in person should be allowed the assistance of a *McKenzie* friend unless the interest of fairness and justice require otherwise. Where proceedings are being conducted in private, the nature of those proceedings which make it appropriate for them to be heard in private may make it undesirable in the interest of justice for a *McKenzie* friend to assist. A judge should give reasons for refusing to allow a litigant in person the assistance of a *McKenzie* friend. For the avoidance of doubt, it is worth emphasising that, although a litigant may have a right to a *McKenzie* friend, a *McKenzie* friend never has a right of audience unless, for example, the court hearing the proceedings grants him or her such rights (see below).

Persons authorised by the court

1.021   Section 27 of the Courts and Legal Services Act confirms the power of the court to grant rights of audience in respect of particular proceedings to a person who does not otherwise have such rights. See *Re D (a child)* (representation: *McKenzie* friend) [2005] EWCA Civ 347; (2005) L.T.L. March 15. Everyday examples are cases in which a husband, wife or other close relative is allowed to speak for a litigant in person and officers and employees of company litigants who are allowed to speak for the company. In the first example the litigant in person should, in normal circumstances, explain to the court himself or herself why such permission was appropriate; if it is granted, the litigant in person should normally remain in court while the rights of audience are being exercised (*Clarkson v Gilbert, The Times*, July 4, 2000, CA). As to companies, r.39.6 provides for representation "at trial" by an employee if the employee has been authorised by the company to appear at trial on its behalf and if the court gives permission. The practice direction to that rule sets out the information to be given to the court in such circumstances, states that such permission should be sought in advance and states that such permission may be obtained informally and without notice to the other parties. Although r.39.6 concerns representation at trial, the practice direction provisions concern representations at any hearing (see *White Book* 39PD.5).

THE COURT FILE

In order to meet its obligation to manage cases, the court opens and maintains a file in every case commenced under the CPR. Many documents on that file will be prepared by the parties, for example, the claim form (see Ch.9), statements of case (see Ch.12), application notices and witness statements (see Ch.14). Any judgment or order made in a case will be drawn up by the court unless the court orders a party to draw it up, or a party, with the permission of the court agrees to draw it up, or the court dispenses with the need to draw it up, or it is a consent order (r.40.3(1)). Orders to be drawn up by parties must be drawn up and filed within seven days (r.40.3(3)) with as many copies as there are parties affected by that order (r.40.4(1)). The order and copies must not be illegible or in any other way unsatisfactory (e.g. containing blasphemies; r.5.2(2)). The court will usually serve sealed copies of the Order on all parties unless it has directed a party to serve them (r.40.4(1)).

1.022

A party to proceedings may, unless the court orders otherwise, obtain from the records of the court a copy of most of the documents on the court's file. These include a certificate of suitability of a litigation friend (see para.7.005); a notice of funding (see para.2.023); a claim form or other statement of case together with any documents filed with or attached to it (see Ch.12); an allocation questionnaire (see para.9.028); a list of documents (see para.30.008); an application notice and any written evidence filed in relation to an application (see Chs 13 and 14), other than an application by a solicitor for an order declaring that he has ceased to be the solicitor acting for a party or an application for an order that the identity of a party or witness should not be disclosed. See further r.5.4B.

The general rule is that a person who is not a party to proceedings (e.g. a journalist) may obtain from the court records a copy of a statement of case (but not any documents filed with or attached to it) and a judgment or order given or made in public (whether made at a hearing or without a hearing). For a copy of any other document, an application must be made to the court. On what basis will the court make a decision? On one hand there is the need for open justice (see *Dain AO v Davis, Frankel and Mead* [2005] 1 All E.R. 1087). But, to prevent the floodgates opening, the applicant must show a legitimate interest in documents that have been judicially employed. The fact that an action is complex and the statements of case long and detailed will not lead to an application being refused (see *Cleveland Bridge UK Ltd v Multiplex Constructors UK (Ltd) sub nom in the matter of an application by Curnow and the Australian Broadcasting Corp* [2005] EWHC 2101, (2005) L.T.L. October 24). That the party opposing the application might suffer damage is a relevant consideration (see *Chan U Seek v Alvis Vehicles Ltd and Guardian Newspapers Ltd* [2004] EWHC 3092, [2005] 1 W.L.R. 2965). See further r.5.4C and note that the position was slightly different before October 2, 2006 (as to which see PD 5 para.4.A1).

Where can you find the judgments of the High Court and county court? These are officially recorded on the Register of Judgments, Orders and Fines. Usually

15

the registration lasts for six years and it may seriously affect an individual's creditworthiness. Details can be found at *www.registry-trust.org.uk*.

HUMAN RIGHTS ACT 1998

1.023 The Human Rights Act 1998 carries into domestic law rights under various ECHR Articles and other rights, collectively called "the Convention rights": the full text of the Act is set out in the *White Book* at para.3D–1 onwards. The Act deserves mention in a book on civil procedure for a variety of reasons. First and foremost is the requirement which it places on courts to interpret and apply English law in a way which is compatible with the Convention rights so far as it is possible to do so (s.3). Thus the Act, like the overriding objective which partly duplicates it, transcends most if not all procedural law.

Where a public authority commits or threatens a breach of a Convention right a person who is or would be a victim of that breach may bring proceedings for remedies and/or may rely on the Act in legal proceedings (see especially ss.6, 7 and 8). The definition of "public authority" is wide and includes the courts themselves. Thus proceedings may be taken in respect of "judicial acts" in respect of which an award of damages may be made against the Crown (s.9).

The Act enables the High Court and superior courts to determine whether any legislation is compatible with the Act and, if appropriate, make a "declaration of incompatibility". The declaration does not by itself affect the validity, continuing operation or enforcement of the legislation. However, it may enable a Minister of the Crown to make an order amending that legislation (see ss.4 and 10).

Jurisdiction and procedure in HRA cases

1.024 A party who seeks to rely on any provision of or right arising under the Act or seeks a remedy available under the Act must state that fact in his statement of case (see, para.12.027) and must give various details including a statement whether the relief sought includes a declaration of incompatibility or damages in respect of a judicial act (see *White Book* 16PD.15). In respect of such claims notice must usually be given to the Crown or the Lord Chancellor respectively (see further *White Book* 19PD.6). When interpreting Convention rights the court must take into account any judgment of the European Court of Human Rights and certain other matters (see s.2): as to the procedure for citing such authorities, see *White Book* 39PD.8.

The county court has no jurisdiction to hear applications for a declaration of incompatibility (s.3). If the making of such a declaration arises in a county court case, it may be possible to transfer the case to the High Court (as to which see r.30.3(g). Similarly, claims in respect of a judicial act may be brought only in the High Courts (r.7.11). If such a claim were commenced in the county court it may be possible to transfer it to the High Court. County courts do have jurisdiction in respect of other HRA cases: for example, proceedings against an education authority or against the police.

Jurisdictional limitations apart, the normal rules apply in deciding in which court and specialist list an HRA case should be started. They also apply in deciding which procedure to use to start the claim. Very often that will be the judicial review procedure (i.e. in the High Court under Pt 54, see para.24.001). Some cases may be commenced by a Pt 7 claim (see para.9.001) or a Pt 8 claim (see para.10.001). The final trial or hearing of a claim for a declaration of incompatibility a claim in respect of a judicial act must be before a full time High Court judge: deputy High Court judges, Masters and district judges have no jurisdiction in such cases (*White Book* 2BPD.15).

CHAPTER 2

Funding Civil Litigation

2.001　Most litigants retain solicitors to conduct their litigation for them. In this chapter we describe the main funding arrangements and also several related topics. Although in recent years the law in this area has been extremely complex and turbulent, most aspects of it now have become settled again. For many clients, the main types of funding arrangement are referrals by claims management companies and conditional fee agreements. However, before we describe these, there are two general topics we must explain: the relevant professional conduct requirements for solicitors and the topic of legal expenses insurance.

SOLICITORS' CODE OF CONDUCT 2007

2.002　With effect from July 2007, the Solicitors' Code of Conduct 2007, published by the Solicitors' Regulation Authority, replaces the Solicitors' Practice Rules 1990 and the Solicitors' Costs Information and Client Care Code. Rule 1 of the new Code ("Core Duties") sets out what should be at the heart of what it means to be a solicitor. Solicitors must uphold the rule of law, act with integrity, not allow their independence to be compromised, act in the best interests of each client, provide a good service to their clients, and not behave in a way that is likely to diminish the trust which the public places in them or the profession. These core duties are the overarching framework within which the other twenty-four rules can be understood. The other rules deal in more detail with specific aspects of practice. What follows is a brief summary of some of the main points to be found in r.2 "Client Relations".

Information about the firm

2.003　A client must be given the name and status of the person who will deal with his case and the name of the person responsible for overall supervision. The client must also be told, in writing, at the outset, not only that they have a right to complain in the event of a problem but also the person to whom they should direct that complaint. Each firm must have a written complaints procedure, a copy of which must be given to the client on request.

　　Making clear the status of the fee earners involved should avoid the problem which arose in *Pilbrow v Pearless de Rougemont & Co.* [1999] 3 All E.R. 355.

In that case, the client was not told that the fee earner who dealt with his case was not a solicitor. The solicitors' claim for costs against that client was dismissed. See further at para.6.001.

Costs information at the outset

2.004 The solicitor must give the client the best information possible about the likely overall costs of a matter. In particular, clients must be told the basis and terms on which the firm's charges will be calculated and whether charging rates may later be increased. The different methods of funding must be discussed (see below) and, if appropriate, the client advised that there are circumstances in which the solicitor may be entitled to exercise a lien for unpaid costs. Any information about costs and funding methods must be clear and must be confirmed in writing.

Information about the case

2.005 The solicitor must clearly identify the client's objectives in relation to the work to be done, give a clear explanation of the issues involved and the options available to the client, and must agree with the client the next steps to be taken. In doing so the solicitor must agree an appropriate level of service for the matter, and explain the responsibilities of both client and firm. Clients must be advised of their potential liability for any other party's costs and (a very important point) the solicitor must discuss with the client whether the potential outcomes of any legal case will justify the expense or risk involved.

Information about funding methods

2.006 The solicitor must discuss with the client how the client will pay. This involves considering whether legal aid is available, whether legal expenses insurance should be obtained and whether the client already has such insurance (e.g., under a motor insurance policy or a house contents policy) or can obtain financial assistance from another person such as an employer or trade union.

Updating costs information

2.007 In CFA cases and legal aid cases some additional matters must be explained both at the outset and, when appropriate, as the matter progresses (see further on this, below).

The requirement to give the client the best information possible about the likely overall costs of a matter applies not only at the outset but also "when appropriate, as the matter progresses". The new code does not repeat the former obligation to give costs information at regular intervals, at least every six months. Instead, it places emphasis on agreeing an appropriate level of service at the outset. This allows solicitors much greater flexibility to respond to their clients' needs. The guidance to r.2 indicates that frequent reports may increase the projected costs of a matter. Whilst some clients may want regular written reports, others may be content to provide initial instructions and then hear no more until an agreed point has been reached.

LEGAL EXPENSES INSURANCE

Before the Event Insurance

2.008 Legal expenses insurance covers the insured in respect of legal costs and expenses he or she may incur pursuing or defending claims arising out of litigation. "Before the Event" ("BTE") insurance is not, or should not, be taken out with any particular piece of litigation in mind. Instead, it relates to any litigation of the types specified in the policy which arise out of any event occurring during the insured period. Most such policies are in fact "add-on" benefits in some other insurance, for example, motor insurance or a house contents policy, but they are also available as stand alone insurance policies. The possible variations between one type of BTE policy and another are legion. Some are limited to particular types of litigation, some cover all except matrimonial litigation. Some cover litigation as a defendant only, some cover litigation whether as a claimant or defendant. Most will specify the maximum amount of cover available, whether in respect of the insured's own costs or in respect of the costs of any opponent which the insured is ordered to pay.

There can be little argument that BTE insurance is the best form of LEI available. It is very much cheaper than its alternative (ATE insurance, see below). Most insurers provide a legal helpline giving advice to the insured at the outset of trouble, before litigation begins. It is easy to find a solicitor of one's choice to take on the litigation once proceedings start; in most cases, the insurer cannot restrict the insured's freedom of choice (see reg.6 of the Insurance Companies (Legal Expenses Insurance) Regulations 1990 (SI 1990/1159).

After the Event Insurance

2.009 "After the Event" ("ATE") insurance is an insurance policy taken out when embarking on a particular piece of litigation and covers the insured against the risk of losing that litigation. Most clients agreeing conditional fee terms with their solicitors will wish to take out ATE insurance covering their opponent's costs should the case be unsuccessful. Without such cover, an unsuccessful client is likely to be reduced to homelessness and/or bankruptcy in order to pay his opponent's costs. The fact that the conditional fee agreement means that he does not also have to pay his own lawyers will be of very little consequence. ATE insurance arranged in conjunction with a conditional fee agreement normally also provides cover in respect of the client's disbursements. This cover may extend to disbursements on counsel's fees. However, often it does not. A client who arranges conditional fee terms with his solicitor will often expect the solicitor to arrange conditional fee terms with counsel also. This gives a mutuality of interest between the insurer, solicitor and counsel. If the case is unsuccessful, the insurer, the solicitor and counsel will all lose money.

ATE insurance is not limited to providing cover in support of conditional fee agreements. Policies can be readily obtained which cover both sides' costs should the case be unsuccessful. The cost of the premium under such policies is of course much higher since the insurer is shouldering all the risk. The client's own solicitor and counsel will be paid whether the case is won or lost.

Insurance premiums for ATE cover may be very expensive. Clients often have to pay a premium exceeding 25 per cent of the insurance cover they seek (BTE insurance premiums rarely exceed 1 per cent). Clients may avoid the cashflow difficulties of financing such premiums in various ways. The policy may provide for a staged premium, i.e. a premium payable in instalments as the case proceeds to trial (see *Rogers v Merthyr Tydfil County BC* [2007] 1 All E.R. 354). Whether it is for a single premium or a staged premium, the insurer may agree that no payment need be made until the case is concluded. Alternatively, the insured may finance the premium by taking out a loan to pay for disbursements including, of course, the insurance premium. In some schemes linked with disbursements loans the premium is itself regarded as a disbursement, i.e. is not payable if the case is lost. However, in most such schemes, the client must still pay interest on the disbursement loan during the period of the litigation; the rates of interest charged are sometimes high.

Although our preference runs in favour of BTE insurance on grounds of price and simplicity, there is one respect in which ATE insurance may be advantageous: reasonable ATE insurance premiums are recoverable as part of the costs recoverable in the litigation. BTE insurance premiums (and the interest payable on disbursement loans) are not recoverable (see the definition of "insurance premium" given in r.43.2).

The Solicitors' Code of Conduct 2007 requires solicitors to discuss the issue of insurance with clients at the outset of their instructions. In particular, the solicitor must discuss with the client whether the client's liability for their own costs may be covered by insurance and whether the client's liability for another party's costs may be covered by pre-purchased insurance and, if not, whether it would be advisable for the client's liability for another party's costs to be covered by ATE insurance (and see further para.2.009).

Insurance cover gives the client peace of mind. If the case is lost, the financial burden the client must shoulder is limited to the cost of any insurance cover he must pay and interest on any loan arranged to finance the disbursements. However, there also remains one risk which may disturb that peace of mind. Insurance cover will be subject to a maximum limit. Before arranging the insurance, the client should seek the best information possible about the cover he is likely to need. His solicitor has a professional conduct obligation to give him such advice (Solicitors' Code of Conduct 2007) but in very many cases the best information will still leave the matter in doubt. The client will remain at risk of paying some costs if, by the conclusion of the proceedings, the total costs payable exceed the insurance cover arranged.

BASIC CHARGING AGREEMENTS

How much is payable?

2.010   The simplest agreement between solicitor and client may be completely open-ended. It could oblige the client to pay "such costs as are in all the circumstances fair and reasonable". An agreement such as this falls a long way short of the professional conduct requirements about costs information (see above). However, such agreements were commonplace until recent years and no doubt will continue to be made for some years to come.

In an effort to comply with the Solicitors' Code of Conduct 2007 most solicitors will make basic charging agreements in writing which specify the hourly rate or rates of the fee earners employed. Rates vary according to the grade of the earner in question and according to the locality in which the work was done. The Guide to the Summary Assessment of Costs issued by the Senior Costs Judge (see para.13.010) gives some basic guidance as to hourly rates for different grades of fee earner in most localities in England and Wales. However, these rates are broad approximations only and many solicitors claim that they are too low. Given the nature of a solicitor's job it is unwise to choose them solely on price. Clients are often willing to pay premium rates for firms which are highly recommended and which deserve that recommendation.

In order to identify the factors determining the reasonableness of a bill delivered under a basic charging agreement, one must first identify whether the work done was "contentious business" or "non-contentious business". Do not assume that all the work done in a solicitor's litigation department is "contentious business". The expression is defined by the Solicitors' Act 1974, s.87 as:

> "business done, whether as solicitor or advocate, in or for the purposes of proceedings begun before a court or before an arbitrator, not being business which falls within the definition of non-contentious or common form probate business contained in Section 128 of the Supreme Court Act 1981."

The important word in this definition is "begun". Assume that a solicitor is consulted by a potential defendant who has been threatened with proceedings claiming compensation. Further assume that the solicitor applies a relevant pre-action protocol and investigates the allegations and negotiates a settlement before any claim form is issued. That is not "contentious business" because no proceedings were "begun".

Factors determining reasonableness of bills

In seeking to justify the reasonableness of a bill concerning contentious business the solicitor must refer to CPR r.44.5. In respect of any item of costs relating to proceedings in a county court, the amount allowed can exceed the amount reasonable to allow as between litigants only if the solicitor and client have entered into a written agreement which expressly permits payment to the solicitor of an amount of costs greater than that which the client could have recovered from another party to the proceeding (Solicitors' Act 1974, s.74(3) and CPR r.48.8(1A)). 2.011

In seeking to justify the reasonableness of a bill concerning non-contentious business the solicitor should refer to the Solicitors Remuneration Order 1994 which sets out factors similar to these listed in r.44.5.

At present, it is not customary for solicitors undertaking civil litigation to stipulate for a fixed fee. However, if a fixed sum is agreed, the reasonableness of that sum would still have to be justified by way of comparison with similar agreements treating time spent as a relevant factor.

When is money payable?

A solicitor who accepts instructions to conduct proceedings makes an entire contract. In the absence of special agreement or unusual circumstances he or she cannot terminate those instructions or deliver a bill until the conclusion of the proceedings except for good cause and on reasonable notice to the client. That said, it is nowadays common practice to make special agreement. The effect of this agreement must be explained to the client at the outset (Solicitors' Code of Conduct 2007). Also, s.65(2) of the Solicitors' Act 1974 enables a solicitor retained to conduct contentious business to request a client to make a payment of money being a reasonable sum on account of costs incurred in the conduct of that business. If the client refuses or fails to pay that is deemed to be good cause whereby the solicitor may give reasonable notice to the client and withdraw. 2.012

REFERRALS BY CLAIMS MANAGEMENT COMPANIES

Claims management companies supply solicitors on their panels with clients in return for a commission paid by the solicitor or by an ATE insurer. Many firms of solicitors now receive work in this way. It is not difficult to see how this state of affairs has come about. Most claims for damages are personal injury claims. In times past most personal injury claimants expected to get or at any rate hoped to get legal help financed by the Legal Aid scheme. In order to find a solicitor, they would seek a recommendation from friends, colleagues or from organisations such as the Citizens Advice Bureau. In recent years, the numbers of people covered by the Legal Aid scheme began to shrink. Ultimately, in April 2.013

2000, the scheme was largely abolished (see para.2.020 below). These changes led to the growth and success of claims management companies which actively market litigation services which are extremely attractive to the average, inexperienced, litigant. "No win, no fee", "where there's blame, there's a claim" and similar slogans, heavily advertised on TV, radio and in the press, encourage thousands of potential claimants to dial contact numbers each week. The successful ones will then receive a home-visit from a "claims investigator" and ultimately will be referred to a firm of solicitors on the company's panel.

The Compensation Act 2006 brought in a scheme for the regulation of claims management companies. The primary aims of the scheme are to curb malpractice and bring in better safeguards for consumers. Some of the worst excesses of claims management companies in recent years include the reliance upon cold-calling for business and upon deceptive advertising and misleading contracts. Today, solicitors face disciplinary and criminal sanctions if they deal with unauthorised claims management companies. In order to obtain authorisation a company must, amongst other things, comply with new rules of conduct covering advertising, marketing, complaints, information to clients and soliciting business.

Many referrals by claims management companies to solicitors involve the purchase of ATE insurance covering liability for the costs of the client and/or the opponent. Although such insurance is arranged before the case is referred to a solicitor, the insurance is usually conditional upon a solicitor agreeing to accept instructions on CFA terms. If a case is accepted and is subsequently successful the client will receive the compensation agreed or awarded in his favour less any disbursement loan interest he agreed to pay and any other costs he agreed to pay which are not recoverable from the opponent. If the case is lost, the client will be liable only for the interest on any disbursement loan obtained. In practice, most cases taken on by claims management companies and their solicitors succeed. Why then do these claimants buy ATE insurance? The reason cannot be gullibility or ignorance. The Solicitors' Code of Conduct 2007 obliges the solicitor involved to consider with them what insurance cover they need and what pre-existing insurance cover they may already have. In most cases the clients are hooked by the benefits the referral brings: speedy action and the will and finance to carry it through. One should not discount the power of advertising. The client is mentally sold on the product before he makes that first phone call.

CONDITIONAL FEE AGREEMENTS

2.014 Current law as to Conditional Fee Agreements is set out in the Courts and Legal Services Act 1990, s.58 as amended (see *White Book*, Vol.2, para.9B–110) and various Regulations made thereunder (see *White Book*, Vol.2, para.7A–1 onwards which also contains specimen forms of agreement). To be valid, a Conditional Fee Agreement ("CFA") between solicitor and client must be in writing, signed by both parties and must not relate to certain types of family proceedings or to any criminal proceedings other than proceedings under s.82 of the Environmental Protection Act 1990. There are various types of CFA. We must briefly describe each one, summarising the main formal and procedural requirements associated with it.

CFA without success fee

Under a CFA without success fee the client must pay ordinary costs if he wins and either no costs or reduced costs if he loses. What amounts to winning or losing for this purpose must be defined in the agreement. The most advantageous terms from the client's point of view will limit his liability for costs to the exact extent to which costs and other sums are actually paid on behalf of the opposing party or are actually recovered or agreed (even though, perhaps, not paid). 2.015

The regulations which used to bedevil CFA law have been revoked by the Conditional Fee Agreements (Revocation) Regulations 2005 in respect of all CFAs (and CCFAs, see below) made in or after November 2005. In revoking the regulations Parliament decided that the consumer protection the regulations were intended to provide can now be left to be dealt with by (what is now) the Solicitors' Code of Conduct 2007. Rule 2.03(2) of that Code provides that a solicitor acting for a client under any form of CFA must explain two matters both at the outset and, when appropriate, as the matter progresses. First, the circumstances in which the client may be liable for the solicitor's costs and whether the solicitor will seek payment of those costs from the client if entitled to do so. Secondly, if the solicitor intends to seek payment of any or all of his costs from the client, the solicitor must advise the client of his right to an assessment of those costs. (The rule also requires an explanation of a third matter which is relevant only when the solicitor is undertaking *pro bono* work on CFA terms.)

A client who agrees "no win, no fee" terms will not usually agree to pay any sums on account. However, if the terms are "no win, reduced fees" it is likely that the agreement will require the client to pay fees at the reduced rate regularly as the case progresses. In either case, the client may also be required to pay disbursements as incurred during the progress of the case. In most cases, the largest disbursements are fees for counsel and fees for expert witnesses. Fees for counsel may be on conditional fee terms (this is considered further below). However, fees for experts are usually not on such terms. A CFA with an expert might imperil the credibility of the expert's evidence. As a matter of professional conduct, solicitors must not instruct experts on fee terms depending upon the outcome of the case (Solicitors' Code of Conduct 2007, r.11.07; contrast terms deferring payment until the conclusion of the case).

In the case of a claimant, the costs of expert witnesses and other disbursements may be financed out of applications for interim payments (see Ch.25). In all cases, these disbursements may be financed by means of a loan secured by an insurance policy taken out to cover the risk that these costs may not be recoverable from the opponent. As we have seen (para.2.009, above) the cost of such insurance may itself be recoverable from the opponent and therefore rules of court require the client to give the opponent advance notice of this potential cost (see para.2.023).

CFAs without success fees are often drafted so as to provide that, if the client obtains an interim order for costs against his opponent, the maximum fees are payable to the extent that they are in fact paid by the opponent.

CFA with success fee

2.016 In this form of agreement the maximum fees payable to the solicitor comprise two ingredients; the base fee, probably calculated by reference to hourly rates, and a success fee expressed as a percentage of the base fee. Depending upon the definition of "win" or "loss" which is employed (i.e. the specified circumstances in which the fees or part of them are payable) a client who loses will pay no fees or reduced fees and a client who wins will pay both the base fee and the success fee. The factors relevant in calculating success fees are described in Ch.38. It is necessary here to note that the success fee may itself comprise two elements: The "risk element", i.e. the price payable to the solicitor for running the risk of non-payment or reduced payment if the case is lost: and the "fee determent element", i.e. the price payable to the solicitor for postponing the payment of fees and expenses during the currency of the agreement.

As explained above, the Solicitors' Code of Conduct 2007 requires the solicitor to advise the client of the basis and terms of these charges and the circumstances in which he may be liable to pay them, and to give such advice both at the outset and, when appropriate, as the matter progresses (see paras 2.006 and 2.015, above).

Reasonable success fees, along with the reasonable amount of any ATE insurance in support, can be recovered from an opponent as part of the costs of the action if proper notice of funding is given (see para.2.023). However, the court will not assess these items until the conclusion of the proceedings (r.44.3A). The agreement can be worded so as to entitle the solicitor to full base fees on any interim order for costs. The success fees on those items will be picked up at the end of the proceedings along with any other base fees and success fees awarded.

As with the simpler form of CFA already described, a client under a CFA with success fee who agrees "no win, no fee" terms will not usually agree to pay any sums on account. Disbursements such as counsel's fees and experts' fees may be financed out of interim payments, or LEI, or may be financed by the solicitor (the solicitor is entitled to claim success fees on "fees and expenses", i.e. on profit costs and disbursements).

Proceedings under s.82 of the Environmental Protection Act 1990 cannot be the subject of an enforceable CFA with success fee. In such proceedings (which are in fact criminal proceedings) the client and solicitor may either make a basic charging agreement or a CFA without success fee.

Collective Conditional Fee Agreements

The CFAs just described require a separate agreement on a case by case basis. Collective Conditional Fee Agreements can reduce the administrative burdens of making individual agreements for bulk purchasers of legal services, such as trade unions or large commercial concerns. Trade unions (and many other membership organisations) often take it upon themselves to support their members who have legal problems likely to end up in litigation. Large commercial concerns are often repeat players in particular types of litigation, for example, disputes about contracts, patents or leases.

2.017

A Collective Conditional Fee Agreement ("CCFA") does not refer to specific proceedings but provides for fees to be payable on a common basis in relation to each class of proceedings it covers. Persons receiving legal services under the CCFA need not be named as parties therein. In virtually all respects CCFAs are governed by the CFA law already described, for example, as to the information to be given to opponents.

BARRISTERS' FEES

The barristers' profession has undergone massive change in the last twenty years and is likely to undergo even more change in the next five. In times past, barristers would accept instructions only from solicitors (subject to a few exceptions), those instructions were on non-contractual terms (i.e. the obligation on the solicitor to pay the barrister was a professional conduct obligation only) and the calculation of barristers' fees was subject to a craft and mystery understood by few people other than barristers' clerks. Indeed, at one time it was considered unprofessional even to discuss counsel's fees with counsel. Solicitors who made the mistake of trying to do so would be quickly told "I think that is something you ought to discuss with my clerk." Many changes have been made and more are on the way, stimulated to some extent by the Legal Services Bill, which is designed to substantially deregulate the legal professions so as to provide greater public access to justice.

2.018

There are now three ways in which barristers may accept instructions. *Professional Client Access* which covers instructions from solicitors, Parliamentary agents, patent agents, trademark agents and notaries, European lawyers registered with the Law Society or Bar Council, employed barristers, legal advice centres, licensed conveyancers and other authorised litigators (soon to include Fellows of the Association of Law Costs Draftsmen). *Licensed Access* which covers instructions from individuals and organisations (such as the Academy of Experts, Chartered Institute of Taxation and, at present, Association of Law Costs Draftsmen) Licences are granted by the Bar Council on the basis that the licensees have sufficient expertise in particular areas of the law in order to instruct barristers directly in those areas either on their own affairs or on behalf of their clients. *Public Access* which covers all members of the public but there are restrictions on the terms of the instructions they can give. The barrister is under an obligation to consider the interests of the client and ensure that these are best served by direct instruction.

Until 1990 barristers in independent private practice were not able to enter into contracts for the provision of their services as barristers. Although this was changed by s.61 of the Courts and Legal Services Act 1990, the standard terms of work under which most barristers accepted instructions from solicitors still remained non-contractual. However, most of these arrangements are expected to be put on a contractual footing as from October 2007. The Law Society and the Bar Council are expected to reach an agreement on terms which will be applicable in most cases and will provide for binding arbitration by a joint tribunal where there is a dispute. If a fee determined by the tribunal remains unpaid the barrister will be able to sue the solicitor for the sum.

In cases funded by the Legal Services Commission ("LSC"; and see further, below), counsel's fees are paid by the LSC direct. So long as the solicitor makes it clear to counsel that counsel must look to the LSC as paymaster, the solicitor is under no financial obligation to counsel in respect of those instructions. In other cases the terms agreed by counsel may be on conditional fee terms, either with or without success fees. A standard form CFA between solicitor and counsel (APIL/PIBA 6, for which see *White Book* Vol.2, para.7B–17) will describe counsel's normal fees for advisory work and drafting in accordance with a specified hourly rate and will give specimen brief fees (varying according to the time estimate which the hearing will ultimately be given) and the number of hours of preparation. Such transparency about fees has removed much of the uncertainty that used to complicate fee negotiations with counsel or his clerk.

In Ch.36 of this book, further information about counsel's fees is given, including information on negotiating and agreeing fees and on the position where a case settles after instructions to counsel have been delivered.

COSTS INCURRED BY LITIGANTS IN PERSON

2.019 Many litigants are unable to afford or are unwilling to instruct solicitors and therefore conduct litigation themselves, either in their spare time or, when necessary, by giving up remunerative employment. CPR r.48.6 sets out what costs they are entitled to recover for this work if an order for costs is made in their favour. The court should allow such costs as would have been allowed if the work and disbursements had been done or incurred by a solicitor on the litigant's behalf. However, in the case of what would have been a profit costs item for a solicitor, the court cannot allow more than two-thirds of the sum which it would have allowed a solicitor. Moreover, if the litigant has not actually suffered any pecuniary loss in doing the work to which the costs relate, he will be limited to £9.25 per hour in respect of time reasonably spent by him on the work involved. Where costs are allowed for attending court to conduct his own case, a litigant in person is not entitled to a witness allowance for himself in addition.

COSTS FUNDED BY THE LEGAL SERVICES COMMISSION

The Administration of Justice Act 1999 repealed the Legal Aid Act 1988. The old Legal Aid Scheme, the Legal Aid Board and the Legal Aid Fund have all been replaced by a new funding scheme, the Legal Services Commission ("LSC") and the Community Legal Service Fund. For lawyers the main changes include the contract and other funding mechanisms which are now in place. For litigants, the main changes include the new and complex eligibility criteria which now apply. For both lawyers and litigants the most important change concerns the exclusion of funding for most personal injury cases because, it seems, these are regarded as suitable for conditional fee terms. However some funding may be authorised in personal injury cases where exceptionally high investigative or overall costs are necessary, or where issues of wider public interest are involved (Explanatory Notes to the Access to Justice Act 1999, para.74). 2.020

Rule 2.03(3) of the Solicitors' Code of Conduct 2007 specifies some additional information which solicitors must explain to legally aided clients at the outset of instructions:

(a) the circumstances in which the clients may be liable for costs incurred on their behalf;
(b) the effects of the statutory charge (as to which, see further below);
(c) the client's duty to pay any fixed or periodic contribution assessed and the consequence of failing to do so (see further, below); and
(d) the fact that, even if the client is successful, the other party may not be ordered to pay costs or may not be in a position to pay them.

The contributions referred to in (c) above are the payments which the client may have to make to the LSC. Some clients are financially eligible for legal aid but their income or capital resources take them above the level at which legal aid will be offered with a "nil contribution". A contribution from capital is normally required in a fixed amount at the outset, where as contributions from income are normally payable on a monthly basis during the currency of the legal aid certificate. Legal aid may later be discharged if the client falls behind on any contributions he is required to make.

The LSC has a statutory charge "on any property recovered or preserved by him [i.e., the legally aided party] (whether for himself or any other person) in any proceedings or in any compromise or settlement of any dispute in connection with which the services [funded by the LSC] were provided" (Access to Justice Act 1999, s.10(7)). The charge puts the legally aided client in a similar position to that of an unassisted client. It is a fact of life that the costs recovered from a losing party are usually less than the costs actually incurred by the winning party's side. A shortfall will certainly arise where the winning party did not get a full order for costs. Where that party is legally aided the statutory charge comes into play at this point. Any sums payable in respect of his case by the LSC which are not recovered from the opposing party will be met first out of the client's contributions and then out of any property recovered or preserved for the client even if this should happen to consume all of it. *"Property"* includes all financial compensation awarded, and real or personal property, wherever situated, including all rights under any compromise or settlement and any costs recovered. *"Recovered"* means that the client has successfully claimed or asserted rights to property or to part of it. *"Preserved"* means that the client has warded off another's claim or assertion of rights to property or to part of it.

Because of the statutory charge, any funding paid for by the LSC in excess of any contributions required is in effect a loan repayable only if the legally aided party wins.

Cost protection

2.021   The grant of legal aid or LSC funding to a party greatly reduces the likelihood that other parties will be able to obtain an order for the payment of costs against him. Section 11 of the Access to Justice Act 1999 provides that, against any legally aided party (see Costs Practice Direction, para.22.3) or a party who received certain "levels of service" for which funding was provided by the LSC (see Costs Practice Direction, para.21.5) any order for costs must not exceed the amount which it is reasonable for that person to pay having regard to all the circumstances including the financial resources of all parties to the proceedings and their conduct in connection with the dispute to which the proceedings relate. In determining the resources of a party with such cost protection, there are certain assets which the court must disregard (for a summary, see Costs Practice Direction, paras 21.12–21.14).

The procedure to follow to determine the liability of a party with cost protection is described at para.39.014. Note that cost protection only applies to that part of proceedings funded out of the Community Legal Service Fund. For periods before the funding started or after it ceased, there is no special protection and a full order for costs may be obtained. Moreover, s.11 gives no protection for orders setting off costs against any money or property recovered or preserved in the action. In *Lockley v National Blood Transfusion Service* [1992] 1 W.L.R. 492 the claimant, a legally aided party, was ordered to pay to the defendant the costs of a pre-trial court hearing. The Court of Appeal allowed orders for costs against the claimant, including the costs of appeal, with directions that the sums payable under these orders should be set off against any damages and costs which the legally aided party might in future recover in the action. This practice was confirmed post-CPR by the Court of Appeal in the case of *R. (on the application of Burkett) v London Borough of Hammersmith & Fulham* [2004] EWCA Civ 1342; *The Times*, October 20, 2004.

In certain, very limited, circumstances a party who cannot recover costs because of s.11 may seek an order for costs against the LSC itself. The procedure on such applications is also covered in Ch.39.

COSTS FUNDED BY NON-PARTIES

In many cases the cost of legal representation of one party, claimant or defendant, may be funded by a non-party, for example, a close relative or friend, a trade union, or, especially in road accident cases, an insurer. In these examples, the non-party providing the financial support has a legitimate common interest with the supported party which derives from their relationship, be it family, social, contractual or otherwise. The funded litigant is usually able to recoup the costs of the legal services from an opposing party in the litigation if he obtains an order for costs to that effect. It has always been the case that, so long as the litigant receiving costs is subject to a potential legal obligation to pay costs to the solicitor who acted on his behalf, full reasonable costs can be recovered from the party ordered to pay costs, even if the solicitor never expected to call upon that potential obligation (*R. v Miller* [1983] 1 W.L.R. 1056).

2.022

In some cases, funding arrangements made between a litigant and a non-party are regarded as contrary to public policy. Before 1967, the tort of maintenance dealt with the illegitimate financing of litigation by an intermeddling mischief-maker. The crime of champerty was committed if the illegitimate intermeddler was motivated by a contract with the litigant under which he would share the proceeds of the litigation. In 1967, maintenance and champerty ceased to be tortious or criminal. However, contracts concerning such matters are still treated as contrary to public policy or otherwise illegal (Criminal Law Act 1967, ss.13,14). This illegality renders these contracts unenforceable between the funder and the funded. Accordingly, if the illegally funded litigant obtains an order for costs against another party, he will not be able to recoup those costs which the funder has incurred. This is an aspect of the so-called indemnity principle which is discussed further at para.38.019.

In all cases of non-party funding, whether legitimate or illegitimate, the non-party should expect the court to consider making an order for costs against him if the litigation is unsuccessful. The principles upon which orders for costs are made against non-parties are considered in Ch.39.

PROVIDING INFORMATION ON FUNDING TO OPPONENTS

Notices of funding

The purchase of ATE insurance and the making of CFAs with success fees may increase the opponent's liability for costs if an order for costs is made against him. Therefore, in order to warm the opponent about that, the rules of court require a Notice of Funding (Form N251) to be given on the commencement of proceedings, i.e. if the funding is arranged pre-commencement for a claimant, with a claim form and, if it is arranged pre-commencement for a defendant, with the acknowledgment of service, defence or other first document (such as an application to set aside a default judgment). Parties are also required to serve

2.023

a Notice of Funding, within seven days, where the relevant funding is first arranged after commencement and where relevant changes to such funding are made (e.g. an ATE policy has been cancelled and/or a second policy has been taken out). On these topics see r.44.15 and the Costs Practice Direction, para.19.1 onwards.

Where there has been a failure to disclose required information, the party at fault will be unable to make a full claim for costs. Success fees and ATE premiums are not recoverable for any period in proceedings during which he failed to provide the required information (r.44.3B). The party at fault may, of course, apply for relief from that sanction. The Costs Practice Direction states that he should do so as quickly as possible after he becomes aware of the default (see Cost Practice Direction para.10.1).

Disclosure of the existence of CFAs with success fees and ATE insurance is also required pre-commencement. On this matter, the Costs Practice Direction does not apply (see para.19.2(5) thereof) but the pre-action protocol does apply (see para.4A.1 thereof) to which the sanction in r.44.3B applies. Whilst the Cost Practice Direction is extremely precise about what is required and when, the pre-action protocol is comparatively vague. It merely states that the litigant "should inform other potential parties to the claim". We would suggest that the best policy here is to follow the Cost Practice Direction format, i.e. give extremely prompt notice by way of Form N251, altering its heading to say "in the Intended action in Barnet County Court" or as the case may be. In 2007 there were proposals to amend the personal injury and clinical negligence protocols so as to require that letters of claim or response give notice of any funding arrangements already entered into.

There are three further comments about notices of funding which should be made. First, the disclosure does not have to reveal the percentage increase specified as the success fee or reveal the amount of any ATE premium paid. Because such information may be prejudicial (e.g. may appear to give an opinion as to the party's prospects of success) it never has to be disclosed until it falls for assessment and it can never fall for assessment until the conclusion of the proceedings (r.44.3A). Secondly, the Costs Practice Direction never requires disclosure of a CFA with success fee made between solicitor and counsel. Strictly speaking such disclosure is required where the pre-action protocol applies but, in practice, CFAs between solicitor and counsel are not frequently made until after commencement of proceedings.

The third comment relates to notices of funding concerning ATE insurance in which a staged premium is payable. In *Rogers v Merthyr Tydfil County BC* [2007] 1 All E.R. 354, the Court of Appeal ruled that any party who has taken out an ATE policy containing such a premium should inform his opponent that the policy is staged, and should set out accurately the trigger moments at which the second or later stages will be reached.

> "[116] ... this obligation should be undertaken in addition to the obligations set out in CPR 45.15(1) and in paras. 19.1(1) and 19.4 of the Costs Practice Directions. If this is done, the opponent has been given fair notice of the staging, and unless there are features of the case that are out of the

ordinary, his liability to pay at the second or third stage a higher premium than he would have had to pay if the claim had been settled at the first stage should not prove to be a contentious issue."

Notices under the Legal Aid Regulations

In all legal aid cases and in some cases funded by the LSC (see para.2.020) the litigant funded out of the Community Legal Service Fund may have cost protection (see para.2.021). Therefore, reg.50 of the Civil Legal Aid (General) Regulations 1989 (which is still in force) requires the solicitor to give other parties prescribed notices of issue and/or amendments of the relevant Legal Aid Certificate or LSC Certificate. Breach of these regulations may lead to the making of a wasted costs order against the solicitor (as to which see para.39.002).

2.024

CHAPTER 3

Interest

CLAIMS FOR INTEREST

Interest payable as of right

3.001 The most important example of interest payable as of right is contractual interest. Any contract under which sums of money are payable may include a suitably worded provision for the payment of interest in the event of delayed payment or non-payment. (In drafting such a provision account should be taken of the Consumer Credit Act 1974, as amended, ss.137 to 140A which enable a court to consider whether the relationship between the creditor and debtor arising out of the credit agreement is unfair to the debtor because of the terms of the agreement).

In both the High Court and the county court a creditor under a contract who properly states (see Ch.12) and pursues a claim has a right to that interest, at the rate and for the period specified in the contract, up until judgment or sooner payment. In theory a contractual rate of interest may even continue to be payable until execution of the judgment or sooner payment.

Various statutes provide for what might otherwise be called "contractual interest"; see, for example, the Bills of Exchange Act 1882, interest (described as damages) recoverable in an action upon a dishonoured cheque and the Solicitors' (Non-Contentious Business) Remuneration Order 1994, interest payable on a solicitor's bill of costs in certain, limited, circumstances.

The points made below at paras 3.003 and 3.004 also apply to interest payable as of right.

Interest payable in the court's discretion

3.002 The most important examples of interest payable in the court's discretion stem from SCA 1981, s.35A and CCA 1984, s.69. Under these sections the courts have power to award interest in all "debt or damages actions", whether the sum is specified or not. This interest compensates a claimant for being kept out of his or her money during the proceedings. Under r.36.14(3) (see Ch.29) the court also has power to award interest as a sanction or penalty upon a defendant for unnecessarily prolonging litigation by not accepting a reasonable offer to settle made by the claimant. The court may award both types of interest in the same case, but if it does so, "the total rate of interest may not exceed 10 per cent above base rate" (r.36.14(5).). "Base rate" is defined in the Glossary to the CPR as the interest rate set by the Bank of England which is used as the basis for other banks' rates. You can find it in the Financial Times referred to as the UK clearing bank base lending rate under the section entitled "London Money Rates". Whether interest should be awarded, and if so, at what rate or rates, on what part of any damages and for what period, are all in the discretion of the court. Nowadays one normally expects the court to award interest in any debt or damages case. In a debt case interest will run from when the debt fell due. In a damages case interest will normally start from when the loss is sustained or otherwise ascertainable. This is not always as easy as it sounds. For example, in *Claymore Services Ltd v Nautilus Properties Ltd* [2007] EWHC 805, Jackson J. stated:

> "The date upon which the builders' cause of action accrues in a restitutionary *quantum meruit* claim is not entirely clear . . . Even if, in theory, the cause of action accrues on the date upon which the building is handed over, nevertheless I am quite satisfied that interest should not run from that date. Interest should only run from the date when the sum due is ascertainable. In this regard, most of the relevant information resides with the contractor. In my view, interest should start to run when the contractor has furnished his final account and the building owner has had a reasonable opportunity to assess the final account."

However, the court may, in its discretion, fix a later start date to take account of any inexcusable delay by the claimant in bringing the matter to trial (*Hellenic Industrial Development Bank SA v Atkin* [2002] EWHC 1405 (Q.B.)). In *Claymore Services Ltd v Nautilus Properties Ltd* [2007] EWHC 805, Jackson J., having reviewed the authorities, found the following three propositions.

(1) Where a claimant has delayed unreasonably in commencing or prosecuting proceedings, the court may exercise its discretion either to disallow interest for a period or to reduce the rate of interest.
(2) In exercising that discretion the court must take a realistic view of delay. In the case of business disputes, litigation is for all parties an unwelcome distraction from their proper business. It is not reasonable to expect any party to take every litigious step at the first possible moment, or to concentrate on litigation to the exclusion of all else. Delay should only be characterised as unreasonable for present purposes when, after making due allowance for the circumstances, it can be seen that the claimant has neglected or declined to pursue his claim for a significant period.
(3) When determining what disallowance or reduction of interest should be made to mark a period of unreasonable delay, the court should bear in mind that the defendant has had the use of the money during that period of delay.

Note further that it is not necessary to show that the defendant has been prejudiced by the delay or other circumstance (*Beahan v Stoneham* (2001) L.T.L. May 16). As to the rate of interest, the rate payable on judgment debts (see para 3.009, below) has been adopted in rules of court relating to default judgments (see Ch.15 below). For the sake of uniformity and simplicity this is the rate which the court frequently adopts. Different rates are awarded in cases in the Commercial Court (base rate plus 1 per cent save in exceptional circumstances), cases concerning personal injuries (see Ch.4) and, of course, cases in which a different rate has been contractually agreed (see, e.g. *Watts v Morrow* [1991] 1 W.L.R. 1421 at 1443 and 1446).

The norm is for an award of simple interest. But note that there is an equitable jurisdiction to award compound interest on damages for deceit at common law where money is either obtained and retained by fraud; or withheld or misapplied by a trustee or other fiduciary: see *Black v Davies* [2005] EWCA Civ 531; (2005) L.T.L. May 6. Increasingly the courts have awarded interest at a rate that reflects the ability of the judgment creditor to borrow money. So, for example, in *Brown v KMR Services* [1995] 4 All E.R. 598 and *Deeny v Gooda Walker (No.4)* [1996] L.R.L.R. 168, interest was awarded to Lloyd's names at 2 per cent above base rate, on the basis that this "represented what individual Names were likely to have to pay when borrowing money" (*per* Phillips J.). Also in *Ahmed v Jaura* [2002] EWCA Civ 210, *The Times*, March 18, 2002, interest was awarded at 3 per cent above base rate to reflect the fact that the judgment creditor was a small businessman.

Stating interest

3.003 A party claiming interest (whether under the statutory powers or otherwise) must say so in his statement of case (see para.12.013). If no claim for interest is stated will no interest be awarded unless an amendment is made (which is not always possible: see para.12.050)? In *Ajou v Stern* [2006] EWCA Civ 165, (2006) L.T.L., March 14, the Court of Appeal (citing the Privy Council authority in *Greer v Alstons Engineering Sales and Services Ltd* [2003] UKPC 46) held that interest may be awarded even if it is not stated. The details as to how interest should be stated are set out at para.12.013. It is sufficient to note here that in respect of a specified claim you must state the rate at which interest is claimed (i.e. the contractually agreed rate, if any, or otherwise the judgment debt rate). Then calculate in pounds and pence the sum of interest which has accrued before commencement of action and also the daily rate at which it accrues; this facilitates the entry of a default judgment (see below). There are some additional points to note concerning interest on claims in a foreign currency as to which see PD 16, para.10.1. In all unspecified claims, interest is stated in more general terms to invoke the court's discretion to assess it.

Default judgments

If a money claim ends by default, i.e. the defendant does not respond to the claim, a default judgment can be entered for the debt or damages claimed and also for interest thereon. Where the claim is for an unspecified amount there has to be a hearing (see Ch.17) at which the damages are assessed and, at that hearing, the court will also assess the interest payable. With a specified claim no hearing is necessary to assess the amount of money due plus interest provided that was stated and claimed pursuant to either of SCA 1981, s.35A or CCA 1984, s.69 (see Ch.15).

3.004

Personal injuries claims

In the case of a claim for damages for personal injuries or death the court must award interest if the damages exceed £200 unless there are special reasons to the contrary (ss.35A(2), 69(2)). One special reason for not awarding interest would be that no claim for it had been stated. Other examples and also an account of the detailed principles concerning the rate of interest and the period for which it is allowed are given in Ch.4 (see paras 4.019 to 4.021).

3.005

Statutory interest on commercial contracts

The Late Payment of Commercial Debts (Interest) Act 1998 creates a statutory right to claim interest on the late payment of certain debts arising under commercial contracts for the supply of goods or services. The Act applies wherever all parties to the contracts are businesses or public authorities. It does not apply to a consumer credit agreement, any contract intended to operate by way of mortgage, pledge, charge or other security, and certain other contracts (see SI 1998/2482).

3.006

Section 1 of the Act implies into every relevant contract a provision for simple interest, which the Act describes as "statutory interest". This is to be treated in the same way as interest carried under an express contract term. A debt that arises under the Act is known as a "qualifying debt" (s.3). Generally, statutory interest runs on a qualifying debt from the date agreed for payment of the goods or services (s.4). However, the court may remit all or part of any statutory interest "in the interests of justice" after considering the conduct of the parties at any time (s.5). How should the court apply s.5? In *Banham Marshalls Services Unlimited v Lincolnshire CC* [2007] EWHC 402, Eady J. stated that, "It is no doubt necessary to have in mind that the mischief to which the statute appers to be primarily directed is that of casual or feckless non-payment." On various debts in that case he remitted some or all of the statutory interest having taken into account where the defences were stronger or weaker and how long it had taken the claimant to bring proceedings for the debts. Note that at present the rate of interest is 8 per cent over base rate.

In addition to interest and court costs, the claimant is also entitled to a small amount of statutory compensation for the inconvenience of having to recover the debt (s.5A). The amount is £40 for debts under £1,000, £100 for debts of £10,000 or more and £70 for cases in between those figures.

As to stating a claim for interest under the Act, see Ch.12 (para.12.013).

Interest where part of the claim is paid before judgment

3.007 It frequently happens that a defendant pays the claimant part of the debt or damages claimed before the claimant obtains judgment thereon. Such payments may be made voluntarily, for example, by a debtor wishing to reduce his indebtedness. Alternatively the court may have ordered the defendant to make an interim payment before trial (see Ch.25). In these cases, when judgment is later entered for the balance of the claim, two calculations of interest may have to be made. One, in respect of the sums previously paid, for interest up to the date of payment. Another, in respect of the balance of the claim, for interest up to the date of judgment.

In *I M Properties Plc v Cape & Dalgleish* [1999] Q.B. 297, CA, C sued D for negligence. C's total losses were assessed at just over £700,000 but C gave credit for £430,000 that it had received from a third party in mitigation of its loss. It was held that C was not entitled to interest on the £430,000 up to the date of its receipt: s.35A provides interest on sums recoverable from the defendant in the proceedings; although the £430,000 formed part of C's initial loss, it had been recovered from a third party before proceedings commenced and therefore was not recoverable from D.

Claim for a debt: interest where whole debt paid before judgment

3.008 Under the old law the court had no power to order interest to be paid on sums which had already been paid and which had not been the subject of its judgment. We have seen above that the law has now altered in the case of part payment. It has also altered, in debt cases, where the whole debt is paid after proceedings have been issued (s.35A(3), s.69(3)). But for this change debtors not obliged to pay contractually agreed interest or statutory interest under the 1998 Act (see above) would in effect obtain interest-free credit if they withheld payment until sued but then paid up before the claimant could enter judgment. Such debtors can in fact still obtain some interest-free credit if they withhold payment of their debts until the moment before the claimant commences proceedings.

In relation to proceedings for recovery of a debt it has been held that interest cannot be awarded on late payments made before proceedings were commenced (*President of India v La Pintada Compania Navigacion SA; The La Pintada (No.1)* [1985] A.C. 104).

INTEREST ON JUDGMENTS

Topics covered so far in this chapter have considered what interest may be awarded in a judgment. Such interest runs only to the date of judgment or sooner payment. Interest on the judgment is entirely different. Save only as to the period in which it runs, it is not discretionary or subject to the parties' prior agreement. No statement of case or application to the court is necessary to obtain it. It is payable also on judgments for interest and costs.

In the High Court judgment interest is payable under the Judgments Act 1838, s.17, the rate being that prescribed by statutory instrument (currently 8 per cent) unless the judgment provides for payment at a different rate (e.g. a contractually agreed rate). Judgment interest is also obtainable, at the same rate, on county court judgments of £5,000 and more under CCA 1984, s.74. County court judgments under £5,000 do not carry interest unless the debt attracts contractual or statutory interest for late payment under the 1998 Act.

Although statutory instruments alter the rate from time to time, the rate applicable to any particular judgment is that rate in force when the judgment was made (*Rocco Giuseppe & Figli v Tradax Export SA* [1984] 1 W.L.R. 742).

As originally enacted, the date from which judgment interest was payable was not discretionary (see generally, *Thomas v Bunn* [1991] 1 A.C. 362). In debt and damages it was the date when judgment was given for the specific sum of money owed by the judgment debtor to the judgment creditor. Thus, in a claim for unspecified damages, the judgment creditor's right to judgment interest ran from the date the damages were assessed. For periods before that date the court had a discretion to award interest in the judgment under SCA 1981, s.35A or CCA 1984, s.69. As to judgments for costs, a different rule applied: judgment interest there ran from the first date the costs in question had been awarded even though the amount of costs (and interest) might not have been quantified until an assessment months, if not years, later. The reasons for the different rule for costs were ancient and also highly technical. In *Thomas* (see above) the House of Lords accepted that the rule was anomalous and capable of producing unfair results, but, for the reasons indicated in the judgment of Lord Ackner, the rule was thought to be the best of the limited alternatives available.

In 1998 s.17 of the Judgments Act 1838 was amended by the Civil Procedures (Modification of Enactments) Order 1998 so as to state:

> "Every judgment debt shall carry interest . . . from such time as shall be prescribed by the rules of court until the same shall be satisfied . . ."

Rule 40.8 now provides that interest payable under either the Judgments Act or s.74 of the County Courts Act shall begin to run from the date that judgment is given (i.e. the traditional date) unless a different date is supplied by a rule, Practice Direction or court order. Likewise, r.44.3(6)(g) provides that interest may be payable on costs from or until a certain date, including a date before judgment (and see also para.45.5 of the Costs Practice Direction which does depart from the traditional date for a small part of every judgment on costs).

The change in the law made in 1998 makes little real difference to claims for debts and damages; there is normally no need to defer the commencement of judgment interest, nor, given the court's power to award interest under SCA 1981, s.35A or CCA 1984, s.69, to bring the traditional date forward. The only common example of a departure from the traditional date is where the judgment for debt or damages is made only as a result of a successful appeal (for pre-1998 learning on this subject, see *Nykredit Mortgage Bank Plc v Edward Erdman Group Ltd (No.2)* [1997] 1 W.L.R. 1627 HL).

As to judgment interest on costs, the new discretion to depart from the traditional date for costs is of great significance, given the court's inability to award interest on costs under SCA 1981, s.35A or CCA 1984, s.69. The new law enables the court to look at the dates when costs were incurred and award payments of interest that fit with the justice of the circumstances of the particular case (*Powell v Herefordshire Health Authority* [2003] 2 Costs L.R. 185, concerning an order for costs made in 1994 which did not fall for assessment until 2002).

As yet no authoritative guidance has been given as to the exercise of the new discretion in relation to costs. It seems to us unwise to rely too heavily upon certain cases in which interest has been granted on costs from a date before the judgment on costs was given since, in each of them the court also purported to alter the rate of interest; this is something it has no discretion to do in the case of judgment interest (*Bim Kemi AB v Blackburn Chemicals Ltd* [2004] 2 Costs L.R. 201, CA; *Douglas v Hello! Ltd* [2004] EWHC 63 (Ch); *Lloyd v Svenby* [2006] EWHC 576 (Q.B.). Pending authoritative guidance, we would respectfully caution against moving away from the traditional date unless there is strong reason to do so. The traditional date, despite its imperfections, has the great advantages of simplicity and uniformity. Exercising the discretion to depart from it in respect of costs will often lead to disproportionate enquiries into the exact funding arrangements.

CHAPTER 4

Personal Injury Damages

This Chapter is intended to provide an introduction to the general principles applicable to the classification and calculation of damages in the largest category of compensation claims, namely those concerning personal injury. The first classification to be made is between special damages and general damages. Special damages in this context are items of pecuniary loss which can be quantified precisely, for example, the cost of repairs, medical expenses, travelling expenses and loss of earnings from date of accident to the trial. 4.001

General damages are not capable of precise calculation. They have to be assessed by the trial judge who will be guided, though not of course bound, by earlier cases. General damages include compensation for pain and suffering, loss of amenity, loss of future earnings and earning capacity and compensation for the cost of future expenses such as nursing or medical care.

Personal injury damages, both general and special, usually carry interest. The detailed principles as to calculation of interest are described below and the method of stating a claim, including interest is described in Ch.12.

SPECIAL DAMAGES

Loss of earnings to trial

The general measure of damages is to put the claimant in the position he was in immediately before the accident (restitutio in integrum). Thus, the claimant can claim no more than he has lost. Damages for loss of earnings in this context are not taxable. Therefore, to prevent the claimant being over-compensated, the court takes into the account the tax and national insurance he would have paid (*BTC v Gourley* [1956] A.C. 185; *Cooper v Firth Brown Ltd* [1963] 1 W.L.R. 418) and any compulsory private pension contributions where his pension rights have been left unaffected (*Dews v NCB* [1986] 3 W.L.R. 227). Thus, he is allowed only the net loss and not the gross loss. By this method of assessment the claimant neither gains nor loses. It is the defendant who gains and the Inland Revenue which loses. 4.002

The award may be increased to take into account the likelihood of overtime, promotion, bonuses, etc. A common method of estimating the effect of these factors is to examine the earnings of a comparable employee or employees for a similar period. The court also takes into account the benefit of any income tax rebate the claimant obtains (*Hartley v Sandholme Iron Co.* [1975] Q.B. 600). Since the personal allowances for income tax are calculated on an annual basis a claimant who returns to work after a tax year has started often pays no tax for the first few weeks. This "income tax holiday" also has to be taken into account (*Brayson v Wilmot-Breedon* (1976), unreported).

The effect of these rules is that it is often simpler to calculate damages for past loss of earnings by working on an annual basis. It is necessary to know the claimant's tax position. You then calculate what his earnings would have been if he had worked throughout the tax year (April 6–April 5) and then calculate what his earnings actually were for the period in question. The difference is the net amount attributable to loss of past earnings. Doing the calculation in this way automatically takes into account the tax implications.

Contractual sick pay

4.003 If the claimant has been paid whilst off work as of right under his contract, then of course there is no loss of earnings and none can be claimed. The claimant's right to contractual sick pay thus benefits the defendant rather than the claimant. To meet this, many contracts of employment now guarantee employees a right to sick pay but, in return, the employee is required to pursue a claim for loss of earnings and to reimburse the employer appropriately. This gives an employee a legal entitlement to sick pay and also enables the employee to recover such payments from the defendant. Whether or not an employer is in fact reimbursed is a private matter between the employer and the claimant (as to employer's liability cases, i.e. injuries at work where the employer is the defendant, see *BRB v Franklin* [1993] Law Society's Gazette, June 23, at 8).

State benefits

4.004 The State provides a variety of benefits which may be payable to an injured person. How do such benefits affect the calculation of damages? Some are subject to complex provisions which may lead to refunds being made to the State and deductions being made from the compensation. With others the defendant may benefit at the State's expense by deducting sums from any loss of earnings compensation without having to refund those sums to the State (see para.4.005, below).

The most complicated provisions apply to the State benefits listed in Sch.2 to the Social Security (Recovery of Benefits) Act 1997 ("the listed benefits"). Under the scheme, the defendant (a "compensator") must refund to the State any listed benefits received by the claimant within a certain period (as to which, see below).

In order to protect the claimant the compensator is limited as to the heads of damage (see below) from which he can make deductions. For example, employment related state benefits paid to the claimant are deductible only from certain loss of earnings claims. Attendance allowances paid to the claimant and therefore recoupable by the State are deductible only from compensation claimed for the cost of care incurred during the relevant period. Mobility allowances paid to the claimant and therefore recoupable by the State are deductible only from compensation claimed for loss of mobility during the relevant period. In particular, no deductions can be made from the head of damages known as the "pain and suffering" award (see below). Thus, under the scheme, if the degree of contributory negligence is high the State still gains full recoupment, the claimant gets reduced damages but he will have received full state benefits and it is the defendant who "loses out".

Must a claimant use a listed benefit under the ordinary rules relating to mitigation of loss? In *Eagle v Chambers* [2004] EWCA Civ 1033; [2005] 1 All E.R. 136 the claimant was in receipt of mobility allowance and the question was whether or not she was obliged to invest it in the Government's Motability Scheme. The court answered the question in the negative, stating that mitigation is a rule relating to the assessment of damages. A court cannot insist that any of the benefits listed in Sch.2 should be used in any way to mitigate loss.

The relevant period over which a benefit is paid begins in the case of an accident or injury on the day following the occurrence and in the case of a disease on the day of the first claim for benefit. The period ends five years later or when the final compensation is paid (whichever is sooner). There is, therefore, a definite cut-off point. There is no need to speculate as to the victim's future entitlement to the listed benefits. Obviously, this cut-off point strongly encourages claimants to reach an early compromise of their claims.

Within 14 days of being notified of the claim, the alleged compensator must send a completed Form CRU1 to the Compensation Recovery Unit of the Department for Work and Pensions. This will give personal details of the victim; the accident; the victim's employer, etc. Clearly, it is envisaged that the victim on making a claim must notify the alleged compensator of these details. Some of these are provided for in the letter of claim under the personal injury pre-action protocol (see Ch.6). The claimant's date of birth and national insurance number are to be supplied after the defendant has responded to the letter and confirmed the identity of his insurers (see para.3.4 of the protocol). Thereafter no compensation payment is to be paid until the CRU has furnished the compensator with a certificate of total benefit.

The certificate is obtained by the compensator by the means of Form CRU4. The CRU will acknowledge the application and a certificate will be issued to the compensator stating the amount of the benefit paid or to be paid by a specified date. As the case progresses, clearly more than one certificate may be necessary.

Having now received the certificate the compensator will deduct what he can from the compensation payment and on paying compensation to the victim will provide a certificate of deduction and pay to the CRU an amount equal to the full "listed benefits" within 14 days.

We started this section by asking, how do such benefits affect the calculation of damages? We should end by posing the question, how does an award of damages affect a claimant's entitlement to benefits? The answer is beyond the scope of this book and very much a niche area. However, you might start by considering if a claimant in receipt of means-tested benefits would be assisted by a personal injury trust (see an excellent article in the 2006 *Journal of Personal Injury Law* (JPI Law 2006, 4, 354–360)).

Non-listed benefits

4.005 Other State benefits, including housing benefit and working tax credits, may reduce a claimant's loss of earnings and so lead to a deduction in the compensation otherwise payable even though there is no obligation on the defendant to make any refund to the State (*Clenshaw v Tanner* [2002] EWHC 1848; (2002) L.T.L. September 24, concerning housing benefit.

Section 5 of the AJA 1982 provides that any saving to an injured person which is attributable to his maintenance wholly or partly at the public expense in a hospital, nursing home or other institution is to be calculated and set off against any income lost as a result of the injuries. The saving may be made on food, drink and, in rare cases, rent and council tax. In practice, the calculation is often ignored in the majority of cases as the saving is de minimis. However, in certain cases where the claimant is subject to lengthy detention in hospital the saving may be of some significance.

Redundancy payments are not deducted unless they relate to incapacity to work (*Colledge v Bass Mitchells and Butlers* [1988] 1 All E.R. 536). "Charitable payments" such as money and gifts from friends are not taken into account as a matter of public policy (*Parry v Cleaver* [1970] A.C. 1). Similarly, the claimant is not required to give credit for money received under a policy of insurance where he has paid the premiums (*Bradburn v Great Western Railway Co.* [1874–80] All E.R. 195; *Pirelli General Plc v Gaca* [2004] EWCA Civ 373; [2004] 1 W.L.R. 2683).

Medical expenses

4.006 Section 2(4) of the Law Reform (Personal Injuries) Act 1948 provides that the claimant can claim the cost of private medical treatment. The claimant does not have to show that there were exceptional circumstances to justify private treatment, and the fact that the same treatment may have been available free under the National Health Service is ignored. Defendant's insurers may be willing to finance private medical treatment pre-trial since, if treatment is thereby obtained more quickly, the claimant's claim for damages for pain and suffering (see below) will then be diminished.

A claimant whose need for medical or nursing care is likely to continue after the trial is also entitled to general damages for future medical expenses. The calculation to be made is similar to the calculation made for damages for loss of future earnings (see below).

There must be deducted from any claim in respect of past or future medical expenses any maintenance element those expenses contain (*Lim Poh Choo v*

Camden & Islington Area Health Authority [1980] A.C. 174 and compare AJA 1982, s.5, above, where deductions are made from lost earnings).

In the more catastrophic cases it may be that the claimant's home has to be adapted in order to cope with his disability or even new accommodation may have to be found. All or part of the outlay may be recoverable where necessary based on the multiplier and multiplicand system (for the method of calculation see *Roberts v Johnstone* [1988] 3 W.L.R. 1247).

What is the position if a claimant might receive payments from his local authority in the future towards the cost of his carers? The answer is far from clear. In *Crofton v NHS Litigation Authority* [2007] EWCA Civ 71, *The Times*, February 15, 2007, the Court of Appeal expressed their dismay at the "complexity and labyrinthine nature of the relevant legislation and guidance" (*per* Dyson L.J.). What is clear is that the issue must be raised early by the defendant, normally in the defence, and where appropriate, the local authority should be joined as a party to the proceedings.

Services rendered by third persons

The claimant may claim the value of services provided by third persons (often, in practice, relatives) where those services have been rendered reasonably necessary by the accident. Thus, a claimant may add to a claim for special damages, for example, reasonable expenses incurred and the value of wages reasonably foregone by a relative who visited him in hospital or nursed him back to health (*Hunt v Severs* [1994] 2 A.C. 350 where, in fact, the sums claimed were disallowed on appeal; see further, below). Similarly, general damages may be awarded to cover any future losses and expenses likely to be incurred by third persons.

4.007

In calculating compensation for such services the court awards a capital sum which the claimant will hold upon trust for the voluntary carer. The sum should represent reasonable remuneration taking into account all the circumstances including, in particular, the carer's income or loss of income during the period in question. The amount is likely to be less than the full commercial cost of providing the services rendered by the carer. Also, the services to be rewarded in this way must be nursing, personal or domestic services. No award is appropriate for the voluntary supply of commercial services such as running the claimant's business whilst he is recovering or assisting a blind claimant to resume his working career (*Hardwick v Hudson* [1999] 1 W.L.R. 1770, CA, at 1766 C–D and 1777 D).

In *Hunt v Severs* [1994] 2 A.C. 350 a young couple were injured in a motor cycle accident. The claimant, who had been riding pillion on her boyfriend's bike, was very severely injured. It was held that the accident was caused by his negligence. The trial judge awarded her damages against him exceeding £500,000 which included the following items:

"Special damages: £4,429, reasonable travel costs incurred by the defendant visiting the claimant in hospital and £17,000, the value of nursing care rendered by him up to the date of the trial.
General damages: £60,000, the value of nursing care to be rendered by him in the future."

In the appeal to the House of Lords, all of these sums were disallowed. It was held that the defendant could not be ordered to pay the claimant extra damages simply to enable her to reward him for his generosity. It was said that to award such compensation would be wrong in principle, even though of course, in reality, this principle was protecting the defendant's insurers only and was financially disadvantageous to the defendant himself.

Agreeing special damages

4.008   In practice special damages are normally agreed. The claimant sets out a schedule of losses annexed to the particulars of claim (see para.12.029). Indeed, the exercise may well have occurred under the personal injury pre-action protocol (see para.6.014). Consequently special damages can usually be agreed at an early stage of the action. It is merely a matter of calculation, and the rules are fairly clear. If for some reason the parties cannot agree on the method of calculation, it is best to prepare a statement showing the alternative methods and agree their arithmetic. Then the judge only has to decide the method to adopt and not the actual quantum.

GENERAL DAMAGES

Pain and suffering

4.009   Damages may be awarded for past and future pain and suffering attributable to the injury and to any consequential operations, etc. Such damages are assessed subjectively. The claimant must actually experience pain and suffering for any damages to be awarded under this head. Thus, in *Wise v Kaye* [1962] A.C. 326 the House of Lords held that damages for pain and suffering were not recoverable for a period during which the claimant was unconscious and incapable of experiencing pain and suffering. Similarly, in *Deeley v McCarthy and Leeds Area Health Authority* [1977] C.L.Y. 764 where a boy aged three was seriously injured, the court included nothing for pain and suffering as he was totally unable to appreciate his condition. The award did, however, include a very large sum for loss of amenities.

Damages under this head include compensation for any mental anguish suffered and may take into account any additional, subjective, factors which increase the suffering. Thus, in *Rourke v Barton*, *The Times*, June 23, 1982 the injuries suffered by the claimant prevented her looking after her invalid husband;

the additional distress this caused the claimant was taken into account. If, because of his injuries, the claimant's life expectancy has been reduced, the award for pain and suffering should take into account any suffering caused or likely to be caused by his awareness of that reduction. There is no separate head of damages for loss of expectation of life.

Loss of amenities

The claimant is entitled to compensation for the deprivation of bodily capacity per se (*H. West & Son Ltd v Shephard* [1964] A.C. 326). Thus, an objective element is involved in the assessment. In addition the claimant must also be compensated for being deprived of any recreation or hobbies previously enjoyed. Thus, there is also a subjective element in the assessment. It is therefore necessary to inquire of the claimant what amenities have been lost. For example, a young person who has lost part of their right hand will obviously have suffered some loss of amenity in any case. The damages can be increased where appropriate to take account of the particular circumstances of the case. Thus, the loss of a right arm by a right-handed man whose hobbies include bowling and playing darts will be compensated by a greater award than would have been the case had his sole hobby been watching television. Age is, of course, always a factor, as the younger the claimant, the longer he has to live with the disability.

4.010

Damages for pain and suffering and for loss of amenity are generally assessed together and given as one lump sum. A useful starting point is the guidelines issued by the Judicial Studies Board (*www.jsboard.co.uk*).

Awards of damages under these heads are also available for mental as well as physical impairment including, in particular, damages for nervous shock.

Loss of future earnings

The court will first assess the net annual loss as at the date of trial. It then applies the appropriate "multiplier", and thereby calculates the appropriate lump sum award. What figure should be taken as the multiplier? If the claimant has a life expectancy of, say, 20 years and the net annual loss at the date of trial is, say £10,000, then simply to multiply these two dates together would result in gross over-compensation. The claimant would receive a sum of £200,000 as a lump sum which could then be invested. The interest alone might compensate for actual loss, yet on eventual death of the claimant the capital would still be intact. Thus, the multiplier is far less than the actual expectation of life. The discount to the multiplier also takes account of contingencies, for example, early death or periods of unemployment. This means that in practice multipliers rarely exceed 16 or 17, even if the claimant is young and has a normal life expectancy.

4.011

The objective in setting a multiplier is to arrive at a lump sum which by drawing down both interest and capital will provide exactly the net annual loss or expense in each year of the relevant period. The amount by which a gross figure has to be discounted, to use up capital, can be determined by reference to actuarial tables once the court has decided upon a rate of interest to represent a notional return on capital. The lower the rate adopted, the higher will be the lump sum award which the claimant receives.

Multipliers can be found in a series of tables known as the Ogden tables (named after Sir Michael Ogden Q.C.). The tables are prepared by the Government Actuary's Department and are based on projected future mortality rates. The publication also includes useful explanatory notes as to how the tables should be used. Details can be found at *www.gad.gov.uk*.

Under the Damages Act 1996, s.1, the Lord Chancellor has power to prescribe the notional rate of interest which the courts can use. In 2001 he set a rate of 2.5 per cent and declared his intention not to "tinker with the rate frequently to take account of every transient shift in market conditions". Although the courts have power to adopt a different rate if satisfied that it is appropriate to do so (s.1(2) of the 1996 Act), they have been discouraged from exercising that power save in exceptional circumstances (*Warriner v Warriner* [2002] 1 W.L.R. 1703, CA; *Cooke v United Bristol Healthcare NHS Trust* [2003] EWCA Civ 1370; [2004] 1 All E.R. 7970).

Loss of earnings and loss of marriage prospects

4.012 For most women who marry there is a possibility that, for at least part of their married life, they will cease paid work for a number of years in order to bring up children. This must be taken into account in any compensation for loss of future earnings. But what of the case of a woman or girl who, because of her injuries, is now unlikely ever to work and unlikely ever to marry? She has lost the opportunity to earn, and the chance of happiness which marriage can bring, and the economic support of a husband which would have been important during the child-rearing years. The principles to be applied were considered in *Hughes v McKeown* [1985] 1 W.L.R. 963. Where the prospects of earnings and the prospects of marriage are both nil, a full loss of future earnings award should be made (i.e. without a notional deduction in respect of child-rearing years since there will be none) and an additional sum should be allowed in the pain and suffering and loss of amenity award to cover the loss of comfort and companionship which marriage might have brought. This latter sum should not include any element of economic loss relevant to the loss of prospects of marriage since that has already been allowed for in the loss of earnings award (in the end, the multiplier to be used and the compensation for loss of marriage prospects to be awarded are the same whether the claimant is male or female). In *Housecroft v Burnett* [1986] 1 All E.R. 332 these principles were approved, subject to the qualification that some reduction should be made in the case of a woman who would have received very high earnings.

Loss of earnings and loss of life expectancy

4.013 When a claimant's life expectancy has been shortened by the accident the loss of earnings claim is to be calculated as follows. The relevant multiplier is the pre-accident life expectancy but this is subdivided into two parts: his actual life expectancy (as shortened by the accident) and the remaining balance which is known as the lost years. Each part of the multiplier is subject to its own multiplicand. For the actual life expectancy the multiplicand is the usual one, the net annual loss as at the date of the trial. For the lost years the usual multiplicand is reduced by an estimated sum which is intended to represent what would have been the claimant's living expenses during the lost years (*Pickett v British Rail Engineering Ltd* [1980] A.C. 134). The estimation of living expenses here differs substantially from a superficially similar calculation in Fatal Accidents Act cases (*Harris v Empress Motors Ltd* [1984] 1 W.L.R. 212; *Phipps v Brooks Dry Cleaning Services Ltd*, *The Times*, July 18, 1996). Where a victim of negligence dies (whether instantly, at the time of the accident, or before litigation is completed) his estate may bring proceedings under the Law Reform (Miscellaneous Provisions) Act 1934. The estate is entitled to recover reasonable funeral expenses and any special damages the deceased could have claimed including loss of earnings for the period (if any) between the date of the accident and the date of his death. A claim can also be made for general damages for pain and suffering and loss of amenity, unless, at the time of the accident, the deceased was killed instantly (*Hicks v Chief Constable of South Yorkshire Police* [1992] 2 All E.R. 65). "Lost years" compensation is now restricted to living claimants only. Where the victim of negligence dies instantly, or before litigation is completed, the 1934 Act claim should not include a claim for lost years' compensation. Instead, his dependants will have a claim under the Fatal Accidents Act 1976 (see below).

Loss of earning capacity

4.014 The claimant may be entitled to compensation for loss of earnings capacity even though there is no loss of future earnings. This is to compensate the claimant if he is now at a disadvantage in the labour market were he, for any reason, to lose his job (*Smith v Manchester Corporation* (1974) 17 K.I.R. 1; *Moeliker v Reyrolle* [1977] 1 W.L.R. 132). There are two tests. First, is there a real or substantial risk (rather than a speculative or fanciful risk) that the claimant will at some time before the end of his working life lose his job (or be in some lower paid employment) when but for the persistent effects of the accident, he would be in work (or in better paid work)? If no, then an award will not be made (see, for example, *Johnson v Warren* (2007) L.T.L. May 2). But if yes, then second, the court has to assess this risk and quantify it in damages. How much damages? In *Evans v Tarmac Central Ltd* [2005] EWCA Civ 1820, (2005) L.T.L. December 12, the trial judge had awarded the claimant almost two years loss of full earnings (that figure having become something of a rule of thumb in this area). On appeal this was reduced. Laws L.J. observed:

> "There is no particular evidence whatever to show that this respondent, who continues to work at the quarry, would or will in the course of his working life be thrown on to the labour market ... In the result I do not think that the absence of positive evidence to the effect that the respondent might lose his job is fatal to the Smith v Manchester claim. I would hold, however, that such a claim is likely to be assessed at a much lower figure than where such evidence is available ... There was in my opinion substantial evidence that if the respondent were put on to the market he would be at a disadvantage. The evidence consists in his present and continuing disabilities ... There is no particular evidence as to the risk to the respondent's job and thus his exposure to vulnerability in the job market. On the other hand he would—if in fact thrown on to the market – in my judgment be at a substantial and by no means merely a minimal (far less a theoretical) disadvantage. The absence of any particular reason to suppose that the respondent might be thrown on to the market means in my judgment that the award of £30,000 is much too high. The judge was estimating the prospects of a contingency arising as to which there was no specific evidence. Some allowance had to be made for it as a real and not fanciful vicissitude of life. But the court leans against speculation where there should be proof. In my judgment the appropriate award here would have been £10,000."

Awards of provisional damages and periodical payments for personal injuries (r.41)

Provisional damages

4.015　The basic rule is that the damages to which a claimant is entitled from the defendant in respect of a wrongful act must be recovered once and for all. A claimant cannot bring a second action upon the same facts simply because the injury subsequently proves to be more serious than was thought when the judgment was given (*Fitter v Veal* (1701) 12 Mod. 542). Accordingly, it is crucial to ensure that the evidence before the court is sufficient for the judge to make an appropriate assessment of damages once and for all. Provisional damages are appropriate in cases which might be described as "chance" cases. These are cases where there is a chance, i.e. a possibility which is less than a probability, that the claimant will at some future date suffer very serious additional damage. For example, a claimant who has lost one eye can sometimes suffer later from sympathetic ophthalmia whereby sight is lost in the good eye leading to total blindness. There is a vast difference between the loss of one eye and total blindness. Other examples would be the onset of traumatic epilepsy or certain kinds of mental illness. Previously, if the medical evidence assessed the risk of, say, sympathetic ophthalmia at 5 per cent the claimant would be compensated for that 5 per cent risk. A 5 per cent risk means that for every 100 persons who suffered the injury, 95 would not develop the deterioration that was feared, but five would. Each claimant would be compensated for the 5 per cent risk, thus leading to over-compensation for 95 per cent of the claimants, but gross under-compensation for the unfortunate 5 per cent.

This difficulty can be avoided if the court makes an award of provisional damages under SCA 1981, s.32A, or CCA 1984, s.51. These sections apply to an action for damages for personal injuries in which there is proved or admitted to be a chance that at some definite or indefinite time in the future the injured person will, as a result of the act or omission which gave rise to the cause of action, develop some serious disease or suffer some serious deterioration of his physical or mental condition. The court can award damages on the assumption that the injured person will not develop the disease or suffer the deterioration. These are known as provisional damages. For the majority of claimants the award will also, in practice, turn out to be final. The unfortunate minority of claimants who do then develop the disease or suffer the deterioration can come back to court for further damages at a future date. If such claimants die before the further damages have been agreed or ordered their dependants may commence proceedings under the Fatal Accidents Act 1976 (see Damages Act 1996, s.3).

It is not necessary for the court to make an award for provisional damages in those cases where, although a forecast of future disease or deterioration is given, the court has before it sufficient evidence on which to assess damages once and for all. For example, the medical evidence might forecast that the claimant who has suffered a leg injury will now suffer osteo-arthritis in the injured joint so that by the age of 55 he will not be able to run for a bus, by the age of 60 he will have to walk with a stick, and by the age of 65 he will be in a wheelchair. Although this could be viewed as "a serious deterioration of his physical condition" and there is a "chance" of it occurring, nonetheless this forecast of the claimant's deterioration is a sufficient basis on which damages can be assessed once and for all. This distinguishes a "forecast" case from a "chance" case. In the latter, any assessment (without the ability to award provisional damages) is bound to be wrong.

Example

In *Willson v Ministry of Defence* [1991] 1 All E.R. 638, Baker J. said that "serious deterioration" means a clear risk of deterioration beyond the ordinary deterioration that can normally be expected. C, a naval dockyard fitter, was injured in 1986. He returned to work, but later took voluntary redundancy and opened a store. The injury to his ankle left him with some pain and disability, and medical reports stated that there would be degeneration of the ankle joint with possible arthritis. C claimed provisional damages on the ground that future deterioration might qualify him for a further award. The judge held that the word "chance" in s.32A of SCA 1981 covered a wide range, but the possibility had to be measurable rather than fanciful. "Serious deterioration" denoted a clear risk of deterioration beyond the norm that could be expected, and ruled out pure speculation as to what might happen in the future. The claim for provisional damages failed and a lump sum award was made.

Provisional damages are available in both the High Court and county court. Claims for provisional damages must be stated (see para.12.015). Statements of case are more often than not prepared and served before the claimant's medical condition has stabilised. In all but the most clear-cut cases (where it is obvious that provisional damages are or are not appropriate) practitioners may prefer to include a claim for provisional damages (with a view to not proceeding with it if it turns out to be inappropriate) rather than not state such a claim and then have to seek the court's permission to amend later.

Stating a claim for provisional damages has certain consequences. The claimant cannot later obtain judgment in default (PD 41, para.5.1) but must apply to the court for an order. A defendant may make a Pt 36 offer and agree to the making of an award of provisional damages. The offer must identify the disease or deterioration (see below) in question. If the claimant accepts it he must, within seven days, apply to the court for an order under r.41 (see Ch.29).

An order for provisional damages will specify the disease or deterioration which may occur in the future and will normally specify a period within which the claimant may come back to the court to seek a further award of damages. An application for a further award is governed by r.41.3. It will, of course, be necessary at that subsequent hearing for the claimant to show that the later disease or deterioration in his health is attributable to the tort of the defendant.

The Supreme Court Act 1981, s.32A and CCA 1984, s.51 require that an award of provisional damages must be the subject of an order by the court. Accordingly, where the case has been settled by agreement, application must be made to the court by consent for an order in the form of a consent judgment (see para.34.005). If the claimant is a child or patient, the approval of the court should be sought at the same time (see PD 41, para.4.1). The procedure to be followed where there has been an award of provisional damages both after trial and after settlement is fully explained in PD 41. Amongst other matters it specifies in para.3.2 the documents to be placed on the "case file" which is preserved after an award of provisional damages for use at any subsequent application.

Periodical payments

4.016 As from April 1, 2005, s.100 of the Courts Act 2003 replaced s.2 of the Damages Act 1996 with new ss.2, 2A and 2B. Rules made under the latter provisions can be found in Pt 41, s.II. There is also a separate PD 41B.

Section 2 gives the court the power to order, without the consent of the parties, that damages for future pecuniary loss, namely care costs (see para.4.006) and loss of future earnings (see para.4.011) are wholly or partly to take the form of periodical payments. It requires the court to consider in all cases whether periodical payments are appropriate. In making any decision the court will take into account: the scale of the annual payments after any deduction for contributory negligence; the form of award preferred by the claimant including the reasons for the claimant's preference and the nature of any financial advice in that respect received by the claimant; and the form of award preferred by the defendant including the reasons for the defendant's preference.

The power to make an order without the consent of the parties only relates to awards in respect of future pecuniary loss. The position is unchanged in respect of other damages where the court may only order periodical payments where the parties consent. The court must be satisfied that the continuity of the payments is reasonably secure before it makes a periodical payments order. There is a presumption of this if it is protected by the Financial Services Compensation Scheme or a Ministerial Guarantee given under s.6 of the 1996 Act or where the source of the payments is a government or health service body. In order to try to ensure that the real value of periodical payments is preserved over the whole period for which they are payable, s.2 provides that periodical payments orders will be treated as linking the payments to the Retail Prices Index (RPI). It was expected that periodical payments would be linked to RPI in the great majority of cases. However s.2(9) gives the court power to make a different provision where circumstances make it appropriate and increasingly claimants are asking courts to use different indices, such as the national average earnings index. Why? Because it is said that the real cost of these future losses will not be met by an order linked to the RPI. Whilst such a request is legitimate and a claimant will be allowed to adduce expert evidence at trial on the point (see *Flora v Wakom (Heathrow) Ltd* [2006] EWCA Civ 1103, [2006] 4 All E.R. 982), currently there is no guidance from the Court of Appeal. However, that may well be forthcoming if cases such as *Thompstone v Tameside & Glossop Acute Services NHS Trust* [2006] EWHC 2904, (2006) L.T.L. November 23, are appealed (periodical payments order made linked not to RPI but the Annual Survey of Hours and Earnings). Pending that it may well be that many claimants will prefer to have a lump sum for these future losses, rather than a periodical payments order linked to the RPI, as in *A (a child suing by his father and litigation friend C) v B Hospitals NHS Trust* [2006] EWHC 2833, (2006) L.T.L. November 17.

Can provision be made for a periodical payments order to be varied in the future should the claimant's medical condition significantly alter? Yes, see the Damages (Variation of Periodical Payments) Order 2005 (SI 841/2005).

Structured settlements (PD 40)

In cases of very severe injuries, the claimant may be entitled to compensation sufficient to cover the costs of future earnings loss and future medical and other expenses for the rest of his life. The sums involved, if capitalised, could be huge. The claimant and/or his family may prefer to avoid the immense worry and stress which the investment and management of large sums of money often involves.

Practitioners should always consider advising as to the possibilities of a structured settlement in cases in which the total value of the claim exceeds £500,000. In a structured settlement claimants normally agree a lump sum of damages in respect of past pain and suffering and past expenses and, for the future, a series

4.017

of payments of damages which, from the claimant's point of view, are similar to an annuity guaranteeing a stream of payments for the rest of the claimant's life.

The courts have power to order the payment of damages in this way if the parties consent (Damages Act 1996, s.2). Therefore, structures are arrived at only by settlement, i.e. agreement between the claimant and either the defendant or the defendant's insurers. The structure may well in fact involve the purchase of an annuity, but, for reasons relating to tax avoidance, the annuity will be bought (or sometimes directly financed) by the defendant or his insurers and not by the claimant. Personal injury compensation by way of periodic payments does not give rise to a liability to income tax in the hands of the recipient claimant provided that the agreement is properly drawn up.

The form which is most commonly used provides "indexed terms for life" whereby the claimant will receive until death periodic payments (inflation-proofed by reference to the retail price index) with the option of a pre-set minimum number of payments. This was the form used in the first structured settlement agreement in this country. In *Kelly v Dawes, The Times*, September 27, 1990 the claimant was left permanently brain damaged. Damages worth £410,000 were awarded paid as a lump sum of £110,000, the balance producing an index-linked annuity of £2,130 per month with guaranteed payments for at least 10 years.

For further details of the law relating to structured settlements, see *White Book* 40CPD.1.

Fatal Accidents Act cases

4.018 Under the Fatal Accidents Act 1976, where by any wrongful act a defendant causes the death of a person, an action for damages can be brought against him "for the benefit of the dependants" of the deceased. Although this is a personal action for the dependants and quite separate from any claim made for the benefit of the deceased's estate, the Fatal Accidents claim should be brought by the personal representatives of the deceased. However, if there is no personal representative, or if they fail to sue within six months of the death the action may be brought by all, or any, of the dependants.

The terms "dependants" includes a spouse or former spouse of the deceased; a civil partner or former civil partner of the deceased; a person who was living with the deceased as a husband or wife or civil partner for at least two years immediately before the deceased's death; any parent or other ascendant of the deceased including a person who was treated as a parent; any child or other descendant of the deceased including a child treated as a child of the family by the deceased; and any person who is or is the issue of, a brother, sister, uncle or aunt of the deceased.

The Fatal Accidents Act allows a claim for "damages for bereavement". This claim is only for the benefit of a husband, wife or civil partner of the deceased; or, where the deceased was a minor who never married, for the benefit of his parents. The court awards as damages such sum as may be specified by statutory instrument whether or not the recipient was a dependant of the deceased.

Apart from damages for bereavement, where applicable, the dependant's claim is for loss of their dependency on the deceased. There must be evidence that the deceased contributed to their financial support. This is, of course, usually very simple to prove in the case of a claim by the widow and children, and in such a case the value of their dependency is usually calculated as a proportion of the deceased's earnings. Any benefits which have accrued or will or may accrue to any dependant from the deceased's estate are disregarded.

Compensation for loss of dependency is assessed in two stages: (1) the actual loss to the date of trial; and (2) the estimated future loss, for which a multiplier is used based on the probable length of earning period the deceased would have had. The two assessments are thus similar to the assessment of past and future loss of earnings in personal injury claims. There is one important difference, however. In personal injury claims the multiplier is a figure selected as at the date of the trial. In Fatal Accidents Act cases it is a figure selected as at the date of death minus the number of pre-trial years (*Graham v Dodds* [1983] 1 W.L.R. 808).

Section 4 of the 1976 Act provides that in assessing damages any benefits which have accrued or will or may accrue to any person from his estate or otherwise as a result of his death are disregarded. For an analysis of this provision see *McIntyre v Harland & Wolff Plc* [2006] EWCA Civ 287, [2006] 1 W.L.R. 2577 as applied in *Arnup v MW White Ltd* [2007] EWHC 601, (2007) L.T.L. April 16.

In the case of the death of a non-wage earning wife and mother the court may value the husband's loss by reference to the cost of employing a housekeeper plus the value of "unreplaceable services" (*Regan v Williamson* [1976] 1 W.L.R. 305) or where the husband has reasonably given up work to look after the family, by reference to his lost earnings (*Mehmet v Perry* [1977] 2 All E.R. 529). The loss to any children on the death of the mother must also be quantified. In *Spittle v Bunney* [1988] 1 W.L.R. 847 Croom-Johnson L.J. stated that "where a very young child is orphaned and no substitute is provided, there is a practice of valuing the services of the mother by having regard to the cost of hiring a nanny [but] . . . one cannot value [a mother's services] at a constant figure for the whole of the child's dependency". The Court of Appeal in this case substituted an award of £25,000 for the original "nanny formula" award of £47,500. Does dependency on state benefits mean that there is no financial loss? It will usually be the case that a person in receipt of state benefits will continue to receive them after the death of a partner, thus incurring no loss other than a proportional one to reflect the fact that one person rather than two is now being supported. However, in *Cox v Hockenhull* [2000] 1 W.L.R. 750, CA the claimant was able to prove a loss of dependency: the deceased had received some state benefits which were not taken into account in assessing the couple's income support; on her death these benefits ceased to be payable and therefore the claimant's income dropped back down to the income support level. Is a claim barred if the deceased's claim against one of several concurrent tortfeasors was settled before his death, even if the agreed sum is less than two thirds of his loss? By a majority the House of Lords in *Jameson v Central Electricity Generating Board* [2000] 1 A.C. 455 answered that question in the affirmative. Their Lordships held that a compromise had the effect of fixing the amount of the claimant's claim in the same way as if the matter had gone to trial and judgment had been given in his favour. Where an action was subsequently brought against a concurrent tortfeasor, there was no scope for inquiry as to whether the agreed amount represented the full value of the claim. Consequently, the only question was whether the sum received by the deceased was intended to be in full satisfaction of the cause of action. On the facts it clearly was, and therefore the terms of the settlement extinguished his claim against other concurrent tortfeasors. The date on which the claim was to be treated as having been satisfied was the date on which the settlement was made, unless the claimant was unable to recover the sum due thereunder (*DPP v Turner (John Eric)* [1974] A.C. 357 applied). As the sum due to the deceased under the settlement had been paid in full, his claim against other concurrent tortfeasors was extinguished as from the date of the settlement.

INTEREST ON DAMAGES

4.019   In personal injury actions the court must award interest if the damages exceed £200 unless there are special reasons to the contrary (see Ch.3). Any sums paid by the defendant in respect of interest on personal injury damages are, like the damages themselves, exempt from income tax, whether or not the sums were paid under an order of the court.

Guidelines as to the calculation of interest

4.020   Guidelines, as to the periods for which interest should be allowed and as to the rates of interest which should be used, have been laid down in a series of Court of Appeal and House of Lords cases. Notably, *Jefford v Gee* [1970] 2 Q.B. 130; *Cookson v Knowles* [1979] A.C. 556; *Birkett v Hayes* [1982] 1 W.L.R. 816; *Wright v British Railways Board* [1983] 2 A.C. 773 and *Lawrence v Chief Constable of Staffordshire, The Times*, July 25, 2000. In the last two cases cited it was said that, in the interests of certainty, these guidelines will not in future be subject to frequent change. The guidelines are not rules of law; the trial judge has a discretion (to be exercised judicially) as to whether to follow them. Contrast, for example, *Barry v Ablerex Construction (Midlands) Ltd* [2000] P.I.Q.R. Q263, where a period of delay of five years saw a deduction of two years' interest, with *Eagle v Chambers* [2004] EWCA Civ 1033; [2005] 1 All E.R. 136 where interest was refused for the entire seven years of delay. However, in the interest of simplicity, they are expressed as broad principles to be applied to the generality of cases. The courts are reluctant to depart from them in any particular case unless it is apparent that their application would result in substantial injustice (see *Dexter v Courtaulds Ltd* [1984] 1 W.L.R. 372).

Fatal Accidents Act cases

The damages awarded have to be divided into three categories:

(1) Damages from the date of death to the date of trial carry interest annually for that period at half the average of the special account rates which were in force during that period (see below).
(2) Damages for bereavement carry interest at full special account rate (see *Sharman v Sheppard*, below).
(3) Damages for future loss from the date of trial carry no interest.

Personal injury cases

The damages awarded have to be divided into three categories:

(1) Special damages carry interest annually for the period from the date of accident to the date of trial at half the average of the special account rates which were in force during that period.
(2) Damages for pain and suffering and loss of amenities carry interest at the rate of two per cent per annum from the date of service of court proceedings to the date of trial.
(3) Damages for future loss of earnings, for loss of earnings capacity and for future expenses carry no interest.

Explanation of the guidelines

The "special account rate" is a rate of interest payable in certain, limited, circumstances on money paid into court and invested, for example, on behalf of trustees, children or patients. The current rate (since February 1, 2002) is 6 per cent (see *White Book*, para.7.0.15). In order to calculate what was the average rate for any period it is convenient to consult conversion tables (such as those published from time to time in *The Law Society's Gazette*).

4.021

The reason for awarding interest on certain sums at only half the special account rate is as follows. Most of the sums will have been mounting up at a steady rate over the relevant period but interest is assessed on the total sum for the whole of the period. To simplify the task of calculation the "half rate" guideline should normally be applied even to sums which were not mounting up over the period (e.g. cost of car repairs) or which were not mounting up at a steady rate (e.g. medical bills). However, in a very exceptional case, for example, a claim including a medical bill for an expensive operation which was paid some years before the trial, interest at the full rate may be allowed on that item from the date it was paid (see generally *Dexter v Courtaulds Ltd* [1984] 1 W.L.R. 372; for a case of equal authority to Dexter which suggests a greater readiness to allow the full rate for large items of special damages, see *Prokop v DHSS* [1985] C.L.Y. 1037. You must ensure that the claim is fully stated in the particulars of claim—see Ch.12).

The reasons for allowing interest on pain and suffering and loss of amenity awards at only 2 per cent per annum and from the service of court proceedings (rather than, e.g. the date of the accident) are as follows. A nominal rate of interest is appropriate because the damages in question are assessed by reference to the level of awards as at the date of trial, not as at the date of the accident. Thus the claimant has already been compensated for any depreciation in the value of money which has occurred since the accident: to allow a full rate of interest as well would cause unjustifiable over-compensation. Interest from the date of the accident is said to be inappropriate because, inter alia, at that time the amount of damages to be awarded is not capable of being quantified. The defendant should not normally be required to pay interest in respect of an item, the value of which it is not possible to estimate. Accordingly, a convenient starting point for the award of interest is usually the date of service of court proceedings (see further *Wright v British Railways Board* [1983] A.C. 773 *per* Lord Diplock).

Into which category should one place bereavement damages (see above)? They would appear to be a head of general damages but allowing a nominal rate of 2 per cent per annum seems inappropriate for an item which does not frequently fluctuate in value. If they are to be treated as special damages, the "half rate" guideline seems inappropriate for so large and fixed an item. There is authority for allowing interest at the full rate (*Sharman v Sheppard* [1989] C.L.Y. 1190).

Special reasons for not awarding interest

4.022   There are no guidelines as to what amounts to a "special reason" for not awarding interest. In each case the matter lies in the discretion of the trial judge. In practice, the entitlement to interest has an extremely strong survival rate. In *Davies v Inman* [1999] P.I.Q.R. Q26 a claimant was held entitled to interest on lost earnings even though, in fact, his employers had continued to pay him those earnings on terms that he would repay them from any damages he recovered. Similarly, in *Wadey v Surrey County Council* [2000] 1 W.L.R. 820 the House of Lords held the claimant entitled to interest on that part of his compensation which represented the State benefits he had already received, the value of which the defendant had to pay, not to him, but back to the State (see para.4.004).

ADVISING ON QUANTUM

4.023   How does the solicitor calculate the likely award of general damages? One way is to instruct counsel. This can be a useful practice provided proper use is made of it. Usually, it is better if counsel is asked to give a second opinion or to comment on a specific difficulty that has arisen. As a general rule counsel should not be asked to advise on quantum until the solicitor has first formed a view on the case. The instructions to counsel preferably should not reveal that view.

Counsel's opinion can then be compared with the solicitor's own assessment. It is not essential, however, to instruct counsel in every case. A solicitor doing a large volume of personal injury work will handle far more cases, particularly small ones, than counsel and can often accurately assess damages without the need for a second opinion.

There are several excellent sources for cases on quantum. A useful starting point is provided by the Guidelines for the Assessment of General Damages in *Personal Injury Cases* which is prepared by the Judicial Studies Board and circulated to all judges, recorders and district judges. The main textbook is *Kemp & Kemp, The Quantum of Damages*, which is published in looseleaf format and is regularly updated. There are the monthly publications, *Current Law* and *Halsbury's Monthly Review*. Also, some computer services designed for solicitors are programmed to supply summaries of recent quantum cases. All lawyers specialising in personal injury work develop a "feel" for the case and can instinctively assess the appropriate sum to be awarded as damages for pain and suffering and loss of amenities. Nonetheless, this "feel" is best verified by checking in one of these sources.

CHAPTER 5

Limitation of Actions

INTRODUCTION

5.001   It is of the utmost importance at the first interview to ascertain when the relevant limitation period will expire. The law is set out in the Limitation Act 1980, a consolidating statute which has been amended several times and may undergo further amendment in the future (Law Commission Report on Limitaton of Actions, Law Com. No.270, H.C. 23, July 9, 2001).

We must start by making three important preliminary points. First, a claimant is required only to commence the action within the relevant time period. By PD 7, para.5.1 proceedings are started when the court issues a claim form by dating it. However, if a claim form is received by the court office on an earlier date, the claim is at that point in time "brought" for the purposes of the Limitation Act 1980 and any other relevant statute (*St Helens Metropolitan BC v Barnes* [2006] EWCA Civ 1372).

Our second preliminary point is that, despite the statement in various parts of the Limitation Act 1980 that "an action ... shall not be brought", there is nothing to prevent a claimant starting proceedings out of time. However, unless the case can be brought within one of the extensions of the basic period (see below) the defendant will have an impregnable defence. A defendant must state the defence under the Limitation Act in order to rely on it (see Ch.12, para.12.036).

Finally, it must be remembered that a prospective defendant can waive the right to rely on the limitation defence. To do so there must be a clear, unequivocal, unambiguous and unconditional promise by the prospective defendant that he will not raise the defence that the action is statute barred. The focus is on whether or not he gave up that right. The promise will be construed objectively, not subjectively. The question is whether the correspondence, etc. can reasonably be understood to contain that particular promise. In addition, the prospective claimant must have relied on the promise and altered his position to his detriment; or it must be inequitable or unconscionable not to hold the prospective defendant to his promise (see *Seechurn v Ace Insurance Sa-NV* (2002) 2 Lloyd's Rep. 390).

ORDINARY TIME LIMITS

Actions founded on simple contract or on tort (ss.2 and 5)

Save for those cases to which some other section applies (see below) the basic period is six years from the date when the cause of action accrued, i.e. six years from the date of breach of contract or from the date of commission of the tort. In contract, the cause of action accrues as soon as the contractual duty is broken. However, since negligence is actionable only on proof of damage, an action in negligence accrues only when some damage occurs. This may be a considerably later starting point that the date when the breach of duty occurred (see, e.g. *Dove v Banhams Patent Locks Ltd* [1983] 1 W.L.R. 1436); *Law Society v Sephton & Co.* [2006] 2 A.C. 543). However, personal injury cases apart, most negligence actions are now subject to a long-stop limitation period of 15 years from the date of the defendant's breach of duty (see s.14B of the Act, discussed below).

5.002

The ordinary time limits do not apply to a claim for specific performance of a contract or for an injunction or other equitable relief unless the court, in exercising its equitable discretion, applies them by analogy (see s.36 and see further *Coulthard v Disco Mix Club Ltd* [2000] 1 W.L.R. 707 and P 7) *Nedlloyd BV v Arab Metals Co.* [2006] EWCA Civ 1717).

Defamation cases (s.4A)

For actions for libel or slander the basic period (as amended by the Defamation Act 1996) is reduced to 12 months from the date on which the cause of action accrued. In certain circumstances permission can be granted extending this time limit (see s.32A, below).

5.003

Limitation in respect of certain loans (s.6)

This section applies to any contract of loan which does not make any effective provision as to the time of repayment. In such a case the basic period is six years from the date the lender makes a demand in writing for repayment (instead of six years from the date the loan was made). Section 6 is intended to apply to loans between members of a family or between friends. The section makes good the assumption which is often made in such cases that the time limit applicable to the loan continues indefinitely until a formal demand for repayment is made. In the case of *Boot v Boot, The Times*, May 9, 1996, C had in 1983 agreed to a loan, secured by a promissory note, of £8,000 to his daughter-in-law. No provision was made for the loan to be repaid on demand and no date for repayment was specified. He made a written demand for repayment in 1990 and the Court of Appeal held that the limitation period ran from that date and not when the loan was made.

5.004

Actions on a specialty (s.8)

5.005 For actions on a bond or on a contract under seal the basic period is 12 years unless a shorter period is prescribed by some other section. Under ss.19 and 20 a six-year period is specified for arrears of rent and arrears of mortgage interest.

The term specialty was once defined as "an archaic word of somewhat imprecise meaning: it includes contracts and other obligations in documents under seal, and also, traditionally, obligations arising under statute" *(Franks Limitation of Actions* (1959)) quoted in *Matadeen v Caribbean Insurance Co. Ltd* [2002] U.K.P.C. 69. However, in English limitation law, the latter part of that definition is no longer appropriate. Section 9 of the Limitation Act 1980 provides a six-year limitation period for obligations arising under statute.

Claims for contribution (s.10)

5.006 Where two or more persons are liable in respect of the same damage (e.g. joint tortfeasors, joint covenantors) but only one of them pays or is ordered to pay compensation to the person injured, he is entitled to recover contribution from the other persons liable (Civil Liability (Contribution) Act 1978, s.1). Normally a claim for contribution is raised in the same action in which the person injured seeks compensation (see para.18.004). However, where separate proceedings are contemplated the limitation period is two years from either:

(1) the date on which judgment for the compensation was given, or on which an award was made on an arbitration; or
(2) if there was no judgment or award, the earliest date on which the amount of compensation was agreed between the person being compensated and the person now claiming contribution.

The judgment or award there referred to is judgment or award that ascertains the amount of compensation, not just the existence of liability (*Aer Lingus v Gildacroft Ltd* [2006] 1 W.L.R. 1173, CA).

Personal injury litigation (s.11)

5.007 Where in any action (whether for negligence, nuisance or breach of duty, statutory, contractual or otherwise) the claimant claims damages which "consist of or include damages in respect of personal injuries to the claimant or any other person" the basic period of limitation is only three years. However, this reduced period runs from:

(1) the date on which the cause of action accrued; or
(2) the date (if later) of the claimant's knowledge.

The expression "date of knowledge" is defined in s.14. Basically it is the first date when the claimant knew, or might reasonably be expected to have known, certain specific facts. These include the seriousness of his injury, its cause, and the identity of the defendant. It is important to correctly identify the injury in question: see *H v N & T* [2004] EWCA Civ 526; (2005) P.I.Q.R. P7 When the court is assessing both the significance of the injury and the facts the claimant might reasonably be expected to have known, the tests it must apply are substantially objective (*Adams v Bracknell Forest BC* [2005] 1 A.C. 76 and *McCoubrey v Ministry of Defence* [2007] EWCA Civ 17; see also *Kew v Bettamix Ltd* [2006] EWCA Civ 1535, adopting the test applied in *Haward v Fawcetts* [2006] 1 W.L.R. 682, noted below). Similarly, knowledge or ignorance of the law is irrelevant. However, to cover the exceptional hard case (a claimant who knew the facts but did not know his legal rights, or a claimant who, because of psychological weakness, delayed litigation more than a reasonable person would do) s.33 of the Act provides a discretionary power for the courts to override the time limit where it is equitable to do so. This power is considered at para.5.019.

Although most personal injury claims concern allegations of breach of duty causing personal injury, s.11 is not limited to such cases. Its time limit also applies to claims in respect of personal injuries, not to the claimant, but to another person (*Howe v David Brown Tractors (Retail) Ltd* [1991] 4 All E.R. 30; *Foster v Zott GMBH & Co. Kg* (2000) L.T.L. May 24, CA) and allegations of breach of duty which did not physically cause personal injury to the claimant (*Norman v Ali* [2000] R.T.R. 107; claim following a road accident against a vehicle owner alleged to have caused or permitted uninsured driving).

Section 11 of the Act does not apply to claims for damages for deliberate assault or trespass to the person. Such cases (typically, sexual abuse cases) are subject to the six-year time limit under s.2, a time limit which cannot be extended under s.33 (*Stubbings v Webb* [1993] A.C. 498). In these cases date of knowledge and significance are irrelevant: if the claimant fails to claim within six years of the assault the courts can do nothing further (*A v Hoare* [2006] 1 W.L.R. 2320, CA).

Fatal Accidents Act claims (s.12)

The basic period is three years from the date of death, or the date of knowledge of the person for whose benefit the action is brought, whichever is the later. The s.14 definition of "date of knowledge" applies (see above). Where there is more than one person for whose benefit the action is brought their respective dates of knowledge have to be calculated separately to determine whether any of them should be excluded from the benefit of the action (s.13).

5.008

No Fatal Accidents Act claim can be brought if, when the death occurred, the cause of action of the person injured was already statute barred, whether or not an application by that person under s.33 might have succeeded (s.12(1) of the Act).

Negligence actions in respect of latent damage (s.14A)

5.008A   This section deals with "any action for damages for negligence other than one to which section 11 ... applies" (see above) where facts relevant to the cause of action are not known at the date of accrual. In other words it applies to non-personal injury cases in negligence where, at the time the cause of action accrued, the damage in question was still latent rather than patent. The section provides an alternative limitation period of three years from the date of knowledge of certain material facts (defined in a manner similar to the "date of knowledge" in s.14 (see above). In *Haward v Fawcetts* [2006] 1 W.L.R. 682, the House of Lords held that "knowledge" for the purposes of s.14A meant knowing with sufficient confidence to justify embarking on the preliminaries to the issue of proceedings. Relying on cases dealing with s.14, the law lords held that the limitation period starts to run when a potential claimant had knowledge of the essence of the act or omission to which the injury was attributable and held that the burden of proof as to the earliest date of that knowledge falls upon the claimants.

For the position of subsequent owners of property at a time when damage in respect of that property is still latent, see Latent Damage Act 1986, s.3.

To protect defendants from what would otherwise be a perpetual risk of liability, s.14B provides a long-stop limitation period of 15 years from the date of the alleged breach of duty. Like s.14A, s.14B applies to actions "for damages for negligence, other than one to which section 11 ... applies". However s.14B is wider in ambit than s.14A; the long stop can bar a cause of action before it has accrued (see s.14B(2)).

It is now settled that s.14A applies only to actions for negligence and does not apply to actions in which the claims arise solely in contract (*Société Commerciale de Réassurance v ERAS (International) Ltd* [1992] 2 All E.R. 82 and the cases cited therein). However, it is also now settled that tortious duties and contractual duties with the same content can co-exist. Thus, in a negligence claim against professional advisers the claimant my frame his case in tort simply to obtain the advantageous limitation period it enjoys (see *Henderson v Merrett Syndicates Ltd* [1994] 3 W.L.R. 761, HL, at 781A and 789B and *Nelson v Rye* [1996] 1 W.L.R. 1378 at 1389A–C).

New claims in pending actions (s.35)

5.009   To ascertain whether a claim is statute-barred one must measure the time period between the date the cause of action arose and the date of commencement of proceedings. But some claims can be raised as part of an existing case and thus without the issue of a separate claim form. The claimant may do so by amending the original action (see Ch.12 para.12.050). The defendant may do so by stating a set-off, making an additional counterclaim or bringing an additional third party action (see Ch.18). Section 35 defines when, for limitation purposes, these claims are deemed to be commenced. Claimants' actions made by amendment and all set-offs and counterclaims are deemed to have been commenced on the same date as the original action. All claims made in third party proceedings are deemed to have been commenced on the date the additional claim form was issued.

As far as third party proceedings are concerned the deeming provision of s.35 may not seem very important. The limitation period for claims for contribution (two years) does not begin to run until the main action is determined (see s.10 noted above). The limitation period for claims for indemnity (six years) does not begin to run until the extent of the liability to be indemnified is known (see s.5 and *R. & H. Green & Silley Weir v British Railways Board* [1985] 1 W.L.R. 570). Thus, at first sight, s.35 appears to be saying "claims which are made today must be made before tomorrow". In fact the importance of the provision, and indeed the main purpose of s.35, concerns the making of amendments after the expiry of a limitation period. When is it fair to allow parties to an existing action to raise by way of amendment matters which would be statute-barred if they attempted to raise them in a new action? This aspect of s.35 is dealt with in Ch.12, para.12.053.

Mortgage actions (s.20)

How long does a mortgagee have to sue for the principal and interest? In *Bristol & West v Bartlett* [2002] 4 All E.R. 544, the Court of Appeal reviewed the relevant law and held that claims for a mortgage debt are governed by s.20 even if the mortgagee has exercised the power of sale before issuing proceedings. So there is 12 years from when the cause of action accrues for a mortgagee to sue for the principal but only six years pursuant to s.20(5) to sue for interest. *Bristol & West* was approved by the House of Lords in *West Bromwich Building Society v Wilkinson* [2005] 1 W.L.R. 2303.

5.010

EXTENSION OR EXCLUSION OF ORDINARY TIME LIMITS

The Limitation Act 1980 provides for several exceptional cases in which the basic periods can be extended.

5.011

Disability (ss.28 and 28A)

Limitation periods do not begin to run against a child until he dies or comes of age. They do not begin to run against a patient until the patient dies or recovers. Thus a child born in 1990 who suffered personal injuries in 1995 could commence a valid action at any time until the year 2011 (i.e. three years after attaining the age of 18; see the facts of *Tolley v Morris* [1979] 1 W.L.R. 592, HL).

5.012

Section 28A applies to cases governed by ss.14A and 14B. It provides an extension to the special three-year limit for claimants who are not under a disability when the cause of action accrues, but are when the special limit starts to run. Thus the period will run from the date of cessation of disability or death but subject to the 15-year-long stop period (see above).

SUPERVENING BANKRUPTCY OR LIQUIDATION OF THE DEFENDANT

5.013 This exclusion of ordinary time limits does not arise from the Limitation Act but from the ordinary operation of insolvency law. A debt which is provable in a bankruptcy or liquidation does not become barred by lapse of time if it was not so barred at the date of the bankruptcy order or the date of the winding up order or resolution in question. This is because the insolvency in effect removes the creditor's right to commence litigation against the insolvent, leaving him to claim instead under the trust which is created comprising all of the insolvent's assets.

> "It is not simply that time has stopped running against a creditor; the cause of action itself is destroyed and replaced by other rights." (HH Judge Paul Baker Q.C. in *Re Cases of Taffs Well Ltd* [1992] Ch.179).

These principles can lead to surprising results as the decision in *Financial Services Compensation Scheme Ltd v Larnell (Insurances) Ltd* [2006] Q.B. 808 shows. In that case, certain investors had the right to make claims for damages in respect of alleged negligent pensions advice. The ordinary six-year time limit for their claims expired in June 1995 at the latest but, the damage they alleged being latent, the extended time limit under s.14A did not expire until May 8, 2000. Their claims were assigned to the claimant who did not commence proceedings until September 2004. The Court of Appeal held that the claims were not statute barred. The defendant had been wound up on May 3, 2000, a few days before the extended limitation period had expired. Because time was still running under s.14A at the winding up, the Limitation Act was irrelevant to the proceedings, even though those proceedings had been commenced nearly nine years after expiry of the basic limitation period, four years after expiry of the extended limitation period and nearly two years after expiry of the long stop limitation period under s.14B (15 years from the date of the alleged breach of duty).

In many cases the fact that limitation periods have become irrelevant because of insolvency will bring no comfort at all to an intending creditor. The fact that the proposed defendant has become insolvent means that the intending creditor must now queue up with other creditors and so may have little prospect of recovering more than a fraction of the value of his claim, if that, even if he acts swiftly. Delayed proceedings against insolvents will have practical effect only if some previously undiscovered assets are later located or if, as in *Financial Services*, the insolvent was insured in respect of the claim and the intending claimant wishes to exercise rights under the Third Parties (Rights Against Insurers) Act 1930 (see paras 6.028 and 7.023).

Debts: acknowledgment or part payment (s.29(5))

Where a debtor acknowledges his indebtedness or makes a part payment in respect of the debt the creditor's right of action "shall be deemed to have accrued on and not before the date of the acknowledgment or payment". The policy behind this exception is that a creditor should be given more time to negotiate for the payment of an admitted indebtedness without the fear that the claim will become statute barred. To be effective for the purposes of s.29 an acknowledgment must be "in writing and signed by the person making the acknowledgment" (s.30). In *Bradford & Bingley Plc v Rashid* [2006] 1 W.L.R. 2066, the House of Lords held unanimously that, so long as the acknowledgment admits liability, it need not contain an admission of a definite amount or of an amount ascertainable by mere arithmetic. The House also held, but only by a majority, that an admission made in the course of "without prejudice negotiations" cannot be relied upon as an acknowledgment for the purposes of the Act. For the effect of an acknowledgment or part payment on persons other than the maker or recipient, see s.31.

Section 29(7) provides that a current limitation period may be repeatedly extended by further acknowledgments or payments but a right of action once barred cannot be revived by any subsequent acknowledgment or payment.

5.014

Fraud, concealment or mistake (s.32)

In each of the following cases the relevant limitation period is six years from the date the claimant discovers the fraud, concealment or mistake or could with reasonable diligence have discovered it:

5.015

(1) where the action is based upon the fraud of the defendant or his agent;
(2) where any fact relevant to the claimant's right of action was deliberately concealed from him by any such person;
(3) where the action is for relief from the consequences of a mistake.

Note that the words "reasonable diligence" require only the taking of such steps (if any) as an ordinarily prudent claimant would take (*Peco Arts Inc v Hazlitt Gallery Ltd* [1983] 1 W.L.R. 1315).

For the effect of this section on persons who are innocent third parties see ss.(3) and (4).

In category (2), deliberate concealment, it matters not whether the concealment was made initially or subsequently (*Sheldon v R H M Outhwaite (Underwriting Agencies) Ltd* [1996] A.C. 102). In *Cave v Robinson Jarvis & Rolf (a firm)* [2002] 2 All E.R. 641, the House of Lords posed the question whether the words "deliberate commission of a breach of duty" in s.32(2) of the 1980 Act meant "deliberate commission of an act or omission, being an act or omission which gives rise to a breach of duty" or simply "deliberate breach of duty". The distinction drawn by earlier case law was between intentional wrongdoing on the one hand and negligence or inadvertent wrongdoing on the other. The House held that s.32 deprives a defendant of a limitation defence in two situations: (i) where he takes active steps to conceal his own breach of duty after he has become aware of it; and (ii) where he is guilty of deliberate wrongdoing and conceals or fails to disclose it in circumstances where it is unlikely to be discovered for some time. But it does not deprive a defendant of a limitation defence where he is charged with negligence if, being unaware of his error or that he has failed to take proper care, there has been nothing for him to disclose. See further *Williams v Fanshaw Porter and Hazelhurst* [2004] EWCA Civ 157; [2004] 1 W.L.R. 3185.

However strange it may be, it seems that cases falling within s.32(2) will also fall within s.14A (negligence actions in respect of latent damage, para.5.009, above). But, unlike the s.14A, s.32(2) applies not only to negligence, but to any cause of action and allows a claim six years, rather than three years after the date when the claimant could, with reasonable diligence, have discovered the breach. Most significant of all, claims within s.32 are not subject to the long stop period of 15 years which might otherwise apply (s.32(5)).

Defamation cases (s.32A)

5.016 As already noted, the basic limitation period for actions for libel or slander is only 12 months from the date on which the cause of action accrued (see s.4A, above). In this instance, knowledge (or ignorance) of the accrual is irrelevant: contrast ss.11, 12 and 14A. However, s.32A does give the court a discretion to allow for commencement at a later time. The intending claimant must apply for the exercise of that discretion within one year of the earliest date on which he or she knew "all the facts relevant to" the cause of action. The section does not say which facts are the relevant facts for this purpose, but see further as to this, *C v Mirror Group Newspapers* [1996] 4 All E.R. 511. The application for permission should be made by application notice in the usual way (see Chs 13 and 14) served on the potential defendant to the defamation action (*Oyston v Blaker* [1996] 1 W.L.R. 1326). As to the circumstances in which the court might exercise its discretion, see *Steedman v BBC* [2001] EWCA Civ 1534.

Consumer Protection Act 1987

5.017 This Act renders producers and (in defined circumstances) suppliers of products strictly liable for personal injury, death or damage to "consumer" property (other than the defective product itself) caused by defective products. There is no claim for property damage alone unless the property was for private use and consumption and the damages exceed £275. Schedule 1 introduces s.11A into the Limitation Act 1980. The section imposes a 10-year-long stop on actions for breach of the statutory duty. Time runs from when the defendant supplied the defective product to another. Contrary to the normal rule that the claimant's rights are merely barred and not extinguished, after the 10-year period the right of action is extinguished. For actions for personal injury (including actions which survive for the benefit of the estate under the Law Reform (Miscellaneous Provisions) Act 1934) the basic time limit is otherwise the same as under s.11, i.e. three years from the date when the cause of action accrued (or death) or the date of the injured person's knowledge, whichever is the later. This same basic limit also applies to an action for loss of, or damage to, property. For actions under the Fatal Accidents Act 1976 for death caused by a defective product, the basic limit remains that laid down in s.12 of the Limitation Act 1980 (see above) subject to the 10-year-long stop. The s.33 discretion to disapply the basic time limits (see below) applies to all actions under Pt 1 of the 1987 Act with the important proviso that there is no discretion to disapply the ten-year-long stop period.

Section 28(7) of the Limitation Act deals with the extension of the limitation period in cases of disability: the 10-year-long stop overrides the normal disability provisions in s.28 (see above) which otherwise apply.

Section 32(4A) provides that the 10-year-long stop also overrides the normal provisions concerning deliberate concealment of facts relating to a cause of action under the 1987 Act.

Personal injury and death claims (s.33)

In personal injury and death claims the ordinary time limit is three years from the date the claimant knew he had a cause of action (see ss.11, 12 and 14 noted above). The ordinary time limit does not cover cases where claimants know all the facts but, until too late, do not know the law. Thus, ignorance of the law does not give a right to bring an action late, but in such cases s.33 of the Act gives the court a discretion to disapply the time limit where it thinks it is equitable to do so after taking into account two matters: first, the degree to which the claimant is prejudiced by the provisions of s.11 or s.12, and secondly the degree to which the defendant would be prejudiced if an order disapplying that time limit were made. In acting under this section the court must have regard to all the circumstances of the case and in particular to six specified matters including "(a) the length of and the reasons for the delay on the part of the claimant" and "(f) the steps if any taken by the claimant to obtain medical, legal or other expert advice and the nature of any such advice he may have received". Note that in *KR v Bryn Alyn Community* [2004] 2 All E.R. 716, the Court of Appeal stated that, as a general rule of thumb, the longer the delay after the occurrence of the matters giving rise to the cause of action, the more likely it is that the balance of prejudice will swing against disapplication.

5.018

Applications under s.33 are usually dealt with pre-trial as a preliminary point (see para.33.006). This is because it is essential for the court exercising the discretion to consider each of the matters specified in the section and to systematically take account of each one.

Section 33 gives the court a general discretion to inquire into the merits of many personal injury cases begun outside the limitation period to see whether justice would be better served by denying the defendants the opportunity to take what may well be an arbitrary and unmeritorious defence. But the judge cannot base his judgment on a finding that the claimant had acted "reasonably". That is not the correct statutory test under s.33 (*McGhie v British Telecommunications Plc* [2005] EWCA Civ 48). Of the six factors specified in s.33 the first two factors, length of and reasons for delay and the effect which the delay has had on the evidence available to the defendant, are often the decisive ones. (The other four factors deal with the conduct of the parties and the duration of any period of supervening mental incapacity suffered by the claimant. Note that the court is not limited to considering only these factors. It is also relevant to consider the strength of the claimant's case, i.e. the claimant's chances of success even if the limitation defence is defeated).

Examples

In *Hartley v Birmingham City District Council* [1992] 1 W.L.R. 968, C notified D of her claim within six weeks of the accident. The proceedings were issued one day late. Both parties accepted that, but for the limitation point, C had a cast-iron case on liability against D and that, but for this application, C also had an unanswerable claim against her solicitors. C's application under s.33 was successful.

In *Dobbie v Medway Health Authority* [1994] 1 W.L.R. 1234, in April 1973 C underwent an operation for the removal of a lump from her breast with a view to it being analysed to check whether or not it was malignant. In fact, the surgeon also removed the breast entirely. Shortly afterwards she was told that the lump had not in fact been malignant. In May 1988 C found out from radio and newspaper reports about another case similar to her's in which compensation had been sought. C then contacted solicitors who promptly contacted D and proceedings were issued in May 1989. In 1990, an expert appointed by C's solicitors prepared a report stating that the surgeon who conducted C's operation had not followed the correct procedure. The Court of Appeal held that, for the purposes of s.14 (see above) the three-year limitation period began in 1973, when she had been told that the lump was not in fact malignant. Her application under s.33 failed.

In *Coad v Cornwall Health Authority* [1997] 1 W.L.R. 189, C was a hospital nurse who, in 1983, suffered a significant back injury while at work. Although the injury caused her severe health problems thereafter she continued at work until, in 1990, after yet another relapse, she accepted that her career as a nurse was over. She then sought legal advice and, in 1991, gave notice of her claim to D and, in 1993, commenced proceedings against D. C did not dispute that the three-year limitation period had begun in 1983: the length of her delay therefore exceeded seven years. However, throughout that time she had had an honest and genuine belief that she had no cause of action so long as her employment as a nurse continued. Her application under s.33 was successful. The Court of Appeal held that, under s.33(3)(a) the "reasons for the delay" should be considered subjectively (contrast other parts of s.33(3) and s.14). Therefore, in an application under s.33 ignorance of the law, even a foolish or unreasonable ignorance, can provide a good excuse.

In *Kew v Bettamix Ltd* [2006] EWCA Civ. 1535, the claimant had worked in the building trade for over thirty-five years, first as a labourer and then as an asphalter. He suffered injuries to his hands caused by the vibrating equipment he used at work. In the 1990s he attributed his symptoms to age. In March 2000 he was told by a company doctor that the injuries may have been attributable to his working conditions. This was confirmed by the company doctor in July 2000 when annual medical reviews were recommended. However, these reviews never took place. By 2003 the claimant was aware that other employees had brought claims for compensation and proceedings on his behalf were commenced in April 2004. The Court of Appeal held that the relevant date of knowledge was March 2000 (see further paras 5.007 and 5.019, above) but held that the trial judge's decision to disapply the time limit under s.33 was correct. It was appropriate to take into account the defendants' conduct prior to proceedings (i.e. not arranging the annual reviews which their doctor had recommended). Over the period of delay (about thirteen months) the defendants had received claims for compensation from other employees and so had been put on notice as to the need to investigate and record facts. On the question of proportionality (i.e. the cost of proceedings in comparison to the relatively low amount of damages likely to be awarded if the claim was successful) the court held it was necessary to take into account also the strength of the claimant's claim.

In *Smith v Hampshire County Council* [2007] EWCA Civ. 246, the claimant brought a claim for damages for education neglect, alleging that his school had failed to diagnose or adequately treat his dyslexia. He was educated in the defendants' schools between 1986 and 1993. The limitation period began either in October 1996, on his eighteenth birthday, or later in October 1998 when he consulted his GP. Proceedings commenced in January 2002, just over three years after he had consulted his GP but less than three years after he had obtained a report from the clinical psychologist to whom his GP had referred him. The Court of Appeal upheld the trial judge's decision that the date of knowledge was October 1998 at the latest and that the time limit should not be disapplied. Although the period of delay was short (just over three months) the evidence of prejudice to the defendant was strong because of the absence of documentation after the passage of so much time between the completion of the claimant's schooling with the defendants and the commencement of court proceedings.

Section 33 and "second action cases"

In *Walkley v Precision Forgings Ltd* [1979] 1 W.L.R. 606, the claimant issued proceedings in 1971, just within the limitation period, but that action was dismissed. In 1976 he issued a second set of proceedings and asked the court to disapply the time limit. The House of Lords held that the purpose of (what is now) s.33 is to enable courts to alleviate the prejudice suffered by claimants who do not start proceedings within the relevant limitation period. From this the House concluded that if, as in this case, a claimant does start an action within time but fails to proceed with it, it is not thereafter open to him to take advantage of s.33. The House reasoned that, since the claimant had previously started

5.019

an action within the three-year period, the time limit plainly caused him no prejudice.

Cases subsequent to *Walkley* indicated a marked unwillingness to apply it unless it was plainly indistinguishable. After more than 25 years the House of Lords has decided to depart from (i.e. overturn) their decision in *Walkley*. In *Horton v Sadler* [2007] 1 A.C. 307, the claimant was injured in a road accident. The defendant was not insured and, although proceedings were issued within the limitation period the claimant failed to give the requisite notice to the Motor Insurers' Bureau (MIB), as to which, see para.6.028, below. In order to cure this mistake the claimant issued a second set of proceedings in which the MIB was given appropriate notice but this second set of proceedings was issued outside the limitation period. The House of Lords allowed an appeal against the findings of the lower courts that there was no jurisdiction to hear an application under s.33. The House accepted that the decision in *Walkley* was anomalous: claimants whose solicitors had failed to issue proceedings at all within the limitation period were better off than claimants whose solicitors had issued proceedings but failed to serve them correctly. Further, the *Walkley* decision wrongly restricted the wide and unfettered discretion that Parliament had intended to confer on the courts in s.33. In *Walkley* the House had wrongly construed the words "an action" in s.33 so as to confine them to the first action brought where there was more than one action. Whilst allowing the appeal, the House also upheld the lower court's ruling to disapply the time limit if it had power to do so. In this case, the claimant had a strong claim against his solicitors and their indemnity insurers in respect of the negligent failure to serve the first claim form correctly. However, that did not outweigh other factors: in a straightforward case in which the delay was short and understandable and caused the MIB no forensic prejudice at all, the judge was entitled to take the view that a motor insurer (or in default, the MIB) was the primary source of compensation for the victim of a road traffic accident.

FOREIGN LIMITATION PERIODS

5.020 The Foreign Limitation Periods Act 1984 affects cases in which an English court has to apply foreign law (e.g. a contract action in which the contract validly adopts French law). The limitation period is that provided by the foreign law. English law continues to govern questions as to whether and when proceedings have been commenced. The Act creates exceptions on grounds of public policy and for cases involving undue hardship. For a case illustration see *Gotha City v Sotheby's (No.2), The Times*, October 8, 1998.

CHAPTER 6

The Preliminary Stages of Litigation

THE FIRST INTERVIEW

When the client first makes contact with the firm, brief but important details should be taken. In most offices it is the receptionist who will have the initial contact with the client. Suitable training needs to be given to ensure clients are allocated to the appropriate fee earner and at least some information is collected about the purpose of the appointment. A valuable lesson can be learnt from the case of *Pilbrow v Pearless De Rougemon & Co.* [1999] 3 All E.R. 355. In that matter the client told the receptionist that he wanted to see a solicitor about family law but he was thereafter advised (quite competently it appears) by someone who, unbeknown to him, was not a solicitor. The Court of Appeal held that the defendant was not liable to pay for the services provided as the claimants had failed to perform their contract to provide legal services by a solicitor. A solicitor may be held guilty of negligence if he fails to check to see if his client has the benefit of any before the event (BTE) insurance (*Sarwar v Alam* [2002] 1 W.L.R.125; *Garrett v Halton Borough Council* [2007] 1 W.L.R. 554 at [69]; and see paras 2.006 and 2.008). Similarly, a solicitor may be held guilty of negligence if he fails to consider at the outset whether his client might be eligible for legal aid (*David Truex v Kitchin* [2007] EWCA Civ 618; and see para.2.020). 6.001

Before seeing a new client, ensure you familiarise yourself with any available material. The client may well be nervous and tense, especially if he has not consulted a solicitor before. An initial exchange of pleasantries and a brief discussion of any information you already have will help put the client at ease. Then ask the client why he has consulted you and what he wants you to do for him. It is important to let him tell his story in his own words and manner. Clients are not always clear about what is relevant to their problem but do not be too eager to interrupt. The client will not be satisfied that a topic is unimportant unless you allow him to tell it to you in the first place. Moreover, a point that on first hearing may sound irrelevant, could well be crucial at a later date. Nevertheless, you will have to strike a balance because some clients will talk incessantly if you give them the opportunity.

After the client has had his say, there are six main tasks for you to perform:

Identify the client's agenda

6.002 Ask yourself: what is the client really seeking to achieve, legally or otherwise? You need to manage the case from day one and that includes managing the client's expectations. For example, debt collection to a client means physically recovering the money and not just "winning" the case by securing an order for payment. At the end of the first interview summarise the steps you and the client should take and the reasons for these.

Identify the correct parties

6.003 It is vital to ensure you know who you act for and who are all the potential parties to any action. As a general rule "all persons to be sued should be sued at the same time and in the same action" (*Morris v Wentworth-Stanley* [1999] Q.B. 1004). For further details see Ch.7.

Take the client's statement

6.004 This will, of course, form the basis of the case. You will rely on it to draft the letter of claim (see para.6.008 below) and prepare particulars of claim (see para.12.011) if proceedings are started.

Give general advice on the law

6.005 The key to resolving any legal dispute is to identify from the outset the relevant issues. In a personal injury claim, for example, you must consider how each of the "ingredients" of negligence will be established, i.e. duty of care, breach, causation and damage. As a case develops you should continually review which issues remain in dispute and how those are to be proved. However, at this stage use simple language to explain to the client the general law as it applies to the facts he has described to you.

Emphasise the overriding objective

6.006 The client must appreciate that the court sees litigation as a last resort. Moreover, negotiations and litigation will not be a long, drawn-out game of poker but very much a "cards on the table" exercise. The parties and their solicitors should co-operate with each other. Further, the client who insists that litigation must be conducted "as a matter of principle" and regardless of the fact that costs will outweigh any possible return, must equally be reminded of the court's own principle of proportionality.

Answer the client's questions

"How much will it cost?" Even if the client does not ask, you must address this point (see Ch.2). 6.007

"How much will I get if I win?" Every client with a personal injuries (see Ch.4) or compensation claim will ask this question. Likewise every defendant wants to know what it will cost him if he has to pay.

"How long will the case take?" Tell the client the steps that will have to be taken. Outline the appropriate pre-action protocol timetable (see para.6.013 below) and also how the case will progress if proceedings have to be started.

FIRST STEPS IN THE PREPARATION OF EVIDENCE

The client's statement

Never delay taking a statement. Memory fades and evidence disappears. So if the client has a document dealing with a point, get it now. As the client is telling the story, jot down the main points and ask questions to obtain further relevant information. Some solicitors record the whole interview. Probe, but do not prompt. Bear in mind that the statement should be in your client's own words and not yours. Let the story develop in chronological order and ensure any gaps are filled. If any part of the story is unclear, seek clarification at this stage. 6.008

Prepare a draft of the statement (see Ch.14) and send it to the client for approval. Flag up clearly where any further details are needed. It is best practice to have the client sign and date this first draft before returning it to you. Second and subsequent drafts should also be signed and dated.

Preparing for disclosure

Voluntary pre-action disclosure of documents is dealt with below. Disclosure by court order, both before and during court proceedings, is considered fully in Ch.30. From the outset the client must appreciate the nature of disclosure and the obligations it imposes on him. After identifying the issues in the case you will need to discuss with the client the location of any documents which either support or damage his case. It is important to emphasise to the client that if he knows about a document which undermines his own case in any way he must make you aware of it now. Consideration then needs to be given to retrieving all the relevant documents. After deciding the types of documents it is reasonable for the client to look for, and where he will conduct that search, ask him to carry out that exercise and bring the documents to the next interview. Thereafter you must, as the case develops, review with the client the requirement of disclosure. 6.009

Obtaining official records

Police accident report

6.010　If, in a road accident case, it is likely that the police attended the scene, write to the chief superintendent of the area where the accident happened and ask for a copy of any accident report that is available. You should quote any known police reference number or otherwise give the date, time, place, names of parties, makes of cars, etc. A fee is payable. A standard report contains statements taken from the parties and any witnesses, measurements, a sketch plan and sometimes photographs. In due course you may need to interview the investigating officer. You will need to arrange this and a further fee is payable.

Criminal proceedings

The police will not release any report until any criminal proceedings have been concluded. If proceedings are ongoing you should discuss with your client if anyone is to attend the trial to make notes of the evidence. Where the defendant is convicted, that conviction may be admissible in a civil trial and if properly relied on by the claimant may reverse the burden of proof (see para.12.024).

Inquests

In a fatal accident case you will need to discuss with the client if he wishes you to represent him at any inquest. If so that will allow you to put questions to any witnesses provided that assists the coroner in reaching a verdict as to the cause of death. Even if the client does not want formal representation it is often prudent for someone to attend to make a note of the evidence.

Employer's accident report book

In respect of injuries suffered at work employers are required to keep an accident report book. In addition an inspector from the Health and Safety Executive may have prepared a report. You should obtain these (see further below).

Inspecting and photographing property, etc.

6.011　In many cases you should carry out some form of inspection after receiving the client's initial instructions. You will find that it helps to build a firm mental picture of what the client says happened. For example, the scene of a motor accident should usually be photographed, sooner rather than later, as skid marks disappear, lamp posts get mended, etc. The photographs will show the degree of visibility from a junction; the width left for other vehicles to pass and so on. Where vehicles were involved and there are no police photographs do not rely on the police observations, for example, "front offside wing-dented". What is the size and depth of the dent? Find out where the vehicles are and arrange for photographs to be taken. If six months later, after the dent has been beaten out, a dispute arises over the speed of the vehicles, an expert may be able to assess such from a photograph of the dent.

In the case of an accident at work, any machine concerned should be inspected as soon as possible and certainly before any alterations are carried out. The accident may have brought to the employers attention a danger of which they were previously unaware and they may well wish to modify the machine. You must get in first and have the machine photographed and inspected. Most employers through their insurers agree to facilities for inspection. Try also to obtain any specifications for or brochure about the machine. Contact the manufacturers if the employers do not deal with your request. In cases of difficulty consider making an application for pre-action disclosure of documents (see para.30.024) and/or inspection of property (see para.27.031).

If the client has sustained personal injuries it is advisable to obtain photographic evidence at an early stage. You may have to arrange this in co-operation with the client's medical advisers if any dressings have to be removed.

Interviewing witnesses

Witnesses often say, "But I have already given a statement to the police" or "the man from the insurance company" or whoever. There is no "property" in a witness. Any person is entitled to interview them and sometimes witnesses need to be reassured on this point. 6.012

You need to use tact and persuasion when taking a statement. Always let the witness tell you his version of the story in his own words. Do not prompt or make any challenges until you have heard the whole tale. You may then decide that some parts of the statement are unclear or otherwise appear unreliable. For example, the witness tells you, "The sports car came through the red traffic light at one hell of a speed and knocked down the poor bloke." But what exactly did the witness see? When did he first observe the sports car? When did he look at the traffic light? How did he assess the speed of the car? Where was the victim when he first saw him? Some witnesses reconstruct what they genuinely believe was the cause of the accident. The reality may be that the witness never saw the accident. He may have heard the screech of brakes, looked up at the traffic lights which he noted were red, saw the victim on the road in front of the car and drew his conclusions from that. Beware, very few witnesses deliberately lie but some can try to be too helpful. See our tips on preparing witness statements for trial at para.14.006.

Pre-action protocols

These are procedures which seek to minimise, if not avoid altogether, the delays and expense of litigation. By requiring each side to give timely and sufficient details of their case, they enable potential litigants to negotiate with cards on the table. As litigation is to be a last resort, failure to follow a protocol step or its spirit, without good reason, will usually incur a sanction (see para.33.011) in any proceedings that are taken. 6.013

A practice direction deals with the implementation of pre-action protocols generally. At the time of writing, nine approved protocols have been published: personal injury (which includes a rehabilitation code at annex D), disease and illness, clinical negligence, housing disrepair, possession claims based on rent arrears, construction and engineering disputes, defamation, judicial review and professional negligence. It is anticipated that either further protocols will follow or the approved protocols may each become a schedule to a general pre-action protocol.

Paragraph 1.4 of the Protocols Practice Direction states that the objectives of the protocols are to; (a) encourage the early and full exchange of information about a prospective claim; (b) enable parties to settle claims without litigation; and (c) support the efficient management of any proceedings that are issued. The protocols therefore seek to discourage parties from conducting tactical manoeuvres. For example, most protocols provide that a minor breach by one party does not exempt the other from following the protocol.

If proceedings are issued the court will expect the parties to have complied in substance with the terms of any approved protocol. As and when an additional protocol is approved, a practice direction will specify the date after which compliance or non-compliance with it will be taken into account by the court. However, where no approved protocol exists the court still expects the parties to:

"follow a reasonable procedure, suitable to their particular circumstances, which is intended to avoid litigation. The procedure should not be regarded as a prelude to inevitable litigation. It should normally include (a) the claimant writing to give details of the claim; (b) the defendant acknowledging the claim letter promptly; (c) the defendant giving within a reasonable time a detailed written response; and (d) the parties conducting genuine and reasonable negotiations with a view to settling the claim economically and without court proceedings" (para.4.2).

The Rules enable the court to take into account compliance or otherwise with a protocol when giving directions for the management of a case and making costs orders (see Ch.38). In addition, para.2.3(4) provides that a claimant might be penalised by the award of less interest, or a defendant by having to pay interest at a higher rate, not exceeding 10 per cent above base rate (see Ch.33).

The seven key elements to the protocols are as follows:

(i) content of the letter of claim;
(ii) timetable for acknowledgments and responses from the defendant;
(iii) content of the defendant's response;
(iv) instruction of experts;
(v) disclosure of documents;
(vi) negotiations and ADR; and
(vii) costs.

The standard letter of claim

If no approved pre-action protocol applies, what should you put in the prospective claimant's letter of claim? Set out fully but concisely the legal and factual basis of the claim so that the prospective defendant can investigate it without requiring extensive further information. Ask for a prompt acknowledgment of the letter, usually within 21 days, followed by a full written response within a reasonable period. For many claims the PD suggests that this will be one month. If appropriate, state that court proceedings will be issued if the full response is not received within that time period. The prospective defendant's attention should be drawn to the court's powers to impose sanctions for failure to comply with the PD and a copy of the PD should be enclosed if the prospective defendant is likely to be unrepresented. See further para.4.3.

6.014

The Personal Injury Protocol provides that immediately after collecting sufficient evidence to substantiate a realistic claim, and before addressing issues of quantum in detail, the claimant should send to the proposed defendant two copies of a letter of claim. One copy is for the defendant and the other to pass on to his insurer. If the insurer is known, the letter must also be written to it direct. Sufficient information must be given so the defendant's insurer or solicitor can commence investigations and at least put a broad valuation on the "risk". The letter should therefore briefly summarise the circumstances of the accident and why the defendant was at fault, as well as indicating the nature of the injuries suffered and outlining any financial loss incurred. A standard format of letter should be used. The personal injury protocol has a specimen version and the other protocols provide templates or lists of contents.

Timetable for acknowledgment and response by defendant

The Protocols PD suggests that the prospective defendant is usually given 21 days to acknowledge receipt of the letter of claim and one month to provide a full letter of response. The acknowledgment letter should justify why any longer period for a response is necessary. See further para.4.4.

6.015

The Personal Injury Protocol recommends that the defendant should reply within 21 calendar days of the posting of the letter of claim (or 42 days if the accident occurred outside England, Wales or the defendant is outside the jurisdiction). The claimant may "safely" issue proceedings provided he waits for that period to expire and receives no response. A word of caution is necessary here. There will still remain the possibility of the court imposing a sanction if the claimant has acted unreasonably, for example, by carelessly sending the letter to the wrong address.

The defendant has a maximum of three months from acknowledging the letter of claim to investigate it and respond (or six months if the accident occurred outside England, Wales or the defendant is outside the jurisdiction). However, whilst the protocol recognises that the timetable may have to be varied according to the circumstances of each case, when any proceedings are issued the parties will be asked to justify any variation-see Pt C of the allocation questionnaire which is discussed at para.9.036. Obviously, if you are consulted by a client close to the end of any relevant limitation period (see Ch.5), then you will need to issue sooner, rather than later, but you should still give the defendant as much notice of the intention to issue as is practicable. Once proceedings have been started the parties should consider asking the court for a direction to stay proceedings for a specific period of time whilst the protocol steps are followed.

The defendant's response letter

6.016 How should the prospective defendant respond if he disputes all or part of a claim that is not governed by an approved protocol? The letter of response should identify which of the prospective claimant's contentions, if any, are accepted and which are disputed. Detailed reasons should be given for the latter. See further para.4.6.

Paragraph 2.12 of the Personal Injury Protocol provides that if proceedings are issued the parties' statements of case (see Ch.12) do not have to be limited to the matters contained in the letters. This does not mean that as a claimant's solicitor you can simply fire off letters of claim that have not been carefully prepared. Likewise, a defendant's response should be well thought out and reasoned. Indeed, it is best practice to have the client approve the letter before it is sent to ensure it accurately represents the client's case. The protocol does provide that no point should be taken in any proceedings unless the party who has changed their position (between writing the letter and preparing their statement of case) obviously intended to mislead the other party. However, advocates may well seek to cross-examine a party at trial on such a point with a view to undermining his credibility.

Disclosure of documents

6.017 The Protocols PD provides that the letter of claim should enclose copies of essential documents relied on and ask for disclosure of any key documents that the prospective defendant can supply. Likewise the prospective defendant's letter of response should enclose copies of essential documents which are relied on, along with copies of any documents requested by the prospective claimant, or an explanation for their omission. Disclosure should also be requested of any crucial documents in the prospective claimant's possession who should provide these within a reasonably short time or explain in writing why he is not doing so.

If the defendant denies liability he should send with his response letter any documents in his possession which are material to the issues identified by the letter of claim. The Personal Injury Protocol provides that these documents may be limited to those that the court would be likely to order on an application for pre-action disclosure or disclosure during the proceedings (see Ch.30). Indeed, the protocol sets out a suggested list of documents that are likely to be material in different types of cases, for example, vehicle maintenance records (road traffic accident) and accident book entry (work place accident). The claimant in the letter of claim, or later, may also indicate to the defendant which classes of documents are considered relevant for early disclosure. However, the claimant should note para.2.10 which states that early disclosure of documents by the defendant is to promote the exchange of relevant information to clarify or resolve issues in dispute. The claimant is not thereby given a licence to set out on a "fishing expedition" for documents.

A direct reference to a claimant giving early disclosure of documents is in para.3.13 of the Personal Injury Protocol which provides that a schedule of special damages, with supporting documents, should be provided by the claimant to the defendant as soon as practicable, particularly where liability is admitted. However, as the protocol prevents insurers from giving a bare denial of liability, they will no doubt request further information from the claimant in order to give a "proper" response. In particular insurers may request copies of any statements taken from witnesses. In most cases it will be simple enough to resist this argument on the basis that the insurer must already have sufficient evidence to prepare the response letter. However, the claimant will have to give serious consideration to disclosing his favourable witness statements, such as appear reliable and credible, at this stage. Note that para.10.3 of the Disease and Illness Protocol provides that "prior to proceedings it will be usual for all parties to disclose those expert reports relating to liability and causation upon which they propose to rely".

It should be noted that in June 2006 the Law Society announced that an agreement had been reached with the health sector that there is a rebuttable presumption that no patient records will be requested by a party for claims below £10,000. The agreement does not appear to be well known or, in any event, applied. Most claimant solicitors will want to check the consistency of their client's version against their medical records, as well as ensuring all relevant medical points are addressed. In many cases, regardless of the amount claimed, defendant insurers will wish to scrutinise the claimant's medical records.

Experts

The client will want to know from the outset if he will "win". Very often the answer will be that the advice of a suitably qualified expert is necessary. This presents the client with a choice. Does he get you to instruct that expert immediately to establish the strengths or weaknesses of his case or just wait and see? Getting a favourable report now will allow the client to proceed with confidence. Moreover, if the client is prepared to give early disclosure of the contents of that report to the defendant, it might just lead to a settlement. Should the client unilaterally show the defendant his expert evidence at this stage? It must be recognised that this will allow the defendant plenty of time for his own expert to consider the report and "pick holes in it". This matter is further discussed at para.23.002.

6.018

The protocol encourages the joint selection of, and access to, experts. However, the report still "belongs" to the party that instructs the expert and there is no obligation to disclose its contents. A suggested letter of instruction can be found at Annex C of the protocol. When is a joint expert desirable? See the discussion at para.23.006, but in this context it arises most often in respect of obtaining a medical report from a suitably qualified and experienced expert on the issue of quantum. Before a party instructs an expert ("the first party") he should give the other party ("the second party") a list of the names of one or more experts in the relevant speciality. If within 14 days the second party makes no objection or does not object to all of those suggested, then the first party should proceed to instruct one of the mutually acceptable experts. However, should the second party object to all the listed experts, both parties may instruct experts of their own choice. Where no reasons are given for the objection, press for such since a court may subsequently decide that this was unreasonable conduct during the protocol procedure and penalise your opponent in costs in any proceedings that are taken.

Your client is entitled to impose reasonable terms when agreeing to be examined by the defendant's medical expert. Suitable conditions might include that:

(1) the defendant will pay the costs of the client attending the examination and any loss of earnings involved;
(2) the defendant's doctor will consider only the injuries and will not discuss the accident with the client any more than is necessary for the purpose of preparing the medical report; and
(3) no other person will be present, apart from the client and the doctor carrying out the examination. In some cases, however, bear in mind that the client may wish, or need to have, a relative or helper present.

Can the client refuse to be examined by the defendant's preferred medical expert? In *Starr v National Coal Board* [1977] 1 All E.R. 243 the Court of Appeal upheld a stay of the claimant's action where he had refused to submit to an examination by a named doctor but had agreed to an examination by anyone else. As a general rule it is the defendant's right to nominate the doctor he wishes to use. In certain limited circumstances a claimant might reasonably refuse, for example, a female claimant with an injury who would prefer to be examined by a female doctor. However, if the attack is on the competency of the doctor, then the court must be satisfied that a "just determination of the cause" will be more difficult to achieve with this particular doctor's report compared to that prepared by any other doctor. In such circumstances the claimant's solicitor should remember that medical evidence can be attacked in the same way as other evidence. If the defendant wishes to obtain evidence which is likely to lack credibility and is easily discredited, why should the claimant wish to prevent this?

Is the client entitled to refuse to submit to a medical examination by the defendant's expert which is unpleasant, painful or even risky? In *Aspinall v Sterling Mansell* [1981] 3 All E.R. 866, the court at first instance held that a defendant is not entitled to a stay of proceedings if the claimant's refusal to have the examination is reasonable because it involves a real risk of serious injury. That test was indorsed in another first instance case, namely *Prescott v Bulldog*

Tools [1981] 3 All E.R. 869. However, in that case the judge had to consider the defendant's request to have the claimant examined for a fifth time when it was proposed that three tests would be carried out. The judge found that the claimant reasonably objected to each test and that for two out of the three tests the reasonableness of his objections outweighed the reasonableness of the defendant's requests for such. However, it was held reasonable for the defendant's expert to carry out the third test as the claimant had already had it performed earlier by his own expert. As the judge commented, it was a pity that arrangements had not been made for a joint test to have occurred.

Can the opponent's solicitor insist on viewing your client's injuries himself? In *Francom v Williams* (1999) C.L. May 43, C and D had a car accident and both suffered from personal injuries. C sued D who counterclaimed for her own injuries which included scarring to her left leg. A medical report and photographs had been disclosed. D was willing to be medically examined by C's doctor but she was not prepared to let C's solicitor view her scars as he wished. C's solicitor argued that there was no advantage in a medical person viewing the scarring. The purpose was to form an opinion as to damages and was it more appropriate for a lawyer rather than a medic to do that. C applied for an order that D's action be stayed unless she submitted to an inspection of her scarring by C's solicitor. It was held that an order of this kind with appropriate safeguards was a last resort and should be made only where it had plainly been indicated as being necessary by medical reports on both sides.

It is important to note that if proceedings are subsequently issued and the second party made no objection to an expert nominated under the protocol by the first party, then the second party will not be entitled to rely on their own expert evidence within that particular speciality unless either the first party agrees, or the court so directs, or the first party's expert report has been amended and the first party is not prepared to disclose the original report.

The cost of a report from an agreed expert will usually be paid by the instructing first party. The best practice is to get written instructions to incur the fee and to ensure that you have sufficient funds on account as it is your professional duty to pay the expert. If your client has any relevant insurance cover, check carefully the policy term (see para.2.008).

Either side may send to an agreed expert, via the first party's solicitors, written questions on his report relevant to the issues. As to this topic in the context of court proceedings, see para.23.019. The expert should send his answers separately and directly to each party. The protocol provides at para.3.20 that the cost of the replies will usually be met by the party which asks the questions. We would recommend that the instructing first party should instruct any expert on that basis and any party asking questions might first—sensibly obtain an estimate of cost.

Where the defendant admits liability in whole or in part, any medical report obtained by agreement pursuant to the protocol should be disclosed. The claimant should delay issuing proceedings for 21 days to see if the case is capable of settlement (see below).

THE PRELIMINARY STAGES OF LITIGATION

Negotiations and Alternative Dispute Resolution (ADR)

6.019　The Protocols PD provides that the letters of claim and response should give details of any form of ADR that the prospective party might be prepared to engage in. Moreover, at para.4.7 it provides that the parties should consider whether some form of ADR procedure would be more suitable than litigation, and if so, endeavour to agree which form to adopt. The parties are warned that "if this paragraph is not followed then the court must have regard to such conduct when determining costs." Similar points are made in the approved protocols (e.g. paras 2.16 to 2.19 of the personal injury protocol; paras 5.1 to 5.4 of the clinical disputes protocol; paras 3.7 to 3.9 of the defamation protocol). Paragraph 5 of the construction and engineering disputes protocol requires the parties to arrange a pre-action meeting as soon as possible after the receipt of the defendant's letter of response (or, where there is a counterclaim, after receipt by the defendant of the claimant's letter of response to the counterclaim). The aim of the meeting is for the parties to agree what are the main issues in the case, to identify the root cause of disagreement in respect of each issue, and to consider how best to resolve these disagreements. Everything said at the meeting is to be treated as "without prejudice" (see para.6.024 below) but, if proceedings are later taken, the court may be told whether or not a meeting took place, who attended and who did not attend.

The professional negligence protocol provides for a six-month negotiation period unless the defendant denies the claim in its entirety and makes no proposals for settlement. If proceedings are commenced the active case management by the court includes encouraging them to use an ADR procedure where appropriate (r.1.4(2)(e) and see para.34.002)). Moreover, the parties will be asked in Pt A of the allocation questionnaire if they want the action stayed for one month to attempt to settle (see para.9.028).

As to ADR generally see Ch.34.

Costs

6.020　Paragraph 3.6 of the defamation protocol states that, in formulating both the letter of claim and the response, and in taking any subsequent steps, the party should act reasonably to keep costs proportionate to the nature and gravity of the case and the stage the complaint has reached. An important point relevant to all protocols is set out in para.4A.1 of the Pre-action Protocol Practice Direction. According to this provision, a person who intends to claim from an opponent costs in respect of any success fee he has agreed to pay or in respect of any insurance cover he has obtained should so inform the other potential parties to the claim. The practice direction does not state when the information should be given or what precise information should be given. Best practice is to follow the procedure which will apply if and when proceedings are commenced, i.e. to give information at the earliest opportunity using the prescribed form N251 (see further para.2.023).

What if a prospective claimant fails to send a letter of claim and starts proceedings without giving the prospective defendant any warning? If the claimant loses, he is likely to be ordered to pay the defendant's costs on the indemnity basis. If he wins, the claimant may be deprived of some of his costs: see *Phoenix Finance Ltd v Federation Internationale De L'automobile*, *The Times*, June 27, 2002. However, the court will probably not reduce the costs of a successful claimant if it is more than likely that the situation would not have been any different had a letter before claim been sent: see *Merial Ltd v Sankyo Co. Ltd* [2004] EWHC 3077; (2004) L.T.L. December 16.

Where proceedings occur after one party has been in serious breach of a pre-action protocol, the court may be persuaded to penalise that party in costs at an early stage, for example, if the case is adjourned for mediation to take place: see *Charles Church Developments Ltd v Stent Foundations Ltd* [2007] EWHC 855, (2007) L.T.L., June 18.

Letters of claim in a debt action

At the time of writing there is no pre-action protocol for debt claims. However, a draft protocol suggested the following contents for the letter of claim: 6.021

(a) The identity of the claimant and proposed defendant.
(b) The basis upon which the debt arose, for example, identify the invoice or contract. We recommend that a copy is always enclosed for ease of reference as well as to ensure that the proposed defendant cannot subsequently allege that he never received a copy.
(c) A statement of the principal amount owing.
(d) An indication of when that amount should have been paid.
(e) A statement of the aggregate sum sought.
(f) A date by which the sum must be paid in order to avoid a claim.
(g) The method for making payment. This should be simple and obvious, for example, cheque, postal order, direct debit or standing order. Do not forget to say who the cheque or postal order should be made payable to. In respect of direct debits or standing orders the appropriate bank details need to be included.
(h) A warning of costs and interest penalties if the letter is ignored. Do not claim anything that the client is not entitled to at this stage, for example, interest may not be payable (see Ch.3).
(i) A telephone number and/or address to which queries or reasons for non-payment can be directed.

In addition, we suggest you remind the proposed defendant that he may take independent legal advice if he wishes to do so and that he should pass the letter to his solicitors promptly. The draft protocol recommends that the defendant should reply within such time as is reasonable and not less than seven days after the date of the posting of the letter of claim. It is preferable to specify in the letter the calendar date for a response before court proceedings will be commenced.

NEGOTIATIONS WITH A VIEW TO SETTLEMENT

6.022   Negotiations are conducted throughout the whole of a case, from the defendant's response to the letter of claim until compromise or the trial is reached. Many cases are settled before a claim form is issued and of the claims started, only a small percentage reach trial. A solicitor conducting civil litigation therefore needs to be a skilled negotiator and proceedings can be looked upon as just another stage of negotiation.

Successful negotiations are more desirable than successful litigation. A reasonable compromise saves the client the expense and worry of a trial yet he has still "won". The psychological pressure of litigation on a client must never be underestimated. If the case proceeds to trial usually one party wins which necessarily means that the other loses. How much better if they both win!

What makes a good negotiator? First and foremost, you need to be a good lawyer-to know all the relevant law applicable to the case-so as to be able to assess the strengths and weaknesses not only of the client's case but also that of the other parties. A knowledge of court procedure is also important here. The lawyer needs to know all the steps available to be used if necessary and appropriate, for example, pre-action disclosure (see para.30.024); preservation and inspection of property and interim injunctions (see para.27.031); further information (see para.32.001). At all times you must bear in mind the overriding objective set out in r.1 (see para.1.006). Secondly, you need to know thoroughly the facts of the case in hand and to do the relevant groundwork and preparation. The likely areas of dispute must be identified in advance. Evidence must be obtained and assessed. Always enter negotiations after a realistic assessment of what the client can hope to gain by them and let the client judge his success by how far those aims are achieved.

Compromise

6.023   As a matter of strict law a solicitor has no implied or ostensible authority to compromise a claim before the issue of proceedings. After commencement the solicitor does have ostensible authority if acting bona fide and not contrary to the express instructions of the client of which the other party is aware (see *Waugh v M.B. Clifford & Sons Ltd* [1982] Ch.374). However, compromise is not a matter which should be left to the construction of fine points of law. Unless given express authority, preferably in writing, you should conduct negotiations making it clear that any agreement reached will be provisional only and subject to the client's decision. As to the pitfalls to avoid when drafting settlement terms see Ch.34.

Without prejudice

6.024   Negotiations should normally be conducted "without prejudice". Without prejudice to what? The negotiations are without prejudice to any trial that may ultimately occur. Nothing said or done is admissible in evidence should negotiations fail and the matter proceed to a trial.

In *Unilever Plc v The Procter and Gamble Co.* [2001] 1 All E.R. 783, the Court of Appeal held that the without prejudice rule is wide enough to cover all statements made by each party touching upon the strength or weakness of its own case and its opponent's case and any valuation, for whatever reason, it placed on its or its opponent's rights. The rule covers not only admissions but assertions. This result accords with the policy, which pervades the CPR, of encouraging pre-litigation settlements. In the case, the without prejudice discussions of the parties held before the action commenced were negotiations genuinely aimed at a settlement and therefore such could not be relied upon by the claimant in the action.

The protection is not acquired by stating that a conversation, meeting or letter is "without prejudice". It is the purpose of the activity that holds the key. For example, merely adding the words to a defamatory letter does not prevent it being admissible in a libel action. Conversely, omitting the words from a genuine offer of compromise may not prove fatal if, for example, the letter is clearly written to commence or continue negotiations. In practice always ensure that you make it clear if a telephone conversation, meeting or letter is "without prejudice". The opposite of without prejudice correspondence is known as "open correspondence", i.e. either the sender or recipient may rely on the contents of the letter at trial.

It is immaterial whether the without prejudice negotiations occur before and/or during litigation: See *Barnetson v Framlington Group* [2007] EWCA Civ 502, *The Times*, June 11, 2007.

Example

In *Bradford & Bingley Plc v Rashid* [2006] UKHL 37, [2006] 1 W.L.R. 2066, the trial judge had held that a letter written by an advice centre on the claimant's behalf, explaining that he could not afford to pay the outstanding balance of his mortgage debt, was an open letter. By the time the matter reached the House of Lords the question was simply whether the without prejudice rule applies not merely to attempts to resolve a dispute over the existence or extent of a liability but also to discussions as to how an admitted liability was to be paid. The House held that the rule has no application to open correspondence that is designed only to discuss the repayment of an admitted liability rather than to negotiate and compromise a disputed liability. The letter did not contain statements or offers made with a view to settling a dispute; as the debt was admitted, there was no dispute.

In two circumstances without prejudice statements are admissible in evidence at trial:

(1) If both parties consent, or, expressly or by implication, waive their right to object: for an example of an implied waiver see *Turner v Fenton* [1982] 1 W.L.R. 52.

(2) If, as a result of without prejudice negotiations, the parties reach a concluded contract of compromise. If one party disputes that an

agreement has been made, the court may look at the correspondence to determine the point.

An interesting example of (2) is provided by *Pars Technology Ltd v City Link Transport Holdings Ltd* (1999) L.T.L. July 7, in which the claimant alleged that a binding agreement had been reached with the defendant concerning the mishandling and loss of a consignment of computer materials. The settlement was said to be evidenced in two letters dated February 7, 1996 and February 12, 1996. In the first letter the defendant wrote offering to pay £13,500 together with a full refund of carriage charges of £7.55 plus VAT on the carriage charges. The claimant wrote the second letter in reply stating that the defendant's offer to pay £13,507.55 plus VAT was accepted. The defendant contended that this was not an effective acceptance of their offer since it proposed different terms, i.e. VAT was to be paid on the principal sum as well as the carriage element. After considering the matter the judge concluded that a contract had been reached in accordance with the offer made in the first letter. The Court of Appeal upheld that decision holding that it was plain in reading the two letters, whatever alleged difference there was in the second letter, it did not intend to vary the offer or add new terms but simply repeated the offer in a slightly different way. It was unreasonable to construe the second letter without reading the first letter. The second letter clearly stated that the claimant accepted the offer made in the first letter.

What if a party wishes to refer the court to without prejudice correspondence on the question of costs? For example, the parties may have discussed the reasonableness or otherwise of using ADR in such correspondence. This will only be possible if the correspondence is clearly marked "without prejudice save as to costs": see *Reed Executive plc v Reed Business Information Ltd* [2004] EWCA Civ 887; [2004] 4 All E.R. 942.

Part 36 offers

6.025   As we have seen, before litigation starts the parties are encouraged to negotiate and settle the claim. It is open to the parties to make "without prejudice" offers to settle and Pt 36 formally recognises this.

A claimant can offer to settle a monetary claim for a specified sum (and/or on express terms for any non-monetary claim). If this is not accepted by the defendant, but at trial the claimant is awarded the same or a greater sum than he proposed in his Pt 36 offer, then the defendant is likely to suffer a heavy financial penalty.

A defendant can also make Pt 36 offers. If a defendant's Pt 36 offer is not accepted by the claimant, but at trial the claimant is awarded the same or less than the defendant's Pt 36 offer, then the claimant is likely to suffer a heavy financial penalty.

The clinical disputes protocol outlines the potential use of Pt 36 offers in that area. The claimant may make an offer which generally should be supported by a medical report which deals with the injuries, condition and prognosis, and by a schedule of loss with supporting documentation. The level of detail necessary depends on the value of the claim. Medical reports may not be required where there is no significant continuing injury, and a detailed schedule might be unnecessary in a low value case. The healthcare provider should respond to that offer, preferably with reasons. The provider may make its own offer to settle, either as a counter-offer to the patient's, or of its own accord, but should support it with any medical evidence and/or that relating to the value of the claim which is in its possession.

This topic is dealt with in detail in Ch.29.

Pre-action negotiations as to costs

6.026 Before concluding a pre-action contract of compromise, it is important to deal with costs. A pre-action offer to settle made by a defendant under Pt 36 must include an offer to pay the costs of the offeree incurred up to the date 21 days after the offer was made (see Ch.29). Similarly, an intending claimant who seeks his costs should explicitly say so in any offer to settle he makes. If the parties can agree upon the main relief and remedies claimed, but cannot agree upon costs, it is possible to commence simple costs-only proceedings solely to have the amount of reasonable costs assessed (r.44.12A as to which see para.39.001).

Now consider cases in which the intending claimant has entered into a CFA with success fees or is liable in respect of AEI or similar cover. It will usually be unwise to reveal, for example, the amount of success fee claimed before the defendant has agreed to pay costs in principle. This is because, if no agreement in principle is made, the intending claimant will have to commence the main proceedings solely to obtain an order for costs (*cf. Vehicle & General Insurance Co. Ltd v H & W Christie Ltd* [1976] 1 All E.R. 747). Revealing the success fee contended for may prejudice those proceedings. If the opponent will agree to pay costs in principle, the amount of those costs could be assessed in costs-only proceedings (see above). However, would such costs include the reasonable amount in respect of success fees and insurance premiums? The safest course for the claimant may well be to ensure that the agreement specifically states that the paying party agrees to pay reasonable sums in respect of these items. If the paying party will not agree to that, start the main proceedings and rely on the *Vehicle & General* case.

MOTOR INSURERS

The claimant's policy

6.027 If a client's car, properly parked on the highway, is damaged by another driver but the client has obtained comprehensive insurance for the car, then he may make a claim on that policy. However, there may be three disadvantages of doing this:

(a) He may lose his no-claims bonus (or one or more "steps" of the bonus).
(b) He will have to pay any policy "excess", i.e. the uninsured element such as the first £100 of damage.
(c) He will not get any compensation for loss of or damage to property in the car not covered by insurance.

For these, smaller, sums the client may consider suing a known defendant. If the claim is for £5,000 or less it can be brought in the county court where it should be dealt with fairly informally on the small claims track (see Ch.20). In such a case it may well be that the claimant's insurers are also intending to sue the defendant in order to get back what they can of the sums that they have paid to the claimant. Under the so-called rights of subrogation the insurers can require the claimant to lend his name to such an action. The insurers should not start proceedings until they have informed the claimant, at which time he may tell them to sue also in respect of the uninsured losses (b) and (c) above. Similarly, a claimant should not sue for any uninsured losses without first notifying his insurers in case they wish to bring an action (see *Buckland v Palmer* [1984] 1 W.L.R. 1109).

The defendant's policy

6.028 Consider now a claim against an insured motorist by any person, including a pedestrian or passenger injured in the accident. The claimant has no rights under the defendant's policy directly except where the defendant is made bankrupt and the Third Parties (Rights against Insurers) Act 1930 applies, as fortified by the Road Traffic Act 1988, Pt VI. These rights are very limited and are subject to many restrictions (for further details see Halsbury's Laws (4th edn.), Vol.25, para.768 et seq. and see *Motor and General Insurance Co. Ltd v Pavey* [1994] 1 W.L.R. 462).

A claimant may have statutory rights outside the policy under the Road Traffic Act 1988, s.151. Where the claimant obtains judgment against a driver he can, subject to two limitations, enforce it against any insurer who issued a certificate in respect of the insured vehicle. The claimant can enforce the judgment in this way "notwithstanding that the insurer may be entitled to avoid or cancel, or may have avoided or cancelled the policy". Sometimes the insurers who have to satisfy the claimant's judgment are not even the defendant's insurers.

Example

Nigel's car insurance covers only himself and his wife. Nigel lends his car to a friend, Fred who has no car and consequently no insurance. Fred negligently runs down Liz. Liz can sue Fred and subject to notice having been given (see below), Nigel's insurers will have to satisfy the judgment (s.151(2)(b)).

The two limitations on the claimant's right to enforce under s.151 are:

(1) The section applies only to a judgment "in respect of any such liability as is required to be covered by a policy of insurance under s.145", i.e. liability for: (a) the personal injury or death of any other person; (b) the cost of emergency hospital treatment; and (c) damage to property other than the insured vehicle itself and goods carried in it for hire or reward.

(2) No sum is payable in respect of any judgment unless before or within seven days after the commencement of the proceedings the insurer is given notice of the bringing of the action (s.152).

As to the giving of notice, there is no prescribed form for you to use. Best practice is to write to the insurers giving them notice immediately before a claim form is issued specifying the court in which proceedings are to be commenced and the approximate date of commencement (see *Harrington v Pinkey* [1989] R.T.R. 345). Make this a habit in every road accident case. To be doubly safe also send a follow up letter enclosing a copy of the claim form. In a case where it is not yet clear whether an insurance company or the MIB (see below) will meet the claim it is sensible to give notice to both. In an exceptional case, oral notice given to a legal secretary at the office of the insurer's solicitors may suffice: see *Nawaz v Crowe Insurance Group* [2003] EWCA Civ 316; *The Times*, March 11, 2003.

If you fail to give notice in time you should seriously consider discontinuing the proceedings and starting again, even if this involves applying to set aside a default judgment you have obtained (see *O'Neill v O'Brien*, *The Times*, March 21, 1997). The option of discontinuing and starting again was not open to the claimant in *Wake v Page*, *The Times*, February 9, 2001, where the limitation period had expired before the problem about failure to give notice was appreciated. It was held that any judgment obtained against the defendant would not be enforceable against the insurers even though the insurers had taken several steps in the proceedings including serving a defence and giving disclosure.

THE MOTOR INSURERS' BUREAU (MIB)

The MIB is an independent body voluntarily set up and financed by the motor insurance companies to settle claims brought by injured persons in cases in which the driver is either uninsured or untraced. The Bureau has made two main agreements with the Government. Copies are available from the Stationery Office or the Bureau's website (*www.MIB.org.uk*). The full text should be studied whenever you are dealing with a particular case. In outline, the agreements are as follows.

6.029

MIB (Compensation of Victims of Uninsured Drivers) Agreement

6.030
(1) The agreement applies only to compulsory risks (see above).
(2) The claimant must sue the driver in the usual way.
(3) Especially in the case of an accident occurring on or after October 1, 1999, there is a long list of trip wires to surmount and deadlines to obey in the period from issue to trial. These include giving the MIB "proper notice" of the issue, then service of proceedings, notice of receipt of a defence, of amendments to the particulars of claim and of receipt of a trial date. In most instances "proper notice" is not just a letter. Copies of court documents, correspondence and details of any relevant insurance which the claimant has must also be given. Care is necessary as this part of the MIB agreement is something of a procedural nightmare.
(4) The claimant must obtain judgment against the driver. If it remains unpaid for seven days the MIB will pay it (including costs).
(5) The judgment must be assigned to, or to the order of, the MIB.

MIB (Compensation of Victims of Untraced Drivers) Agreement

6.031
(1) The current agreement came into effect on February 14, 2003.
(2) Like the uninsured drivers' agreement, strict procedural requirements must be followed.
(3) There must be proof that the untraced driver was negligent. The MIB will carry out a full investigation.
(4) The death or injury must not have been caused deliberately by the untraced driver.
(5) If appropriate, the MIB makes an award assessed in a similar way, although with minor differences, as a court would have assessed damages.
(6) There is an appeals procedure, by way of arbitration by a Queen's Counsel.
(7) Any award will include a contribution towards legal costs, as set out in the schedule.

THE CRIMINAL INJURIES COMPENSATION AUTHORITY (CICA)

6.032   The CICA is a statutory body which administers the Criminal Injuries Compensation Scheme. The Scheme provides ex gratia compensation to victims of violence or, if the victim dies, his dependants. For an application to be considered the applicant must have been:

(a) A victim of a crime of violence, or injured in some other way covered by the Scheme, for example, when attempting to apprehend a suspected offender.
(b) Physically and/or mentally injured as a result.
(c) In England, Wales or Scotland at the time when the injury was sustained.
(d) Injured seriously enough to qualify for at least the minimum award of £1,000 available under the Scheme (see below).

The application must be made within two years of the incident for which a claim is made. However, the CICA may waive the time limit if a good reason for the delay can be shown and it is in the interests of justice to do so, for example, the injuries only became apparent some time after the incident which caused them and it is still possible for the Authority to investigate and verify the details of the incident.

Under the Scheme compensation is assessed in a manner similar to that used by the courts when assessing damages for personal injuries but there are some important differences:

(1) A "standard amount" is set according to a detailed tariff running from level 1 (£1,000, e.g. a chipped front tooth requiring crown) to level 25 (£250,000, e.g. quadriplegia/ tetraplegia-the paralysis of all four limbs).
(2) Claims in respect of loss of earnings or earning capacity have certain prescribed limits, for example, none is payable for the first 28 weeks and all claims are capped at earnings equal to one and a half times the gross average industrial earnings at the time when the claim is assessed.
(3) Certain "special expenses" may be payable for practical, medical and care costs provided the applicant has been incapacitated for longer than 28 weeks as a direct result of the injury. Private medical treatment costs are only considered if it can be shown that the treatment was not routinely available under the NHS and that it was a reasonable option.
(4) Compensation is only payable for the three most serious injuries suffered. The full tariff award is paid for the most serious injury, 30 per cent for the second injury and 15 per cent for the third injury.
(5) The total amount payable under the Scheme in respect of the same injury cannot exceed £500,000.

The Scheme itself, various guides and application forms can be obtained free of charge from the CICA at Tay House, 300 Bath Street, Glasgow, G2 4LN (DX GW 379 Glasgow; telephone 0141 331 2726; fax 0141 331 2287, *www.cica.gov.uk* or general enquiries by email at *enquiries.cica@gtnet.gov.uk* or on the freephone helpline telephone number 0800 358 3601).

CHAPTER 7

Parties to Actions

7.001 A solicitor is entitled to act for any person able to instruct him to bring or defend proceedings in court. But does the client have authority to give the solicitor instructions? Is the client the best person to take or defend a case? And with whom or against whom should any proceedings be taken? This chapter summarises the law relating to particular types of litigants, adding or substituting parties to an action and the solicitor's role in all of this.

7.002 TITLE TO THE ACTION

In a simple action the title will read:

Between:

          Mrs Ethel Smythe   Claimant

          and

          Dr Doris Hake   Defendant

PD 7, para.4.2 provides that if there is more than one claimant and/or defendant, the title should read, for example,:

          (1) Mr Stephen Crowley   Claimants

          and

          (1) Dr Doris Hake
          (2) Mrs Mary Clark   Defendants

7.003 TYPE OF LITIGANTS

Adult individuals

7.004 In the case of parties who are individuals all their known forenames and surname should be stated in the heading to the action, including whether Mr, Mrs,

Miss or Ms or any other title (e.g. Dr). If a trading name is used by an individual, that should also be added, for example, Ms Elizabeth Wright trading as Wright's Electrics. These matters are dealt with in the notes on completing the claim form and PD 16 para.2.6.

As to the rules of service of documents see Ch.8.

Can an individual delegate the right to conduct litigation by power of attorney? No, said the Court of Appeal in *Gregory v Turner* [2003] 1 W.L.R. 1149. See further para.1.018 and s.27 of the Courts and Legal Services Act 1990.

Children (Pt 21)

A child is a person under the age of 18, whether married or unmarried. He must have a "litigation friend" to conduct proceedings on his behalf unless the court otherwise orders. Pre-CPR a child could sue for wages due in a county court and defend a debt claim without having the equivalent of a litigation friend. The court expects the litigation friend to be a substantial person; and it is desirable that he should be a relation (parent or guardian) or otherwise a close family friend. The Official Solicitor is appointed to act if no one else is able and willing to do so.

7.005

In order to become a litigation friend on behalf of a child claimant the person who wishes to act must file a certificate of suitability (Form N235) when the claim form is issued. The certificate should confirm that the person: (a) consents to act; (b) knows or believes the claimant to be a child; (c) can fairly and competently conduct the proceedings; and (d) has no interest adverse to that of the child. In addition the person must undertake to pay any costs which the child may be ordered to pay in relation to the proceedings. That certificate must be served on one of the child's parents or guardians or otherwise on the person with whom the child resides or in whose care the child is. A certificate of service must also be filed when the claim is issued.

In order to become a litigation friend on behalf of a child defendant the person who wishes to act should file and serve a certificate of suitability when he first takes a step in the action, usually on filing a defence.

The title to an action involving a litigation friend might be: Stephen Lawson (a child by Ann Lawson his litigation friend). There is no requirement to state the relationship, if any, between the child and the litigation friend.

A person may not, without the permission of the court, make an application against a child until a litigation friend has been appointed. Likewise, a person may not take any step in proceedings, save issuing and serving a claim form, or applying to the court for the appointment of a litigation friend, until the child has a litigation friend. An application for an order appointing a litigation friend may be made by a person who wishes to be appointed or a party.

The litigation friend has a duty to fairly and competently conduct proceedings on behalf of the child. All steps and decisions he takes in the proceedings must be for the benefit of the child. The court may direct that a person may not act as a litigation friend or terminate his appointment.

In *Re A (Minors) (Conjoined twins: Medical treatment) (No.2)* [2000] 4 All E.R. 961 the Court of Appeal held that neither r.4.10(9) of the Family Proceedings Rules nor r.21.7(1) of the Civil Procedure Rules specified any limit on the court's power to terminate the appointment of a guardian ad litem or litigation friend. If such a person did act manifestly contrary to the child's best interests, the court would remove him even though neither his good faith nor his diligence was in issue: see *Re Taylor's Application* [1972] 2 Q.B. 369, 380 and *Re Birchall* [1880] 16 Ch.41, 42.

When a child reaches 18 a litigation friend's appointment ceases. The child must then within 28 days serve a notice on all other parties that the appointment has ceased, give his address for service and state whether or not he intends to carry on the action. If he fails to do so any other party may apply to strike out the child's statements of case. Where the proceedings continue the title to the action becomes: Stephen Lawson (formerly a child but now of full age).

The approval of the court must be obtained before making a voluntary interim payment to a child (see Ch.25). A litigation friend cannot enter into a binding settlement or compromise on behalf of a child. Any agreement as to the whole or part of a claim reached before or during proceedings must be approved by the court (see Chs 10 and 34); *Drinkall v Whitwood* [2003] EWCA Civ 1547; [2004] 4 All E.R. 378 and *Dietz v Lennig Chemicals Ltd* [1969] 1 A.C. 170, HL. Likewise acceptance of a Pt 36 offer must be approved by the court (see Ch.29). As to costs, see Ch.39.

There are other special rules relating to children, including service of documents (see Ch.8), default judgment (see Ch.15) and statements of truth (see Ch.12).

Patients (Pt 21)

7.006   A patient is a person who by reason of mental disorder within the meaning of s.94(2) of the Mental Health Act 1983 (the Act) is incapable of managing and administering his property and affairs. Virtually all the provisions outlined above concerning children apply to patients. Note, however, two important qualifications. First, if a person has been authorised by the Court of Protection pursuant to Pt VII of the Act to conduct legal proceedings in the name of the patient or on his behalf, that person should normally be appointed the litigation friend and must file at the court an official copy of the order or other document that constitutes his authorisation to act. Secondly, when a party ceases to be a patient, the litigant friend's appointment continues until it is ended by a court order. For a detailed discussion of the application of Pt 21 in this area and the approach that should be taken by the court, see the cases of *Masterman-Lister v Jewell & Home Counties Dairies* [2003] EWCA Civ 70; (2002) L.T.L. December 19 and *Folks v Faizey* [2006] EWCA Civ 381, *The Independent*, April 12, 2006.

What steps should a solicitor take if he is unsure whether or not his client falls within the definition of a patient? The solicitor should seek an order of the court directing that the Official Solicitor consider the evidence, appoint a medical expert and appear at the hearing: see *Lindsay v Wood* [2006] EWHC 2895, *The Times*, December 8, 2006.

Companies and other corporate bodies

Companies and other corporate bodies are legal persons and therefore can sue and be sued in their own names. Ensure you check the correct description of the company which may be a "public limited company" or "plc" (the Welsh equivalents are "cwmni cyfyngedig cyhoeddos" or "ccc"); or otherwise "limited". It is best to do a company search to establish the correct and full name. That will also give you other useful information such as the registered office address. See Ch.8 as to the rules of service of documents on a company.

7.007

Partnerships (CPR, r 7.2A, PD 7 and PD 73)

Partnerships are not legal persons. However, if partners carry on business in England or Wales, they may sue in the names of their firm, which is treated as their collective description. PD 7 para.5A.3 provides that where a partnership has a name, unless it is inappropriate to do so, claims must be brought against the name under which that partnership carried on business at the time the cause of action accrued. In either case the title to the action should read, for example, "Bloggers and Co. (a firm)".

7.008

Where a claimant wishes to sue a firm best practice is to make enquiries of the financial standing of the defendant partnership before proceedings are commenced. Especially in debt claims it is better to know in advance whether the members of the firm are worth powder and shot. You can make use of PD 7 para.5B.2. This allows you to obtain from the partnership a written statement of the names and last known places of residence of all the persons who were partners in the partnership at the time when the cause of action accrued.

The advantage of suing partners in their firm's name is the ability to enforce the judgment against partnership property (see s.23 of the Partnership Act 1890 and PD 73 s.III). The disadvantage is the need to seek the court's permission to enforce a judgment against persons not identified in the proceedings as partners.

See Ch.8 as to the rules of service on a firm of partners. Enforcement of judgments is dealt with in Chs 40 and 41.

Limited liability partnerships

A limited liability partnership ("LLP") unites the tax status and organisational flexibility of a partnership with limited liability for its members. LLPs were created by the Limited Liability Partnerships Act 2000. An LLP is a legal person separate from its members. It is a body corporate, formed on incorporation. It must have a registered office. Third parties normally contract directly with a

7.009

LLP, rather than with its individual members. How can you recognise one? Its name will end with "limited liability partnership", "llp" or "LLP" (or where registered in Wales "partneriaeth atebolrwydd cyfngedig", "pac" or "PAC"). See Ch.8 as to the rules for service on corporations.

Estates of deceased persons (Pt 19)

7.010 These rules provide four provisions dealing with litigation concerning the estates of deceased persons.

(1) The basic rule. The estate should be represented by the deceased's personal executors (i.e. executors or administrators) joined in their capacity as such. Note that by r.19.7A a claim may be brought by or against executors (trustees or administrators) in that capacity without adding any persons who have a beneficial interest in the estate (or trust).

(2) Where a litigant dies during an action. The death of an applicant determines an application under the Inheritance (Provision for Family and Dependants) Act 1975 and a defamation action is automatically determined on the death of either party. In other cases the court may order the personal representatives to be joined and that the action is to continue as if they had been substituted for the deceased.

(3) Where a party to an action dies and no personal representatives are appointed. The court may require notice to be given to any person having an interest in the deceased's estate. For example, notice might be given to an insurer or the MIB where the action is against a motorist who is now deceased. The court may then order that the action should proceed in the absence of any person representing the estate or it may appoint a person to represent the estate for the purpose of those proceedings. In either event any judgment given in the action will bind the estate as if a personal representative had been joined.

An order under this provision is futile in debt claims against a litigant who dies because, for all practical purposes, the judgment would be unenforceable. In such cases the creditor himself should take out letters of administration of the deceased's estate if it is large enough to cover his debt and expenses.

(4) Where a prospective defendant dies before proceedings are commenced. Where a grant of probate or administration has been made, the claim must be made by issuing a claim form naming as the defendant "the personal representatives of" the deceased. Within four months after issue the claimant must apply to the court for it to appoint someone to represent the estate under (3) above. If he fails to do so the claim form is no longer valid for service (see para.9.005 and PD 7 para.5.5). If personal representatives are appointed the court will normally substitute them as defendants on the application. See generally r.19.8.

What if probate or letters of administration have not been granted by the time proceedings are issued? The claim must be brought against "the estate of" the deceased and the claimant must apply within four months of issue for an order appointing a person to represent the estate of the deceased in the claim. Again, if he fails to do so, the claim form is no longer valid for service. What if the claimant in error had issued the claim against the "personal representatives" of the deceased but a grant of probate or administration had not yet been made? Or say the defendant was dead when the claim was started? By r.19.8(3) such claims are treated as having been brought against "the estate of" the deceased.

Vexatious litigants (PD 3 and SCA 1981, s.42(1A))

A "vexatious litigant" is a person who habitually and persistently and without any reasonable ground either institutes vexatious civil proceedings or makes vexatious applications in civil proceedings. In *Bhamjee v Forsdick (No.2)* [2003] EWCA Civ 1113; [2003] B.P.I.R. 1252 the Court of Appeal laid down guidelines for making a civil restraint order (previously known as a *Grepe v Loam* order and defined in r.2.3) against a vexatious litigant. The mechanics appear in PD 3C. Such an order will restrain the litigant from making any further applications in those proceedings without first obtaining the permission of the court. Any application issued without such permission will stand dismissed without the need for the other party to respond to it.

7.011

If a litigant exhibits the hallmarks of persistently vexatious behaviour, a judge of the Court of Appeal, High Court or a designated civil judge (or his appointed deputy) in the county court should consider whether to make an extended civil restraint order against him. For an example see *R. (on the application of Ranbir Kumar) v Secretary of State for Constitutional Affairs* [2006] EWCA Civ 990, [2007] 1 W.L.R. 536. Indeed, r.23.12(b) provides that, "If the court dismisses an application and it considers that the application is totally without merit, the court must at the same time consider whether it is appropriate to make a civil restraint order" (and likewise when dismissing an appeal—see r.52.10(5)). This order, which should be made for a period not exceeding two years, will restrain the litigant from instituting proceedings or making applications in the courts identified in the order in or out of or concerning any matters involving or relating to or touching upon or leading to the proceedings in which it is made without the permission of a judge identified in the order. Any application for permission should be made on paper and would be dealt with on paper without any hearing. Is such a limitation lawful? As the right to an oral hearing is not absolute even where ECHR Art.6(1) is engaged: see *Miller v Sweden* (2006) 42 E.H.R.R. 51, this provision was held to be lawful in *R. (on the application of Ewing) v Secretary of State for Constitutional Affairs* [2006] EWHC 504, [2006] 2 All E.R. 993.

If an extended civil restraint order is found not to provide the necessary curb on a litigant's vexatious conduct, a judge of the Court of Appeal, High Court or a designated civil judge (or his deputy) in the county court should consider whether the time has come to make a general civil restraint order against him. Such an order will have the same effect as an extended civil restraint order except that it will cover all proceedings and all applications in the High Court or in the identified county court as the case may be. It too may be for a period not exceeding two years.

If a litigant subject to an extended civil restraint order or a general civil restraint order continues to make applications pursuant to the relevant order which are dismissed as being totally devoid of merit, the court should consider whether it is appropriate to make any subsequent refusals of permission final. Thereafter, any subsequent refusal of permission on the grounds that the application is totally devoid of merit will not be susceptible of appeal unless the judge who refuses permission himself grants permission to appeal.

What if a vexatious litigant bombards the court with telephone calls and faxes? That is precisely what Mr Bhamjee did. This led Mr Justice Collins in *R. (on the application of Bhamjee) v First Secretary of State* [2005] EWHC 350 to make an order that was accompanied with a penal notice that he was prohibited from telephoning any person in the Administrative Court Office, whether lawyer or manager, and that he equally was prohibited from contacting the court by fax.

Note that the other party or parties to the litigation may apply for any of these restraint orders. Also, the Attorney-General can apply for an order pursuant to s.42 of the Supreme Court Act 1981.

Forms are provided for the three kinds of restraint order, namely: N19, N19A and N19B. Does The Human Rights Act 1998 or the European Convention on Human Rights have any effect on the general principles relating to the grant or refusal of permission to appeal to vexatious litigants? No said the Court of Appeal in the case of *Ebert v Official Receiver* [2001] EWCA Civ 340; [2002] 1 W.L.R. 320.

CLAIMS INVOLVING MULTIPLE PARTIES AND/OR CAUSES OF ACTION (R.7.3)

7.012 A single claim form can be used by one or more claimants to start all claims which can be conveniently disposed of in the same proceedings against one or more defendants. In the simplest case, the claim form will be issued by a claimant (C) against a defendant (D). But a single claim form might be used in any of the following circumstances:

(i) Two passengers in a car accident, C1 and C2 bring a claim against the driver of the car, D1.

(ii) A person injured by drinking bad fizzy pop, C brings a claim against the shopkeeper who sold it, D1 and the manufacturer who made it, D2.

(iii) A car passenger, C injured in an accident, brings a claim against the driver, D1 and the rider of the motorcycle, D2 that collided with D1's car.

(iv) As (iii) but in addition C sues D1 to recover a loan that D1 has not yet repaid to C.
(v) As (iv) but in addition C sues D3, a fellow passenger who assaulted C after the accident.

The test under r.7.3 is simply whether the claims "can be conveniently disposed of in the same proceedings". Neither the rule nor PD 7 add to this. The matter is addressed by the court when it exercises its case management powers (see Ch.33). If the court considers it "inconvenient" to proceed with the action as it stands then by r.3.1(2)(e) it can, for example, direct that part of the proceedings should be dealt with separately, or (i) direct a separate trial of any issue, or (j) decide the order in which issues are to be tried, or (k) exclude an issue from consideration.

In examples (i) to (iii) above it would appear convenient for the matters to proceed to trial as they stand. However, the court might decide in any of these cases to order a "split trial", i.e. all questions of liability and breach of duty or contract are to be tried before and separately from any issue as to damages. See, for example, *White v Brunton* [1984] 3 W.L.R. 105 and the discussion of this topic in para.33.006.

In examples (iv) and (v) above there are a totally separate causes of action taken first against D2 for the recovery of a loan and secondly against D3 for assault. Neither of those matters are relevant to each other nor to the facts that constitute the accident involving C, D1 and D2. In both cases the court would probably consider it convenient to order separate trials of each cause.

THE ADDITION AND SUBSTITUTION OF PARTIES (PT 19)

A person cannot be added or substituted as a claimant unless he gives his consent in writing and that is filed with the court. If a person refuses to be a claimant, he must be made a defendant to the action unless the court orders otherwise.

7.013

Example

For some years C had been a member of an international unincorporated religious association ("the association"). He had made certain payments into a bank account that was in the names of himself and two other members, MD and SB. That money was then lent to an English registered charity ("the charity") which was under the control of the association. C now claimed repayment of the loans. The court found that MD and SB, who were not parties to the action, were arguably jointly entitled with C to any relief that he was entitled to in respect of the loans. There were no grounds for directing that they need not be joined as parties to the action. It would be unsatisfactory for the case to come on for trial before their position was clarified, because an order made in C's favour, in proceedings where neither was a party, might leave the charity still exposed to future claims at their suit. The court stayed the action against the charity to allow C to specifically ask MD and SB if they wanted to claim any interest in the moneys in question and whether or not they wished to be joined as parties to the proceedings, either as co-claimants or as defendants. See *Roche v Sherrington* [1982] 1 W.L.R. 599.

All persons that are jointly entitled to a remedy (save in probate proceedings) must be parties to an action, unless the court orders otherwise. However, if the entitlement to a remedy is both joint and several then one person may sue in respect of the several obligations owed.

Example

A husband and wife deposited funds in a joint bank account. The deposit was made according to the terms of an express mandate which required the bank to make payments out of the account only on the joint signatures of both account holders. Subsequently the bank, acting solely on the husband's instructions, negligently transferred funds from the account to him without the wife's knowledge or authority. She brought an action against the bank claiming damages for breach of mandate. In those circumstances the bank was held to owe an obligation separately to the husband and wife not to honour instructions unless signed by each of them. Therefore, the wife was entitled to sue the bank in respect of the several obligations owed to her without joining in her husband. See *Caitlin v Cyprus Finance Corporation (London) Ltd* [1983] Q.B. 759.

By r.19.4A the court may not make a declaration of incompatibility in accordance with s.4 of the Human Rights Act 1998 unless 21 days' notice, or such other period of notice as the court directs, has been given to the Crown. Where such notice has been given to the Crown, a Minister, or other person permitted by the Act, must be joined as a party on giving notice to the court.

Does Pt 19 apply to public law proceedings? No—see *River Thames Society v First Secretary of State* [2006] EWHC 2829, (2006) L.T.L. September 22 (where the court ordered substitution under its inherent jurisdiction).

Can an order be made under r.19 to substitute a party after judgment? Yes, see *Prescott v Dunwoody Sports Marketing* [2007] EWCA Civ 461, (2007) L.T.L. 17 May.

Cases where the limitation period has not expired (r.19.2)

7.014 The court may order a person to be added as a new party if:

(a) It is desirable to do so in order that all matters in dispute can be resolved. For example, in an action for wrongful interference with goods a person may be joined as a second defendant in order to establish that, at the date of the alleged interference, he had a better right to the goods than the claimant (see *de Franco v Metropolitan Police Commissioner*, *The Times*, May 8, 1987). For an example where the court refused to exercise its discretion see *Coal Mining Contractors v Davies* [2006] EWCA Civ 1360, [2007] 1 All E.R. 518.

(b) There is an issue involving the new party and an existing party which is connected to the matters in dispute and it is desirable to add the new party in order to resolve that issue.

Examples

In *Re Blenheim Leisure (Restaurants) Ltd*, *The Times*, August 13, 1999 the company, *BLR* had been struck off the Register of Companies. An application was made by the directors to restore *BLR* to the Register. The directors alleged that the company had been struck off by mistake. The effect of striking off was to vest *BLR*'s assets in the Crown. *Fordingstone Ltd*, F, claimed to be the landlords of premises that had been let to *BLR*. When F learnt that *BLR* had been dissolved it served notices on the Treasury Solicitor under s.24(3) of the Landlord and Tenant Act 1954. Since the Crown was not in occupation of the premises, the effect of those notices was to terminate any tenancies to which *BLR* might have been entitled upon the expiry of the notice period. It was only following service of the notices that the directors applied to restore *BLR* to the register. The effect of restoration, if granted, would be that *BLR* would be deemed to have existed throughout the period of its dissolution, without any of its assets vesting in the Crown, with the result that F's notices would have no effect. F therefore applied to be joined as a party to the application so that it could make submissions as to whether it was just that *BLR* should be restored having regard to: (a) the true circumstances in which it alleged *BLR* had come to be struck off; and (b) the retrospective invalidation of its notices. The Court of Appeal by a majority held that it was desirable that F should be added to the proceedings. In deciding whether to restore *BLR* to the register the court had to consider all the circumstances of the case, which included the nature of the original application to remove the company's name from the register, the reasons for the application to restore, and the intervening substantive rights that had arisen after dissolution.
In contrast, in the case of *Myers v Dortex International Ltd*, *The Times*, March 18, 1999 the claimant sued his employer, D for personal injuries sustained in two accidents at work. At the time of the first accident *AXA* was D's insurer but, by the time of the second accident, D was insured with Lloyd's underwriters who had assumed responsibility for the defence. *AXA* was contractually obliged to indemnify D for any liability to the claimant arising out of the first accident. *AXA* sought to be added as a party on the basis that the trial judge should resolve the question of each insurer's liability. The Court of Appeal held that joinder was not required in order to resolve the issues in dispute between the claimant and defendant. The effect of joining *AXA* would be that the claimant would face two conflicting defences in respect of causation and that was undesirable. In any event, it was reasonable to expect that the trial judge would provide a full and reasoned decision which would enable the insurers to resolve the issue of causation and apportionment of liability between themselves.
In addition, the court may order a new party to be substituted for an existing one if: (a) the existing party's interest or liability has passed to the new party; and (b) it is desirable to substitute the new party so that the court can resolve the matters in dispute in the proceedings.

It should be noted that the court can make an order of its own initiative even if there is no cause of action against the party being joined. In *TSB Private Bank International SA v Chabra* [1992] 1 W.L.R. 231 the claimant bank took proceedings to enforce a written guarantee given by the defendant. It obtained a freezing order (see para.27.025) restraining him from removing his assets, and those of a company called BHL, out the jurisdiction. In fact, the defendant had already left the jurisdiction but had claimed to have assets in the jurisdiction in respect of this company. He was the majority shareholder in the company. The court of its own initiative joined BHL as a party as there was credible evidence, not contested by the defendant, that assets that appeared to be the company's property might, in fact, be assets of the defendant that therefore were available to satisfy any judgment obtained against him.

Case where the relevant limitation period has expired (r.19.5)

7.015 If the limitation period has expired at the time the application is made, the court may add or substitute a party only if:

(a) The relevant limitation period (see Ch.5) was current when the proceedings started; and
(b) The addition or substitution is necessary. Rule 19.5(3) sets out three possible grounds of necessity, namely:

  (i) The new party is to be substituted for a party who was named in the claim form in mistake for the new party. See, for example, *Adelson and Another v Associated Newspapers Ltd* [2007] EWCA Civ 701, *The Times*, July 18, 2007. The person who made the mistake must be the person responsible, directly or through an agent, for the issue of the claim form. He must demonstrate that, had the mistake not been made, the new party would have been named in the pleading. The mistake has to be as to the name of the party, rather than as to the identity of the party. Note that the court held that the test set out in the pre-CPR case of The Sardinia Sulcis [1991] 1 Lloyd's L.R. 201 should still be followed.
  (ii) The claim cannot properly be carried on by or against the original party unless the new party is added or substituted as claimant or defendant.

Example

X Co. sues D in 1996. Y Co. sues D in 1997. In 1999 X Co., an Italian company ceases to exist on merging with Y Co., another Italian company which under Italian law succeeds to X Co.'s rights and liabilities. For X Co.'s action against D to continue it is necessary for Y Co. to be substituted as the claimant. See *Industrie Chimiche Italia Centrale v Alexander G. Tsavliris & Sons Maritime Co.; The Choko Star* (1995) [1996] 1 W.L.R. 774.

(iii) The original party has died or had a bankruptcy order made against him and his interest or liability has passed to the new party. See *Three Rivers District Council v Governor and Company of the Bank of England* [1996] Q.B. 292.

Whilst in *R. (on the application of Johnson) v Secretary of State for Health* [2006] EWHC 288 the court found that no interest had passed to the applicant, the court did consider the possibility that a party might be joined under the court's case management powers in r.3.1(2)(m)—see Ch.1.

In addition r.19.5(4) provides that in a personal injuries claim the court may add or substitute a party where it directs that ss.11 or 12 of the Limitation Act 1980 shall not apply to the claim by or against the new party. See Ch.4 and the case of *Liff v Peasley* [1980] 1 W.L.R. 781.

Do rr.19.5(3) and (4) provide an exhaustive list of the court's jurisdiction to add or substitute a party when the limitation period has expired? Arguably, yes. Rule 19.5(3) states that "the addition or substitution of a party is necessary only if [our emphasis] the court is satisfied that" one of the three grounds is established. Rule 19.5(4) then commences, "In addition [to r.19.5(3)], in a claim for personal injuries the court may add or substitute a party" where it gives one of the statutory directions.

It may well be that the first issue the court has to determine on the application is whether or not the relevant limitation period has actually expired before proceedings were issued such that the action is statute-barred. This question arose in the case of *Virk v Gan Life Holdings Plc* (2000) 52 B.M.L.R. 207. The claim was for judgment under an insurance policy of which *Gan Life and Pensions Plc* ("*GLP*") had succeeded as the insurer. Under the policy the claimant was to receive a "critical illness benefit" if he suffered a stroke and survived for 30 days. On August 11, 1992 the claimant suffered a stroke. In 1993 liability was repudiated under the policy for non-disclosure. The action was commenced on August 21, 1998. It was common ground that the action had been taken against the defendant by mistake, the claimant being mistaken as to which of *GLP* and the defendant had succeeded as insurer under the policy. *GLP* was one of the defendant's associated companies. The claimant applied to substitute *GLP* for the defendant. Both the district judge and judge held that the cause of action accrued on August 11, 1992 when the claimant suffered his stroke and dismissed the application as the relevant limitation period was not current when the proceedings had been started. The claimant contended that the 30-day survival clause was a condition precedent to liability under the policy and so the cause of action did not accrue until September 11, 1992. The Court of Appeal agreed with that interpretation and held that the action had not been statute-barred. Whilst the defendant had made a careless error in naming the wrong defendant there had been no prejudice as a result of that to *GLP*. Accordingly, the court allowed the amendment as being both necessary and proper in the circumstances.

Should a party ever be re-joined to proceedings under r.19(2)? See *Kent (as executrix for Chapper, deceased) v M&L Management & Legal Ltd* [2005] EWHC 2546.

CONSOLIDATION (R.3.1(2)(G) AND (H))

7.016 The court may of its own initiative, or on the application of any party, consolidate two or more actions into one action. The court may consolidate proceedings, or try two or more claims on the same occasion, as part of its general powers of management (see Ch.33). If the proceedings are not pending in the same division of the High Court or in the same county court an order for transfer can be made (see Ch.9). The main purpose of consolidation is to save costs and time pursuant to r.1(2)(b), (d) and (e). The circumstances in which cases may be consolidated are similar to those where parties may be added (see above).

INTERVENERS

7.017 Any person may apply to the court for its permission to be added as a party to proceedings. As seen the court may do so pursuant to r.19.2(2)(b) if there is an issue involving the person and an existing party which is connected to the matters in dispute and it is desirable to add the person in order to resolve that issue. Hence, in *Astro Exito Navegacion SA v Southland Enterprise Co. (No.2)* [1983] 2 A.C. 787 a London bank which had confirmed the letter of credit payment of the delivery of a vessel in Taiwan was allowed to intervene to challenge the validity of interim mandatory orders. However, the rule does not appear to be wide enough to permit joinder of a party who is merely interested in the case in so far as it determines a question of law (see *Spelling Goldberg Productions Inc v BPC Publishing Ltd* [1981] R.P.C. 280).

REPRESENTATIVE PROCEEDINGS (PT 19, S.II)

7.018 Sometimes, there are so many potential claimants or defendants to an action that it would be inconvenient to join all of them. Rule 19.6 therefore allows a representative action where numerous persons have the "same interest". Although this is not a rigid limitation, representation is not allowed where the interests or liabilities of the group are too diverse such that the overriding objective cannot be met. Also representative proceedings will not be permitted where no individual can be identified as a representative of the association in question: see *EDO MBM Technology Limited v Campaign to Smash EDO* [2005] EWHC 837 and *Oxford University v Webb* [2006] EWHC 2490.

Examples

Representative proceedings were allowed where 11 out of 12 tenants decided to sue their landlord for failing to carry out repairs (see *Moon v Atherton* [1972] 2 Q.B. 435) and where a claimant sought to override the provisions of a restrictive covenant where a number of people had the benefit of that covenant (see *Guardians of Tendring Union v Downton* (1880) 45 Ch.584).

A single claim form may be issued by or against a group. If a person is not part of the group this must be clearly shown in the title to the action, for example, "Glennys Moon suing on behalf of herself and the tenants of a block of flats known as Petherton Court, Gayton Road, Harrow (except Catherine Eluned Roberts)" see the case of Moon above. The members of a group being represented are regarded as parties but not full parties. This means that they are not primarily liable for costs or subject to disclosure (see, e.g. *Ventouris v Mountain* [1990] 1 W.L.R. 170). If some of them object to being represented they can apply to be excepted from the representation and join as parties separately, either in their own names, or by their own representative if they are numerous (see, e.g. *John v Rees* [1970] Ch.35). Where the representative wishes to discontinue the action one or more of the group can apply to be added as full parties as if they had been substituted for the representative (see, e.g., the case of Moon above).

Any judgment is binding on all persons represented (see *Howells v Dominion Insurance Co. Ltd* (2005) L.T.L. April 4). The courts avoid any injustice this might cause in two ways. First, by allowing representative actions only where it is sure that the proceedings are for the benefit of the group represented and the proceedings are being fully and properly argued in accordance with the overriding objective. Secondly, where the claimant seeks to enforce a judgment against a represented person, by allowing that person to dispute liability on the grounds of his own special circumstances. This is done by requiring the claimant to obtain the court's permission before enforcing the judgment.

Example

On January 18, 2001 C, an employee at a club known as the "Blue's Club", fell down some stairs at the club and was injured. C sues D and E, the treasurer and secretary of the club "on their own behalf and on behalf of all other members of the Blue's club on January 18, 2001". C obtains judgment. When seeking permission to enforce that against F, F might argue (1) that he was not a member of the club at the time C was injured and/or (2) that C owes him a debt in respect of an entirely different matter. F is not entitled to deny the judgment nor allege contributory negligence by C (see, e.g. *Campbell v Thompson* [1953] 1 Q.B. 445).

Although a claimant can enforce the judgment against a person represented, the representative himself cannot. If, for example, the representative is not insured in respect of a claim and he wishes to claim a contribution from other members of the group he represents he should make an additional claim (see, e.g. *Choudhury v Hussain, The Times*, October 10, 1989, Ch.18).

Can a judgment against an unincorporated association be enforced against a person who was not a party to the proceedings? No, not unless the court gives it permission (r.19.6(4)(b)). See, for example, the representative proceedings of *Huntingdon Life Sciences Group Plc, Huntingdon Life Sciences Ltd (1) Brian Cass (as representative of the Employees of the First Claimants) (2) v Stop*

Huntingdon Animal Cruelty (SHAC) (an unincorporated association by its representative Dr. Max Gastone) [2007] EWHC 522, (2007) L.T.L. April 19. Whilst an injunction was made against the defendant protest group, the court would not grant the claimants permission to enforce it against any persons not named.

REPRESENTATION OF INTERESTED PERSONS WHO CANNOT BE ASCERTAINED, ETC. (R.19.7)

7.019 What if you are acting in a case concerning the rights of an unborn child or where any interested party cannot be found? Rule 19.7(1) applies to claims about the estate of a deceased person; property subject to a trust and the meaning of a document, including a statute. How can the court assist? It may make an order appointing a person to represent any other person or persons in the claim where the person or persons to be represented are unborn, cannot be found or easily traced, or are a class of persons who have the same interest in a claim and one or more members of that class are unborn, etc. So a court application will be necessary. This should be made by anyone who wishes to be appointed or any party to the claim. The application can be made at any time before or after the claim has started.

What if such a claim is settled? By r.19.7(5) the court's approval will be necessary. This will be given if the court is satisfied that the settlement is for the benefit of all the represented persons. On whom is any judgment or order binding? Unless the court otherwise directs, it binds all persons represented in the claim but it may only be enforced by or against a person who is not a party to the claim with the permission of the court.

GROUP LITIGATION ORDERS (PT 19, S.III)

7.020 Rule 19.11 details the procedures under the CPR which apply where numerous proceedings are brought in relation to similar or related facts ("group litigation"). The basic scheme is as follows. The court may make a Group Litigation Order ("GLO") "where there are or are likely to be a number of claims giving rise to the GLO issues". Any GLO must:

(a) contain directions about the establishment of a register (the "group register") on which the claims managed under the GLO will be entered;

(b) specify the GLO issues which will identify the claims to be managed as a group under the GLO. For example, "is this particular drug capable of causing this particular illness?"; and

(c) specify the court (the "management court") which will manage the claims on the group register.

What if there are already claims which raise one or more of the GLO issues? The GLO may direct their transfer to the management court or order their stay until further order. In addition it may direct their entry on the group register or that from a specified date they should be started in the management court and entered on the register. Directions are normally given for publicising the GLO by supplying copies to the Law Society and the Senior Master, Queen's Bench Division at the Royal Courts of Justice.

In *Taylor v Nugent Care Society* [2004] EWCA Civ 51; [2004] 1 W.L.R. 1129, the claimant had commenced proceedings which raised an issue covered by a GLO but he had been refused permission to join the GLO out of time. Was it an abuse of process for him to proceed with his claim? The Court of Appeal indicated that to dismiss the claimant's case must be a proportionate response to his failure to take the steps which he should have taken at an earlier date which would have resulted in his becoming part of the group litigation. In addition, it is necessary to consider whether his claim could have been dismissed if he had commenced his proceedings and not then applied to join the group litigation. Also the court should consider whether other action could be taken by the courts to protect the position of the defendant if he was faced with separate and parallel proceedings by the claimant. In particular the court may make an order staying the claimant's action until after the completion of the group action (or at least until after the completion of part of that action). As to costs, the court might make an order to protect a defendant (in the event that a costs order was made against the defendant) from having to pay any costs in addition to those which the defendant would have had to pay even if the claimant had been a party to the group action.

What is the effect of any GLO judgment or order? Where such is given or made in a claim on the group register in relation to one or more GLO issues it is binding on the parties to all other claims that are on the register at that time (unless the court orders otherwise). In addition the court may give directions as to the extent to which that judgment or order is binding on the parties to any claim which is subsequently entered on the register. See further PD 19B Q.B.D. Court Guide and the comments of Lord Woolf in *Boake Allen Ltd v HMRC* [2007] UKHL 25, [2007] 1 W.L.R. 1386. A list of current GLOs can be found on the Court Service website.

DERIVATIVE CLAIMS (R.19.9)

This is an action by a minority shareholder in a company on behalf of the company to prosecute a cause of action vested in it, for example, fraud at common law, or the abuse or misuse of power by the majority whether acting as directors or shareholders. See *Eastmanco (Kilner House) Ltd v Greater London Council* [1982] 1 W.L.R. 2. 7.021

Where a defendant responds to the particulars of claim, the claimant must apply to the court for permission to continue the claim. That application may include a request to be indemnified in costs out of the assets of the company. If the claimant fails to apply then any defendant who has responded may apply for an order to dismiss the proceedings. In *Jafari-Fini v Skillglass Ltd* [2005] EWCA Civ 356; (2005) L.T.L. March 16, the Court of Appeal held that permission to make a derivative action on behalf of a company will be refused in circumstances where if the applicant was successful in claims in his personal capacity he would be in a position to ensure that the company's claims were pursued and if he was unsuccessful the company's claims would be finally determined.

MISCELLANEOUS ACTIONS

7.022　CPR, Schs 1 and 2 contain other rules about parties, for example, RSC Ord.54 concerns applications for a writ of habeus corpus.

WHOM TO SUE?

7.023　When advising a claimant a key consideration is whom the client should sue. The following notes consider some of the possibilities.

Retailer and manufacturer? Wherever possible proceedings may be taken against both. There are three causes of action to consider. A claim in negligence against any person who puts defective goods in circulation, if it is proved that that person knew or ought to have known of the defect and if loss was suffered which was foreseeable: on this cause of action a claimant cannot normally recover damages if the only losses are purely economic. Secondly, under the Consumer Protection Act 1987 against a "producer" (as defined therein) of goods which were defective and cause loss; although it is largely based on strict liability principles, this cause of action is limited in a variety of ways. In particular, it applies only to goods which cause loss to a "customer" (as defined in the Act). Thirdly, as between the injured buyer and the immediate seller, a claim in contract. Subject to the terms of the contract, this claim may well impose strict liability on the seller and avoid the other limitations placed on the two causes of action just mentioned. Under the doctrine of privity of contract the claim will not be available unless the person injured was the buyer and the person sued is the seller from whom he bought the goods. However, a check should be made to see if the Contracts (Rights of Third Parties) Act 1999 applies. In general the Act sets out the circumstances in which a third party has a right to enforce a term of a contract (s.1); the situations in which such a term may be varied or rescinded (s.2); and the defences available to the promisor when the third party seeks to enforce the term (s.3). Section 1 does not affect the promisee's rights, or any rights that the third party may have which are independent of the Act (ss.4 and 7(1)). However, the Act does not apply to certain contracts (s.6).

Employer and employee? Where a tort is committed by an employee (or agent) acting in the course of his employment it is usual to sue both the employee and his employer; the latter will be vicariously liable for the former.

Motorist and insurer? Where a tort is committed by an insured person the victim has no right at common law to sue the insurer directly since he is not privy to the contract of insurance (see *Post Office v Norwich Union Fire Insurance Society* [1967] 2 Q.B. 363). Note, however, that:

(1) the insurer usually has the contractual right, as against the defendant, to conduct the defence on his behalf;
(2) in an action against a motorist the claimant usually has a statutory right to enforce against the insurer any judgment he obtains against the defendant;
(3) in an action against a bankrupt see the restricted rights given by the Third Parties (Right against Insurers) Act 1930;
(4) if the accident is in an EC or EFTA country, it may be possible to take proceedings there under Council Directive 2000/26/EC (see an useful article by D.J. Hickman, *Law Society's Gazette*, January 30, 2003).

Trustee and beneficiaries? Suppose a stranger to a trust wishes to sue the trustees to enforce a contract for the sale of land or an executor sues the trustee of an inter vivos trust to determine the validity of a legacy in favour of their trust. In both these cases it is unnecessary to join the beneficiaries as additional defendants. A judgment given in any action involving trustees is binding on all the beneficiaries, unless the court orders otherwise (see CPR, Pt 64).

Persons unknown? PD 7 para.4.1(1) provides that a claim form "should state ... the full name of each party ...". But what if the claimant does not know the name of a party? A description can be used provided it is sufficiently certain as to identify both those who are included and those who are not. If that test is satisfied then it does not seem to matter that the description may apply to no one or to more than one person nor that there is no further element of subsequent identification whether by service or otherwise. In *Bloomsbury Publishing Plc v News Group Newspapers Ltd* [2003] EWHC 1205; [2003] 3 All E.R. 736, the fifth book in the Harry Potter series was stolen by persons unknown from the printers and offered to certain newspapers. An order was made against "the person or persons who have offered the publishers of the Sun, the Daily Mail, and the Daily Mirror newspapers a copy of the book 'Harry Potter and the order of the Phoenix' by J K Rowling" requiring them to deliver up all copies of the book. Also see *South Cambridgeshire DC v Persons Unknown* [2004] EWCA Civ 1280; *The Times*, November 11, 2004.

THE SOLICITOR'S ROLE GENERALLY

A solicitor warrants his authority to take any positive step in proceedings, for example, to issue a claim form or serve a defence (see, e.g. *Donsland Ltd v Hoogstraten* (2002) P.N.L.R. 26). A solicitor may be ordered to pay personally the costs that are incurred where any steps are taken without authority, even if he does not know that he lacks authority.

7.024

Examples

The client gives the solicitor instructions on behalf of a non-existent company (see *Simmons v Liberal Opinion Ltd* [1911] 1 K.B. 966) or is a person not properly authorised to give instructions on behalf of a company (see *West End Hotels Syndicate v Bayer* (1912) 29 T.L.R. 92). Unknown to his solicitors, the client is of unsound mind and therefore lacks capacity to instruct the solicitors to defend proceedings on his behalf (see *Yonge v Toynbee* [1910] 1 K.B. 215). Does a solicitor warrant that in bringing the proceedings his client is solvent or that he has correctly named his client in the proceedings? No, held the Court of Appeal in *Nelson v Nelson* [1997] 1 W.L.R. 233 and *Seb Trygg Liv Holding Aktiebolag v Manches* [2005] EWCA Civ 1237, [2006] 1 All E.R. 437 respectively.

CHAPTER 8

Service of Documents

THE GENERAL RULE—SERVE ON SOLICITORS WHERE POSSIBLE

Rule 6 and PD 6 provide a comprehensive code for the service of documents. Intricate provisions are made as to the who, the how and the where of service and some irrebuttable presumptions are provided as to when service takes effect. It is easy to get lost in the detail and, indeed, the rules themselves are difficult to rationalise and are incoherent on some points. We start by stating an implied general rule underlying this difficult code: where a party or his agent has indicated that a solicitor is acting or will act for him in the proceedings, all documents to be served on that party should be served on that solicitor. Service on solicitors is the method most likely to advance the overriding objective of getting cases dealt with promptly and in a proper form without intervention and possible loss or misunderstanding on the part of the lay client (*Nanglegan v Royal Free Hampstead NHS Trust* [2002] 1 W.L.R. 1043, CA, para.19). The main exceptions to this general rule are the service of claim forms on registered companies (alternative methods of service are available here) and documents which must be served personally on a party in order to be in full support against him (e.g. an injunction indorsed with a penal notice; see further Ch.27). A minor exception, which usually arises in the context of service of a claim form, permits personal service of a document on a party who has a solicitor if that solicitor has not given written notice to the party serving that he is so authorised (r.6.4(2); see para.8.002).

8.001

When, and in what circumstances, can a party assume that his opponent has a solicitor acting for him? In defended proceedings this will always become clear as a result of the opening stages of court proceedings, if not earlier. The claim form must state the claimant's "address for service" (as to which, see further para.8.009). Similarly, a defendant must state his address for service in his Acknowledgment of Service or Defence. In both cases if these parties wish to act by solicitor their addresses for service will be their solicitors' business address. That solicitor is said to be "on the record" for his client in those proceedings and will remain so, even if his instructions to act are later terminated, unless and until a notice of change is validly served or an order is made removing the solicitor from the record (see later, Ch.28).

In practice the involvement of a solicitor for a party usually becomes clear during the negotiations made pre-action. Indeed, many, if not most, claims are negotiated and settled without the need for any court proceedings being issued. In these cases of course there is no need for service of any court documents. In the cases that do not settle early a solicitor may be nominated to accept service of any claim form on behalf of an intended defendant. A valid nomination may be made by the defendant himself or by his insurer (see *Collier v Williams* [2006] EWCA Civ 20, [2006] 1 W.L.R. 1945; or a solicitor acting for an intended defendant may nominate himself for the purpose of accepting service. Knowledge that a solicitor has been authorised to accept service renders irregular any service by post, DX, fax or email if the document is sent or transmitted to an address personal to the defendant. You can of course send or transmit the document to the defendant's solicitor (*Nanglegan v Royal Free Hampstead NHS Trust* [2002] 1 W.L.R. 1043, CA). Where a solicitor has been authorised to accept service, personal service on that party (as to which, see para.8.002) is also ruled out if the authorised solicitor has given the party serving written notice that they are instructed. In this instance documents must be served (whether by post, DX or the other permitted methods) only upon that solicitor (r.6.4(2)).

Do not underestimate the importance of obtaining from a solicitor acting for an intended defendant written notice making clear whether or not he is authorised to accept service. A failure to do so is perilous. The fact that a solicitor is negotiating on behalf of a party does not by itself prove that that solicitor is authorised to accept service. He may not be, in which case service directed towards him rather than his client will be bad (*Smith v Probyn*, *The Times*, March 29, 2000 and *Marshall Rankine v Maggs* [2006] EWCA Civ 20, [2006] 1 W.L.R. 1945). A solicitor's express confirmation of instructions to accept service sent to an intending claimant does not by itself prove that that solicitor is authorised to accept service relating to proceedings brought by that intending claimant's assignee (*Firstdale Ltd v Quinton* [2004] 1 All E.R. 639).

METHODS OF SERVICE

Personal service (r.6.4)

8.002 A document is served personally on an individual by "leaving it with" that person. Solicitors often employ an enquiry agent or process server to undertake the task. The server should hand the document to the person and tell him what it is. If he will not take it the server should explain what the document contains and leave it as nearly in his possession as he can. It suffices if the document is dropped at the feet of the person being served.

Where a partnership is sued in the firm's name, personal service is effected by leaving the document with any partner. Pre-CPR that partner could be served anywhere. However, PD 6, para.4.1 is headed "personal service on partners" and provides that "where partners are sued in the name of a partnership, service should be effected in accordance with r.6.4(5) and the table set out in r.6.5(5) where it refers to an 'individual who is suing or being sued in the name of a firm'". However, the table appears in r.6.5(6) rather than 6.5(5) as set out below. If that is to be followed it appears personal service should be at the partner's residence or on him at the firm's principal place of business. If a partner is served at say the local theatre we fail to see that he can or should seek to argue that such service was ineffective. In the alternative, proceedings may be left with any person who, at the time of service, has the control or management of the partnership business at its principal or last known place of business. Arguably, an office manager could be served but not the receptionist. To avoid any potential arguments it is best practice to always serve a partner.

If the partnership has more than one place of business, it is a question of fact as to which constitutes the principal office. The headed notepaper of the firm might state this. Otherwise it may be said to be where any central administration is carried out. Whoever is served must also be handed a notice in Form N218 stating whether he is being served as a partner, or as a person having control or management of the partnership business, or as both (PD 6, para.4.2). The process server should explain the notice to ensure the correct person is being served.

A document is personally served on a company or other corporation by leaving it with a person holding a "senior position". By PD 6, para.6.2, in respect of a registered company or corporation that is a director, the treasurer, secretary, chief executive, manager or other officer; and for a corporation which is not a registered company includes, in addition, the mayor, chairman, president, town clerk or similar officer; this list is not exhaustive. In *Gregson v Channel Four Television Corporation*, *The Times*, August 19, 2000 there was uncontradicted evidence that the person with whom the document was left was employed by the defendant corporation as a senior business executive. The Court of Appeal held that this was personal service on " a company or other corporation" under r.6.4(4).

Postal service (r.6.2(1)(b))

According to the rules service by post will be effective only if first-class post is used or any alternative service which provides for delivery on the next working day. So the rules do not permit service by second-class post save where the party to be served is a registered company (see further, para.8.010).

8.003

If it is effected correctly (e.g. the document is enclosed in an envelope which is properly addressed, stamped and posted) service by post will give rise to an irrebuttable presumption of service even if in fact the document never reaches the addressee (see further at para.8.013). Irrebuttable presumptions also arise in respect of each of the next four methods of service if they are effected correctly.

Leaving the document at "the place of service" (rr.6.2(1)(c) and 6.5(4)(b))

8.004 This method of service is a variation on service by post. Instead of employing a postman to deliver the document to the recipient's address, the party serving can take the document there himself, or employ another agent, for example, a courier or enquiry agent.

Document exchange (DX) (PD 6, para.2.1)

8.005 The DX is a private post retrieval system used by many businesses and professions including most firms of solicitors. Each subscriber has a box which has a distinct box number and which is located at the DX office nearest to them. Letters and parcels delivered to that DX office or any other DX office in the country will be delivered to that box, usually within 24 hours. Service by DX is permitted if the party to be served includes his DX number in his address for service (see para.8.009) or in his or his solicitors' writing paper. In the (perhaps unlikely) event that a DX subscriber is or later becomes unwilling to accept service by DX, he can prevent it by so informing other parties in writing (e.g. altering his writing paper to say "service by DX not accepted").

Facsmile (Fax) (PD 6, para.3.1)

8.006 Service may be effected by fax only if the party to be served or his legal representative has previously indicated that he is willing to accept service by fax and has stated the fax number to which the document should be sent. However, the existence of a fax number on a legal representative's writing paper will constitute such notice as will the inclusion of the fax number in a statement of case, acknowledgment of service or similar document. The inclusion of a fax number in the writing paper of the party to be served does not by itself authorise service by fax. Parties (unlike legal representatives) must expressly indicate in writing their willingness to accept service by this means, either by letter ("in writing") or by including the fax number in the statement of case, acknowledgment or similar document. For a cautionary tale see *Hart Investments Ltd v Fidler* [2006] EWHC 2857, (2007) L.T.L., January 18.

PD 6, para.3.3 states that any fax number given by a party "must be at the address for service". The PD does not make clear what happens if, in fact, the number relates to a telephone line at a different address or is a mobile phone number. Will an attempted service by fax fail if the fax is received at a different address? It is difficult to believe that a party who fails to comply with the Practice Direction will be permitted to rely upon his own wrong in order to invalidate any service by fax he later receives. PD 6, para.3.3 gives clearer guidance in the case of service by email or other electronic identification (as to which see below). An email address or electronic identification is deemed to be at the correct address (even if, in fact, it is not).

PD 6, paras 3.1 to 3.4 does not contain an express provision permitting a party or solicitor who has authorised service by fax to countermand that authority later (e.g. by stating in writing "service by fax not accepted"). Possibly he can still so state but he should ensure that he brings this to the attention of the other parties. Where a document is served by fax, the party serving it need not in addition send a hard copy by post or DX. However, in practice, a hard copy is usually sent. Fax numbers can be misdialled thereby sending faxes astray. Sending another copy by post or DX is a quick and easy way of making double sure of service. Keeping a copy of a copy sent by post or DX provides on the file a simple and familiar form of proof of good service. Such proof may be important if the party served later applies to set aside a default judgment and/or later denies that the document was served.

Email and similar electronic means of service (PD 6, para.3.1)

Service may be effected by email or other similar means only if the party to be served or his legal representative has previously indicated in writing a willingness to accept such service and has stated the email address or other electronic identification to which documents may be sent. Inclusion of the email address or electronic identification in a statement of claim, Acknowledgment of Service or similar document, will constitute such notice. However, the inclusion of, for example, an email address in the writing paper of the party or his legal representative does not by itself authorise service by email. The rule makers appreciate that most parties and solicitors are unwilling to accept service by email. The email addresses most solicitors use are personal to them. Problems may arise if documents are served by email at a time when the solicitor in question is absent from his office, whether on holiday or on business elsewhere.   8.007

Assume that a party has expressly authorised service by email. A party seeking so to serve should first seek to clarify with his opponent whether there are any limitations he should be aware of, such as the format in which documents are to be sent and the maximum size of attachments that may be received (PD 6, para.3.2). Having served a document by email it is not necessary to send a hard copy by post or fax. However, sending a hard copy may in fact be easier and cheaper than, for example, requesting the recipient to send a "read" receipt and then remembering to look out to see whether he does so. Also, sending another copy by post or DX is a quick and easy way of making double sure of service. Keeping a copy of a copy sent by post or DX provides on the file a simple and familiar form of proof of good service. Such proof may be important if the party served later applies to set aside a default judgment and/or later denies that the document was served.

WHO IS TO SERVE (R.6.3)

As a general rule if the court has issued or prepared a document it will also serve it. However, the court can order the parties to both prepare and serve   8.008

documents. Some courts appear to take the view that where the party applying for an order has prepared it on disk, there is a saving in time and costs if that party files and serves the order in the form that it is finally made. Local practice varies and you should find out what your courts require.

Whilst r.6.3(2) provides that the court can serve a document by any of the prescribed methods, PD 6, para.8.1 states that it will normally use the first-class post. If you want a document personally served you will have to arrange this yourself as there is no provision in the rules for service by a court officer. The key document that you will want served personally is a claim form where the limitation period has already expired or will shortly expire. In these circumstances it is sensible to attend at the court office to have the claim form issued and to take it away with you along with the response pack. If you ever send a document to the court to be issued but you wish to serve it yourself you must make that abundantly clear in your covering letter to ensure that the court does return it to you. Where the court issues and serves the claim form it will give notice to the claimant on a prescribed form—N205A (specified claim) or B (unspecified claim). This also states the date of deemed service (see further, para.8.013, below). If after posting a claim form to the address given it is returned to the court, you will receive a notice to that effect from the court (see r.6.11).

Address for service (r.6.5)

8.009 A party's address for service is the address which other parties must use for the purposes of service if they wish to serve documents by post, DX, fax, email or other electronic means. A party must give an address for service within the jurisdiction. (As to service out of the jurisdiction, see Ch.11). The claimant must give an address for service on the claim form itself. A defendant must state his address for service on any acknowledgment of service or defence. Where a party is represented by a solicitor, the solicitor's business address is that party's address for service for virtually all purposes (for exceptions, see para.8.001, above). A party who resides or carries on business within the jurisdiction who is not represented by a solicitor must give his residence or place of business as his address for service. Where a party has no solicitor acting for him and has not given an address for service the service of documents on him can be effected either by personal service (which may be expensive) or by taking or posting the document to one of the places specified by r.6.5(6) which provides as follows:

(a) An individual can be served at his usual or last known residence.
(b) A proprietor of a business can be served at his usual or last known residence; or at his place of business or last known place of business.
(c) An individual who is suing or being sued in the name of a firm can be served at his usual or last known residence; or at the principal or last known place of business of the firm.
(d) A corporation incorporated in England and Wales other than a company can be served at its principal office; or at any place within the

jurisdiction where it carries on its activities and which has a real connection with the claim.

(e) A company registered in England and Wales can be served at its principal office; or at any place of business within the jurisdiction which has a real connection with the claim.

(f) Any other corporation or company can be served at any place within the jurisdiction where the corporation carries on its activities; or at any place of business of the company within the jurisdiction.

Unless it fails for some other reason, service via an address for service given by the party to be served is valid even if that party no longer resides or carries on business at that address and even if, if it is a solicitor's address, that solicitor no longer carries on business there or has been disinstructed (r.6.5(4)). PD 6, para.7 states that:

"A party or his legal representative who changes his address for service shall give notice in writing of the change as soon as it has taken place to the court and every other party".

It appears that a person's "usual ... residence" (see (a), (b) and (c) above) has to be determined objectively, without reference to the state of knowledge of the party serving the document. It is a question of fact: see *Cherney v Deripaska* [2007] EWHC 965, (2007) L.T.L., May 10. A more important question is what constitutes a person's "last known residence". There are three possible approaches to determine this question: the narrow approach (considering only the knowledge of the party serving the document or his agents); the wide view (considering the knowledge available to the general public, whether or not it was known to the party serving the document or his agents); or the middle view (considering the actual knowledge of the party serving at his agents but also imputing to them knowledge they could or should have acquired by taking reasonable steps to ascertain or check the address). Case law runs in favour of the middle view (see *Cranfield v Bridgegrove Ltd* [2003] 1 W.L.R. 2441, CA, para.103; *Mersey Docks Property Holdings v Kilgour* [2004] EWHC 1638 (TCC) and *Marshall Rankine v Maggs* [2006] EWCA Civ 20, [2006] 1 W.L.R. 1945). But note that service is not effective at an address where the defendant has never lived as decided in *Marshall Rankine*.

Can proceedings that are issued for service within the jurisdiction be properly served at a defendant's last known residence when, at the time of deemed service, the defendant is resident out of the jurisdiction? No, held Evans-Lombe J. in *Fairmays (formerly Palmer Cowen) (a firm) v Palmer* [2006] EWHC 96, (2006) L.T.L., January 31. In the case the defendant had until May 2003 been residing in England. He then left to live in Addis Ababa, Ethiopia, on a three year consultancy contract. In July 2003 he wrote to the claimant informing it that he was working abroad and no longer living at his former address in England. This case should be contrasted with *Kamali v City & Country Properties Ltd* [2006] EWCA Civ 1879, (2007) L.T.L., January 31. There the claimant was served at his place of business in England but he was temporarily out of the jurisdiction at the time. The Court of Appeal held that the service was valid. So how should a claimant overcome the difficulties of seeking to serve proceedings on a defendant for whom they did not have an accepted address for service but who they suspect may be absent abroad or become so? As the court suggested in *Fairmays* the solution may be to issue concurrent proceedings for service abroad in respect of which an order for alternative service on the last known address of the defendant within the jurisdiction can be obtained.

No difficulty arises with the expression "real connection with the claim" (see (d) and (e) above). The notes on completing a claim form state that, in respect of a company, the address for service may be given as "any place of business that has a real, or the most connection with the claim, for example, the shop where the goods were bought". It has been held that the place where a foreign corporation or company "carries on its activities" or has "any place of business" (see (f) above) is effectively the same: documents can be sent or taken to any place within the jurisdiction which has a connection with the foreign corporation or company which is more than a transient or irregular connection (*Lakah Group v Al Jazeera Satellite Channel* [2003] EWCA Civ 781).

For service on the Crown see 24.018

SERVICE ON COMPANIES

8.010 We use the term companies here to cover both companies and corporations. The CPR provisions just covered as to personal service, postal service and the other permitted methods of service are not limited to service on individuals. They also apply to service on companies, including foreign companies if they give an address for service in the UK, or authorise a solicitor to accept service or have a place of business in the UK. There are also provisions in the Companies Act 1985 which, as r.6.2(2) makes clear, may offer additional methods of service in some cases. In the case of foreign companies, the additional methods available are in fact more restrictive than the CPR methods. Accordingly, they have little practical value except where, by mistake, the serving party has failed to comply with the CPR provisions. For example, a serving party might turn to them if he has overlooked the fact that the foreign company previously authorised a solicitor to accept service, or gave an address for service in this country, or if the party serving has posted the document other than by way of first-class post. Section 694A of the 1985 Act provides for the service on a foreign company which has a branch in Great Britain but only if the claim "is in respect of the business of that branch" (and see *Saab v Saudi American Bank* [1999] 1 W.L.R. 1861, CA). Section 695 of the 1985 Act covers foreign companies which do not have a branch here in the UK: it permits service on the company if it has an established place of business here (as to which see *Adams v Cape Industries* [1990] 1 Ch.433, CA).

Section 725 applies to companies registered under the Companies Act 1985. It also relaxed the restriction on using first class post and does not adopt the CPR provisions as to deemed service (as to which see para.8.013, below). Under s.725 any document can be served on a company registered under the Act by leaving it at or sending it by post to the registered office of the company, i.e. even if that is not its "place of business". In the case of service by post it is immaterial whether first-class post, second-class post, recorded delivery or registered post is used. Delivery is presumed "in the ordinary course of post" if there is proof of proper addressing, prepaying and posting (Interpretation Act 1978, s.7). The presumed date of service depends upon the class of post used. Pre-CPR the presumed date of service was the second business day after posting if first-class post was used or the fourth business day after posting if second-class post was used. The presumption of delivery will be rebutted if the letter is returned by the post office undelivered to the company. Due service on a registered company under s.725 is valid even where the company has solicitors acting for it who have written to the party serving confirming that they have instructions to accept service (*Cranfield v Bridgegrove Ltd* [2003] 1 W.L.R. 2441, CA, para.86).

SERVICE OF DOCUMENTS ON CHILDREN AND PATIENTS

Rule 6.6 prescribes the methods of service according to the type of document that is to be served as follows: 8.011

(a) A claim form issued against a child who is not also a patient is to be served on one of the child's parents or guardians; or if there is none, the person with whom the child resides or in whose care the child is at the time.
(b) A claim form issued against a patient is to be served on the person authorised under Pt VII of the Mental Health Act 1983 to conduct the proceedings in the name of the patient or on his behalf; or if there is no person so authorised, the person with whom he resides or in whose care he is at the time.
(c) As to service of an application for an order appointing a litigation friend, see Ch.7.
(d) Any other document is to be served on the litigation friend.

SERVICE OF DOCUMENTS ON MEMBERS OF THE FORCES

PD 6, para.5 and the Annex to the PD set out the detailed requirements as to service of documents on members of HM Forces and the United States Air Force. 8.012

DEEMED SERVICE (R.6.7)

8.013 A court order that requires a party to take a step in the proceedings should state the last day on which this can be done. In all other cases where a document is served that requires a response from the recipient within a specified time it is necessary to work out when that period begins. The method of service of the document determines when it is deemed to have been received. The rule provides that a document served by:

(a) first-class post (or any alternative service which provides for delivery on the next working day) is deemed to be served the second day after it was posted;

(b) document exchange is deemed to be served the second day after it was left at the document exchange;

(c) delivering it to, or leaving it at, a permitted address is deemed to be served the day after it was delivered to, or left at, the permitted address;

(d) fax is deemed to be served that day if it is transmitted on a business day before 4pm; but in any other case on the business day after it was transmitted (note that r.6.7(3) defines a business day as any day that is not a Saturday, Sunday or a bank holiday and the latter is said to include Christmas Day and Good Friday);

(e) other electronic means are deemed to be served the second day after it was transmitted;

(f) personal service after 5pm on a business day or at any time on a non-business day is deemed ("treated") as being served on the next business day.

As a result of a series of decisions culminating in the cases reported as *Cranfield v Bridgegrove Ltd* [2003] 1 W.L.R. 2441, CA, this rule has been interpreted in a way which is both revolutionary and surprising. The importance which the date of service has in the calculation of many other time periods in the rules has led to the conclusion that the deeming provisions in r.6.7 should be treated as irrebuttable. In an effort to provide certainty and to limit the scope for factual disputes the rule is taken to focus only upon the sending or transmission of the document, not its receipt. Proof of sending or transmission gives rise to an irrebuttable presumption that the document was served on the day indicated by the rule even if it can be proved as a fact that the document never came to the attention of the intended recipient. Fiction not fact now governs the date of service. For example, a claim form may be sent to an address which, as the claimant well knows, is an address at which the defendant is no longer living (Cranfield para.102) or a claim form claiming possession of a tenanted room in a house is sent by post to the address of the house (in which the claimant also lived) is valid even if it is not delivered to the defendant's room (*Akram v Adam* [2005] 1 All E.R. 741, CA, see further Ch.15). The day of service indicated by the rule applies no matter what evidence there is as to non-delivery of the document or delivery upon an earlier day or a later day. In almost all cases, any injustice the fiction may cause for the party serving can be avoided by the exercise of the court's discretion to extend the time for service (but see further, para.9.009). In order to limit injustice for the party served, the fiction of deemed service does not determine whether any default judgment a claimant obtains should be set aside (see further Ch.15). Unhappily, the possibility remains that the fiction will not provide the desired certainty, at least in the case of documents served by the parties rather than by the court. For example, a defendant wishing to challenge the service of a claim form within a relevant limitation period may dispute that the claim form was ever sent or may dispute the date upon which the claimant says the claim form was posted to him or the hour upon which the claimant says the document was served by fax or personally served.

In a further, and even more disquieting twist, the Court of Appeal has ruled that, in calculating the day of deemed service, Saturdays, Sundays and other non-business days should be included in the reckoning except in the case of service by fax (because there the rule expressly limits the calculation to business days; see (d) above). Rule 6.7(1) includes a cross-reference to r.2.8 (as to which, see para.1.018, above). However, the judgment of the court in one case states:

> "if it had been intended to exclude Saturdays and Sundays from the calculation of the deemed day of service by first-class post, the draftsman would probably have used, and if he wanted to make the position clear he ought to have used, the specially defined expressed "business day" to be found in and used in other parts of Rule 6.7."

The illogical mismatch of deemed dates according to the method of service used (some examples are given below) was noted as was the possibility of an amendment being made to the rule (*Anderton v Clwyd County Council (No.2)* [2002] 1 W.L.R. 3174, paras 44 and 45).

Examples

Assume that a claimant takes steps to serve a claim form on the first Friday in the month of February (i.e. a month which has no bank holidays). The day of service is:

(a) Friday if service by fax is used before 4pm or if personal service is used before 5pm.
(b) Saturday if service by delivery to a place of service is used.
(c) Sunday if service by post, DX or email is used.
(d) Monday if service by fax is used after 4pm or if personal service is used after 5pm.

Now assume that the claimant takes steps to serve a claim form on the first Tuesday in the month of February. The day of service is:

(a) Tuesday if service by fax is used before 4pm or if personal service is used before 5pm.

(b) Wednesday if delivery to a place of service is used.

(c) Thursday if service by post, DX or email is used or if service by fax is used after 4pm or if personal service is used after 5pm.

In all of these cases, might it not be preferable for r.6.7 to state the deemed day of service to be the second business day after posting if service by post is used otherwise the next business day after the date any other method of service was initiated? (Two days not one is appropriate for service by post in order to accommodate delays in the post and the possibility that the document may be put into a pillar box after the last collection has been made for that pillar box that day.)

SERVICE BY AN ALTERNATIVE METHOD (R.6.8)

8.014 If there is some impediment or difficulty in effecting service by the primary methods permitted by the CPR, an application can be made to the court to permit service by an alternative method. The applicant must demonstrate to the court "that there is a good reason to authorise service by a method not permitted by these Rules" (r.6.8(1)). If an order is made it must specify the method of service to be used and the date when the document will be deemed to be served (see para.8.013, above).

On what basis will an order be made? In *Albon v Naza Motor Trading SDN BHD (No.2)* [2007] EWHC 327, (2007) L.T.L., April 11, Lightman J. stated:

"the provisions of CPR Part 6.8 and the requirement of a good reason for authorising an alternative method of service must be interpreted and applied in a manner which gives effect to the overriding objective. In particular the court must have in mind the horrendous cost of litigation today, the hurdles thereby created in the way of obtaining justice on the part of those with limited means (and in particular those with limited means facing litigants with abundant means) and the need to ensure that cases proceed expeditiously. The question whether there is good reason is a matter to be determined by the judge at the date of the application on the particular facts of the case before him. It is not a precondition of the making of the order that service by a method permitted by the Rules is impracticable: it is only necessary that there is a good reason to make the order. In deciding what is a good reason the court will have in mind the overriding objective and whether the making of the order will enable the court to deal with the case justly. There is no good reason if the application is made to achieve a collateral object which the Rule is not designed to confer e.g. a step ahead in a race to commence proceedings in this jurisdiction before they are commenced elsewhere. The court will have in mind in circumscribing the ambit of what is a good reason that a finding of its existence is only the first stage in the process: the second stage must then be gone through of deciding whether the court's discretion should be exercised having regard to all the facts including the parties' conduct."

In times past the "good reasons" most often relied upon were that a defendant was evading service or was untraceable. Today these facts do not amount to any sort of problem if the claimant has a "last known address" for the defendant. The document can be served on that address thereby giving rise to an irrebuttable presumption of service even if the document never reaches its intended recipient (see para.8.013). An order for service by an alternative method might still be needed in the following cases.

(1) A negligence claim in which the claimant knows the name of the defendant and has details of the defendant's insurer but has no address for the defendant, whether current or past, or where the address the claimant has no longer exists because, for example, it has been demolished. The claimant has invited the insurer to nominate solicitors to act for the defendant but they have failed to do so. The court may allow service by post on the insurers or the Motor Insurers' Bureau (MIB) (*cf Gurtner v Circuit* [1968] 2 Q.B. 587 and the procedure agreed between the official solicitor and the MIB approved by the Senior Master on March 11, 2003 and *Abbey National Plc v Frost* [1999] 1 W.L.R. 1080).

(2) Proceedings brought by a local authority to obtain injunctions (interim and final) to prevent persons unknown converting land into and using a caravan site in breach of planning control. An Order was made under r.6.8 authorising service of the claim form by way of documents in plastic bags nailed to posts placed in prominent positions on the site (*South Cambridgeshire DC v Persons Unknown* [2004] EWCA Civ 1280 and see: *cf Bloomsbury Publishing Group Plc v News Group Newspapers Ltd* [2003] 1 W.L.R. 1633).

Two further cases provide examples of circumstances in which the court held it was not appropriate to allow service by an alternative method. In *Elmes v Hygrade Food Products Plc* [2001] EWCA Civ 121 the claim form was served in time but was incorrectly served on the defendant's insurers instead of on the defendant. It was now too late to serve the defendant because the relevant limitation period had expired. The claimant was refused an order which would have given retrospective authority to the incorrect service on the insurer. In *Knauf UK GmbH v British Gypsum Ltd* [2002] 1 W.L.R. 907, CA, the claimant wished to serve a claim form on an EU defendant via its solicitors in England even though they had not been nominated to accept service. The claimant's purpose was to use a speedier method of service than the methods otherwise available so as to obtain priority for the English courts. Such priority was unlikely to be obtained otherwise. It was held that a desire to subvert the normal rules allocating jurisdiction between EC courts was not a "good reason" for making an Order under r.6.8.

ORDER TO DISPENSE WITH SERVICE (R.6.9)

8.015　This power is most commonly exercised to dispense with reservice of documents, for example, if an amended statement of case is filed and served when the application to amend it is made, then on granting the application the court may well dispense with service of that document. Amending statements of case are dealt with in Ch.14.

In a series of decisions culminating in the cases reported as *Cranfield v Bridgegrove Ltd* [2003] 1 W.L.R. 2441 claimants have sought an order dispensing with service of a claim form in circumstances in which they have failed to make good service earlier and it was now too late to apply for an extension of time for service (as to which, see para.9.006, below). The cases have come to be divided into two categories: cases in which no attempt at all was made to effect service (category 1); and cases in which good service was attempted but not achieved (category 2). The strong message from Cranfield is that the court has no power to dispense with the service in category 1 cases and should be very slow to do so in all but the most exceptional category 2 cases. The court gave examples of exceptional circumstances which might justify an Order dispensing with service:

(i) Claim form sent to the correct person at the correct address and actually arrives in time but is irrebuttably deemed to arrive late (Cranfield paras 10 and 11).

(ii) Claim form sent to the correct person at the correct address and arrives in time but was sent by second-class post when first class post should have been used (Cranfield para.32).

(iii) Claimant served a photocopy of a claim form as issued by the court (instead of a court copy) which reaches the correct person at the correct address and arrives in time (Cranfield para.88).

The judgment, at para.32, anticipates that there may well be other circumstances in which it is proper to dispense with service of a claim form retrospectively. Such occurred in *Olafsson v Gissurarson (No.2)* [2006] EWHC 3214, (2007) L.T.L., January 4. Whilst the proceedings were personally served on the defendant in Iceland, the consul did not ask the defendant to sign a copy of the claim to acknowledge receipt as required by Icelandic law. Mackay J. held that "the failure to achieve valid service was for want of the merest of technicalities, in circumstances where the fact of service is accepted. The only defect was as to evidence of service, and the best evidence is now available in that the defendant accepts and has always accepted that he did indeed receive all the relevant documents in appropriate form at the appropriate time". Contrast that with the refusal to dispense with service in *Kuenyehia v International Hospitals Group Ltd* [2006] EWCA Civ 21, (2006) L.T.L. 15 December. There the claimants' solicitors purported to serve a copy of the claim form by fax to the legal department of the defendant on the fax number recorded in the defendant's letters. The failure to first obtain the defendant's written consent to service by fax (see para.8.006) meant that the method of service employed was not permitted by the CPR.

SPECIAL PROVISIONS ABOUT SERVICE OF THE CLAIM FORM

Service by a contractually agreed method (r.6.15)

In order to avoid or minimise problems of service, some contracts specify a particular method of service which may be used should a claim in relation to the contract later be issued. A typical method is service upon nominated firms of solicitors in England. Rule 6.15 provides that, in such cases, the claim form will be deemed to be served on the defendant if it is served by the method specified provided that the claim form is issued only in respect of a claim under that contract. If (unusually) the specified method involves service out of the jurisdiction r.6.15 does not dispense with the need to obtain any permission otherwise needed (r.6.15(2) and see para.11.008, below).

8.016

Ad hoc agreements for service

In *Kenneth Allison Ltd v A. E. Limehouse & Co.* [1992] 2 A.C. 105 proceedings issued against a firm of chartered accountants was served at the firm's principal place of business on a personal assistant who, immediately before service, was authorised to accept service by one of the partners who was in another part of the premises. The service was held to be effective even though it was not one of the methods permitted by the rules of court, (there had been no personal service on a partner and the personal assistant was not a person in control of the business). It is arguable that the CPR prohibit ad hoc agreements for service which are not permitted by the rules (see rr.6.1, 6.13 and 6.16). The point was raised in *Cranfield v Bridgegrove Ltd* [2003] 1 W.L.R. 2441, CA but was not decided upon (see especially, para.85). In our view, if such an argument ever succeeded, a claimant who had served a claim form in accordance with an ad hoc agreement should be granted an order dispensing the service under the rules (as to which see para.8.015, above).

8.017

Service on an agent of a principal who is overseas (r.6.16)

If a principal resides and carries on business out of the jurisdiction, but he entered into a contract with the claimant by or through an agent who resides or carries on business within the jurisdiction, the court may order service of the claim form on that agent. The claimant must apply to the court for its permission with supporting evidence dealing with the following:

8.018

(a) Full details of the contract including that it was entered into within the jurisdiction by an agent who was also acting within the jurisdiction.
(b) That the principal is, and was at the time of the contract, out of the jurisdiction.
(c) Why service out of the jurisdiction cannot be effected. It is this last provision that limits the usefulness of r.6.16. Although, a century ago, service out of the jurisdiction was often expensive and difficult, today it usually is not (see further, Ch.11).
(d) That at the time of the application the agent's authority has not been terminated or that he is still in business relations with his principal.

Where the court make an order it must state the period within which the defendant must respond to the particulars of the claim.

CERTIFICATES OF SERVICE (R.6.10)

8.019 A party who serves a document must also file at court a certificate of service in Form N215 if such a certificate is required by any rule, practice direction or court order. The foremost example of such a requirement is r.6.14(2)(a) which states that where a claim form is served by the claimant he must file a certificate of service within seven days. Until he has done so he is not entitled to enter judgment in default (see Ch.15).

CHAPTER 9

From Issue to Allocation

INTRODUCTION

This Chapter follows the progress of an action from commencement (whether in the High Court or a county court) through to allocation to one of the three case management tracks. Most actions can be started by completing a Form N1, a claim form generally known as a Pt 7 Claim. You then send it (with copies for the court and for each defendant named) usually to the court of your choice together with the issue fee. In some cases a different claim form is used (for example, N2, Probate Claim, N5, Possession of Property and N8, Arbitration).

This Chapter does not cover the various methods of service (as to which see Ch.8), the alternative procedure for claims under Pt 8 (as to which see Ch.10) or the topic of drafting statements of case (as to which see Ch.12).

9.001

HIGH COURT OR COUNTY COURT?

As a general rule if both the High Court and county court have jurisdiction to deal with a case you can consider issuing in either court. However, there are limitations. For example, proceedings cannot be commenced in a county court for libel or slander, or in respect of any toll, fair, market or franchise unless the parties agree in writing. Most possession claims (i.e. claims for the recovery of possession of land, see further para.24.005) must be started in the county court for the district in which the land is situated. Only in exceptional cases can the claim be started in the High Court and, in such cases, the claimant must file a certificate stating the reasons for bringing the claim in that court (r.55.3). PD 55, para.1.3 lists circumstances which may, in an appropriate case, justify starting a possession claim in the High Court: complicated disputes of fact, points of law of general importance or claims against trespassers with a substantial risk of public disturbance or serious harm to persons or property which require immediate determination. Although the value of the land and the amount of any financial claim may be relevant, these factors alone will not normally justify starting an action in the High Court (PD 55, para.1.4).

9.002

There are financial restrictions on starting money claims in the High Court (r.7.1 and PD 7, paras 2.1 and 2.2). A claim must be worth more than certain prescribed amounts before it can be taken in the High Court. Proceedings for either a specified or unspecified amount of money that do not include a claim for personal injuries may not be started in the High Court unless the value of the claim is more than £15,000. Where proceedings include a claim for personal injury damages the value of the claim must be £50,000 or more. A "claim for personal injuries" is defined in r.2.3(1) as a claim for damages in respect of personal injuries to the claimant or any other person or in respect of a person's death, and "personal injuries" includes any disease and any impairment of a person's physical or mental condition.

Rule 16.3 explains how a claimant should calculate the value of a money claim. The claim form must contain a statement of value and this will normally make clear the amount of money the claimant is claiming (if it is a fixed sum) or the amount he "expects to recover" (if the amount claimed is not a fixed sum). The perils of exaggerating one's expectations in order to get into the High Court and/or to avoid the small claims track or the fast track are dealt with later in this Chapter. The statement of value should not be increased by taking into account interest or costs or any sums that may be payable under the Social Security (Recovery of Benefits) Act 1997 (as to which see para.4.004) and should not be decreased on account of any possible finding of contributory negligence. A statement of value in a claim brought by two or more claimants usually aggregates the amounts each claimant expects to recover. It is important to note here two respects in which the court may calculate the value of a claim differently from a claimant. When it is deciding whether to allocate the claim to a particular track, the court will disregard any amount which is not in dispute and, where there are two or more claimants, will consider the claim of each claimant separately (r.26.8, and see further para.9.034, below).

Claims below the financial hurdles just described must be commenced in a county court. Claims above them may be commenced in either the High Court or the county court. In these, larger, cases PD 7, para.2.4 gives a steer in favour of a county court. It provides that a claimant should start his claim in the High Court if he believes that "it ought to be dealt with by a High Court Judge". The basis upon which he should form this opinion appears to be, first, a recognition that the case might go to trial (district judges and masters deal with most cases before that stage) and then taking into account three matters listed in para.2.4:

(1) the financial value of the claim and the amount in dispute, and/or
(2) the complexity of facts, legal issues, remedies or procedures involved, and/or
(3) the importance of the outcome of the claim to the public in general.

Similar matters will be considered by the court when it considers (if it does) whether to transfer a case (see further para.9.023) and when it considers allocation to track (see further para.9.034).

WHICH COURT OFFICE?

Once past the decision as to the type of court (High Court or county court) there is generally no restriction as to which locality in England and Wales the claimant can start proceedings. Most claimants will want to issue out of the county court office or the High Court Central Office or district registry which is most conveniently located to themselves or to their solicitors. However, there are some types of claim where restrictions are imposed, for example, consumer credit claims and some actions for the recovery of land (see further, Ch.24). Bear in mind also that some claims for a specified amount of money may later be automatically transferred to the "defendant's home court" (see further para.9.024). In other cases the defendant might later apply for transfer of the case to a different court (see further para.9.025).

9.003

Are the parties bound by a contractual agreement to start proceedings in a particular court in England and Wales? In *Snookes v Jani-King (GB) Ltd* [2006] EWHC 289, (2006) L.T.L. February 23, it was a term of a contract between the parties that, "Save as provided herein any proceedings arising out of or in connection with this Agreement shall be brought in a court of competent jurisdiction in London". The claimant issued proceedings in the Swansea District Registry of the High Court. Silber J. held that the term was binding and set aside the claim form.

WHEN ARE PROCEEDINGS COMMENCED? (R.7.2)

Proceedings are started when the court issues a claim form by dating it. However, if a claim form is received by the court office on an earlier date, the claim is at that point in time "brought" for the purposes of the Limitation Act 1980 and any other relevant statute: see PD 7 para.5.1 and *St Helens Metropolitan BC v Barnes* [2006] EWCA Civ 1372, [2007] 1 W.L.R. 879. The court should record when the claim form was received by means of the date being stamped either on the claim form held on the court file or on the letter that accompanied it. If you intend to issue proceedings towards the end of the relevant limitation period it is essential to have someone attend in person at the court office to do this and obtain a dated receipt if the court cannot immediately process the documentation.

9.004

SERVICE OF CLAIM FORM

Time for service

Rule 7.5 states a general rule that the claim form must be served on the defendant within four months of the date of issue or, where it is to be served out of the jurisdiction (see Ch.11) within six months of the date of issue. The last day upon which service or deemed service must be effected is the corresponding day of the relevant month, or the last day of that month if there is no corresponding day.

9.005

Examples

A claim form to be served within the jurisdiction is issued on August 17, 2007. The last date for service or deemed service under r.7.5 is December 17, 2007.

A claim form to be served outside the jurisdiction is issued on August 17, 2007. The last day for service or deemed service under r.7.5 is February 17, 2008.

A claim form for service within the jurisdiction is issued on October 31, 2007. The last date for service or deemed service under r.7.5 is February 29, 2008.

Rule 7.5 states a general rule to which there are, of course, exceptions. The most notable perhaps concerns claims for a new tenancy under s.24 and for the termination of a tenancy under s.29(2) of the Landlord and Tenant Act 1954 where the time for service is two months "and rules 7.5 and 7.6 are modified accordingly" (r.56.3).

In *Vinos v Marks & Spencer Plc* [2001] 3 All E.R. 784 the Court of Appeal explained that serving a claim form later than the last day permitted is a problem for the claimant which the court cannot remedy by granting an extension of time under its general powers (under r.3.1, as to which see para.33.002) or under its general power to rectify errors of procedure (r.3.10, as to which see para.1.015). Moreover, in *Cranfield v Bridgegrove Ltd* [2003] 1 W.L.R. 2441 the Court of Appeal explained why another possible solution, an order dispensing with service, will be available only in the most exceptional of cases (see further para.8.015). This means that the only available methods of obtaining more time for service are: (i) to issue a new claim form, but this would be futile if the relevant limitation period has now expired (see further Ch.5); or (ii) to apply for an extension of time for service under the rule to which we now turn.

Application for extension of time for service

9.006   Applications for an extension of time for service under r.7.6 are usually made without notice and should be supported by evidence stating (at PD 7, para.8.1 and 8.2):

   (i)   all the circumstances relied on;
   (ii) the date of issue of the claim;
   (iii) the expiry date of any time extension previously ordered; and
   (iv) a full explanation as to why the claim has not been served.

If it is successful, a copy of the order granting an extension will be served on the defendant together with the claim form and other documents. The defendant will then have (usually) seven days in which to apply (on notice) to have the order set aside under r.23.10 (see further para.13.005, below).

If the time limit to service the claim form is about to expire, the warning in *Collier v Williams* [2006] EWCA Civ 20, [2006] 1 W.L.R. 1945, should be heeded.

"An application for an extension of time for service of the claim form is potentially of critical importance, especially where the application is made shortly before the end of the 4 months period for service and where the cause of action has become time-barred since the date on which the claim form was issued. If the application is allowed and an extension of time is given, the defendant can always apply under CPR 23.10 for the order to be set aside, in which case the applicant may be worse off than if it had been refused in the first place. It is highly desirable that on the without notice application, full consideration (with proper testing of the argument) is given to the issue of whether the relief sought should be granted. Equally, if an application is made late in the day and refused on paper when proper argument would have made it proper to grant, a great deal of heart-ache can be saved. We think that applications of this kind, where time limits are running out, should normally be dealt with by an urgent hearing. We accept, however, that owing to time constraints, pressure of business and the like, it will sometimes not be possible to deal with such an application other than on paper. Even in such cases, however, consideration should be given to dealing with the application by telephone" (*per* Dyson L.J.).

Rule 7.6 makes significantly different provisions for two types of application for extension: Applications made before expiry of the original period or any extended period previously ordered; and applications made after expiry of the original period and any extended period previously ordered. Before describing the different provisions it is as well to state now that most applications under r.7.6 will fail. The time requirements laid down by the rules are important and must be observed. Because they are imposed in pursuit of the legitimate aim of the good administration of justice, they do not impair the claimant's right to a fair trial under ECHR Art.6 (*Anderton v Clwyd County Council (No.2)* [2002] 1 W.L.R. 3174, CA, para.31).

A claimant who applies before the time limit has expired is not required to show that he has at all times taken all reasonable steps to effect service. The court will take a calibrated approach: the better his conduct the more likely it is that an extension will be allowed; the worse his conduct the more likely it is that the court will refuse to grant the extension. Just how good his conduct has to be is demonstrated by the facts of *Hashtroodi v Hancock* [2004] 1 W.L.R. 3206 in which the Court of Appeal explained the principles. In that case the claimant suffered catastrophic injuries in a road accident and instructed solicitors to take proceedings against the defendant. Although negotiations began within a few months of the accident the claim form was not issued until just one week before the relevant limitation period expired. The claimant's solicitor did not attempt to serve the claim form until the last month for service when he wrote to the defendant's insurers inviting them to nominate solicitors to accept service, and stated that, otherwise, the defendant would be served personally. That letter, which was sent to the wrong address, never received a written reply. The claimant's solicitor did not in fact attempt to serve the claim form on the defendant personally. Instead, on the day before the expiry of the four month time limit, he made a without notice application for a three week extension of time which was granted. Within the next week solicitors were nominated to accept service, did so accept and applied to set aside the extension of time that had been granted. The extension was set aside by the Court of Appeal.

"[35] It follows that this is a case where there is no reason for the failure to serve other than the incompetence of the claimant's legal representatives. Although this is not an absolute bar, it is a powerful reason for refusing to grant an extension of time. Despite this, [counsel for the claimant] submits that an extension should be granted. In relation to the application of the overriding objective, he relies on the following factors. First, the claim is very substantial. Secondly, the issues in the case were identified early on, so that a short extension of time would not undermine the case management process. Thirdly, the extension of time would not put the parties on a more or less equal footing than they would have been if the extension were not granted. Fourthly, the extension would not increase the cost of the litigation. Fifthly, it would be disproportionate to refuse the extension. Finally, the defendant has not suffered any prejudice as a result of the extension, since at the date of the claimant's application, the defendant had not yet acquired an accrued limitation defence.

'[36] We are in no doubt that the time for serving the claim form should not be extended in this case. The absence of any explanation for the failure to serve is, on the facts of this case, decisive. Sadly, the errors on the part of [the claimant's solicitor] were particularly egregious. The other facts identified by [counsel for the claimant] are not sufficient to outweigh the complete absence of any reason which might go some way to excusing the failure to serve in time. If we were to grant an extension of time in the present case, it seems to us that the rule stated in CPR r.7.5 would cease to be the general rule. Moreover, there would be a real risk that statements made by this court about the importance of the need to observe time limits would not be taken seriously. That would be most unfortunate'". (Dyson L.J.).

In *Leeson v Marsden* [2006] EWCA Civ 20, [2006] 1 W.L.R. 1945, the Court of Appeal stressed that without any good reason to explain the failure to serve the claim form in time, normally an order under r.7.6(2) should be refused.

"It is true that in *Hashtroodi's* case, the court said at para 18 that the power in CPR 7.6(2) had to be exercised in accordance with the overriding objective. But it went on to say that this means that it will always be relevant for the court to determine and evaluate the reason why the claimant did not serve the claim form within the specified period. That is the critical inquiry that the court must undertake in these cases. The strength or the weakness of the reason for the failure to serve is not one of a number of factors of roughly equal importance to be weighed in the balance. The exercise of going through the check list of factors set out in CPR 1.1(2) will often not be necessary. If, as in the present case, there is no reason to justify the failure to serve the claim form in time, it should normally not be necessary to go further" (*per* Dyson L.J.).

It is vital to remember that the claim form does not have to contain full details of the claim. All that is required is a concise statement of the nature of the claim (see para.12.009). So the court will not extend the time for service of the claim form if the claimant is awaiting receipt of documentation he requires in order to complete the particulars of claim (see *Glass v Surrendran* [2006] EWCA Civ 20, [2006] 1 W.L.R. 1945).

The road is rockier still for applicants in the second group. Rule 7.6(3) states that if the time for service (whether fixed by rule or by a previous order) has expired the court may grant an extension only if:

(a) the court has been unable to serve the claim form (this has been held to include cases where, by oversight, the court has not attempted to serve; *Cranfield v Bridgegrove Ltd* [2003] 1 W.L.R. 2441, para.29);
(b) the claimant has taken all reasonable steps to serve the claim form but has been unable to do so; and
(c) in either case, the claimant has acted promptly in making the application.

The difference between the two sub-rules was explained by the Court of Appeal in *Marshall Rankine v Maggs* [2006] EWCA Civ 20, [2006] 1 W.L.R. 1945.

"CPR 7.6(3) is subject to pre-conditions: relief *cannot* be granted if the conditions are not satisfied. Under CPR 7.6(2), there are no pre-conditions, so that relief can be granted under that rule even if the court is not satisfied that the claimant has taken all reasonable steps to serve and has acted promptly. The decision in *Hashtroodi's* case highlights the importance of the reason why the claim form was not (if it was not) served within the 4 months period. We would agree that the CPR 7.6(3) requirements are *relevant* to the exercise of the discretion given by CPR 7.6(2). But the fact that the pre-conditions stated in CPR 7.6(3)(b) and (c) are not satisfied is not necessarily determinative of the outcome of an application under CPR 7.6(2). That is clear from the passages set out at para 87 above. When deciding whether to grant an extension of time under CPR 7.6(2), the court is required to consider how good a reason there was for the failure to serve in time (assuming that the application is dealt with after the end of the 4 months period): the stronger the reason, the more likely the court will be to extend time; and the weaker the reason, the less likely. This involves making a judgment about the reason why service has not been effected within the 4 months period. It is a more subtle exercise that that required under CPR 7.6(3) which provides that unless *all* reasonable steps have been taken, the court *cannot* extend time" *per* Dyson L.J.

If a claimant purports to serve proceedings on an address which he mistakenly believes is the last known residence of the defendant (see para.8.009), it is necessary to consider the reasonableness of that belief. In the *Marshall Rankine v Maggs* case, the court stated that if the claimant is misled by the defendant as to his residence, then the court is likely to hold that the claimant had reasonable grounds for his belief. In such circumstances, the court is likely to hold that there is a very good reason for the claimant's failure to serve within the four months period and to grant an extension of time. In such a case the defendant may even be estopped from denying that the address to which the document is sent is his last known residence.

> "But it is incumbent on a claimant to take reasonable steps to ascertain a defendant's last known residence. What that involves must depend on the circumstances of the case. In many cases, the claimant will know the address for certain. Where the position is less clear, a direct request of the defendant, or his legal representatives (if they do not have instructions to accept service) may yield an answer. Other enquiries may have to be made. But the present case shows how dangerous it can be to make assumptions. In our judgment, the first claimant did not have a reasonable basis for concluding that 47 Hays Mews was the defendant's last known residence. He did not *know* that it was his last known residence. He assumed that it was. He had no real basis for believing that it was the defendant's residence" (*per* Dyson L.J.).

Further guidance as to sub-rule (b) was given by the Court of Appeal in *Carnegie v Drury* [2007] EWCA Civ 497, *The Times*, June 11, 2007. This only requires the judge to consider whether all reasonable steps were taken to serve the defendant during the four month period allowed. Attempts made after that time are irrelevant and must not be taken into account. Note also that in the case a 10 week delay in making the application was held not to meet sub-rule (c).

DEFENDANT'S RIGHT TO CALL FOR SERVICE

9.007   Rule 7.7 provides that, where a claim form has been issued against the defendant but has not yet been served on him, he may serve a notice requiring the claimant either to discontinue the claim or serve it within a period specified in the notice (which must be at least 14 days after service of the notice). If the claimant fails to comply with that notice the defendant may then apply to the court for the dismissal of the claim or some other sanction. In practice defendants rarely exercise their right to call for service. It is of course entirely possible that the claimant's delay in service could cause problems for the defendant especially if publicity about the claim was damaging his reputation. However, even in that case, most defendants would prefer to sit it out and hope that the claimant never validly served.

Defendants often find out that a claim form has been issued before it is served upon them. The intention to commence proceedings will have been mentioned during the pre-action protocol stage. Indeed, in several of the cases recently before the Court of Appeal, the claimant's solicitors had sent the defendant's solicitor or insurer a copy of the claim form (for information only, not by way of service). By doing so, they sought to avoid starting off the timetable for the service of statements of case. This, of course, proved to be a most dangerous practice. It is far better for claimants to serve proceedings and either agree an extension of time to serve particulars of claim, or obtain an order for one (see para.9.010, below).

PARTICULARS OF CLAIM (R.7.4)

The claimant must "state his case" by way of particulars. As to drafting the claim form, particulars of claim and other statements of case, see Ch.12. 9.008

Particulars of claim may appear on the claim form itself or they can be prepared and served as a separate document. PD 16, para.3.1 provides that particulars should be set out in the claim form if that is practicable. Where you have adequately investigated the case under the pre-action protocol procedures, the particulars of claim should be served with the claim form. However, there is no prohibition on issuing a claim form without particulars.

When must particulars be served? (r.7.4)

Where the particulars of claim are included on the claim form, or are ready as a separate document at the time of issue, you should send such to the court along with the issue fee and sufficient copies of each document (one for the court file and one for each defendant). Remember that you can ask the court to serve the proceedings or return the service copies to you for you to effect service (see Ch.8). 9.009

If a claim form is issued without particulars of claim it must contain a statement that the particulars will follow. In these circumstances the court will return the service copy of the claim form to you for you to serve it on the defendant either with or without particulars of claim. If you serve it without particulars it is important to note that the defendant is not required to take any action whatsoever. By rr.7.4(1) and (2) you must serve the particulars within 14 days of service of the claim form provided that is no later than the latest time for service of the claim form, i.e. four months from the date of issue of the claim form (or six months where the claim form is to be served out of the jurisdiction—see Ch.11).

Example

A claim form issued for service within the jurisdiction on August 17, 2007 must be served by December 17, 2007. If it is served without particulars on December 10, 2007 the claimant will have less than fourteen days left in which to serve the particulars, i.e. only until December 17, 2007.

Note that r.7.4(2) specifically refers to the latest date for service of the claim form as required by r.7.5 and there is no reference to any extension of time for service that may have been ordered under r.7.6.

Therefore, a claim form that is served pursuant to an ordered extension must be accompanied by particulars of claim.

If particulars are served on the defendant after the claim form, the claimant must within the next seven days file a copy at the court along with a certificate of service (see Ch.8).

What if particulars are served late?

9.010 Although the time for service of particulars of claim is short the parties may make an agreement in writing extending the time limit if they so wish (see r.2.11; contrast agreements deferring the filing of a defence as to which, see para.9.017). If the defendant will not consent to an extension of time, the claimant could apply to the court under its general powers (r.3.1 as to which see para.33.002). In *Robert v Momentum Services Ltd* [2003] 1 W.L.R. 1577 the Court of Appeal gave guidance as to the way such applications should be dealt with. If the application is made before the time for service has expired the court should determine it simply having regard to the overriding objective and to the prejudice if any that will be caused to the defendant by the delay in service. The court should not embark upon any investigation of prejudice caused by delay at earlier stages. Only rarely will it be appropriate to dismiss an application on the grounds that the claim is weak unless the court is able to conclude that the defendant could successfully apply for summary judgment or an order striking out the particulars (as to which see Ch.19 and para.33.008 respectively).

If the application for an extension of time is made after the time limit has expired the court may treat it as an application for relief from a sanction and go through the checklist of factors set out in r.3.9 (as to which, see further para.33.011). In practice, applications for an extension are not normally made after the time for service has expired. Instead, the claimant just serves the particulars late, perhaps hoping that the defendant will not take the point. In *Totty v Snowden* [2002] 1 W.L.R. 1384 the claimant did serve late and the defendant did take the point and applied for an Order setting aside the service. The Court of Appeal held that, in such circumstances, the court does have power to extend the time limit retrospectively. The very strict regime which applies to delays in the service of claim forms (see para.9.006, above) does not apply to delays in the service of particulars of claim.

What if particulars are never served?

9.011 Rule 9.1(2) provides that a defendant need not respond to a claim until the particulars of claim have been served on him. What if, after serving a claim form without particulars, the claimant fails to serve any? It does not appear that a r.15.11 automatic stay will occur (see para.9.017 below) as that is only triggered six months after the expiry of the time for filing a defence and a defence is not required until after particulars of claim have been served. The court may of its own initiative, strike out the claim form pursuant to r.3.4(2)(c) given the claimant's failure to comply with r.7.4(2)(b). The defendant is unlikely to apply for such an Order unless and until the relevant limitation period has expired.

DOCUMENTS TO BE SERVED ON THE DEFENDANT

If a claim form without particulars is served, the defendant receives a sealed copy and explanatory notes that state that he should not reply until he receives the particulars of claim. When particulars are served they must be accompanied by a "response pack". These are forms prepared by the court which allow the defendant to: (a) acknowledge service of the particulars of claim; (b) admit the whole or part of the claim; (c) defend the whole or part of the claim; and (d) counterclaim.

9.012

Acknowledgment of service (Pt 10)

The defendant may file an acknowledgment of service if he is unable to file his defence within the 14 days as required by r.15.4 or if he wishes to dispute the court's jurisdiction. An acknowledgment must be filed within 14 days after service of either a claim form with particulars or any particulars that are served separately later.

9.013

Example

A claim form with particulars is deemed to be served on Thursday December 6, 2007. The last day the defendant has to file his acknowledgment is Thursday December 20, 2007 (see para.8.013 as to calculating the day of deemed service).

Note that if the claim form is served out of the jurisdiction, the practice direction to Pt 6 specifies the period for the filing of an acknowledgment (see Ch.11).

The acknowledgment form must be completed with the defendant's address for service (see Ch.8). It must be signed by the defendant or his legal representative instructed to accept service on his behalf. If a solicitor signs the acknowledgment, the address for service must be his business address.

In addition, the defendant's full name should appear on the form correcting any error that may have been made on the claim form, for example, "Jonathan Patrick Maryland described as John Maryland". If you are instructed by two or more co-defendants you may use a single acknowledgment form or both or all of them. Whilst there are boxes on the form for a defendant to indicate an intention to contest all or part of the claim, there is no obligation imposed by r.10 to tick either box. However, r.11(2) provides that a defendant who wishes to contest the court's jurisdiction must file an acknowledgment.

The completed acknowledgment of service form should not be sent to the claimant's solicitors. It must be filed at the court where the proceedings were started. Rule 2.3 provides that this can be done by "delivering it, by post or otherwise, to the court office". Hence, it appears the defendant can choose any method he pleases, including fax where the court has a fax number. The vital thing is to ensure that the court receives the acknowledgment within the prescribed period. If time is short deliver it to the court and get a receipt. If it is faxed we recommend that a hard copy is put in the post that night but ensure

Consequences of failing to acknowledge

9.014 Acknowledging service of the particulars of claim is optional unless the client wishes to challenge the court's jurisdiction. Filing an acknowledgment within the prescribed period prevents the claimant obtaining judgment. However, unless the defendant goes on to file a defence the claimant will still be able to obtain judgment in default (see Ch.15).

Amending or withdrawing an acknowledgment

9.015 An acknowledgment of service is not a statement of case (a term defined in r.2.3(1)). It can be amended or withdrawn only with the permission of the court (PD 10, para.5.4).

Admissions

9.016 If the defendant is prepared to admit all or part of the claim he should complete the form of admission (see Ch.16).

Defence

9.017 If the defendant wishes to challenge the jurisdiction of the court he must say so in his acknowledgment and then apply to the court. There is no need to serve a defence unless the application is unsuccessful.

If the defendant acknowledges service and the claimant applies for summary judgment (see Ch.19), there is no need to file a defence. Of course a response should be made to the application which may include, as part of the evidence, a draft defence. If the application is unsuccessful the court usually gives directions as to the filing of a defence.

In all other cases where the defendant has been served within the jurisdiction, he must file a defence within 14 days after service of the particulars of claim; or, if he filed an acknowledgment, within 28 days (r.15.4(1)). If the defendant was served out of the jurisdiction see Ch.11.

Example

The defendant is served within the jurisdiction with particulars of claim on Thursday November 1, 2007. If he is ready to file a defence he must do so by Thursday November 15, 2007. If he wants to acquire extra time he needs to file an acknowledgment by that date. He will then have until Thursday November 29, 2007 to file a defence.

What if a defendant still has insufficient time to file a proper defence? As soon as he is aware of the difficulties he should ask the claimant's solicitors to agree to a 28 days' extension pursuant to r.15.5. The parties are able to agree up to a maximum of 28 additional for service of the defence. The defendant must notify the court in writing of any extension that is agreed. If the defendant requires further time, even if the claimant's solicitor's agree, an application must be made to the court. Obviously, it should be made by consent, if possible, but the court may well insist on a hearing if it is not satisfied with the reasons given.

Rule 15.6 provides that "a copy of the defence must be served on every other party". The rules are silent as to who should do this. If you wish the court to serve it, a copy or copies for service will have to be enclosed. Otherwise, when filing the defence, you could serve all other parties and inform the court accordingly.

What if the defence is never served?

If a defence is filed the case will proceed to the allocation stage (see para.9.027, below). If no defence is filed the claimant may be able to obtain a default judgment (see Ch.15). What happens if the claim does not proceed to the allocation stage and the claimant does not apply for a default judgment or summary judgment? Rule 15.11 provides that the claim is automatically stayed six months after the end of the permitted period for filing a defence. If either party later wishes to bring the action back to life they must apply to the court for the stay to be lifted.

DOCUMENTS SERVED AFTER THE DEFENCE

Counterclaim

If the defendant wishes to bring an action against the claimant it is usually best to do it by way of counterclaim. The counterclaim should form part of the defence. See Chs 12 and 18 as to drafting and making the counterclaim. It is possible to obtain default judgment on a counterclaim (see Ch.18). In order to enter default judgment the defendant has to prove the counterclaim was served and where the defendant effected service of the document he must file a certificate of service (see Ch.8). 9.018

Reply to Defence and Defence to Counterclaim

If a claimant wishes to respond to facts raised in the defence he must do so by way of a Reply. When a counterclaim has been raised, the claimant must file a defence as otherwise default judgment is usually available (see Ch.15). 9.019

See Ch.12 as to drafting this statement of case. However, at this stage note that PD 15, para.3.2 states that where a claimant serves a reply and defence to counterclaim, these should form one document. Rule 15.8 provides that if a claimant wishes to file a reply he must do so with his allocation questionnaire. By r.26.3(6) the date for filing a completed allocation questionnaire is at least 14 days after the date it is served by the court. However, any defence to counterclaim must be filed within 14 days of service of the counterclaim. How can these different time scales for reply and defence to counterclaim be harmonised? The answer is to be found in PD 15, para.3.2A which provides that:

> "where the date by which the claimant must file his allocation questionnaire is later than the date by which he must file his defence to counterclaim (because the time for filing the allocation questionnaire under Rule 26.3(6) is more than 14 days after the date on which it is deemed to be served), the court will normally order that the defence to counterclaim must be filed by the same date as the reply. Where the court does not make such an order the reply and defence to counterclaim may form separate documents."

FIXED DATE CLAIMS

9.020 In a possession claim (see further, para.9.002) the date for the hearing is fixed when the claim form is issued (r.55.5). In possession claims the particulars of claim must be filed and served with the claim form (r.55.4).

A similar regime applies to proceedings under the Consumer Credit Act 1974, as amended (e.g. claims by a creditor to enforce a regulated agreement relating to goods under s.141). PD 7B (the Practice Direction supplementing r.7.9) specifies the location of the particular county court where certain actions must be started (e.g. proceedings for the recovery of goods under a regulated hire purchase agreement may be commenced only in the county court for the district in which the debtor resides or carries on business or where he so resided or carried on business when he last made a payment under the agreement). The practice direction also states that the court will fix a hearing date when the claim form is issued and requires the particulars of claim (the contents of which are—prescribed) to be served with the claim form.

PRODUCTION CENTRE CASES (R.7.10 AND PD 7C)

9.021 Certain claimants such as water companies, finance companies, mail order firms, etc. often wish to issue hundreds, sometimes thousands, of claim forms at one go. This would place a considerable strain on a particular court. Accordingly, a "Production Centre" has been in existence since 1989 specifically to cater for the bulk issue of claim forms in county court matters. The Centre is deemed to be part of the office of the county court whose name appears on the issued claim form. If the court chosen is Northampton County Court the Centre also has jurisdiction to deal with subsequent stages including the entry and enforcement of default judgments. The claimants or their solicitors prepare the documents for issue in the usual way and submit them electronically to the Centre. A single statement of truth may accompany each batch of claim forms. The Centre will then issue each claim form on behalf of the named county court and notify it.

The Centre will only issue a claim form if the claim is for a specified sum of money less than £100,000. It cannot be used to issue High Court claims nor, for example, claims against more than two defendants. Permission must be obtained to use the Centre and each user must agree to comply with the Code of Practice that forms part of the accompanying practice direction.

MONEY CLAIM ONLINE ("MCOL")

It is now possible for individuals, businesses and government departments to issue a claim for a fixed amount of money of less than £100,000 online at *www.hmcourts-service.gov.uk/onlineservices/mcol/index.htm* (see generally, r.7.12 and PD 7E). Note that the claim must be against no more than two defendants who each have an address for service in England and Wales. It is not possible to use MCOL to start proceedings against a child or patient or the Crown. In addition, the claimant must have a valid credit or debit card in order to pay court fees. It is not possible to claim any exemption or remission of fees here. All MCOL claims are issued in the name of Northampton County Court, to take advantage of its existing technology and the staff's experience of administering the Production Centre (see para.9.021 above). 9.022

How does a claim made using MCOL differ from the usual Pt 7 procedure? The main point to note is that the particulars of claim must be set out in no more than 1080 characters (including spaces and punctuation). Fortunately the MCOL screen has a character counter. So how is a statement of truth completed online? By typing the name of the person working online, and where appropriate, his position or office held if signing on behalf of a company or firm. That person thereby certifies that the information provided is true.

Once all the information required by MCOL is completed and the court fee paid online, the system will display the claim number. MCOL submits the claim to the Northampton County Court to be issued. The court then sends the claim form and response pack to the defendant. The defendant has 14 days from the date of service of the claim to respond. For MCOL purposes the date of service is calculated to be five days from the date the claim is issued. If the defendant ignores the claim, a request for judgment by default can be made online. At the same time the claimant can request a warrant of execution. If the defendant wishes to acknowledge service and/or file a defence (plus any counterclaim) he may do so online or by filling out the acknowledgment of service form and/or defence in the claim pack and faxing or posting it to the court. When a defence is filed and the defendant is an individual, the case is transferred to the defendant's home court, otherwise it is transferred to the claimant's home court. In any event, the claim can no longer be handled by the MCOL system. MCOL sends the parties notice of transfer, an allocation questionnaire, and where the amount claimed exceeds £1,000 a request for the allocation questionnaire fee.

Note that PD 55B sets out a scheme known as "Possession Claims Online" where in certain county courts some Pt 55 possession claims (see para.24.005) can be dealt with initially via the website *www.possessionclaim.gov.uk*.

TRANSFER OF PROCEEDINGS (PT 30)

9.023 In certain circumstances, dealt with below, the proceedings commenced in one court may be transferred to another court. The transfer may occur automatically, most commonly on the filing of a defence, or by the court of its own initiative, or on the application of a party. Also note that by r.30.6 a court may specify the place where the trial or some other hearing is to take place without ordering the transfer of the proceedings. Further, r.2.7 permits the court to deal with a case at "any place" that it considers appropriate. So it might hold a hearing in a non-court location such as the house of a claimant that is the subject of a building dispute.

Automatic transfer (r.26.2)

9.024 If a claim has been commenced: (a) for a specified amount of money; (b) otherwise than out of the "defendant's home court"; (c) not in a specialist list; and (d) against a defendant who is an individual, the claim will be automatically transferred to the defendant's home court if either:

> (i) the defendant applies to set aside or vary a default judgment pursuant to r.13.4 (see Ch.15); or
> (ii) a judge is to determine the time and rate of payment of a judgment obtained after a r.14 admission has been filed (see Ch.16); or
> (iii) a defence is filed.

If a claim is proceeding in the county court, the "defendant's home court" is the county court for the district in which the defendant resides or carries on business. In respect of a High Court claim, that address is the district registry for the district in which the defendant resides or carries on business or otherwise the Royal Courts of Justice.

What if the claim is against two or more defendants with different home courts? The rule provides that if the defendant who files a defence first is an individual the proceedings will be transferred to his home court. It should be noted that an automatic transfer may occur only once in each case.

Example

C issues a claim out of the Hastings County Court against a Mr Roberts, Ms Wallace and Mega Rich (Mythshire) Ltd for a specified sum of money. Each defendant has a different home court, namely Eastbourne, Canterbury and Newcastle respectively. If Mr Roberts files the first defence, the case will automatically be transferred to Eastbourne County Court. If instead Ms Wallace files the first defence the case will be automatically transferred to Canterbury County Court. However, if Mega Rich (Mythshire) Ltd files the first defence, the case will remain at the Hastings County Court regardless of any defences subsequently filed by the other two defendants.

Application for a transfer

Transfer between county courts and within the High Court (r.30.2)

Where an enactment, other than the Rules, requires proceedings to be started in a particular county court, the court has no power to order a transfer to a different court nor to allow them to continue in the wrong court. Otherwise, if proceedings have been started in the wrong county court, the court may of its own initiative or on application order that the proceedings should either: (a) be transferred to the correct county court; or (b) continue in the current county court; or (c) be struck out. Striking out a claim would of course be disproportionate in most cases save the most exceptional (see further *Restick v Crickmore* [1994] 1 W.L.R. 420, noted below).

9.025

If proceedings have been started in the correct county court, the court may of its own initiative or on application order a transfer to another county court if either: (a) it is satisfied that transfer is appropriate having regard to the criteria in r.30.3 (see below); or (b) it is dealing with proceedings for the detailed assessment of costs (see Ch.38); or the enforcement of a judgment (see Chs 40 and 41) that could be more conveniently or fairly dealt with at another county court.

The High Court may, having regard to the r.30.3 criteria order the transfer of proceedings between High Court offices (i.e. to or from the Royal Courts of Justice and any district registry). A district registry may order that proceedings for the detailed assessment of costs should be transferred to another district registry if it is satisfied that those proceedings could be more conveniently or fairly dealt with at the other district registry. It is important to bear in mind that when a county court or a High Court exercise this power it can limit the transfer to a part of the proceedings, such as a defendant's counterclaim or an application (e.g. summary judgment) made in the proceedings.

Transfer between divisions of the High Court and to and from a specialist list (r.30.5)

The High Court may order that proceedings in any Division should be transferred to another. Only a judge dealing with cases on a specialist list may order the transfer of proceedings to or from that list.

Transfer between High Court and county court

Section 40(1) of the County Courts Act 1984 provides that if proceedings of a type required to be brought in a county court (e.g. a money claim under £15,000) are in fact brought in the High Court, the High Court must either transfer them to a county court or strike them out. The alternative of striking out is available only if the claimant knew or ought to have known of the requirement that the proceedings should be in a county court. What sort of claimant faces having his claim struck out? In *Restick v Crickmore* [1994] 1 W.L.R. 420 Stuart-Smith L.J. answered that question by saying:

> "Where the action . . . can be seen as an attempt to harass a defendant, deliberately run up unnecessary costs, be taken in defiance of a warning of the defendants as to the proper venue or where a party, or more likely his solicitor persistently starts actions in the wrong court . . . It may also be in a particularly blatant case where the value of the [claimant's] claim is so obviously of a very low order the action should be struck out if there are no extenuating circumstances".

Another power to send cases from the High Court to a county court is provided by s.40(2) of the County Courts Act 1984. This gives the High Court a general discretion to order transfer of proceedings to a county court even though they were not required to be started there.

The transfer criteria under r.30.3

9.026 When considering a transfer of proceedings the court must have regard to the following:

(a) The financial value of the claim and the amount in dispute, if different.
(b) Whether it would be more convenient or fair for hearings (including the trial) to be held in some other court.
(c) The availability of a judge specialising in the type of claim in question.
(d) Whether the facts, legal issues, remedies or procedures involved are simple or complex.
(e) The importance of the outcome of the claim to the public in general.
(f) The facilities available at the court where the claim is being dealt with and whether they may be inadequate because of any disabilities of a party or potential witness.
(g) Whether or not there is a real prospect of a declaration of incompatibility under s.4 of the Human Rights Act 1998 being made (PD 30, para.7).

The criteria list is not exhaustive. Obviously the court will consider the overriding objective and the matters specified in rr.1.1(2) and 1.4(2). Also, PD 30, para.2 draws attention to PD 29, para.2 which indicates when orders for transfer will be made in High Court cases issued in London (see further, para.22.014).

ALLOCATION TO A PARTICULAR TRACK

The court allocates a defended claim to one of the three tracks: the small claims track (see Ch.20), the fast track (see Ch.21) or the multi-track (see Ch.22). The court first sends to each party an allocation questionnaire in Form N150 and in most cases makes a decision without holding a hearing. (Note that if the claim falls within the financial scope of the small claims track (see Ch.20) a slightly different allocation questionnaire in Form N149 is sent to the parties). As a general rule the court serves an allocation questionnaire on each party when a defendant files a defence. However, if the defence is that money claimed has been paid (see r.15.10) or the defendant makes an admission of part of a claim for a specified amount of money (see Ch.16) the court will not serve questionnaires until the claimant returns a notice indicating his wish that the proceedings should continue.

9.027

What if there are two or more defendants? Provided at least one of them files a defence, the court serves questionnaires when either all the defendants have each filed a defence or when the period for the filing of the last defence has expired, whichever is the sooner. In any circumstances where the case is to be automatically transferred to defendant's home court the court serves questionnaires before transferring the proceedings.

The claimant may apply to the court for the questionnaires to be served earlier than the court would otherwise normally do so. In practice, if all the parties are ready, willing and able to proceed quickly a consent application should be filed with the defence. In addition, the court may dispense with the need for questionnaires. This is most likely to occur when a pre-allocation hearing takes place, for example, an application for an interim injunction (see Ch.27) or for summary judgment (see Ch.19).

A court fee is payable at the allocation stage whether or not allocation questionnaires are dispensed with. The fee is payable by the claimant unless the action is proceeding on a counterclaim alone, in which case it is payable by the defendant (see *White Book*, Vol. 2, paras 10–10 and 10–22).

PD 26, para.4.1 spells out the court's general approach in relation to allocation (achieving the overriding objective, as far as possible in cooperation with the parties and their legal representatives). PD 26, para.4.2 provides that in most cases the court expects the statements of case and allocation questionnaires to contain sufficient information to enable it to allocate the claim to a track and to give case management directions. If the court does not have enough information to allocate the claim, it will generally make an order requiring one or more parties to provide further information within fourteen days (r.26.5(3)).

Completing the allocation questionnaire Form N150

9.028   Whilst you are not obliged to serve a copy of your completed questionnaire on any other party, PD 26, para.2.3 provides that the parties should consult with one another and co-operate in completing the questionnaires. In addition you should try and agree upon the case management directions which you intend to ask the court to make. However, please bear in mind two points. First, that this consultation period must not delay the filing of the questionnaires. Secondly, do not put anything in the questionnaire that you do not wish any other party to see since after allocation the court sends each party copies of the other parties' completed questionnaires.

The questionnaire Form N150 is divided into the following sections: settlement, location of trial, pre-action protocols, case management information, time estimate for trial, proposed directions, costs and other information. Some brief notes on each of these topics is set out below.

A. *Settlement*: Any party may request a stay of proceedings for one month to settle the claim either by informal discussion or by alternative dispute resolution. The court will so direct if all parties request it to and, in other cases, may so direct at the request of one party or of its own initiative if it considers that such a stay would be appropriate (r.26.4(2)). The glossary defines alternative dispute resolution ("ADR") as a collective description of methods of resolving disputes otherwise than through the normal trial process. In practice references to ADR are usually understood as being references to some form of mediation by a third party. Whilst the court will often encourage the parties to attempt ADR and sometimes will encourage them in the strongest terms, it has no power to order them to submit to mediation (*Halsey v Milton Keynes General NHS Trust* [2004] 1 W.L.R. 3002, CA). However, there may be costs penalties for a party who later wins at trial who acted unreasonably in refusing ADR (see further para.34.002).

Once granted, the court may extend a stay until a specified date or for such period as it considers appropriate.

However, the parties have to convince the court that a settlement is actively being pursued. PD 26, para.3.1 provides that a letter is generally acceptable as an application to extend a stay and should: (i) confirm that all parties agree to the extension; and (ii) explain the steps being taken and identify any mediator or expert who is assisting in the process. Any extension is not normally longer than four weeks unless clear reasons are given to justify more time. The court may demand a timetable of the steps taken so far and those that are proposed. In addition the court may require notification of compliance or otherwise with each timetable step; or it may limit the length of a stay to carrying out just the next step.

By r.26.4(4) the claimant must tell the court if any settlement is reached during the period of a stay. The parties should apply for a consent order (see Ch.34) or for approval of a settlement where any party is a child or a patient (see Ch.10). If no request is made for a further extension of a stay or the court is not informed of any settlement by the end of the period of a stay, it may either allocate the case, or require a party to give further information, or fix an allocation hearing.

B. *Location of trial*: If you require the trial to occur at a particular court you should identify it and give your reasons, for example,. the convenience of witnesses or that particular facilities are required for a disabled party or witness.

C. *Pre-action protocols*: If an approved pre-action protocol (see Ch.6) applies to the claim, you must state whether or not you have complied with it. Where no such protocol applies, you must state whether or not you have "exchanged information and/or documents (evidence) with the other party in order to assist in settling the claim". Where the answer is given in the negative, an explanation as to the extent of, and reasons for, any non-compliance must be given on a separate sheet. We would also recommend that you take this opportunity to place on record any poor pre-action conduct by any other party.

D. *Case Management Information*: First you are asked to state if the amount of the claim is still in dispute. Next state whether you have made any interim applications and if so state what for and the relevant hearing date. (This is because the outcome of a pending application may well affect the case management directions the court should give. If you intend to make an interim application in the future see H, below). This section of the questionnaire also deals with the evidence expert and non-expert the party intends to call at the trial. Under the pre-action protocol procedures there may have been some discussion and disclosure of this evidence already. The form asks "So far as you know at this stage, what witnesses of fact do you intend to call at the trial or final hearing including, if appropriate, yourself?" Space is then given for the names of the witnesses and a description of the facts about which they may give evidence. Next come some tick boxes which enable you to indicate whether you wish to use expert evidence at the trial, whether you have already copied any experts' reports to other parties, and whether you consider the case suitable for a single joint expert in any field. Space is then given for you to list any single joint experts you propose to use and any other experts you wish to rely on. You are invited to identify single joint experts with the initials "SJ" after their names. Beside each name you should also state the expert's field of expertise. There are more tick boxes to indicate whether you wish your experts to give evidence orally at the trial (see generally as to expert evidence, Ch.23, below).

Finally, you must indicate the track you consider to be the most suitable for the case. Brief reasons must be given if you request allocation to a track that is not the normal one for the case given its financial value (see below). If you request the multi-track you should state whether you consider the claim should be managed and tried at the Royal Courts of Justice and, if so, why (PD 29, para.2.6, and see further para.22.014).

E. *Trial estimate*: An estimate as to how long the trial will take is required. If there are any known dates to avoid, these should also be stated. It also makes sense to say why any dates should be avoided, for example, that an essential witness has a holiday booked or an expert is already due to give evidence at the trial of another case.

F. *Proposed directions*: You should attach a list of directions that are appropriate for the management of the case and indicate whether or not these are agreed by the other parties. As to the fast track (see Ch.21) you should consider the directions outlined in PD 28. As to the multi-track (see Ch.22) and the Queen's Bench Division Practice Form, PF52.

G. *Costs incurred by legal representatives*: Unless he has indicated that the matter should be allocated to the small claims track, a represented party must state the legal costs incurred to date and the likely overall costs. In addition, PD 43, para.6.4 provides that unless the court directs otherwise a represented party must file and serve an estimate of costs (see Ch.13). This must be done at the same time as filing the completed allocation questionnaire.

H. *Other information*: You may attach to the questionnaire any document you wish the judge to take into account when allocating the case. However, PD 26, para.2.2(2) provides that generally the court will not consider it unless it has been agreed between all the parties or a copy has been served on them. In addition to documents that deal with the matters raised in the questionnaire, you should provide the court with any information that may affect the timetable it will set or which may make it desirable to hold an allocation hearing.

You must state if you intend to make an interim application, for example, for summary judgment (see Ch.19) or for the court's permission to issue a claim not previously made (see Ch.18). Details of such should be given and ideally the application should be filed with the completed questionnaire.

Do not try to squeeze detailed answers into the relatively small boxes on the form. Use separate sheets of paper and clearly identify the part of the questionnaire you are dealing with. Remember to write the claim number on these, as well as on any documents you file at the same time, and ensure that all extra pages are securely attached to the questionnaire.

Time for filing questionnaires

9.029 By r.26.3(6) each party must file a completed allocation questionnaire by no later than the date the court has specified on it. (The last day to file the document must be at least 14 days after the date when it is deemed to have been served on the party, as to which, see para.8.013, above). Can the parties vary that date by agreement? No, says r.26.3(6A). Rule 26.5(5) then provides that where a party fails to file a questionnaire the court may give any direction it considers appropriate. Usually, the court directs that the party in default must file the questionnaire by a specified date otherwise his statement of case is struck out. If all the parties fail to file responses the court file will be referred to a judge who will normally direct that unless a questionnaire is filed within three days of service of the order the claim and any counterclaim will be struck out. If at least one party files a questionnaire, the court may order that an allocation hearing takes place and that all parties must attend or otherwise allocate the claim if it has sufficient information.

Identifying the "normal track"

The general rule is that a claim is allocated to its "normal track". These are identified by r.26.6 as follows.

9.030

The small claims track

The small claims track is dealt with in Ch.20. By 26.6(1) this is the normal track for the following cases:

9.031

Any claim for personal injuries where both:

(i) the financial value of the whole claim is not more than £5,000; and
(ii) the financial value of any claim for damages for personal injuries is not more than £1,000. It should be noted that in this context "damages for personal injuries" means damages as compensation for pain, suffering and loss of amenity (i.e. general damages only; see Ch.4) and does not include any other damages.

Examples

(1) C sues D expecting to be awarded £3,000 in general damages and £2,500 in special damages. As the financial value of the whole claim exceeds £5,000 (it is worth £5,500) the small claims track is not the normal track.
(2) C sues D expecting to be awarded £1,250 in general damages and £2,500 in special damages. Whilst the financial value of the whole claim does not exceed £5,000 (it is worth £3,750), the value of the general damages exceeds £1,000 and so the small claims track is not the normal track.
(3) C sues D expecting to be awarded £750 in general damages and £3,900 in special damages. The small claims track is the normal track for the claim as the financial value of the whole claim is not more than £5,000 (it is worth £4,650) and the general damages part is valued at less than £1,000.

Any claim which includes a claim by a tenant of residential premises against his landlord where:

(i) the tenant is seeking an order requiring the landlord to carry out repairs or other work to the premises (whether or not the tenant is also seeking some other remedy);

(ii) the cost of repairs or other works to the premises is estimated to be not more than £1,000; and
(iii) the financial value of any other claim for damages is not more than £1,000.

Examples

(1) C sues D claiming £1,950 for repairs and £1,250 in compensation. As the financial value of the repairs and the damages claimed each exceed £1,000 the small claims track is clearly not the normal track.
(2) C sues D claiming £1,950 for repairs and £750 in compensation. As the financial value of the repairs exceeds £1,000 can it be said that the small claims track is not the normal track? The answer is, yes. PD 7A, para.3.9 provides that if either of the amounts exceeds £1,000, the small claims track is not the normal track.

Note also that the court will not allocate a claim to the small claims track if it includes a claim by a tenant of residential premises against his landlord for a remedy in respect of harassment or unlawful eviction.

All other claims which have a financial value of not more than £5,000

PD 26, para.8.1 states that this track is intended to provide a proportionate procedure by which the most straightforward claims with a financial value of not more than £5,000 can be decided, without the need for substantial pre-hearing preparation and the formalities of a traditional trial, and without incurring large legal costs. Indeed, the small claims procedure has been designed so that litigants can conduct their own case without legal representation if they so wish. Cases that are said to be generally suitable for this track include consumer disputes, accident claims, disputes about ownership of goods and most disputes between landlord and tenant other than those for possession. A case involving a disputed allegation of dishonesty is not usually suitable.

The fast track

9.032   The fast track is dealt with in Ch.21. It the normal track for any claim for which the small claims track is not the normal track and which has a financial value of not more than £15,000. In addition, the fast track is only the normal track for such claims if the court considers that:

(a) the trial is likely to last for no longer than one day (i.e. five hours); and
(b) oral expert evidence at trial will be limited to: (i) one expert per party in relation to any expert field; and (ii) expert evidence in two expert fields.

PD 26, para.9.1 provides that where the fast track is the normal track for a case but the court is considering allocating it to the multi-track, it should allocate it to the fast track unless it believes that it cannot be dealt with "justly" on that track. This will require the court to take into account the limits likely to be placed on disclosure (see Ch.30), the extent to which expert evidence may be necessary (see above and Ch.23) and whether the trial is likely to last more than a day.

In order to hear a case in five hours the court may order separate trials of the issues of liability and quantum (see Ch.33) since if each will last a day the claim as a whole may be allocated to the fast track. Indeed, PD 26, para.9.1(3)(c) provides that the possibility that a trial might last longer than one day is not necessarily a conclusive reason for the court to allocate it to the multi-track. However, the court may not allocate a case to the fast track where it involves a counterclaim or other additional claim (see Ch.18) that is to be heard at the same time as the claim itself and as a consequence the trial will last longer than a day.

The multi-track

The multi-track is the normal track for any claim for which the small claims track or fast track is not the normal track. It is dealt with in Ch.22. The allocation of a case to the multi-track may well affect the view the court and the parties should take as to the amount of time and money it is reasonable and proportionate to spend on the case. The multi-track is intended for cases which are likely to need detailed procedural stages before trial and/or a lengthy trial hearing. Such things can be expensive. The fast track is intended as a limited procedure designed for straightforward cases the financial value of which does not exceed £15,000. It provides a short but reasonable timescale bringing such cases to a trial which should be concluded within one day and with limited use of expert evidence.

9.033

> "[30] The upshot of this is that a defendant to a claim that has been allocated to the fast track knows that the trial is likely to be short, expert evidence limited, and that if he is successful he is likely to be awarded only comparatively modest fixed costs for the trial itself. These factors are intended to influence his decision as to the resources that he will deploy in defending a claim, and are likely to do so. Where a defendant is defending a claim that has been allocated to the multi-track, very different considerations apply. This is the clear purpose and effect of the rules. The different treatment accorded to fast track and multi-track claims is intended to bring about an approach to the conduct of litigation that is proportionate to what is at stake". (Dyson L.J. in *Maguire v Molin* [2002] EWCA Civ 1083 noted in para.9.041, below)

Assessing the financial value

When the court assesses the financial value of a claim it ignores the following:

9.034

    (a) Any amount not in dispute. By PD 26, para.7.4 the court apply these general principles:

(i) any amount for which the defendant does not admit liability is in dispute;
(ii) any sum in respect of an item forming part of the claim for which judgment has been entered (e.g. by way of summary judgment) is not in dispute;
(iii) any specific sum claimed as a distinct item and which the defendant admits he is liable to pay is not in dispute;
(iv) any sum offered by the defendant which has been accepted by the claimant in satisfaction of any item that forms a distinct part of the claim is not in dispute.

(b) Any claim for interest whether made pursuant to contract and/or statute.
(c) Costs.
(d) Any contributory negligence.

What if two or more claimants have started a claim against the same defendant using the same claim form but each claimant has a separate claim? In those circumstances the financial value of all the claims are assessed individually. If the financial value of each claim places it in a different track it is possible for the matters to be so allocated provided this meets the overriding objective (see Ch.33).

Exaggerated claims

9.035　In order to allocate it to the appropriate track, the court will make its own assessment of the value of a claim (r.26.8(2)) having regard to the views expressed by the parties (r.26.8(1)(h)). If you feel that your opponent has exaggerated the size of his claim make sure that you express that view in your defence or in your allocation questionnaire. In a personal injury case you should make direct reference to any relevant points that appear from the claimant's medical report that is attached to the particulars of claim. If the court believes that the amount the claimant is seeking exceeds what he may reasonably expect to recover it may make an order under r.26.5(3) directing the claimant to justify the amount (PD 26, para.7.3(2)).

What should happen if the exaggeration is not detected until later, at the trial or settlement? The exaggerator may be penalised in costs in either of two ways. If nothing else happens, the court which later assesses his costs should limit them taking into account the consequences of his exaggeration (*Booth v Britannia Hotels Ltd* [2002] EWCA Civ 579, as to which, see para.38.018, below). In fact, something else may happen. If the exaggeration is made plain to the court at the time costs are awarded (as it will be if the claim is tried) that court may deprive the exaggerator of some or all of his costs. Rule 44.3(4) states that, when deciding what order (if any) to make about costs, the court must have regard to, amongst other things, the conduct of all the parties. Rule 44.3(5) provides that the conduct of the parties includes: "(b) whether a claimant who has succeeded in his claim, in whole or in part, exaggerated his claim". Helpful guidance on this topic was given by Neuberger J. (as he then was) in *Harrison v Bloom Camillin* (2000) L.T.L., February 4.

> "Why should the fact that a claim has been exaggerated result in an order for costs less favourable to the successful claimant than if it had not been exaggerated? I think there are a number of reasons. The first is that if a claimant exaggerates a claim it is less likely that the defendant will be persuaded to settle or, indeed, that the claimant will be persuaded to settle. Secondly, if a claim is in fact worth far less than the statement of claim suggests, then it is likely that the amount of costs and court time that will be expended on the case will be likely to be in excess, and possibly far in excess, of (a) what is justified in terms of proportionality and, (b) what would have been spent if the claim had not been exaggerated. Thirdly, there is an element of pour encourager les autres in relation to depriving a successful plaintiff, who has exaggerated his claim, of some of his costs".
>
> "... The word "exaggerated" is difficult to define in any mathematical way. A claim where a claimant gets 10 per cent less than he sought is plainly not exaggerated save, I suppose, on the most unusual facts. A claim where the claimant gets two per cent of what he sought is plainly exaggerated save on unusual facts. In the present case one is talking of a recovery in the region of 25 per cent of what was claimed. To my mind that is capable of being exaggeration on appropriate facts".

In that case Neuberger J. took into account the conduct of the defendant and came to the conclusion that the claim was not exaggerated or, if it was, the exaggeration had not significantly added to the costs or time involved in the proceedings.

In *Devine v Franklin* [2002] EWHC 1846, Q.B. a claim in respect of personal injuries was brought by one neighbour against another. The claimant sought general damages in excess of £1,000 and the claim was allocated to the fast track. At the trial the claimant won on liability but was found to have overstated his injuries. General damages of £500 were awarded and special damages of £195 were agreed. On appeal, Gray J. held that in these circumstances the claimant should be confined to the costs he would have recovered had the claim been allocated to the small claims track (as to which see para.20.003 and see *Voice and Script International Ltd v Alghafar* [2003] EWCA Civ 736, noted in para.20.013, below).

In *Painting v University of Oxford* [2005] EWCA Civ 161 a claim for personal injury damages of about £400,000 was later conceded to be "deliberately misleading". Some months before trial the defendants made a Pt 36 offer of over £184,000 but had then realised, belatedly, that they had video evidence which would undermine the claim and had reduced the offer to £10,000. The claimant never attempted to accept the first offer, or the reduced offer or to make a Pt 36 offer or any offer. At trial the claimant was awarded a little over £25,000. The Court of Appeal held that, even though she had beaten the reduced Pt 36 offer, the claimant should be penalised in costs. The court made the order sought by the defendants: that they should pay the claimant's costs down to the date they reduced their Pt 36 offer, and she should pay their costs thereafter. In all the circumstances the defendants were the effective overall winners.

In *Hooper v Biddle & Co. (a firm)* [2006] EWHC 2995, (2006) L.T.L., October 11, the claimant's claim at the outset was for approximately £3.75m. It was subsequently reduced to £350,000 plus interest, and the claimants eventually accepted £38,000 inclusive of interest which was 1 per cent of the original amount and little over 10 per cent of the stated claim. Miss Prevezer Q.C. stated:

> "It is quite clear that the value pleaded in the Points of Claim of £350,000 was not one properly based on expert evidence. The [expert's report] which I have been shown and which was relied upon the Claimants, firstly does not support that value and secondly, and more importantly, as [counsel for the Claimants] accepts, was obtained for a different purpose. It was only after [the joint expert's] report was produced that the Claimants sought specific advice from [their expert] to support the claim. I find that the Claimants' claim was grossly exaggerated at the protocol stage ... It was then exaggerated when the proceedings were commenced in 2005, and these factors, in my view, were bound to affect the way the Defence was run."

RULE 26.8(1) ALLOCATION FACTORS

9.036   When deciding the track for a claim, the court must take into account the following factors:

(a) The financial value, if any, of the claim (see above). If a claim has no financial value, for example, an application for an injunction, the court allocates the claim to the track it considers most suitable having regard to the matters that follow. The claim to be considered here is the amount the claimant seeks to recover through the court. There is nothing objectionable in a claimant limiting his claim so as to bring it within the financial limits of the small claims track even where this does not reflect the full value of his claim (*Khiaban v Beard* [2003] 1 W.L.R. 1626, CA).

(b) The nature of the remedy sought. In *Afzal v Ford Motor Co. Ltd* [1994] 4 All E.R. 720 the Court of Appeal gave the example of a claim for damages for trespass that might have a financial value falling within the small claims limit but allocation to a different track would be justified where the result might have far reaching consequences for the rights of the parties. In addition the court felt claims involving ownership of family heirlooms might be inappropriate for the small claims procedure.

(c) The likely complexity of the facts, law or evidence.

(d) The number of parties or likely parties. If the defendant is considering making an additional claim he should state this on his allocation questionnaire (see above).
(e) The value of any counterclaim or other additional claim and the complexity of any matters relating to it. PD 26, para.7.7 states that as a general rule the courts will not aggregate all the claims together but will usually regard the largest of them as determining the financial value of the claims.

Example

C sues D for £4,000. D counterclaims for £3,500. D makes a third party claim against T for £4,000. As the financial value of each claim is below £5,000 the court may regard the small claims track as the normal track. However, whilst as a general rule the court do not aggregate the claims, it might do so where they are truly separate matters, for example, the defendant counterclaims alleging non-payment of a debt after the claimant sues him for personal injuries. In addition, if the choice is between the fast track and multi-track and the case involves a counterclaim or other additional claim that is to be heard at the same time as the claim itself and as a consequence the trial will last longer than a day, the court may not allocate it to the fast track (see above).

(f) The amount of oral evidence which may be required.
(g) The importance of the claim to persons who are not parties to the proceedings, for example, a test case.
(h) The views expressed by the parties. PD 26, para.7.5 provides that the court will treat these as an important factor, but emphasises that the decision is the court's and it is not bound by any agreement or common view of the parties.
(i) The circumstances of the parties.

Allocation hearings (r.26.5(4))

PD 26, para.6.1 states that as a general principle the court will only hold an allocation hearing if it thinks it is necessary. The court gives the parties at least seven days' notice in Form N153 and this includes a brief explanation of the decision to hold a hearing, for example, that the court is seeking the parties' consent to allocate a claim to the fast track rather than the multi-track (see below).

9.037

It is important to bear in mind that at an allocation hearing the court exercises its case management powers. PD 26, para.6.5 therefore provides that a legal representative who attends should, if possible, be the person responsible for the case and must in any event be familiar with the case so as to be able to provide the court with the information it needs to both allocate the case and manage it. Moreover, the representative must have sufficient authority to deal with any issues that are likely to arise at the hearing. In many cases this means that at least an assistant solicitor or legal executive should attend with the client. Sending the trainee that morning with a file he has never read simply will not do.

The court will usually impose a costs penalty if it has to hold an allocation hearing due to the failure of a party to file a questionnaire or to provide further information which the court has ordered. The court may require the defaulting party to pay on the indemnity basis (see Ch.38) the costs of any other party who attends the hearing. Normally there is a summary assessment of those costs and the order provides for their immediate payment or within a specified period of time (see Ch.13). In addition the court may order that non-payment will lead to the party's statement of case being struck out. What if a defaulting party fails to attend the hearing? If the judge is satisfied that notice of the hearing was properly served he will usually order what steps that party is required to take and provide that unless such are taken by a specified date his statement of case is struck out. As to relief from sanctions see Ch.33.

Allocation to a different track by consent (r.26.7(3))

9.038 The court cannot allocate a claim to a track if the financial value exceeds the limit for that track unless all the parties consent. However, PD 26, para.8.1(2) provides that the court will not allocate a case by consent to the small claims track that would otherwise be allocated to the fast track unless it is satisfied that it is suitable for that track. In that respect note that the court does not normally allow longer than one day for a small claims track hearing.

Should a claimant consent to a claim being dealt with in a "lower track", i.e. fast track instead of multi-track or small claims track rather than fast track? Important considerations will include: the amount of disclosure already given and how much more you feel you realistically need; whether oral evidence from expert witnesses will be required; the length of the trial and the ability to recover costs. As to the latter point r.27.14(5) provides that for most costs purposes a claim that would normally be allocated to the fast track, but which is allocated to the small claims track by consent, will be treated as a fast track case only if all the parties agree (see Ch.38).

Different claims and different tracks?

9.039 The rules do not provide for different claims or parts of claims to be allocated to different tracks simultaneously, for example, a claim of £13,000 may well be allocated to the multi-track (rather than the fast track) where a counterclaim of £30,000 is made. If the court feel that both matters can be tried together in one day it may allocate the case to the fast track. Alternatively, if the court orders that the claim and counterclaim should be tried separately and it is apparent that each matter could be heard in a day, the court might suggest to the parties that a fast track allocation should occur.

What if a substantial claim is relatively straightforward as to liability but complex as to quantum? The court may direct that each issue should be tried separately and invite the parties to consent to liability being dealt with on the fast track. If the claimant is successful, the case can then be re-allocated to the multi-track to deal with the question of quantum.

Notice of allocation (r.26.9)

After it has allocated a claim to a track, the court serves notice of allocation on every party. It also serves a copy of the allocation questionnaires filed by the other parties and a copy of any further information supplied. Where there has been no allocation hearing the notice will be in Forms N154 (fast track), N155 (multi-track) or N157–160 (small claims track). As a general rule the court gives brief reasons for its decision and these are set out in the notice. However, no reasons are given if the claim has been allocated to the track requested in all the filed questionnaires. The notice of allocation after a hearing is given in Forms N154, 155 or 157.

9.040

Appeals and re-allocation

Allocation decisions made at a hearing may be challenged on appeal if permission is given (as to which, see Ch.44). Sometimes, a dissatisfied party can instead apply to the court for re-allocation, i.e. where the decision was made without a hearing or at a hearing at which the party was not present or represented and for which he was not given due notice (PD 26, para.11.1).

9.041

Parties can also apply for re-allocation where there has been a change of circumstances since the allocation decision was made, for example, permitted amendments which increase the financial value of the claim beyond the normal range of the track to which it was allocated. If the revised financial value exceeds the normal range by only a small amount, it will usually be wrong to re-allocate if that will cause substantial disruption to the progress of the litigation. However, if the excess is substantial, there should usually be a re-allocation, even if that will cause considerable delay to the completion of the litigation: *Maguire v Molin* [2002] EWCA Civ 1083. In that case the claim was allocated to the fast track and proceeded to a trial on liability which was adjourned part heard. The claimant then applied for permission to amend the particulars of claim so as to increase the amount of the damages sought to about £80,000. That application was listed for hearing at the start of the resumed trial on liability and was dismissed. The Court of Appeal upheld the district judge's decision that the application was made too late and that the delays and additional costs of aborting the trial on liability were such that, in the interests of justice, the amendment should not be allowed (and see further, para.9.033, above).

CHAPTER 10

Part 8 Claims

INTRODUCTION

10.001 Part 8 is described as an "alternative procedure for claims". The main differences with Pt 7 are that no defence is required, default judgment is not available and each claim is automatically allocated to the multi-track. The claimant should file any written evidence he intends to rely on with his claim form. The defendant should file any written evidence he intends to rely on with his acknowledgment of service. In practice, this early date for filing evidence is not as burdensome as it might appear. A Pt 8 claim is appropriate if the claimant is seeking "the court's decision on a question which is unlikely to involve a substantial question of fact" (r.8.1(2)(a)). The absence of any factual dispute should mean that extensive witness statements are unnecessary.

Typical examples of Pt 8 claims include applications for declarations as to the construction of documents and applications in the administration of estates and trusts. In such cases there may well be no controversy between claimant and defendant. Indeed, sometimes, a claimant may successfully apply for permission under r.8.2A to issue the claim form without naming any defendants (e.g. applications to the court for directions by trustees, as to which see PD 64B, para.4.2). In other cases, the controversy between claimant and defendant may have been resolved at the pre-action stage and the Pt 8 claim merely concerns consequential matters. Here are some examples: a claim by or against a child which has been settled before the commencement of Pt 7 proceedings and the application is made solely to obtain the court's approval of that settlement (r.21.10); where parties to a dispute have reached an agreement on all issues (including which party is to pay costs) but have failed to agree the amount of those costs and the application is made for an order for those costs to be determined by detailed assessment (r.44.12A). Another group of cases to which the Pt 8 procedure is mandatory is set out in s.B of PD 8. This, with additions and modifications in s.C, bring together miscellaneous applications under various statutes. All of them are relics of the RSC and CCR which have not yet been expressly provided for in the CPR.

THE PART 8 CLAIM FORM (R.8.2)

As a general rule you need to complete claim form N208 by stating the following: 10.002

(a) That Pt 8 applies. PD 8, para.4.2 says, "In particular, the claim form must state that Part 8 applies; a Pt 8 claim form means a claim form which so states". Whilst form N208 is entitled "Claim Form (CPR, Pt 8)" we suggest you remove any doubts that perhaps the wrong form has been used by stating, "Part 8 of the Civil Procedure Rules applies to this claim".
(b) The question the claimant wants the court to decide or the remedy the claimant is seeking and its legal basis (see below).
(c) The enactment, rule or practice direction under which any claim is being made (see below).
(d) Any representative capacity of the claimant and/or defendant. Pt 8 is often used in cases involving wills or trusts and it is important to ensure the parties are accurately described (see Ch.7).

The claim form simply requires you to give details of the claim dealing with (b) and (c) above and to include a statement of truth and an address for service. In practice, the full details of the claim are set out in the witness statement(s) that are to be filed with the claim form. Do not clutter up the claim form with background facts unless you intend to rely on matters set out in the claim form instead of filing witness statements (see r.32.6 and PD 8, para.7.2).

A Pt 8 claim is issued and served in the same way as a Pt 7 claim (see Chs 8 and 9). However, where statute sets the time limit for issuing and serving proceedings (e.g. s.287(4) Town and Country Planning Act 1990 as in *Corus UK Ltd v Erewash BC* [2006] EWCA Civ 1175, (2006) L.T.L., June 22) any extension of time for service of the claim form will fall under r.3.1(2)(a) rather than r.7.6 (see paras 33.002 and 9.006 respectively). The claimant receives from the court a notice of issue form N209. Whether you issue in the High Court or county court may well be a question of jurisdiction (see Ch.9). As all cases are allocated to the multi-track a statement of value is unnecessary.

We have set out below a suggested version of a Pt 8 claim.

Suggested Pt 8 details of claim

1. Pt 8 of the Civil Procedure Rules 1998 applies to this claim.
2. This claim is made under the Inheritance (Provision for Family and Dependants) Act 1975.
3. The remedy sought by the claimant is an order for provision to be made for him out of the estate of Emma Jane Lacey deceased ("the Deceased").
4. The legal basis for the claim is that:

(a) The claimant is the widower of the Deceased who died on May 6, 2007.
(b) Probate of the Deceased's will dated January 2, 2002 was granted to all of the defendants on September 7, 2007.
(c) The Deceased failed to make any financial provision for the claimant in her will.
(d) The claimant has been left in need as particularised in his witness statement dated October 8, 2007.
(e) The Deceased should have made reasonable financial provision for the claimant.

ACKNOWLEDGMENT OF SERVICE (R.8.3)

10.003   A defendant served with a Pt 8 claim should also receive some guidance notes in Form N208C and an acknowledgment of service in Form N210 (or Form N210A which is for use in costs only proceedings under r.44.12A). If the defendant wishes to respond to the claim he must do so within 14 days after deemed service of the claim form. It is important to note that the defendant must file at the court and serve on all other parties both the acknowledgment of service and the witness statement(s) he intends to rely on. (Contrast Pt 7 claims where it is the court office, not the defendant, which sends a copy of the filed acknowledgment of service to the claimant.)

The acknowledgment in Form N210 is divided into seven lettered sections, namely:

A. *Not contesting the claim.* Where a defendant does not wish to contest the claim he should tick this box. However, if the defendant requires any specific direction or court order he must set out the details here.

B. *Contesting the claim.* If the defendant wishes to contest the claim he must tick the box. His reasons for doing so should be made clear in the written evidence filed and served with the acknowledgment. Where a defendant is seeking a remedy different to that sought by the claimant he must set out details in the box.

C. *Disputing the court's jurisdiction.* Again, all the defendant has to do is to tick the box. However, he must file an application within 14 days of filing the acknowledgment at the court.

D. *Objecting to the use of the procedure.* If the defendant contends that the Pt 8 procedure should not have been used by the claimant he must tick this box and then state his reasons for objecting.

Rule 8.8(1) provides that where the defendant contends that the Pt 8 procedure should not be used because: (a) there is a substantial dispute of fact; and (b) the use of the procedure is not required or permitted by a rule or practice direction, he must state his reasons when he files his acknowledgment of service.

An important provision in PD 8, para.5.3 should not be overlooked. Any statement of reasons that includes matters of evidence must be verified by a statement of truth.

An acknowledgment of service stating objections may cause the court to hold a hearing to determine them. If the objections are upheld the court may direct that the claim should continue as if the claimant had not used the Pt 8 procedure. The court will allocate the claim to a track and give case management directions.

E. *Written evidence.* If the defendant intends to rely on written evidence (see below) he must tick this box and should file that evidence with the acknowledgment. Where the other parties have agreed in writing to extend the time for taking that step by up to 14 days, a copy of the agreement must be filed at the same time as the acknowledgment.

F. *Full name of defendant.* The full name of the defendant filing the acknowledgment must be stated.

G. *Formal parts.* These include giving a statement of truth as to the facts stated in the form and an address for service.

What if the defendant fails to file an acknowledgment of service within the specified time? He may still attend the hearing of the claim but he may not take any part unless the court gives its permission. It appears, therefore, that the rule applies even if the acknowledgment is filed a few days late. In those circumstances a defendant should not wait and rely on the trial judge exercising his discretion. He should make an application under r.3.9 for relief from the sanction (see para.33.011). This is necessary as r.8.3 requires the defendant to acknowledge within a specific period of time and r.8.4 specifies the consequences of failing to do so. This also means that a claimant cannot effectively agree with the defendant pursuant to r.2.11 (see Ch.33) to extend the time for filing the acknowledgment. See below as to agreements to extend the time to serve evidence.

Where the Pt 8 procedure is used, no Pt 20 claim (see Ch.18) may be made without the court's permission. The court usually refuses permission unless any counterclaim or third party proceedings fall within the scope of the Pt 8 procedure.

FILING EVIDENCE (RR.8.5 AND 8.6)

The general rule is that a claimant must file any written evidence on which he intends to rely with his claim form. But what if the limitation period is about to expire and more time is needed to obtain that evidence? In those circumstances you should apply to the court to issue the claim and for an extension of time to file and serve the written evidence (see PD 8, para.7.4). Ensure that a witness statement is filed in support of the application detailing the reasons for the delay. Where the defendant wishes to rely on written evidence, he must file it with his acknowledgment and, at the same time, serve it on all other parties. What if

10.004

the evidence is not available? The claimant may agree in writing with the defendant to extend his time to serve his written evidence in reply. However, this extension cannot be for longer than 14 days after the defendant files his acknowledgment. Moreover, do not forget that the defendant must file the agreement when he files the acknowledgment (see above and PD 8, para.7.5(2)). If the claimant will not agree to an extension or such is insufficient, the defendant must apply to the court (see Ch.33).

Within 14 days of service of the defendant's evidence, the claimant may file and serve further written evidence in reply. The defendant can agree in writing to extend the claimant's time for filing and serving his further written evidence in reply but that extension cannot be for longer than 28 days after service of the defendant's evidence on the claimant. If the parties cannot come to an agreement and/or further time is needed, an application should be made to the court. There is no right for the defendant to file any further evidence and if he wishes to do so he must apply to the court for its permission.

The court controls the evidence used at trial (see para.33.012). In particular, r.8.6 provides that evidence may not be relied on at the hearing of the claim unless it was filed and served in accordance with the rules, or the court gives its permission. Oral evidence may be given at the hearing only if the court requires or permits it and the court may give directions requiring the attendance for cross-examination of a witness who has given written evidence. Once the court has been able to assess the type and amount of evidence required at trial it may well decide that the Pt 8 procedure is no longer appropriate if substantial cross examination on disputed facts is necessary.

CASE MANAGEMENT

10.005   Since a Pt 8 claim is automatically allocated to the multi-track there is no requirement to complete allocation questionnaires. The court may give directions either on application or of its own initiative immediately a Pt 8 claim is issued. Often this includes fixing a hearing date when it can be conveniently set at the outset, for example, in mortgage possession claims; or the appointment of trustees; or where there is no dispute whatsoever, such as in child and patient settlements. Certain applications may not require a hearing at all, for example, costs only proceedings under r.44.12A. Where directions are later required these are normally made after either the acknowledgment of service has been filed or the time for doing so has expired. If necessary, the court holds a directions-hearing.

What if Pt 8 is tactically used by a claimant, for example, as a way to avoid allocation to either the small claims track or the fast track? Can a defendant challenge the use of the procedure first and only if that fails then file his written evidence? If the claimant has clearly got it wrong, whether deliberately or not, it is to be hoped that the court will pick this up before service of the Pt 8 claim form and direct that the action should proceed as if the claimant had not issued a Pt 8 claim. If there has been a clear abuse of process, the court may strike out the claim under r.3.4 (see para.33.008).Indeed, PD 8 para.3.4 provides that the court will certainly take that conduct into account when considering costs in due course (see Ch.38). However, the dilemma for the defendant is that r.8.5 provides that if he fails to file and serve his written evidence in accordance with the rules he must secure the court's permission to rely on any evidence at trial if the matter does indeed proceed under Pt 8. We suggest that if the court has not seen any clear misuse of the Pt 8 procedure, the safest course for the defendant is to; (a) acknowledge; (b) object to the procedure; and (c) file his written evidence.

CHAPTER 11

Cases With a Foreign Element

11.001   This Chapter covers service outside the jurisdiction, for example, the service of English proceedings on defendants who are based overseas, and three related topics: applications for a stay of English proceedings on the basis that the English courts are not the most appropriate forum (forum non conveniens); applications for injunctions restraining the commencement or continuation of actions in foreign courts (anti-suit injunctions); and English proceedings to obtain a declaration of non-liability (a "negative declaration").

Rule 2.3(1) provides that "jurisdiction" means, unless the context requires otherwise, England and Wales and any part of the territorial waters of the United Kingdom adjoining England and Wales. There are two basic sets of procedural rules concerning service of a claim form outside the jurisdiction: cases governed by the Civil Jurisdiction and Judgments Acts 1982 and 1991 (CJJA 1982 and 1991) in which service is permissible without the prior permission of the court; and other cases, in which permission to serve is required.

THE COUNTRIES OF THE EUROPEAN UNION (EU) AND THE EUROPEAN FREE TRADE ASSOCIATION (EFTA)

11.002   In 1968 the members of the then European Economic Community signed a Convention at Brussels on civil jurisdiction and the enforcement of judgements. The UK acceded to the Convention in 1978 and it is part of UK law pursuant to the CJJA 1982. The Convention unifies to a large extent the private law applicable in the EC countries over a wide range of civil proceedings. The CJJA 1991 gave effect to the later Lugano Convention where the same system applies to Poland and the EFTA countries of Iceland, Norway and Switzerland. The Brussels Convention has been superseded by EC Regulation No.44/2001 ("the Regulation"). The countries currently governed by the Regulation are: Austria, Belgium, Denmark, Finland, France, Germany, Greece, Ireland, Italy, Luxembourg, Netherlands, Portugal, Spain, Sweden and the UK. UK in this context means England and Wales, Scotland and Northern Ireland; s.16 of the CJJA 1982 allocates jurisdiction between these parts of the UK by means of a set of rules which are substantially the same as the Regulation.

The two Conventions, the Regulation and the system relevant to the different parts of the UK are all very similar in content. For ease of reference we shall refer only to the Regulation and shall refer to all the relevant countries as Contracting States.

Scope of the Regulation

Although the Regulation covers a wide range of civil proceedings it does not apply to all. Proceedings outside its scope include proceedings concerning revenue, customs, administrative matters, legal status, rights in matrimonial property, wills and succession, insolvency, social security and arbitration. Permission to serve outside the jurisdiction in cases such as these is required even if the defendant is domiciled in a Contracting State.

11.003

The "first seised" rule

A court in which proceedings covered by the Regulation are commenced must, of its own initiative, examine whether it has jurisdiction (Regulation, Art.25). Further, a court must decline jurisdiction if proceedings involving the same cause of action and between the same parties has already been commenced in the courts of another Contracting State (Regulation, Art.27). The rule is that the court "first seised" of a matter should try it. The doctrine of forum non conveniens cannot be applied in order to stay proceedings in the courts of a Contracting State in favour of similar proceedings in the courts of another State. It is immaterial whether or not the other State is within the EU or EFTA (*Owusu v Jackson* [2005] 2 W.L.R. 942, E.C.J.).

11.004

What amounts to seisin depends upon the national law of the court in question. In *WPP Holdings Italy Srl v Benatti* [2007] EWCA Civ 263, *The Times*, April 16, 2007, the Court of Appeal held that an English court is seised of a case when the claim form is lodged with the court provided the claimant does not subsequently fail to take the requisite steps to serve the claim on the defendant. Whilst the claim form must be capable of service, invalid service does not prevent seisin. However, in *Miles Platt Ltd v Townroe Ltd* [2003] EWCA Civ 145, (2003) L.T.L., February 13, it was held that a French court was not seised of a claim where, as a preliminary to litigation, it had appointed an expert to investigate and report. Accordingly, the Court of Appeal refused to stay the English proceedings under Art.27 (see also *Boss Group Ltd v Boss France SA* [1997] 1 W.L.R. 351, CA).

Litigants in an action before the courts in one Contracting State may seek provisional and protective measures from the courts in another Contracting State (Art.31 of the Regulation). However, the measures must be of a provisional nature (as opposed to final) and there must be some territorial connection between the relief sought and the territorial jurisdiction of the court in which the application is made (*Van Uden Maritime BV v KG Deco-Line* [1999] Q.B. 1225, E.C.J., a claim for an interim payment to be paid out of assets located in the state of the court hearing the application). The remedy more frequently sought under Art.31 is an interim injunction, especially a freezing injunction (as to which, see para.27.015).

Contracting States: the domicile rule

11.005 By Sch.1, Art.2 of the CJJA 1982 the general rule is that a defendant must be sued in the courts of the Contracting State in which he is domiciled. Indeed, Sch.1, Art.3 excludes the application of the particular provisions of law of the various Contracting States as against persons domiciled in other Contracting States. Thus the jurisdiction claimed by the English courts based on transient presence within this country (see para.11.015, below) is not available against defendants domiciled in a contracting state. "Domiciled in the United Kingdom" is defined by s.41 of the CJJA 1982 as meaning resident in the UK, the nature and circumstances of such residence indicating a substantial connection with the UK. For example, the defendant's home and place of work is London or Cardiff or—Edinburgh or Belfast, etc. There is a presumption of domicile after three months' residence. Section 42 of the CJJA 1982 Act determines that a company's domicile is the contracting state where it has its "seat". For the purposes of UK law a company has its seat in the UK if it was incorporated or formed under part of the UK law and has its registered office or some other official address in the UK; or if its central management and control is exercised in the UK (see *Ministry of Defence and Support of the Armed Forces for the Islamic Republic of Iran v Faz Aviation Ltd* [2007] EWHC 1042, (2007) L.T.L. 16 May).

What if there are multiple defendants? Article 6.1 of the Regulation provides that in these circumstances a defendant domiciled in a Contracting State may also be sued in the court for the place where any one of the defendants is domiciled provided the claims are so closely connected that it is expedient to hear and determine them together to avoid the risk of irreconcilable judgments resulting from separate proceedings. In this context the words "defendants" and "claims" are wide enough to encompass defendants and claims in more than one action: see *Masri v Consolidated Contractors International (UK) Ltd* [2005] EWCA Civ 1436, *The Times*, October 27, 2005.

Exclusive jurisdiction

11.006 By Sch.1, Art.22 jurisdiction concerning rights in and tenancies of land; the validity of constitutions and decisions of companies or other legal persons or their dissolution; entries in public registers; the registration or validity of patents or other registerable industrial property rights, is given exclusively to the Contracting State where the land, legal person or register is situate. See, for example, *FKI Engineering Ltd v Dewind Holdings Ltd* [2007] EWHC 72, (2007) L.T.L., January 25. There is no power to depart from this Article by agreement and any other court is bound to decline jurisdiction.

Some of the special jurisdiction rules

11.007 Unless an alternative basis of jurisdiction applies, a defendant who is domiciled in a Contracting State must be used in the courts of that state. However, there are several alternative bases of jurisdiction, including matters relating to claims in contract, tort and agreements to submit to a particular jurisdiction.

Contract

By Sch.1, Art.5(1) proceedings relating to a contract are to be dealt with in the court of the place of performance of the obligation in question. Unless otherwise agreed, in the case of the sale of goods and/or supply of services, that is the place in a Contracting State where, under the contract, the goods or services were delivered or provided, or where such should have been delivered or provided. Where there are a number of obligations arising under the same contract, jurisdiction under the Regulation is determined by the principal obligation; *Union Transport Group Plc v Continental Lines SA* [1992] 1 W.L.R. 15, HL. In that case the claimant charterers agreed a fixture with defendant ship owners in London for the charter of a ship of suitable tonnage to be nominated by the defendants for the carriage of a cargo from Florida to Bangladesh. The House of Lords held the obligation to nominate a vessel to be the principal one since it was an essential pre-requisite to the performance of the other obligations. See also *Color Drack GmbH v Lexx International Vertriebs GmbH* (Case C-386/05), [2007] W.L.R. (D) 117.

Tort

By Sch.1, Art.5(3) tortious claims can be taken in the courts for the place where either the harmful event was committed or the damage occurred. Where a libel is published in more than one country the courts of each country have jurisdiction to rule in respect of the harm caused in that country. If instead the claimant sues in the courts of the Contracting State in which the defendant is domiciled (see para.11.005, above) the courts of that State have jurisdiction toward damages in respect of all the harm caused by the libel (*Shevill v Presse Alliance SA* [1996] A.C. 959).

Agreement

Article 23 of the Regulation provides that if one or more of the parties are domiciled in a Contracting State they may agree that the courts of a nominated Contracting State shall have exclusive jurisdiction to settle any disputes that may arise. The agreement must be either in writing or evidence in writing or, in international trade or commerce, in a form which accords with the practices in that trade.

Accepting the jurisdiction

Article 24 of the Regulation provides that the courts of a Contracting State have jurisdiction where the defendant participates in the proceedings, unless that is solely to contest jurisdiction (see below).

Commencement of proceedings

Rule 6.19(1) provides that a claim form may be served out of the jurisdiction on a defendant without the permission of the court provided that:

(a) each claim against that defendant is a claim which by virtue of the CJJA 1982 the court has power to hear and determine; and

(b) each claim is made in proceedings to which the following conditions apply—

   (i) no proceedings between the parties concerning the same cause of action are pending in the courts of any other part of the UK or of any other Convention territory; and

   (ii) either the defendant is domiciled in a part of the UK or in any other Regulation territory, or the proceedings begun by the claim form are proceedings to which Art.22 refers (see above), or the defendant is a party to an agreement conferring jurisdiction to which Art.23 applies (see above); or

(c) in a non-CJJA case, the court is given jurisdiction by a specific enactment, for example, the Civil Aviation (Euro Control) Act 1962.

Rule 6.19(3) provides that where a claim is to be served out the jurisdiction pursuant to the rule the claim form and, where they are contained in a separate document, the particulars of claim must be endorsed with a statement that the court has power under the Act to deal with the claim and that no proceedings based on the claim are pending between the parties in Scotland, Northern Ireland or another Regulation territory.

Practice direction 6B sets out at paras 1.1 to 1.3C the wording of the certificate to be used in each case. If it is omitted the court will issue the claim form but mark it: "Not for service out of the jurisdiction." This means you will either have to effect service in England or Wales (see Ch.8) or amend the claim form (see Ch.12). However, what if the claimant omits to include the statement and the court fails to notice the error? Does that invalidate service of the claim form? Mr Justice Rimer was faced with that situation in the case of *Trustor AB v Barclays Bank Plc & Another, The Times*, November 22, 2000. He held that the court on issue should have noticed the error and marked the claim form as not being for service out of the jurisdiction. It was not and as a result the claim form was served in Luxembourg on the third party. He observed that r.6.19(3) was a mandatory provision and non-compliance with it was not trifling, but it did not justify the court in saying that there had been no service at all. Failure to include the statement was an irregularity which had not caused any prejudice to the third party. It could therefore be remedied by the court under its general power under r.3.10 (as to which, see para.1.015, above).

NON-CJJA 1982 CASES

If the CJJA 1982 does not apply, the first question to consider is whether the action falls within the jurisdiction of the English courts. It is convenient to mention here three general matters: **11.008**

(1) The courts can claim jurisdiction over, and therefore a claim form can be served without the court's permission, if the defendant is present in England and Wales, even temporarily. However, if the English courts are not the most appropriate forum for the action the defendant can apply for a stay (see below), thereby compelling the claimant to start proceedings elsewhere.

(2) If the defendant is not present in England and Wales the courts have jurisdiction over him only if:

   (a) the court is given jurisdiction by a specific enactment, for example, the Civil Aviation (Eurocontrol) Act 1962; or
   (b) the defendant voluntarily submits to the jurisdiction, for example, by instructing English solicitors to accept service on his behalf; or
   (c) the court assumes jurisdiction over the defendant on the grounds set out in r.6.20 and it gives the claimant permission to serve the claim form outside the jurisdiction.

(3) Where permission is given to serve the claim form outside England and Wales the defendant can still object to the court's assumption of jurisdiction over him and apply to set aside the order granting permission. On such an application the claimant must prove that the permission was correctly given and that England is clearly the most appropriate forum (see *Spiliada Maritime Corp. v Cansulex Ltd* [1987] A.C. 460 discussed below).

Applying for permission to serve

In order to apply (under r.6.21) for permission to serve a claim form out of the jurisdiction the claimant must adduce written evidence stating: **11.009**

(a) the paragraph or paragraphs of r.6.20 relied on and the matters relied on in support of them;
(b) the belief of the claimant that his claim has a reasonable prospect of success;
(c) the defendant's address or, if not known, the place or country where the defendant is or is likely to be found;
(d) the facts and circumstances demonstrating that "England and Wales is the proper place in which to bring the claim" (i.e. demonstrating that England and Wales is clearly the most appropriate forum).

As the application is made without notice and may well not require a hearing, it is important to make full disclosure of all relevant facts. This includes drawing the court's attention to any features that might reasonably be thought to weigh against the making of the order sought.

What if a claim form is served out of the jurisdiction but the court's permission was necessary and it was not obtained? Consider first whether you can issue a new claim form and begin again. If, because of the law of limitation, it is too late to do that, the claimant's next best course is to obtain the missing permission and serve again. If, as is likely, he will need an extension of time for service his prospects of obtaining such an extension are poor (see para.9.006). Those prospects become virtually non-existent if the time for service has already expired (*Cranfield v Bridgegrove Ltd* [2003] 1 W.L.R. 2441). It will not improve his prospects to seek instead an order for service by an alternative method under r.6.8 or an order dispensing the service under r.6.9 or an order remedying his error of procedure under r.3.10 (see *Nanglegan v Royal Free Hampstead NHS Trust* [2002] 1 W.L.R. 1043 see especially para.14 which cites an earlier case).

The deadline for service of a claim form depends upon whether it was issued for service within the jurisdiction or outside it. The deadline is four months if it is for service within the jurisdiction or six months if it is for service outside. Which deadline applies where the claim form was issued for service within the jurisdiction but the claimant now wishes to serve it outside the jurisdiction? In one of the cases reported under the name *Anderton v Clwyd County Council (No.2)* [2002] 1 W.L.R. 3174 it was held that the six month deadline applies (see paras 85 to 99). Thus, a claimant who spots his mistake early may just squeak home if, within six months of issue of the claim form, he applies for permission to serve outside the jurisdiction and for an extension of time for doing so.

CHALLENGING THE COURT'S JURISDICTION (R.11)

11.010 If a defendant is served with a claim form and he wishes to dispute the court's jurisdiction he must take the following steps:

(1) File an acknowledgment of service stating this (see Ch.9). The defendant does not accept the court's jurisdiction by filing the acknowledgment. However, he should not file a defence as that is likely to be construed as accepting the jurisdiction (or waiving any irregularity that might be challenged).

(2) Make an application for a declaration that the court has no jurisdiction (or that it should not exercise its jurisdiction). The application must be made within the period for filing a defence (see below) and must be supported by evidence. If the defendant fails to make that application within the stipulated period he is deemed to have accepted the court's jurisdiction.

The defendant is required within the prescribed time to "apply to the court for an order" (r.11.1(1)). Rule 23.5 provides that the application is treated as having been made when it is received by the court, rather than when the court actually gets round to issuing it.

The court will normally deal with the application without a hearing. The trial of such a preliminary issue is costly and it is only ordered if such furthers the overriding objective. If the application is successful the court may make any order sought, for example, setting aside the claim form or service of such; discharging any pre-action order or staying the proceedings (see Ch.33). If the application is refused the acknowledgment of service ceases to have effect. The defendant must file a further one within 14 days or such other period as the court directs. Provided the defendant files that acknowledgment, he must then meet the court direction as to the time to file his defence. He must take both steps to prevent the claimant obtaining default judgment (see Ch.15).

Time for service of claim form (r.7.7(3))

Where a claim form is to be served out of the jurisdiction it must be served within six months of the date of issue (see para.9.007) 11.011

Does the court have power to retrospectively extend the time for service of the claim out of the jurisdiction? In *Nesheim v Kosa* [2006] EWHC 2710, (2006) L.T.L., October 4, Briggs J., relying on the pre-CPR authority of *National Justice Compania Naviera SA v Prudential Assurance Co. Ltd (The Ikarian Reefer (No.2))* (2000) 1 W.L.R. 603 answered that question in the affirmative.

METHODS OF SERVICE

Rule 6.24 and subsequent rules make general provisions for the method of service of documents out of the jurisdiction, whether or not the party serving requires permission so to serve. A claim form to be served out of the jurisdiction may be served by any method permitted by the law of the country in which it is to be served. Alternatively, the claimant may request service through official channels, for example, under the Hague Convention of 1965 or the Judgments Regulation (EC1348/2000). Such Conventions involve an officially designated transmitting agency passing relevant documents to an officially designated receiving agency which arranges service and then provides a certificate of service. The official channels are foreign governments, judicial authorities and British Consulate authorities. In order to serve through official channels a claimant in a High Court or county court case must file the appropriate documentation in the court office in which the case is proceeding. In respect of each defendant who is to be served, the appropriate documentation is as follows: 11.012

(a) A request for service. This must include an undertaking to be responsible for all the expenses incurred by the Foreign and Commonwealth Office in effecting service and to pay those on being informed of the amount.
(b) The sealed original and duplicate copy of the claim form and any accompanying documents.
(c) Copies of the particulars of claim.
(d) The response pack suitably amended.
(e) Translations of the documents where required and a translator's statement.

You should arrange service direct in respect of a defendant in Scotland, Northern Ireland, the Isle of Man, the Channel Islands, any independent Commonwealth country, any associated state, any colony or the Republic of Ireland.

Note that if a party makes a pre-action application for example, under r.25.4(1)(b) for an order for inspection (see Ch.27) or r.31.16 for a disclosure order (see Ch.30), the same service rules apply in relation to the application notice and order.

THE PERIOD FOR RESPONDING TO A CLAIM FORM

11.013 In EU matters, provided service occurs in the European territory of a Contracting State, the defendant has 21 days after service of the claim form indorsed with or accompanied by particulars to acknowledge service; or 21 days after service of separate particulars. If service is not in the European part of a Contracting State the period is extended to 31 days.

In EU matters the time period for filing a defence where service occurs in the European territory of a Contracting State is within 21 days after service of particulars of claim; or 35 days if an acknowledgment has been filed. If service is not in the European part of a Contracting State, the periods are extended to 31 days and 45 days respectively.

In non-EU matters particulars of claim must be included on or accompany the claim form on service. The table at the end of PD 6B sets out the periods for filing an acknowledgment (or admission) and/or a defence. For example, where a defendant has been served with a claim form in Abu Dhabi the period for acknowledging service or admitting the claim is 22 days after service. If the defendant chooses to acknowledge, he obtains an extra 14 days to file a defence, for example, in the case of a defendant in Abu Dhabi who acknowledges service, the period for filing a defence is 36 days after service of the claim form.

Note that where an application notice or order is to be served out of the jurisdiction, then in all matters the period for responding to service is seven days less than the number of days listed in the table. When you apply for any hearing date you must allow adequate time for the service of any response.

For further information concerning service out of the jurisdiction you should contact the Foreign Process Section, Room E02 at the Royal Courts of Justice.

COUNTERCLAIMS AND ADDITIONAL CLAIMS

It should never be necessary to serve a counterclaim on a claimant out of the jurisdiction. Every claimant must specify in the claim form an address for service which is within the jurisdiction. By commencing proceedings in this country he is deemed to submit to its jurisdiction in regard to any counterclaim (*Derby & Co. v Lassson* [1976] 1 W.L.R. 202, HL) unless, for example, the CJJA 1982 applies and the court of some other Contracting State is already seised of the case.

11.014

Consider now an additional claim to be served on a person other than the claimant. Rule 20.3 provides that an additional claim is to be treated as a claim for the purposes of the CPR unless any particular rule is excluded. The service rules in Pt 6 are not excluded by Pt 20. Accordingly, if the additional claim is to be served out of a jurisdiction permission for such service must be obtained unless, for example, the party to be served is domiciled within a Contracting State and the relevant treaties apply (see above).

FORUM NON CONVENIENS

Subject to the provisions of the CJJA 1982 (as to which see further below) the court will grant a stay of action if it is satisfied that there is another available forum which is clearly or distinctly more appropriate than the English forum; the disadvantages, if any, which the claimant may suffer if prevented from invoking the English jurisdiction will not normally be determinative provided that the court is satisfied that substantial justice will be done in that forum. The fact that some proceedings have already been commenced in the foreign court (lis alibi pendens) is an additional factor to be taken into account but not a conclusive factor. This doctrine was fully considered by the House of Lords in the case of *Spiliada Maritime Corp. v Cansulex Ltd; The Spiliada* [1987] A.C. 460, Lord Goff described a two-stage test, i.e. the defendant must first show that England is not the natural or appropriate forum for the trial and satisfy the court that there is another available forum which is clearly or distinctly more appropriate than the English forum. The court looks for the forum with which the action has the most real and substantial connection, for example, in terms of convenience or expense, availability of witnesses, the law governing the relevant transaction, and the places where the parties reside or carry on business. If the court concludes that there is no other available forum which is more appropriate than the English court it normally refuses a stay. However, if the court determines that there is another forum which is prima facie more

11.015

appropriate it will normally grant a stay unless, under the second part of the test, the claimant can show that there are circumstances by reason of which justice requires that a stay should not be imposed. In this inquiry, the court will consider all the circumstances of the case, including circumstances which go beyond those taken into account when considering connecting factors with other jurisdictions. One such factor can be the fact, if established objectively by cogent evidence, that the claimant will not obtain justice in the foreign jurisdiction.

The fact that granting a stay (or refusing permission to serve under r.6.20 see above) may deprive the claimant of a legitimate personal or juridical advantage available to him under the English jurisdiction does not, as a general rule, deter the court from grant a stay (or refusing permission) if it is satisfied that substantial justice will be done to all the parties in the available appropriate forum. Accordingly, the fact that a foreign forum has a more limited system of disclosure or lower awards of damages will not necessarily deter the court from granting a stay (or refusing permission).

Can the availability of financial assistance be a relevant factor? In *Connelly v RTZ Corp. Plc (No.2)* [1998] A.C. 854 C appealed against a Court of Appeal ruling that his action against D should be stayed. The court had found that the case should be heard in Namibia and it was not possible to take into account C's eligibility for legal aid in England when determining the most appropriate forum. D appealed against a subsequent Court of Appeal decision to lift the stay after C undertook not to apply for legal aid and his solicitors agreed to continue to act for him under a conditional fee arrangement. The House of Lords allowed C's appeal and dismissed D's. Where the possibility of either Community Legal Service Funding or a conditional fee arrangement was an issue, the general principle was said to be that if a more appropriate forum had been identified, the stay would not be refused simply because the claimant would not have financial assistance to him overseas which would be available to him here. However, exceptionally, the question of the availability of financial assistance could be a relevant factor if the claimant could show that substantial justice would not be done if he had to proceed in a forum where no assistance was available to him.

As we have seen the doctrine of forum non conveniens does not apply to cases to which the EU or EFTA Conventions apply (see para.11.004 above). At present there is still controversy as to whether the doctrine applies where the choice falls between different courts of the UK (see further *White Book*, para.6.19.25).

Thus far we have considered the doctrine of forum non conveniens only in relation to defence applications for a stay of proceedings. Such applications are made where the claim form has been validly served within the jurisdiction and, in such cases, the burden is upon the defendant to show that a foreign court is more appropriate. However, the doctrine more frequently arises in cases in which the claimant seeks permission to serve out of the jurisdiction. It is a matter he must deal with in his evidence in support (see para.11.009, above). If the defendant later applies to set aside the order permitting service out of the jurisdiction, the burden will be upon the claimant to show that the English court is the most appropriate.

ANTI-SUIT INJUNCTIONS

This section deals with applications for injunctions restraining the commencement or continuation of actions in foreign courts. For example, an English case where proceedings (on a matter not covered by the CJJA 1982) have been commenced, or threatened, in a foreign court and the defendant, or potential defendant in those proceedings asks the English court for an injunction which in effect requires his opponent to stay, or not commence, the foreign action. Here, it is not enough for the applicant (the defendant or potential defendant in the foreign proceedings) to show that England is the more appropriate forum. He must also satisfy the court as to two matters:

11.016

(1) that the foreign proceedings complained of are in the circumstances vexatious or oppressive; and
(2) that the injunction will not deprive the claimant in the foreign proceedings of any advantages in that forum of which it would be unjust to provide him.

See generally *Societé Nationale Industrielle Aerospatiale v Lee Kui Jak* [1987] A.C. 871, PC.

As a general rule the English court will not grant an anti-suit injunction to restrain proceedings in a foreign court unless the English court has a sufficient interest in, or connection with, the matter in question to justify such interference (*Airbus Industrie G.I.E v Patel* [1999] 1 W.L.R. 119, HL); unsuccessful application for an injunction to restrain proceedings in Texas where the natural forum for proceedings was India).

In CJJA 1982 cases, the Conventions and Regulation preclude the grant of an anti-suit injunction against the commencement or continuation of proceedings before the court of another Contracting State, even where the proceedings in the other State were taken for no purpose other than to harass or oppress the applicant (*Turner v Grovit* (C159/02) [2004] 1. L.Pr. 25). But is it consistent with the Conventions and Regulation for a court of a Contracting State to make an order restraining a person from commencing or continuing proceedings in another Contracting State on the ground that such proceedings were in breach of an arbitration agreement (see generally para.33.003)? As the House of Lords considered the answer was not obvious, it referred the question to the ECJ: see *West Tankers Inc v Ras Riunione Adriatica Di Sicurita Spa* [2007] UKHL 4, (2007) 1 Lloyd's Rep 391.

CLAIM FOR A NEGATIVE DECLARATION

Most actions are started by claimants seeking remedies such as debt or damages. Potential defendants usually have to wait to be sued. In the waiting, their opponent might start proceedings in a foreign court which the potential defendant thinks is less convenient to him than the English courts. In fact, potential

11.017

defendants do sometimes take the initiative. In a claim for a negative declaration the claimant seeks a ruling that he is not liable to the persons joined as defendants, i.e. he has not committed the breach of contract or other civil wrong of which they may have accused him. Seeking a negative declaration is obviously a device by which procedural advantages may be obtained but that does not by itself make it illegitimate or improper. It is an accepted device in the courts of virtually all the EU and EFTA member states (see *White Book*, para.6.19.22). In CJJA 1982 cases the "first seised" rule (see para.11.004) gives priority to the first EU or EFTA court in which proceedings are commenced. Thus, starting a claim for a negative declaration in England may prevent the opposing party starting the claim he wishes to bring in some other *Contracting State (Boss Group Ltd v Boss France SA* [1997] 1 W.L.R. 351, CA). It is—otherwise of course if the opponent starts first. In those circumstances priority will go to the court in which he started proceedings.

In non-CJJA 1982 cases a claim for a negative declaration may offer advantages whether or not proceedings have been commenced elsewhere. Bringing such a claim is an alternative to applying for an anti-suit injunction (see above). Of course, the claim will not live long before the English court if the English court's jurisdiction is challenged and the court is not satisfied that England is clearly the most appropriate forum.

In *Smyth v Behbehani, The Times*, April 9, 1999, B, a Kuwaiti national started proceedings in Sharjah against S, a British citizen. B claimed to be entitled to the repayment of three money transfers from S. The Sharjah court held that it had jurisdiction to hear B's claim in respect of only one of the transfers. S commenced proceedings in England, challenging the Sharjah court's jurisdiction and seeking a negative declaration of non liability in respect of the repayment of all the transfers. B applied for a stay of those proceedings on the ground of forum non conveniens, but it was held that there was an important procedural advantage to S in having all three transfers examined by a single court and that England was the most appropriate forum. B appealed. The Court of Appeal said that it must approach claims for negative declarations with great care in order to ensure that they were not brought to gain illegitimate procedural advantage. The judge had been right to find that there was an important procedural advantage to S, and in the interests of justice, of allowing proceedings involving comparable transactions to be tried at the same time. In the context of an application for a stay on the ground of forum non conveniens, as opposed to an application to strike out, the judge had been entitled to conclude that S's claim for a negative declaration did not deprive her of the right to pursue her action in the UK.

CHAPTER 12

Drafting Statements of Case

INTRODUCTION

Statements of case (previously called "pleadings") are the formal documents by which the parties are required to concisely set out the facts on which they intend to rely. The claimant starts by completing a claim form and preparing "particulars of claim". If the defendant wishes to contest the claim he must respond with a "defence". If the defendant also wishes to make a claim against the claimant, his statement of case is called a "defence and counterclaim". The claimant may respond to the defence by way of a "reply" and defend the counterclaim by way of a "defence to counterclaim". In addition to claiming against the claimant, a defendant can make a claim against a third party. Counterclaims and third party claims are known as additional claims and are dealt with in Pt 20 (see Ch.18). Additional statements of case should be drafted in exactly the same way as those in the main action. Rule 2.3(1) provides the full definition, namely that a "statement of case" means: (i) a claim form, particulars of claim where these are not included in a claim form, defence, additional (Pt 20) claim, or reply to defence; and (ii) includes any further information given in relation to them under r.18 (as to which see para.32.001).

12.001

Part 16 sets out the rules and practices to be followed when drafting statements of case and these are dealt with below. However, it should be noted that Pt 16 does not generally apply to Pt 8 claims (see Ch.10) nor certain specialist proceedings (see Ch.24).

THE FUNCTION OF STATEMENTS OF CASE

In the case of *McPhilemy v Times Newspapers Ltd* [1999] 3 All E.R. 775, Lord Woolf M.R. said:

12.002

> "The need for extensive pleadings including particulars should be reduced by the requirement that witness statements are now exchanged. In the majority of proceedings identification of the documents upon which a party relies, together with copies of that party's witness statements, will make the detail of the nature of the case the other side has to meet obvious.

This reduces the need for particulars in order to avoid being taken by surprise. This does not mean that pleadings are now superfluous. Pleadings are still required to mark out the parameters of the case that is being advanced by each party. In particular they are still crucial to identify the issues and the extent of the dispute between the parties. What is important is that the pleadings should make clear the general nature of the case of the pleader. ... No more than a concise statement of facts is required. As well as their expense, excessive particulars can achieve directly the opposite result from that which is intended. They can obscure the issues rather than providing clarification. In addition, after disclosure and exchange of witness statements pleadings frequently become of only historical interest.... [This] case is overburdened with particulars and simpler and shorter statements of case would have been sufficient."

The most important function of statements of case is to enable the court and the parties to identify and define the issues in dispute. Judicial case management (see Ch.33) means that the court will scrutinise the statements of case to ensure that the parties have concisely, but precisely stated the factual ingredients that are necessary to establish a case. If a statement of case does not disclose any reasonable grounds for bringing or defending a case, the court may strike it out. The court can also require a party to provide further information if the statement of case is insufficient. Further, if the court determines that an issue raised by a statement of case is irrelevant or that it would be disproportionate to pursue it, the court may exclude that issue from consideration (see para.1.006, above). A statement of case should be thought of as a "skeleton". You are putting together the bones of the case. For example, the particulars of claim in respect of a negligence action should deal with the essential facts that will establish a duty of care situation, breach of that duty, causation and damage. It is important to bear in mind that the witness statements served later in the proceedings by the claimant and on which he intends to rely on at trial will "flesh out" the detail of the incident complained of, how it was caused by the defendant and the damage suffered. See further below.

Example

Extract from particulars of claim:

> "On 26 July, 2007, at the claimant's home address of 16 Coppin Lane, Border Town, Mythshire ('the Property'), the claimant and the defendant entered into an oral contract ('the Contract') for the defendant to build an extension to the Property.
> It was a term of the Contract, stated in the conversation by the claimant and agreed by the defendant, that the defendant would build the extension for £15,000 plus VAT in accordance with a specification prepared by the claimant's architect dated February 1, 2007, a copy of which is attached".

The claimant's witness statement dealing with the above might read:

"On July 26, 2007 I telephoned the defendant at 9am and asked him if he would be interested in building an extension to my house. I told him that my architect, Tom Robinson had recommended him to me. He arrived that evening at about 6.30 pm. He had a look round and I went over Mr Robinson's specification dated February 1, 2007 with him. He sat with a calculator and after about 10 minutes he said he could do the job for £15,000 plus VAT. I readily agreed as Mr Robinson had suggested anything under £20,000 would be reasonable. I asked him if that included everything in the specification and he said, 'Yep, down to the last nail.'"

GENERAL FORMALITIES

Every statement of case should include the following matters: 12.003

(1) *The name of the court.* On the claim form this needs to be written in the box at the top right-hand corner. When drawing up any other statement of case it should appear at the top left-hand corner of the document. In the High Court the name of the division and any appropriate district registry must be stated, for example,

"In the High Court of Justice Queen's Bench Division Brighton District Registry"

or

"In the High Court of Justice Chancery Division Royal Courts of Justice".

(2) *The claim number.* When the court issues the claim form it will insert a reference number in the box at the top right-hand corner. The claim number must then appear on all future statements of case in that position. (Indeed, it is vital to ensure that you quote that number whenever you write to the court).

(3) *The title to the action.* See Ch.7.

(4) *The description of the statement of case.* Particulars of claim can either be typed directly on to the reverse side of the claim form or they can be prepared as a separate document. Where a defence and counterclaim form one document it should bear that title.

(5) *A statement of truth.* A party is required to confirm that the facts stated are true. The claim form has set out on it the required wording. All other statements of case should contain a statement of truth. A statement of case which does not do so is bad but it can subsequently be made good: PD 22, para.2.3 makes provision for the statement to appear in a separate document.

(6) *An address for service.* The claimant's address for service (see Ch.8) must be set out on the claim form. If particulars of claim are served separately the address must also appear there. Although an acknowledgment of service is not a statement of case, it should be noted that

DRAFTING STATEMENTS OF CASE

where a defendant files such it must contain his address for service. If no acknowledgment is filed the defendant's address for service must appear on the defence. Any address for service given by a party should include the postcode. Note also that a defendant should provide his date of birth (see PD 16 para.10.7).

(7) *The name of counsel, if the statement of case is settled by him.* Although it does not appear as a formal requirement under the rules it remains the practice that counsel's name is put at the end of a statement of case that he has prepared. The Chancery Guide provides that if solicitors or counsel drafted the statement of case, their name should appear at the end. The Commercial Court Guide says that the document must be signed by the individual person or persons who drafted it.

STATEMENTS OF TRUTH

12.004 Statements of case must be verified by a statement of truth such as "I believe that the facts stated in [described document] are true." Its purpose is to eliminate allegations in which a party has no honest belief and to discourage parties advancing cases which are unsupported by evidence in the hope that some evidence might turn up on disclosure or at the trial (*Clarke v Marlborough Fine Art (London) Ltd* [2002] 1 W.L.R. 1731). A statement of truth must be signed by either the party to the action, his litigation friend if he is a child or patient, or a legal representative on behalf of that person. However, r.22.1(8) provides that it may be made by two parties jointly or a person who is not a party to the proceedings if this is permitted by a relevant practice direction, for example, PD 22, para.3.6(2) allows a person having the control or management of a partnership's business to sign on behalf of the partnership.

If you are the solicitor for a party, should you sign on behalf of the client? What exactly are you asserting? PD 22, para.3.7 is the starting point. It provides that you are referring to the client's belief that the factual content of the statement of case is true and not your own. So far so good. However, what steps must you take to be in a position to make such a statement? PD 22, para.3.8 provides that your signature is taken by the court as your statement that:

(a) You were authorised by the client to sign. This begs the question as to how you should obtain and record that authority. If you are acting for a large company issuing numerous claims one simple letter of authority signed by the client will suffice. But if you are acting for an individual what is the point in getting an authority signed? You might just as well get the client to sign the statement of truth.

(b) Before signing you explained to the client that the effect would be to confirm his belief that the facts stated in the statement of case were true.

(c) Before signing you informed the client that he could be prosecuted for contempt of court if he made a statement that turned out to be false and he did not have an honest belief in its truth.

What is the practical effect of PD 22, paras 3.7 and 3.8? It is clear that you are not in contempt of court simply because you make a statement of truth on behalf of a client who is acting dishonestly. But para.3.8 says that your "signature will be taken by the court as [your] statement" that you had authority to sign, etc. We take the view that you are indeed making a statement of truth, but on your own behalf. You are making a statement to the court that you have acted in accordance with para.3.8. It is contempt to make such a statement falsely (r.32.14) and disciplinary proceedings may well be inevitable. Whether a solicitor signs or not he will still have to explain to the client the consequences of making a false statement. There should not be any problems with established commercial clients who are familiar with this matter. But in respect of the client who walks in off the street, we would recommend that he always sees, and approves, the statements of case and signs the statements of truth.

We suggest that the real purpose of the statement of truth is to ensure that someone takes responsibility for the contents of the statement of case, even if he does not have direct knowledge of the facts. As that person is "fronting" the litigation he needs to make it his business to find out. This is the reason why the statement can be signed on behalf of a registered company or corporation by a "person holding a senior position", namely a director, the treasurer, secretary, chief executive, manager or other officer of the company or corporation. Solicitors should discuss with their commercial clients any relevant insurance in this respect-not to cover any contempt but possibly the costs of proceedings for such. If the corporation is not a registered company the mayor, chairman, president or town clerk or other similar officer my sign (PD 22, para.3.5). PD 22, para.3.11 contains useful examples of who may sign in cases involving managing agents, trustees, insurers and the MIB, companies and in-house legal representatives.

Whoever signs the statement of truth must print his full name beneath his signature. If a solicitor signs then he must put his name and not that of his firm.

What steps should be taken if you consider that your opponent has made a false statement of truth? Practice Direction 32, para.27 provides that you should refer the allegation to the court dealing with the claim. The court will usually initiate steps to consider if there is a contempt of court and may direct you to refer the matter to the Attorney General with a request to him to consider whether he wishes to bring proceedings for contempt of court. Further details are set out in the Practice Direction.

What if a statement of truth is omitted? Rule 22.2 provides that the statement of case remains valid but it cannot be used as evidence at any interim hearing. However, the court may strike it out either of its own initiative or on the application of any other party. We suspect that the court will only exercise its powers of strike out where there has been a persistent failure to make statements of truth by a party. If you are served with a statement of case that lacks a statement of truth we suggest you write requiring it to be provided within seven days and that you copy that letter to the court. The court may well make an order of its own initiative directing that the step should be taken within a specified period but imposing the sanction that otherwise the statement of case is struck out. If you do have to make a court application in this respect it is worth remembering that PD 22, para.4.3 provides that the defaulting party should usually pay the costs forthwith (see Ch.13 as to making the application and costs).

FORMAT OF A STATEMENT OF CASE

12.005 The rules do not dictate the actual format of a statement of case. Contrast this with a witness statement (see Ch.14) where PD 32, para.19.1 even suggests the size and quality of the paper that should be used. For our part we feel that there is much to be said for adopting the provisions of that practice direction and the guidelines offered in the Chancery and Commercial Court Guides. In particular, the statement of case should:

(1) follow a chronological sequence of events;
(2) be divided into numbered paragraphs and each paragraph should be confined to one allegation;
(3) deal with the case on a point-by-point basis, to allow a point by point response.

It is a matter of taste as to whether or not each paragraph should have a heading. We favour their use in lengthy documents as they clearly flag up for the court and the parties the different areas of facts. Headings also assist in drafting the document in the first place as they form the skeleton for the statement of case itself. Wherever possible, use non-contentious headings which can be adopted without issue by the other parties.

An excellent way of shortening the length of any statement of case is to use definitions for phrases that will regularly appear. Whilst we have rarely seen an actual "definition clause" in a statement of case, it could be useful in a complex case. In addition, where the case consists of multiple parties, it will simplify matters not to call each repeatedly "the first claimant", "the second defendant", etc. but to have an introductory paragraph. That should refer instead to each by a shortened version of their name, for example, the first claimant (Mrs Hilary Catlin) will be known as "Mrs Catlin", etc. This will often be necessary in additional proceedings (see Ch.18).

The decision of Morritt L.J. in *Morris v Bank of America National Trust* [2000] 1 All E.R. 954, CA, contains useful practical advice about the presentation of lengthy statements of claim in complex cases.

"The Amended Points of Claim cover 150 A4 pages. Although there are only 228 paragraphs, a number of them are sub-divided and sub-sub-divided. Paragraph 159, for instance, has 17 sub-paragraphs and covers four pages. Paragraph 170 (with six sub-paragraphs, most of them spawning sub-sub-paragraphs) covers nearly 13 pages. It is rivalled by Paragraph 187, which covers 12. Paragraph 188 covers only six, but has no less than 28 sub-paragraphs. The Points of Defence is a somewhat slimmer document, containing only 93 pages, with 436 paragraphs and fewer sub-paragraphs. No use is made of headers or footers to make it easier for a judge to find his way round these massive pleadings. It is he who is under a duty to control the case, and it is the duty of the parties and their representatives to help him.

There is no reason why the judge should not be provided with material in electronic form, such as pleadings, skeleton arguments and statements of issues, supported by hypertext (or other) links enabling him to move rapidly from what the claimant says about a matter to what a defendant says about a matter, or enabling him to take up a cross-reference to an earlier part of a document (or to another document) instantaneously."

Occasionally, the rules require certain documents to be attached to a statement of case, for example, a copy of a written contract that is being relied on. However, in many other cases it is convenient to prepare and attach a separate document, such as a schedule of debts and interest, rather than to clutter up the statement of case with a long list.

Pre-CPR a statement of case had to end with a "prayer for relief", i.e. a list of what the party wanted. As parties no longer "plead" their case, equally it is not a requirement of the rules that they have to end up praying! If the statement of case is necessarily lengthy and numerous remedies are sought, then a summary at the end may prove useful.

PRINCIPLES OF DRAFTING STATEMENTS OF CASE

Sufficient facts should be stated concisely, yet precisely

Each party must state clearly the facts he is coming to court to prove, not the legal consequences he intends to draw and not the detailed evidence he intends to call. If litigants were allowed to only state law they would conceal the facts in issue. If a claimant could merely allege that "The defendant owes me £15,000" the defendant would be left to guess what facts the claimant was intending to prove at trial. Does such an allegation relate to a contract or to a trust? Does it refer to something that happened days ago or years ago? The claimant should make these matters clear by stating the facts he relies on, not just the legal conclusion he draws from them. For example, if the claim relates

12.006

to goods sold and delivered he should give the details of the contract, the date of delivery of the goods, etc. Now assume that in such a case the defendant simply answered the claim in his defence saying, "The defendant denies that he is liable to pay". The claimant is then left to guess. The defendant's defence might be that there was no agreement, or that it was invalid, or that no goods were delivered, or that he has already paid. The point is that if the defendant were allowed to merely state the legal result he contends for he would hide the facts upon which his defence is based.

A good statement of case strikes a balance between the need to give enough detail to inform both the court and the other parties of the issues being raised and the need to omit details which would only obscure those issues. Of course, the degree of detail necessarily varies with the nature of the case. In *McPhilemy v Times Newspapers Ltd*, above, the claimant sued the defendant newspaper alleging libel. The defence was 38 pages long. Lord Justice May commented that it was no longer tolerable in libel cases to have excessively long particulars of justification. "Rather perhaps should the particulars succinctly set out the scope of the intended justification, leaving the detail to be given once only in witness statements".

It is always tempting when drafting a statement of case that alleges negligence to first copy the examples given in any relevant precedent and then to add all those that you can think of drawing on the particular facts of the case. This just pads out the document with lots of irrelevant material and even worse, it will obscure the claimant's real case. Simply list all the ways the loss or damage complained of can be explained as being caused by the opponent's negligence on the facts of the case and leave it at that.

When dealing with a claim for an unspecified amount of financial loss you should give enough information to enable the opponent to evaluate the claim should he wish to make a Pt 36 offer (see Ch.29). Minute accuracy is not essential: the loss may be described as "estimated" or "approximate". The larger the claim, the greater the need for a breakdown or statement of the figures upon which the claim is based. As Simon Brown L.J. said in *QPS Consultants Ltd v Kruger Tissue (Manufacturing) Ltd* [1999] B.L.R. 366:

> "Given the huge size of the suggested [counter]claim (some £14 million) and the obvious inter-relation between the losses said to be accruing through under-production and the costs of modifications such as would curtail or modify such losses (including considerations as to mitigation of loss), it seems . . . wholly inexcusable that the defendants gave nothing whatever by particulars to crystallise this claim."

If you fail to do so the defendant can seek further information (see the *QPS* case and Ch.32).

Reference may be made to a point of law (PD 16, para.13.3(1))

12.007 As a general rule there is no need to state any English law. But if a claim is based on propositions of foreign law, then the party who advances that should refer to the system of law on which he relies: see *Global Multimedia International Ltd v Ara Media Services* [2006] EWHC 3612, *The Times*, August 1, 2006. It will normally be a defendant, however, who will wish to raise a point of English law as a defence, for example, that the claim discloses no cause of action because it alleges a promise unsupported by consideration or because special damage is essential to the cause of action and none is alleged. It is vital that any such legal issue becomes clear at an early stage since the objection might dispose of the whole action if it can be heard as a preliminary point (see Ch.33). Note, in addition that PD 16 para.13.1 provides that a defendant must give details of the expiry of any relevant limitation period that he relies on in his defence.

There is no requirement to state any provision of the Compensation Act 2006. However, under s.1, a court when considering a claim in negligence or breach of statutory duty may, in determining whether the defendant should have taken particular steps to meet a standard of care (whether by taking precautions against a risk or otherwise), have regard to certain matters. These include whether a requirement to take those steps might either prevent a desirable activity from being undertaken at all, to a particular extent or in a particular way, or discourage persons from undertaking functions in connection with a desirable activity. In answering a claimant's allegation that certain steps were not taken, a defendant may wish to rely on these particular defences.

The name of an intended witness may be stated (PD 16, para.13.3(2))

Whilst excessive factual details should not be given in a statement of case, a party can state "the name of any witness he proposes to call". By this we assume a party can choose to indicate if he has any particular witness in mind who will prove a particular fact. We see little advantage to this. As there is "no property in a witness" the opponent would be free to interview the named person. If a party is prepared to go so far as to "name names" then why not reveal that person's evidence by attaching their witness statement to the statement of case or voluntarily disclosing it? 12.007A

However, there may be occasions where a party should "name names" in putting forward his version of events. If, for example, in an industrial accident claim, part of the defendant's case is that the machinery in question was regularly checked, arguably he should say by whom and when.

Documentary evidence may be attached (PD 16, para.13.3(3))

A party can attach to a statement of case any document he considers "necessary" to his claim or defence. There are some documents that must be attached, for example, a medical report that is being relied on in a personal injury case (see below). We feel that this provision should be used as a way of ensuring that the court has the fullest possible knowledge of relevant facts from the outset. So if a party has voluntarily disclosed a document before proceedings were issued or has 12.008

received a document from the other side that fundamentally assists his case, and it is admissible, we take the view that it may be appropriate to attach it.

DRAFTING A CLAIM

The claim form

12.009 On the front page of the claim form, after the formal parts, the claimant must first give "a concise statement of the nature of the claim" and, secondly, "specify the remedy which the claimant seeks" (r.16.2). As to the former the only guidance given on the claim form itself is that the facts and full details about the claim, including interest, should appear in the particulars of claim. So would the following be adequate?

> "Damages for negligent misstatement and/or negligence and/or breaches of duty arising out of the defendant's financial models and/or projections and/or advice and/or information provided to the claimant between about October 1999 and June 2000 and in reliance upon which the claimant agreed to and did provide £860 million of loan finance to Box Clever Finance Limited to fund the merger of the businesses of UK Consumer Electronics Limited (formerly Granada TV Rental Limited) and TUK Holdings Limited (formerly Thorn UK Limited)."

This was the concise statement in *Nomura International Plc v Granada Group Ltd* [2007] EWHC 642, (2007) L.T.L., March 30. Cooke J. held that these were inadequate, stating,

> "Insofar as it sought to make any claim in contract, it would be necessary for it to be able to identify the particular contract and the alleged breach. In the case of any breach of tortious duty, it would be necessary for it to be in a position to identify the essential acts or omissions which constituted the breach of duty, negligence or negligent misstatement. For the purposes of negligent misstatement, Nomura would have to be able to identify what advice or information was inaccurate and what was given negligently, at least in essence." He went on to strike out the proceedings as an abuse of process (see para.33.008, below).

The examples given in the notes on completing the claim form in respect of the remedy sought are: payment of money; an order for return of goods or their value; an order to prevent a person doing an act; damages for personal injuries. If their basic requirements are not met or the details are garbled or abusive, the matter is likely to be referred to a judge and struck out.

The addresses of both the claimant and defendant on the claim form must include their postcodes (details can be obtained from www.royalmail.com or the Royal Mail Address Management Guide) It is important to note that if a postcode is omitted, whilst the court will issue the claim form, it will keep it and will not permit it to be served until the claimant supplies the details or the court dispenses with this requirement. See PD 16 para.2.5. A claimant must not be slow in sorting this out as the claim form must usually be served within four months of being issued (see para.9.007). Rule 16.2(1)(cc) requires that where the claimant's only claim is for a specified sum of money, the claim form must contain a statement of the interest accrued on that sum (see further Ch.3 and para.12.013, below).

Hidden away in r.16.2(5) is a provision that allows the court to grant to the claimant any remedy that he is entitled to even if it is not specified in the claim form. This should not be seen as a charter for sloppy drafting. Whilst it will allow the court to ignore any technical arguments by a defendant that a claim was "not properly made out", we anticipate that this provision is primarily aimed at litigants in person who may find it difficult to state their claims with legal accuracy.

If proceedings are taken against the Crown, see 24.018.

The statement of value

An important feature of the claim form is the statement of value that must appear next on the front page. The information will be used as part of the allocation process (see Ch.9). If the claimant is suing for a specified sum you put that amount. Then in the box at the bottom right-hand corner handily labelled "amount claimed" insert the amount claimed. Where the claimant is seeking an unspecified amount you must state the amount that he reasonably expects to recover within the financial bands covered by the three tracks, i.e. "not more than £5,000" (small claims); "more than £5,000 but not more than £15,000" (fast track) or "more than £15,000" (multi-track). See Ch.9.

12.010

Do not forget that there are different rules for personal injury and housing disrepair or similar cases if the financial value of the whole claim is below £5,000 (see Ch.9). The appropriate statements are:

> Personal injuries—"My claim includes a claim for personal injuries and the amount I expect to recover as damages for pain, suffering and loss of amenity is (a) not more than £1,000 or (b) more than £1,000".
>
> Housing disrepair, etc.—"My claim includes a claim against my landlord for housing disrepair relating to residential premises. The cost of the repairs or other work is estimated to be (a) not more than £1,000 or (b) more than £1,000". If the client is also making any other claim for damages it must be stated whether or not those damages are expected to be more than £1,000.

If there is no value you can put on your money claim at present you simply state, "I cannot say how much I expect to recover".

Rule 16.3(7) makes clear that statements of value are not conclusive, i.e. they do not limit the power of the court to give judgment for a higher or lower amount.

Where the claim form is to be issued out of the High Court (see Ch.9) a statement of the ground relied on must be put at the foot of the front page. Of course, the usual ground will be that the claimant expects to recover more than £15,000 but the others to choose from are: "By law, my claim must be issued in the High Court. The Act which provides for this is (specify appropriate Act)"; or "My claim includes a claim for personal injuries and the value of the claim is £50,000 or more"; or "My claim needs to be in a specialist High Court list, namely (specify list)". The statement should commence, "I wish my claim to issue in the High Court because (state ground)".

The prescribed forms, N7 (Pt 7) and N207 (Pt 8) require the claimant to state whether or not the action raises any issue under the Human Rights Act 1998. If so, details must be given in the particulars of claim (see para.12.027).

The particulars of claim

12.011 The particulars of claim can either be typed on the reverse side of the claim form or prepared as a separate document. PD 16, para.3.1 states that if it is practicable to do so the particulars of claim should be set out on the claim form. The claim form must state "Particulars of claim to follow" if the particulars are not going to be served with the claim form.

Rule 16.4 provides that the particulars of claim must include:

(a) a concise statement of the facts on which the claimant relies;
(b) any claim for interest, aggravated damages, exemplary damages or provisional damages with certain prescribed information;
(c) such matters as may be set out in a practice direction.

A concise statement of the facts on which the claimant relies

12.012 The particulars of claim should state all the facts necessary for the purpose of formulating a complete cause of action. For example, a claim in negligence will cover at least three areas: the incident complained of; that it was caused by the defendant's negligence; and the loss or damage the claimant has suffered thereby. A claim alleging the breach of a term of a contract will cover at least four areas: the agreement; the term alleged to have been broken; breach of that term; and the consequences of that breach including the loss the claimant has suffered thereby. On both of these examples, see further para.12.032, below. As to the additional restrictions which apply to particulars of claim in claims issued online, see para.9.022, above.

Claims for interest

12.013 As to the entitlement to interest, see Ch.3.

Rule 16.4 provides that interest must be claimed in the particulars of claim and the basis for it must be detailed, i.e. whether the claim is made pursuant to the terms of a contract, statute or otherwise. Where the claim is for a specified amount of money the following details must be set out:

(a) the percentage rate at which interest is claimed;
(b) the date from which it is claimed;
(c) the date to which it is calculated. This must not be later that the date on which the claim form is issued;
(d) the total amount of interest claimed to the date of calculation;
(e) the daily rate of interest claimed after that date.

Examples

(1) SCA 1981, s.35 or CCA 1984, s.69.
(a) A claim for a specified amount of money

"The claimant claims interest under [s.69 of the County Courts Act 1984] [s.35A of the Supreme Court Act 1981] at the rate of 8 per cent per annum, from [date when the money became due] to [date of issue] of £...And also interest at the same rate up to the date of judgment or earlier payment at a daily rate of £..."

Assume the claim is for £12,500. The following steps need to be taken:

Step 1—work out the daily rate of interest at 8 per cent per annum by multiplying the amount claimed by 0.08 and dividing by 365, i.e. £12,500 3 0.08 4 365 5 £2.74.

Step 2—calculate the number of days that have arisen from, but not including, the day the money fell due up to and including the day of issue. Hence, if the debt became owed on August 1, 2007 and the claim form is completed on September 13, 2007, then 43 days have passed (30 in August and 13 in September).

Step 3—multiply the number of days by the daily rate, for example, 43 3 £2.74 5 £117.82.

(b) Unspecified claim

"In respect of damages awarded to him the claimant is entitled to interest pursuant to [s.69 of the County Courts Act 1984] [s.35A of the Supreme Court Act 1981] for such periods and at such rates as the court see fit".

(2) Late Payment of Commercial Debts (Interest) Act 1998

"The claimant claims interest under the Late Payment of Commercial Debts (Interest) Act 1998 at the rate of ... per cent per annum (i.e. 8 per cent over the base rate which is ... per cent) from [date when the money became due] to [date of issue] of £... and also interest at the same rate up to the date of judgment or earlier payment at a daily rate of £..."

The three steps outlined above should then be followed to calculate interest payable up to the date of issue and the daily rate payable thereafter.

(3) Contractual interest

"By clause 3 of the Contract the defendant agreed to pay interest on the Debt, or any part that remained outstanding after the Repayment Day, at the rate of 15 per cent per annum, and until payment, whether that occurs before or after any judgment".

See Ch.3 for further details.

Claims for aggravated or exemplary damages

12.014 Aggravated damages are awarded by the court as compensation for the defendant's objectionable behaviour. On the other hand, exemplary damages go beyond compensating for actual loss and are awarded to show the court's disapproval of the defendant's behaviour. The facts said to establish the grounds for each claim must be stated.

For a review of this topic see *Kuddus v Chief Constable of Leicestershire Constabulary* [2002] 2 A.C. 122.

Claims for provisional damages

12.015 As to this topic generally see para.4.015. PD 16, para.4.4 requires that the particulars of claim must state if the award is sought under s.32A of the Supreme Court Act 1981 or s.51 of the County Courts Act 1984 and that there is a chance that at some future time the claimant will develop a specified serious disease or suffer some type of serious deterioration in his physical or mental condition.

Claims for wrongful interference with goods

12.016 Rule 19.5A(1) provides that in a claim for wrongful interference with goods, the particulars of claim must state the name and address of every person who, to the claimant's knowledge, has or claims to have an interest in the goods and who is not a party to the claim.

Defamation claims

12.017 See Pt 53 and PD 53 for matters that should be included in the claim form and particulars of claim.

Matters Required by PD 16

12.018 Practice Direction 16 sets out certain matters that must be included in particulars of claim in certain circumstances. We have summarised these below:

Injunction or declaration (para.7.1)

Where the claim is made for an injunction or declaration concerning land or the possession, occupation, use or enjoyment of land, the particulars of claim must state if residential premises are involved and identify the land (by reference to a plan where necessary).   **12.019**

Examples

> "The claimant is the owner of the residential premises known as 'Dunrunin', Westbourne, Mythshire".

> "The claimant is the owner of the commercial premises in Malt Street, Westbourne, Mythshire as outlined in red on the attached plan".

Recovery of goods (para.7.2)

If a claim is brought to enforce the right to recover possession of goods the particulars of claim must contain a statement showing the value of the goods.   **12.020**

Example

The goods should, of course, have already been defined in the particulars of claim (see above). On the assumption that they have been called "the Electronic Equipment", a suitable statement might read, "The value of the Electronic Equipment is £. . .".

Written agreement (para.7.3)

Where a claim is based upon a written agreement, a copy of the contract or documents constituting the agreement should be attached or served with the particulars of claim. The originals should be available at the hearing. In addition, any general conditions of sale incorporated in the contract should also be attached. However, if any document is too bulky it is sufficient to attach or serve relevant extracts.   **12.021**

Examples

> "By a written contract ('the Contract') dated April 10, 2007, the claimant agreed to buy from the defendant . . . A copy of the Contract is attached".

> "By an agreement in writing ('the Contract') contained in emails from the claimant to the defendant dated . . . and from the defendant to the claimant dated . . . it was agreed that . . . Copies of the emails are served with this statement of case".

Oral agreement (para.7.4)

Where a claim is based upon an oral agreement, the particulars of claim should set out the contractual words used and state by whom, to whom, when and where they were spoken.

Example

"On September 27, 2007, at the defendant's house at 6 The Drive, Westbourne, Mythshire, the claimant and the defendant made an oral contract ('the Contract') by which the claimant agreed to buy the defendant's motor home for £16,000. It was a term of the Contract, stated by the claimant and agreed by the defendant in the conversation, that the motor home was sold as it stood including all the contents".

Agreement by conduct (para.7.5)

12.022 Where a claim is based upon an agreement by conduct, the particulars of claim must specify the conduct relied on and state by whom, when and where the acts constituting the conduct were done. Few contracts arise out of conduct alone. An agreement may be formed partly in writing and/or orally and partly by conduct, for example, as the result of a previous course of dealings. In such a case it is important to identify the course of dealings relied on in order that the defendant knows the case against him.

High Court consumer credit agreement cases (para.7.6)

12.023 As outlined in Ch.9 most actions relating to Consumer Credit Agreement fall to be dealt with in the county court. If a claim is issued in the High Court it must contain a statement that the action is not one to which s.141 of the Consumer Credit Act 1974 applies.

Civil Evidence Act 1968, ss.11 and 12 statements (para.8.1)

12.024 These two sections of the 1968 Act provide that a person's conviction for a criminal offence (s.11) or a finding or adjudication of adultery or paternity (s.12) can be used in civil proceedings as evidence that the person committed the offence, etc. For example, in a road accident case the claimant might prove negligence on the part of the defendant simply by proving that as a result of the accident in question the defendant was convicted of careless driving. By stating the conviction the burden of proof passes to the defendant. Negligence will be presumed unless the defendant can prove the contrary. The particulars of claim must include the following details:

(a) The type of conviction, finding or adjudication and its date.
(b) The court or Court-Martial which made the decision.

(c) The issue in the claim to which it relates.
(d) A statement that the party intends to rely on the conviction.

Example

"The claimant intends to rely on evidence of the defendant's conviction for driving without due care and attention contrary to s.3 of the Road Traffic Act 1988 on January 11, 2007 at Canterbury Magistrates' Court. This conviction relates to the issue of the defendant's negligence".

If the defendant wishes to deny the matter or allege that it is erroneous or irrelevant, he must do so in his defence (see below). If it is denied then the claimant can prove it by producing a certificate of conviction (see Ch.6). In most cases a defendant will allege that the conviction was erroneous. The burden of doing so may be discharged on the balance of probabilities (see *Wauchope v Mordecai* [1970] 1 W.L.R. 317). He will be able to state that it is irrelevant if the conviction relied on does not relate to the issue before the court (e.g. a conviction for income tax fraud relied on in a simple RTA claim).

Clinical negligence (para.9.3)

In clinical negligence claims, the words "clinical negligence" should be inserted at the top of every statement of case. 12.025

Competition Act 1998 (para.14)

If a party wishes to rely on any finding of the Director General of Fair Trading provided pursuant to s.58 of the Competition Act 1998 he must include a statement to that effect and identify the Director's finding on which reliance is placed. 12.026

Human rights (para.15.1)

If a party wishes to rely on any provision of, or right arising under, the Human Rights Act 1998, or seeks a remedy available under that Act, he must state that fact. Precise details of the Convention right which it is alleged has been infringed and particulars of the infringement must be given. In addition, the relief sought must be specified along with any declaration of incompatibility in accordance with s.4 of the Act or damages in respect of a judicial act to which s.9(3) of the Act applies. If a declaration of incompatibility is sought, precise information of the legislative provision alleged to be incompatible and details of the alleged incompatibility must be given. Where the claim is founded on a finding of unlawfulness by another court or tribunal, details of the finding must be set out. If the claim is founded on a judicial act which is alleged to have 12.027

DRAFTING STATEMENTS OF CASE

infringed a Convention right of the party, the party must state the judicial act complained of and the court or tribunal which is alleged to have made it.

Miscellaneous matters

12.028 Paragraph 8.2 lists certain matters that a claimant must specifically set out in his particulars of claim where he intends to rely on them in support of his action. These are:

(1) Any allegation of fraud. The seriousness of this matter means that full and precise particulars of the allegations must be given. It is not permissible to leave fraud to be inferred from the facts stated and so fraudulent conduct must be distinctly alleged (*Davy v Garrett* (1878) 8, Ch. D. 473 and see *Medcalf v Mardell* [2003] 1 A.C. 120).

(2) The facts of any illegality. The claimant might seek a declaration of non-liability on the grounds of illegality. However, it is far more usual for a defendant to rely on illegality, for example, that the contract being sued on is void under statute.

(3) Details of any misrepresentation. The particulars of claim must show the nature and extent of each alleged misrepresentation and state by whom and to whom it was made, and whether it was made orally or in writing.

(4) Details of all breaches of trust. "It is not the practice of the Court where one breach is proved to direct a roving inquiry with a view of ascertaining whether there are any other breaches of trust.... The [claimants] are not entitled to relief at trial, except in regard to that which is alleged in the pleadings and proved at the trial" (*per* Warrington J. in Re Wrightson [1908] 1 Ch.789 at 799).

(5) Notice or knowledge of a fact. The claimant should state any specific facts, documents or other overt acts on which he intends to rely in support of his allegation that the defendant had notice or knowledge of some fact. It is insufficient to state that the defendant "ought to know" or "ought to have known" some fact. In those circumstances the defendant could seek further information about the allegation (see Ch.32).

(6) Details of unsoundness of mind or undue influence. These two matters often arise in probate actions. Particulars of the nature of the unsoundness, the character of the undue influence and the acts alleged in the exercise of it, with necessary dates, must be stated.

(7) Details of wilful default. Consideration needs to be given as to how the defendant's duty arose and the acts said to constitute the wilful refusal to carry it out.

(8) Any facts relating to mitigation of loss or damage. Generally speaking, a claim should not include facts which anticipate a particular point that might be taken in the defence (see below). However, it is sometimes necessary to describe steps which, although taken in order to mitigate loss, have actually increased that loss.

PERSONAL INJURY CLAIMS

Practice Direction 16 prescribes some of the contents of the particulars of claim for certain specified proceedings, namely personal injuries, recovery of land, hire purchase claims and defamation. We now look in detail at the provisions dealing with personal injury claims. The particulars of claim must deal with the following: **12.029**

(a) The claimant's date of birth must be stated. This is sensible as it may well affect the issue of quantum of certain damages.
(b) Brief details of the claimant's personal injuries must be stated.
(c) A schedule of any past and future expenses and losses claimed must be attached.
(d) The claimant must also attach to or serve with the particulars any report from a medical practitioner he relies on which deals with the injuries alleged.

As to (b) above, how brief the details should be will depend upon whether or not you are relying upon a medical report. If you are, very short details may be given and you should include an express reference to the report.

As to (c) above, there is no requirement to produce evidence in support of the expenses and losses claimed. However, that will often have been done already, i.e. voluntarily under the pre-action protocol. Where any figures have been agreed, this should be stated. However, do ensure that you only refer to those matters which the defendant was prepared to bind himself to as part of the protocol procedure.

As to (d) above, an example of a substantial claim commenced without a medical report would be a claim commenced towards the end of the relevant limitation period (see further para.6.015, above).

INCONSISTENT STATEMENTS OF CASE (PD 16, PARA.9.2)

A statement of case may itself contain alternative and therefore inconsistent allegations. For example, in a contract case the claimant may allege that a promise he says the defendant made became a term of the main contract, or alternatively that if formed the subject matter of a collateral contract. In his defence, the defendant might allege in the alternative: (1) that he never made the promise; (2) that if it was made, the promise was not broken; (3) that the claimant's cause of action is statute-barred. If the alternatives are clearly pleaded as such, the claimant is entitled to give a statement of truth asserting an honest belief that one of the set of facts relied on is true (*Clarke v Marlborough Fine Art (London) Ltd* [2002] 1 W.L.R. 1731). Sometimes the claimant denies facts alleged by the defendant but nevertheless wishes to assert that his claim should prevail even if the defendant's allegations of facts are upheld. In such circumstances, it is possible to rely on a statement of truth which   **12.030** makes it clear that while the claimant's primary case challenges the defendant's account, if the court finds that to be the truth, the claimant will seek to rely upon it as an alternative basis for liability (*Binks v Securicor Omega Express Ltd* [2003] 1 W.L.R. 2557, CA; cf *Goode v Martin* [2002] 1 All E.R. 620).

If a statement of case contains too many inconsistencies it will fail to clarify the issues in dispute. The court is likely to penalise the party in costs and prohibit him from pursuing certain issues (see Ch.33). In extreme cases where the inconsistencies show the allegations to be fictitious or unsustainable the court will strike out the statement of case (*Remmington v Scoles* [1897] 2 Ch.1).

However, a subsequent statement of case must not contradict or be inconsistent with an earlier one; for example, a reply to a defence must not bring in a new claim. Where new matters have come to light the appropriate course will usually be to seek the court's permission to amend the statement of case (see below).

ANTICIPATING A PARTICULAR DEFENCE

12.031   Generally speaking, a claim should not include facts which anticipate a particular defence. It is best to wait and see what the defence actually contains. Answering allegations before they are raised is "like leaping before you come to the stile" (Sir Ralph *Bovey's Case* (1684) Vent 217, *per* Hale C.J.). Assume, for example, that a claimant seeks damages for breach of a contract containing an exclusion clause which he thinks is invalid or inapplicable. To state the clause and then to explain it away would look weak. It is far better to see if the defendant takes the point in his defence (see below) and then answer any allegations in the reply.

By way of exception it is usual to anticipate defences under the Limitation Act (see Ch.5). It is poor tactics to allege a debt which accrued seven years ago without stating the facts which, it is alleged, take the case out of the ordinary limitation period, for example, the debt was acknowledged two years ago. In these cases the particulars of claim would look weak if it did not anticipate. The important difference here is that until these additional matters are dealt with the claimant does not appear to have a valid cause of action (see generally, *Busch v Stevens* [1963] 1 Q.B. 1).

TEMPLATES FOR CLAIMS

12.032   The particulars of claim tell a story. Let us consider that of the claimant who purchased a washing machine from a local shop. Several weeks later due to an alleged electrical fault it leaked over her kitchen floor ruining the carpet. If you think of each chapter of the story as being a paragraph in the particulars of claim, then in respect of this claim alleging breach of a contractual term there will be the following chapter headings:

(1) The contract (attach a copy of it if written).
(2) The relevant contractual term.
(3) How that term was broken by the defendant.
(4) The consequences for the claimant.
(5) The loss and damage suffered as a result.
(6) The interest sought on the claim.

Hence, you end up with a template that can be used to draft the claim. Another example might concern a road traffic accident. Assume the claimant and the defendant are driving their cars along a road in opposite directions. Suddenly, the defendant allegedly swerves in front of the claimant who cannot avoid the collision. The claimant ends up in hospital with multiple injuries. The basic structure of the particulars of claim will be:

(1) Details of the date, time and place of the accident.
(2) A description of the defendant's negligence (include any relevant conviction imposed by the criminal courts).
(3) The loss and damage suffered by the claimant as a result (include a schedule of such and a medical report).
(4) The interest sought on the claim.

Obviously, the number of paragraphs needed to set out any claim will depend upon its complexity. Where the claimant relies on two or more causes of action arising out of the same facts the familiar items should be woven together to avoid unnecessary repetition. However, if the claimant is raising causes of action based on different facts it is more convenient to keep separate the facts applicable to each.

DRAFTING A DEFENCE

A defence must comment on the facts stated in the particulars of claim, admitting or denying them as the case may be. In addition, any facts relied on by the defendant must be stated. 12.033

When a fact is admitted it ceases to be in issue and neither party is required or permitted to advance evidence about it at trial. The defendant is duty-bound to further the overriding objective (see para.1.003, above) by admitting any fact which it would be unreasonable to deny. If he fails to do so he can expect to be penalised in costs whatever the outcome of the trial. A claimant may be able to put pressure on a defendant to make admissions by serving a notice to admit (see para.32.007).

Rule 16.5 requires that a defence must address each allegation made in the particulars of claim and state if it is:

(a) Denied. If so the defendant must give his reasons and where he intends to put forward a different version of events he must state it.

(b) Admitted.
(c) Neither admitted nor denied because he has no knowledge about the issue and requires the claimant to prove it, for example, loss and damage allegedly suffered. These are often called "non-admissions".

Rule 16.5(6) provides that if you dispute the claimant's statement of value you must state why and give your own value where possible. In a personal injury case you should make direct reference to any relevant points that appear from the claimant's medical report that is attached to the particulars of claim.

As a general rule if a defendant fails to address an allegation he is deemed to admit it. However, if he has set out in his defence the nature of his case in relation to that issue he is taken to have required the claimant to prove it. In addition, where a claim includes a money claim, a defendant is always assumed to require any allegation relating to its amount to be proved unless he expressly admits it (see, generally, r.16.5(3), (4) and (5)). The best way to draft a defence is to answer the claim paragraph by paragraph. In other words deal in turn with each of the claimant's allegations, admitting or denying them according to the defendant's own case. Any additional facts representing the defendant's version of events can be inserted in their appropriate place in the story. Where two or more paragraphs can be safely admitted in their entirety you should do this in one paragraph in response, for example, "Paragraphs 1, 2 and 3 of the particulars of claim are admitted".

The following are common examples of cases where the defendant will often put forward a different version of events to that stated by the claimant:

(1) In contract actions: facts showing that the contract has been discharged or released or varied or was made only as agent for another.
(2) In debt actions: the defence of tender before claim (see below).
(3) In damages actions: facts showing that the defendant acted without negligence or that the injury was caused wholly or in part by the claimant or some third person.
(4) In assault and battery cases: facts showing that the defendant acted in self defence.

When this method is followed it is possible to compare the particulars of claim and defence and so locate precisely the facts in issue between the parties at this stage. The position may be slightly altered by any reply (see below). The alternative method of drafting a defence is to strike out on your own separate path: stating in chronological order all the relevant facts and denying the claimant's major allegations. This will be necessary where you are faced with a claim that is either too short or too long. Whichever method is used the defence must provide a complete account of the defendant's case.

Although a well-drafted claim should set out only one allegation per paragraph you must take care to spot any paragraphs that contain two or more points and to answer each and every one of them clearly and unambiguously.

Example

Paragraph 3 of the particulars of claim reads:

> "The defendant placed the order for the goods on July 20, 2007 and on July 21, 2007 the claimant delivered the goods to the defendant's storage depot".

Which of the following is the best response if the defendant says that the order was placed on July 20, 2007 but the claimant did not deliver them as he collected them from the claimant's shop on July 21, 2007?

(1) "Paragraph 3 is denied".
(2) "As to paragraph 3, the defendant admits that the claimant placed the order for the goods on 20 July 2007 but denies that on 21 July the claimant delivered the goods to the defendant's storage depot".
(3) "As to paragraph 3, the defendant admits that the claimant placed the order for the goods on July 20, 2007 but denies that the claimant ever delivered the goods to the defendant's storage depot. The defendant asserts that he collected the goods from the claimant's shop on July 21, 2007".

(1) is wrong as it fails to address both points. Whilst the placing of the order is admitted, the delivery by the claimant is denied. At first sight (2) appears correct. However, it could be construed as meaning that the goods were delivered but on a different day. The confusion arises because the defendant's own case is not stated. Therefore only (3) correctly addresses the substance of the claimant's allegations and puts the issue of delivery beyond any doubt by stating the defendant's version.

Sample defences

To illustrate further how the defendant should state his own version of events, we have set out below four typical types of defences.

12.034

Tender before claim (r.37.3)

In this defence the defendant alleges that before the claimant started the action he unconditionally offered the claimant the amount due, or, if no specified amount is claimed, an amount sufficient to satisfy the claim. The defence carries the implication that the commencement of the action was unnecessary and the claimant should pay the whole costs. In order to rely on the defence the defendant must make a payment into court of the amount he says was tendered.

12.035

At first sight it may seem odd that a defence of tender should ever be raised. One might ask, if the defendant had offered payment surely the claimant would have accepted it. In practice the real dispute between the parties concerns the amount of money due.

Example

C sells and delivers wine to D for an agreed price of £75 per case. C says that 200 cases were delivered and sends D an invoice for £15,000. D says that only 120 cases were delivered and sends C a cheque for £9,000. C returns the cheque and sues D for £15,000. In this example the claimant will defeat the defence of tender before action if he can prove any of the following:

(a) The debt due exceeded the amount tendered.
(b) He was not obliged to accept payment by cheque and, in returning the cheque, he did not waive his objection. Strictly speaking a cheque is not legal tender but in *Jones v Arthur* (1840) 8 Dowl 442 the claimant was held to have waived his right to object when he returned the cheque complaining only that it was not for the full sum due.
(c) The tender was made conditional on the claimant acknowledging that no more was due, i.e. the cheque was sent in "full and final settlement" or with some similar words. Even if the full amount was tendered the defendant cannot require the claimant to give up his right to query the calculation. However, if in the example the defendant tendered £9,000 unconditionally or "under protest that this is the full amount due" the claimant should have accepted it and sued only for the balance.

Defences under the Limitation Act (PD 16, para.13.1)

12.036 The defendant must give details of the expiry of any limitation period that he relies on. For example, "The alleged cause of action did not arise within six years before the commencement of this action and is barred by (s.2—if a claim in tort) (s.5—if a contract claim) of the Limitation Act 1980".

As to limitation generally see Ch.5.

Defence of set-off (r.16.6)

12.037 A set-off is a money claim the defendant has against the claimant. It has a dual effect. First, it is a claim that can be made in a separate action or by counterclaim (see Ch.18). Secondly, if raised in the claimant's action it has the additional effect of extinguishing his claim up to its value. Rule 16.6 provides that a set-off may be included in a defence, whether or not it is also an additional claim.

There are three matters set out below which, in common parlance, lawyers usually call "set-offs". Strictly speaking, only the first is a true set-off. The second was originally only a defence. The third was originally a cross-action in the courts of equity. These two have become set-offs because of the reform of the courts and procedure made by the Judicature Acts 1873–75.

Mutual debt set-off. Ever since the so-called Statutes of Set-off in 1729 and 1735 a claim for a debt can be set-off against or extinguished by a debt the claimant owes the defendant "in the same right". Both claim and set-off must be for specified amounts.

Example

C and D supply goods to each other. On May 31, 2007 C owed D £60,000 and D owed C £50,000. If C starts an action against D his claim would be totally extinguished by the set-off; D would also make a counterclaim to obtain the balance of £10,000. If D started proceedings first his claim could be partially extinguished.

Assume D dies and X, another trader, is appointed his executor. X personally owes C £10,000. If, as executor, X sues C for the £60,000 C could still set-off £50,000 but not X's personal debt since that is not due "in the same right". However, C could raise an ordinary counterclaim (*Re Richardson* [1933] W.N. 90 *per* Romer L.J.).

Common law defence of abatement. From early times where the claimant sues for the price of goods or services supplied the defendant has been able to "set up", in reduction of the price, any claim he has for defects in the quality of the goods or services supplied (*King v Boston* (1789) 7 East 481; *Mondel v Steel* (1841) 8 M&W 858). Although this is not a true set-off at common law (since it is for damages rather than a debt) it is treated as a defence in abatement of the claimant's claim. Since 1873 the defendant has also been able to put such forward as a counterclaim, and therefore nowadays it has no significant difference from a true set-off. For sale of goods cases the matter has been made statutory (Sale of Goods Act 1979, s.53).

Equitable set-off. Before 1875 equity would grant an injunction to restrain a claimant from insisting on his legal rights where it would be unconscionable for him to do so without taking into account any cross-claims the defendant had arising out of the same subject matter. Since 1875 the administration of law and equity has fused, and nowadays rather than issue an injunction the court will treat related cross-claims as defences extinguishing the claimant's claim up to the value of the cross-claim.

Examples

C, a warehouseman, sued D for the agreed charges for storing D's goods. D claimed that, because of C's negligence, some of the goods had been lost or stolen from the warehouse. This cross-claim for negligence amounted to an equitable defence thereby defeating an application for summary judgment (*Morgan v Martin Johnson* [1949] 1 K.B. 107).

C, a householder, sued D, a builder, for damages for failing to complete a building contract. D raised three cross-claims, namely quantum meruit for extra work done, damages for breach of contract by C and damages for trespass to D's tools (thrown away by C). All the cross-claims were held to be equitable set-offs. The cross-claims exceeded C's claim by £10. C's claim was dismissed and judgment for £10 was given on the counterclaim (Hanak v Green [1958] 2 Q.B. 9).

C, a landlord, sued D, its tenant, for rent. D successfully stated, by way of set-off, damages for breach by C of its covenant for quiet enjoyment even though D's rent covenant provided for payment of rent "without any deduction" (*Connaught Restaurants Ltd v Indoor Leisure Ltd* [1994] 1 W.L.R. 501; contrast *Coca-Cola Financial Corporation v Finsat International Ltd* [1996] 3 W.L.R. 849 in which it was held that there was a clear contractual exclusion of the right to set-off).

The exact scope of the common law defence of abatement can now be regarded as of academic interest only (see *Sim v Rotherham Metropolitan Borough Council* [1987] Ch.216 *per* Scott J.). It is a narrow common law version of the wide doctrine of equitable set-off. If equitable set-off is available, abatement is not needed (and see further, *Aectra Refining and Manufacturing Inc v Exmar NV* [1994] 1 W.L.R. 1634). If, in the circumstances, equitable set-off is not available then it will also be impossible to establish abatement. There are certain exceptional types of transactions in which the law withholds both matters, for example, cheque actions (see Ch.19) and actions for freight under a contract of carriage (see *United Carriers Ltd v Heritage Food Group (UK) Ltd* [1996] 1 W.L.R. 371 and the cases cited therein).

In some cases equitable set-off may also be available as a defence to a non-money claim, for example, forfeiture or specific performance (*BICC Plc v Burndy Corporation* [1985] Ch.232) or to a non-litigious remedy, for example, a landlord's right to distrain for rent (*Eller v Grovecrest Investments Ltd* [1995] 2 W.L.R. 278).

It is usual to state a set-off both as a defence and counterclaim. To do so the last paragraph of the defence might read:

> "If necessary, the defendant will rely upon his counterclaim in this action by way of set-off in reduction or extinction of the claimant's claim".

Contributory negligence

12.038   In many cases the defendant will allege that the claimant contributed towards his own misfortune. It is important that the defendant should set out his allegations in the defence and include details of any duty that the claimant failed to discharge. Why? So factual and expert witnesses can, where appropriate, deal with it in their evidence and the trial issues are clear—see *Dziennik v CTO Gesellschaft Fur Containertransport MBH and Co.* [2006] EWCA Civ 1456, (2006) L.T.L., November 13.

Example

In the case of *Spiller v Brown* (1999) L.T.L., July 20, the claimant was hit by the defendant's car whilst she was crossing the road in front of a stationary bus. The defendant was driving in the same direction as the bus, he overtook it and did not see the claimant in time. As part of his defence the defendant relied on para.30 of the Green Cross Code (as detailed in the Highway Code). This provides that a pedestrian should never cross the road directly behind or in front of a bus but should wait until the bus has moved off and the road can be clearly seen in both directions. The Court of Appeal held that the Code neatly put the case so far as contributory negligence was concerned and assessed it at 50 per cent.

Specific proceedings

Just as PD 16 prescribes the contents of the particulars of claim for certain specified proceedings (see above), it equally sets out what is required in any defence. For personal injury cases these are as follows: 12.039

(a) In respect of each matter contained in any medical report attached the defendant should state if he:
  (i) agrees such;
  (ii) disputes such and if so, says why;
  (iii) neither agrees nor disputes such as he has no knowledge of the facts.
(b) Where the defendant has obtained his own medical report on which he intends to rely he must attach it to his defence.
(c) In respect of each item in any schedule of past and future losses attached the defendant should prepare a counter-schedule which should state if he:
  (i) agrees such;
  (ii) disputes such and if so, gives an alternative figure, where appropriate;
  (iii) neither agrees nor disputes such as he has no knowledge of the facts.

Note also that where a defendant wishes to contradict the particulars of claim on the basis of medical records or reports, he should indicate that intention in his defence (or by amending it should the information only be obtained subsequently) or at the very least by informal notice: see *Field v Denton Hall Services* [2006] EWCA Civ 169, *The Times,* March 22, 2006 (also discussed at para.31.019).

DRAFTING A COUNTERCLAIM

Normally, the defence and counterclaim are included in the same document, which is given that title. Then comes a subheading "Defence" and the paragraphs of the defence. Next comes a subheading "Counterclaim" and beneath it the 12.040

paragraphs of the counterclaim. The paragraphs are numbered in ascending sequence from the defence: if the last paragraph of the defence was numbered 6, the first paragraph of the counterclaim will be numbered 7.

The facts of a counterclaim should be drafted in the same way as the facts of particulars of claim. Two additional points to bear in mind are:

(a) Many of the facts will already have been stated in the defence and so there is no need to set them out again. They can be incorporated into the counterclaim by simply stating "paragraphs ... to ... (inclusive) are repeated".

(b) If the action has been issued out of the county court you must include a statement of value (see above and r.20.3(2)(b)).

FORMS OF ADMISSION, DEFENCE AND COUNTERCLAIM

12.041 When the defendant receives the particulars of claim he will also be served with the "response pack" which contains these forms (see Ch.9). Many litigants in person use the forms but solicitors tend to draw up their own statements of case.

DRAFTING A REPLY AND/OR DEFENCE TO COUNTERCLAIM

12.042 The claimant should file a reply if he wishes to respond to the defences raised. There is no need to do so simply to deny the defences. Rule 16.7 provides that a claimant who does not file a reply is not taken to admit the matters raised in the defence. Moreover, if a reply fails to address a matter raised in the defence it is still assumed that the claimant requires that point to be proved by the defendant. A reply should be limited to stating any new facts the claimant intends to prove to defeat a defence.

However, as previously noted (para.12.030, above) the facts in the reply should not be inconsistent with the facts alleged in the claim. If after seeing the defence the claimant wishes to change his story he should do so by amending his particulars of claim.

Filing a defence to counterclaim is compulsory in so far as the defendant may otherwise obtain default judgment (see Ch.15). The defence to counterclaim should be drafted in exactly the same way as an ordinary defence. Where a claimant files both a reply and defence to counterclaim they should usually be included in the same document which bears that heading with the two subheadings thereafter.

FURTHER STATEMENTS OF CASE?

A party may not file or serve any statement of case after a reply without the court's permission (r.15.9). The court will usually direct that the party amends its existing statements of case rather than add to them. The pre-CPR case of *Tito v Waddell* (No.2) [1977] Ch.106 is an example of a rare case where subsequent statements of case were allowed.

12.043

SUGGESTED DOCUMENTS

We have set out below some suggested statements of case. We hope that each side's case is sufficiently well stated that we do not need to explain it. However, you should note the following background facts:

12.044

(1) The defendant's employees have not been joined as co defendants since prior to proceedings being issued the defendant's insurers indicated that vicarious liability was not disputed.

(2) During the pre-action protocol procedure the parties agreed on a joint expert to prepare the medical evidence and his report is attached to the particulars of claim.

(3) Liability is contested and the insurers have argued in correspondence that the claimant was contributorily negligent and also failed to mitigate his loss by refusing to undergo surgery (see *Selvanayagam v University of the West Indies* [1983] 1 All E.R. 824).

(4) The claim form contained the following statement of value: "I expect to recover more than £15,000". The claim has been issued in the county court as the claimant does not expect to recover more than £50,000.

(5) The particulars of claim are a separate document but will be served with the claim form.

(6) The parties have attached to their respective statements of case a schedule and counter schedule of losses and expenses. These are not reproduced.

(7) No acknowledgment of service was filed and so the defence contains the defendant's address for service.

Suggested particulars of claim

12.045 IN THE WESTBOURNE COUNTY COURT Claim No. WB07879

BETWEEN:
    Mr Charles Darling   Claimant
    and
    Downtown Buses (Mythshire) Limited   Defendant

12.046

PARTICULARS OF CLAIM

1. On February 7, 2005 at about 8a.m. the claimant was standing at a bus stop in the High Street, Westbourne, Mythshire when a bus owned by the defendant and driven by their employee in the course of his employment stopped at the bus stop.
2. The claimant attempted to board the bus as a prospective paying passenger. While he was doing so the conductor, acting in the course of his employment, sounded the bell as a signal for the driver to move the bus forward. The bus moved forward suddenly and the claimant fell into the road.
3. The claimant fell into the road due to the negligence of the defendant and its employees.

12.047

PARTICULARS

The conductor of the bus was negligent in that he:

(1) Sounded the bell without first ensuring that the claimant was in a safe position.
(2) Failed to give any warning to the claimant that the bus was about to move.

The driver of the bus was negligent in that he:

(1) Drove away from the bus stop without ensuring that the claimant was in a safe position.
(2) Drove off too fast and with a sudden jerk.

4. By reason of this negligence the claimant has suffered pain, injury, loss and damage. Full particulars are set out in the attached medical report and schedule of losses and expenses. The claimant's date of birth is December 26, 1980.
5. The claimant has on medical advice reasonably refused to undergo surgery on his neck. Further details are contained in the medical report attached hereto.

6. In respect of damages awarded to him the claimant is entitled to interest pursuant to s.69 of the County Courts Act 1984 for such periods and at such rates as the court sees fit.

I believe that the facts stated in these particulars of claim are true.
Signed: C. Darling
Full name: Charles Darling
Date: June 29, 2007.

Suggested defence

IN THE WESTBOURNE COUNTY COURT Claim No. WB07879

BETWEEN

Mr Charles Darling   Claimant
and
Downtown Buses (Mythshire) Limited   Defendant

DEFENCE

1. It is admitted that on February 7, 2005 at about 8a.m. a bus owned by the defendant and driven by their employee stopped at the bus stop in the High Street, Westbourne, Mythshire. It is not admitted that the claimant was standing at that bus stop as the defendant has no knowledge of that fact. Neither the defendant's bus driver nor conductor saw the defendant standing at the bus stop.
2. It is admitted that the conductor, the defendant's employee, sounded the bell as a signal for the driver to move the bus forward. At the time the bell was sounded the claimant had not boarded the bus. It is denied that the bus moved forward suddenly. the bus moved forward slowly and smoothly. It is admitted that the claimant fell into the road.
3. It is denied that the claimant fell into the road due to any negligence of the defendant or its employees.

PARTICULARS

The conductor of the bus was not negligent as he:

(1) Sounded the bell before the claimant attempted to board the bus.
(2) Warned the claimant not to board the bus as it was already moving. He shouted, "You can't get on, we're going".

The driver of the bus was not negligent as he:

(1) Had already started to drive away from the bus stop when the claimant attempted to board the bus.
(2) Drove slowly and smoothly.

4. It is denied that the injuries and losses complained of in the particulars of claim were caused in any way by the defendant or its employees. Further, or alternatively, such were caused wholly or in part by the claimant's negligence. The claimant was negligent in that he attempted to board the bus while it was in motion and he ignored the warning of the defendant's bus conductor.
5. No admissions are made as to the pain, injury, loss and damage allegedly suffered by the claimant. The defentdant's counter schedule to the claimant's schedule of losses and expenses is attached. The medical report attached to the particulars of claim is agreed save as stated in the next paragraph.
6. It is denied that the claimant has acted reasonably in refusing to have surgery on his neck. It is not admitted that the claimant relied on any medical advice when refusing to have surgery prior to seeing Mr Smart, the Consultant Neo-surgeon who prepared the medical report attached to the claimant's particulars of claim. It is not admitted that the claimant relied on Mr Smart's advice. It is further denied that Mr Smart's advice, as disclosed in his report, reasonably enitles the defendant to refuse to have surgery. The defendant asserts that the claimant has failed to mitigate his loss as a consequence of unreasonably refusing surgery on his neck.

I believe that the facts stated in this defence are true. I am duly authorised by the defendant to sign this statement.

Signed: A. Downtown
Full name: Alan Patrick Downtown
Position or office held: Director of the defendant company
Name of defendant's solicitor's firm: Brisk & Co.
Defendant's solicitor's address to which documents should be sent:
16 Old Town, Westbourne, Mythshire. DX 7003 Westbourne.
Date: July 30, 2007.

AMENDING STATEMENTS OF CASE

12.050   In many cases there will be no need to amend a statement of case if proper consideration is given to drafting it in the first place. However, a party may change his mind; new facts may arise; the opponent's statement of case may surprise you or simple typographical errors may have been made. Rule 17 and PD 17 deal with how and when a statement of case may be amended.

Amendments before service (r.17.1(1))

Any party may amend his statement of case at any time before it has been served on any other party. So, in a multi-party action once one party has been served the right to amend is lost. Let us briefly review the requirements as to filing and serving statements of case in order to see where last minute changes might be possible.

12.051

(a) A claim form with particulars of claim. After issue you can ask the court to serve it or you can do so. Hence if you have decided to serve it there may be a chance to deal with any amendments beforehand. If so you will need to file an amended version at the court (see below) and obviously effect service of the amended document. However, you must bear in mind that any amendment which has the effect of adding, substituting or removing a party requires the court's permission (see Ch.7).

(b) Separate particulars of claim. You are required to file these and a certificate of service within seven days of serving them (see Ch.9). Hence, you can serve the final version of the document that you are satisfied with but thereafter will need the court's permission to make any amendments.

(c) A defence. Rule 15.6 simply provides that "a copy of the defence must be served on every other party" (see Ch.9). When filing a defence it appears you can request the court to effect service or you may do that yourself. If you have asked the court to do it there might just be time before they serve it to make an amendment.

(d) A reply. This must be filed with your allocation questionnaire and served on all other parties "at the same time" (see r.15.8(b), Ch.9). In this instance there is no time then to amend.

Can you challenge amendments that have been made without the need for the court's permission? Rule 17.2 provides for this. An application must be made to the court within 14 days of service of the amended document. The most likely grounds are that the amendment is futile, frivolous, made in bad faith or has the effect of adding or substituting a totally new claim (see below). If the court's permission was necessary in the first place because the amendment adds or substitutes a party (see Ch.7) you should apply to strike it out (see Ch.33).

Amending after service (r.17.1(2))

Once you have served the statement of case you can only make an amendment with either the written consent of all the other parties (r.17.1(2)(a)) or the court's permission (r.17.1(2)(b)).

12.052

Should the parties agree to amendments? Obviously you must see the proposed amendment first. Correction of typographical errors and minor changes to the party's story should be tolerated as the court will undoubtedly allow such. Moreover, you should point out technical defects to your opponent. In the case of *Hannigan v Hannigan* (2000) I.L.R., July 3, Brooke L.J. in the Court of Appeal said, "the overriding objective is not furthered by arid squabbles about technicalities". In *McPhilemy v Times Newspapers Ltd* [1999] 3 All E.R. 775, Lord Woolf stated "Unless there is some obvious purpose to be served by fighting over the precise terms of a pleading, contests over their terms are to be discouraged".

Where an agreement to amend is reached between the parties there is no requirement that the written consent should be filed. It will, however, be reflected in the way the amendment is made (see below). Further, the parties who agree to the amendment need to consider if their own statements of case will need to be amended as a result and if so, who is to pay the costs. It is usual for the party who wishes to amend to pay the costs of any consequential amendments (see below) and if all matters can be agreed, a consent application should be made.

Does a party have a right to amend his statement of case to present his case as he thinks best? No. If a proposed amendment falls foul of the balancing act required by the overriding objective, it will not be allowed. Judicial case management (see Ch.33) means that the court will seek to ascertain from the statements of case what issues need to be addressed. If matters are unclear the court and any other party can demand further information (see also Ch.32).

What if after disclosure (see Ch.30) or the exchange of evidence (see Ch.31) a new issue emerges. Is there a general presumption in favour of permission to amend? No. The party wishing to address the issue should formulate a proposal to amend his statement of case and notify the other parties promptly. See *Edo Technology Ltd v Hills* [2006] EWHC 589, *The Times*, May 24, 2006.

It is clear that the later the application is made, the less chance it will have of success. However, if after rigorously evaluating their case on a proposed new issue that would be likely to delay trial, a party decides that it is so important that it ought to be advanced, an application to amend should be made with proposed directions that will enable a manageable trial date to be re-arranged. That will not necessarily guarantee success. In the *McPhilemy* case it was said by May L.J. that late amendments which cause a fixed trial date to be vacated should only be rarely allowed. This is consistent with the court's general approach to postponing a trial (see Ch.36).

Amendments after the expiry of the limitation period

12.053 Section 35 of the Limitation Act 1980 and rr.17.4 and 19.5 which gives effect to it, permit the court to grant permission for late amendments in three limited circumstances. However, they do not apply where a contractual or substantive time limit (e.g. the Hague Rules) has expired (see *Payabi v Armstel Shipping Corp.* [1992] 2 W.L.R. 898). Where the relevant limitation period has expired after the claim form was issued, the court may allow an amendment to:

(a) Add or substitute a new cause of action which arises out of the same facts or substantially the same facts as the cause of action which has already been started.

Examples

In *Lloyds Bank Plc v Rogers* (1999) 38 E.G. 187 the claimant commenced possession proceedings against the defendants in April 1992 following a formal demand in August 1991. No money claim was made. In May 1998 the claimant's application to amend the claim to add a money claim was allowed. The defendants appealed relying on s.35 of the 1980 Act. In the Court of Appeal Auld L.J. held that the original claim stated all the essential matters of fact necessary for the new remedy and so there was no new cause of action since nothing was sought to be added to the "factual situation" already stated. However, Evans L.J. held that the money claim was conspicuous by its absence and the attempt to add the new remedy was, in the circumstances, an attempt to add a new cause of action. However, the court agreed to dismiss the appeal holding that the facts relied on in support of the money claim were undoubtedly the same, or substantially the same, as those already claimed, and the judge was therefore correct to allow the amendment.

In *Alliance and Leicester Plc v Pellys* (1999) L.T.L., June 9 the claimant originally alleged breach of two duties against the defendant solicitors: (a) a contractual duty under the implied terms of the retainer; and (b) a common law duty of care in negligence. Breach of duty was alleged in three ways, all of which amounted to an alleged failure to pass on pertinent information. By the amendments the claimant sought to introduce: (i) a new contractual duty based on the express terms of a contractual document; (ii) a further nine alleged breaches of the implied contractual duty; and (iii) six additional fiduciary duties, the alleged breaches of which were said to be found in the "new" breaches at (ii) above. The defendants objected to the amendments on the ground that the limitation period had expired in 1996. Park J. disallowed all the amendments. The new contractual duty clearly asserted a new cause of action and arose from facts newly stated, i.e. the existence and terms of the contractual document. The nine further allegations of breach were to be treated as a package. Both their number and their terms justified the conclusion that new causes of action were being asserted which arose from new facts. The same reasoning applied to the additional fiduciary duties. For similar cases where amendments were refused by the Court of Appeal see *Paragon Finance plc v D. B. Thakerar & Co. (a firm)* [1999] 1 All E.R. 399 and *Del Grosso v Payne & Payne (a firm)* [2007] EWCA Civ 340, (2007) L.T.L., March 1.

The provision must be interpreted in accordance with the Human Rights Act 1998. In *Goode v Martin* [2001] EWCA Civ 1899, [2002] All E.R. 620, the claimant alleged negligence in relation to an accident suffered on a yacht. She had no memory of the accident and alleged one way in which the accident had occurred. The defendant filed a detailed defence saying it occurred in another way. Outside the limitation period she sought leave to amend her particulars of claim to say that, even if it happened in the way the defendant alleged, the defendant was negligent. The argument on behalf of the defendant resisting the amendment was that, if one followed the language in CPR 17.4 which related to "facts or substantially the same facts as a claim in respect of which the party applying for permission was already claiming a remedy in the proceedings", then permission to amend should not be given. The Court of Appeal accepted the submission of counsel for the claimant in that case saying that the CPR should be interpreted so as to contain additional words which would allow the claimant to bring her claim outside the limitation period. It held that CPR 17.4(2) should be read, so far as material, in the following way:

> "The Court may allow an amendment whose effect will be to add a new claim, but only if the new claim arises out of the same facts or substantially the same facts as are already in issue on the claim in respect of which the party applying for permission has already claimed a remedy in the proceedings." See also *Charles Church Developments Ltd v Stent Foundations Ltd* [2006] EWHC 3158, *The Times*, January 4, 2007.

(b) Correct a mistake in the naming or joinder of parties. Mistakes as to names ("mere misnomers") are curable under r.17.4. Simple examples are cases in which the claimant intends to sue X, serves the proceedings on X, but misnames him in the claim form as Y; also, a case in which the claimant transposes the names of the claimant and the defendant on the claim form (see *Teltscher Brothers Ltd v London and India Dock Investments Ltd* [1989] 1 W.L.R. 770. In *Gregson v Channel Four Television Cororation*, *The Times*, August 11, 2000, CA, C intended to sue in libel the well known broadcasting company, but, by mistake, did so by using the name of a dormant company which was similar to the name of the intended defendant; he was allowed permission to amend.

Mistakes which do involve the joinder of a different party after expiry of a limitation period are curable, if at all, only under r.19.5. The claimant will have to show that the addition or substitution of the new party is "necessary" in either of the following senses:

(a) "the new party is substituted for a party whose name was given in any claim made in the original action in mistake for the new party's name; or

(b) any claim made in the original action cannot be maintained by or against an existing party unless the new party is joined or substituted as [claimant] or defendant in that action" (Limitation Act 1980 s.35(6)).

In *Morgan Est (Scotland) Ltd v Hanson Concrete Products Ltd* [2005] 3 All E.R. 135 C, an engineering contractor, sued D, a pipe manufacturer, for breach of contract. In fact the contract for the purchase of the pipes from D was made by company A who had assigned it to C who had subsequently reassigned it to E. C was allowed to join A and E in substitution for itself (see also *Adelson v*

Associated Newspapers Ltd [2007] EWCA Civ 701, *The Times*, July 18 2007).

In *Weston v Gribben* [2006] EWCA Civ 1425, *The Independent*, November 8, 2006, Lloyd L.J. suggested that "it may be a convenient working test to ask whether you can change the identity of the claimant or, as the case may be, the defendant without significantly changing the claim."

(c) Alter the capacity in which a party claims if the new capacity is one which that party had when proceedings started or he has since acquired. "Capacity" is used in the sense of legal competence or status to bring or defend a claim. A change of capacity is an alteration from a personal capacity to a representative capacity, or an alteration from a representative capacity to another representative capacity or to a personal capacity (*Haq v Singh* [2001] 1 W.L.R. 1594, CA).

Making an application for permission

The application notice (see Ch.13) should be filed at court with a copy of the statement of case with the proposed amendments. No hearing will be necessary if the application is made by consent or all the parties agree to the matter being dealt with in their absence. The court may also take the view that a hearing is unnecessary. There is no specific requirement to file any evidence in support but where the matter is being contested it is sensible to do so.   12.054

If permission is given, the court will need to consider if amendments should be made to any other statements of case (see below). In addition, the court will usually order that the applicant should file and serve the amended document within a specified period, usually 14 days. The court may also direct that the applicant should serve a copy of the order on all other parties.

On an appeal, the Court of Appeal (see Ch.44) may allow a party to amend his statement of case, even if no application was made in the lower court: see *London Borough of Islington v UCKAC* [2006] EWCA Civ 340, [2006] 1 W.L.R. 1303.

Consequential amendments

When a statement of case is amended the other parties to the action may have to make consequential amendments to any subsequent statement of case they have already served. The court will give a direction to that effect if it agrees that the consequential amendments are necessary. The order will specify the date the parties have to file and serve their amended documents failing which they will be assumed to be relying on their original statement of case.   12.055

Costs of amendments

12.056 Interim costs are dealt with in Ch.13. It should be remembered that any consent application needs to provide for costs otherwise none will be recoverable in respect of that application. The usual order will be for the applicant to pay the other parties "costs of and caused by" his application, i.e. the costs of preparing and attending any hearing and the costs of any permitted consequential amendment to their own statements of case. However, if the application is necessary and it is clear that the respondent should have consented to the application, the respondent may be ordered to pay costs: see *La Chemise Lacoste SA v Sketchers USA Ltd* [2006] EWHC 3642, (2006) L.T.L., May 24.

Practice on amending

12.057 Rule 22.1(2) provides that where a statement of case is amended, the amendment must be verified by a statement of truth unless the court orders otherwise. Note that PD 17, para.1.4 provides that if the substance of the statement of case is changed as a result of an amendment, the amended document should be re-verified by a statement of truth. So what is the position of documents attached to a statement of case, for example, a schedule of expenses and losses in a personal injury claim? It is usually necessary to up date this as the case develops. Normally, the parties will agree to the schedule and counter schedule being amended. However, if substantial changes occur, for example, significant losses are claimed for the first time, we take the view that the document itself should be re-verified with a statement of truth.

Where the court's permission is not required to make an amendment, the amended statement of case should be endorsed: "Amended [specify document] under CPR r.17.1(1) or (2)(a) dated . . .". If permission was given by order the endorsement should read: "Amended [specify document] by Order of [specify judge] dated . . .". The amended document does not have to show the original text. However, if the court considers it desirable it may direct that both the original and the new text should be shown either by coloured amendments (in manuscript or computer generated) or by use of a numerical code in a monochrome computer generated document. Where colour is used, the text should be struck through in that colour and any text replacing it inserted or underlined in the same colour. In rare cases where several amendments are permitted the appropriate order of colours is red, green, violet and yellow.

CHAPTER 13

Interim Applications

TYPES OF APPLICATION

Part 23 sets out general rules about applications for court orders during the course of proceedings. Out go the old terms ex parte and inter partes (although you may still hear these in some courts). Instead, there are applications without notice and applications with notice. Each of these can be further sub-divided into applications without hearings and applications with hearings. Before studying the details of Pt 23 and its practice direction, it is helpful to have in mind a few examples of each of the four types: 13.001

(1) Applications without notice and without a hearing. Examples are applications to district judges concerning merely administrative or preliminary matters. For example, applications for an extension of time for service of a claim form (see para.9.006) and applications for permission to serve a claim form overseas (see para.11.009 and, for further examples, see the Queen's Bench Guide at *White Book*, para.1A–53).

(2) Applications without notice but with a hearing. Examples are applications for interim injunctions, freezing injunctions and search orders (see Ch.27) i.e. applications to a circuit judge or a High Court judge which are not of a formal or administrative nature and which are urgent and/or the circumstances of the application require secrecy.

(3) Applications with notice and with a hearing. This is the largest category. Examples include an application to set aside default judgments (see para.15.011) or to enter summary judgment (see Ch.19). The hearing will be conducted in court, either in a court room or in a private room, or may be conducted by telephone or by video conferencing.

(4) Applications with notice but without a hearing. The best example of this category is a case in which all parties agree the terms in which an order should be made. Although, at present, this is the smallest category, it has the potential for rapid growth. The rules suggest two further examples within this category: cases when the parties agree that a hearing is not required and cases which the court does not consider that a hearing would be appropriate. At present, these examples are common only in cases on the small claims track.

APPLICATION NOTICES

13.002 An application notice is a document in which the applicant states his intention to seek a court order (r.23.1). Save in very exceptional circumstances, this document has to be prepared and filed in court even if the application is to be made without giving notice to the other parties (r.23.3). In the case of urgent applications, for example, for an interim injunction, an application may be made before an application notice has been filed but, in such cases, the application notice must be filed with the court on the same or next working day, or as ordered by the court (see PD 25, Interim Injunctions, para.4.3).

Formal requirements for application notices (the title of the claim, the full name of the applicant, etc.) are set out in PD 23, para.2.1 which also refers to the practice Form N244 which may be used. The practice form invites the applicant:

(i) to state whether he wishes the application to be dealt with at a hearing, at a telephone conference or without a hearing; and
(ii) if relevant, stating a time estimate for the hearing or conference indicating whether this estimate is agreed by all parties; and
(iii) to specify the level of judge by whom the application should be decided.

Masters and district judges have jurisdiction to deal with virtually all interim applications. Certain matters, however, are reserved to a judge (i.e. a circuit judge in a county court or the High Court Judge in the High Court, see generally PD 2). Examples of matters reserved to a judge are:

(i) applications relating to the liberty of the subject;
(ii) applications under certain statutes such as the Supreme Court Act 1981, s.42 (see para.7.011);
(iii) applications for injunctions: the jurisdiction of the master or district judge is limited to granting injunctions in terms of agreed by the parties and granting injunctions which are ancillary to certain methods of enforcement of judgments (see further Ch.41).

If the level of judge is not specified in the application, it will be treated as an application to a master or district judge (see PD 23, para.2.6). However, a master or district judge may refer an application to a judge instead of dealing with it himself (PD 2 and see PD 23, para.1).

The application notice must state what order the applicant seeks and must give brief reasons for the application (r.23.6). It must also be signed (PD 23, para.2.1) presumably by the applicant, his litigation friend or solicitor (compare PD 22, para.3.1).

An application notice should be filed in the court office for the court in which the application is to be made (see below). A fee is payable unless the applicant can obtain exemption on grounds of financial hardship (see *White Book*, paras 10–6 and 10–18). Applications should be made in the court in which the claim is proceeding, i.e. the court where the claim started or, if it has been transferred to another court, to the court to which the claim has been transferred. There are three special cases. Applications made before commencement of proceedings (e.g. applications for freezing injunctions or search orders) should usually be made to the court where it is likely that the claim to which the application relates will be started (r.23.2(4)). Application made after the court has notified the parties of a fixed date for trial should be made to the court where the trial is to take place (r.23.2(3)). Applications made after proceedings for enforcement of judgment have begun should usually be made to the court which is dealing with the enforcement of the judgment (r.23.2(5)).

If there is a time limit within which an application must be made, the application is treated as being made on the day the application notice is received by the court (see r.23.5).

DOCUMENTS IN SUPPORT OF AN APPLICATION

He who alleges must prove. The court will need to be satisfied by evidence of any facts relied on in support of the application. On interim applications, parties cannot rely upon oral evidence unless the court, a practice direction or some other enactment so permits (r.32.6). Instead, the parties must rely upon written evidence. The applicant can rely upon written evidence set out in his application notice or his statement of case or in a witness statement. Each item of written evidence relied on must contain a statement of truth (see para.14.005). There is no requirement to give notice of intention to rely on hearsay evidence at interim applications (r.33.3) and therefore the applicant may also rely upon written hearsay, for example, correspondence received and copies of correspondence sent. In some exceptional cases, evidence in support must be given by affidavit (e.g. on applications for search orders and freezing injunctions, PD 25, Interim Injunctions, para.3.1). In other cases, an applicant may rely upon affidavit evidence if he so wishes. However, if he does so, he may not recover any additional costs thereby incurred unless the court otherwise orders (r.32.15).

13.003

Part C of the practice form of application notice, N244, enables the applicant to identify the evidence relied on in support of his application. This is a convenient practice in all cases and a requirement in some (see, e.g. summary judgment applications, PD 24, para.2(4) and see para.19.018).

All evidence relied on in support of an application must be filed in court, ideally at the same time the application notice is filed. However, the practice direction provides that exhibits (not defined, presumably documents or articles referred to in witness statements of affidavits) should not be filed in court unless the court otherwise directs (see generally PD 23, para 9.6).

Unless it is the most simple application, in an application which proceeds to a hearing, the applicant should produce to the court a draft of the order he seeks. If the case is proceeding in the Royal Courts of Justice (i.e. London High Court) and the order is unusually long or complex, it should also be supplied on disk for use by the court office (PD 23, para.12.1).

In applications which are to be made with notice, the applicant must serve with the application notice a copy of his evidence in support and a copy of any draft order attached to his application. Details of these obligations and details of the procedure for evidence in response and further evidence in reply is given below.

APPLICATIONS WITHOUT NOTICE

13.004 PD 23, para.3 sets out a list of occasions when an application may be made without serving an application notice on the respondent:

(1) where there is exceptional urgency;
(2) where the overriding objective is best furthered by doing so;
(3) by consent of all parties;
(4) with the permission of the court;
(5) where para.2.10 above applies (this is explained below);
(6) where a court order, rule or practice direction permits.

On some applications to a judge, there may be exceptional urgency (i.e. applications for interim injunctions) or the circumstances of the application may require secrecy (e.g. applications for freezing injunctions or search orders). Except where secrecy is essential, an applicant who does not have time to give formal notice to the respondent must, nevertheless, give as much informal notice as he can (PD 23, para.4.2 and PD 25, Interim Injunctions, para.4.3(3)).

Applications to a master or district judge may be made if they are of a preliminary or administrative nature or if, although a hearing may have been requested, the master or district judge does not consider that a hearing would be appropriate (see r.23.8(c)). Consider, for example, an application for an extension of time where the extension requested is short and the evidence in support is persuasive. The master or district judge may consider that a hearing of this application would be disproportionate to the matter in controversy. The respondent can challenge the extension granted if he wishes (see r.23.10, summarised below). As a general rule an application to extend the time for service of a claim form where the time limit is running out should be heard: see *Collier v Williams* [2006] EWCA Civ 20, [2006] 1 W.L.R. 1945, discussed at para.9.006.

PD 23, para.2.10 provides for the case in which a date for a hearing has been fixed and shortly before that date one party wishes to make an application at that hearing, but does not now have sufficient time to serve an application notice on his opponent. Paragraph 2.10 states that he should inform his opponent and the court (if possible in writing) as soon as he can of the nature of his application and the reason for it and should then make the application orally at the hearing. Paragraph 2.10 does not by itself authorise non-compliance with the rules about giving notice. At the hearing, the court may direct that, in the circumstances of the case, sufficient notice has been given and hear the application (r.23.7(4)). Equally, however, the court may refuse to hear the application or may adjourn the appointment to a later date to give the respondent more time to prepare for it.

Serving orders made without notice

Rule 23.9 states that where the court makes an order on an application made without notice, copies of the following documents must be served on the respondent: (i) the application notice; (ii) the evidence in support; and (iii) the order made (whether that order granted or dismissed the application). Save for interim injunctions and similar orders, the court will in most cases draw up the order (r.40.3) and serve it (r.40.4). Where this is to happen, the applicant should submit to the court as many copies of the application notice and evidence and support as there are respondents.

13.005

Rule 23.9(3) requires that an order made without notice must contain a statement of the right the respondent has to make an application to set aside or vary the order under r.23.10. Rule 23.10 gives the respondent this right, usually referred to as a liberty to apply, if he makes his application to set aside or vary the order within seven days of it being served upon him. Rule 23.10 does not apply to the applicant. However, a court which deals with an application without a hearing and which is unwilling to grant the applicant the full order he seeks will give the applicant some other right to be heard. It may either list the application for a hearing (with or without notice to the respondent) or make an order of its own initiative under r.3.3. An order under that rule gives all parties affected by the order the right to apply to have it set aside, varied or stayed: see r.3.3(5). Note that in *Collier v Williams* [2006] EWCA Civ 20, [2006] 1 W.L.R. 1945, the Court of Appeal indicated that it was good practice for any such application to be dealt with at a hearing rather than on paper.

APPLICATIONS WITH NOTICE

The general rule is that a copy of the application notice must be served on each respondent (r.23.4). It should be served as soon as practicable after it has been filed and, except where another time limit is specified in the rules or practice directions, at least three days before the date of which the court will deal with it (r.23.7(1)). If a hearing is requested, the court will notify the applicant of the time and date fixed for the hearing. If, as is usual, the applicant wants the court to serve the respondent, he must file his written evidence in support with his application notice (r.23.7(2)) plus copies of the evidence in support, the application notice and any draft order attached to it. The court will then serve all these together with a notice of the date and time fixed for the hearing.

13.006

If the respondent wishes to rely upon evidence in reply and, thereafter, if the applicant wishes to rely upon further evidence, such evidence in reply and further evidence should be both filed and served as soon as possible (PD 23, paras 9.4–9.6). Sometimes, the court may give timetable directions for the filing and service of this evidence in which case the parties must in any event comply with these directions (PD 23, para.9.2).

Hearing the application

13.007　In all cases, especially cases on the multi-track, there may be one or more hearings in court before the trial; allocation hearings, case management conferences, listing hearings and pre-trial reviews. Wherever possible, applications should be made so that they can be considered at any other hearing for which a date has already been fixed or is about to be fixed (PD 23, para.2.8). Also, at any hearing, the parties should anticipate the possibility that the court may wish to review the conduct of the case as a whole and give any necessary case management directions. Parties should therefore be ready to assist the court in doing so and to answer questions the court may ask for this purpose (PD 23, para.2.9). The combined effect of these provisions (paras 2.8 and 2.9) is that, today, in contrast to the position under the previous rules, pre-trial hearings are fewer in number, endure for longer, and require the attendance of more senior fee earners than pre-trial hearings under the previous rules.

Although the general rule is that all hearings in the civil courts are in public (r.39.2) PD 39, para.1.5 gives a list of 10 hearings which, unless the court otherwise orders, will be listed as hearings in private:

(1) a claim by a mortgagee against one or more individuals for an order for possession of land;

(2) a claim by a landlord against one or more tenants or former tenants for the repossession of a dwelling house based on the non-payment of rent;

(3) an application to suspend a warrant of execution or a warrant of possession or to stay execution where the court is being invited to consider the ability of a party to make payments to another party;

(4) a re-determination under r.14.13 or an application to vary or suspend the payment of a judgment debt by instalments;

(5) an application for a charging order (including an application to enforce a charging order), garnishee order, attachment of earnings order, administration order, or the appointment of a receiver;

(6) an order to attend court for questioning;

(7) the determination of an assisted person's liability for costs (as to this, see further, Ch.39);

(8) an application for security for costs under s.726(1) of the Companies Act 1985;

(9) proceedings brought under the Consumer Credit Act 1974, the Inheritance (Provision for Family and Dependants) Act 1975, or the Protection from Harassment Act 1997;

(10) an application by a trustee or personal representative for directions as to bringing or defending legal proceedings.

At a hearing in private (ie a hearing in "secret", see *Economic Department of the City of Moscow v Bankers Trust Company* [2004] EWCA Civ 314, [2005] 1 Q.B. 202) members of the public who are not parties to the proceedings will not be admitted unless the court so permits (PD 39, para.1.9). The factors which may justify the conduct of a hearing in private are set out in r.39.2(3): see *Three Rivers DC v The Governor and Company of the Bank of England* [2005] EWCA Civ 933, (2005) L.T.L., August 18. What standard of proof applies on an application for a matter to be heard in private? Is it the criminal (beyond reasonable doubt) or civil (balance of probabilities) standard? The issue remains unresolved: see *British Broadcasting Corp. v Her Majesty's Attorney General* [2007] EWCA Civ 280, (2007) L.T.L., March 12.

In practice, most pre-trial applications to masters and district judges are conducted in public, but no members of the public seek admission. The conduct of a hearing in public does not require the court to make special arrangement for accommodating members of the public (r.39.2(2)). Members of the public will be admitted where practicable. Of course the master or district judge may, if he thinks it appropriate, adjourn the proceedings to a larger room or court (see generally PD 39, para.1.10).

Most district registries of the High Court and county courts have facilities to deal with interim applications by telephone conferencing. A list of these, known as "telephone conference enabled courts", can be found on HM Court Service website. What sort of interim matters are heard this way? By PD 23 para.6.2 this general rule is that. At a telephone conference enabled court, all allocation hearings (see para.9.037), listing hearings (see para.36.002), interim applications, case management conferences (see para.22.004) and pre-trial reviews (see para.36.003) with a time estimate of less than one hour will be conducted by telephone. The exceptions are any hearing of an application made without notice to the other party, or where all the parties are unrepresented, or where more than four parties wish to make representations at the hearing (for this purpose where two or more parties are represented by the same person, they are treated as one party). Note that neither a party, nor a party's legal representative, can attend the judge in person while the application is being heard, unless every other party to the application has agreed.

It is obviously essential that the time estimate given by the parties for a telephone hearing is accurate. The court will normally have to schedule a number of calls and any party who gets it wrong is likely to be penalised in costs (see Ch.38). It is also vital that the judge has a complete court file in front of him and, indeed, all the parties have all the relevant documents to hand. "The judge who is conducting the hearing should have available before him the appropriate documentary material in a form which the parties to the proceedings are able to duplicate so that their submissions are readily intelligible" *per* Lord Phillips in *Heyward v Plymouth Hospital NHS Trust* [2005] EWCA Civ 939, *The Times*, August 1, 2005. PD 23 para.6 sets out what documents should be produced for the hearing.

What if a party wants the hearing in front of the judge? Any party can simply write to the court and request this. A full explanation should be given as to why a telephone hearing is unsuitable. That request will be determined by the court without any hearing at all.

What about other hearings? Can these be made by telephone? The applicant should make that request on the application notice. Any other party can apply. Normally the court will only make such an order and give directions as to how the telephone hearing is to occur if all the parties consent.

The mechanics of how a telephone conference call takes place are detailed in PD 23.

At present, video conferencing facilities are extremely scarce. However, where they are used, they more exactly recreate the advantages of a face-to-face hearing; the court and the parties have the advantage of seeing and hearing everyone involved. In addition, significant costs may be saved. These advantages led the Court of Appeal (see Ch.44) in *Black v Pastouna* [2005] EWCA Civ 1389, *The Independent,* December 2, 2005, to direct that in cases lasting less than 30 minutes the parties should seriously consider using this facility. Indeed, it is possible that within the next 10 or so years, every lawyer's office will become equipped with video conferencing facilities. If that happens, video conference hearings may well replace telephone hearings and indeed may well replace hearings in court in most cases. Currently, if any party wishes to use video conferencing facilities, and those facilities are available in court, they should apply to the Master or district judge for directions. Guidance can be found in para.29 and Annex 3 of PD 32.

Application with notice but without a hearing

13.008   Rule 23.8 states that the court may deal with an application without a hearing if—

> (a)   the parties agree to the terms of the order sought;
> (b)   the parties agree that the court should dispose of the application without a hearing, or
> (c)   the court does not consider that a hearing would be appropriate.

Application notices containing a request that the application be dealt with without a hearing are sent to a master or district judge for him to decide whether to grant the request. If he does so, the master or district judge will so inform the applicant and the respondent and may give directions for the filing of evidence (see generally PD 23, paras 2.2 to 2.4).

The best example of para.(a) is an application made jointly by all parties. PD 23, para.10 covers a somewhat similar position. Where parties agree the terms of the order sought only after a hearing date has been fixed they can write to the court consenting to the making of an order (a copy of which must be filed). If the court makes the order, it will vacate the hearing.

The best example of para.(c) is the case in which the court makes an order immediately upon receipt of the application notice (see para.13.001, an example concerning applications for an extension of a time period).

Examples of (b), opposed paper applications, are at present rare. However, it is possible that this type of application will become more common once parties and their advisers become more cooperative with each other and less combative in their approach to interim applications. The court's duty to further the overriding objective by active case management includes encouraging the parties to cooperate with each other in the conduct of the proceedings (r.1.4(2)(a)).

COSTS IN INTERIM APPLICATIONS

Once it has dealt with an interim application, the court has a discretion as to whether to make an order for the costs of that application. The general rule is that "costs should follow the event", i.e. the loser should pay the winner's costs. Under the CPR, this is in fact merely the starting point from which the court may in its discretion readily depart. The principles upon which that discretion is exercised and the basis upon which an assessment of costs will be conducted (indemnity basis or standard basis) are considered further in Ch.38. In this Chapter, we consider a collection of rules about costs in interim applications and the procedure by which those costs will be assessed, summary assessment or detailed assessment.

13.009

Paragraph 8.5 of the Costs Practice Direction ("CPD") sets out in tabular form a list of orders commonly made in interim applications and states the general effect of each order. The list includes "costs", "costs in the case", "costs thrown away" and various other orders. No such orders are likely to be made in cases allocated to the small claims track; r.27.14 places a restriction on costs in such cases (see further Ch.20 para.20.010).

If an order for costs is made, r.44.2 places an obligation upon a solicitor to give his client written notice within seven days of the making of any order for costs against the client which is made in the client's absence. The purpose of this rule is to ensure that an unsuccessful litigant is informed about his costs liability as soon as possible. The letter informing him must also explain why the order came to be made (CPD, para.7.2).

Last in the list of orders for costs set out in CPD, para.8.5 are "no order as to costs" and its equivalent "each party to pay his own costs". These orders are defined as meaning what they say. Similarly, r.44.13(1) states that if, in its order, the court says nothing about costs, no party is entitled to costs in relation to that order. However, this is modified by r.44.13(1A) where the court makes an order granting permission to appeal (see Ch.44); an order granting permission to apply for judicial review (see Ch.24); or any other order or direction sought by a party on an application without notice (see para.13.004, above). If the order does not mention costs, it will be deemed to include an order for applicant's costs in the case. What can a dissatisfied respondent do? By r.44.13(1B) he may apply at any time to vary the order.

Summary assessment

13.010 Summary assessment is the procedure by which the court, when making an order about costs, orders payment of a sum of money instead of fixed costs or costs to be assessed by way of detailed assessment (r.43.3; and see para.38.014). In *Contractreal Ltd v Davies* (2001) L.T.L., May 17, Arden L.J. emphasized the importance of summary assessment as follows:

> "Summary assessment is an essential part of the Civil Procedure Reforms. It allows a party who has won an application to receive reimbursement of his costs in the amount awarded by the court within a very short period of time indeed, usually 14 days. It avoids the need for a full blown detailed assessment. The fact that the court has this power tends to focus the mind of the well advised parties and helps avoid unmeritorious, tactical applications and contentions.
>
> On the other hand, it must be accepted that the process is not as detailed as would occur on an assessment by a Costs Judge over a period of time. Summary assessment is a relatively rough and ready process. It is there because as Voltaire said the best can be the enemy of good, but it is a rough and ready process. The margin for which disagreement is possible must, in my judgment, be a large margin".

As a general rule, costs will be summarily assessed in all hearings (whether interim hearings or trial hearings) which last less than one day. The main exceptions to summary assessment relevant to short interim applications are as follows:

(1) Where the party awarded costs is funded by the LSC. (CPD, para.13.9) There would be no point in summarily assessing these costs as there may still have to be a detailed assessment anyway for the purposes of the Legal Services Commission ("LSC"). It is obviously undesirable for the court to assess the same costs twice. Where this exception applies, note the court's power to order a payment on account. A summary assessment of costs can be made against an LSC funded client. However, such an order is not by itself a determination of the liability of the LSC funded client to pay those costs (as to which see further Ch.39).

(2) Costs other than base costs. The exception here applies to "additional liability", for example, recoverable success fees and insurance costs. Conditional fee agreements and after the event insurance are described in Ch.2. Rule 44.3A prevents the court from making any assessment of an additional liability before the conclusion of the proceedings or part of the proceedings to which it relates. However, the existence of a conditional fee agreement or similar funding arrangement is not by itself a sufficient reason for not carrying out summary assessments (CPD, para.14.1). Any base costs assessed before the conclusion of proceedings will not be payable unless the receiving party's

solicitor or counsel is entitled to require such payment. Accordingly, the form of agreement recommended by the Law Society does entitle solicitors to payment of costs on all successful interim applications, whatever the outcome of the proceedings at trial. The court will usually accept an appropriately worded certificate by the solicitor as proof of this entitlement (CPD, para.14.3). If the lawyers are not entitled to immediate payment, the court may order payment of the base costs into court to await the outcome of the case (CPD, para.14.4).

(3) Where the paying party shows substantial grounds for disputing the sum claimed for costs that cannot be dealt with summarily or there is insufficient time to carry out a summary assessment. (CPD, para.13.2) Not all cases are suitable for summary assessment. The court should order the costs to be assessed by detailed assessment if the paying party can raise issues which will require full investigation or where the claim for costs is open to multiple challenges which are genuine.

(4) Where the parties have agreed the amount of costs. (CPD, para.13.13(a)) For this exception to apply, the parties must agree the amount of costs, not just the entitlement. In other words, the court is not bound to accept an agreement between parties that a consent order should be made for a detailed assessment. Special provision is made for applications which settle before the hearing. The costs of such an application may be dealt with in one of three ways:

(i) the parties may agree a figure to be inserted into a consent order, or
(ii) the parties may agree that there should be no order for costs, or
(iii) the parties may attend upon the appointment simply to argue costs.

If (iii) occurs, no costs will be allowed for the appointment unless some good reason is shown for the failure to deal with costs as set out at (i) or (ii) (CPD, para.13.4).

Each party who is represented and who intends to claim costs must file and serve a statement of those costs as soon as possible and in any event, not less than 24 hours before the date fixed for the hearing (CPD, para.13.5(4)). The statement of costs should follow form N260 as closely as possible (CPD, para.13.5(3); as to the consequences of breach of para.13.5, see below para.13.016). The purpose of filing statements is so that the parties may "assist the judge in making a summary assessment of the costs". Paragraph 13.5(3) makes clear that statements of costs must also be filed on behalf of LSC-funded clients even though the court will not assess their costs summarily. A statement of costs by an LSC-funded client may assist the court to assess the reasonable costs of the opponent. It will also assist the solicitor who drew it to obtain an order for payment on account (see further, below).

In deciding what figure to allow the court will obviously hear argument from both sides and will pay particular attention to the statement of costs filed by the opponent and the judge's own experience as to what costs are reasonable. At present, all judges in the civil courts are provided with a guide to the summary assessment of costs prepared by the senior costs judge. The guide includes some recommended fees for counsel and recommended hourly rates to allow in respect of different grades of fee earners working in different localities in England and Wales. These guidelines rates are included as a starting point only. In order to simplify the process of summarily assessing costs in the future, there are also plans for the senior costs judge to publish "benchmark costs", i.e. fixed amounts of costs for the court to award in specified types of hearing and in other hearings which are analogous to them.

When are summarily assessed costs payable? The court has a discretion as to the time of payment (r.44.3(1)(c)). If no time of payment is stated in the order, the costs are payable within 14 days (r.44.8). Of course, the court may later extend, or even shorten that time limit on an application under r.3.1(2)(a) (see para.33.002). But what if the costs are not paid? The receiving party should apply to the court for an "unless order" (see *Crystal Decisions (UK) Ltd v Vedatech Corp* [2006] EWHC 3500 and para.33.007, below).

What happens if you fail to file and serve a statement of costs? CPD, para.13.6 states that failure without reasonable excuse may affect the party's entitlement to costs and may affect the party's liability for the costs of any further hearings or proceedings caused by that failure (e.g. the costs of an adjourned hearing or the costs of a detailed assessment). The penalty imposed must of course be proportionate to the harm done. As a general rule, a party at fault should not be deprived of all his costs if there are no aggravating factors (*MacDonald v Taree Holdings Ltd, The Times*, December 28, 2000).

In current practice, solicitors regularly breach the rules intentionally in respect of the costs of hearings which they believe will end in an order for "costs in the case". Many courts overlook this breach because they do not desire to assess costs in the case: obviously, to do so would require an assessment of both sides' costs. On this point these solicitors and courts must note that CPD does not exclude summary assessment following orders for costs in the case.

Detailed assessment

13.011 Detailed assessment is the procedure by which the amount of costs is decided by a costs officer in accordance with Pt 47 (r.43.4). Chapter 38 covers the procedure to be followed on detailed assessments. Detailed assessments are laborious and expensive procedures. If they must be undertaken it is usually more economic to defer them to take place at the same time as the detailed assessment of other orders for costs at the conclusion of the proceedings in question. In order to achieve this, r.47.1 states that detailed assessments must be delayed until the conclusion of proceedings unless the court orders the costs to be assessed immediately. Rather than order an early detailed assessment, the court may prefer to exercise its power under r.48.3(8). This enables the court awarding costs to order the paying party to pay an amount on account before the costs are assessed. Indeed, litigants should expect that whenever the court awards costs to be assessed by way of detailed assessment, it will also make an order for a payment on account of those costs (see CPD, para.12.3).

Given the rules and practice as to summary assessments, the court is more likely to order a detailed assessment of interim orders for costs only where the application was heavy, unusual or lasted more than one day. These are the cases in which litigants often instruct counsel. Instructing counsel may substantially increase the costs of an application if, for example, a senior solicitor also attends the hearing or if more than one counsel is instructed. In any particular case, it may be obvious to the court awarding costs that the winning party's decision to instruct one or more counsel was an extreme extravagance or alternatively was entirely reasonable. If either party thinks the costs officer may not be in an equally good position to decide this question, they may ask the court awarding costs to state its opinion in its order. Thus, the order may state whether or not, in the court's opinion, the hearing was fit for the instruction of one or more counsel. CPD, para.8.7 states that where the order states such an opinion "the costs officer conducting a detailed assessment of [those] costs . . . will have regard to the opinion stated". Under the previous rules this was called "giving a certificate for counsel". However, that expression is not wholly appropriate today. The expression "certificate as to counsel" covers the possibility that the court may state its opinion that the hearing was not fit for counsel.

CHAPTER 14

Drafting Applications, Witness Statements and Affidavits

DRAFTING APPLICATION NOTICES

14.001   The procedure on interim applications is described in Ch.13. A practice form of application, N244, has been published. You are not required to use the form but given the amount of different information that is needed we would recommend that you do. It is important to complete the box at the top left-hand corner of the form in order that the court can quickly and correctly process the application. If you want the judge to consider the matter without a hearing you must say so. If you require a hearing or telephone conference you should give a time estimate that is agreed by the other parties where possible. You need to identify the level of judge required to deal with the hearing (see PD 2B and para.13.002) and confirm which of the other parties are to be served with the application.

The body of the form is divided into three lettered parts, namely:

Part A: Here you must set out the order sought and the grounds, including any rule or statutory provision. A draft of the proposed order should be attached. Remember to include an order for costs otherwise none may be recoverable in respect of the application (see r.44.13(1)).

Part B: Here you must indicate what type of evidence the applicant intends to rely on at the interim hearing. Most applications require supporting evidence. Even if it is not prescribed by the appropriate rule or practice direction you should still consider what factual evidence the court will want if the applicant is going to be successful. You have a choice as to the format of the evidence. It can be either:

(a) a witness statement or affidavit (see below); or
(b) the party's statement of case provided it has been verified by a statement of truth (see para.12.004); or
(c) the evidence set out in Pt C provided that it is verified by a statement of truth.

Part C: This is really just a page of the application where a witness statement can be typed.

The form ends being signed by the applicant, his legal representative, or any litigation friend and is followed by the applicant's address for service.

USE OF WITNESS STATEMENTS AND AFFIDAVITS

Witness statements and affidavits have only one significant difference in that an affidavit is sworn or affirmed before a person authorised to take it. All practising solicitors may do so (see PD 32, para.9.1). It is important to note, however, that an affidavit must be sworn or affirmed before a person who is independent of the parties and his representatives. **14.002**

As a general rule evidence used at any hearing other than trial is by way of witness statement. The use of affidavits is mandatory in only a few areas, for example, in support of an application for a search order or freezing injunction (see Ch.27). A witness may, for religious or other reasons, consider that his evidence is only acceptable if sworn. In these circumstances, if you use an affidavit and in order to obtain an order for costs you should invite the court to direct that the additional costs incurred because the evidence was an affidavit are recoverable. Without such a direction the additional costs incurred will not be recoverable.

By r.32.12, a witness statement may be used only for the purpose of the proceedings in which it is served. However, there are three exceptions, namely, that the witness gives consent in writing to some other use of it; the witness statement has been put in evidence at a hearing held in public; or the court gives permission for some other use. As to the last exception, will the court give permission for witness statements relied on in previous proceedings by party A to be used by party B in later proceedings? Not unless the statements are relevant beyond an attempt to discredit the witnesses of party A by party B in the subsequent action: see *L'Oreal SA v Bellure NV* [2006] EWHC 1503.

Note that a person who swears or affirms his evidence by way of affidavit is called a deponent.

WITNESS STATEMENTS AND AFFIDAVITS: GENERAL FORMALITIES

A witness statement or affidavit should always include the following: **14.003**

(a) "Identity details". In the top right-hand corner you must put some basic information that allows the judge to quickly find the document. You must state: (1) the party on whose behalf it is made; (2) the initials and surname of the witness or deponent; (3) the number of the statement or affidavit in relation to that person; (4) the identifying initials and number of each exhibit referred to; and

(5) the date the statement was made or the affidavit sworn. In respect of an affidavit that information must also appear on the backsheet.

Example

On behalf of the claimant
M. Flanders
2nd
Exhibits "MF4 to MF7"
Dated: July 23, 2007

This would be the second statement of M. Flanders made on behalf of the claimant on July 23, 2007. Note that each exhibit is numbered and marked with the initials of the maker of the statement. Where a witness has made more than one statement, the numbering of the exhibits runs consecutively throughout and does not start again with each statement. Hence, there were three exhibits to M. Flanders' first statement.

(b) The title to the action. See para.7.001 but note that PD 32, para.17.1 allows for a shortened form to be used where several parties have the same status in the proceedings, for example:

Number:

   A.B. (and others)   Claimants/Applicants

   C.D. (and others)   Defendants/Respondents

(c) The witness's or deponent's details. It is desirable to identify the document by giving it a title, such as "Witness statement of Michael Flanders". The first paragraph of a statement or affidavit should set out the full name and address of the witness or deponent. As an affidavit must be sworn or affirmed it is usual to introduce the deponent by stating, "I (full name) of (address) state on oath (or do solemnly and sincerely affirm)". The address should be the person's private residence unless the evidence is being given by him in a professional, business or other occupational capacity when his work address, the position he holds and the name of his employer should be given. What if a person who should state his home address is too afraid to do so? You will need to get to the bottom of this potential problem and consider if he is reliable, credible and likely to be prepared to give oral evidence if required to do so at any hearing. If you are satisfied that there is a good reason you should seek the court's permission to file a defective witness statement or affidavit (see PD 32, para.25.2). The application can be made without notice to any other party and you should produce supporting evidence justifying the request that the address is withheld. We have seen addresses given "care of" solicitor's offices which is wrong unless authorised by the court.

In addition, the witness's or deponent's occupation or "his description" (such as retired etc.,) should be stated. Finally, if the person is a party or the employee of a party this should be recorded. It is also traditional, and we consider that it remains good practice, to say if the person is related in any way to a party.

Example

"My full name is Michael Flanders and I live at 9 Chelsea Drive, Westbourne, Mythshire. I am a retired gas fitter. I am the claimant's father."

(d) Exhibit any relevant documents. The first page of each exhibit must set out the "identity details" referred to in (a) above and the exhibit must be numbered, for example, "MF3". It is permissible to exhibit a photocopy of a document provided you allow the other parties to inspect the original should they wish to do so before the hearing. Also ensure you take the originals to the hearing as the judge may wish to look at them. If you exhibit numerous documents, such as letters, put them in suitable bundles in chronological order with the earliest at the top. Each bundle should have a front page with an index. Where an exhibit contains more than one document the bundle should not be stapled but otherwise securely fastened to ensure the documents can be easily read. The pages should be numbered consecutively at bottom centre. If a page is illegible a typed copy should be included after the document bearing the same page number but prefixed with an "a".

There is no need to exhibit court documents as these should already be on the court file and an official copy is always admissible evidence.

In the body of a witness statement the maker should refer to each exhibit. He must also sign a declaration attached to each exhibit, for example, "I verify that this is the exhibit marked 'MF3' to my statement dated (date)".

In the body of an affidavit the deponent should refer to each exhibit stating, "There is now shown to me marked 'AB1' the (give a description of the document)". When an affidavit is sworn or affirmed each exhibit must be verified by the deponent and identified by a declaration completed by the person who takes the affidavit. The declaration might read, "This is the exhibit marked 'AB1' to the affidavit of Alice Bright sworn before me this (date)".

(e) Ending. Affidavits and witness statements differ here also. Affidavits should conclude with a jurat which is the statement at the end of an affidavit authenticating it. It bears the deponent's signature and usually reads, "Sworn (or affirmed) this (date) at (full address) before me (signature of person taking the affidavit followed by his name and qualifications printed)". It is important to note that there must be no space between the end of the text and the jurat and so, in addition, it must not appear on a separate page.

What if the deponent is unable to read or sign? In these circumstances the person who is taking the affidavit should read the document to him and if he is satisfied that it was understood and approved a certificate to that effect should be endorsed. The full requirements are set out in PD 32, paras 7 and 21. The form of certificate appears in Annex 1 of the practice direction.

Witness statements should end with a statement of truth. PD 32, para.20.2 states that this should read: "I believe that the facts stated in this witness statement are true". Like an affidavit, there are similar provisions for a certificate to be given in respect of a person who cannot read or sign. See PD 22 para.3A. The form of certificate appears in Annex 1 of that practice direction.

SOLICITORS' DUTIES

14.004   Witness statements and affidavits must contain the truth, the whole truth and nothing but the truth. A solicitor must take great care when preparing such a document. No pressure of any kind should be placed on a witness to give anything but a true and complete account of his evidence. It is improper to serve a witness statement or affidavit that a solicitor knows to be false or which the maker does not in all respects believe to be true. In addition, a solicitor is under a professional obligation to check where practicable the truth of the facts stated if he is put on enquiry as to their truth. If a solicitor discovers that he has served a document that is incorrect he must inform the other parties, and where appropriate the court, immediately. See generally *ZYX Music GmbH v King* [1995] 3 All E.R. 1.

Neither a solicitor nor counsel should allow the cost of preparation of witness statements or affidavits to be unnecessarily increased by over-elaboration. Such will be penalised in costs (see Chs 38 and 39).

DRAFTING EVIDENCE FOR USE AT AN INTERIM HEARING

14.005   Most applications require some evidence. Occasionally, that may be limited to the contents of the statements of case but it must be remembered that these can only be used in evidence if verified by a statement of truth. However, in most cases a witness statement appearing either at Pt C of the application form (see above) or separately needs to be prepared. The contents of the statement are dictated by the nature of the application and many practice directions prescribe what evidence is required, for example, PD 24, para.2 as to summary judgment (see Ch.19).

There are, however, six general points that you might bear in mind when preparing a witness statement to be used at an interim hearing.

   (1) List the important points to be brought to the court's attention. In contrast to statements of case (see Ch.12), witness statements should state the detailed evidence relied on and should anticipate the opponent's case.
   (2) Then decide who should be the deponent: the person who can speak to most of the points from personal knowledge. This will usually be the party. If not, it is appropriate to state the maker's relationship with the party, for example, director, employee, solicitor, etc.

(3) Then divide up the important points into numbered paragraphs with headings. The information should appear in chronological order. Use headings to emphasise the key points to be brought to the court's attention. Ensure you focus on the relevant facts. For example, a witness statement in support of an application to set aside a default judgment (see para.15.011) needs at least two important factual matters to be addressed, namely why the proceedings did not come to the defendant's attention and why the court should set aside the default judgment.

(4) In the case of hearsay evidence, state the source of the information. A witness statement must indicate which of the contents derive from the maker's own knowledge and which are matters of information he has received and those that are his own belief. The source of any matters of information or belief must also be given. According to the case of *Deutsche Ruckversichering AG v Walbrook Insurance Co. Ltd* [1995] 1 W.L.R. 1017 it does not have to be the original source. However, evidence is far less persuasive the more distant it is from the original source. As to multiple hearsay, see Ch.31.

(5) Set out the relevant facts in a logical order, state the maker's means of knowledge and exhibit any supporting documents. The amount of relevant detail contained in a witness statement from a person with first hand knowledge of the facts marks the distinction between bare allegation and persuasive presentation. Unless the means of knowledge are obvious, always explain how the maker came to learn the facts he states, for example, "I am advised by Mr Jones who inspected the vehicle immediately after the accident that . . .". If any of the facts arise from, or are supported by documents, these should be exhibited. However, take care not to produce irrelevant exhibits and always ensure that your have read the entire document. Do not leave it to the advocate at the hearing to try and explain away any ambiguities.

(6) Address only essential matters of law. A party is not a lawyer. Legal arguments are best left to the advocates at the hearing (and see further, para.14.008). However, the maker of the statement may have to express a legal opinion. For example, when applying for summary judgment there must be a statement of belief that on the evidence the respondent has no real prospect of succeeding. It is usual to begin this with the statement, "I am advised by my solicitor and believe that . . .".

DRAFTING WITNESS STATEMENTS FOR USE AT TRIAL

Chapter 31 sets out the law of hearsay and the procedure to follow on exchange of witness statements. Before you set out to draft the statement of any witness who a party intends to call at trial or to rely on as hearsay evidence it is as well

14.006

DRAFTING APPLICATIONS, WITNESS STATEMENTS AND AFFIDAVITS

to bear in mind its purpose and likely effect. The purpose, in pursuance of the overriding objective (r.1.1) is to save expense and ensure that the case is dealt with expeditiously and fairly. Exchanging before trial all of the evidence a party intends to rely on enables all the parties to the action to evaluate their prospects of success earlier than they otherwise could. By analysing the exchanged documents, each side can see the final extent of the dispute over a particular issue; what evidence they face and therefore what the result is likely to be. The cards have now all been played. Any bluff has been called The exchange therefore increases the chances that a case will settle, so avoiding a trial. If no settlement is reached, the exchange enables the parties to plan and develop fully their retaliation to their opponent's case (see Ch.32).

It is vital to remember that a witness statement will be the maker's evidence at trial (see para.31.010). As a general rule he will enter the witness box, take the oath or affirm and give his name and address. He will be given a copy of his statement and confirm that it is true. He will then be cross examined by the other side. There are a few exceptions to this rule but none will rescue a party if the inadequacies in the statement were caused by sloppy drafting. Let us put it this way. Imagine a civil trial as an invitation to the judge to watch two different films, "The Claimant's Story" and "The Defendant's Story". But the judge is in an unusual cinema as there are two screens and he has to watch them both at the same time. He must listen to the narrator of each story who has the annoying habit of also interjecting commentary into the other film. He will try to work out who to believe and who to disbelieve amongst the range of characters who appear, especially those with the leading roles. As the stories move further and further apart he will begin to ask himself which plot is more plausible. Finally, as the credits roll, he will have the final say in the epilogue where he will review the storylines and pass judgment on the performances.

The role of a witness statement at trial is to tell a story. The facts should run in chronological order. There must be no confusing flashbacks. The witness must tell his own tale, in his own words, frame by frame. However, in telling it he must leave no gaps, no empty frames, no blurred pictures. Consider the example below. The case concerns a personal injury claim by a nurse who hurt her back at work whilst lifting a patient. Read what she says and try to visualise how she lifted the patient. In fact, you might get a colleague to play the patient and another to take the role of the claimant. Now you read out what follows and see how the story unfolds.

Example

"I went to see Mr Jones, the patient in the shower. I helped him wash himself but then, all of a sudden, his leg went into a spasm. I sat him on the shower chair. I had to get him out of the shower so I used the lifting technique shown to me by Mrs Smith, the matron. I put my left hand under Mr Jones' leg and my right hand under his shoulder. I lifted him and the chair out of the shower. The chair had no wheels and the shower tray was about 10 cm high. It was then that my back gave out."

In the example, the nurse will no doubt be able to clarify which of Mr Jones' legs went into spasm when cross examined at trial. But will she be able to explain either why, or indeed how, she allegedly lifted both Mr Jones and the chair out of the shower?

You might take the following steps when preparing a witness statement for use at trial:

Identify all the issues upon which the party needs to adduce evidence

Only the issues in dispute between the parties should be addressed. Do not deal with other matters merely because they may arise in the course of the trial. We will deal with issue analysis in detail in Ch.22 when considering the initial preparation of a multi-track case for case management but it applies equally to all cases. **14.007**

Take particular care when preparing the witness statement of the claimant in a personal injury case if his medical condition has not stabilised. In *Baron v Lovell* (2000) P.I.Q.R. P20; *The Times*, September 14, 1999, CA, Lord Justice Brooke said:

> "Pre-trial disclosure obliges the parties to disclose to each other the substance of the evidence on which they intend to rely at the trial. If a claimant's symptoms are continuing, this must be made clear in the witness statements served on his side. It is not legitimate to serve out of date statements and then hope to be allowed to update them in a radical way just before the trial".

In respect of each witness whom it would be reasonable to call on these issues, carefully interview them and then list all the important points they can make

In many instances you will have interviewed potential witnesses before the proceedings commenced. If you have adequate information on file to prepare a complete, clear and logical witness statement then you can safely go ahead and do so. Otherwise reinterview the witness. If possible you should prepare a first draft of the statement and send it to him highlighting the areas you need to speak to him about.

In an ideal world two people would interview a witness. The old saying that two heads are better than one is very true in this respect. Listening, as well as questioning, are your basic tools. It is often best to tape-record the interview but explain that to the witness first to ensure he has no objections. Let the witness tell the story in his own words. Make a note of any gaps and ensure that you go back and cover those later. At the end summarise for the witness what you have grasped as the key parts of his story to ensure that there are no fundamental misunderstandings. Always try to prepare the statement whilst it is fresh in your mind. Reflect on your list of important points and prepare an outline of the statement by way of paragraph headings.

If a witness has already made a statement, for example, to the police in a road traffic accident case, ensure you re-read it. Look out for any inconsistencies when you now interview that person. For example, assume the witness said in his statement to the police that the defendant was driving "just over the middle white line of the road". Now, perhaps many months later, he tells you it was "way over the middle". You will need to establish two things: (a) what he is actually saying; and (b) why his recollection is now apparently different from what he told the police. If you fail to ask these questions (and include any explanation in the witness's statement) then the other side no doubt will do so to good effect by way of cross examination at trial.

As a general rule, you should not interview anyone in the opponent's camp, for example, his relatives or employees. Such people will normally be unwilling to give you an interview anyway. However, the more important reason is that it is far better to have these people called by the other side so that they can cross-examined. You may have an idea as to whether or not they will be called from the details given on the opponent's allocation questionnaire (see Ch.9). Of course, if the person is an important witness and he is not called by the opponent that fact will speak for itself at trial.

Concentrate upon first-hand evidence, rather than hearsay. Cut out all irrelevancies and inadmissible opinions (see para.31.009). Ensure that any relevant allegations against an opponent are supported. An example of the dangers of including unsupported allegations can be found in *Assi v Dina Foods Ltd* [2005] EWHC 1099, (2005) L.T.L. May, 20. In his statement the Claimant alleged that the defendant's managing director, Mr. Haddad, had previously been dismissed from a job for theft. However, at trial:

> "in cross-examination he admitted that he had no idea whether or not this was true. It was just something which, so the Claimant said, he had heard. He agreed that it was nothing more than a rumour. Mr. Haddad, when he gave evidence, made plain that it was nonsense. However, the Claimant's elevation of a rumour into what he called, on oath, 'a fact', typified what I regard as his cavalier approach to giving evidence on oath to the Court. In another attack he accused Mr. Haddad of 'lying and cheating everybody' whilst accepting in the same breath that he had no evidence to support such serious allegations" (*per* Coulson J.).

If you have several witness who can deal with the same point then you must ask if it is disproportionate to call all of them. It is best to choose the ones who can also give important evidence on the other issues that will have to be decided at trial. You might decide with any other witness to serve their statement and rely on it as hearsay (see para.31.012).

For each witness prepare a statement in the proper form

14.008 "The witness statement must, if practicable, be in the intended witness's own words, the statement should be expressed in the first person" (see PD 32, para.18.1). This requirement must be borne in mind when actually interviewing the witness in the first place. If your notes of the interview do not record at least the actual key words said you will end up drafting your version of the statement. Further, do not include legal argument in the document. In the case of *Alex Lawrie Factors Ltd v Morgan, Morgan and Turner, The Times*, August 18, 1999, the Court of Appeal warned against the grave dangers of "lawyers putting their sophisticated legal arguments into a witness' mouth". The court held that the purpose of an affidavit or witness statement was for the witness to say, in his or her own words, what the relevant evidence was. It was not to be used by the lawyer who prepared it as a vehicle for complex legal argument to which the witness would not be readily able to speak if cross-examined on the document. In the case the second defendant, Mrs Morgan was seeking to avoid liability to the claimant under a deed of indemnity. She had averred that the reason why her signature appeared on the deed was due to her former husband's fraudulent actions and misrepresentations.

The claimant applied for summary judgment (see Ch.19) and in her evidence in reply Mrs Morgan stated that she had had the opportunity of studying the decision of the House of Lords in *Barclays Bank Plc v O'Brien* [1994] 1 A.C. 180 in some detail. She made a number of points in reliance on that decision. The judge said that Mrs Morgan was clearly, from her evidence, a woman not without intelligence. He concluded that her evidence as to how she came to sign the deed of indemnity was simply not credible and he awarded summary judgment.

On the appeal, Mrs Morgan's counsel had sought permission to put in new evidence going to her intelligence. The court allowed such because the situation was susceptible of injustice if the matter proceeded on the basis on which the judge had considered it, which would derive from his interpretation of the kind of woman Mrs Morgan must be from a perusal of her evidence. The court said that the case was a very good warning of the grave dangers which could occur when lawyers put into witness' mouths a sophisticated legal argument which in effect represents the lawyers' arguments in the case to which the witnesses themselves would not be able to speak if cross-examined on. Having had the benefit of further evidence, the court did not consider that this was a case in which it was appropriate to disregard Mr Morgan's evidence as incredible and it allowed the appeal.

We go along with the recommendation to be found in PD 32, para.19.2 that you should set out the relevant events in a chronological order and ensure that each paragraph is confined to a distinct portion of the subject. In addition, suitable paragraph headings allow the trial advocate and the judge to quickly pick out important topics.

Send the draft statement to the witness for checking

Ask the witness to read through it carefully and add to it and/or amend it as and where necessary. If only minor corrections are made the witness should be told to initial these and then to sign and date the statement and return it to you. If substantial alterations are required it may be appropriate to re-interview

14.009

the witness. Once the final version is prepared (see below) send it off to be signed.

Additional formalities if the witness is being called to give oral hearsay

14.010 For a definition of hearsay and a description of the procedural requirements which apply to it, see paras 31.012–31.014.

Review the evidence

14.011 Before exchange occurs you need to review all the statements that have been taken. Is there enough evidence to intimidate the opposition and/or discharge the relevant burdens of proof? How might the other parties respond to each statement? Are there any significant inconsistencies that have appeared between the statements themselves and/or other available evidence and/or the client's stated case? As to the witnesses themselves, what, if any, mud can be thrown at them by the opponents, for example, criminal convictions or other matters suggesting dishonesty or unreliability? As "cards on the table litigation" cases are often won or lost on paper do not underestimate the importance of this review.

THE FINAL VERSION

14.012 The final version of a witness statement or affidavit should:

    (a) be produced on durable quality A4 paper with a 3.5cm margin;
    (b) be fully legible and should normally only be typed on one side of the paper;
    (c) where possible, be bound securely;
    (d) have the pages numbered consecutively;
    (e) be divided into numbered paragraphs;
    (f) have all numbers, including dates, expressed in figures;
    (g) give in the margin the reference to any document mentioned.

It is important to ensure that any amendments to a witness statement are initialled by the maker. Alterations to an affidavit must be initialled by both the deponent and the person who took the affidavit. Failure to do this will mean that the document can only be used in evidence with the court's permission. A rather novel situation arose in the case of *Mealey Horgan Plc v Horgan, The Times,* July 6, 1999. The claimant's solicitors sent their client's statements to the defendant's solicitors on the day required by a court direction. It appears they did not check that the defendant was in fact ready to exchange. The defendant's solicitors some days later were told by a witness that he needed to amend his statement. Although the witness had not been shown the claimant's statements, the claimant was suspicious that he had discussed the contents with the defendant. On counsel's advice the witness's statement was amended by crossing out certain parts and the additions were highlighted. Further parts were blanked out as the witness's new employers objected that these were confidential. The witness statement was then served with a covering letter which gave some indication as to the contents of the deleted passages. The defendant then applied for permission to retrospectively extend the time for service of the witness statement.

The parties agreed that the matter of the deletion should be left to the trial judge (see Ch.37). Buckley J., sitting in the Queen's Bench Division, held that until a witness statement was filed or served it may be amended. The method of amendment adopted by the defendant was entirely appropriate and sensible in the circumstances. There was no prejudice to the claimant since both the original and the amended versions were available for use in cross examination in such manner as the trial judge thought fit.

The exchange of witness statements is dealt with at para.31.005. We have set out below a suggested version of a witness statement to be used at the trial of the action.

Suggested witness statement 14.013

On behalf of the defendant
A. J. George
1st
Exhibits "AJG1" to "AJG3"
Dated: October 23, 2007

IN THE HIGH COURT OF JUSTICE   HQ 2005 01554
QUEEN'S BENCH DIVISION
WESTBOURNE DISTRICT REGISTRY
BETWEEN

    Workgear (Mythshire) Limited   Claimant
    and
    Safety Shoes (Mythshire) Limited   Defendant

WITNESS STATEMENT OF AMY JULIET GEORGE

<u>Background</u>

1. My full name is Miss Amy Juliet George. I am employed as the Head of Quality Control of the defendant company at its factory premises in Swann Industrial Estate, Westbourne, Mythshire.

2. I have been employed by the defendant for the last 12 years. I have always worked in quality control and was appointed Head of the department in April 2000. I supervise 5 full-time and 2 part-time quality controllers.

Claimant's complaints

3. I first learnt of the claimant's complaints about the leather uppers of the shoes supplied on December 14, 2003 when I telephoned Mr Alexander Thomas, the claimant's Sales manager. I have corresponded with, and spoken to, Mr Thomas on the telephone on numerous occasions since I became Head of department. I would say we have spoken at least 5 times a year when he has placed orders.

4. In my telephone conversation with Mr Thomas on December 14, 2003 he told me that the complaints which the claimant was making in respect of the shoes received from the defendant also applied to several other shoes received from other suppliers. He also said that all the affected shoes had been stored together in the same part of the claimant's warehouse in Westbourne.

Quality control measures

5. Leather uppers of shoes produced at the defendant's factory are subjected to 3 quality control measures.

6. The first measure is in respect of raw materials. Shoe leather is purchased in the form of cured hides and each hide is subject to a visual check by the cutting machine operators. This check has proved very effective in the past. I refer to my exhibited records of the results of those checks over the last 12 months marked "AJG1". It can be seen at the bottom of page 3 that the average rejection rate is approximately 5 per cent of all hides which are then returned to the supplying tannery.

7. Thereafter 2 further tests are carried out on completed shoes before packaging. The checks are made in respect of batches. An average batch is 25,000 pairs.

8. A 10 per cent sample of each batch is subjected to what is known as a "Ballisto Scan". This is an industrial test to identify defective stitching, damage to soles and tears to, or thinning of, the leather uppers. The test is carried out by my staff. Where a problem is identified that is not unique to the item scanned the whole batch is returned to the Stitching Department for sorting.

9. The final quality control measure affecting leather uppers is a visual appraisal of each batch. This appraisal is also made by my staff. Where a problem is identified that is not unique to the item appraised, the quality controller either subjects a further batch to a Ballisto Scan and/or returns the whole batch to the Stitching Department for sorting.

10. I refer to my exhibited records of the results of the Ballisto Scan and the final visual checks made in the last 12 months marked "AJG2". It can be seen at the bottom of pages 7 and 9 that the average number of whole batches returned to the Stitching Department for sorting after the Ballisto Scan and visual checks were approximately 3 per cent and 1 per cent respectively.

Quality control records

11. My department maintains full quality control records of all products sold during the last 6 years. From these records I note that the shoes which are the subject of this action came from batch number WWW 9876. I refer to my exhibited records for that batch marked "AJG3". It can be seen that it was subject to each of the quality control measures I have described without any problems whatsoever.

12. Batch number WWW 9876 comprised in total 26,500 pairs of shoes. So far as I am aware no complaints have been received about this batch other than the complaints now made by the claimant in this action.

Statement of truth

13. I believe that the facts stated in this witness statement are true.

Signed: *Amy George*
Dated: *23rd October 2007*

CHAPTER 15

Default Judgment

THE GENERAL PICTURE

15.001 A defendant who fails to file an acknowledgment of service and/or a defence within the time limits provided is at risk of having a default judgment entered against him. The danger zone does not begin until 14 days after the particulars of claim have been served. It can be delayed for another 14 days (i.e. until 28 days after service of the particulars of claim) if he files an acknowledgment of service.

Example

A claim form containing particulars of claim is deemed to have been served in England and Wales on Thursday September 6, 2007. The last day the defendant may file his acknowledgment of service or, in the alternative, a defence, is Thursday September 20 (i.e. 14 days after service of the particulars of claim). If he fails to acknowledge or defend, the claimant may obtain judgment in default of acknowledgment on Friday September 21.

If the defendant does file an acknowledgment of service the last day he has to file a defence is Thursday October 4, 20075 (i.e. 28 days after service of the particulars of claim). If he fails to do so the claimant may obtain judgment in default of defence on Friday October 5.

In practice most defendants who are going to default do not file an acknowledgment of service first and most defendants who file an acknowledgment of service do later serve their defence in time. Thus, most default judgments are entered in default of acknowledgment of service (i.e. failure to file that document or a defence within the time allowed, r.12.3(1)). Judgments in default of defence (i.e. defendant files an acknowledgment of service but nevertheless fails to file a defence in the extended period thereby obtained, r.12.3(2)) are comparatively rare.

In most money claims and delivery of goods claims the default judgment is obtained without a hearing ("on request", see para.15.005, below). In some exceptional money claims and in claims for other remedies (e.g. an injunction) a default judgment can be obtained only "on application" (see para.15.009).

What is a defence?

For the purposes of the default judgment rules it is the act of filing a defence which is significant, not its quality. This is confirmed by PD 12, para.1.1 which states that, for present purposes, a defence includes any document "purporting to be a defence". Thus, a default judgment cannot be obtained even if the defendant has written something fairly meaningless on the defence form. However, the court may well strike that out of its own initiative under r.3.4(2) or the claimant could apply for a strikeout (see para.33.008) or, alternatively, apply for summary judgment (see Ch.19).

15.002

Filing an acknowledgment of service or defence late

Assume that the danger zone has begun but the claimant has not yet entered a default judgment. If the defendant filed his defence today, would that prevent the claimant obtaining a default judgment even though the defence was filed late? Could the defendant file an acknowledgment of service so gaining any outstanding balance of the 14 day extension of time such a document can secure? The CPR are quite unclear on this point. This is in contrast to the rules on admissions (as to which see Ch.16). Rule 14.2 expressly provides that a defendant may file or return an admission late if he does so before a default judgment is entered and, in such cases, the admission is treated as if it had been filed or returned in time.

15.003

There is authority for saying that a late defence or acknowledgment of service may not prevent the claimant from obtaining a default judgment (*Coll v Tattum Neuberger J.,The Times*, December 3, 2001). However, in that case, the point was largely academic; the claimant was claiming an injunction and therefore had to "apply" for judgment which application the court considered along with the defendant's cross application for an extension of time. The judge granted the extension of time sought but invited the claimant to apply for directions should they wish to seek summary judgment, an interim injunction or other interlocutory relief.

> "In my view, where there has been no application to seek judgment in default of defence or judgment in default of acknowledgment of service, the claimant can frequently be expected to accept late acknowledgment of service or a late defence. However, in my judgment the claimant, and indeed the court, would be entitled to insist, in an appropriate case, on the defendant seeking an extension of time. The rules are there to be observed, and it seems to me that the general thrust of the rules is such that where there is no defence or acknowledgment of service or where it is served late, the claimant should have the right to apply for judgment in default, without the defendant automatically 'trumping' such an application by the service of a late defence. Having said that, I think that if an application for

judgment in default were made after a late acknowledgment of service, or after a late defence, it may very well be dismissed, even though technically justified."

We take the message here to be as follows: the claimant can in theory obtain a default judgment but should not normally attempt it in practice.

Consider now delay by a claimant in obtaining a default judgment. Extreme delay will prevent him from obtaining it, and will also prevent the defendant filing a late defence, save upon an application to the court. By r.15.11 the claim is automatically stayed six months after the end of the permitted period for filing a defence if no admission, defence or counterclaim has been filed and the claimant has neither obtained judgment in default nor made an application for summary judgment (see further Chs 19 and 33).

CLAIMS IN WHICH DEFAULT JUDGMENT IS NOT AVAILABLE (RR.12.2 AND 12.3(3) AND PD 12, PARAS 1.2 AND 1.3)

15.004 A claimant cannot obtain default judgment in any of the following instances:

(a) Where the claim is for the delivery of goods that are subject to a regulated agreement under the Consumer Credit Act 1974, as amended, since this is a fixed date action (see Ch.9).
(b) Where a Pt 8 claim has been made (see Ch.10).
(c) Admiralty, arbitration, contentious probate, possession and provisional damages claims and other specialist proceedings.
(d) Where the defendant has applied to strike out the claimant's statement of case or for summary judgment and the application has not been determined.
(e) Where the defendant has satisfied the whole claim, including any costs.
(f) Where the claimant is seeking judgment on a claim for money and the defendant has served or filed an admission under r.14.4 or 14.7 together with a request for time to pay (see Ch.16).

DEFAULT JUDGMENT ON REQUEST (R.12.4)

15.005 In most cases it is possible to obtain default judgment by simply filling in the appropriate practice form and sending it to the court. If you arranged service of the claim form, you must also file a certificate of service (see para.8.019). There will be no hearing. As a general rule a request can be made where the claim is for:

(a) A specified or unspecified amount of money. Forms N205A (or N225) and N205B (or N227), respectively, should be completed.
(b) Delivery of goods where the claim form has given the defendant the alternative of paying their value. If no such alternative was given then an application for default judgment must be made (see below). Further, do not forget that default judgment will not be available if the claim concerns an agreement that is regulated by the Consumer Credit Act 1974 (see above).
(c) Any combination of the above remedies. If he has claimed other remedies, for example, possession of land, an injunction or specific performance, the claimant must make an application for a default judgment (see para.15.009, below). However, he can still obtain a default judgment on request if he now wishes to abandon any remedy for which a request cannot be made. The abandonment of the remedy must be stated on the request form. You will have to write it in as there is no box to tick.

For the exceptions to the general rule see para.15.009.

As to obtaining default judgment against the Crown, see para.24.018.

Claim for a specified amount of money (r.12.5(1))

If a specified amount of money was claimed the judgment will be for that amount less any payments made plus fixed costs (as to which see para.38.010). The judgment may also specify the amount of interest payable if the claim for interest was properly stated in the particulars of claim (see para.12.013) and, in the case of discretionary interest, the rate claimed is no higher than the judgment debt rate. In other cases (for example, where the claim for interest was not properly stated) the judgment may specify the amount, the fixed costs and "an amount of interest to be decided by the court" (r.12.6). The procedure for deciding the amount of interest in such a case is set out in r.12.7, as to which, see below.

15.006

The amounts specified in the judgment are payable immediately unless the judgment states a different date for payment or states a rate of payment, for example, by weekly or monthly instalments. Which date or rate of payment applies depends upon the request the claimant makes. Most claimants will request immediate payment so as to enable them to proceed straight away to enforcement proceedings. In the majority of claims for specified sums, the entry of a judgment in default is the easy part. It is the enforcement of that judgment that requires skill and expertise (as to which see Ch.40).

What if the defendant has paid everything apart from the fixed costs? In such a case the claimant can simply request a default judgment for those fixed costs.

Claim for an unspecified amount of money

15.007 If an unspecified amount of money was claimed the default judgment obtained in respect of it will be for "an amount to be decided by the court and costs" (r.12.5(2)). Rule 12.7 provides that, on entering such a judgment, the court will give any directions it considers appropriate and, if it considers it appropriate, will also allocate the case to a particular case management track. In most cases the court will fix a date for a disposal hearing, as to which, see Ch.17. Until the amount payable has been decided by the court, the claimant cannot proceed to enforce this judgment. However, the judgment is conclusive on liability in respect of the matters stated in the particulars of claim at the time they were served (see further para.17.005, below).

Claim for delivery of goods or payment of their value

15.008 If the claim was for the delivery of goods and the claim form gave the defendant the alternative of paying their value, the default judgment available on request is a judgment requiring the defendant to either: (a) deliver the goods; or (b) pay the value of the goods as decided by the court; and (c) pay costs. The procedure for deciding the value of the goods is set out in r.12.7 (see above). If the claimant now wishes to obtain an order for delivery of goods without giving the defendant the option of paying their value he cannot obtain a default judgment by request and should instead make an application (as to which see below).

A special rule applies where the claimant is only a part owner of the goods in question: he is entitled to a money remedy only unless he has the written authority of every other part owner of the goods to make a claim on behalf of both or all of them (see generally r.40.14).

Request in claim against two or more defendants (r.12.8(1))

What should happen if the claimant has sued two or more defendants and one files a defence but the other or others fail to do so? Rule 12.8(1) provides that remedies otherwise obtainable on request (i.e. claims for money or delivery of goods) can still be obtained by request against the defendant or defendants in default and the claimant may proceed with his claim against the other or others. However, in respect of a claim for the delivery of goods, the claimant cannot enforce the judgment without the court's permission unless and until judgment has been obtained against all of the defendants.

DEFAULT JUDGMENT ON APPLICATION

15.009 In some cases the rules do not permit the claimant to obtain a default judgment on request. Instead, he must make an application to the court. As to the procedure on applications see Chs. 13 and 14.

An application is necessary if the claimant wishes to obtain an order other than an order for the payment of money or for the delivery of goods or payment of their value. Most other remedies are discretionary only. The requirement for an application gives the court an opportunity to decide whether to exercise its discretion to grant the order sought and, if so, in what terms. Remember also that in some cases no default judgment is obtainable at all (see para.15.004, above).

Rule 12.10 makes an application necessary even to obtain the simple remedies of money or delivery of goods or payment of value in any case in which the claim is made against any of the following persons.

(1) A child or patient (see further Ch.7): an application here gives the court an opportunity to ensure that the defendant is properly represented by a litigation friend. If the defendant does not have a litigation friend the claimant must first apply for someone to be appointed (see r.21.6).

(2) In tort by one spouse or civil partner against the other: the court has power to stay the action if it appears that no substantial benefit would accrued either party from its continuance or if it could be more conveniently disposed of by other means.

(3) Against a foreign State (as defined in the State Immunity Act 1978) or against certain other persons or bodies which have diplomatic or similar immunity: the requirement for an application gives the court the opportunity to determine whether proceedings against these defendants are properly brought.

(4) Against a defendant served without leave outside the jurisdiction or against a defendant domiciled in Scotland, Northern Ireland or in another EU or EFTA State whether or not served outside the jurisdiction: the requirement for an application here gives the court an opportunity to determine whether the English court should assume jurisdiction in the claim in question (see further Ch.11).

In all of the above cases except (4) the application must be made on notice to the defendant. In (4) the application can be made without notice and without service of the evidence and support in advance. In claims against a foreign State or in (4) above the evidence and support must be by affidavit, not by witness statement.

Application for default judgment against two or more defendants (r.12.8(2))

If the claim against a defaulting defendant can be dealt with separately from the claim against the others, the court may enter default judgment against that defendant and the claimant may continue the proceedings against the rest. However, a claim for the delivery of goods may not be enforced without the court's permission until judgment has been obtained against all the defendants

15.010

to the claim. Where the claim against a defaulting defendant cannot be dealt with separately from the claim against others, the court will not enter default judgment and it must deal with the application at the same time as it disposes of the claims against the others.

SETTING ASIDE A DEFAULT JUDGMENT

15.011 CPR Pt 13 sets out the procedure for applications to set aside or vary judgments entered in default of an acknowledgment of service or in default of defence. As we have seen, most such judgments are obtained merely by filing a request. There is no consideration by the court of the merits of the claim on the question of liability or, sometimes, on the question of quantum either. The absence of any decision on the merits means that the defendant has no right of appeal. Instead he can apply under CPR Pt 13 for an Order setting aside or varying the default judgment.

Where the default judgment was obtained "on application" (e.g. in a claim for an injunction) the normal route of challenge is by way of appeal. Although such appeals are rare, set aside applications in such cases are rarer still. The defendant would have to show some change of circumstance likely to produce a more favourable outcome for him the existence of which or evidence of which was not available to him earlier.

Where the court must set aside a default judgment

15.012 Rule 13.2 states that the court must set aside a default judgment which was wrongly entered because of one or more of the following reasons.

(1) It was obtained prematurely, i.e. before the time for acknowledgment of service and/or defence had expired.
(2) It was obtained after the defendant had applied to have the particulars of claim struck out under r.3.4 or the claim summarily dismissed under Pt 24 but before such application(s) had been disposed of.
(3) It was obtained even though the whole claim (including interest and costs) had already been paid or satisfied.
(4) On a claim for money it was obtained after the defendant had filed or served an admission with a request for time to pay.

Where a default judgment is set aside under r.13.2 it is not usual for the court to impose conditions upon the defendant and it is usual for the court to award costs against the claimant. Note that r.13.2 does not cover all cases in which a default judgment was "wrongly entered"; for example, a default judgment obtained in a possession action or a default judgment for an injunction obtained on request. In these cases, the defendant must apply under r.13.3 to which we now turn.

In cases falling outside r.13.2, r.13.3 gives the court a discretion to set aside a default judgment but only if the defendant can show either

(a) that he has a real prospect of successfully defending the claim, or
(b) there is some other good reason why the judgment should be set aside or the defendant permitted to defend the claim.

We shall look at each of those alternatives separately (see below). A defendant who wishes to apply under r.13.3 should act quickly since one factor the court takes into account in deciding whether or not to exercise its discretion is the promptness or otherwise of the application (r.13.3(2)). Promptness is of course an extremely flexible concept. In many cases it will be a make-weight factor only. It will not by itself justify granting an application which is otherwise weak or justify refusing an application which is otherwise strong (for an example, see *National Westminster Bank Plc v Bowles* L.T.L., February 23, 2005).

Is there "a real prospect of successfully defending the claim"?

The test under r.13.3(1)(a) as to whether there is a real prospect of success is the same as on a summary judgment application under Pt 24 (as to which see Ch.19). The only significant difference between them concerns the burden of proof. Although, in both cases, the burden falls upon the applicant, on set aside applications the applicant is always the defendant. Summary judgment applications can be made by either the claimant or the defendant. Under r.13.3(1)(a) the defendant must show that his prospects of successfully defending the claim are "real" as opposed to "fanciful". However, the proper disposal of the application does not involve the court conducting a mini-trial. In *Royal Brompton Hospital NHS Trust v Hammond*, *The Times*, May 11, 2001, CA it was held that, when deciding whether a defence has a real prospect of success, the court should not apply the same standard as would be applicable at the trial, namely the balance of probabilities on the evidence presented. Instead, the court should also consider the evidence that could reasonably be expected to be available at trial.

15.013

How the court decides whether a defence is real without conducting a mini-trial has lead to a series of unsatisfactory cases now largely concluded by the clear statements of authority in *Three Rivers District Council v Bank of England (No.3)* [2001] 2 All E.R. 513, HL (a summary judgment application) and *ED&F Man Liquid Products Ltd v Patel* [2003] EWCA Civ 472 (a set aside application) (see below). The defence relied on must be more than merely arguable: it must carry some degree of conviction.

> "[94] ... the question ... whether the claim has no real prospect of succeeding at trial ... has to be answered having regard to the overriding objective of dealing with the case justly. But the point which is of crucial importance lies in the answer to the further question that then needs to be asked, which is—what is to be the scope of that inquiry?

[95] I would approach that further question in this way. The method by which issues of fact are tried in our courts is well settled. After the normal processes of [disclosure and requests for information] have been completed, the parties are allowed to lead their evidence so that the trial judge can determine where the truth lies in the light of that evidence. To that rule there are some well-recognised exceptions. For example, it may be clear as a matter of law at the outset that even if a party were to succeed in proving all the facts that he offers to prove he will not be entitled to the remedy that he seeks. In that event a trial of the facts would be a waste of time and money, and it is proper that the action should be taken out of court as soon as possible. In other cases, it may be possible to say with confidence before trial that the factual basis for the claim is fanciful because it is entirely without substance. It may be clear beyond question that the statement of facts is contradicted by all the documents or other material on which it is based. The simpler the case the easier it is likely to be to take that view and resort to what is properly called summary judgment. But more complex cases are unlikely to be capable of being resolved in that way without conducting a mini-trial on the documents without [disclosure] and without oral evidence . . ..That is not the object of the rule. It is designed to deal with cases that are not fit for trial at all." (Lord Hope of Craighead in *Three Rivers District Council v Bank of England (No.3)* [2001] 2 All E.R. 513, HL (a summary judgment application).

"[9] In my view, the only significant difference between the provisions of CPR 24.2 and 13.3(1), is that under the former the overall burden of proof rests upon the claimant to establish that there are grounds for his belief that the respondent has no real prospect of success. Whereas, under the latter, the burden rests upon the defendant to satisfy the court that there is good reason why a judgment regularly obtained should be set aside. That being so, although generally the burden of proof is in practice of only marginal importance in relation to the assessment of evidence, it seems almost inevitable that, in particular cases, a defendant applying under CPR 13.3(1) may encounter a court less receptive to applying for test in his favour than if he were a defendant advancing a timely ground of resistance to summary judgment under CPR 24.2.

[10] It is certainly the case that under both rules, where there are significant differences between the parties so far as factual issues are concerned, the court is in no position to conduct a mini-trial . . . however, that does not mean that the court has to accept without analysis everything said by a party in his statements before the court. In some cases, it may be clear that there is no real substance in factual assertions made, particularly if contradicted by contemporary documents. If so, issues which are dependent upon those factual assertions may be susceptible of disposal at an early stage so as to save the cost and delay of trying an issue the outcome of which is inevitable . . .

[11] I would only add that, where there is claim or judgment for monies due and issues of fact are raised by a defendant for the first time which, standing alone would demonstrate a triable issue, if it is apparent that, with full knowledge of the facts raised, the defendant has previously admitted the debt and/or made payment on account of it, a judge will be justified in taking such acknowledgments into account as an indication of the likely substance of the issues raised and the ultimate success of the defence belatedly advanced.

[52] Mr Thomas [counsel for the defendant] has powerfully submitted that, in deciding as he did, the judge in effect conducted a mini-trial of the issues in a manner impermissible on an application to set aside judgment under CPR 13.3(1)(a)). He said that there were plainly issues of fact as to whether and, if so, when [the defendant's liability ceased]. He further submits that the judge was wrong to reject the explanation of the first defendant for the series of admissions made that the debt was due.

[53] I would accept, as the judge accepted, that without the written admissions that would plainly be correct. However, in a case where, with knowledge of the material facts, clear admissions in writing are unambiguously made by a sophisticated businessman who has ample opportunity to advance his defence prior to judgment [being] signed, a judge is in my view entitled to look at the case 'in the round', in the sense that, if satisfied of the genuineness of the admissions, issues of fact which might otherwise require to be resolved at trial may fall away. Here, the broad issue was clear. [Was this a simple sale, as the claimant alleged or a joint venture as the first defendant alleged?] The series of written admissions, if informed and genuine, were a clear indication that the former was the case. In that respect, I consider that the judge was entitled to reject as devoid of substance or conviction such explanation as was advanced for the making of those admissions and in my view he was entitled to conclude that the first defendant lacked any real prospect of successfully defending the claim." (Potter L.J. in *ED&F Man Liquid Products Ltd v Patel* [2003] EWCA Civ 472).

In our experience the different burden of proof mentioned by Potter L.J. (see [9] above) can affect the outcome in some cases. If your defence is weak, it is easier to survive a summary judgment attack than it is to win a set-aside application. Thus, the weaker your defence is, the more important it is not to let the case go by default if you wish to oppose it. A weak defence will be weakened further if the defendant defaults in filing it and will be weakened further still if he fails to commence his set aside application promptly.

Is there some other good reason to set aside?

Rule 13.3(1)(b) leaves open the possibility that, even if a defendant has no real prospect of successfully defending the claim, the court may still set it aside if

15.014

there is some other good reason why: (i) the judgment should be set aside or varied: or (ii) the defendant should be allowed to defend the claim. (i) and (ii) are, in effect, two sides of the same coin. A judgment should be set aside if the defendant ought to be allowed to defend it and the defendant will be allowed to defend a judgment which is set aside. However, although the distinction does not have a difference, it does show the two ways in which the defendant may direct his application. He may, either, point to some vice in the judgment obtained or dwell upon his own good behaviour, despite the default, or, of course, he may attempt both.

If the judgment is "regular", in the sense that the proceedings were served in accordance with the CPR, the fact that the defendant had no knowledge of the claim before judgment in default was entered is not by itself a sufficiently good reason for setting that judgment aside: see *Akram v Adam* [2005] 1 All E.R. 741, CA. In that case the defendant's usual or last known address was a room in a house in which the claimant, his landlord, also lived. The claim form was correctly posted to the house thereby raising the irrebuttable presumption of deemed service (see Ch.8). The claimant later obtained judgment in his absence and it was held on appeal that the defendant was not entitled to have that judgment set aside. Since, in all the circumstances, he had no real prospects of successfully defending the claim, setting the judgment aside simply because he had failed to receive prior notice of the claim would have been pointless and compelling the claimant to obtain summary judgment would merely waste time and money (*cf* the extract from the decision in *Three Rivers District Council*, set out above).

But if the judgment is "irregular" in the sense of being obtained without service of the claim form in accordance with the rules, the Court of Appeal in *Nelson v Clearsprings (Management Ltd)* [2006] EWCA Civ 1252, *The Times*, October 5, 2006, indicated that the following steps should be taken:

i) If the defendant can show he has not been served (or is not deemed to have been served) with the claim form at all, then he would normally be entitled to an order setting the judgment aside and to his costs in making the application.

ii) If, when the claimant is served with an application to set aside such a judgment, he believes that he can show that the defendant has no real prospect of successfully defending the claim, then he may apply to the court for orders dispensing with service of the claim form, permission (under CPR 24.4(1)) to apply forthwith for summary judgment, and for summary judgment on his claim.

iii) If such an application and cross-application are made the court should make such order as it considers just.

iv) If the claimant can show that the defendant has been guilty of inexcusable delay since learning that the judgment has been entered against him, the court would be entitled to make no order on the defendant's application for that reason. The judgment would then stand (subject to any direction made by the court, whether in relation to statutory interest accruing due on the judgment or otherwise).

Both *Akram* and *Nelson* were possession cases to which Pt 13 does not apply. The court in *Nelson* indicated that it considered the irregular judgment to be an error of procedure capable of being corrected under r.3.10 (see para.1.015). The court also expressed the hope that the Civil Rules Committee may in due course review the provisions concerning service of proceedings and also those relating to setting aside a judgment obtained in default or by the failure of a party to attend trial (see further paras 37.007 and 43.002).

Can a claimant apply under this ground? Why might a claimant want to apply? In *Messer Griesheim GmbH v Goyal MG Gases PVT Ltd* [2006] EWHC 79, *The Times*, February 14, 2006, the claimant successfully applied to set aside its default judgment. It was also granted at the same time summary judgment on the same claim for the same amount. It did so because a summary judgment would be enforceable in India against the defendant company but a default judgment would not. The defendant was an Indian company with no, or at least no known, significant assets in England or Wales or, it would appear, anywhere else except in India.

Conditions the court may impose

By r.3.1(3) when the court makes an order setting aside a default judgment, it may attach conditions, including the payment of a sum of money into court. A cross-reference to this power is included as a footnote to r.13.3 but not to r.13.2 since it is not usual to impose conditions in successful applications under that rule. 15.015

Where a judgment is set aside under r.13.3(1)(a) (real prospect of successfully defending) but the court takes the view that that defence will probably fail it may make the same conditional order as it would have made had the claimant applied for summary judgment. Conditional orders are considered further at para.19.014, below.

Practice on applications

Chapter 13 describes the procedure on making applications and filing evidence in support and evidence in reply. Chapter 14 describes drafting applications and witness statements. If the claimant will be asking the court to make a conditional order if the application succeeds, he should warn the defendant of that in advance. If he intends to seek a condition involving a payment of money into court he should also warn the defendant as to the amount. That will give the defendant an opportunity to provide evidence of his means if he wishes to argue that such a condition would stifle his defence. 15.016

If, despite being given such a warning, he fails to put in full and frank evidence of his means, the court may refuse him a further opportunity to do so later (*Olatawura v Abiloye* [2003] 1 W.L.R. 275, CA and *Kamal v Redcliffe Close (Old Brompton Road) Management Ltd*, L.T.L., January 21, 2005, Ch.D).

In certain claims for a specified sum of money, an application to set aside a default judgment will lead to an automatic transfer of the claim to the defendant's home court if it is not already being dealt with there (see r.13.4 which applies where: (a) the claim is for a specified sum of money; (b) which is not in a specialist list; and (c) the defendant is an individual; and (d) the claim has not already been automatically transferred to another defendant's home court).

Rule 13.6 makes a special provision for cases in which the claimant abandoned a claim for certain remedies in order to obtain a default judgment on request (see above). It states that if the default judgment is set aside the abandoned claim is automatically restored.

VARYING A DEFAULT JUDGMENT

15.017 Consider a default judgment in a claim in respect of two or more separate matters where, on a set aside application under r.13.3 the court decides there is no real prospect of successfully defending part of the claim nor any other good reason for setting aside the judgment in respect of that part. In such a case it may be appropriate to vary the default judgment so as to make it judgment in part only.

Another example of the variation of a default judgment is in respect of the rate at which the judgment debt is to be paid. In both the High Court and the county court a default judgment can be entered for a sum payable immediately, or by a set date, or by periodical instalments (r.12.5(2) and r.40.11(a)). The county court has a set procedure by which either party, claimant or defendant, can later apply to vary the date or rate of payment (CCR 22.10). In respect of a default judgment obtained under Pt 12 the defendant (but not the claimant) could also apply for a variation of a money judgment, or indeed any other judgment, by relying upon r.13.3.

DEFAULT JUDGMENT AND ADDITIONAL CLAIMS

15.018 The expression "additional claim" covers counterclaims (i.e. claims by a defendant against the claimant or against the claimant and some other person) claims for contribution, indemnity or some other remedy against any person (whether or not already a party) and consequential claims (e.g. counterclaims and claims for contribution made by a defendant). For further details see Ch.18. Part 12 (default judgment) applies only to a counterclaim (r.20.3(3)). The defendant can enter judgment in default of defence to counterclaim if the claimant fails to file his defence to counterclaim within the time allowed for doing so (r.12.3(2)(b)). For additional claims which are not counterclaims the person against whom they are brought will be bound by the outcome of the proceedings whether they participate or not. In most cases a non-participant will be deemed to admit the additional claim against him and if the main proceedings end in a default judgment under Pt 12, the additional proceedings may sometimes end in a default judgment under r.20.11 (see further para.18.009).

CHAPTER 16

Admissions and Requests for Time to Pay

WHAT IS AN ADMISSION?

A party may admit the truth of the whole or any part of another party's case. This may be done before or after the commencement of proceedings. How can a party make an admission? The answer is by giving notice in writing, for example, by letter or, during proceedings, formally in a statement of case. When a fact is admitted neither party will have to incur further expense on it. The overriding objective is served (see para.1.006). What facts should be admitted? A party ought to admit any fact which it is neither to his interest nor in his power to disprove. If he fails to do so he can expect to be penalised in costs whatever the outcome of the trial. Sometimes, the opponent can make this costs penalty automatic by serving a notice to admit (see further para.32.008, below).

16.001

The first time consideration needs to be given to making any written admissions is during the pre-action protocol stages. Much of the negotiations will be conducted on a without prejudice basis and if admissions are made the parties need to be clear as to whether or not the maker intends to be bound by them. If you are dealing with a matter under the personal injury pre-action protocol, or those concerning clinical disputes or disease and illness claims (see Ch.6), special attention needs to be paid to r.14.1A and PD 14 para.1.1. If proceedings are subsequently started, any party can apply for judgment on a pre-action admission or a party can apply apply to withdraw such an admission (see para.16.009, below).

Note also that by s.2 of the Compensation Act 2006 an apology, an offer of treatment or other redress, does not of itself amount to an admission of negligence or breach of statutory duty.

The second time a defendant needs to consider making an admission is upon receiving the response pack (see Ch.9). Where the only remedy which the claimant is seeking is the payment of money, the defendant can complete the appropriate Form N9A (specified amount claimed) or N9C (unspecified amount claimed) to take one of the following steps:

(a) By r.14.4 he may admit the whole of the claim for a specified amount of money.

(b) By r.14.5 he may admit part of the claim for a specified amount of money and in addition file a defence.
(c) By r.14.6 he may admit liability to pay the whole of a claim for an unspecified amount of money.
(d) By r.14.7 he may admit liability to pay a claim for an unspecified amount of money and offer a sum in satisfaction of that claim.

In all other cases the defendant will need to consider making any suitable admissions as part of his defence (see Ch.12).

In a personal injury case it is important to remember that an admission of negligence, without an admission that the claimant suffered injury as a result, is not an admission of liability (see *Blundell v Rimmer* [1971] 1 W.L.R. 123). However, in these circumstances the claimant might be able to obtain summary judgment (see Ch.19 and see further *White Book*, para.14.3.4).

JUDGMENT ON A WRITTEN ADMISSION

16.002 Assume that, although proceedings have commenced, the parties have continued to negotiate and your opponent now makes an admission. If he does so orally ask him to repeat it in writing. If or when it is in writing, invite him to consent to judgment being entered on that admission (as to consent orders see, Ch.34). If that is refused ask why. Is the admission disputed? Is the opponent purporting to withdraw it (see below)? If by this stage you are confident that it is a clear and unambiguous admission which ought to conclude the matter it deals with, you can apply to the court for judgment under r.14.3. If it is not sufficiently clear and unambiguous consider seeking further information by way of clarification and/or serving a notice to admit facts (see Ch.32).

How can a defendant who is prepared to admit the claimant's claim protect himself if he also wishes to make a counterclaim against the claimant that exceeds the amount of the claim? The answer is to agree to the claimant entering judgment on condition that he is not to enforce it until the counterclaim has been tried. A claimant in these circumstances should consider the merits of the counterclaim and whether summary judgment might be obtained on the basis that the defendant has no real prospect of succeeding on the counterclaim (see Ch.19). A better condition for a claimant is that the defendant should pay the amount due into court pending determination of the counterclaim.

ADMISSIONS IN FORM N9A OR N9C

16.003 A defendant served with a Pt 7 claim form should receive a response pack, i.e. forms prepared by the court allowing him to acknowledge service, make admissions and/or state his defence and/or counterclaim. Where the only remedy claimed is the payment of money, the response pack will include Form N9A if the amount claimed is specified or N9C if the amount claimed is unspecified.

If the defendant wishes to admit the claim in whole or in part, he may use the form provided and return it to the claimant or file it in court, whichever is appropriate (as to which, see below).

That step must be taken within 14 days after service of the claim form if it has on it, or is accompanied by, particulars of claim. However, where the particulars are served after the claim form, the form of admission must be returned to the claimant or filed at the court within 14 days after service of the particulars of claim.

By r.14.2(3) a defendant may return his r.14.4 admission to the claimant or file any other r.14 admission with the court even after the prescribed period for doing so has expired provided the claimant has not already obtained default judgment pursuant to r.12 (see Ch.15). The admission is then treated as having been received within the required time period.

The four ways in which the defendant may use these forms to make admissions are set out in para.16.001 above by reference to the rule numbers, rr.14.4 to 14.7. Where the defendant makes an admission under any of these rules, the claimant has a right to enter judgment unless the defendant is a child or patient, or the claimant is a child or patient and the admission is made under rr.14.5 or 14.7 (see below). Rule 21.10 provides that, where a claim is made by or on behalf of a child or patient, or against such a person, no settlement, compromise or payment is valid unless approved by the court. The procedure for obtaining such is described in Ch.10.

Admission of whole of claim for a specified amount of money (r.14.4)

The defendant must send the form of admission N9A direct to the claimant (in all other cases the defendant must file the form at the court). The claimant can then obtain judgment by filing a request in Form N205A (this is, in fact, the bottom half of the notice of issue of the claim) or Form N225. If the defendant has not requested any time to pay (see below) the claimant's request should deal with the following matters: 16.004

(a) The amount due must be specified. Judgment is for the "whole" of the debt inclusive of fixed costs and interest. Note that by r.14.14 the claim for interest must have been properly stated in the particulars of claim (see Ch.12). The request must set out an up to date calculation of interest. If it has been claimed otherwise than pursuant to s.35A of the Supreme Court Act 1981 or s.69 of the County Courts Act 1984 (see Ch.3) the judgment is for the court to assess the amount of interest payable.

(b) When the amount due is to be paid. The claimant may state that the whole of the judgment debt should be paid immediately, or by a set date, or by monthly instalments at a figure the claimant is prepared to accept. Presumably, as the defendant has not asked for time to pay most claimants will want judgment to be entered for immediate and full payment. If the claimant does not specify a date for payment the judgment is payable immediately.

Upon receiving the request the court will enter judgment and produce an order in Form N30(1). The order is sent to the parties and officially recorded in the Register of Judgments, Orders and Fines. Registration of the judgment will normally have a deleterious effect upon the defendant's credit rating. One way of avoiding registration is to pay the claimant the whole of the claim, including fixed commencement costs stated in the claim form, within 14 days of service of the particulars of claim. If he does this the claimant will not be entitled to enter judgment under rule 14.4 or a default judgment see para.15.004, above). Furthermore, the defendant will not be liable for any further costs other than the fixed commencement costs unless the court so orders (r.45.3(1)).

Admission of part of claim for a specified amount of money (r.14.5)

16.005 The defendant must file the form of admission N9A at the court. The court then sends the claimant a notice of the part admission in Form N225A. The claimant then has 14 days to complete the document and return it to the court. The notice itself specifies the last date to do this. Once the 14 days have expired the claim is stayed. However, the stay is automatically lifted when a completed notice is filed. The claimant may accept or reject the amount admitted in satisfaction of his claim. If he accepts it judgment is entered following the procedure outlined above. See below as to any request made by the defendant for time to pay.

If the amount is rejected the case proceeds as a defended claim and may be transferred automatically to the defendant's home court (see Ch.15).

Rule 45.3(2) provides a means by which the defendant can limit his liability for any of the claimant's costs in excess of the fixed commencement costs. If, within 14 days after service of the particulars of claim, he pays into court the sum he admits plus the fixed costs stated in the claim form and the claimant later gives notice of acceptance of that payment in satisfaction of the whole claim, the defendant will not be liable for any further costs unless the court orders otherwise.

Admission of liability to pay whole of claim for an unspecified amount of money (r.14.6)

The defendant must file the form of admission N9C at the court. The court will send the claimant a copy of that document and a request for judgment in Form N226. The claimant then has 14 days to complete the document and return it to the court. The notice itself will specify the last date to do this. Once the 14 days has expired the claim is stayed. However, it is automatically lifted by filing the completed notice and judgment is entered for an amount to be decided by the court at a disposal hearing (see Ch.17).

Defendant's offer to satisfy a claim for unspecified amount of money (r.14.7)

The defendant must file the form of admission N9C at the court. The court will send the claimant a notice of the admission and offer in Form N226. The claimant then has 14 days to complete the document and return it to the court. The notice itself will specify the last date to do this. Once the 14 days have expired the claim is stayed. However, the stay is automatically lifted when a completed notice is filed. The claimant may accept or reject the amount offered in satisfaction of his claim. If he accepts it then judgment will be entered following the procedure outlined in para.16.004 save the judgment figure will be for the amount offered, court fees and solicitor's costs on issuing the claim form and on entering judgment. Also, see below as to any request made by the defendant for time to pay. If the claimant rejects the amount offered judgment will be entered for an amount to be decided by the court at a disposal hearing.

16.006

If the defendant wishes to make a "without prejudice" offer to settle the claim he should do so by way of a Pt 36 offer (see Ch.29).

DEFENDANT'S REQUEST FOR TIME TO PAY (R.14.9)

If a defendant is unable to make immediate payment of the amount he has admitted he can request to pay it at a future date and/or by way of weekly or monthly instalments. By PD 14, para.2.2 he should complete as fully as possible the statement of means contained in the admission form or otherwise give that information in writing. If the details are incomplete the court may of its own initiative make an order requiring him to do so. Otherwise, the claimant should always draw the court's attention to any defects in the statement of means form and ask that the defendant is directed to give the information. How else can the claimant be expected to decide whether or not to accept the proposal? Do not forget that if the admission was made under r.14.4 (i.e. of the whole claim for a specified amount of money-see above) the admission form will have been received by the claimant direct from the defendant. If the claimant feels the information is inadequate he should send a copy to the court and ask it to direct that the defendant fully completes it.

16.007

Determination of rate of payment (rr.14.10 to 14.12)

There is little economic sense in any claimant commencing proceedings for a money claim unless the defendant has the means of paying any judgment (or unless someone else will have to meet the judgment, e.g. an insurer). If the claimant was prepared at the outset to accept payment by instalments then this should have figured in the pre-action negotiations. The claimant must take a

16.008

realistic view of the weekly or monthly amount the defendant is now offering to pay. It is better to accept an offer of £20 a week that the defendant will probably pay regularly, as opposed to pressing for a higher figure on which the defendant may repeatedly default.

In respect of a r.14.4 admission the claimant must file a copy of the defendant's admission and request for time to pay when filing the request. In all cases where the defendant's request for time to pay is rejected the court enters judgment for the amount admitted and for it to be paid at the time and rate of payment that the court will subsequently determine.

Who makes the determination? By r.14.11 a court officer may determine the rate of payment where the amount of the judgment outstanding is not more than £50,000 including fixed costs and (in our opinion) interest. This is a paper exercise and there is no hearing. The court officer uses certain prescribed guidelines, including by PD 14, para.5.1 taking into account the statement of means supplied by the defendant and any observations made by the claimant. Notice of the determination is then served on the parties. However, the court officer may feel unable to make a determination himself because, for example, the defendant's disclosed means are inadequate to pay the amount that he has proposed. In those circumstances he may well consult with a judge before taking any action and the judge may decide to deal with the determination instead (see r.3.2). A judge will also determine the rate of payment if the amount outstanding is more than £50,000.

Wherever possible a judge makes a determination without a hearing but if one is required the parties must be given at least seven days' notice. The judge might order, for example, that the judgment debtor should bring certain specified documents to the hearing.

Where the judge is to make a determination the matter will be transferred automatically to the defendant's home court if: (a) the only claim is for a specified sum of money; (b) it is not in a specialist list; (c) the defendant is an individual; and (d) the claim has not already been automatically transferred to any other defendant's home court. Presumably, the defendant's home court in this context is determined by the address for service he gives on the admission form.

What if either party does not like the determination? If it was made without a hearing (whether by a court officer or a judge) an aggrieved party has a short time to apply for the decision to be re-determined by a judge. The application must be made within 14 days after service of the determination on the applicant and leads to the automatic transfer of the matter to the defendant's home court if the conditions outlined above exist. If the determination was made at a hearing an aggrieved party can either bring an appeal, if he gets permission (see further Ch.44) or apply for an Order varying the rate of payment, if he can show a relevant change in circumstances since the date of the decision (PD 14, para.6.1). A further alternative is, of course, to seek the opposing party's consent to a variation in the rate of payment and, if it is forthcoming, to lodge a consent order (see Ch.34).

AMENDING OR WITHDRAWING AN ADMISSION

If a party makes a pre-action admission (see above) he may withdraw it before proceedings commence if the person to whom the admission was made agrees or, after proceedings start, if all parties consent or the court gives permission. See generally r.14.1A.

16.009

The permission of the court is required to amend or withdraw an admission made during proceedings (r.14.1(5)). In deciding whether to exercise its discretion the court will consider all the circumstances of the case, including the following matters set out in PD 14, para.7.2.

(a) the grounds upon which the applicant seeks to withdraw the admission including whether or not new evidence has come to light which was not available at the time the admission was made;
(b) the conduct of the parties, including any conduct which led the party making the admission to do so;
(c) the prejudice that may be caused to any person if the admission is withdrawn;
(d) the prejudice that may be caused to any person if the application is refused;
(e) the stage in the proceedings at which the application to withdraw is made, in particular in relation to the date or period fixed for trial;
(f) the prospects of success (if the admission is withdrawn) of the claim or part of the claim in relation to which the offer was made; and
(g) the interests of the administration of justice.

Some case examples of the factors are given below and others are to be found in the *White Book*, para.17.3.5.

In *Sollitt v Broady Ltd.*, February 23, 2000, CA (technically a pre-CPR case) the claimant suffered injuries at work. In between the date of the accident and the commencement of proceedings the claimant's employer changed its name and transferred its assets to a new company, which new company later adopted the employer's old name. The claimant issued and served proceedings upon the new company which served a defence admitting that the accident occurred and that the claimant was its employee but denied or refused to admit negligence, causation and loss and damage. Subsequently, when the mix up over company names was appreciated, the new company sought permission to withdraw its admissions and to have the claimant's employer joined in substitution. By that time the claimant's employer was a company with no assets and no insurance cover. Had the mix up been pointed out earlier the claimant might have been able to secure the ability to enforce any judgment he later obtained. The new company was not permitted to withdraw its admission, the defendant's employer was added as a co-defendant and, subsequently, judgment was entered against them both for a sum exceeding £10,000. The appeal to the Court of Appeal was dismissed.

In *Flaviis v Pauley* [2002] EWHC 2886, (Q.B., Nelson J.) the claimant suffered severe injuries because of the unroadworthy condition of a motorbike he had hired from the defendant. The front wheel of the motorbike had become detached whilst he was riding it on a motorway. At first the defendant sought to argue in correspondence that the claimant was guilty of contributory negligence. This was rejected by the claimant and, shortly thereafter, the defendants informed the claimant's solicitors that liability for the accident was no longer in dispute. The defendants later offered under Pt 36 a sum exceeding £700,000 which the claimant sought to accept six days later. In the meantime the defendants discovered that the claimant had lied about his name, his age, his career prospects and his entitlement to be in the UK. In fact he was an illegal immigrant who, for several years, had overstayed his limited permission to remain here. He had obtained a stolen Italian passport which he purported to be his. The defendants applied to re-open the issue of liability and withdraw their offer. On the basis of the new information about the claimant they wished to argue that: (i) the contract of hire was void and unenforceable as a result of fraud or illegality (including driving without a valid driving licence or valid insurance); and (ii) the accident was caused wholly or partly by the claimant's own negligence. Nelson J. considered the illegality defence arguable (at the trial the court would have to determine whether it would be an "affront to the public conscience" to grant the claimant relief) but the defence of negligence or contributory negligence to be unarguable. The defendants were permitted to withdraw their admission of liability only to the extent necessary to enable them to put forward a defence of fraud or illegality. They were not permitted to withdraw their admission of liability so as to reopen the issue of either negligence or contributory negligence.

In *Hamilton v Hertfordshire County Council* [2003] EWHC 3018, Q.B., a claim was made for injuries suffered in an accident at work. The accident occurred in May 1998. The letter before claim was sent in September 2000 and liability was admitted in January 2001 on which basis proceedings were commenced in April 2001. In February 2002 the defendants applied to withdraw their admission of liability and this application was adjourned to be heard at the same time as the trial in April 2003. The trial judge refused to allow the defendant to withdraw its admission but her decision was reversed on appeal. Keith J. held that the application was made in good faith: the admission had been made in the mistaken belief that all accounts of the accident demonstrated that it must have occurred only because of a breach of statutory duty. Having reconsidered the facts they now wished to defend the claim on the basis that the accident was caused wholly by the fault of the claimant. That defence had a realistic prospect of success. In considering the prejudice which the admission would cause to the claimant, the court was entitled to take into account the disappointment the claimant would feel. However, in this case, that did not outweigh the injustice to the defendant if they were not allowed to raise the defence.

Also see *White v Greensnad Homes* [2007] EWCA Civ 643, *The Times*, July 19, 2007, where the second defendant was granted permission to amend its defence to withdraw an admission made in both the defence and in a letter of response to the letter of claim.

STAY OF PROCEEDINGS AFTER SIX MONTHS' INACTIVITY (R.15.11)

A claim is automatically stayed six months after the end of the permitted period for filing a defence if no admission, defence or counterclaim has been filed and the claimant has neither obtained judgment in default nor made an application for summary judgment (see Ch.19). In light of r.14.2(3) dealt with above, the court will accept the late filing of an admission up until a stay has been imposed.

16.010

CHAPTER 17

Disposal Hearings

17.001 Practice Direction 26, para.12 governs the procedure which applies where a party obtains a judgment for an unspecified amount of money (other than costs). Whenever such a judgment is entered or made, the court must give directions providing for the assessment of the sum payable. A disposal hearing is the main procedure for assessment. It applies in most cases in which the judgment was obtained before allocation. However, it is not the only possibility and, strictly speaking, it is not relevant at all where the judgment is obtained after allocation. In order to explain the full range of alternatives provided by PD 26, para.12, it is convenient to start by defining "relevant orders" and then to deal separately with judgments obtained before allocation and judgments obtained after allocation.

RELEVANT ORDERS

17.002 The classic example of a judgment for an unspecified amount of money is a judgment for "damages and interest to be assessed". However, PD 26, para.12 is not limited to such orders. Paragraph 12.1 defines a relevant order as any order or judgment of the court which requires the amount of money to be paid by one party to another to be decided by the court. Thus, it includes an order for the taking of an account or the making of an inquiry as to any sum due and other similar orders. There are two types of judgment for an unspecified amount of money which PD 26, para.12 does not apply to: orders for costs which the court, in its discretion, has awarded between litigants and orders for costs payable under a contract between a solicitor and client for legal services (PD 26, para.12.1(4)).

JUDGMENT OBTAINED BEFORE ALLOCATION

17.003 Examples of judgments for an unspecified amount of money obtained before allocation include judgments in default under Pt 12 (see para.15.001), judgments on admissions under Pt 14 (see para.16.002), judgment obtained on the striking out of a statement of case under Pt 3 (see para.33.008) or on a summary judgment application under Pt 24 (see para.19.001). Whether or not such judgment was obtained at a hearing, the court will give the appropriate directions of its own motion. It may allocate the claim, fix a disposal hearing or give other directions.

Allocation

If the financial value of the claim is such that the claim would, if defended, be allocated to the small claims track, the court will normally allocate it to that track as soon as the judgment is entered. Allocating a claim to the small claims track will bring into operation the special rules restricting the recovery of costs between litigants (r.27.14; see further para.20.010). 17.004

In cases in which the financial value exceeds the small claims limit, it will not normally be appropriate to allocate it to a track. Such cases, if suitable, are usually best dealt with at a disposal hearing (see below). Allocation to a track is appropriate only if a case should proceed to a trial with all the delay and expense that that may involve. Given the judgment already obtained, a trial would be inappropriate "unless the amount payable appears to be genuinely disputed on substantial grounds" (PD 26, para.12.3), for example, a case likely to involve a prolonged investigation of facts suitable for determination by a circuit judge or High Court judge.

Disposal hearing

In most cases the court will fix a date for a disposal hearing to be conducted by a master or district judge (see further below). If the judgment leading to the disposal hearing is a default judgment, it is reasonable to presume that the disposal hearing also will not be contested. In such cases, the judgment creditor should serve his evidence on the opponent at least three days before the hearing. It is convenient also to ask the opponent to indicate whether the hearing will be opposed. If the court is satisfied that the evidence was properly served, it has power to decide the amount payable at the disposal hearing. 17.005

It is open to the judgment creditor to serve evidence in advance even if the hearing is likely to be contested. However, in such cases, the court may, instead of deciding the amount payable, give timetable directions permitting the opponent more time to respond to the evidence, to file evidence in reply and to prepare for a further hearing on a subsequent date. Indeed, if at the first hearing it appears that the dispute between the parties should be determined by way of trial, the court may allocate the claim to a track or give directions for the filing of allocation questionnaires.

At an assessment on a disposal hearing, the judgment debtor cannot challenge the question of liability since that has already been determined in the judgment already obtained. He can, however, challenge issues of quantum including, if relevant, issues of contributory negligence (*Maes Finance Ltd v A. L.*

Phillips & Co., The Times, March 25, 1999) or causation (*Lunnun v Singh* [1999] L.S.G., August 11).

Who should conduct a disposal hearing? In the case of *Sandry v Jones, The Times*, August 3, 2000, Thomas L.J. sitting in the Court of Appeal said:

> "Although the case involved an assessment of damages only, it was, at least on the papers, a substantial claim and it involved contested medical and accountancy issues. Consultant orthopaedic surgeons were called on both sides and accountants were also called. Having heard that evidence and a volume of lay evidence, the judge's judgment ran to some three and a half pages only. There may have been some compelling reason why it was necessary for this particular case to be tried by a district judge, in which case any comments that I make will be inappropriate. However, if there was no such compelling reason, I do think, as does the learned lord justice who gave leave to appeal, that it is more appropriate that a case of this complexity should be tried by a circuit judge rather than by a district judge. It appears (and it was, in so far as he was able to do so, confirmed by Mr Moody, counsel for the defendant) that trial by a district judge was a course taken with the consent of both parties. Again, it seems to me that it is incumbent on advisers to parties also to give careful consideration to the appropriate level of judicial expertise necessary to try a particular case."

The costs of a disposal hearing are in the discretion of the court. The judgment creditor will usually be entitled to the costs, but the court will take into account all the circumstances including each parties' conduct and may allow him only part of his costs or may make some other order (see generally Ch.38). If the hearing lasted less than one day, the court will make a summary assessment of the costs unless there is good reason not to do so (see further para.13.010). For this purpose, each party intending to apply for costs should file and serve a statement of those costs not less than 24 hours before the date fixed for the hearing. If the court does not summarily assess the costs, it will leave the costs to be determined by detailed assessment (i.e. by a costs officer, see para.38.015) and then decide whether to exercise the power in r.44.3(8) to order the paying party to pay a sum on account of those costs.

Other directions

17.006 If a case appears suitable for allocation but the court does not have sufficient information upon which to make that allocation, the directions may be for the filing of allocation questionnaires or for the conduct of an allocation hearing. A further possibility is an order that the claim be stayed while the parties try to settle the case by alternative dispute resolution or other means.

JUDGMENT OBTAINED AFTER ALLOCATION

Examples of judgments for an unspecified amount of money obtained after allocation include judgments given on determination of a preliminary issue or on a split trial as to liability or indeed judgments obtained at the trial itself. In all such cases the court should, of its own motion, give directions appropriate for determining the amount payable. It may be appropriate to re-allocate the claim to a different case management track. It may be appropriate to order that the claim be stayed while the parties try to settle the case by alternative dispute resolution or other means. In most cases, the most appropriate order will be to fix a date for a further hearing. In this instance, directions may; (i) specify the level or type of judge before whom the further hearing will take place; (ii) specify the nature and purpose of that hearing; and (iii) give any timetable directions appropriate as to the filing and serving of evidence for that hearing. Save, perhaps, where the judgment was obtained at trial, it may also be necessary to give directions as to disclosure and expert evidence. All decisions as to the amount payable may be referred to a master or district judge irrespective of the financial value of the claim and irrespective of the track to which the claim has been allocated (PD 26, para.12.10).

17.007

If the purpose of the hearing just described is to decide the amount payable in accordance with the order, the difference between this hearing and disposal hearing is a difference in name only. At such a hearing, the judgment debtor could not challenge the question of liability, but could challenge issues of quantum including issues of contributory negligence and causation, unless rulings on these issues had already been made (see the case law on these topics cited above in relation to disposal hearings).

CHAPTER 18

Counterclaims and Additional Claims (Pt 20)

18.001 This Chapter will focus on acting for a defendant. Apart from serving a defence, what else can he do? You should always ask the following questions.

(a) Is there a claim against the claimant and/or anyone else?
(b) Is any co-defendant more or less liable?
(c) Is any third party responsible for the claimant's losses?

An additional matter, dealt with in Ch.26, concerns the possibility of seeking security for costs against the claimant.

COUNTERCLAIM BY A DEFENDANT AGAINST A CLAIMANT (R.20.4)

18.002 The defendant can add causes of action to the proceedings that have been commenced by the claimant by raising a counterclaim against the claimant. This can be for any relief or remedy, in respect of any matter, whenever and however it arose. Any counterclaim does not have to be limited to a money claim nor need it be related to the claimant's action.

Example

C sues D for the price of goods delivered. D defends stating that the goods were defective and counterclaims for damages. In addition, D might counterclaim for money C owes him under an entirely separate contract. He could even counterclaim for personal injuries if say C's employee had negligently run over his foot when delivering the goods!

For most purposes a claim and a counterclaim are treated as two independent actions. Indeed they may well be tried separately (see Ch.7 and Ch.33). You might also cross-refer to: Ch.12 (drafting statements of case); Ch.15 (default judgment); Ch.19 (summary judgment) and Ch.29 (Pt 36 offers). However, as to costs where both the claim and counterclaim succeed, see para.18.011, below and para.38.008)

There is also some difference in respect of periods of limitation (see generally Ch.5). However, let us briefly consider here the position if the defendant fails to make a counterclaim until several years after the claimant's action has begun and when the limitation period has already expired. In *JFS (UK) Ltd v Dw'r Cymru Cyf* [1999] 1 W.L.R. 231 the claimants, C, brought an action against the defendant, D, claiming for work not paid for, loss of profit and interest arising out of a contract that had been concluded in 1991. C issued proceedings in 1996 within the limitation period. D served a defence but made no counterclaim. C amended its claim in January 1998 and D applied for permission to amend its defence and add a counterclaim after the limitation period had expired. The proposed counterclaim alleged that C had made substantial and material misrepresentations which had induced D to enter into the contract. The judge granted D permission. C appealed and the main issues for the court were whether D had "previously made any claim in the action" within the meaning of the Limitation Act 1980, s.35(3), so that the court was precluded from permitting D to make a claim against C in respect of a cause that was now statute barred. Also, whether the court had power to allow the amendment under what is now r.17.4. The Court of Appeal dismissed the appeal. The court held that a "claim" in s.35(3) had to be construed as a "claim for relief". Whilst the defendant's positive averments in his defence might loosely be said to be making a claim that the debt was not due because the claimant had extended the time limit for payment, that was not a claim in the legal sense. The court therefore had a discretion in the matter. The judge had not erred in exercising his discretion on the facts to allow the amended defence and the making of the counterclaim.

How does a defendant make a counterclaim? It is, of course, a statement of case and must be prepared as such (see Ch.12). If the claim has been issued in the county court you must remember to include a statement of value (see Ch.9). You should prepare particulars of the counterclaim at same time as drafting the defence. The defendant will not need the court's permission to bring the counterclaim provided it is filed with the defence. A defendant needs to carefully consider any possible counterclaim that he might realistically make at the same time as he defends the action. If he only discovers the existence of a counterclaim after filing his defence or then decides to make one, he will incur the additional expense of a court application for its permission to proceed (see below). In order to avoid default judgment, the claimant must file a defence to the counterclaim (see Ch.15).

COUNTERCLAIM BY A DEFENDANT AGAINST SOMEONE OTHER THAN A CLAIMANT (R.20.5)

Pre-CPR a defendant could add a defendant to his counterclaim, in addition to the claimant, provided the relief or remedies sought related to, or were connected with, the claimant's claim. By r.20.5(1) if the defendant wishes to counterclaim against a person other than a claimant he must apply to the court for an order that that person is added as a defendant to the counterclaim. The application can

18.003

be made without notice to any other party unless the court directs otherwise. Whilst there is no prescribed test, it is our view that the "old" one is likely to prevail as it ensures that the case between claimant and defendant is expeditiously and fairly dealt with in accordance with the overriding objective (r.1.2(d): see para.1.006).

Example

D employed H as a management contractor for a very substantial project. It fell well behind and the whole programme fell into disarray. A commercial settlement was reached whereby D paid £83.9 million to H, and H agreed to complete by a new date and to meet all the costs of doing so. The sum was not apportioned in any way as to the works it covered or the contractors involved. C and Y had been part of D's professional advisory team for the project. C sued D for fees due, and D counterclaimed against C and Y in respect of the delays (see *P&O Developments Ltd v Guy's and St Thomas NHS Trust* (1999) 89 B.L.R. 3).

There is no particular provision in the rules for a defendant who wishes to add a "co-counterclaimant", i.e. a person with whom he would counterclaim against the claimant. In an appropriate case the defendant could apply under r.19 for the court to exercise its power to add a party (see para.7.013).

Example

X employed C to ship goods to London. D, who was X's selling agent, received the goods by depositing the freight charge with the warehouseman. C sought a declaration against D that the freight charge belonged to C. D wanted to rely on the contract between X and C as the basis of his defence and to counterclaim for short delivery and damage to the cargo. The court ordered that X should be added as a party in order to raise these claims. This was appropriate because X was the person ultimately responsible to pay the freight charge that C was claiming (see *Montgomery v Foy* [1895] 2 Q.B. 321).

In either case if the court allow the application it will give directions as to the management of the case (see para.18.010, below).

CO-DEFENDANT'S CONTRIBUTION AND INDEMNITY CLAIMS AGAINST EACH OTHER (R.20.6)

18.004   A defendant who has filed an acknowledgment of service or a defence may make an additional claim for contribution or indemnity against another defendant. A claim for contribution relies on the right to recover all or part of the amount that the defendant is found liable to pay. An indemnity is the right to recover the whole amount.

Where two or more defendants are held liable for the same damage (whether their liability is in tort, contract, breach of trust or otherwise) the trial court has power under the Civil Liability (Contribution) Act 1978 to apportion the liability between them. Because of this power a defendant who wishes to claim a contribution is not generally obliged to serve a formal notice on his co-defendants. However, he must do so if the right to the contribution is regulated by a contract between the defendants (see s.7(3) of the 1978 Act) or, of course, if he wishes to claim for a full indemnity. In addition, the defendant should consider the tactical step of making a Pt 36 offer to his fellow co-defendants on the question of the apportionment of liability (see Ch.29).

What sort of notice is required? Currently there is no prescribed form (but see Q.B.D. PF 22). The claim is made by filing a notice that contains a statement of the nature and grounds of the claim. As the defendant is making an additional claim the notice must be prepared as a statement of case (see Ch.12) and so it must be verified by a statement of truth. The notice must be filed and the defendant should arrange for service of it (see Ch.8). Permission is not required to file and serve the notice provided those steps are taken at the same time that defendant's defence is filed. What if the claim for contribution or indemnity is against a defendant added to the claim later? In those circumstances the notice must be filed and served within 28 days after that new defendant files his defence. The co-defendant may respond in the usual way, for example, acknowledgment, admission or defence. (He can also file and serve his own notice.) However, whilst the defendant cannot obtain default judgment he may be able to enter judgment on any admission that is made. The case will, of course, already have been allocated to a track but on the filing of a defence by a co-defendant the court will arrange a hearing to ensure that suitable directions are given for the management of the whole proceedings.

Example

D1 was a cleaning company. It had a contract to clean D2's premises. A storeroom was set aside by D2 for D1 to keep its cleaning materials and equipment. C was an employee of D1. She was injured in August 1998 when a sink in the storeroom, into which she had been emptying a carpet cleaner, became detached from the wall causing her to fall. D1 had a supervisor on site to ensure that the equipment was properly maintained. In addition D1 employed a services engineer to visit the premises every six months. His evidence was that the sink had always been loose but he had not reported that fact to a representative of D2. The recorder found that D2 used the storeroom to some extent and that both defendants owed duties under the Occupier's Liability Act. He also found that D1's duty to its employees was owed even when they worked at a third party's premises. The recorder asked who had been the principal occupier and who therefore had the greater responsibility for the safety of the sink. He found that: (1) D2 owned the sink; (2) responsibility for maintaining it had not passed to D1; (3) D2 maintained control of the storeroom as it held the key; and (4) D2's employees used the storeroom. Upon those findings of fact he concluded that a special onus of responsibility was cast on D2 and he apportioned liability 75 per cent to D2 and 25 per cent to D1.

D2 appealed. The Court of Appeal held that the recorder did not seem to have found that D2's responsible officers had been aware of the defect given his finding that, had they known, the sink would have been promptly repaired.

Although he had started by considering the occupation of the storeroom, he seemed later to have equated occupation with ownership. This was inappropriate. The first and third factors he had relied on were misconceived. To retain the responsibility to maintain did not necessarily involve a responsibility for a defect in equipment used for activities carried on at the premises. The overwhelming responsibility fell on D1 as C's employer and as the party carrying on the operations in the storeroom. In those circumstances the court adjudged D2's contribution at 25 per cent and D1's at 75 per cent. See *Andrew v Initial Cleaning Services Ltd and McDougalls Catering Foods Ltd*, The Times, August 18, 1999.

Finally, it should be noted that if the defendant wishes to make a claim against a co-defendant that is neither for a contribution nor an indemnity, he must issue an additional claim form (see below).

CLAIMS BY A DEFENDANT AGAINST A NON-PARTY

18.005   What if the defendant wishes to make a claim against someone who is not already a party to the proceedings? To do so he must issue an additional claim form. He can do this without the court's permission provided it is issued before or at the same time as he files his defence. If permission is needed, see below. Particulars of the additional claim must be contained in or served with the claim form. The particulars cannot be served later. The claim form and particulars should be prepared as statements of case in the usual way (see Ch.12) and so must be verified by a statement of truth. The additional claim is issued and served as if the claim had commenced by way of a Pt 7 claim form. Likewise the third party may respond in the usual way, for example, acknowledgment, admission, defence and counterclaim. The procedural steps are described below.

Why should the defendant bring this type of additional claim as an alternative to issuing separate proceedings? Assume D is a firm of book manufacturers. Last year it sold 500,000 books to C and C has issued a claim form against D alleging breach of contract on the basis that the books are defective due to poor binding. D refutes this allegation. The senior partner has seen where the books were stored and he considers the adverse conditions there caused the bindings to break. However, D accepts that there may also have been some problem with the glue used to bind the books. D wishes to defend the action, counterclaim against C for non-payment and wonders if a claim should also be made against T. T was D's supplier of the glue which was used in the manufacturing process that might have been solely or partly to blame for any defect in the binding. If D issues a claim form against T for breach of contract the issue will be whether or not the glue supplied to bind the books was defective. But the issue between C and D is very similar, i.e. whether or not the binding was defective and the cause of it (glue or otherwise). There will be a considerable amount of duplication of work in each action, namely as to witness statements, experts and preparation for trial. Hence, one reason for third party proceedings is to save costs. Moreover, it is possible that C might win his action, the trial judge determining that the books were indeed defective due to poor binding. He might even conclude the main or only problem with the binding was the glue. But if there is a separate trial between D and T a different judge might decide that the glue was satisfactory. Therefore, the second reason for third party proceedings is to ensure that the claims are decided uniformly.

Examples

(1) C sued D, a solicitor, alleging professional misconduct. D notified T, his insurers, but they said that C's claim was not covered by the terms of their policy. D issued an additional claim against T seeking an indemnity in respect of any damages awarded to C. See *Walker & Knight v Donne, The Times*, November 9, 1976.

(2) C engaged D, a firm of chartered surveyors, as advisers and development consultant for a new shopping centre. T was the site developer. T agreed with C to share the development costs. Part of D's duties was to check and authorise payment of T's claims for C's share of the development costs. Between December 1989 and June 1992 T submitted a number of claims to C, including in each a figure for notional interest. D recommended that C pay those sums which it did. C sued D alleging that it had negligently and in breach of contract failed to advise C that notional interest was not in fact payable. C claimed damages equal to the amount of interest it had paid T. D issued an additional claim against T claiming contribution pursuant to s.1 of the 1978 Act on the basis that T was liable in respect of the damage C had allegedly suffered. D also argued that s.6 of the Act provided that the entitlement to compensation operated "whatever the legal basis of his liability, whether tort, breach of contract, breach of trust or otherwise". The judge struck out D's claim.

The Court of Appeal, in allowing the appeal, held that the Act was broadly formulated to provide for contribution in circumstances spanning a variety of causes of action, forms of damage and remedies. The wide language of s.6 made it clear that liability to contribute was not dependent on any breach of duty or default. Both claims for restitution and for damages could be a claim for compensation in respect of damage under ss.1 and 6 of the Act. Therefore, a restitutory claim by C against T for repayment of the notional interest, whether because it was paid under a mistake of fact or for no consideration, was a claim in respect of the same "damage" alleged by C against D so as to enable D to claim a contribution or indemnity against T under s.1 of the Act. Note that C had sued T for recovery of the interest but T was in financial difficulties and the claim was settled by C abandoning it and T giving up most of its interest in the development (*Friends Provident Life Office v Hillier Parker May and Rowden* [1996] 2 W.L.R. 123). Also see *Hurstwood Developments Ltd v Motor & General & Aldersley & Co. Insurance Services Ltd* (2002) P.N.L.R. 10.

The title to the action should be:

C   Claimant
D   Defendant
T   Third Party

You should think of the action between the claimant and the defendant as the "main claim" and that between the defendant and the third party as the "consequential claim". As we have seen, in the "consequential claim" the defendant is effectively saying to the third party, "if the claimant proves this against me I will then claim the following against you". The usual claims made are for contribution or an indemnity. However, the defendant may seek other remedies against the third party and/or ask the court to determine questions or issues that arise out of the main claim but which also concern the sub action. As part of its case management powers the court will have to decide if it is convenient to allow the third party claim to be made (where its permission is necessary) or to continue. This topic is dealt with below.

What if the main claim is compromised? It is sensible for the defendant to try and settle both the main claim and the consequential claim at the same time but this is not always possible. The third party proceedings will continue to trial without the benefit of any findings of fact in the main claim. Moreover, the defendant may lose at that trial or otherwise may find that it is held that he overpaid the claimant. In *J. Sainsbury Plc v Broadway Malyan* [1999] P.N.L.R. 286 a fire took place at one of C's stores. D had been the architects retained by C to design and supervise the construction of the store. This included a fire compartment wall. T were the consulting engineers retained by C to advise on structural questions. A girder in the fire compartment wall failed during the fire and C's claim against D was that the store could have been substantially saved if the girder had not failed. D joined in T as a third party. D settled the dispute with C at £7,125,000. Judge Humphrey Lloyd Q.C. held that D's claim against T failed because it had not been part of T's responsibility to C to advise on the fire protection required for the girder. The judge considered what the position would have been if he was wrong about liability and concluded that in those circumstances not only would T have only a small contribution, but that it was open to T to challenge the settlement figure. Moreover, T had done that successfully, thereby reducing the damages which would have been awarded if liability had been established by D.

CLAIMS BY A THIRD PARTY AGAINST A FOURTH PARTY, ETC.

18.006 The third party can raise a counterclaim against the defendant and/or bring in a fourth party. The fourth and subsequent parties can do the same.

Example

V, the hirer of a car under a hire purchase agreement with B Ltd, sold it to F, a motor dealer before she had paid all the instalments due or exercised the option to purchase. F resold the car to T and on the same day T sold it on to D. Shortly afterwards C bought the car from D only to get a letter a few months later from B Ltd informing him that the car was their property under the HP agreement with V. C wrote to D asking for the return of the purchase price. In the meantime V paid to B Ltd the outstanding instalments and exercised her option to purchase the car. C sued D to recover his purchase money alleging a total failure of consideration. D issued an additional claim against T and there were similar fourth and fifth party proceedings issued by T against F and F against V respectively. The substance of each of the claims against the third, fourth and fifth parties was for damages for breach of the implied condition that the seller had a right to sell. See *Butterworth v Kingsway Motors; Hayton, Kennedy and Rudolph* [1954] 1 W.L.R. 1286. The title in the case would have been:

C   Claimant
D   Defendant
T   Third Party
F   Fourth Party
V   Fifth Party

The statements of case in an action like this soon become unintelligible if the parties are referred to by their respective titles. Hence, in these circumstances PD 20, paras 7.4, 7.10 and 7.11 contain some sensible advice on how to refer to parties and the use of suitable abbreviations.

APPLYING FOR PERMISSION TO ISSUE AN ADDITIONAL CLAIM

To summarise, the court's permission is needed if the defendant wishes to: 18.007

(a) counterclaim against the claimant after filing the defence;
(b) claim against a co-defendant for any remedy other than contribution and/or an indemnity;
(c) claim against a third party after filing the defence in the main action.

Permission is also needed for any other additional claim.

Rule 20.9(2) sets out some of the factors that the court may take into account when it considers an application to issue an additional claim:

(1) The connection between the additional claim and the claim made by the claimant against the defendant.

Examples

In a road accident case, D sued C for damages for personal injury. D denied the claim but alleged that the accident may have been caused by the car being unroadworthy. D therefore issued an additional claim against T, the dealer from whom D had recently purchased the car. D claimed damages against T for breach of the implied term of satisfactory quality. As D's claim arose out of the same facts as the claimant's, i.e. the unroadworthiness only became apparent when the accident happened, the court may decide that there is a sufficient connection between the two matters such that it is just and convenient to deal with them both at the same time. As T may also be a tortfeasor, C could ask the court under r.19 to join T as a co-defendant (see para.7.013). If T does become a co-defendant, D could seek a contribution or indemnity (see generally *Andrews v Hopkinson* [1957] 1 Q.B. 229).

In the case of *Sterling Credit Ltd v Rahman* [2001] 1 W.L.R. 496 C had a possession order against D's property and was taking enforcement proceedings. D required the permission of the court to make a counterclaim seeking to re-open the loan transaction with C under s.139 of the Consumer Credit Act 1974 (as it was then). The Court of Appeal granted permission. Mummery L.J. said:

> "In deciding whether that claim should be dealt with in separate proceedings the court may have regard to the matters specified in CPR 20.9 These provisions are subject to the overriding objective in CPR Part 1. In my judgment, this is a case in which it is appropriate to grant permission to make a counterclaim rather than to direct that the issue of the section 139 application be made by separate action. There is a connection between the claim for the enforcement of the charge taken to secure the money advanced under the credit bargain in respect of which Mr Rahman seeks relief. The credit bargain, which is the subject matter of the proposed counterclaim, is also part of the subject matter of the mortgagees' claim for enforcement of their security rights in order to secure payment of the sums due under that agreement. The counterclaim will be more effective than a separate action in enabling the court to deal with the case justly in the interests of both parties, having regard to saving expense and ensuring expeditious and fair dealing with the case."

(2) Whether the additional claimant is seeking substantially the same remedy which some other party is claiming from him.

Example

A hospital, C settled its claim for damages for delay and repayment of loss and expense in arbitration proceedings against a contractor, T. C then sued 16 defendants. The eighth defendant, WGI instituted additional proceedings against T alleging that it was bound to contribute to any damages awarded against WGI in favour of C. Since the hospital had indemnified T as part of the compromise in the arbitration, the result of this would be a reduction in any damages awarded to C. The additional claim was brought under ss.1 and 6 of the 1978 Act on the alleged grounds that T was liable to C in respect of the same damage as was being claimed against WGI. T argued that it was not the same damage and requested that the additional proceedings be struck out. The House of Lords held that C's claim against WGI was based on WGI's breach of duty in that its conduct had weakened the case for the hospital in the arbitration, making it less able to negotiate a proper compromise. In those circumstances the main claim and additional claim were not in respect of the same damage and the additional proceedings were struck out (see *Royal Brompton Hospital National Health Trust v Hammond and Taylor Woodrow Construction Holdings Ltd* [2002] 2 All E.R. 801.)

(3) Whether the additional claimant wants the court to decide any question connected with the subject matter of the proceedings:

(i) not only between existing parties but also between existing parties and a person not already a party;

Example

C sues D, a builder, for an injunction to restrain him from building on certain land. When D tells T, his customer about C's claim, T says that if D stops building he will bring a claim for breach of contract. The purpose of D's additional claim against T will not be to seek any remedy against him but to ensure that T is bound by the findings of fact made in C's claim against him.

(ii) against an existing party not only in a capacity in which he is already a party but also in some further capacity.

Rimer J. in *Re a Debtor (No.87 of 1999), The Times,* February 14, 2000 said:

> "There is nothing in Part 20 of the Civil Procedure Rules 1998 which indicates that a claimant suing personally cannot be made the object of a counterclaim against him in some different capacity, although I of course accept that the provisions of Part 20.9 indicate that that particular feature of a counterclaim will be a factor to which the court should have regard in considering whether to dismiss the counterclaim or to require it to be dealt with separately from the main claim. It would, however, in my view, be surprising if the CPR were so rigid as to place a complete bar on such counterclaims, particularly when there was not such rigidity under the former practice: see In re: Richardson, Richardson v Nicholson [1933] W.N., 90. It appears to me that it may well in many cases be convenient and just to permit such a counterclaim to be raised in the same proceedings as the claim; and I cannot see that there ought to be any presumption that there is anything intrinsically impossible or inconvenient about permitting both such claims to proceed and to be tried together. At the end of the proceedings the court will of course have every opportunity to give such judgment as is just having regard to the different nature of the two claims. It will not be compelled, for example, to set the claim and counterclaim off against each other and merely give judgment to one party for the balance. In many cases that might produce a great injustice. In other cases it might perhaps be a just order to make."

Note that these factors are also taken into account by the court when it decides whether or not to dismiss an additional claim (see below) or order separate trials (see Ch.33).

If permission is needed, the application must be supported by evidence that states:

(a) The stage which the action has reached. If possible, the applicant should set out a timetable of the action to date.
(b) The nature of the additional claim or details of the question or issue which needs to be decided. We recommend that a draft of the proposed additional claim is exhibited to the evidence.
(c) A summary of the facts on which the additional claim is based.
(d) The name and address of the proposed additional party.

If delay has contributed to the need for the application, this should also be explained by the applicant. However, in many cases a late application will be refused: see *Powell v Pallisters of Hereford Ltd* (2002) L.T.L., July 1.

SERVICE OF AN ADDITIONAL CLAIM FORM (RR.20.8 AND 20.12)

18.008 If a defendant has issued an additional claim form without needing the court's permission he must arrange for it to be served within 14 days of filing his defence. He can either ask the court to serve it or do this himself (see Ch.8). Where the court gives permission to make the additional claim it also makes directions as to its service.

What is served with an additional claim form? The additional party receives a revised form of the response pack. However, in addition the party effecting service must include a copy of every statement of case which has already been served in the proceedings and any other documents as the court may direct. Note that a copy of the additional claim form must also be served on existing parties.

CONSEQUENCES OF A NON-PARTY FAILING TO ACKNOWLEDGE AND/OR DEFEND (R.20.11)

18.009 What if the additional party fails to acknowledge and/or defend? He will be deemed to admit the additional claim and will be bound by the outcome of the proceedings in so far as such are relevant. . But what if a main claim is lost due to the defendant's own default? Can that defendant request judgment in default of the additional party responding to the additional proceedings? Yes, provided he has either satisfied the default judgment given against him or he wishes to obtain judgment for any remedy other than a contribution or indemnity.

CASE MANAGEMENT OF ADDITIONAL CLAIMS

Where a defence to the additional claim is filed the court arranges a hearing to consider making directions for the future conduct of the proceedings. PD 20, para.5.3 provides that at the hearing the court may: **18.010**

(1) Treat it as a summary judgment hearing (see Ch.19). For example, the court may decide that a third party has no real prospect of successfully defending that additional claim.
(2) Dismiss the additional proceedings. For example, the claim may not reveal any cause of action or, applying the overriding objective, the court may decide that the claim has been commenced unfairly late for tactical reasons (see *Ernst & Young (a firm) v Butte Mining Plc (No.2)* [1997] 2 All E.R. 470 which concerned a defendant's counterclaim against a claimant).
(3) Give directions about the way any claim, question or issue set out in, or arising from, the additional claim should be dealt with. For example, the court may add or substitute a third party as a defendant or permit a third party to defend the claimant's action. The court may order disclosure (see Ch.30) of certain specified classes of documents between the claimant and the third party. As to judicial case management generally, see Ch.33.
(4) Give directions as to the role, if any, the additional party will take at the trial of the main claim and the extent to which he will be bound by any judgment. The usual direction is for a third party to be allowed to appear at the trial of the main action, to take such part as the trial judge directs and to be bound by the result. In many cases a trial timetable is drawn up in advance of the hearing and so the third party will be significantly involved in the pre-trial steps (see Ch.37).

ADDITIONAL CLAIMS AND COSTS

The general rule is that the loser should pay the winner's costs. Additional proceedings demand close attention. For example, a claim and a counterclaim may both "succeed". In third party proceedings, the defendant to the main claim is in the unenviable position of having run up costs in both defending the main claim and making his own third party consequential claim. If the main claim fails, the claimant will normally be ordered to pay the defendant's costs and the defendant ordered to pay the third party's costs. However, so long as the defendant acted reasonably in joining in the third party, the amount of costs that the defendant has to pay the third party can normally be included in the defendant's own claim for costs against the claimant. But what if the main claim succeeds and thereby the third party claim fails? What if a counterclaim by the defendant also succeeds? For a detailed discussion see para.38.008. **18.011**

CHAPTER 19

Summary Judgment

SCOPE AND EFFECT OF CPR, PT 24

19.001 CPR, Pt 24 allows the court to enter judgment early, i.e. granting or dismissing claims in whole or in part, without the delay and expense of a trial. Summary judgment is appropriate where the claim or defence attacked has no real prospect of success and there is no other compelling reason for a trial. Pt 24 enables the court to carry out its duty of active case management (r.1.4(1)) which includes "(b) Identifying the issues at an early stage [and] (c) deciding promptly which issues need further investigation and trial and accordingly disposing summarily of the others" (r.1.4(2)). With very few exceptions (listed below) Pt 24 covers all cases whichever track they are on and whomsoever is the applicant, whether claimant, defendant, counterclaimant or parties to an additional claim.

The summary judgment may dispose of a whole claim, i.e. granting the remedies sought therein, or dismissing the claim as the case may be. Alternatively, the summary judgment may dispose of only part of a claim, i.e. dealing with only one or some of several causes of action raised in a claim, or dealing with only one or some of the defences raised therein. The summary judgment may dispose merely of one or some discrete issues of fact or law. These may be any issues "on which the claim in whole or part depends" (PD 24, para.1.2(2)). Although, ordinarily, these will be preliminary issues, they need not be. In exceptional cases, the early decision on, for example, some aspects of the issue of quantum might facilitate settlement between the parties. Early decision of such issues may therefore help "the parties to settle the whole or part of the case" (r.1.4(2)(f)) and thereby further the overriding objective (see para.1.006).

If the issue raised in a case is a pure point of construction of a document, then that can be determined on a summary application. There is normally no need for a full trial (or a trial of a preliminary issue) because the case is not affected by evidence.

> "It seems to me that if at the end of the argument the court comes to a clear view as to the correct construction, the court has jurisdiction to grant summary judgment under CPR 24.2 on the basis that a trial would have no realistic prospect of causing it to reach a different judgment" (*per* Toulson

L.J. in *BBC Worldwide Ltd v Bee Load Ltd* [2007] EWHC 134, *The Times*, March 15, 2007).

So what sort of case has no real prospect of success?

> "The words 'no real prospect of being successful or succeeding' do not need any amplification, they speak for themselves. The word 'real' distinguishes fanciful prospects of success and directs the court to the need to see whether there is a 'realistic' as opposed to a 'fanciful' prospect of success. It is important that a judge in appropriate cases should make use of the powers contained in Pt 24. In doing so he or she gives effect to the overriding objectives contained in Pt 1. It saves expense; it achieves expedition; it avoids the court's resources being used up on cases where this serves no purpose, and I would add, generally, that it is in the interests of justice. If a claimant has a case which is bound to fail, then it is in the claimant's interests to know as soon as possible that that is the position. Likewise, if a claim is bound to succeed, a claimant should know that as soon as possible". (Lord Woolf M.R. in *Swain v Hillman* [2001] 1 All E.R. 91.

Exceptions to Pt 24

19.002 The main exceptions to Pt 24 are set out in r.24.3(2). The court cannot give summary judgment against a defendant in certain types of proceedings for possession of residential premises and proceedings for an admiralty claim in rem. Note that there is no restriction on giving summary judgment against a claimant in these exceptional types of case.

Whilst an application for summary judgment can be made against the Crown, such cannot occur until after expiry of the period for filing a defence.

Summary judgment in cases with a right to jury trial

19.003 Can summary judgment be granted where there is a right to jury trial, for example, claims for libel, slander, malicious prosecution and false imprisonment by virtue of SCA 1981, s.69 and CCA 1984, s.66? In *Safeway Stores Plc v Tate* [2001] 2 W.L.R. 1377, the Court of Appeal held that the right to trial by jury, and in particular the function of the jury to determine certain issues, was not a matter of mere procedure. It was an important and substantive legal right. Therefore it was beyond the power of the Civil Procedure Rules Committee to abolish or limit such by its general powers to reform the rules of practice and procedure. Although the right might be amended by statute, this could not be done by subordinate legislation. Since neither the Civil Procedure Act 1997 nor CPR r.24.2 made express reference to defamation actions, the general provision in the rule did not override the specific statutory provisions. Note however that in *Alexander v Arts Council of Wales* [2001] 1 W.L.R. 1840 the Court of Appeal held that it is open to a judge, in a defamation action, to discharge the jury and grant summary judgment where there is no evidence upon which a reasonable jury, properly directed, could find for the applicant.

The Court of Appeal in the Safeway case was concerned with a libel claim. The court pointed to the Defamation Act 1996 which came into force on February 28, 2000. That Act specifically provides for the summary disposal of libel actions without a jury subject to specific limitations on the amount of damages which can be recovered (currently £10,000). Those provisions are now embodied in CPR Pt 53.

Overlap with r.3.4

19.004 Applications under Pt 24 may dispose of cases where the claim or defence attacked has no real prospect of success. Many cases falling within Pt 24 also fall within r.3.4, the court's power to strike out statements of case which disclose no reasonable grounds for bringing or defending the claim, or which are an abuse of the court's process or otherwise likely to obstruct the just disposal of the proceedings. In many cases, applications under Pt 24 will be combined with applications under r.3.4. There are, of course, substantial differences between the two provisions. In particular, orders under r.3.4 focus upon statements of case or part thereof and so are sometimes not apt to dispose of preliminary issues only. Also, there are procedural requirements under Pt 24 which do not apply to r.3.4.

Summary judgment not summary trial

19.005 Although the civil courts may grant summary judgment they should not conduct a summary trial. There are regular statements to the effect that Pt 24 does not entitle the court to embark upon a "mini-trial" or to resolve issues which ought to be tried properly by way of an "informal trial" on an interim application.

> "Useful though the power is under Pt 24, it is important that it is kept to its proper role. It is not meant to dispense with the need for a trial where there are issues which should be investigated at the trial . . . the proper disposal of an issue under Pt 24 does not involve the judge conducting a mini-trial, that is not the object of the provision; it is to enable cases, where there is no real prospect of success either way, to be disposed of summarily".
> (Lord Woolf M.R. in *Swain v Hillman* [2001] 1 All E.R. 91).

At a trial the criterion to be applied by the court is probability: victory goes to the party whose case is the more probable (taking into account the burden of proof). This is not true of a summary judgment application.

"The criterion which the judge has to apply under CPR Pt 24 is not one of probability; it is absence of reality." (Lord Hobhouse of Woodborough in *Three Rivers District Council v Bank of England (No.3)* [2001] 2 All E.R. 513. "It may be clear as a matter of law at the outset that even if a party were to succeed in proving all the facts that he offers to prove he will not be entitled to the remedy that he seeks. In that event a trial of the facts would be a waste of time and money, and it is proper that the action should be taken out of court as soon as possible. In other cases it may be possible to say with confidence before trial that the factual basis for the claim is fanciful because it is entirely without substance. It may be clear beyond question that the statement of facts is contradicted by all the documents or other material on which it is based. The simpler the case the easier it is likely to be take that view and resort to what is properly called summary judgment. But more complex cases are unlikely to be capable of being resolved in that way without conducting a mini-trial on the documents without [disclosure] and without oral evidence" (*per* Lord Hope of Craighead in the *Three Rivers District Council* case).

In *The Bolton Pharmaceutical Co. 100 Ltd v Doncaster Pharmaceticals Group Ltd* [2006] EWCA Civ 661, (2006) L.T.L. May 26, Mummery L.J. observed that:

"Everyone would agree that the summary disposal of rubbishy defences is in the interests of justice. The court has to be alert to the defendant, who seeks to avoid summary judgment by making a case look more complicated or difficult than it really is. The court also has to guard against the cocky claimant, who, having decided to go for summary judgment, confidently presents the factual and legal issues as simpler and easier than they really are and urges the court to be "efficient" ie produce a rapid result in the claimant's favour. In handling all applications for summary judgment the court's duty is to keep considerations of procedural justice in proper perspective. Appropriate procedures must be used for the disposal of cases. Otherwise there is a serious risk of injustice." Summary judgment at trial

In very exceptional cases the court may grant summary judgment at the trial (e.g. *Evans v James* [1999] EWCA Civ 1759, judgment for the claimant; and *Alexander v Arts Council of Wales* [2001] 1 W.L.R. 1840, judgment for the defendant). In practice claimants rarely seek summary judgment at this stage: it is easier for them to establish the trial criterion (probability) rather than the summary judgment criterion (opponent's case is unreal). An application for summary dismissal by a defendant may well be refused because the court treats the fact that the case has reached trial as a compelling reason why there ought to be a trial (see below). However, it may well be that an earlier summary judgment application is adjourned for case management reasons until trial: see, for example, *Monsanto Technology LLC v Cargill International SA* [2006] EWHC 2864, (2006) L.T.L., November 13.

There is an alternative application which the defendant can make: a submission of no case to answer (as to which see para.37.005, below). Almost invariably he will not be allowed to develop that submission unless he elects not to call evidence if it fails. If he does so elect the trial court will determine the question according to the trial criterion and not the summary judgment criterion (see *Benham Ltd v Kythira Investments Ltd* [2003] EWCA Civ 1794 discussed at para.37.007).

THE "NO REAL PROSPECTS" TEST

19.006   We have already outlined the principles underlying this test when describing the law in relation to certain applications to set aside default judgments (see Ch.15 which also contains lengthy statements of authority taken from *Three Rivers District Council v Bank of England (No.3)* [2001] 2 All E.R. 513, a summary judgment case, and *E D & F Man Liquid Products Ltd v Patel* [2003] EWCA Civ 472, a set aside case). The test is expressed here in the negative, "no real prospect", because the burden of demonstrating that falls upon the applicant, the person attacking the claim or defence in question. In set aside applications the applicant is always the defendant who has to show the strength of his own case, not the weakness of his opponent's.

Because a summary judgment application is not a trial, or even a mini-trial, it is not necessary to consider at this stage which party has the stronger case. The only question for the court to consider is whether the case attacked has some real prospects of success (or whether, for some other compelling reason, there ought to be a trial, see further below). The following cases make this distinction clear.

In *Swain v Hillman* [2001] 1 All E.R. 91 a scaffolding plank, left upright on a building site, fell upon the claimant causing him severe injuries. According to his statement of case and supporting witness statements the plank had been so placed some three days prior to him sustaining his injury. He alleged that the defendants had failed to remove the plank, permitted the plank to be positioned where it was and failed to have a sufficient system of inspection and maintenance on the site. Save to say that no one else was present at the time the accident occurred the claimant offered no explanation as to who or what had dislodged the plank. It was held that the claimant had raised genuine issues which should be investigated at the trial: (i) was someone other than the claimant responsible for the accident and was that person negligent? And (ii) was the defendant negligent to leave the plank in a position which was inappropriate as a result of which it was interfered with thus resulting in the accident?

In *Three Rivers District Council v Bank of England (No.3)* [2001] 2 All E.R. 513 the claim arose out of the collapse of the Bank of Credit and Commerce International SA (BCCI). The claimants sought damages for misfeasance in a public office alleging that the defendant had authorised BCCI to carry on the business of banking. The House of Lords held by a majority of three to two that this highly complex case should not be decided on documents without hearing oral evidence but should go to trial.

In *Merchantbridge & Co. Ltd v Safron General Partner I Ltd* [2006] EWCA Civ 158, (2006) L.T.L., February 14, the parties had entered into a contract for the defendant to provide the claimant with investment advice. Upon termination of that contract by the defendant discussions were commenced as to a possible settlement. The judge granted the defendant summary judgment, holding that during those discussions the claimant had orally promised that it would not pursue any claim that might have arisen out of the defendant's termination of the contract. The claimant had disputed making that promise. On appeal, the Court held that the judge "came to a too robust hasty decision on the documentation that an oral agreement forgoing any right to sue for wrongful termination had been made" and that was an issue which should go for trial.

In *Miller v Garton Shires (a firm)* [2006] EWCA Civ 1386 (2006) L.T.L., October 31, the claimant had been injured in a road traffic accident. A police accident investigator reported that it had been the claimant's car that had lost control and caused an accident. However, there was eyewitness evidence potentially supporting the claimant's version that the other car had crossed onto the wrong side of the road. The defendant solicitors had acted for the claimant in his personal injury claim but had not issued proceedings in time. When sued in negligence the defendant was granted summary judgment on the ground that, on careful examination of the written evidence, the district judge was confident that it was the claimant who had been at fault and, accordingly, his claims against the defendant had no real prospect of success. The Court of Appeal observed that whilst summary judgment should not amount to summary trial (see para.19.005) that does not mean that summary relief is only rarely to be available or is to be used only in exceptional circumstances or where the facts or the material facts are entirely free of dispute. The impropriety of a mini trial at the summary stage is not a principle or practice such that *any* evaluation of a conflict of evidence discernible on the available paper evidence amounts to a mini trial and is, without more, on that score such as to deny summary relief. This was a case where the evidence was so clear that no testing of live witnesses was needed. The eyewitness' evidence said to support the claimant was at best an interesting hypothesis and theory.

These cases show that the respondent to a summary judgment application is not required to prove his case to a very high standard. It will suffice to show that his case may succeed even though it is improbable that it will do so. There is, however, a substantial disadvantage in showing only a case which is "shadowy and unsatisfactory" (per the Vice-Chancellor, Sir Richard Scott in *Bates v Microstar Ltd* (2000) L.T.L., July 4, CA, para.78). If the respondent fails to show a stronger case, the court may make a conditional order against him, for example, an order requiring him to pay money into court and providing that judgment will be given against him if he does not comply (see para.19.015, below).

Some other compelling reason for a trial

19.007 A respondent to a summary judgment application who cannot show any real prospect of success may still avoid summary judgment against him by showing some other compelling reason for a trial. This is because the requirements under paras (a) and (b) of r.24.2 are cumulative and "the rules envisage circumstances in which there is a compelling reason why the claim should proceed to trial notwithstanding that, at the time of the hearing of the application for summary judgment, the claimant has no real prospect of succeeding on the claim" (*per* Schiemann L.J. in *Parker v Snyder* (2003) L.T.L., April 1). For example, because the applicant's conduct is in some way unmeritorious, i.e. devious and crafty rather than plain and straightforward (*Miles v Bull* [1969] 1 Q.B. 258), or harsh and unconscionable (*Bank fur Gemeinwirtschaft AG v City of London Garages* [1971] 1 W.L.R. 149). Another reason for a trial may be to enable a respondent who is a defendant some time to investigate the claim where he has not previously had an opportunity to do so and where there are grounds for believing that such investigation may provide him with real prospects of success (*Harrison v Bottenheim* [1878] 26 W.R. 362).

Effect of a set-off

19.008 A set-off is a mandatory cross claim which a defendant can raise against a claimant and which is also a defence to the claim (see CPR, r.16.6 and see further Ch.12).

A set-off which has real prospects of success will prevent the claimant obtaining summary judgment on his claim. It may be, however, that the claimant could still obtain summary judgment in the form of rulings upon his claim. This would be worthwhile if, in addition to raising the set-off, the defendant denied substantial issues of fact or law concerning the claim and if those issues were discrete from the set-off. Summarily disposing of such issues might avoid some of the expense and delay of a trial and might help the parties to settle the remainder of the case. The summary judgment suggested here would be judgment for the claimant subject only to the determination of the defence of set off or further order and with a stay of execution pending trial of the defence of set off or further order.

No set-off in cheque actions

19.009 Traditionally, the courts treat cheques, bills of exchange and promissory notes as cash. If a defendant had paid cash, it would be too late for him now to raise a set-off or counterclaim to avoid payment. Accordingly, if he pays by cheque, etc., which is dishonoured the court will not permit any set-off or counterclaim either to prevent summary judgment (*Fielding & Platt v Selim Najjar* [1969] 1 W.L.R. 357) or to stay execution of it (*Cebora v SIP (Industrial Products)* [1976]

1 Lloyd's Rep. 271) unless there are exceptional circumstances. Examples of exceptional circumstances include:

(1) a bona fide denial of the validity of the cheque, for example, denying the signature, or alleging that the amount of the cheque had been improperly altered;
(2) a bona fide allegation that the cheque was obtained by fraud;
(3) a bona fide allegation that the cheque relates to an illegal transaction, for example, a gambling debt; and
(4) a bona fide allegation of a total failure of consideration, or a quantified partial failure of consideration.

The special rules for cheque actions also apply to direct debit mandates, which are the modern equivalent of cheques, see *Esso Petroleum Co. Ltd v Milton* [1977] 1 W.L.R. 938.

WHEN TO APPLY

Application by claimant

Unless the court otherwise orders or unless a practice direction otherwise provides, a claimant cannot apply for summary judgment until two hurdles have been cleared; the claimant must have served his particulars of claim and the defendant must have filed an acknowledgment of service or a defence (r.24.4(1)). Service of the particulars of claim is essential because, until it is served, the time for the second hurdle, the defendant's response, does not begin (r.10.3 and 15.4). Some claimants may hope that the second hurdle will not be surmounted. If the defendant does not acknowledge service or file a defence, the claimant may be entitled to enter judgment in default (see Ch.15).

19.010

Once the two hurdles have been surmounted, the claimant could, in theory, apply for summary judgment at any time. In practice, the ideal time to apply is before or when filling the allocation questionnaire. If he does so the court will not normally allocate the claim before the hearing of the application (PD 26, para.5.3).

If the claimant applies for summary judgment before a defence is filed (e.g. immediately after the defendant has filed an acknowledgment of service) the defendant need not file a defence before the hearing of the summary judgment application (r.24.4(2)).

The exceptional cases in which the two hurdles do not arise are claims in which a practice direction otherwise provides, claims under Pt 8 and, of course, claims in which the court otherwise orders. A practice direction does otherwise provide in specific performance cases and certain similar cases. PD 24, para.7 states that, if in his claim form, a claimant seeks specific performance of an agreement relating to property, or the rescission of such an agreement or the forfeiture or return of a deposit made under such an agreement, he may do so at any time after the claim form has been served. This exception is made because, in these cases, the claimant cannot obtain judgment in default except upon an application to the court (r.12.4(2)). In a specific performance claim, if the claimant waits until the defendant is in default, he would be able to combine his application under r.24.4 with an application under r.12.4.

In claims in which the Pt 8 procedure has been used (see Ch.10) there is no provision for particulars of claim, defences or judgments in default. In Pt 8 cases, if the defendant acknowledges service, the claimant can immediately seek summary judgment. If the defendant defaults in acknowledging service, the claimant may seek the court's permission to apply for summary judgment.

If a claimant fails to comply with any relevant pre-action protocol (see para.6.013), the court will not normally deal with the application before a defence has been filed or, alternatively, the time for doing so has expired (PD 24, para 2(6)).

Application by defendant

19.011　A defendant can apply for summary judgment in his favour on the claimant's claim at any time. There are no hurdles to clear. If he applies before filing an acknowledgment of service or defence, the claimant cannot obtain a default judgment until the summary judgment application has been disposed of (r.12.3(3)). The ideal time is before or when filing his allocation questionnaire, thereby delaying allocation (PD 26, para 5.3). But it is not a compelling reason for a trial that the application is made later. In *James E McCabe Ltd v Scottish Courage Ltd* [2006] EWHC 538, (2006) L.T.L., April 5, summary judgment was granted

> "notwithstanding the late stage reached in these proceedings, the issues raised are questions of construction or law and that, since disclosure is virtually complete, there is no reason why these matters should not be dealt with in order to obviate the need for a trial or at least eliminate significant issues at it" (*per* Cooke J.).

Turning now to a defendant's application for summary judgment on a counterclaim or on any other additional claim (see Ch.18) Pt 24 applies (see r.20.3) and there are no hurdles to clear. However, as in other circumstances, the ideal is for applications for summary judgment to be made before the allocation stage.

HOW TO APPLY

19.012　An application under Pt 24 is for a hearing before a master or district judge, save for applications for an injunction which must be heard by a circuit judge or

High Court judge as the case may be (PD 24, para.3 and PD 2, Allocation of Cases to Levels of Judiciary, para.2).

The application must include or identify the written evidence upon which the applicant relies, unless no evidence is relied on (PD 24, para.2(4)). That evidence must be filed and further copies of it must be served with the application notice (r.23.7 and PD 23, paras 9.3 and 9.6).

The application notice must include a statement that it is an application for summary judgment made under Pt 24 (PD 24, para.2(2)) and should draw the respondent's attention to r.24.5(1) (which sets out the time limit for the respondent's evidence, see below). The application notice or the evidence in support must identify concisely any point of law or provision in a document on which the applicant relies and/or state that the applicant believes that the respondent has no real prospect of success on the claims, defences or issues to which the application relates. In either case the application notice or evidence in support must state that the applicant knows of no other reason why the disposal of the claim, defence or issue should await trial (see generally PD 24, para.2(3)).

The application notice and any written evidence must be served on the respondent at least 14 days before the date fixed for the hearing (r.24.4(3)). However, the court may direct that shorter notice is sufficient: see *Phillips v Avena* [2006] EWHC 3333, *The Times* November 22, 2005. Summary judgment applications can also be fixed by the court acting upon its own initiative. An example of this is given in PD 26, para.5. On receipt of allocation questionnaires, the court may, instead of allocating the claim to a track, fix a hearing and give the parties at least 14 days' notice of the date of that hearing. The court must also give notice of the issues which it is proposed the court will decide at that hearing.

EVIDENCE IN RESPONSE AND FURTHER EVIDENCE IN REPLY

Rule 24.5 sets out procedural requirements for evidence relied on by a respondent to an application and also for evidence relied on by any party where the summary judgment hearing was fixed by the court of its own initiative. At least seven days before the hearing any written evidence relied on must be filed and copies served on all other parties to the application. If, on receiving evidence in response, a party who wishes to file and serve further evidence in reply to that evidence must do so at least three days before the hearing. As to the content of evidence in response and further evidence in reply, the parties should consider the burden of proof in summary judgment applications (see above).

19.013

ORDERS MADE IN SUMMARY JUDGMENT APPLICATIONS

Granting summary judgment

19.014 If a claimant's application is successful, the court will enter judgment. Where a specified amount of money was claimed, the judgment will be final and the claimant can proceed to enforcement (see Ch.40). For an unspecified claim, if quantum remains fully in dispute, the judgment will be for damages to be assessed at a later "disposal" hearing (see Ch.17). Can the court give summary judgment for part of the damages? Yes, but only if the court is satisfied that such part of the damages can be clearly identified and quantified and that such ascertained part of the damages is undisputedly due: see *Sinclair Investment Holdings SA v Cushnie* [2006] EWHC 219, (2006) L.T.L., February 6. In the alternative, the court may award an interim payment: see Ch. 25. In addition to granting summary judgment the court may make any consequential orders which are appropriate (see para.19.015).

Success upon a preliminary issue or upon a claim subject to a set-off will be in the form of declaratory relief describing the issue or claim determined. In some cases, for example, equitable set-off (see Ch.12) the court may give judgment on the claim with a stay of execution pending trial of the defendant's cross claim.

Where a defendant's application for summary judgment in his favour on a claimant's claim is successful, the court will strike out or dismiss the claim or give a ruling upon the relevant issue. If the decision disposes of the whole of the claimant's claim, the only further order for the court to make may be for costs of that claim and in respect of any counterclaim.

Any summary judgment given against a defendant who does not attend the hearing may later be set aside or varied on just terms (PD 24, para.8).

Refusing summary judgment

19.015 Obviously, if the applicant fails to establish his application, the application must fail. However, this does not necessarily mean that the application will be dismissed. If it "appears to the court possible that a claim or defence may succeed but improbable that it will do so" (PD 24, para.4), the court may make a conditional order, i.e. an order requiring the respondent to pay a sum of money into court or to take a specified step in relation to his claim or defence as the case may be. In either case, the order will be subject to the condition that his claim will be dismissed or his statement of case will be struck out if he does not comply.

Example

In *Homebase Ltd v LSS Services Ltd* [2004] EWHC 3182, Ch.D, C claimed from D sums equivalent to rent for D's occupation of certain premises. D's case was that no such fees were payable because of an oral agreement to that effect expressly made by representatives of C and D. C denied that any such agreement had been made and sought summary judgment. It was held that, although the evidence relied on by D was not incredible, sufficient doubts as to it had been raised so as to justify the making of a conditional order requiring D to pay into court the whole sum claimed by C.

As to requiring a payment into court, the court must decide the amount of the payment having regard to the overriding objective, in particular the amount of money claimed and the financial position of each party (rr.1.1 and 1.2). The court should not impose a financial condition upon a party which is impossible for him to fulfil. However, this does not mean that a person on supplementary benefit and receiving legal aid with a nil contribution can never be ordered to pay substantial sums into court (*M.V. Yorke Motors v Edwards* [1982] 1 W.L.R. 444 and see further Ch.33). Money paid into court provides security for any sum payable to any other party in the proceedings (r.3.1(6)). As such, it will not form part of the respondent's general assets should he later become insolvent *Re Ford* [1900] 2 Q.B. 211. Although the making of a payment into court is the usual step specified in a conditional order, the court has power to order the respondent to make a payment direct to the applicant or it may give the respondent the option of either paying money into court or providing a satisfactory bank guarantee for the same sum.

If the applicant will be asking the court to make a conditional order against the respondent should the application for summary judgment fail, then he should warn the respondent in advance: see *Anglo-Eastern Trust Ltd v Kermanshahchi* [2002] EWCA Civ 198. In that case the Court of Appeal accepted that the warning need not appear in the Application Notice but could be done informally by letter. In those circumstances the respondent should then prepare a witness statement setting out his means to be produced to the court if it intends to make a conditional order.

If a defendant wishes to pursue an improbable defence, the proper penalty to impose on him (after giving due notice) is the payment of money. What penalty is appropriate in respect of a claimant wishing to pursue an improbable claim? In *Olatawura v Abiloye* [2003] 1 W.L.R. 275 a claimant was ordered to give £5,000 by way of security for the defendant's costs and this was upheld by the Court of Appeal. The court must of course ensure that the making of such an order will not stifle the claim.

> "Whether or not the person concerned has (or can raise) the money will always be a prime consideration, not least since article 6 of the European Convention for the Protection of Human Rights and Fundamental Freedoms became incorporated into domestic law. Paradoxically, of course, the more difficult it appears to be for the person concerned to raise the money, the more obvious becomes the need for an order for security to protect the other party against the risk of incurring irrecoverable costs. The court will have to resolve that conundrum as best it may" (Simon Brown L.J. in *Olatawura*; see also *Ali v Hudson* [2003] EWCA Civ 1793 noted in Ch.26).

Consequential orders

19.016 If summary judgment is given for an unspecified amount of money, the court may:

    (i) direct a disposal hearing (see Ch.17); or
    (ii) immediately allocate the claim to the small claims track if appropriate (this will affect the recoverability of costs for subsequent stages of the proceedings; see further Ch.20); or
    (iii) if the amount payable appears to be genuinely disputed on grounds which appear to be substantial, allocate the claim to the fast track or multi-track as appropriate (see generally PD 26, para.12 and see further, Chs 21 and 22).

Where the court dismisses the application or makes an order that does not completely dispose of the claim, the court may give case management directions as to the future conduct of the case (PD 24, para.10). For example, the court may give directions as to the filing and service of a defence or treat the hearing as if it was an allocation hearing (see r.24.6 and see Ch.9).

In all cases, whether summary judgment is granted or refused, the court may make an order for costs and either summarily assess those costs or order a detailed assessment to be made, possibly ordering a payment on account in the meantime (see further Ch.13 which also explains the obligation to file and serve statements of costs of hearings lasting less than one day).

There is a further alternative if a claimant obtains summary judgment in proceedings in which the only claim made is for a specified sum of money or a Consumer Credit Act claim. If the value of the claim exceeds £25, the court may award fixed costs (see Pt 45).

CHAPTER 20

The Small Claims Track (Pt 27)

TYPES OF CASES

Most cases dealt with on this track can be described as follows: 20.001

(a) Straightforward claims with a financial value of not more than £5,000.
(b) Cases that do not need a substantial amount of pre-hearing preparation.
(c) Cases that should not involve the parties in large legal costs. PD 26, para.8.1 states that "the small claims procedure has been designed so that litigants can conduct their own case without legal representation if they so wish" (as to the restrictions on orders for costs, see para.20.011, below).

These three points are cumulative. Cases likely to satisfy all three include consumer disputes, accident claims, disputes about ownership of goods and most disputes between landlord and tenant other than those for possession. Possession claims can be allocated to the small claims track if all parties agree (r.55.9) as can any claim exceeding the financial limits of the track (r.26.7). Similarly, there is nothing objectionable in a claimant limiting his claims so as to bring it within the financial limits of the small claims track even where this does not reflect the full value of his claim (*Khiaban v Beard* [2003] 1 W.L.R. 1626 CA: RTA claim which was restricted to the loss of no claims bonus and miscellaneous expenses totalling £155.73, the parties' insurers having agreed to abide by the court's decision as to liability when settling the full claim).

It is important to remember that personal injury and landlord and tenant cases have their own special allocation rules. These are generally as follows:

A personal injury claim will be allocated to the small claims track where: (i) the financial value of the whole claim is not more than £5,000; and (ii) the financial value of any claim for general damages for personal injuries is not more than £1,000.

A claim will be allocated to the small claims track if it includes a claim by a tenant of residential premises against his landlord where: (i) the tenant is seeking an order requiring the landlord to carry out repairs or other work to the premises (whether or not the tenant is also seeking some other remedy); (ii) the cost of repairs or other works to the premises is estimated to be not more than £1,000; and (iii) the financial value of any other claim for damages is not more than £1,000. However, the court will not allocate the case to this track if it includes a claim by a tenant of residential premises against his landlord for a remedy in respect of harassment or unlawful eviction.

For the detailed rules as to allocation on this track see Ch.9.

Once allocated to the small claims track the following parts of the CPR do not apply: Pt 31 (disclosure and inspection), Pt 33 (miscellaneous rules about evidence), Pt 36 (offers to settle). Whilst Pt 18 (further information) does not apply, r.27.2(3) provides that the court of its own initiative may order a party to provide further information if it considers it appropriate to do so.

Most of Pts 25, 32, 35 and 39 are also excluded, but not rules about interim injunctions, the power of the court to control evidence, various rules about expert evidence and the general rule that hearings are to be in public.

RETAINING SOLICITORS TO CONDUCT SMALL CLAIMS

20.002   Few small claims cases are conducted by a solicitor from the very beginning to the end. Most clients want initial advice about the merits of the bringing or defending a case and advice about quantum. Some firms are prepared to do this for a fixed fee offering an hour or perhaps half an hour's consultation. At this stage you can help the client construct his case and in particular you might consider the following practical questions:

(a)   Are photographs and/or a video available or do they need to be taken?
(b)   Have all relevant documents been obtained, for example, invoices, estimates, sketch plans, contracts, brochures, booking forms, letters, etc?
(c)   Is an expert's report needed? If so, what issues need to be addressed? Would it make sense to seek the appointment of a joint expert? Is the case really suitable for this track?
(d)   What witnesses are available? Are any statements already available, for example, in a police accident report or as letters written to the client? Is it possible to use blank proforma statements for the client and other witnesses to complete by hand?

If you are instructed to prepare a document for a litigant in person it is vital to remember that he will be using it as a focal point of his case. Whilst it should be drawn up in accordance with the rules, keep it simple. Consider with the client attaching to a claim form or defence his witness statement(s), any expert's report and other evidence. The more direction you can give to the client's case the easier it is for him to carry on conducting it himself. You will also, of course, make life a lot easier for the district judge and there is a lot to be said for that on this track.

One dilemma you may sometimes face is being asked by a client who has prepared his own statements of case and evidence to represent him at the hearing.

Many people remain intimidated by the courts and opt to see a solicitor at the last minute. Whilst small claims hearings are a good opportunity for young advocates to gain experience, the preparation time may be considerable. Firms need to have a policy. Will they take on such cases? If so, on what terms and who will deal with it? The most important thing of all is to spell out clearly to the client the costs involved.

ALLOCATION

Note that where a claim falls within the financial scope of the small claims track, a slightly different allocation questionnaire in Form N149 is sent to the parties (rather than the usual Form N150: see para.9.027). The main difference is that the parties are asked whether or not they agree that the small claims track is the most suitable track for the claim. Any reasons for disagreeing should be given. 20.003

There are four possible types of allocation to the small claims track. These are:

(1) Allocation with directions.
(2) Allocation followed by a preliminary hearing.
(3) Allocation followed by a "paper disposal".
(4) Allocation by consent.

Allocation with directions (Form N157)

In most small claims track cases there is only one hearing and that is the trial itself. On allocation to the track the district judge usually issues standard directions that are incorporated into or attached to the notice of allocation (Form 157). This is then sent to all the parties. The standard directions are: 20.004

(1) That each party should file and serve copies of all documents (including any expert's report) that he intends to rely on at the hearing by a specified date. This is the only form of "disclosure and inspection" of documents that exists on the small claims track. Contrast disclosure on the other tracks (see Chs 21, 22 and 31).
(2) That the original of those documents must be brought to the hearing.
(3) The date of the hearing and time.
(4) The court must be informed immediately if the case is settled by agreement before the hearing.

The above represent the directions that are used if the district judge does not specify any other. However, App.A to r.27 provides a list of standard directions that can be made in relation to particular types of claims, for example, road accidents (Form B); building disputes, vehicle repairs and similar contractual claims (Form C); tenant's claims for the return of deposits or landlord's claims for damage caused (Form D) and holiday and wedding claims (Form E). These standard directions seek to assist the parties in preparing the case. For example, lists are given of documents that a party might wish to rely on and the parties are told which of those the court will find very helpful, for example, sketch plans and photographs in a road accident claim.

There are some special directions that the court can issue. These include:

(a) That a party must clarify his case by filing and serving a prescribed list of items or certain details. A litigant in person faced with this direction often seeks legal advice. It is to be hoped that the direction is clear but if there is any doubt we would suggest that a telephone call or faxed letter to the court should quickly resolve any ambiguity. Moreover, the solicitor should consider the whole of the case with the client and not just any matter picked up on by the district judge. See generally, para.20.002 above.

(b) That the hearing is to occur at a specified place other than the court. It is not that unusual for district judges to deal with small claims concerning building disputes in the home of the owner.

(c) That expert evidence is necessary in relation to a particular issue and that it should be given by a single expert (see below).

Allocation followed by a preliminary hearing (Form N158)

20.005 Rule 27.6 makes it clear that preliminary hearings are not to be encouraged. The time and expense involved means the district judge only orders such if he feels that special directions are required and that these should be explained to the parties in person; or that an order for summary judgment or striking out a statement of case can be made.

District judges are often faced with poorly prepared statements of case. Rules 27.6(1)(b) and (c) provide that he can hold a preliminary hearing "to enable" him to dispose of the case summarily, either because a party's stated case shows no real prospect of success or discloses no real grounds for bringing or defending the claim. In practice the court tends to use the hearing as an opportunity for the party to explain his case, a sort of "mini-trial". The matter can then either be struck out or the party directed as to what steps need to be taken to clarify his case. Otherwise, district judges will normally hold a preliminary hearing where they feel that expert evidence is necessary (see below).

Allocation followed by a "paper disposal" (Form N159)

20.006 If after reading the statements of case the district judge feels that he can decide on the issues without anything further he can invite the parties to agree to the case being disposed of without a hearing. We doubt that this occurs very often. Only where the issues are narrow, clearly defined and addressed by the statements of case is a district judge likely to consider himself able to rely on the parties' paperwork. Moreover, what litigant is going to agree?

Allocation by consent (Form N160)

20.007 A case that exceeds the financial limit for the small claims track (see above and Ch.9) cannot be allocated to the track unless all the parties consent. When might a party with a claim that would normally be dealt with in the fast track consent to it being dealt with in the small claims track? It is a difficult question to answer positively where the party wants legal representation and he can arrange suitable funding. But if the party is going to deal with post-allocation matters himself, then the advantages of the small claims track should be pointed out. Note, however, that all the parties must agree and no one party can insist on allocation to the track.

EXPERT EVIDENCE (R.27.5)

20.008 Expert evidence in any form is not admissible at a small claims hearing unless the court gives its permission. In most cases the court gives a simple, standard direction that any party intending to rely on an expert's written report at the hearing must file and serve it by a specified date. Note the direction is for one report only. As outlined above, in a very limited number of cases the district judge may give a special direction for the joint appointment of a single expert in relation to an identified issue. This might read, for example:

> "It appears to the court that expert evidence is necessary on the issue of whether the claimant's losses were caused by the defendant's breach of contract (as alleged in para.3 of the particulars of claim) or the claimant's failure to follow the defendant's instructions (as alleged in para.2 of the defence) and that that evidence should be given by a single expert to be instructed by the parties jointly. If the parties cannot agree about who to choose and what arrangement to make about paying his fee, either party may apply to the court for further directions".

In many cases where this type of direction is thought necessary by the district judge he orders the attendance of the parties at a preliminary hearing. This gives him the opportunity not only to explain the proposed direction but also to sort out the practical arrangements of appointment, payment, etc. there and then. It should be noted that the detailed rules concerning experts in Pt 35 (see Ch.23) do not generally apply to this track. For example, there is no right for any party to put written questions to the expert about his report. Of course, once the report is available the case may settle. Where the court can be persuaded that settlement is more likely if certain written questions are put to the expert, a direction to that effect may be made. In any event, failing a settlement, consideration has to be given as to whether or not the expert should give oral evidence at trial. In most cases this happens but with strict time limits placed on his evidence (see below).

THE HEARING OF A SMALL TRACK CLAIM

20.009 The hearing date is usually set out on the allocation form or as part of the directions order. At least 21 days' notice is given to the parties unless they agree to accept less. If a party cannot make the hearing date because, for example, he has an urgent hospital appointment, he should immediately ask the court to fix a new date. The consent of all other parties should be sought. If the party is prepared for the court to make a decision in his absence, he can give written notice to that effect at least seven days before the hearing. A party must appreciate that if he does nothing then the court will probably strike out his statement of case. It will be very difficult to set aside that order if he received legal advice on the point. Rule 27.11(3) provides that the court may set it aside only if the applicant "had a good reason" for not attending or failing to give notice of non-attendance.

Most district judges are familiar with conducting a small claims hearing and each has their own way of doing so. The strict rules of evidence do not apply and the hearing is quite informal. Usually the District Judge will identify the issues that have to be resolved by him and outline his proposed timetable for the hearing, for example:

> Claimant's evidence (45 minutes): claimant, witnesses A and B.
> Defendant's evidence (45 minutes): defendant, witness C.
> Oral evidence from jointly appointed expert (30 minutes).
> Reasons for decision (10 minutes).

By PD 27, para.4.3 the district judge can adopt any method of proceeding that he considers fair. Our experience is that the court goes out of its way to ensure the parties feel that they have had a "fair crack of the whip". A solicitor should ensure that he knows his local courts' practice so that he can pass on that information to any client who is conducting the hearing himself.

The ordinary restrictions on rights of audience (as to which, see Ch.1) are relaxed for hearings on the small claims track. PD 27 para.3 provides that a litigant may present his own case at the hearing (via any of its officers or employees in the case of a corporate party) or may authorise a barrister, solicitor, legal executive employed by a solicitor or a lay representative to present his case for him. A lay representative may not exercise any right of audience where the client does not attend the hearing, at any stage after judgment, or on any appeal. However, the court, exercising its general discretion to hear anybody, may hear a lay representative even where he has no right of audience. In *Avinue Ltd v Sunrule Ltd* [2003] EWCA Civ 1942 a corporate defendant was represented at the hearing by a director (whose first language was not English) and a lay representative. The district judge refused to let the lay representative present the case or cross-examine the claimant's witnesses. The Court of Appeal held that that refusal had resulted in an unfair trial and a retrial was ordered.

COSTS (R.27.14)

Routine award of costs

Unless an exception applies (see paras 20.011 and 20.012, below) an award of costs in cases in the small claims track is restricted by r.27.14. The restrictions indicate the extent to which the costs of legal advice and assistance can be considered justifiable and proportionate in ordinary circumstances. Normally, only the fixed costs of actually issuing the claim are recoverable. However, bear in mind that if you are advising a client in respect of a claim for an injunction or for an order for specific performance, a sum not exceeding £260 in respect of your costs may be recoverable. In addition, the court has a discretion to order payment of court fees, travelling expenses, loss of earnings or leave (up to £50 per day) and experts' fees (not exceeding £200 per report). For a fuller discussion of r.27.14 and the complicated rules that apply concerning costs incurred before allocation and also costs in cases subsequently allocated to a different track, see para.38.021 below.

20.010

Costs where a party has behaved unreasonably

Rule 27.14(2)(d) gives the court power to order a party to pay further costs if that party has behaved unreasonably. What sort of behaviour is likely to attract an order under this part of the rule? For a claimant making a claim which is dishonest, or making a claim which is deliberately vague and imprecise and then failing to comply with a court order to clarify it will usually lead to an adverse order. Failing to beat a reasonable offer of compromise made by the defendant will not usually lead to an adverse order for costs but will probably disentitle the claimant to some of the costs he would otherwise have received. For a defendant contesting a case unsuccessfully will not by itself lead to an adverse order but dishonestly telling lies and/or contesting a claim up to a late stage with no real intention of pursuing it to a hearing usually will.

20.011

Cases allocated to the small claims track by consent

The cost restriction in r.27.14 will apply to cases which were outside the financial scope of the small claims track but were allocated to it by consent unless the parties agree that the fast track provisions should apply instead see para.38.021, below).

20.012

For costs purposes, some possession claims can end up as a hybrid between the small claims track and the fast track. Rule 55.9 provides that the court can only allocate possession claims to the small claims track if all parties agree. Such agreement does not by itself bring the costs restriction of r.27.14 into play unless the parties further agree the court should make an order specifically having that effect.

SUMMARY JUDGMENT (PT 24)

20.013   A party who faces a hopeless small claim or who has been served with a spurious defence has a choice. He can either let the case run on to allocation and a hearing or he can apply for summary judgment. The latter course, if successful, might achieve for him a swifter conclusion than he would otherwise reach. However, he is unlikely to achieve a better order for costs by this route. In *Voice and Script Ltd v Alghafar* [2003] EWCA Civ 736 the Court of Appeal held that, in cases which, if allocated, would have been allocated to the small claims track, the normal rule should be that the small claim costs regime should apply. That case concluded by way of a default judgment on liability rather than summary judgment. At the disposal hearing (as to which, see Ch.17) it became apparent that, because of errors of calculation, a claim originally set at over £9,000 should have been set at around £4,000. Although the defendant, acting in person, pointed out that this was below the small claims limit, the district judge awarded costs because the claim had never been allocated to any track. The Court of Appeal disagreed.

APPEAL

20.014   Appeals against small claims judgments are dealt with in Pt 52 of the CPR (see Ch.44). However, the following should be noted in particular:

   (a)   Rule 27.14(2) (see para.20.010) applies to costs incurred on an appeal.
   (b)   Pursuant to r.52.3(6) many appeals from the small claims track are likely to be refused permission to appeal on the basis that the court considers that it does not have a real prospect of success and there is no other compelling reason why the appeal should be heard. The overriding objective and the concept of proportionality will be very influential here.
   (c)   The court's power under r.52.3(7) to grant permission to appeal but limiting the issues to be heard and imposing conditions, including security for costs under r.25.25, may also deter many appeals from being made or pursued.

CHAPTER 21

The Fast Track (Pt 28)

TYPICAL CASES

Fast track cases occupy the middle, rather than the outside lane of the litigation motorway, i.e. sandwiched between simple small claims and much more complex multi-track cases. Matters dealt with on this track can be summarised as follows:

21.001

(a) Relatively straightforward claims with a financial value of more than £5,000 but less than £15,000.
(b) Cases that require some, but not substantial, pre-hearing preparation.
(c) Cases that can be tried in one day or less.
(d) The majority of cases in which oral expert evidence will be limited to one per party in any field and expert evidence in no more than two fields.

It is important to remember that personal injury and landlord and tenant cases have their own special rules. These are generally as follows:

Personal injuries: even if the financial value of the whole claim does not exceed £5,000 the case is usually allocated to the fast track if the financial value of any claim for general damages is more than £1,000.

Claim by a tenant of residential premises against his landlord seeking an order requiring the landlord to carry out repairs or other work to the premises: even if the financial value of the whole claim does not exceed £5,000 the case is usually allocated to the fast track if: (i) the cost of repairs or other works to the premises is estimated to be more than £1,000; and (ii) the financial value of any other claim for damages is more than £1,000. In addition the court will usually allocate to the fast track a claim by a tenant of residential premises against his landlord for a remedy in respect of harassment or unlawful eviction.

For the detailed rules as to allocation on this track see Ch.9.

HOW FAST IS "FAST"?

A fast track case is expected to proceed from the directions given on allocation to a trial in not more than 30 weeks. Fast means fast. The track is underpinned

21.002

by the overriding objective and in particular by r.1.1(2) which provides that cases should be dealt with: (c)(i) in ways that are proportionate to the amount of money involved, (d) expeditiously and (e) by allotting an appropriate share of the court's resources.

If you are going to effectively make a claim on a fast track case it is vital to "front load" your preparation. Get full statements from all potential witnesses. Sort out the documentary evidence and consider pre-action disclosure (see Ch.30). It is essential to follow the pre-action protocols (see Ch.6), particularly in relation to personal injury cases where the protocol is primarily designed for fast track cases. The court expects the parties to have taken the appropriate protocols steps. If there has not been time to do so because, for example, proceedings are issued due to limitation problems, you should ask for the action to be stayed so that the protocol procedures can be undertaken.

THE NEED FOR A CASEPLAN

21.003 Litigation is expensive. Especially in fast track cases there is a danger that each side may incur costs exceeding the value of the claim. It is vitally important to ensure at all stages that, as far as possible, the costs are kept proportionate to the benefits gained by the proceedings. By the end of the pre-action protocol stage, if not before, each party should make an assessment of the likely value, importance and complexity of the case. They should then draw up a caseplan in advance indicating the necessary work, the appropriate level of fee earner to carry it out and the overall time likely to be needed on the various stages in getting the case to trial. You may of course be compelled subsequently to revise your caseplan, for example, unforseen problems may arise or your opponents may take an unreasonably awkward and expensive approach to the case.

If ultimately you win the case plus costs on the standard basis, the court assessing them will allow costs which appear disproportionate ony to the extent that they are shown to have been necessary (see further para.38.017). Being able to justify your costs claim by reference to a caseplan and to the revisions to it which you were compelled to make, will greatly assist your recovery of costs. A party without such a caseplan will encounter a court much less receptive to allowing the full costs claimed.

DIRECTIONS ON ALLOCATION (R.28.2)

21.004 When it allocates a case to the fast track the court gives directions for the management of the case and sets a timetable for certain steps to be taken up to trial. A typical timetable to run from the date of allocation will be:

Disclosure:	4 weeks
Exchange of witness statements:	10 weeks
Exchange of experts' reports:	14 weeks

Sending of pre-trial checklists by the court: 20 weeks
Filing of completed pre-trial checklists: 22 weeks
Hearing: 30 weeks

The expectation is that the court does not have to hold a hearing to do this. The parties are required to co-operate with each other to achieve that goal. If a hearing is necessary because a party or his legal representative fails to provide the court with adequate information, he can expect the court to impose a costs sanction.

Typical directions, outlined in the Appendix to r.28, cover the following matters: disclosure, exchange of witness statements, exchange of experts' reports, and fixing the trial date or trial window.

Disclosure

The court usually directs that standard disclosure (see Ch.30) should take place. However, r.28.3(2) provides that the court may direct that no disclosure should be given at all. Bearing in mind that in small track cases (see Ch.20) disclosure does occur, albeit limited to documents that a party intends to produce in support of his case, it is our view that the court should not make such a direction unless either: (i) substantial pre-action disclosure has taken place; or (ii) the parties agree that there should be no disclosure. In the alternative the court may direct that disclosure should be given of certain specified documents or classes of documents. This power can be used to ensure that litigants in person give adequate disclosure and in those circumstances the court might direct that the parties simply exchange copies of certain documents rather than initially make a formal list. However, PD 28, para.3.6(4)(b) slightly complicates matters as it provides that the parties must serve a disclosure statement with the copies or record that they have agreed to give disclosure without that statement.

21.005

Exchange of witness statements

There is always a direction for the exchange of witness statements that the parties intend to rely on at trial. The exchange is usually simultaneous. As to drafting witness statements, see Ch.14 and as to exchange and evidence generally, see Ch.31.

21.006

Exchange of experts' reports

As a general rule a case is not allocated to the fast track if extensive expert evidence is required. Oral expert evidence at a fast track trial is limited to: (a) one expert per party in relation to any field; and (b) no more than two expert fields. In other words no more than two experts per party. Of course, the court always

21.007

endeavours to minimise the amount of expert evidence by requiring the joint appointment of a single expert (see Ch.23) where this is possible.

On allocation, or subsequently the district judge may direct that no expert evidence is necessary at all. He usually makes this order when all the parties have indicated in the allocation questionnaires, or otherwise, that they do not wish to use expert evidence. He may give such a direction even if a party does want to adduce expert evidence if satisfied that such evidence is not needed and the case can be fairly argued on a common-sense basis without experts.

If the court decides that expert evidence is necessary, the normal direction is for the appointment of a single expert. If that is not possible the parties are allowed to obtain their own expert evidence but the court limits the number and provides for the exchange of written reports that the parties intend to rely on. In addition, where the parties have their own experts the court usually directs that the experts have a "without prejudice" discussion and prepare and file a statement of issues on which they agree and disagree, with a summary of their reasons.

By r.35.5(2) if a case is proceeding on the fast track the court will not direct that any expert should attend a hearing "unless it is necessary to do so in the interests of justice". When might it be said to be in the interests of justice to allow oral expert evidence at a fast track trial? We suggest that the following are possibilities:

(1) Where a single joint expert has been appointed and one party wishes to show that his report is ambiguous or inadequate. To show up any failings in the report it is vital to exercise the right to ask the expert written questions within 28 days of receiving the report (see Ch.23). Then complete the pre-trial checklist (see Ch.36), enclose a copy of the report and the expert's replies to your questions and explain why you want the expert called at trial.

(2) When the difference of opinion between the parties' own experts is so wide and technical that the trial judge will require the experts' assistance beyond the joint written statement of agreed and disputed issues.

Where oral evidence is required from experts on the issues of both liability and quantum, the court sometimes orders a split trial (see below) to ensure that each issue can be heard in one day. This does at least make it easier for you to arrange the attendance of suitable experts. It has always been difficult to find a time for a trial that is convenient for everyone concerned, especially busy experts. The advantages of fast tracking is that you can instruct an expert who will know the exact (or approximate) trial date and who will therefore only take on the case on the basis of being able to attend the trial.

Expert evidence is dealt with in detail in Ch.23.

Trial date

One of the key directions made on allocation is the fixing of the trial date or a period of time when this is to take place. As we have seen the aim is for the trial to occur within 30 weeks.

21.008

Split trials are often ordered in the hope and expectation that the case will settle after the first hearing. If it does not and a second full day becomes necessary the case might be re-allocated to the multi-track.

The great danger is, of course, that an order for a split trial may increase the costs rather than reduce or avoid them. This is almost bound to happen where the witnesses called at the first hearing will have to be called again at the second hearing. The topic of split trials and the case law thereon is set out in para.33.006, below.

Implications for the parties

The parties should endeavour to agree directions and file these for the court to consider on allocation. You should work from the standard directions set out in the Appendix to r.28. In addition to the above-mentioned matters, the parties should also consider if any additional directions are required. There are two possibilities to consider at this stage:

21.009

(a) If there is an outstanding request for further information arising from a party's statement of case (see Ch.32) it is sensible to incorporate an order for that to be done.
(b) If a party wishes to amend his statement of case (see Ch.14) that should be dealt with now.

What should you do if you are dissatisfied with a direction made at a hearing you attended? The simple answer is to appeal it (see Ch.44). And what if, as is more likely, the direction was made by the court of its own initiative? Within 14 days you must apply to the court for it to reconsider the matter. It is important to clearly state why the court should reconsider the particular direction. Perhaps there were facts the court did not know about, although you must remember that you had the opportunity in the allocation questionnaire to provide the court with all relevant information. If you fail to appeal or seek a reconsideration, as appropriate, it is assumed that you are content with the direction and any later application for a variation will have to show a change in circumstances since the order was made.

Can the parties vary the fast track timetable? Rule 2.11 allows the parties to vary a date by written agreement unless a rule or court order prohibits it. There is no objection to the parties agreeing to extend the time for disclosure and exchanging evidence provided this does not alter the timetable for dealing with pre-trial checklists and trial (see below). Problems may arise in dealing with evidence, for example, a witness may fall ill or an expert may not deliver his report on time. It is important to keep the other parties informed of developments and make a prompt application to the court as soon as it is clear that the balance of the timetable cannot be met. Do not leave it until the last minute.

Failure to comply with directions

21.010 The best approach to a fast track case is to be fully prepared before proceedings are issued and to ask the court on allocation for suitable directions. Then promptly obey the timetable. Adequate preparation of the case is the key. If you fail to meet a direction you can expect the other side to apply for an order to enforce it with a sanction (see Ch.33). PD 28, para.5.2 says any application should be made promptly and with prior warning. So if your opponent has not given disclosure on time or is late in exchanging evidence, fire off a letter immediately and apply to the court three days later. We think it reasonable to wait that number of days. The court often makes an order of its own initiative.

Adjourning the trial

21.011 Do not feel that you will be able to eventually persuade the court to put back a trial date. The fast-track means what it says; the adherence to a fixed timetable is all important. PD 28, para.5.4(6) says, "Litigants and lawyers must be in no doubt that the court will regard the postponement of a trial as an order of last resort." Hence, if a party has disclosed and exchanged enough information so that say one out of the three issues in dispute can be determined in the case, he can expect the court to order that the trial of that issue should proceed. The court will also order that when the remaining two issues are tried the defaulting party, even if he wins, will not be able to recover any costs. Where both sides are at fault the court may order that neither party should be entitled to costs.

There can be no doubt that in the past a minority of applications for adjournments were made by solicitors who had failed to properly conduct the action. The client had invariably been kept in the dark. There is, of course, a professional obligation on solicitors to keep their clients fully informed of all developments and the court has power under PD 28, para.5.4(6) to require a party, as well as his solicitor, to attend the hearing of an adjournment application.

PRE-TRIAL CHECKLIST

21.012 The court sends out a pre-trial checklist for you to complete and return by a date that is specified on the form but that is not more than eight weeks before the trial. Although there is no obligation to exchange copies with other parties PD 28, para.6.1(4) encourages you to do so in order that the court is not given conflicting or incomplete information. If you want the court to give any particular directions, try to agree these first with the other parties but in any event you should file a draft order. See Ch.36 for more details.

After the pre-trial checklists have been returned or the time for their return has expired, the court file is referred to a judge who may issue final directions or convene a hearing. The court wishes to avoid a hearing and penalises in costs any party who makes a hearing necessary. Ultimately you will receive a notice in Form N172 confirming or fixing the trial date and specifying any directions made. If you are dissatisfied with a direction made, it is essential to appeal it or ask for a reconsideration, as appropriate, since the trial judge is not going to make last-minute changes.

The most common directions at this stage are:

(a) Expert evidence to be given orally or by way of written reports filed with the listing questionnaire.
(b) Preparation of a trial bundle (see Ch.36).
(c) A trial timetable and time estimate. Bearing in mind that the longest period of time any fast track hearing should take is one day (or five hours), a typical example is as follows:

Claimant's opening speech:	10 minutes.
Defendant's opening speech:	10 minutes.
Cross examination and re-examination of claimant's witnesses	90 minutes
Cross examination and re-examination of defendant's witnesses:	90 minutes
Defendant's closing submissions:	20 minutes.
Claimant's closing submissions:	20 minutes.
Judge preparing and delivering judgment:	40 minutes.
Summary assessment of costs:	20 minutes.

As to conducting a trial on the fast track, see Ch.37. At the end of the trial the judge normally carries out a summary assessment of costs and it is vital that you attend the hearing prepared for this (see Chs 13 and 38).

CHAPTER 22

The Multi-Track (Pt 29)

TYPICAL CASES

22.001 Cases allocated to the multi-track are those which are unsuitable for the fast track (see Ch.21). As a general rule that means a case on the multi-track has a financial value of more than £15,000; and/or a trial estimate of longer than one day; and/or a requirement for oral expert evidence at trial exceeding one expert per party in more than two expert fields. All Pt 8 claims (see Ch.10) are allocated to the multi-track.

PD 29, para.3.2 states that the hallmarks of the multi-track are the ability of the court to deal with cases of widely differing values and complexity; and the flexibility given to the court to manage the case in a way appropriate to its particular needs. This judicial case management (detailed in Ch.33) occurs primarily at two stages, namely on allocation and pre-trial. Your ability to influence the judge's decisions depends initially therefore on how you complete the allocation questionnaire and the pre-trial checklist.

The allocation questionnaire is dealt with in Ch.9. You should state in the questionnaire if you consider a case management conference is necessary, give your reasons (e.g. you want the court to order an early trial with a fixed hearing date) and a time estimate for it (which should include the master or district judge's reading time). Try to get the agreement of all the other parties on those matters. Also send to the court a list of the dates when any participant at the proposed hearing will be unavailable. In Q.B.D. cases, the court will send out Form PF49 on which you should state convenient dates for a case management conference or any other hearing.

Case management normally takes place at the appropriate Civil Trial Centre. A conference is generally conducted by a master or district judge.

CASE MANAGEMENT AT THE OUTSET

The need for a caseplan

22.002 Litigation is expensive. Unless some control is imposed, there is a danger that the total amount of costs reasonably spent by all parties will equal if not exceed the value of the claim. It is vitally important to ensure at all stages that, as far as possible, the costs are kept proportionate to the benefits to be gained by proceedings. By the end of the pre-action protocol stage, if not before, each side should make an assessment of the likely value, importance and complexity of the case. They should then draw up a caseplan in advance indicating the necessary work, the appropriate level of fee earners to carry it out and the overall time likely to be needed on the various stages in getting the case to trial. You may of course be compelled subsequently to revise your caseplan, for example, unforeseen problems may arise or your opponents may take an unreasonably awkward and expensive approach to the case.

If ultimately you win the case plus costs on the standard basis the court assessing them will allow costs which appear disproportionate only to the extent that they are shown to have been necessary (see further para.38.017). Being able to justify your costs by reference to a caseplan and to the revisions to it which you were compelled to make will greatly assist your recovery of costs. A party without such a caseplan will encounter a court much less receptive to allowing the full costs claimed.

Issue identification

When the court considers what directions to make on allocation its first concern is to ensure that the issues between the parties have been identified and the necessary evidence prepared and disclosed (see PD 29, para.4.3).

22.003

If the statements of case have been properly drafted (see Ch.12) you should be able to compare the particulars of claim, the defence (and counterclaim) and any reply (and defence to counterclaim) to work out what issues are agreed and those that remain in dispute. We would suggest that you start with the claimant's claim and annotate the particulars of claim by writing in the margin beside each paragraph the letters "A" (for Admitted), "D" (for Denied) and "NA" (for Not Admitted). Then go through the defence duplicating these annotations against the relevant paragraphs. Where the defendant states his own version of events mark these "E" (for Extra) unless the assertions have been addressed in the claimant's reply, in which case the paragraphs can be annotated accordingly. If the claimant has raised any extra factual points in the reply mark these "R".

The claim, defence and any reply will now be annotated with the letters A, D, NA, E and R. Later on, similar treatment will have to be given to a counterclaim or other additional proceedings (see Ch.18). However, it is best to delay this task for the time being or you will end up with a totally confusing alphabet soup!

Applying the maxim "He who alleges must prove" (see Ch.31) the claimant should prepare to prove the NA, D and R paragraphs. He should also consider what evidence he has contradicting the E paragraphs. In negligence claims, for example, these are likely to be topics such as contributory negligence and failure to mitigate loss, topics upon which a failure by the claimant to lead evidence is bound to invite adverse comment. The defendant should fully prepare to contradict the D paragraphs and prove the E paragraphs. He should also consider what, if anything, he can add by way of evidence to improve his case in respect of the NA paragraphs.

No party needs to dwell on the A paragraphs. No evidence is required at trial on an issue that is admitted.

The judge will carefully scrutinise the statements of case and may direct at this stage that a party should clarify any matter which appears to be in dispute or provide further information. The objective, pursuant to r.1.4(2)(c), is to decide promptly which issues need full investigation and trial and those which can be disposed of summarily.

Case management conference

22.004 The purpose of a case management conference is to set out an agenda before significant costs are incurred. That agenda will be dictated totally by the judge unless you: (a) fully complete the allocation questionnaire; and (b) propose directions that can be justified. You must anticipate the questions the judge will ask about the case and the procedural steps he is likely to be considering. We suggest that you ask yourself the following questions:

(1) What are the real issues in dispute? If there is to be a case management hearing it may assist the court to better understand the case if the claimant prepares a case summary. By PD 29, para.5.7 this should set out a brief chronology of the claim, the issues of fact which are agreed or in dispute and the evidence needed to decide them. It should not normally exceed 500 words and the other parties should be invited to agree it.

Example

IN THE HIGH COURT OF JUSTICE   HQ 2007 00654
QUEENS BENCH DIVISION
WESTBOURNE DISTRICT REGISTRY
BETWEEN

	(1) -Mrs Jane Walker	
	(2) -Mr Robin Walker	Claimants
	and	
	Ashtons (a firm)	Defendants

AGREED CASE SUMMARY

1. Chronology of claimants' case:

On June 11, 2005 the claimants orally instructed the defendants to carry out a full structural survey on "Ovedene", 12 Turner Drive, Westbourne, Mythshire ("the Property").

The defendants' written structural survey report on the Property was dated June 29, 2005 and stated that there were "no unusual hazards".

The claimants purchased the Property on September 15, 2005.

2. <u>Agreed issues of fact:</u>

   (i) The contract provided for the defendants to advise as to whether or not the agreed purchase price of £355,000 for the Property was reasonable and as to the condition and value of the Property.
   (ii) The defendants had a duty to exercise reasonable care and skill when inspecting the Property and preparing the report.
   (iii) The claimants relied on the report in deciding to purchase the Property.
   (iv) The Property was constructed by a method known as "Ground Base" and that such is an "unusual hazard".

3. <u>Disputed issues of fact:</u>

   (i) That the defendants knew or ought to have known in 2005 of the "Ground Base" method of construction.
   (ii) That the defendants overstated the value of the Property.
   (iii) That the defendants caused loss or damage to the claimants.
   (iv) The quantum of damages claimed.

4. <u>Evidence needed to determine the issues:</u>

   The claimants will give evidence as to the distress, inconvenience and consequential losses they have suffered as a result of being unable to sell the Property and move.
   Mr Ashton will give evidence of his inspection, report and state of knowledge in 2005.
   Each party intends to rely on the expert evidence of its own chartered surveyor as to the issues of liability, causation and quantum.

   (2) Are any of the issues suitable for trial as preliminary issues or might there be a split trial? Should the issues be heard in any particular order? See generally Ch.33.
   (3) Do you need to amend your statement(s) of case? Can this by done by consent or is a court order necessary (see Ch.12).
   (4) Do you need further information about another party's case? Has such been requested and ignored or refused?
   (5) Can you make any further admissions? Should further admissions be sought from any other party? See Ch.32.
   (6) Might some form of ADR be appropriate for the whole case or any particular issue? Has the question been explored with the other parties? Are any special directions needed from the court to facilitate ADR? See in particular PD 29 para 4.10(9) detailed at para.34.004).

(7) By what date can you give standard disclosure (see below and Ch.30)? Are you going to contend that to search for any category or class of document is unreasonable? Can you specify that category or class and justify your decision? Is specific disclosure required on any issue and if so, which? Is any special disclosure order appropriate?

(8) Are there any reasons to extend the time periods for inspection (see Ch.30) and if so, until when?

(9) Have all potential witnesses of fact been interviewed? If not, when is this going to take place? Which of the current witnesses will you definitely rely on at trial? What enquiries need to be made about the others? By what date will you be able to serve signed witness statements? Will any witness summaries be necessary? Are interpreters needed for any witness? Will any witness need to give evidence by video link? See generally below and Ch.31.

(10) On what issues is expert evidence required? Can a single joint expert be agreed on any issue? How many experts are needed? Have reports already been obtained and disclosed? Have you identified at least the field or fields of expertise required? By what date will you be able to serve signed expert reports? When are the experts available to discuss the matter after service of their reports? What oral expert evidence is required and can you justify it? Are interpreters needed for any expert? Will any expert need to give evidence by video link? See generally below and Ch.23.

(11) When will you be able to return the pre-trial checklist? Is a further case management conference and/or a pre-trial review necessary?

(12) What are your current estimates of the maximum and minimum lengths of the trial? What is the earliest date by which your case and evidence will be ready for trial? Have you checked the availability of all witnesses and experts? Do you require the use of information technology at trial? See generally Ch.36.

(13) Are there, or are there likely to be, any additional claims (see Ch.18) to be considered?

(14) How much is all of this going to cost? Should the court impose costs budgets on some or all of the parties (see further, para.33.013)? Is each step cost-effective? And who should take it and when? We come back yet again to the overriding objective, for example, in order to ensure the parties are on an equal footing you need to ask if a party should be given longer to take a particular step, such as disclosure? See generally Ch.33.

Disclosure

22.005 The following notes should be read in conjunction with Ch.30 where this topic is dealt with.

It is important to bear in mind that documentary evidence may well be the key to success or failure in a case. A judge may place far more weight on the contents of a piece of paper rather than the oral evidence of a witness. However, many multi-track cases by their very nature involve a potentially huge number of documents. How are those documents to be managed? The judge considers whether to:

(a) Dispense with or limit standard disclosure (r.31.5(2)).
(b) Order standard disclosure (r.31.5(1)).
(c) Order specific disclosure (r.31.12).

The judge seeks to tailor the disclosure order to the case before him. After isolating the issues he must consider if standard disclosure is required across the whole spectrum of the case or whether more, or less, is justified bearing in mind the overriding objective. Where numerous documents of a similar type are involved he may ask you to consider if disclosure might:

(1) Be limited by the use of sampling methods.
(2) Occur in stages.

When might you justify seeking a direction under r.31.12(2) that a party must carry out a particular type of search and disclose documents located as a result? In the Commercial Court the following categories of cases are given by way of example: where fraud, dishonesty or misrepresentation is alleged; or where knowledge or the lack of it, or disclosure or non-disclosure, is in issue. In such instances you may be able to persuade the judge that a fuller understanding of the history of events in the case, or of the states of mind of those concerned, is vital to enable the court to dispose of the case justly. Obviously, you will have to convince the court that the likely costs of this are proportionate to the amount of money involved and the importance of the case. We have set out below a suggested order.

(1) On or before (date) (each/specify) party shall carry out a thorough search for all documents relevant to (the issues listed in the Schedule to this Order/the issues in the case), including for the avoidance of doubt, all documents which may lead to a train of inquiry enabling a party to advance his own case or damage that of his opponent.
(2) On or before (date) (each/specify) party shall disclose by list:
   (a) any documents located as a result of the search, and
   (b) any other documents relevant to (the issues listed in the Schedule to this Order/the issues in the case) that were once, but are no longer, in his control.

Experts

The following notes should be read in conjunction with Ch.23 where this topic is dealt with.   22.006

The judge must consider at the outset what expert evidence you and the other parties are proposing to call and whether that meets the overriding objective. Cases on the multi-track frequently are of such complexity or nature and size that the use of single joint experts is inappropriate. However, you should be prepared for the judge to ask if a single joint expert might be appointed to:

(a) Carry out an examination at this point in time.
(b) Chair and facilitate meetings of the parties' own experts. This may occur occasionally in complex multi-track cases where a meeting of the parties' own experts is likely to involve unusual difficulties or complexities.

If reports from experts in a number of disciplines or fields are necessary you must define such and obtain the court's approval. This can be a source of disagreement between the parties that the judge must endeavour to resolve. In such circumstances you might obtain a short opinion from a leading expert in the dominant discipline who you intend to instruct.

Trial date

22.007 By r.29.2(2) the court aims to fix the trial date or the period in which the trial is to take place as soon as practicable (see below).

Outside the Royal Courts of Justice ("RCJ"), a trial date or trial period will usually be specified in the directions on allocation. In cases proceeding in the RCJ, the directions on allocation will set a trial window only and will direct the claimant to obtain a listing appointment from the Clerk of the Lists within the next few days. Notice of that appointment must be given to the other parties and, at the appointment, the Clerk will set a trial period within the window having regard to the parties' representations.

Conducting a case management conference

22.008 A conference is akin to a business meeting. The judge wants to ascertain the issues in the case that need to be addressed and how that is then to happen pretrial. Where possible the advocate who is to conduct the trial should attend the conference. R.29.3(2) makes it clear that any legal representative who attends must be familiar with the case and possess sufficient authority to deal with any issues that are likely to arise. PD 29, para.5.2(2) adds that such a person must be personally involved in the case and able to deal with such matters as evidence, fixing the timetable and identifying the issues.

Should a represented party attend with his solicitor? We would suggest that in most cases, the answer must be yes. (Although note that in the Commercial Court the client is not required unless the court so directs). If the judge suggests a timetable that is different from that proposed, the client can immediately either confirm his agreement or explain why it cannot be met. In addition, some conferences have seen parties reach a settlement. See further below as to attendance at the pre-trial review.

Directions on allocation

You are in the best position to know what directions are required from the court for the case to proceed to trial. Reflect on what happened before proceedings commenced and decide what steps need to be taken next. As to completing the allocation questionnaire, see above and Ch.9.

PD 29, para.4.6 encourages you to co-operate with the other parties and agree directions to avoid a hearing. By para.4.7 any agreed directions must:

(a) Set out a timetable by reference to calendar dates for the taking of steps for the preparation of the case.
(b) Include a date or a period (the trial period) when it is proposed that the trial will take place.
(c) Include provision about disclosure of documents and both factual and expert evidence.

We have set out below a suggested set of possible directions concerning disclosure and evidence that might be proposed by you; or otherwise made on allocation or subsequently. A word of caution here. PD 29, para.5.8(1) requires you to issue and serve an application for any direction not routinely made at a case management conference which you believe will be opposed.

22.009

Suggested directions

Disclosure

Standard disclosure is to be made by (date), with inspection (number) days after notice.
Standard disclosure is to be made by (date) in relation to the following issues (issues defined), with inspection (number) days after notice.
Special disclosure order is to be complied with by (date), with inspection (number) days after notice.

22.010

Witness statements

Signed statements of witnesses of fact, and hearsay notices where required by r.33.2, are to be exchanged not later than (date).
Unless otherwise ordered, witness statements are to stand as the evidence in chief of the witness at trial.

Experts

Signed reports of experts:
are to be confined to one expert for each party from each of the following fields of expertise (fields defined); or

are to be confined to the following issues (issues defined); or
are to be exchanged (sequentially/simultaneously) not later than (date for each report in each field of expertise).

The meeting of experts is to be by (date).

The joint statement of the experts is to be completed by (date).
Any short supplemental expert reports are to be exchanged (sequentially/ simultaneously) by not later than (date for each report in each field of expertise).
If the experts' reports cannot be agreed, the parties are to be at liberty to call expert witnesses at the trial, limited to those experts whose reports have been exchanged pursuant to this Order.
The parties are to be at liberty to apply to call expert witnesses at the trial, limited to those experts whose reports have been exchanged pursuant to this Order.

Variation of directions

22.011 What should you do if you are dissatisfied with a direction made at a hearing you attended? The simple answer is to appeal it (see Ch.44). And what if the direction was made by the court of its own initiative? Within 14 days you must apply to the court for it to reconsider the matter. It is important to clearly state why the court should reconsider the particular direction. Perhaps there were facts the court did not know about, although you must remember that you did have the opportunity in the allocation questionnaire to provide the court with relevant information. If you fail to appeal or seek a reconsideration, as appropriate, it is assumed that you are content with the direction and any later application for a variation will have to show a change in circumstances since the order was made.

Can the parties vary the timetable(s) set on the multi-track? Rule 2.11 allows the parties to vary a date by written agreement unless a rule or court order prohibits it. There is no objection to the parties agreeing to extend the time for disclosure and exchanging evidence provided this does not alter the timetable for completing and returning the pre-trial checklists (see below). Problems may arise in dealing with evidence, for example, a witness may fall ill or an expert may not deliver his report on time. It is important to keep the other parties informed of developments and make a prompt application to the court as soon as it is clear that the balance of the timetable cannot be met. Do not leave it until the last minute.

Failure to comply with directions

22.012 The best approach to any case is to be fully prepared before proceedings are issued and to ask the court on allocation for directions that suit you. Then promptly obey the timetable. If you fail to meet a direction you can expect the other side to apply for an order to enforce it with a sanction (see Ch.33). PD 29, para.7.2 says any application should be made promptly and with prior warning. So if, for example, your opponent has not given disclosure on time, fire off a letter immediately and apply to the court three days later.

Adjourning the trial

Do not feel that you will be able to eventually persuade the court to put back a trial date. PD 29, para.7.4(6) says, "Litigants and lawyers must be in no doubt that the court will regard the postponement of a trial as an order of last resort." Hence, if a party has disclosed and exchanged enough information so that say two out of the four issues in dispute can be determined in the case, he can expect the court to order that the trial of those issues should proceed. The court will also order that when the remaining two issues are tried the defaulting party will not be able to recover any costs even if he wins. Where both sides are at fault the court may order that neither party should be entitled to costs.

There can be no doubt that in the past a minority of applications for adjournments were made by solicitors who had failed to properly conduct the action. The client had invariably been kept in the dark. There is, of course, a professional obligation on solicitors to keep their clients fully informed of all developments and the court has power under PD 29, para.7.4(6) to require a party, as well as his solicitor, to attend the hearing of an adjournment application.

22.013

Case management in the Royal Courts of Justice

As a general rule a non-personal injury claim with an estimated value of more than £15,000 may be commenced in the Central Office of the Royal Courts of Justice ("RCJ"). However, before doing so you should consider PD 29, para.2.2 which provides that most claims with a financial value of less than £50,000 will be transferred to a county court. Even if a claim exceeds £50,000 the court may order its transfer to a county court if it appears straightforward with no complex facts, legal issues, remedies or procedures involved.

PD 29, para.2.6 provides a list of matters considered suitable to be managed and tried at the RCJ even if their value may not exceed £50,000:

22.014

(1) Professional negligence claims.
(2) Fatal Accident claims.
(3) Fraud or undue influence claims.
(4) Defamation claims.
(5) Claims for malicious prosecution or false imprisonment.
(6) Claims against the police.
(7) Contentious probate claims.

CASE MANAGEMENT PRE-TRIAL

The pre-trial checklist

22.015 The court sends out the pre-trial checklist for you to complete and return by a date that is specified on the form which is not less than eight weeks before the trial. Although there is no obligation to exchange copies with other parties PD 29, para.8.1(5) encourages you to do so in order that the court are not given conflicting or incomplete information. If you want the court to give any particular directions, try to agree these first with the other parties but in any event you should file a draft order. See para.36.001 for more details.

After the pre-trial checklists have been returned or the time for their return has expired, the court file is referred to a judge who may issue final directions or convene a directions hearing. The court wishes to avoid a hearing and penalises in costs any party who makes one necessary. Ultimately, you will receive a notice in Form N172 confirming or fixing the trial date and specifying any directions made. If you are dissatisfied with a direction made on listing it is essential to appeal it or ask for a reconsideration, as appropriate, since the trial judge is not going to make last minute changes.

The most common directions at this stage are:

(a) Expert evidence to be given orally or by way of written reports filed with the listing questionnaire.
(b) Preparation of a trial bundle (see Ch.36).
(c) A trial timetable and time estimate (see Ch.36).

Pre-trial review

22.016 The court may hold a pre-trial review when dealing with complex cases involving numerous parties and/or those that are likely to last a significant period of time. In the Commercial Court trials estimated to last eight days or more usually have a pre-trial review. In respect of Chancery matters it is those cases estimated to last more than ten days. The pre-trial review is normally fixed to take place between eight and four weeks before the trial date. It may occur instead of, or in addition to, a listing hearing (see above).

A pre-trial review is normally dealt with by the trial judge. In addition to the directions outlined above, the following questions may also need to be addressed:

(a) Are there any preliminary issues to be dealt with?
(b) What issues are to be determined and in what order?
(c) Do any of the parties require the use of information technology at trial?
(d) In what order are witnesses to be called?

(e) Is the evidence of experts (or of experts on a particular issue) to be taken together at the same time and after factual evidence has been given?

(f) How are the trial documents to be organised?

The advocate who is to conduct the trial should attend the review. Rule 29.3(2) also applies, i.e. where a party is represented a person familiar with the case and with sufficient authority to deal with any issues that are likely to arise must attend. The client or a representative of a client company may be present. In the case of *Baron v Lovell, The Times*, September 14, 1999, CA the judge directed that a pre-trial review should occur and that "advocates and clients must attend the hearing. Advocates attending the hearing must have authority to make decisions concerning the case".

Lord Justice Brooke explained why such a direction had been given and warned of the price to be paid for its breach. He said:

"If ever there was a case which ought to have been settled at the pre-trial review, [. . .] it was this one. If it had, there would have been a saving of six sets of professional fees (orthopaedic, advocate and solicitor on both sides) for a full day's hearing at the trial [. . .]. Mr Baron would have been relieved of the continuing anxiety of these proceedings. This is the reason why a court may make it obligatory, as it did in this case, for the client to attend such a hearing, accompanied by an advocate who has authority to make decisions concerning the case. If a defendant's lawyers choose not to send a representative with appropriate authority to attend a pre-trial review and choose not to ensure that the client (who in this case should be equated with the defendant's insurer) attends the review, the judge, who is likely to be the trial judge, is likely to note their absence. If he considers that that party has acted unreasonably in this way in connection with the litigation in breach of a direction of the court, there may come a time when he decides that it is appropriate to make an order for indemnity costs against that party, or to exercise his power to award interest on damages at a much higher rate than what is usual, if those powers are available to him. The whole thrust of the CPR regime is to require the parties to behave reasonably towards each other in the conduct of the litigation."

Further details about this case are given in para.23.008, below.

INFORMATION TECHNOLOGY (IT)

The use of IT in litigation is increasing. For example, parties need to consider if disclosure can be given or evidence served and filed by use of IT. Note however the word of caution introduced by the Chancery Guide that the "use of IT is acceptable only if no party to the case will be unfairly prejudiced and its use will save time and money". 22.017

The following direction might be made at a case management conference or a pre-trial review:

> "The parties are to consult with each other and the court with a view to arranging service and filing of statements of case, disclosure lists, witness statements, experts' reports, trial bundle and other documents in computer readable form as well as in hard copy. The format for court disks is (specify format)."

TRIAL

22.018 Claims for damages for defamation, fraud, malicious prosecution and false imprisonment are tried by a judge and jury unless the court orders trial by a judge alone. Where a jury trial is to occur, it is essential that the time estimate given to the court should be accurate and realistic so as to ensure that the jury do not suffer hardship and inconvenience. When preparing for a jury trial, remember to copy sufficient bundles of documents for the use of the jury. If there are any outstanding procedural matters or applications, these should normally be dealt with before the jury is sworn in. For further guidance, see the Q.B.D. Court Guide.

As to preparing for trial and conducting it on the multi-track, see Chs 36 and 37.

CHAPTER 23

Experts

INTRODUCTION

There is no such thing as a "claimant's" or "defendant's" expert—or at least there should not be. By r.35.3 it is the duty of an expert to help the court on the matters within his expertise. This duty overrides any obligation to the party that has instructed him and/or is paying him. It is not for a party or any legal representative to literally dictate what the expert puts in his report:

23.001

> "Whilst some degree of consultation between experts and legal advisers is entirely proper, it is necessary that expert evidence presented to the court should be, and should be seen to be, the independent product of the expert, uninfluenced as to form or content by the exigencies of litigation. To the extent that it is not, the evidence is likely to be not only incorrect but self defeating" (*per* Lord Wilberforce in *Whitehouse v Jordan* [1981] 1 W.L.R. 246 at 256).

There is a CPR Protocol for the Instruction of Experts in Civil Cases ("PIE"). This is annexed to PD 35. We will refer to it during the course of this chapter.

Section 3 of the Civil Evidence Act 1972 sets out the test for calling an expert witness in civil proceedings as follows:

(a) The expert may give his opinion on any relevant matter. If an issue is irrelevant the court can exclude it from consideration under r.3.1(2)(k). The effect of such a direction is to prohibit the calling of expert evidence on a matter which would otherwise be admissible (see para.33.012).
(b) The expert must be qualified to give the opinion. What if your opponent chooses an expert who you believe is not suitably qualified? Whilst you can seek a court ruling on the point is there any advantage in doing so? If another party makes a poor selection, surely that is his problem?

In the case of *Sansom v Metcalfe Hambleton and Co.* (1995) Law Society's Gazette, February 4, the claimants sued the defendant, a firm of chartered surveyors, claiming professional negligence. The claimants alleged that the

323

defendants had failed to draw their attention to a crack in a wing wall which abutted a retaining wall but which had no structural significance. At the trial a structural engineer gave evidence for the claimants and a chartered surveyor for the defendant. The judge found the defendant liable and awarded damages.

However, the Court of Appeal allowed the defendant's appeal and dismissed the claim. The court held that it should be slow to find a professionally qualified person guilty of a breach of his duty of skill and care without evidence from those within the same profession as to the standard to be expected on the facts of the case and the failure of the qualified person to measure up to that standard. Whilst it is not an absolute rule, unless it was an obvious case, in the absence of the relevant expert evidence the claim would not be proved.

This case was far from open and shut. The evidence of the structural engineer was not expert evidence admissible in accordance with s.3 of the 1972 Act on the issue of the chartered surveyor's negligence. Accordingly, the judge had not had relevant and admissible evidence to show a failure by the chartered surveyor to comply with the standard of skill and care to be exercised by a competent surveyor.

A trial judge is not bound to accept the evidence of an expert. In *Dover District Council v Sherred*, *The Times*, February 11, 1997, Lord Justice Evans said:

> "Where expert evidence was admissible in order to enable the judge to reach a properly informed decision on a technical matter, then he could not set his own lay opinion against the expert evidence that he had heard. But he was not bound to accept the evidence even of an expert witness, if there was a proper basis for rejecting it in the other evidence that he had heard, or the expert evidence was such that he did not believe it or for whatever reason was not convinced by it."

Also see *Fuller v Strum* [2002] 2 All E.R. 87 where the trial judge declined to follow the evidence of a renowned handwriting expert (see further para.23.006).

Equally, the trial judge is not bound to accept the evidence of a single joint expert appointed and instructed by both parties to the litigation (see *Armstrong v First York* [2005] EWCA Civ 277; *The Times*, January 19, 2005 and para.23.008).

PRE-ACTION MATTERS

23.002 From the first interview with his solicitor a client will want an assessment of his chances of successfully suing or defending a claim. In technical mattes, unless the solicitor has specialist knowledge, he will be no better placed than a trial judge. Indeed, at this stage he is in a worse position as he probably has little or no idea of the other side's case. The solicitor will have to inform the client that the advice of a suitably qualified expert is necessary. When should this be obtained? Each case will turn on its own unique facts. There are two very simple rules. First, do not rush to instruct an expert. As we have seen it is vital that the correct expert is chosen. But, secondly, do not leave it too late. Select a suitable expert and ask him what information he needs in order to give the fullest possible and accurate opinion. Sound him out as to whether he feels the case might ultimately justify his attendance at trial and if so his general availability in the future.

If a report is obtained and it is favourable, do you show the contents to the other side? It might just lead to a settlement but will the other side really cave in? The unilateral disclosure of expert evidence will give the other side plenty of time to instruct their own expert to consider the report and "pick holes in it". Of course, in personal injury matters if proceedings are issued the rules require the claimant to attach to his particulars of claim any medical report he intends to rely on (see para.12.029). However, the usual rule during proceedings is for the simultaneous exchange of experts reports that the parties intend to rely on. Where this is both desirable and possible we recommend that it should take place during pre-action negotiations.

Whilst the current pre-action protocols (see para.6.013) encourage the joint selection of and access to experts, the report still "belongs" to the party who instructs the expert. There is no obligation to disclose it to the other side (see *Carlson v Townsend* [2001] 3 All E.R. 663). Contrast this with the appointment of a single joint expert in court proceedings (see para.23.006). However, an important restriction on the right to call expert evidence in personal injury cases can arise under the personal injury pre-action protocol. Where a party nominates an expert for agreement and no objection is made, the party who did not object will be prohibited from relying on their own expert evidence within that particular speciality unless either: (a) the other party agrees: or (b) the court so directs, or (c) the report from the expert has been amended and the instructing party is not prepared to disclose the original report.

RESTRICTIONS ON EXPERT EVIDENCE IN COURT PROCEEDINGS

The calling of oral or written expert evidence in all cases is controlled by the court. Its main powers are as follows.

23.003

Expert evidence must be reasonably required

Rule 35.1 provides that expert evidence should be restricted to that which is reasonably required to resolve the proceedings.

23.004

Example
In *May v Woollcombe Beer & Watts* [1998] 51 E.G. 88, the defendants (D) were a firm of solicitors who acted for the claimant (C) when he purchased his house. Prior to the purchase a modification order had been made by the local

authority in respect of two rights of way near the house, upgrading them from footpaths to bridlepaths, open to all traffic, and making a diversion. The local authority had submitted the order to the Secretary of State for confirmation. D had been informed by the seller's solicitors of the details of the order. However, D made no additional enquiry of the local authority concerning the status of the confirmation request with the Secretary of State.

Following completion of the purchase, a public enquiry was held and rights of way were confirmed as byways open to all traffic. C commenced proceedings against D alleging that he had only been told by D that the paths were footpaths that had been diverted. C claimed that D had been negligent in failing to ascertain whether the Secretary of State had been asked to confirm the rights of way as byways. C wanted to call expert evidence at trial from a solicitor experienced in conveyancing on the issue of whether further enquiries should have been made by D, and if so, what enquiries.

Judge Jack Q.C., sitting in the Mercantile Court, held that before making an order for expert evidence the court should be fully satisfied that an issue had arisen on which evidence of proper practice was necessary to allow the court to make its decision. In this case expert evidence was not required on the straightforward issue as to whether D should have made an additional enquiry of the local authority. However, having discovered the existence of the modification order, the issue arose as to whether D should have made enquiries to ascertain whether the local authority had sought confirmation of the order from the Secretary of State. That question could not be answered through textbooks or Law Society Guidance, and it was a matter on which the court would be assisted by evidence from an experienced conveyancer as to proper practice.

Case management of issues and evidence

23.005 By r.35.4(1) no party may call an expert or put in evidence an expert's report without the court's permission. In managing a case the court determines the issues on which it requires evidence, the nature of that evidence and the way that it is to be placed before the court (see r.32.1, para.33.012 and the decision of Aikens J. in *JP Morgan Chase Bank v Springwell Navigation Corp* [2006] EWHC 2755, (2006) L.T.L, December 4). Rule 35.5(1) provides that if the court requires expert evidence the presumption is that it will be given in a written report unless the court directs otherwise. The court normally considers the need for oral expert evidence on allocation and listing. Experts appointed by the parties are required to narrow down and explain their differences (see para.23.018 below) before the court will consider allowing them to give oral evidence at trial.

When a party wants the court's permission to call an expert or rely on his report he must either identify the actual expert or the field in which he wishes to rely on expert evidence. This is dealt with to a large extent in the allocation and pre-trial checklists, listing questionnaires (see Chs 9 and 36 respectively). As to case management on the multi track see Ch.22.

Experts' fees and expenses can form a significant part of the costs in many cases. By r.35.4(4) the court may limit the amount that is recoverable. In particular the court will consider the parties' conduct in the use of experts both before and during proceedings (see Ch.38).

Single jointly appointed expert

Rule 35.7(1) allows the court to direct the appointment of a single joint expert rather than each party instructing their own expert. The direction is made in relatively few small claims cases (see Ch.20). It is common in fast track cases (see Ch.21) that require expert evidence. This is because fast track matters are by their very nature relatively straightforward and concern one, or at most two issues that need expert evidence. As to the multi-track, see Ch.22.

23.006

A single expert is said to be sufficient where the case is concerned with a substantially established area of knowledge and it is not necessary for the court directly to sample a range of opinions. Obviously, the overriding objective and especially the aspects of saving expense and proportionately are important considerations. So, for example, in medical negligence cases, any non-medical expert evidence should usually be given by a single joint expert (see *Peet v Mid-Kent Healthcare NHS Trust* [2002] 3 All E.R. 688).

Both the Q.B.D. and the Chancery Court Guides provide that:

> "In very many cases it is possible for the question of expert evidence to be dealt with by a single expert. Single experts are, for example, often appropriate to deal with questions of quantum in cases where the primary issues are as to liability. Likewise, where expert evidence is required in order to acquaint the court with matters of expert fact, as opposed to opinion, a single expert will usually be appropriate. There remains, however, a body of cases where liability will turn upon expert opinion evidence and where it will be appropriate for the parties to instruct their own experts. For example, in cases where the issue for determination is as to whether a party acted in accordance with proper professional standards, it will often be of value to the court to hear the opinions of more than one expert as to the proper standard in order that the court becomes acquainted with the range of views existing upon the question and in order that the evidence can be tested in cross examination."

How do you instruct a single joint expert? The court normally directs that the parties should agree on the appointment between themselves. Failing that the court may make the appointment from any list the parties can agree or otherwise request the appropriate expert's professional body to make the appointment. Rule 35.8 provides that all the parties may instruct the expert and imposes no obligation to prepare joint instructions. In order to avoid the expert receiving instructions that might be thought to be conflicting, incomplete or inadequate we take the view that it is desirable to agree joint instructions to a single expert if at all possible. The parties must anticipate any problems (e.g. each party asking the expert to proceed on different assumptions) and should endeavour to resolve these. Otherwise such issues should be raised with the court in writing in the allocation questionnaire or pre-trial checklist or by way of application. If the parties separately instruct the expert they must send a copy of those instructions to all other parties at the same time (see PIE para.17.7). This may lead a party to feel that he should send additional instructions to the expert, for example, "the claimant has suggested that you carry out test X. In light of this we suggest you carry out test Y at the same time" or "the defendant has asked that you carry out test X. Our client will not consent to that test being carried out". The correspondence could continue to ridiculous lengths. Whilst it must be acceptable to clarify a point with an expert in the instructions received from another party, any substantial problems should be referred to the court. Indeed, r.35.8(3)(b) gives the court power to direct what inspections, examinations or experiments should be carried out by the expert. These matters should be considered at the time of the appointment of the single expert and not later. See further *Yorke v Katra* [2003] EWCA Civ 867; (2003) L.T.L., June 9.

What if expert evidence is required from different areas of expertise? PD 35, para.6 provides the solution by requiring that a leading expert is appointed in the dominant discipline. Other experts should then be appointed in the other relevant disciplines. The leading expert should prepare the general part of the report and annex or incorporate the contents of the reports from the other experts.

As to payment of a single joint expert's fees the instructing parties are jointly and severally liable unless the court directs otherwise. Before the expert is instructed the court may limit the amount he can be paid and direct that the instructing parties pay that amount into court. There appears to be no alteration to the basic rule that a solicitor who instructs an expert is personally liable to pay him unless a different agreement is reached. It therefore makes sense for a solicitor to come to some arrangement with the expert and the other instructing parties, especially if one or more of them is acting in person.

If you do not agree with the direction you should appeal it or ask for it be reconsidered, as appropriate. Failing that a party may decide to foot the costs of retaining his own expert adviser to deal with such matters as: the instructions that should be given to the single joint expert; drafting written questions (see below) and attending at trial to assist the advocate cross examine the expert. As the Chancery guide states, "An order for a single joint expert does not prevent a party from having his or her own expert to advise him or her, but he or she may well be unable to recover the cost of employing his or her own expert from the other party". As to costs, see Ch.38.

What if the expert fails to follow instructions and a party feels that his case has been prejudiced as a result? By analogy with the case law concerning expert determination: "if the mistake made was that the expert departed from his instructions in a material respect . . . either party would be able to say that the certificate was not binding because the expert had not done what he was appointed to do" (see *Jones v Sherwood Computer Plc* [1992] 1 W.L.R. 277). So if an expert uses a computer package for mapping the contours of strata of rock under the seabed that is different from that agreed by the parties and thereby places one party at a disadvantage, the court may terminate the appointment (see *Shell UK Ltd v Enterprise Oil Plc*, *The Times*, June 17, 1999).

In one of the earliest reported CPR cases, that of *Knight v Sage Group Plc* (1999) L.T.L., April 28, the Court of Appeal dealt with a personal injury matter. The claimant had attached only a preliminary medical report to her particulars of claim and was refusing to disclose two other medical reports. The court said that it had considered whether to direct that a joint expert should be appointed to report on the claimant's medical condition but declined to do so as the defendant was unwilling to accede to that course. However, the court anticipated that any judge who heard a future application concerning the service of a medical report would want to know whether the defendant had been willing to co-operate or maintained its present attitude not to agree to a joint medical expert being appointed.

When should a single joint expert attend trial? Mr Justice Colman in the shipping case of *Voaden v Champion* (2001) Lloyd's Rep.739, said:

"Certainly, in relation to trials in the Commercial Court and the Admiralty Court it will only be in cases where the sole expert is to report on discrete and substantially non-controversial matters, collateral to the main issues, that it should be assumed that the sole expert will not have to be present at the trial to explain the contents of his report. In any other case the absence of a sole expert may well prejudice the fair resolution of the expert issues in question and make it more difficult for the court to resolve those issues in the light of all the other evidence before it."

In the case of *Fuller v Strum* [2002] 2 All E.R. 87, the defendant challenged the validity of his late father's will. Each side had consulted his own handwriting expert and each expert had come up with a different answer. In the result, the master ordered that a single joint expert should be appointed. The reports of the other experts were not put in evidence. The joint expert concluded that there was very strong evidence that the will was a forgery. The trial judge commented:

"[The joint expert] did not give evidence orally. This was, I am told, in the interests of saving costs. However, in a case where factual evidence is in conflict with the expert's conclusions, the judge is faced with a dilemma, and it would have assisted me greatly to have had the opportunity to put this dilemma to [the joint expert], and to have obtained as much assistance as I could from her evidence. As it was, I was presented with a paper report coupled with a series of further limited questions, and even more limited and guarded answers, which were not of much assistance to me. While the dispassionate opinion of a court appointed expert would have been of great assistance had she been called to give oral evidence, I think that in the absence of such oral evidence, examination and cross-examination of the original two experts would have assisted me more."

What if you disagree with a single joint expert's report? The Court of Appeal had to consider this point in the case of *Walker v Daniels* (2000) 1 W.L.R. 1382. Lord Woolf M.R. said:

> "In a substantial case such as this [serious personal injuries sustained by claimant], the correct approach is to regard the instruction of an expert jointly by the parties as the first step in obtaining expert evidence on a particular issue. It is to be hoped that in the majority of cases it will not only be the first step but the last step. If, having obtained a joint expert's report, a party, for reasons which are not fanciful, wishes to obtain further information before making a decision as to whether or not there is a particular part (or indeed the whole) of the expert's report which he or she may wish to challenge, then they should, subject to the discretion of the court, be permitted to obtain that evidence. In the majority of cases, the sensible approach will not be to ask the court straight away to allow the dissatisfied party to call a second expert. In many cases it would be wrong to make a decision until one is in a position to consider the position in the round. You cannot make generalisations, but in a case where there is a modest sum involved a court may take a more rigorous approach. It may be said in a case where there is a modest amount involved that it would be disproportionate to obtain a second report in any circumstances. At most what should be allowed is merely to put a question to the expert who has already prepared a report. In a case where there is a substantial sum involved, one starts, as I have indicated, from the position that, wherever possible, a joint report is obtained. If there is disagreement on that report, then there would be an issue as to whether to ask questions or whether to get your own expert's report. If questions do not resolve the matter and a party, or both parties, obtain their own expert's reports, then that will result in a decision having to be reached as to what evidence should be called. That decision should not be taken until there has been a meeting between the experts involved. It may be that agreement could then be reached; it may be that agreement is reached as a result of asking the appropriate questions. It is only as a last resort that you accept that it is necessary for oral evidence to be given by the experts before the court. The expense of cross examination of expert witnesses at the hearing, even in a substantial case, can be very expensive. The great advantage of adopting the course of instructing a joint expert at the outset is that in the majority of cases it will have the effect of narrowing the issues. The fact that additional experts may have to be involved is regrettable, but in the majority of cases the expert issues will already have been reduced. Even if you have the unfortunate result that there are three different views as to the right outcome on a particular issue, the expense which will be incurred as result of that is justified by the prospects of it being avoided in the majority of cases".

The *Daniels'* case was considered by Neuberger J. in *Cosgrove v Pattison* (2001) L.T.L., February 7. There the parties owned adjoining houses and surrounding land. There was a boundary dispute involving related issues over a party wall and building of a shared driveway. A joint expert was appointed. However, the defendants were unhappy with his report and applied for permission to rely on an expert of their own who was already a witness of fact in the proceedings and had supplied a report criticising that of the joint expert. The application was refused but allowed on appeal. It was held that in determining whether to allow the evidence of a second expert, in addition to the evidence of an expert instructed jointly under Pt 35, the court had to consider:

(i) the nature of the issue or issues in dispute;
(ii) the number of issues in dispute on which the expert evidence was relevant;
(iii) the reason for requiring the second report;
(iv) the amount at stake and/or the nature of the issues at stake and their importance;
(v) the effect on the conduct of the trial of permitting a second expert to be called;
(vi) the delay, if any, in making the application;
(vii) the delay that instructing and calling the second expert might cause;
(viii) any other special features of the case;
(ix) the overall justice to the parties in the context of the litigation.

Should the judge dealing with an application to rely on a new expert's report see it? In the *Cosgrove* case Neuberger J. was happy not to. He commented:

"By tacit agreement between counsel I have not seen a copy of his report, and that may well be right. It may be embarrassing if I carried out some sort of weighing exercise between two expert reports, when neither expert is being called at this stage."

Where a single joint expert is appointed by the parties pursuant to a court order, can one party meet that expert without the other party being present? No, held the Court of Appeal in the case of *Peet v Mid-Kent Healthcare Trust* [2002] 3 All E.R. 688. The court stated that the framework of the Rules was designed to promote an open process so that both sides could be aware of what information was placed before the single expert. A single joint expert should not attend a conference with just one party unless that was expressly agreed in writing by all the parties. In *Childs v Vernon* [2007] EWCA Civ 305, (2007) L.T.L, March 16, the Court of Appeal stressed that it would be wholly improper for one party to have any discussion about the case with a joint expert in the absence of the other party unless the other party gave his fully informed consent. Where a party is a litigant in person he can only give such consent if he knows his rights.

EXPERT EVIDENCE OBTAINED BY EACH PARTY

23.007 "The general rule is that, whilst a party is entitled to privacy in seeking out the 'cards' for his hand, once he has put his hand together, the litigation is to be conducted with all the cards face up on the table. Furthermore, most of the cards have to be put down well before the hearing. This is not the product of a change of fashion or even recognition that professional judges approach their duties on the basis of mental equipment, training and attitudes of mind which are far removed from those of juries. It is the product of a growing appreciation that the public interest demands that justice is provided as swiftly and as economically as possible" (*per* Sir John Donaldson M.R., *Naylor v Preston Area Health Authority* [1987] 2 All E.R. 353 at 359).

If the parties are permitted by the court to obtain their own expert evidence, r.35.13 provides that failure to disclose an expert's report will mean that the party cannot use it at trial nor call the expert to give evidence unless the court gives permission. Consider the example below.

Example

The claimant is suing the defendant in negligence. In order to decide whether or not to take legal advice she obtains a report from expert X. This is favourable only in parts and although it also lacks any detailed analysis she goes to see a solicitor for advice. Following a letter of claim and subsequent negotiations liability was denied. The claimant cannot agree with the defendant on the appointment of a joint expert and she decides to instruct her solicitor to obtain a further report. The solicitor gets this from expert Y. It is satisfactory and proceedings are issued. A defence is filed and the case is allocated to the multi-track. The court directs that standard disclosure (see Ch.30) should occur. The claimant decides to retain the privilege from inspection that exists for both reports. However, in accordance with the direction to exchange the report of any expert she intends to rely on at trial, her solicitors subsequently send the defendant a copy of Y's report.

Think of it this way. The claimant has collected two "cards", the reports from X and Y, that she might play during the action. However, she is entitled not to throw down either card as it attracts legal professional privilege. The first time the procedural rules require her to disclose the cards is at standard disclosure. This she does by disclosing the existence of the documents ("experts reports prepared for taking legal advice in contemplation of these proceedings") but as each is privileged from inspection, and she chooses not to waive that privilege, neither document needs to be specifically identified. The next time she has to deal with the documents procedurally is to comply with the direction to exchange experts reports that she intends to rely on at trial, i.e. to now play a card before the trial. She will play Y's report but never play X's. Subject to what we say immediately below, the defendant will never see the report from X and certainly will not have to pay the costs associated with it even if he loses.

Conditional permission and refusal of permission

23.008 In *Vasiliou v Hajigeorgiou* [2005] EWCA Civ 236 [2005] All E.R. (D) 179 (Mar), the court directed that: "Both parties do have permission, if so advised, to instruct one expert each in the specialism of restaurant valuation and profitability". D instructed expert X to inspect the property and prepare a report. D then wanted to instruct expert Y instead. Did D need the court's permission to instruct expert Y instead of X? No, held the Court of Appeal. But, had the direction been that D had permission to instruct one expert and named that person as expert X, then in those circumstances permission would have been required. And would the court have granted it? Yes, said the Court of Appeal but in order to prevent expert shopping and as a check against possible abuse, disclosure of the abandoned expert's report will normally be imposed as a condition. See also *Beck v Ministry of Defence* [2003] EWCA Civ 1043; *The Times*, July 21, 2003.

What if a party obtains a report from an expert before proceedings start but during the litigation it seeks the court's permission to rely on a different expert at trial? In what circumstances might the court require the first report to be disclosed as a condition of granting permission to the party to rely on another expert in the same field? In *Carruthers v MP Fireworks Ltd* (2007) L.T.L., February 6, a decision of Mr Recorder Browne Q.C. at the Bristol County Court, the first expert had performed tests on the firework in issue. The court therefore felt that if the claimant wanted to rely on a different expert, the results of those initial tests should be put before other experts and the court. This was especially so as the first expert's tests may have caused some physical alteration to the exhibit in question.

The court may refuse to allow a party to call certain expert evidence. In *Baron v Lovell* (1999), *The Times*, September 14, 1999, the parties were obliged by court order to disclose their expert evidence by November 20, 1998. However, the defendant's medical expert did not examine the claimant until January 6, 1999. His report was received by the defendant's solicitors on February 24, 1999 but they failed to disclose it to the claimant's solicitors who assumed that the defendant did not intend to rely on the report at trial. A pre-trial review occurred but the defendant did not attend and the defendant's solicitors instructed agents. The agents were able to hand the report to the judge but they could offer no explanation as to why it had not been disclosed earlier. The judge noticed that there was a large measurement of agreement between the parties' experts and he dismissed as nonsense the defendant's expert's statement that the claimant's employment would not be prejudiced. The judge refused to permit the defendant to call their expert since the case would be further delayed by the need for the experts to discuss the case and file a joint statement. He further directed that the claimant's expert evidence was to be limited to the two written reports previously disclosed and there was to be no oral expert evidence at trial. This was upheld by the Court of Appeal. Lord Justice Brooke said: "Everyone therefore knows where they stand, and there will be a great saving of time, expense and uncertainty as a result". Also see *Calenti v North Middlesex NHS Trust* (2001) L.T.L., April 10.

Expert's duties and format of report (PD 35, paras 1 and 2) (PIE para.4)

23.009 Any expert that is instructed to give or prepare evidence for the purpose of court proceedings must prepare his report in accordance with Pt 35. It is the duty of an expert to help the court on matters within his own expertise. This duty is paramount and overrides all other obligations, including those owed to the person from whom he receives instructions or payment. Expert evidence must be the independent product of the expert that is not influenced by the pressures of litigation. An expert is required to assist the court by providing an objective and unbiased opinion on matters within his expertise. He should not assume the role of an advocate. He should consider all material facts, including those that might detract from his opinion. An expert should make it clear when a question or issue falls outside his expertise and when he is not able to reach a definite opinion, for example, because he has insufficient information. If, after producing a report, an expert changes his view on any material matter, this must be communicated to all the parties without delay, and when appropriate to the court.

Any expert's report must:

(a) be addressed to the court and not you;
(b) give details of the expert's qualifications and any literature or other materials which he has relied on in compiling the report. For example, if an expert refers to research evidence in his report, he must identify it in the report, so that it will be available to be considered by the other side without delay (and not merely four days before the trial starts as happened in *DN (by his father and litigation friend RN) v London Borough of Greenwich* [2004] EWCA Civ 1659; [2005] 1 F.C.R. 112);
(c) state what test or experiments he carried out or supervised;
(d) summarise any range of opinions and give reasons for the conclusions he has reached;
(e) contain a statement that he has understood and discharged his duty to the court;
(f) contain a statement setting out the substance of all material instructions (whether written or oral). The statement should summarise the facts and instructions given to the expert which are material to the opinions expressed in the report or upon which those opinions are based; and
(g) be verified by a statement of truth. The wording prescribed by PD 35, para.1.4 is,

> "I confirm that insofar as the facts stated in my report are within my own knowledge I have made clear which they are and I believe them to be true, and that the opinions I have expressed represent my true and complete professional opinion." This wording is mandatory and must not be modified (PIE para.13.5).

Will an expert witness be permitted to depart substantially from his written report in his evidence-in-chief at trial? No, held the Court of Appeal in *DN (by his father and litigation friend RN) v London Borough of Greenwich* [2004] EWCA Civ 1659; [2005] 1 F.C.R. 112, not unless the trial judge is satisfied that no injustice will result in the circumstances of the particular case.

When is an "expert" not an expert?

In *Stevens v Gullis and Pile* [2000] 1 All E.R. 527, C was a builder who sued D, his former customer for an unpaid bill. D counterclaimed alleging the work had been delayed, incomplete and defective. D joined in T as a Pt 20 third party (see Ch.18). T was D's architect who had supervised the works and approved them. D instructed as an expert, I. The parties' experts were directed to meet and file a joint memoranda. I attended a meeting but overlooked drawing up the memoranda despite numerous reminders. The judge directed that I had to set out in writing the details required by PD 35, para.1.2 (see above) failing which D would not be able to call I as an expert in the third party proceedings. I wrote to the court a letter headed "SI Architecture" indicating that his relevant qualification was a BSc (Hons) Building Surveying and setting out details of his experience. He failed to give any statement of truth, saying instead that he had submitted his reports to the best of his ability and that each was a true and accurate account of the condition of the building at the time of his inspections.

The judge was not impressed with I. Not only had he omitted a statement of truth but he had not set out the substance of his instructions and this was of particular concern as there were suspicions that I was taking instructions directly from D. The judge also noted that there had been no application for relief from the sanction he had imposed (see para.33.015)). The judge concluded: "In my view it is in the interests of the administration of justice that (I) should not give his evidence . . . It is essential in a complicated case such as this that the court should have a competent expert dealing with matters which are in issue". On appeal, Lord Woolf M.R. said that the requirements of PD 35, para.1 are intended to focus the mind of an expert on his responsibilities in order that litigation can progress in accordance with the overriding principles set out in Pt 1. However, I had demonstrated that he had no conception of those requirements and the judge had been correct to exclude him from giving expert evidence. The judge had directed that I could give evidence as to fact. The Court of Appeal revoked that order since I had not inspected the building until about three and a half years after C had finished his works and by that time further works had been carried out. Moreover, it would be extraordinarily difficult, if not impossible, for him to give evidence as to fact without giving evidence as an expert.

C and D had agreed that I should act as an expert witness in the main claim provided he complied with the formalities required by PD 35 by a specified date. They invited the court to make an order to that effect by consent. Lord Woolf said that it would be quite wrong for the court to do so. It was not known if I would obey the order but moreover it would be wholly wrong to impose I as an

23.010

expert upon the judge who had very properly indicated his view that I was not an appropriate person to give expert evidence. The parties could not override judicial discretion to exclude expert evidence.

If an expert fails to discharge his duty to the court, it is likely that the judge will report him to his professional body: see *Pearce v Ove Arup Partnership* (2001) L.T.L., November 8. Note that in this case the expert's governing body did not agree with the judge (see *The Lawyer*, February 10, 2003). That professional regulatory bodies have a disciplinary role in respect of their members who act as expert witnesses was confirmed by the Court of Appeal in *Meadow v General Medical Council* [2006] EWCA Civ 1390, [2007] 2 W.L.R. 286. Can a wasted costs order be made against an expert? Yes, held Mr Justice Peter Smith in *Phillips v Symes* [2004] EWHC 2330; *The Times*, November 5, 2004. He stated:

> "It seems to me that in the administration of justice, especially, in spite of the clearly defined duties now enshrined in CPR 35 and PD 35, it would be quite wrong of the court to remove from itself the power to make a costs order if appropriate against an expert who, by his evidence, causes significant expense to be incurred, and does so in flagrant reckless disregard of his duties to the Court." Also see PIE para.4.7.

Legal professional privilege and the instructions to an expert

23.011 As noted above, where parties jointly instruct a single expert in court proceedings they will each see the instructions given by the other to the nominated expert. But what is the status of oral and written instructions given by a solicitor to an expert solely instructed on behalf of a client? Rule 35.10(3) provides that the expert's report must state the substance of all material instructions, whether written or oral, on the basis of which the report was written. Or, as PD 35 para.2.1(3) puts it, the report must "contain a statement setting out the substance of all facts and instructions given to the expert which are material to the opinions expressed in the report or upon which those opinions are based".

So, has legal professional privilege in relation to instructions to an expert gone? Rule 35.10(4) states that whilst the instructions shall not be privileged against disclosure, the court will not generally order disclosure of any specific document referred to in the instructions nor permit the expert to be questioned on his instructions save by the person who instructed him. An exception will be made only if the court is satisfied that there are reasonable grounds to consider that the statement of instructions given by the expert in his report is "inaccurate or incomplete". This is qualified by PD 35, para.4 which provides that such cross examination will only be permitted where it is in the "interests of justice". Of course, a client can always waive privilege if he wishes to do so. Indeed, there are many occasions when solicitors might use a standard format for instructions to an expert similar to the pre-action personal injury protocol version. In such a case there should be no objection to the expert exhibiting those to his report. There is no question of confidential information concerning the merits of the case having to be disclosed.

We take the view that the court will not readily entertain any applications for disclosure or cross examination in this context. After reports have been exchanged it should be routine for you to send a copy of the other side's report(s) to your own expert(s) for comment. Obviously, one point that can be looked for is whether any reports are based on inaccurate or incomplete instructions. If there are doubts the matter should be raised in correspondence and/or an interim application made for directions concerning the "suspicious" report. If you leave the matter until trial the court are unlikely to be sympathetic because you may be seen as trying to ambush your opponent.

The scope of r.35.10(4) was addressed by the Court of Appeal in *Lucas v Barking, Havering & Redbridge Hospitals NHS Trust* [2003] EWCA Civ 1102; [2004] 1 W.L.R. 220.

> "There is a plain impact on the scope of legal professional privilege, and thus a degree of protection against the loss of privilege is given by the restrictions on disclosure provided for by 35.10(4). I think it a premise of the arrangements constituted by 35.10(3) and (4) that in the ordinary way the expert is to be trusted to comply with 35.10(3): the effect of the 35.10(4) restrictions is that the party on the other side may not as a matter of course call for disclosure of documents constituting the expert's instructions as a check to see that 35.10(3) has been fulfilled. There must be some concrete fact giving rise to 'reasonable grounds' within the closing words of 35.10(4). It is unsurprising that the expert is thus to be trusted; it is of a piece with his overriding duty to help the court (CPR 35.3). Overall, 35.10(4) in my view strikes an important balance between on the one hand the protection of the party whose privilege is lost, and on the other the vindication of 35.10(3) where there is a real question-mark as to its fulfilment" (*per* Laws L.J.).

There must be transparency in the instructions given to an expert so that he can be seen to have acted impartially, independently and in full compliance with his duty to the court. Never put pressure on an expert to give favourable evidence. Likewise, the temptation to ask an expert to edit or re-write parts of his report should be resisted. If you telephone him up and "suggest" that he removes or substantially re-writes one of his conclusions, that oral instruction is clearly material to the report and he should include it (see PIE paras.13.15 and 15.2). What about the more subtler approach of asking the expert to "fine tune" his report-to edit out a bit here, add a bit there and change a few words? Provided the expert agrees and his opinions remain unchanged, technically there is no problem. But the bottom line is surely that the expert should express himself in his report in his own words. After all, he is supposed to be communicating with the court.

If an expert makes an early report to his client before he makes the report which is later disclosed in the litigation as being the evidence he intends to give at trial, does the law require that the earlier report should also be open to inspection? No, held the Court of Appeal in *Jackson v Marley Davenport Ltd* [2004] EWCA Civ 1225; [2004] 1 W.L.R. 2926. The early report is usually protected from inspection by legal professional privilege (see para.30.013).

Directions sought by an expert (r.35.14)

23.012 An expert can make a written request to the court for any direction that will assist him in carrying out his task. It appearst that a single jointly appointed expert uses this provision the most. This is likely because he receives instructions from any number of parties, all of whom have competing interests. So in a multi-party action this might be a considerable number of solicitors' letters. He may receive instructions that he considers are inadequate or incomplete despite his best attempts to ask for clarification. His instructions may conflict and he may be unable to find any acceptable solution. He may know that one of the parties has a document that he needs to look at but the party refuses to hand it over or denies that he has it. In rare cases he is going to be asked by a party to act contrary to his duty to the court. Whatever the problem, the answer is for the expert to obtain a court direction (see PIE para.11). In some instances the threat of such might resolve the issue. Otherwise, the expert can apply without notifying any party.

If you instruct your own expert can you make it a term of his retainer that he must raise any matter with you first before he asks the court for a direction? Rule 35.14 is entitled: "Expert's right to ask the court for directions". Sub-paragraph (2) specifically provides that an expert must, unless the court orders otherwise, provide a copy of any proposed request for directions to the party instructing him. This must be done at least seven days before the request is filed. Further, notice must also be given to all other parties at least four days before the request is filed. The intention is to reduce the risk of the expert accidentally informing the court about without prejudice or privileged matters by allowing any party to approach the court first if it considers such matters will be disclosed as a result of the expert's request.

An expert must feel confident that he can discharge his duty to the court. In respect of a single joint expert it may well be that some of the problems that arise will illustrate that the direction for his appointment was inappropriate and in those circumstances the court are likely to revoke the order. What you can be certain about is that the court will penalise a party whose conduct is deemed to be inappropriate. This is usually by way of the imposition of sanctions and/or costs (see Chs 33 and 38 respectively).

The provision of information (r.35.9)

23.013 What if a claimant takes an action against say a hospital in a complex clinical dispute and his expert requires certain information from the hospital in order to prepare a proper report? The first step is to ask the hospital to voluntarily disclose the information. Failing that, you should apply in the usual way on notice to the court for a direction that the hospital must file a document containing this information. By PD 35, para.3 the document should set out sufficient details of any facts, tests, or experiments which constitute the information to enable the expert to make an assessment and obtain an understanding of the significance of the information.

Such a direction is only made in furtherance of the overriding objective. Obviously, r.1.1(2)(a) is of importance as the applicant will claim that the information is necessary to put the parties on an equal footing. See further para.1.009. We recommend that the applicant's expert makes a witness statement in support stating what information is required and why. If the information is only otherwise available after time-consuming and expensive research details of such should be given. The court are concerned to determine if the proposed exercise is cost effective and whether it is required to fairly deal with the issues in question. In certain circumstances a respondent may resist the application on the basis of commercial confidentiality.

How many experts?

On the fast track the parties are limited to a maximum of two experts giving oral evidence, i.e.: (a) one expert per party in relation to any field; and (b) no more than two expert fields. There is no limit imposed on the number of written expert reports. There are no prescribed limits on the multi-track. Obviously, the overriding objective and especially the concept of proportionality will be upper most in the judge's mind when considering this point. See, for example, *S v Chesterfield & North Derbyshire Royal Hospital NHS Trust* [2003] EWCA Civ 1284; (2004) Lloyd's Rep.Med 90. 23.014

Whilst the starting point is that each party should be allowed the same number of experts, the overriding objective does not require that to ultimately be the court's order. "The desirability for equality of arms was not intended to result in an absolute rule that, in every case, the parties must be limited to calling the same number of experts" *per* Smith L.J. in *Kirkman v Euro Exide Corp (CMP Batteries) Ltd* [2007] EWCA Civ 66, *The Times*, February 6, 2007.

Impartiality and proportionality

Can a party, his former or current employees or so-called "in house" experts give expert evidence? Rule 35.2 defines an "expert" for the purposes of Pt 35 as an expert who has been instructed to give or prepare evidence for the purpose of court proceedings. Such an expert owes a duty to the court and his report must be prepared in accordance with Pt 35. Whilst, therefore, the appointment of an independent expert should always occur there is no objection to the client or his employees or in-house experts making a witness statement that contains factual evidence. But can a party's employee or in-house expert give expert evidence? In *Field v Leeds* CC (2000) 17 E.G. 165, the Court of Appeal held that it may be appropriate for an expert to be called who is an employee of a party 23.015

provided that person is properly qualified to give evidence. The court must be supplied with a proper report so the judge can assess:

(i) what the issues in the case are likely to be; and
(ii) the expert's ability to deal with those issues.

How can a party's employees or in-house experts meet with the requirements of Pt 35? Lord Woolf in the Field case said:

"If the City Council wishes to use a witness such as Mr Broadbent [an officer in its Claims Investigation Section], it is important that they show that he has full knowledge of the requirements for an expert to give evidence before the court, and that he is fully familiar with the need for objectivity. In the future I would encourage, if a person such as Mr Broadbent is to give evidence, the authority concerned provides some training for such a person to which they can point to show that he has the necessary awareness of the difficult role of an expert, particularly in relation to claims such as these. I would not agree with the approach of the judge, while understanding why he adopted that approach on the material which was before him".

Waller L.J. added:

"The question whether someone should be able to give expert evidence should depend on whether:

(i) it can be demonstrated whether that person has relevant expertise in an area in issue in the case; and
(ii) that it can be demonstrated that he or she is aware of their primary duty to the court if they give expert evidence."

Those tests were applied by Aikens J. in *Gallaher International Ltd v Tlais Enterprises Ltd (No.2)* [2007] EWHC 464, (2007) L.T.L., April 19. He allowed the claimant to rely on the expert evidence of an employee of an associate company. Why? Because the relationship was openly declared; the expert had been isolated from the rest of the company during the period of his instruction; the expert had shown that he was willing and able to carry out his duty to the court; the expert could give relevant evidence in a field where expertise was scarce and the defendant would be able to cross-examine the expert on the issue of his independence at trial.

Is an expert who has a close personal and professional relationship with a litigant precluded as a matter of law from acting as the litigant's expert? Neuberger J. sitting in the Chancery Division in the case of *Liverpool Roman Catholic Archdiocesan Trustees Inc. v Goldberg, The Times*, March 9, 2001, answered that question in the negative. In his Lordship's judgment, when considering an application to exclude expert evidence, the court should have in mind the following factors:

(a) If the expert evidence was said to be inadmissible then the point should be raised as soon as possible. The parties and the court should know where they were sooner rather than later and a determination of the point early would save costs and assist case management generally. Moreover, the decision on admissibility might be challenged in the Court of Appeal. If the decision on admissibility was reached only very shortly before the trial then, particularly if the decision was that the evidence was inadmissible, if the decision turned out to be wrong the trial would go ahead on a false basis and the Court of Appeal might feel that there was no option but to order a retrial; or the trial date would be lost while the question of admissibility went to the Court of Appeal, or the appeal would have to be rushed on inconveniencing the Court of Appeal and causing unfair delay to other litigants.

(b) If the objection was raised early, the court should normally determine it unless the court was satisfied that the trial judge would be in a better position to decide the point.

(c) If the objection was raised later then the court should be slower to determine the application rather than leaving it to the trial judge. However, that did not mean that the court should not determine it if it thought it appropriate to do so.

(d) The court should be particularly slow to determine an application to exclude evidence when the application was made so late that the case was coming on for trial.

(e) If there was any real doubt whether expert evidence was admissible the issue should be determined in favour of admissibility.

Note, however, that when the matter reached trial, Evans-Lombe J. ruled that the evidence should be disregarded on the basis that:

"where it is demonstrated that there exists a relationship between the proposed expert and the party calling him which a reasonable observer might think was capable of affecting the views of the expert so as to make them unduly favourable to that party, his evidence should not be admitted however unbiased the conclusions of the expert might probably be" (see [2001] 1 W.L.R. 2337).

However, the Court of Appeal in *Factortame (R. on the application of) v Secretary of State for Transport* [2002] 4 All E.R. 97 observed that:

"This passage seems to us to be applying to an expert witness the same test of apparent bias that would be applicable to the tribunal. We do not believe that this approach is correct. It would inevitably exclude an employee from giving expert evidence on behalf of an employer. Expert evidence comes in many forms and in relation to many different types of issue. It is always desirable that an expert should have no actual or apparent interest in the outcome of the proceedings in which he gives evidence, but such disinterest is not automatically a precondition to the admissibility of his evidence. Where an expert has an interest of one kind or another in the outcome of the case, this fact should be made known to the court as soon as possible. The question of whether the proposed expert should be permitted to give evidence should then be determined in the course of case management. In considering that question the judge will have to weigh the alternative choices open if the expert's evidence is excluded, having regard to the overriding objective of the Civil Procedure Rules" (*per* Lord Phillips M.R.).

What about a party acting as his own expert? In *DN (by his father and litigation friend RN) v London Borough of Greenwich* [2004] EWCA Civ 1659; [2005] 1 F.C.R. 112 the Court of Appeal observed that it very often happens in professional negligence cases that a defendant will give evidence to a judge which constitutes the reason why he considers that his conduct did not fall below the standard of care reasonably to be expected of him. He may do this by reference to the professional literature that was reasonably available to him as a busy practitioner or by reference to the reasonable limits of his professional experience; or he may seek to rebut, as one professional man against another, the criticisms made of him by the claimant's expert(s). Such evidence is common and admissible. But, of course, a defendant's evidence on matters of this kind may lack the objectivity to be accorded to the evidence of an independent expert and this consideration goes to the cogency of the evidence, not to its admissibility (see also *ES v Chesterfield and North Derbyshire Royal Hospital NHS Trust* [2003] EWCA Civ 1284; [2004] Lloyd's Rep.Med 90). In any event such a defendant should normally call an independent expert.

What about any other potential or actual conflict of interest? In *Toth v Jarman* [2006] EWCA Civ 1028, [2006] 4 All E.R. 1276, the defendant doctor was sued for clinical negligence. One of his experts was a member of the Cases Committee of the Medical Defence Union (MDU). The claimant argued that this raised an undisclosed conflict of interest between the expert's duty of objectivity as an expert and his interest in assisting in the defence of a member of the MDU. The Court of Appeal held that whilst the presence of a conflict of interest does not automatically disqualify an expert, the key question is whether the expert's opinion is independent. The court stressed that it is not for the parties to decide the issue. This is because where an expert has a material or significant conflict of interest, the court is likely to refuse the party permission to rely on that evidence or otherwise the trial judge may well decline to accept it. It is therefore important that a party who wishes to call an expert with a potential conflict of interest should disclose details of that conflict to both the court and the other parties at as early a stage in the proceedings as possible. In any event an expert should produce his curriculum vitae when he provides his report and this should give details of any employment or activity that raises a possible conflict of interest.

When will exchange occur?

The usual direction is for the parties to exchange reports setting out the substance of any expert evidence on which they intend to rely by a specified date. In most cases the exchange will be simultaneous. When you are ready to exchange your report(s) you should advise your expert(s) (see PIE para.14.1) and contact the other parties to see if they are also in a position to do so. The usual practice is for solicitors to undertake to put the report(s) in that night's post or DX. If a solicitor gives such an undertaking he must ensure that it is carried out.

23.016

What if you cannot make the deadline to exchange? Normally, this happens because an expert has let you down, although it is only fair to say that usually it is due to the expert being ill. However, as soon as it becomes clear that you will be unable to exchange in accordance with the direction you should contact all the other parties and seek their agreement to an extension of time for the exchange. Check with the expert when he can realistically guarantee that you will get the report and propose that date. Any agreement reached must be recorded in writing but remember that the parties cannot alter the case management dates set in fast track or multi-track cases (see Chs 21 and 22 respectively). If no agreement is reached or if a case management date will not be met, ensure you make an immediate application to the court.

What if you are ready to exchange within the deadline but your opponent is not? If a good reason is given for an extension you should agree to it, subject to what we have said above. But what if there has been no request or application for an extension? If you comply with the direction and serve the report(s) your opponent will gain an advantage. This is of far greater significance in relation to witness statements (see the analysis on this point at para.31.005). We recommend that you file the report(s) with the court, explain the situation in a covering letter and ask the court to make an order of its own initiative. If your court's practice is to make orders of its own initiative when receiving such information from a party, we see no need to make a formal application for the defaulting party to be prevented from relying on expert evidence at trial. In any event, we would expect the court to normally allow a further short period of time to comply with the direction before effectively depriving the party of a significant part of its case.

Sequential exchange

The court will normally direct a simultaneous exchange of experts' reports. However, if the defendant is unable to address an issue properly because the claimant alone knows the relevant facts or if costs will be saved, a sequential exchange may be ordered.

23.017

Examples

The claimant brought an action against the defendants, his employers, claiming damages for personal injuries. He alleged that he had become deaf as a result of being exposed since 1952 to excessive noise in the course of his employment with the defendants at their railway workshops. The Court of Appeal held that in the majority of cases, where the area of inquiry was comparatively limited, it might be just and convenient that there should be simultaneous disclosure of non-medical expert's reports. In this case, however, the inquiry went back to 1952 and it was likely that at the trial the claimant's only witnesses would be himself and his expert. In addition it would be for the claimant to say where and under what conditions he had been working. Until the claimant had given that evidence, the defendants could not direct their minds either to the precautions which they had or ought to have taken, or the degree of noise at any particular place at any particular time. In those circumstances the fair way of dealing with the expert evidence was that there should be sequential exchange of reports. Otherwise, the defendants would be called upon to write a thesis on noise generally in engineering workshops and that would be of no value to anyone. See *Kirkup v British Railways Engineering Ltd* [1983] 3 All E.R. 147.

In *Rayment v Ministry of Defence, The Times*, July 6, 1998, the Master ordered disclosure of the defendant's report as to quantum to be made two months after the claimant's. He made an order for mutual exchange relating to negligence, causation and prognosis. Mr Justice Harrison upheld the Master's order. He said that there was a significant potentially for duplication and waste of costs if there were to be a simultaneous exchange of experts' reports on quantum. However, it would not necessarily be right to make that order as a matter of course in each case.

Discussions between experts (r.35.12)

23.018 The court will not permit oral expert evidence unless it is necessary. Where each party has been allowed to appoint its own expert the court will usually direct that the experts identify and discuss the expert issues to try and reach agreement and to narrow down those issues. If it is convenient and cost effective most experts will meet face to face but a direction to discuss the matter could also be complied with by telephone or video conference. Following the discussion the experts are normally directed to prepare a statement "for the court" showing those issues on which they agree and disagree with a summary of their reasons for disagreeing. If the experts have a fundamental difference of opinion as to the correct approach to be taken in respect of an issue, that would clearly justify a direction for each to attend the trial to give oral evidence. As the statement is prepared for the court it may be used by any party as the basis on which to cross examine an opponent's expert (see *Robin Ellis Ltd v Malwright* (1999) C.L. June). But does it become a privileged statement if it is used in a mediation? No, not any more than would the statements of case in the action, if they were so used. This was the decision of the Court of Appeal in *Aird v Prime Meridian Ltd* [2006] EWCA Civ 1866, *The Times*, February 14, 2007. However, it is important to note that the case, stayed so mediation could be attempted, did not follow the usual sequence of events. As Smith L.J. stated:

"In the course of argument, I observed that in my experience it was unusual for a joint statement to be ordered, as it was here, before expert reports had been exchanged. We were told that this is not an uncommon practice in the Technology and Construction Court. It seems to me that there are dangers inherent in producing a joint statement until after expert reports have been exchanged. There is a danger that one expert might express agreement with the other expert which, on taking full instructions from his client after production of his report, he wishes to resile from. It appears that that is what has happened here."

It is important to ensure that any discussion between experts correctly identifies the issues that need to be resolved in the case. The court may specify the issues that must be discussed and a party may assist his expert in drawing up the agenda. However, the parties and their lawyers must appreciate that it is generally recognised that the most productive discussions between experts occur in their absence. As the Commercial Court Guide states:

"Neither the parties nor their legal representatives should seek to restrict the freedom of experts to identify and acknowledge the expert issues on which they agree (i.e. on which they share the same expert opinion) at (or following further consideration after) meeting of experts".

Your client is protected by the fact that the content of the discussion cannot be referred to at trial, unless all the parties agree, as the discussion is "without prejudice" (see para.6.024).

Any agreement reached as a consequence of a discussion between experts will not be binding on the parties unless they expressly decide to accept it. Obviously, a party may not be best pleased if his expert has a change of view as a result of the discussion. The party will have to decide whether or not to accept the expert's new position and what room he has left to manoeuvre. So if a party's own expert now agrees wholly or mainly with the opponent's expert, will that party be given the court's permission to rely on alternative expert evidence? The answer is only in rare cases where the party can demonstrate a good reason, such as the expert acting outside his instructions or expertise, or otherwise shown to have acted incompetently. The obvious starting point should be to ask the expert why he has changed his views: see *Stallwood v David* [2006] EWHC 2600, [2007] 1 All E.R. 206. The problem that arose in this case would have been avoided had the expert followed PIE paras 15.4 and 15.5 and given his reasons for his change of views.

Is an expert immune from suit? In *Stanton v Callaghan* [1998] 4 All E.R. 961, the Court of Appeal held that an expert who prepared a joint statement, in conjunction with the expert instructed by another party, for the purpose of indicating what matters were or were not in issue between them, was immune from suit by the party who had retained him in respect of that statement. That was so, notwithstanding that he did not in the event give evidence at trial, either because it did not take place or because he was not called as a witness. Such immunity was justified because the public interest in facilitating full and frank discussion between experts before trial required that each should be free to make proper concessions without fear that any departure from advice previously given to the party who had retained him would be seen as evidence of negligence, and it was needed in order to avoid the tension between a desire to assist the court and fear of the consequences of a departure from previous advice. Does a case management direction that each parties' expert should attend a without prejudice meeting breach Art.6 of the ECHR? No, said the Court of Appeal in *Hubbard v Lambeth Southwark & Lewisham Health Authority* (2002) Lloyd's Rep. Med. 8. The court indicated that a private pre-trial meeting of both parties' expert witnesses can usefully identify and narrow the issues, notwithstanding that in this particular case the claimants' experts were criticising the professional competence of a distinguished colleague at such a meeting. As the court pointed out, the experts had already committed themselves on paper in criticising their distinguished colleague. The court said the real fear was that the experts might be tempted to sell their clients down the river. However, as the court observed, it would be perfectly proper for them to make concessions if they thought concessions should be made.

> "If they are made, it is in the interests of justice that they should be made before the trial rather than dragged out in the trial process with the inevitable time and cost consequences which that would entail" (*per* Tuckey L.J.).

Should lawyers attend the without prejudice meetings of experts? There is no hard and fast answer said the Court of Appeal in Hubbard. Tuckey L.J. listed the arguments for having lawyers as:

> "(1) it would give clients confidence; (2) lawyers will be able to assist on law and facts if there was some misunderstanding about those matters in the course of discussion, and (3) they will be able to assess the real effect of the expert debate. The arguments against are: (1) it adds unnecessarily to the costs because there is no real benefit in having lawyers present if they are to keep out of the debate, which they must; and (2) there is a risk that they will influence the experts at the meeting".

Hale L.J. suggested that;

> "It seems worthwhile for consideration to be given by those who are working on practice guidelines, either in the clinical negligence area or in civil cases generally, to the possibility of appointing an independent neutral person to chair these meetings in appropriate cases. Such person would probably be legally qualified and have experience in the field of litigation involved."

Disclosed reports as evidence (r.35.12)

By exchanging a report in accordance with the directions order you preserve the right to use that report or call the expert at trial, such as may be permitted by the court. However, it must be borne in mind that any party may now use the report in evidence, even if you ultimately decide not to do so. In those circumstances you should be notified as to which parts of the report your opponent considers are particularly important, and why they want to use them. See *Gurney Consulting Engineers (a firm) v Gleeds Health & Safety Ltd* [2006] EWHC 43, *The Times*, April 24, 2007.

23.019

Written questions to experts (r.35.6)

You may put written questions to an expert instructed by another party or a single joint expert about his report. Unless the court orders or the other party agrees, only one set of questions may be asked and they must be served within 28 days of service of the expert's report. What sort of questions can you ask? Rule 35.6(2)(c) states that they must be for the purpose only of clarification of the report. So an acceptable question might be:

23.020

> "As to para.31, where you state that 'the safety switch was missing on inspection', please clarify the following: (a) which safety switch? For ease of reference please identify it on a copy of the specification that appears on p.87 of your report; and (b) was this first seen by you on your inspection of July 16 or August 14?".

Indeed, the parties have a duty to assist the court to further the overriding objective (see para.1.011) by spotting any manifest ambiguities or errrors in the report of a single joint expert and resolving these by asking one or more suitable questions (see *Woolley v Essex CC* [2006] EWCA Civ 753, (2006) L.T.L., May 17).

It is often going to be beyond your ability to draft these questions. Where there is a single joint expert you will have to decide if it is worth employing your own expert to consider the report and prepare any relevant questions (see above). Where you have instructed your own expert you must promptly send him a copy of the other party's report after exchange and ask him to draft any suitable questions. What must be remembered is that this procedure cannot be used as a means of cross-examining the expert. When any other party sends written questions to your expert, they should send you a copy as well. Ensure that your expert is content to answer all the questions. If any questions go beyond seeking verification of his report, the expert should decline to answer the question and say why. In extreme cases the expert could apply to the court for a direction.

The courts pay close attention to the use of this procedure, especially where each side has its own expert(s). As the Commercial Court Guide says, it must be used as:

"an instrument for the helpful exchange of information. The court will not allow it to interfere with the procedure for an exchange of professional opinion at a meeting of experts, or to inhibit that exchange of professional opinion. In cases where, for example, questions oppressive in number or content are put, or questions are put (without permission) for any purpose other than clarification of an expert's report, the court will not hesitate to disallow the questions and to make an appropriate order for costs against the party putting the questions".

What sort of questions beyond clarification might be allowed? In the case of *Mutch v Allen* [2001] EWCA Civ 76; (2001) L.T.L., January 22, C had issued proceedings claiming damages for personal injuries. He had been a backseat passenger in D's car which had been involved in a road traffic accident. C accepted that he had not worn a seat belt and D alleged contributory negligence on that basis. D's solicitors wrote to C's medical experts following receipt of their reports asking if C's injuries would have been materially reduced, if not prevented, had he worn a seat belt. C's solicitors objected. However, in August 2000, an order was made which gave D permission to request that information and the Court of Appeal ultimately upheld this. Note that in the case the answers given by C's orthopaedic expert were unhelpful to his case. In those circumstances the Court directed that it was appropriate that the expert should give oral evidence at trial and each side were to be permitted to cross-examine him.

Equally, it was open to either side to consider seeking permission before trial to call some other expert on the issue.

It is important to ensure that the expert is aware that if he fails to answer a question then the party that puts it can apply for a court order (see PIE para.16.1 which emphasises that "experts have a duty to provide answers to questions properly put."). The court has no power to require an answer. However, it may order that a party cannot rely on that expert's evidence. Such a draconia measure is usually only imposed when the court is of the opinion that the failure to answer constitutes a significant breach of the expert's overriding duty to the court and thereby his evidence at trial will not assist the court. The more usual order is that the party is not to recover all or part of that expert's fees whatever may happen in the future.

Finally, who pays the expert for answering questions? PD 23, para.5.3 provides that the party or parties instructing them must pay any fees charged. However, this does not affect any decision of the court as to the party who is ultimately to bear the expert's costs.

Inspection of documents in an expert's report

23.021   Rule 31.14(2) provides that subject to r.35.10 (see above) a party may inspect a document mentioned in an expert's report. In technical multi-track cases an expert's report frequently lists all or many of the relevant previous papers (published or unpublished) or books written by the expert or to which the expert has contributed. Requiring inspection of this material is often unrealistic, and the potential collating and copying burdens huge. If you want such a document and it is not voluntarily supplied, you should try to obtain it from another source before making an application to the court. The court are unlikely to make the order unless you can show that inspection of the document is appropriate for dealing with the case justly and it is not reasonably available to you from an alternative source. See PD 31, para.7.

Photographs, plans, analyses, measurements, survey reports and other similar documents relied on by an expert form part of his report and therefore copies should accompany it on exchange. Different rules apply where such documents do not form part of the report of an expert, see para.31.022.

Expert evidence in low-velocity collision claims

D's car hits the back of C's car at a slow speed. C says that as a result he suffered whiplash. What if D denies causing C's personal injury? Some experts believe that one can never say definitively that, below a certain inmpact, injury is impossible or even very unlikely. They say that there are too many imponderables. Other experts take a different view and say that below a certain impact injury is impossible or at any rate very unlikely. With such divergence of expert opinion, many low value road traffic claims find there way into the multi-track (see Ch.22) rather than the fast track (see Ch.21). In *Casey v Cartwright* [2006] EWCA Civ 1280, *The Times*, October 10, 2006, the Court of Appeal gave the following guidance (*per* Dyson L.J.):

23.022

"29. It is not controversial that in ordinary run-of-the-mill road traffic whiplash injury cases, there will be no need for expert medical evidence on the causation issue. The question of whether such evidence should be permitted only arises where the defendant contends that the nature of the impact was such that it was impossible or very unlikely that the claimant suffered any injury or any more than trivial injury as a result of the collision and that accordingly the claimant has fabricated the claim. It is only in such a case that the causation issue arises.

30. We think that it is desirable that, if a defendant wishes to raise the causation issue, he should satisfy certain formalities. In this way, the risk of confusion and delay to the proceedings should be minimised. Accordingly, where in a particular case a defendant wishes to raise the causation issue, he should notify all other parties in writing that he considers this to be a low impact case and that he intends to raise the causation issue. For the reasons set out at para 33 below, he should do so within three months of receipt of the letter of claim. The issue should be expressly identified in the defence, supported in the usual way by a statement of truth. Within 21 days of serving a defence raising the causation issue, the defendant should serve on the court and the other parties a witness statement which clearly

identifies the grounds on which the issue is raised. Such a witness statement would be expected to deal with the defendant's evidence relating to the issue, including the circumstances of the impact and any resultant damage.

31. Upon receipt of the witness statement, the court will, if satisfied that the issue has been properly identified and raised, generally give permission for the claimant to be examined by a medical expert nominated by the defendant.

32. If upon receipt of any medical evidence served by the defendant following such examination, the court is satisfied on the entirety of the evidence submitted by the defendant that he has properly identified a case on the causation issue which has a real prospect of success, then the court will generally give the defendant permission to rely on such evidence at trial.

33. We believe that what we have just said reflects the tenor of the judgment in *Kearsley*. There will, however, be circumstances where the judge decides that, even though the evidence submitted by the defendant shows that his case on the causation issue has real prospects of success, the overriding objective nevertheless requires permission for expert evidence to be refused. It is not possible or desirable to produce an exhaustive list of such circumstances. They include the following. First, the timing of notification by the defendant that he intends to raise the causation issue. Unless the defendant notifies the claimant of his intention to raise the issue within 3 months of receipt of the letter of claim, permission to rely on expert evidence should usually be denied to the defendant. It is important that the issue be raised at an early stage so as to avoid causing delay to the prosecution of the proceedings. The period of 3 months is consistent with para 2.11 of the Pre-Action Protocol for Personal Injury Claims which provides that a defendant be given 3 months to investigate and respond to a claim before proceedings are issued.

34. Secondly, if there is a factual dispute the resolution of which one way or the other is likely to resolve the causation issue, that is a factor which militates against the granting of permission to rely on expert evidence on the causation issue. In such a case, expert evidence is likely to serve little or no purpose.

35. Thirdly, there may be cases where the injury alleged and the damages claimed are so small and the nature of the expert evidence that the defendant wishes to adduce so extensive and complex that considerations of proportionality demand that permission to rely on the evidence should be refused. This must be left to the good sense of the judge. It does not detract from the general guidance given at para 32 above.

36. We should say something about single joint experts. They have an invaluable role to play in litigation generally, especially in low value litigation. But we accept the submission of Mr Turner [counsel for the claimant] that, at any rate until some test cases have been

decided at high court level, judges should be slow to direct that expert evidence on the causation issue be given by a single joint expert. This is because the causation issue is controversial.

Evidence of expert opinion or fact?

In *Kirkman v Euro Exide Corp (CMP Batteries) Ltd* [2007] EWCA Civ 66, *The Times,* February 6, 2007, the Court of Appeal sought to discern the distinction between evidence of fact and expert opinion in the context of a personal injury action. In the case the claimant's solicitors initially instructed the claimant's doctor, Mr Banks as an expert. His early reports consisted of a mixture of factual matters of which he, as the treating doctor, had personal knowledge, and also of his expert opinion. But, for reasons of their own, the claimant's solicitors considered that they did not wish to rely upon him as their expert. They still wanted, and felt that they needed, to call him because as the treating doctor, his evidence would be central to the judge's finding. As the Court pointed out, in these circumstances there was a good argument in favour of relaxing the usual rule that each side should only have permission to call the same number of experts (see para.23.014 above). However, that course was not followed. Instead the claimant's solicitors took the view that the important aspects of Mr Banks' evidence were factual and set about the rather artificial process of separating the factual aspects of his report from the expert ones in a witness statement (see Ch.14). The kernel of Mr Banks' proposed evidence was the statement that if the claimant had presented himself in October 2001 and had not recently had an accident he, Mr Banks, would not have advised the claimant to undergo a ligament reconstruction. In the court's view, that was clearly a statement of fact.

23.023

> "He is there saying what he would have done in a set of circumstances which did not in fact happen. True, in saying that, Mr Banks is relying upon his knowledge and his experience as a professional person. But he is not expressing an expert opinion" (*per* Smith L.J.). See also paras 1.009 and 31.011.

CHAPTER 24

Cases Not Governed by Standard Track Allocation

JUDICIAL REVIEW (PT 54)

24.001 Judicial review is exclusively within the jurisdiction of the High Court (CCA 1984, s.38). Claims are dealt with by the Administrative Court (previously known as the Crown Office). The High Court has a supervisory jurisdiction over inferior courts, tribunals and other bodies and persons charged with the performance of public duties and acts. Judicial review is quite different from an appeal. It is concerned with the legality rather than the merits of the decision, with the jurisdiction of the decision-maker and the fairness of the decision-making process rather than whether the decision was correct (*per* Lord Hoffman in *Kemper Reinsurance Co. v Minister of Finance* [1998] 3 W.L.R. 630 at 638; for a fuller description of judicial review see *per* Lord Clyde in *Reid v Secretary of State for Scotland* [1999] 2 W.L.R. 28 at 54).

By r.54.1(2)(a) a "claim for judicial review" is defined as "a claim to review the lawfulness of an enactment; or a decision, action or failure to act in relation to the exercise of a public function". The judicial review procedure is governed by Pt 8 (see Ch.10) save as modified by Pt 54.

The judicial review procedure must be used in any claim where the claimant is seeking:

(a) a mandatory order (previously known as an order of mandamus);
(b) a prohibiting order (previously known as an order of prohibition);
(c) a quashing order (previously known as an order of certiorari); or
(d) an injunction under s.30 of the Supreme Court Act 1981, i.e. restraining a person from acting in any office in which he is not entitled to act.

What if the claimant requires other remedies? The procedure can be used where the claimant is seeking a declaration or an injunction against a public authority: see s.31(2) of the Supreme Court Act 1981. However, if such is in addition to one of the above remedies, the judicial review procedure must be used. Section 31(4) of the Supreme Court Act sets out the circumstances in which the court may award restitution, recovery of a sum due and damages on a claim.

Before taking judicial review proceedings, the prospective claimant should consider taking the steps outlined in the approved pre-action protocol. However, these will not apply if the prospective defendant is say, a tribunal that has no legal power to change the decision being challenged or the matter is urgent, like the refusal of a local housing authority to provide a homeless person with interim accommodation. Yet even in emergency cases, it is good practice to fax to the prospective defendant a draft of the proposed claim form. Where the use of the protocol is appropriate, the court will normally expect all parties to have complied with it. The court will take into account any non-compliance when giving case management directions or when making orders for costs.

The judicial review pre-action protocol sets out a standard suggested format for the letter of claim and its response (Annexes A and B). The letter of claim should identify the issues in dispute and establish whether litigation can be avoided. It should contain the date and details of the decision, act or omission being challenged and a clear summary of the facts on which the claim is based. It should give details of any relevant information that the claimant is seeking and an explanation of why this is considered relevant. The prospective defendant should usually be allowed at least 14 days to respond.

Part 54 provides a speedy means for determining issues of public and administrative law subject to certain protections (summarised below) which are given to statutory tribunals and public authorities and which are necessary for reasons of public policy. Where the applicant has rights under public and private law, judicial review is appropriate only in respect of the former. As a general rule it is an abuse of the process of the court to raise by way of an ordinary action claims which should be brought under Pt 54 (*O'Reilly v Mackman* [1983] 2 A.C. 237). However, claims may be properly brought by ordinary action where issues of public law are raised only collaterally or peripherally (*Davy v Spelthorne Borough Council* [1984] A.C. 262) or where, although the principal issue is one of public law, the case also concerns private rights, thus making proceedings under Pt 54 inappropriate (*Wandsworth London Borough Council v Winder* [1985] A.C. 461). If it is not clear whether judicial review or an ordinary action is the correct procedure, it will be safer to make an application for judicial review. If appropriate the court may later change the case into an ordinary action or direct that it should be heard by a judge who is not nominated to hear judicial review cases (*Trustees of the Dennis Rye Pension Fund v Sheffield City Council* [1998] 1 W.L.R. 840).

Further, in the case of *Clark v University of Lincolnshire and Humbershire* [2000] 3 All E.R. 752, Lord Woolf M.R. said:

> "The courts' approach to what is an abuse of process has to be considered today in the light of the changes brought about by the CPR . . . While in the past, it would not be appropriate to look at delay of a party commencing proceedings other than by judicial review within the limitation period in deciding whether the proceedings are abusive this is no longer the position. While to commence proceedings within a limitation period is not in itself an abuse, delay in commencing proceedings is a factor which can be taken into account in deciding whether the proceedings are abusive. If

proceedings of a type which would normally be brought by judicial review are instead brought by bringing an ordinary claim, the court in deciding whether the commencement of the proceedings is an abuse of process can take into account whether there has been unjustified delay in initiating the proceedings. When considering whether proceedings can continue the nature of the claim can be relevant. If the court is required to perform a reviewing role or what is being claimed is a discretionary remedy, whether it be a prerogative remedy or an injunction or a declaration the position is different from when the claim is for damages or a sum of money for breach of contract or a tort irrespective of the procedure adopted ... . Where a student has, as here, a claim in contract, the court will not strike out a claim which could more appropriately be made under [Pt 54] solely because of the procedure which has been adopted. It may however do so, if it comes to the conclusion that in all the circumstances, including the delay in initiating the proceedings, there has been an abuse of the process of the court under the CPR. The same approach will be adopted on an application under Part 24. The emphasis can therefore be said to have changed since O'Reilly v Mackman. What is likely to be important when proceedings are not brought by a student against a new university under [Pt 54], will not be whether the right procedure has been adopted but whether the protection provided by [Pt 54] has been flouted in circumstances which are inconsistent with the proceedings being able to be conducted justly in accordance with the general principles contained in Part 1."

Judicial review is best considered as a remedy of last resort. The intending applicant should first exhaust any right of appeal or other means provided for challenging the decision. Until that has been done, judicial review is not appropriate save in exceptional circumstances, for example, where a point of principle needs to be determined which, in some cases, can most conveniently be done upon judicial review (*R. v Sandwell MBC Ex p. Wilkinson* [1999] 31 H.L.R. 22. However, that does not mean that the parties should ignore ADR. As Lord Woolf indicated in *Cowl v Plymouth* CC [2002] 1 W.L.R. 803:

"The parties do not today, under the CPR, have a right to have a resolution of their respective contentions by judicial review in the absence of an alternative procedure which would cover exactly the same ground as judicial review. The courts should not permit, except for good reason, proceedings for judicial review to proceed if a significant part of the issues between the parties could be resolved outside the litigation process. The disadvantages of doing so are limited. If subsequently it becomes apparent that there is a legal issue to be resolved, that can thereafter be examined by the courts which may be considerably assisted by the findings made by the complaints panel."

Apart from the subject-matter of the claim, the judicial review procedure has the unusual feature of two separate stages. First, the claimant must lodge the claim and permission to proceed with it must be granted. Secondly, after parties have filed various documents, a full judicial review hearing takes place. As to the first stage, by r.54.5 the permission of the Administrative Court is required before a claim can proceed, whether it was started under Pt 54 or transferred to that court. This hurdle is intended to eliminate at the outset frivolous or obviously untenable claims. It is made by filing a N461 claim form. Where the claim is proceeding in the Administrative Court in London, documents must be filed at the Administrative Court Office, the Royal Courts of Justice, Strand, London, WC2A 2LL. If the claim is proceeding in the Administrative Court in Wales (because it relates to say a devolution issue or an issue concerning the National Assembly for Wales, the Welsh executive, or any Welsh public body), documents must be filed at the Law Courts, Cathays Park, Cardiff, CF10 3PG. Extremely urgent claims for judicial review can exceptionally be commenced outside London or Cardiff but the Administrative Court Office in London must be consulted first, if necessary by telephone, prior to filing the claim form.

The claim form must be filed promptly and in any event not later than three months after the grounds to make the claim first arose. This time limit may not be extended by agreement between the parties and does not apply when any other enactment specifies a shorter time limit for making the claim. However, the court may extend time on application. In *R. v Customs & Excise Commissioners Ex p. British Sky Broadcasting Group Plc* (2000) L.T.L. July 14, Langley J. said:

> "The question is when did grounds [to make the claim] first arise. It is not when did the applicant first know of the existence of such grounds. Knowledge or the lack of it are relevant to the discretion to extend time. There is no dispute that the focus is on the real substance of the claim made to decide when grounds for an application first arose. That may differ from the specific decision which an applicant seeks to impugn."

Note that PD 54, para.4.1 provides that where the claim is for a quashing order in respect of a judgment, order or conviction, the date when the grounds to make the claim first arose is the date of that judgment, order or conviction.

Is the requirement to apply promptly, read with the three-month time limit, compatible with Art.6 of the ECHR? Lord Steyn expressed doubts in the case of *R. v Hammersmith & Fulham LBC Ex p. Burkett* [2002] 1 W.L.R. 1593.

What must the claim form contain? In addition to the matters set out in r.8.2 (see Ch.10) the claimant must also state:

(a) the name and address of any person he considers to be an interested party, i.e. any person (other than the claimant and defendant) who is directly affected by the claim. Where the claim for judicial review relates to proceedings in a court or tribunal, any other parties to those proceedings must be named in the claim form as interested parties. For example, in a claim by a defendant in a criminal case in the magistrates' or Crown Court for judicial review of a decision in that case, the prosecution must always be named as an interested party;

24.002

(b) that he is requesting permission to proceed with a claim for judicial review; and
(c) any remedy (including any interim remedy: see Ch.27) claimed.

PD 54, paras 5.6 and 5.7 provide that when the claim form is filed at the Administrative Court, the following must be included:

(a) a detailed statement of the grounds for bringing the claim for judicial review;
(b) a statement of the facts relied on;
(c) any application to extend the time limit for filing the claim form (see generally *R. v Bromley LBC Ex p. Barker* (2000) E.G.C.S. 51);
(d) any application for directions;
(e) a time estimate for the hearing;
(f) any written evidence in support of the claim or application to extend time;
(g) a copy of any order sought to have quashed;
(h) where the claim relates to a decision of a court or tribunal, an approved copy of the reasons for reaching that decision;
(i) copies of any documents the claimant proposes to rely on;
(j) copies of any relevant statutory material; and
(k) a list of essential documents for advance reading by the court (with page references to the passages relied on).

The claimant must file two copies of a paginated and indexed bundle containing all these documents. Where it is not possible to file a document, the claimant must explain why it is not currently available.

The claim form must be served by the claimant (the court will not do so) on the defendant and, unless the court otherwise directs, any person the claimant considers to be an interested party. This must be done within seven days after the date of issue. Any person served with the claim form who wishes to take part in the judicial review must file an acknowledgment of service (Form N462) within 21 days. It must also be served on the claimant and, subject to any court direction, any other person named in the claim form as soon as practicable. In any event, that must not be later than seven days after it is filed. These time limits may not be extended by agreement between the parties.

What should the acknowledgment of service deal with if the person filing it intends to contest the claim? It must set out a summary of his grounds for doing so, state the name and address of any person considered to be an interested party and may include, or be accompanied by, an application for directions. What if no acknowledgment is given? That party may not take part in a hearing to decide whether permission should be given unless the court allows him to do so. However, if permission to proceed is given, he may take part in the hearing of the judicial review provided he complies with r.54.14 (see below) or any other direction of the court regarding the filing and service of grounds and evidence. Where that person does take part in the hearing of the judicial review, the court may take his failure to file an acknowledgment of service into account when deciding what order to make about costs. Note that in the case of *R. v The Advertising Standards Authority Ltd Ex p. Rath* (2001) H.R.L.R. 22 the defendants had filed evidence and appeared at the permission hearing by counsel. However, they had not filed an acknowledgment of service. Turner J. held that it was too late for the claimants to contend that the defendants had not acknowledged service within Pt 54. In the circumstances, either the defendants would be treated as having acknowledged or the claimants as having waived the requirement to do so.

As a general rule the court will consider whether or not to grant permission to proceed without a hearing (PD 54, para.8.4). Neither the defendant nor any other interested party need attend the hearing unless the court directs otherwise. However, should the defendant or any party attend, the court will not generally make an order for costs against the claimant save in exceptional circumstances: see *R. (on the application of Payne) v Caerphilly CBC (Costs)* [2004] EWCA Civ 433; (2004) L.T.L., March 17, and *R. (on the application of Mount Cook Ltd) v Westminster CC* [2003] EWCA Civ 1346; *The Times*, October 16, 2003. What may constitute exceptional circumstances?

> "The hopelessness of the claim; the persistence in it by the claimant after having been alerted to facts and/or of the law demonstrating its hopelessness; the extent to which the court considers that the claimant, in the pursuit of his application, has sought to abuse the process of judicial review for collateral ends—a relevant consideration as to costs at the permission stage, as well as when considering discretionary refusal of relief at the stage of substantive hearing, if there is one; and whether, as a result of the deployment of full argument and documentary evidence by both sides at the hearing of a contested application, the unsuccessful claimant has had, in effect, the advantage of an early substantive hearing of the claim" (*per* Auld L.J. in the Mount Cook case).

In *Ewing v Office of the Deputy Prime Minister* [2005] EWCA Civ 1583, [2006] 1 W.L.R. 1260, the court recommended that where a proposed defendant or interested party wishes to seek costs at the permission stage, the acknowledgement of service should include an application for costs and it should be accompanied by a schedule setting out the amount claimed. The judge refusing permission should include in the refusal a decision whether to award costs in principle, and (if so) an indication of the amount which he proposes to assess summarily. The claimant should be given 14 days to respond in writing and should serve a copy on the defendant. The defendant will have seven days to reply in writing to any such response, and to the amount proposed by the judge. The judge will then decide and make an award on the papers.

What approach does the court take at the permission hearing? Part 54 is silent but obviously the overriding objective set out in r.1 (see para.1.006) applies. Pre-CPR an application for permission was normally disposed of without a hearing and based only on documents filed by the claimant. In those circumstances the claimant had to show a case which was "arguable": see *R. v Inland Revenue Commissioners Ex p. National Federation of Self-Employed and Small*

Businesses Ltd [1982] A.C. 617. However, if the judge had heard argument from the parties and there was unlikely to be a substantially greater number of points taken at the judicial review hearing, a much higher threshold of arguability was required namely that the claim was not merely arguable but was strong, that is to say, likely to succeed: see *Mass Energy Ltd v Birmingham CC* (1994) Env.L.R. 289. As already noted, Pt 54 requires the claimant to fully state his case, albeit with a limited response from any other parties. The court apply a similar test in light of the overriding objective and require the claimant to show reasonable grounds for believing that:

(1) there has been a failure of public duty; and
(2) the applicant has sufficient interest or locus standi in the matter; and
(3) the application has been made with great urgency and in any event within three months from the date when grounds for the claim arose, or the case is one in which a late application should be allowed.

The requirement to apply with great urgency, the requirement to obtain permission to proceed and the requirement to support the application by written evidence comprise the main protections afforded to statutory tribunals and public authorities by judicial review proceedings which they would not have in ordinary proceedings.

When permission to proceed is granted the court usually gives case management directions. By PD 54, para.12.1 there will be no direction for disclosure of documents (see Ch.30) unless the court orders otherwise. The pre-action protocol dealing with judicial review makes it clear in para.6 that it does not impose a greater obligation on a public body to disclose documents (or indeed give reasons for its decision) than that already provided for by statute or common law. It stresses, however, that where the court considers that a public body should have provided relevant documents (and/or information), particularly where this failure is a breach of a statutory or common law requirement, then the court may impose sanctions (see Ch.33). See *R. (on the application of Quark Fishing Ltd) v Secretary of State for Foreign and Commonwealth Affairs* [2002] EWCA Civ 1409; (2002) L.T.L. October 30, where Laws L.J. stated:

> "there is no duty of general disclosure in judicial review proceedings. However there is—of course—a very high duty on public authority respondents, not least central government, to assist the court with full and accurate explanations of all the facts relevant to the issue the court must decide".

24.003   Human rights cases raising issues of proportionality may lead to an order for disclosure of specific documents being made.

> "Such applications are likely to increase in frequency, since human rights decisions under the Convention tend to be very fact-specific and any judgment on the proportionality of a public authority's interference with a protected Convention right is likely to call for a careful and accurate evaluation of the facts. But even in these cases, orders for disclosure should

not be automatic. The test will always be whether, in the given case, disclosure appears to be necessary in order to resolve the matter fairly and justly" *per* Lord Bingham of Cornhill in *Tweed v Parades Commission of Northern Ireland* [2006] UKHL 53, [2007] 2 W.L.R. 1.

Case management directions may concern the service of the claim form and any evidence on other persons. Where a claim is made under the Human Rights Act 1998, a direction may be made for giving notice to the Crown or joining the Crown as a party. A direction can also be made for the hearing of the claim for judicial review to be held outside London or Cardiff. Before making any such direction the judge will consult the judge in charge of the Administrative Court as to its feasibility. Additionally, the court may direct a stay of proceedings to which the claim relates or grant interim relief.

As to the principles upon which interim relief should be granted in judicial review cases, see *R. v Ministry of Agriculture Fisheries and Food Ex p. Monsanto Plc* [1998] 4 All E.R. 321. The ideal time to apply for interim remedies is, of course, at the time when permission is granted.

The court serves the order giving or refusing permission and any directions on the claimant, the defendant and any other person who filed an acknowledgment of service. Where there has not been a hearing but the court either refuses permission to proceed or gives it subject to conditions or on certain grounds only, the court will serve its reasons for making the decision with the order. The claimant may not appeal that decision but can request that it is reconsidered at a hearing. Any such request must be filed within seven days after service of the court's reasons. The claimant, defendant and any other person who has filed an acknowledgment of service will be given at least two days' notice of the hearing date. If permission to proceed is subsequently refused, the claimant may seek permission to appeal to the Court of Appeal under Pt 52 (see Ch.44 and *R. v SOS for Home Department Ex p. Harris* (2002) L.T.L. February 1). If permission to appeal is refused by the Court of Appeal, the claimant has no right to appeal to the House of Lords: see *R. v Secretary of State for Trade and Industry Ex p. Eastaway* [2000] 1 W.L.R. 2222. Neither the defendant nor any other person served with the claim form may apply to set aside an order giving permission to proceed.

What steps must now be taken if a defendant (or any other person served with the claim form) wishes to contest the claim or support it on additional grounds? By r.54.14 that party must, within 35 days after service of the order giving permission, file and serve detailed grounds for contesting the claim or supporting it on additional grounds, along with any written evidence. Permission to proceed with the judicial review claim is granted on specific grounds. The court's permission is required to rely on any other grounds and the claimant must apply for this on notice to the court, and to any other person served with the claim form, no later than seven clear days before the hearing (or the warned date, where appropriate).

How should a claimant prepare for the judicial review hearing? The claimant must file and serve a skeleton argument not less than 21 working days before the date of the hearing of the judicial review (or the warned date). The defendant and any other party wishing to make representations at the hearing must file and serve a skeleton argument not less than 14 working days before the date of the hearing (or the warned date). Skeleton arguments must contain the following:

(a) a time estimate for the complete hearing, including delivery of judgment;
(b) a list of issues;
(c) a list of the legal points to be taken (together with any relevant authorities with page references to the passages relied on);
(d) a chronology of events with page references to the bundle of documents (see below);
(e) a list of essential documents for the advance reading of the court (with page references to the passages relied on), if that is different from the list filed with the claim form, along with a time estimate for that reading; and
(f) a list of persons referred to in the proceedings.

The claimant must also file a paginated and indexed bundle of all relevant documents required for the hearing when he files his skeleton argument. The bundle must include those documents required by the defendant and any other party who is to make representations at the hearing. At the judicial review hearing, no written evidence may be relied on unless it has been served in accordance with Pt 54, or a court direction, or the court gives its permission. Any person may apply for permission to file evidence; or make representations at the hearing of the judicial review. See, for example, *R. v Bow Street Metropolitan Stipendiary Magistrate Ex p. Pinochet Ugarte (No.3)* [1999] 2 W.L.R. 827. However, any such application must be made promptly. It is often appropriate, and sometimes essential, that the court hears oral evidence, including the cross-examination of witnesses: *R. (Wilkinson) v Broadmoor Special Hospital Authority* [2002] 1 W.L.R. 419.

Can a respondent argue at both the permission stage and at the substantive hearing that there has been undue delay by the applicant in making the claim? In the case of *R. v Lichfield DC Ex p. Lichfield Securities Ltd, The Times,* March 30, 2001, the Court of Appeal held that while ultimately it is a matter for the judge hearing the substantive application, the appropriate course is that the respondent should be permitted to recanvass, by way of undue delay, an issue of promptness which has been decided at the permission stage in the applicant's favour only if:

(i) the judge hearing the initial application has expressly so indicated;
(ii) new and relevant material is introduced on the substantive hearing;
(iii) exceptionally, the issues as they have developed at the full hearing put a different aspect on the question of promptness; or
(iv) the first judge has plainly overlooked some relevant matter or otherwise reached a decision per incuriam.

Can the court decide the claim for judicial review without a hearing? The answer is yes, but only if all the parties agree. What if the parties reach agreement before the hearing date? The claimant must file at the court a document (with two copies) signed by all the parties setting out the terms of the proposed agreed order together with a short statement of the matters relied on as justifying the proposed agreed order and copies of any authorities or statutory provisions relied on. The court will consider the filed documents and, if satisfied, make the order. Otherwise a hearing date is set. If an agreement relates just to costs, the parties need only file a document signed by all of them setting out the terms of the proposed order.

Rule 38.6 will apply if the applicant discontinues the application, that is, unless the court orders otherwise the applicant will be ordered to pay the respondent's costs (see further Ch.35). But those costs may be reduced where the respondent fails to follow the pre-action protocol: see *Aegis Group Plc v Inland Revenue* (2005) L.T.L., May 13.

What costs order should be made if the judicial review claim is settled without a full hearing? In *Boxhall v Waltham Forest LBC* (2001) L.T.L., January 5, the claimants applied for judicial review on the grounds that the defendant had failed to assess their accommodation, community care and welfare needs, and had not provided them with suitable accommodation. The claim was adjourned by consent for the defendant to carry out assessments but without an order for costs. Permission to proceed was subsequently granted on a contested application by the claimants and the judge ordered costs in the case. The defendant completed a carer's assessment on the first claimant and produced a care plan which concluded that neither claimant was in need of accommodation. The judicial review was brought to a conclusion when the defendant offered the claimants new accommodation on the basis that they were the most suitable applicants at the time. Baker J. held that the starting point was the court's wide discretion under r.44.3 (see para.38.008) to depart from the pre-CPR rule that the unsuccessful party should usually pay the costs of the successful party. In his view the authorities established the following principles:

(a) the court had power to make a costs order when the substantive proceedings had been resolved without a trial but the parties had not agreed about costs;

(b) ordinarily it was irrelevant that the claimant was legally aided;

(c) the overriding objective was to do justice between the parties without incurring unnecessary court time and consequently additional costs;

(d) the extent to which the court would look into unresolved substantive issues depended on the circumstances of the case, not least the amount of costs at stake and the conduct of the parties;

(e) in the absence of a good reason to make any other order, the fall back position was to make no order as to costs (see *R. v Southwark London BC, ex p Kuzeva* [2002] EWCA Civ 781; (2002) L.T.L. May 30,); and

(f) the court should take care to ensure that it did not discourage parties from settling judicial review proceedings, e.g. by a local authority making a concession at an early stage.

Baker J. concluded that the claimants had made a number of requests for an assessment before commencing proceedings. The first permission hearing was adjourned by consent on the defendant's agreement to carry out an assessment. The defendant contested the adjourned permission hearing unsuccessfully then, shortly afterwards, carried out a carer's assessment. There was little doubt that the defendant would have been found to have acted unlawfully if the substantive issues had been contested at a hearing. Accordingly, the claimants were entitled to their costs as sought. But note the warning given by Munby J. in *R. (on the application of MB by her litigation friend) v Lambeth London BC* [2006] EWHC 639, (2006) L.T.L., April 19.

What are the court's powers in respect of making a quashing order? The court may remit the matter to the decision-maker, direct it to reconsider the matter and reach a decision in accordance with the judgment of the court. Where the court considers that there is no purpose to be served in remitting the matter to the decision-maker it may, subject to any statutory provision, take the decision itself. Where a statutory power is given to a tribunal, person or other body it may be the case that the court cannot take the decision itself. If a declaration, an injunction or damages are sought, the court may instead of refusing the application, order the proceedings to continue as if begun by claim form under CPR, Pt 7 and may give directions either allocating the proceedings to a case management track, or providing for allocation questionnaires or an allocation hearing.

INTERPLEADER PROCEEDINGS

24.004 Interpleader proceedings are appropriate where a person holding money, goods or chattels is, or expects to be, sued by two or more rival claimants to the property. If he has no interest in the dispute, he can apply for relief by way of interpleader, that is, a hearing at which the rival claimants will be made to interplead, argue against each other and not against him. Here are some typical examples:

(1) A car is left with a repairer. The customer now claims it back, but so does a finance company, saying that it is subject to a hire-purchase agreement with them.
(2) A solicitor receives a sum of money as the deposit on a contract for the sale of land. The money is now claimed by both the buyer and the seller.
(3) (the most frequent example) A High Court Enforcement Officer ("HCEO") enforcing a money judgment takes goods from a judgment debtor (see para.40.004), but a claim to the goods is made by some other person. The HCEO will notify the judgment creditor of the claim and, unless that person admits the claim, will start interpleader proceedings.

Interpleader proceedings have two unusual features. First, the role played by the applicant: he must be truly a disinterested party. Indeed, he must provide written evidence confirming that he claims no interest in the money, goods or chattels (other than for his charges or costs), does not collude with any of the rivals and is willing to dispose of the property as the court may direct. (A HCEO is not usually required to provide such evidence). Secondly, the proceedings can either form the subject of a separate action brought for the purpose, or can be raised as an interim application in an existing action. The latter alternative is appropriate where the applicant has already been sued by one or more of the rivals: notice of the application should be given to the parties to those proceedings and all other rival claimants. The court will then stay all proceedings in the action other than the interpleader proceedings.

In the High Court, the procedure is governed by RSC, Ord.17, scheduled to CPR, Pt 50. The application is made by claim form under Pt 8 (see PD 8B, s.A). Most interpleader proceedings are summarily determined by the master or district judge (PD 2, Allocation of Cases to Levels of Judiciary, para.4.1).

The county court's jurisdiction to hear interpleader proceedings derives from two sections of the CCA 1984, s.38 in the case of a "stakeholder's interpleader" (see examples (1) and (2) above); and s.101 in the case of any goods (or the proceeds of sale thereof) seized under a warrant of execution. The procedure is governed by CCR, Ord.33 and special forms of application are provided, see Forms N88, N88(1) and N89 (PD 4, table 3). A stakeholder's interpleader can be determined by the district judge (PD 8, s.B and PD 2, Allocation of Cases to Levels of Judiciary, para.11.1). However, an interpleader in respect of goods seized in execution is sought by the district judge in person issuing a summons and therefore must be determined a circuit judge. On what basis should the district judge issue such a summons? In the case of *Newman (t/a Mantella Publishing) v Modern Bookbinders Ltd* [2000] 2 All E.R. 814, the Court of Appeal observed that:

> "What the district judge undoubtedly does have is the obligation to consider whether the claim is on the face of it sufficient in detail and credible in substance, and a corresponding area of judgment; but once a claim meets these elementary tests, it appears to us that the district judge will have no option but to issue an interpleader summons" (*per* Sedley L.J.).

ACTIONS FOR THE RECOVERY OF LAND

Part 55 of the CPR deals with "possession claims", i.e. a claim for the recovery of possession of land, including buildings or parts of buildings. The procedure prescribed in Pt I must be followed where the claim is brought either by a landlord (or former landlord); a mortgagee; a licensor (or former licensor); against trespassers; or by a tenant seeking relief from forfeiture. Note that by r.55.1 "a possession claim against trespassers" is defined as a claim for the recovery of land which the claimant alleges is occupied only by a person or persons who entered or remained on the land without the consent of a person entitled to possession of that land but does not include a claim against a tenant or sub-tenant whether his tenancy has been terminated or not.

24.005

CASES NOT GOVERNED BY STANDARD TRACK ALLOCATION

As a general rule a possession claim must be started in the county court for the district in which the land is situated. However, it may be commenced in the High Court if the claimant files with his claim form a certificate stating the reasons for bringing the claim in that court verified by a statement of truth. PD 55 refers to circumstances which may justify starting the claim in the High Court. Who are the defendants to a claim made against trespassers? Where the claimant does not know the name of a person in occupation or possession of the land, the claim must be brought against "persons unknown" in addition to any named defendants. The claim form and form of defence sent with it must be in the format required by the relevant PD. Also note that unlike Pt 7 proceedings, the particulars of claim must be filed and served with the claim form.

Possession claims are a form of fixed date actions, i.e. the court will fix a date for the hearing when it issues the claim form. In all cases, apart from actions against trespassers, the defendant must be served with the claim form and particulars of claim not less than 21 days before the hearing date. If the evidence of witnesses is to be relied on at the hearing, their witness statements must usually be filed in advance of the hearing. However, in a possession claim against trespassers the defendant must be served with the claim form, particulars of claim and any witness statements in the case of residential property, not less than five days before the hearing date and in the case of other land, not less than two days before the hearing. In all other possession claims the hearing date will be not less than 28 days from the date of issue of the claim form. Rule 55.5 provides that the standard period between the issue of the claim form and the hearing will be not more than eight weeks.

As to the methods of service of proceedings, see Ch.8. But what if the possession claim is against trespassers and has been issued against "persons unknown"? In those circumstances the claim form, particulars of claim and any witness statements must be served on those persons by attaching copies of those documents to the main door or some other part of the land so that they are clearly visible and if practicable, inserting copies in a sealed transparent envelope addressed to "the occupiers" through the letter box. In the alternative, if there are no premises, for example, caravans trespassing in a field, service is effected by placing stakes in the land in places where they are clearly visible and attaching to each stake copies of the claim form, particulars of claim and any witness statements in a sealed transparent envelope addressed to "the occupiers".

How should a defendant respond? First, note that there is no form of acknowledgment of service and Pt 10 does not apply (see Ch.7). In a possession claim against trespassers r.15.2 does not apply (also see Ch.7) and the defendant need not file a defence. So what is the effect in any other possession claim of the defendant failing to file a defence within the time specified in r.15.4? The answer is that the claimant cannot enter default judgment (see Ch.12) and the defendant may take part in any hearing. However, the court will most likely take his failure to file a defence into account when deciding what order to make about costs.

What steps must be taken before the hearing? All witness statements must be filed and served at least two days before the hearing. However, in a possession claim against trespassers all witness statements on which the claimant intends to rely must be filed and served with the claim form (see above). Further, in a mortgage possession case, not less than 14 days before the hearing the claimant must send a notice to the property addressed to "the occupiers". This notice must state that a possession claim for the property has started; give the name and address of the claimant, the defendant and the court which issued the claim form; and provide details of the hearing. The claimant must produce at the hearing a copy of the notice and evidence that he has served it.

Very often a defendant does not attend the hearing. If you served the claim form and particulars of claim, the matter will not proceed unless you can produce at the hearing a certificate of service of those documents. At the hearing the court can often decide the claim. However, if the judge considers that the action is genuinely disputed on grounds which appear to be substantial, he will give case management directions. These include the allocation of the claim to a track or directions to enable it to be allocated. How does the court determine the appropriate track? Rule 55.9 provides that the court should consider:

(a) the matters set out in r.26.6 (see para.9.030) as modified by the relevant practice direction;
(b) the amount of any arrears of rent or mortgage instalments;
(c) the importance to the defendant of retaining possession of the land; and
(d) the importance of vacant possession to the claimant.

Whilst the court may make a possession order it can also fix a date for possession, thereby postponing it and make it conditional: see *Bristol CC v Hassan* [2006] EWCA Civ 656, [2006] 1 W.L.R. 2582 and PD 55 para.10.

Note that the court will only allocate a possession claim to the small claims track if all the parties agree. If you agree to such an allocation does the usual "no costs" rule (see Ch.20) apply? The answer is no, since for the purposes of costs the case is treated as if it were proceeding on the fast track save in respect of trial costs. Those costs are at the court's discretion but cannot exceed the amount recoverable under r.46.2 (see Ch.21) on the assumption that the claim had a financial value up to £3,000. However, if you would prefer the usual small claims costs rules to apply instead, the court will order this if all the parties agree.

Mortgage possession proceedings

The Administration of Justice Act 1970, s.36 as amended in 1973 gives the court certain powers, if it appears to the court that in the event of exercising one of them, the mortgagor is likely to be able within a reasonable period to pay off any arrears of capital and interest which have accrued. If so satisfied, the court could then adjourn the proceedings or, in giving judgment, stay or suspend execution of the judgment or postpone the date for delivery of possession for such period as the court thinks reasonable. Any such adjournment or suspension, etc. can be made subject to conditions with regard to payment by the mortgagor

24.006

as the court thinks fit, and the court has express power to vary or revoke any condition. Because of the 1973 amendment, the court is concerned only with the actual arrears in instalments and should ignore the effect of any mortgage clause which makes the whole outstanding balance due and payable.

Sadly, many defendants to mortgage possession actions are not aware of the court's ability and willingness to help them avoid eviction and therefore fail to attend the hearing. In the absence of any evidence of ability to pay, the court's power to suspend or postpone under AJA 1970, s.36 does not arise. If the claimant has prepared evidence in due form and has given sufficient notice of it to the defendant, the court is likely to make an order in Form N29 giving possession in 28 days. As to the court's power to specify the date for possession, see PD 40, para.8.1. When selecting the date to specify, the court should consider the overriding objective (r.1.2 and cf. *Six Arlington Street Investments v Persons Unknown* [1987] 1 W.L.R. 188).

In an exceptional case, where the defendant does attend and raises some substantial dispute about the claimant's claim, the court can give case management directions such as requiring the filing of allocation questionnaires or actually allocating the case and giving suitable directions. In practice, however, the defendant does not normally dispute the claimant's claim or deny that there are any arrears, but simply asks for time to pay. This raises the possibility that the court may suspend or postpone the proceedings for a reasonable period under its powers in AJA 1970, s.36. What period should be regarded as a reasonable period for this purpose? The first point to establish is whether the defendant has the ability to discharge the arrears by means of instalments paid over the remaining term of the mortgage. If so, that period may well be the reasonable period to allow (*Cheltenham & Gloucester Building Society v Norgan* [1996] 1 W.L.R. 343). If, however, the defendant can discharge the arrears only by way of sale, various other factors will come into play including the extent to which the mortgage debt and arrears were secured by the value of the property and the effect of time on that security (*National & Provincial Building Society v Lloyd* [1996] 1 All E.R. 630 and *Bristol & West Building Society v Ellis* [1996] 1 All E.R. 21).

In *Cheltenham & Gloucester Plc v Krausz* [1997] 1 All E.R. 21 the Court of Appeal held that if a lender is entitled to possession and seeks an order for possession, the court has no jurisdiction to withhold that remedy except (generally speaking) under s.36 of the AJA 1970 just described (i.e. on being satisfied that the mortgage debt and arrears will be paid off in full within a reasonable period). This decision seems almost wholly to negate the earlier decision in *Palk v Mortgage Services Funding Plc* [1993] Ch.330, the court's power under LPA 1925, s.91 to order a sale by a borrower at a price insufficient to discharge the mortgage debt and arrears. It now seems that the Palk ruling is relevant only if, for example, the lender consents or decides not to seek an order for possession.

If a suspended order is made this will be in Form N31. It grants possession but suspends it so long as the current instalments plus so much per month off the arrears are paid.

Lenders in possession actions rarely seek an order for costs preferring instead to rely on the provisions in the mortgage deed which entitle them to add all legal costs to the amount of the outstanding debt. This contractual provision means that the full amount of the bill rendered by the lenders' solicitor will be added to the debt. If the lender does rely on its contractual entitlement to costs, the court cannot unilaterally make a costs order and summarily assess those costs: see *Bank of Ireland Home Mortgages Ltd v Bissett* (1999) C.L. 409. Some district judges therefore include in the order made a provision requiring that the lender should notify the borrower within a stated period of time the amount of costs which they propose to add to the mortgage debt. If the defendant considers that the amount of these costs are unreasonable, he could invite the court to order a detailed assessment of these costs either in these proceedings (*Gomba Holdings v Minories Finance Ltd (No.2)* [1993] Ch.171) or, more likely, by means of an application under s.71 of the Solicitors Act 1974 (as to the procedure under s.70 of the Solicitors Act 1974, which is analogous, see Ch.39).

Second mortgagors securing loans not exceeding £15,000, made by secondary banks and finance houses are usually regulated agreements within the meaning of s.8 of the Consumer Credit Act 1974. In such cases, the criteria of the AJA 1970 do not apply and instead the court must consider whether it is appropriate to make a time order under s.129 of the Consumer Credit Act 1974. The court can order such instalments, payable at such times as the court, having regard to the means of the debtor, considers reasonable. Time orders often allow a period exceeding the remaining period of the loan.

Mortgagees today prefer to seek an order for possession rather than issue foreclosure proceedings. Under an order for possession, once the mortgage and the costs of sale have been recouped by the lender, any balance still remaining is paid to the borrower. This is not so under a foreclosure order because the whole equity of redemption is extinguished and the legal title will vest fully in the lender. Because of the draconian nature of foreclosure, the courts are reluctant to grant it. Rather than abolishing the remedy outright, procedural obstacles were placed on the path of foreclosure as long ago as 1925. In particular, where a claim for foreclosure is brought, the court has power under s.91 of the LPA 1925, on the application of a person interested, to order sale instead of foreclosure. There is even power to re-open a foreclosure after an order absolute. Consequently, foreclosure is no longer usually sought by most lenders and even those who still persist in seeking it, cannot seriously expect to obtain it. Foreclosure is not possible in any event in the case of a regulated agreement under the Consumer Credit Act 1974 as s.113 prevents a lender from obtaining any greater benefit by enforcing security than he would have obtained if no security had been given.

Interim possession orders

In the county court (but not the High Court) certain applicants who are entitled to proceed under Pt 55 (see above) may also seek an interim possession order under CCR, Ord.24, Pt II. This provides a remedy similar to a mandatory interim injunction (see Ch.27 and see the undertakings which the court must consider imposing on the applicant if the order is made, CCR, Ord.24, r.12(4)). The order compels the respondent to vacate the specified premises within 24

24.007

hours of the service of the order upon them. The order (see Form N134) will also specify a return date for a hearing (i.e. the second hearing) which the court may (amongst other things) make a final order for possession or discharge the interim possession order and allow the proceedings to continue as if it had not included a claim or an interim possession order.

There are several limitations on applications for interim possession orders in addition to those applicable to proceedings under Pt 55 (e.g. that the respondent is not a tenant or ex-tenant). The three most important are: (i) the term "premises" is defined to exclude open land; (ii) the proceedings must not include a claim by the applicant for any remedy other than recovery of land; (iii) the claimant must commence the application within 28 days of the date on which he first knew, or reasonably to have known, that the respondent or any of the respondents was in occupation.

Subject to those limitations, the proceedings should be commenced by a claim form in Form N130 which includes a form of affidavit in support to be completed and sworn by the applicant. (CCR, Ord.24, r.10(2) permits the use of either a witness statement or an affidavit in support and does not specify who must be the deponent of that statement or affidavit.) Within 24 hours of issue, a copy of certain documentation including a note stating the date of the first hearing must be served by the applicant or his agent by fixing it to the main door or other conspicuous part of the premises.

Interim possession orders are enforceable by police action (i.e. by arrest and prosecution; see the prescribed form of order, Form N134 and the prescribed form of affidavit of service, Form N135, which the applicant may take together with a copy of the interim possession order to the local police station). They are not enforceable by bailiffs (CCR, Ord.24, r.13).

Other possession proceedings

24.008 Claims for possession against tenants and former tenants are usually brought in the county court local to the premises and are governed by much the same procedure as applies to mortgage possession proceedings (i.e. PD 8B, s.B applies; see para.B.1(2)). The claim form (Form N5) will be for a fixed date hearing before a district judge. Claims concerning a dwelling house and based on rent arrears will initially be listed as hearings in private (PD 39, para.1.5(2)). The claim form must be served on the defendant at least 21 days before the hearing. Although there is no requirement to file or serve evidence in advance, the claimant should, nevertheless, do so if, at the hearing, he intends to ask the district judge for judgment. As in mortgage possession proceedings, the district judge may, instead of giving judgment, adjourn the proceedings, or give case management directions. If the case merits full investigation and trial, he may allocate the proceedings to a case management track. Disputes between landlord and tenant on claims for possession are not likely to be allocated to the small claims track (see Ch.20 and PD 26, para.8.1(1)(c)). Instead, if the claim appears to be straightforward, the court will probably allocate the case to the fast track, direct the exchange of witness statements and fix a final hearing date.

In some cases under the Housing Act 1988 there is an accelerated procedure for possession. CCR, Ord.49, r.6 applies to assured tenancies and Pt II of Pt 55 applies to assured short-hold tenancies. In respect of the latter, r.55.12 sets out the conditions that must be satisfied before the procedure can be used. There is a prescribed form of claim form and a defendant who wishes to defend or seek a postponement of possession must file a defence within 14 days of service of the claim form. If that step is not taken the claimant can file a written request for possession which is referred to a judge.

Other landlord and tenant matters

Section I of Pt 56 deals with claims under the Landlord and Tenant Act 1927, the Leasehold Property (Repairs) Act 1938, the Landlord and Tenant Act 1954, the Landlord and Tenant Act 1985 and the Landlord and Tenant Act 1987.   24.009

In s.II you will find details for making claims under the Access to Neighbouring Land Act 1992, Chancel Repairs Act 1932, Leasehold Reform Act 1967 and the Leasehold Reform, Housing and Urban Development Act 1933.

Probate and inheritance claims (Pt 57)

Section I of Pt 57 deals with what are commonly known as contentious probate claims, namely claims for the grant of probate of a will (or letters of administration of the estate), the revocation of such a grant, or for a decree pronouncing for or against the validity of an alleged will. See s.128 of the Supreme Court Act 1981, which defines non-contentious probate business (and also the Non-Contentious Probate Rules 1987). In the High Court the matter is assigned to the Chancery Division. There are Chancery district registries at Birmingham, Bristol, Cardiff, Leeds, Liverpool, Manchester, Newcastle upon Tyne and Preston. Only county courts there have jurisdiction to deal with a claim. See s.32 of the County Courts Act 1984 as to which probate claims may be heard in a county court. The Pt 7 procedure applies save as set out in Pt 57. The claim form and all subsequent court documents relating to the claim must be marked at the top, "In the estate of [name] deceased (Probate)". Note that the commencement of a probate claim will, unless a court otherwise directs, prevent any grant of probate or letters of administration being made until the claim has been disposed of. All claims are allocated to the multi-track.   24.010

Section II deals with applications to rectify a will and s.III contains the Rules for substituting and removing personal representatives (see further Ch.7).

Claims under the Inheritance (Provision for Family and Dependants) Act 1975 are dealt with in s.IV. Rule 57.16(1) requires all claims to be made using the Pt 8 procedure (see Ch.10). Does the former partner of a deceased who was to receive nothing either under his contested will or on intestacy, but who had a right to bring a claim under the 1975 Act, have an interest in the estate for the purposes of Pt 57 and so is entitled to bring a probate action? Yes, see *O'Brien v Seagrave* [2007] EWHC 788, *The Times*, May 2, 2007.

Technology and Construction Court (TCC) (Pt 60)

24.011   The Technology and Construction Court is the name for the court previously known as the Official Referees' Court, the original of which dates back to the Judicature Acts 1873–1875. A TCC claim is a claim which involves issues or questions which are technically complex or for which a trial by a judge of the TCC is for any other reason desirable. Typical examples are cases concerning civil or mechanical engineering, building or other construction work, most professional negligence claims (save those concerning doctors and lawyers), landlord and tenant disputes concerning repairing covenants, claims relating to the supply and use of computers and claims arising out of fires. Most cases involve complicated questions of fact, often of a scientific or technical nature. A high proportion of them concern numerous contracts and sub-contracts so giving rise to a multiplicity of defendants and third parties.

Allocation to the TCC is equivalent to the allocation to the multi-track and therefore there is no need to file allocation questionnaires. The practice direction also excludes the need to file pre-trial checklists (listing questionnaires). In the TCC, these documents are replaced by specialist care management questionnaires and a pre-trial review questionnaire annexed to the practice direction.

A claimant can commence a TCC claim by marking the words "Technology and Construction Court" beneath the name of the High Court or county court in which it is issued. A High Court claim can be issued in the court office in St Dunstan's House, 133–137 Fetter Lane, London EC4A 1PT. A claim form can also be issued in the office of the Central London County Court, or in any county court office where there is also a High Court district registry. See PD 60 paras 3.3 and 3.4. Claims can also be transferred to the TCC if the parties consent or if a successful application for transfer is made at which all parties have had an opportunity to be heard.

Unless the proceedings end in a default judgment, the court will fix a case management conference within 14 days after the defendant has filed an acknowledgment of service or a defence (whichever is the earlier). To assist the parties to prepare for that appointment, the court will send each party a case management information sheet (see Appendix A to PD 60) and a case management directions form (Appendix B) which the parties must complete, exchange and file in court not less than two days before the hearing. At the first case management conference, the court will usually fix the date for trial of the case and of any preliminary issue that it orders to be tried and will also give case management directions, including, usually, the fixing of a date for a pre-trial review. In order to assist the parties to prepare for that pre-trial review, the court will send to each party a pre-trial review questionnaire (Appendix C) and a pre-trial review directions form (Appendix D) which they must complete, exchange and file in court not less than two days before the date of the pre-trial review.

The case management directions form (and, to a lesser extent, the pre-trial review directions form) indicate some of the special orders and directions which are made in the TCC so as to reduce each case to manageable proportions. For example:

"Claimant/defendant to serve a Scott Schedule [of defects and damages] [under paragraph . . . of the particulars of claim/defence] by . . . am/pm on . . . Column headings to be as follows:"

A Scott Schedule is a document divided into columns. Some columns are for completion by the claimants, listing their claims item by item; other columns are for the defendants, answering the claims item by item. Further columns may be included to state cases arising as between defendants or as between defendants and third parties. See generally the Court of Appeal guidance given in *Weet v Packer* (1999) L.T.L. December 1.

The Commercial Court (Pt 58)

A specialist procedure for commercial and mercantile disputes has been in existence since 1895. The Commercial Court forms part of the High Court, Queen's Bench Division in London. Its practice and procedures are set out in Pt 58 and in the Commercial Court Guide. Rule 58.1(2) defines a commercial claim as "any claim arising out of the transaction trade or commerce" and 11 examples are given including the export or import of goods, insurance and reinsurance and banking and financial services. Outside London courts equivalent of the Commercial Court are allocated in those district registries which have a Mercantile Court (Manchester, Liverpool, Birmingham, Bristol, Leeds, Newcastle-upon-Tyne and Cardiff). The county court equivalent is the Business List maintained in the Central London County Court. There is a separate practice direction defining mercantile claims in terms similar to the definition of a commercial claim and, as noted above, a Mercantile Court Guide has been produced. Procedure in the Mercantile Court and the Business List are similar, but not identical to Commercial Court procedure.

24.012

A claim form NI(CC) for Pt 7 claims or N208(CC) for Pt 8 claims marked "Queen's Bench Division, Commercial Court" can be issued out of the Admiralty and Commercial Court registry in Room E200 in The Royal Courts of Justice. Existing proceedings may be transferred to the Commercial Court by order of the court where the proceedings are being dealt with, or by order of a judge of the Commercial Court. All cases in the Commercial Court are allocated to the multi-track and there is no requirement for allocation questionnaires or indeed pre-trial checklists (listing questionnaires).

Service of the claim form and other documents is to be effected by the parties and not by the court. The claimant must serve the defendant's response pack with the claim form not with the particulars of claim. An acknowledgment of service is required in all cases concerned in the Commercial Court. In default, the claimant may obtain judgment even if he has not served his particulars of claim (see r.58.8).

Part 58 and the Commercial Court Guide contain various provisions concerning statements of case, including regulations as to drafting them and a requirement to prepare a summary (not exceeding five pages) of any particulars of claim, defence or reply which exceeds 25 pages in length. Parties may agree extension of time for the filing of a defence exceeding 28 days. Where this is agreed, the defendant must notify the court in writing.

After service of the defence, the parties should prepare an agreed case memorandum containing a short and uncontroversial description of what the case is about and of its material case history, as well as a list of issues, with a section listing important matters which are not in dispute. The parties must apply for a case management conference within 14 days after all defendants who intend to serve a defence have done so. The claimant's solicitor must prepare and lodge a case management bundle for use at that hearing containing the claim form, the case memorandum, a list of issues and various other documents. At least seven days before the case management conference, all parties must exchange and file copies of their case management information sheet, a document similar to a pre-trial checklist (allocation questionnaire). At the case management conference, the court will endeavour to provide a pre-trial timetable, i.e. directions fixing the time for disclosure and the exchange of witness statements and expert reports and fixing a progress monitoring date (usually, a date after the date for exchange of witness statements and expert reports) and the fixed date for trial or the trial period.

At least three days before the progress monitoring date, each party must exchange and file a progress monitoring information sheet which will indicate the extent to which they have complied with the pre-trial timetable. Problems indicated by these sheets may lead to a reconvening of the case management conference.

The Commercial Court Guide in s.E also makes important alterations to the standard rules as to disclosure of documents. Where standard disclosure has been given, the disclosure statement must be amplified so as to identify any respects in which the search has been limited, to set out in detail the facts considered at arriving at the decision that it was reasonable to limit the search in those respects and to specify by whom the search was conducted. These additions will make it easier for the court and for the opponents to check that full and proper disclosure has been made. See the revised list of documents from N265(CC). The Commercial Court Guide accepts that there is no presumption in the Commercial Court in favour of the appointment of single joint experts (see para.H2.2). Indeed, in view of the complexity and value of cases in the Commercial Court, such appointments are likely to be rare save where both parties consent.

Mercantile Courts (Pt 59)

24.013 The Mercantile Court is a specialist list established within the High Court district Registries at Birmingham, Bristol, Cardiff, Chester, Leeds, Liverpool, Manchester and Newcastle, as well as the Central London County Court (previously called the Business List and now called the Mercantile List). What claims can be started in this court? Rule 59.1 indicates that the action must relate to a commercial or business matter in a broad sense and it must not otherwise be required to proceed in the Chancery Division or in another specialist

list. The usual Pt 7 procedure applies save as set out in this Part. The claim form must be marked in the top, right-hand corner "Queen's Bench Division, (appropriate) District Registry, Mercantile Court" or "Central London County Court, Mercantile List".

There are two particular matters to note about the Mercantile List at the Central London County Court. First, proceedings should only be started there if it has some connection with the South Eastern Circuit. For example, because it is convenient for the claim to be dealt with in that court, or the claim arises out of a transaction which took place within that circuit or one of the parties resides or carries on business within that circuit. Secondly, a claim for less than £15,000 may not be issued without the permission of the court.

Note that like the Commercial Court (see para.24.012), this court also makes use of a case management information sheet (PD 59, Annex A), standard directions (Annex B) and a pre-trial checklist (Annex C).

Admiralty claims (Pt 61)

Those dealing with claims involving damage done by a ship, the ownership of a ship, salvage and the like, will need to consult this Part. Equally, reference should be made to the Admiralty Court Guide (which is part of the Commercial Court Guide). 24.014

Arbitration claims (Pt 62)

Section I of this Part deals with the following applications: 24.015

(a) to determine whether there is a valid arbitration agreement;
(b) to establish whether an arbitration tribunal is properly constituted;
(c) to decide what matters have been submitted to arbitration in accordance with an arbitration agreement;
(d) to declare that an award by an arbitral tribunal is not binding on a party; and
(e) to determine any matter under the 1996 Arbitration Act.

Generally the Pt 8 procedure applies (see Ch.10). As to the content of the claim form, see r.62.4. Note that if a defendant to existing litigation wishes to apply under s.9 of the 1996 Act to stay the proceedings he made file an application notice at the court dealing with those proceedings (see para.33.004).

Section II of this Part deals with any other arbitration claims. As to enforcing an arbitration award, see s.III.

Patents and other intellectual property claims (Pt 63)

The Patents Court and a Patents County Court are part of the specialist lists and have jurisdiction under Section I of this Part to determine any matter arising 24.016

CASES NOT GOVERNED BY STANDARD TRACK ALLOCATION

under the 1977 Patents Act including infringement actions, revocation actions, threats under s.70 of the 1977 Act and disputes as to ownership. In addition the Court may hear claims concerning registered designs, Community registered designs and semiconductor topography rights. The usual Pt 7 procedure applies save as modified by this Part and all cases are automatically allocated to the multi-track. Registered trade marks and other intellectual property rights are dealt with in s.II.

Estates, trusts and charities (Pt 64)

Section I of this Part is concerned with claims relating to the administration of estates and trusts. It covers the following actions to which the Pt 8 procedure (see Ch.10) applies:

(a) for the court to determine any question arising in the administration of the estate of a deceased person or the execution of a trust;
(b) for an order for the administration of the estate of a deceased person, or the execution of a trust, to be carried out under the direction of the court;
(c) under the Variation of Trusts Act 1958; and
(d) under s.48 of the Administration of Justice Act 1985.

Section II applies to charity proceedings as defined by s.33(8) of the Charities Act 1993. Rule 64.6 sets out the requirements for an application to the High Court under s.33(5) of the Act for permission to start proceedings.

Proceedings relating to anti-social behaviour and harrassment (Pt 65)

24.017 This Part is divided into six sections dealing with the following:

(a) injunctions under the Housing Act 1996;
(b) applications by local authorities under s.91(3) of the Anti-social Behaviour Act 2003 for a power of arrest to be attached to an injunction;
(c) claims for demotion orders under the Housing Act 1985 and Housing Act 1988 and proceedings relating to demoted tenancies;
(d) anti-social behaviour orders under the Crime and Disorder Act 1998; and
(e) claims under s.3 of the Protection from Harassment Act 1997.

Crown Proceedings (Pt 66)

24.018 This Part sets out the rules for civil proceedings by or against the Crown, and other civil proceedings to which the Crown is a party. These matters are defined by the Crown Proceedings Act 1947. The following practical points should be noted.

(a) By r.16.2(1A) in civil proceedings against the Crown, the claim form (see para.12.009) must contain the names of the government departments and officers of the Crown concerned and brief details of the circumstances in which it is alleged that the liability of the Crown arose;
(b) By r 6.5(8) the service of documents (see Ch.8) on the Attorney General must be effected on the Treasury Solicitor and service on a government department must be effected on the solicitor acting for that department as listed in PD 66.
(c) Rule 66.4 deals with counterclaims, additional claims and any defence of set-off made against the Crown.
(d) Whilst in civil proceedings against the Crown a request for a default judgment can be made (see para.15.005), that must be considered by a Master or district judge, who must in particular be satisfied that the claim form and particulars of claim have been properly served on the Crown. See r.12.4(4).
(e) Rules 66.6 and 66.7 deal with what enforcement action (see Chs 40 and 41) may not be taken against the Crown.

Proceedings relating to solicitors (Pt 67)

This Part contains rules about certain types of proceedings relating to solicitors, namely: 24.019

(a) proceedings to obtain an order for a solicitor to deliver a bill or cash account and proceedings in relation to money or papers received by a solicitor;
(b) proceedings under Pt III of the Solicitors Act 1974 relating to the remuneration of solicitors (see para.39.003); and
(c) proceedings under Sch.1 to the Solicitors Act 1974 arising out of the Law Society's intervention in a solicitor's practice.

References to the European Court (Pt 68)

This part deals with references to the European Court. It briefly describes how an order may be applied for, admitted and transmitted to the European Court. The PD considers how the court might word any references and has annexed to it a useful note issued by the European Court.   24.020

CHAPTER 25

Interim Payments

THE OBJECT OF THE RULES

25.001 An interim payment is an advance payment on account of any damages, debt or other sum (except costs) which a defendant, or the claimant to a counterclaim, may be held liable to pay. Part 25 deals with interim remedies generally and rr.25.6 to 25.9 deal specifically with interim payments. The object of the rules is twofold:

(1) In all money claims (save those allocated to the small claims track) to enable the claimant who has a strong case on liability (see the grounds for applying, below) to avoid the financial hardship which might otherwise be suffered because of any delay during the period between the issue of the claim form and the completion of any negotiation or adjudication on quantum.
(2) In possession claims to require the defendant to pay compensation to the claimant for his occupation of the land where such payment would be appropriate even if the claim for possession fails (e.g. it is a forfeiture action and the defendant obtains relief against forfeiture).

CONDITIONS TO BE SATISFIED

25.002 No claimant has a right to an interim payment. If he can establish one or more grounds for applying (see below) the court will then exercise its discretion as to two questions: (i) Whether it would be appropriate in principle to make an order; and (ii) if so the amount if any it is appropriate to award.

On question (i) the court may decide that it is not appropriate to order an interim payment if the application is made too close to the trial, or for too small an amount of money for it to be worthwhile, or if, in some other way, it would delay or prejudice the fair conduct of the trial (*Campbell v Mylchreest* [1998] EWCA Civ 60, (1998) L.T.L., January 26, and *Tinsley v Sarkar* [2004] EWCA Civ 1098, (2004) L.T.L., July 23 discussed at para.25.009 below).

On question (ii) the court must not order a sum which is "more than a reasonable proportion of a likely amount of the final judgment" (r.25.7(4)). "There is no rule (of law or thumb) as to what is a reasonable proportion" *per* Langley

J. in *Spillman v Bradfield Riding Centre* [2007] EWHC 89 (although 75 per cent is a common figure that found some favour in *Dolman v Rowe* [2005] EWCA Civ 715 as cited in *Spillman*). The court must also take into account "contributory negligence; and ... any relevant set-off or counterclaim" (r.25.7(5)). Additionally it must take into account "the financial position of each party" (r.1.1(2)(c)). In *British and Commonwealth Holdings Plc v Quadrex Holdings Inc* [1989] Q.B. 842 the Court of Appeal held that an order for an interim payment of £75 million would have had a severe adverse impact on the business of the defendant which would have been irremediable: it reduced the amount to £5 million. The court must also take into account the risk that, because of impecuniosity, a claimant who receives too large an interim payment may later be unable to pay the excess back (*Harmon CFEM Facades (UK Ltd) (in liquidation) v The Corporate Officer of the House of Commons* [2000] EWHC Technology 84.

The grounds upon which an interim payment may be ordered are set out in r.25.7, which states as follows:

"The court may only make an order for an interim payment where any of the following conditions are satisfied—

(a) the defendant against whom the order is sought has admitted liability to pay damages or some other sum of money to the claimant;

(b) the claimant has obtained judgment against that defendant for damages to be assessed or for a sum of money (other than costs) to be assessed;

(c) it is satisfied that, if the claim went to trial, the claimant would obtain judgment for a substantial amount of money (other than costs) against the defendant from whom he is seeking an order for an interim payment whether or not that defendant is the only defendant or one of a number of defendants to the claim;

(d) the following conditions are satisfied—

  (i) the claimant is seeking an order for possession of land (whether or not any other order is also sought); and

  (ii) the court is satisfied that, if the case went to trial, the defendant would be held liable (even if the claim for possession fails) to pay the claimant a sum of money for the defendant's occupation and use of the land while the claim for possession was pending; or

(e) in a claim in which there are two or more defendants and the order is sought against any one or more of those defendants, the following conditions are satisfied—

  (i) the court is satisfied that, if the claim went to trial the claimant would obtain judgment for a substantial amount of money (other than costs) against at least one of the defendants (but the court cannot determine which); and

  (ii) all the defendants are either—

(a) a defendant that is insured in respect of the claim;
(b) a defendant whose liability will be met by an insurer under s.151 of the Road Traffic Act 1988 or an insurer acting under the Motor Insurers' Bureau Agreement, or the Motor Insurers' Bureau where it is acting itself; or
(c) a defendant that is a public body"

Admission of liability: ground (a)

25.003 Given the ability to obtain judgment on admissions this ground largely duplicates ground (b) so far as admissions are concerned. It does however have some independent value. The claimant may be unwilling to enter judgment on admissions because the admission relates to a secondary claim he made in the alternative and he still wishes to pursue his primary claim (*cf. Shearson Lehman Brothers Inc v Maclaine, Watson & Co. Ltd* [1987] 1 W.L.R. 480, CA.

The reasonable proportion to be allowed here may well be 100 per cent of the highest sum indisputably due to the claimant. If the defendant has put a value on his admission the interim payment is likely to be at least that value. In *Shearson Lehman Brothers Inc v Maclaine, Watson & Co. Ltd* [1987] 1 W.L.R. 480, CA the primary claim was for the full contract price of goods delivered, namely £23.9 million. There was also an alternative claim for damages for non-acceptance which was calculated at a minimum figure of £7.2 million. The defendants denied liability in respect of both claims and further stated that the true value of the damages claim would not exceed £5.2 million. On the claimant's establishing what is now ground (c) (see below) an interim payment of £5.2 million was ordered.

Judgment for a sum to be assessed: ground (b)

25.004 The judgment obtained may be a default judgment (see Ch.15), a judgment on admissions (see Ch.16) or a summary judgment (see Ch.19). As with ground (a), the reasonable proportion to be allowed may well be 100 per cent of the value of the judgment if that value is assessed as the highest sum indisputably due to the claimant (*Harmon CFEM Facades (UK Ltd) (in Liquidation) v The Corporate Officer of the House of Commons* [2000] EWHC Technology 84). If that sum is too small to merit the making of an order the application may be dismissed (*Campbell v Mylchreest* [1998] EWCA Civ 60, Auld L.J.).

At trial the claimant will obtain judgment for a substantial sum against the respondent: ground (c)

25.005 To establish this ground the claimant must show that: (i) at trial, he is bound to win; (ii) his win will be against the respondent to the application (whether or not he also wins against any other defendants); and (iii) that the win will be for a substantial amount of money. (As to the incorrect use of the word "that" in ground (c), see *Harmon CFEM Facades (UK Ltd) (in Liquidation) v The Corporate Officer of the House of Commons* [2000] EWHC Technology 84).

As to (i) it is not enough to show that the claimant is likely to succeed at trial: the court must be satisfied that he is bound to succeed, at least in respect of the claims upon which he seeks an interim payment (see generally *British and Commonwealth Holdings Plc v Quadrex Holdings Inc* [1989] Q.B. 842. Given the ability to obtain a summary judgment in such circumstances ground (c) (like ground (a)) largely duplicates ground (b). *British and Commonwealth Holdings Plc* demonstrates that it does have some independent value: if on the summary judgment application it appears to the court possible that the defendant's defence may succeed but improbable that it will do so the court may make a conditional order (see para.19.014, above) and/or make an order for an interim payment.

As to (ii) if there is more than one defendant and the claimant cannot say against which one he is bound to win, this ground is not available to him: instead he must seek to get through the somewhat narrower doors of ground (e) (see below).

As to (iii) what is a substantial amount of money? Certainly, anything in six figures is substantial and anything within the small claims limit is not (the interim payment rules do not apply to cases allocated to the small claims track). In between those figures the court will assess whether the amount is substantial in the light of the overriding objective, taking into account, for example, the financial position of both parties (see r.1.1(2)(c)). Turning now to the court's general discretion, it will consider also how long the delay is likely to be until the trial is concluded (r.1.1(2)(d)) and will also take into account any contributory negligence, relevant set-off or counterclaim (r.25.7(5)). The value of a counterclaim which has a reasonable prospect of success may preclude the court from saying that it is satisfied the claimant will obtain a substantial sum at trial (*Bovis Lend Lease Ltd v Braehead Glasgow Ltd* [2000] EWHC Technology 108).

Claim for occupation and use of land: ground (d)

This ground applies where the claimant claims possession of land and the defendant resists the claim saying that he is entitled to remain, for example, as a tenant paying rent. In such a case the court may order an interim payment if it is satisfied that, whether or not the claim for possession fails, if the case goes to trial, the defendant will have to pay the claimant something for the defendant's use and occupation of the land whilst the claim for possession was pending.

25.006

At trial the claimant will obtain judgment for a substantial sum against one or more of the defendants: ground (e)

In very many cases, particularly personal injury cases, a claimant who sues several defendants in the alternative is able to say that he is bound to win at trial

25.007

against one or more of them. However, unfortunately, until trial he cannot satisfy the court as to which one or more of them that will be. On this ground the requirement to point the finger of liability at a particular defendant or defendants is replaced by a requirement to show that all of them are sufficiently secured whether by insurance or its equivalent or by governmental finance; this ground is available only if all of the defendants are public bodies, or persons whose liability is covered by an insurer or by the MIB. The rationale here is that, since one or more of them is bound to lose, all of them can be made to take an appropriate share in funding the interim payment. Given the financial backing which is available to them, being ordered to make an interim payment will not cause any of them any personal hardship. At the trial, the court, having determined which of them are liable will make an appropriate adjustment order under which the losing defendants must pay the balance of compensation to the claimant and must refund any interim payments made by other defendants (as to adjustment orders, see below).

VOLUNTARY PAYMENTS

25.008 Before making an application to the court the claimant should ask the defendant to make a voluntary payment. A well-advised defendant will often grant voluntarily anything the claimant can obtain by order anyway. If the voluntary interim payment is in respect of a child or patient some court proceedings will still be necessary. The payment will not be valid without the approval of the court (r.21.10). PD 25B, para.1.2 provides that such permission should be obtained before the payment is made.

APPLICATIONS FOR INTERIM PAYMENTS

Making the application

25.009 A claimant may apply for an interim payment at any time after the claim form has been served on the respondent to the application and the time limited for that person to file an acknowledgment of service has expired (see Ch.9). The application is often combined with an application for judgment on admissions or summary judgment. The claimant thereby hopes to obtain an order for a sum of money to be assessed and, pending that assessment, an order for an interim payment to be made immediately.

In all cases an application notice must be issued and served at least 14 days before the hearing and by PD 25b para.2.1 must be supported by evidence which deals with the following:

  (1) the sum of money sought;
  (2) the items or matters in respect of which the payment is sought;
  (3) the sum of money for which final judgment is likely to be given;

(4) the reasons for believing that one of the grounds exists;
(5) any other relevant matters;
(6) in claims for personal injuries, details of special damages and past and future losses (see Ch.4); and
(7) in a claim under the Fatal Accidents Act 1976, details of the person(s) on whose behalf the claim is made and the nature of the claim.

The applicant should exhibit all relevant documents in support of the claim (e.g. police accident report and any expert's report already disclosed but not filed at court) including any medical reports on which the applicant wishes to rely.

Strictly, the rules do not require the applicant to show any need for the interim payment or that he will suffer prejudice if he does not receive it. However, if the delay in assessment of damages is unlikely to be substantial, the court may be reluctant to exercise its discretion to make an order unless the claimant has some special reason for requiring it, for example, the payment of private medical treatment or hardship caused by loss of earnings. We take the view that where the applicant has any particular need for an interim payment there is no harm in giving the details of it in the witness statement made in support of the application. Indeed, PD 25b para.2.1(2) set out above requires evidence to be given of the items or matters in respect of which the payment is sought. It is only one logical step further to explain why. In exercising its discretion the court may be assisted by this information: see *Wade v Turfrey* (2007) L.T.L., March 22. Indeed, in our experience this is particularly true when the litigation friend applies on behalf of a child or patient asking the court to direct immediate payment of the interim payment to himself.

However, this is far from an uncontraversial area. Whilst in general the court is not concerned as to the desirability of the expenditure intended to be met with the proposed interim payment (*Stringman v McArdle* [1994] 1 W.L.R. 1653), it is a relevant consideration, which may lead to the court declining to exercise its discretion to order an interim payment, that the payment may prejudice the trial or the position of the defendant in the proceedings or prejudge an issue to be determined at the trial (*Campbell v Mylchreest* [1998] EWCA Civ 60, (1998) L.T.L., January 26 and *Tinsley v Sarkar* [2004] EWCA Civ 1098, (2004) L.T.L., July 23. Both of these cases involved applications for an interim payment to be spent on the claimant's care regime that the defendant intended to challenge at trial. The same issue was raised but rejected in *Wade v Turfrey* (2007) L.T.L. March 22).

Opposing the application

The defendant is unlikely to get very far relying upon some error in procedure, for example, the application was not served at least 14 days before the hearing; such errors will not invalidate the application and the court may make an order remedying the error (r.3.10, see further para.1.015, above). The defendant might seek to challenge whether any grounds for applying have been established.

25.010

There is probably little chance of disproving grounds (a), (b) or (d) if relied on by the claimant. However, on grounds (c) and (e) he might succeed in showing that the claimant is not bound to win or that the win will not be for a "substantial amount of money" or, on ground (e), that not all of the defendants are backed by the government, or by an insurer or the MIB.

The most fertile ground for opposing the application is on whether the court, in its discretion, should make an order and, if it does so, the amount it should allow (see in particular para.25.009 above).

If the respondent wishes to rely on written evidence at the hearing he must file a witness statement and serve copies on every other party to the application at least seven days before the hearing. (If the applicant then wishes to rely on further evidence in reply he must file it and serve a copy on the respondent at least three days before the hearing). The respondent will know from the claimant's evidence how much the claimant is seeking. If the respondent wishes the court to take into account his ability to pay that sum (or indeed any sum) when deciding whether or not to exercise its discretion, he should give sufficient details of his financial position in his evidence.

The order for an interim payment

25.011 If the court makes an order for an interim payment it will state the amount and will usually require it to be paid within a specified number of days in one lump sum. However, the order may provide for payment by instalments, for example, in the case of payments for the occupation of land the court will usually order periodical payments as if they were of payments of rent. Any instalment order must state the total amount of the payment and of each instalment, as well as the number of instalments and the date each is to be paid. The payment is normally made direct to the applicant, via his solicitor. However, if the order is made in favour of a child or patient the court will direct to whom the money is to be paid or otherwise invested (see r.21.11 and PD 21, para.8).

Further, by reg.20(3) of the Community Legal Service (Costs) Regulations 2000 (SI 2000/441) if a solicitor's client is funded by the Community Legal Service (see Ch.2), "any money received by way of any interim payment made in accordance with an order made under CPR r.25.6, or in accordance with an agreement having the same effect as such an order" can only be paid direct to the client "where [the Regional CLS Director] considers it essential to protect the client's interests or welfare".

If the court refuses to order an interim payment the claimant may appeal. Whether he loses or wins on an application or an appeal, r.25.6(2) provides that a claimant may make more than one application for an interim payment order. As always the overriding objective needs to be considered carefully. If the court has previously refused an application it will require a significant change in circumstances to justify asking for more of the court's time—r.1.1(2)(e).

In personal injury cases affected by the law on recovery of social security benefits (see Ch.4) PD 25B, para.4.1 provides that the defendant should obtain and file at the hearing a certificate of recoverable benefits if: (a) the application is other than by consent; (b) the claim falls under the heads of damage set out in column 1 of Sch.2 to the Social Security (Recovery of Benefits) Act 1997 in respect of recoverable benefits received by a claimant set out in column 2 of that Schedule, and (c) the defendant is liable to pay recoverable benefits to the Secretary of State. If an order is made it will state the amount by which it has been reduced according to the Act and the Social Security (Recovery of Benefits) Regulations 1997 (SI 1997/2205). The claimant will receive the net amount but any adjustment subsequently made (see below) will take into account the gross figure.

FURTHER CONDUCT OF THE ACTION

Some rules affect the conduct of the parties after an interim payment has been made: 25.012

(1) Rule 38.2(2)(b) provides that where the claimant has received an interim payment either voluntarily or pursuant to a court order in respect of a claim he is only allowed to discontinue (see Ch.35) that claim if the defendant who made the interim payment consents in writing or the court gives its permission.
(2) If the defendant later wishes to make a Pt 36 offer (see Ch.29) his offer should state that he has taken the interim payment into account.
(3) Rule 25.9 provides that unless the defendant agrees, the fact that an interim payment has been made voluntarily and/or under a court order shall not be disclosed to the trial judge until he has dealt with all questions of liability and quantum.
(4) When final judgment is given, the court can make such orders in respect of an interim payment as may be necessary to give effect to the trial court's determination, for example, judgment for the balance and/or an order that one defendant refund moneys to another defendant (r.25.8). It sometimes happens that although a claimant is awarded an interim payment he wholly loses at trial or secures a judgment for less than the amount paid. In these circumstances the court may award the defendant interest on the overpaid amount from the date when he made the interim payment (*Manotta v London United Busways Ltd* (2000) C.L. June).

CHAPTER 26

Security For Costs

INTRODUCTION

26.001 An order for security for costs seeks to protect the party in whose favour it is made against the risk of being unable to enforce any costs order he may later obtain. The order, if complied with, will provide the party in whose favour it is made with funds normally held in court available for the payment of any costs the court later awards him. There are three major types of security for costs applications which we shall describe separately below; applications against claimants and appellants (rr.25.12, 25.13 and 25.15): defence applications against someone other than the claimant (r.25.14) and applications against any party who has failed to comply with a rule, practice direction or a relevant pre-action protocol (r.3.1). Further, an order may be made as an alternative to granting summary judgment to a defendant (see paras 26.006 and 19.014).

APPLICATIONS AGAINST CLAIMANTS AND APPELLANTS

26.002 The general rules can provide security for the costs of opposing claims, Pt 20 claims (see Ch.18) and appeals. Thus, applications can be made by defendants to claims, defendants to counterclaims, respondents to appeals and by appellants in respect of cross appeals. They can also be made by third parties against the defendants who commenced the third party proceedings.

In order to obtain an order for security for costs the applicant must show:

(i) that one or more grounds for security exist (see the list given below): and
(ii) that, in all the circumstances of the case, it is just to make such an order.

As to question (i) r.25.13 lists the following grounds:

(a) The opponent is resident outside England and Wales and is not resident in a Brussels Contracting State, a Lugano Contracting State or a Regulation State (see the list of these countries at para.11.002).

(b) The opponent is a company or other body (whether incorporated inside or outside Great Britain) and there is reason to believe that it will be unable to pay the applicant's costs if ordered to do so.

(c) The opponent has changed his address since the claim (or appeal) was commenced with a view to evading the consequences of the litigation.

(d) The opponent failed to give his address in the claim form or appellant's notice or gave an incorrect address in that form.

(e) The opponent (not being a litigant who is suing in a representative capacity) is a nominal claimant or appellant and there is reason to believe that he will be unable to pay the applicant's costs if ordered to do so.

(f) The opponent has taken steps in relation to his assets that would make it difficult to enforce an order for costs against him.

(g) A statute permits the court to require security for costs (r.25.13(1)(b)(ii)). The primary examples here are the Companies Act 1985, s.726 (insolvent companies registered in England, Wales or Scotland) and the Arbitration Act 1996, s.70(6) (applications challenging an award on grounds of jurisdiction or serious irregularity or appealing on a point of law: for further details see *White Book*, para.25.13.16).

As to question (ii) (is it just to make the order?) there are many factors which may have to be considered. For example, where solvency is a relevant issue (see (b) and (g) above) the court will take into account the strength of his claim or appeal, whether it is alleged that his insolvency was brought about by the conduct of the applicant, delay by the applicant in making the application and whether the order for security is being sought oppressively in order to stifle a claim or appeal. Difficult Human Rights Act 1998 questions may arise here: a requirement to raise funds which he is unable to raise may amount to a breach of his rights to a fair trial (ECHR Art.6(1)); on the other hand the court must not allow an insolvent claimant or appellant to put unfair pressure on a prosperous defendant or respondent (see further *White Book* paras 25.12.7, 25.13.1 and 25.13.10). The court may also take into account open offers of compromise made by the applicant, payments into court and offers to settle, but not other statements made in negotiations conducted "without prejudice" (*Simaan General Contracting Co. v Pilkington Glass Ltd* [1987] 1 W.L.R. 516).

If residence is a relevant issue (see (a) above) the court will take into account the value of any property within the countries of the EU and EFTA (e.g. a statue, the subject matter of the action, lodged in a bank to the order of both parties' solicitors *De Bry v Fitzgerald* [1990] 1 W.L.R. 552; for the list of EU and EFTA States, see para.11.002, above), and the presence of co-claimants or co-appellants who are resident here (*Slazengers Ltd v Seaspeed Ferries International Ltd* [1988] 1 W.L.R. 221).

An order for security for costs may infringe the defendant's right under ECHR Art.6 (which includes effective access to the courts). Article 14 requires that the enjoyment of rights under the convention must be secured without discrimination on any grounds such as race, language, national or social origin, birth or other status. Whilst ground (a) prevents discrimination as between UK claimants and claimants resident elsewhere in the EU and EFTA, the Human Rights Act 1998 requires courts to exercise their discretion in security for costs applications so as not to discriminate between any claimants because of their country of residence. Thus, where ground (a) (but no other ground) is established, the court should not exercise its discretion to order security for costs unless it does so on grounds relating to obstacles to, or to the burden of enforcement of, a subsequent order for costs in the context of the particular foreign claimant or country concerned. It is discriminatory and wrong to take into account the impecuniosity of an individual foreign claimant: *Nasser v United Bank of Kuwait* [2002] 1 W.L.R. 1868, CA. In that case the applicant's likely costs up to the end of the proceedings in question was £10,000. There being no obstacle to or difficulty about enforcing orders for costs in that case the amount of security was limited to the amount needed to cover the extra burden in terms of costs and delay likely to be involved in seeking to enforce an order for costs overseas. The extra burden was assessed at £5,000 and that was the sum ordered as security.

No formal evidence is required in order to prove the obstacles to or difficulties of enforcement which may arise, or the extra costs the applicant may be put to. Whilst there must be a proper basis for considering that such problems exist the court will take note of obvious realities (*Thistle Hotels Ltd v Gamma Four Ltd* [2004] EWHC 322). In *De Beer v Kanaar & Co.* [2003] 1 W.L.R. 38, CA the obstacles or difficulties relied on including a lack of probity on the part of the claimant, the fact that his assets were easily movable and the risk that an order for costs against him would be difficult or even impossible to enforce: in all the circumstances the amount of security it was appropriate to award was £130,000, the full amount of the applicant's likely costs up to the end of the proceedings.

Whichever ground for security is relied upon, special questions of discretion arise where the proceedings comprise a claim and linked counterclaim.

Example

In a contract action the claimant is an impecunious company and the defendant is an American company which raises a counterclaim arising out of the same matter or transaction as the claim. The court may well refuse to grant the claimant security for the costs of defending the counterclaim if it considers that the counterclaim does not raise issues which go beyond the defence of the claim (*Neck v Taylor* [1893] 1 Q.B. 560 and *Thistle Hotels Ltd v Gamma Four Ltd* [2004] EWHC 322). Similarly, the court may refuse to grant the defendant any security for his costs of defending the claim. If both claim and counterclaim are going to be litigated anyway, ordering security which the claimant failed to pay would serve no purpose other than to hamper the claimant's conduct of the case and to give the counterclaiming defendant the right to begin (*B J Crabtree (Insulations) Ltd v GPT Communication Systems Ltd* [1990] 59 B.L.R. 46, CA).

How to apply

Although this is not expressly required by the rules, the best practice is for the applicant not to apply to the court until he has requested the claimant or appellant to provide security by consent.

26.003

Applications for security for costs will normally be heard by a master or district judge. There is a practice form of application (Form PF43). Part 23 makes general provisions concerning evidence in support, evidence in reply and further evidence. The application should be supported by written evidence which sets out the applicant's case as to questions (i) and (ii) above and which exhibits a draft bill of costs. As the usual order is that proceedings are stayed pending the payment of security, the later the application is made, the less likely it will be successful: see *Vedatech Corporation v Seagate Software Information (No.2)* [2002] EWCA Civ 54 (application shortly before trial meant judge made an unless order dismissing the claim if the security was not provided. The Court of Appeal held that this was oppressive and disproportionate).

Applications under s.726 of the Companies Act 1985 will be listed as a hearing in private in the first instance (PD 39, para.1.5(8); see further Ch.13). In some cases the company claimant's impecuniosity will be admitted or easily proved (e.g. by proof of the existence of insolvency proceedings). In other cases insolvency may be established by means of the expert evidence of accounts. Such evidence is expensive. In an appropriate case the court will appoint a single expert to provide such evidence (*Guinle v Kirreh Kinstreet Ltd v Balmargo Corporation Ltd*, Arden J., (1999) L.T.L., December 3; see further as to expert evidence, Ch.23).

In determining the amount of security, the court must take into account the amount which the claimant or appellant is likely to be able to raise. The court should not normally make continuation of his claim or appeal dependent upon a condition which it is impossible for him to fulfil. An impairment of his right of access to the courts which is disproportionate to the need to protect other parties is likely to be a breach of ECHR Art.6(1). However, in considering this issue, the court should consider, not only the resources of the claimant or appellant, but also the prospects of him being able to raise the amount needed from outside sources. A claimant or appellant who seeks to limit the amount of security he must give is under an obligation to put in proper and sufficient evidence not only as to his own resources, but also as to the prospects of funds being available and forthcoming from any outside source (*Kufaan Publishing Ltd v Al-Warrack Bookshop Ltd*, March 1, 2000, CA).

If security is ordered the court will specify the sum considered appropriate. For a practice form of order, see Form PF 44 (as to which, see *Radu v Houston* [2006] EWCA Civ 1575 and para.33.007, below). Usually an order for the sum to be paid into court is more convenient than an order requiring the provision and agreement of a bond. The practice form of order specifies a reasonable time for the payment in or other compliance, stays the proceedings in the meantime and provides for automatic dismissal of the proceedings if security is not provided. Alternatively, the security may take the form of a personal undertaking given by the claimant's solicitor (*A Ltd v B Ltd* [1996] 1 W.L.R. 665). In all cases, the amount of security ordered may later be increased or reduced on proof of a material change of circumstances (*Gordano Building Contractors Ltd v Burgess* [1988] 1 W.L.R. 890).

Can a claimant who is insured against liability for the defendant's costs in the event of the action failing rely on the existence of such insurance as sufficient security itself? The Court of Appeal in *Nasser v United Bank of Kuwait* [2002] 1 W.L.R. 1868 indicated that this was a possibility. However, the defendant would be entitled, at the very least, to some assurance as to the scope of cover, that it was not liable to be avoided for misrepresentation or non-disclosure and that its proceeds could not be diverted elsewhere (and see further *Al-Koronky v Time Life Entertainment Group Ltd* [2006] EWCA Civ 1123).

DEFENCE APPLICATIONS AGAINST SOMEONE OTHER THAN THE CLAIMANT

26.004   Rule 25.14 is new. It does not apply to appeals. It permits applications by defendants (including defendants to additional claims, see Ch.18) against certain persons behind or connected with the claimant. To obtain an order for security under r.25.14 the defendant must show:

(i) that in all the circumstances, it will be just to make an order: and
(ii) either:

(a) the claimant's right to make the claim was assigned to him by the person against whom the order for security is sought with a view to avoiding the possibility of a costs order being made against him; or
(b) the person against whom the order is sought has contributed or agreed to contribute to the claimant's costs in return for a share of any money or property which the claimant may recover in the proceedings.

Orders under r.25.14 are not encountered frequently in practice. Persons who assign the right to make a claim do not normally do so with a view to avoiding adverse costs orders. In practice the assignment is made because the assignor has simply run out of the finance or the energy to continue the fight. As to ground (b), the agreement to fund the litigation may well amount to a champertous agreement and, as such, may amount to an abuse of the process of the court. This may entitle the defendant to obtain a general stay of proceedings, not just security for costs (*Stocznia Gdanska SA v Latreefers Inc* [2000] EWCA Civ 36).

The application under this rule will often be combined with an application to join the person against whom the order is sought as a party to the action. It may also be combined with other applications. For example, if the circumstances so warrant, the defendant might also seek security for costs against the claimant under the general rules. Rule 25.14 does not spell out the consequences if a person ordered to give security under this rule fails to do so. Should an order under this rule provide for the claim to be struck out if it is not complied with, thereby terminating the current claimant's claim? For a case illustration (in which it seems no application was made under r.25.14 expressly) see *Compagnie Noga d'Importation et Exportation SA v Australian and New Zealand Banking Group Ltd* [2004] EWHC 2601 Comm, especially para.130).

SECURITY FOR COSTS ORDERS UNDER R.3.1

Rule 3.1 sets out the court's case management powers including powers to deal with recalcitrant parties, i.e. parties who fail to comply with obligations imposed on them by rules, practice directions, relevant pre-action protocols or orders of the court. These powers contain wholly new grounds for security for costs orders. The relevant parts of r.3.1 are as follows: 26.005

> "(3) when the court makes an order, it may
>
> (a) make it subject to conditions including a condition to pay a sum of money into court; and
>
> (b) specify the consequence of failure to comply with the order or a condition.
>
> (5) the court may order a party to pay a sum of money into court if that party has, without good reason, failed to comply with a rule, practice direction or a relevant pre-action protocol.
>
> (6) when exercising its power under paragraph (5) the court must have regard to-
>
> (a) the amount in dispute; and
>
> (b) the costs which the parties have incurred or which they may incur.
>
> (6A) where a party pays money into court following an order under paragraph (3) or (5) the money shall be security for any sum payable by that party to any other party in the proceedings."

In cases to which these provisions apply, an application for security for costs can be made against any party, whether English-based or foreign-based, whether claimant, defendant, appellant or respondent to an appeal. An example of para.(3) could be an order terminating an action unless security for costs is given made against a party who had previously failed to comply with an order which did not contain conditions. Paragraph (5) permits the making of security for costs orders against a party who is not in breach of a court order, but is in breach of a rule, practice direction or a relevant pre-action protocol. Moreover, orders under r.3.1 are not limited to orders for security for costs. Where the party against whom the order is made is a defendant or defendant to counterclaim, the court may also order him to give security for any money remedy claimed against him (see para.(6)).

Assume that some relevant wrongful conduct is proved or admitted. What factors should the court take into account in the exercise of its discretion to order security for costs under this rule? In *Ali v Hudson* [2003] EWCA Civ 1793 Clark L.J. summarised the correct general approach as follows:

"(i) It would only be in an exceptional case (if ever) that a court would order security for costs if the order would stifle a claim or an appeal;

(ii) In any event, (a) an order should not ordinarily be made unless the party concerned can be shown to be regularly flouting proper court procedures or otherwise to be demonstrating a want of good faith; good faith being understood to consist . . . of a will to litigate a genuine claim or defence (or appeal) as economically and expeditiously as reasonably possible in accordance with the overriding objective; and (b) an order will not be appropriate in every case where a party has a weak case. The weakness of the party's case will ordinarily be relevant only where he has no real prospect of succeeding."

SECURITY FOR COSTS UNDER CPR 24

26.006 Under Pt 24 a defendant can apply for a claim to be summarily dismissed on the grounds that the claimant has no real prospect of succeeding and there is no other compelling reason why the case should be disposed of at a trial. If the court considers that it is possible that the claim will succeed but it is improbable that it will do so the court may make a conditional order, terminating the claim unless security for costs is given. Do not make the mistake of thinking that such an order is appropriate in every case where a party appears to have a weak claim. In *Olatawura v Abiloye* [2003] 1 W.L.R. 275 Simon Brown L.J. gave the following guidance:

"The last thing this judgment should be seen as encouraging is the making by either side of exorbitant applications for summary judgment under r.24.2 in a misguided attempt to obtain conditional orders providing security for costs. On the contrary, the court will be reluctant to be drawn into an assessment of the merits beyond what is necessary to establish whether the person concerned has 'no real prospect of succeeding' and the occasions when security for costs is ordered solely because the case appears weak may be expected to be few and far between."

CHAPTER 27

Interim Injunctions

INTRODUCTION

An injunction is an order of the court either compelling a party to take specified steps (a mandatory injunction) or restraining him from taking specified steps (a prohibitory or negative injunction). An injunction granted after a trial is often called a final or perpetual injunction. An interim injunction is an order made before trial, if necessary even before the issue of proceedings, and is usually granted to maintain existing conditions (the "status quo") until the trial can be heard. An injunction, whether mandatory or prohibitory, whether final or interim, can be granted to remedy an injury already suffered or to prevent an injury occurring (e.g. *Cambridge Nutrition Ltd v BBC* [1990] 3 All E.R. 523, CA; interim injunction to restrain the broadcast of a programme listed for broadcast within the next few days).

27.001

A full interim injunction may continue in force until "judgment in the action or further order". An interim injunction granted without notice of the application continues in force only for a short time and will usually specify the date of a further hearing (the "return day") at which the matter will be reconsidered. Even before the without notice order expires the respondent may apply on notice for it to be discharged.

An interim injunction is usually a temporary version of the type of injunction the applicant will seek at the trial and is thus only a provisional remedy. However, many injunction cases never get beyond the interim stage. The parties are often content to accept the court's decision as a fair indication of what the trial judge would order. In addition the applicant might seek summary judgment (see Ch.19) as well as an interim injunction (see *L.A. Gear Inc v Hi-Tec Sports Plc* [1992] F.S.R. 121). In exceptional cases the interim order may amount to the full remedy sought by the claimant (*Cambridge Nutrition Ltd v BBC* [1990] 3 All E.R. 523, CA, noted above) or may give the applicant a remedy which is a collateral to his trial remedies (e.g. freezing injunctions and search orders: see paras 27.015 and 27.023 below). The principles applicable to the grant of these exceptional types of interim injunction differ from the general principles laid down in *American Cyanamid v Ethicon* [1975] A.C. 396 (see para.27.003) below).

In disputes between neighbours about building works, can a claimant obtain a final injunction restraining the use of the building or even compelling its demolition if he did not previously seek an interim injunction? In *Mortimer v Bailey* [2004] EWCA Civ 1514, the Court of Appeal answered this question affirmatively holding that it was enough for the claimants simply to warn the defendants of their intention to seek a final injunction. They were not required to take the risk of applying for an interim injunction bearing in mind the dangers that would come with it (costs and undertakings in damages, as to which, see below). It had been open to the defendants to seek declaratory relief if they wished to have the question determined before erecting the building. Nevertheless, the court accepted that delay in seeking injunctive relief is a factor which can be taken into account in deciding whether an injunction should be granted. It may strengthen an argument that the injury to the claimant is small and that damages rather than an injunction will provide an adequate remedy (*Jaggard v Sawyer* [1995] 1 W.L.R. 269, CA).

UNDERTAKING AS TO DAMAGES (PD 25, PARA.5.1A)

27.002 Since every interim injunction is granted before trial and therefore before the merits of the case have been finally determined, the applicant is required to give an "undertaking as to damages", i.e. a promise to pay his opponent compensation if the applicant later fails to establish his right to the injunction. The undertaking is often referred to as a "cross-undertaking" so as to indicate that it is given by the applicant. If the applicant does later fail to establish his right to the injunction the undertaking is enforced by an inquiry into what loss the respondent suffered because of the injunction. The assessment of damages is made on the premise that the applicant has covenanted with the respondent not to prevent the respondent doing that which he was restrained from doing by the terms of the injunction (*per* Lord Diplock in *Hoffman-La Roche v Secretary of State for Trade and Industry* [1975] A.C. 295). The undertaking is also enforceable by co-defendants who were not directly subject to the injunction but who have suffered loss because of it (*Dubai Bank Ltd v Galadari (No.2)*, *The Times*, October 11, 1989). However, a person who is not a party to the proceedings may not recover damages for any losses sustained due to the injunction and a party to the proceedings may not claim that person's losses as third party losses pursuant to the cross-undertaking. Whilst the court has jurisdiction to require an applicant to give an undertaking for the benefit of a non-party, the principles for doing so are far from clear: see *Smithkline Beecham Plc v Apotex Europe Ltd* [2006] EWCA Civ 658, [2006] 3 W.L.R. 1146.

The undertaking is given, not to the respondent, but to the court, which has a discretion as to whether or not to enforce it. The presumption is that it will unless there are special circumstances: see *Lunn Poly Ltd v Tui UK Ltd* [2006] EWCA Civ 430, *The Times*, April 18, 2007.

Damages include the costs incurred and these are recoverable on the standard basis: see *Apex Frozen Foods Ltd v Ali* [2007] EWHC 469, (2007) L.T.L., April 11.

The court has a discretion not to require an undertaking where the interim injunction is sought by the Crown, local authorities and similar law enforcement agencies acting in the public interest to enforce the law (*Hoffman-La Roche v Secretary of State for Trade and Industry* [1975] A.C. 295, above, *Kirklees BC v Wickes Building Supplies Ltd* [1993] A.C. 227 and the cases cited therein, and *Customs and Excise Commissioners v Anchor Foods Ltd* [1999] 1 W.L.R. 1139 in which an undertaking was in fact required).

GENERAL PRINCIPLES UPON WHICH GRANTED: *AMERICAN CYANAMID V ETHICON*

In *American Cyanamid v Ethicon* [1975] A.C. 396 the House of Lords declared that so long as an action was not frivolous or vexatious the only substantial factor the court takes into account is the balance of convenience. In other words it should not pre-judge the merits of the case, but should simply consider the nature of the injunction sought and ask: would it hurt the claimant more to go without the injunction pending trial than it would hurt the defendant to suffer it? The matters for the court's attention and the order in which they are dealt with may be listed as follows:

27.003

Whether there is a serious issue to be tried

The claim must not be frivolous or vexatious and must have some prospect of succeeding.

27.004

> "It is no part of the court's function at this stage to try to resolve conflicts of evidence on affidavits as to fact on which the claims of either party may ultimately depend nor to decide difficult questions of law which call for detailed argument and mature considerations. These are matters to be dealt with at the trial" (*per* Lord Diplock in *American Cyanamid*).

In practice, if questions of law do arise in proceedings before them, most judges cannot resist answering them (see *per* Lord Jauncey in *R. v Secretary of State for Transport Ex p. Factortame Ltd (No.2)* [1991] 1 A.C. 603). In *Bristol & West Building Society v Marks and Spencer Plc* [1991] 41 E.G. 139 an interim injunction was refused on this factor (and other factors, see below) because of the construction which the learned judge made of the meaning of the leasehold covenant upon which the claimant was suing.

Which way the balance of convenience lies

(1) Are damages an adequate remedy for the claimant and is the defendant able to pay them? *Shelfer v City of London Electric Lighting Company* [1895] 1 Ch.287 has for over a century been the leading case. It is authority for the following propositions, as found by the

27.005

Court of Appeal in *Regan v Paul Properties Ltd* [2006] EWCA Civ 1391, [2006] 3 W.L.R. 1131:

(1) A claimant is prima facie entitled to an injunction against a person committing a wrongful act, such as continuing nuisance, which invades the claimant's legal right.
(2) The wrongdoer is not entitled to ask the court to sanction his wrongdoing by purchasing the claimant's rights on payment of damages assessed by the court.
(3) The court has jurisdiction to award damages instead of an injunction, even in cases of a continuing nuisance; but the jurisdiction does not mean that the court is "a tribunal for legalising wrongful acts" by a defendant, who is able and willing to pay damages.
(4) The judicial discretion to award damages in lieu should pay attention to well settled principles and should not be exercised to deprive a claimant of his prima facie right "except under very exceptional circumstances."
(5) Although it is not possible to specify all the circumstances relevant to the exercise of the discretion or to lay down rules for its exercise, the judgments indicated that it was relevant to consider the following factors: whether the injury to the claimant's legal rights was small; whether the injury could be estimated in money; whether it could be adequately compensated by a small money payment; whether it would be oppressive to the defendant to grant an injunction; whether the claimant had shown that he only wanted money; whether the conduct of the claimant rendered it unjust to give him more than pecuniary relief; and whether there were any other circumstances which justified the refusal of an injunction.

This factor may not be relevant in cases where damage is not the main issue, for example, where the use or misuse of a property right is in question (*Smithkline Beecham Plc v Apotex Europe Ltd* [2003] EWCA Civ 137, patent rights) or in judicial review cases where the claimant has no right to damages (*R. v Secretary of State for Transport ex parte Factortame Ltd (No.2)* [1991] 1 A.C. 603 (Lord Goff).

In *Bath & North East Somerset District Council v Mowlem Plc* [2004] EWCA Civ 115 damages were held not to be an adequate remedy for the claimant in the following circumstances: disputes as to certain aspects of a development project had arisen; if the defendant builder was at fault the contract provided for liquidated damages only and, unless an injunction was granted the claimant would be unable to employ a new builder to re-undertake the disputed work; an interim injunction was granted restraining the defendant builder from refusing entry to the site to any new builder employed. (In *Bath & North East Somerset District Council* and elsewhere it is suggested that factors concerning the adequacy of damages precede questions as to the balance of convenience but do not form part of them. For a contrary view see the dictum of Lord Bridge set out in para.27.010, below.)

Is the burden on the claimant to show why damages should not be awarded instead of an injunction? No, held the Court of Appeal in *Regan v Paul Properties Ltd* [2006] EWCA Civ 1391, [2006] 3 W.L.R. 1131.

If damages are an adequate remedy for the claimant, an injunction will be refused; if not, you must next consider:

(2) Is the undertaking as to damages adequate protection for the defendant and is the claimant able to honour it? The claimant may be ordered to put up some security in case he fails to honour it, for example, a bank guarantee or the payment of a specified sum into an account held in joint names of the parties' solicitors (see further below). If the answer to question (2) is yes, the injunction will be granted: if no, you must next consider:

(3) The maintenance of the status quo (the existing conditions). Where the other factors are evenly balanced the court prefers to maintain the status quo, i.e. the state of affairs prevailing before the last change if the claimant applies promptly after that change (*Garden Cottage Foods Ltd v Milk Marketing Board* [1984] A.C. 130 *per* Lord Diplock). Accordingly, this factor is normally in the claimant's favour. But note that, unlike (1) and (2), it is never by itself conclusive and the relevant status quo will change if the claimant delays his application to the court.

(4) Other factors, including social and economic factors. In *American Cyanamid* itself, where an injunction was granted to restrain a threatened infringement of a patent, the court took into account the fact that "no factories would be closed and no workpeople would be thrown out of work" because of the injunction. The court will also take into account the public interest in cases in which the injunctions will have some public or political significance going beyond the protection of merely private rights (*Beaverbrook Newspapers v Keys* [1978] I.C.R. 582). There is no rule that, in such cases, the claimant is required to show more than a serious question to be tried (*R. v Secretary for State for Transport Ex p. Factortame Ltd (No.2)* [1991] A.C. 603).

(5) The relative strength of the parties' cases, i.e. the prediction which side will win. This is the factor of last resort and even then should be used only if the strength of one case is disproportionate. This factor has always been controversial. It underlies most of the exceptions to *American Cynamid* which have been recognised (see para.27.011 below). In *Series 5 Software Ltd v Clarke* [1996] 1 All E.R. 853 Laddie J. strongly asserted that Lord Diplock's famous dicta on this factor in *American Cyanamid* have not been properly understood. This assertion is supported by what Lord Diplock stated in *NWL Ltd v Woods* [1979] 1 W.L.R. 1294 (see para.27.007) below) and by certain

dicta of Lord Goff in *R. v Secretary of State for Transport Ex p. Factortame Ltd (No.2)* [1991] 1 A.C. 603. In the case of *Guardian Media Group Plc v Associated Newspapers Ltd* (2000) L.T.L. January 20, CA, Robert Walker L.J. commented:

> "The American Cyanamid principles have a degree of flexibility and they do not prevent the court from giving proper weight to any clear view which the court can form at the time of the application for interim relief (and without the need for a mini-trial on copious affidavit evidence) as to the likely outcome at trial. That is particularly so when the grant or withholding of interim relief may influence the ultimate commercial outcome. it is not necessary to consider today whether the court's entitlement to give effect to its provisional view of the merits goes quite so far as Laddie J. sought in Series 5 Software v Clarke [1996] 1 All E.R. 853."

The expression "balance of convenience" has been criticised. In *Francome v Mirror Group Newspapers Ltd* [1984] 1 W.L.R. 892 Sir John Donaldson M.R. described it as:

> "an unfortunate expression. Our business is justice, not convenience. We can and must disregard fanciful claims by either party. Subject to that, we must contemplate the possibility that either party may succeed and must do our best to ensure that nothing occurs pending the trial which will prejudice his rights. Since the parties are usually asserting wholly inconsistent claims, this is difficult, but we have to do our best. In doing so we are seeking a balance of justice, not of convenience."

In *Cayne v Global Natural Resources Plc* [1984] 1 All E.R. 225 May L.J. described the expression "balance of convenience" as a useful shorthand:

> "but in truth . . . the balance that one is seeking to make is more fundamental, more weighty, than mere 'convenience' . . . [A]lthough the phrase may well be substantially less elegant, the 'balance of the risk of doing an injustice' better describes the process involved."

In *R. v Secretary for Transport Ex p. Factortame Ltd (No.2)* [1991] 1 A.C. 603 in which the House of Lords reaffirmed the American Cyanamid principles, Lord Bridge's speech included the following dictum:

> "Questions as to the adequacy of an alternative remedy in damages to the party claiming injunctive relief and of a cross-undertaking in damages to the party against whom the relief is sought play a primary role in assisting the court to determine which course offers the best prospect that injustice may be avoided or minimised."

EXCEPTIONS TO AMERICAN CYANAMID

Several exceptions to the *American Cyanamid* principles as originally enunciated have been recognised or suggested. In our view several of them are really just varieties of the same exception; in cases where the injunction will pre-empt or obviate the need for a trial, the court should take into account the strength of the claimant's case. Although we list them as exceptions it has been explained that "when properly understood" the *American Cyanamid* principles as originally enunciated cover at least the first two of them (see *per* Lord Diplock in *NWL Ltd v Woods* [1979] 1 W.L.R. 1294).

27.006

Likelihood of defence under Trade Union and Labour Relations (Consolidation) Act 1992, ss.219–220

This is a statutory exception first made in 1975 shortly after *American Cyanamid* was reported. Under ss.219–220 of the Act certain conduct which would otherwise give rise to an action in tort is protected from such action if done "in contemplation or furtherance of a trade dispute". Section 221 as amended provides that if the respondent to an application for an interim injunction claims a defence under ss.219–220 "the court shall, in exercising its discretion whether or not to grant the injunction, have regard to the likelihood" of his establishing the defence at the trial. This provision is one of the factors the court should consider when deciding which way the balance of convenience lies. It is not an overriding or paramount factor (*NWL Ltd v Woods* [1979] 1 W.L.R. 1294). The weight to be attached to it depends upon the degree of likelihood that the defence will be established, i.e. the stronger the defence the less likely it is that an interim injunction will be granted (see *Hadmor Productions Ltd v Hamilton* [1983] 1 A.C. 191 and *Anglian Windows Ltd v GMB* [2007] EWHC 917, (2007) L.T.L., May 8). The rationale behind s.221 may be explained as follows: industrial action is used by the defendant as a bargaining counter in negotiations with an employer; its effectiveness depends upon it being promoted immediately; if it is postponed the defendant is unlikely to be able to mobilise support later, once the initial furore has died down. Thus s.221 enables the court to take account of the fact that the grant of an injunction is tantamount to giving final judgment against the defendant (*per* Lord Diplock in *NWL Ltd v Woods*, above).

Where the injunction will finally dispose of the action

Interim injunction applications are decided without a full investigation of the merits of either party's case. Thus, the court is reluctant to give a claimant interim relief which pre-empts the defendant's right to a trial.

27.007

> "Cases of this kind are exceptional, but when they do occur they bring into the balance of convenience an important additional element" (*per* Lord Diplock in *NWL Ltd v Woods* [1979] 1 W.L.R. 1294).

In such cases, factor (5) (see above) is given increased importance (although it must not be treated as the sole consideration; *Lansing Linde Ltd v Kerr* [1991] 1 W.L.R. 251). To obtain interim relief the claimant must show a "more than arguable case" or "more than merely a serious issued to be tried".

Examples
Parnass/Pelly v Hodges [1982] F.S.R. 329: a passing-off action in which an interim injunction would force the defendant to permanently damage his marketing strategy.

Lansing Linde Ltd v Kerr [1991] 1 W.L.R. 251: an interim injunction to enforce a restrictive covenant in an employment contract in an action which could not be tried before the covenant had expired or almost expired. But if such an action can be tried speedily, the general principles of *American Cyanamid* should be applied; see *Lawrence David Ltd v Ashton* [1989] I.C.R. 123.

Where the injunction will restrict freedom of expression

27.008 Many cases falling within this exception concern interim injunctions sought against newspapers or other media. The grant of an injunction would restrict the defendant's rights under ECHR Art.10 (freedom of expression). In such cases the principles to be applied have been restated in s.12 of the Human Rights Act 1998 (for the full text, see *White Book*, vol.2, para.3D–18). Section 12(3) states as follows:

> "No such relief [i.e. relief that might restrict a right to freedom of expression] is to be granted so as to restrain publication before trial unless the court is satisfied that the applicant is likely to establish that publication should not be allowed."

In *Cream Holdings Ltd v Banerjee* [2005] 1 A.C. 253, it was held that the meaning of the word "likely" must depend upon the circumstances. In general it should be taken to mean "more likely than not" i.e. a test which is higher than the normal "reasonable prospects of success" test and which is the same as the test which will be applied at trial should the case get that far. However, some flexibility is essential. In many cases the urgency of an application may lead the court to apply a lower test at the outset. If an applicant only has a few hours or days in which to obtain an injunction he may not have sufficient time in which to assemble all the evidence he needs to show the strength of his case. In other cases the seriousness of the possible adverse consequences if no injunction is obtained may lead the court to apply the lower test throughout the interim stage. For example, in some notorious criminal trials, threats of personal injury or even death may be made against some of the participants. This may justify the court restraining disclosure of their whereabouts even in cases where it cannot be said their claim for relief is "more likely than not" to prevail at trial.

In *A v B Plc* [2003] Q.B. 195, the Court of Appeal gave guidelines as to the law relating to interim injunction applications where issues concerning actions for breach of confidence and/or the protection of rights under ECHR Art.8 (right to respect for private and family life). In that case, the claimant was a professional footballer seeking to restrain a national newspaper from publishing lurid articles about his sexual encounters. It was held that the claimant was not entitled to any interim injunction. The guidelines should now be read in the light of *Cream Holdings Ltd v Banerjee* [2005] 1 A.C. 253, as to the strength of case to be shown.

Interim mandatory injunctions

The leading authority on interim mandatory injunctions is *Zockoll Group Ltd v Mercury Communications Ltd* [1998] F.S.R. 354, CA citing with approval the summary of the law given by Chadwick J. in *Nottingham Building Society v Eurodynamics Systems* [1993] F.S.R. 468 at 474.

27.009

> "In my view the principles to be applied are these. First this being an interlocutory matter, the overriding consideration is which course is likely to involve the least risk of injustice if it turns out to be 'wrong' in the sense described by Hoffman J. [i.e. granting an injunction to a party who fails to establish his right at the trial (or would fail if there was a trial) or alternatively, in failing to grant an injunction to a party who succeeds (or would succeed) at trial; see Rover Ltd v Cannon Film Sales Ltd [1987] 1 W.L.R. 670].
>
> Secondly, in considering whether to grant mandatory injunction the court must keep in mind that an order which requires a party to take some positive step at an interlocutory stage, may well carry a greater risk of injustice if it turns out to have been wrongly made than an order which merely prohibits action, thereby preserving the status quo.
>
> Thirdly, it is legitimate, where a mandatory injunction is sought, to consider whether the court does feel a high degree of assurance that the [claimant] will be able to establish this right at a trial. That is because the greater the degree of assurance the [claimant] will ultimately establish his right, the less will be the risk of injustice if the injunction is granted.
>
> But, finally, even where the court is unable to feel any high degree of assurance that the [claimant] will establish his right, there may still be circumstances in which it is appropriate to grant a mandatory injunction at an interlocutory stage. Those circumstances will exist where the risk of injustice if this injunction is refused sufficiently outweigh the risk of injustice if it is granted."

In many cases in which an interim mandatory injunction is granted, the injunction is worded in negative form even though it is positive in effect. In *Rover International v Cannon Film Sales Ltd* [1987] 1 W.L.R. 670, Hoffman J. described cases such as these as being cases having a "dynamic status quo": an order was granted in respect of a distribution agreement relating to seventeen films requiring the defendant to deliver to the claimant's solicitors forthwith certain negatives and other materials relevant to three of the films.

Where the defendant has no arguable defence

27.010   In *Official Custodian for Charities v Mackey* [1985] Ch.168, Scott J. said that the *American Cyanamid* principles were not applicable in a case in which there is no arguable defence to the claimant's claim. Instead he placed reliance upon a nineteenth-century dictum of James L.J.:

> "Balance of convenience has nothing to do with a case of this kind; it can only be considered where there is some question which must be decided at the hearing" (*Stocker v Planet Building Society* (1879) 27 W.R. 877).

In *Patel v W. H. Smith (Eziot) Ltd* [1987] 1 W.L.R. 853 the claimant, whose title to the land in question was not disputed, obtained an interim injunction to restrain trespass even though the acts complained of did not harm him:

> "If there is no arguable case, as I believe there is not, then questions of balance of convenience, status quo and damages being an adequate remedy do not arise" (per Balcombe L.J.).

This approach appears to conflict with *American Cyanamid* factor (5): relative strength of parties' cases to be a factor (of last resort) in weighing the balance of convenience. Properly understood however there is no conflict. If there is no arguable defence the claimant is entitled to summary judgment (see Ch.19) and, therefore, is entitled to an injunction which is final. To seek an interim injunction in such a case merely gives the defendant two occasions, not one, on which to raise a defence.

Defamation and malicious falsehood

27.011   Where a claimant seeks an injunction to restrain defamation or malicious falsehood two basic rights conflict: the claimant's right to protection from unlawful injury to his reputation and the defendant's right to freedom of speech. For many years now the courts have resolved this conflict by holding that if the defendant bona fide intends to state a defence of justification or fair comment on a matter of public interest the claimant cannot obtain an interim injunction however strong his case unless it is clear that no defence will succeed at trial (*cf.* para.27.014, above). The severity of this rule against claimants does not infringe their rights under ECHR Art.6 (right to a fair trial) or Art.8 (right to respect for private life): *Greene v Associated Newspapers Ltd* [2005] 1 All E.R. 30. Instead the claimant is left to claim remedies at the trial only, i.e. damages and a final injunction. A claimant can sometimes obtain an interim injunction to restrain publication of confidential information (see *A v B Plc* [2003] Q.B. 195, CA, noted in para.27.008, above) and in cases of conspiracy to injure (*Gulf Oil (Great Britain) Ltd v Page* [1987] Ch.327; *Femis-Bank (Anguilla) Ltd v Lazar* [1991] Ch.391). For examples of recent attempts to show that no defence will succeed at trial see *Greene v Associated Newspapers Ltd* [2005] 1 All E.R. 30 and the cases cited therein: virtually all the attempts are unsuccessful. For a case in which an interim injunction was obtained see *Kaye v Robertson, The Times,* March 21, 1990.

PROCEDURE ON APPLICATIONS

Applications without notice

An application can be made without giving any formal notice to the opponent if "it appears to the court that there are good reasons for not giving notice" (r.25.3(1) and also see Ch.13). The evidence in support of the application must set out the reasons relied on (r.25.3(3)). An application without notice is appropriate if two conditions are satisfied: that the giving of notice to the opponent would cause injustice to the applicant because of the urgency of the matter or because of the need to obtain a provisional remedy by surprise; and that the risk of damages to the opponent is either compensatable by damages or is clearly outweighed by the risk of injustice to the applicant if an order is not made without notice (*Re First Express Ltd, The Times,* October, 10, 1991).

27.012

Urgent applications and those made without notice are provided for in PD 25, para.4. If the claim form has already been issued, the application notice, evidence in support and a draft order (also on disk) should, wherever possible, be filed with the court two hours before the hearing. If the claim form has not been issued, the applicant is also normally required to undertake to do that immediately or otherwise as directed by the court. If a hearing cannot be arranged an application can be made by telephone (see PD 25, para.4.5).

Under the Trade Union and Labour Relations (Consolidation) Act 1992, s.221(1) no application can be made without notice against a person likely to raise the "furtherance of a trade dispute" defence unless all reasonable steps have been taken to give that person notice and an opportunity to be heard. In other cases informal notice of the application should be given to the opponent unless secrecy is essential (see PD 25, para.4.3(3)). Similar provision is made for injunctions which might affect rights of freedom of expression (Human Rights Act 1998, s.12(2) and see further, para.27.008, above). The injunction should specify precisely the acts the respondent must do or must abstain from doing (PD 25, para.5.3). The standard form text makes clear that a defendant who is an individual "who is ordered not to do something must not do it himself or in any other way. He must not do it through others acting on his behalf or on his instructions or with his encouragement." A similar explanation is also given for a defendant which is a corporation.

A party seeking an injunction owes a duty to disclose to the court "all material facts of which the court should be made aware" (PD 25, para.3.3). This is particularly important when the application is made without notice.

"The urgency of the application and the absence of the other side necessarily mean that the court is even more reliant than it normally is on the scrupulous and meticulous assistance of the advocate in deciding whether or not to make extreme orders of this kind [a freezing injunction, see below] in the circumstances of the particular case" (*per* Mummery L.J. in *Memory Corp Plc v Sidhu (No.1)* [2000] 1 W.L.R. 1443, CA). As to the penalties for non-disclosure, see para.27.020, below.

Applications made on notice

27.013   These applications are made in cases which are not urgent and also in other cases as a follow up to the original application where it was made without notice. Orders made on a without notice hearing are usually for a limited time only (seldom more than seven days) and will usually specify the date of a further hearing (the "return day") when the matter comes back before the court for reconsideration.

Before the hearing date for the application arrives each party files in court and serves copies of all the written evidence on which he intends to rely. PD 25, para.2.2 provides that the application notice and evidence in support must be served as soon as practicable after issue and in any event not less than three days before the hearing date. A draft order (also on disk) should be filed with the application.

As to the value and enforceability of the applicant's undertakings as to damages (see para.27.002) above) the court will take into account the applicant's financial standing. If he is not able to show assets within the jurisdiction to provide substance to the undertakings given, particularly the undertakings in damages, the applicant may be required as a condition of the grant of the remedy to back up his undertakings by providing some readily available security within the jurisdiction. This may consist of a payment into court, the provision of a bond by an insurance company or standby credit by a bank. Alternatively, the judge may order a payment by way of such security to the applicant's solicitors to be held by them as officers of the court pending further order. Sometimes the undertaking of a parent company may be acceptable. If the applicant is an insolvent company the liquidators may be required to give a personal undertaking perhaps up to a limited amount; in *Re DPR Futures Ltd* [1989] 1 W.L.R. 778 the court accepted personal undertakings by the liquidators limited to £2 million, the estimated net assets of the company.

Non-disclosure of all material facts

27.014   As to the applicant's duty to disclose all material facts of which the court should be made aware, see para.27.012 above. If, after an order has been obtained, a claimant becomes aware of a material non-disclosure, he must bring it to the attention of the court and, if appropriate, seek a discharge of the order obtained.

At a hearing on notice, the respondent may ask the court to rule upon allegations that the applicant did not fulfil his duty to disclose all material facts. If those allegations are proved the court has a discretion to discharge the injunction and refuse to reimpose it. In exercising that discretion the court will bear in mind the overriding objective and the need for proportionality (*Memory Corp Plc v Sidhu (No.1)* [2000] 1 W.L.R. 1443, CA). The court will consider the seriousness of the non-disclosure, the harm done to the respondent, the relative culpability of the applicant and his lawyers and the prejudice the applicant will suffer if the interim injunction is lost.

A further consequence of a finding of material non-disclosure is the entitlement it will give the respondent to claim compensation under the applicant's undertaking as to damages (see above). An inquiry into what loss has been suffered may be deferred to be decided at or after the trial. (Compare and contrast *Lock International Plc v Beswick* [1989] 1 W.L.R. 1268 and *Columbia Picture Industries Inc v Robinson* [1987] Ch.38 where an award of £10,000 aggravated damages was made, at trial, subject to rights of set-off which the claimants had for damages and costs ordered against the defendant).

Serving the injunction

Both mandatory and prohibitory injunctions have to be drawn up, indorsed with a penal notice (see PD 25) and personally served on the respondent or, if a company, on the officers of the company against whom enforcement proceedings may later be taken (see generally CPR, Sch.1 and 2; RSC, Ord.45, r.7; CCR, Ord.29, r.1). Breach of an injunction is a contempt for which the respondent can be committed (as to the liability of directors and other officers of a company, see *Att-Gen of Tuvalu v Philatelic Distribution Corp. Ltd* [1990] 1 W.L.R. 926). A prohibitory injunction may be enforced by committal even before it has been served if the respondent was present when the injunction was made or was notified of it "whether by telephone . . . or otherwise" (CPR, Schs 1 and 2; RSC, Ord.45, r.7(6); CCR, Ord.29, r.1(6)). 27.014A

Where an on notice application is compromised on the basis of an undertaking given by the respondent in lieu of an injunction (see further Ch.34) it is nevertheless advisable for the applicant to have a formal order drawn up, indorsed with a suitable penal notice and served on the respondent (see *Hussain v Hussain* [1986] Fam. 134).

As to the need to serve full notes of a without notice application which applies in the case of freezing injunctions and, possibly in other cases also, see para.27.020, below.

FREEZING INJUNCTIONS (R.25.1(f))

Supreme Court Act 1981, s.37 enables the High Court to grant injunctions "in all cases in which it appears to the court to be just and convenient to do so". A 27.015

common example is a freezing injunction imposed to restrain a party from: (a) removing from the jurisdiction assets located there; or (b) dealing with any assets whether located in the jurisdiction or not. The history of this form of remedy goes back to the case of *Mareva Compañia Naviera SA v International Bulkcarriers SA* [1975] 2 Lloyd's Rep. 509 where an injunction was granted restraining a defendant from improperly disposing of his assets, or concealing, or moving them abroad thereby making himself "judgment proof" and stultifying an action brought against him. The remedy is now available wherever there is a real risk of dissipation of assets: the applicant does not have to show that the respondent intends to deal with his assets with the specific intention of stultifying the proceedings (see further para.27.017).

County courts have no general jurisdiction to grant freezing injunctions (see generally County Courts Remedies Regulations 1991 noted in the *White Book*, vol.2, para.9B–81). They may grant them only:

(i) in family proceedings,
(ii) in order to secure the preservation, custody or detention of property which forms or may form the subject-matter of proceedings,
(iii) in aid of execution of a county court judgment.

Exceptions are also made for any county court held by a judge who is a judge of the High Court or the Court of Appeal, and for certain proceedings in a patents county court and proceedings which will be or which are already included in the Central London County Court Business List (as to which, see para.24.013, above).

Importance of freezing injunctions

27.016 The amount of court time spent on applications for a freezing injunction of one sort or another, and the amount of case law they have produced, is enormous. It is easy to see why this should be so. In many cases the grant or refusal or discharge of a freezing injunction is determinative of the action. If the injunction is refused, or granted but later discharged, a claimant may perceive little point in continuing with the litigation. If the injunction is granted, and survives an on notice hearing, the defendant may well concede defeat; the paralysing effect the injunction has on his business, and the injury to his reputation, may render futile any further opposition to the claimant's claim. It is not the purpose of a freezing injunction to provide the claimant with a means of exerting pressure on a defendant to settle an action (*Camdex International Ltd v Bank of Zambia (No.2)* [1997] 1 All E.R. 728). However, in practice, that is often its effect.

With its growth of importance to litigants, so the freezing injunction has grown in size. In the following four respects its availability has been increased over the years. The injunction can be granted:

(1) pre-trial or post-trial;
(2) against any defendant whether foreign-based or English based;

(3) against a claimant in respect of orders for costs (*Jet West Ltd v Haddican* [1992] 1 W.L.R. 487 as to which see para.27.020, below);
(4) in respect of assets in this country or assets worldwide;
(5) in proceedings brought here solely in aid of foreign proceedings being taken anywhere else in the world (see para.27.019, below).

Applying for a freezing injunction

The application must be made to a High Court judge or any other judge duly authorised (PD 25, para.1.1). It is usually made without notice and possibly even before the action has commenced.

27.017

Three main issues arise on the application:

(1) whether the claimant has a good arguable case;
(2) whether the claimant can adduce sufficient evidence as to the existence and location of assets which the injunction, if made, would affect; and
(3) whether there is a real risk that the defendant may deal with those assets so as to render nugatory any judgment which the claimant may obtain.

As to (1), the difference between "good arguable case" and the *American Cyanamid* test of "serious question to be tried" has been described as being "incapable of definition" (*per* Parker L.J. in *Derby & Co. Ltd v Weldon* [1990] Ch.48). Mustill J. once described "a good arguable case" as "one which is more than barely capable of serious argument, but not necessarily one which the judge considers would have a better than 50 per cent chance of success" (*Ninemia Maritime Corporation v Trave S GmbH* [1983] 2 Lloyd's Rep. 660, a point which was not taken on the appeal, [1983] 1 W.L.R. 142; cf. the test for interim injunctions restricting freedom of expression, para.27.008, above).

It is very difficult to visualise a case where the grant of a freezing order, made without notice, could be said to have been properly made in the absence of any formulation of the case for substantive relief that the applicant for the order intended to institute. See *Fourie v Le Roux* [2007] UKHL 1, [2007] 1 W.L.R. 320. This is further demonstrated by the obligation on the court to include directions about the institution of proceedings for substantive relief.

As to (2), the order sought should identify as precisely as possible the bank accounts or other assets to be affected by the injunction. The order will be confined to assets within England and Wales if they are of sufficient value to protect the claimant's claim. The injunction can be extended to cover bank accounts standing in the name of another person, for example, the defendant's spouse, if there is evidence that the money held in the account belongs to the defendant (*SCF Finance Co. Ltd v Masri* [1985] 1 W.L.R. 876 and also see *C Inc. Plc v L, The Times*, May 4, 2001). If the defendant is the majority shareholder of a company which has substantial assets the injunction can also be made against that company which should be added as co-defendant in the action (*TSB Private Bank International SA v Chabra* [1992] 1 W.L.R. 231).

The standard form of order does not freeze assets which the defendant holds only as an executor or trustee and not as beneficial owner (*Federal Bank of the Middle East v Hadkinson (No.2)* [2000] 1 W.L.R. 1695, CA).

As to (3), a risk of dissipation, etc. may be shown in a variety of different ways, for example, evidence of dishonest behaviour by the defendant, unreliability in the past, evasiveness in these proceedings (such as a willingness to retract admissions and/or rely upon implausible defences), statements of intent by the defendant, a lack of any established business reputation, or the possession of a poor reputation such as some types of off-shore companies have, a propensity to change domicile and/or move assets regularly and/or at short notice, having only weak or non-existent links with this country save for assets invested here, or being based in a country in which it is difficult to enforce English judgments.

In *Gulf Interstate Oil Co. v ANT Trade and Transport Ltd of Malta; The Giovanna* [1999] 1 Lloyd's Rep. 867, Rix J. held that if the defendant has already made an offer of security, no without notice application for a freezing injunction should be brought without at least some mention of that if it was still current at the date the claimants went to court. This is because such an offer, even if subject to qualification, runs counter to the implicit appeal by an applicant for the court's help in challenging a real risk that assets might be dissipated.

Cases on the risk of dissipation, etc. which are legion, depend solely upon their own particular facts. The risk of dissipation may be established without proof of any wrongdoing or deviousness by the respondent (*Ninemia Maritime Corporation v Trave S GmbH* [1983] 1 W.L.R. 142, CA; *Customs and Excise Commissioners v Anchor Foods Ltd* [1999] 1 W.L.R. 1139). On the other hand, proof of deviousness may not by itself establish the risk of dissipation (*Aragchinchi v Araghchinchi* [1997] 2 F.L.R. 142, CA).

Applying for a freezing injunction in aid of foreign proceedings

27.018 Section 25 of the CJJA 1982 empowers the court to grant all forms of interim relief in aid of foreign courts unless "in the opinion of the court, the fact that the court has no jurisdiction apart from this section in relation to the subject matter of the proceedings in question makes it inexpedient for the court to grant it". The power was originally applicable only to foreign proceedings pending in the court of an EU state where the subject matter of the proceedings was within the scope of the Brussels Convention (as to which see Ch.11). Since April 1997 the power extends to foreign proceedings in all countries, including non-EU and EFTA countries and to proceedings outside the scope of the Brussels or Lugano Conventions (see further *White Book* vol.2, para.5–160). If the proceedings are governed by the conventions no permission is needed to serve overseas. If the conventions do not apply permission to serve overseas can be obtained under r.6.20(4) (see generally Ch.11).

In many respects an application for a freezing injunction under s.25 is the same as it would be if the main proceedings were in this country: it should be made to a High Court judge who will not make an order unless the basic requirements are satisfied, namely that the claimant has a good arguable case and there is a real risk of dissipation. Additional points of principle arise where the application under s.25 is in respect of a worldwide freezing order in circumstances where the defendant in question is neither domiciled nor resident in this country and there is no substantial connection between the relief sought and the territorial jurisdiction of the English court. The principles to be applied in such cases were considered by the Court of Appeal in *Motorola Credit Corpn v Uzan (No.2)* [2004] 1 W.L.R. 113. In that case the claimants showed a good arguable case that the defendants were involved in an international fraud and conspiracy. The defendants were members of a wealthy and powerful Turkish family: D1 and D3 were the sons of D2 and D4 was his daughter. D1, D2 and D3 were not resident here but D1 owned a valuable house in London. D4 was ordinarily resident in England. The claimants had already obtained orders against the defendants in proceedings taken in New York but the courts in New York lacked jurisdiction to make orders freezing assets which were located outside the State of New York. At all times all four defendants had denied the jurisdiction of the courts of England and New York to make orders in respect of this dispute and, indeed, they obtained anti-suit injunctions in Turkey restraining the claimants from continuing the proceedings in New York or in England. In these proceedings the defendants sought to appeal against the worldwide freezing injunctions made against them under s.25, and against consequential orders for disclosure and cross-examination that had been made against them, and against orders of committal made against them for breach of those orders. None of the defendants were present in this country and all were believed to be in Turkey. All of them made clear that they did not intend to comply with any order against them made by the English courts. The Court of Appeal exercised its discretion to hear their appeals, notwithstanding their contempt. Since the appeals were against the very orders the breach of which had placed them in contempt it was "necessary to satisfy conditions of fairness" to hear them. The court listed five considerations to be born in mind when considering whether it is inexpedient to make an order under s.25.

> "[115] . . . First, whether the making of the order will interfere with the management of the case in the primary court e.g., where the order is inconsistent with an order in the primary court or overlaps with it. That consideration does not arise in the present case. Second, whether it is the policy in the primary jurisdiction not itself to make worldwide freezing/disclosure orders. Third, whether there is a danger that the orders made will give rise to disharmony or confusion and/or risk of conflicting inconsistency of overlapping orders in other jurisdictions, in particular the courts of the State where the person enjoined resides or where the assets affected are located. If so, then respect for the territorial jurisdiction of that State should discourage the English court from using its unusually wide powers against a foreign defendant. Fourth, whether at the time the order is sought there is likely to be a potential conflict as to jurisdiction rendering it inappropriate and inexpedient to make a worldwide order. Fifth, whether, in a

case where jurisdiction is resisted and disobedience to be expected, the court will be making an order which it cannot enforce."

In this case the second consideration listed was not by itself determinative: the court drew a distinction between cases in which the primary court simply lacked jurisdiction to grant relief and cases where the primary court had such jurisdiction but would refuse to exercise it on the merits or for other substantial reasons (see [119]). In the result it was held that it was not expedient to grant orders under s.25 against D2 and D3 and to that extent some of the appeals were allowed. It was expedient to make orders under s.25 against D1 and D4 and, to that extent, the appeals were dismissed. See also *Amedeo Hotels Ltd Partnership v Zaman* [2007] EWHC 295, (2007) L.T.L., April 2.

Terms of a freezing injunction

27.019 The Practice Direction to Pt 25 contains standard forms of freezing injunctions and search orders for use in all cases unless the judge hearing a particular application considers there is a good reason for adopting a different form. The standard forms of freezing injunction have three main components: certain undertakings given by the claimant; the order restraining the defendant from disposing of his assets (describing them in so far as the claimant can); and various provisos and limitations. The order does not by itself give the claimant any property rights over the assets in question. Thus, if the defendant later becomes insolvent, a freezing order granted pre-trial will not make the claimant a secured creditor (*Flightline Ltd v Edwards* [2003] 1 W.L.R. 1200, CA).

The undertakings will include, amongst others, an undertaking to indemnify any person upon whom notice of the order is served, in respect of any expenses and liabilities they may incur in seeking to comply with the order and the claimant's cross-undertaking to the defendant as to damages (see para.27.003, above). In *RBG Resources Plc v Rastogi* [2002] L.T.L., May 31, Laddie J. accepted a limited cross-undertaking where the claimant had shown an extremely strong case of serious and extensive wrongdoing by the defendants which, it was alleged, had made the claimant financially weak.

While a freezing injunction is in force there is a continuing obligation on the claimant not only to be willing to honour the cross-undertaking as to damages, but also to draw at least the defendant's attention to any material change for the worse in his financial position. This would enable the defendant to then seek either a voluntary release of or reduction in the freezing order or to apply to the court for such relief (*Staines v Walsh* L.T.L., June 10, 2003, ChD).

The restriction on the disposal of assets is worded so as to cover all assets (i.e. whether or not described) except to the extent that their total unencumbered value exceeds a specified amount. The value specified should take into account the value of the claimant's claim plus interest and costs (*Atlas Maritime Co. SA v Avalon Maritime Ltd (No.3)* [1991] 1 W.L.R. 917). If an excessive amount is specified the claimant may later become liable to pay damages to the defendant under the undertaking damages which must be given.

"[There] comes a point at which, if you open your mouth too wide, you run a substantial risk that there may be a claim against your client under the counter-indemnity" (*per* Lord Donaldson M.R. in *Jet West Ltd v Haddican* [1992] 1 W.L.R. 487).

The standard forms of injunction state the date up to and including which the order will remain in force ("the return date"). These are, of course, orders made on a without notice application. An order made on notice may endure until judgment or further order, or even sometimes "until two weeks after the trial in this action or further order" (*Allied Arab Bank Ltd v Hajjar* [1998] Q.B. 787).

The provisos and limitations will acknowledge any prior right any bank may have to set off against any of the defendant's assets they hold, the value of any loans they may have made to the defendant before the date of the injunction. They will also allow the defendant to draw reasonable living expenses and/or to pay debts in the ordinary course of business. They will give the defendant and anyone else affected by the order, liberty to apply (on notice) to set aside or vary the order, or to seek further directions. A worldwide freezing injunction in standard form sets out certain limitations on its operation overseas.

The injunction may also include various orders for disclosure (see below).

Serving freezing injunctions

As to service on the defendant, see para.27.015, above. In *Interoute Telecommunications UK Ltd v Fashion Gossip Ltd*, *The Times*, November 10, 1999, Lightman J. held that an applicant who obtains relief on a without notice application (including in particular a freezing injunction) is under a duty to provide full notes of the hearing with all expedition to any party that would be affected by the order made. The notes must be supplied whether or not any party requests them (*Thane Investments Ltd v Tomlinson*, *The Times*, December 10, 2002, Neuberger J.). 27.020

A curious feature of a freezing injunction is that, although it is made against the defendant, it may be effective only if notice of it is given to the bank, or some other person in possession of assets. Can banks, and perhaps other persons, become liable to the claimant if, after receiving notice, they fail to prevent the defendant dissipating assets in breach of the injunction? Can they be sued in negligence? No, banks do not owe a duty of care to preserve assets in these circumstances: see *Commissioners of Customs & Excise v Barclays Bank Plc* [2006] UKHL 28, (2006) 3 W.L.R. 1. But there is a form of liability in contempt proceedings. Persons given notice of a freezing injunction are guilty of a contempt of court if they knowingly assist in the disposal of the assets, whether or not the defendant has any knowledge of the injunction. Merely paying or handing over the asset in question to the defendant does not by itself amount to a contempt, even if it is done with notice of the injunction; to amount to a contempt, the bank or possessor of the asset must have notice of a probability that the asset would then be disposed of in breach of the injunction (*Bank Mellat v Kazmi* [1989] Q.B. 541).

In one case, a conveyancing solicitor, given notice of a freezing injunction which had been served on his client, failed to countermand two cheques which he had drawn on a client account and despatched to his client on the previous day. He was found guilty of contempt of court, ordered to pay £8,000 in compensation and suspended from practice for five years (see (1989) 39 L.S.G. 48).

How can one enforce an order in respect of overseas assets, against a defendant who is himself overseas, and who has no assets in this country? It is unlikely that a foreign court would recognise and enforce an injunction made without notice; our courts will not recognise and enforce a foreign injunction (*EMI Records Ltd v Modern Music Karl-Ulrich Walterbach GmbH* [1992] 1 Q.B. 115). Instead one should seek protective measures in the court local to the assets (i.e. seek to invoke their equivalent to our CJJA 1982, s.25; see above). The fact that an order is not enforceable in this country and is likely to be disobeyed will often persuade the English court not to grant a freezing injunction (*Motorola Credit Corpn v Uzan (No.2)* [20041] 1 W.L.R. 113, paras 109, 122 and 125).

For guidelines as to how the court should exercise its discretion to permit a party to enforce a worldwide freezing injunction see *Dadourian Group Int Inc v Simms* [2006] EWCA Civ 399, [2006] 1 W.L.R. 2499.

Applications to discharge or vary the order

27.021 The injunction will be discharged if, at a hearing on notice, the defendant provides sufficient security for the claim (*Allen v Jambo Holdings Ltd* [1980] 1 W.L.R. 1252) or if the judge is satisfied that there is no sufficient risk of default (as in *Ninemia Maritime Corporation v Trave S GmbH* [1983] 1 W.L.R. 142) or that it was obtained as a result of material non-disclosure (see para.27.014, above). The claimant himself should apply for a discharge if he later decides not to proceed with his claim.

Once a freezing injunction has been granted, the claimant is under a duty to press on with his claim so that the defendant is subject to the order for the minimum amount of time necessary, and not kept in limbo.

Alternatively, the defendant may apply to vary the provisions made for reasonable living expenses, or to allow the payment of outstanding debts and payment of legal fees incurred in defending the proceedings. Before allowing such variations the court may require evidence that there are no other assets out of which the payments could reasonably be made (*A. v C. (No.2)* [1981] Q.B. 961). There is a possibility that, once some assets are caught, the defendant may take steps to prevent further assets coming to England and may try to discharge out of the caught assets all subsequent trading debts, living expenses and legal costs. In order to check up on this, the court is willing to inquire into all the defendant's financial dealings including those made with subsidiary companies and parent companies (see *Atlas Maritime Co. SA v Avalon Maritime Ltd (No.3)* [1991] 1 W.L.R. 917; and see *D. B. Deniz Nakliyati TAS v Yugopetrol* [1992] 1 W.L.R. 437). The court will not consent to any variation being made unless and until the defendant complies with any such disclosure order (*Prekookeanska Plovidba v LNT Lines SRL* [1989] 1 W.L.R. 753).

Variations may also be applied for by third parties intervening in the action such as persons whose claims the defendant has admitted in good faith and wishes to pay (*Iraqi Ministry of Defence v Arcepey Shipping Co. SA* [1981] Q.B. 65) or directors of a defendant company who apply to be added as co-defendants if, for example, the defendant company can no longer afford legal representation (*ALI Finance Ltd v Havelet Leasing Ltd* [1992] 1 W.L.R. 455).

Applications for variation or discharge are properly made to the High Court judge even if the without notice order was first made by the Court of Appeal (*Ocean Software Ltd v Kay* [1992] 2 Q.B. 583). In county court cases, the county court has power to vary an injunction made by the High Court if all parties are agreed on the terms of variation. See generally PD 2B.

Rights of third parties in the property attached

A person may apply as intervener to discharge or vary the injunction, for example, by showing title paramount to the defendant (*Cretanor Maritime Co. Ltd v Irish Marine Management Ltd* [1978] 1 W.L.R. 966) or by showing that the order substantially interferes with their business rights (*Galaxia Maritim SA v Mineral Importexport* [1982] 1 W.L.R. 539, the owners of a ship which was prevented from sailing because of an injunction in respect of the defendant's cargo on board). Successful interveners may be awarded their costs against the claimant on the indemnity basis (*Project Development Co. Ltd v KMK Securities Ltd* [1982] 1 W.L.R. 1470). The definition of the indemnity basis of costs has changed over the years (see Ch.38). In our view successful interveners should today be awarded their costs on the standard basis only. Indeed, if the order made in *Project Development Co. Ltd* was made today it would be converted into an order for costs on the standard basis by r.44.4(4). The order made in *Project Development Co. Ltd* was repeated in *Westminster City Council v Porter* [2003] EWHC 2373 (CL), in circumstances not dissimilar from the grant of a freezing injunction. However, it does not appear that r.44.4(4) was drawn to the court's attention in that case.

27.022

SEARCH ORDERS (R.25.1(h))

In disputes one party may suspect that the other party is about to destroy documents or conceal information which is, or may be, relevant to legal proceedings. The concern is that such action will prevent the court from properly determining the party's rights. It may be very tempting for that party to take documents and photocopy them or, these days, take a computer and copy its hard drive. Such measures of self help are fraught with potential civil and criminal liability. See, for example, *L v L* [2007] EWHC 140, (2007) EWHC 1 February. Instead a party should apply to the court for an order to be made for the preservation and obtaining of evidence for the purpose of future legal proceedings.

27.023

A search order compels the defendant to "permit" the claimant's agents to enter the defendant's premises, search for and (in most cases) seize certain documents or property. The object of the order is to preserve evidence and it is a special form of mandatory injunction. It does not amount to a search warrant and therefore no forcible entry of premises can be made. However, if a defendant fails to comply with the order he can be committed for contempt. Orders in this form are uniquely British; they are unknown in the rest of Europe and in the United States; see (1990) 106 L.Q.R. 173. Although in a particular case they may infringe rights under ECHR, Arts 6 (fair trial) or 8 (privacy), they do not do so in principle (see cases cited in *White Book*, para.25.1.29). The Civil Procedure Act 1997, s.7 places the courts' jurisdiction to make these orders on a statutory footing.

How to apply

27.024 The application must be made to a High Court judge or any other judge duly authorised (PD 25, para.1.1). The county court jurisdiction to make search orders is subject to limitations similar to those which apply in the case of freezing injunctions (see para.27.017, above). Most applications must therefore be made to the High Court; proceedings may be transferred to a county court after the application has been disposed of.

In order to secure the advantage of taking the defendant by surprise the application is invariably made without notice, often before the main action is commenced. The application must be supported by evidence. It should describe the premises and the relevant documents or property and show a strong case that serious harm or serious injustice will be suffered if the order is not made. The applicant will be required to give the usual undertaking as to damages.

As with freezing injunctions, search orders are usually made pre-trial but can also be granted post-trial if necessary as an aid to execution of the judgment: see *Distributori Automatici Italia SpA v Holford General Trading Co. Ltd* [1985] 1 W.L.R. 1066.

Examples

In *Anton Piller KG v Manufacturing Processes Ltd* [1976] Ch.55 C applied without notice and before proceedings had commenced showing that D had documents dishonestly acquired from C which would prove C's claim for heavy damages for breach of copyright and wrongful use of confidential information. There being strong evidence that these documents were likely to be copied and/or sent abroad an order authorising their seizure was made.

In *CBS United Kingdom Ltd v Lambert* [1983] Ch.37 there was strong evidence that the defendants, a husband and a wife, were involved in the production and sale of pirate records and cassettes and the claimant believed that the first defendant had recently bought several expensive cars which he intended to hide from his creditors and dispose of for cash if the need arose. The Court of Appeal granted; (1) a search order; (2) a freezing injunction; (3) an order requiring the defendants to disclose forthwith full details as to all their assets whether in this country or abroad including in particular details of all bank accounts and motor vehicles; and (4) an order to deliver up forthwith to the claimant's solicitor three cars which were specified in the order.

Search orders can be used in any type of action if the circumstances so warrant (see, e.g. *Yousif v Salama* [1980] 1 W.L.R. 1540, claim for commission under an agency agreement; *Emanuel v Emanuel* [1982] 1 W.L.R. 669, ancillary relief in divorce proceedings). However, in practice, they are most commonly sought against alleged infringers of copyright, patents, trade marks and the like.

Form of order

The standard form of search order provides for it to be served by a supervising solicitor, an experienced solicitor familiar with search orders who is independent of the claimant and the claimant's solicitors. The supervising solicitor must also (amongst many duties) "explain the terms and effect of the order to the respondent in everyday language", supervise the entry and search and later supply a written report to the claimant's solicitor (this is for the use of the judge on the return date). Where the supervising solicitor is a man and the respondent is likely to be an unaccompanied woman, at least one other person named in the order must be a woman and must accompany the supervising solicitor. In all cases, unless the court otherwise orders, the order must be served between 9.30a.m. and 5.30p.m. on a week day. See PD 25, paras 7.2 to 7.5.   27.025

If, before any search begins, the person served with the order wishes to seek legal advice and/or apply to the court to vary or discharge the order, he should still permit the supervising solicitor and the claimant's solicitors to enter the premises but otherwise may refuse entry to others and may in certain circumstances refuse permission for the search to begin for a short time, not to exceed two hours unless the supervising solicitor agrees to a longer period.

Any publicity about the order and its execution could be extremely damaging to the defendant's reputation. Because this is so, the standard form of search order contains an undertaking by the claimant not to inform third parties about the proceedings until after the return date.

DISCLOSURE OF INFORMATION BY THE DEFENDANT

The standard forms of freezing injunctions and search orders require the defendant to disclose immediately, and later verify by affidavit, certain information. As to a freezing injunction this is the whereabouts of all his assets in England and Wales (whether in his own name or not and whether solely or jointly owned, giving the value, location and details of all such assets). The making of such orders ancillary to a freezing injunction is expressly provided for by r.25.1(1)(g) as a general rule a respondent will be compelled to give such disclosure before the conclusion of any hearing or appeal at which he seeks to challenge   27.026

the freezing injunction (*Motorola Credit Corp v Uzan (No.2)* [2004] 1 W.L.R. 113. Rule 25.1(1)(g) should not be used to fish for information to determine whether the applicant should apply for a freezing injunction (*Parker v C S Structured Credit Fund Ltd* [2003] EWHC 391 (Ch)).

In the case of a search order, the respondent must supply the following information as to items listed in the order (so far as he is aware): where all such items are, the name and address of everyone who has supplied him or offered to supply him with such items, the name and address of everyone to whom he has supplied or offered to supply them and full details of the date and quantities of every such supply and offer. The court's power to make such orders derives from s.7 of the Civil Procedure Act 1997 rather than from r.25.1(1)(g).

Privilege against self-incrimination

27.027 In some cases a defendant may be entitled to refuse to disclose information on the grounds that it may incriminate him. The privilege against self-incrimination has been removed in High Court "infringement cases" (see SCA 1981, s.72, the types of proceedings being closely defined therein). Claims of privilege against self-incrimination are also restricted by the Theft Act 1968, s.31 in respect of all cases in which there is a real risk of a prosecution under that Act. In other cases, however, if the privilege is likely to arise the standard form of freezing injunction states:

> "If the provision of any of this information is likely to incriminate the Respondent, he may be entitled to refuse to provide it, but is recommended to take legal advice before refusing to provide the information. Wrongful refusal to provide the information is contempt of court and may render the Respondent liable to be imprisoned, fined or have his assets seized".

In respect of a search order the respondent must hand to the supervising solicitor any document he believes may be incriminating and if the supervising solicitor concludes that it may be incriminating, or he has any doubts, he must retain the documents and refer the matter to the court. Whilst the validity of this provision was doubted by Waller L.J. in *Den Norske Bank ASA v Antonatos* [1999] Q.B. 271. Does the privilege against self-incrimination include material constituting free-standing evidence that was not created by a respondent to a search order under compulsion? No, held the Court of Appeal in *C Plc v P* [2007] EWCA Civ 493, (2007) L.T.L., May 23. In the case an independent computer expert applied for directions from the court as to what to do with offending material that he had uncovered while imaging the contents from computers retrieved in the course of the execution of a search order. The court ordered that the material should be passed to the police.

There is no privilege in respect of the risk of criminal proceedings in the courts of a foreign state. Also, proof that compliance with the order puts the defendant at serious risk of violent assault by his associates does not necessarily justify the discharge of the order (*Coca-Cola Company v Gilbey* [1995] 4 All E.R. 711).

Enforcing orders for disclosure

27.028 Freezing injunctions in particular will often be ineffective unless and until the defendant has made sufficient disclosure of his assets. What can be done to enforce orders for disclosure? Only in exceptional circumstances will cross-examination be ordered on an affidavit sworn pursuant to a freezing injunction (*House of Spring Gardens Ltd v Waite* [1991] 1 Q.B. 241: if cross-examination is ordered, see PD 2B, para.7).

In *Bayer AG v Winter* [1986] 1 W.L.R. 497, injunctions were granted restraining a defendant from leaving the country and requiring him to deliver up his passports. In *B v B (Passport Surrender: Jurisdiction)*, *The Times*, April 1, 1997 the court refused to make such orders where they were sought as enforcement measures in their own right, i.e. additional means of exerting pressure on the defendant to pay sums owed. These orders are perhaps the modern equivalent of the ancient writ of ne exeat regno which in most cases will be of too narrow a compass to be of any use (see further *Allied Arab Bank Ltd v Hajjar* [1988] Q.B. 787; *Ali v Naseem*, *The Times*, October 3, 2003).

In *Belgolaise SA v Deepak Lal Purchandani* [1999] Lloyd's Rep. Bank 116, Coleman J. commented upon the overuse of applications for committal for contempt on the grounds of alleged breaches of the disclosure orders on the grounds of failure to include fine details of assets and accounts and movements of funds or failure to explain suspicious account entries or other matters arising out of the affidavit.

He emphasised that in commercial litigation proceedings to commit for contempt should be treated as a last resort, to be used only in cases of flagrant refusal to disclose assets or to respond to further requests for a more explicit account of assets or for disclosure of documents relevant to the whereabouts of assets. In the ordinary way the correct course for a claimant's advisers who are not satisfied that the affidavit or subsequent statements have made adequate disclosure is to write to the defendant setting out clearly and precisely what additional information is required and setting a reasonable time limit for that to be fully provided, but making it clear that if an adequate response is not received within that time, the claimant will apply to the court for committal for contempt. Alternatively, if at the time of non-compliance with the disclosure order a defence has already been served, a further remedy is available, namely the striking out of the defence.

In *Canada Trust Co. v Stolzenberg*, *The Times*, November 10, 1997, Neuberger J. held that where a foreign defendant, with no assets in the UK, failed to comply with an order for disclosure made by the High Court pursuant to a freezing injunction, and there was a strong case against that defendant, it may be appropriate to debar him from defending the case, if he failed to adhere to the order within a reasonable time limit. The defendants' claim that the disclosure requirements of the order would compel him to breach the law of another jurisdiction, while a factor to be taken into consideration, did not outweigh the claimant's urgent need for the specified evidence.

EFFECT OF A R.3.7 STRIKE OUT (R.25.11)

27.029 The practice direction supplementing r.3.7 provides that where a claim is struck out for non-payment of a court fee, the court will send a notice that it has been struck out to the defendant. The notice explains that the interim injunction will cease to have effect 14 days after the date the claim is struck out under r.3.7. Rule 25.11(2) provides that if the claimant applies to reinstate the claim before the interim injunction ceases to have effect, the injunction will continue until the hearing of the application unless the court orders otherwise. If the claimant makes such an application, the defendant is given notice in the ordinary way under r.23.4.

INTERIM RECEIVERSHIP ORDERS

27.030 Supreme Court Act 1981, s.37 (referred to above in connection with freezing injunctions) also enables the High Court to make interim orders appointing receivers "in all cases in which it appears to the court to be just and convenient to do so". In *Hart v Emelkirk Ltd* [1983] 1 W.L.R. 1289, an interim order was made appointing a receiver in respect of two blocks of flats. The flats were let on long leases under which the landlord had certain obligations to repair and insure and the tenants were required to pay ground rents and contribute to the costs of repair via a service charge. There was evidence that the current beneficial owner of the reversions to the leases had made no attempt to manage the block of flats, to collect rents and service charges, or to effect repairs or insurance for several years past and the properties had fallen into a condition which demanded urgent attention. Similar receivership orders have been made in *Daiches v Bluelake Investments Ltd* (1985) 82 L.S.G. 3258 and in another case which has been reported on two related points; registration of a caution to protect the receivership order (*Clayhope Properties Ltd v Evans* [1986] 1 W.L.R. 1223) and payment of remuneration to a receiver (*Evans v Clayhope Properties Ltd* [1987] 1 W.L.R. 225). In *Parker v Camden London Borough Council* [1986] Ch.162, it was held that, in view of (what is now) Housing Act 1985, s.21 a receivership order should not be made against a local authority; however the council tenants were held to be entitled instead to an interim mandatory injunction.

In our view, the principles applied to these cases fully comply with the principles we described above as relevant to interim mandatory injunctions. In other words, if the receivership order will not finally dispose of the dispute between the parties (for an example see Hart, above) the ordinary principles of *American Cyanamid* should be applied. However, if the receivership order will have consequences which are irreversible at a later trial (as in *Parker*, see below) the claimants should be required to show a strong case.

In *Hart* the order which was granted merely filled the vacuum in estate management that had arisen. In *Parker* the relief granted related to a specific, short-term, problem: the local authority landlord's unwillingness to hire outside engineers to repair heating boilers which had broken down during a strike of its boilermen. It is also worthy of note that in both cases the persons liable as landlords appear not to have had any arguable defence (see above).

In *Derby & Co. Ltd v Weldon (Nos 3 and 4)* [1990] Ch.65, interim receivership was ordered in aid of a freezing injunction and in *Derby & Co. Ltd v Weldon (No.6)* [1990] 1 W.L.R. 1139 further orders were made requiring the transfer of certain assets into the sole name of the receiver.

In *International Credit and Investment Co. (Overseas) Ltd v Adham (Appointment of Receiver)* [1998] B.C.C. 134 it was held that the court was entitled to pierce the corporate veil to appoint a receiver over the property in cases where a worldwide freezing injunction had been granted over property and where there was a real risk that the orders might be breached.

INTERIM ORDERS RELATING TO RELEVANT PROPERTY

Both the High Court and the county court can make a variety of orders relating to "relevant property", that is property (including land) which is the subject-matter of the action or as to which any question has arisen. These include orders for detention, custody, preservation, inspection, the taking of samples and experimentation or the delivery up of goods under the Torts (Interference with Goods) Act 1977, s.4 and orders for the sale of relevant property which is perishable or which for any other good reason it is desirable to sell quickly: see generally r.25.1. Rule 25.1(1)(l) enables the court to make "an order for a specified fund to be paid into court or otherwise secured, where there is a dispute over a party's right to the fund". An order under this paragraph is akin to the appointment of a trustee or receiver of a fund pending resolution of some dispute concerning it. It does not enable the court to direct a defendant in a simple debt claim to create a fund in court, thereby securing the claimant's claim (*Myers v Design Inc International) Ltd* [2003] 1 W.L.R. 1642, Ch., the claimant in that case was invited instead to seek relief by way of a freezing injunction or an application for summary judgment).

27.031

Applications for these orders are made to a master or district judge and, normally on notice. Orders for detention, etc. may also authorise a person to enter upon any land or building in the possession of a party to the action.

CHAPTER 28

Change of Solicitors

28.001 A solicitor goes on the record by stating in correspondence with another party or in a statement of case that he is authorised to accept service on behalf of the client (see Ch.8). He will remain on the record and will continue to be served with documents and will be expected to attend court hearings until such time as a notice or order is served which takes him off the record (see r.42.1). In *Gloag & Son Ltd v Welsh Distillers Ltd* (1999) L.T.L., June 11, Pumfrey J. said that it was regrettable and wrong in principle for solicitors to remain on record and not appear in any form when the order being made involved serious consequences for the client. We are aware that some judges telephone solicitors who are on the record and ask them to explain their absence. In addition the court may exercise its power under r.3.1(2)(b) and require a solicitor to attend court to give an explanation.

If a solicitor ceases to be instructed in the matter and the former client instructs new solicitors, they should prepare and serve a notice of change in Form N434 giving their address as the new address for service. If the former client intends to act in person in future then, technically, he should prepare and serve the form, which we now call a notice of acting. In practice former clients often overlook this formality. Accordingly, it is usually advantageous for the former solicitor to prepare the notice of acting for him, then get him to sign it, and then see to its service and filing. The solicitor may also warn the former client that, if he refuses to cooperate in this, the solicitor may apply for an order that he has ceased to act together with an order for the costs of the application.

If a solicitor acts for a client under a CLS Funding certificate that is revoked or discharged the retainer with the client comes to an end (see reg.4 of the Community Legal Services (Costs) Regulations 2000) (SI 2000/441). The solicitor will come off record by simply filing a notice of revocation or discharge at the court. No further notice is required by the rules. However, PD 42, para.2.2 says that in these circumstances if the former assisted person wishes either to act in person or appoint another solicitor to act on his behalf "a notice of the change giving the last known address of the former assisted person must also be filed and served on every other party". Hence it appears that whilst the former client is responsible for either giving notice that he is acting in person or appointing solicitors who should go on record, the solicitor must still file and serve this additional notice unless he is absolutely certain that the proceedings have come to an end.

The procedure by which a solicitor can obtain an order declaring that he has ceased to act in the matter is as follows (see generally r.42.3). Unless the court directs otherwise the application notice and supporting evidence must be served on the former client (but not upon other parties in the action). It is of course inappropriate to use the solicitor's business address for the purpose of service of this document. Since the solicitor is not acting for the party now reliance can be placed upon the address prescribed by r.6.5(6) (see Ch.8). In a simple matter it will normally be appropriate to request that the application should be dealt with without a hearing (*Miller v Allied Sainif (UK) Ltd, The Times*, October 31, 2000). Requiring the attendance of the solicitor and former client will simply take up court time and lead to an increase in costs. Nevertheless, if the case is complex, or if a hearing date is close, solicitors who wish to come off the record are advised to attend court. In *Roshdi v Thames Trains Ltd* [2002] EWCA Civ 284, the claimant's solicitors applied for removal from the record on the first day of trial and an order was made by consent. The Court of Appeal upheld the trial judge's refusal to adjourn the trial.

Whilst the court has a discretion as to whether or not to make the order it usually does and it should then be served on every party to the proceedings. Note that the order only takes effect on service. Thereafter the party's address for service will be the address (if any) stated in the order or (more likely) the address for service indicated by r.6.5(6) (see Ch.8).

Rule 42.4 deals with the rare occurrence of a solicitor who ceases to act for a party due to death, bankruptcy, ceasing to practice or disappearing without trace and no notice of change has been served. In such circumstances an order declaring that the solicitor has ceased to act may be made on the application of any other party, or, indeed, may be made by the court acting upon its own initiative.

CHAPTER 29

Part 36 offers to settle

THE RATIONALE OF PT 36

29.001 The new Pt 36 (in force from April 2007) makes provision for the parties to an action to make offers to each other in settlement of that action. In most cases steps taken under Pt 36 are the most important tactical steps those parties will take. An offer to settle governed by Pt 36 constitutes an attempt by the party making it to *force* the other party into a compromise. The compromise element is clear enough. Once made the other party has a short time within which to accept the offer. If he does so, the relevant cause of action will come to an end and (usually) the claimant will be entitled to his reasonable costs to date in respect of that cause of action. The forcing element becomes apparent if the offer to settle is not accepted. Thereafter, the parties are taking a heavy risk as to costs and interest.

A Pt 36 offer is treated as being made "without prejudice except as to costs" (r.36.13). These words mean that the offer to settle is not an admission or concession by the party making the offer. If it is not accepted and the case proceeds to trial the trial judge will not be told about it until the end. For example, in a personal injury claim, it is permissible for a defendant to deny all liability and invite the trial judge to dismiss the claim even though he has made a Pt 36 offer to pay many thousands of pounds to the claimant.

Consider first an offer to settle made by the defendant. If the claimant fails to accept it and pushes his claim on to trial but then fails to obtain a judgment more advantageous to him than the offer, the trial judge is likely to make two orders for costs. The first order will deal with costs incurred in the period up to a date usually within 21 days of service of the offer. These costs will be awarded to the claimant. However, the second order will award to the defendant the costs from that date. The claimant thus ends up paying a substantial proportion of both parties' costs even though he has won the action. By failing to beat the defendant's offer to settle it is he, not the defendant who is regarded as the losing party from the date shortly after that offer was made.

Making a well estimated offer to settle prevents a claimant pursuing inordinate or exaggerated claims at the defendant's expense. If the offer to settle is accepted the defendant pays the costs to date and the litigation ceases as to that claim. If the claimant unsuccessfully seeks a more advantageous award, he will have to pay most of the costs incurred after the offer was made. The earlier the defendant makes a good offer, the greater the costs penalty on the claimant. Bear in mind that offers to settle can even be made before the commencement of proceedings.

Consider now an offer to settle made by a claimant. Assume that the defendant does not accept it and lets the case proceed to trial. If the claimant obtains a judgment which is at least as advantageous to him as he proposed in his offer, the court will make in his favour a more generous order as to costs and may also award more interest than it would otherwise have done. Although costs before the offer was made will be assessed on the standard basis, most of the costs incurred after the offer was made will be assessed on the indemnity basis (as to the difference, see Ch.38). The court may also allow an enhanced rate of interest on any debt or damages awarded to the claimant and on the costs incurred after the date of the offer. The enhanced costs and interest are in effect bonuses awarded to the claimant for making what turns out to be a well judged offer of compromise. There are no equivalent bonuses for defendants who make well judged offers. The reason for this divergence was explained by Lord Woolf M.R. in *Petrotrade Inc. v Texaco Ltd* [2003] 1 W.L.R. 947, CA: they create an incentive for the claimant to make a Pt 36 offer. Without them, Pt 36 offers would be of no value to the claimant: if he wins the case he will obtain his ordinary costs anyway; if there were no incentive why should he volunteer to accept terms of compromise which may be less advantageous to him than the court might award?

A claimant who makes a successful Pt 36 offer usually obtains advantages as to costs and interest. A defendant who makes a successful Pt 36 offer avoids liability to pay the claimant's costs for the period shortly after his offer and, indeed, may end up receiving costs for that period. Since Pt 36 provides these advantages in order to encourage parties to make genuine attempts at settlement, the parties should not be deprived of the advantages unless there are strong reasons for doing so. However, do not deduce from this that a litigant who has made a genuine attempt at settlement is thereby licensed to litigate unreasonably in the future. Claimants who maintain an expensive argument that has no reasonable prospects of success may end up with no order for costs even though the defendants lose the claim on an alternative argument and also fail to beat a Pt 36 offer (*Kastor Navigation Co. Ltd v Axa Global Risks (UK) Ltd* [2004] EWCA Civ 277). Defendants who make successful Pt 36 offers will lose the normal costs advantages if they have obstructed the claimant's opportunity to assess whether or not to accept the offer (r.36.14(4): *Ford v G.K.R. Construction Ltd* [2002] 1 W.L.R. 1397, CA in which the defendants failed to make prompt disclosure of their case to the claimant).

What has happened to payments into court?

In earlier times the courts refused to take into account the offers to settle system we now have (*Walker v Wilsher* (1889) 23 Q.B.D. 335). Instead, for money claims only, a system was developed which required payments into court. A defendant wanting to compromise a money claim on terms lower than the

29.002

claimant would accept was not permitted simply to offer them money. He had to demonstrate the genuineness of his offer, and his ability to pay it, by paying the money into court. Claimants who failed to accept the payment and also failed to recover more at trial were penalised in costs. Defendants who offered such monies but did not pay it into court were not given such advantages. However, the offers to settle system we now have was developed in arbitration law (the "sealed offers" system) and were ultimately adopted by the civil courts in cases which were not simply about debt and damages claims. In *Calderbank v Calderbank* [1976] Fam 93, the Court of Appeal approved the general use of offers to settle in matrimonial proceedings. In *Cutts v Head* [1984] Ch.290, the Court of Appeal extended their use to all non-money claims.

Subsequently the payment into court system was perceived as just one aspect of a larger principle which holds that parties must not pursue litigation unreasonably, for its own sake (Access to Justice Report, Interim Report, 1995: Ch.24, para.5, *Crouch v Kings Healthcare NHS Trust* [2005] 1 W.L.R 2015). This led to the implementation of Pt 36 in the form we now have. There are of course many cases still going through the courts in which payments into court were made before April 2007. These are taken care of by certain transitional provisions which are elaborated in a separate practice direction to Pt 36. Guidance as to the old payments into court system may also be found in earlier editions of this book.

Of course, the concept of making payments into court has not been abolished for all purposes. The convenience of using the court as a collecting bank for the parties is so great that there remain several other uses for it which have nothing to do with offers of compromise. For example, a defendant who wishes to raise a defence of "tender before claim" (as to which, see para.12.035, above) must make a payment into court of the amount he says was tendered (r.37.3). The claimant cannot get the money out of court unless he concedes defeat which will usually involve him paying all of the defendant's costs. If at the trial the claimant fails to disprove the defence, his action will be dismissed and although he can now take the money out of court, before he does so he will usually have to pay all of the defendant's costs. Other examples of payments into court include payments made under conditional orders made by the court (see para.19.014, above and para.33.007, below), under orders for security for costs (see para.26.003, above), control of money recovered by or on behalf of a child or patient (r.21.11) and the payment into court of trust funds (r.37.4 and the Practice Direction thereto).

Pt 36 and the small claims track

29.003   Before launching into the detail of Pt 36 it may be important to recall that this part of the CPR does not apply to cases allocated to the small claims track (see Ch.20).

MAKING OFFERS TO SETTLE

When to offer

There are no time limits on the making of offers to settle and no limit on the number of offers that can be made if earlier offers are not accepted. Unless earlier offers have been accepted, each party can make offers at any time including before the commencement of proceedings, and even after judgment, if the case goes on appeal (CPR 36.3(2)). Each side has little to lose and much to gain by making an offer to settle on any terms he is willing to agree to and the sooner he makes an offer, the better the potential advantages will be. Of course, it is often difficult to sufficiently investigate the facts in order to make an early offer other than an offer which is unduly cautious (claimants offering to settle for too much and defendants offering to settle for too little). However, if they are not accepted, such offers can easily be refined later (claimants later asking for less and defendants later offering more).

29.004

Making offers to settle as early as possible advances the vital date for cost purposes, thereby maximising the costs pressure put upon the opponent. There is a tactic which some defence lawyers use that takes maximum advantage of the pressure which an offer to settle places on the claimant: an offer of a sum which is less than the claimant is entitled to but which is, they estimate, more than he dares refuse—a "sub-minimum offer". Many claimants will accept such an offer if it is finally judged. All civil litigation and civil negotiations are conducted under pressure of costs. Usually such pressure bears most heavily on the weaker party, who is usually the claimant. Defence lawyers who recommend sub-minimum offers calculate that, should they meet a claimant of above average bravery who does not accept a sub-minimum offer, they could always make an increase later on. Herein lies the weakness inherent in sub-minimum offers. An increase is always disadvantageous to the defence. It delays the vital date for cost consequences. It gives the claimant the upper hand in negotiations: by increasing the offer the defence appears to be crumbling and the claimant feels his decision to reject the earlier offer has been proved right.

What to offer

By making an offer to settle the offeror is proposing to the offeree the terms upon which he is prepared to compromise litigation or intended litigation between them. Such terms should be set out as clearly as they would be in a consent order, with this exception: it is not necessary to deal with costs since all Pt 36 offers carry within them certain implied offers as to costs (see para.29.016, below). No harm is done if an offer expressly sets these out or refers to them. However, problems may arise if the offer makes provision for costs which is inconsistent with what would otherwise be implied. In *Mitchell v James* [2004] 1 W.L.R. 158, CA, it was said that the draftsman of Pt 36 had not intended terms as to costs to be included in a Pt 36 offer and therefore, such terms may

29.005

fall outside the scope of a valid offer. Although a Pt 36 offer may contain terms as to costs, as to which the court would have regard in exercising its discretion at the end of the trial, such terms could not be used to obtain an order for costs on an indemnity basis. The facts of this case are summarised in para.29.022, below. Also outside the scope of a valid offer are terms which make no concessions other than as to enhanced interest which might otherwise be awarded (*Ali Reza-Delta Transport Co. Ltd v United Arab Shipping Co.* [2004] 1 W.L.R. 165.

Form and content of offers

29.006   Rule 36.2 states as follows:

> (1) An offer to settle which is made in accordance with this rule is called a Pt 36 offer.
> (2) A Pt 36 offer must—
>   (a) be in writing;
>   (b) state on its face that it is intended to have the consequences of Pt 36;
>   (c) specify a period of not less than 21 days within which the defendant will be liable for the claimant's costs in accordance with r.36.10 if the offer is accepted;
>   (d) state whether it relates to the whole of the claim or to part of it or to an issue that arises in it and if so to which part or issue; and
>   (e) state whether it takes into account any counterclaim.

(Rule 36.7 makes provision for when a Pt 36 offer is made.)

> (3) Rule 36.2(2)(c) does not apply if the offer is made less than 21 days before the start of the trial.
> (4) In appropriate cases, a Pt 36 offer must contain such further information as is required by r.36.5 (Personal injury claims for future pecuniary loss), r.36.6 (Offers to settle a claim for provisional damages), and r.36.15 (Deduction of benefits).
> (5) An offeror may make a Pt 36 offer solely in relation to liability.

Paragraph (c) requires Pt 36 offers to be explicit as to the initial period in which the offeree is allowed to consider whether to accept the offer. This is the period referred to elsewhere in Pt 36 as "the relevant period", a key provision in the Pt 36 system. A Pt 36 offer is made when it is served on the offeree (CPR 36.7) and is accepted by the offeree when notice of acceptance is served on the offeror (CPR 36.9). As to the available methods of service and deemed dates of service, see Ch.8. The relevant period commences on the day the offer is served rather than the day the offer is written. (Whilst this may not be clear from para.(c), it is made clear in the practice form quoted below.) However, minor errors as to the date specified in the notice may not be fatal to the effectiveness of the offer (see para.29.010, below).

In some circumstances the "relevant period" can be longer or shorter than the period specified in the offer: for example, if the offer was made less than 21 days before trial, the relevant period is a period up to the end of a trial or such other period as the court determines. In other cases the relevant period may be longer than the period specified, if the parties so agree (see generally CPR 36.3(1)(c)).

The "relevant period" which applies to a particular offer is important in at least three ways. During this period all parties should, as far as possible, avoid taking steps incurring further costs in the action. It is a cease-fire period during which further preparations for battle should not be made (unless they are urgent or essential) whilst one party is considering the other party's peace proposal (see further para.29.012, below). Secondly, the defendant will be obliged to pay the claimant's costs if the offeree (whether claimant or defendant) accepts the offer before the relevant period expires. Thirdly, the offeree (whether claimant or defendant) will usually be obliged to pay the offeror's costs incurred after the relevant period if the offeree either accepts the offer late or pushes on to judgment but fails to obtain a result more favourable to him than was offered.

As to paragraphs (a), (b), (c) and (d), there is no prescribed form for Pt 36 offers although parties may use Form N242A. After setting out the title of the proceedings (including the name of the court if proceedings have already been issued in court) and the offeree's address for service it states as follows:

> "**Take notice** the (defendant) (claimant) offers to settle the claim. This offer is intended to have the consequences of Part 36. If the offer is accepted within____ days (must be at least 21 days) of service of this notice the defendant will be liable for the claimant's costs in accordance with Rule 36.10 of the Civil Procedure Rules.
>
> The offer is to settle . . ."

The form then sets out several tick boxes specifying "the whole of the claim", "part of the claim *(give details below)*", "a certain issue or issues in the claim *(give details below)*" and also contains passages dealing with the complexities of periodical payments of damages, provisional damages and the deduction of State benefits (as to all of which, see below).

Paragraph (d) of r.36.2(2) enables the offeror to make one global offer in respect of the whole claim or a series of separate offers each dealing with separate parts or issues in the claim, for example, some but not all causes of action and some but not all of the issues which arise. Most offerors prefer to keep it simple and make one global offer. As to the offeree's right to request clarification of that offer, see para.29.012, below.

As to counterclaims (see r.36.2(2)(e), above) the offer must be explicit as to whether the counterclaim is included (i.e., it will end if the offer is accepted) or excluded (i.e., it may continue whether or not the offer is accepted). The "keep it simple" principle inclines most offerors to include the counterclaim.

Defence offers to pay money

29.007 Rule 36.4 sets out a general rule that a Pt 36 offer by a defendant to pay a sum of money in settlement of a claim must be an offer to pay a single sum of money. This means that if the defendant wishes to depart from the "keep it simple" principle and offer different sums in respect of different causes of action he must use different offers to settle. The general rule does not apply to Pt 36 offers made by claimants; they can make their offers as complicated as they wish. Also, the general rule does not apply in all personal injury claims. A defendant can offer to settle *a future pecuniary loss claim* either by way of a lump sum, or by way of periodical payments (as to which his offer must be explicit) or by way of both a lump sum and periodical payments. If a claim includes *a claim for provisional damages* an offer to settle must specify whether or not the offeror is offering to agree to the making of an award for provisional damages. If he is, the offer must also state relevant details (e.g. the disease or deterioration to be specified in an award and the limited period within which further claims can be made).

If a defendant's money offer is accepted, the claimant is entitled to expect that, after a period of (usually) 14 days he will either receive the money or can enter judgment for it (r.36.11(6) and (7)). Rule 36.4(2) seeks to discourage a defendant from making an offer which includes an offer to pay all or part of the money later than 14 days after acceptance. Such an offer will not be treated as a Pt 36 offer unless the offeree accepts it (as to this, see further, para.29.010, below).

As to interest on debts and damages, note that a defendant's offer to pay a sum (and, indeed, a claimant's offer to accept a sum) is treated as inclusive of interest until the date on which the period specified in the offer expires or (if the offer was made less than 21 days before the start of a trial) a date 21 days after the date the offer was made (r.36.3(3)).

We have already described the aggressive tactic employed by some defendants of making sub-minimum offers in the first instance (see para.29.004 above). A non-aggressive strategy is to try to predict what a trial court would award and then include some safety margin to guard against mishaps. For example, in a case where liability is admitted, the defendant should consider paying in, say, ten percent more than he thinks the claim is worth. Similarly, a claimant may be prepared to accept, or offer to accept, 90 per cent of his valuation of the claim. Sometimes, these safety margins will have the beneficial effect of bringing the parties to a compromise which neither of them would otherwise have considered.

Example

At the stage after allocation C values his claim at £15,000 and D values it at £12,250. C may well be advised to make an offer to settle for £13,500 and to accept any offer made by the defendant for that or a larger sum. Allowing him the same ten percent safety margin, D ought to be prepared to offer up to £13,750 and to accept any offer to settle made by the claimant for that or a lower sum.

In this example each party's evaluation of the claim is within 20 percent of the other party's valuation and, therefore, they are likely to reach a compromise. The cases which still go to trial after substantial offers to settle have been made are usually those where the parties disagree over some fundamental element such as remoteness, contributory negligence or the like.

So far we have suggested a safety margin of ten percent. But is this enough or too much? What further discount is appropriate if liability is not admitted? Also, how accurately can the party determine what sum the trial court may award? These matters will depend upon the particular circumstances of each case. And they are matters on which the litigants are entitled to skilled advice from their solicitors (see further para.6.022).

Defence offers affected by the Social Security (Recovery of Benefits) Act 1997

This is an important topic in most personal injury claims. As to the general law of state benefits see para.4.004, above. Because of the complex rules which govern deductions Pt 36 makes special provision which: (i) defines how defendants must make Pt 36 offers; (ii) defines when such offers are beaten; and (iii) makes provision for cases in which offers are accepted late. 29.008

Under the Act a person paying compensation to certain claimants must refund to the State certain listed benefits paid to those claimants. The refund must be made within 14 days after the claim for compensation ends. A compensator must pay the full amount of the relevant benefits whether or not the claimant was guilty of contributory negligence. Although the compensator has a right to make deductions in respect of those benefits from the compensation he would otherwise have to pay, deductions can be made only in respect of particular heads of damage. For example, attendance allowances recoupable by the State are deductible only from compensation for loss of care incurred during the relevant period. In a particular case the compensator may have to refund more to the State than the amount he can deduct from the compensation. Section 15 of the Act provides that the court must specify the compensation attributable to each head of damage.

Under r.36.15 defendants in these cases are given a choice of two types of offer to settle, and must indicate in the notice which one they have chosen. This is done by stating either that the offer is made *without regard to any liability for recoverable benefits*, or that it is *intended to include any deductible benefits*.

We shall refer to the first of these as a gross offer and the second as a net offer. Our preference runs firmly in favour of net offers. A defendant can make a net offer only if he has already applied to the Department of Work and Pensions for a certificate of recoverable benefits. His offer must state the amount of gross compensation, the name and amount of any deductible benefit by which that gross amount is reduced, and the net amount after such deduction. A net offer tells the claimant how much he will actually receive if he accepts it.

Rule 36.15(7) gives a defendant a short time within which to "clarify" a net offer if he makes it before he has received the certificate of recoverable benefits he has applied for. The practice form, N242A indicates what this clarification amounts to. Being unable to specify the net figure being offered to the claimant, the defendant can state "I have not yet received a certificate of recoverable benefits". Once he has received the certificate, the defendant gets just seven days to specify the name and amount of any deductible benefit by which the gross amount is reduced, and the net amount after such deduction.

On the acceptance of a net offer the claimant is entitled to receive the net sum and the defendant will be left to sort out his obligations to make additional payments to the State. If that offer is not accepted, the question whether it is subsequently beaten at judgment depends upon the net amount the claimant will recover not the gross amount (r.36.15(8); for a case illustration under the old Pt 36, see *Williams v Devon* [2003] EWCA Civ. 365). If the case terminates not by judgment but by the claimant's late acceptance of the offer, the court may permit the defendant to make further deductions from the offer in order to take into account further deductible benefits which have accrued since the offer was made (r.36.15(9)).

A gross offer is an offer to settle for a sum expressly stating that the offer is made without regard to any liability for recoverable benefits. "Without any" in this context means "before having". Such an offer does not avoid the need to obtain a certificate of recoverable benefits. A claimant who accepts a gross offer will not find out how much he will actually receive until the certificate has been obtained. Even then there may be a dispute as to how to apportion the compensation. A certificate is also needed in order to calculate the net sum payable if the offer is not accepted and the case proceeds to judgment. At that stage the question whether or not a gross offer has been beaten will depend solely on the gross value of the claim as shown in the judgment. How much of that sum can be kept by the claimant and how much must go to the State and what other monies must go to the State will be irrelevant. The deductions from damages which the defendant can make will be in respect of all relevant benefits, not just those benefits which had accrued before the date the gross offer was made.

In our view gross offers merely enable defendants to make rudimentary offers to settle; offers which, since the net amount payable is unknown, are in fact unlikely to achieve settlement. Defendants should make them only as a preliminary to making a net offer, which they can do immediately after writing off for a certificate of recoverable benefits.

Offers solely in relation to liability

29.009 In all claims, including money claims, either side can make a valid Pt 36 offer solely in relation to liability (r.36.2(5)). This provision is best illustrated by case law. In *Huck v Robson* [2003] 1 W.L.R. 1340, CA. the claimant in a two-car road accident claim made a Pt 36 offer as a tactic placing extra pressure on the defendant to settle the issue of liability. Although her pleaded case was that the defendant was 100 per cent liable, she offered to settle on a 95/5 per cent basis. The offer was not accepted, the claim was tried on liability and the defendant was held 100 per cent liable. Although the trial judge considered the offer to settle was "not an offer of anything" and that it was "derisory" and "meaningless" the Court of Appeal disagreed and awarded the claimant enhanced costs because of it. In *Read v Edmed* [2004] EWHC 3274 (Q.B.), a claim was made in respect of a collision between a bicycle ridden by the claimant and a car driven by the defendant. The claimant's Pt 36 offer to settle the question of liability on a 50/50 basis was not accepted. At the trial both parties were held equally at fault. The claimant was awarded her costs post-offer on the indemnity basis and the question of interest was deferred to the court which would later assess the quantum issue.

In both of these cases the claimants made offers to settle inviting the defendants to accept liability at a percentage less than 100 per cent. In order to avoid liability for enhanced costs and interest, the defendants were required either to accept the offer or prove that their liability was less than was offered. Does the same principle apply if the claimant's offer to settle invites the defendant to accept 100 per cent liability? In that instance we would share the view taken by the trial judge in *Huck v Robson* [2003] 1 W.L.R. 1340, CA. The offer is in effect a demand to the defendant to give in or pay enhanced costs and interest. In our view the trial judge in such cases should exercise his discretion not to allow the claimants the advantages which successful offers usually have.

Offers to settle which are outside Pt 36

Rule 36.1(2) states as follows:

> "Nothing in this Part prevents a party making an offer to settle in whatever way he chooses, but if the offer is not made in accordance with rule 36.2, it will not have the consequences specified in rules 36.10, 36.11 and 36.14.
>
> (Rule 44.3 requires the court to consider an offer to settle that does not have the cost consequences set out in this Part in deciding what order to make about costs.)"

29.010

Similar warnings of the need to comply with the requirements of Pt 36 are given in r.36.4(2) (offers to pay some at a date later than 14 days following acceptance), and r.36.5(2) (concerning offers to settle claims for future pecuniary loss). Other rules make mandatory requirements without stating the consequences of non-compliance (see r.36.4(1) (a defendant's offer to pay money must normally be an offer to pay a single sum of money) and r.36.6(2) (an offer to settle a claim including a claim for provisional damages must specify whether or not the offeror is proposing that the settlement shall include an award of provisional damages). Do not assume that offers which in some minor respects fall outside the requirements of Pt 36 will never be accorded the benefits which Pt 36 would have offered. We would explain the rationale of these provisions as follows. In order to encourage genuine attempts at settlement which are clear, comprehensive and timely, Pt 36 lays down rules which, in some instances, are somewhat technical. Parties wishing to be sure of the benefits of these rules must be punctilious in their compliance with them. Nevertheless, Pt 36 remains just one aspect of the larger principle which holds that parties must not pursue litigation unreasonably, for its own sake. Just as the court has power to withhold the benefits of Pt 36 from parties whose conduct is unreasonable even if they have punctiliously followed the procedures (see para.29.001, above) so in other cases minor errors committed by an offeror which cause no prejudice to the offeree may not be fatal to the effectiveness of the offer. For example, in *Hertsmere Primary Care Trust v Rabindra-Anandh* [2005] 3 All E.R. 274, the claimant had obtained an order for an account to be taken of payments it had made to the defendant. The claimant made an offer to settle for a specified sum plus costs but, by mistake, the offer letter was not explicit as to the period within which the defendant could accept that offer. The defendant's legal team spotted the error immediately but did not point it out to the claimant. The offer was not accepted and, on the taking of the account, the defendant was ordered to pay a sum larger than the settlement offer. The Master's decision to award the claimant enhanced interest and costs on the indemnity basis despite the non-compliance was upheld on appeal. The error was a pure technicality: by failing to draw it to the claimant's attention the defendant's legal team had deprived the claimant of an opportunity to rectify it, thereby failing in their duty to help the court to further the overriding objective (r.1.3).

Withdrawing or altering a Pt 36 offer

29.011 An offeror withdraws or alters an offer to settle by serving on the offeree written notice of the withdrawal or change of terms (r.36.3(7)). Such notice can be given at any time in order to make an increased offer (i.e., an offer more favourable to the offeree) similarly, offers to settle can be readily withdrawn or reduced after the expiry of the relevant period (usually with the 21 day period specified in the offer, see further para.29.006, above) provided that the offeree has not previously served notice of acceptance (r.36.3(6)). Once an offer has been validly withdrawn or changed so that its terms are less favourable to the offeree, the offeree can no longer accept the old offer and, if the matter goes to judgment, the offeror will not be entitled to the benefits of enhanced interest or costs which the old offer might otherwise have brought him (r.36.14(6)).

We must now explain a restriction which applies on withdrawing offers or changing them to terms which are less favourable to the offeree before the expiry of the relevant period. At this early stage a notice of withdrawal or change has effect only if the court gives permission (r.36.3(5)). Applications for permission must not be made to the judge allocated to conduct the trial unless all parties agree (Practice Directions supplementing Pt 36, para.2.2). In what circumstances will such an application be granted? In *Flynn v Scougall (Practice Note)* [2004] 1 W.L.R. 3069, the Court of Appeal adopted with approval the guidance given in several previous cases, including some pre-CPR cases. In order to obtain permission the offeror should show matters such as fraud or mistake affecting the offer or some sufficient change of circumstance since it was made, for example, a change in the law relevant to the claim or the discovery of new evidence.

Flynn concerned a defendant's offer to settle a money claim made at a time when such offers had to be paid into court. The defendant made a payment exceeding £24,000. At that stage she had seen the expert report relied upon by the claimant. Within one week she had received the report made by her own expert which caused her to seek permission to reduce the payment to £10,000. Before that application was heard and within the period which today would be regarded as the relevant period, the claimant purported to serve notice of acceptance. The Court of Appeal considered that the difference between the experts' reports was nothing out of the ordinary in personal injury litigation. It held that, although the claimant's acceptance did not prevent the court from granting the permission sought, it was nevertheless an important consideration to be taken into account and refused permission.

> "[42] The defendant chose to make the Pt 36 payment before [her expert's] report arrived. In doing so, she secured the advantage of an earlier payment into court and took the risk that [her expert's] report might improve her evidential position. The fact that it may have done so was not, in my view, even close to a sufficient change of circumstance... it was not based on the discovery of new evidence nor a change in legal outlook. Rather, the defendant was relying on a further review of available information by a fresh expert. I do not consider that the defendant has shown that she should in justice be permitted to reduce her Pt 36 payment so as to deny the claimant's otherwise unfettered right to accept full payment within 21 days." [May L.J., with whom Potter L.J. and Brooke L.J. agreed]

ACCEPTING OFFERS TO SETTLE

Clarification of offers to settle

In most cases a party who receives a Pt 36 offer is allowed a short time (the "relevant period", as to which, see para.29.006, above) in which to consider whether to accept. His decision either way may have enormous repercussions: if he rejects the offer, the battle will go on with enhanced risks as to costs and interest; if he accepts the offer the battle will cease for now but, if he has accepted on the wrong terms, other dangers and pitfalls may arise. In most cases the decision is his and his alone but he is entitled to expect appropriate advice (strong advice where necessary) from his advisors.

29.012

During the relevant period both sides should, as far as possible, avoid taking any steps incurring further costs. Further preparations for battle should not be made (unless they are urgent or essential) while one side is considering the other side's peace proposal. However, there are some steps which it may be reasonable for an offeree to take in order to help him make his decision. First, he may seek professional advice, sometimes including counsel's advice and the advice of expert witnesses as to whether to accept. Instead of that, or, sometimes, in addition, he may spend money asking the offeror to clarify the meaning of the offer to settle which has been made. A procedure for this has been laid down in the rule next mentioned but, as yet, there is little post-CPR case authority upon it.

Rule 36.8 states that an offeree may, within seven days of a Pt 36 offer being made, request the offeror to clarify the offer. The rule does not require the request to be made in writing but, as a matter of common sense, we think that it should be. Further, no indication is given as to what matters the offeree may legitimately ask to be clarified. We would suggest that specific reference should be made to any defect in the offer the offeree has spotted, for example, failure to state if a counterclaim has been taken into account. If the offer to settle is thought to be ambiguous, the request for clarification should spell out the ambiguity and ask the offeror to state which is the correct interpretation.

Offers to settle are often made globally in respect of several causes of action or issues. In our view an offeree is not normally entitled to seek clarification which sub-divides that which the offeror has summed up together. The sub-division would enable him to pick and choose which parts to accept and which to reject. In *Factortame Ltd v Secretary of State for the Environment, Transport and the Regions* [2002] 1 W.L.R. 2438, CA, the judge in the lower court (His Honour Judge Toulmin Q.C.), held that a party is not entitled to interrogate another party as to his thinking behind the making of a Pt 36 offer (this point was not taken on the appeal). The parties may well value different aspects of the case differently. To prevent his opponent cherry-picking an offeror ought to be allowed to make a global offer on a "take it or leave it" basis. Indeed, r.36.4(1) provides that an offer by a defendant to pay money must usually be an offer to pay a single sum of money (no such compulsion is placed upon claimants). However, an exception allowing the offeree to obtain a sub-division of a global offer might be appropriate where the global offer causes the offeree real difficulty or embarrassment. In *Walker v Turpin* [1994] 1 W.L.R. 196, CA, two claimants raised separate causes of action against the same defendant in the same proceedings. The defendant made a lump sum offer in respect of both causes and, in accordance with the then rules, paid that lump sum into court. Depending upon how that sum was divided one claimant was prepared to accept it but the other claimant was unlikely to do so. The defendant was ordered to apportion his payment between the two claimants.

> "...if a defendant wishes to have the advantages flowing from a payment into court, he must make a payment in the form which does not embarrass the [claimants]. In this case, where there are separate [claimants], each pursuing his own separate causes of action, the payment should be in a form which enables each [claimant] to know where he stands, so that he can accept the payment and bow out if he wishes." (Sir Donald Nicholls V.C.)

If the facts of this case recurred today a claimant wishing to accept the sum allotted to him could either do so, if the defendant so agreed, or could serve his own offer to settle in respect of it.

Rule 36.8 further provides that where the offeror does not give the clarification requested within seven days the offeree may, unless the trial has already started, apply for an Order that he does so. If the court makes an Order it must specify the date when (i.e., from which) the Pt 36 offer is to be treated as having been made. The wording of this Pt of the rule is difficult to follow. Presumably, the intention is that the court can direct that, once the offer has been clarified, the relevant period allotted to the claimant to consider it recommences from the date the court specifies.

When and how to accept

A Pt 36 offer can be accepted at any time, whether or not he has subsequently made a different offer, unless the offeror has served Notice of Withdrawal on the offeree (r.36.9(2)) or unless the trial has concluded (whether or not judgment has been given: r.36.9(5)). As explained below there are potential costs penalties and other penalties to be aware of if an offer is accepted after the expiry of the relevant period (as to which, see para.29.006).

29.013

In order to accept a Pt 36 offer, the offeree must serve written notice of acceptance on the offeror. The Practice Directions supplementing Pt 36 provides that a copy of the Notice of Acceptance must be filed in the court where the case is proceeding and states that, if the offeror is legally represented, the Notice of Acceptance must be served on the legal representatives. If either party is a child or patient (see Ch.7, above) the Notice of Acceptance will not lead to a valid settlement of the claim unless it is approved by the court (r.21.10).

Permission to accept a Pt 36 offer is required in the following cases (r.36.9(3)):

(i) In cases involving compensation recovery payments (see para.29.008, above) where the defendant has made a net offer which the claimant does not accept until after the relevant period has expired. In this instance the claimant may suffer more than just a penalty in costs. He may also suffer further deductions in respect of recoverable benefits accrued to him since the Pt 36 offer was made.

(ii) In a claim under the Fatal Accidents Act 1976 and the Law Reform (Miscellaneous Provisions) Act 1934 where an apportionment of compensation is required under r.41.3A. In such a case the court will apportion the money as between, for example, the deceased's estate, the widow and the children.

(iii) Where the trial has started. This is a case in which the standard orders for costs (see below) may not be appropriate.

Applications for permission to accept should not be made to the judge allocated to conduct the trial, unless all parties agree. In compensation recovery cases the application must give full details including details of deductible benefits subsequently accrued and must be accompanied by a copy of the current certificate of recoverable benefits (PD36, para.3.2).

Save as explained below, permission to accept a Pt 36 offer is also required where it was made by some, but not all, of the defendants and they were sued jointly or in the alternative. Before the claimant can get his hands on the money the court may make orders for costs protecting the other defendants; for example, orders for their costs to be paid by the claimant and/or by the defendant who made the Pt 36 offer. In many cases it will be obvious what orders for costs the court will make if asked. Consider, for example, an RTA claim against D1 (a driver) and D2 (a vehicle repairer) and it later transpires that only D2 is liable and it is he who makes the Pt 36 offer. To cover such cases r.36.12(2) permits a claimant to accept the offer without permission if—

> "(a) he discontinues his claim against those defendants who have not made the offer; and
> (b) those defendants give written consent to the acceptance of the offer."

Compare and contrast the position which obtains where a Pt 36 offer was made by one or more, but not all, defendants who are sued "severally" (see para.29.015, below).

The effect of acceptance

29.014   The acceptance of an offer to settle usually has triple effect: a stay of all relevant proceedings, provision for the costs of those proceedings, and the implementation of the terms agreed. In particular cases there may also be further consequences. We deal with each of these effects and consequences below.

Stay of all relevant proceedings

29.015   If a Pt 36 offer related to the whole of the claim and included the counterclaim and is accepted, the whole claim and counterclaim will be stayed. If it related to the whole claim but not the counterclaim, the claim only will be stayed and the counterclaim may continue. If the offer related to part only of the claim and is accepted the claim is stayed only as to that part and, unless the parties have agreed costs, the liability for costs has to be decided by the court. In cases involving children or patients, where the approval of the court is required before a settlement can be binding, a stay takes effect only when that approval is given (see generally r.36.11). The fact that proceedings are stayed under this rule does not, of course, affect the power of the court to deal with costs and other related matters that remain outstanding.

Consider what should happen in the following example:

In respect of a building project which went horribly wrong, C sues D1 (an architect), D2 (a builder), D3 (a sub-contractor) and D4 (the manufacturer of steel joists used in the project). The defendants are sued "severally" in respect of multiple causes of action, the damages claimed against each are not precisely the same and a finding of liability against one of them will not, in C's submission, preclude further findings against the others. C values his total claim at £1 million. D4 makes a Pt 36 payment of £200,000 in settlement of D4's liability and C wishes to accept that payment.

Rule 36.12(3) provides that, in circumstances such as these, the claimant may accept the Pt 36 offer and continue with his claims against the other defendants "if he is entitled to do so". The question arises, however, is he entitled to do so? If the other defendants will not admit that he is, it would be advisable to get the court's ruling on the matter before proceeding further. As to such rulings, see para. 33.006, below. Rule 36.12(4) provides that, if he is not so entitled, the claimant must apply to the court for an order permitting him to accept the Pt 36 offer. Such an order would enable the court to protect the costs position of the other defendants.

Provision for the costs of proceedings

Rules 36.9, 36.10 and 36.11 set out the costs consequences following acceptance. These rules are as dry and technical as rules about costs usually are. In order to explain them, we will divide the different possibilities into three groups: (i) cases in which the offeree accepts a Pt 36 offer promptly (i.e., within the relevant period, as to which see para.29.006) and served the Notice of Acceptance without needing the court's permission; (ii) cases in which the offeree needed the court's permission to accept; and (iii) cases in which acceptance is made late (i.e. after expiry of the relevant period).

29.016

Prompt acceptance, no permission needed

This group sub-divides into four. (We did indicate that these rules are dry and technical.) The simplest case, which is also the most frequent, is where the prompt acceptance made without permission leads to a stay of the whole proceedings. In such a case the claimant (whether offeree or offeror) is entitled to his costs of the proceedings up to the date upon which the Notice of Acceptance was served on the offeror. This timeline allows the claimant (where he is the offeree) to recover his reasonable costs of steps taken to determine whether he should accept; for example, he may reasonably need the advice of his solicitor or counsel. The claimant's costs here will include any costs attributable to defending a counterclaim if that counterclaim was taken into account as part of the Pt 36 offer.

Secondly, a special provision is made where the Pt 36 offer was made by the defendant, related only to part of the claim, but, on acceptance, the claimant abandons the balance. For example, if C sues D alleging breach of contract and negligence and D makes a Pt 36 offer in respect of the contract claim only, C could accept it and abandon his claim in tort. Where this provision applies the claimant is entitled to his costs of the entire proceedings, including costs incurred in respect of the abandoned claim, unless the court otherwise orders. If the court is asked to "otherwise order" it will take into account the claimant's conduct, namely whether or not it was reasonable for him to have pursued the part of the claim which he subsequently abandoned.

In the two circumstances just described, which will lead to a stay of all proceedings, an order for costs in favour of the claimant is deemed to be made (r.44.12). If the costs it covers cannot be agreed the claimant can apply for detailed assessment, as to which see Ch.38.

In the next two cases dealt with in this division prompt acceptance does not lead to an automatic provision for costs. Unless the parties can agree costs, the liability for costs will have to be decided by the court. These instances are where the Notice of Acceptance stays only part of the proceedings whilst the other parts continue (in this instance an order for costs may deal also with the costs of the continuing proceedings); next, where the Pt 36 offer was made less than 21 days before the start of the trial (if, by the time of the prompt acceptance the trial has already begun, the parties will inform the trial judge that the matter is resolved and each side can then make submissions as to who should pay what costs and upon what basis (standard or indemnity)).

Acceptance with court's permission

29.017   Where the court's permission is required to accept the Pt 36 offer (as to which, see para.29.013) and such permission is given the parties may then agree costs or, if not, the court will make an order dealing with them and may order "that the consequences set out in r.36.10 will apply". Such an order would be appropriate only if acceptance leads to a stay of all proceedings. The consequences would be those set out in the previous section (prompt acceptance) or those set out in the next alternative, to which we now turn.

Late acceptance without permission

Here we consider a Pt 36 offer where the Notice of Acceptance is made after the relevant period has expired. Given his failure to accept earlier, why is the offeree wanting to accept now? Very often this comes about, not because of any change in circumstance in the case, but merely because the offeree has lost confidence in what he previously thought he could achieve at trial and/or becomes fearful of the costs consequences if he fails to achieve a result more favourable for himself at trial. In such cases the offeror will usually remain willing to settle the action on the terms he previously offered so long as a suitable arrangement is reached as to who pays what costs for the period after the relevant period expired. If these points can be agreed (and they usually can) the parties should draw up and enter an appropriately worded consent order (see Ch.34). What follows is a summary of what the court is likely to award if the parties cannot agree costs.

Consider first a defendant who wishes to accept a claimant's Pt 36 offer. The claimant is likely to be allowed all his costs of the relevant proceedings up to the date of the Notice of Acceptance. It will normally be unwise for him to hold out for more, e.g. costs on the indemnity basis from the date of the Pt 36 offer. Enhanced costs are provided as an encouragement to claimants to make good offers; they are not provided as an encouragement to make offers early (c.f. *Dyson Ltd v Hoover Ltd* [2002] EWHC 2229).

Next consider a claimant who wishes to accept late a Pt 36 offer made by the defendant. If the parties cannot agree on costs, one may presume as a starting point an order on the following lines:

(i) the defendant to pay the claimant's costs up to the date on which the relevant period expired; and
(ii) the claimant to pay the defendant's costs thereafter.

> "But that presumption may be dislodged in special circumstances, e.g., where the judge takes the view that a defendant has withheld material and not allowed a claimant to make a proper appraisal of the defendant's case. . ." (Waller L.J.)

The quotation just made comes from *Factortame Ltd v Secretary of State for the Environment, Transport and the Regions* [2002] 1 W.L.R. 2438. In that case the court postponed the date from which the party's liability to costs switched from January 7, 2000 to February 7, 2000 or, in some cases, February 14, 2000: this was done on the basis that, in litigation as complex as theirs, it had been unfair to hold the claimants to the normal 21 day period. Secondly, some claimants could show that the defendants had wrongfully withheld information about certain aspects of their defence for a considerable period.

In the absence of special circumstances, the court should not deprive a defendant of the costs benefits that a successful offer usually brings. In *Matthews v Metal Improvements Co. Inc* [2007] EWCA Civ. 215, C suffered injuries at work which rendered him a patient. In a claim against his employers, brought by his litigation friend, C claimed damages including a substantial sum for loss of future earnings based on a normal life expectancy. D made an offer to settle and, in accordance with the rules in force at that time, paid the money offered into court. That offer was not accepted but, shortly after the 21 day period had expired, the claimant's medical condition worsened so reducing his life expectancy. The litigation friend now decided to accept the offer and sought the court's approval. At first such approval was granted and D was ordered to pay all C's costs. The judge took the view that C's original decision to refuse the offer to settle was reasonable. However, the Court of Appeal held that the judge's approach was based on a misunderstanding of the function of a Pt 36 offer, which was to place the claimant on risk as to costs if, as a result of the contingencies of litigation, the claimant failed to achieve a more favourable result. The Court of Appeal varied the order for costs to limit the claimant's costs to the date 21 days after the payment into court was made plus the costs of the approval hearing (which was required in any event) and ordered C to pay D's other costs from that date.

Implementation of the terms agreed

Where the terms agreed relate to or include non-monetary terms (e.g. terms settling a claim for an injunction, or specific performance of possession of land), 29.018

the cause of action which the claimant may have once had is now replaced by the contractual rights which arise from the accepted Pt 36 offer. If he alleges that the defendant has not honoured these terms he can seek to enforce his new contractual rights by applying to the court without the need to start a new claim (r.36.11(8)). If the contractual rights are dependent upon the existence of a single signed document stating all the terms the court has power to order the parties to sign such a document (*Orton v Collins* [2007] EWHC 803 (Ch), which concerned the disposition of an interest in land and the Law of Property (Miscellaneous Provisions) Act 1989, s. 2).

As to the procedure on applications to implement such terms, which will normally be made on notice to the defendant, see Chs 13 and 14.

In most cases the terms agreed relate to the payment of money by the defendant to the claimant. If the money is not paid promptly the claimant can apply to the court to enforce payment. Where the Pt 36 offer which has led to the settlement was made by the claimant, an application on notice to the defendant is again appropriate.

Rule 36.11(6) and (7) states that, in certain circumstances, a claimant can "enter judgment for the unpaid sum". The circumstances are where the Pt 36 offer was made by the defendant but the defendant does not pay the sum offered within 14 days. In most cases the 14 days runs from the date of acceptance. However, sometimes it is 14 days from the date of the making of an order in cases where an order for provisional damages has to be made or an order for periodical payments has to be made. At present the CPR does not contain any provision permitting a claimant to whom this special procedure applies to "enter judgment" merely by filing a request for judgment under r.36.11(6) and (7). We would therefore suggest that, in these cases, which are likely to arise very frequently, the claimant should make an application to the court but invite the court to deal with it without a hearing (see further para.13.004).

Further consequences

29.019 Where the accepted offer makes provision for periodical payments of damages or provisional damages, the claimant must, within seven days of the date of acceptance,, apply to the court for a suitable order under r.41.8 or r.41.2, as the case may be which will give effect to such provision (rr.36.5(7) and 36.6(5)).

A claimant wishing to accept a Pt 36 offer in settlement of a claim for libel or slander may apply to the court for permission to make a "statement" in open court which he hopes will be widely reported, so vindicating his good name (see further PD 53, para.6.1). In *Phillipps v Associated Newspapers Ltd* [2004] 1 W.L.R. 2106, Eady J. held that the claimant's costs of an incidental to making the statement fall to be paid by the defendant. We respectfully suggest that, if the defendant will not agree to the making of a consent order to cover such costs (to be assessed if not agreed) the claimant would be well advised to apply for an order expressly dealing with them.

A defendant who has withheld sums in respect of certain state benefits must, within 14 days of making a payment, make a further payment to the

Department of Work and Pensions of the sum withheld from the gross compensation and must furnish the claimant with a certificate of deduction (see further para.4.004, above).

WHERE OFFERS TO SETTLE ARE NOT ACCEPTED

The rule of secrecy

Rule 36.13(1) states "a Part 36 offer will be treated as 'without prejudice' except as to costs". This means that, if it is not accepted and the matter proceeds to a trial, the Pt 36 offer is not admissible in evidence (see further para.6.024, above). Rule 36.13(2) clarifies this as follows:

29.020

> "The fact that a Part 36 offer has been made must not be communicated to the trial judge or to the judge (if any) allocated in advance to conduct the trial until the case has been decided."

Three exceptions are made to r.36.13(2):

(a) Where the defence of "tender before claim" has been raised (see further para.29.002, above);
(b) Where the proceedings have been stayed following the acceptance of a Pt 36 offer (see para.29.015, above);
(c) Where the offeror and the offeree agree in writing that the rule of secrecy should not apply.

The current rules do not repeat an exception made under the old rules the absence of which we rather regret. Under the old rules where there had been a split trial and the issue of liability had been determined in favour of the claimant, the defendant was allowed to mention the existence of any offer to settle he had made in order to persuade the court to make an order reserving the cost of the split trial until all remaining issues had been determined (for a case example see *HSS Hire Services Group Plc v BMB Builders Merchants Ltd* [2005] 1 W.L.R. 3158, CA). We would be sorry to see a return to the ancient practice on split trials where defence counsel used to use nods and winks to persuade the court to reserve the costs ("I will invite your lordship to reserve costs in this case. I regret to say that circumstances prevent me from disclosing the grounds upon which I make that submission but my learned friend well knows those grounds"). The new rule does enable the learned friend to agree that the rule of secrecy should not apply. However, if he does not, and the court makes an order for costs against the defendant, the defendant will have to hope that he can later apply for that order to be revoked once the issues as to amount have been decided and his offer to settle can be seen to have been a good offer (as to revocation of cost orders, see CL.43).

Note that it is only communications to the trial judge which are prohibited by r.36.13. There is nothing to prevent a claimant mentioning a defendant's

Pt 36 offer on an interim application before a different judge, for example, mentioning it in support of an application for an interim payment (see Ch.25) or to defeat an application for security for costs (see Ch.26).

As to appeals, r.52.12 makes similar provision for secrecy: The fact that a Pt 36 offer has been made must not be disclosed to any judge of the appeal court who is to hear or determine an application for permission to appeal or the appeal itself until all questions (other than costs) have been determined. This rule is subject to express exceptions for cases where disclosure is either necessary or proper for the determination of the appeal or any application in the appeal (for example, where the appeal concerns the Pt 36 offer itself or where the respondent to the appeal has sought security for costs).

The underlying purpose of the rule of secrecy is to prevent a premature disclosure which might unfairly prejudice the trial court's opinion of a claim or an appeal court's opinion of an appeal. The fact that offers to settle have been made and by whom does not truly show the strength or weakness of a case. It mainly shows the strength or weakness of each side's confidence in their case.

If the rule is broken the judge has a discretion whether to continue with the hearing or to recuse himself (i.e. adjourn and order a retrial before a different judge). In *H. v A, The Times,* July 13, 1983, CA, the solicitor broke the rules by failing to delete references to offers to settle which were made in the documents used on the appeal; the appeal was adjourned so as to come before different judges and the solicitor was personally penalised in the costs thrown away (as to the current law of wasted costs orders, see Ch.39). However, in many cases the judge will decide that the breach of the rule has not made a fair trial before him impossible. An important factor against recusal is the delay and extra cost this will cause (*Garratt v Saxby (Practice Note)* [2004] 1 W.L.R. 2152, CA). Another factor is how and why the rule of broken. Parties cannot be permitted to break the rule deliberately simply to get a re-trial (*Gaskins v British Aluminum* [1976] Q.B. 524, CA).

Orders for costs following judgment

29.021 At the end of a trial, or a summary judgment application, the judge will announce his decision, indicating who he thinks has won and who has lost. At this point the claimant's advocate may announce, joyfully or sorrowfully as the case may be, that Pt 36 offers have been made and have or have not been bettered. There are several possibilities: failure to beat the defendant's Pt 36 offers may lead to cost penalties for the claimant; failing to beat the claimant's Pt 36 offers may lead to cost penalties and possibly interest penalties for the defendant. Do not overlook also those circumstances in which the Pt 36 tactics will be irrelevant, for example, where the claim is dismissed or where the claimant is awarded remedies which are worth less than those listed in his offers to settle but are worth more than those listed in the defendant's offers to settle. In these cases the standard orders for costs are likely to be made (as to which, see para.38.008, below).

Where claimant made an offer which was not beaten

29.022 Has the claimant achieved for himself a result which is as good as or is better than the terms he invited the defendant to accept? Sometimes this will be easy to see. For example, *Huck v Robson* [2003] 1 W.L.R. 1340, CA, the defendant rejected the claimant's offer to split liability 95 per cent/5 per cent but the trial judge held the defendant 100 percent liable. In the case of money remedies that include interest some arithmetic may be necessary. Part 36 offers to pay or accept a sum of money are treated as inclusive of interest until the expiry of the relevant period (as to which, see para.29.006). If the court later awarding debt or damages also awards interest it will be necessary to calculate what that interest would have been if the case had settled at the end of the relevant period (*Blackham v Entrepose UK* [2004] EWCA Civ 1109).

In the case of non-money claims it may be more difficult to determine whether the claimant has bettered his own offer. In doing so, the court should not take into account any terms as to costs which the claimant may have offered. In *Mitchell v James* [2004] 1 W.L.R. 158, CA, the claimant sued the defendant for specific performance of an agreement concerning an existing partnership (a firm of accountants) which was later joined as a third party. The claimant made a Pt 36 offer setting out terms including liability for costs—claimant and defendant each to pay their own costs and one-half of the third party's costs. The offer was not accepted and the case went to trial at which the claimant was awarded remedies that were different from those set out in his offer to settle. It was unclear whether the trial award, which the claimant had obtained was better than the terms he had offered unless one brought into account his offer as to costs. The claimant argued that, if his offer as to costs was taken into account, it was plain that the defendant was worse off than he would have been had he accepted the Pt 36 offer. The claimant therefore sought the beneficial orders as to costs and interests which are characteristic of a successful offer by the claimant (see below). The trial judge refused so to order and so did the Court of Appeal.

Enhanced interest and costs

29.023 If the claimant has achieved for himself a result which is as good as or is better than he proposed in his offer the court may award him interest at a rate not exceeding 10 per cent above base rate on the whole or Pt of any sum of money (excluding interest) awarded to him for some or all of the period starting with the date on which the relevant period expired (see generally r.36.14). This is often referred to as "enhanced interest". In addition, the court may also award the claimant his costs on the indemnity basis (for a definition of which, see Ch.38) from the same date and may also award enhanced interest on those costs.

In *Petrotrade Inc v Texaco Ltd* [2002] 1 W.L.R. 947, CA, the Court of Appeal emphasised the importance of awarding these incentives to claimants where it is appropriate to do so. As to the rate of enhanced interest to allow, the court made it clear that 10 per cent is the maximum enhancement, it is not the starting point. In deciding what rate to allow the court should take into account the value of the claim.

> "If a claim is small, enhanced interest has to be at a higher rate than if the claim is large, otherwise the additional advantage for the claimant will not be achieved" (*per* Lord Woolf M.R.)

This was a Commercial Court case in which, at the time, the normal rate of interest was one percent above base rate. The claimant offered to accept approximately US$143,000 and later obtained judgment for approximately US$150,000. The Court of Appeal allowed interest at 4 per cent above base rate for the appropriate period and costs on the indemnity basis. In *R. v Bryn Alyn Community (Holdings) Ltd* [2003] EWCA Civ 383, the Court of Appeal applied the same principles to enhanced interest on costs. As a general rule, the claimant should be allowed interest at the appropriate rate (in this case also 4 per cent above base rate) from the date the costs were incurred (which will usually be treated as the date when the work was done or the liability for disbursements was incurred). The enhanced interest awarded on the money compensation and the costs should run only until the date of the judgment. From that date judgment interest will begin (see further Ch.3).

Special factors arise where the claim is for libel or slander or where the claim is funded by a CFA with success fees (as to which, see Ch.38). In *McPhilemy v Times Newspapers Ltd (No.2)* [2003] 1 W.L.R. 934 CA, the claimants, suing for libel, offered to accept £50,000 and the case went to trial by jury who awarded £145,000. It was held that a jury award should be treated as inclusive of interest and therefore it would be unjust to order interest on that award at an enhanced rate or at any rate. However, the claimant was allowed costs on the indemnity basis with interest on those costs at the rate of 4 per cent over base rate from the date the costs were incurred until the date of judgment.

If the claim was funded by a CFA with success fees, any enhanced interest on costs will also be payable on the success fee. Since, in the nature of things, that will not have been paid in advance, the court should not award interest from the date before the date of the order or, if it does so, the existence of the success fee should be taken into account in fixing the rate (*Montlake v Lambert Smith Hampton Group Ltd* [2004] EWHC 1503 (Comm); *CEL Group Ltd v Nedlloyd Lines UK Ltd* [2003] EWCA Civ 1716(2), in which the enhanced interest was reduced to two percent above base rate.

It is convenient to mention here two cases in which the court will not award enhanced interest or enhanced costs. Rule 36.3(4) states that a Pt 36 offer shall have the consequences set out in Pt 36 only in relation to the costs of proceedings in respect of which it is made, and not in relation to costs any appeal from the final decision in those proceedings. Thus, for example, where a claimant who has received enhanced interest and enhanced costs in respect of a trial decision will not receive the same advantages in respect of an unsuccessful appeal against that decision unless he made a new offer to settle the appeal proceedings.

Secondly, the court will not award enhanced costs or interest where "it considers it unjust to do so" (r.36.14(3)). Rule 36.14(4) states that, when considering whether it will be unjust to award such enhancements the court will take into account all the circumstances of the case including:

"(a) the terms of any Part 36 offer;
(b) the stage in the proceedings when any Part 36 offer was made, including in particular how long before the trial started the offer was made;
(c) the information available to the parties at the time when the Part 36 offer was made; and
(d) the conduct of the parties with regards to the giving or refusing to give information for the purposes of enabling the offer to be made or evaluated."

In *Kastor Navigation Co. Ltd v Axa Global Risks UK Ltd* [2004] EWCA Civ 277, the claimants recovered at trial the full amount of their claim (over US$3 million) having previously offered to settle for a lesser sum (US$2.8 million). Nevertheless, most of the case had been taken up by their pursuing an expensive argument which the trial judge considered had never had any serious prospects of success. The Court of Appeal held that the proper order to make was no order for costs thereby leaving each side to bear its own costs of the trial.

Where defendant made an offer which was not beaten

As to what is meant by beating an offer to pay money (e.g. the need to calculate interest thereon) see para.29.022, above. If, despite the offer of compromise he received, the claimant goes on to judgment, wins but does not win more than he was offered, the claimant is regarded, for the purposes of costs, as the loser for the latter part of the proceedings. The court will normally order him to pay the defendant's costs incurred from the last day of the relevant period (as to which see para.29.006, above) and interest on those costs (see generally r.36.14(2)). Although this is not mentioned in the rules, the court will usually order the defendant to pay the claimant's costs incurred in the earlier part of the proceedings. Since these two costs orders are made together and cover the whole period of the proceedings they are sometimes referred to collectively as "a split order for costs".

The court will not order the claimant to pay any of the defendant's costs if "it considers it unjust to do so" and r.36.14(4) states that, when considering whether to withhold the benefits, the court will take into account all the circumstances of the case including four specified circumstances which we have quoted in para.29.023, above. Paragraph (a) "the terms of any Pt 36 offer" is illustrated by *Factortame Ltd v Secretary of State for the Environment, Transport and the Regions* [2002] 1 W.L.R. 2438, in which it was said that, in heavy and complex litigation it may be unfair to expect a claimant to be able to properly consider an offer to settle within the normal 21 day period.

29.024

Factortame and *Ford v G.K.R. Construction Ltd* [2000] 1 W.L.R. 1397, CA, both illustrate paras (d) "the conduct of the parties with regard to the giving or refusing of information". In *Ford* a claimant was allowed to recover her costs in full even though she had failed to accept a defendant's offer (paid into court) which was some £6,000 to £10,000 more than she was eventually awarded. She had honestly overestimated the value of her claim and the defendant did not seek the evidence by which they reduced her award until an extremely late stage, during an adjournment of the trial.

Paragraph (b) of r.36.14(4) "the stage in the proceedings in which any Pt 36 offer was made, including in particular how long before the trial started the offer was made" indicates that the rule makers think that the standard split order for costs may not be appropriate in the case of offers made at a very late stage. Consider, for example, a claimant who fails to accept what turns out to be a high offer which was made just before the trial began. He is likely to say that his refusal or failure to consider that offer properly at that stage was reasonable. He will no doubt seek to poor scorn on the defendant's policy of leaving it so late before making such a good offer. On the other hand, the defendant may seek to show that the claimant would not have accepted the offer even if it had been made earlier (for a pre-CPR authority, see *King v Weston Howell* [1989] 1 W.L.R. 579, CA, and consider also the detailed facts of *Charles v NTL Group Ltd* [2002] EWCA Civ 2004).

Even if the court does consider it just to make a costs order against the claimant, it need not order him to pay all of the defendant's costs. In *Johnson v Gore Wood & Co. (No.2)* [2004] EWCA Civ 14, the defendants made a Pt 36 offer of (and, in accordance with the rules then in force, paid into court) £750,000 and the claimant failed to recover more than £170,000. Nevertheless, the Court of Appeal ordered the defendants to pay the claimant's costs up to the last day of the relevant period and ordered the claimant to pay only 50 per cent of the defendants' costs from that date. This was so even though the claimant had grossly exaggerated his claim right from the beginning (he valued it in millions).

> "[16] However, we are satisfied that it would be unjust to order Mr Johnson to pay all Gore Wood's costs after the date of payment in... we take account of the way in which Gore Wood conducted the trial. The judge noted that every issue had been contested. For instance, the terms of the loans, which had not been an issue in the Company action, were disputed in these proceedings albeit that the proceedings were effectively between the same parties. [Counsel for the claimant] also referred to the cross-examination of, for instance, Mr Johnson's wife. We note that the trial timetable was considerably extended by the cross-examination of Mr Johnson's witnesses... we also take account of the circumstances of the claim and the litigation history. In all the circumstances, doing the best we can, we consider that the right order would be for Mr Johnson to pay only 50 percent of Gore Wood's costs as from the last date [of the relevant period]." (Arden L.J., giving the judgment of the court)

CHAPTER 30

Disclosure and Inspection

INTRODUCTION

"In plain language, litigation in this country is conducted 'cards face up on the table'. Some people from other lands regard this as incomprehensible. 'Why', they ask, 'should I be expected to provide my opponent with the means of defeating me?' The answer, of course, is that litigation is not a war or even a game. It is designed to do real justice between opposing parties and, if the court does not have all the relevant information, it cannot achieve this object" (per Sir John Donaldson M.R. in *Davies v Eli Lilly & Co.* [1987] 1 W.L.R. 428).

30.001

The pre-action protocols (see para.6.013) require the parties to prospective litigation to consider at a very early stage the documentary evidence that is available. However, there is no obligation on a party to place any "cards face up on the table" that are adverse to his own position. The claimant can request that the defendant disclose documents that he would normally show during court proceedings but the only way to compel that disclosure is by way of court order (see para.30.024 below). Therefore, prior to a claim form being issued, the parties can to a large extent select those cards they wish to play and keep all the others hidden.

Disclosure and inspection, as part of the litigation process, provide for far more that just the pre-trial revelation of evidence that each party intends to rely on at the trial itself. As a general rule, a party must disclose those documents he has or has had under his control that he intends to rely on or which adversely affect his own case. He must place these "face up on the table" by specifically describing each in a prescribed list. He must then allow the other side the opportunity to inspect the contents of those documents or to take copies. The main purpose of disclosure is to enable the parties to evaluate better the strength of their case in advance of the trial and so to promote the compromise of disputes and the saving of costs. Many actions settle after disclosure has taken place. The process causes the parties to concentrate their minds on the issues in question and often gives their solicitors an opportunity to meet and talk casually about settlement.

The following are exceptions, dealt with below, to the general rule of disclosure:

(1) The court may order that a party can withhold disclosure of a document on the ground that disclosure would damage the public interest.
(2) A party may claim that it would be disproportionate to the issues in the case to permit inspection of certain documents.
(3) A party may claim that a document is privileged from inspection.

THE MEANING OF DISCLOSURE (R.31.2).

30.002 A party discloses a document by stating that the document exists or has existed. However, there are two possible ways of disclosing the existence of a document, namely generally or specifically. Let us continue with the analogy of playing cards. Imagine a pack of cards is spread out over a table face down. You can see 52 cards. You would describe each generally as "a playing card". Only when a card is turned over to be face up do you know its actual value. You can then specifically describe it as, for example, "the two of diamonds" or whatever.

STANDARD DISCLOSURE (R.31.5)

30.003 Claims dealt with on the small claims track have their own basic disclosure rules (see para.20.004).

When a case is allocated to the fast track (see Ch.21) or multi-track (see Ch.22) the court may order that the parties give "standard disclosure". Rule 31.6 provides that standard disclosure requires a party to disclose the following types of documents:

(a) The documents on which he relies.
(b) The documents which:

1. Adversely affect his own case.

Example

In *Board v Thomas Hedley & Co.* [1951] 2 All E.R. 431 the claimant sought damages from the defendants, alleging that they had manufactured and sold a dangerous cleaning product which she had used and as a result had contracted dermatitis on both hands. The defendants disclosed all complaints received by them about the product up to May 18, 1950, the date when the claimant bought the product (see further below).

2. Adversely affect another party's case. Most of these documents will usually advance the party's own case, but not always.
3. Support another party's case.

Examples

In *Board v Thomas Hedley & Co.* (see above) the claimant sought specific disclosure (see below) of the complaints received by the defendants after May 18, 1950. The Court of Appeal held that an important issue was whether the product was dangerous. On that issue evidence that subsequent users had suffered from dermatitis would be admissible, and, therefore, documents relating to such later complaints might enable the claimant to advance her case, and so were relevant and ought to be disclosed insofar as they related to "complaints of personal injuries". Lord Denning said:

> "The relevant information with regard to [the complaints] is all in the hands of the defendants, and justice requires that the [claimant] should be put in possession of it also so that she can present her case on equal terms".

In *Manatee Towing Company v Oceanbulk Maritime SA and McQuilling Brokerage Partners Inc.*, [1999] 1 Lloyd's Rep. 876, *McQuilling* had assisted in negotiations for the purchase of a ship by the defendants from the claimants. The defendants alleged that a contract had resulted at an advantageous price. The claimants' action was for a declaration that there had been no concluded contract. The defendants counterclaimed for a declaration and alternatively against *McQuilling* for damages for breach of warranty of authority. The claimants made no quantified claim against *McQuilling* at that stage. McQuilling wished to put the defendants to proof of their loss and applied for disclosure from the claimants as de facto owners of the ship, of documents relating to the ship's condition. Mr Justice Rix said that it was common ground that there was no issue of quantum between the claimants and *McQuilling*, only between *McQuilling* and the defendants. However, the documents requested were relevant to the issue of quantum between the defendants and *McQuilling*. The documents could support *McQuilling*'s case and *McQuilling* was entitled to be put in a position where it could defend itself on quantum.

To decide if a document falls within the scope of standard disclosure a party must ascertain what issues are in dispute in the case. As to issue identification see para.22.003.

(c) The documents that he is required to disclose by any relevant practice direction. We understand that in due course PD 31 may specify what particular documents should be disclosed in particular types of cases. The personal injury pre-action protocol already provides some suggested lists of documents to be disclosed in certain cases (see para.6.017).

As a general rule standard disclosure is obtainable only against persons who are properly joined as parties to an action. Information cannot be obtained from strangers to the dispute except by calling them as witnesses at the trial. This is often called the "mere witness rule". However, there are two major exceptions to the rule, namely (1) disclosure of documents required from non-parties pursuant to SCA 1981, s.34 and CCA 1984, s.53; and (2) disclosure of information under the principle established in the case of *Norwich Pharmacal v Customs and Excise* [1974] A.C. 133. Both of these matters are dealt with below at paras 30.023 and 30.025, respectively.

WHAT IS A "DOCUMENT"? (R.31.4)

30.004   A document is anything in which information of any description is recorded, for example, audio tape (*Grant v Southwestern and County Properties* [1975] Ch.185) a computer database (*Derby & Co. Ltd v Weldon (No.9)* [1991] 1 W.L.R. 652) and a video tape (see *Rall v Hume* [2001] 3 All E.R. 248).

What everyday electronic documents do most of us already take for granted? Emails, DVDs, CCTV footage, CD-ROMS, digital camera pictures, voicemail messages, instant messages received on-line? But do we understand the technology behind these? How is electronic documentation created and stored? Parties to litigation and their solicitors must grapple with this question. Here are a just few pointers. When you look at a computer screen you are observing what is called active or online data. This is ultimately stored, such as the material that you put in a file or the contents of your inbox and sent items in the e-mail system. Embedded or metadata is what you cannot normally see, even when an electronic document is printed. But the computer program will normally store information about when each file was created, when it was edited, by whom, and who has accessed it. Replicant data is automatically created by a computer, it's the automatic back up feature. In addition there is back-up data held in a storage system. Most organisations (and many individuals these days) use a back-up system to preserve information in case of a disaster. Finally, residual data is the material you thought you had got rid of! Hitting the delete button will only remove a file or e-mail etc from your active data. You will find that it is stored elsewhere on the database and can usually be retrieved.

Note that by r.31.10 a party does not have to disclose more than one copy of a document. Rule 31.4 defines a copy of a document as being anything onto which information recorded in the document has been copied, by whatever means and whether directly or indirectly. However, where a copy of a document contains a modification, obliteration or other feature on which a party intends to rely; or which adversely affects his own case or another party's case or supports another party's case; that must be treated as a separate disclosable document.

DOCUMENTS UNDER A PARTY'S "CONTROL" (R.31.8)

A party only has to disclose a document that is, or has been, under his "control", that is to say: 30.005

   (a)   It is or was in his physical possession. This, arguably, includes documents of a company held by a director or an employee.

   (b)   He has or has had a right to possession of it. This includes documents in the possession of a bailee or agent. A principal also has a right to documents relating to acts done in his name during an agency and after it has terminated in the absence of any express exclusion to the contrary (see *Yasuda Fire & Marine Co. of Europe Ltd v Orion Marine Insurance Underwriting Agency Ltd* [1995] Q.B. 174).

   (c)   He has or has had a right to inspect or take copies of it, for example, medical records.

THE SOLICITOR'S ROLE IN DISCLOSURE

From the very outset the solicitor must consider and advise upon disclosure (see para.6.009). The client must appreciate the extent of his obligation and the importance of not destroying documents that might have to be disclosed. In *Rockwell Machine Tool Co. Ltd v E. P. Barrus (Concessionaires) Ltd* [1968] 1 W.L.R. 693 Megarry J. who heard the case said: 30.005A

> "Two matters which in particular disturbed me were these. First, there was a witness for a defendant who, in response to a question in cross-examination, readily undertook to make a transatlantic call and the next day announced that documents of prima facie relevance were being dispatched by airmail. This at least suggests that the process of [disclosure] had not been complete. No doubt last-minute disclosure is better than none at all: but the [claimants] were entitled to see the documents and consider their effect in advance of the hearing, and not be reduced to prising information out of witnesses under cross-examination and then considering what was disclosed after the [claimants] had closed their case and some ten days of the hearing had elapsed. Secondly, it appeared from evidence for the defendants that between the issue of [proceedings] and the hearing, one of the defendants had been carrying on with its routine process of destroying documents seven years old, even though these probably included documents which ought to have been disclosed".

Indeed, the solicitor owes a duty to the court to examine his client's documents himself to ensure that proper disclosure is made and not leave the matter to a clerk (see *Woods v Martin's Bank* [1959] 1 Q.B. 55). If the client will not permit this, or insists on giving imperfect disclosure, the solicitor must withdraw from the case (see *Myers v Elman* [1940] A.C. 282). It is important for a solicitor to emphasise to a client that if he destroys disclosable documents deliberately and contumaciously or such that a fair trial is rendered impossible, his statement of case is likely to be struck out(see *Douglas v Hello! Ltd (No.3)* [2003] EWHC 55; [2003] 1 All E.R. 1087) and/or contempt of court proceedings may be taken (see *Prest v Marc Rich & Co. Investment AG* [2006] EWHC 927).

SEARCHING FOR STANDARD DISCLOSURE DOCUMENTS (R.31.7)

30.006 In order to give standard disclosure a party is required to make a "reasonable search" for documents falling within r.31.6(b) and (c). The factors relevant in deciding the reasonableness of a search include:

(a) the number of documents involved;
(b) the nature and complexity of the proceedings;
(c) the ease and expense of retrieval of any particular document; and
(d) the significance of any document which is likely to be located during the search.

PD 31, para.2 reminds parties to bear in mind the overriding principle of proportionality. It may therefore be reasonable to decide not to search for documents coming into existence before some particular date, or to limit the search to documents in some particular place or places, or to documents falling into particular categories. Consider the case of *Forrester v British Railways Board, The Times*, April 8, 1996, where C claimed damages in negligence against D following the death of her nine-year-old daughter when she fell onto the track from a moving train. C sought specific disclosure (see para.30.021 below) of: (1) investigations by D into 324 deaths and non-fatal accidents due to falls from trains between 1972 and 1990; (2) the papers, reports, and memoranda provided to the Health and Safety Executive and another company in relation to the compilation of reports by them into the safety of the door mechanisms; (3) the documents concerning all maintenance, repairs and service records on all doors on all Inter-City trains; (4) reports of incidents involving the opening of doors while trains were in motion, be they suicides or not; (5) reports on failures of all doors, hinge equipment and securing devices; and (6) reports of claims by passengers or staff who had fallen from moving trains.

The Court of Appeal said that the width of C's request was staggering. The classes of documents sought were far too wide, in other words, there was no need for D to search for them in the first place. D did not have to disclose documents relating to different hinges from the one involved in the incident nor documents relating to incidents of a different nature, including suicide attempts.

With increasing amount of documents being stored electronically, it is often neither feasible or possible for most parties to litigation to review all data from their computer systems for disclosure purposes. Individuals, firms and companies need to consider what management systems they use and the way in which records are stored. So how should a party set about complying with its disclosure obligations in relation to electronic documents? Start by identifying how many documents have been created by electronic means. Then see if these have been preserved and where they are stored. The key task then is to retrieve, and search for, any further relevant electronic documents. A key word search can often be used to narrow down the number of documents to be searched.

Beware that the following are typical areas of dispute between parties. The number of individuals to be included in the search; how many replicated versions of a document should be searched for; what key words should be used for the search; whether a party should search just in its email folders, or whether the search should extend to word document systems, accounting and other databases, lap top computers and PDAs; how many business locations and departments should be searched; what back-up tapes should be selected; how a search for residual data should be carried out.

See further para.30.008 below.

LIMITED OR EXTENDED DISCLOSURE?

The court seeks to ensure that any disclosure ordered is tailored to the requirements of the case and is no wider than appropriate. Anything more extensive than standard disclosure must always be justified (see below). But the court may consider that even standard disclosure across the whole spectrum of a case is wider than required. The parties and the court need to consider if it is feasible to limit disclosure by use of sampling methods or by requiring disclosure simply of a sufficient number of documents to show a specified matter. Also, the court asks if disclosure can be avoided by requiring a party to provide information under Pt 18 (see para.32.001). 30.007

The overriding objective (see Ch.1) includes, so far as is practicable, dealing with a case in a way that is proportionate to four factors: (a) the amount of money involved; (b) the importance of the case; (c) the complexity of the issues; and (d) the financial position of each party. A limited or extended amount of disclosure may be proportionate by reference to such matters.

In a road traffic accident case the court often orders, or the parties agree, that there is no need for the defendant to give any disclosure as he is unlikely to have any relevant documents, save those that are privileged from inspection (see para.30.013 below). However, if there is a dispute about the point of impact, the defendant's documents identifying the nature, extent and location of damage to his vehicle normally form part of standard disclosure. Likewise, if the claimant alleges that the defendant's vehicle was defective, or the defendant claims that an unforeseen defect caused or contributed to the accident, the defendant's vehicle maintenance records are disclosable.

Problems as to the extent of disclosure of the claimant's medical records in a personal injury action sometimes arise. However, it appears to have become fairly settled practice that all the records must be disclosed if that is necessary for the fair disposal of the action (see *Steele v Moule* (1999) C.L. May 23 and the cases cited therein). Note that such disclosure may be on terms (see para.30.016 below) and account should be taken of the Law Society agreement to limit the request for medical records (see para.6.017).

When is it appropriate for the court to order more than standard disclosure? The following categories of cases are given in the Commercial Court Guide by way of example: where fraud, dishonesty or misrepresentation is alleged; or where knowledge or the lack of it, or disclosure or non-disclosure, is in issue. In such instances a party may be able persuade the judge that a fuller understanding of the history of events in the case, or of the states of mind of those concerned, is vital to enable the court to dispose of the case justly.

By r.31.12(2) the court may direct that a party must carry out a particular type of search and disclose all documents located as a result, for example:

> "on or before September 12, 2007 the defendant shall carry out a thorough search for all documents relevant to the issues in the case, including for the avoidance of doubt, all documents which may lead to a train of inquiry enabling a party to advance his own case or damage that of his opponent".

This type of order is rare and derives from the very wide definition given to disclosure pre-CPR established by the case of *Cie Financiére et Commerciale du Pacifique v Peruvian Guano Co.* (1883) 11 Q.B.D. 55. Contrast this order, which, in effect, directs a party to search for any document that might shed light upon an issue in the case with rr.31.6 and 31.7.

DRAFTING A STANDARD DISCLOSURE LIST OF DOCUMENTS

30.008 The relevant practice form is N265. On the first page it commences with a "Disclosure Statement" which reads:

> "I state that I have carried out a reasonable and proportionate search to locate all the documents which I am required to disclose under the order made by the court on (date)."

We discussed above the duty to search. If a party did not search for particular documents created before a certain date or did not search in a particular location or category, he must say so, for example,

> "I did not search for documents—
> 1. pre-dating 2003;
> 2. located elsewhere than the defendant's records office at 2 The Wishing Tree, Westbourne, Mythshire;
> 3. in categories other than maintenance and repair records required for the defendant's operator's licence."

Practice Direction 31, para.4.2(2) provides that when setting out the extent of the search a party should:

> "draw attention to any particular limitations ... which were adopted for proportionality reasons and give the reasons why the limitations were adopted, for example, the difficulty or expense that a search not subject to those limitations would have entailed or the marginal relevance of categories of documents omitted from the search".

The form also requires the party to state the extent to which it has searched for electronic documents. The details of any key word search used to narrow down the number of documents searched for must be given.

The maker of the statement must then certify that he understands the duty of disclosure, that such has been discharged and that the list is complete. Note that proceedings for contempt of court may be brought against a person if he makes, or causes to be made, a false disclosure statement, without an honest belief in its truth.

Who should sign the statement? It must be the party or his litigation friend. A party's solicitor cannot sign. By PD 31, para.4.7 an insurer or the MIB may sign a disclosure statement on behalf of a party where it has a financial interest in the result of the proceedings brought wholly or partially by or against that party. Where the party is a company, firm, association or other organisation (including an insurer or the MIB), the statement must identify who has signed and explain why he is the appropriate person to do so. There is no reason why that should not be a person who can make a statement of truth (see para.12.004).

Solicitors should discuss with their commercial clients the need to appoint "disclosure officers" who are suitably trained to identify and collect the required documents and thereby able to make the disclosure statement that to the best of their knowledge the duty of disclosure has been discharged.

The final page of the practice form is divided into three separate lists of documents:

The first list. Here the party must list and number, in a convenient order, the documents in his control which he does not object to being inspected. As to the grounds for objecting to inspection, see below. If documents are of a similar nature, for example, letters, invoices, etc. they should be bundled together. The party should specifically disclose each document or bundle by giving it a short description so that it can be identified. The party receiving the list can then decide whether or not they wish to inspect the document or have a copy of it. If the document is being kept elsewhere, for example, with a bank or solicitors, this should also be stated. PD 31, para.3.2 states that the documents should normally be listed in date order, numbered consecutively and given a concise description, for example, "letter, claimant to defendant [dated]". Note that for over 100 years now parties have been penalised in costs if their descriptions of documents were unnecessarily long-winded (*Hill v Hart-Davis* (1884) 4 Q.B.D. 470).

What if a party does not wish a part of a document that is irrelevant to be inspected? That part may be blanked out but this should be stated in the list, for example, "entries in defendant's sales ledger for March 27, 2005 save those which are blanked out" (see *GE Capital Corporate Finance Group v Bankers Trust Co.* [1995] 1 W.L.R. 172).

The second list. Here, the party must first list and number the documents in his control which he objects to being inspected. The party should generally disclose these documents, for example, "confidential correspondence between the claimant and his solicitors"; "various experts reports and witness statements", etc. It is quite proper to do this. The existence of the document has been disclosed and so the duty to give disclosure is thereby discharged. However, the general description ensures that the contents are not indirectly revealed.

The objections to inspection must be stated. A legitimate ground must be claimed. It is not a ground of objection that the document is adverse to the party's case. For examples of different possible grounds, see below. In practice, the most common objection is based on legal professional privilege. For example, as to the confidential correspondence between the claimant and his solicitors, the objection might be stated as "these documents were created for the sole purpose of giving or obtaining legal advice and are by their nature privileged from inspection". If different grounds are relied on for different documents they should be arranged and listed in separate bundles.

Should the parties group all the "without prejudice" (see para.6.024) letters and copy letters together and list them here? In most cases there is no advantage in doing so; all the parties to the action will have participated in such correspondence and so will have a complete set of letters and copy letters on file. There is an advantage to listing them here if you want to keep the contents of them secret from any other parties to the action who have not participated in that correspondence.

Examples

In *Rush & Tompkins Ltd v Greater London Council* [1989] A.C. 1280 the claimants negotiated a compromise with the first defendant but the action was still proceedings against a second defendant. The claimants listed their "without prejudice" correspondence with the first defendant in this part of their list claiming privilege from inspection by the second defendant. That was upheld on appeal.

In the multi-party action of *Vickers Shipbuilding & Engineering Ltd v Cape Contracts Plc* (1998) C.L.Y. 338, V issued third party proceedings (see Ch.18) against both N and C. A confidential compromise was reached between V and N and that led to a stay of the proceedings between them. C applied for an order for disclosure of that compromise. V resisted the application, arguing that the agreement was privileged from inspection by C and, in any event, irrelevant. Judge Kershaw Q.C., sitting in the Queen's Bench Division, dismissed the application. The judge held that whilst the compromise was not irrelevant, without prejudice communications between parties should be protected from inspection by other parties in the same litigation. C could claim a contribution (see Ch.18) from N, who remained a party to the action, and N would not be able to rely against C on its agreement with V.

Should disclosure be given of documents in respect of which a genuine doubt arises as to whether or not they fall within r.31.6? In complex multi-party litigation it may well be difficult to say if a document does, for example, adversely affect or support another party's case. The most advisable course is to give disclosure of every document unless it clearly does not fall within the definition of standard disclosure. Group any doubtful documents together in convenient bundles, list them here and specify the claim of irrelevancy. The solicitor's duty to the court has been described above. Moreover, if a party is silent now what response can he make to an application for specific disclosure (see para.30.021 below) of such documents? His failure to deal with these matters in his list of documents is going to appear suspicious, possibly even slippery.

The third list. Here the party should list and number the documents that have been, but are not now, in his control. This often comprises little more than the original letters, written by or on behalf of the party, copies of which have already been detailed in the first list. In respect of each document it is necessary to state when it was last in the party's control and where it is now. The purpose is to enable the parties receiving the list to continue their investigations elsewhere. If they can locate the present whereabouts of the documents they may be able to obtain copies on an application for disclosure by a non-party (see below). See further *Punjab National Bank v Jain* [2004] EWCA Civ 589; [2004] All E.R. (D) 01 (May).

A CONTINUING DUTY (R.31.33 AND PD 31, PARA.3.3)

The duty of disclosure continues until the proceedings in which the order was made are concluded. If after serving his list a party becomes aware of further documents that should have been disclosed, he must immediately notify all the other parties by preparing and serving a supplemental list of those documents. We recommend that the last page of Form N265 is adapted for this purpose.

30.009

Example

In *Vernon v Bosley (No.2)* [1997] 3 W.L.R. 683, the claimant had witnessed unsuccessful attempts to rescue his two daughters from a motor car which had plunged into a river while being driven by the defendant, their nanny. After the accident his mental condition deteriorated, his business failed, he was unable to obtain any other employment and his marriage broke down. He brought an action against the defendant claiming damages in respect of nervous shock or psychiatric injury sustained when he witnessed the aftermath of the accident. The judge found the defendant liable although he rejected the claim for failure of the business on the basis that it would have failed in any event. The defendant appealed. The Court of Appeal affirmed the decision although it reduced the award. However, the defendant's counsel then received anonymously through the post copies of a county court judgment in earlier family proceedings between the claimant and his wife which included two medical reports which stated that the claimant's psychiatric health had dramatically improved and that he was substantially, if not fully, recovered. The claimant's advisers knew of the changed prognosis before the judge gave judgment in the personal injury claim, although on their advice that prognosis was not communicated to the judge nor to the Court of Appeal and it was unknown to the defendant's advisers.

The Court of Appeal held that a party to civil litigation was under a continuing obligation until the conclusion of proceedings to disclose all relevant documents whenever they came into his possession, unless they were clearly privileged from disclosure, notwithstanding that disclosure by list had already been made. Where, therefore, a document was disclosed to a party after he had closed his case, or the evidence as a whole was concluded, he should apply to the court to reopen the case in the light of the disclosure if the document was of real significance and there was otherwise a risk of injustice. It followed that the existence of the two medical reports should have been disclosed to the defendant's advisers before the judge gave judgment. Also see *Stocznia Gdanska SA v Latvian Shipping Co.* (2001) L.T.L. February 12.

PRIVILEGE FROM DISCLOSURE (R.31.19(1))

30.010 Any person may apply to the court, without notice to any party, for an order permitting him to withhold disclosure of a document on the ground that its disclosure would damage the public interest. The starting point is whether or not disclosure is necessary for either the fair disposal of the case or to save costs. If so the judge should then examine the documents before making any order. He should then consider whether the documents belong to a class protected by public interest immunity (see *Kelly v Commissioner of Police of the Metropolis, The Times*, August 20, 1997). Where the documents fall within a protected class, the court should consider if the documents contain something of real use to a party. Where they do, the court should examine the documents to decide whether the need to do justice between the parties outweighs the need for the proper protection of the public interest (see *Goodridge v Chief Constable of Hampshire Constabulary* [1999] 1 All E.R. 896 also discussed at para.30.015). See also *Carnduff v Inspector Rook* (2001) L.T.L. May 11.

INSPECTION

30.011 A party is entitled to inspect the contents of the documents in the first list of the other parties. "Inspection" means examination and is not confined to mere ocular inspection (*Grant v Southwestern and County Properties* [1975] Ch.185). By r.31.15 a party must give written notice of his wish to inspect a document to the disclosing party who, in return, must permit inspection within seven days after the date of receiving the notice. In addition, if a party requests a copy of a document and undertakes to pay the reasonable copying costs, the disclosing party must provide that copy within seven days after receiving the request.

If another party wishes to physically inspect documents ensure you carefully make available only those which were in your first list and not any for which privilege from inspection was claimed. Ideally the person carrying out inspection should be supervised at all times.

Should you simply request that the disclosing party sends to you copies of all documents that are open to inspection? Unless the documents are very few in number, arguably not. But careful consideration must be given as to whether it is reasonable to incur the cost of inspection by a solicitor, agents or a party. However, you need to also bear in mind that when inspecting a document things may be apparent that would not otherwise be seen on a photocopy, for example, creases, punctures made by pins, staples or paper clips which indicate that another document may have been attached at one time. In addition, the person given the task of preparing photocopies may not carry it out meticulously; parts of the document may be omitted or words written on the reverse side may be accidentally missed.

When you are reviewing electronic documents that the other side will be entitled to inspect you should at the same time consider how inspection will take place. Should the electronic documents be printed onto paper? If so, should the embedded data (the creation date, author, edit dates etc) be included? Alternatively, should the documents be produced electronically? But is your opponent's system compatible? If the documents are produced electronically, how are you going to eliminate irrelevant, confidential or privileged parts of documents?

The key is to anticipate potential problems. Prior to allocation, discuss any issues that may arise regarding searches for and the preservation of electronic documents with the other side. Swap information about the categories of electronic documents within your control, the computer systems, electronic devices and media on which any relevant documents may be held, the storage systems used and document retention policies. Where difficulties or disagreement arise, refer these to a judge for directions at the earliest practical date.

As a general rule there is no obligation on a party giving disclosure of a document in a foreign language to provide a translation of it (see *Bayer AG v Harris Pharmaceuticals Ltd* [1991] F.S.R. 170). However, in light of *Maltez v Lewis*, *The Times*, April 28, 1999, if the party giving that disclosure has a disproportionately deeper pocket than the recipient, the court might place upon him the burden of providing translations. See further *Sumitomo Corp. v Credit Lyonnais Rouse Ltd* [2002] 4 All E.R. 68, where the court had to determine whether the claimant had a claim to legal professional privilege in order to withhold from inspection some 700 documents that were English translations of Japanese originals. The Japanese originals were in the control of the claimant and unprivileged. Whilst the translations had been made to assist its lawyers, the court ordered disclosure of the translations (also see para.30.013 below).

LIMITING INSPECTION ("THE DISPROPORTIONATE GROUND") (R.31.3(2))

30.012 A party is not required to permit inspection of any category or class of documents that he considers would be disproportionate to the issues in the case. However, he must state that ground in his disclosure statement (see above). It is not necessary to give any supporting arguments but any other party may challenge the claim on application to the court for specific inspection (see para.30.021 below). How might the ground be justified?

Example

(1) The documents are of negligible probative value: (2) the documents are of no or negligible relevance: (3) inspection is unnecessary for the fair determination of any of the issues in the case: (4) to permit inspection will be onerous as it will involve extensive editing of a great deal of the material if it is relevant: and (5) the documents are confidential (see *Dolling-Baker v Merrett* [1991] 2 All E.R. 890 at 897).

PRIVILEGE FROM INSPECTION

30.013 Even if a document is disclosable, it may be possible to claim a privilege from inspection. There is no privilege simply because the document is unfavourable.

Legal professional privilege

It has long been established that "individuals should be able to consult their lawyers in the certain knowledge that what they tell their lawyers and the advice they receive from their lawyers, whether orally or in writing, will be immune from compulsory disclosure" (*per* Sir Richard Scott V.C. in *Re Barings Plc* [1998] 1 All E.R. 673 and see the cases cited therein). The rule that confidential communications between a client and his legal advisers are privileged is not confined to communications between lay persons and their solicitors. It extends to communications with salaried legal advisers and foreign lawyers and can apply to communications between officers of Customs and Excise and their own internal legal department (see *Alfred Crompton Amusement Machines Ltd v Customs and Excise (No.2)* [1973] 2 All E.R. 1169).

The scope of what is often called legal advice privilege was clarified to some extent by the House of Lords in *Three Rivers District Council v Governor and Company of the Bank of England (No.4)* [2004] UKHL 48; [2004] 3 W.L.R. 1274. The House accepted that legal advice is not confined to telling the client the law; it must include advice as to what should prudently and sensibly be done in the relevant legal (public or private law) context. There must be a "relevant legal context" in order for the advice to attract legal professional privilege. As Lord Scott explained (at para.38).

"If a solicitor becomes the client's 'man of business', and some solicitors do, responsible for advising the client on all matters of business, including investment policy, finance policy and other business matters, the advice may lack a relevant legal context. There is, in my opinion, no way of avoiding difficulty in deciding in marginal cases whether the seeking of advice from or the giving of advice by lawyers does or does not take place in a relevant legal context so as to attract legal advice privilege. In cases of doubt the judge called upon to make the decision should ask whether the advice relates to the rights, liabilities, obligations or remedies of the client either under private law or under public law. If it does not, then, in my opinion, legal advice privilege would not apply. If it does so relate then, in my opinion, the judge should ask himself whether the communication falls within the policy underlying the justification for legal advice privilege in our law. Is the occasion on which the communication takes place and is the purpose for which it takes place such as to make it reasonable to expect the privilege to apply? The criterion must, in my opinion, be an objective one."

Who is the solicitor's "client" for the purposes of legal advice privilege? One of the matters debated at the Court of Appeal hearing that led to the *Three Rivers (No.4)* judgment was whether, or which, communications between the Bank's solicitors and the Bank employees or ex-employees, or officers or ex-officers, could qualify for legal advice privilege. It was accepted that communications between the lawyers and third parties could not qualify. The Court of Appeal held that only communications between the Bank's solicitors and the Bank's Bingham Inquiry Unit could qualify. All other communications had to be disclosed. This was not an issue which arose for decision on the appeal to the House of Lords and their Lordships declined to address it.

It is well established that the privilege does not operate where the documents are part of, or relevant to, criminal or fraudulent acts: "No one doubts that a claim for professional privilege does not apply to documents which have been brought into existence in the course of or furtherance of a fraud to which both solicitor and client are parties" (*per* Lord Sumner in *O'Rourke v Darbishire* [1920] A.C. 581). But what if solicitors employ private investigators for the purposes of litigation and they obtain evidence by engaging in criminal or fraudulent acts? In *Dubai Aluminium Co. Ltd v Al Alawi* [1999] 1 All E.R. 703, Rix J. sitting in the Queen's Bench Division held that the documents and reports created as a result are susceptible to disclosure and inspection as they fall outside the proper scope of legal professional privilege.

What is the status of communications between a client or his lawyers and third parties? These attract legal professional privilege if the sole or dominant purpose of the document being brought into existence was to use it as evidence in contemplated or actual proceedings; or as part of the material on which to make a decision as to whether or not to commence or defend proceedings. This is often called "litigation privilege." Hence, no privilege attaches to documents if they were brought into existence before the possibility of litigation ever arose (e.g. pre-accident maintenance reports on vehicles) or by strangers to any possible litigation (e.g. medical reports made by the casualty department at which a road accident victim received treatment). If these documents later come into the control of a party they are disclosable even though that party obtained such solely for the purposes of the present litigation (see *Ventouris v Mountain* [1991] 1 W.L.R. 607). An exception is made for a collection of documents obtained by a solicitor, the inspection of which would betray the trend of advice given about the litigation (see *Ventouris*, above, obiter; *Dubai Bank Ltd v Galadari (No.7)* [1992] 1 W.L.R. 106 and *Sumitomo Corp. v Credit Lyonnais Rouse Ltd* (2001) L.T.L. July 20). Subject to that exception, a non-privileged document does not become privileged merely because it is handed to a solicitor for the purposes of an action. See also *Re Barings Plc* [1998] 1 All E.R. 673 where Sir Richard Scott V.C. reviews and comments on the relevant case law in this area.

Note that the fraud exception dealt with above applies to both advice and litigation privilege: see *Kuwait Airways Corporation v Iraqi Airways Co. (No.6)* [2005] EWCA Civ 286; *The Times*, April 25, 2005. In what circumstances will the exception apply?

> "It can only be used in cases in which the issue of fraud is one of the issues in the action where there is a strong (I would myself use the words 'very strong') prima facie case of fraud" but "where the issue of fraud is not one of the issues in the action, a prima facie case of fraud may be enough" (*per* Longmore L.J.).

Privilege against self-incrimination

30.014   See generally *Renworth Ltd v Stephansen* [1996] 3 All E.R. 244 where the Court of Appeal held that it would uphold a claim for privilege against disclosure on the ground of incrimination in a civil case where it was satisfied that disclosure would tend to expose the person concerned to proceedings for a criminal offence or offences. In deciding whether such a claim should be upheld, the court would examine: (i) the existence of any link between the answers sought and the offence or offences to which the claimant would be exposed: and (ii) whether, in respect of any possible offences, the privilege had been removed and replaced by a more limited statutory protection. Where it had, the court would consider whether exposure to proceedings for that offence would realistically expose the claimant to the risk of separate and distinct proceedings for other offences in respect of which the privilege had not been so abrogated.

Challenging a claim to privilege

30.015   Your opponent may have disclosed the existence of a document but objected to you inspecting it. This can be challenged by an application to the court with supporting evidence in the usual way (see Chs 13 and 14). The court may require that the document is produced for it to inspect privately for the purpose of deciding whether the claim or objection is valid. Unhappily for the applicant, a claim of privilege is normally upheld if the documents are clearly described and the claim appears soundly based. Claims of public interest immunity and irrelevancy are slightly easier to attack but the applicant must still satisfy the test that there is a real, and not merely a fanciful possibility that the document might contain something useful. If so, the court should not refuse the application without first examining the document itself. The court must consider it in light of other material already available and then decide whether or not the need to do justice between the parties outweighs the need for proper protection of the public interest (see *Goodridge v Chief Constable of Hampshire Constabulary* [1999] 1 All E.R. 896 and *Atos Consulting Ltd v Avis Plc (No.2)* [2007] EWHC 323). If a claim to privilege is well founded, that is the end of the matter: considerations of convenience and the savings of time and costs are irrelevant: see *General Mediterranean Holdings SA v Patel* [1999] 3 All E.R. 673.

DISCLOSURE IN STAGES (R.31.13)

The parties may agree in writing, or the court may direct, that disclosure or inspection or both should take place in stages. This most commonly occurs when a split trial (see Ch.33 para.33.006) is agreed or directed to take place. As a general rule where the issue of liability is to be tried first, disclosure is also limited to that issue. The parties should not unnecessarily be put to the cost and obligation of disclosure in respect of the issue of quantum that may prove academic (see *Buchanan-Michaelson v Rubinstein* [1965] 1 W.L.R. 390). In *Baldock v Addison* [1995] 1 W.L.R. 158, Lightman J., sitting in the Chancery Division, held that only very special circumstances would justify an order for disclosure relating to quantum; a mere interest in learning the amount in issue in the litigation was not sufficient; nor was the fact that the applicant was legally aided and required the information in order to make a meaningful report to the legal aid authorities or to ensure that legal aid was granted or continued. But what if a party wishes to make a well-assessed Pt 36 offer? In *Kapur v J.W. Francis and Co.*, The Times, March 4, 1998, the Court of Appeal held that if a defendant wished to ask a court to impose as a term of separate trials an order for disclosure of information as to quantum, to enable him to make a realistic offer of settlement, he had to specify the information he required and justify the request by satisfying the court that such an order was not wasteful of costs and would be of real assistance to him in making a realistic and sensible offer. Millett L.J. said that it was difficult to conceive of a situation where it would be right to order general disclosure of a claimant's documents relating to quantum to enable a defendant to ascertain the strength of the claimant's case.

In light of the overriding objective, the court has a wide discretion as to when to order disclosure. Generally, it is inexpedient and unnecessary to do so until the issues have been defined by the statements of case (see *RHM Foods Ltd v Bovril Ltd* [1982] 1 W.L.R. 661). However, disclosure may be ordered early where it assists in properly defining the issues (see *C Shippam Ltd v Princes-Buitoni Ltd* (1983) C.L.Y. 3027: disclosure of drawings was ordered prior to the

30.016

defendant serving a defence where the defendant challenged the claimant's monopoly in fluted jars; and *Dun & Bradstreet Ltd v Typesetting Facilities Ltd* (1992) C.L.Y. 579: inspection of the defendant's database by the claimant was held to be essential in order that the claimant could fully and properly prepare its particulars of claim).

INSPECTION OF DOCUMENTS REFERRED TO IN STATEMENTS OF CASE, ETC. (R.31.14)

30.017 A party may inspect a document mentioned in a statement of case, witness statement, witness summary or an affidavit. The exercise of this power in respect of, for example, affidavits in supports of an interim application, might in some circumstances be justifiable on the basis that the reference to the document renders prior disclosure of it unnecessary: important examples here are the affidavits filed in respect of applications for freezing injunctions and search orders (see Ch.27) since these applications are made many months before disclosure by list is likely to take place. In some circumstances it might be justifiable as a way of giving other parties the same advantage they would have received if the document referred to had been fully set out in the statement of case, etc. It enables the other parties to check for themselves whether the reference to the document was full enough to be fair and whether any inference or conclusion drawn by the reference was justifiable. It follows that, in such circumstances, the court has power to order inspection even if the document is not yet in the control of the respondent (*Rafidain Bank v Agom Universal Sugar Trading Co. Ltd* [1987] 1 W.L.R. 1606). There must, however, be a direct allusion to the document (*Dubai Bank Ltd v Galadari (No.2)* [1990] 1 W.L.R. 731).

Can a party resist inspection of a document under r.31.14 on the basis of legal professional privilege (see para.30.013 above)? Arguably yes as it seems unlikely that the CPR would have intended to abolish privilege at a stroke under this provision: see *Lucas v Barking, Havering & Redbridge Hospitals NHS Trust* [2003] EWCA Civ 1102; [2004] 1 W.L.R. 220.

In addition, and subject to r.35.10(4), a party may inspect a document referred to by an expert in his report (see para.23.021).

INSPECTION ON TERMS

30.018 In the case of a document over which the respondent claims a lien, although the court has power to order inspection, the order may be conditional on the applicant paying into court a sum equal to the value of the lien (*Woodworth v Conroy* [1976] Q.B. 884, where, in fact, no such condition was imposed).

In the case of a computer database, Vinelott J. in *Derby & Co. Ltd v Weldon (No.9)* [1991] 1 W.L.R. 652 listed several difficulties which the court should have regard to before fixing the terms upon which inspection may be ordered, for example, safeguards will be necessary to exclude inspection of irrelevant or privileged material; to avoid corruption of information stored and to minimise interference with the respondent's everyday use of the computer.

In the case of confidential documents which are not privileged, can the court impose terms limiting who may inspection them? The making of confidential reports, especially hospital reports and records may be inhibited if it were thought that non-professional eyes might later read them. In *McIvor v Southern Health Board* [1978] 1 W.L.R. 757 the House of Lords overruled earlier Court of Appeal cases which limited disclosure of medical reports to the applicant's medical advisers. As a general rule medical records are disclosed to both the applicant's medical and legal advisers on condition that they are not disclosed to the respondent nor his insurers (see *Steele v Moule* (1999) C.L. May 23 and the cases cited therein). See also the standard orders made for pre-action and non-party disclosure detailed at paras 30.023 and 30.024 below.

Orders preventing the disclosure of information to a party direct have also been made in other cases: *Church of Scientology v DHSS* [1979] 1 W.L.R. 723 (to protect informers from harassment); and see *Ventouris v Mountain* [1991] 1 W.L.R. 607 (allegations that inspection could lead to violence, intimidation, interference with witnesses and destruction of evidence); *Arab Monetary Fund v Hashim* [1989] 1 W.L.R. 565 (to conceal the identities of persons overseas implicated in currency offences said to be punishable by death); *Black & Decker Inc v Flymo Ltd* [1991] 1 W.L.R. 753 (to prevent a business rival gaining commercial advantage from inspecting the design documents and drawings of an intended new product); and *Helitune Ltd v Stewart Hughes Ltd* (1995) C.L.Y. 4156 (where it was held that a notebook containing the results of tests carried out in the course of development of a new product was likely to contain important trade secrets such that the applicant's interests were adequately served if there was disclosure to an independent expert). In each of these cases the purpose of the restrictions imposed was to prevent confidential information which a party had been compelled to disclose being used for a purpose extraneous to the action. See also *Simba-Tola v Elizabeth Fry Hostel* (2001) L.T.L. July 30.

INADVERTENT INSPECTION (R.31.20)

Where a party inadvertently allows a privileged document to be inspected, the party who has inspected the document may only use it or its contents with the permission of the court.   30.019

In *Breeze v John Stacey and Sons Ltd*, *The Times*, July 8, 1999, the Court of Appeal held that a solicitor had no duty, in the face of a mistake which was less than obvious, to inquire of the party supplying privileged documents whether privilege had been waived deliberately. In the case the defendant's solicitor had exhibited by mistake to an affidavit certain privileged material, namely 127 out of 440 paginated pages. The court found that this abundance of privileged material meant that it was entirely reasonable for the claimant's solicitor to conclude, as he did, that the decision to include such was deliberate. The fact that the privileged documents had not been expressly referred to in the affidavit did not assist the defendant, as there was also no reference to some of the other documents that were not privileged.

In *Al Fayed v Commissioner of Police of the Metropolis* [2002] EWCA Civ 780; *The Times*, June 17, 2002 the Court of Appeal stated that the following principles apply.

(i) A party giving inspection of documents must decide before doing so what privileged documents he wishes to allow the other party to see and what he does not.

(ii) Although the privilege is that of the client and not the solicitor, a party clothes his solicitor with ostensible authority (if not implied or express authority) to waive privilege in respect of relevant documents.

(iii) A solicitor considering documents made available by the other party to litigation owes no duty of care to that party and is in general entitled to assume that any privilege which might otherwise have been claimed for such documents has been waived.

(iv) In these circumstances, where a party has given inspection of documents, including privileged documents which he has allowed the other party to inspect by mistake, it will in general be too late for him to claim privilege in order to attempt to correct the mistake by obtaining injunctive relief.

(v) However, the court has jurisdiction to intervene to prevent the use of documents made available for inspection by mistake where justice requires—as, for example, in the case of inspection procured by fraud.

(vi) In the absence of fraud, all will depend upon the circumstances, but the court may grant an injunction if the documents have been made available for inspection as a result of an obvious mistake.

(vii) A mistake is likely to be held to be obvious and an injunction granted where the documents are received by a solicitor and:

(a) the solicitor appreciates that a mistake has been made before making some use of the documents; or

(b) it would be obvious to a reasonable solicitor in his position that a mistake has been made;

and, in either case, there are no other circumstances which would make it unjust or inequitable to grant relief.

(viii) Where a solicitor gives detailed consideration to the question whether the documents have been made available for inspection by mistake and honestly concludes that they have not, that fact will be a relevant (and in many cases an important) pointer to the conclusion that it would not be obvious to the reasonable solicitor that a mistake had been made, but is not conclusive; the decision remains a matter for the court.

(ix) In both the cases identified in vii) a) and b) above there are many circumstances in which it may nevertheless be held to be inequitable or unjust to grant relief, but all will depend upon the particular circumstances.

(x) Since the court is exercising an equitable jurisdiction, there are no rigid rules.

SUBSEQUENT USE OF DISCLOSED DOCUMENTS (R.31.22)

A party to whom a document has been disclosed may use the document only for the purpose of the proceedings in which it is disclosed, except where:

(a) It has been read to or by the court, or referred to, at a hearing that has been held in public. However, the court may still make an order restricting or prohibiting the use of that document.

30.020

Example

In *Smithkline Beecham Biologicals SA v Connaught Laboratories Inc* [1999] 4 All E.R. 498 the Court of Appeal held that the current practice was to invite the judge to familiarise himself with material out of court to which, in open court, economic reference, falling far short of verbatim citation, was made. In this context, the important private rights of the litigant must command continuing respect but so must the no less important value that justice was administered in public and was the subject of proper public scrutiny. Even though a document was not read in open court it would be treated as such if it was pre-read by the court and referred to by counsel in a skeleton argument which was incorporated in submissions in open court, or if the document was referred to (even though not read aloud) by counsel or by the court. That rule might not apply if any document contained a trade secret or truly secret information. See also *Lilly Icos Ltd v Pfizer Ltd (No.2)* [2002] 1 All E.R. 842 and *Smithline Beecham Plc v Generics (UK) Ltd* [2003] EWCA Civ 1109; [2004] 1 W.L.R. 1479.

(b) The court gives its permission.

Examples

In *Crest Homes Plc v Marks* [1987] A.C. 829 the House of Lords said that in exceptional circumstances it would permit the applicant to use documents disclosed in one action for the purposes of other proceedings if there were "cogent and persuasive reasons" that will not occasion injustice to the person giving disclosure. In the case the claimants had commenced two actions against the defendant, the first in 1984 and the second in 1985. In both actions the claimants obtained search orders plus related disclosure orders (see Ch.27). As a result of the search order in the 1985 action the claimants obtained documents which, they alleged, should have been disclosed to them in the 1984 action. The court permitted them to use information obtained in the 1985 action in support of proceedings for contempt of court in the 1984 action.

In *Apple Corp Ltd v Apple Computer Inc*. (1991) Law Society's Gazette, May 22, there were parallel proceedings in relation to the same dispute before the High Court and before the European Commission. The desirability of ensuring each tribunal should have the same materials for consideration constituted "cogent and persuasive reasons" and an order was made permitting the applicant to use in the European Commission case certain documents which had been disclosed in the English proceedings.

(c) The party who disclosed it and the person to whom it belongs agree.

SPECIFIC DISCLOSURE (R.31.12 AND PD 31, PARA.5)

30.021 When you receive your opponent's list you should check not only to see what documents you will wish to inspect but also to ensure that it is complete. For example, a letter may be disclosed that begins, "Further to your letter of March 1" but the letter of March 1, is not itself disclosed. But what can you do if you suspect that your opponent will not, or has not, made proper disclosure in accordance with the court order, or is objecting to produce for inspection documents you have a right to inspect? The first step will usually be to raise this matter in correspondence. Otherwise, if you still believe that the disclosure of documents given by a disclosing party is inadequate, you can make an application to the court for specific disclosure.

The application notice must specify the order sought and annex a draft version. The particular document or class of document for which disclosure is required should be described. Care must be taken in giving that description. In *Multigroup Bulgaria Holding AD v Oxford Analytica Ltd* (1999) L.T.L. August 17, C was ordered to give specific disclosure of certain documents relating to its "subsidiaries". On a subsequent application Eady J., sitting in the Queen's Bench Division, held that there was genuine scope for misunderstanding as to the extent of the obligations imposed by the order. He went on to define the term "subsidiary" for the purposes of the order as not being limited to those companies in which C owned 51 per cent or more of the shares, but that it extended to all those companies over which it enjoyed de facto control. Finally, note that the application must be supported by evidence and the grounds must be set out in the notice or the supporting evidence.

The court may order that a party must:

(a) disclose certain specified documents or classes of documents;
(b) carry out a search to the extent stated and disclose any documents located as a result.

In deciding whether or not to make an order the court will take into account all the circumstances of the case and, in particular, the overriding objective. But if the court concludes that a party from whom specific disclosure is sought has failed adequately to comply with the obligations imposed by an order for disclosure, whether by failing to make a sufficient search for documents otherwise, the court usually makes such order as is necessary in the judge's opinion to ensure that those obligations are properly complied with.

Examples

In *Jones v Greavison* (1998) C.L.Y. 327, C brought an action against D for damages arising from a road traffic accident. C's claim arose out of a credit hire agreement entered into with X, a credit hire company. D's enquiries revealed that the hire vehicle was owned by a company called Z. D requested a copy of the contract between C and X as well as a copy of the contract between X and Z. D believed that the rates charged by X were excessive having contacted Z direct and obtained a considerably cheaper quote for an identical vehicle. C refused to provide any documentation or information. D applied for specific disclosure of both documents on the ground that such were relevant to the issue of quantum and, in particular, the reasonableness of the daily rate charged by X. The application was granted, including disclosure of the contract between X and Z as C's solicitors were also acting under instructions from X.

In *Forum (Holdings) Ltd v Brook Street Computers Ltd* (1999) C.L. March, C issued proceedings against D alleging repudiatory breach of contract for the supply of computer software and hardware. D had represented that the software would meet 90 per cent of C's needs with the balance being provided by bespoke programming. D further represented that the software was then in use at 800 other sites thereby impliedly representing that those users were satisfied with the product. These representations became part of a contractual document. C complained that the software was unsuitable and applied for disclosure of documentation from D in relation to the supply of such to other customers. At first instance the application was refused. The Court of Appeal allowed the appeal in part. The court held that C was entitled to disclosure that would enable it to establish whether or not it had received a standard package in line with D's representations. The judge had wrongly refused disclosure of documents relating to the supply of standard specification and bespoke additions to other sites. C was entitled to the information as to the suitability of the software supplied to those sites, but the court drew a distinction between pre-contractual issues and matters arising after the contract date. The court said that disclosure after the contract was to be limited to the standard specification of upgraded and revised software supplied to the other sites. Documents as to claims made against D by other customers should be restricted to issues arising before the date of contract.

Where an application is made for specific disclosure of electronic data that has been deleted from a party's systems, but not permanently destroyed, the remedy may be to require that party to conduct a search for residual data or even for the court to direct that an independent expert carries out such a search.

FAILURE TO DISCLOSE OR ALLOW INSPECTION (R.31.21)

A party may not rely on any document that he fails to disclose or in respect of which he fails to permit inspection unless the court gives it permission. Hence, if a party is not prepared to put a particular card on the table (face up or face down) at this stage then he is not allowed to play it later at the trial so as to take

30.022

the other parties by surprise. Of course, the failure may lead to more dire consequences, e.g. a refusal to obey an order to give specific disclosure of a document within the time limit imposed may result in the defaulting party's statement of case being struck out. As to the court imposing a sanction and relief from such, see para.33.011.

DISCLOSURE AGAINST A NON-PARTY (R.31.17)

30.023 As we noted at the beginning of this chapter the general rule is that disclosure is not to be ordered against a "mere witness". However, this application for disclosure forms a significant exception to that rule. The application for disclosure against a person who is not a party to proceedings is permitted under s.34 of the Supreme Court Act 1981 or s.53 of the County Courts Act 1984. The court may only make an order where:

(a) the documents of which disclosure is sought are likely to support the case of the applicant or adversely affect the case of one of the other parties to the proceedings; and
(b) disclosure is necessary in order to dispose fairly of the claim or to save costs.

Assume that C is injured whilst working. The Health and Safety Executive are known to have inspected the premises both before and after the accident and may well have records of other accidents involving similar machinery to that C was using at the time. An application could be made against the Health and Safety Executive for it to disclose their records on the basis that such would be likely to support C's case on the issues of causation and liability. However, for the court to make the order, the following five hurdles as set up by the Court of Appeal in *Three Rivers DC v HM Treasury* [2002] 4 All E.R. 881 must be cleared.

(1) The Rule gives no power to order a non-party to disclose documents which do not meet the threshold conditions (a) and (b) above and that cannot be circumvented by including documents which do not meet that threshold condition in a class which also includes documents which do meet that condition.
(2) The test under the threshold condition is whether the document is likely to support the case for the applicant or adversely affect the case of one of the other parties. In this context likely means "may well" as opposed to "more probable than not".
(3) When applying that test it has to be accepted (and is not material) that some documents which may then appear likely to support the case of the applicant or adversely affect the case of one of the other parties will turn out, in the event, not do so.

(4) In applying the test to individual documents, it is necessary to have in mind that each document has to be read in context; so that a document which, considered in isolation, might appear not to satisfy the test, may do so if viewed as one of a class.

(5) There is no objection to an order for disclosure of a class of documents provided that the court is satisfied that all the documents in the class do meet the threshold condition. In particular, if the court is satisfied that all the documents in the class (viewed individually and as members of the class) do meet that condition-in the sense that there are no documents within the class which cannot be said to be "likely to support ... or adversely affect" then it is immaterial that some of the documents in the class will turn out, in the event, not to support the case of the applicant or adversely affect the case of one of the other parties.

Only in very exceptional factual situations will the court order disclosure of a non-party's confidential medical data: see *A v X & B (Non party)* [2004] EWHC 447; (2004) L.T.L. April 6.

An order under the Rule must specify the documents or the classes of documents that the respondent must disclose. It should require the respondent, when making disclosure, to specify any of those documents which are no longer in his control or in respect of which he claims a right or duty to withhold inspection. In addition, the order may require the respondent to indicate what has happened to any documents which are no longer in his control and to specify the time and place for disclosure and inspection.

Example

In *AXA Equity & Law Life Assurance Society Plc v National Westminster Bank Plc* (1998) C.L.Y. 332, C relied on statements made by a firm of auditors, X when it subscribed £19 million of mortgage debenture stock issued by a company, Z, following which Z went into administrative receivership. It became apparent that the stock issue was part of a fraud by F, who had been Z's managing director. C issued proceedings agains X claiming negligent misstatement and/or liability under the Financial Services Act 1986. However, C did not serve the proceedings. C alleged that it was unable to adequately state its case against X unless it had disclosure of documents from certain non-parties, i.e. Z's bankers, Z, F, F's solicitors relating to those parties' relationship with X in the placing of stock, the audit of the accounts and the financial position of Z at the time of the stock being placed. None of those parties resisted the application and we suspect that the order would now be made. (Pre-CPR the order could not be made in a non-personal injury action and a Norwich Pharmacal (see para.30.041 below) order was inappropriate in the case, as C knew the identity of the defendant). For further examples see the cases of In the *Matter of Howglen Ltd* [2001] 1 All E.R. 376 and *Clark v Ardington Electrical Services* [2001] EWCA Civ 585; (2001) L.T.L. April 4.

Who pays the costs of the application and complying with any order made? Rule 48.1(2) provides that the general rule is that the court will award the respondent his costs. The court may, however, make a different order, having regard to all the circumstances, including the extent to which it was reasonable for the respondent to oppose the application and whether the parties to the application have complied with any relevant pre-action protocol.

PRE-ACTION DISCLOSURE (R.31.16)

30.024   An application for disclosure before proceedings have started is permitted under s.33 of the Supreme Court Act 1981 or s.52 of the County Courts Act 1984. The purpose of the rule is to allow the applicant to find out without undue delay whether or not he has a cause of action (see *M. v Plymouth HA* (1994) C.L.Y. 3668: where the order was limited to a list of documents in particular categories concerning C that were in D's possession, rather than a list of every document relating to C that was in D's possession). When hearing an application under r.31.16 the court should not normally determine any of the substantive issues in the anticipated proceedings. It is sufficient for the substantive claim to be properly arguable and to have a real prospect of success: *Rose v Lynx Express Ltd* [2004] EWCA Civ 447; *The Times*, April 22, 2004.

The court may only make an order where:

(a) The applicant and respondent are both likely to be a party to subsequent proceedings. In *Dunning v Board of Governors of United Liverpool Hospitals* [1973] 2 All E.R. 454 (cited and approved by the Court of Appeal in *Three Rivers DC v HM Treasury* [2002] 4 All E.R. 881). This was interpreted as proceedings that "may" or "may well be made" if, on examination, the documents in question indicated that the applicant had a good cause of action; and

(b) if proceedings had started, the respondent's obligation to give standard disclosure would include the documents or classes of documents of which the applicant seeks disclosure; and

(c) it is desirable to either dispose fairly of the anticipated proceedings or assist the dispute to be resolved without proceedings or save costs.

As to (c), in *Total E & P Soudan SA v Edmonds* [2007] EWCA Civ 50, (2007) L.T.L., January 31, Tuckey L.J. ordered pre-action disclosure, stating:

"I think that Total would be able to plead a case along the lines which have been indicated on the material it now has. But I have little doubt that with the documents it seeks it would be able to plead a more focused case. In what is potentially a large and complex claim it is obviously preferable from the point of view of both parties to have a properly pleaded case from the outset. It seems to me therefore that disclosure of these documents in advance of proceedings is desirable in order to dispose fairly of any future proceedings."

In *SES Contracting Ltd v UK Coal Plc* [2007] EWHC 161, (2007) L.T.L., April 16, the parties had already spent around a quarter of a million pounds. Seymour J. observed

> "It is obvious that, if any proceedings are to be commenced on behalf of the Applicants, the cost of those proceedings, if bitterly fought to a conclusion, are likely to be very great. Therefore, simply as a matter of common sense, it seems overwhelmingly probable that [counsel for the Applicants] is right when he says that the Applicants wish to consider all available information before making a decision as to whether to commence litigation. If [counsel for the Applicants] took any other view, he would be like the punk in *Dirty Harry* responding positively to Clint Eastwood's question whether he felt lucky, and thereby being exposed to the same unfavourable outcome."

However, purely tactical applications simply fishing for material to support a claim will be refused: see *Meretz Investments NV v First Penthouse Ltd* [2003] EWHC 2324; (2003) L.T.L. October 16.

The application should specify the document or class of documents for which pre-action discovery is sought and the supporting evidence should detail the grounds and facts relied on. In addition, the applicant should set out the nature of the claim he intends to make and show not only the intention of making it but also that there is a reasonable basis for making it (see the case of Dunning referred to above, where the court said that ill-founded, irresponsible and speculative allegations or allegations based merely on hope would not be a reasonable basis for an intended claim in subsequent proceedings). The key principles to bear in mind when making an application were laid down by the Court of Appeal in *Black v Sumitomo* [2001] EWCA Civ 1919; [2003] 3 All E.R. 643, as follows:

(a) CPR 31.16 does not require that the proceedings are likely, but rather that the respondent is likely to be a party if proceedings are issued, where "likely" means "may well";

(b) because disclosure will only be ordered in relation to documents which would be the subject of standard disclosure the court must be clear what the issues in the litigation are likely to be;

(c) the court is only permitted to consider a grant of pre-action disclosure where there is a real prospect in principle of such an order being fair to the parties if litigation is commenced, or of assisting the parties to avoid litigation, or of saving costs in any event;

(d) if there is such a real prospect the court should go on to consider the question of discretion which has to be considered on all the facts and not merely in principle but also in detail;

(e) pre-action disclosure should not be ordered as a matter of course, at any rate where the parties at the pre-action stage have been acting reasonably, especially in relation to pre-action protocol requirements (see in particular *Marshall v Allotts (a firm)* [2004] EWHC 1964; (2005) P.N.L.R. 11);

(f) the discretionary elements include the clarity and identification of the issues raised by the complaint, the nature of the documents requested, and the opportunity which the complainant has to make its case without pre-action disclosure;

(g) the more focused the complaint and the more limited the disclosure sought, the easier it is for the court to exercise its discretion in favour of an order on the basis that transparency was what the interests of justice and proportionality most required.

In *Burns v Shuttlehurst* [1992] 2 All E.R. 27, C obtained judgment against D, his former employers, however, D went into liquidation. D's insurers, X refused to indemnify D and C applied for pre-action disclosure against X in respect of a proposed claim under the Third Parties (Rights against Insurers) Act 1930 (see Ch.7). The Court of Appeal held that the application should be refused as a claim against X was not "likely" until the measure of C's damages had been ascertained, at which time the documents would clearly be disclosable under s.2 of the 1930 Act.

If documents otherwise generally available have been collected together in the form of a report, disclosure may be ordered of that report if it would thereby save costs (see, e.g. *Barings Plc v Secretary of State for Trade and Industry* [1998] 1 All E.R. 673). It should also be noted that the rule specifically provides for disclosure to "assist the dispute to be resolved without proceedings". So it appears that there is no reason, as long as the rest of the test is met, why an order should not be made for the disclosure of documents that will assist the resolving of the dispute.

Is an argument about appropriate forum relevant on an application for pre-action disclosure? No, held the Court of Appeal in the *Total E & P Soudan SA* case.

An order under the Rule must specify the documents or the classes of documents which the respondent must disclose; and require the respondent, when making disclosure, to specify any of those documents which are no longer in his control or in respect of which he claims a right or duty to withhold inspection. In addition, the order may require the respondent to indicate what has happened to any documents which are no longer in his control and to specify the time and place for disclosure and inspection.

Who pays the costs of the application and complying with any order made? The starting-point is r.48.1(2) as discussed above. Further, in *Bermuda International Securities Ltd v KPMG (a Firm)* [2001] EWCA Civ 269; The Times, March 14, 2001, Waller L.J. said:

"As the judge recognised there is clearly a presumption in favour of [the defendant, KPMG] in relation to both the costs of the application and the costs of complying with any order made. In the argument before him little distinction may have been made between the costs of the application and the costs of complying. The judge's attitude was that KPMG should not have dug their heels in to the extent that they did, and that thus a costs order should not be made in their favour. Before us when it was put to [the claimant's counsel] on what basis it was proper for KPMG to be deprived of the costs of complying with any order, he was quick to accept that he could think of none. In my view it is important that it is recognised that in relation to pre-action disclosure, the cost of the actual exercise will be paid by the applicant for that disclosure. But so far as the application is concerned if it has been unreasonably resisted, those are the very circumstances contemplated where the order for costs may be different. In this case KPMG were really resisting the production of documents root and branch. Their reference in their letter to 'particular' documents does not assist them since they clearly meant only 'particular' documents. They were obviously concerned about the precedent that might be set, but in circumstances where the issue is in fact a narrow one and readily ascertainable, and where they themselves have already reviewed the documents and it was no burden to hand them over, it was certainly open to the judge to make the order for costs that he did. Once again it does not seem to me possible to impugn the exercise of his discretion in that regard". Also see the observations on costs made by Seymour J. in the *SES Contracting Ltd* case.

THE RULE IN NORWICH PHARMACAL

This is a form of disclosure of a very special but exceptional kind. It derives from the inherent jurisdiction of the court rather than the rules. It has been preserved by r.31.18. It was established in the case of *Norwich Pharmacal v Commissioners of Customs and Excise* [1974] A.C. 133. It relates to the disclosure of information (names and addresses of alleged wrongdoers) relevant to a future action. It can be sought against a person whether or not he is personally liable for the wrong complained of so long as he has become "mixed up" in the wrongdoing, albeit innocently, so as to facilitate its commission. Such an order is commonly made as part of a search order (see Ch.27 para.27.023). Otherwise, an application should be made in the usual way with supporting evidence.

30.025

To summarise there are three conditions that must be satisfied before an order will be made, namely:

a) A wrong must have been carried out or arguably carried out by an ultimate wrongdoer;

b) There must be a need for an order to enable action to be brought against the ultimate wrongdoer. The information in question in the *Norwich Pharmacal* case was such that without it "no action can ever be begun because the appellants do not know who are the wrongdoers who have infringed their patent" (*per* Lord Reid at p.174);

c) The person against whom the order is sought must be mixed up in the wrongdoing so as to have facilitated it and be able or likely to be able to provide the information necessary to enable the ultimate wrongdoer to be sued.

Is the rule restricted to tort? In the case of *Ashworth Security Hospital v MGN Ltd* [2002] 4 All E.R. 193, the House of Lords held that the court had jurisdiction to order disclosure of the identity of wrongdoers wherever the person against whom disclosure was sought had become mixed up in wrongful, albeit not tortious, conduct that infringed a claimant's legal rights. Even if the jurisdiction only arose where the wrongdoing was tortious, the restriction against ordering disclosure did not apply where the defendant was a party to the wrongdoing. Accordingly, where medical information held on a hospital database had been supplied by an unidentified hospital employee to a newspaper in breach of confidence and breach of contract, through an intermediary, and the intermediary and the newspaper knew that the information was disclosed in breach of confidence, the court had jurisdiction to order the newspaper to disclose its source.

Does it make any difference if the claimant does not know if a tort has been committed or not but believes that it has taken place? In *P. v T. Ltd* [1997] 4 All E.R. 200 the managing director of the defendant company informed C, a senior employee, that serious allegations had been made against him by a third party. C was subsequently dismissed after a disciplinary hearing. At all times D refused to identify the third party who had accused C. Sir Richard Scott V.C., sitting in the Chancery Division, held that where justice required the granting of relief, the court would make an order for disclosure to assist a prospective claimant to obtain the information and documents necessary to bring an action in tort against a third party, notwithstanding that, without such information, the claimant could not ascertain whether the unidentified third party had in fact committed a tort against him. Moreover, the tort of which the claimant complained about did not necessarily have to be criminal in nature. In the case, it was not possible for the claimant to know for certain whether he had a viable cause of action in libel or malicious falsehood against the informant without disclosure. Justice therefore demanded that he should be placed in a position to clear his name if the allegations made against him were without foundation.

According to Lightman J. in *Mitsui & Co. Ltd v Nexen Petroleum UK Ltd* [2005] EWHC 625; (2005) L.T.L. May 10, the exercise of the jurisdiction of the court against third parties who are mere witnesses, innocent of any participation in the wrongdoing being investigated, is only to be exercised if the innocent third parties are the only practicable source of information. The whole basis of the jurisdiction against them is that unless and until they disclose what they know, there can be no litigation in which they can give evidence.

Who should bear the costs of disclosure under a Norwich Pharmacal order? As a general rule it is the applicant. But see *Totalise Plc v Motley Fool Ltd* [2001] EWCA Civ 1897; [2002] 1 W.L.R. 1233, where a different order was made.

No order should be made if the disclosure will not assist the claimant in deciding whether or not he should bring a claim, and if so on what basis; nor where the claimant's claim is very weak and highly speculative (see *Re Murphy's Settlements* [1998] 3 All E.R. 1). It is also refused if the interests of the person against whom it is sought outweigh the interests of the applicant and if the order would otherwise be oppressive (see the decision of Alan Steinfield Q.C.

sitting in the Chancery Division in the case of *Microsoft Corp. v Plato Technology Ltd* (1999) L.T.L. March 11). A claimant should exhaust all other avenues before applying for an order. In *Nikitin v Richards Butler LLP* [2007] EWHC 173, (2007) L.T.L., February 19, Langley J. stated

> "it remains the basic principle that disclosure of information occurs by the familiar procedures applicable to proceedings commenced between the relevant parties. Rule 31.16 provides for the exceptional circumstances to which it refers, but again in an adversarial or potentially adversarial context between applicant and respondent. Norwich Pharmacal relief is the third and last port of call."

CHAPTER 31

Evidence

KEY QUESTIONS

31.001　The key questions that arise in any case are:

(1) What facts must be proved?
(2) How will that be done?

The first question is answered by having a thorough understanding of the relevant substantive law. The law of evidence and procedure determines the answer to the second question. Evidential law specifies which party must prove the facts in issue and the types of evidence admissible to prove them. The procedural rules dictate the way in which the evidence may or may not be adduced.

This Chapter is concerned with non-expert evidence. The topic of expert evidence is dealt with in Ch.23.

THE LEGAL BURDEN

31.002　The general rule is that a party who asserts a fact must prove it, unless it is admitted.

Example

C buys a washing machine from D. C issues a claim form alleging that the machine was defective because the door seal was missing and this led to C's kitchen floor being flooded. In the defence, D denies the seal was missing and states that C caused the flood by not installing the machine correctly.

The legal burden of proof is on C as C is asserting that the machine was defective and that the defect caused the flood damage.

Subject to certain procedural requirements, the legal burden of proof is reversed in some circumstances. See, for example, ss.11 and 12 of the Civil Evidence Act 1968 discussed at para.12.024.

THE EVIDENTIAL BURDEN

The party with the legal burden of proof initially bears the evidential burden. 31.003
  Above example continued
C must adduce sufficient evidence at trial that the washing machine was defective due to the missing door seal and that this caused the damage to his kitchen for the judge to find in his favour "on the balance of probabilities". (Part of C's case will also be to establish how the machine was installed and that this was done correctly). If C adduces evidence in support of his case on all relevant issues an evidential burden passes to D. If he does not adduce any evidence contradicting C's evidence he must lose. However, D's evidence, no doubt, will be to the effect that the seal was present (or perhaps, even if it was missing, that such would not have caused the damage complained of by C) and that C incorrectly installed the machine. If the judge is undecided as to which version of events he accepts, C must fail as he has the legal burden of proof throughout.

THE STANDARD OF PROOF

The standard of proof in civil cases is said to be "on the balance of probabilities". However, the balance is not fixed in any arithmetical way. In *Re H (minors) (sexual abuse)* [1996] 1 All E.R. 1 at 16 Lord Nicholls of Birkenhead said: 31.004

> "The balance of probability standard means that a court is satisfied an event occurred if the court considers that, on the evidence, the occurrence of the event was more likely than not. When assessing the probabilities the court will have in mind as a factor, to whatever extent is appropriate in the particular case, that the more serious the allegation the less likely it is that the event occurred and, hence, the stronger should be the evidence before the court concludes that the allegation is established on the balance of probability. Fraud is usually less likely than negligence. Deliberate physical injury is usually less likely than accidental physical injury . . . Built into the preponderance of probability standard is a generous degree of flexibility in respect of the seriousness of the allegation. Although the result is much the same, this does not mean that where a serious allegation is in issue the standard of proof required is higher. It means only that the inherent probability or improbability of an event is itself a matter to be taken into account when weighing the probabilities and deciding whether, on balance, the event occurred. The more improbable the event, the stronger must be the evidence that it did occur before, on the balance of probability, its occurrence will be established".

What tips this balance one way or another? Bear in mind that a trial judge endeavours to make findings of fact from the evidence presented. He draws inferences from facts. In particular, if the judge is asked to disbelieve a witness, that witness should be cross-examined. Moreover, the failure to cross-examine a witness on some material part of his evidence or at all, may be treated as an acceptance of the truth of that part or the whole of his evidence (see *Markem Corporation v Zipher Ltd* [2005] EWCA Civ 267, (2005) L.T.L. 22 March).

What if a party fails to call evidence? Can an adverse inference be drawn? In *Benham Limited v Kythira Investments Ltd* [2003] EWCA Civ 1794; (2003) L.T.L. December 15, the Court of Appeal approved the following guidance given by Brooke L.J. in *Wisniewski v Central Manchester Health Authority* [1987] P.I.Q.R. P324; [1998] Lloyd's Rep. Med 223, namely:

> "(1) In certain circumstances a court may be entitled to draw adverse inferences from the absence or silence of a witness who might be expected to have material evidence to give on an issue in an action.
> (2) If a court is willing to draw such inferences they may go to strengthen the evidence adduced on that issue by the other party or to weaken the evidence, if any, adduced by the party who might reasonably have been expected to call the witness.
> (3) There must, however, have been some evidence, however weak, adduced by the former on the matter in question before the court is entitled to draw the desired inference: in other words, there must be a case to answer on that issue.
> (4) If the reason for the witness's absence or silence satisfies the court then no such adverse inference may be drawn. If, on the other hand, there is some credible explanation given, even if it is not wholly satisfactory, the potentially detrimental effect of his/her absence or silence may be reduced or nullified."

Is it only when a party fails to call a relevant witness who is either the party himself or a witness within the party's control that a court should draw an adverse inference? No, held Mann J. in *Fulham Leisure Holdings Ltd v Nicholson Graham & Jones* [2006] EWHC 2017, [2006] 4 All E.R. 1397 "The absence of a relevant witness is taken to be part of the evidential picture, and I do not see why control should be a necessary element. The reasoning ought to apply if the missing witness is demonstrated to be willing even if not controlled."

The trial judge assesses the overall credibility of a party's case having heard oral evidence and read any documentary evidence. If he then cannot decide which side of the line the decision ought to be, the burden of proof comes into play and the claimant fails (see *Morris v London Iron and Steel Co. Ltd* [1988] Q.B. 493).

In what circumstances can a trial judge decide a disputed issue of fact by resorting to the burden of proof? In *Stephens v Cannon* [2005] EWCA Civ 222; *The Times*, May 2, 2005, the Court of Appeal held that the circumstances must be exceptional.

> "Nevertheless the issue does not have to be of any particular type. A legitimate state of agnosticism can logically arise following enquiry into any

type of disputed issue. It may be more likely to arise following an enquiry into, for example, the identity of the aggressor in an unwitnessed fight; but it can arise even after an enquiry, aided by good experts, into, for example, the cause of the sinking of a ship. The exceptional situation which entitles the court to resort to the burden of proof is that, notwithstanding that it has striven to do so; it cannot reasonably make a finding in relation to a disputed issue. A court which resorts to the burden of proof must ensure that others can discern that it has striven to make a finding in relation to a disputed issue and can understand the reasons why it has concluded that it cannot do so. The parties must be able to discern the court's endeavour and to understand its reasons in order to be able to perceive why they have won and lost. An appellate court must also be able to do so because otherwise it will not be able to accept that the court below was in the exceptional situation of being entitled to resort to the burden of proof. In a few cases the fact of the endeavour and the reasons for the conclusion will readily be inferred from the circumstances and so there will be no need for the court to demonstrate the endeavour and to explain the reasons in any detail in its judgment. In most cases, however, a more detailed demonstration and explanation in judgment will be necessary" (*per* Wilson J.).

EXCHANGE OF WITNESS STATEMENTS

Rule 32.2(1)(a) provides that as a general rule any fact which needs to be proved by the evidence of a witness at trial has to be proved by that witness giving oral evidence. However, as part of the "cards on the table" approach to modern litigation, no witness can be called to give evidence at trial unless either: (a) his statement setting out the oral evidence intended to be relied on at trial has been exchanged earlier in accordance with the court's direction; or (b) the court otherwise grants its permission. As to the court's control of evidence, see para.33.012. 31.005

On the small claims track (see Ch.20) and the fast track (see Ch.21) an order for exchange by a specified time is normally made on allocation. In respect of multi-track cases (see Ch.22) the order is made as part of the overall case management. We dealt with drafting witness statements for use at trial in Ch.14.

Will the exchange be simultaneous or sequential?

"The normal rule should be that the exchange of witness statements shall be simultaneous... But if either party shows any reluctance to 'come clean', the district judge has power to order that the exchange of witness statements be wholly or partially sequential... hereby tying the party to a particular case... before the other party has to prepare his own witness statements" (*per* Lord Donaldson M.R. in *Mercer v Chief Constable of the Lancashire Constabulary* [1991] 1 W.L.R. 367).

Sequential exchange may also be ordered where a party is allowed to serve supplemental statements in order to improve or add to the statements he has already made (see below and also *Williams v Alpha Mechanical Handling and National Power* (1996) C.L.Y. 994).

When a party is ready to exchange the witness statements he intends to rely on at trial he should contact the other parties to see if they are also in a position to do so. The normal practice is for solicitors representing parties to undertake to put the statements in that night's post or DX. Obviously different arrangements are made if any party is acting as a litigant in person. A personal exchange is probably the best solution. The matter needs to be addressed at the time the court makes the order.

What if you cannot make the deadline to exchange? As soon as that becomes clear you should contact all other parties and seek an agreement to an extension. Try to find out when the witness can realistically guarantee that you will get their signed statement or can otherwise make arrangements to provide you with a statement and propose that date. Any agreement reached must be recorded in writing but remember that the parties cannot alter the case management dates set in fast track or multi-track cases (see Chs 21 and 22, respectively). If no agreement is reached or if a case management date will not be met, ensure that you make an immediate application to the court.

What if you are ready to exchange within the deadline but your opponent is not? If a good reason is given for an extension you should agree it, subject to what we have said above. But what if there has been no request or application for an extension? If you comply with the direction and serve the statements your opponent potentially gains an advantage in that he will see your evidence first and could tailor his own evidence accordingly. We recommend that you file the statements with the court and explain the situation in a covering letter. If your court's practice is to make orders of its own initiative when receiving such information from a party we see no need for you to make any formal application. In any event the court normally allows a further short period of time to comply with the direction before effectively depriving a party of a significant part of its case (see below).

Once exchange has taken place a party needs to review the opponent's statements. Has enough evidence been adduced to seriously challenge your version and/or discharge the relevant burdens of proof? What needs to be responded to in each statement and how is that to be done? Are supplemental statements justified (see below)? Will permission be needed for more examination in chief at trial? Are there any significant inconsistencies between the statements themselves and/or other available evidence and/or the opponent's stated case? As to the witnesses themselves, what, if any, mud can be thrown at them, for example, criminal convictions or other matters suggesting dishonesty or unreliability? Do not underestimate the importance of this review. All the cards have now been placed face up on the table. A party needs to sort out his hand and see where the high cards and trump cards are placed. Instead of waiting to puncture the opponent's evidence by cross-examination a party should consider seeking further information to attack the statements (see para.32.001).

Supplemental witness statements

31.006
What if after statements have been served you want a witness to give additional evidence, for example, to deal with events occurring, or matters discovered, after his statement was served, or in response to matters raised by another party's statements? The rules are silent as to parties serving supplemental statements. As a general rule it does not save costs to allow such. However, the Chancery Guide provides that such can be served and permission then sought to rely on the evidence at trial. The Commercial Court Guide provides that permission must be obtained to serve additional statements.

In *St Albans Court Ltd v Daldorch Estates Ltd, The Times,* May 24, 1999, Mrs Justice Arden ordered that the witness statements already served were to stand as evidence-in-chief and that there was to be no further evidence in chief unless permission was given at trial (see para.31.010 below). However, she went on to direct "that supplementary witness statements should be provided in this event". This seems an eminently sensible practice since any additional examination in chief that is permitted can then be given by the witness adopting his supplemental statement. However, the danger is that the trial judge might not give his permission. We take the view that rather than run that risk an interim application for a direction to serve supplemental statements should be made.

Serving witness statements late

31.007
What can you do if you discover a new favourable witness after witness statements have already been exchanged? You will need to make an interim application for the court's permission to serve the statement and to be allowed to rely on it at trial. The court will carefully scrutinise why the discovery was made so late in the day and only in exceptional cases is it likely that you will be successful. In *Stroh v London Borough of Haringey* (1999) L.T.L. July 13, the defendant in a personal injury action delayed investigating most of the basic facts for over three years during the litigation. Two weeks before the trial it sought to adduce the evidence of four maintenance personnel. The judge refused to allow the defendant to adduce the evidence. He held that the claimant would suffer prejudice as she was now faced with a battery of four witnesses with special knowledge. The Court of Appeal upheld that decision. It was clear that the judge had had in mind the overriding objective and was entitled to conclude that the prejudice to the claimant outweighed the prejudice to the defendant.

Can you delay exchanging to make last minute amendments? Remember that you can agree to extend the date for exchange with the other parties provided that does not alter any date fixed for the filing of listing questionnaires or a trial date. Otherwise you should exchange those statements that do not require amending and apply promptly to the court in respect of those that do. You should not, in our opinion, rely on the case of *Mealey Horgan Plc v Horgan, The Times,* July 6, 1999, which turns on its own unique facts. We dealt with the case in some detail at para.14.012. The additional points we would stress in this context are that the claimant had received the statements six weeks before the trial date and given their nature it was said that the claimant could still properly prepare for trial notwithstanding the defendant's delay. It was the lack of any prejudice to the claimant in the case which convinced the court that it would be disproportionate to exclude the defendant's evidence.

Witness summaries

31.008 Sometimes, a potential witness may move away without telling you and cannot be traced. Occasionally, you know precisely where to find a witness who is thought to be favourable but he refuses to co-operate in giving you a statement. You should endeavour to find out why he is being so difficult. Always suggest that he obtains advice from an independent solicitor if he has any doubts about his legal position. You will then need to consider how important and credible the person's evidence is likely to be and the possibility that the witness will be unfavourable, if not outright hostile, at trial. If you decide that you wish to keep open the possibility of calling the witness you must apply under r.32.9 for permission to serve a witness summary. (Also do not forget before the trial to serve a witness summons on the witness—see para.36.003). The application can be made without notice to any other party but should be made before the deadline to exchange witness statements has expired. We recommend that a copy of the proposed summary should accompany the application. The summary must either set out the evidence you expect the witness to give or otherwise list the matters on which you propose asking the witness questions. It must be prepared in the format of a witness statement insofar as that is possible.

Example

In *Harrison and Harrison v Bloom Camillin (a firm)* (1999) L.T.L. March 30 the claimants alleged that the defendants, a firm of solicitors, had been negligent in failing to serve proceedings against their former accountants, Touche Ross, within the limitation period. The defendants sought permission to serve witness summaries from various people, including the claimants' father and an employee of Touche Ross. On the evidence Neuberger J. was persuaded that there was a real risk of injustice or would be a reasonably justified sense of injustice by the defendants if they were not allowed to call the witnesses in issue. He granted permission for witness summaries to be served.

Objections to contents

31.009 What should you do if your opponent serves on you witness statements that contain irrelevant or inadmissible evidence? Best practice is to immediately raise this in correspondence. The Chancery Guide says it should be done within 28 days. You should then seek to resolve the matter with your opponent or otherwise raise the matter on application at any pre-trial review or at trial itself.

Should a case management judge deal with the question of admissibility of evidence proposed to be used at an interim hearing at an earlier preliminary hearing? Should a question of admissibility of evidence proposed to be used at trial be heard as a preliminary issue before the trial? "No" answered the Court of Appeal in *Stroude v Beazer Homes Ltd* [2005] EWCA Civ 265; *The Times*, April 28, 2005. "In general, disputes about the admissibility of evidence in civil proceedings are best left to be resolved by the judge at the substantive hearing of the application or at the trial of the action, rather than at a separate preliminary hearing. The judge at a preliminary hearing on admissibility will usually be less well informed about the case. Preliminary hearings can also cause unnecessary costs and delays. In the present case [summary judgment application] no good reason is apparent nor has one been advanced for departing from the usual practice. It has not been suggested that this is one of those cases in which the ruling on admissibility would dispose of or abbreviate the substantive application. The practical effect of a split proceeding seeking a pre-emptive ruling has been to hold up the hearing of the summary judgment application. It may well have increased the costs of proceedings. I cannot see what advantage there was in it for anyone" (*per* Mummery L.J.).

Use at trial

By serving a witness statement in accordance with the court order a party preserves the right to call the witness at trial or, in certain circumstances, may rely on the statement as hearsay evidence (see below). It appears that the court cannot compel you to rely on the evidence should you subsequently decide not to do so (Society of *Lloyd's v Jaffray*, *The Times*, August 3, 2000). But as a matter of common sense, where a party serves a witness statement but does not rely on that evidence at trial, the judge may draw an adverse inference from the "missing" evidence. However, r.32.5(5) permits any other party to use the statement as hearsay evidence. This means that it is imperative to make the right decision in the first place. If you subsequently decide not to call a witness you should notify the other parties and say whether or not you will be relying on the statement as hearsay evidence at trial. 31.010

Where you are not relying on the statement at all but it has already been placed in the trial bundle (see para.36.006), you should notify the court so the trial judge can decide whether or not to read it (see Society of Lloyd's above). But what if another party does rely on the statement as hearsay, can he rely on part or none of it and otherwise dispute its contents? No, held the Court of Appeal in *McPhilemy v Times Newspapers Ltd* [2000] 1 W.L.R. 1732. Brooke L.J. stated that there is "no principle of the law of evidence by which a party may put in evidence a written statement of a witness knowing that his evidence conflicts to a substantial degree with the case he is seeking to place before the [court/jury], on the basis that he will say straightaway in the witness's absence that the [court/jury] should disbelieve as untrue a substantial part of that evidence."

Usually, a witness whose statement has been served will be called to give evidence at trial. As a general rule the whole of his statement stands as his evidence in chief. This means that the statement must comprehensively address the relevant issues. The witness enters the witness box and takes the oath or affirms. He then states his name and address, is shown a copy of his statement and confirms that it is true. No further questioning by you is possible unless the court considers that there is a good reason to grant permission pursuant to r.32.5(3) so that the witness can:

(1) Amplify his evidence. This does not mean give totally new evidence. If the witness statement has been so poorly prepared that the proposed evidence will unfairly take the other side by surprise, permission is not normally given. If, however, it amounts to no more than filling in minor gaps or clarifying apparent ambiguities or inconsistencies, permission is usually granted. If in the circumstances the court is minded to grant the other side an adjournment then no doubt it will be on terms providing for you to pay the costs of and occasioned by such.
(2) Give evidence in relation to new matters that have arisen since the witness statement was served.

Whether or nor the whole or part of a witness's statement is ordered to stand as his evidence in chief once he has been called to give evidence he may be cross examined on any part of it (r.32.11). Of course, cross-examination is not limited just to the statement. See para.37.012.

OPINION EVIDENCE

31.011 As a general rule only a suitably qualified expert witness may give opinion evidence. However, s.3(2) of the Civil Evidence Act 1972 (confirming the common law position) permits a non-expert witness to give opinion evidence on any matter "as a way of conveying relevant facts personally perceived by him". First, it must be noted that the evidence must be relevant. Secondly, the opinion is limited to matters within the personal knowledge of the witness.

Example

Bob is in a pub. He observes that D's face is very red and his eyes are glazed. He hears D slur his words. He watches D stagger out of the pub and fall into his car. He hears the car start up and sees it disappear out of his sight, around a corner, within a matter of a few seconds. Bob then hears a crash. He runs along the road and observes that D's car has apparently hit C's car. C sues D. C's solicitor takes a witness statement from Bob and exchanges it. Bob is called to give evidence for C at trial.

As to drafting witness statements, see Ch.14. The question we want to consider here is how far can Bob's statement go, assuming he is not an expert on the issue whether or not D drove negligently. D's demeanour, how far he drove and in what manner are relevant matters. Based on what he saw and heard, Bob can give his opinions that D was (a) "drunk", (b) "drove away very fast" and (c) "drove only a few hundred metres before the crash". What Bob cannot express is an admissible opinion as to who caused the accident. It is not admissible for Bob to say that because D was drunk, etc., D must have caused the accident. It is for the trial judge to decide the issue of causation.

Other examples of opinion evidence that will be admissible in these circumstances include an opinion as to road, weather and lighting conditions, as well as the age and identity of an individual and his handwriting. A further example in a personal injury claim was given by the Court of Appeal in *Kirkman v Euro Exide Corp (CMP Batteries) Ltd* [2007] EWCA Civ 66, *The Times*, February 6, 2007, in respect of:

> "the evidence of the employer, who states that if his employee (the claimant) had not been injured, he (the employer) would have promoted him to a more senior position within, say, two years. No-one would suggest that such evidence is inadmissible; no-one would suggest that it is expert evidence, although it is founded upon the witness's knowledge, experience and expertise. The usefulness of the employer's statement is that he has sufficient knowledge of the claimant's qualities and the needs of his own business to be able to give a credible statement as to what would have happened if the claimant had not been injured. But although the evidence depends upon a degree of expertise, it is not expert evidence" (*per* Smith L.J.). See also para.23.023.

HEARSAY EVIDENCE

Hearsay is defined by s.1(2)(a) of the Civil Evidence Act 1995 and r.33.1(a) as "a statement made, otherwise than by a person while giving oral evidence in proceedings, which is tendered as evidence of the matters stated".   31.012

What is it in practice?

Hearsay to the lay person usually means the simple repetition by one person of what another person said or wrote. However, for legal purposes a statement is only hearsay if it is being relied on in a court as evidence of the truth of its contents. The purpose of the repetition is crucial.

Example

In a road traffic case witness A says (in his witness statement and) at trial; "the defendant got out of his car and sobbed, 'I was in the middle of the road . . .. I wasn't looking'. He then got back into his car." What is the purpose of A repeating in court what the defendant said earlier out of court? It will be to prove the truth of its contents, namely that the defendant was driving in a   31.013

negligent fashion, i.e. driving in the middle of the road and not looking where he was going.

But what if in the same case, witness B says (in his witness statement and) at trial; "the claimant got out of his car and yelled at the defendant, 'You're a fat bastard'." What is the purpose of B repeating that to the court? It will not be to prove that the defendant is (a) overweight and (b) illegitimate! At most it will be to show the claimant's state of mind, namely that he was angry. Equally, if the defendant was claiming that those words were slanderous, B's repetition would be for the purpose of showing that they were spoken and not that they were true.

Formalities

31.014 Section 2 of the 1995 Act provides that if a party intends to adduce hearsay evidence he should give (a) details and (b) notice of that to the other parties. The Civil Procedure Rules outline how this is to be achieved in practice.

Rule 33.2(1)(a) provides that if the hearsay evidence a party intends to rely on at trial is to be given by a witness giving oral evidence, then the party complies with s.2 by serving that person's witness statement on the other parties in accordance with the court's order.

By r.33.2(2) where a party intends to rely on hearsay evidence at trial that is contained in a witness statement of a person who is not being called to give oral evidence, the party must, when serving that witness statement, inform the other parties (in the covering letter) that the witness is not being called to give oral evidence and give the reason why the witness will not be called.

Rule 33.2(3) states that in all other cases, a party should serve a notice which:

(1) identifies the hearsay evidence, for example, what paragraph it appears in if it is contained in a witness statement;
(2) states that the party serving the notice proposes to rely on the hearsay evidence at trial; and
(3) gives the reason why the witness will not be called.

However, r.33.3 provides that no hearsay notice is required in respect of:

(a) evidence given at hearing other than a trial, i.e. interim hearings and post-trial hearings;
(b) an affidavit or witness statement that is to be used at trial but which does not contain hearsay evidence. Instead, the party relying on the affidavit or witness statement must give notice under r.33.2(2) (see above);
(c) a statement in a probate action alleged to have been made by the person whose estate is the subject-matter of the proceedings; and
(d) where the requirement is excluded by a practice direction.

If a hearsay notice is required when must it be served? The answer is no later than the latest date for serving witness statements as ordered by the court. In addition, if the hearsay evidence is a document, a copy must be supplied to any party who requests it.

Section 2(4) of the 1995 Act provides that the failure to serve a hearsay notice does not affect the admissibility of the evidence. However, r.32.1(2) gives the court power to exclude evidence that would otherwise be admissible. Non-compliance with the rules may well see the trial judge exclude the hearsay evidence. The courts are reluctant to adjourn any trial and will always carefully weigh up the prejudice to the parties. If it is proportionate to adjourn, the defaulting party is likely to be heavily penalised in costs. In addition, the weight of the evidence may be seriously reduced (see below).

Calling the maker of a hearsay statement (r.33.4)

How might you respond to your opponent's indication that he intends to rely on hearsay evidence at trial? If there are any advantages in requiring the maker of the hearsay statement to attend to be cross-examined by you then you must apply to the court within 14 days for permission to do so. Is this very likely? Consider first the position of your opponent. If the evidence is important and the witness is available his first instinct should be to call the maker. Why is he relying on second-hand evidence? If the reason is that the evidence will be destroyed by cross-examination then your careful reading of the statement in light of the other available evidence should tell you to make the application. However, you must always carefully consider whether you can actually diminish or destroy the evidence by cross-examination. There is a real danger that if you call the maker but the cross-examination is ineffective you will improve, rather than weaken, the opponent's case. If, on balance, you decide against calling the maker for cross-examination, consider if evidence can be given to discredit him (see below).

31.015

What is the scope of cross-examination under r.33.4? In *Douglas v Hello! Ltd* [2003] EWCA Civ 332; (2003) L.T.L. March 3, the Lord Chief Justice observed that:

> "it is to allow the maker of the statement to be cross-examined as to its contents. That provision does not enable [a party] to cross-examine the witness when she is called as to matters that do not arise out of the statement. Reference to the 'contents' of the statement confines it to matters dealt with in the statement. But a reasonable approach has to be adopted to determine what are the contents of the statement for that purpose. The trial judge has a considerable discretion over the extent of the cross-examination. If he considers that the cross-examination is going beyond proper bounds, then his powers to control evidence enable him to limit the evidence in an appropriate manner. The judge can be relied upon to see that no unreasonable use is made of the powers of cross-examination".

Attacking the credibility of hearsay evidence (r.33.5)

31.016 If you wish to attack the credibility of the maker of a hearsay statement relied on by your opponent you must serve notice of that intention within 14 days of receiving the hearsay notice. A simple letter will suffice. The usual ways of attacking credibility involve making allegations of bias, previous convictions or a previous inconsistent statement. However, what admissible evidence can you adduce of this at trial? It is too late to include it in any witness statements as they have already been served. We recommend that you apply for permission to serve supplemental or additional statements. If you leave the matter for the trial judge to determine your opponent may claim that he has been ambushed and that the evidence should be excluded, or the matter adjourned, at your expense, so that the fresh evidence can be considered.

Weight and credibility of hearsay evidence

31.017 By s.4 of the 1995 Act when estimating the weight, if any, the trial judge may give to hearsay evidence, he should have regard to any circumstances from which the reliability or otherwise of the evidence can be assessed. An obvious example are words or actions tantamount to an admission. These always carry extra probative force on the basis that people do not usually speak falsely against themselves. Section 4(2) sets out guidelines to the judge in estimating weight, namely:

(a) Whether it would have been reasonable and practicable to have called the maker of the hearsay statement that is being relied on. The best possible reason will be that the maker is dead. But other reasons may include that the maker is abroad and unwilling to return; unfit to attend trial; untraceable; unlikely to remember the details of his statement (e.g. routine business records made by various people); or is the opponent, the opponent's spouse or employee.

Take care when relying on the hearsay evidence of a person who is abroad. Will the witness's failure to return for the trial or give evidence by video link (see para.31.018, below) damage his credibility? In *Dunn International Ltd v CDE* (1998) C.L.Y. 819, Judge Lloyd Q.C. observed that when hearsay evidence was relied on where the witnesses were in Europe and no explanation had been provided as to why the witnesses were not called, the court would give little weight to the statements of these witnesses where the evidence had been contradicted by witnesses who had appeared and had been cross-examined.

(b) Whether the original statement was made contemporaneously with the occurrence or existence of the matters stated. Arguably, a statement is more accurate the closer in time that it is made to the matter in question.

(c) Whether the evidence is multiple hearsay. If A tells B something and B repeats it in court to prove the truth as to what A said then that is first hand hearsay. If A tells B and B tells C and C tells the court, that is second hand, multiple hearsay. Obviously, the more times something is repeated the more likely it is to change. If we work our way through an alphabet of people by the time A's message reaches Z it may well be unrecognisable to A.

(d) Whether any person involved had any motive to conceal or misrepresent the facts.

(e) Whether the original statement was an edited account, or made in collaboration with another person or for a particular purpose. A statement made by a person trained to make it, or record it, may be more reliable than a statement made by, or to, someone not so trained.

(f) Whether the circumstances in which the evidence is adduced suggest an attempt to prevent the proper evaluation of its weight. This would include late disclosure of the hearsay to the opponent, or total failure to serve a s.2 notice, or perhaps serving a defective notice.

At first sight it may be thought that hearsay evidence is preferable to first hand oral evidence. After all hearsay evidence is "cut and dried": it has no surprises; and if it is contained in a document it usually saves the expense of calling a witness. In practice the preference lies entirely the other way. The value of first-hand evidence is the weight and credibility the courts traditionally attach to it. Hearsay evidence by its very nature is second-hand evidence. First-hand evidence from a witness who can be tested by cross-examination is always more persuasive. A trial judge faced with conflicting evidence has to decide which is probably the more accurate. If he has received predominantly first-hand evidence from, say, the claimant, but mainly hearsay evidence from the defendant, he may feel compelled to give judgment for the claimant. Do not therefore assume that it is correct to put in a hearsay statement wherever it is possible to do so. It will usually be better to call the witness.

Evidence sworn out of court and video conferencing

What can be done if one of your proposed witnesses will be unable to attend the trial? Perhaps he is going into hospital or intends to go abroad. If his evidence is of marginal value only or merely supports other evidence, it is sensible to put it in as a hearsay statement. But if the evidence is vital (and cannot be agreed with the other parties) it is best to try and call him. You need to promptly ask the court to adjourn the trial until he is available. Where he has far to travel the party wishing to call him should offer to pay his travelling expenses. There are two other possibilities. Often, the easiest and cheapest option is to obtain the court's permission to allow the witness to give evidence through a video link (r.32.3). This is a developing area. In *Rowland v Norgen* [2002] EWHC 692; [2002] 4 All E.R. 370, Newman J. held that no defined limit

31.018

or set of circumstances should be placed upon the discretionary power to permit evidence by video link. In the case the Master had said that it should be limited to cases where there was a pressing need, for example, where the witness was too ill to attend in person and his evidence was crucial in determining the issues. Also see the video conferencing guidance notes in PD 32, Annex 3. If the witness is going to be unavailable whilst having lengthy medical treatment it may instead be appropriate to seek the court's permission to put in the evidence by way of deposition (see Pt 34).

In the case of *Polanski v Conde Nast Publications Ltd* [2005] UKHL 10; [2005] 1 W.L.R. 637, the claimant sought permission to give evidence in his libel claim by video conference link from France so as to avoid coming to the UK where he might be arrested and extradited to America. The House of Lords held that the use of video conferencing would be likely to be beneficial to the efficient, fair and economic disposal of the litigation and would not prejudice the defendant to any significant extent. Giving evidence by video link was an entirely satisfactory method of giving evidence if there was a sufficient reason for departing from the normal rule that witnesses gave evidence in person before the court. If the claimant could not give evidence by video link he would be gravely handicapped in the conduct of the proceedings but it would not alter his status as a fugitive. The consequences for the parties were one of the factors the court would take into account when deciding whether an order would bring the administration of justice into disrepute. A fugitive from justice was entitled to invoke the assistance of the court and its procedures in protection of his civil rights. It would be inconsistent if a fugitive was entitled to bring his proceedings in the UK but could not take advantage of a procedural facility flowing from a modern technological development which had become readily available to all litigants. The general rule was that in respect of proceedings properly brought in the UK, a claimant's unwillingness to come to the UK because he was a fugitive from justice was a valid reason, and could be a sufficient reason, for making a video conferencing order.

If the court refuses to make a video conferencing order, the applicant may seek to have his witness statement admitted as hearsay evidence (see para.31.013) at trial rather than attend trial to give oral evidence. This could well see the opponent apply for an order requiring the applicant to attend trial to be cross-examined (see para.31.015). In the Polanski case Lord Nicholls indicated that the court would not be bound in those circumstances to make an order excluding the witness statement from evidence.

> "Such an exclusionary order should not be made automatically in respect of the non-attendance of a party or other witness for cross-examination. Such an order should be made only if, exceptionally, justice so requires. The overriding objective of the Civil Procedure Rules is to enable the court to deal with cases justly. The principle underlying the Civil Evidence Act 1995 is that in general the preferable course is to admit hearsay evidence, and let the court attach to the evidence whatever weight may be appropriate, rather than exclude it altogether" (at para.36).

Previous statements of witnesses

31.019 This topic is covered by s.6 of the 1995 Act. Subsection (2) states that, subject to exceptions: "A party who has called or intends to call a person as a witness in civil proceedings may not in those proceedings adduce evidence of a previous statement made by that person". Why? Because ordinarily the duplication of sworn testimony and previous statements adds nothing of value. The main exception to the rule is where in cross-examination it is suggested to the witness that his evidence has been fabricated. In re-examination an earlier written statement may be put to the witness to rebut that allegation.

What if you are served with a statement made by a witness that is inconsistent with a statement previously made by the same witness, for example, in a police accident report or a medical report? Of course, your opponent should have addressed such inconsistencies when preparing the statement but what if he has failed to do so? Provided the existence of the previous inconsistent statement is known to the opponent before the trial you can safely put it to the witness in cross-examination without any fear of objection or a request for an adjournment. The purpose of the cross-examination will be to neutralise or destroy the evidence but it appears that the trial judge may not rely on the previous inconsistent statement as evidence of its truth: see *Field v Denton Hall Services* [2006] EWCA Civ 169, *The Times*, March 22, 2006.

DOCUMENTARY EVIDENCE

31.020 In practice, the parties will usually agree on the documentary evidence that is to be adduced at trial. However, in addition to questions of hearsay dealt with above, three other matters may arise: the authenticity, availability and admissibility of a document.

Rule 32.19 provides that when you disclose a document in accordance with Pt 31 (see Ch.30) the other party is deemed to admit that it is authentic unless he serves on you a notice (Form N268) requiring you to prove it at trial. That notice must be served by the latest time for serving witness statements or within seven days of disclosure of the document, whichever is the later. There are few cases where such a notice is served. What if you receive one? You should consider applying to the court for a direction as to what steps should be taken in light of the overriding objective. If the court holds that the authenticity of the document is not an issue it needs to be concerned with at trial then it can exclude that issue from consideration and, in effect, revoke the notice.

Is it essential to produce the original of a document: the so-called "best evidence rule"? No, said the Court of Appeal in *Springsteen v Flute International Ltd* (2001) L.T.L. April 10. If a party seeks to adduce secondary evidence of the contents of a document then it is a matter for the court to decide, in the light of all the circumstances of the case, what weight, if any, to attach to that evidence. Also see *Post Office Counters Limited v Mahida* [2003] EWCA Civ 1583; *The Times*, October 31, 2003.

What if the original of a document is not in a party's possession but he wants to produce it at the trial? The simple answer is to serve a witness summons on the person holding the document requiring him to produce it to the court (see Ch.36).

What about the admissibility of video evidence said by a defendant to undermine a claimant's personal injury claim to an extent that it would substantially reduce any award? As a general rule it is usually in the interests of justice to permit the defendant to cross-examine the claimant and his medical advisers on that evidence, so long as that does not amount to trial by ambush. The video is a document and should be disclosed in the usual way (see para.30.004 and *Rall v Hume* [2001] 3 All E.R. 248).

But what if the defendant obtains such video evidence covertly? In *Jones v University of Warwick* [2003] EWCA Civ 151; [2003] 1 W.L.R. 954, an enquiry agent, acting for the defendant insurers obtained access to the claimant's home twice by posing as a market researcher. She used a hidden camera and the claimant had no idea that she was being filmed. The film was disclosed to the claimant's solicitors after proceedings for personal injury to the claimant's right hand had been commenced. The defendant's expert, after seeing the films taken in the claimant's home, was of the opinion that the claimant had an entirely satisfactory function in her right hand. The claimant's medical experts came to a different conclusion. Before the Court of Appeal it was not disputed that the enquiry agent was guilty of trespass and that she would not have been given permission to enter had she not misled the claimant as to her identity. As the medical experts had seen what was recorded in the films taken at the claimant's home, if the film was not admitted in evidence, those experts would not be able to give evidence. New medical experts would have to be instructed and the existence of the recordings would have to be concealed from the court and the new experts.

The court accepted in *Jones* that it had a difficult balancing act to perform. The parties' right to a fair hearing was important but it could not ignore the fact that the video recording was obtained as a result of the defendant's representative having trespassed and infringed the claimant's right of privacy. The court felt that if the conduct of the insurers in the case went uncensured, there would be a significant risk that such practices would be encouraged. In extreme cases this behaviour might be so outrageous that the defence should be struck out. Otherwise the court will reflect its disapproval in the order for costs, perhaps on the indemnity basis (see para.38.016) for the entire case.

REAL EVIDENCE

31.021   Real evidence is concerned with matters other than documents, for example, the machine at which the claimant factory worker was injured. Usually, the parties will agree to preserve such evidence until trial but failing such, an injunction can be obtained (see Ch.27). Arguably, real evidence also includes the judge attending the scene of an accident or watching a video or the reconstruction of an accident. On the latter point, the court can compel parties to supply facilities to enable a reconstruction to be made (see *Ash v Buxted Poultry Ltd*, *The Times*, November 29, 1989: defendant-employer ordered to allow the claimant to make a video recording showing the nature of the work done by the claimant, in respect of which he claimed damages for personal injuries).

PLANS, PHOTOGRAPHS, MODELS, ETC.

Rule 33.6 makes special provision for admitting plans, photographs, models and the like as evidence at trial if such are not contained in a witness statement or expert's report not to be given orally at trial nor otherwise the subject of a hearsay notice. For such to be admissible the party intending to rely on the plan, etc., must serve a notice to that effect no later that the latest date for serving witness statements. Where the evidence does form part of an expert's report he must give this notice at the same time as serving the report. After serving notice the party must allow any other party to inspect the evidence should they wish to do so with a view to agreeing it.

31.022

SIMILAR FACT EVIDENCE

As Lord Bingham of Cornhill said in *O'Brien v Chief Constable of South Wales Police* [2005] UKHL 26; *The Times*, April 29, 2005, "That evidence of what happened on an earlier occasion may make the occurrence of what happened on the occasion in question more or less probable can scarcely be denied". This is called similar fact evidence. On what basis is it admissible? The House of Lords held that two questions must be answered in the affirmative.

31.023

First, assuming the evidence (provisionally) to be true, is it "probative"? As Lord Simon of Glaisdale observed in *Director of Public Prosecutions v Kilbourne* [1973] A.C. 729, 756,

> "Evidence is relevant if it is logically probative or disprobative of some matter which requires proof . . . relevant (i.e. logically probative or disprobative) evidence is evidence which makes the matter which requires proof more or less probable".

Secondly, should it be admitted? In making that decision the case management or trial judge should consider such questions as: Does justice require the evidence to be admitted? What is the potential significance of the evidence, assuming it to be true, in the context of the case as a whole? Is it likely that admission of the evidence will distort the trial and distract the attention of the decision-maker by focusing attention on issues collateral to the issue to be decided? Does the potential probative value of the evidence outweigh its potential for causing unfair prejudice? What is the burden in time, cost and personnel resources of disclosure of the evidence? What is the effect on the lengthening of the trial, with the increased cost and stress inevitably involved and the potential prejudice to witnesses called upon to recall matters long closed, or thought to be closed; the loss of documentation; the fading of recollections?

For an example of a case where similar fact evidence was excluded at the case management stage, see *JP Morgan Chase Bank v Springwell Navigation Corp* [2005] EWCA Civ 1602, (2005) L.T.L., December 20.

RECONSTRUCTION EVIDENCE

31.024 A witness may well not be able to remember events that happened several years ago. Can he try to persuade the court that as his usual practice was to take a certain step then he must have taken that step in this particular case? The answer is, yes. In *Pesskin v Mischon de Reya* [2003] EWHC 1745 the defendant solicitors did not have a recollection of the critical events in question, one of which was the giving of advice to the client. Etherton J. found that they had given that advice. In making that finding he relied on the fact that it would be surprising for a solicitor not to have advised the client on the facts of the case. The defendants had give some evidence that their own practice was to explain, and in the case of that particular client it was their practice to explain orally (and not in writing) and to record matters for the benefit of themselves (and not their client) in order to explain the absence of attendance notes of advice.

But what sort of weight will a trial judge gives this evidence? In *Fulham Leisure Holdings Ltd v Nicholson Graham & Jones* [2006] EWHC 2017, [2006] 4 All E.R. 1397, the partner in the defendant firm, Mr Talbot had conduct of the transaction in issue at the critical time and his acts were said to amount to negligence. Mann J. found him to be a careful and conscientious man.

> "He obviously goes about his work, and his evidence, in a methodical way. His recollection of actual events in relation to the history of this action is (again understandably) very thin. Most of his evidence is reconstruction, based mainly on the premise that the consequences of what he did as a matter of drafting are so obvious that viewing the matter realistically he cannot have done them accidentally and cannot have done them without instructions. In other words, if it was a mistake it was so obvious that he cannot have made it. His approach is, in my view, coloured by his expressed view that he does not make what he calls 'material mistakes', by which he meant mistakes which had 'material adverse consequences to a client'. From that he reconstructs that he must have had instructions, that the relevant changes must have been deliberate and that they were done on the basis of what was agreed with the other side . . .
>
> His great firmness in the witness box in his reconstruction of events in a manner which presents the relevant drafting as deliberate and properly approved was in my view coloured by his unwillingness to accept that he might have made a mistake and his strong desire to construct an edifice

consistent with that theory. I therefore have to approach his evidence with a certain amount of caution . . .

He reconstructs on the basis that being a careful solicitor who is unlikely to have made a mistake, he would have done X or Y. Mr Talbot was entitled to put forward his actual recollection, and his recollection as refreshed from his own notes and the notes of others. This last process will be likely to involve a reconstruction exercise going beyond the actual notes. He is also entitled to put forward his own practices, and to interpret the notes that he made on drafts. In addition, he can seek to demonstrate himself as being a careful and competent solicitor, because that may go to the probabilities of his having made a mistake of the nature alleged as opposed to his having done the acts deliberately. All this will be against the background of real events in which the witness participated, and he is entitled to give a flavour of those events too. It is inevitable at that point that his evidence would spill over to an expression of what he believed happened, which is a further stage in a reconstruction exercise. It is inevitable that any competently conducted cross-examination will end up with his giving answers which amount to that, because such a cross-examination would have to put the negligence case to him and invite him to deal with it. There is nothing wrong with his doing that in answer to the inevitable questions, and therefore nothing wrong with his anticipating them (so far as he does) in his evidence in chief. The objected to parts are therefore an inevitable, or an almost inevitable, continuation of a reconstruction exercise which the witness is clearly entitled to do at least some of, and to characterise this end point as inadmissible is unrealistic (whether or not technically correct). Its weight is, of course, a different matter, and the greater the extent of his theorising, and the farther it moves from established facts or plainly admissible evidence, the less weight it probably has."

ADVICE ON EVIDENCE

It is in respect of substantial multi-track cases that a solicitor usually instructs counsel to appear at the trial. If so it is often desirable to let counsel prepare the statements of case and to consult with him as to the case management directions. Once disclosure and the exchange of evidence has taken place it is usual to obtain a written advice from counsel on evidence. It is just as important to obtain a detailed and comprehensive survey of all the evidence even if the solicitor or someone else in the firm intends to conduct the case. In large or difficult matters it is often appropriate to seek a second opinion on evidence.

31.025

It is not enough for a solicitor to have his secretary copy every document in sight and to send them to counsel saying, "Here are the papers—please advise on evidence". The solicitor must sift through the documentation on file isolating those that may be relevant and include:

(1) witness statements of the client and all potential witnesses;
(2) medical and other expert evidence;
(3) all the evidence received from the other parties;
(4) statements of case;
(5) any replies to requests for further information;
(6) correspondence;
(7) any interim orders;
(8) any photographs, plans, etc.; and
(9) opinions previously received from counsel.

The instructions should summarise the issues and state clearly what it is necessary to prove and how at this stage it is proposed to prove it. Any questions for counsel to consider should be well signposted. Ask counsel if he requires a conference with the client before advising in writing. You might also ask counsel to telephone you for a chat first.

The advice must be carefully studied. It is sensible to tick off each paragraph as you deal with it. Always go back to counsel for further advice if anything happens which may cause counsel to change his view of the case, for example, if evidence subsequently disclosed by the other side contains points which were not anticipated. If counsel does not conduct any case management hearing and directions are given in terms that differ from counsel's recommendations you should refer the matter back to him immediately to consider an appeal against the order.

CHAPTER 32

Fact Management

FURTHER INFORMATION (Pt 18)

Rule 18.1 provides that the court may at any time order a party to: (a) clarify any matter which is in dispute in the proceedings; or (b) give additional information in relation to any such matter, whether or not the matter is contained or referred to in a statement of case (see Ch.12). As to the court exercising this power of its own initiative, see para.33.001. In this Chapter we will be concerned with the parties managing the facts in the case.

32.001

If a party, whether claimant or defendant, fails to state his case with sufficient detail or serves inadequate witness statements, his opponent may seek clarification. He has a right to know what case he will have to meet at trial. This will avoid unnecessary expense and avoid him being taken by surprise.

Assume that the claimants are a firm of property managing agents. The claimants bring an action against the defendants, a group of 42 property companies, for terminating their appointment as the defendants' managing agents without giving the notice required by the contract. In the defence, the defendants state that they were entitled to terminate the agreement by reason of the failure of the claimants to exercise due care, skill and diligence in managing the properties. The following particulars are given of those allegations:

> "(i) The claimants failed to collect on the defendants' behalf monies due to the defendants in respect of rents, maintenance charges, insurance premiums and the like. (ii) The claimants failed regularly or at all to inspect the defendants' properties. (iii) The claimants failed to carry out or have carried out sufficiently or at all any necessary repairs renewals or general maintenance of the defendants' properties. (iv) The claimants failed to ensure that leases or the like which they negotiated on behalf of the defendants, (a) contained the normal tenants' covenants; (b) provided for the payment of rent at the market rate; (c) contained rent revision clauses; (d) were so drawn that management expenses incurred by the defendants would be as low as possible. (v) The claimants failed to ensure that shops and the like with residential accommodation above were let to one and the same tenant. (vi) The claimants failed to enforce on behalf of the defendants various tenants' covenants in respect of which tenants were in breach".

"What the defendants have done by way of particulars is to enumerate every obligation which managing agents of property would be expected to have and to say quite generally that the [claimants] failed to comply with it" (per Plowman J. in *Cyril Leonard & Co. v Simo Securities Ltd* [1971] 3 All E.R. 1318). As the claimants did not know the substance of the case alleged against them the defendants were ordered to give further information by answering the following request:

> "Of the allegations that the defendants were entitled to terminate the agreement by reason of the failure of the claimants to exercise due care, skill and diligence, specify all such failures of the claimants relied upon by the defendants as entitling them to terminate the agreement, stating in relation to each such failure (a) the property in question (b) all facts and matters relied upon as constituting such failure".

WHEN TO ASK

32.002 Practice Direction 18, para.1.3 provides that requests for further information should be made as far as possible in a single comprehensive request and not piecemeal. Any application concerning statements of case should be outlined in or ideally accompany the allocation questionnaire. As a general rule, however, the court will not order particulars until after disclosure and inspection (see generally Ch.30). Ordering the opponent to supply now that which he will supply anyway later inevitably increases costs. The order is not justifiable unless it serves some litigious purpose.

Early clarification may be required where the party alone is in possession of the information. In *Monk v Redwing Aircraft Co. Ltd* [1942] 1 All E.R. 133 clarification of the claimant's claim was ordered before the defendant served his defence. The claimant had sought damages for wrongful dismissal. The information ordered to be given was as to: (a) the length of notice the claimant alleged as being reasonable notice: (b) the employments he had been engaged in since the dismissal: and (c) the salary which he had received since his dismissal. These facts were, of course, matters entirely within the knowledge of the claimant himself. In addition, the defendants required the information in order to consider making a Pt 36 offer (see Ch.29).

In *Jones v Swift Structures* (1995) C.L.Y. 4160, the claimant commenced proceedings against two defendants for damages in respect of an injury he sustained at work on a construction site. After service of the first defendant's defence but before disclosure, the claimant asked eight short questions by way of clarification. The court ordered that these should be answered as whether or not the claimant continued or discontinued (see Ch.35) his action against the first defendant depended on the replies given. All the parties would needlessly incur costs if the claimant was forced to wait until after disclosure before being able to properly consider discontinuance (see Ch.35).

Early clarification of the claimant's case was also ordered in *Honey v Newman* (1997) C.L.Y. 634 in order to assist the defendant make a realistic and informed assessment of the claim for the purposes of a Pt 36 offer. Proceedings were commenced following a road traffic accident. Liability was not disputed. The claimant's action included claims for: (a) cost of repair of his motor car; (b) diminution in its value: and (c) hire charges. The defendant requested clarification of various aspects of the claim. The circuit judge required the claimant to answer certain questions including; (a) as to the date of repair of the vehicle as that was relevant to the interest calculation; (b) as to whether the vehicle had been involved in any other accident and if so details of the repairs, as that was relevant to the claim for diminution in value; (c) as to the particular make and model of the vehicle as that was relevant to the claim for diminution in value; (d) as to the date of disposal of the vehicle and details of the sum paid and to whom it was disposed as that was relevant to the claim for diminution in value; and (e) as to the recorded mileage at the date of sale as this was relevant to the issue of diminution in value.

In *Corporation Nacional del Cobre de Chile v Metallgesellschaft AG Ltd, The Times*, January 6, 1999 it was held that further information might be ordered to assist a party make an application for summary judgment (see Ch.19) even if disclosure had not been completed. The judge said that the case must have the makings of a Pt 24 case and the exercise must not be a fishing expedition. Whilst the questions put in the case were numerous, he held that they were not oppressive as most were capable of short answers. Further, it was reasonably conceivable that the answers might shorten or dispense with a full trial, or at least reduce further disclosure.

HOW TO ASK

Practice Direction 18, para.1.1 provides that the party seeking clarification or information should first serve a Request for such. A reasonable time should be specified for a response. A letter can be used if the Request and reply are likely to be brief. Any such letter must identify itself as a Pt 18 Request and it must not deal with any other matter. 32.003

Normally, the Request forms a separate document. PD 18, para.1.6 provides that any Request must:

(a) be headed with the name of the court, title and number;
(b) in its heading state that it is a Request made under Pt 18, identify the parties concerned and state the date on which it is made;
(c) set out in a separate numbered paragraph each request for information or clarification;
(d) where a Request relates to a document, identify that document and (if relevant) the paragraph or words to which it relates;
(e) state the date by which a response is expected.

A Request may set out the questions on the left-hand side of the page and leave room for the answers on the right. If this practice is adopted the request should be sent in duplicate.

WHAT NOT TO ASK

32.004 Practice Direction 18, para.1.2 provides that a Request for clarification or information should be concise and strictly confined to matters which are reasonably necessary and proportionate to enable the questioner to prepare his own case or to understand the case he has to meet.

In addition to the cases cited above, useful guidance as to the sort of questions that should generally be avoided was given in the case of *Det Danske Hedelskabet v KDM International Plc* [1994] 2 Lloyd's Rep. 534. A dispute had arisen as to whether Christmas trees delivered by the claimant to the defendant had excessive needle drop. One hundred and six questions were asked by the defendant of the claimant who refused to answer them. Some questions related to information obtainable from the claimant's suppliers whilst others related to average prices paid by the claimant. The court held that information which will lead only to further inquiry is not essential information. Requests which can only be answered by detailed research or investigation, which the party being questioned would not otherwise have undertaken for trial, will hardly ever be necessary. Hypothetical questions should normally be avoided. The claimant's suppliers were not its agents and the claimant was entitled to reply that it did not know answers to questions directed at its suppliers. It was oppressive for the claimant to be asked to prepare statistical information which required a substantial investigatory exercise and which would yield a marginal evidentiary contribution.

You cannot seek further information to "fish" for a case. In *Rofe v Kevorkian* [1936] 2 All E.R. 1334, D denied that he was liable for the price of certain drawings sold to him by C as originals on the ground that they were merely copies. The Court of Appeal refused to allow a Request asking C when, where and from whom he had acquired the drawings. The Request was held to be a fishing expedition "by a man who is trying to make a case and has not already the evidence which would justify him in making the case" (*per* Greer L.J.). Likewise, the Court of Appeal in *Best v Charter Medical of England Ltd*, *The Times*, November 19, 2001, held that unless there was evidence of a good cause of action in defamation, an order for further information under Pt 18 would be a fishing expedition. However, if the claimant could meet that test, the precise words might be ascertained by such an order. Also note that r.53.3 provides that unless the court orders otherwise, a party will not be required in defamation proceedings to answer a Pt 18 request about the identity of the defendant's sources of information.

RESPONDING TO A REQUEST

Where the questions are put by letter the response may be in the same way. If the Request was provided in duplicate with space for the answers on the right-hand side that document should be used. Otherwise, the formalities are similar to a formal Request, namely: 32.005

(a) be headed with the name of the court, title and number;
(b) in its heading identify itself as a response to the request;
(c) repeat the text of each paragraph of the Request and set out under each paragraph the answer; and
(d) refer to and have attached to it a copy of any document not already in the possession of the questioner which forms part of the response.

However, note two important additional matters:

(a) the response must be verified by a statement of truth (see generally para.12.004); and
(b) a party serving a response must also file it with the court along with a copy of the Request.

If a party objects to complying with the Request or part of it, or is unable to do so at all, or within the time stated, he must inform the questioner promptly and in any event within the time stated. A letter will suffice. Reasons for the response should be given, for example, the request can only be complied with at disproportionate expense. If appropriate, he should give the date by which he expects to be able to reply. There is no need for the responding party to do anything else. But it is vital that some sort of response is made in time (see below). If the questioner wants to take the matter further he must apply to the court for an order.

APPLYING FOR AN ORDER

If after serving a Request there is no response in the time stated or the questioner disagrees with any response given, he should apply for a court order. The simplest method is to attach a copy of the Request to the application notice along with a draft order. Supporting evidence should be prepared consisting of a witness statement exhibiting any response. There is no need to serve any other party provided 14 days have passed since the Request was served and the time stated for a response has come and gone without any being received. In such circumstances the court may make an order without a hearing. 32.006

If the court is satisfied that the questions meet the Pt 18 criteria it normally orders that answers should be given by a specified time and date otherwise a sanction is imposed, for example, the defaulting party's statement of case is struck out (see para.33.008). In *Parkin v Brew* (1999) C.L. May 38, the claimant brought an action for damages for multiple personal injuries. The defendant sought clarification of certain aspects of her claim for care and business losses estimated at £577,000. The claimant's solicitors failed to comply with an order to answer the Request and a sanction was imposed striking out her claim for the care and business losses. The solicitors applied for relief from the sanction on the ground that the default had been due to the delay of the claimant's accountant in preparing a report on the special damages. It was held that there was no compelling excuse for the default. If the accountant's report was necessary to enable the Request to be answered then the claimant's solicitors should have taken action to withdraw instructions from the accountants who had delayed in preparing the report. The defendant and his solicitors had been prejudiced in that the claimant's claim could not be properly evaluated until the Request had been answered. The judge said that the larger the claim the greater should be the diligence of a claimant's solicitors rather than the indulgence of the court.

NOTICES TO ADMIT (R.32.18)

32.007 Significant costs can be incurred when preparing witness statements and in calling witnesses at trial. What can be done if a party refuses to make reasonable admissions in his statements of case and therefore forces the other parties to incur expense? The rules make three provisions: first, further information (see above). Secondly, costs sanctions are imposed on a party if he behaves unreasonably. Thirdly, the notice to admit procedure. This is often the best method to try although unfortunately it has never been used frequently enough in practice.

Any party may, without needing the permission of the court, serve on his opponent a notice (Form N266) specifying certain facts or specifying a certain part of his case. The notice calls upon the opponent to deliver a written admission of the facts, or the part of the case. No time limit is placed on a reply being given. Any admission so made is for the purposes of the action only, can be used only by the person serving the notice and can be amended or withdrawn if the court so allows (see para.16.009).

The sanction behind the notice is that, if the recipient does not admit the matters it specifies within a reasonable time he may be penalised in costs even if he wins the case overall.

Example

In a road accident case D has a good defence on negligence but decides also to deny that he was involved in the accident. C serves a notice to admit facts establishing that D was involved in the accident. D does not admit them. At trial the judge finds that D was involved but that he was not negligent. The judge therefore dismisses C's claim with costs. However, C should point out D's unreasonable conduct in refusing to admit his involvement in the accident and request a special order for costs which penalises D for his unreasonableness (see further para.38.018, below).

When to serve

A notice to admit must be served at least 21 days before the trial. As to the methods of service, see Ch.8. 32.008

CHAPTER 33

Judicial Case Management

COURT'S POWER TO MAKE AN ORDER OF ITS OWN INITIATIVE (R.3.3)

33.001 Unless a rule or some other enactment provides otherwise, the court may exercise its powers on an application or of its own initiative. Where the court proposes to act it may, as a matter of its discretion, give any person likely to be affected by the order an opportunity to make representations, often limited to written submissions. However, if the court makes an order without any hearing or representations, any party affected by it may apply in the usual way (see Chs 13 and 14) to have the order set aside, or varied, or stayed. The order should specify the time limit in which the application should be made.

In very limited circumstances the court may exercise this power to strike out a claim after the claimant has called all his evidence. In *Bentley v Jones Harris & Co.* [2001] EWCA Civ 1724, (2001) L.T.L., November 2, Latham L.J. observed:

> "If a judge concludes at the end of a claimant's evidence, whether on the application of the defendant or of his own motion, that the claimant has no real prospect of success or, in other words, is bound to fail, on his assessment of the evidence before him at that stage, he is in my view entitled to give judgment for the defendant, in the same way as if there had been an application at an earlier stage in the proceedings for summary judgment under CPR part 24.2. In that way, he will be giving effect, in the circumstances of the trial, to the overriding objective and in particular to the need to contain within limits the expenditure of time and costs on the particular case before him".

If the court does consider striking out the claim before the defendant has called any evidence, it will take into account similar factors as to those concerning a submission of no case to answer (see para.37.005).

> "Thus it will be necessary to have regard not only to the weakness of the claimant's case taken in isolation on the basis of the evidence so far called, but to the availability of so far uncalled evidence from either party which if called might increase the strength of the claimant's case sufficiently to

clear the bundle of the no realistic prospect of success test and to the possible availability of inferences adverse to the defendant and therefore capable of sustaining the claimant's case which might be drawn from the defendant's encouragement of the court's termination of the trial by striking out the whole or part of the claim" (*per* Mr Justice Colman in *National Westminster Bank Plc v Rabobank Nederland* [2006] EWHC 2959, (2006) L.T.L. December 1).

Extending or shortening time for compliance (r.3.1(2)(a))

The court may extend, and indeed shorten, the time for compliance with any rule, practice direction or court order. A retrospective extension of time may be granted, i.e. an application for an extension can be made after the time for compliance has expired. 33.002

The Court of Appeal gave general guidance in the case of *Mortgage Corp Ltd v Sandoes* [1996] T.L.R. 751 as follows:

(a) Time requirements laid down by the rules and directions given by the court are not merely targets to be attempted; they are rules to be observed.
(b) At the same time the overriding objective is that justice must be done.
(c) Litigants are entitled to have their cases resolved with reasonable expedition. The non-compliance with time limits can cause prejudice to one or more of the parties.
(d) The vacation or adjournment of the date of trial prejudices other litigants and disrupts the administration of justice.
(e) Extensions of time which involve the vacation or adjournment of trial dates are granted as a last resort.
(f) Where time limits have not been complied with the parties should co-operate in reaching an agreement as to new time limits that do not involve the date of trial being postponed.
(g) The courts will not look with favour on a party who seeks only to take tactical advantage from the failure of another party to comply with time limits.
(h) In considering whether to grant an extension of time to a party who is in default, the court will look at all the circumstances of the case.

As to granting a retrospective extension of time to serve witness statements see *Stroh v London Borough of Haringey* (1999) L.T.L. July 13 and *Mealey Horgan Plc v Horgan, The Times*, July 6, 1999, discussed at para.31.007.

Any application made for an extension of time, particularly for a retrospective extension, should in our view be supported by evidence that sets out the reasons for the delay, even if they are not good ones. In *Southwark LBC v Nejad, The Times*, January 28, 1999, the Court of Appeal stated that whilst the court should not fetter itself from exercising a discretion to extend time simply because there was no explanation for the delay and in particular no acceptable reason for such, the explanation given, or the lack of it, or the frankness of it, were factors which the court was entitled to take into account. The exercise was said to be one of balancing all the relevant factors and where the result of not granting an extension would be draconian, the court was concerned to assess the proportionality of the resulting penalty to the applicant to his failure or failures. In other words, the punishment should fit the crime.

Where the court is considering a retrospective, rather than a prospective, application to extend time, it should have regard to the checklist of factors in r.3.9 (see para.33.011): *Sayers v Clarke-Walker (a firm)* [2002] 1 W.L.R. 3095 and *Robert v Momentum Services Ltd, The Times*, February 13, 2003.

Is it ever appropriate for the court to dismiss an application for an extension of time on the ground that the claim is weak? In the Robert case the Court of Appeal held that such should only occur in exceptional cases. The court would have to be able to conclude that an application to strike out the claim under r.3.4 (see para.33.008) or an application for summary judgment (see Ch.19) by the defendant under r.24 would succeed. To refuse a prospective application for an extension of time on the ground that the claim is weak but the tests under rr.3.4 and 24.2 are not met, would be a truly draconian step to take that might well infringe a claimant's rights to a fair trial under Art.6 of the ECHR. Where appropriate the defendant should cross-apply under either or both of those Rules. In any event, if a defendant does wish to argue a lack of merits of the claim as a reason for refusing an extension of time, notice should be given to the claimant.

Finally, it must be remembered that r.2.11 allows the parties to vary a date for taking a step in proceedings by written agreement unless a rule or court order prohibits it. We have already seen examples of such prohibitory Rules (paras 9.029, 21.009 and 22.011). But does the fact that a rule imposing a time limit is expressed in mandatory terms (i.e. "must") mean that it falls within r.2.11? We would say not. The prohibitory Rules are explicit, for example, rr.28.4 and 29.5 state that "A party must apply to the court if he wishes to vary [certain dates in the case management timetable] and further adds that "Any date set by the court or these Rules for doing any act may not be varied by the parties if the variation would make it necessary to vary any of the dates". Equally, r.3.8(3) provides that "the time for doing the act in question may not be extended by agreement between the parties".

STAY OF PROCEEDINGS (R.3.1(2)(F))

33.003   A stay imposes a halt on proceedings, apart from taking any steps allowed by the rules or the terms of the stay. Proceedings can be continued if the stay is lifted. The court may stay the whole or part of any proceedings or judgment either generally or until a specified date. Some stays arise as a result of particular rules, for example, after six months' inactivity (see para.16.010) or after acceptance of a Pt 36 offer (see para.29.015). But in all circumstances a stay must be a proportionate order (*James v Baily Gibson & Co. (a firm)* (2002) L.T.L. October 30: an order staying the whole proceedings on the ground that the claimant had failed to comply with orders for psychiatric tests was disproportionate as it denied her the opportunity to claim for heads of damage not affected by the lack of psychiatric evidence). We have outlined below the more general grounds for the imposition of a stay.

Stay pending appeal in another decision

In *Nixon v F. J. Morris Contracting Ltd* (1999) L.T.L. August 31 C claimed damages for personal injuries which led to multiple sclerosis ("MS"). The trial of some preliminary issues was fixed for October 4, 1999. Meanwhile the issue of whether symptoms of MS could be triggered by trauma to the head and/or neck had been considered in a Scottish case and the House of Lords were due to hear an appeal in that matter in February 2000 in which they would undertake a detailed examination of the scientific evidence on the point. The Court of Appeal stayed the action pending that appeal. The court held that it would not be right to require C to incur the expense of a ten-day trial in October 1999, going over much of the same evidence as had been before the Scottish courts, before the House of Lords decision on that evidence was known.

33.003A

Stay pending arbitration

Domestic arbitration proceedings: in *Halki Shipping Corporation v Sopex Oils Ltd*, *The Times*, January 19, 1998, the Court of Appeal held that a defendant who was a party to an arbitration agreement was entitled to a stay of court proceedings unless the court was satisfied that the action was not brought in respect of the matter referred to arbitration or was bought under an agreement which was null and void, inoperative or incapable of being performed. See s.9 of the Arbitration Act 1996.

33.004

In *Patel v Patel, The Times*, April 9, 1999, D acknowledged service of court proceedings and indicated an intent to contest them. This was required before an application for a stay of those proceedings could be made under the Arbitration Act 1996, s.9. However, he failed to serve a defence in time and C entered judgment in default. D then applied to set aside the default judgment, for an order to be allowed to defend the claim and to make a counterclaim and for directions. C argued that this amounted to taking a step in the substantive proceedings and that as a result D was barred from seeking a stay. The Court of Appeal held that D's application did not help C since without it there would have been no proceedings to stay. D did not need permission to defend and counterclaim if his application was successful. By requesting something surplus to the relief actually required D had not taken a substantive step in the proceedings. The application for consequential directions was ambivalent, as one of these could have been for a stay. The court said that to refuse a stay would be contrary to the spirit of the Act itself.

If a defendant applies for a stay but subsequently issues an application for summary judgment, does he thereby accept the court's jurisdiction? Yes, answered the Court of Appeal in *Capital Trust Investment Ltd v Radio Design AB* [2002] 2 All E.R. 159 unless, when making the summary judgment application, the defendant makes it perfectly clear that it is conditional on the stay application failing.

Third party proceedings (see para.18.005) may be stayed under s.9 pursuant to an arbitration agreement (see *Wealand v CLC Contractors Ltd* (1998) C.L.Y. 251).

Where proceedings are stayed the claimant will normally be ordered to pay the defendant's costs on the indemnity basis.

In exceptional circumstances, if the court has no jurisdiction under s.9 because there is an issue whether or not an arbitration agreement has been concluded, the court may exercise its inherent jurisdiction to order a stay: see *Albon v Naza Motor Trading SDN BHD* [2007] EWHC 665, (2007) L.T.L., April 11.

Where only one of several defendants to litigation is entitled to a stay of proceedings in favour of arbitration, the court will only grant a stay in rare and compelling cases: see *Mabey and Johnson Ltd v Danos* [2007] EWHC 1094, (2007) L.T.L. May 14.

Foreign arbitration proceedings: in *Reichhold Norway ASA v Goldman Sachs International* [2000] 2 All E.R. 679, the Court of Appeal held that where claimants, who were engaged in a foreign arbitration against a company that was not a party to relevant English proceedings, brought an action in England in respect of claims which arose out of the same subject-matter the court might properly stay the action pending final determination of the abitration.

Other grounds for a stay

33.005　Stay pending payment of costs in earlier proceedings: where a party has been unsuccessful in one action and commences a further action in respect of the same or substantially the same subject-matter the action will be stayed until he has paid the costs of the first set of proceedings (see *Society of Lloyd's v Jaffray* (1999) C.L. June and *Investment Invoice Financing Ltd v Limehouse Board Mills Ltd* [2006] EWCA Civ 9, [2006] 1 W.L.R. 985). See also r.3.4(4).

Stay pending criminal proceedings: in *Secretary of State for Trade and Industry v Pollock* (1998) C.L.Y. 681 it was held that there was no general rule that civil proceedings should await the outcome of criminal proceedings. It was for the applicant to show that there was a real risk of serious prejudice or injustice by demonstrating that if he was cross-examined during criminal proceedings on the basis of his testimony given during the civil action he was at risk of serious prejudice. Such a risk was recognised by the general principle that a person facing a criminal charge was not required to give a detailed account of his affairs in advance of criminal proceedings. However, in *Surrey Oaklands NHS Trust v Hurley* (1999) L.T.L., June 25 it was held that a defendant was not to be excused from taking any procedural step in civil proceedings merely because that step would have the effect of disclosing his defence in the criminal proceedings. This was particularly so where recent changes in the criminal law permitted adverse inferences to be drawn from a defendant's silence. Moreover, there was no reason in principle why an application for summary judgment (see Ch.19) should have to await the outcome of concurrent criminal proceedings. See also *Zambia v Meer Care & Desai* [2006] EWCA Civ 390, (2006) L.T.L., March 7. As to the procedural requirements, see PD 23, para.11.

SPLIT TRIALS AND PRELIMINARY ISSUES

The court may direct a separate trial of any issue and dismiss or give judgment on a claim after a decision on a preliminary issue—see r.3.1(2)(i) and (l). 33.006

It is sometimes advantageous to try the issue of liability first or some other factual question. The court seeks at an early stage to identify any potentially decisive issues and may order that these are to be tried first. Indeed, the decision on one particular issue often leads to the parties settling the remainder of the dispute.

In multi-track cases (see Ch.22) consideration is usually given at the case management conference and again at the pre-trial review as to the possibility of the trial of a preliminary issue or issues the resolution of which is likely to shorten the proceedings.

G K R Karate (UK) Ltd v Yorkshire Post Newspapers Ltd [2000] 2 All E.R. 931 concerned a claim for libel in which the defences raised included justification and fair comment. The time estimate for a full trial was four to six weeks whereas a trial limited to the defence of fair comment would last approximately three days. At a pre-trial review the judge ordered a split trial with the defence of fair comment being tried first. This decision was upheld by the Court of Appeal as being fair, sensible and economic. Contrast with *DHL Air Limited v Wells* [2003] EWCA Civ 1743; *The Times*, November 14, 2003.

In *Tilling v Whiteman* [1979] 1 All E.R. 737 the House of Lords warned of the dangers of allowing preliminary points of law to be decided on hypothetical facts. In the case the claimants were the joint owners of a dwelling-house. They let the property but subsequently sought to recover possession. On a preliminary point the judge held that since the house was required as a residence for only one of the claimants the application did not fall within the statutory ground claimed. The Court of Appeal dismissed the appeal but the House of Lords allowed it. Lord Scarman said that the decision in the county court on a preliminary point of law was a disturbing feature of the case. He commented that:

> "Had an extra half an hour or so been used to hear the evidence, one of two consequences would have ensued. Either [the first claimant] would have been believed when she said she required the house as a residence, or she would not. If the latter, that would have been the end of the case. If the former, your Lordships' decision allowing the appeal would now be final. As it is, the case has to go back to the county court to be tried. Preliminary points of law are too often treacherous short cuts. Their price can be, as here, delay, anxiety and expense".

In *McLoughlin v Grovers (a firm)* [2002] 2 W.L.R. 1279, the Court of Appeal indicated that the correct approach to preliminary issues was:

(a) only issues that were decisive or potentially decisive should be identified;
(b) the questions should usually be questions of law;
(c) they should be decided on the basis of a schedule of agreed or assumed facts;
(d) they should be triable without significant delay, making full allowance for the implications of a possible appeal; and
(e) any order should be made by the court after a case management conference.

In personal injury cases, orders for a split trial of liability and quantum are frequently ordered where the applicant can show that it is likely to lead to economies in time and costs. However, such an order is not appropriate in every personal injury case. Sometimes, the witnesses likely to be called on both issues are largely the same and therefore a split trial might just lead to increased costs and delay. In *Cullen v London Fire & Civil Defence Authority* (1999) L.T.L. August 8, C was a fireman. He claimed damages for psychiatric injury caused by shock as a result of D's alleged negligence. The judge refused to order a split trial as to whether D was under a duty to C and whether that duty was breached. The Court of Appeal held that it could find no error in the judge's reasoning and was not persuaded that a split trial would be economic in time or costs.

CONDITIONAL ORDERS (R.3.1(3))

33.007 When the court makes an order it may impose conditions, including that of a payment into court and also specify the consequences of failure to comply with the order or condition, for example, that the party's statement of case is struck out. The purpose of such orders is not so much to punish bad behaviour but to encourage good behaviour in the future. A party who has failed or refused to allow inspection of a document may be ordered to produce it by a certain deadline or the proceedings will be terminated in favour of his opponent (see further, para.30.022). If past non-compliance has led to the entry of a default judgment, the court may require a payment into court as a condition for setting that judgment aside: this prevents the guilty party from using further proceedings merely as a delaying tactic. Conditional orders must be expressed clearly and precisely and the condition must be one which is capable of being complied with. An impecunious party should not be ordered to pay into court a sum of money which he is unlikely to be able to raise (*M. V Yorke Motors v Edwards* [1982] 1 W.L.R. 444, HL and *Chapple v Williams* (1999) L.T.L. December 8).

Often a party will be given one final chance to meet the terms of an order, including any conditions previously imposed. This is known as an "unless order". Why? Because the order will normally automatically debar the defaulting party from pursuing his claim, defence or counterclaim *unless* within a specified period of time he meets the terms of the order. Indeed, PD 3 para.1.9 makes it clear that where a court order states "shall be struck out or dismissed" or "will be struck out or dismissed" this means that the striking out or dismissal will be automatic and that no further order of the court is required. This was confirmed by the Court of Appeal in *Marcan Shipping (London) Ltd v Kefalas* [2007] EWCA Civ 463, [2007] 3 All E.R. 365.

A typical example of an unless order can be seen in the case of *Jani-King (GB) Ltd v Prodger* [2007] EWHC 712, (2007) L.T.L. April 10. There the defendant failed to comply with a specific disclosure order in respect of his counterclaim (see para.30.021). Subsequently the order was made an unless order. Whilst the defendant disclosed various documents within the time limit, there were omissions. What could the defendant do? The general test in respect of unless orders is whether there has been complete compliance with the order, subject only to any de minimis exceptions: see *Hytec Information Systems Ltd v Coventry CC* [1997] 1 W.L.R. 1666. As the defendant accepted that, based on that test, he could not argue that there had been compliance, he could not pursue an appeal. He did apply for relief from the sanction (see para.33.011) and this was granted.

An unless order should not normally be made if permission to appeal the original order was granted on the grounds of the respondent's impecuniousity: see *Radu v Houston* [2006] EWCA Civ 1575, *The Times*, January 1, 2007. In the same case the Court of Appeal also observed that a security for costs order (see Ch.26) should not normally be made on an unless basis on the first occasion.

STRIKING OUT A STATEMENT OF CASE (R.3.4)

By r.3.4(2) the court may, of its own initiative or on application, strike out a statement of case, or any part of it, if it appears to the court that: 33.008

(a) The statement of case discloses no reasonable grounds for bringing or defending the claim

What if particulars of claim or a defence merely state, "Money owed £5,000" or "I deny that I owe the money" (i.e. a bare denial); or are incoherent and make no sense; or contain a coherent set of facts but even if those facts are true no legally recognisable claim or defence is disclosed? These are examples given in PD 3.4, paras 1.4 and 1.6 as to when the claim or defence might be struck out as disclosing no reasonable grounds for bringing or defending the action.

If a party believes that he can show without a trial that his opponent's case has no real prospect of success on the facts, or that the matter is bound to succeed or fail, as the case may be, because of a point of law (including the construction of a document), that party may apply under r.3.4 and/or for summary judgment under Pt 24 (see Ch.19; *Taylor v Midland Bank Trust Co. Ltd* (1999) L.T.L., August 21). A statement of case is not suitable for striking out if it raises a serious live issue of fact which can only properly be determined by hearing oral evidence (*Bridgeman v McAlpine-Brown* (2000) L.T.L. January 19). As to the principles upon which a court may strike out an allegation of fraud or dishonesty see *Three Rivers DC v Governor and Company of the Bank of England* (No.3) [2001] 2 All E.R. 513.

(b) That the statement of case is an abuse of the court's process or is otherwise likely to obstruct the just disposal of the proceedings, for example, it is vexatious, scurrilous or obviously ill-founded (see PD 3.4, para.1.5).

Proceedings will be struck out as an abuse of process if the issues could and should have been dealt with in earlier litigation between the parties: see *Joseph v Joseph* (2003) L.T.L. February 27. So this applies where C sues D twice in respect of the same issues. Moreover, it also applies where C sues D, D takes additional proceedings against TP and then subsequently C sues TP making the same allegations: see *Aldi Stores Ltd v WSP Group Plc* [2007] EWHC 55, (2007) L.T.L., February 8.

If parties to later civil proceedings were not parties to, or privies of those who were parties to the earlier proceedings, then it will only be an abuse of the process of the court to challenge the factual findings and conclusions of the judge or jury in the earlier action if: (i) it would be manifestly unfair to a party to the later proceedings that the same issues should be relitigated; or (ii) to permit such litigation would bring the administration of justice into disrepute: see *Nesbitt v Wilf Holt of the Citizens Advice Burea* [2007] EWCA Civ 249, (2007) L.T.L., March 26.

If a claimant commences proceedings when he has no known basis for making a claim, it is likely to be struck out.

> "If a claimant cannot point to any particular instance of negligence, breach of duty, negligent misstatement or negligent misrepresentation at the time of the issue of the Claim Form, he cannot have any valid basis for his claim at that point and has no business issuing a Claim Form to stop the running of time in respect of some claim which he hopes in the future to be able to formulate. That is the key element of abuse in this case" (*per* Cooke J. in *Nomura International Plc v Granada Group Ltd* [2007] EWHC 642, (2007) L.T.L. 30 March. The case is discussed at para.12.014).

A Pt 8 claim (see Ch.10) made to avoid the time limits for judicial review proceedings (see Ch.24) under Pt 54 is likely to be struck out as an abuse of process: see *Carter Commercial Developments v Bedford BC* (2001) 34 E.G.C.S. 99. Similarly, if a judge strikes out the allegation of publication of a defamatory statement to all but the claimant's partner, the judge may then dismiss the claim as an abuse on the basis that any damages awarded would be nominal and disproportionate to the costs involved: see *Wallis v Valentine, The Times,* August 9, 2002. However, a statement of case in an area of developing jurisprudence should not be struck out where it raises a serious issue of fact that can only be properly determined by hearing oral evidence: see *Partco Group Ltd v Wragg* (2002) 2 Lloyd's Rep. 343.

For a full discussion of abuse of process see the House of Lords case of *Johnson v Gore Wood & Co. (a firm) (No.1)* [2001] 1 All E.R. 481.

Proceedings are vexatious if they comprise two or more sets of proceedings in respect of the same subject-matter and amount to harassment of the defendant in order to make him fight the same battle more than once with the attendant multiplication of costs, time and stress. In addition to striking out the statement of cases in such proceedings, the court may make an order prohibiting new proceedings being commenced without the court's permission (*Ebert v Venvil* [2000] Ch. 484). Indeed, whenever an action is struck out for wrongful conduct by the claimant and that claimant then commences a second action in respect of the same subject-matter, the court should start with the assumption that some special reason has to be identified to justify a second action being allowed to proceed (*Securum Finance Ltd v Ashton* [2000] 3 W.L.R. 1400).

Alternatively, if the second action is not struck out and costs were ordered in the first action but have not yet been paid, the second action may be stayed until the costs of the first action have been paid (r.3.4(3)).

(c) That there has been a failure to comply with a rule, practice direction or court order

In *Biguzzi v Rank Leisure Plc* [1999] 1 W.L.R. 1926, Lord Woolf, M.R. gave useful guidance on this matter. He said that under the CPR the keeping of time limits was far more important than under the previous rules of court. The clearest reflection of such can be found in the overriding objective and this unqualified, discretionary power to strike out a statement of case for failure to comply with a rule, etc. However, the fact that a judge has this power does not mean that in applying the overriding objective the initial approach should be to strike out the statement of case. In many cases there will be alternatives which enable a case to be dealt with justly without taking the draconian step of striking the case out (see para.33.011 below). If delays do occur the court must ensure that the default does not go unmarked. The courts need to show by their conduct that they will not tolerate the parties' failure to comply with dates. Striking out must produce a just result and in making that decision the court are not confined to considering the relative positions of the parties. The effect on the administration of justice must be taken into account, including the effect of the court's ability to hear other cases if such defaults are allowed to occur.

The decision in Biguzzi makes clear that it would not be just to strike out a claim or defence merely because of some minor or technical breach which caused the other parties no harm or harm which could be compensated for in other ways (*Hannigan v Hannigan* (2000) L.T.L., May 18: use of obsolete and defective claim form; claimant ordered to correct the defects and *Walsh v Misseldine* (2000) L.T.L., March 1 substantial delay by the claimant, claim allowed to proceed to trial on the basis that the judge would assess compensation which would have been payable had the trial not suffered delay).

Where an application to strike out a claim is based on the claimant's delay in pursuing the claim, what is the correct test? According to the Court of Appeal, the court should only strike out the claim if there is a substantial risk that a fair trial is no longer possible: see *Taylor v Anderson, The Times*, November 22, 2002.

Whilst the courts have not taken the very strict approach to failures to adhere to time limits which practitioners feared they would when the Rules were implemented, the courts will always strive to carefully balance delay against prejudice. See, for example, *Moy v Pettman Smith* [2005] UKHL 7; [2005] 1 W.L.R. 581, where Lord Carswell observed:

> "It must no doubt be frustrating for district judges who have charge of case management of actions before trial to be faced constantly with delays which result from inefficiency, incompetence or downright neglect on the part of the practitioners whose duty it is to prepare them. One is left with the very clear impression, however, that Deputy District Judge Stary either was over-influenced by the defects on the part of the solicitors in preparing the case and by the imperative of efficiency in managing a stream of actions for trial, or else she failed to appreciate how considerable an effect on the value of the claim the new medical evidence would have. She did not at any stage go into the question of the degree of prejudice which would be sustained by the health authority, which could readily be met by an order for costs. She either failed to carry out any balancing exercise or misunderstood the profound effect of the medical evidence which the claimant wished to adduce. Whatever the reason, the result of her decision was a drastic reduction in the amount which the claimant was likely to recover at trial, which the claimant and his advisers may justifiably have regarded as a serious injustice."

In addition to the three grounds for striking out listed in r.3.4, the court also has an inherent jurisdiction to strike out any document or strike out, dismiss or stay any proceedings which amount to an abuse of the court's process. For example, it may strike out vexatious applications made in proceedings (*Ebert v Venvil* [2000] Ch.484). Also, the court may strike out a claim which the claimant had commenced or continued with no intention of bringing it to a conclusion (*Grovit v Doctor* [1997] 1 W.L.R. 640, HL and *Habib Bank Ltd v Jaffer, The Times*, April 5, 2000).

Court acting of its own initiative

33.009   PD 3.4, para.2 provides that if a court officer is asked to issue a claim form which he believes may fall within r.3.4(2)(a) and (b), as above, he should issue it but may consult a judge before returning it to the claimant or serving the defendant. The judge may make any order as he sees fit, for example, set a hearing for the claimant to make representations or staying the proceedings until the claimant files a witness statement or amended particulars of claim. Paragraph 3 makes similar provisions in respect of a "suspect" defence.

Consequences of strike out

33.010   Where the court strikes out the whole of a claim or defence, it may enter such judgment for the other party as that party appears entitled to. Where the strike out relates only to part of a claim or defence, the court may also give directions for the management of any remaining parts of the proceedings, for example, allocating them to a case management track. Where a strike out occurs automatically because of non-compliance with the terms of an order previously made (e.g. an "unless order" – see para.33.007) the other party may obtain judgment with costs under r.3.5. This can be done by filing a request for judgment which states that the right has arisen due to non-compliance with the court order. A request can be made where the claim was for either a specified amount of money, or an amount to be decided by the court, or delivery of goods where the claim form gave the defendant the alternative of paying their value, or any combination of these remedies. In any other case an application must be made to the court. The procedure is similar to entering default judgment, as to which see Ch.15.

Where the party has obtained a judgment under r.3.5 the other party has an opportunity to apply to set it aside if he applies within 14 days of service of the judgment itself (r.3.6). The court must set it aside if there was no entitlement to the judgment. Otherwise r.3.9 applies (relief from sanctions-see immediately below).

SANCTIONS AND RELIEF FROM SANCTIONS (RR.3.7, 3.8 AND 3.9)

Rule 3.7 provides for the circumstances in which a claim is automatically struck out for the non-payment of certain fees and how the action might be reinstated. As to how any interim injunction is affected, see para.27.029. 33.011

In *Biguzzi v Rank Leisure Plc* [1999] 1 W.L.R. 1926, see above, Lord Woolf M.R. reviewed the possible sanctions a court might impose, short of striking out a statement of case, where a party has failed to comply with a rule, practice direction or court order. He drew attention to the practice direction as to protocols and the sanctions specified there, namely:

(a) An order that the defaulting party should pay all or part of the costs of the proceedings;
(b) An order that those costs should be paid on an indemnity basis (see Ch.38 para.38.016). The order may provide for immediate payment after a summary assessment (see Ch.13 para.13.010). Lord Woolf considered that this sanction was particularly valuable in bringing home to the solicitor and the party the consequences of default.
(c) Where the claimant is at fault, an order that the payment of damages or any specified sum awarded should not carry any interest at all, or interest for any period as limited by the court, or interest at such reduced rate or rates as specified by the court.
(d) Where the defendant is at fault, an order that the payment of damages or any specified sum awarded against him should carry interest at a higher rate (not exceeding 10 per cent above base rate) for such period as specified by the court.

One or more of these orders can be made at the same time. Lord Woolf indicated that their use should also have the advantage of reducing the number of appeals which themselves generate huge disproportionate costs.

Rule 3.8 provides that where a party fails to comply with a rule, practice direction or court order, any sanction for that failure has effect unless the party in default applies for and obtains relief from the sanction. It is important to note:

(a) that where the sanction is the payment of costs the payee can only obtain relief by appealing the costs order;
(b) that where a rule, practice direction or court order requires a party to do something within a specified time and it specifies the consequences of failure to comply, the parties cannot agree to extend the time for compliance;
(c) that if a party does not apply for relief, the court may still grant it of their own initiative: see *Keen Philips v Field* [2006] EWCA Civ 1524, [2007] 1 W.L.R. 686.

On an application for relief from a sanction the court pursuant to r.3.9 considers all the circumstances including:

(a) the interests of the administration of justice;
(b) whether the application for relief was made promptly;
(c) whether the failure to comply was intentional;
(d) whether there is a good explanation for the failure;
(e) the extent to which the party in default has complied with other rules, practice directions, court orders and any relevant pre-action protocol;
(f) whether the failure to comply was caused by the party or his legal representative;
(g) whether the trial date or the likely trial date can still be met if relief is granted;
(h) the effect which the failure to comply has had on each party;
(i) the effect which granting relief would have on each party.

Any application for relief must be supported by evidence. The witness statement made in support should carefully and fully address each of the above matters because the court must work through the checklist systematically *(Bansal v Cheema* (2001) L.T.L., September 13; *Woodhouse v Consignia Plc* [2002] 2 All E.R. 737 and *Sayer v Clarke-Walker* cited at para.33.002) and no single factor is necessarily conclusive. The court must stand back and assess the significance and weight of all relevant circumstances: see *Hansom v Makin* [2003] EWCA Civ 1801; (2003) L.T.L., December 18. The checklist given above is not exhaustive; the court must consider "all the circumstances". Thus, when considering whether to grant relief to a defendant, the court is entitled to consider the merits of the defence (*Chapple v Williams* (1999) L.T.L., December 8). But it is important that the court only takes into account relevant considerations (*Gall v The Chief Constable of the West Midlands* [2006] EWCA Civ 2638, (2006) L.T.L., November 1).

When considering if any delay was caused by a claimant's lawyers, the court should consider any right of redress the claimant has against those lawyers and its merits. See *Welsh v Parnianzadeh* [2004] EWCA Civ 1832; [2004] All E.R. (D) 170 (Dec) where the Court of Appeal indicated that "a claimant who is reduced to a claim which would perforce be on a percentage basis for loss of chance against her legal advisers is not only suffering a real loss in the sense of being caused further delay and expense, but is also suffering a real reduction in the value of her claim" (*per* Mance L.J.).

When granting relief from a sanction, the court may impose terms. For example, the payment of costs and a sum of money into court (see *Primus Telecommunications Netherlands BV v Pan European Ltd* [2005] EWCA Civ 273, (2005) L.T.L., February 23).

CONTROLLING EVIDENCE

"As with all actions, libel actions should by proper case management be confined within manageable and economic bounds. They should not descend into uncontrolled and wide-ranging investigations akin to public inquiries, where that is not necessary to determine the real issues between the parties. The court will ... strive to manage the case so as to minimise the burden on litigants of slender means. This includes excluding all peripheral material which is not essential to the just determination of the real issues between the parties, and whose examination would be disproportionate to its importance to those issues", *per* May L.J. in *McPhilemy v Times Newspapers Ltd*, [1999] 3 All E.R. 775. 33.012

By r.1.4(2) active case management by the court includes (b) identifying the issues at an early stage; (c) deciding promptly which issues need full investigation and trial and accordingly disposing summarily of the others and (d) deciding the order in which issues are resolved. As to issue identification generally see para.22.003.

If the parties fail to identify the legal and factual issues that are in dispute, the court will do so. In *St Albans Court Ltd v Daldorch Estates Ltd, The Times,* May 24, 1999, Mrs Justice Arden listed the following nine provisional issues for the parties to work from:

"1. Was Mr Haq a shadow or de facto director of SA.C. on 11 February 1994?
2. Did the non-disclosure by Mr. Haq of his interests in Desgold cause SA.C. to enter into the Desgold agreement?
3. Did the shareholders of SA.C. approve the Desgold agreement?
4. Was clause 8 of the special conditions forming part of the Desgold agreement a penalty clause?

5. Has the claimant's claim (if any) to the Desgold payment already been compromised? (There is also an issue raised by the 9th defendant as to whether the judgment obtained against the claimant in respect of the Desgold payment makes the payment res judicata, but this does not require evidence).
6. Did the directors of SA.C. make the Desgold payment on advice?
7. Was the Daldorch agreement valid and binding?
8. Did the directors of SA.C. act in good faith in what they considered to be the best interests of SA.C. in entering into the Daldorch agreement?
9. If the Daldorch payment was made without consideration, has Daldorch changed its position?"

Rule 32.1 allows the court to give directions as to: (a) the issues on which it requires evidence; (b) the nature of the evidence which it requires to decide those issues; and (c) the way in which the evidence is to be placed before the court. Subparagraph 2 makes it clear that the court may use its power under this rule to exclude evidence that would otherwise be admissible. In *Post Office Counters Limited v Mahida* [2003] EWCA Civ 1583; *The Times*, October 31, 2003, the Court of Appeal indicated that "The power in the Civil Procedure Rules r 31.1(2) to exclude evidence even if it is admissible is principally a case management power designed to allow the court to stop cases getting out of hand and hearings becoming interminable because more and more admissible evidence, especially hearsay evidence, is sought to be adduced" (*per* Hale L.J.). In *JP Morgan Chase Bank v Springwell Navigation Corp* [2005] EWCA Civ 1602, (2005) L.T.L. 20 December, the Court of Appeal agreed that admissible similar fact evidence (see para.31.023) should be excluded to avoid overburdening the trial.

This power to control evidence must, of course, be exercised in accordance with the overriding objective of dealing with cases justly. A party should not be prevented from putting forward evidence which is central to a legitimate substantial claim or defence he raises (*McPhilemy v Times Newspapers Ltd* [1999] 3 All E.R. 775). However, the court can control the manner in which such evidence is put forward and thus limit the costs involved (see *per* Lord Woolf M.R. in *McPhilemy* and see further *G K R Karate (UK) Ltd v Yorkshire Post Newspapers Ltd* [2000] 2 All E.R. 931 which is noted in para.33.006, above).

A trial judge's decision to limit cross-examination of a witness should usually be given in advance and must not impose too strict a timetable: see *Hayes v Tansco Plc* [2003] EWCA Civ 1261; (2003) L.T.L., September 17 and *Three Rivers DC v Bank of England* [2005] EWCA Civ 889, (2005) L.T.L, August 23. If a party's advocate has already cross-examined a witness, that party will not be allowed to cross-examine the same witness again himself after dispensing with the services of his advocate: see *Sharma v Sood* [2006] EWCA Civ 1480, (2006) L.T.L., October 13.

CONTROLLING COSTS

There have been several cases in recent years in which the courts have shown a willingness to exercise greater control over the costs of litigation in two new ways: by requiring costs estimates; and by imposing costs caps. Estimates state the amount of recoverable costs which the parties expect they will incur. Costs caps state the amount of recoverable costs which the court will allow them to incur.

33.013

The Costs Practice Direction already places an obligation on represented parties to file and serve, at certain stages in the proceedings, estimates of the base costs they have incurred and the base costs likely to be incurred (Costs Practice Direction, s.6; as to the meaning of "base costs" see para.38.007, below). Represented litigants are required to file and serve estimates at the allocation stage, at the listing stage and also at any other stage when required to do so by the court. The original purpose in requiring estimates seems to have been to bring home to the parties the costs likely to be incurred in the proceedings. Estimates also have the salutary effect of educating procedural judges as to the expense of litigation. The Costs Practice Direction provides that, on any assessment of costs, the court may have regard to any estimate previously filed by that party or by any other party in the same proceedings. "Such an estimate may be taken into account as a factor, among others, when assessing the reasonableness of any costs claimed" (para.6.6). The Court of Appeal decision in *Leigh v Michelin Tyre Plc* [2004] 2 All E.R. 175 explains how estimates might affect any subsequent detailed assessment of costs. If there is a substantial difference, 20 per cent or more according to Costs PD para.6.5A, between the estimated costs and the costs claimed, the difference calls for an explanation. Secondly, a low estimate may cap the amount of costs recoverable if the paying party can show he relied upon it, for example, by carrying on with the litigation rather than settling. Lastly, a low estimate may also provide a cap if the court relied upon it and would have given different case management directions had a realistic estimate been given.

Since 1996 orders setting costs budgets have become a familiar feature in the law of arbitration. Section 65 of the Arbitration Act 1996 expressly permits arbitrators to set costs budgets, i.e. to limit in advance the amount which can be incurred by the parties in a particular case as costs. This provision is widely used and is generally regarded as beneficial in creating "equality of arms" (a rich party cannot blackmail a poorer party by threatening to cause or recover substantial costs) and in promoting proportionality (making sure that the costs bear some proportion to the amount or value in dispute). Before making his final report, Lord Woolf considered whether it was appropriate for the courts to set costs budgets for each party at case management conferences, and reviewing those budgets if necessary as the case proceeded. These proposals produced a general outcry from the legal profession (see Woolf Final Report paras 16 and 17) and so were dropped. However, costs cap orders have been made in cases in which Group Litigation Orders had previously been made: *AB v Leeds Teaching Hospitals NHS Trust* [2003] EWHC 1034 (Q.B.) and *Various*

Ledward Claimants v Kent & Medway Health Authority [2003] EWHC 2551 (Q.B.). They have also been made in other Court of Appeal cases: *King v Telegraph Group Ltd* [2004] EWCA Civ 613 (in defamation cases initiated under a CFA without ATE cover the court should consider making a costs capping order if there was a danger that, unless a cap was imposed, the freedom of the press would be jeopardised); and *R. (Corner House Research) v Sec of State for Trade and Industry* [2005] EWCA Civ 192 (if, on grounds of public interest, the court makes a prospective costs order in favour of the applicant, it may be appropriate to set a budget on the applicant's costs in that case).

In *Leigh v Michelin Tyre Plc* [2004] 2 All E.R. 175 and *Willis v Nicholson* [2007] EWCA Civ 199, (2007) L.T.L., March 13, the Court of Appeal again repeated invitations to the Civil Procedure Rule Committee to consider as a matter of urgency what general provisions to make for rules as to costs caps. Ultimately costs caps may become a standard practice in all very large cases. (The costs incurred in setting caps may be disproportionate in smaller cases which, many practitioners believe, should be made subject to fixed costs instead.) Each order is likely to contain provision for the court to review the cap where it is shown that it has become inappropriate due to circumstances that could not reasonably have been foreseen at the time the order was made. Do not underestimate the difficulty of forecasting accurately what costs will be reasonably incurred in large cases. For example, consider the facts of *Arkin v Borchard Lines* [2005] EWCA Civ 655 (noted in para.39.015, below). In that case professional funders estimated that their total outlay on expert evidence up to the end of the trial might amount to some £600,000. In fact they spent £1.3 million.

CHAPTER 34

Termination of an Action by Consent

REACHING A BINDING SETTLEMENT OUTSIDE COURT PROCEEDINGS

Negotiations

For the solicitor, civil litigation commences when the client first seeks advice. Sometimes, the most difficult job a solicitor has is to persuade the client not to fight an action. Often this advice will be unpalatable. The clients' price or principles will not let them back down. But the old maxim is as true today as it has always been: don't go to law. Losing is not the only risk taken. Cases can take months, often years to complete and time can sap confidence. As the trial draws nearer doubts creep in, costs mount up and the nervous strain can become unbearable. Even if successful, a party may still be out of pocket. The costs order in his favour will not cover all the expenses suffered. For example, a party cannot recover expenses or loss of earnings involved in attending a solicitor to give instructions: such losses can be recovered only when attending court as a witness. Further, a victory may be worthless if the opponent becomes bankrupt, dies or simply disappears.

34.001

The solicitor's paramount duty in conducting civil litigation is to keep the door open for negotiations. Both before a case starts and throughout the interim stages the solicitor must endeavour to compromise the claim on the best terms practicable for the client. How far does a solicitor's duty extend in negotiations? Does it include telling an opposing solicitor that you have previously made an offer that is lower than the one he is now making? For a review of this area and the answer to the question posed (albeit on the unique facts of the case) see *Thames Trains Ltd v Adams* [2006] EWHC 3291, (2007) L.T.L., January 3.

Litigation has never been an end in itself, it is a means to an end. The end here referred to is an enforceable result. In the past, claimants often started actions as a prelude to seeking a negotiated settlement, an enforceable contract setting out the parties' rights. There are several other means of achieving the same end, the two main ones being arbitration (in the hope of obtaining an "award" which can later be registered as a judgment of the High Court) and mediation (in the hope of reaching an agreed settlement). As we have seen in earlier chapters, the courts recognise the importance of ADR and encourage its use (see, for example, paras 6.019, 9.028 and 22.004, above).

As to conducting "without prejudice" negotiations, see Ch.6.

Alternative dispute resolution (ADR)

34.002   Although the different methods of ADR are described as being "alternatives" to litigation, they can sometimes be employed in addition to it. For example, parties who need the litigious remedies of an interim injunction and/or disclosure can start an action, get the remedies and only then turn to ADR.

Arbitration has one important feature in common with litigation. In litigation the judge gives a judgment which is binding on the parties. An arbitrator's decision (called an award) is likewise binding on the parties. Thus instead of going to court to have the judge impose a solution on the parties, the parties have gone before an arbitrator who has imposed a solution on them.

Unless an agreement provides to the contrary an arbitration is before one arbitrator. However, a contract with an arbitration clause can provide for however many arbitrators the parties think would be appropriate in the event of dispute (e.g. in a two-party contract, one arbitrator appointed by each party and an umpire appointed by the arbitrators).

Arbitration is thus very similar to having a contract dispute resolved before the courts, particularly if the dispute would have been assigned to the Commercial Court (see para.24.012). Indeed provision is made under s.93 of the Arbitration Act 1996 for judges of the Commercial Court to act as arbitrators. At an arbitration hearing, unless the parties have agreed otherwise, the rules of evidence apply and because of the further need to state a case in writing arbitration is often considered to be a specialist form of litigation.

The great advantage to the parties of arbitration over litigation is privacy. Trials are conducted in public; arbitration is in private. Large companies which are household names and therefore always newsworthy often find it more convenient for the company image to resolve disputes privately behind closed doors rather than in the public forum of a courtroom. Indeed many consider privacy to be the only advantage of arbitration. Often it is not cheaper for the work involved is much the same and indeed the arbitrator will also have to be paid (if the arbitrator is a judge the fees are taken in the High Court).

Another advantage which arbitration may offer is the possibility of appointing as arbitrator a person who is skilled in the subject-matter of the dispute, for example, a surveyor to arbitrate a rent review or a shipbroker to arbitrate a charterparty dispute.

Note that in the Commercial Court a facility exists for a without prejudice, non-binding, early neutral evaluation by a Commercial Judge of a dispute, or of particular issues in it (see Commercial Court Guide G2).

Mediation differs significantly from litigation or arbitration in that no solution is imposed on the parties. Mediation is a form of assisted without prejudice negotiation where a mediator seeks to facilitate a compromise between the parties themselves. Sometimes both sides attend mediation simply to explore whether there is any prospect of compromise and without any real expectation of achieving one. Nevertheless, a compromise can still emerge.

The mediation usually begins in a meeting at which both parties state their cases to the mediator and exchange views. They then move to separate rooms. The mediator visits each in turn reporting on offers and counter-offers, proposals and counter-proposals and obviously has to visit each side several times. If both sides are, or become, genuinely concerned to achieve a compromise, then one will usually be achieved.

A particular advantage which mediation may offer over litigation is the possibility of preserving or restoring goodwill between the parties to the dispute. Often, it is just as important to preserve a long-term business relationship as it is to insist upon strict legal rights.

In *Halsey v Milton Keynes General NHS Trust* [2004] 1 W.L.R. 3002, the Court of Appeal held that, whilst the court will often encourage the parties to attempt ADR, it has no power to order them to submit to it. The judgment explains the circumstances in which the court should impose a costs sanction on a successful litigant on the ground that he had refused to take part in ADR. The general rule is that the party who loses litigation should pay the winner's costs. In order to displace that rule in a particular case the burden is upon the loser to show that the winner acted unreasonably in refusing to take part in ADR. Various factors for consideration are listed: the nature of the dispute, the merits of the case, whether other settlement methods have been attempted, whether the costs of mediation would be disproportionately high, whether mediation would delay the trial, whether the mediation has a reasonable prospect of success, and whether the court has encouraged mediation. As to the last it was said that the stronger the encouragement given by the court, the easier it will be for the loser to discharge the burden of showing that the winner's refusal was unreasonable. The court also considered various forms of court encouragement and expressed approval of a standard form of order which now forms part of PD 29 para.4.10(9).

"The party shall ... consider whether the case is capable of resolution by ADR. If any party considers that the case is unsuitable for resolution by ADR, the party shall be prepared to justify that decision at the conclusion of the trial, should the trial judge consider that such means of resolution were appropriate, when he is considering the appropriate costs ordered to make. The party considering the case unsuitable for ADR shall, not less than 28 days before the commencement of the trial, file with the court a witness statement without prejudice save as to costs, giving the reasons upon which they rely for saying that the case was unsuitable."

See further *Burchell v Bullard* [2005] EWCA Civ 358 discussed at para.38.018, below.

UNDERTAKINGS

34.003 Often, an application for an injunction (see Ch.27) is compromised on the basis of an undertaking given by the respondent in lieu of the injunction. It is nevertheless advisable for the applicant to have a formal order drawn up, indorsed with a suitable penal notice and served on the respondent (see *Hussain v Hussain* [1986] Fam. 134).

If, as part of a commercial settlement, party A agrees with party B to give an undertaking to the court, party A will at the same time be treated as agreeing with party B that they are not going to do what they are promising the court not to do. So if there is a breach of the undertaking to the court by A, such will be an actionable as breach of contract by B against A. See *Independiente Ltd v Music Tarding Online (HK) Ltd* [2007] EWCA Civ 111, (2007) L.T.L., January 26.

COURT APPROVAL OF SETTLEMENT

34.004 If a prospective claim is settled on behalf of a child or patient (see Ch.7) the agreement is not binding until it is approved by the court. An application should be made to a master or district judge for such approval under Pt 8 (see Ch.10). A draft of the proposed order in Practice Form N292 should be attached to the application. PD 21, paras 6.2 and 6.3 provide that the court should be given the following information:

(a) whether and to what extent the defendant admits liability;
(b) the age and occupation, if any, of the child or patient;
(c) the litigation friend's approval;
(d) in a personal injury case, the circumstances of the accident; any medical reports; a schedule of any past and future expenses and if considerations of liability are raised any evidence (e.g. police accident report) and details of any prosecution brought;
(e) except in very clear cases, a copy of counsel or the solicitor's opinion on the merits of the settlement; and
(f) a copy of the instructions that led to the opinion unless these are sufficiently set out in it.

If a settlement or compromise is reached during proceedings, an application should be made for approval in a similar fashion.

What if a settlement is reached but it is then alleged that at that time the claimant was a patient and the settlement was not in his best interests? See *Bailey v Warren* [2006] EWCA Civ 51, *The Times*, February 20, 2006.

CONSENT ORDERS AND JUDGMENTS

Where the parties reach agreement during proceedings they can draw up a consent judgment or order to be entered on the court's records. Rule 40.6 provides that this may be done by a court officer simply sealing the order and entering it into the records provided: 34.005

(a) none of the parties is a litigant in person;
(b) the court's approval is not required;
(c) the judgment or order is for:
   (i) the payment of an amount of money (including damages or the value of goods to be decided by the court);
   (ii) the delivery up of goods with or without the option of paying the value of the goods or the agreed value;
   (iii) the dismissal of any proceedings, wholly or in part;
   (iv) the stay of the whole of the proceedings on agreed terms (a "Tomlin order"—see below);
   (v) the stay of enforcement of a judgment, either unconditionally or on condition that the money due is paid by instalments specified in the order;
   (vi) the setting aside under Pt 13 of a default judgment (see Ch.15) that has not been satisfied;
   (vii) the payment out of money which has been paid into court;
   (viii) the discharge from liability of any party; and
   (ix) the payment, assessment or waiver of costs, or such other provision for costs as may be agreed.

Practice Direction 40B, para.3.2 provides that if the court officer considers that the order is unclear or incorrect he may refer it to a judge for consideration.

In all other cases the parties should apply to the court for judgment to be given or the order to be made in the agreed terms. Normally, the court will deal with the application without any hearing. A draft of the proposed consent judgment or order should be attached to the application.

Any consent judgment or order must be expressed as being "By Consent". It must be drawn so that the judge's name and judicial title can be inserted and should be signed by any solicitor or counsel acting for a party.

It is vital to ensure that when negotiating terms of settlement the key facts have been obtained and understood. A salutary lesson can be found in the case of *Kyle Bay Ltd t/a Astons Nightclub v Underwriters Subscribing under Policy No.019057/08/01* [2007] EWCA Civ 57, (2007) L.T.L., February 7. There the claimant failed in its attempt to re-open, on the grounds of mistake and misrepresentation, a compromise of an insurance claim that it had made against its defendant underwriters. The claimant's contention was that the policy it had taken out with the defendant was "declaration-linked", and was not therefore subject to average, whereas the settlement of the business interruption component of its insurance claim following a fire was based on the common mistaken assumption and/or a misrepresentation by the defendant. That assumption or misrepresentation was to the effect that the policy was not declaration-linked, but was on a "gross profits basis" and was accordingly subject to average. As a result, the claimant agreed with, and received from, the defendant £205,500, whereas, on the basis that the policy was declaration-linked, the claimant should have received approximately £100,000 more.

It is also important to tie up all loose ends when negotiating the terms of a settlement, especially in respect of costs. If interim costs were previously reserved, it needs to be decided if any of the parties will now pay those costs. Indeed, it must be asked if the parties are content to abide by all previous interim costs orders or whether a party who was ordered earlier in the proceedings to pay the opponent's costs in any event should now be permitted to escape liability as part of the settlement.

"Tomlin Orders"

34.006 What if the parties wish to agree certain matters that are beyond the ability of the court to order, for example, as to the parties entering into a contract? The solution is to draw up a schedule of the agreed terms and to either annex such to a consent order or directly refer to its existence. Historically, these orders are known as Tomlin Orders.

It is important to ensure that the agreed terms are enforceable and adequate, for example, provision should be made for the payment of money out of court, for costs and for interest to date on any money remedy and for further interest should a party default on a payment. Provisions for the payment of money out of court, or the payment and assessment of costs must appear in the body of the order and not in the schedule (see PD 40B, para.3.5). This is because a payment out of court or an assessment of costs can only take place pursuant to a court order.

Given the ability of a non-party to obtain a copy of a judgment from the court file (see para.1.022), if the parties want the terms of settlement to be confidential, the schedule should simply refer to another document that records the agreement. Normally that agreement is held by the parties' solicitors.

A suggested Tomlin order that includes the terms in a schedule appears below.

BY CONSENT IT IS ORDERED:

1. That all further proceedings in this claim are stayed upon the terms set out in the Schedule except for the purpose of carrying the terms into effect.
2. That the parties have permission to apply to carry the terms into effect.
3. That the defendant is to pay the claimant's costs to be assessed by a detailed assessment if not agreed.

SCHEDULE

1. The defendant will pay to the claimant the sum of £76,843 on or before (date).

IN THE EVENT OF DEFAULT BY THE DEFENDANT:

    1.1 the claimant may immediately file a request for judgment for the amount due and owing;
    1.2 the sum shall carry interest until payment is made in full at a daily rate equal to (figure) per cent above the base rate as at (date).

2. As part of the compromise of this action the claimant and defendant shall forthwith enter into a Distribution Agreement (which shall be on the same terms as their Distribution Agreement dated [date] [save in the following respects . . .])

DATED this [date]

CHAPTER 35

Discontinuance

INTRODUCTION

35.001   Part 38 permits a claimant to discontinue all or any part of his claim. "Claimant" here includes a defendant who has brought a counterclaim or a claim against a third party (r.20.3 and see Ch.18). "Part of a claim" means a separate cause of action in a claim which covers two or more causes of action. Discontinuance must be distinguished from a reduction in the number of remedies listed in a claim. A formal reduction in the number of remedies claimed requires an amendment to the Statement of Case (see para.12.050) whilst discontinuance is effected by notice, by consent or by court order (see below).

Why discontinue? Perhaps the party proposing to do so finds that he has overstated his case, or sued the wrong defendant, or simply cannot produce the evidence which will prove his claim. Before discontinuing it is usually best to try to negotiate some sort of settlement, for example, a claimant may propose a "drop hands" settlement, that is to say each side withdraws their respective claims and pays their own costs.

A solicitor should advise a client about the costs consequences of discontinuance before proceedings are started since as a general rule the discontinuing party ends up paying the other parties' costs (see below). If a client discontinues it should not come as a shock to him that he will have to pay for the privilege of doing so.

DISCONTINUANCE BY NOTICE (R.38.3)

35.002   In most cases a claimant can discontinue by filing and serving a notice in Form N279. The notice must specify the part of any claim that is being discontinued. It must be served on all other parties to the proceedings and confirm that such has been done. If there is more than one defendant, the claimant may discontinue against all or any of them and the notice must specify which defendant or defendants.

Where other parties' consent is needed

Where the claimant has already received an interim payment in relation to a claim, whether that was paid voluntarily or by court order (see Ch.25), he can discontinue that claim only if the defendant who made the payment consents in writing (or the court otherwise gives its permission—see below).

What if there is more than one claimant but all of them do not wish to discontinue? Unless every other claimant gives their written consent those seeking to discontinue must obtain the court's permission to do so.

Where the claimant needs the written consent of some other party, a copy of it must be attached to the notice of discontinuance (r.38.3(3)).

35.003

Where permission of the court is needed

The claimant must first obtain the permission of the court before discontinuing all or part of a claim in relation to which:

35.004

(a) the court has granted an interim injunction (see Ch.27) against a defendant who will now cease to be a defendant;
(b) a defendant who has made to the claimant an interim payment refuses to give his consent;
(c) any other claimant refuses to consent.

The purpose of the permission requirement here is to enable the court to consider what orders to make in respect of any interim relief already granted, to secure an appropriate order for costs (as to which see para.35.016, below) and, very occasionally, to prevent a discontinuance which would be an abuse of process (as to which, see the examples given in para.35.008).

When serving a notice of discontinuance the name of the judge who granted the permission and the date of the order must be stated on Form N279.

Setting aside notice of discontinuance (r.38.4)

Where the claimant discontinues by filing and serving a notice, the defendant can apply within 28 days of service to set aside the notice. The right to set aside will not be permitted if it is an abuse of process.

35.005

Examples

In *Castanho v Brown & Root (U.K.) Ltd* [1980] 1 W.L.R. 833, the claimant sought damages for personal injuries and interim payments were made to him. It was later realised that a better result might be obtained if proceedings were brought in Texas and proceedings were started there. The claimant's English solicitors then served notice of discontinuance after a defence had been recently served admitting liability. Further proceedings were started in the United States

Federal Court in Texas and the earlier proceedings ended. Parker J. struck out the notice of discontinuance in the English proceedings as an abuse of process and granted an injunction restraining proceedings (see Ch.11) in the US. He held that the abuses of process were to use the machinery of discontinuance to improve the claimant's position in the American proceedings and that the claimant had received interim payments that he could not repay. The House of Lords subsequently agreed with his decision holding that the notice of discontinuance was an abuse of process because the court would not have allowed the claimant, who had secured interim payments and an admission of liability in England, to discontinue his action in order to obtain advantages by suing in a foreign court without being put on terms.

In *Ernst & Young v Butte Mining Plc* [1996] 1 W.L.R. 1605, C's solicitor misled D's solicitor into believing that C was not going to discontinue the action in the near future. By tactical use of the then court rules, C served notice of discontinuance before D had managed to make a counterclaim that otherwise was statute-barred. Robert Walker J., sitting in the Chancery Division, said:

> "Heavy, hostile commercial litigation is a serious business. It is not a form of indoor sport and litigation solicitors do not owe each other duties to be friendly (so far as that goes beyond politeness) or to be chivalrous or sportsmanlike (so far as that goes beyond being fair). Nevertheless, even in the most hostile litigation (indeed, especially in the most hostile litigation) solicitors must be scrupulously fair and not take unfair advantage of obvious mistakes . . . The duty not to take unfair advantage of an obvious mistake is intensified if the solicitor in question has been a major contributing cause of the mistake."

In *Gilham v Browning* [1998] 1 W.L.R. 682 C sued D and D made a counterclaim. C died and D failed to serve its expert's report in accordance with a court direction. D was refused permission to rely on expert evidence as they had offered no proper explanation for the late service of that evidence and it would result in considerable prejudice to the claim which was now being conducted by C's executrix. D did not appeal that order but discontinued the counterclaim instead. C applied to set aside the notice on the basis that D was seeking to escape the effect of the order disallowing their evidence by abandoning their counterclaim so that they might bring new proceedings in which the disallowed evidence could be called. The Court of Appeal held that D had sought to escape by the side door from the first action where their counterclaim was evidentially hopeless in order to start a new action where the evidential problem would not arise. In circumstances where a long overdue date for trial of the first action was fixed and imminent, D's actions constituted an abuse of process.

Liability for costs (r.38.6)

35.006 As a general rule, a claimant who discontinues by notice against a defendant is liable for that defendant's costs which were incurred on or before the date of service of the notice. This rule does not apply to claims allocated to the small claims track (r.38.6(3) and see Ch.20). Normally, payment of costs will be on the standard basis but it may exceptionally be on the more favourable indemnity basis. See, for example, *Naskaris v ANS Plc* [2002] EWHC 1782 (Ch.D) where discontinuance occurred after unreasonable delay; *Wates Construction Ltd v HGP Greentre All Church Evans Ltd* [2005] EWHC 2174, (2005) L.T.L., November 4, where indemnity costs were awarded from the date that it became clear beyond any doubt that it was impossible for the claim to succeeed; and *Three Rivers DC v Governor and Company of the Bank of England* [2006] EWHC 816, (2006) L.T.L., April 24, where the claimant had discontinued during the course of trial having persued a hopeless case in what was described as an extraordinary manner. As to the basis of assessment of costs, see para.38.016).

What if proceedings are only partly discontinued? The claimant is then liable for the costs that relate only to the part of the proceedings which have been discontinued and those costs are assessed at the conclusion of the balance of the action. Rule 38.8 makes provision for a case in which an earlier assessment of costs has been agreed or ordered; if those costs are not paid within 14 days of any date agreed by the parties, or ordered by the court, the defendant can apply to stay (see Ch.33) the remainder of the proceedings until those costs are paid (r.38.8).

If a claimant wishes to avoid paying costs under the general rule he must make an application to the court in the usual way (see Chs 13 and 14). When might he escape from the costs sanction?

Examples

In *Amoco (UK) Exploration Co. v British American Offshore Ltd* (2000) L.T.L., December 13, A sought to restrain B from continuing proceedings in the courts of Texas. At first B opposed A's claim but later withdrew from the Texas proceedings. Langley J. held that an order for costs against B fairly reflected the overall merits.

In *Everton v WPBSA Promotions Ltd*, December 13, 2001 (Gray J.) the claimant wished to discontinue his claim against one of several defendants solely because further proceedings against that defendant would be fruitless; he had become bankrupt because of reasons wholly unconnected with the litigation: discontinuance was permitted with no order as to costs.

In *Walker v Walker* [2005] EWCA Civ 247 a claim for compensation exceeding £200,000 with allegations of fraud had become complex and protracted. By this stage each side had incurred over £100,000 in costs, one of the defendants had committed suicide and the other had assets which were unlikely to exceed his own costs and the claimant's costs if the matter continued to trial. The claimant now wished to discontinue with no order as to costs. The Court of Appeal accepted that the litigation was probably commercially worthless but held that this had been so since commencement: therefore the claimant should pay costs to the defendants.

"[36] . . . Plainly, under [r.38.6] the court has to be persuaded that it is just to depart from the normal rule. The rule recognises that justice will normally lead to the conclusion that a defendant who defends himself at substantial expense against a [claimant] who changes his mind in the middle of the action for no good reason – other than that he has re-evaluated the factors that have remained unchanged – should be compensated for his costs". (Chadwick L.J.).

SUBSEQUENT PROCEEDINGS (R.38.7)

35.007 A claimant who discontinues a claim after the defendant has filed a defence requires the court's permission if he subsequently wishes to issue another claim against the same defendant that arises out of the same or substantially the same facts. The subsequent claim must of course be issued within the relevant limitation period (see Ch.5). As to the procedure on the application for permission, see r.23.2(4) and PD 23, para.5. Applications for permission are sometimes made where the claimant was misled or tricked by the defendant, where new evidence has come to light or where there has been a favourable change in the law. Depending upon the circumstances the grant of permission may be conditional upon the claimant satisfying any order for costs outstanding from the previous proceedings. The court's power to refuse permission or impose terms cannot be circumvented by assigning the causes of action to a new claimant. The court has an inherent jurisdiction to make such orders against the new claimant as it would have made against the original claimant had he started the subsequent proceedings (*Sinclair v British Telecommunications Plc* [2001] 1 W.L.R. 38 and consider an application for security for costs against the original claimant; r.25.14 described in para.26.004).

CHAPTER 36

Preparations for Trial

COMPLETING THE PRE-TRIAL CHECKLIST

In fast track (see Ch.21) and multi-track (see Ch.22) cases the court sends out the pre-trial checklist in Form N170 for you to complete and return by a date that is specified on the form (usually not more than eight weeks before the trial). 36.001

The objectives of the pre-trial checklist are to:

(a) ensure all directions have been complied with to date or otherwise fresh directions are speedily sought;
(b) fix a date for trial or confirm the date and time already given;
(c) confirm the estimated length of trial;
(d) set a timetable for the trial; and
(e) decide whether or not to hold a pre-trial review in a multi-track case (see below).

The form is divided into five lettered parts:

A: Directions complied with. If any directions remain outstanding you must say why and it is best to state when those will be met. If you wish the court to give any particular further directions you should try to agree these first with the other parties but in any event you should file a draft order.

B: Non-expert witnesses. The number of witnesses being called to give evidence for the party at trial must be stated. Where the trial date has not yet been fixed, any dates that a witness will be unavailable to attend court during the trial period and the reason for such must be given. Any special facilities or arrangements needed at the trial court by any witness must be detailed along with an indication as to whether or not an interpreter will be provided for any witness.

C: Experts. This topic is dealt with in detail in Ch.23. The checklist first reminds the party that he cannot rely on expert evidence unless the court has already given its permission. If permission is still required, then an application must be attached. As to each expert, the party must state the expert's name, field of expertise, whether joint or own expert, whether the report is agreed or not and whether permission has already been given by the court for the expert to give oral evidence at trial. Further, the party must indicate if there has been a discussion between experts and a joint statement filed. Where an expert is giving oral evidence at trial and the trial date is not yet fixed, any dates the expert will be unavailable to attend court during the trial period and the reason for such must be given.

D: Legal representation. An indication must be given as to whether the party will be acting in person or by a legal representative. Any dates when such people are unavailable during the trial period and the reason must be stated.

E: The trial. The party must indicate whether or not the time estimate for trial already provided has changed and, if so, set out the new estimate in days, hours and minutes, as appropriate. It must be made clear whether or not the new estimate is agreed. Moreover, a trial timetable must be attached in a multi-track case and, if possible, also agreed. It is sensible to indicate any areas of disagreement and the reasons for these. If a hearing has to be adjourned because of an inaccurate time estimate, the party responsible for the error is likely to be ordered to pay the costs thrown away. An estimate must also be given of the number of pages of evidence likely to be included in the trial bundle (see para.36.012, below).

F: Document and fee checklist. The form reminds the party to attach relevant documents, for example, any application notice with draft order and the appropriate fee, the proposed trial timetable in a multi-track case, an estimate of costs and the listing fee. Where a party is legally represented he must attach a separate estimate of base costs incurred to date and to be incurred if the case proceeds to trial (see further para.33.013, above and para.38.007, below).

What if no party files the completed pre-trial checklist by the date specified? The court will order that unless a completed pre-trial checklist is filed within seven days from service of that order, the claim, defence and any counterclaim will be struck out without further order of the court.

Directions on listing

36.002 After the time has expired for returning the pre-trial checklists the court confirms any trial date previously given or fixes one. You receive notification on Form N172. The file is referred to a judge who may issue final directions or hold a hearing to give these. The court wishes to avoid any unnecessary hearings and may financially penalise any party who files an inadequate listing questionnaire.

The most common directions on listing are:

(a) Expert evidence to be given orally or by way of written reports filed with the pre-trial checklist.
(b) Preparation of a trial bundle.
(c) A trial timetable and time estimate.

PRE-TRIAL REVIEW

The court may hold a pre-trial review when dealing with complex cases involving numerous parties and cases estimated to last more than 10 days (*White Book*, para.29.7.1). The hearing is normally fixed to take place between eight and four weeks before the trial date. It may occur instead of, or in addition to, a listing hearing (see above).

36.002A

The trial judge normally deals with a pre-trial review. As to possible directions, see Ch.22.

If a party wishes to use any form of information technology at trial or arrange evidence by video link, directions should be obtained for this. See further para.31.018.

If possible, the advocate who is to conduct the trial should attend the pre-trial review. Where a party is represented a person must attend who is familiar with the case and possesses sufficient authority to deal with any issues that are likely to arise. The client or a representative of a client company may be present. See further the case of *Baron v Lovell, The Times*, September 14, 1999, CA referred to in para.23.008.

Rule 29.8 requires the court "if practicable" to fix a trial timetable as soon as the listing stage is complete. Such timetables are often set at pre-trial reviews. The trial advocates should seek to agree a draft timetable for the judge to consider which schedules the oral submissions, witness evidence and expert evidence over the course of the trial. Ideally, it will allot times at each stage to each party. Such a timetable will give the trial judge firm control over the progress of the trial and may focus the advocates' minds on the best method of using time. The timetable should be included in the trial bundle (see para.36.006). Of course, the trial judge is not bound to follow the trial timetable: he has full power to conduct the trial in the manner he considers best to enable him to deal with the case justly (r.29.9).

ORGANISING WITNESSES

Witness summons (r.34.3)

How do you ensure that a witness attends trial? The answer is to have the court where the case is proceeding (or where the relevant hearing is to occur) issue a witness summons in Practice Form N20. There must be a separate summons for each witness. As a general rule, the court's permission is not necessary unless the summons is to be issued:

36.003

(a) less than seven days before the date of trial; or
(b) for the witness to attend on any date except the date fixed for trial; or
(c) for the witness to attend a hearing other than the trial.

In our view you should make it your general practice to use witness summonses in the case of almost every witness (except experts) as an aid to persuasion. And you should tell witnesses that the summons is an order issued by the court to guarantee the availability of all the important witnesses whose evidence the parties wish to rely on. In other words, you should put the responsibility for the forcing element of the summons where it belongs, i.e. on the legal system. Even if you do not adopt this strategy, there are three important instances where a summons should be served, even on a willing witness. Police officers, who by convention, do not take sides in a civil dispute and therefore will not give evidence unless compelled to do so. Witnesses who may otherwise have difficulty getting time off work. And expert witnesses if they require such.

Unless the court directs otherwise, a witness summons is only binding if it is served at least seven days before the date on which the witness is required to attend court. The witness is bound until the conclusion of the hearing. However, if after the witness has given evidence his attendance is no longer required, the judge may release him.

Two copies of the witness summons should be filed at the court for sealing. One copy is kept on the court file. The court serves the witness summons by post. If you wish to serve it you should make that clear in your covering letter to the court. As to the methods of service see Ch.8. At the time of service the witness must be offered or paid a sum reasonably sufficient to cover his travelling expenses to the court and in returning to his home or place of work. In addition, a sum must also be offered or paid by way of compensation for loss of earnings, leave or benefit, or such lesser sum as it may be proved that the witness will lose which is equivalent to the amount paid to a witness who attends the Crown Court. If the court is to serve the summons you must lodge these funds.

Can a witness apply to set aside a summons? In *Harrison and Harrison v Bloom Camillin (a firm)* (1999) L.T.L., May 14, C's father applied to have a witness summons served on him by D set aside. Neuberger J. held that it was clear that r.34.3(4) allows the court to set aside or vary a witness summons and should do so if, on balancing the value of the evidence to the applicant against the burden on the witness, and the degree of intrusiveness of the proposed questioning and all the other circumstances, it seems to the court that the summons is oppressive. The judge held that it was clear that D was trying to conduct a fishing or speculative exercise and it was therefore right that the witness summons should be struck out.

In *Brown v Bennett, The Times*, November 2, 2000, C wished to call X as an expert witness but was unable to afford her fee. C being unwilling to give evidence without a fee, C served a witness summons upon her. Neuberger J. had no hesitation in setting that witness summons aside.

How do you get a non-party to produce documents to the court before or at a trial? Again, the answer is to issue a witness summons in Form N20 listing the documents that are required. What documents can the witness be summoned to produce? Rule 34.2(5) states that such are limited to those which the person could be required to produce at the hearing itself. The usual practice is for production to occur before the trial since this is likely to save costs and further the interests of justice. If production only occurs at trial, lengthy or numerous documents of crucial importance might be disclosed requiring the case to be adjourned whilst the parties read and consider them. Moreover, sight of the documents is often desirable before witness statements are prepared, or before a party decides whether or not to accept a Pt 36 offer (see Ch.29) or settle on particular terms.

Normally, the non-party on whom the witness summons is served does not object to producing the documents and it is usually possible to arrange a time convenient to him. You must not confuse this production of documents with disclosure under Pt 31 (see Ch.30). The witness summons must list the documents that are to be produced. They should be identified individually or by a compendious description that enables each one to be specifically identified: see *Tajik Aluminium Plant v Hydro Aluminium AS* [2005] EWCA Civ 1218, [2006] 1 W.L.R. 767. The production is to the court and not the parties. The judge can therefore rule on which documents should be made available to the parties for inspection or copying, and the arrangements that should be made for the safe keeping of the documents.

What if the witness is likely to be unavailable to give evidence at trial? A deposition may be taken pursuant to r.34.8. If he is out of the country, see r.34.13. However, serious consideration needs to be given to using video evidence (see generally Ch.31).

Unavailable witnesses

On allocation the court are concerned to set a realistic hearing date. Part H of the allocation questionnaire (see Ch.9) and Pts B and D of the pre-trial checklist ask if there are any dates when the party, his representatives, experts or other essential witnesses will not be able to attend court. It is essential that this information is obtained and given to the court. Also ensure that you record the reasons why a person cannot attend at a particular time.

36.004

If you instruct an expert after proceedings have been issued you must first check that he will be available to attend trial. In *Rollinson v Kimberley Clark Ltd, The Times*, June 22, 1999, the Court of Appeal held that when a trial date is imminent, it is not acceptable to seek to instruct an expert witness without checking his availability or, if instructions have been given, to go ahead when there is no reasonable prospect of the expert being available. A check should be made and if the expert is not available another should be instructed. When a trial date was set it was said that neither of the defendant's experts were available. The judge and the Court of Appeal refused an adjournment. The defendant's approach to instructing the consultant was said to "lack the appropriate sense of urgency or elementary precaution". Moreover, there was insufficient evidence before the court that the first expert was unavailable and unable to alter his commitments on the dates fixed for the trial.

In *Matthews v Tarmac Bricks & Tiles Ltd, The Times*, July 1, 1999, the trial judge held a pre-trial review. However, whilst the defendant was represented by a barrister, no member of the staff of her instructing solicitors was present and she only had a list of dates when the defendant's two experts were unavailable without any reasons for such. The judge fixed a trial date but unbeknown to him one expert would be out of the country and the other had been summoned to give evidence at a different court at that time. Both the judge and the Court of Appeal refused to alter the trial date. Lord Woolf M.R. said,

> "The approach which was being adopted by the lawyers before the judge was wholly inappropriate. . . .They were regarding it as the responsibility of the court to defer the hearing to a date which could, with convenience, be met by the doctors. It was apparently thought that all that was required was to tell the court the dates the doctors had indicated would not be convenient and the court would thereupon find a date which would allow the case to be heard to meet their convenience . . . The right course for the parties to have adopted in this case was to attempt to reach agreement themselves as to the dates which could be met, to have consulted with the court, and with the court's co-operation to find a date within a reasonable time for the hearing".

He went on to stress that parties must make all the relevant information available to the court.

The judge had also ordered that the parties' experts should meet but that had not occurred by the time of the appeal. The defendant submitted that no date could be arranged. Lord Woolf commented, "I do not for one moment accept that is so, particularly having regard to the sensible suggestion made by the judge about the use of the telephone for that purpose". The defendant was also criticised for pursuing the appeal rather than exploring the question of videoing evidence. Whilst that might prove expensive it was preferable to vacating the trial date or incurring the expense of an appeal. In addition, it was said that the defendant should have contacted the court where the expert was summoned to appear to make it aware of the situation. The court would then have ensured that a time was given to enable the witness to give evidence in this case.

Whilst Lord Woolf accepted that it was preferable for the defendant to be able to call its doctors at trial he was satisfied that the case could be tried justly if that did not happen. The judge would have their written reports and "could properly form a judgment as to the right result without those doctors being called". His Lordship did not rule out the possibility of the defendant being able to obtain alternative expert evidence even at that late stage. Lord Justice Clarke concurred and stated that he also expected the trial judge to admit the written reports if either or both of the doctors could not attend the trial. He also pointed out that the trial judge retained the power to adjourn the trial if it should for any reason appear appropriate to do so. Finally, Lord Justice Mance also agreed stating,

> "Even now there may be a possibility of a pre-recorded video. Failing all else. . .the existing experts' evidence is in writing. Steps may even be taken now leading to [the defendant's] experts appearing in person on the

relevant dates. It will be open to [the defendant] to ask the judge for such further directions as may assist in that regard".

Getting everybody to court

Ensure that you remind all the witnesses, at the very latest, one week before the hearing date arrives. This is probably best done by telephone, fax, email or personal messenger, as well as by letter. 36.005

THE TRIAL BUNDLE

Documents need to be prepared for the trial judge, advocates and witnesses to use at trial. PD 39, para.3.1 directs that unless the court orders otherwise, the claimant must prepare and file a "trial bundle" of documents not more than seven days and not less than three days before the start of the trial. As a general rule the bundle should include a copy of each of the following: 36.006

(1) the claim form and all statements of case (see Ch.12);
(2) a case summary and/or chronology where appropriate (see below);
(3) requests for further information and responses to the requests (see Ch.32);
(4) all witness statements to be relied on as evidence and any witness summaries (see Ch.31);
(5) any notices of intention to rely on hearsay evidence under r.32.2 and any notices of intention to rely on evidence (such as a plan, photograph, etc.) under r.33.6 (see Ch.31);
(6) any medical reports and responses to them;
(7) any experts' reports and responses to them (see Ch.23);
(8) any order giving directions as to the conduct of the trial (e.g. the trial timetable, see para.36.002, above); and
(9) any other necessary documents.

What should you do with the original documents? These, together with copies of any other court orders should be available at the trial. Should a solicitor delegate the task? He can but the preparation and production of the trial bundle, even where it is delegated to another person, is the responsibility of the legal representative who has conduct of the claim on behalf of the claimant.

The trial bundle should be paginated (continuously) throughout, and indexed with a description of each document and the page number. Ensure that the pagination can be clearly distinguished from any existing pagination on a document. Contemporaneous documents and correspondence should be included in chronological order. If a document has to be read across rather than down the page, it should be put in the bundle so as to ensure that the top of the text starts nearest the spine.

Where the total number of pages is more than 100, numbered dividers should be placed at intervals between groups of documents. The bundle should normally be contained in a ring binder or lever arch file. Where more than one bundle is necessary, they should be clearly distinguishable, for example, by different colours or letters. If there are numerous bundles, a core bundle (see below) should also be prepared. Where more than one file is used, include a clear and comprehensive index covering all the files at the beginning of the first one. Then prepare a separate index for each file. This will ensure that a document can be easily found during the trial.

For convenience, experts' reports may be contained in a separate bundle and cross-referenced in the main bundle. Large documents, such as plans, should be placed into an easily accessible file.

What if a document that should be included in the trial bundle is illegible? The answer is to have a typed copy prepared and this should be included in the bundle next to it, suitably cross-referenced. Likewise, if a foreign document has been translated, the translation should be marked and placed adjacent to it.

You should try to agree the contents of the bundle with the other parties. This should include any agreement that the documents contained in the bundle are authentic even if not disclosed under Pt 31 (see Ch.31), and that documents in the bundle may be treated as evidence of the facts stated in them even if a notice under the Civil Evidence Act 1995 has not been served. If it is not possible to agree the contents of the bundle a summary of the points in dispute should be included.

The party responsible for preparing the trial bundle should start early enough to enable agreement to be reached as far as possible and in order that the case summary can refer to the bundle. Bundles that are properly prepared make it easier for the judge to understand the case and for the advocates to present it, thus saving time and costs. However, if a party copies unnecessary documents or poorly prepares the bundle, costs penalties may be imposed.

As to a "case summary and/or chronology where appropriate" see para.22.004 and the example given there. These documents should be non-contentious and agreed with the other parties if possible. Any material dispute about an event stated in them should be noted.

Finally, the party filing the trial bundle should supply identical bundles to all the parties to the proceedings and for the use of the witnesses.

Core bundles

36.007 If the trial bundle documentation runs to several lever arch files, the party should prepare a core bundle containing only those documents which are essential to the proceedings (PD 39, para.3.6).

Skeleton arguments

36.007A Although not required by the rules themselves, skeleton arguments are required by the Chancery Guide (para.8.31) the Queen's Bench Guide (para.7.11.5) and by the Commercial Court Guide (para.16). Each of these guides gives deadlines for delivery and also guidance as to content (*cf.* Form N163 for use on appeals). Skeleton arguments, for any court hearing, should contain a brief description of the issues in the case, a summary of the relevant facts, a summary of the legal principles and a reference to the leading cases on those principles. The skeleton argument is an invitation to the judge to inform himself in advance about the issues he will have to decide. It is an invitation that the judge is expected to accept. Listing officers are instructed to place the trial bundle, skeleton arguments and other papers before the judge in sufficient time to enable him to do the necessary pre-reading.

Skeleton arguments will of course state any case authority relied on. The *Practice Direction (Citation of Authority)* [2001] 1 W.L.R. 1001 lays down a number of rules as to what authorities may be cited and the manner in which the citation should be made. For example, a decision on an application that only decided that the application was arguable should not be cited unless it clearly indicates that it purports to establish a new principle or to extend the present law. In judgments decided after April 2001 that indication must take the form of an express statement to that effect. Advocates should also be wary of citing any judgment which contains an indication that the court delivering the judgment considered that it was merely applying decided law to the facts or otherwise was not extending or adding to the existing law. Having chosen which cases to cite, the advocate must (amongst other things) state in respect of each of them the proposition of law that the authority demonstrates, and the parts of the judgment that support that proposition. If it is sought to cite more than one authority in support of a given proposition, the advocate must state the reason for taking that course.

What if you wish to rely on human rights cases? PD 39, para.8.1 states that where it is necessary for a party to give evidence at a hearing of an authority referred to in s.2 of the Human Rights Act 1998, then the authority to be cited should be an authoritative and complete report and the party must give to the court and any other party a list of those authorities and copies of the reports not less than three days before the hearing. You can use written reports of the complete original texts issued by the European Court and Commission, including those from the Court's judgment database available on the internet at *www.echr.coe.int*.

In most cases skeleton arguments are exchanged, i.e. served by each side simultaneously. However, in complicated cases it may be appropriate for the court to order sequential service with the claimant serving his argument first. This would enable the defendants to prepare a skeleton argument which dealt with the issues in the same order in which the claimant had dealt with them (*Brown v Bennett, The Times*, June 13, 2000).

Reading lists and time estimates

For trials in the High Court (both Chancery and Queen's Bench Division) the claimant must file with the trial bundle a reading list together with an estimate

36.008

of the length of reading time required and an estimate of the length of the hearing (see generally *Practice Direction (RCJ Reading Lists and Time Estimates)* [2000] 1 W.L.R. 208.

The document must be signed by all advocates, beneath whose signatures should appear their names, business addresses and telephone numbers.

CHOICE OF ADVOCATE

36.009 Where a party is legally represented, the question arises as to who should be chosen to conduct the case on behalf of the client at the trial; the solicitor who conducted the litigation leading to trial, another advocate from the same firm, or a barrister or a solicitor-advocate from another firm? When advising on this question the solicitor is under a duty to act in the best interests of the client. Solicitors should not make it a condition of providing litigation services that advocacy services must also be provided by that solicitor or by the solicitor's firm or the solicitor's agent. This ensures that the advocacy services provided by a firm have to be a bonus which clients of that firm can use if they want to, not a burden they have to put up with.

A solicitor who provides both litigation and advocacy services should, as soon as practicable after receiving instructions, and from time to time, consider and advise the client whether his best interests would be served by the solicitor, another advocate from the solicitor's firm, or some other advocate providing the advocacy services. The solicitor should have regard to the following circumstances:

(i)   the gravity, complexity and likely cost of the case;
(ii) the nature of the solicitor's practice;
(iii) the solicitor's ability and experience; and
(iv) the solicitor's relationship with the client.

Two matters should be emphasised to the client, namely: (i) who to choose and (ii) the likely cost. It also makes sense for the advice to the client to be recorded by a note on the file and in a letter to the client.

Drafting the brief for trial

36.010 The brief for trial is perhaps the most important document that the solicitor has to draft. It is the set of instructions that will be sent to the advocate chosen to present the case at trial. It must inform that advocate about every aspect of the case that may be mentioned at the trial. The trial is the culmination of all the effort that has gone into the case, and the brief is the final document in preparation for the trial. It must therefore be given detailed thought, time and attention.

Implicit in the act of drafting a brief is the assumption that the advocate chosen to conduct the case at trial is not the same person who previously had the conduct of the case. Does this assumption still hold good now that the vast majority of civil trials are conducted in the county courts, courts in which solicitors have full rights of audience? In our opinion it does. The skills needed by a trial lawyer are not likely to be needed or studied by most litigators even if they regularly undertake advocacy in interim hearings. Furthermore, even if the same lawyer is going to both prepare and present a case we still think that a "brief" of sorts should be drafted if only as part of the lawyer's preparation for trial.

A brief should begin by listing all the copy documents sent with it, i.e. witness statements, statements of case, medical reports, other experts' reports, agreed bundles of documents, all opinions of counsel previously received and all relevant notices and orders.

Do not send original documents to your advocate. It used to be said of barristers that "Those [documents] they don't lose, they scribble on". Instead, your advocate should be supplied with good copies. Keep the originals, and also copies of every new document you send so that you can discuss the case intelligently with the advocate over the telephone if necessary and, of course, so that you are still able to conduct last minute negotiations.

The number of documents sent with the brief is usually extremely large. Gone are the days when it was possible to enclose them all within large sheets of paper tied up in pink ribbon. These days the documents are usually sent in one or more ringbinder files arranged with cardboard dividers for ease of reference. Some of the documents may have been sent to the advocate previously (e.g. medical reports with instructions to advise on quantum) and so may already be housed in a ringbinder file. Other documents will have to be copied now, for example, opinions and notes previously delivered by the advocate and witness statements.

Usually, all the evidence which you intend to rely upon will have been disclosed to your opponent, in the form of witness statements and expert's reports, several weeks before you draft the brief. However, it is still often necessary for you to prepare further evidence for each of your witnesses either by obtaining their comments upon the witness statements and reports relied upon by the opponent and/or by taking supplementary witness statements (see Ch.31).

Office practice varies as to whether the brief itself is included in the ringbinder file. It is more convenient for the administrative staff if it is and their convenience is important if high efficiency is to be maintained. However, this should not be the decisive factor. The convenience of the advocate is the more important, even at the expense of causing the administrative staff some inconvenience. Most advocates prefer the brief to be kept separate, i.e. a bundle of pages stapled together, the pages being either A4 ISO or A3 ISO, which is twice the size of A4 ISO. The advantages of the large paper are that it is readily identifiable and it prevents the brief from being of inordinate length and yet still leaves ample margins for the advocate to make manuscript notes and comments.

PREPARATIONS FOR TRIAL

The brief should be as full and as explicit as the circumstances demand. If there are any matters as to which you are unsure whether you should put them in or leave them out, the wisest course is to put them in. This leaves it to the advocate to decide their relevance and importance.

Delivering a brief to counsel

36.011 If a party is being funded by the Legal Services Commission, the backsheet should be indorsed with the appropriate reference number and a copy of any certificate should be included together with any amendments thereof or any specific authorities to incur costs (Civil Legal Aid (General) Regulations 1989, reg.59). Otherwise, it is advisable to negotiate the fee in advance with counsel or with counsel's clerk.

The Bar's "Written Standards for the Conduct of Professional Work: General Standards" states that "3.2 A barrister is not considered to have accepted a brief or instructions unless he has had an opportunity to consider it and has expressly accepted it". Thus, a day or two after delivering the brief the solicitor should telephone counsel's chambers to agree the fee. Under the Code of Conduct of the Bar of England and Wales (1990) it is not necessary for brief fees to be agreed in advance or marked on the brief. However, in our view it will usually be wiser to agree it in advance, and to get the client's approval of it and (bearing in mind para.3.2 quoted above) get counsel or his clerk to confirm expressly acceptance of the brief at that fee.

In an ideal world briefs would always be delivered at least two weeks before the date fixed for trial.

There used to be a rule that, once the brief has been delivered, the full fee was payable even if the case should subsequently settle. Since 1967 it has been agreed that, in such a case "counsel may accept no fee or less than the agreed fee". Today, the old rule is not applied rigidly: instead the court expects counsel to agree a reduced fee taking into account work already done on the brief since delivery and the prospect that counsel will have a gap in his diary which may be difficult to fill (*Martin v Holland & Barrett* [2002] 3 Costs L.R. 530; *Miller v Hales* [2006] EWHC 1717 (Q.B.)). However, the fact remains that some fee will still be payable. This can provide a useful negotiating point for the claimant. It enables him to impose a deadline on offers of compromise "after which date the brief for trial will have to be delivered"; those acting for the defendant will appreciate what this means.

The brief fee covers only the first day of the trial and thereafter counsel will be entitled to a "refresher" for each subsequent day. Thus refreshers should also be agreed in advance where the case has been estimated to last more than one day. A refresher usually amounts to one half or two thirds of the brief fee unless the brief fee is very substantial. Think of it like this; the refresher fee is counsel's daily rate. If it is half the brief fee, the brief will cover two day's work, one for preparation, the other for presentation. If it is two-thirds of the brief fee, the brief covers one and half day's work; a half-day of preparation and the first day of the trial.

RECUSAL OF JUDGE

In *AWG Group Ltd v Sir Alexander Morrison* [2007] EWCA Civ 6, [2006] 1 W.L.R. 1163, the trial judge stated, "in the course of my pre-reading into the case I noticed that it was intended to call as a witness for *AWG Group Ltd* ("*AWG*") Mr Richard Jewson ("Mr Jewson") who, at all material times until March 2002 was a director of *AWG* and chairman of the audit sub-committee of its board. Alerted by the name I then discovered that Mr Jewson is well known to me of which fact I then alerted the parties on the November 29. The response of the claimants was to indicate that, rather than risk my withdrawal and the consequent delay in obtaining another judge and his completing the pre-reading process on which I had already spent a week, they would not call him to give evidence since they did not regard him as other than a relatively peripheral witness. The response of the defendants is contained in a letter from Messrs Dechert LLP of the November 30, the conclusion of which was to ask me to withdraw. Inconvenience, costs and delay do not, however, count in a case where the principle of judicial impartiality is properly invoked. This is because it is *the* fundamental principle of justice, both at common law and under Art.6 of the European Convention for the Protection of Human Rights. If, on an assessment of all the relevant circumstances, the conclusion is that the principle either has been, or will be, breached, the judge is automatically disqualified from hearing the case. It is not a discretionary case management decision reached by weighing various relevant factors in the balance."

36.012

The test for apparent bias is that, having ascertained all the circumstances bearing on the suggestion that the judge was or would be biased, the court must ask "whether those circumstances would lead a fair-minded and informed observer to conclude that there was a real possibility. . .that the tribunal was biased": see *Taylor v. Lawrence* [2003] Q.B. 528 at para.60. See also *R. v Gough* [1993] A.C. 646; *Re Medicaments and Related Classes of Goods (No.2)* [2001] 1 W.L.R. 700; *Porter v Magill* [2002] 2 A.C. 357; and *Lawal v Northern Spirit Ltd* [2004] 1 All E.R. 187.

When might there be a real possibility of bias? The following examples were given in *Locabail (UK) Ltd v Bayfield Properties Ltd* [2000] Q.B. 451 at 480:

"By contrast, a real danger of bias might well be thought to arise if there were personal friendship or animosity between the judge and any member of the public involved in the case; or if the judge were closely acquainted with any member of the public involved in the case, particularly if the credibility of that individual could be significant in the decision of the case. . .or if, for any other reason, there were real ground for doubting the ability of the judge to ignore extraneous considerations, prejudices and predilections and bring an objective judgment to bear on the issues before him. . .In most cases, we think, the answer, one way or the other, will be obvious. But if in any case there is real ground for doubt, that doubt should be resolved in favour of recusal."

What if a judge has dealt with a party before and been critical of that party? In *Drury v BBC* [2007] All E.R. (D) 205 (May), the claimant applied for the recusal of one of the judges from hearing an appeal, on the ground that he had, on a previous occasion, refused permission to appeal in another matter in which the claimant had acted as a McKenzie friend, and in the process had made some criticisms of the claimant. The Court of Appeal held that the fact that a judge had made a finding against a party on a previous occasion, even if he had been critical to that party, did not found a later objection to the judge sitting in another matter. It was, however, also plain that where there was any room for doubt as to which course to adopt, that doubt should be resolved in favour of recusal.

Should a judge hear a case in which one or more of the advocates are members of his chambers? In what circumstances will a party waive his rights to object? What steps should both the trial judge and counsel take? These issues were to some extent considered in *Smith v Kvaerner Cementation Foundations Ltd* [2006] EWCA Civ 242, [2007] 1 W.L.R. 370. See also *Gillies v Secretary of State for Work and Pensions* [2006] UKHL 2, [2006] 1 W.L.R. 781.

CHAPTER 37

Trial

SITTING BEHIND COUNSEL

The solicitor's professional conduct rules, as amended from July 1, 2007, provide that, where a barrister has been instructed, the instructing solicitor will need to decide whether it is in the interests of his client and the interests of justice to attend the proceedings with counsel. In reaching this decision the solicitor will need to consider what is necessary for the proper conduct of the case, taking into account the nature and complexity of the case and the capacity of the client to understand the proceedings (r.11).

37.001

In trials in cases allocated to the multi-track, there should always be at least one person sitting behind counsel (or, if leading counsel is instructed, sitting in front). What is the role of that person? Their first task is to ensure that everyone is at the right court at the right time. The client and witnesses will probably be nervous. The second task is to tell them what to expect and to set about quietly reassuring them. In civil cases this task can be shared with the specialist advocate, whether that person is a solicitor or a barrister. Barristers are permitted to discuss cases with a potential witness if, inter alia, the witness is the lay client, a character witness, an expert witness or a witness in respect of whom the barrister has been supplied with a proper proof of evidence (Code of Conduct of the Bar of England and Wales 1990, para.607; the above is a brief summary of the gist of this paragraph only; as to barristers interviewing witnesses and taking proofs of evidence in the absence of a solicitor or clerk, see paras 607 and 609).

WITNESSES

It is particularly important to tell a witness what will happen when he enters the witness box. The clerk of the court will administer the oath or, if preferred, the form of solemn affirmation. The first advocate to ask him questions will be the one who wanted this witness to attend. The witness will be handed a copy of the statement he made previously and asked to say whether its contents are true. Usually, the witness is then asked questions by the advocate for the other party.

37.002

A witness should therefore re-read his statement shortly before being called to give evidence.

A witness should be told that whenever he is asked a question, whether by an advocate or by the judge he should give as short an answer as possible. A "yes" or "no" is ideal, but, if the question cannot be answered in such simple terms, he should use as short a sentence as he can manage. Follow-up questions will be asked if necessary. It is vitally important that the witness giving evidence should not lose his temper and become embroiled in an argument with an advocate. This can never do any good and may cause serious harm. It is a good idea to tell the witness to keep his eye on the judge, who is usually taking a note of the evidence. In any event, even when the question is not from the judge the answer should always be given to the judge.

Witnesses often worry about what to call the judge. In the High Court the judge should be addressed as "My Lord" or "My Lady"; in the county court the circuit judge should be addressed as "Your Honour". If you think this sort of formality would over-worry the witness just tell him to call the judge "sir" or "madam"; no judge would object to this from a witness. Indeed, county court district judges should be addressed simply as "sir" or "madam". Always explain the layout of the court to the client and witnesses so that they know who is who among the court officers and what functions they will carry out. Unlike criminal trials, whilst the case is going on there is no reason why the witnesses should not sit in the court. The other side will object if they do not want this to happen, but will have to have cogent reasons for excluding the witnesses. Most witnesses prefer to sit in rather than wait outside. Obviously, the client will be present throughout anyway. Whilst the case is going on, the solicitor or representative should take a verbatim note of the evidence given. This is particularly important when the advocate is conducting a cross-examination and is unable to take his own verbatim notes. So far as is possible, take a verbatim note of everything that happens, and record the times.

Although the client will want to be present throughout the trial, a witness may not. When such a witness has given his evidence the advocate should ask the court to release him. It is necessary to find out in advance whether the witness will wish to be released. The solicitor will also have told the witness beforehand to send a note of his net losses and expenses in attending court. Expert witnesses do not usually need reminding.

PROCEDURE AT TRIAL

Small claims track and Pt 8 claims

37.003   Hearings in cases allocated to the small claims track are fairly informal. The strict rules of evidence do not apply. By PD 27, para.4.3 the district judge can adopt any method of proceeding that he considers to be fair at a small claims hearing (see Ch.20). Part 8 hearings are mainly determined on the filed evidence (see Ch.10). In both types of cases the judge will identify the issues that have to be resolved by him and outline his proposed timetable for the hearing if this has not already been set.

Fast track and multi-track

See Chs 21 and 22 respectively. 37.004
Unless a suitable trial timetable (see Ch.36) has already been laid down, the judge will give directions as to which party should speak first and as to the order of oral submissions if there are more than two parties. Directions may be made dispensing with opening submissions or, more usually, putting strict time limits on them. It is possible for proceedings to be conducted very briskly indeed; the judge first putting questions to each advocate in turn and then immediately requiring them to call their witnesses.

The following is a typical fast track timetable where the case will last the whole day:

Judge's reading time:	30 minutes
Opening statement:	10 minutes
Cross examination and re-examination of claimant's witnesses:	90 minutes
Cross examination and re-examination of defendant's witnesses:	90 minutes
Defendant's closing statement:	15 minutes
Claimant's closing statement:	15 minutes
Judge preparing and delivering judgment:	30 minutes
Summary assessment of costs:	20 minutes

The claimant's advocate will usually open the proceedings unless the burden of proof (see para.31.002) of all the issues lies on the defendant. The advocate begins by making opening submissions outlining the facts and indicating areas of dispute, the legal principles involved, and the areas where a ruling will have to be made. Only the essential parts of the statements of case, the agreed photographs, plan and documents should be gone through. The claimant's advocate will rely heavily upon his case summary (see Ch.36). The defendant's advocate may then be invited to address the court. The first witness for the claimant is then called. It is customary (though not essential) to call the claimant first. Each adult witness will take the oath or make a solemn affirmation. Child witnesses are at first questioned by the judge to determine whether they are competent to give evidence, either sworn (*R. v Hayes* [1997] 1 W.L.R. 234) or unsworn (Children Act 1989, s.96).

Unless the court orders otherwise, a witness statement stands as the evidence of that witness. Once the first question session, the examination-in-chief, is concluded, the witness will be cross-examined by the defence advocate and then, if necessary, re-examined by the claimant's advocate (see below). This procedure is then repeated with the other witnesses the claimant calls. In a lengthy multi-track case the order in which the witnesses are called will usually have already been decided upon at the pre-trial review. When all the claimant's witnesses have been called the defendant's witnesses are usually called in the same way, i.e. the defendant first and then other witnesses, each being examined, cross-examined and, if necessary, re-examined. As to varying the order of witnesses, see below. At the conclusion of the evidence the defendant's advocate and then normally the claimant's advocate will make closing submissions.

Submission of no case to answer

37.005 At the close of the claimant's case, the defendant may invite the court to consider a submission that no case has been made out that needs to be answered. In a trial by jury the submission is made to the judge in the absence of the jury. The judge will determine whether there is any real or reasonable prospect that the claimant's case might be made out or whether there is any case fit to go before a jury. In doing so the judge will have regard to the possibility that the way the defence case is later conducted may improve the claimant's case. For example, the claimant may be able to score worthwhile points in cross-examining the defendant's witnesses or maybe able to invite inferences from the defendant's failure to call particular witnesses. If the submission of no case to answer fails the jury will later give a verdict on all the evidence; the possible strengthening in the claimant's case the judge made allowance for may not in fact materialise.

If the case is being tried without a jury a defendant who makes a submission of no case to answer is almost invariably barred from calling evidence (see *Benham Ltd v Kythira Investments Ltd* [2003] EWCA Civ 1794 and *Graham v Chorley BC* [2006] EWCA Civ 92, *The Times*, March 20, 2006). Were this not so the judge might be embarrassed by having to make a premature ruling on the claimant's evidence and then a second ruling later upon all the evidence if the submission fails. Only in the most exceptional circumstances should a judge hear an application without putting the defendant to his election. If the defendant does elect not to call evidence his submission of no case will be determined on the balance of probabilities only. The claimant will win so long as he has adduced some evidence to support each material fact of his claim, however weak that evidence might be. The claimant will also be entitled to invite the court to draw adverse inferences from the defendant's decision not to call a witness who might be expected to have material evidence to give on the issues. Because this is so the judge in a non-jury trial should always warn the defendant that if he proceeds with his submission he will be taken to have elected not to call evidence. The defendant will normally be unwise to make that election unless he was not intending to call evidence anyway (see further as to when adverse inferences can properly be drawn from a party's failure to give evidence at para.31.004).

If, quite exceptionally, a trial judge is willing to entertain a submission of no case to answer without putting the defendants to their election, the judgments in *Benham* and *Graham* make it quite clear that if the defendants have material evidence that they are ready to give on a central issue the trial judge should not assess the merits of the claimant's case at this half-way stage on the balance of probabilities. Instead the judge should ask himself whether the claimant has

> "advanced a *prima facie* case, a case to answer, a scintilla of evidence to support the inference for which they contend, sufficient evidence to call for an explanation from the defendants? That it may be a weak case and unlikely to succeed unless assisted, rather than contradicted, by the defendant's evidence, or by adverse inferences to be drawn from the defendants' not calling any evidence, would not allow it to be dismissed on a no case submission" (*per* Brown L.J. in *Benham*).

Order of witnesses

Should the witnesses always be grouped according to the party calling them? Given that expert reports and witness statements have already been exchanged, everybody will know what every witness is expected to say. Thus, the witnesses may be grouped according to the issues instead. For example, assume that, in a building dispute which is likely to last six weeks, one issue turns upon the chemical analysis of the cement mix used. Each side is intending to call an expert witness on this issue and expert reports have been exchanged. There is nothing to be gained by dividing the testimony of these two witnesses by three or more weeks. It is much more convenient if one expert follows the other one into the witness box. 37.006

Failure to attend trial (r.39.3)

If the defendant fails to attend the trial the court may hear the claimant's evidence and where the case is proved it usually awards judgment and costs. In addition, the court is likely to strike out any counterclaim. Where the claimant fails to attend the defendant may prove any counterclaim and secure a judgment with costs. The claim itself is normally struck out. Should both parties fail to attend the court usually strikes out the whole proceedings. 37.007

Orders made because of a party's failure to attend may later be set aside under r.39.3(5). This gives the court a discretion where three grounds are satisfied: prompt application, good reason for not attending, and a reasonable prospect of success at the trial. There is no residual discretion for the court (*Barclays Bank Plc v Ellis* [2001] C.P.Rep.50 CA).

THE ART OF ADVOCACY

What follows in this section is only a short introduction to a very large topic. No one should think that advocacy can ever be properly learned from books. You should attend court as much as possible where you will see how it should 37.008

be done; and, unfortunately, sometimes, how it should not be done. Also, start off with the easy cases, particularly short interim applications.

Preparation

37.009 The key to successful advocacy is preparation. Thus, the litigation solicitor, even if he has no intention of ever appearing as an advocate, must know something of the art of advocacy otherwise he will not be able to brief his chosen advocate properly.

The advocate must get his points across. However, he must have decided beforehand which points he wants to make and the order in which he must make them. To do this adequate time must be spent preparing the case summary (see Ch.36). By the time of the trial the legal and factual issues in dispute should have become clear. Do not be tempted to stray from that path. Do not indulge in over-elaboration. A trial advocate should never be pressed into making every point conceivable and inconceivable without judgment or discrimination. The trial advocate should "assist the judge by simplification and concentration and not advance a multitude of ingenious arguments in the hope that out of ten bad points the judge will be capable of fashioning a winner" (*per* Lord Templeman in *Ashmore v Corp of Lloyd's* [1992] 2 All E.R. 486).

Opening and closing statements

37.010 The parties oral opening statements should be no longer than the circumstances require and even in a heavy case may be very short. Unless the judge asks, these should not be developed. It should be possible for the claimant to explain the case and the issues to be tried fairly concisely. If there are any outstanding procedural matters to be dealt with, it is usually best for the claimant to raise these in opening.

Advocates should avoid reading out aloud any document unless it is absolutely necessary. In some cases the judge may have already read the material. In other cases, the reading of documents may be left until witnesses of fact give oral evidence. To assist the court the parties should prepare for the judge a core reading list (see Ch.36). At the conclusion of the claimant's opening statement, advocates for other parties will usually be invited to make a short opening statement.

In substantial cases the court may require written summaries of opening and closing statements, insofar as any points are not covered in the case summaries. Normally, the claimant will make the final closing statement, although in the Commercial Court the defendant usually makes the last statement but the claimant has a right of reply.

Examination-in-chief

37.011 Start with questions as to the witness's name, address, relationship to the parties or proceedings and, if an expert witness, qualifications. Show the witness a copy of his statement, get him to confirm that it is his statement and to authenticate any documents referred to in the statement. You will need the judge's permission to use any supplemental witness statement or ask any additional questions in order to amplify the original statement (see para.31.010). If you are permitted to ask extra questions then you will have to obey the golden rule of examination-in-chief, i.e. on disputed matters you cannot ask your own witness leading questions. A leading question is one that prompts the witness or assumes a fact not yet proved. Thus, you cannot normally ask a landlord-client the question "Did the tenant last November pick up a hammer and smash the furniture in your presence?" Neither can you ask "what did the tenant do after he had picked up a hammer and smashed the furniture?" The technique is to briefly lead the witness through any undisputed matters (e.g. "did you visit the premises last November?") and then ask a general question (such as "what do you remember particularly about that occasion?"). If that does not obtain the desired response try another general question such as "what complaint do you now make against this tenant?" Once the witness has started upon the desired topic you should keep him there by asking how, when, why, type questions: How did you react to that? When did that happen? Why did you do that? The questions most frequently asked once the witness is giving relevant evidence is "And then what happened?"

During the examination-in-chief the opposing advocates should remain seated and silent. They should listen carefully for any questions which are objectionable, for example, questions which lead the witness or questions raising irrelevant issues (questions about other persons, other places, other times or questions about the witness's non-expert opinions). If a question is asked which you wish to object to, or if the witness strays into irrelevance, how should you make an objection? Please do not use the Hollywood method (Objection, your Honour!). Simply stand up and state politely "That is not evidence". The other advocate should then at least pause. When he or she does so you should resume your seat, unless the judge addresses you.

Cross-examination

37.012 The true test of an advocate is his or her proficiency in the skill, or art, of deadly cross-examination; the ability to destroy the evidence of an opposing witness by asking a series of piercing, puncturing, pulverising questions. An experienced advocate will execute a staged campaign which has frequently been tried and tested on other witnesses and which has been thoroughly adapted and prepared so as to undermine this particular witness. The opening shots are aimed at his confidence; next, several barrages of questions will cause the witness to accept a series of facts damaging to his previous testimony; the final round is often the question "And you still say . . ." which receives a doubtful, embarrassed, and crestfallen reply. Proficiency in this skill requires years of practice even though, because of exchange of witness statements, it is now so much easier to plan most questions in advance.

When planning your questions for cross-examination, try to identify the aspects of this witness's evidence that are most vulnerable to attack. Generally speaking the weaknesses that the evidence may have, and which it is your job to expose, are ambiguity, insincerity, faulty perception and erroneous memory. In practice most of your best scores will come from the weaknesses of faulty perception and erroneous memory. The most likely weaknesses in the evidence of experts are somewhat different: ambiguity (i.e. more than one opinion on the matter is tenable); insincerity (the expert is not stating honest independent opinions but has descended into the arena); and faulty perception (look for omissions in his report; it is normally easier to cross-examine on what is not there rather than on something which is there).

Beginners usually find that the skill of cross-examining is, at first anyway, the easier skill to acquire. This is because, in cross-examining, you are allowed to ask leading questions. Cross-examination is essential because a failure to challenge evidence given in chief implies acceptance of it. There is a danger in cross-examining someone whose evidence is unshakeable. Although cross-examination is essential it may appear to strengthen rather than weaken your opponent's case.

You can minimise the danger by formulating the question "I put it to you that ...". Thus "I put it to you that an important part of the evidence you have given here today is untrue. I put it to you that, in the claimant's presence, you did pick up a hammer and smash the furniture". This formulation does challenge the evidence strongly but prevents you becoming embroiled in an argument you may not win and, therefore may appear to lose.

Everyone will agree that the "I put it to you" formulation is nowadays considered old-fashioned and stagey but these are not necessarily fatal faults. Its staginess makes it more uncomfortable for the witness to answer than for you to ask. On the other hand, one common weakness of this formulation is that it almost invariably compels the witness to stick to what he said before. In the result, he just repeats his evidence.

An alternative method is to say, for example, "You know that my client has said". If nothing else it will involve a repetition of your own side's evidence rather than the other side's evidence. It also puts pressure on the witness to find some middle ground to adopt, i.e. to retract or qualify what he previously said. This formulation is, however, best confined to putting your client's case to a witness. On the whole, questions in cross-examination should be just that: questions, not statements. Also, it is unprofessional to seek to browbeat the opposing witness or to subject them to an argumentative and overbearing assault.

A common mistake of beginners is to try to comment on the evidence as each point is scored. The proper place for comment is in your closing statement. And do not do what so many do; seek to get in some comment indirectly by asking the witness that one question too many; the one which explains away any comment you may otherwise have been able to make.

Examples

In a contract action: Was that letter the first time you complained? (Yes.) You didn't complain before, then? (I tried to telephone many many times but your client's phone has been disconnected.)

In a road accident case: Your mother was also a passenger, wasn't she? (Yes.) But she hasn't come to give evidence for you today has she? (She wanted to. But she suffered a massive stroke three weeks ago. She's still in hospital.)

On a claim for a debt which the defendant says he repaid, in cash, on meeting the claimant in the street: Do you often walk about with £4,000 in cash in your wallet? (Yes.) Show me how much you've got in your wallet today. (Witness produces over £4,000 in cash.)

Re-examination

Re-examination of your witness has two purposes. It can be used to restore your own witness's credibility. For example, where it has been suggested in cross-examination that he would not have had a clear observation of certain matters, you can ask questions demonstrating the amount of detail he can recall. Re-examination can also be used to allow your witness to explain points made in cross-examination which seem adverse but in fact are not; you see this especially when the cross-examiner has insisted upon a yes or no answer and your witness replied "Yes but". Re-examination must be confined to matters arising out of the cross-examination. Leading questions should not be asked.

THE ROLE OF THE TRIAL JUDGE

In *Southwark LBC v Kofi-Adu* [2006] EWCA Civ 281, *The Times*, June 1, 2006, Parker L.J. examined the role of the trial judge as follows:

> "It is important to stress at the outset that, within the bounds set by the Civil Procedure Rules, a first instance judge is entitled to a wide degree of latitude in the way in which he conducts proceedings in his court. However, that latitude is not unlimited. Ultimately, the process must always be the servant of the judicial function of dealing with cases justly (see the overriding objective expressed in CPR 1.1). In an adversarial system such as we have developed in this jurisdiction the discharge of that function requires the first instance judge (as Lord Denning MR put it in *Jones v. National Coal Board* [1957] 2 QB 55 at 63):
>
>> '... to hear and determine the issues raised by the parties, not to conduct an investigation or examination on behalf of society at large....'"

As Lord Denning MR went on to explain, that does not mean the judge is "a mere umpire to answer the question 'How's that?'". Lord Denning MR continued:

"His object, after all, is to find out the truth, and to do justice according to law; and in the daily pursuit of it the advocate plays an honourable and necessary role. Was it not Lord Eldon LC who said in a notable passage that 'truth is best discovered by powerful statements on both sides of the question'? ... And Lord Greene MR who explained that justice is best done by a judge who holds the balance between the contending parties without himself taking part in their disputations? If a judge, said Lord Greene, should himself conduct the examination of witnesses, 'he, so to speak, descends into the arena and is liable to have his vision clouded by the dust of conflict': see *Yuill v. Yuill* [[1945] P 15 at 20]."

Under the CPR first instance judges rightly tend to be very much more proactive and interventionist than their predecessors. But it remains the case that interventions by the judge in the course of oral evidence (as opposed to interventions during counsel's submissions) must inevitably carry the risk so graphically described by Lord Greene MR. The greater the frequency of the interventions, the greater the risk; and where the interventions take the form of lengthy interrogation of the witnesses, the risk becomes a serious one.

In the case the court were left in no doubt that the judge's constant (and frequently contentious) interventions during the oral evidence, served to cloud his vision and his judgment to the point where he was unable to subject the oral evidence to proper scrutiny and evaluation. The flaw was not so much in the decisions he made but in the way he reached them, in that he allowed himself not merely to descend into the arena but, once there, to play a substantial part in the interrogation of the witnesses. In effect, he arrogated to himself a quasi-inquisitorial role which is entirely at odds with the adversarial system.

It is well recognised not only that a trial judge may, and commonly will, begin forming views about the evidence as it goes along, but that he may legitimately give assistance to the parties by telling them what is presently in his mind (see *Hart v Relentless Records Ltd* [2002] EWHC 1984). Therefore, a trial judge may, before reaching the defendant's case, indicate that he did not think much of the claimant's evidence. What is not acceptable is for the judge to form, or to give the impression of having formed, a firm view in favour of one side's credibility when the other side has not yet called evidence which is intended to impugn it (see *Steadman-Byrne v Amjad* [2007] EWCA Civ 625, (2007) L.T.L., June 27).

JUDGMENT

37.016   After the closing statements the judge will deliver his judgment. He will sometimes adjourn to the following day before doing so, particularly if the hour is late, and in complex multi-track cases he may expressly reserve judgment, in which case the parties will be told at a later date when to attend to hear the judgment delivered. Where judgment is reserved (see generally PD 40E), the parties must inform the court if there are meaningful settlement discussions between them (*Gurney Consulting Engineers (a firm) v Gleeds Health and Safety Ltd (No.2)* [2006] EWHC 536, *The Times*, April 24, 2006) or any agreement is reached that makes it unnecessary for the judgment to be delivered (*HFC Bank Plc v HSBC Bank Plc (formerly Midland Bank Plc)* (2000) L.T.L., April 3). However, the parties cannot prevent the judge from still handing down his judgment if he considers that to be in the public interest (*Prudential Assurance Co. Ltd v McBains Cooper (a firm)* [2000] 1 W.L.R. 2000, CA).

After judgment has been given there are several formal applications which may be made:

(a) On a claim for debt or damages interest may be awarded in the judgment (see generally Ch.3). The calculations are best done immediately: you should take a pocket calculator along for this purpose.

(b) The successful advocate will ask for costs. Costs are limited on the small claims track (see para.20.010). On the fast track and in simple multi-track matters there is usually a summary assessment of costs there and then (see para.38.014). Otherwise, a detailed assessment will be ordered if the parties cannot agree in the meantime (see para.38.015). If a party ordered to pay costs wants to rely on the conduct or misconduct of the non-paying party in order to seek a reduction in the costs to be paid, should he raise that factor at the end of the trial or later before the costs judge at the time of a detailed assessment? In *Northstar Systems Ltd v Fielding* [2006] EWCA Civ 1660, *The Times*, January 8, 2007, Waller L.J. stated,

> "It seems to me that consideration of a party's conduct should normally take place both at the stage when the judge is considering what order for costs he should make, and then during assessment. But the court will want to ensure that dishonesty is penalised but that the party is not placed in double jeopardy. Ultimately, the question is one of the proper construction of the order made by the judge. Thus it will be important for the judge, who is asked to take dishonesty into account at the end of a trial when considering the order as to costs, to consider what is likely to occur on assessment. Where dishonest conduct is being reflected in an order made by the trial judge, it must be wise for the future for judges to make clear whether they are making the order on the basis that, on the assessment, the paying party will still be entitled to raise the dishonesty in arguing that costs incurred in supporting the particular dishonesty were unreasonably incurred. Judges may also want to consider whether to make an order under rule 44.14 and it would be wise to do that before considering precisely what order to make in relation to the costs of a trial generally."

See further para.38.018.

(c) A ruling may now be sought in respect of the costs of any interim application which were "reserved" (see Ch.13).

(d) Any advocate appearing for a party funded by the L.S.C. should apply for a detailed assessment of the costs payable out of the Community Legal Service Fund (see Ch.39).

In many cases where judgment is reserved it is now the practice for a draft of the judgment to be sent to the lawyers for the parties (or to the parties themselves if unrepresented) on a confidential basis before the date upon which it is to be given formally. In order to save time at that hearing the draft usually requires the parties' lawyers to submit to the court written suggestions about typing errors, wrong case references and other minor corrections. Full details of this practice are given in a series of Practice Statements (see *White Book*, vol.1, paras B5–001 to B7–001 and *Director of Public Prosecutions v P* [2007] All E.R. (D) 246). Sending out a draft judgment may enable the parties to agree any consequential matters such as the form of order, interest, costs, etc., and so obviate the need for the further hearing. At the very least it will enable the parties properly to prepare for that hearing and reduce the time it will take. The draft judgment is confidential and its publication may lead to contempt of court proceedings: see *Baigent v Random House and "The Lawyer"* [2006] EWHC 1131, *The Times*, May 24, 2006.

At the later hearing the final judgment is generally made available in written form and is not read out in open court. Even if the parties will not attend, the judge cannot, or rather should not, dispense completely with the formality of pronouncing his judgment. If the prior hearing was in public he should make his judgment available to the parties in public also, whether or not they attend. The formality also fixes the time for appealing that judgment (see generally *Owusu v Jackson* [2002] EWCA Civ 877, (2002) L.T.L. June 19).

CHAPTER 38

Costs Payable by One Party to Another

DEFINITION OF COSTS

Rule 43.2(1) states as follows: 38.001

"In Parts 44 to 48, unless the context otherwise requires—

(a) 'costs' includes fees, charges, disbursements, expenses, remuneration, reimbursement allowed to a litigant in person under Rule 48.6, any additional liability incurred under a funding arrangement and any fee or reward charged by a lay representative for acting on behalf of a party in proceedings allocated to the small claims track;"

Before studying different aspects of this definition, it is necessary to consider the scope of an order for costs.

What does an order for costs cover?

In most cases, the costs payable by one party to another mainly comprise of court fees, remuneration for solicitors and counsel and sums payable to witnesses. All of these items fall within the definition of costs. However, a party may not be able to recover all of these items under an order for costs he obtains. It is always necessary to define the context in which the question of costs arises. Is the order intended to cover the whole of the expenditure made by the receiving party or only a part, and if so, which part? For example, the court fees incurred by a claimant on issuing the claim form are not usually recoverable under an order for costs made in his favour on an interim application which did not terminate the proceedings in question. Such fees will be recoverable if the claimant obtains an order for costs at the trial. However, an order at trial may not cover any costs incurred in relation to interim applications (see generally Ch.13 and r.44.13(1)).   38.002

Costs usually refers to legal costs

38.003   Pre-eminent examples of costs are the bills payable for work done and expenses incurred by solicitors, counsel, and other persons authorised to conduct litigation or provide advocacy services. There is a general rule of longstanding that allowable costs are, and are limited to, remuneration for the exercise of professional legal skill (*Buckland v Watts* [1970] 1 Q.B. 27). The origins of the rule lie in the desire of the old common-law courts to exclude unquantifiable elements from the definition of costs. "Professional skill and labour are recognised and can be measured by the law; private expenditure of labour and trouble by a layman cannot be measured. It depends on the zeal, the assiduity, or the nervousness of the individual. Professional skill, when it is bestowed, is accordingly allowed for in taxing a bill of costs . . ." (Danckwerts L.J., in *Buckland*). In *R. v Legal Aid Board Ex p. Eccleston* [1998] 1 W.L.R. 1279, Sedley J. criticised the logic of this rule because it also excludes expenses which would be easy to quantify, such as expenses incurred traveling to consult legal, medical or other advisors in connection with the litigation. He suggested that the exclusion of non-legal costs is better regarded today as a policy limitation rather than as a legal distinction.

The decision in *Buckland* led to the passing of the Litigants in Person (Costs and Expenses) Act 1975 which makes specific provision for the remuneration of litigants in person. However, that statute is of no assistance to a litigant who has instructed a solicitor but, perhaps to minimise his own liability for costs, wishes to undertake some of the preparation of the case himself. Tasks such as interviewing witnesses or preparing a list of documents to be disclosed to the opponent can be extremely time-consuming and the hourly rate lawyers' charge may be such that the litigant would make a substantial saving if he did the work himself or directed an employee to do it. In the "Access to Justice Final Report", Lord Woolf M.R., referred to the

> "desirability of promoting arrangements whereby litigants could undertake much of the preparation of their case but with access to legal advice and representation as necessary. This is known as 'unbundling'".

However, this proposed change in the law has not yet been implemented. In *Sisu Capital Fund Ltd v Tucker* [2006] 1 All E.R. 167, the liquidators and administrators of a company which was awarded costs were not allowed to recover anything in respect of time spent by them and their employees on matters which, if undertaken by their lawyers, would have been recoverable as costs. Similarly, in *Agassi v Robinson (Inspector of Taxes)* [2006] 1 All E.R. 900, a litigant in person (the famous tennis player, see further below) was not allowed to recover the modest fees of an accountant who had instructed counsel under the Bar's Licensed Access Scheme. In this case, the Court of Appeal suggested that the reason for limiting costs to legal costs was the need to control the activities of unskilled and unregulated persons who might otherwise conduct litigation (see para.81 of the judgment).

Litigants in person

38.004 The definition of costs in r.43.2(1) includes "reimbursement allowed to a litigant in person under Rule 48.6". Neither that rule nor the statute from which it, in part, derives (Litigants in Person (Costs and Expenses Act (1975)) contains an exhaustive definition of the term "litigant in person" but r.48.6 does state that it includes "a company or other corporation which is acting without a legal representative". A more exhaustive definition of the term "litigant in person" was given by the Court of Appeal in *Agassi v Robinson (Inspector of Taxes)* [2006] 1 All E.R. 900. This case demonstrates that a litigant in person refers to any litigant who is not represented by a person authorised to conduct litigation. The case concerned the UK income tax affairs of the famous tennis player. Mr Agassi lost before the Special Commissioners, and before the High Court Judge and, ultimately, before the House of Lords. However, in the Court of Appeal he won his case and was awarded costs. In the appeal, as in all earlier stages, he had been advised and assisted by a firm of accountants who had been advising and assisting him in tax matters for many years. In respect of the court hearings the accountants instructed barristers under the Bar's Licensed Access Scheme. The accountants and barristers above mentioned, in common with most accountants and barristers, were not authorised to conduct litigation and Mr Agassi did not retain in this matter any solicitor or other person authorised to conduct the litigation for him. Mr Agassi was held to be a litigant in person even though, of course, he had never sought to prepare his case or represent himself in this matter.

In practice, of course, most litigants in person are litigants who act and speak for themselves. They either cannot afford to, or do not wish to, pay for legal representation and legal aid is not available to them.

Rule 48.6 permits litigants in person to recover costs for "work" and "disbursements" subject to severe restrictions. First, both work and disbursements are limited to what would have been allowed if the work had been done or the disbursements had been made by a legal representative on the litigant's behalf. This restriction disentitles the litigant to any work he would have done even if represented, such as digging out the facts in order to instruct his lawyers *Richards & Wallington (Plant Hire) Ltd* (1984) Costs L.R. (Core) 79. Similarly, disbursements incurred which a legal representative would not have incurred are not recoverable. This restriction prevents the litigant recovering the costs of any advice and assistance he obtains from non-lawyers. In *Agassi* the fees of the accountants were not recoverable save possibly to the extent they could be characterised as being out of pocket expenses or expert witness allowances (see further, below).

Next, the amount recoverable for work (as opposed to disbursements) is subject to two further tight restrictions. First, the amount allowed must take into account any financial loss proved by the litigant in person, or, if no financial loss is proved, an amount calculated at an hourly rate of £9.25 in respect of time reasonably spent. Secondly, the amount allowed cannot exceed two-thirds of the amount which would have been allowed if the litigant had been represented by a legal representative.

The restrictions on costs imposed by r.48.6 do not apply to a solicitor who, instead of acting for himself, is represented in the proceedings by his firm or by himself in his firm name (PD48, para.52.5 and *Malkinson v Trim* [2003] 1 W.L.R. 463, CA).

In-house solicitors

38.005   Many large companies which become involved in litigation do not retain independent solicitors but are represented instead by their in-house legal departments. Similarly, the government is almost invariably represented by its in-house team, the Treasury Solicitors' Office. For the purposes of assessment, the expense of using an in-house team rather than an independent solicitor is presumed to be not less than the fees an independent solicitor would have charged (*Re Eastwood* [1975] 1 Ch.112, CA). This approach is based more upon pragmatism than it is upon principle. The alternative method of assessment would be to require the receiving party to produce figures to demonstrate the cost of the in-house team which is attributable solely to the litigation. To make that method compulsory in all cases "would, as it seems to us, simply be to introduce a rule unworkable in practice and to push abstract principle to a point at which it ceases to give results consistent with justice" (Russell L.J., and see further, para.38.020, below).

Expenses and witness allowances

38.006   The definition of costs in r.43.2(1) includes "expenses", a term to which plainly includes out of expenses which have always been allowed to all litigants whether they are represented or in person. There are many case references to litigants being entitled to recover these (see, for example, *Buckland v Watts* [1970] 1 Q.B. 27). "Out of pocket expenses" cover sums incurred on couriers, telephone and fax and court filing fees (*Mealing-McLeod v Common Professional Examination Board (Assessment of Costs)* [2000] 2 Costs L.R. 223, and see *Agassi* at para.65).

Litigants are also entitled to recover reasonable expenses incurred on witnesses. In calculating the reasonable amount the court takes into account the witness's earnings level, the time engaged in travelling to and from, and attending at, the trial and reasonable travelling and hotel expenses etc. An expert witness is also entitled to reasonable fees compensating him for time spent familiarising himself with the facts of the case so as to enable him to express an expert opinion on them. Rule 48.6(5) provides that a litigant in person who is allowed costs for attending at court to conduct his case is not entitled to claim also a witness allowance in respect of such attendance.

Additional liability

The definition of costs given in r.43.2 includes "any *additional liability* incurred under a *funding arrangement*". The words here shown in italics are themselves defined in r.43.2. In order to get the complete picture you also need to take on board the practice direction definition of base costs.

38.007

In most cases additional liability means that part of a success fee under a conditional fee agreement which is recoverable from the paying party (see para.2.016, above) and/or a reasonable sum in respect of an insurance premium paid or payable for a relevant "After the Event" (ATE) insurance policy (see para.2.009, above). It also means an additional amount which is sometimes recoverable in respect of "self insurance" notionally incurred by a litigant whose case is funded by a trade union or similar "membership organisation". These three forms of additional liability are the items about which the opponent should have received a Notice of Funding at the outset (see para.2.023, above). A party who is ordered to pay costs is not liable to pay any additional liability for any period during which the receiving party was in breach of the requirement to give Notice of Funding, unless the court otherwise orders (r.44.3B).

Once you have grasped the definition of additional liability, it is easy to understand the term base costs. Paragraph 2.2 of the Costs Practice Direction (CPD) defines these as "costs other than the amount of any additional liability". There is no obligation to give any Notice of Funding in respect of base costs unless they are funded out of the Community Legal Service fund to a litigant who has cost protection (see paras 2.021 and 2.024, above). However, represented parties do have to give estimates of costs in certain circumstances (see para.33.013). Estimates should state the base costs incurred and to be incurred, but need not give any estimate of any additional liability thereon (CPD, para.6.2).

A feature which is unique to an additional liability is the fact that the court will never make any assessment of it until the conclusion of the proceedings, or the part of the proceedings, to which it relates (r.44.3A). In the case of a success fee, its recoverability may well depend upon who ultimately wins the case. As regards all forms of additional liability, the prohibition on early assessment lessens the likelihood that potentially embarrassing information (the percentage increase specified as a success fee or the amount of any premium for ATE insurance) will be revealed at a time when it could damage the prospects of success.

The procedure on assessment of an additional liability is described later in this Chapter (see especially paras 38.023 and 38.025) as are the factors which are relevant when assessing the reasonableness of additional liability claims.

DISCRETIONARY NATURE OF COSTS

38.008 Rule 44.3 gives the court a discretion whether to order one party to pay another's costs, the amount of those costs, and the time for payment. Sub-rule (2) confirms, with modifications, the general principle that "costs follow the event", i.e. that the losing litigant will be ordered to pay the winning litigant's costs and will be left to bear his own. The modifications to this general rule were summarised and explained by Lord Woolf M.R. in *AEI Rediffusion Music Ltd v Phonographic Performance Ltd* [1999] 1 W.L.R. 1507 as follows:

> ". . . the 'follow the event principle' [is] a starting point from which a court can readily depart. . . . The . . . rules . . . require courts to be more ready to make separate orders which reflect the outcome of different issues . . . It is now clear that a too robust application of the 'follow the event principle' encourages litigants to increase the cost of litigation, since it discourages litigants from being selective as to the points they take. If you recover all your costs as long as you win, you are encouraged to leave no stone unturned in your effort to do so".

A somewhat chilling example of the new approach is provided by *Irvine v Commissioner of Police for the Metropolis* [2005] EWCA Civ 129: the claimant, a police officer, tripped on a stair carpet at work and was seriously injured. He sued his employer for negligence and breach of statutory duty. Later he joined two further defendants, the company which managed the building and the company responsible for fitting the carpet in question. Before proceedings commenced the first defendant encouraged the claimant to sue the second defendant instead of himself and later, in his defence, suggested that any liability lay with the second and third defendants. The case went to trial. All claims of negligence were lost but the claimant won his claim for breach of statutory duty against the first defendant. The damages awarded were approximately £26,000. The costs of all four parties were approximately £100,000. Although the first defendant was ordered to pay the costs incurred by the claimant in bringing his successful claim against him, the claimant was ordered to pay the costs of the other two defendants. It seems likely that these costs will exceed the damages he recovered.

Pre-CPR it is likely that, in a case such as this, the court would have made the losing defendant responsible for all defendant's costs either directly (a "Sanderson Order") or indirectly (a "Bullock Order") i.e. an order under which the claimant would have to pay the successful defendants' costs but could then add them to his own costs and recover them from the losing defendant). Post CPR claimants must give careful thought to how they are going to pursue their claims. They should not assume that, where one party seeks to lay the blame at the door of another, they are entitled to pursue that other party at the expense of the one who is pointing the finger.

Rule 44.3(4) states that, in deciding what order (if any) to make about costs, the court must have regard to all the circumstances including the conduct of all parties, the degree of success and failure each party has achieved and the effect of any payment into court or admissible offer to settle (whether or not made in accordance with Pt 36) The "conduct of the parties" is widely defined in sub-rule (5) as including:

> "(a) conduct before, as well as during, the proceedings, and in particular the extent to which the parties followed any relevant pre-action protocol;
> (b) whether it was reasonable for a party to raise, pursue or contest a particular allegation or issue;
> (c) the manner in which a party has pursued or defended his case or a particular allegation or issue;
> (d) whether a claimant who has succeeded in his claim, in whole or in part, exaggerated his claim."

Rule 44.3(6) sets out a list (which is not exhaustive) of orders for costs which the court may make which will give the receiving party only a partial indemnity in respect of his reasonable expenditure. The court may order that a party must pay:

(a) a proportion of another party's costs;
(b) a stated amount in respect of another party's costs;
(c) costs from or until a certain date only;
(d) costs incurred before proceedings have begun;
(e) costs relating to particular steps taken in the proceedings;
(f) costs relating only to a distinct part of the proceedings; and
(g) interest on costs from or until a certain date, including a date before judgment.

Paragraph (f) in that list indicates that the court may award costs by dividing entitlement according to which party has won on each issue in the case. Orders for "costs of issues" can often prove difficult, if not impossible, to carry into effect. Rule 44.3(7) provides that if the court is minded to make an order under para.(f), it must instead, if practicable, make an order under paras (a) or (c). For example, if each side wins some issues but loses others, the court may make a single order for costs in favour of the overall winner allowing him only a part or percentage of his costs (*Burchell v Bullard* [2005] EWCA Civ 358). A percentage order for costs may also be appropriate where the winner is guilty of conduct falling within the other parts of the definition set out in r.44.3(5) (and see further para.38.018).

METHODS OF ASSESSMENT

The amount of costs payable by one party to another may be fixed by rules or determined by way of a summary assessment or a detailed assessment. 38.009

Fixed costs on early judgments

38.010 Fixed costs may be applicable where a default judgment, a judgment on admissions, summary judgment or default costs certificate is obtained in proceedings in which the only claim made is a claim made for a specified sum of money. The amount of fixed costs payable in these cases (and in a few others, e.g. certain Consumer Credit Act claims) are set out in Pt 45. However, the award of costs or the amount thereof is not made compulsory by Pt 45. If it so wishes, the court may award no costs or may award a sum to be assessed by summary assessment or by detailed assessment (r.45.1(1)).

The fixed costs here described are always added in to an order which otherwise provides for the payment of money. The time for payment of a judgment for money (including costs) is within 14 days after the date of the judgment unless a different date is specified in the judgment or in the CPR, or unless the court has stayed the proceedings or judgment (r.40.11).

Note that, when fixed costs are awarded, the amount allowed is the amount set out in the relevant rule or practice direction. The amount is the same whether or not the recipient is entitled to claim an additional liability.

Fixed costs in fast track trials

38.011 Part 46 provides sums equivalent to fixed costs for fast track trials. Unless it decides not to award any fast track trial costs, the court may not award more or less than the sums shown in the table to r.46.2 (likely to be amended in October 2007) and any other disbursements unless the court apportions the amount awarded between the parties to reflect their respective degrees of success on the issues at trial, or unless r.46.3 applies.

Rule 46.3 provides:

(1) An additional sum in respect of a legal representative whose attendance at trial was necessary to give assistance to the advocate.

(2) An additional amount in respect of any separate trial which the court considered it was necessary to direct.

(3) An additional amount where the party paying costs has behaved improperly during the trial.

(4) A reduced amount where the party receiving costs has behaved unreasonably or improperly during the trial.

(5) A reduced amount where the party receiving costs is a litigant in person. Fast track trials do not often involve multiple parties. Where they do, only one award of fast track trial costs can be made in respect of each advocate who appears, regardless of how many parties that advocate represented (r.46.4).

Fixed costs in some RTA claims which settle pre-issue

A fixed cost regime applies to road traffic accident claims in which the accident occurs after October 5, 2003 and in which all questions of compensation and costs are agreed, save possibly the amount of costs payable (r.44.12A and rr.45.7 to 45.14). The regime is not limited to personal injury claims: the agreed compensation may relate to personal injury, damage to property, or both (r.45.7(2)(b) and see r.45.7(4)(a)). The regime has top and bottom financial limits. It does not apply if the agreed damages exceed £10,000. It does not apply if the small claims track would have been the normal track for the claim had a claim been issued for the amount of damages agreed. For cases within these limits, the amount payable depends upon, amongst other things, the amount of agreed damages. The minimum sum (i.e. where the agreed damages are £1,000) is "fixed recoverable costs" of £1,000 plus 12.5 per cent for London Weighting where appropriate, plus a success fee of 12.5 per cent on the sum excluding London weighting if the solicitor was retained on a CFA with success fee, plus certain allowable disbursements, plus VAT where payable. Claimants may be entitled to a larger sum if the circumstances are exceptional. However, they will be heavily penalised in costs if they persuade the court to entertain a claim for a larger sum but fail to get an increase of 20 per cent or more (rr.45.13 and 45.14).

38.012

Fixed success fees in some RTA claims and employers' liability claims

CPR 45 ss.III, IV and V derive from industry wide agreements as to success fees which were achieved through the good offices of the Civil Justice Council. None of them apply to claims for which the small claims track is the normal track (as to which, see Ch.20).

38.013

Section III applies to RTA claims in respect of accidents occurring after October 5, 2003. It provides a two-stage success fee for solicitors: 100 per cent for cases which actually reach a trial and 12.5 per cent for all other RTA cases. For counsel, a three-stage success fee is provided: 100 per cent for cases reaching trial; a reduced figure (75 per cent multi-track or 50 per cent fast track) for cases which settle within 21 days pre-trial (multi-track) or 14 days pre-trial (fast track); and 12.5 per cent for all other RTA cases. In this context "trial" is a reference to the final contested hearing or to the contested hearing of any issue ordered to be tried separately. Thus, 100 per cent success fees may be payable even if the defendant has at all times admitted liability but the case is fought solely as to the assessment of damages. More curiously still 100 per cent is also payable where, at the final hearing, the claimant fails to beat an offer to settle which was previously made by the defendant: although he will thereby be deprived of his costs incurred in the period after the offer was made, he will still receive a 100 per cent success fee on his earlier costs even though, had he accepted the offer when it was made, he would only have received 12.5 per cent (*Lamont v Burton* [2007] EWCA Civ 429).

Section III provides for certain exceptional circumstances in which different success fees may be payable; RTA claims which have a value (before any reduction for contributory negligence which exceeds £500,000 and in which the applicant can show that the appropriate success fee is either substantially higher or substantially lower than the fixed success fee. Woe will betide a claimant who applies whose success fee is assessed at no greater than 20 per cent, or a defendant who applies and who fails to get the claimant's success fee assessed at less than 7.5 per cent. In these cases, the fixed success fee of 12.5 per cent will continue to apply and the costs of the application and the assessment will be ordered against the applicant.

CPR 45 s.IV applies to employers' liability, accident claims which do not arise from a road traffic accident and in which the injury was sustained after September 2004. CPR 45 s.V applies to employers' liability, disease claims in which the letter before claim containing the main allegations of fault was sent after September 2005. Both of these sections provide a regime which is basically the same as in RTA claims (a two-stage success fee for solicitors, a three-stage success fee for Counsel and an opportunity to seek higher or lower fix success fees in claims worth £500,000 before any reduction for contributory negligence). There are, of course, differences; for example, the lowest success fee for counsel is 25 per cent and the lowest success fee for solicitors is 25 per cent or 27.5 per cent if the claimant has the benefit of notional ATE cover provided by a trade union or similar membership organisation (as to which, see para.38.007, above). In some employers' liability disease cases, the lowest success fee is much higher than the percentages just mentioned. In claims worth £500,000 before any reduction for contributory negligence, provision is made for applications for a higher or lower success fee, with penalties if the application is not sufficiently successful.

Summary assessment

38.014 Summary assessment is the procedure by which the court when making an award of costs immediately calculates and specifies the sum of costs it allows. As a general rule the court will summarily assess costs in cases tried on the fast track, hearings which have lasted less than one day certain hearings in the Court of Appeal (Costs Practice Direction (CPD), para.13.2), and in detailed assessment hearings where costs are awarded to the paying party (CPD, para.45.2, see below). Chapter 13 contains an account of summary assessment including a list of exceptional cases and the procedure to follow, i.e. filing and serving a statement of costs. Costs which have been summarily assessed are payable within 14 days of the assessment unless the court specifies some other time period either when making the order for costs (r.44.8) or upon a later application (r.3.1(2)(a)). Consider now a summary assessment where the receiving party claims an additional liability (see para.38.007, above). On a summary assessment before the conclusion of the proceedings r.44.3A usually prevents any assessment of the additional liability. On a summary assessment at the conclusion of the proceedings, the receiving party will have already filed and served a statement of costs (no doubt limited to the base costs claimed, see CPD, para.13.5(5)). The court may decide not to do a summary assessment and send the whole question for detailed assessment. Alternatively, it may conduct a summary assessment of the base costs only or a summary assessment of all the costs. The one option not open to it is to make a summary assessment of the additional liability only (see generally r.44.3A). In order to help the court, the party seeking an additional liability must prepare and have available for the court a bundle of documents including:

(1) copies of any Notice of Funding (Form N251) filed by him (r.44.3B disentitles him to any additional liability for periods during which he was in breach of the requirement to give notice);
(2) copies of every estimate of costs filed by him (these and the estimates filed by other parties can be taken into account as a factor, amongst others when assessing the reasonableness of any costs claimed: CPD, para.6.6);
(3) copies of any statements of costs filed by him for this hearing and previous hearings (the costs now being assessed should include an additional liability on any base costs summarily assessed by the court at previous hearings); and
(4) if a success fee is claimed, a copy of the risk assessment prepared at the time the CFA was entered into (as to assessing the reasonableness of success fees and other additional liability claims, see paras 38.026 and 38.028).

Detailed assessment

Detailed assessment is a procedure by which the amount of costs is decided, not by the court awarding costs, but by a costs officer in accordance with Pt 47, which is summarised below. On completion of the proceedings before him, the costs officer will issue a final costs certificate which will include an order to pay the costs to which it relates (unless the court otherwise orders). Costs determined by detailed assessment must be paid within 14 days of the date of the certificate (r.44.8). There are, however, two ways in which the party receiving costs may obtain some of those costs at an earlier stage. A court which orders a party to pay costs may also order an amount to be paid on account of those costs before they are assessed (r.44.3(8)). The costs practice direction indicates that every court making an order for detailed assessment will also consider whether to exercise this power and require the paying party to pay such sum of money as it thinks just on account (CPD, para.12.3). The principles to be applied here were considered by Laddie J. in *Dyson Ltd v Hoover Ltd* [2004] 1 W.L.R. 1264. A trial court should normally order a sum at least equal to the minimum sum the receiving party is likely to recover on the detailed assessment and, if it is possible to calculate it, a sum close to the figure the costs officer would arrive at. The court will also take into account all the circumstances, including the financial strength of the parties and the possibility of an appeal.

38.015

The second way of obtaining payment of costs before the conclusion of detailed assessment proceedings is for the receiving party to apply to the court conducting those proceedings for an interim costs certificate (r.47.15 which is summarised below).

BASIS OF ASSESSMENT

38.016 There are two bases upon which the court may assess the amount of costs recoverable (whether by summary assessment or detailed assessment): the indemnity basis and the standard basis (see generally r.44.4). Neither basis permits the recovery of costs which have been unreasonably incurred or which are unreasonable in amount. In other respects, however, the bases are defined differently.

Where costs are to be assessed on the indemnity basis, the court will give the receiving party the benefit of any doubt as to whether the costs were reasonably incurred or were reasonable in amount. In many cases, doubts will arise as to the quantum of counsel's fees and as to the number and length of attendances on client and witnesses. From the receiving party's point of view, the indemnity basis is always to be preferred since it will give him the benefit of those doubts. However, in practice, this basis is awarded only in exceptional cases, for example, cases in which the paying party's conduct has been unreasonable to a high degree (*Kiam v MGN Ltd* [2003] Q.B. 281, CA; *Excelsior Commercial & Industrial Holdings Ltd v Salisbury Hamer Aspden & Johnson* [2002] EWCA Civ 879) and cases in which the paying party is a defendant who has failed to accept the claimant's reasonable offer to settle (see r.36.14(3): see para.29.023). In most cases, the standard basis is one which, as its name implies, will ordinarily apply.

When assessing costs on the standard basis, the court will disallow any costs which are disproportionate to the matters in issue and any costs as to which doubts arise as to whether they are reasonable or proportionate. From the paying party's point of view, the standard basis is to be preferred since that is the one which gives him the benefit of any doubts. The extent to which standard basis costs can be further downgraded by the reference to proportionality is considered separately below.

Rule 44.4(4) makes the definitions of basis "judge-proof": costs between parties will be assessed on the indemnity basis only if that basis is specified; in all other cases, costs between parties will be assessed on the standard basis.

In determining what costs are reasonable and (in standard basis cases, proportionate) r.44.5 directs the court to have regard to "all the circumstances" and must also have regard to:

"(a) the conduct of all the parties, including in particular—

    (i) conduct before, as well as during, the proceedings; and

    (ii) the efforts made, if any, before and during the proceedings in order to try to resolve the dispute;

(b) the amount of value of any money or property involved;
(c) the importance of the matter to all the parties;
(d) the particular complexity of the matter or the difficulty or novelty of the questions raised;
(e) the skill, effort, specialised knowledge and responsibility involved;
(f) the time spent on the case; and
(g) the place where and the circumstances in which work or any part of it was done."

Experienced practitioners will recognise this list as a restatement of the old "seven pillars of wisdom" with substantial modifications, including the addition of "conduct of all parties" which is placed first in the list.

Proportionality

Costs awarded on the standard basis must be proportionate as well as reasonable. In *Lownds v Home Office* [2002] 1 W.L.R. 2450, the Court of Appeal gave the following guidance on proportionality:

38.017

(1) In a case where proportionality is likely to be an issue, the court assessing costs must undertake a two-stage approach. First, it must consider the totality of the costs claimed in comparison with the benefit gained by the proceedings. If the costs as a whole are not disproportionate according to that test then the second stage is for the assessment to proceed in the usual way, i.e. a consideration of the reasonableness of each item. If, on the other hand, the total costs appear disproportionate, the court must, at the second stage, proceed to assess them, item by item, applying a test of necessity rather than reasonableness.

(2) In considering the question of proportionality the court assessing costs must have regard to whether the appropriate level of fee-earner or counsel was deployed, whether offers to settle were made, whether unnecessary experts were instructed and the other matters set out in r.4.5(3) (see para.38.016, above).

In *Giambrone v JMC Holidays Ltd* [2003] 1 All E.R. 982, Morland J. upheld a ruling by a costs judge that a claim for costs in a multi-party holiday claim was disproportionate. The bill of costs claimed over £1 million in respect of a judgment on liability obtained by 652 claimants who suffered injuries and losses during holidays organised by the defendants. Liability was admitted within two years of the letter before claim. In this appeal the learned judge also decided that, when comparing the amount claimed against the benefit gained, the court should ignore any VAT claimed. Another point taken was whether the proportionality test should be applied to costs incurred before April 26, 1999 (the start date for the CPR). He ruled that all costs claimed should be taken into account but, if the total claimed is disproportionate, the necessity test should be applied only to costs incurred after April 26, 1999.

Once the first-stage decision is made that the costs are or appear to be disproportionate, the items which are at most at risk of being disallowed (as unnecessary even if in fact reasonable) are the instruction of solicitors in expensive city areas if the work could have been undertaken equally well by less expensive solicitors, the instruction of leading counsel and the number and length of attendances on counsel, client and others. Claiming success fees and ATE insurance premiums in addition to base costs will not, by itself, render a claim for costs disproportionate. When considering proportionality the assessing court should consider base costs separately from any additional liability claimed and should not, for example, reduce a success fee simply on the ground that, when added to the base costs, the total appears disproportionate (CPD, paras 11.5 and 11.9).

Conduct of the parties

38.018   The conduct of the parties is referred to in two places in the Costs Rules. The first is r.44.3 which is quoted and discussed in para.38.007, above in connection with the factors relevant to the court awarding costs. The second mention is in r.44.5 which is headed "Factors to be taken into account in deciding the amount of costs" and is quoted in para.38.016, above. It would of course be utterly wrong for the court assessing costs to take into account conduct which the court awarding costs has already considered and perhaps, because of it, awarded a percentage order (see para.38.007, above). In *Northstar Systems Ltd v Fielding* [2006] EWCA Civ 1660, the Court of Appeal overruled the guidance given in an earlier case (*Aaron v Shelton* [2004] 3 All E.R. S61) which held that a paying party cannot raise issues of conduct at a detailed assessment if those matters could and should have been raised at the time the costs awarded. *Northstar* concerned an order for costs made following a 99 day trial of certain preliminary issues in a property dispute. The defendants, who were the overall winners, had been guilty of serious dishonesty. Having considered whether to disallow their costs, and indeed to order them to pay costs to the losers, the trial judge decided not to do so on the basis that the dishonesty did not go to the heart of the court's process; it had no legal, as opposed to evidential, relevance to the remedies claimed. He therefore awarded costs to the defendants, limited to 80 per cent. This was done partly in order to penalise the defendants and partly to take into account a reasonable sum in respect of the expense to which the claimants had been put because of the dishonesty. The main issues on the appeal were whether the order for costs allowed the defendants 80 per cent of all their costs, including costs incurred in advancing their dishonest allegations; and, if it did, whether a costs judge conducting a detailed assessment could disallow those costs as being unreasonable. The appeal largely came to an end once the defendants conceded that they were entitled only to 80 per cent of their reasonable costs excluding any costs incurred in respect of the dishonesty allegations.

"[34] It seems to me that consideration of a party's conduct should normally take place both at the stage when the judge is considering what order for costs he should make, and then during assessment. But the court will want to ensure that dishonesty is penalised but that the party is not placed in double jeopardy. Ultimately, the question is one of the proper construction of the order made by the judge. Thus, it will be important for the judge, who is asked to take dishonesty into account at the end of a trial when considering the order as to costs, to consider what is likely to occur on assessment. Where dishonest conduct is being reflected in an order made by the trial judge, it must be wise for the future for judges to make clear whether they are making the order on the basis that, on the assessment, the paying party will still be entitled to raise the dishonesty in arguing that costs incurred in supporting the particular dishonesty were unreasonably incurred . . ."

Cases on conduct or misconduct affecting costs are legion. Conduct of which complaint is made may be conduct before, as well as during, the proceedings (r.44.3(5)(a) and r.44.5(3)(a)(i)). A successful defendant may be deprived of the whole or part of his costs if some misguided or dishonest behaviour by him brought about the litigation (*Groupama Insurance Co. Ltd v Overseas Partners Re Ltd* [2003] EWCA Civ 1846). Whether a failure to submit to mediation should disentitle a successful party from all or part of his costs was considered at length in *Halsey v Milton Keynes General NHS Trust* [2004] 1 W.L.R. 3002, see further para.34.002; and see *Burchell v Bullard* [2005] EWCA Civ 358).

A problem regularly encountered at detailed assessment hearings concerns the bills of receiving parties who have excessively exaggerated the value of their claims. The court awarding costs may award a claimant only a percentage order if it considers that he has so exaggerated his case as to lead to "an obvious and substantial escalation in the costs over and above those which it was reasonable for the claimant to incur" (*Purfleet Farms Ltd v Secretary of State for Transport, Local Government and the Regions* [2002] EWCA Civ 1430). But what is the position if the court making the order said nothing about the exaggeration or if the order for costs is a deemed order made following acceptance of an offer to settle? Useful guidance on this was provided by the Court of Appeal in *Booth v Britannia Hotels Ltd* [2002] EWCA Civ 579. In that case a claim for personal injury damages of £617,000 later settled for £2,500 plus costs after the disclosure of video evidence. On assessing the claimant's bill of costs (which totalled £96,000) the district judge allowed all reasonable costs on the issue of liability and 60 per cent of the costs on the issue of quantum. This led to an assessment of approximately £35,000 and two further appeals. In the Court of Appeal it was held that, rather than adopt a percentage approach, the district judge should have asked herself which items of costs were reasonably incurred and what would be a reasonable amount to allow in respect to each of those items in order to establish quantum which, it appeared from all the circumstances, was worth not much more than £2,500.

"In the context of this case that, to my mind, means the district judge should have started by going through the bill of costs and ruling out all of those items she considered to be unjustified (for example, almost all of the medical fees, cost of retaining leading counsel, etc). That would, no doubt, have left some items which were plainly reasonable as items, even if questionable in amount, and other items where it would be difficult if not impossible to disentangle what was reasonable from what was unreasonable even having regard to the way in which Rule 12(1) required that doubts be resolved. At that stage, but not at any earlier stage, it would, in my judgment, be appropriate for the district judge to consider awarding a percentage of the sum claimed, but the percentage awarded would have to be such that at the end of the exercise the total sum awarded by way of costs could be regarded as reasonable having regard to the amount of damages obtained. In other words, the district judge must give herself an opportunity to look at the results in the round before concluding her arithmetic. In the present case her approach was wrong because in particular it deprived her of that opportunity and resulted in a conclusion that it was reasonable for the claimant to expend about £57,000 in order to recover £2,500 and to require the defendants to pay 60 per cent of the sum expended. That, in my judgment, must be nonsense" (Kennedy L.J.).

The matter was remitted to the district judge for re-assessment downwards.

An alternative solution to the problem of exaggeration was suggested by the Court of Appeal in *Lahey v Pirelli Tyres Ltd* [2007] EWCA Civ 91, which concerned a claim for £150,000 in which the claimant rejected a pre-issue offer to settle of £5,000 but later settled on a payment of £4,000 with an order for costs to date. The claimant claimed costs exceeding £27,000 including success fees and VAT. The base profit costs alone were over £11,000. On detailed assessment the district judge held that he had no jurisdiction to impose a 25 percent penalty or any other penalty since to do so would be to depart from the order for costs already made. He assessed the costs at £15,182.71 inclusive of VAT, a decision which was upheld by the circuit judge and by the Court of Appeal. However, the Court of Appeal pointed out certain arguments the defendant should have raised at the detailed assessment. The claimant was entitled to 100 per cent of his reasonable costs which is rarely the same as 100 per cent of his total costs. Had the defendant argued that it was not reasonable for the claimant to reject the pre-issue offer of £5,000 the district judge could have disallowed all the post-issue costs as being unreasonable.

THE INDEMNITY PRINCIPLE

38.019 An order for costs between parties allows the receiving party to claim from the paying party only an indemnity in respect of the costs covered by the order. The indemnity is often imperfect in that it may not cover every item which the receiving party is bound (by contract) to pay to his own legal representative. The court's order for costs may have expressly excluded some items (see r.44.3(6)). Other costs may be unreasonable or disproportionate. The paying party is often required to pay the receiving party a sum which is less than the sum the winner has to pay his own legal representative. Because of the indemnity principle, the total sums payable by the receiving party to his own legal representatives are the maximum which the paying party may be required to pay him. The paying party can never be required to pay the receiving party more than the receiving party is himself obliged to pay. This is because the order for costs belongs to the receiving party, not to his legal representatives.

Example

In *Gundry v Sainsbury* [1910] 1 K.B. 645 the claimant, a labourer, was awarded £15 damages for injuries sustained by the bite of a dog. The claimant had expressly agreed with this solicitors that he would not have to pay them any costs. It was held that, having incurred no costs in pursuing his claim, the claimant could recover none.

38.020

There are several important inroads or exceptions to the indemnity principle. First, it has always been the case that, so long as the receiving party is subject to a potential legal obligation to pay his solicitor's costs, full costs can be recovered from the paying party even if the solicitor never expected to call upon that potential obligation (*R. v Glennie: R. v Miller* [1983] 1 W.L.R. 1056). As to the costs of in-house lawyers, the conventional approach taken in *Re Eastwood* [1975] 1 Ch.112 (see para.38.005, above) requires an assumption that the indemnity principle is not being infringed. Although *Re Eastwood* left room for a more exact calculation of costs in "special" cases, courts are extremely reluctant to find other cases sufficiently special to merit such a calculation (*Cole v BT* [2000] EWCA Civ 208.

The indemnity principle does not prevent the recovery of full costs where the receiving party has entered into a conditional fee agreement with his legal representatives (see Ch.2). There are also statutory exceptions to the principle allowing full recovery of costs incurred on behalf of a legally aided party where the legal representative is entitled only to legal aid prescribed rates (Civil Legal Aid (General) Regulations 1989 (SI 1989/339), reg.107B) and to allow litigants in person costs at a rate of £9.25 per hour for time reasonably spent even where they suffer no financial loss (Litigants in Person (Costs and Expenses) Act 1975, summarised above). The principle does not apply to fixed costs, for example, fixed recoverable costs in RTA claims which settle pre-issue (*Nizami v Butt* [2006] 2 All E.R.) or fixed success fees in certain RTA claims and employers' liability claims (*Lamont v Burton* [2007] EWCA 429).

In times past the primary value of the indemnity principle was that it prevented receiving parties making a profit on costs at the expense of paying parties. In recent years that value has been greatly eroded by the introduction of conditional fee agreements under which litigants do not expect to pay any costs, win or lose, and therefore have no more than a notional interest in the sums a paying party may later have to pay. Today, the principle is relied upon more often than not as a means by which the paying party can avoid making any payment at all because of, for example, defects in the validity of the charging arrangements between the receiving party and his lawyers (*Hollins v Russell* [2003] 1 W.L.R. 2487). The Law Society and others regularly call for the abolition of the principle. For several years now, the Civil Justice Council has had a working party researching how this could be achieved and what, if any, controls on costs should take its place.

RESTRICTIONS ON COURT'S DISCRETION AS TO COSTS

Small claims

38.021   The court's discretion to award costs in cases allocated to the small claims track is severely restricted. In such cases, r.27.14 applies, of which sub-rule 2 and 3 are set out in full below:

> "(2) The court may not order a party to pay a sum to another party in respect of that other party's costs, fees and expenses including those relating to an appeal, except—
>
> (a)   the fixed costs attributable to issuing the claim which—
>   (i)   are payable under Part 45; or
>   (ii) would be payable under Part 45 if that part applied to the claim.
> (b)   in proceedings which included a claim for an injunction or an order for specific performance a sum not exceeding the amount specified in the relevant practice direction for legal advice and assistance relating to that claim [£260];
> (c)   any court fees paid by that other party;
> (d)   expenses which a party or witness has reasonably incurred in travelling to and from a hearing or in staying away from home for the purposes of attending a hearing;
> (e)   a sum not exceeding the amount specified in the relevant practice direction for any loss of earnings or loss of leave by a party or witness due to attending a hearing or to staying away from home for the purpose of attending a hearing [up to £50 per day for each person];
> (f)   a sum not exceeding the amount specified in the relevant practice direction for an expert's fees [up to £200 for each expert]; and
> (g)   such further costs as the court may assess by the summary procedure and order to be paid by a party who has behaved unreasonably.
>
> (3) A party's rejection of an offer in settlement will not of itself constitute unreasonable behaviour under paragraph (2)(g) but the court may take it into consideration when it is applying the unreasonableness test."

The sums of money shown in square brackets above are taken from PD 26, para.7.

The opening words of sub-rule (2) make clear that it applies not only to costs relating to the small claim itself but also to costs relating to any appeal therefrom. The first two exceptions listed in sub-rule (2) indicate the extent to which the cost of legal advice and assistance is considered justifiable in cases allocated to the small claims track. The costs of legal services are considered disproportionate to the extent they go beyond help as to commencement, advice concerning equitable remedies and help as to appeals unless exception (2)(g) applies. Exception (2)(g) concerns unreasonable conduct by the opponent, for example, disgraceful, vexatious, harassing behaviour which unnecessarily complicates and delays the proceedings. Sub-rule (3) provides that a failure to accept an offer to settle which turns out to be a good offer does not by itself justify an order for costs under exception (2)(g).

Allocation to the small claims track does not remove the litigants' right to use legal representation, at their own expense, if they so wish. Alternatively, they may employ and pay a "lay representative" to present their case for them at a hearing. A "lay representative" is any person other than the litigant, a barrister, a solicitor or a legal executive employed by a solicitor (PD 27, para.3.1). Fees charged by such a person are expressly included in the definition of costs given in r.43.2. However, r.27.14(4) makes clear that such fees are not recoverable from any other party unless an order is made under sub-rule (2)(g).

Once a claim is allocated to the small claims track, the r.27.14 restriction on costs applies to the period before, as well as the period after, allocation except where the court or a practice direction provides otherwise (r.44.9 as to which see CPD, para.15.1(3), summarised below). However, the restriction does not affect any order for costs made before allocation and does not affect any subsequent costs if the court subsequently re-allocates the claim to a different track (r.44.11).

The Costs Practice Direction makes provision for claims outside the financial scope of the small claims track which are allocated to that track only because of an admission of part of the claim by the defendant reduces the amount in dispute to a sum within the scope of that track. On entering judgment for the admitted part before allocation of the balance of the claim, the court may allow costs in respect of the proceedings down to date (CPD, para.15.1(3)). The judgment mentioned could be a judgment requested by the claimant under r.14.7(9) (see Ch.16) or, arguably, an order for an interim payment where r.25.7(a) applied. When allocating the balance of the claim to a track, the court will disregard (amongst other things) "any amount not in dispute" (r.26.8(2)).

Finally, we must describe two cases to which the r.27.14 restriction on costs does not apply even though these cases are allocated to the small claims track. The restriction on costs does not apply to claims which, although outside the financial scope of the small claims track, are allocated to it by consent. These cases are treated, for the purposes of costs, as if they were proceeding on the fast track (r.27.14(5)). The second exceptional case concerns possession claims which are allocated to the small claims track. Rule 55.9 treats these cases, for the purposes of costs, as a hybrid between the small claims track and the fast track (see further, para.20.012).

Statutory restrictions

38.022 Under the Slander of Women Act 1891, words spoken or published which impute unchastity or adultery to any woman or girl are actionable without proof of special damage. But the claimant can recover no more costs than damages unless the judge certifies that there were reasonable grounds for bringing the proceedings.

Under Access to Justice Act 1999, s.11, costs payable by a party funded by the LSC cannot exceed the amount (if any) which it is reasonable for him to pay having regard to all the circumstances including the means of both parties and their conduct in connection with the dispute (see further on this, Ch.2 and note also the court's power to award costs against the LSC in certain circumstances, see Ch.39).

The Rent Act 1977, s.141, and the Housing Act 1985, s.110, provide that a person who takes proceedings under those Acts in the High Court which could have been brought in the county court is not entitled to recover any costs.

ASSESSING THE REASONABLENESS OF SUCCESS FEES

38.023 A success fee may comprise two elements: the risk element and the fee deferment element. Both of these are described further below. The total of the two must not exceed 100 per cent. A CFA specifying a success fee exceeding 100 per cent is unenforceable (*Jones v Caradon Catnic Ltd* [2005] EWCA Civ 1821). Because the success fee must be specified in the CFA itself, the solicitor must make his assessment of the risk element and the fee deferment element at the outset. The court will not be called upon to assess the reasonableness of that assessment until the conclusion of proceedings. However, CPD, para.11.7 provides that when doing so, the court "will have regard to the fact and circumstances as they reasonably appeared to the solicitor or counsel when the funding arrangement was entered into and at the time of any variation of the arrangement". In other words, since the lawyers cannot use hindsight, the court must not use it either.

Risk element: assessment by solicitor

38.024 The solicitor must first identify the prospects of success of the claim or defence in question and then convert those prospects into a success fee. The prospects of the success will depend upon:

- The perceived legal risks (e.g. is the law favourable and/or is it likely to change?)
- The perceived factual risks (e.g. is liability admitted or easy to establish? If not, what is the strength and credibility of the supporting evidence? Is expert evidence required?)
- And the perceived procedural risks (e.g. limitation defences)

Having calculated the prospects of success (e.g. 80 per cent) the arithmetical way of calculating the appropriate success fee is to divide the percentage chance of losing by the percentage chance of winning and then multiply it by 100 (e.g. 20 ÷ 80 3 100 5 25 per cent). Most practitioners avoid the arithmetic by using ready-reckoners such as follows:

Prospects of success (expressed as a %)	Success fee %
100	0
90	11
80	25
75	33
70	43
65	54
60	67
50	100

So far we have considered only the success fee appropriate for a loss of the legal representative's own fees. A further calculation has to be made for any solicitor who is funding counsel's fees and other disbursements and, therefore, risks losing them as well as his own fees if the case is lost. The further calculation involves considering the likely total cost of disbursements in comparison with the total amount of base fee profit costs likely to be incurred. For example, if the success fee on profit costs only should be 33 per cent and if the disbursements funded by the solicitor are likely to amount to about one-half of the likely base fee profit costs, the supplement is about 17 per cent and therefore the total success fee for risk element alone is 50 per cent.

Experience shows that, in most cases, it is wholly impossible for a legal representative to assess a single stage success fee accurately before the end of the pre-action protocol stage. At that early stage (and, probably, for some considerable time thereafter) the legal representative normally lacks sufficient information about the case even to make an informed guess about what will happen if it is fought to trial. Although risk assessments in other contexts can be scientific, risk assessments for the purpose of CFA's can never be. They are no more than subjective expressions of confidence in a case by the person making the assessment. They can never be scientific because, in the world of CFA's the assessor never has an opportunity to review risk and adjust accordingly.

Something which approximates reviewing risk is the stipulation of a discounted success fee, i.e. a fee which allows for a worst case scenario (i.e. 100 per cent) but discounts that to a lower fee or lower fees if, in fact, the case settles early. The Civil Procedure Rule Committee has now provided discounted success fees as between the parties in certain RTA claims and employers' liability claims (see para.38.013, above). The facts of *Atack v Lee* [2005] 1 W.L.R. 2643 provide a clear demonstration of the advantage of a discounted fee. That was an RTA claim which, because of the early date of the accident, was not governed by the fixed success fee regime of CPR 45 s.3. The claimant's solicitor stipulated for a single stage success fee (100 per cent) but the court ruled that any fee in excess of 50 per cent would be unreasonable and this was upheld by the Court of Appeal. This was so even though the solicitors' worst case scenario actually occurred: the case went to a two day trial on liability. Had the solicitors stipulated for a discounted success fee similar to the fixed success fees now available in RTA cases, they would have received 100 per cent. The Court of Appeal held impliedly in that case, and expressly in *U v Liverpool City Council* [2005] 1 W.L.R. 2657, that if a CFA does not contain a discounted success fee it is not permissible for the court to justify a high single stage success fee by saying "had this solicitor and client agreed a two stage success fee, it would have been reasonable for them to specify a second stage fee which is as high as if not higher than the fee now being claimed."

Risk element: assessment by the court

38.025 CPD, para.11.8 states that, in deciding whether the risk element of the success fee is reasonable, the relevant factors which may be taken into account include:

(a) the risk that the circumstances in which the costs, fees or expenses would be payable might or might not occur;
(b) the legal representative's liability for any disbursements;
(c) what other methods of financing the costs were available to the receiving party.

Items (a) and (b) above refer to the success fee calculation and possible supplement described in para.38.024. As to item (c) the other methods of financing the costs may include litigation funded by an employer or trade union, or out of pre-existing insurance cover (e.g. "Before the Event" (BTE) cover). As to the steps a prospective claimant's solicitors should take to investigate the existence of BTE cover, see para.2.008, above.

Decisions on the amount of success fee

38.026 The earliest case authorities concerned modest value personal injury claims which were simple enough to make them likely to settle pre-issue. The first case finished in a House of Lords decision (*Callery v Gray* [2002] 1 W.L.R. 2000) which cast doubt upon the ruling made by the Court of Appeal but, nevertheless, held that it was for the Court of Appeal, not the House of Lords, to supervise the developing practice of CFA law. The next Court of Appeal case on this point (*Halloran v Delaney* [2003] 1 W.L.R. 28) departed from the *Callery* benchmark of 20 per cent allowing instead success fees of only 5 per cent. Legal professional uproar continued for many months until the fixed success fee regime now provided by the CPR came into force (see further, para.38.013).

More recent case authorities deal with claims which did not appear to be stone-cold certain winners from the outset. They include high value claims, allocated to the multi-track which are fought all the way to a trial on liability. All of them have concerned single stage success fees, usually claimed at 100 per cent. In most, if not all of them the courts appear to be increasing the pressure upon claimant's lawyers to move away from single stage success fees towards the CPR style discounted success fees (*Atack v Lee* [2005] 1W.L.R. 2643, noted in para.38.024; *U v Liverpool City Council* [2005] 1 W.L.R. 2657, tripping case in which liability was strongly denied at first, 50 per cent was appropriate; and *Burton v Kingsley* [2005] EWHC 1034 (Q.B.), very large RTA claim fought to trial on liability; CFA specified base success fee of 100 per cent; the fixed success fee regime did not apply; a success fee of only 50 per cent was allowed).

There is as yet no case law on the reasonableness of discounted success fees fixed by contract rather than by the CPR. When such cases come the paying parties are likely to argue that the CPR models should be adopted under which the discount will apply to all parts of a case before trial. Receiving parties are likely to oppose this saying that the CPR approach (informed by an industry wide agreement) does not take into account the individual facts of each particular case. A discounted success fee fixed by agreement is likely to provide for a staged increase or several staged increases beginning from an earlier date in the proceedings, for example, on the filing of a defence and/or on the filing of pre-trial checklists. The receiving parties are likely to pray in aid the words of Lord Woolf C.J. in the Court of Appeal decision in *Callery v Gray* [2001] 1 W.L.R. 2112):

> "108 The logic behind a two-stage success fee is that, in calculating the success fee, it can properly be assumed that if, notwithstanding the compliance with the protocol, the other party is not prepared to settle, or not prepared to settle upon reasonable terms, there is a serious defence. By the end of the protocol period, both parties should have decided upon their positions. If they are prepared to settle, they should make an offer setting out their position clearly and providing the level of cost protection which they determine is appropriate.
>
> 109 A further advantage of a two-stage success fee would be the knowledge that if a claim was not settled, the full success fee would be payable. This knowledge would encourage rigorous consideration of the merits of the claim during the protocol period and therefore accord with the intent of the CPR.
>
> . . .
>
> 111 A two-stage success fee would have the advantage that the uplift would more nearly reflect the risks of the individual case, so that where a claimant's solicitor had to pursue legal proceedings, this would be in the knowledge that, although a significant risk of failure existed, the reward of success would be that much greater. Where, on the other hand, the claim settled as a consequence of an offer by the defendant, he or his insurer would have the satisfaction of knowing that he had ensured that the success fee would be reduced to a modest proportion of the costs."

The fee deferment element

38.027 The fee deferment element is intended to compensate the lawyer for the loss of the benefit of payments on account. The industry standard for this element (not yet tested by case law) is an extra 5 per cent on the success fee for every complete year the case is likely to last as perceived when the agreement was made. Five per cent is justifiable if the average cost of borrowing over the period is likely to be 10 per cent and the fees on which the sum is payable are accruing at a steady rate throughout the period. To the extent that it is reasonable this element will always be borne by the litigant who made the CFA; r.44.3B(1)(a) provides that the fee deferment element is never recoverable from a paying party.

Greater experience with CFAs has led more and more legal representatives not to attribute any part of their success fee to the fee deferment element. They may well take the view that, in cases which settle early, the attributable amount is too small to bother about and, in cases which settle late, they will usually be able to justify a maximum 100 per cent success fee solely relying upon the risk of losing. This practice is perhaps encouraged by the CPR regime of fixed success fees in certain cases. Under those rules success fees of 100 per cent are payable in cases which go to trial. Plainly, since the full amount is payable by the opposing party, no part of those success fees is attributed to the fee deferment element.

38.028 ### Assessing the reasonableness of insurance cover costs

The insurance market

From time to time the magazine entitled Litigation Funding produces charts which describe and compare different insurance products which are available on the market. The charts provide valuable guidance for solicitors anxious to ensure that they are recommending to their clients the best and most economical insurance products. However, the premiums shown are indicative only and may vary depending on a number of factors including the stage the case has reached, whether liability is in dispute and the prospects of success. This makes the charts of much less value in a detailed assessment in order to prove or disprove the reasonableness of the insurance costs actually incurred in a particular case (see further *Rogers v Merthyr Tydfil County BC* [2007] 1 All E.R. 354.

Factors for the court

38.029 CPD, para.11.10 states that in deciding whether the cost of insurance cover is reasonable, the relevant factors to be taken into account include:

  (1) where the insurance cover is not purchased in support of a conditional fee agreement with a success fee, how its cost compares with the likely cost of funding the case with a conditional fee agreement with a success fee and supporting insurance cover;

(2) the level and extent of the cover provided;
(3) the availability of any pre-existing insurance cover;
(4) whether any part of the premium would be rebated in the event of early settlements;
(5) the amount of commission payable to the receiving party or his legal representatives or other agents.

Decisions on ATE premiums

In *Callery v Gray (No.2)* [2001] 1 W.L.R. 2143, a premium of £367.50 was allowed in full. In the matter of Claims Direct Test Cases [2003] EWCA Civ 136, claims of £1,525 per policy were allowed at £621 per policy. In The Accident Group Test Cases (2003) (SCCO transcript) claims of £997.50 per policy were allowed at sums between £425 and £525 depending upon the year of purchase.

In *Pirie v Ayling* (2003) (SCCO transcript) Master Hurst held that an ATE premium expressed to be "20% of the compensation received" was unreasonable in any simple personal injury claim where the compensation exceeded £2,000. In this case the claimant had received £13,000 and was therefore seeking to recover a premium of £2,600. Master Hurst allowed £367.50.

In *Rogers v Merthyr Tydfil County BC* [2007] 1 All E.R. 354, the Court of Appeal considered and upheld the legitimacy of an ATE premium which is payable in two or more instalments depending upon how far the claim proceeded. The court held that there is in principle no difference between a two-stage success fee and a staged ATE premium. The financial risk to which the ATE provider is exposed inevitably rises as a case proceeds towards trial. While defendants may be liable to pay a higher premium if they take a case to trial and lose, the situation is no different from that facing them in relation to their liability to pay a higher success fee when claims are resolved against them at or shortly before a trial. The court also upheld in full the amount claimed for the premium. *Rogers* was a tripping case in which the damages were agreed at just over £3,000 subject to liability and which went to a trial on liability. The claimant had purchased a staged premium policy from DAS: (1) £450 payable at the outset; (2) £900 payable on issue of proceedings; and (3) a further £3,510 if the case got within 60 days of trial; on each stage a further 5 per cent was payable in respect of insurance premium tax. The costs of getting this modest case to trial were claimed at £18,632 including the premium of £5,103 and a success fee of 100 per cent. The Court of Appeal allowed the premium in full. The fact that by itself it exceeded the compensation recovered did not mean it was disproportionate. The insurance market was such as to lead the court to conclude that it was *necessary* to incur the staged premium and all necessary expenses should be adjudged as proportionate (para.105). The court stated that, in the future, any party who has an ATE insurance premium incorporating two or more staged premiums should inform his opponent that the policy is staged, and should set out accurately the trigger moments at which the second or later stages will be reached (para.116).

38.030

The decisions summarised above all concern modest value personal injury claims. In commercial cases ATE cover often costs as much as 25–40 per cent of the amount of cover bought. On detailed assessments of such premiums in the Supreme Court Costs Office paying parties often do not challenge the quantum claimed. Receiving parties do not normally buy too much cover and will often obtain two or three quotations before placing the insurance. In some cases the paying party will have purchased similar cover no doubt for a similar price. If he challenges the amount the receiving party paid he should expect to be called upon to explain how much he paid.

DETAILED ASSESSMENT PROCEEDINGS

Earliest time for detailed assessment

38.031 All orders for costs are treated as orders for costs to be decided by detailed assessment unless they otherwise provide (e.g. by specifying the amount allowed or describing it as fixed costs). Rule 47.1 states a general rule that the costs of any proceedings or any part of proceedings are not to be assessed by the detailed procedure until the conclusion of those proceedings unless the court otherwise directs. This has the effect of delaying the assessment of some orders for costs made at interim hearings. Such costs have to be left to be assessed along with the general costs of the proceedings unless the court summarily assesses them or makes an order for them to be assessed by detailed assessment "forthwith" or "immediately".

PD 47, para.1.1 states what amounts to the conclusion of proceedings for the purposes of r.47.1 and gives the court power to make an order allowing detailed assessment proceedings earlier in cases where there is no realistic prospect of the claim continuing.

Form of bill

38.032 The Costs Practice Direction contains several precedents of bills. The use of the precedents is not compulsory but is recommended and when a different format is used, a short explanation of why it has been adopted should appear in the narrative towards the beginning. The format of the first three precedents largely reverts to the format which was prescribed pre-CPR. Precedent A is the one which will be used most frequently in practice. It starts with the full title of the proceedings and some background information about the case including a brief description of the proceedings, a statement of the status of the fee earners in respect of whom costs are claimed and the rates claimed for each such person and a brief explanation of any agreement or arrangement between the receiving party and his solicitors which affects the costs claimed in the bill. The actual costs claimed are set out on paper divided into five columns headed as follows:

Item No., description of work done, VAT, disbursements, profit costs. Precedent A shows how to claim success fees on profit costs and counsel's fees. Such fees have to be shown separately either in the appropriate arithmetic column or in the narrative column. In Precedent A they appear as four separate items in the bill: solicitor's success fees on interim orders for costs, counsel's success fees on interim orders for costs, solicitor's success fees on other base fees, and counsel's success fees on other base fees.

The second bill precedent, Precedent B, shows how to claim success fees and insurance premiums in cases where all other costs (i.e. the base costs) have been summarily assessed during the proceedings. Precedent C is for use where the receiving party was funded by the Legal Services Commission ("LSC"). It includes multiple columns to enable the draftsman to set out "LSC only" items alongside items payable by the losing party. Precedent D has been criticised and is not now commonly used.

As the precedents demonstrate, all items must be consecutively numbered and must be divided under such of the following heads as may be appropriate:

(1) Attendances on the court and counsel up to the date of the notice of commencement.
(2) Attendances on and communications with the receiving party.
(3) Attendances on and communications with witnesses, including any expert witness.
(4) Attendances to inspect any property or place for the purposes of the proceedings.
(5) Attendances on and communications with other persons, including.
(6) Communications with the court and with counsel.
(7) Work done on documents: preparing and considering documentation including documentation relating to pre-action protocols where appropriate, work done in connection with arithmetical calculations of compensation and/or interest and time spent collating documents.
(8) Work done in connection with negotiations with a view to settlement if not already covered in the heads listed above.
(9) Attendances on and communications with London and other agents and work done by them.
(10) Other work done which was of or incidental to the proceedings and which is not already covered in any of the heads listed above.

Head (1) should also set out, in chronological order with dates, all the relevant events in the proceedings including events which do not constitute chargeable items and including all orders for costs which the court has made (whether or not a claim is made in respect of those costs in this bill).

Bills are often divided into separate parts, each part containing such of the 10 heads as are appropriate. Division into parts is necessary or convenient to show, for example, work done by different solicitors, costs claimed under different orders against different paying parties, and costs before and after a change in the rate of VAT.

The bill should conclude with a summary showing the total costs claimed and the total VAT claimed. Finally comes such of the prescribed certificates as are appropriate to the case and then the signature of the receiving party or his solicitor. These certificates give information on matters such as any rulings made as to entitlement to interest on costs (e.g. a ruling under r.36.14(3), see Ch.29), any payments made by the paying party on account of costs included in the bill and as to the receiving party's entitlement to recover from the paying party the VAT he is or has been liable to pay on the costs claimed. The text of the certificates is set out in Costs Precedent F.

If the bill of costs is capable of being copied onto a computer disk, the paying party is entitled to demand a disk copy free of charge (CPD, para.32.11).

Notice of commencement

38.033 In order to commence detailed assessment proceedings, the receiving party must serve a variety of documents on the paying party and, in some cases, other parties (e.g. any person who has given the receiving party notice in writing that he has a financial interest in the outcome of the assessment and wishes to be a party accordingly). The documents are a copy of the bill of costs, copies of the fee notes of counsel and of any expert in respect of whom fees are claimed in the bill, written evidence as to any other disbursement which is claimed and which exceeds £250 and a notice of commencement in Form N252. This notice states the amount of costs claimed, requires the paying party to serve points of dispute (see below) by a specified date and warns that, if points of dispute are not received by that date, the receiving party may ask the court to issue a default costs certificate (see below). If notices of commencement are to be served on more than one person, the receiving party must also serve a statement giving the name and address for service of each such person.

The commencement of detailed assessment proceedings does not involve any step taken in the court. Thus, the notice of commencement does not have to be sealed or produced to the court at this stage. Similarly, the paying party's points of dispute should be served only on the receiving party and other relevant persons. They should not be filed in court at this stage.

Latest time for commencement

38.034 The deadline for commencement of detailed assessment proceedings is within three months of the date of the order for costs or other event under which the right to costs arose (r.47.7). The bringing of an appeal does not stay or extend that time unless the court so orders (r.47.2). However, if detailed assessment proceedings are stayed pending an appeal, the deadline for commencement becomes three months after the date of the order lifting that stay (r.47.7). The parties may agree to extend or shorten the deadline or alternatively, either party may apply to the court for an order extending or shortening the time (CPD, paras 33.1 and 33.2).

Permission to commence detailed assessment proceedings out of time is not required. In most cases in which this occurs, the only sanction the court may impose will be to disallow all or part of the interest otherwise payable on costs (r.47.8(3)) and/or disallow the costs of the assessment proceedings (r.47.18). A paying party seeking greater sanctions than these must take the initiative by applying to the court before the sleeping dog wakes requesting an order disallowing all the costs previously ordered unless the receiving party commences detailed assessment proceedings within such further time as the court permits (r.47.8(1)).

Points of dispute: general practice

Any party wishing to challenge the amount of costs claimed must serve on the receiving party and on every other party to the detailed assessment proceedings brief points of dispute identifying each item in the bill which is disputed and, in each case, stating concisely the nature and grounds of that dispute, and, where practical, suggesting a figure to be allowed for each item in respect of which a reduction is sought. Precedent G in the Costs Practice Direction is a model form of points of dispute which is on paper divided into two columns. The second column is for any annotations which the receiving party may later wish to make (see below). 38.035

The normal period for serving points of dispute is 21 days after the date of service of the notice of commencement. A longer period is appropriate where the notice of commencement is served on a party outside England and Wales (see CPD, para.35.4). The parties may agree to extend or shorten the time for service or indeed a party may apply to the court for an order extending or shortening that time.

If the points of dispute are capable of being copied onto a computer disk, the receiving party is entitled to demand a disk copy free of charge (CPD, para.35.6).

On receipt of points of dispute the receiving party may, if he wishes, serve a reply within the next 21 days. The reply may take the form of an annotation to the points of dispute or may be set out on a separate document. Serving a reply on a separate document does not avoid the obligation to file points of dispute annotated as required under CPD, para.40.2(d) (as to which, see below).

Points of dispute challenging success fees

Section 20 of the Costs Practice Direction provides complex provisions to deal with cases in which a paying party wishes to challenge the amount of a success fee where the CFA in question is governed by the Conditional Fee Agreements Regulations 2000 or the Collective Conditional Fee Agreements Regulations 2000. In such cases if any amounts of a success fee payable to solicitor or Counsel is disallowed on assessment, that amount ceases to be payable under the CFA unless the court is satisfied that it should continue to be so payable. 38.036

The provisions set out in s.20 of the Costs Practice Direction are designed to ensure that both counsel and client will be told in advance of any relevant challenge to success fees and will be told the date of the detailed assessment should they wish to attend and make representations. Both sets of regulations mentioned above were revoked by the Conditional Fee Agreements (Revocation) Regulations 2005 but continue to have effect in relation to CFA agreements and CCFA agreements entered into before November 2005.

Default costs certificates

38.037   If the paying party fails to serve points of dispute within the time allowed, the receiving party can file in court a request for a default costs certificate. The form of request is prescribed (Form N254). The default costs certificate itself (Form N255) includes an order to pay a total sum comprising the costs claimed in the bill, fixed costs of £80 (CPD, para.25.1) and the amount of any court fee payable. The paying party must pay that sum within 14 days (r.44.8) unless he successfully applies to have the certificate set aside. The principles which will be applied on an application to set aside are set out in r.47.12 and CPD, paras 38.1 to 38.4. The principles are very similar to those which apply on applications to set aside default judgments (see Ch.15). Standard forms of orders on set-aside applications are published in the SCCO Guide (see *White Book* para.48.111). A default costs certificate does not entitle the receiving party to take further steps, for example, for enforcement, if he subsequently discovers the notice of commencement was not validly served on the paying party before the default costs certificate was issued (see generally r.47.12(3) and (4)). Instead, the receiving party must file a request for the default costs certificate to be set aside (which can be done by a court clerk without any hearing; CPD, para.38.1) or must apply to the court for directions.

Where the receiving party is funded by the Legal Services Commission (LSC), the issue of a default costs certificate does not prohibit, govern, or affect any detailed assessment of the same costs which may have to be made to determine the sum payable out of the Community Legal Service fund (CPD, para.37.5). Default costs certificates are addressed to the litigant ordered to pay costs. If the LSC funded client's solicitor wishes to seek payment from the Community Legal Service fund, it is still necessary to complete a request for a detailed assessment hearing in order to obtain a sealed Community Legal Service assessment certificate (see further Ch.39).

Request for a hearing

38.038   If points of dispute are served, the receiving party must file a request for a detailed assessment hearing (Form N258) within six months of the date of the order or other event giving rise to the right to costs claimed (r.47.14). The sanctions for delay in filing a request are identical to those applicable to delay in commencing detailed assessment proceedings (see above "latest time for commencement").

The appropriate office for filing the request, and indeed for making any other application in detailed assessment proceedings including requests for default costs certificates, is defined in the Costs Practice Direction at para.31.1. It is the county court office or district registry for the court in which the order for costs was made or, in all other cases, the Supreme Court Costs Office ("SCCO"). The SCCO also acts as the detailed assessment hearing centre for all London county courts (Costs Practice Direction, para.31.1A).

In addition to filing the request for a detailed assessment hearing, the receiving party must also file voluminous documentation including copies of the documents served on the paying party at the commencement of the detailed assessment proceedings, above and including:

"(d) a copy of the points of dispute, annotated as necessary in order to show which items have been agreed and their value and to show which items remain in dispute and their value" (see generally CPD, para.40.2).

The primary purpose for this annotation is to facilitate the issue of an interim costs certificate (see below). The receiving party may also use the annotation so as to avoid the need to serve a separate reply to the points of dispute.

On receipt of the request for a detailed assessment hearing, the court will usually fix a date for the hearing and give all parties at least 14 days' notice of that date. In exceptional cases, it may be appropriate to fix a preliminary appointment first, for which notice of less than 14 days may be given (see generally CPD, paras 40.5 and 40.6).

If the proceedings later settle, the receiving party should give notice of that fact to the court immediately, preferably by fax (CPD, para.40.9).

A party wishing to vary his bill of costs, points of dispute or reply may file in court and serve on his other parties an amended or supplementary document. Permission to do so is not required, but the court may later disallow any variation or permit it only upon conditions including conditions as to the payment of any costs caused or wasted by the variation (CPD, para.40.10).

Interim costs certificates

A receiving party who has filed a request for a detailed assessment hearing may apply for an interim costs certificate for such sum as the court considered appropriate (r.47.15, CPD, para.41.1). In deciding whether to grant such a certificate and if so in deciding the amount, the court will no doubt have regard to the documents filed with the request for the detailed assessment hearing, including in particular the points of dispute annotated by the receiving party. It will also determine what, if any, payments have already been made by the paying party either voluntarily or under an order for a payment on account made by the court awarding costs (see r.44.3(8)). Unless some good reason to the contrary is shown, the court is likely to allow an interim costs certificate in such amount as will bring the total payments up to an amount equal to the minimum sum which the receiving party is almost certain to recover at the

38.039

detailed assessment hearing (*cf.* Dyson Ltd v Hoover Ltd [2004] 1 W.L.R. 1264).

Parties who are compelled to consider, or alternatively pay, an interim certificate, will almost always reflect upon what their total costs liability is likely to be. Thus, interim certificates and applications for interim certificates often provoke the parties into a settlement of the total costs claimed. In the hope that it will save costs, some courts now issue interim certificates on their own initiative immediately upon receipt of the request for a hearing. The certificate has to be appropriately worded so that the sum ordered to be paid is net of any payments voluntarily made to date.

Conduct of the hearing

38.040 Unless the court directs otherwise, the receiving party must file with the court the papers in support of the bill not less than seven days before the date for the detailed assessment hearing and not more than 14 days before that date (see generally CPD, paras 40.11 and 40.12). These papers comprise most of the papers the receiving party has relevant to the conduct of the case except those of which copies have already been filed in court (e.g. statements of case, allocation questionnaires, listing questionnaires, orders and directions made and papers filed on requesting the detailed assessment hearing).

In detailed assessments proceeding in a county court or district registry, the assessment will be made by a district judge however large or small the bill. In the SCCO, assessments of bills which exceed £50,000 (excluding VAT) will be made by a costs judge. Smaller bills are assessed by authorised court officers unless a request or application for a hearing by a costs judge is made (CPD, para.30.1).

Rule 47.14 states that no person other than the receiving party and parties who have served points of dispute may be heard at the detailed assessment hearing unless the court gives permission. Rule 47.14 also provides that only items specified in the points of dispute may be raised at the hearing unless the court gives permission. Although in theory, paying parties may amend their points of dispute at any time without permission, the court is unlikely to allow parties to use that route to circumvent r.47.14 except where it is just or appropriate to do so. Any late amendments made may be disallowed or permitted only upon conditions (CPD, para.40.10).

As to each item of costs in dispute, the court must decide at least three questions:

(1) Was that cost actually incurred?
(2) If so, was it reasonable to incur it?
(3) If so, is the sum claimed for it reasonable in amount?

As to question (1), the burden of proof is on the party receiving costs whichever basis of assessment applies. The item of costs will be disallowed if the court is not persuaded that that item was incurred or if the court is satisfied that the item did not cause the party any expense, for example, the solicitor waived his fee in respect of it. A litigant cannot recover from another litigant more money than he is liable to pay (see above "the indemnity principle").

As to questions (2) and (3), the burden of proof is on the party receiving costs if the standard basis applies, but is on the party paying costs if the indemnity basis applies. On the indemnity basis, the item will be allowed in full unless the court is persuaded that the item is unreasonable or is persuaded that the amount claimed for it is unreasonable. On the standard basis the court must take the two-stage approach described in para.38.017, above. Unless the totality appears disproportionate, each item will be allowed only if the receiving party shows it was reasonable to incur that item and it is reasonable in amount. If the totality appears disproportionate each item will be allowed only if the receiving party shows it was necessary to incur it and it is reasonable in amount.

> "[37] Although we emphasise the need, when costs are disproportionate, to determine what was necessary, we also emphasise that a sensible standard of necessity has to be adopted. This is a standard which takes fully into account the need to make allowances for the different judgments which those responsible for litigation can sensibly come to as to what is required. The danger of setting too high a standard with the benefit of hindsight has to be avoided. While the threshold required to meet necessity is higher than that of reasonableness, it is still a standard that a competent practitioner should be able to achieve without undue difficulty. When a practitioner incurs expenses which are reasonable but not necessary, he may be able to recover his fees and disbursements from his client, but extra expense which results from conducting litigation in a disproportionate manner cannot be recovered from the other party.
>
> [38] In deciding what is necessary, the conduct of the other party is highly relevant. The other party by cooperation can reduce costs, by being uncooperative he can increase costs. If he is uncooperative, that may render necessary costs which would otherwise be unnecessary, and that he should pay the costs for the expense which he has made necessary is perfectly acceptable. Access to justice would be impeded if lawyers felt they could not afford to do what is necessary to conduct the litigation. Giving appropriate weight to the requirements of proportionality and reasonableness will not make the conduction of litigation uneconomic if on the assessment there is allowed a reasonable sum for the work carried out which was necessary" (Lord Woolf C.J. in *Lownds v Home Office* [2002] 1 W.L.R. 2450).

As to proportionality, the comparison must always be made with the costs incurred and the benefit gained. Even if the totality is not considered disproportionate, individual items may be (*Giambrone v JMC Holidays Ltd* [2003] 1 All E.R. 982 at [28]).

Production of documents at the hearing

38.040A The papers the receiving party must file with the court in support of his bill (see para.38.038) will contain many documents which are confidential and sensitive. In times past the paying party had no right to see these documents unless, in an exceptional case, the court (the costs judge or district judge) thought it right to permit inspection. This meant the paying party had to rely on the court's good sense and fairness in reaching the right result and the receiving party had to rely on the court's discretion in not revealing documents which were unduly sensitive. In *South Coast Shipping Co. Ltd v Havant Borough Council* [2002] 3 All E.R. 779, Ch.D., the former practice was held to infringe the paying party's right to a fair trial under ECHR Art.6. Instead, the court should make much greater use of CPD, para.40.14. On each item as to which the paying party raises a genuine dispute the court will inspect the documents the receiving party wishes to rely on and will make a provisional ruling. If the paying party is unwilling to accept a provisional ruling which is adverse to him the court will put the receiving party to an election whether to disclose the documents to the paying party or to withdraw them and rely instead on other evidence. The costs judge or district judge would then have to put the documents he had seen "out of his head, but that is not a difficult task" (Pumfrey J. at [57]). More details of the procedure to follow, and of steps that may be taken to avoid or minimise their expense, are set out in the SCCO Guide (*White Book* para.48.122). If the costs claimed include a success fee paying parties frequently ask to see the CFA under which it arises to check its validity. Non-compliance with the relevant CFA regulations may disentitle the receiving party to claim any solicitor's charges under the CFA. In *Hollins v Russell* [2003] 1 W.L.R. 2487 the Court of Appeal made clear that, in most CFA cases, a paying party who challenges the receiving party's entitlement to claim solicitors' charges will be permitted to inspect the agreements under which they are said to be payable.

Costs of detailed assessment proceedings

38.041 As a general rule, an order for costs to be determined by detailed assessment carries with it the costs of conducting that detailed assessment (*Ross v Bowbelle (Owners)* [1997] 1 W.L.R. 1159). Thus, r.47.18 states that the party receiving costs is entitled to the costs the detailed assessment proceedings unless the court otherwise orders. In deciding whether to make some other order, the court must have regard to all the circumstances including the conduct of the parties, the amount, if any, by which the bill of costs has been reduced, and whether it was reasonable for a party to claim the costs of a particular item or to dispute that item.

Rule 47.19 provides for the making of offers to settle the costs of proceedings which give rise to assessment proceedings. If either party makes an offer expressed to be "without prejudice save as to the costs of the detailed assessment proceedings" the court will take that offer into account in deciding who should pay the costs of the detailed assessment proceedings. The fact of the offer must not, of course, be communicated to the court until the question of costs of the detailed assessment proceedings falls to be decided.

Although r.47.19 does not specify a time within which offers to settle should be made, the Costs Practice Direction states that offers made by a paying party should usually be made within 14 days after service of the notice of commencement on that party and that offers to settle made by the receiving party should normally be made within 14 days after the service of points of dispute by the paying party. Offers made after these periods are likely to be given less weight by the court when deciding what order as to costs to make unless there is good reason for the offer not being made until the later time.

In contrast to offers to settle under Pt 36, r.47.19 does not contain any mechanism for deciding how the costs of assessment proceedings should fall if the offer is accepted. It has sometimes been argued that, because of the *Ross v Bowbelle (Owners)*, above, an offer to settle detailed assessment proceedings should be treated as inclusive of the costs of the detailed assessment. However, in *Crosbie v Munroe* [2003] 2 All E.R. 856, CA, it was held that an offer to settle under r.47.19 was not so inclusive and, unless agreement could be reached as to the costs of detailed assessment, the court would make an order as to them. In that case the claimant commenced costs-only proceedings (see para.39.001, below) in the course of which the defendant made an offer to settle for "the all-inclusive sum of £2,650 in respect of your profit costs, disbursements, VAT and interest . . . pursuant to CPR Part 47.19 . . .". The claimant accepted that offer before any order for costs was made in the proceedings and the dispute before the Court of Appeal was as to the costs of those proceedings. We respectfully suggest that the Court of Appeal in that case reached the right decision for the wrong reasons. Despite the expressed terms of the offer, r.47.19 did not apply to it, Pt 36 did and r.36.13 entitled the claimant to the additional costs he was seeking. Also, in that case, the *Ross v Bowbelle (Owners)* point does not appear to have been argued.

Does the new Pt 36 apply to detailed assessment proceedings? There is nothing in the new Pt 36 which expressly excludes them. Some of its terminology is, of course, difficult to apply to detailed assessment proceedings (e.g. references to the trial, and to the trial judge) especially where the receiving party is the defendant (acceptance gives rise to an automatic order for costs in favour of the claimant!). But these problems are equally present in the application of Pt 36 to appeals. If Pt 36 does apply to detailed assessment proceedings, it would largely duplicate r.47.19 but with important additional provisions (e.g. enhanced costs and interest in certain circumstances).

Can offers to settle be made where the costs in question relate to a party funded by the LSC? There are several problems here. For example, where the paying party makes what turns out to be an accurate offer which is turned down, it may be difficult to determine who is responsible for that offer being turned down, solicitor, counsel or the LSC funded client in person? CPD, para.46.4 provides that where the receiving party is an LSC funded client, offers to settle will not have the consequences specified under r.47.19 unless the court so orders. There is no difficulty about so ordering where the offer to settle was made on behalf of the LSC funded client. Where the offer was made by the paying party and was for a sum which is higher than the sum assessed by the court, it may be unfair to make the LSC funded client shoulder responsibility for the paying party's costs (i.e. by setting them off against other costs allowed, thereby swelling the statutory charge) and it is possible to penalise the solicitor or counsel only where their conduct was unreasonable or improper (see r.44.14).

Final costs certificates

38.042 After the hearing, the receiving party is given a period of 14 days in which to file a completed bill, i.e. a bill calculated to show the amount due following the detailed assessment of the costs (r.47.16). The receiving party must also produce to the court evidence of payment of all items allowed in the bill other than payments ("profit costs") to any solicitors instructed in the litigation. Thus, when filing the completed bill, the receiving party must also produce receipted fee notes and receipted accounts in respect of all sums paid except solicitors' charges. Some of these payments will of course be very small. Save for counsel's fees, the receiving party can avoid the obligation to produce receipts for payments which do not individually exceed £500 by including a suitably worded certificate in the bill (see Costs Precedent F). It sometimes happens that impecunious receiving parties cannot get receipts until they get costs from the paying party. To solve this cashflow problem, they should first seek an interim certificate in respect of costs for which they do not need to produce receipts.

Once the completed bill and the receipts have been filed and checked, the court will issue a final costs certificate (Form N356) specifying the total costs allowed, the sums already paid and specifying the balance payable and ordering payment of it, usually within 14 days (r.44.8). A paying party who seeks more time to pay and who cannot agree terms with the receiving party can apply for an order staying enforcement. Such an application can be made to a costs judge or district judge of the court office which issued the certificate or to the court (if different) which has general jurisdiction to enforce the certificate (CPD, para.42.11).

Agreed costs certificates

38.043 Sometimes, the costs payable in detailed assessment proceedings are agreed, but the receiving party nevertheless wishes to obtain a certificate so as to enable him to use enforcement proceedings if necessary. Where all parties consent, a certificate (whether interim or final) which is drawn up by the parties and expressed to be "by consent" can be obtained under r.40.6 (see PD 47, para.2.18 and see Ch.34).

If the receiving party alleges that costs have been agreed but the paying party will not consent to the issue of a certificate, an application can be made on notice supported by evidence filed and served at least two days before the hearing date (r.47.10, CPD, paras 36.1 and 36.2).

Appeals

Rules 47.20 to 47.23 deal with appeals from the decisions of an authorised court officer. Any party to the detailed assessment proceedings has a right of appeal, without permission, which lies to a costs judge or district judge. The appellant's notice (Form N161) must be filed within 14 days after the decision in question. The court then serves copies of the notice on all other parties. CPD, para.48.3 states that the appellant's notice should, if possible, be accompanied by a suitable record of the decision appealed against. If there is no written decision or official transcript the suitable record might be the officer's comments written on the bill or an advocate's notes agreed by the opponent and approved by the authorised court officer where appropriate. As to the duty of an advocate to assist an unrepresented opponent in providing a note of the decision, see CPD, para.48.3(3)).

38.044

On an appeal from an authorised court officer, the costs judge or district judge will rehear the proceedings which gave rise to the decision appealed against and make any order and give any directions which he considers appropriate. This is a significant difference between appeals from authorised court officers and appeals from judges, such as costs judges (see below).

Part 52 deals with appeals from the decisions of costs judges and district judges not only where the judge conducted the detailed assessment proceedings but also where he was hearing an appeal from an authorised court officer. The general practice and procedure on appeals from costs judges and district judges is considered in Ch.44. The right of appeal, which is subject to a permission requirement, lies, in a High Court case to a High Court judge and, in a county court case to a circuit judge. At the hearing it is customary for the judge to sit with two assessors, one of whom will be a costs judge or district judge and the other will be a practising barrister or solicitor. Any remuneration paid to the second assessor for his services may be determined by the court and awarded as part of the costs of the appeal (r.35.15). In practice the remuneration is based on the daily rate of fees payable to a deputy district judge.

An appeal from a costs judge or district judge will be limited to a review of the decision appealed against unless the court considers that, in the circumstances of an individual appeal, it would be in the interest of justice to hold a re-hearing (r.52.11).

CHAPTER 39

Costs: Special Cases

COSTS ONLY PROCEEDINGS

39.001 Rule 44.12A sets out the procedure to be followed where parties to a dispute have reached an agreement on all issues, including which party is to pay costs, but have been unable to agree the amount of those costs. If no proceedings have been started, either party can start simple Pt 8 proceedings under this rule to obtain an order for detailed assessment. For this rule to apply, the agreement to pay costs must have been made or confirmed in writing. The court fee payable on such application is £30 in the county court and £50 in the High Court. However, this rule cannot be used as a means of starting ordinary actions on the cheap. CPD, para.17.9 makes clear that, if the application is opposed, it will be dismissed and the parties will be left to recommence proceedings under Pt 7 or Pt 8.

Costs only proceedings should be commenced in the court in which the main proceedings would have been heard if that had been necessary (see generally CPD, paras 17.1 to 17.11). The claim form must:

(1) identify the claim or dispute to which the agreement to pay costs relates;
(2) state the date and terms of the agreement on which the claimant relies;
(3) set out or have attached to it a draft of the order which the claimant seeks (see below);
(4) state the amount of the costs claimed; and
(5) state whether the costs are claimed on the standard or indemnity basis. If no basis is specified the costs will be treated as being claimed on the standard basis.

The Supreme Court Costs Office Guide sets out a standard form of order (see *White Book* vol.1, para.48.285).

WASTED COSTS ORDERS

Section 51(6) of the SCA 1981 gives the court power, at any stage of proceedings, to "disallow or (as the case may be) order the legal or other representative concerned to meet the whole [or part] of any wasted costs". Subsection (7) defines "wasted costs" as meaning: 39.002

> "Any costs incurred by a party—
>
> (a) As a result of any improper, unreasonable or negligent act of omission on the part of any legal or other representative or any employee of such a representative; or
> (b) which in the light of any such act or omission occurring after they were incurred, the court considers it unreasonable to expect that party to pay."

The purpose of s.51(6) is not to punish the solicitor or other legal representative for his wrong doing but to protect his client from the cost consequences of it and, similarly, to protect the other parties to the action. The jurisdiction is easy to apply if the applicant is the lawyer's dissatisfied client. However, applications can also be made by another party to the action (*Medcalf v Mardell* [2003] 1 A.C. 120). If such an application is made there are several dangers and cross-currents of which to be aware. Is the applicant simply attempting to circumvent an inability to obtain effective cost orders against an LSC-funded opponent? Is the lawyer attacked able to present a full defence bearing in mind the legal professional privilege which his client may insist upon, to the disadvantage of the lawyer? Is the application under s.51(6) itself an abuse of the system, seeking to intimidate or harass the opposing lawyers, or seeking to undermine their ability to give their clients objective advice and assistance?

Applications for wasted cost orders are often made at the end of a trial or other conclusion of proceedings. Indeed it has been said that applications are best left until this stage (*Ridehalgh v Horsefield* [1994] Ch.205; CPD, para.53.1). Only in limited circumstances can an application be made after the final hearing in the main proceedings (*Gray v Going Places Leisure Travel Ltd* [2005] EWCA Civ 189). If a case terminates without a hearing, for example, on acceptance of a Pt 36 offer an application for a wasted costs order can be made to a cost judge or district judge conducting detailed assessment proceedings (*Burrows v Vauxhall Motors Ltd* [1998] P.I.Q.R. P48). Trial judges and other judges can also direct a cost judge or district judge to enquire into a matter and report to the court as a preliminary to the court making a wasted cost order (r.48.7(6)) or, alternatively, can delegate the whole question of making a wasted cost order to a cost judge or district judge (r.48.7(7)).

Even where the court considers making a wasted cost order of its own initiative it must give the legal representative a reasonable opportunity to attend a hearing and give reasons why it should not make such an order (r.48.7(2)). A party may apply for a wasted costs order by filing an application notice in accordance with Pt 23 (see Ch.13) or by making an application orally in the course of any hearing (CPD, para.23.3). In order to ensure that the legal representative's client is properly informed about wasted costs allegations, the court may direct that notice must be given to the client of any proceedings concerning wasted costs orders and of any order made.

As a general rule the court will consider whether to make a wasted costs order in two stages (see generally CPD, para.53.6). In the first stage the court must be satisfied that it has before it evidence or other material which, if unanswered, would be likely to lead to a wasted costs order being made, and must be satisfied that the wasted costs proceedings are justified having regard to the likely costs involved. The procedure followed should be a summary procedure for use in simple and obvious cases only. Further proceedings would be inappropriate if they would result in complex proceedings involving detailed investigation of facts or where the time likely to be spent upon them is disproportionate to the time spent on the substantive proceedings (*White Book*, para.48.7.14).

At the second stage the court will reconsider the evidence or other material before it, will consider any evidence or submissions put forward by the legal representative and will then decide whether it is appropriate to make a wasted cost order.

CPD, para.53.4 states that it is appropriate for the court to make a wasted costs order against a legal representative only if—

"(a) He has acted improperly, unreasonably or negligently,
(b) his conduct has caused a party to incur unnecessary costs, and
(c) it is just in all the circumstances to order him to compensate that party for the whole or part of those costs."

That provision plainly derives from the guidance given by the court of appeal in a pre-CPR case, *Ridehalgh v Horsefield* [1994] Ch.205 which also stated that terms such as "improper", "unreasonable" and "negligent" should be given common-sense definitions and include (respectively) conduct which is disgraceful whether or not it amounts to professional misconduct, conduct which is vexatious, i.e. designed to harass the opponents rather than advance the resolution of the issue, and conduct which is negligent as normally understood whether or not there exists a duty of care between the persons involved. However, it has to be borne in mind that it is often reasonable for an applicant to represent unreasonable clients, i.e. to present hopeless cases (*White Book*, para.48.7.5). The court must also make full allowance for the fact that applicants often have to make decisions quickly, in the heat of battle.

APPLICATIONS UNDER S.70 OF THE SOLICITORS ACT 1974

39.003 Part III of the Solicitors Act 1974 is entitled Remuneration of Solicitors and deals with a variety of disputes between solicitor and client which the civil courts can determine. The most frequently used provision is s.70 which, where it applies (see below) enables a client to seek a detailed assessment of the solicitor's bill. An application under s.70 can be commenced in the Supreme Court Costs Office in London. A High Court district registry only has jurisdiction in respect of contentious business done in that registry, contentious business done in a county court within its district, and non-contentious business, wherever done (r.67.3; as to the meaning of contentious business and non-contentious business, see para.2.010, above). A county court has virtually no jurisdiction under s.70. It is limited to costs in respect of contentious business done in that county court and, even then, only if the amount of the bill in question does not exceed £5,000 (Solicitors Act 1974, s.69).

A party wishing to apply under s.70 must use the alternative procedure for claims provided by Pt 8 (PD 8, s.A and s.B; see further Ch.10). Solicitors rarely apply under s.70. For them, the better route to adopt usually is to commence simple money claim (under Pt 7) leading to a default judgment or summary judgment on terms requiring detailed assessment of the bill and giving the solicitor judgment for the sum claimed if the defendant fails to comply with those directions (see Form PF 15). If the client (or rather former client) seeks an order under s.70, there are various time limits which have to be observed. He has a right to an order only if he applies within one calendar month of the delivery of the bill. In other cases, the court has a discretion whether to make an order, i.e. may allow it only on terms (for example, terms as to part payment of the bill) and in some cases, the court has a discretion only if "special circumstances apply". In one case, no order can be made against the solicitor; where the bill in question was paid more than 12 months before the commencement of proceedings (*Harrison v Tew* [1990] 2 A.C. 523). As to the difference between a retention of monies by the solicitor and a payment by the client, see *White Book*, vol.2, para.7C–118.

Rule 48.10 sets out the procedure to be followed if an order is made under s.70 unless that order otherwise provides. Within 28 days of the order, the solicitor must serve a breakdown of the bill. This is a document giving details of the work done which is drawn up in a form similar to a bill of costs payable by one party to another under an order for costs. The breakdown must also include an account showing money received by the solicitor to the credit of the client and sums paid out of that money on behalf of the client other than payments made in satisfaction of the bill itself or any items included in it. This is known as the "cash account". In addition to the breakdown, the solicitor must at the same time serve copies of counsel's and experts' fee notes in respect of all fees claimed in the bill and written evidence of all disbursements exceeding £250 and claimed in the bill. The client must serve points of dispute within 14 days of being served with the breakdown and, if the solicitor wishes to serve a reply, he must do so within 14 days thereafter. Failure to comply with these requirements entitles the other party to apply under r.48.8 seeking some order adverse to the party in default. Either party can request a hearing date for the assessment (in Form N258C) once points of dispute have been served if they do so within three months of the date of the order under s.70. The court will then fix a hearing date and, unless otherwise directed, the solicitor must file with the court the papers in support of the bill not less than seven days before and not more than 14 days before the day fixed for the hearing.

At the hearing, the bill will be assessed on the indemnity basis modified by three presumptions (r.48.8):

(1) Costs are presumed to have been reasonably incurred if they were incurred with the express or implied approval of the client.
(2) Costs are presumed to be reasonable in amount if their amount was expressly or impliedly approved by the client.
(3) Costs are presumed to have been unreasonably incurred if they are of an unusual nature unless the client was warned in advance that he might not recover all of these costs from another party.

Assessing the bill on the indemnity basis suggests that the burden of proof as to reasonableness will normally fall upon the former client. In fact, his position is much better than that. The items of costs he is most likely to challenge are the unusual items. With them, the burden of proof is on the solicitor to show that they were reasonably incurred or that he properly warned the client of the risk involved.

Subject to rights of appeal, the outcome of the detailed assessment will be the production by the court of a final costs certificate. The sum specified in that certificate is arrived at in three stages. It specifies the balance found due on taking the cash account, plus or minus the costs allowed in the detailed assessment and plus or minus the costs of the assessment procedure itself. These costs are governed by the so-called "one-fifth rule" to which we now turn.

Awarding costs in proceedings under Solicitors Act 1974, s.70

39.004 Costs of the proceedings before the commencement of the detailed assessment will be provided for, if at all, in the order for assessment. Where that order was obtained without any substantial dispute, the court frequently awards the costs "in the assessment" in other words, they will be dealt with in the same way as the costs of the assessment proceedings.

Section 70(7) states that every order for the taxation of a bill shall require the taxing officer to tax not only the bill, but also the costs of the taxation. The word "taxation" is the old term for what, in the CPR, is referred to as detailed assessment. Sections 70(9) and 70(10) set out the "one-fifth rule". Under this rule, the costs of the detailed assessment are to be paid by the former client except in four circumstances:

(1) The solicitor sought the order for assessment and the assessment has not been opposed by the former client.
(2) The order for detailed assessment provides otherwise.
(3) The costs officer certifies that there are "special circumstances" (see below).
(4) One-fifth or more of the bill has been disallowed. In this case, unless points (2) and/or (3) apply, it is the solicitor who must pay the costs of the detailed assessment proceedings.

The origins of the one-fifth rule lie in the belief that former clients who exercise their rights to challenge a solicitor's bill do so at their own expense unless they can persuade the court that the bill should be disallowed by a substantial amount. For this purpose, anything less than one-fifth is not regarded as substantial unless there are "special circumstances". Perhaps the simplest and best way to show special circumstances and thereby avoid the harshness of this rule is for the former client to make an offer to settle before or shortly after commencing proceedings. If such an offer is made in accordance with Pt 36 (see Ch.29) and if the former client does better than he proposed in his Pt 36 offer, the court may consider this a special circumstance entitling him to the costs and indeed may award those costs on the indemnity basis and with additional interest (r.36.14(3)). A former client can also minimise his risks as to the one-fifth rule by requesting the court to exclude from the order for assessment all the profit costs, or alternatively, all the disbursements (see s.70(5) and (6)). This would be appropriate if he does not wish to challenge the amounts claimed for the excluded items.

In respect of disbursements, there is another rule which can operate very severely against the solicitor whether or not the disbursements are unusual. If the bill includes disbursements which, at the time of delivery of the bill, the solicitor had not then paid, the court will disallow those disbursements unless they were described in the bill as being unpaid (Solicitors Act 1974, s.67). However, the court has power to permit the solicitor to withdraw the bill and deliver a new one, or to amend the bill to insert the words "not yet paid" (for case authorities, see *White Book*, vol.2, para.7C–107).

OTHER METHODS OF CHALLENGING SOLICITORS' BILLS

Non-contentious business; remuneration certificates

In non-contentious business (for the definition, see para.2.010, above) where the bill does not exceed £50,000, the solicitor must inform the client in writing of the right to require the solicitor to obtain a certificate from The Law Society. If the client exercises his right within one month of being advised of his rights, The Law Society will peruse the solicitor's file and issue a certificate stating what sum, in their opinion, would be fair and reasonable (whether the sum charged or a lesser sum). In order to make this challenge, clients must (usually) pay to the solicitor all the VAT and paid disbursements shown in the bill and also half the profit costs claimed (see generally Solicitors' Remuneration Order 1994 (SI 1994/2616) set out in the *White Book*, para.7–188). Instead of applying to The Law Society or, after having done so, the client may also apply to the court for a detailed assessment of the bill (see para.39.003, above). Whether or not a "non-contentious business" bill exceeds £50,000, the solicitor must, before suing for his costs, also inform the client of his rights under s.70 of the Solicitors' Act 1974. These two methods of challenge are excluded in respect of

39.005

non-contentious business only if the solicitor and client have entered into a non-contentious business agreement under s.57 of the Solicitors' Act 1974, which is described separately below. In the case of contentious business, clients can never require a certificate from The Law Society. Such clients do usually have the right to challenge the bill under s.70 of the Solicitors' Act 1974. However, this right will be excluded if the parties enter into a contentious business agreement under s.59 of the Solicitors' Act 1974, described below. Also, even if the challenge has not been excluded, there is no obligation upon the solicitor to inform the client of his rights under s.70.

Contentious business agreements

39.006 The term "contentious business agreement' is defined by the Solicitors Act 1974, s.59. Most contentious business agreements fix remuneration by reference to hourly rates. To be valid, the agreement must define precisely how much is payable per hour of work done and should also contain terms as to when it is payable. Because of the need for precision, it is not usually possible for the agreement to permit the solicitor to review hourly rates each year. Instead, agreements may be made for, for example, 12 months with automatic expiry if by then, no agreement has been reached as to rates for subsequent periods. CFAs may be contentious business agreements (see *Hollins v Russell* [2003] 1 W.L.R. 2487 at [23] and [93]).

A special rule applies to contentious business agreements made with a client acting in the capacity of a guardian, trustee or receiver of property. In these cases the agreement must be approved by the courts, before any payment is made under it (1974 Act, s.62).

A contentious business agreement does not prevent the client terminating the retainer (e.g. sacking the solicitor) at any time. In such a case, s.63 of the 1974 Act makes provision for payment. Section 63 also applies in the case of death or incapacity of the solicitor.

For the solicitor, the main purpose of entering into a contentious business agreement is to exclude the client's right to the challenge the bill under s.70 (see s.60(1)). Nevertheless, the solicitor's remuneration still remains subject to judicial supervision (see below).

If work is done under a contentious business agreement, an unpaid solicitor cannot commence simple debt proceedings against his former client. Instead, he must apply to the court in which the contentious business was done for that court to determine the validity or effect of the agreement and enforce it or set it aside as appropriate (s.61(1) and (2); for contentious business concerning arbitration, see s.61(6)(b) and (c)). Before allowing enforcement, the court will examine the agreement and consider whether it is fair and reasonable. The agreement is unfair if the client did not fully understand and appreciate its effect before making it; it is unreasonable if it constitutes excessive profiteering by the solicitor.

If the remuneration is fixed by reference to an hourly rate, the solicitor cannot start proceedings on the agreement before the expiration of one calendar month from the date on which a bill of these costs was delivered:

(a) to the client either personally or by being left or posted to his place of business or last known place of abode,
(b) signed by the solicitor or enclosed with a letter so signed (Solicitors' Act 1974, s.60(1) and s.69).

It is noticeable that the court is required to consider the fairness and reasonableness of the agreement made, rather than the sum payable under it. Contrast an assessment under s.70 which will enquire into the fairness and reasonableness of each and every item in a bill. Conversely, when considering a contentious business agreement, the court's primary enquiry is as to the circumstances at the time of the agreement. However, if, as is usual, the remuneration is fixed by reference to an hourly rate, the court does have power to enquire into the number of hours worked and into whether that number of hours was excessive (1974 Act, s.61(4B)). If the solicitor's time records are not believed, or are considered excessive, the solicitor will not obtain full enforcement of the agreement. As to the somewhat mystifying reference to taxation, the old term for detailed assessment, in s.61(4B), which also appears in s.57(5) and (7), see the dictum of Mustill J. in *Walton v Egan* [1982] 2 Q.B. 1232 set out, below.

A solicitor who receives payment in advance will not need to enforce his contentious business agreement. Indeed, s.61(5) provides that, if an agreed amount has been paid, a client wishing to challenge the agreement or calculation must apply to the court within 12 months of the date of payment or within such further time as appears to the court to be reasonable. (As to what facts amount to payment, see *White Book*, vol.2, para.7C–118.)

Non-contentious business agreements

A solicitor and client may enter into a non-contentious business agreement as defined in s.57 of the Solicitors' Act 1974. As with contentious business agreements, this definition emphasises that the agreement must make crystal clear what the client's financial obligations are. However, unlike contentious business agreements, remuneration here can be fixed as a commission or percentage. These methods of charging are of course common in the case of probate and conveyancing matters. However, commission terms are of little relevance to charging agreements made by litigators.

A non-contentious business agreement restricts the client's right to require assessment under s.70 of the Solicitors' Act 1974 except in two respects (1974 Act, s.57(5) and (7)):

(i) Where the agreement is shown to be unfair or unreasonable:

39.007

(ii) Where the agreement fixes the remuneration by reference to an hourly rate and the client persuades the court to enquire as to the number of hours worked and as to whether that number was excessive.

The principles underlying the reference to taxation (the old word for detailed assessment) in s.57(5) and, in our view, s.57(7) and s.61(4B) which was first enacted in 1990 are clearly explained in *Walton v Egan* [1982] 2 Q.B. 1232:

"Where there is a special agreement under section 57, the ... solicitor's right of action is founded on the agreement not the bill; indeed, so far as section 57 is concerned, there is no need for the solicitor to render a bill at all. Nor is there any room for taxation under section 70, for this is concerned with bills not agreements. It is true that section 57(5) seems to contemplate that a taxation may occur, but this is in my view a procedure initiated by the court pursuant to its own inherent powers to supervise solicitors as officers of the court; it is not a procedure exercised as a right by the client. When an action on a special agreement comes before the court [e.g. a solicitor's simple debt claim] the matter may be sent to the [costs judge] so that he can enquire into the facts and report back to the court. When doing so, he is acting as a delegate of the powers exercised by the court, and he is not exercising his own originating powers of taxation" (*per* Mustill J.).

A non-contentious business agreement also excludes the rights which the client would otherwise have to require a solicitor to obtain a remuneration certificate (see above and see the Solicitors' Remuneration Order 1994 (SI 1994/2616), Art.9).

Non-contentious business agreements differ from contentious business agreements in that, to enforce a non-contentious business agreement, the solicitor can commence simple debt proceedings. Before doing so, however, the solicitor must comply with s.69 of the 1974 Act (i.e. deliver a signed bill and wait at least one month).

COSTS FUNDED BY THE LSC

39.008 In this section we look at the cost position between the Legal Services Commission (LSC) and the solicitor acting for the LSC funded client. The position is governed by the Access to Justice Act 1999 and the Civil Legal Aid (General) Regulations 1989 (SI 1989/339) (the latter being hereinafter called "the regulations"). The solicitor is not allowed to seek remuneration for any work done in the proceedings covered by a funding certificate whether or not that work falls within the scope of that certificate (reg.64 and see *Littaur v*

Steggles Palmer [1986] 1 W.L.R. 287 as to the effect of certificates which only cover part of the proceedings involving the LSC-funded client).

In certain cases the costs may be assessed by the LSC regional director rather than by the court (see regs 105 and 106A), the most important examples being cases in which the solicitor believes that the total amount payable to the solicitor and counsel (if any) will not exceed £2,500 plus VAT.

Unless assessment of costs by the regional director is possible a solicitor wishing to obtain payment from the LSC must, in most cases, obtain an order from the courts for a detailed assessment; see reg.107. This regulation (or reg.107A where applicable) specifies the basis of assessment as the standard basis. At first sight this appears to promise an agreeable amount of similarity between LSC-funded costs and costs between litigants. In fact the two assessments are significantly different. A detailed assessment of LSC-funded costs deals with the costs covered by the certificate in respect of which prescribed rates of remuneration may apply; a detailed assessment of costs between litigants deals only with the cost of action and remunerates that work at normal rates. Consider first the difference between costs of certificates and costs of action. Assume, for example, that the LSC-funded client has won the action with costs. The loser will not be required to pay for the following items since these are not costs of action:

(1) Work done to secure the continuation or extension of the certificate (such as writing to the client encouraging him not to default in instalments of contribution or obtaining counsel's opinion so as to enable the removal of a limitation).
(2) Work done for which the prior approval of the regional director was obtained but which is disallowed as being unreasonable in the detailed assessment between litigants.
(3) Work done in respect of matters for which no award of costs was made or, indeed, matters for which costs were awarded against the LSC-funded client.

(As to costs incurred in giving opponents notices of issue of a funding certificate and similar notices, these are to be treated as costs of the action: see reg.111.)

How does the difference between costs of certificates and costs of action affect the assessment of the LSC-funded costs? The answer depends upon whether or not the LSC-funded client was awarded costs payable by the other party, i.e. whether he won or lost, and the date upon which the funding certificate was first issued, i.e. whether or not it was before February 26, 1994. The practice relating to winners' and losers' bills in cases where the certificate was first issued on or after February 26, 1994 is summarised below. As to the practice to be followed in cases in which the certificate was first issued before February 26, 1994, see earlier editions of this book.

The winner's bill

39.009 If the LSC-funded client is awarded costs two assessments may be necessary and two certificates may be issued. One assessment is to determine how much the loser must pay to the LSC funded client's solicitor (see para.38.013) and this will lead to a default cost certificate or a final costs certificate (see para.38.037). The other assessment is to determine how much will be paid by the LSC to the solicitor and counsel; this assessment will lead to a Community Legal Service assessment certificate. The same bill will be used for both assessments. Costs payable only by the LSC will be shown in separate columns of that bill. A second document may also be prepared, an LSC schedule to the bill which sets out all the items in the bill which are claimed against other parties calculated at the LSC prescribed rates with or without any claims for enhancements (see Precedents C and E and see generally CPD, paras 40.2(c) and 49.1 to 49.8). It is not necessary to serve a copy of the LSC schedule on the paying party. Its contents are of no relevance to him. The bill and the schedule enable the winner's solicitor to set forth three overlapping calculations of his costs.

(1) Costs recoverable against the LSC only. These are set out in separate parts of the bill and will be assessed at the prescribed rates applicable, if any. At present there are no prescribed rates for work done in the Court of Appeal or House of Lords or for counsel's fees for non-matrimonial work. In most county court cases the hourly rate for work done by solicitors or their employees is £65.00 plus VAT (£28.75 plus VAT for travelling and waiting). The hourly rate is the same whether the work is done by a partner or by a trainee. However, in exceptional cases some "enhancement" is possible; see further para.39.011.

(2) Costs recoverable from another party. These will be assessed at normal rates. Solicitor's normal rates depend upon two factors; the grade of fee earner it was reasonable to employ and the hourly rate it is reasonable to claim for that fee earner. Hourly rates for each grade of fee earner depend on the locality in which the work is done.

(3) Costs payable by the LSC in respect of costs recoverable from another party. These are set out in the schedule or may be included in the LSC-only columns of the bill. The sums claimed for these items may be quite different from the sums claimed for them against the opponent. Against the LSC the solicitor can claim the relevant prescribed rates only and these are usually lower than normal rates. From the solicitor's point of view the prescribed rates are merely the first instalment, payable by the LSC, possibly in advance of any payment being made by the loser. In respect of these items, the LSC funded client's solicitor hopes to receive the second instalment when the full costs are paid by the loser.

What happens if the paying party successfully challenges some of the items in the parts of the bill he must pay and the assisted person's solicitor therefore wishes to claim those items against the LSC? Having disallowed the items as between the parties the costs officer will indicate that disallowance in the bill by making an appropriate note thereon and will delete those items from the LSC schedule. The question now arises, should those items be restored to LSC only columns in the bill? The costs officer would have to be persuaded that, although the item was unreasonable so far as the paying party is concerned, it was nevertheless reasonable so far as the funding certificate is concerned.

At the completion of the assessment the LSC-funded client's solicitor will have to draw up a third document specifying the sums allowed on the assessment; counsel's fees, other disbursements, the sums allowed as against the paying party at normal rates, the same items but calculated at prescribed rates, the items allowed only against the LSC and the costs of the assessment proceedings. This summary when sealed by the courts becomes the Community Legal Service assessment certificate (see Form Ex80A). Assume that the losing party was insured and so the costs assessed at normal rates will be paid in full. The Community Legal Service assessment certificate would then be used for accounting purposes as between the solicitor and the LSC. For example, the LSC may have made disbursements to the solicitor before trial and these must now be repaid.

The loser's bill

If the LSC-funded client is not awarded costs there still has to be an LSC only assessment. If this is done by the courts it is always kept quite separately from any assessment of costs between litigants which the opponent may be entitled to seek. In most cases a provisional assessment will be made, i.e. the costs officer notifies the solicitor of the sum he proposes to allow and requires the solicitor to so inform the court office within 14 days if he wishes to be heard on the assessment. 39.010

In addition to the prescribed rates, there are two other ways in which the legal aid costs differ from costs payable by a fee-paying client. First, being assessed on the standard basis means that, for any costs as to which there is a doubt, the LSC rather than the solicitor is given the benefit of that doubt (contrast solicitor and client assessments which are made on the indemnity basis, see para.39.003). Secondly, the solicitor is allowed no remuneration, either against the LSC for against the client in person for any work in respect of unreasonable steps which the client authorised or caused (e.g. visits to the solicitor's office by the client in excess of the number of visits which it was reasonable for him to make; a fee paying client can be required to pay for such visits if his solicitor gave him prior warning of the consequences of such extravagance, see further para.39.003).

Enhancements

39.011　Where costs funded by the LSC are subject to prescribed rates the solicitor may be allowed some or all of the fees at enhanced rates if:

(1) the work was done with exceptional competence, skill or expertise;
(2) the work was done with exceptional despatch;
(3) the case involves exceptional circumstances or complexity.

The meaning of this, the so-called "threshold test" has yet to be fully explored in reported cases. For example, what does "exceptional" mean? Does it mean all cases which are not standard or only a tiny minority of cases? Is all work done competently by a senior partner work done with exceptional competence, skill or expertise? Is all work done concerning freezing injunctions, work done with exceptional despatch, involving exceptional circumstances or complexity?

Once the threshold test is passed the enhancement is by a percentage uplift of the prescribed rate having regard to the degree of responsibility accepted by the solicitor, the care, speed and economy which the case was prepared and the novelty, weight and complexity of the case. This, the quantum test, sounds rather like another re-statement of the "seven pillars" of wisdom (see para.38.016). In county court cases the enhancement may not exceed 100 per cent. In very exceptional High Court cases an enhancement up to 200 per cent is possible. This again raises the question, what is meant by exceptional?

Reduction

39.012　A court may also award costs at a level lower than the prescribed rates "where it appears reasonable to do so having regards to the competence or dispatch with which the item or class of work was done" (see generally on enhancements and reduction, Legal Aid in Civil Proceedings (Remuneration) Regulations 1994 (SI 1994/339).

LSC-funded client's involvement in assessment proceedings

39.013　Regulations 105A and 119 make provisions concerning LSC funded clients who have an interest in any assessment of costs, for example, clients who have made a contribution which may not be refunded or who have recovered or preserved any money or property over which the LSC may have a statutory charge.

If the LSC-funded client has such a financial interest the solicitor must supply him with a copy of the bill, explain what his financial interest is, how the assessment may affect it, and how he can protect it (e.g. by making written representations or by attending any hearing). To ensure that proper compliance is made, all bills including costs funded by the LSC must be endorsed with a certificate referring to the relevant regulations (CPD, para.4.1(6) and, for the form of certificate, see Precedent F).

ORDERS FOR COSTS AGAINST LSC-FUNDED CLIENTS AND/OR THE LSC

Any costs ordered to be paid by an LSC-funded client must not exceed the amount which is a reasonable one for him to pay having regard to the circumstances including the financial resources of all parties to the proceedings and their conduct in connection with the dispute to which the proceedings relates (Access to Justice Act, s.11(1) as to which see further para.2.021, above). Regulations made under the Act set out a procedural code governing orders for costs against LSC-funded clients and against the LSC itself. The ordinary rules governing the assessment of costs do not apply to the assessment of such costs (r.44.17). The procedure to be followed in such cases is set out in ss.21 to 23 of the Costs Practice Direction. Since June 5, 2000 this procedure also applies to applications against assisted persons and against the LSC in respect of old legal aid certificates (Access to Justice Act 1999 (Commencement No.3: Transitional Provisions and Savings) Order 2000, para.8.3). Section 11 does not prevent another party obtaining a detailed assessment of costs awarded against an LSC funded party in order to set those costs off against any costs or damages awarded in the LSC funded party's favour in *Hill v Bailey* [2004] 1 All E.R. 1210).

39.014

The Costs Practice Direction states that the court awarding costs can either make "an order for costs to be determined" or an order "specifying the costs payable". The former is defined as an order for costs under s.11(1) under which the amount of costs payable by the LSC-funded client is to be determined by a costs judge or district judge. An "order specifying the costs payable" means an order for costs pursuant to s.11(1) which specifies the amount which the funded client is to pay. The court awarding costs will not make an order specifying the costs payable unless (amongst other things) it considers that it has sufficient information before it to decide what amount is a reasonable amount for the LSC-funded client to pay. If the court awarding costs makes "an order for costs to be determined" it may also; (i) state the amount of "full costs"; or (ii) make findings of fact, for example, concerning the conduct of all parties, which are to be taken into account by the court in the subsequent determination proceedings. Those proceedings should be commenced by way of an application in Form N244 to the cost judge or district judge of the court in which the order for costs was made. As to the documentation to accompany the application, see CPD, para.23.3. The application should be made within three months of the order for costs to be determined but, in certain limited cases, it is possible to apply late (see CPD, para.23.14).

If, as is usual, the LSC-funded client is of very limited means, how much will be the "amount which is a reasonable one for him to pay"? Very often that amount will be nil or only a nominal amount. Moreover, in calculating the resources of the LSC-funded client, there are certain assets which the court must disregard (for a summary of the regulations, see CPD, paras 21.12 to 21.14). A successful party who was not himself funded by the LSC (a "non-funded party") who is deprived of his costs because of s.11(1) may turn for help to the

Community Legal Service (Cost Protection) Regulations 2000 (SI 2000/824 as amended) which allows the court in certain circumstances to order payment of all or part of the costs against the LSC.

Regulation 5 of the Cost Protection Regulations sets out several conditions which must be satisfied if an order for costs is to be made against the LSC:

(a) a s.11(1) costs order must have been made against the funded client and the amount (if any) which he is required to pay under that order must be less than the amount of the full costs;

(b) the non-funded party must make a "request" (i.e. an application in Form N244) to a costs judge or district judge within three months of the making of the s.11(1) costs order;

(c) as regards costs incurred in a court of first instance, the proceedings must have been instituted by the funded client and the court must be satisfied that the non-funded party is an individual who will suffer financial hardship unless the order is made; and

(d) the court must be satisfied that it is just and equitable in the circumstances that provision for the costs should be made out of the public funds.

As to (a) and (b) an application against the LSC will often be combined in the application against the LSC-funded client (see above). As to (d), costs judges and district judges have jurisdiction to decide what is just and equitable. The Court of Appeal has held that, in most cases, it is just and equitable for the LSC to pay that part of the full costs which is not payable by the funded party (*R. (Gunn) v Secretary of State for the Home Department* [2001] 1 W.L.R. 1634).

As to (c) orders for costs against the LSC cannot be obtained by a claimant in first instance proceedings. However, they can be obtained by a defendant in such proceedings (subject to the "individual who will suffer financial hardship" condition) and by parties to appeals (whether appellants or respondents).

COSTS ORDERS IN FAVOUR OF OR AGAINST NON-PARTIES

39.015   Rule 48.2 provides for the exercise of the court's power to order costs for or against non-parties. Where the court is considering whether to exercise its power the non-party must be added as a party for the purposes of costs only and must be given a reasonable opportunity to attend a hearing at which the court will consider the matter further. There is no need to add the Legal Services Commission as a party when making an order under the CLS (Cost Protection Regulations 2000 (see para.39.014, above) or a legal representative when making a wasted costs order (see para.39.002, above). Nor does it apply in proceedings seeking pre-commencement disclosure or orders for disclosure against a person who is not a party; in these cases r.48.1 makes full provision.

Orders against non-parties have been litigated in dozens of cases in recent years. The two principal authorities today are *Symphony Group Plc v Hodgson* [1994] Q.B. 179, in which Balcombe L.J. set forth nine principles to apply, and *Arkin v Borchard Lines Ltd* [2005] 1 W.L.R. 3055, CA which reviewed and restated some of the principles to be applied. It seems there are three broad categories of cases in which the court will make an order for costs against non-parties.

(i) Where the non-party's conduct amounts to champerty, or maintenance (i.e. officious intermeddling) or is otherwise unmeritorious or self-seeking.
(ii) Where the non-party is under a clear contractual obligation to indemnify the unsuccessful party in the litigation (e.g. an insurer whose contractual liability exceeds the claim and costs in question or a trade union which has funded a member's claim).
(iii) Where the non-party is a "professional funder", i.e., someone other than those persons listed above who finances the whole or part of a litigant's costs for reward. Persons falling into this category are now potentially liable for the costs of all opposing parties but only up to the extent of the funding they provided.

In *Arkin*, a professional funder ("MPC") agreed to arrange and pay for the expert evidence which a claimant needed in return for 25 per cent of any damages he was later awarded. Although MPC were kept well informed about the litigation they did not participate in the conduct of the claim and did not attempt to control the litigation and so their agreement was held not to be champertous. The claim failed. MPC had spent £1.3 million on the claimant's expert evidence and so were ordered to pay another £1.3 million towards the defendants' costs.

Are there any non-party funders who will not be ordered to pay costs? In *Arkin* the Court of Appeal recognized an exception in favour of "pure funders", persons with no personal interest in the litigation, who do not stand to benefit from it (save for the return of their money if it is successful) who are not funding it as a matter of business and who in no way seek to control its course. The term is not limited to relatives, moved by natural affection, but includes, for example, persons who respond to a fund-raising campaign in order to prevent a claimant's claim from being lost by default or by inadequate presentation. The court does not overlook the injustice this causes to the defendant. Although, having won the case, he cannot recover costs from them he would have been liable to reimburse them if he had lost the case. The greater good of the community (access to justice for impecunious litigants) prevails over the considerations of justice to the individuals concerned.

We would suggest another category of non-party funders who will not be ordered to pay costs: legal representatives acting properly in litigation in which they have agreed CFA terms with their clients. Although this category is not expressly mentioned in *Arkin*, no applications were made against the unsuccessful claimant's legal representatives in that case. In *Hodgson v Imperial Tobacco Ltd* [1998] 1 W.L.R. 1056 the Court of Appeal held that solicitors were at no greater risk of a costs order when acting under a CFA than when acting under any other funding arrangement.

COSTS WHERE A GROUP LITIGATION ORDER HAS BEEN MADE

39.016 Group litigation orders are described in para.7.020, above. Rule 48.6A sets out the ground rules affecting costs in such cases. A distinction must be made between "individual costs" and "common costs". The latter, which used to be called generic costs, includes costs incurred in relation to any GLO issue. If an order for costs is made against a group litigant, his liability for common costs is several rather than joint. This prevents him having to pay the shares of other group litigants. The size of each share (of the opponent's common costs and of the group's common costs) depends upon the date his claim was removed from the group register. The date his claim joined the register is not normally regarded as significant since those who joined the register late take the benefit of the conduct of proceedings up to that date.

Rule 48.6A and the Practice Direction (Group Litigation) supplementing Pt 19 deal with apportionments between individual costs and common costs. Where an order for costs covers both types, either the court awarding costs or the court later assessing them has power to direct how they should be apportioned.

PROTECTIVE COSTS ORDERS

39.017 Protective costs orders are orders made pre-trial which anticipate the costs orders which may be made at trial. They indemnify the applicant out of a particular fund or estate against both his own costs of litigation and against any costs he might be ordered to pay to another party. They are clearly established where the litigation is a derivative claim brought by a minority shareholder (r.19.9(7) and see further para.7.026, above). They are also made in analogous proceedings, for example, where a trustee or beneficiary seeks guidance on the disposal of a trust fund (*McDonald v Horn* [1995] 1 All E.R. 961 or where a policyholder objects to a scheme of arrangement affecting insurance funds held by the insurer (*Re Axa Equity and Law Life Assurance Society Plc (No.2)* [2001] 1 All E.R. (Comm.) 1010).

Fertile ground for applications for protective costs orders is the field of public law cases, concerning issues of general public importance where the applicant has no private interest in the outcome. The principles to apply were considered in *R. (Corner House Research) v Secretary of State for Trade and Industry* [2005] EWCA Civ 192 which concerned a challenge made by a pressure group to the effectiveness of certain anti-corruption procedures proposed by the

British Government with regard to international trade. The governing principles (summarised above) were stated in para.74. In para.75, the court gave examples of different forms of protective costs order. The simplest, where the applicant's lawyers are acting pro bono, is for an order that there shall be no order for costs in the main proceedings, whatever the outcome. Where the lawyers are not acting pro bono, the applicant may seek an order limiting or extinguishing its liability to pay the opponent's costs if it later loses but without any corresponding restriction upon its own right to recover costs if it later wins. In such cases the applicant should expect the court to make a capping order which will restrict its recoverable costs to solicitors' fees and a fee for a single advocate of junior counsel status which are no more than modest. The judgment also makes provision as to how and when a protective costs order should be sought and, if appropriate, resisted by the opposing party (paras 78 and 79).

In two subsequent cases the Court of Appeal have expressed doubts as to the validity of the criterion that an applicant for a protective costs order must be shown to have no private interest in the outcome of the case. In *Wilkinson v Kitzinger* [2006] EWCA 2022 (Fam), in which the petitioner sought a declaration that her same sex marriage which was valid under the Law of British Columbia was also valid in the United Kingdom, a protective costs order was refused but a costs cap of £25,000 was imposed on the respondent. In *R. (England) v Tower Hamlets LBC* [2006] EWCA Civ 1742, a judicial review application concerning an historic building, the Court of Appeal expressed the hope that the Rule Committee would take the opportunity in the near future to review the public interest criterion.

PROSPECTIVE COSTS ORDERS

Prospective costs orders are defined in a Practice Statement ([2001] 1 W.L.R. 1082) which sets out a model form of order. They may be made in respect of "the costs of applications by trustees, or beneficiaries or other persons concerned in relation to the administration of a trust including questions of construction, questions relating to the exercise of powers confined by the trust or questions as to the validity of the trust". An order in the model form directs the trustees: 39.018

(i) to pay the reasonable costs of another party;
(ii) to make payments on account on a monthly basis during the proceedings; and
(iii) to indemnify the party whose costs are paid in respect of any other party's costs which he may be ordered to pay.

Applications for prospective costs orders will normally be made on paper without a hearing unless, for example, one party wishes to oppose the making of the order.

ASSESSMENT OF COSTS PAYABLE PURSUANT TO A CONTRACT

39.019   Rule 48.3 is one of the most mysterious rules in the CPR. In what circumstances will the court assess "(whether by the summary or by detailed procedure) costs which are payable by the paying party to the receiving party under the terms of the contract"? The two most likely examples are both excluded; contracts between solicitor and client (r.48.3(2)) and mortgagees' costs unless the court orders an account of those costs (CPD, paras 50.1 to 50.4). The next most likely example, applications under s.71 of the Solicitors Act 1974 appear to be covered by r.48.8 (see in particular CPD, paras 56.1 and 56.5).

In our view r.48.3 is largely, if not totally, obsolete. Cases which it previously covered now fall within r.44.12A (as to which, see para.39.001, above). One case which may still fall within r.48.3 arises in certain Chancery actions where trustees exercise a power given to them in a trust deed to agree to pay the costs of some other party to the proceedings. In such a case a prospective costs order (see para.39.018, above) is not required. Instead the Practice Direction supplementing CPR 64 states that r.48.3 applies (see *White Book*, vol.1, para.64PD.6).

CHAPTER 40

Enforcement of Money Judgments

INTRODUCTION

A money judgment is not enforced by the court automatically. It is always for the successful party (the judgment creditor) to decide when and how best to enforce it. If the judgment debtor is insured in respect of the claim and the defence has been conducted by his insurers, the enforcement of the judgment is unlikely to arise; the insurers will usually settle up without a fight. In other cases, the correct time to consider enforcement is before proceedings are even begun. Is the debtor worth suing? If he is not, litigation will just be sending good money after bad.

40.001

Given that the decision to sue has been taken, there are three questions for the judgment creditor to consider: (i) Can he find the debtor? (ii) Can he find out what assets the debtor has? (iii) Can he take those assets from him? The court cannot help with the first: consider employing an inquiry agent. The courts can help on the second and third questions, although as to the second, it may be preferable to use an inquiry agent instead of, or as well as, the courts (see below).

HIGH COURT ENFORCEMENT OF COUNTY COURT JUDGMENTS

In respect of county court judgments where the amount recoverable exceeds £600 (High Court and County Courts Jurisdiction (Amendment) Order 1999 (SI 1999/724)) it will often be advantageous to seek enforcement in the High Court. On registration in the High Court, the judgment will attract interest under the Judgments Act 1838. This statute provides a regime for judgment interest which, from the creditor's point of view, is better than the regime applicable in the county courts in up to two respects. Under the county court regime, no interest is payable on judgments for less than £5,000 save where the Late Payment of Commercial Debts (Rate of Interest) Order 1998 applies (see para.3.006). Also, even where interest is payable, it ceases to be payable as soon as the judgment creditor commences any enforcement proceedings in the county court (including information hearing, third party debt proceedings or a

40.002

615

judgment summons, see below) unless those proceedings fail to produce any payment from the debtor. In the High Court interest does not cease to accrue during enforcement proceedings. In our opinion, once judgment has been registered in the High Court, interest under the 1838 Act will continue to accrue even if, later, third party debt proceedings or equitable execution (see below) is sought in the county court (see CCA 1984, s.42(5)).

In order to obtain enforcement in the High Court, the county court judgment creditor must obtain a certificate of judgment from the county court and deliver it to the High Court (see CCR, Ord.25, r.13 and the Queen's Bench Guide paras 11.2.5 to 11.2.8). Once registered, any application for a stay of execution has to be made in the High Court. However, applications to set aside, correct, vary or quash the judgment must still be made in the county court.

INFORMATION HEARING (PT 71)

40.003 If, after judgment has been obtained, the debtor does not pay immediately, the creditor can apply without notice for an order bringing the debtor before the court in order to examine him as to his means. If the judgment debtor is a body corporate, the order can be made against an officer of the company. The order provides for the production of all relevant books or documents.

How is the application made? The judgment creditor must complete and file an application notice in Form N316, if the debtor is an individual, and N316A if an officer of a company or other corporation is to be questioned. The notice must include the name and address of the judgment debtor, the judgment or order sought to be enforced and the amount then owed. The judgment creditor should identify any particular documents he wishes the judgment debtor to bring to court.

On filing the application notice the court issue an order for the judgment debtor to attend court at a specified time. He is warned that if he fails to attend that he may be sent to prison for contempt. The order must, unless the court orders otherwise, be served personally at least 14 days before the information hearing. If the judgment creditor attempts to serve the order but fails, he must notify the court at least seven days before the hearing. If he successfully serves the order, he must file an affidavit of service not less than two days before the hearing or otherwise produce it at the hearing.

Can the judgment debtor demand in advance his expenses of travelling to and from the information hearing? Yes, by r.71.4 the judgment debtor can within seven days of service of the order require the judgment creditor to pay a sum reasonably sufficient to cover those expenses. The judgment creditor must file an affidavit or produce it at the hearing stating whether or not a request for travelling expenses was made and if so, the amount paid, as well as the amount of the judgment debt outstanding. This information can be included, where appropriate, in the affidavit of service.

The information hearing usually takes place in the court for the area where the judgment debtor resides or carries on business. An officer of the court conducts the examination, but a judge may do so if that is considered appropriate. Note that if the judgment creditor wishes the examination to be conducted by a judge this must be stated in the application notice, together with reasons. Where the examination is conducted by a court officer standard questions as set out in Appendices A and B to PD 71 are asked. The judgment creditor may attend the hearing and ask additional questions but these should first be set out in the application notice. The officer makes a written record of the responses given by the judgment debtor who is invited to read and sign it at the end of the hearing. Where the hearing is conducted before a judge, the standard questions are not used. The questions are asked by the judgment creditor and the hearing is tape recorded.

If the judgment debtor fails to attend court or having attended court refuses to take the oath or affirm or otherwise refuses to answer questions, a committal order may be made against him. It is essential that the judgment creditor files an affidavit giving a statement as to the position in respect of the travelling expenses allowed to the judgment debtor otherwise a committal order cannot be made: see r.71.8(3) and *Pelling v Bow County Court* [2005] EWCA Civ 384; (2005) L.T.L. February 25.

WRIT OF FIERI FACIAS (HIGH COURT); WARRANT OF EXECUTION (COUNTY COURT)

This is the form of enforcement against the debtor's goods and chattels. Article 8 of the High Court and County Courts Jurisdiction Order 1991 (SI 1991/724) allocates all proceedings for enforcement against chattels to the High Court where the sum which it is sought to enforce is £5,000 or more (unless the proceedings in question arose out of an agreement regulated by the Consumer Credit Act 1974). Enforcement against chattels where the sum which it is sought to enforce is less than £600 (see above) can be taken in the High Court only in respect of a High Court judgment. If the sum which it is sought to enforce is £600 or more but less than £5,000, enforcement against chattels is available in both courts. There are said to be two powerful advantages in transferring judgments for £600 or more to the High Court for enforcement; interest on judgment may then become payable; also, execution by a High Court Enforcement officer ("HCEO") is often considered to be more effective than execution by county court bailiffs. As to the procedure on transfer.

40.004

The High Court form is usually referred to as a writ of fi fa (the Latin is pronounced to rhyme with by bay). It is directed to the HCEO of the county in which the debtor's goods are situated. It is issued by the appropriate court office on production of:

(1) a praecipe with the court fee imprinted thereon (Practice Form 86)
(2) the judgment or an office copy; and
(3) the order granting permission to issue (where required, see below).

In order to facilitate issue, the judgment creditor will normally also produce two copies of the writ form duly completed. One form of writ is sealed and returned to the judgment creditor who forwards it to the HCEO who will acknowledge receipt and send the writ to his officer for execution (see generally RSC, Ord.46, r.6).

If the judgment is expressed in a foreign currency the praecipe and the writ must state the sterling equivalent of the sum at the date of the issue of the writ (Queen's Bench Guide, para.11.2.4).

In the county court, the warrant of execution (see Form N42) is issued on the payment of the fee prescribed and on filing a request in Form N323. The warrant is executed by the bailiff of the court for the district in which it is to be executed (if this is a different county court, see Form N53). Where the debtor is in breach of an instalment order, the warrant may be issued either for the whole of the judgment debt and costs remaining unpaid or for any part thereof. However, in the case of enforcement of part of the total sums remaining unpaid, that part must not be less than £50 or one monthly instalment (or, as the case may be, four weekly instalments) whichever is the greater. Before executing the warrant the court sends a notice in Form N326 to the debtor (see generally CCR, Ord.26, r.1).

Where a judgment orders the debtor to pay a sum of money and to pay costs to be determined by a detailed assessment of costs (see para.38.015) the judgment creditor need not delay enforcement until those costs have been assessed. A writ or warrant may be issued before the detailed assessment and a separate writ or warrant for costs may be issued later (RSC, Ord.47, r.3; CCR, Ord.26, r.1(5)).

Permission to issue the writ or warrant is not usually required, but note four important exceptions:

(1) Where six or more years have elapsed since the date of the judgment (RSC, Ord.46, r.2; CCR, Ord.26, r.5). As to the Limitation Act 1980, see *Lowsley v Forbes* [1999] 1 A.C. 329; *Patel v Singh* (2002) L.T.L. December 13; *Duer v Frazer* [2001] 1 W.L.R. 919 concerning foreign judgments and *Re a Debtor (No.50A–SD–1995)* [1997] Ch.310 concerning stale statutory demands.

(2) Where any change has taken place, whether by death or otherwise, in the parties entitled to or liable to execution (RSC, Ord.46, r.2; CCR, Ord.26, r.5).

(3) Whilst a county court attachment of earnings order is in force (Attachment of Earnings Act 1971, s.8(2)(b); see generally below).

(4) In certain actions against partners (CPR Pt 73).

In each of these cases except (4) permission can be sought on application without notice to the debtor.

In executing the writ or warrant, the HCEO or bailiff can seize such of the debtor's goods and chattels in his county or district as may be sufficient to realise the judgment debt and expenses. The items seized are then sold, usually by public auction. After deducting the expenses of execution, the judgment creditor is paid off and any surplus proceeds are returned to the debtor. It is always helpful to inform the HCEO or bailiff of specific items which could be seized, for example, tell him the make, type and registration number of the debtor's car, if known. In practice, the debtor's goods are not usually removed immediately. The debtor and the HCEO or bailiff will enter into an agreement for "walking possession" whereby, in consideration of the goods not being removed at once, the debtor agrees not to dispose of them nor permit them to be moved (and see further, *White Book* 2001, vol.2, para.10–66 and, the county court, Form N42). As to the penalties for rescuing goods seized in execution, see the crime of "pound breach", CCA 1984, s.92 and *Newman v Modern Bookbinders Ltd* [2000] 1 W.L.R. 2559. Only goods belonging to the debtor are liable to execution; it is not permissible to seize goods on hire or hire-purchase to the debtor (and see interpleader proceedings, Ch.24). Certain goods belonging to the debtor are exempt from seizure; such tools, books, vehicles and other items of equipment as are necessary to the debtor for personal use by him in his employment, business or vocation; also, such clothing, bedding, furniture, household equipment and provisions as are necessary for satisfying the basic domestic needs of the debtor and his family (see generally *White Book* commentary to RSC, Ord.45, r.1 and CCA, 1984, s.89). The HCEO or bailiff must not effect forcible entry to any premises unless and until he has taken possession of any goods or chattels therein (see generally *McLeod v Butterwick* [1998] 1 W.L.R. 1603).

It is possible for a judgment creditor to seek remedies against the HCEO or bailiff for any alleged dereliction of duty (in the county court, see CCA, 1984, s.124).

THIRD PART DEBT PROCEEDINGS (PT 72)

If the judgment debtor is himself the creditor of another, it is possible to obtain an order that his debtor should pay the judgment creditor. This is known as a third party debt order and is obtained in two stages. The application is made without notice on Form N349. This should set out, amongst other matters, the name and address of the judgment debtor, details of the judgment or order sought to be enforced, the amount due, the name and address of the third party and confirmation that he is within the jurisdiction. See further PD 72, para.1.2. 40.005

The hearing will be before a judge. If successful the judge will make an interim third party debt order. This will direct that until the next hearing, when the judge will decide whether or not to make the order final, the third party must not make any payment which reduces the amount he owes the judgment debtor to less than the amount specified in the order, namely the amount of money remaining due to the judgment creditor under the judgment or order plus fixed costs.

The interim third party debt order only becomes binding on a third party when it is served on him. Copies of an interim third party debt order, the application notice and any documents filed in support of it must be served on the third party, not less than 21 days before the date fixed for the hearing. Those documents must be served on the judgment debtor not less than seven days after a copy has been served on the third party and seven days before the date fixed for the hearing. What if the third party claims not to owe any money to the judgment debtor or less than the amount specified in the order? He must notify the court and the judgment creditor in writing of that within seven days of being served with the order. If this is disputed by the judgment creditor then he must file and serve written evidence setting out the grounds of dispute.

What if the judgment debtor or the third party objects to the court making a final third party debt order? He must file and serve written evidence stating the grounds for his objections. Equally, if the judgment debtor or the third party knows or believes that a person other than the judgment debtor has any claim to the money specified in the interim order, he must file and serve written evidence stating his knowledge of that matter. In the latter circumstances, the court will serve on that person notice of the application and the hearing.

What order might the court make at the hearing? The court may make a final third party debt order; discharge the interim third party debt order and dismiss the application; decide any issues in dispute between the parties, or between any of the parties and any other person who has a claim to the money specified in the interim order or direct a trial of any such issues, and if necessary give directions. What is the effect of the order being made final? It is then enforceable as an order to pay money and so any of the enforcement steps outlined in this chapter can be taken against the third party. This form of enforcement is discretionary. The court may refuse to make the final order if, for example, the debtor is insolvent and, bankruptcy or similar proceedings being imminent, the effect of the order would merely be giving the judgment creditor priority over the other unsecured creditors: see *Roberts Petroleum Ltd v Bernard Kenny Ltd* [1983] A.C. 192 (concerning a charging order to which similar principles apply). See also *Fraser v Oystertec Plc* [2004] EWHC 2225; [2004] All E.R. (D) 253 (Nov). Third party debt proceedings cannot be taken on a judgment for a sum less than £50 or its foreign equivalent.

A bank account is an obvious target for third party debt proceedings. However, the order made will bite only upon the credit balance in the account (if any) at the time of service of the interim order; a further order is needed to attach money paid in subsequently (*Heppenstall v Jackson and Barclays Bank Ltd (Garnishees)* [1939] 1 K.B. 585). Also, a joint bank account is not attachable in respect of a debt owed by one of two account holders, even if either of them has authority to draw on the account (*Hirschorn v Evans* [1938] 2 K.B. 801).

There are several points to bear in mind if third party debt proceedings are taken against a "deposit-taker", i.e. a person who may, in the course of his business, lawfully accept deposits in the UK, such as a bank, building society, etc. (see s.40(6) of the SCA 1981).

(1) The application notice must state whether the deponent knows the name and address of the branch at which the account is held and the account number and must state such information thereto as he has. PD 72, para.1.3 stresses that the court will not grant speculative appli-

cations for third party debt orders, and will only make an interim third party debt order against a bank or building society if the judgment creditor's application notice contains evidence to substantiate his belief that the judgment debtor has an account with the bank or building society in question.

(2) The order must be served on the registered or head office and it is also desirable to serve a copy on the branch office concerned. How should a bank or building society respond? It is required to retain money in accounts held solely by the judgment debtor (or, if there are joint judgment debtors, accounts held jointly by them or solely by either or any of them) and to search for and disclose information about such accounts. Are there any limitations? Note that it is not required to retain money in, or disclose information about, accounts that are either in the joint names of the judgment debtor and another person or accounts in the names of individual members of a firm where the interim order has been made against a firm.

(3) In making an order, any conditions applicable to the account in question purporting to restrict withdrawals are to be disregarded (e.g. conditions requiring an account holder to give notice or to produce a deposit book or share-account book; SCA 1981, s.40, CCA 1984, s.108).

(4) An order against a building society or credit union cannot require a payment which would reduce the account to a sum less than £1.

(5) Deposit-taking institutions do not usually attend the hearing. Instead, they merely write to the court agreeing to comply with any order made.

(6) Before paying the judgment creditor, the deposit-taker is entitled to deduct a prescribed sum (currently £55) in respect of administrative and clerical expenses (SCA 1981, s.40A; CCA 1984, s.109).

(7) What if the judgment debtor or his family suffers hardship in meeting ordinary living expenses as a result of the third party debt order? By r.72.7 the court may, on an application by the judgment debtor, make an order permitting the bank or building society to make a payment or payments out of the account. The application notice must include detailed evidence explaining why the judgment debtor needs a payment of the amount requested. See further PD 72, para.5.

Judgment creditors who are self-employed often have trade debts due to them. It is possible to find out an information hearing what these debts are and then take third party debt proceedings accordingly. It is not uncommon for solicitors to be served with a third party debt order, as solicitors of course often hold money on behalf of clients. Also an insurance company that has underwritten an endowment policy may be served with such an order.

A claimant cannot obtain a third party debt order in respect of a debt situated in an EC country because the national courts of EC countries have exclusive jurisdiction in enforcement: see Ch.11 and *Kuwait Oil Tanker Co. Sak v Qabazard* [2003] UKHL 31; (2004) 1 A.C. 300. As to non-EC based debts, an

English court will not make a third party payment order regarding a debt situated abroad, unless it appears that the English order will be recognised under the foreign law as discharging the liability of the third party: see *Societe Eram Shipping Co. Ltd v Compagnie Internationale De Navigation* [2003] UKHL 30; [2004] 1 A.C. 260.

ATTACHMENT OF EARNINGS

40.006   This is governed by the Attachment of Earnings Act 1971 and CCR, Ord.27. In a sense, the Act provides a form of third party debt proceedings to attach future debts which are payable by an employer. An order is made compelling an employer to make regular deductions from the debtor's earnings and pay them into court.

"Earnings" is defined to include sums payable by way of wages or salary (including, e.g. overtime pay) and by way of pension (but not state pensions and other state benefits). The Act does not apply to pay or allowances payable to a debtor as a member of Her Majesty's Armed Forces (but see analogous remedies under the Armed Forces Act 1971).

To obtain an attachment of earnings order, the judgment creditor must complete Form N337 and send it to the county court for the district in which the debtor resides. Where the judgment was obtained in a different county court, the proceedings must be transferred. Except in certain Family Division cases, the High Court has no power to make an attachment of earnings order. A High Court judgment creditor has to apply to the appropriate county court and file, amongst other things, an office copy of the judgment (CCR, Ord.25, r.11).

A notice of application for an attachment of earnings order (in Form N55) is served on the debtor (usually by the court) together with Form N56, a questionnaire which the debtor must complete so providing a statement of means. At any stage of the proceedings, the court may also require information as to earnings from any person appearing to have the debtor in his employment (see Forms N338 and N61A). If the debtor completes and returns Form N56 (the statement of means) the court staff may make an attachment of earnings order (in Form N60) and send copies of it to the parties and to the debtor's employer. No hearing is convened unless the court staff consider that they lack sufficient information to make an order or unless either party objects to an order made.

If the debtor does not send the court a statement of means within the time allowed, the court staff will automatically issue an order compelling him to do so. The order will be in Form N61, indorsed with a penal notice, to be served on the debtor personally by the county court bailiff. Continued disobedience leads, via further notices, to hearings and adjourned hearings, and ultimately to arrest and imprisonment (see Forms N63, N112, N112A).

All hearings and adjourned hearings usually take place before a district judge, who will seek the information relevant to the making of an attachment of earnings order. Such an order will be made only if the district judge is satisfied that the debtor has sufficient means.

An attachment of earnings order, whether made by the court staff or by the district judge, will specify the "normal deduction rate" and the "protected earning rate", the latter being the amount which the court decides the debtor must be allowed to retain out of his earnings in any event. It will normally be a sum equal to the sum which the debtor would receive for himself and his family if he were on income support.

Example

If the protected earnings rate is £110 per week and the normal deduction rate is £15 per week, then, in any week in which the debtor earns £125 or more, the creditor will receive the full £15. If in one week the debtor earns a sum between £110 and £125, the creditor will receive the excess over £110. If in one week the debtor earns £110 or less then, for that week, the creditor receives nothing. If in one week the debtor receives advance pay (e.g. holiday pay) the normal deduction rate will apply to each pay period covered by the payment. Thus, from a payment comprising £125 per week or more for a three-week period, a sum of £45 would be deducted.

40.007

The costs of the application (as to which see CCR, Ord.27, r.9) may be summarily assessed. The order is served on the debtor and on the employer by ordinary first-class post. The employer is usually given an explanatory booklet giving details as to how an attachment of earnings order operates. In respect of each deduction he has to make, he is entitled to deduct an additional sum (at present £1) in respect of his clerical and administrative expenses (see Attachment of Earnings Act 1971, s.7). The smallest sum for which an attachment of earnings order can be made is £50 or the amount remaining payable under a judgment for not less than £50.

It is the duty of both the debtor and the employer to notify the court of any cessation of the debtor's employment. Similarly, if the debtor obtains another job, he must inform the court and the order can then be redirected to the new employer. The court can convene further hearings during the currency of the order, for example, to compel the debtor to give information as to any change in employment.

In theory, an attachment of earnings order secures the whole amount of the judgment debt outstanding. Thus, once it has been made, the judgment creditor cannot use any other method of enforcement without first drawing the attachment of earnings order to the court's attention. For this reason, judgment creditors often turn to attachment of earnings orders as a method of final resort rather than a method of first resort. An attachment of earnings order also affects any entitlement to interest under the County Courts (Interest on Judgment Debts) Order 1991 (SI 1991/1184) (see Art.4(3)); no such interest accrues whilst an attachment of earnings order is in force.

CHARGING ORDER ON LAND (PT 73)

40.008 This method of enforcement provides the judgment creditor with the equivalent of a mortgage over land specified in the order. Thus, subject to any prior mortgages and charges affecting that land, the judgment creditor becomes a secured creditor. The charging order does not affect the accrual of any judgment interest payable on High Court judgments or on county court judgments on which interest is payable (see County Courts (Interest on Judgment Debts) Order 1991 (SI 1991/1184), Art.4(2)). Subsequently, if the judgment debt remains unpaid, the judgment creditor can apply for an order for the sale of the land charged so that the judgment may be satisfied out of the proceeds of sale remaining after discharge of any prior mortgage or charge (see, for example, *Harlow & Milner Ltd v Teasdale* [2006] EWHC 1708, (2007) L.T.L. January 26, where it is noted that orders for sale of a defendant's home are exceptional whilst sales of second homes and investment properties are more common). The charging order secures all judgment interest due and accruing due, including interest accruing more than six years before the eventual sale of the property (*Ezekiel v Orakpo* [1997] 1 W.L.R. 340; contrast applications to enforce judgments, *Lowsley v Forbes* [1999] 1 A.C. 329).

Jurisdiction of the High Court and county court

40.009 The High Court has jurisdiction to make a charging order over land only if the judgment in question is a High Court maintenance order, or is a judgment for a sum exceeding £5,000 and which either was made by the High Court or has been transferred to the High Court under CCA 1984, s.42 (see ss.(5) and see generally Charging Orders Act 1979, s.1).

The jurisdiction of the county court to make a charging order over land is unlimited. If the judgment in question is a High Court judgment, proceedings should be taken in the county court local to the debtor. If the judgment in question is a county court judgment, proceedings should be taken in the county court in which the proceedings are presently being conducted.

Charging order procedure

40.010 The procedure for obtaining a charging order is similar to the third party debt procedure. An application notice in Form N379 must be filed. As to its contents see PD 73, para.1.2. An interim charging order is usually made without notice to the judgment debtor and a date set for the final hearing. The interim order should be registered against the land and copies of the order and application notice must of course be served. If, at the hearing, the order is made final, that too should be registered. If it should be necessary to enforce the charge, this is done by commencing a Pt 8 claim in the Chancery Division or, in the county court, by applying to the court for the district in which the land is situated by a claim form to which PD 8B, s.B applies (compare county court mortgage possession proceedings, Ch.24). The county court has jurisdiction to order sale only if the judgment debt remaining unpaid does not exceed £30,000 (CCA 1984, s.23(c); as to the order for sale see Form N436). See further r.73.10.

A charging order can be made in respect of land which the debtor owns jointly with another person (e.g. a spouse, see *National Westminster Bank Ltd v Stockman* [1981] 1 W.L.R. 67). However, the order ranks as a charge upon the debtor's beneficial interest rather than upon the land itself. Thus, it will not inhibit a sale by two trustees or a trust corporation (see *Perry v Phoenix Assurance Plc* [1988] 1 W.L.R. 940). To obtain an order for sale, proceedings would have to be taken under s.14 of the Trusts of Land and Appointment of Trustees Act 1996 (as to which the county court has unlimited jurisdiction; see the High Court and County Courts Jurisdiction Order 1991 (SI 1991/724), Art.2(1)(p) and see *Midland Bank Plc v Pike* [1988] 2 All E.R. 434). As a general rule, on any contest between a judgment creditor and a joint proprietor of the property or any adult or child resident therein, the interests of the judgment creditor will, sooner or later, prevail (see *Harman v Glencross* [1986] Fam. 81; *Austin-Fell v Austin-Fell* [1990] Fam. 172; *Re Citro (a bankrupt)* [1991] Ch.142 and *Lloyds Bank Plc v Byrne & Byrne* [1991] 23 H.L.R. 472).

In exercising its discretion whether to grant a charging order, the court will take into account the position of other creditors of the judgment debtor and also any trustee or person beneficially entitled to the land in question: see, for example, *Lewis v Eliades* [2005] EWHC 488; [2005] All E.R. (D) 345 (Apr). To facilitate this, the application notice should state whether the applicant knows of any such persons, giving the names and addresses known. The court may then require that notice of the interim order should be given to these persons. In the proceedings made without notice to the debtor, the creditor has a duty to make full and frank disclosure of all the relevant circumstances of which he is aware. In the High Court, a master or a district judge has jurisdiction to grant an injunction (called a "stop notice") in connection with or ancillary to a charging order. See r.73, Pt III.

Does enforcement of a foreign currency judgment by means of a charging order require the judgment debt to be converted into sterling before enforcement is completed? No, held the Court of Appeal in *Carnegie v Giessen* [2005] EWCA Civ 191; *The Times*, March 14, 2005.

CHARGING ORDER ON SECURITIES (PT 73)

By similar procedures, a judgment creditor can also obtain a charging order on a judgment debtor's beneficial interest in securities of any of the following kinds (1979 Act, s.2(2)): 40.011

(1) government stock;
(2) stock of anybody (other than a building society) incorporated within England and Wales;

(3) stock of anybody incorporated outside England and Wales or of any state or territory outside the UK, being stock registered in a register kept at any place within England and Wales;
(4) units of any unit trust in respect of which a register of the unit trust holders is kept at any place within England and Wales.

Section 2 further states that the order may provide for the charge to extend to any interest or dividend payable in respect of the assets (thus removing the need to appoint a receiver). A copy of the order obtained must be served on the Bank of England or the company concerned. Pending sale, the creditor's interest may be protected by an ancillary injunction called a stop order (see r.73 Pt II).

EQUITABLE EXECUTION: APPOINTMENT OF A RECEIVER (PT 69)

40.012 This is a long stop-method of enforcement which reaches property which other methods cannot reach, such as a legacy, income under a trust fund, income from a business the debtor owns in partnership with others, and debts likely to accrue to the debtor in the future (see, e.g. *Soinco SACI v Novokuznetsk Aluminium Plant* [1998] Q.B. 406). The application is made to a master or district judge and, save in very urgent cases, by application notice. In the High Court, if there is a danger that the property may be disposed of before the hearing, the master or district judge may grant an ancillary injunction (PD 2, application of cases to levels of judiciary, para.2.3(c)).

Receivership is often cumbersome and expensive. It should not be sought if there are no impediments to legal execution.

CHARGING ORDER ON DEBTOR'S INTEREST IN PARTNERSHIP PROPERTY

40.013 A judgment creditor of a partner can apply for an order under s.23 of the Partnership Act 1890 charging that partner's interest in the partnership property and profits with payment of the amount of the judgment debt and interest thereon and may by the same or subsequent order appoint a receiver of that partner's share of profits (whether already declared or accruing) and certain other orders. The application is made by claim form to which Pt 8 applies and which must be served on the debtor and on the other partners in England and Wales (see s.III of PD 73). If an order is made, the other partners are at liberty to redeem the interest charged or can purchase it if a sale is ordered.

SEQUESTRATION

40.014 This is a form of contempt proceedings which is available in both the High Court and the county court. Sequestration can be used only in respect of orders in the nature of an injunction and therefore only rarely concerns money judgments. An application in accordance with Pt 23 (see Ch.13) is made to a judge seeking permission to issue a writ of sequestration, i.e. a writ appointing four sequestrators and directing them to take possession of all the real and personal property of the contemnor and to keep the same until the contempt is cleared (see generally RSC, Ord.46, r.5). The court may apply the property for the benefit of the judgment creditor; for an example, see *Mir v Mir* [1992] Fam. 79, wardship proceedings in which an order was made for the sale of land previously sequestrated in order to finance further litigation overseas.

In the county court, the jurisdiction to order sequestration falls within the ancillary jurisdiction of the court (see CCA 1984, s.38 and *Rose v Lastington* [1990] 1 Q.B. 562).

JUDGMENT SUMMONS

40.015 This method of enforcement is available only in the case of the High Court or county court maintenance orders and judgments or orders of any court or payment of certain taxes or other sums of contributions due to the state. It is a means of obtaining an order for imprisonment which is suspended so long as stated instalments are paid. In order to obtain such an order the applicant (i.e. a person awarded maintenance or the state) must show that the debtor has the means to pay, but has failed to pay (see generally CCR, Ord.28).

BANKRUPTCY AND WINDING UP OF COMPANIES

40.015A These are not strictly methods of enforcement. They are considered separately in Ch.42.

ENFORCEMENT OF FOREIGN JUDGMENTS (PT 74)

40.016 There are a variety of provisions under which the English courts will recognise and enforce foreign judgments. The three main provisions are summarised below.

At common law, an action upon the judgment can be brought, i.e. a simple money claim; there are however many defences which can be raised to such a claim.

Under AJA 1920 and the Foreign Judgments (Reciprocal Enforcement) Act 1933, money judgments obtained in certain countries may be registered here.

Broadly speaking, registration makes the judgment enforceable as if it were an English judgment. Costs of and incidental to the application (including costs of translation, etc.) may be awarded and, unless the registration is set aside, added to the judgment as registered. Under the statute there are several grounds upon which registration may be refused (see, e.g. *Habib Bank Ltd v Ahmed*, *The Times*, November 2, 2000).

Under CJJA 1982, applying Council Regulation (EC) No.44/2001, many judgments, whether for the payment of money or otherwise, are registerable in the High Court if they were obtained in another EU Member State or elsewhere in the UK. Under the CJJA 1982, the grounds upon which registration may be refused are severely limited (for an example see *Tavoulareas v Tsavliris* [2006] EWCA Civ 1772, *The Times*, January 5, 2007. It is important to note that, under this Part of the CJJA 1982, it is immaterial whether the defendant to the proceedings is or was domiciled inside or outside the EU. Indeed (subject to the 1968 European Judgments Convention, Art.59, see below) as against a non-EU defendant, the judgment sought to be registered may have been obtained by reliance upon the "exorbitant jurisdiction" of the judgment court.

Example

40.017   A Frenchman will be entitled to register in England a French judgment which he obtained against an American defendant who has assets here, the French court having assumed jurisdiction because of the French nationality of the claimant.

Article 59 of the European Judgments Convention enables each member state to enter judgment conventions with non-EU states agreeing not to recognise judgments based upon the exorbitant jurisdictions so far as concerns defendants domiciled in their states. Australia, Canada and the USA have indicated interest in agreeing such conventions with the UK, but as yet, no such conventions have been concluded.

The procedure by which to register an EU but non-UK judgment under the CJJA 1982 is set out in Pt IV of r.74. In outline, it requires the following.

(1) An application for registration made to a master or district judge without notice being served on any other party but with supporting evidence: see, for example, *La Caisse Regional Du CreditAgricole Nord de France v Ashdown* [2007] EWCA Civ 574 (2007) L.T.L. May 15. Note that the court hearing the application may direct a claim form under Pt 8 to be filed and served (see Ch.10).

(2) An order giving permission to register will state a time limit for appeal (see below) and will stay execution of the judgment until that time limit expires. (In the meantime, the applicant should consider whether to seek, e.g. a freezing injunction; see para.27.015).

(3) Notice of registration must be served on the respondent informing him of his right to appeal and specifying the time limit imposed.

(4) An appeal against registration must be made under r.74.8 to a judge by application in accordance with Pt 23 (see Ch.13). There is some

authority to the effect that the court has no power to extend the time for appealing (*TSN Kunstoff Recycling Gmbh v Jurgens* (2001) L.T.L., February 22).

(5) No orders for security for costs can be made solely upon the grounds that the party applying for registration is not domiciled or resident within England and Wales (security for costs may, of course, be ordered on other grounds; see further r.74.5 and para.26.002.)

(6) In exceptional cases, registration can be refused on public policy grounds: see *Maronier v Larmer* [2003] 1 All E.R. (Comm.) 225 (Court of Appeal refused registration where the procedure of the court first seised had resulted in a defendant being prevented from putting his case to the court such that he had manifestly not received a fair trial as required by ECHR Art.6).

In the case of a non-money judgment made elsewhere in the UK, the procedure outlined above applies by virtue of r.74.16 save that the challenge to registration must be made by an application to set aside the order, and so is made to a master or district judge not to a High Court judge.

In the case of a money judgment made elsewhere in the UK, a much simpler procedure is laid down by r.74.15; lodging at the High Court a certificate of judgment issued by the original court not more than six months previously. The judgment creditor must also produce a certified copy of the certificate which the court clerk will seal and return to him. No application to a master or district judge is required.

The effect of registration under CJJA 1982 is that the judgment can now be enforced as if it were a judgment of the High Court (see CJJA 1982, s.4(2); Sch.6, para.6; Sch.7, para.6). The reasonable costs and expenses of and incidental to obtaining the certificate or certified copy of the judgment and registration are recoverable. Interest on the original judgment runs in accordance with the registered details. Interest on the costs and expenses of and incidental to obtaining this certificate and registration accrues as if they were the subject of an order for costs and expenses made by the High Court on the date of registration of the certificate (see CJJA 1982, s.7; Sch.6, para.8; Sch.7, para.7). The court has a discretion to stay proceedings for enforcement if it is satisfied that a valid challenge to the original judgment has been or will be commenced in the court in which the judgment was originally made (see CJJA 1982, Sch.1, para.38; Sch.6, para.9; Sch.7, para.8; and see further *Petereit v Babcock International Holdings Ltd* [1990] 1 W.L.R. 350). Application for a stay can sometimes take the proceedings into a serpentine maze of hearings before the English court, the judgment court and the Court of Justice of the European Communities (see further, an article by Jonathan Goodliffe, New Law Journal, May 17, 1996, p.717).

Under CJJA 1991, a regime equivalent to that which applies to judgments made in the courts of EU Member States has been introduced for judgments made in the courts of EFTA States who have ratified the Lugano Convention; for a list of the relevant EFTA States, see CJJA 1982, s.1(3) as amended.

ENFORCEMENT OUTSIDE ENGLAND AND WALES

40.018 If a debtor has assets outside the jurisdiction of the English court, the first point to consider is whether the proceedings themselves should be commenced outside the jurisdiction. If proceedings are taken in England, the next point to consider is whether the court for the country in which it is intended to enforce any English judgment will recognise that judgment. Also, what attitude might they take to a default judgment or any judgment made in proceedings in which the defendant took no part?

The statutes, conventions and treaties under which the English High Court registers foreign judgments are, of course, reciprocal. Before approaching the foreign court it will usually be necessary to obtain a certificate of the English judgment from the High Court or county court which awarded it (see r.74, Pt II). Once registered the judgment can be enforced as if it were a judgment of the foreign court.

If there is no reciprocal enforcement procedure in the country concerned then, to enforce an English judgment in such a country, fresh proceedings on the judgment would have to be taken there.

ADVISING THE JUDGMENT DEBTOR

40.019 Solicitors are not often called upon to advise a judgment debtor. However, it would be wrong to think that nothing can be done for such a client. Usually, the most sensible and practical course to take is to negotiate with the judgment creditor for payment of the debt by instalments of a realistic amount. Often, the judgment creditor will insist on taking some steps to protect his interest, for example, he may insist upon obtaining and registering a final charging order, but will then agree that no steps be taken to enforce the order so long as the debt is paid by specified monthly instalments. It is not uncommon for an attachment of earnings order to be obtained by consent, the creditor agreeing not to register the order with the debtor's employer, thus saving possible embarrassment, so long as the debtor voluntarily pays the instalments regularly (see Form N64). Instead of or in addition to negotiating, consider the following points:

(1) Whether there are any grounds for setting the judgment aside; see Ch.43.
(2) In the county court by CCR, Ord.22, r.10, a judgment debtor who is unable to pay the judgment debt forthwith may apply for an instalment order. Alternatively, if the order is already for payment by instalments, he or she may ask the court staff to reduce the instalments. After notifying the creditor, the court staff may make such an order. Either party may then apply for a reconsideration by the district judge. In the High Court the equivalent application is to apply for a stay of execution on terms (see RSC, Ord.45, r.11 and RSC, Ord.47, r.1).

(3) Where two or more attachment of earnings orders are in force. The judgment debtor can apply for a consolidated order and thereafter the sums deducted from his earnings will be apportioned between the creditors entitled thereto. Consolidated attachment of earnings orders may also be made on the application of a creditor, or the employer or indeed without any application, the court staff simply making the arrangements after giving all persons affected an opportunity to submitting written submissions (see generally CCR, Ord.27, r.18 to 22).

(4) A person against whom a judgment has been obtained in the High Court or county court, may apply to the county court for an administration order. A schedule of creditors is prepared detailing the amounts owing to each. The debtor is ordered to pay the total amount due by instalments. The amount received by the court is then apportioned between the creditors in proportion to the amounts due and from time to time the creditors will receive an appropriate remittance. When an administration order has been made, it is not possible for any creditor involved to issue enforcement proceedings. The duty to do this now rests on the court manager (i.e. the Senior Clerk of the Court) making the administration order (see generally CCR, Ord.39). Whilst an administration order is in force, no interest will accrue on county court judgments under the County Courts (Interest on Judgment Debts) Order 1991 (see Art.4(3)).

(5) For a client to petition for his own bankruptcy is a drastic step but, on a rare occasion, it may be appropriate. However, before taking such a step, it is always appropriate to consider whether the debtor should try to put together some voluntary arrangement compounding his debts which is acceptable to the majority of his creditors. To give him time to do so without further threat of proceedings, he may seek a moratorium against enforcement of debts (see para.42.003).

CHAPTER 41

Enforcement of Other Judgments

RECOVERY OF LAND

41.001　Judgments for the recovery of land are enforced in the High Court by a writ of possession and in the county court by a warrant of possession.

Procedure in the High Court is to prepare a praecipe in Form PF88 and the writ of possession itself in Form 66. Except in mortgage possession cases or a case under RSC, Ord.113 the permission of the master or district judge is needed to issue the writ. The application (to which Pt 23 applies) is usually made without notice. Permission will not be granted unless every person in possession of the whole or any part of the land has been given notice sufficient to enable him to apply for any relief to which he is entitled (see generally RSC, Ord.45, r.3). The writ will be executed by the HCEO, using force if necessary. In practice, it is essential for a representative of the claimant to be on hand to receive possession from the HCEO, and it is a sensible precaution to seal up the premises and change the locks immediately thereafter.

The same writ may also direct the HCEO to levy execution on the judgment debtor's goods in respect of any money judgment given in the same action, for example, for mesne profits and costs.

In the county court the claimant cannot apply for enforcement until the date fixed for possession has passed (*Bell v Tuohy* [2002] 1 W.L.R. 2703, CA. In order to enforce he should file in court Form N325 which is a request for the issue of a warrant for possession. In most cases no permission is necessary (see generally CCR, Ord.26, r.17). The absence of any judicial intervention at this stage does not infringe the defendant's ECHR rights (*Southwark LBC v St Brice* [2002] 1 W.L.R. 1537, CA). The warrant is then executed by the court bailiff and, as in the High Court, someone should be present to receive possession of the property. The warrant may also direct the bailiff to levy execution in respect of any money judgment obtained.

Knowingly impeding an officer of the court, such as a bailiff executing a warrant for possession, constitutes a contempt of court punishable by committal (*Bell v Tuohy* [2002] 1 W.L.R. 2703, CA, and, as to committal, see para.41.003).

Recovery of goods

Judgments for the recovery of goods are enforced in the High Court by a writ of delivery and in the county court by a warrant of delivery. The form of enforcement has to comply with the form of judgment. Sometimes the judgment debtor is ordered to return specific goods. Sometimes he is given the option of either returning the goods or paying their value. In either case he usually has to pay damages and costs (and see para.15.008).

41.002

The High Court and county court rules are similar (see generally RSC, Ord.45, r.4; CCR, Ord.26, r.16). Where the judgment is for the delivery of goods without the option of paying their value a writ or warrant directing specific delivery may be issued without permission. This form directs the HCEO or bailiff to cause the goods to be delivered to the claimant. Alternatively the claimant may enforce the judgment by committal or sequestration (see para.40.014).

Where the judgment does give the defendant the option of paying the value of the goods the claimant may obtain:

(1) without permission, an ordinary writ or warrant of delivery: this directs the HCEO or bailiff to cause the goods to be delivered to the claimant, or, if he cannot obtain possession of them, to levy execution for their assessed value; or
(2) if the court so orders (on an application by summons or on notice) a writ or warrant directing specific delivery.

Any writ or warrant may include a clause directing execution of any money judgment the claimant obtained.

Injunctions

Injunctions, both mandatory and prohibitory, can be enforced by committal proceedings (see generally RSC, Ord.52; CCR, Ord.29) and CPR Practice Direction-Committal Proceedings), and by sequestration (in the High Court a writ, in the county court an order; see para.40.014). A mandatory injunction, for example, to take down a wall, may also be enforced by the court directing the claimant to do the act required to be done, and allowing him a money judgment in respect of his expenses so incurred (RSC, Ord.45, r.8; CCA 1984, s.38).

41.003

If an injunction is endorsed with a penal notice (PD 40B, para.9.1) and served on the defendant subsequent disobedience may be punished by an application for committal to prison for contempt of court. In the case of an interim injunction the application can be made under Pt 23. In the case of a final injunction the application must be made by commencing fresh proceedings under Pt 8. The standard of proof which applies is the criminal standard, proof beyond all reasonable doubt (*Dean v Dean* [1987] F.L.R. 517). However, it is not necessary to prove that the disobedience was deliberate (*Gulf Azov Shipping Co. Ltd v Idisi* [2001] EWCA Civ 505). The application must be supported by evidence on affidavit and the application notice or claim form plus copy affidavit must be served on the defendant by way of personal service (see Ch.8). However, in a very exceptional case, procedural defects in service (or other matters) may be waived by the court if satisfied that no injustice has been caused to the respondent by the defect (Practice Direction Committal Proceedings, para.10; *Bell v Taohy* [2002] 1 W.L.R. 2703, CA).

The defendant should attend at the hearing of the application in person (see *Irtelli v Squatriti* [1993] Q.B. 83) and take a full part therein even if the application is under Pt 8 and he has failed to acknowledge service (r.8.4 does not apply: Practice Direction-Committal Proceedings, para.2.5(4)). The court's primary desire is to encourage obedience, not merely punish disobedience. Usually, even if breach of injunction is proved the defendant is, at first, given a stern warning only. He will be sent to prison only if further hearings become necessary. Imprisonment for contempt of court must be for a fixed term (without prejudice to the power of the court to order earlier release). Subject to any specific statutory provision (e.g. Attachment of Earnings Act 1971, s.23; CCA 1984, ss.110 and 118) the maximum period is two years (Contempt of Court Act 1981, s.14; County Courts (Penalties for Contempt) Act 1983, s.1). In *Enfield LBC v Mahoney* [1983] 1 W.L.R. 749 the Court of Appeal considered what should be done in the case of a contemnor who proves to be unshakable in his determination to flout the court's order. Once such a contemnor has been sufficiently punished he should be released if it is clear that further imprisonment will have no coercive effect.

The threat of imprisonment and imprisonment itself may have little coercive effect on a contemnor who is already in prison. In *Raja v Van Hoogstraten* (2002) L.T.L. October 11, a defendant who had previously been sent to prison on serious criminal charges, was carrying on a policy of wilfully disobeying disclosure orders made in a freezing injunction. He was fined £200,000, suspended for 28 days. The fine was set to increase every week by 10 per cent of the previous week's fine until compliance.

An undertaking given to the court in lieu of an injunction is enforceable in the same way as an injunction (*Gandolfo v Gandolfo* [1981] Q.B. 359 and the cases cited therein and CCR Ord.29, 1A).

Masters and district judges have no jurisdiction in contempt proceedings in the High Court. In the county court district judges have jurisdiction in committals in respect of assaults on staff and contempts in the face of the court (CCA 1984, ss.14 and 118) committals under the Attachment of Earnings Act 1971, s.23 and the Protection from Harassment Act 1997, s.3 and to any application for the discharge of a committal order, unless the order in question specifically reserves such applications to a circuit judge (CCR, Ord.29, r.3 and see generally Practice Direction 2—Allocation of Cases to Levels of Judiciary).

Breach of an injunction granted under the Protection from Harassment Act 1997 may amount to a criminal offence. Breach "without reasonable excuse" is punishable with up to five years imprisonment (s.3(6)).

Specific performance

An order for specific performance can be enforced in the same manner as a mandatory injunction. Alternatively, in the case of a defendant who refuses to execute a conveyance or other document the court can appoint some other person to execute it. A conveyance or document so executed is treated for all purposes as if it had been executed by the defendant (SCA 1981, s.39; CCA 1984, s.38). The order may be made at the time specific performance is granted or later on an application to the master or district judge to which Pt 23 applies. It is usual for the master or district judge to be appointed.

41.004

CHAPTER 42

Insolvency

INTRODUCTION

42.001   Every textbook on civil litigation is required to cover at least some aspects of insolvency law. However, these topics never sit easily in such a book. There is too much conflict between the aims of the law of insolvency (which are noble) and the objectives of most creditors (which seem selfish). The law of insolvency deals with and settles problems concerning individuals and companies whose debts cannot be paid as and when they fall due. Its aims are to avoid insolvencies occurring where possible; otherwise to achieve an orderly realisation and distribution of assets for the benefit of all the creditors, to investigate financial delinquencies and frauds in order to remedy them or impose penalties in respect of them as appropriate, and, in the case of individuals only, to provide for the insolvent's rehabilitation in the future (contrast corporate insolvents: they will be dissolved).

None of the aims just listed may seem important to persons who are unlucky enough to have lent money to or otherwise given credit to an individual or company which is now insolvent. A creditor's primary objective is to get his money back, or his invoices paid, as soon as possible and preferably in advance of anyone else who might make similar claims upon the insolvent. It will often be in the creditor's best interest to defeat any "orderly realisation and distribution of assets" by executing a "me first" policy instead.

However, insolvency law does offer one big attraction to creditors. To help them achieve their just ends, payment, it provides them with a sometimes powerful means; the ability to threaten the debtor with social disgrace, the loss of financial reputation and, in the case of companies only, dissolution. "There is, and will always be, stigma and pain associated with bankruptcy" (a quote from the Insolvency Service website: *www.insolvency.gov.uk*). The threat of insolvency proceedings will often induce a debtor to pay up, even if he has to borrow from someone else in order to do so. The use of insolvency law as a threat appears to be an exception to a general rule of civil litigation that you should never make empty threats. A creditor who does threaten to commence insolvency proceedings can in truth add to his threat the following words: "Don't make me do this. It will probably be bad for both of us if I do."

Our aims in this chapter are twofold. We want to provide a short account of the whole of the law of insolvency from start to finish. Whilst so doing we want to describe in greater detail three important procedural matters; the use and service of statutory demands; the procedures by which to challenge statutory demands; and the presentation of petitions. At the end of this chapter (at para.42.022) we list a variety of specialist topics in the law and practice of insolvency proceedings all of which lie beyond the scope of this book. The main purpose of this list is to encourage the beginner to appreciate the complexity of insolvency law.

References to IA 1986 and IR 1986 are respectively references to the Insolvency Act 1986 and the Insolvency Rules 1986. References to PDIP is a reference to the Practice Direction Insolvency Proceedings (*White Book*, vol.2, para.3E–1).

What is insolvency?

The terminology and consequences differ as between individuals and companies. As to winding up a partnership see the Insolvent Partnerships Order 1995. An individual is insolvent as a matter of law when a bankruptcy order is made against him by a court of competent authority. The order brings about a variety of divestings, disabilities and disqualifications unless and until it is rescinded or discharged. An undischarged bankrupt is divested of ownership of assets which belonged to him beneficially before bankruptcy, is disabled from the management of any company (unless the permission of the court is obtained) and may, in certain circumstances, be disqualified from holding certain positions of trust such as being a practising solicitor, member of Parliament, local councillor or magistrate.

42.002

A company is insolvent as a matter of law when a winding-up order is made in respect of it by a court of competent authority. The winding-up order, unless later declared void (see Companies Act 1985, s.651) will lead ultimately to the termination of the company's legal personality and, therefore, existence.

In proceedings commenced by a creditor the court will not make a bankruptcy order or a winding-up order as the case may be unless there is proof in one form or another that the debtor in question is insolvent, i.e. evidence proving or, more usually, giving rise to a presumption that, the debtor is unable to pay his debts, either presently, as they fall due (practical insolvency or negative cash flow) or potentially, taking into account all future and contingent liabilities (balance sheet insolvency).

Although, before making any order, the court looks at facts, the legal concept of insolvency remains separate and independent from the factual concept of insolvency. There are many people who are insolvent in fact but who have never been adjudged to be insolvent, for example, people with debts but no assets at all. Also, because the court will sometimes presume factual insolvency from, for example, failure to pay in compliance with a statutory demand, a person who has assets greatly exceeding his debts could be adjudged insolvent, for example, a wealthy person who wilfully refuses to pay a debt. The fact that the legal concept of insolvency and the factual concept of insolvency may be inconsistent helps explain the relevance of insolvency law to a creditor seeking payment. If the debtor is factually solvent, a creditor who has the means of establishing legal grounds for insolvency proceedings may well threaten the debtor that he will do so unless payment is made. Contrast the case where the debtor is factually insolvent. Here, the creditor will often rush to complete his debt proceedings before any other creditor brings insolvency proceedings. If the debtor is factually insolvent the prospect of somebody else commencing insolvency proceedings threatens debtor and creditor alike.

Insolvency law as an aid to debtors

42.003 An individual or company oppressed by debts may seek help from the law of insolvency in one of two ways. First, the debtor himself may commence the relevant insolvency proceedings so relieving him of the need to continue responding to any debt proceedings already commenced against him. In the case of an individual the making of a bankruptcy order will start the slow process towards rehabilitation. In the case of a company a winding-up order in proceedings commenced by the company is a form of suicide.

The second way in which insolvency law can help debtors is aimed in the opposite direction. The law may give the debtor a moratorium on the enforcement of debts; a breathing space in which to put together some voluntary arrangement acceptable to the majority of the creditors. In the case of an individual, also see county court administration orders and interim orders. The former strictly fall outside the insolvency regime. An order is a mechanism for dealing with an individual with multiple debts to give him respite from enforcement proceedings whilst he pays off his debts. Only an individual with a county court judgment, at least one other debt and total debts of less than £5,000 can apply for such an order. In the case of companies see administration orders and the wide discretion given to the court on hearing a winding-up petition (IA 1986, s.125 and para.42.020).

STATUTORY DEMANDS

42.004 Serving a statutory demand is now the primary method by which a creditor threatens a debtor with bankruptcy or winding-up proceedings as the case may be. The prescribed form of demand gives details of the debt in question and contains a demand that the recipient should "pay the above debt or secure or compound for it to the Creditor's satisfaction". Notes to the form give a warning to the recipient that the demand must be "dealt with" (see below) within 21 days after service or insolvency proceedings may follow. In the case of a demand served upon an individual, the debt in question must equal or exceed £750 (IA 1986, s.267(4)). In the case of a demand served upon a company the debt in question must exceed £750 (IA 1986, s.123). In either case the debt in question must be just that, a debt, not damages. In this context the term "debt" includes a sum payable under a contract or under a judgment where the amount payable is specified by that contact or judgment. If the sum is payable under a contract the creditor should consider whether to serve a statutory demand first or to sue to judgment first. This is considered further at para.42.010.

In the case of a statutory demand served on a company, the debt in question must be immediately payable (IA 1986, s.123 "indebted in a sum exceeding £750 then due"): in the case of a company, only one form of statutory demand is prescribed.

In the case of a statutory demand served on an individual, the debt in question must be unsecured; if some security is held the debt in question is that sum which the creditor is prepared to regard as unsecured and full details must be given of the value which the creditor puts on the security and of the total debt which is alleged by the creditor (IR 1986, r.6.1(5)). In the case of an individual, the debt in question may be a future debt which the debtor appears to have no reasonable prospect of being able to pay. In the case of an individual there are three prescribed forms of statutory demand for a non-judgment debt which is immediately payable, for judgment debts and for future debts. However, a failure to use the correct form will not necessarily invalidate the demand (*Re a Debtor (No.1 of 1987)* [1989] 1 W.L.R. 271 noted at para.42.006).

When completing a statutory demand it is important to check, amongst other things, that it is dated and signed by an individual whose name and (if appropriate) position with or relationship to the creditor is stated. The signing need not be done by the individual named: the form may be signed by, for example, an authorised member of his staff (*Re Horne* [2000] 4 All E.R. 550). The form must also specify the name and address of at least one individual to whom the recipient of the demand may direct any communications concerning it.

Statutory demands are not issued or sealed by a court. It is for the creditor or his advisers to obtain and complete the form and then effect service.

Service and proof of service

In the case of a statutory demand to be served on an individual, personal service (see para.8.002) should be effected if practicable. If it is not practicable, careful study must be made of PDIP, para.11 which gives guidance as to possible alternative methods of service which may be used. If a bankruptcy petition is later issued, proof of service of the statutory demand will be made by an affidavit or witness statement (Forms 6.11 and 6.12). This evidence and a copy of the statutory demand must be filed in court when the bankruptcy petition is issued (IR 1986, r.6.11).

Service of a statutory demand on a company is effected "by leaving it at the company's registered office" (IA 1986, s.123(1)(a)). The statute makes no reference to service by post but it is possible that this method of "leaving" a document at a particular address will be effective (*Re a Company No.008790 of 1990* [1992] B.C.L.C. 561, not following a decision reported in 1985). In practice until the case law becomes more clearly settled, it is safer to ensure that service is effected by a process server. The facts of service will be set out in the winding-up

42.004A

petition and will be proved by a standard form affidavit verifying the petition (see IR 1986, r.4.12).

Responses to a statutory demand

42.005 On receiving a statutory demand the alleged debtor may make one of two responses, i.e. may challenge it or attempt to comply with it. Alternatively, the debtor may make no response, i.e. may attempt to ignore it. The correct method of challenging a statutory demand depends upon whether the recipient of the demand is an individual or a company.

Challenge made by an individual

42.006 In the case of a statutory demand served upon an individual the method of challenge is simple and clear cut; an application in prescribed form plus affidavit or witness statement in support (Form 6.4) made in the appropriate bankruptcy court (as to which see para.42.012 and IR 1986, rr.6.4 and 6.40). The application must be made within 18 days of service of the demand. Unless the court immediately dismisses the application (see IR 1986, r.6.5) it will fix a time and place for a hearing and give notice thereof to the applicant, to the creditor and to the person named as contact in the statutory demand (see above). At that hearing the application may be determined summarily or, if appropriate, it may be adjourned to a later date for which directions may be given.

IR 1986, r.6.5(4) sets out four grounds upon which the statutory demand may be set aside:

> "(a) the debtor appears to have a counterclaim, set-off or cross demand which equals or exceeds the amount of the debt or debts specified in the statutory demand; or
> (b) the debt is disputed on grounds which appear to the court to be substantial; or
> (c) it appears that the creditor holds some security in respect of the debt claimed by the demand, and either Rule 6.1(5) [see para.42.004] is not complied with in respect of it, or the court is satisfied that the value of the security equals or exceeds the full amount of the debt; or
> (d) the court is satisfied, on other grounds, that the demand ought to be set aside."

Grounds (a) and (b) are the grounds most frequently relied on. To obtain a setting aside the applicant need not show more than a genuine triable issue PDIP, para.12.4. The applicant may be entitled to a setting aside even if he does not have a case strong enough to oppose an application for summary judgment. This is because the making of a bankruptcy order is a draconian step. Creditors are not encouraged to abandon the summary judgment procedure in favour of the statutory demand procedure (cf. Re a Company (No.0012209 of 1991) [1992]

1 W.L.R. 351 noted below at para.42.011). In *Re a Debtor (No.490–SD–1991)* [1992] 1 W.L.R. 507 Knox J. Held that there is no "grey area" in statutory demand cases such as exists in summary judgment cases, i.e. cases in which a conditional order will be made (see Ch.19).

Where the statutory demand is made in respect of a judgment debt ground (a) but not ground (b) is available even in respect of matter which could have been raised in the action in which that judgment was obtained; see PDIP, para.12.3 which states:

> "Where a statutory demand is based on a judgment or order, the Court will not at this stage go beyond the judgment or order and enquire into the validity of the debt [save in respect of counterclaims, etc. see para.12.4] nor, as a general rule will it adjourn the application to await the result of an application to set aside the judgment or order."

An exception to this is made in some county court cases where the same district judge can be asked to set aside both the statutory demand and the default judgment upon which it is based. In such a case the court may adjourn the application if it is satisfied that an application to set aside the judgment will in fact be made. Indeed, often, the two applications can be determined at the same subsequent hearing. If an adjournment of the setting aside application is refused the applicant should immediately apply for a stay of execution of the money judgment pending a setting aside application. A stay of execution of the money judgment will prevent the presentation of a bankruptcy petition. However, it is not enough merely to stay the issue of a writ of fi fa: that merely stays one method of enforcement, not the judgment itself.

To establish ground (b) the applicant must show a dispute which extends to the full amount of the debt. If he disputes only part of the debt there can be no setting aside unless he first pays the other part, i.e. the undisputed part of the debt (*Re a Debtor (No.490–SD–1991)* [1992] 1 W.L.R. 507).

As to ground (c) "security" refers to rights over property rather than rights over other persons, such as a guarantor (*Re a Debtor (No.310 of 1988)* [1989] 1 W.L.R. 452). If the court is satisfied that the security is under valued in the statutory demand but its true value is still less than the full amount of the debt, see IR 1986, r.6.5(5).

As to ground (d) it will not suffice for the applicant to show merely technical defects in the statutory demand, such as the misstatement of the true debt or the use of an incorrect form, even where such defects are perplexing. A defective statutory demand will be set aside only if the mistakes made have caused or will cause prejudice to the applicant (*Re a Debtor (No.1 of 1987)* [1989] 1 W.L.R. 271 and *Coulter v Chief Constable of Dorset Police* [2004] EWCA Civ 1259; The Times, October 22, 2004).

A solicitor may serve a statutory demand on a former client for unpaid fees, even within one month of delivering the bill (*Re a Debtor (No.88 of 1991)* [1993] Ch.286). However, it will usually be unwise to do so. The demand will be set aside if there is a genuine dispute as to quantum or if there is a genuine allegation of negligence unless, for example, a sum of costs exceeding £750 is undisputed (*Re a Debtor (Nos 49 and 50 of 1992)* [1995] Ch.66.

Do not serve a statutory demand in respect of a judgment debt which is over six years old; consider instead resurrecting enforcement proceedings in the original action (see *Re a Debtor (No.50A–SD–1995)* [1997] Ch.310 and see Ch.40).

An application for setting aside which is made within the 18–day time limit will prevent the creditor from presenting a bankruptcy petition in respect of that statutory demand unless and until the application is dismissed (IR 1986, r.6.4(3) and r.6.5(6)). If the 18–day deadline has expired the recipient of the statutory demand can apply for an extension of time together with (if necessary) an injunction restraining the presentation of a bankruptcy petition (see further PDIP, para.12.5).

If an order setting aside a statutory demand is made penalty orders for costs may be made against the creditor or his advisers (*cf. Re a Company (No.0012209 of 1991)* [1992] 1 W.L.R. 351, noted below). As to consent orders granting dismissing, or withdrawing applications, see PDIP, para.16.3.

If the court refuses to set aside a statutory demand and a petition is later issued, the debtor cannot re-argue on that petition the same issues visited in the set aside application unless there is a real change of circumstances (*Turner v Royal Bank of Scotland PLL* (2000) L.T.L., June 30).

Challenge made by a company

42.007 In the case of a statutory demand served upon a company the method of challenge which the company may adopt is to apply for an injunction restraining the presentation of a petition, or, if already presented, restraining the advertisement of that petition. The injunction will be granted if it appears that: (1) the company has some prospect of defeating the claim made against it; and (2) the company is solvent. If both of these matters are proved the creditor may be ordered to pay costs on an indemnity basis (see Ch.38). The reason for awarding costs on this exceptional basis is explained in two cases *Re a Company (No.00122209 of 1991)* [1992] 1 W.L.R. 351 and *Re a Company (No.006798 of 1995)* [1996] 1 W.L.R. 491. In the latter case a wasted costs order (see Ch.39) was also made against the petitioner's solicitor.

It seems to me that a tendency has developed . . . to present petitions against solvent companies as a way of putting pressure on them to make payments of money which is bona fide disputed rather than to invoke the procedures which the rules provide for summary judgment . . . [If a solvent company has no grounds at all for refusing to pay a debt or] if the court comes to the conclusion that a solvent company is not putting forward any defence in good faith and is merely seeking to take for itself credit which it is not allowed under the contract, then the court would not be inclined to restrain presentation of the petition. But if, as in this case, it appears that the defence has a prospect of success and the company is solvent, then I think that the court should give the company the benefit of the doubt and not do anything which would encourage the use of the Companies Court as an alternative to the RSC, Ord.14 procedure [see now CPR, Pt 24].

For these reasons the injunction will go. The basis upon which the injunction is granted is that presentation of the petition is an abuse of the process of the court. I think that it should be made clear that abuse of the petition procedure in these circumstances is a high risk strategy, and consequently I think the appropriate order is that [the party who threatened to present a petition] should pay the company's costs on an indemnity basis (*Re a Company (No.0012209 of 1991)* [1992] 1 W.L.R. 351 per Hoffman J.).

If the company allows the petition to be advertised then there is a serious danger that the damage that will be done to the company by the advertisement will far outweigh any commercial advantage in disputing a genuinely disputed debt. Those facts lead to the opportunity for abuse. The presentation of the petition, or the threat to present the petition, imposes on the company a commercial pressure which is different in kind from the issue of a claim form. It is of course that opportunity to exert commercial pressure which leads to the creditor's decision to present a petition rather than to take proceedings in the official referees' corridor [now named the Technology and Construction Court, see Ch.24] (*Re a Company (No.006798 of 1995)* [1996] 1 W.L.R. 491 per Chadwick J.).

An injunction will not be granted if the genuine dispute relates only to part of the debt alleged, unless the company pays off the undisputed part (*Re Trinity Insurance Ltd* [1990] B.C.C. 235).

Will inaccuracies in a statutory demand served upon a company invalidate that demand? As yet there is no English case law on the point. It is possible that a stricter attitude will be taken in respect of mistakes made in statutory demands served upon companies than is taken in the case of statutory demands served upon individuals (as to which see para.42.004).

Complying with a statutory demand

If the recipient of the statutory demand (whether an individual or a company) pays up within the three weeks specified then, presumably, the matter is at an end as between the parties involved. The statutory demand also invites the recipient to "secure or compound for the debt to the Creditor's satisfaction" and it also identifies an individual to whom any communication regarding the demand may be sent. A creditor who rejects a reasonable offer to secure or compound the debt will not be able to prove his grounds for insolvency proceedings (IA 1986, s.271(3) and s.125 as to which see para.42.018). A debtor seeking to compound his debt with one creditor may also seek to make a voluntary arrangement (see p.613) with all his creditors; as to making an offer to compound which is also a proposal to enter a voluntary arrangement, see *Re a Debtor (No.2389 of 1989)* [1991] Ch.326. In considering whether an offer is reasonable the creditor, and later perhaps the court, should take into account the amounts promised, the prospects of that promise being kept and the history of any previous promises made (and see further Muir Hunter on Personal Insolvency, para.3–095/1).

42.008

If in compliance with the demand the debtor makes payments reducing his debt to £750 or below (if a company) or below £750 (if an individual) the creditor will not be entitled to bring or pursue insolvency proceedings based on that statutory demand (*Re Patel* [1986] 1 W.L.R. 221).

No response to a statutory demand

42.009 If the recipient of the statutory demand fails to make any response at all the creditor may, after expiry of 21 days, commence bankruptcy proceedings or winding-up proceedings as the case may be. However, if he does so, the alleged debtor has full right to defend those proceedings on the basis that he does not owe any money to the creditor. A failure to respond to the statutory demand does not give rise to any implied admission of indebtedness.

A failure to respond to the statutory demand does, however, have some adverse consequences for a debtor who is an individual. He cannot defeat the petition merely by quibbling about the amount of his indebtedness. A bankruptcy petition cannot be dismissed solely upon the ground that the debt was over-stated in the demand unless, within 21 days of service of the demand the debtor "gave notice" to the creditor disputing the validity of the demand on that ground [or] "paid the correct amount" (IR 1986, r.6.25(3)).

Demand first or sue to judgment first?

42.010 How should you advise a client wishing to commence proceedings in respect of a debt? Is it best for that client to threaten insolvency proceedings first? The threat alone often produces payment. But what dangers are there in making this threat? If it does not produce payment, should you carry out the threat?

Alternatively, is it best to commence debt proceedings? The letter before claim may produce payment. If it does not, any debt proceedings commenced will probably end in a default judgment and the services of sheriff's officers or bailiffs can be employed. What are the dangers in suing to judgment first?

In the further alternative, is it safe to serve either a statutory demand or a letter before claim? In some cases the use of either procedure may lead to the immediate disposal and/or concealment of known assets. In this sort of case the creditor should consider applying without notice for a freezing injunction (see further para.27.015).

There are no easy answers to the questions we have posed. There are many factors to be taken into account and their relative importance in any particular case may be difficult or even impossible to gauge. The tables set out on pp.655 to 658 indicate our opinions on three matters:

(1) The advantages and disadvantages of adopting the insolvency route or the debt route.
(2) Factors to take instructions upon before advising the client.

(3) A list of cases in which we say that the insolvency route must not be used.

Some of the points made are matters of opinion and some people may not share the opinions which we express. Also, the text set out in the tables is not exhaustive of all the matters which may have to be taken into account in any particular case; it is provided by way of introduction to a complex topic.

PERSONAL INSOLVENCY: BANKRUPTCY

Grounds for a creditor's petition

A creditor to whom the debtor owes £750 or more is entitled to present a bankruptcy petition in three circumstances. If the debtor has failed to comply with a statutory demand and the time allowed for doing so has now expired (IA 1986, s.268). If the debt is payable under a judgment and execution or other process has been issued to enforce that judgment, but has been returned unsatisfied (also IA 1986, s.268). Or, where a voluntary arrangement has been made which binds the creditor, if the debtor has, amongst other things, failed to comply with his obligations under that arrangement or has given false or misleading information (IA 1986, s.276).

42.011

Presentation of bankruptcy petition

The appropriate court in which to commence proceedings is defined in IR 1986, r.6.9. Usually it will be the court for the district in which the debtor has resided or carried on business for the longest period during the previous six months. In the London insolvency district the appropriate court will be the High Court and the proceedings will be issued out of the Bankruptcy Registry which forms part of the Chancery Division. Outside London it will be a county court which has bankruptcy jurisdiction for the relevant area. Special provision is made for proceedings brought against non-resident or untraced debtors (London) petitions issued by a minister of the Crown or a government department (also London) and petitions issued whilst a voluntary arrangement is in force (see IR 1986, r.6.9(4A)).

42.012

Before issuing a petition it is advisable and normally essential to commission a Land Charges Search against the name of the debtor and also to inquire of the relevant court whether any interim order has been made or whether any application to set aside a relevant statutory demand has been made.

To what extent, if at all, will a bankruptcy petition based upon a judgment debt be affected by any stay of execution in the action in which that judgment was given? If there is a general stay of execution, for example, pending an appeal, the judgment debt is not "payable" and so a bankruptcy petition should not be issued in respect of it. However, if as is more usual, there is a stay of execution only under RSC, Ord.47, r.1 (i.e. stay of execution by writ of fi fa) a bankruptcy petition can be issued but is likely to be adjourned so long as the stay persists.

There are four prescribed forms of bankruptcy petition. The most frequently used is the form for use in the case of non-compliance with a statutory demand concerning a debt immediately payable. The other forms are for use in cases of non-compliance with a statutory demand concerning a future debt, or an unsatisfied judgment, or default concerning an approved voluntary arrangement. Useful guidance on drafting petitions is given in PDIP, para.15. You should prepare at least four forms of petition; one for the court, one for service, one to be exhibited to an affidavit of service and the fourth for your own file.

The following documentation must be lodged at court on presentation (i.e. issue).

(1) Three forms of petition: the court keeps one and seals the other two.
(2) An extra form of petition if it is based upon default concerning an approved voluntary arrangement; this is for service on the supervisor of the arrangement and will be sealed by the court.
(3) If the petition is based upon non-compliance with a statutory demand, a prescribed form of affidavit of service of the demand exhibiting a copy of it.
(4) An affidavit in prescribed form verifying the petition; as to who should be the deponent see IR 1986, r.6.12.
(5) The court fee.
(6) The deposit payable in respect of the Official Receiver's fee (currently £370; Insolvency Fees Order 1986, Art.9).

On issue the court office will insert the time, date and place of the hearing, register a pending action against the name of the respondent, "the debtor", in the Land Charges Department and transmit the deposit paid in respect of the Official Receiver's fee.

IR 1986, r.6.14 requires personal service upon the debtor (whether by the court, the petitioning creditor or his agent) and, as to (2) above postal service on the supervisor (by the petitioning creditor or his agent). If necessary an order for substituted service (see further PDIP, para.11.4) can be obtained. Service must be effected (usually) at least 14 days before the hearing date and an affidavit of service exhibiting a sealed copy of the petition must be filed in court immediately after service (forms are prescribed).

If the petition is not served an application for an extension of time for service must be made prior to the hearing date, and you should at the same time get a new hearing date. If, unluckily for you, you make your application on the original hearing date you will pay a larger court fee and you will get no costs of the hearing.

The debtor's responses

The debtor's response, or lack of response, to the service of petition will affect any subsequent hearing of the petition. The debtor may: 42.013

(1) Pay off the debt. If despite payment the petition goes to a hearing (see IR 1986, r.6.32 and see below as to consent orders) the petition will be dismissed unless another creditor properly applies to be substituted as petitioner (see IR 1986, rr.6.30 and 6.31).
(2) Offer to compound the debt. Any such offer must be carefully considered. If it is refused the petitioner's solicitor should seek to gather evidence demonstrating that such refusal is reasonable (see further below). The court may dismiss the petition if offers are unreasonably refused. If the offer is accepted see PDIP, para.16.3 as to obtaining consent orders.
(3) Apply for an interim order. This would give the debtor a moratorium, a breathing space in which to put together some voluntary arrangement acceptable to the majority of creditors. An interim order will stay the bankruptcy proceedings, and other proceedings (IA 1986, s.252). Even an application for an interim order may lead to a stay (IA 1986, s.254).
(4) File notice of intention to oppose the petition. A form of notice is prescribed. It should be filed at least seven days before the hearing and a copy must be served upon the petitioner or his solicitor (IR 1986, r.6.21). For example, if the petition is based upon non-compliance with a statutory demand the debtor may wish to raise a triable defence to the allegation of debt. He is not precluded from doing so merely because he did not apply to set aside the statutory demand. However, if he did so apply, but was unsuccessful he cannot re-argue the same issues again unless there has been a real change of circumstances (Turner v Royal Bank of Scotland PLC (2000) L.T.L. June 30).
(5) Make no response. This does not in fact preclude him from raising any objection at the hearing.

Hearing of bankruptcy petition

The petition is heard by a bankruptcy registrar (High Court, London) or a district judge (county court). Usually only the petitioner or his solicitor will attend although, of course, the debtor may, as may any creditor who has given prior notice to the petitioner or to whom the court grants permission. Bankruptcy petitions are not advertised (contrast winding-up petitions) and therefore creditors who do not make credit searches (unlike banks and some credit agencies) will not normally know of the petition unless, for example, they have been contacted by the debtor in an attempt to put together some voluntary arrangement. 42.014

As to evidence, the petition and service thereof are proved by affidavits already filed. In order to prove that the debt is still outstanding the court will normally accept a certificate signed by the person representing the petitioner. The text of the certificate is set out in PDIP, para.15.9. In London the certificate is printed on the attendance slips and must be filed after the hearing. A fresh certificate is required at every adjourned hearing. The petitioner may also adduce evidence in relation to any issues raised by the debtor (see responses (2), (4) and (5) above). The court is willing to investigate a judgment debt upon which a petition is based if it is shown that the judgment was obtained by fraud, collusion or represents a miscarriage of justice (*Dawodu v American Express* [2001] B.P.I.R. 983, Etherton J.).

At the hearing the petition may be dismissed or adjourned. Alternatively, a bankruptcy order may be made. The order requires the debtor to attend before the Official Receiver. In practice, the court will also contact the Official Receiver's office by telephone. That office will then register the bankruptcy order in the Land Charges Department and will advertise the order in the London Gazette and in a newspaper. As to the possibility of postponing publicity, for example, pending an appeal, see IR 1986, r.6.34.

Effect of bankruptcy on enforcement procedures in other actions

42.015 The commencement of bankruptcy proceedings gives a power to stay any pending actions against the debtor: the power is exercisable by the bankruptcy court or by the court in which the action is pending (if different). After the making of a bankruptcy order any person claiming that the bankrupt owes them any debt or liability must, instead of commencing or pursuing litigation, prove in the bankruptcy unless given permission to the contrary (see generally IA 1986, s.285). A claimant who does not learn of the bankruptcy order until after he has commenced his action may be given retrospective leave to commence proceedings (*Re Saunders (A Bankrupt)* [1997] Ch.60).

Contrast the position of a litigant who had already obtained judgment against the debtor. He is entitled to keep the benefits of any enforcement procedures taken so long as the enforcement in question was "completed" before the date of the bankruptcy order (see generally IA 1986, ss.278 and 346). Execution against goods is completed by seizure and sale and (usually) the expiry of a further fourteen days unless, before that deadline, the sheriff or bailiff is given notice of a bankruptcy petition already presented. Execution against land is completed by seizure or by the appointment of a receiver or the making of a charging order. However, as to charging orders, note that, in the case of an order nisi the enforcement court may later refuse to make the order absolute. Attachment of a debt is completed by receipt of the debt.

Procedure following the bankruptcy order

42.016 On the making of a bankruptcy order the bankrupt is deprived of the power to deal with any property beneficially belonging to him. The Official Receiver is constituted trustee of the bankrupt's estate until such time as another trustee in bankruptcy is appointed. The Official Receiver's function is to protect the estate and commence investigations into the conduct and affairs of the bankrupt. He must also summon a creditor's meeting for the purpose of appointing a trustee (unless the value of the estate is too small to justify such a step). The bankrupt must collaborate fully with the Official Receiver, must deliver up all property including books, papers and records and must complete a Statement of Affairs in the prescribed forms supplied by the Official Receiver. In certain very limited circumstances the bankrupt can apply for an annulment of the bankruptcy order. Subject to that, it is too late now for the bankrupt to seek to set aside a default judgment upon which the petition was founded (*Sebuliba v Dagenham Motors* (2002) L.T.L., November 12). The task of applying for the set aside, if it is appropriate, falls to the Official Receiver or the trustee.

Ultimately all the bankrupt's estate will be collected in, sold and the proceeds distributed. This includes the bankrupt's home if it belongs to him or belongs to him jointly with another person, for example, his spouse. Unless the circumstances are exceptional the maximum period of delay before sale will be one year from the date of the bankruptcy order.

Certain chattels such as tools, clothing, bedding, etc. are exempt from the estate vesting in the trustee (the list is the same as that given on para.40.004 concerning execution against goods). The bankrupt is also entitled to keep any income received after bankruptcy subject, however, to the effect of any "income payments order" which may be made by the court on the application of the trustee. As to after-acquired property, such as a legacy, the trustee has 42 days in which to claim it after receiving notice of it from the bankrupt. The claim is made by notice under IA 1986, s.307 the service of which automatically vests the property in the trustee.

In the case of most bankrupts, unless they commit some breach or default in the obligations imposed upon them to assist the Official Receiver and trustee, the bankruptcy order will be discharged 12 months after the date upon which it was made. Usually the discharge is automatic, i.e. no court order is necessary. To obtain formal evidence of discharge in such a case the court will if requested issue a certificate of discharge. Also the discharged bankrupt may, at his own expense, require the Official Receiver to advertise the discharge in the London Gazette and in a newspaper. Discharge releases the former bankrupt from liability in respect of most bankruptcy debts and may bring to an end the disqualifications and disabilities previously imposed (see para.42.001). However, it has no effect on the functions of the trustee or upon the bankrupt's obligation to assist the trustee. More time may be needed before a final distribution can be made to the creditors who have proved in the bankruptcy.

If, the Official Receiver decides that the bankrupt has been dishonest either before or during the bankruptcy or that he is otherwise to blame for his position, the Official Receiver can apply to the court for a Bankruptcy Restrictions Order ("BRO"). The court may make a BRO against a bankrupt for between two and 15 years and this order will mean that the bankrupt continues to be subject to the restrictions of bankruptcy described above. See further PDIP para.16A and an article by D.J. Exton in the *Law Society's*

Gazette on October 26, 2006 (103/41). To avoid court proceedings the bankrupt can give a bankruptcy restrictions undertaking which will have the same effect as a BRO.

CORPORATE INSOLVENCY: WINDING UP

Grounds for a creditor's petition

42.017   There are seven grounds upon which a company may be wound up (IA 1986, s.122). The ground most important to most creditors is ground (f) "the company is unable to pay its debts". This ground is defined in IA 1986, s.123. Leaving aside references to steps taken in Scotland or Northern Ireland, this section indicates four ways in which ground (f) may be established.

(1) Non-compliance with a statutory demand served by the petitioner (see para.42.004).
(2) Unsatisfied judgment debt upon which the petitioner has sought enforcement.
(3) Other evidence of inability to pay debts as they fall due (i.e. practical insolvency or negative cash flow).
(4) Evidence that the company's assets are less than its liabilities, present, contingent and prospective (i.e. balance sheet insolvency).

Presentation of winding-up petition

42.018   Most winding-up petitions are issued out of the High Court, Chancery Division, (the so-called "Companies Court") either in London or in one of the eight Chancery District Registries. The jurisdiction of the High Court at any of these offices is unlimited in all respects, value and territorial. A relatively small number of petitions are issued out of county courts. Not all of them have jurisdiction; none of the London county courts have. Even if the county court has jurisdiction, that jurisdiction is limited in value (share capital paid up or credited as paid up not exceeding £120,000) and is limited territorially (the registered office of the company must be situated in the district of the court; see generally IA 1986, s.117).

Is a winding up petition "an action upon a judgment" for the purposes of s.24 of the Limitation Act 1980 such that it is subject to the six year limitation period? No, held the Court of Appeal in *Ridgeway Motors (Isleworth) Ltd v ALTS Ltd* [2005] EWCA Civ 92; [2005] 2 All E.R. 304.

Before issuing a petition it is vital to effect a search of the Central Index of Petitions which is maintained by the Companies Court in London. It may be that a petition has already been issued by another person.

The prescribed form of winding-up petition is very brief. You should prepare at least four forms of petition; one for the court, one for service, one to be exhibited to an affidavit of service and one for your own file. The following documentation should be lodged at court on presentation (i.e. issue).

(1) Three forms of petition: the court keeps one and seals and returns the other two.
(2) Additional copies of the petition for service upon any administrator, administrative receiver or supervisor of a voluntary arrangement, who has been appointed or any liquidator appointed if the company is already in voluntary liquidation (and see further examples concerning companies authorised within the meaning of the Banking Act 1987: IR 1986, r.4.7). These copies also are sealed and returned to the petitioner.
(3) A prescribed form of affidavit verifying the petition (as to who should be the deponent see IR 1986, r.4.12).
(4) The court fee.
(5) The deposit payable in respect of the Official Receiver's fee.

On issue the court will allocate a hearing date, usually about six weeks ahead so as to allow time for the petitioner to effect service and advertisement.

The petitioner must arrange service of the petition; ideally, personal service at the registered office of the company, on a director or other officer or employee (and see further IR 1986, r.4.8). An affidavit of service in prescribed form must be filed immediately after service and any additional copies of the petition required (see (2) above) must be sent to the office holder in question on the next business day following the day on which the petition was served on the company.

In order to notify any other creditors of the date fixed for the hearing of the petition, the petitioner must arrange an advertisement in prescribed form in (usually) the London Gazette. The effect of such publicity may be devastating to the financial reputation of the company and any related companies and also the company's bank is likely to freeze its accounts with the company. Because this is so there are fixed time limits within which the advertisement must be made; not less than seven business days after service on the company and not more than seven business days before the hearing (as to the meaning of business day in this context see para.1.018 and IR 1986, r.4.11 and r.13.13). On being served with a petition, or indeed with a statutory demand, the company may seek an injunction restraining the advertisement if it considers that the presentation of the petition is/would be an abuse of the process of the court (see further para.42.007).

Certificate of compliance

At least five days before the hearing the petitioner's solicitor must file in court a prescribed form certifying that the rules relating to service and advertisement have been complied with. At about the same time the solicitor should consider

42.019

preparing and getting instructions upon a list of the names and addresses of persons who have given notice of their intention to appear at the hearing. The prescribed form of list also shows which creditors in the list will support the petition and which will oppose it. The list should be filed with the court office on the Friday before the hearing. We recommend getting instructions as to it some days earlier because it is possible that some creditors will have given notice to the petitioner directly rather than to the solicitor.

Hearing of winding-up petition

42.020 In the High Court, the hearing will take place in open court before the registrar (London) or district judge unless it is opposed in which case it will be listed as adjourned for hearing before a High Court judge. If the company intends to oppose the petition it should file its affidavit in opposition and send a copy to the petitioner, not less than seven days before the hearing. Any hearing which is not ready for determination may be adjourned but the court is reluctant to allow many or substantial adjournments because of the deleterious effect which the proceedings usually have on the company's ability to trade. Adjournments do not involve further advertisement unless the court so orders.

IA 1986, s.125 gives the court a wide discretion to dismiss, adjourn, grant interim relief or make any other order it thinks fit. The petition may be dismissed if substantial errors in procedure have been made, or if no grounds can be established or if the majority of the creditors oppose the petition. Also in an appropriate case the court may order that another creditor be substituted as petitioner if, for example, the petitioner fails to appear or no longer seeks a winding up.

If a winding-up order is made the court forthwith gives notice to the Official Receiver who must, amongst other things, notify the registrar of companies and arrange for the order to be advertised in the London Gazette and in a newspaper.

Effect of a winding-up order

42.021 The winding up of a company is deemed to commence, i.e. the operation of a winding-up order is backdated to, the time of presentation of the petition, or, if the company was then already in voluntary liquidation, to the time when the resolution for winding up was passed (see generally IA 1986, s.129). This doctrine of relating back explains why the petition has to be advertised, and why the petition may have such a devastating effect on the company's business. It upsets any contracts entered into, any dispositions of assets made or any enforcement proceedings "completed" (see para.42.015) since the earlier date.

After the making of a winding-up order no action against the company can be commenced or continued unless the court grants permission (IA 1986, s.130).

The procedures following the order (investigations, realisation of assets and distribution amongst creditors) are largely the same as the procedures following the making of a bankruptcy order. There are however three major differences. The person appointed by the creditors to conduct the winding up is called the liquidator (the Official Receiver is the liquidator until such appointment). The liquidator acts as agent of the company with, for example, a power of sale; legal title to company assets is not usually transferred to him. Thirdly, the final stages of winding up are not discharge (rehabilitation of a defaulter), but dissolution (death of the company).

Specialist topics in insolvency law and practice

    Personal insolvency: bankruptcy   42.022
    Secured debts
    Future debts
    Individual Voluntary Arrangements
    Fast Track Voluntary Arrangements
    Cases with a foreign element
    Recognition of insolvency proceedings taken elsewhere in the EC
    Summary administration of small bankruptcies
    Death or disability of the debtor
    Death or removal of the trustee
    Powers and duties of the trustees
    Remuneration and costs
    Preferential and deferred debts and claims
    Proof of debts
    Disclaimers, etc.
    Setting aside or adjusting prior transactions including fraudulent transactions and voidable preferences
    Interim receivership
    Insolvent partnerships
    Second bankruptcy
    Criminal bankruptcy
    Discharge of orders
    Annulment or rescission of orders

Corporate insolvency: winding-up proceedings

    Administration   42.023
    Administrative receivership
    Company Voluntary Arrangements
    Moratoriums under the Insolvency Act 2000
    Winding up foreign companies
    Insolvency under EC Regulation 1346/2000
    Death, release, removal, etc. of liquidator
    Powers and duties of liquidators
    Remuneration and costs
    Proof of debts
    Preferential and deferred debts and claims

Provisional liquidators
Special managers
Secured creditors' rights
Disclaimers, etc.
Malpractice before and during liquidation
Setting aside or adjusting prior transactions including fraudulent transactions and voidable preferences
Company Directors Disqualification Act 1986
Compulsory winding up after commencement of voluntary winding up
Rescission of winding-up orders
Dissolution of company
Restoration to the register

Table 1: Threatening and/or suing: advantages and disadvantages

Route taken	Advantages	Disadvantages
Insolvency, *i.e.* statutory demand to be followed by petition in the case of non-payment	1 Imposes the maximum threat pressure upon most debtors 2 Only minimal costs are incurred if the statutory demand produces payment 3 The creditor can change to the debt route (see below) if the statutory demand does not produce payment 4 Enables the trustee or liquidator to reopen fraudulent or other transactions previously made and to commence various types of misfeasance proceedings against the debtor, directors agents, etc.	1 May cause the hard pressed debtor to commence insolvency proceedings himself and/or seek a moratorium 2 Heavy costs penalty if recipient successfully challenges the demand or gets a subsequent petition dismissed 3 Presenting a petition usually kills any chance of the debtor arranging a loan to pay off this creditor 4 Insolvency proceedings are expensive and in practice the costs may not be fully recoverable by the petitioner 5 The existence of secured creditors, and creditors with priority debts may leave little for distribution to the unsecured creditors 6 The equality of treatment accorded to all unsecured creditors (whether petitioners or not) may reduce the amount recoverable by the petitioner

Route taken	Advantages	Disadvantages
Debts, *i.e.* letter of claim to be followed if necessary by a claim form, entry of judgment, and execution thereof	1 A letter of claim carries some threat pressure 2 If the debtor is factually insolvent, proceedings in debt may bring the claimant full repayment in advance of (and possibly at the expense of) other creditors 3 This is the safest route where the creditor suspects that the debtor will dispute any proceedings taken against him	1 Low threat pressure makes it more likely that litigation will have to be commenced 2 This route may become slow and expensive if the debtor vigorously defends and/or seeks to set aside any default judgment or unopposed summary judgment obtained 3 Litigation costs incurred may be wasted because of conflicting proceedings, *e.g.* execution of judgments obtained by other creditors, insolvency proceedings and/or a moratorium

Table 2: Threatening and/or suing: factors upon which instructions are needed

1	What assets does the debtor have?	If none, neither route is worthwhile except perhaps the making of a threat if it causes the debtor to borrow
2	What other creditors are there?	Information is needed on the number of creditors, the size of their debts, and the likelihood of them bringing conflicting proceedings, and their position in the pecking order relative to your client (*i.e.* whether their debts are secured or rank in priority). If your client's chances are likely to be postponed or swamped, are there any particular assets (see above) which you can identify and attack via the debt route? Speed is essential: you may get only one chance
3	What information is there as to fraudulent and other transactions which may be reopened?	Usually such proceedings are not practicable unless and until insolvency proceedings have been commenced and appropriate orders made therein
4	Is it appropriate to seek a freezing injunction?	Can the creditor (*a*) show a good arguable case, (*b*) sufficiently identify assets belonging to the debtor and (*c*) show that there is a real risk that the debtor will try to arrange the dissipation or secretion of assets so as to frustrate any litigious remedies the creditor may obtain?
5	Are there any alternative remedies available?	*e.g.* under *Romalpa* clauses in the case of sale of goods, or remedies of forfeiture or distress in the case of non-payment of rent

Table 3: When not to use insolvency proceedings

Don't use a statutory demand if:
1 The claim is not a debt claim (*e.g.* it is a claim for damages)
2 The debtor has a triable defence to the claim
3 You do not know or are not sure whether the debtor has a triable defence to the claim
4 The undisputed debt is £750 or less (companies) or less than £750 (individuals)
5 Immediate protection in the form of a freezing injunction is appropriate
Don't present a petition if:
1 The debtor is making a genuine attempt to borrow to repay this debt
2 Someone else has already commenced proceedings (see below paras 42.016 and 42.024)
3 Your purpose in doing so is merely to increase the threat pressure. The remedy claimed in a bankruptcy petition or winding-up order is in effect a class remedy for the benefit of all creditors. Therefore the proceedings may continue even after your debt is paid. Indeed a main purpose of the subsequent proceedings may be to reclaim that payment. A petitioner needs permission to withdraw a petition. Instead of granting permission the court may make an order putting some other creditor into the petitioner's place. If subsequently the petition is successful the payment to the original petitioner may then be avoided (see generally, *Smith v Ian Simpson & Co.* [2001] Ch. 239).

CHAPTER 43

Applications to Set Aside or Vary Orders

43.001 We are not concerned in this chapter with the power of a higher court to set aside or vary the judgment or order of a lower court. Instead we consider in what circumstances a party affected by an order can apply or reapply to the court which made it asking that court to set aside or vary it. Although we have sought to classify various examples under the following headings, these headings are not mutually exclusive. Some examples could be placed under more than one heading.

ORDERS MADE IN THE ABSENCE OF ONE PARTY

43.002 Rule 23.10 applies to orders made in interim applications. A party served with such an order who was not served with a copy of the application notice may apply to the court for the order to be set aside or varied if he makes his application within seven days of being served with the order (r.23.10(2)) or within such extended time as the court may permit him (r.3.1(2)(a)).

Rule 23.11 applies to orders made on interim applications where the applicant or respondent fails to attend the hearing. The court may proceed in his absence but may later, on application or of its own initiative, re-list the application. Similarly, wherever the courts makes an order of its own initiative (r.3.3) or an interim order without a hearing (PD 23, para.11(2)) a party affected by that order has the right to apply to have it set aside, varied or stayed, and, indeed, the order must contain a statement of that right (r.3.3(5)(b)). Orders made without notice or without a hearing are essentially provisional orders only, one or more parties not having had a full opportunity to make submissions or adduce evidence.

Rule 39.3 deals with the failure of a party to attend the trial. The court may proceed in the absence of one party or may make an order striking out the claim, counterclaim or defence of the absentee, or, if no one attends, strike out the whole proceedings. An application may later be made for an order setting aside any orders made at trial and/or restoring the proceedings. The Rule contemplates a trial in the absence of a party who has been served with proceedings under the rules (including deemed service) or in respect of whom service has been dispensed with (see Ch.8). It does not apply to applications to set aside judgments "irregularly" obtained, in the sense of being obtained without service of the claim form in accordance with the rules. As to the latter see para.15.014.

An application under r.39.3 must be supported by evidence showing that the applicant:

> "(a) acted promptly when he found out that the court had exercised its power to strike out or to enter judgment or make an order against him;
> (b) had a good reason for not attending the trial; and
> (c) has a reasonable prospect of success at the trial" (r.39.3(5)).

As to (b), in *Estate Acquisitions and Development Ltd v Wiltshire* [2006] EWCA Civ 533, *The Times*, June 12, 2006, Dyson L.J. stated:

> "if the reason for a party's non-attendance is that he did not know that the hearing was taking place on the day when it did take place, it will usually be necessary to ask why the party was not aware that the hearing was taking place on that day . . . .. The mere assertion that the party was unaware of the hearing date is unlikely to be sufficient to constitute a good reason. It will usually be relevant to inquire whether the party was aware that proceedings had been issued and served. Once a party is aware that proceedings have been served, he knows that it is likely that steps will be taken in the proceedings and that there will be a hearing or hearings. Unless he has nominated a solicitor to act on his behalf, he must be taken to expect to receive communications personally from the opposing party and/or the court. These will include notifications of hearing dates. If he does not have a system in place for ensuring that such communications are received by him, he is unlikely to be able to rely on the absence of such a system to say that he had a good reason for not attending the hearing.
> Similarly, if a party is aware that proceedings are imminent and he has not established a system for ensuring, so far as practicable, that communications relating to the impending litigation are received by him. It will be particularly difficult for a party to argue that he had a good reason for not attending if the court concludes that he deliberately avoided receiving such communications in order to frustrate the litigation process.
> But what if a party is unaware of the existence or imminence of proceedings and he does not have a system in place to ensure that documents relating to litigation are brought to his notice? Mr Blaker [counsel for the claimant] submits that the fact that the party is unaware of the existence or imminence of litigation is irrelevant. The mere fact that he does not have in place a system which will, so far as practicable, ensure that documents relating to litigation are brought to his notice is of itself determinative of the question whether he had good reason for not being aware of, and therefore not attending, a hearing date fixed in the course of such proceedings. I do not agree . . . A person is under no obligation to make him-

self amenable to potential claims of which he has no notice. It must follow that, if he fails to attend a hearing in proceedings of which he is unaware, he has a good reason for failing to attend."

If an applicant satisfies conditions (a) and (b) above, it appears that the burden may pass to the respondent to demonstrate (c) that the applicant has no reasonable prospect of succeeding at trial: see *Gaydamak v UBS Bahamas Ltd* [2006] UKPC 8, *The Times*, March 7, 2006.

Finally under this heading consider default judgments in respect of which rules specifically provide for applications to set aside or vary: Pt 13, setting aside or varying default judgments (see Ch.15) and r.47.12, setting aside default cost certificates (see Ch.38).

ORDERS DIRECTLY AFFECTING NON-PARTIES

Rule 40.9 states that a person who is not a party but who is directly affected by a judgment or order may apply to have the judgment or order set aside or varied. An application under this rule might be made by non-parties such as banks who are given notice of a freezing injunction.

43.003

ORDERS WORKING OUT, SUPPLEMENTING OR ENFORCING ORDERS PREVIOUSLY MADE

The making of an order, even a final order, does not thereby terminate the jurisdiction of the court which made that order. Either party may apply to the court to determine any subsidiary or consequential issues which may arise between them, for example, issues relating to the costs payable (see Ch.38), the methods of enforcement available (see Chs 40 and 41) and the amount of judgment interest payable (Electricity Supply *Nominees Ltd v Farrell* [1997] 2 All E.R. 498). The principles here are sometimes summarised by saying that all orders carry with them an implied "liberty to apply". In the case of interim orders the words "liberty to apply" are often expressly included in the order so as to remove or minimise doubts thereto. The liberty to apply, whether express or implied, can be invoked for all purposes necessary to give effect to the court's order.

43.004

COURT'S POWER UNDER CPR 3.1(7)

Rule 3.1(7) gives the court a very general power to vary or revoke any order made "under these Rules". Most orders so made are case management directions, i.e. orders made to secure the just disposal of a claim. Directions such as these should never be regarded as final. Further applications on the same matter may be made if there has been a material change in circumstances. For

43.005

example, any time limits imposed by an order can later be altered by another order. Where orders on matters such as disclosure of documents and security for costs have been made or refused the court may subsequently discharge an order which it previously made or grant an application which it previously refused. In the case of interim injunctions (see Ch.27) the express terms of an injunction made on notice (or in the presence of all parties to be bound by it) usually indicate that further orders can be made, i.e. the injunction states that it is effective until trial or further order (PD 25 Interim Injunctions, para.5.2).

The court's power under r.3.1(7) was considered by Patten J. in *Lloyds Investment (Scandinavia) Ltd v Christen Ager-Hanssen* [2003] EWHC 1740 (Ch). In that case, the claimant had entered judgment against the defendant after he had failed to comply with conditions imposed on him by an order setting aside an earlier judgment obtained in default of defence. The defendant applied to vary the terms of the order setting aside the first judgment. In dismissing the application, pursuant to CPR 3.1(7), the judge stated:

> "Although this is not intended to be an exhaustive definition of the circumstances in which the power under CPR Part 3.1(7) is exercisable, it seems to me that, for the High Court to revisit one of its earlier orders, the Applicant must either show some material change of circumstances or that the judge who made the earlier order was misled in some way, whether innocently or otherwise, as to the correct factual position before him. The latter type of case would include, for example, a case of material non-disclosure on an application for an injunction. If all that is sought is a reconsideration of the order on the basis of the same material, then that can only be done, in my judgment, in the context of an appeal. Similarly it is not, I think, open to a party to the earlier application to seek in effect to re-argue that application by relying on submissions and evidence which were available to him at the time of the earlier hearing, but which, for whatever reason, he or his legal representatives chose not to employ."

In *Collier v Williams* [2006] 1 W.L.R. 1945. the Court of Appeal cited Patten J.'s decision with approval, stating that the circumstances he had outlined "are the only ones in which the power to revoke or vary an order already made should be exercised under rule 3.1(7)" (para.40 of the judgment). These principles are applied less strictly where a party who makes an unsuccessful interim application later re-applies for the same relief, based on material which was not, but could have been, deployed in support of the first application. Although there is a public interest in discouraging a party from seeking to fight over again a battle he has already lost it may be necessary to allow him to do so in order to give effect tto the overriding objective (as to which, see Ch.1)

> "To take an example: suppose that an application for summary judgment in a substantial multi-track case under CPR 24 is dismissed, and the unsuccessful party then makes a second application based on material that was available at the time of the first application, but which through incompetence was not deployed at that time. The new material makes the case for

summary judgment unanswerable on the merits. In so extreme a case, it could not be right to dismiss the second application solely because it was a second bite at the cherry. In those circumstances, the overriding objective of dealing with cases justly, having regard to the various factors mentioned in CPR 1.1(2), would surely demand that the second application should succeed, and that the proceedings be disposed of summarily. In such a case, the failure to deploy the new material at the time of the first application can properly and proportionately be reflected by suitable orders for costs, and (if appropriate) interest. The judge would, of course be perfectly entitled to dismiss the second application without ceremony unless it could be speedily and categorically demonstrated that the new material was indeed conclusive of the case." (*Woodhouse v Consignia Plc* [2002] 1 W.L.R. 2558, para.57).

Rule 3.1(7) is not limited to purely procedural orders (Patten J. in *Lloyds Investment (Scandinavia) Ltd v Christen Ager-Hanssen* [2003] EWHC 1740 (Ch) at para.7, just before the passage quoted above). The rule was relied on in *Latimer Management Consultants Ltd v Ellingham Investments Ltd* [2006] EWHC 3662 (Ch), in order to vary a costs order which had been made at the end of a trial. In that case the trial judge, had ordered the first defendant to pay costs to the claimant but refused to make any order in favour of or against the second defendant. Subsequently the judge ordered the second defendant to pay the claimant's costs on the basis that he had been misled as to the financial position of the first defendant and it had subsequently become apparent that the second defendant had funded and controlled the proceedings and had benefited from them.

RELIEF FROM SANCTIONS

The court has power under Pt 3 to make various orders imposing sanctions on a party who has failed to comply with a rule, practice direction or court order (see, e.g. r.3.1(3), r.3.1(5), r.3.4 and r.3.7). Rule 3.9 sets out the court's general discretion to grant relief from such sanctions. Our commentary on r.3.9 is set out in para.33.011, above.

43.006

CORRECTING ACCIDENTAL SLIPS OR OMISSIONS IN JUDGMENTS AND ORDERS

Rule 40.12(1) states that "The court may at any time correct an accidental slip or omission in a judgment or order". This rule, known as the "slip rule", is mainly used to correct typographical mistakes. It can also be used to correct other more substantial errors and omissions in expressing the manifest intention of the court. But the rule cannot be used to correct errors of substance, nor in an attempt to add to or detract from the original order made by the judge:

43.007

see *R+V Versicherung AG v Risk Insurance and Reinsurance Solutions SA* [2007] EWHC 79, *The Times*, February 26, 2007.

The court also has "an inherent power to vary its own orders to make the meaning and the intention of the court clear" (PD 40B, para.4, which see generally). Is it open to a court under the slip rule to amend an order which gave effect to the intention which it had at the time that the order was made on the ground that, on further consideration after the order was made, the court had had second thoughts? No, held the Court of Appeal in *Roadrunner Properties Ltd v Dean* [2004] EWCA Civ 376; (2004) 11 E.G. 140. The court stated that the purpose of CPR 40.12 is to enable the court to amend an order which has been perfected but which fails to give effect to the intention of the court at the time when it was made. Typically, that occurs where there has been some drafting error, or the omission of material words; but it may include a case where the court had intended the order to contain the form of words which it does contain, but had misunderstood the legal effect of that form of words.

An application under this rule may be made informally, for example, by letter, or under Pt 23. The application may be dealt with without a hearing if the applicant so requests, with the consent of the parties, or where the court does not consider that a hearing would be appropriate. However, if the application is opposed, it should if practicable be listed for hearing, ideally, before the judge who gave the judgment or made the order in question.

OTHER AMENDMENTS TO JUDGMENTS AND ORDERS MADE BEFORE SEALING

43.008 In most cases the giving of judgment is a two stage process. The first stage occurs when the judge speaks out his decision or hands down a written judgment. The second stage occurs when a formal order of the court is sealed by the court office and copies of it are made available to the parties. In most cases the period of time between the two stages will be at least several days and, sometimes, may extend to several weeks.

The date of the first stage is the vital one for most purposes. The judgment takes effect from that date (r.40.7) and the time for appealing the judgment begins then (r.52.4) unless, as to either matter, the court otherwise orders. The date of the first stage should be shown in the formal order drawn up at the second stage (r.40.2(2)).

We have already seen that, under r.40.12, the court has power at any time (i.e. before or after stage 2) to correct accidental slips or omissions in the judgment. Before stage two arrives the judge also has a discretion to alter, or indeed to reverse, his decision but should exercise that discretion only in exceptional circumstances (*Stewart v Engel* [2000] 1 W.L.R. 2268). As Arden L.J. stated in *Venture Finance Plc v Mead* [2005] EWCA Civ 325; [2005] All E.R. (D) 376 (Mar):

"It occasionally happens that, after a judge has given judgment, the advocate or party who has lost jumps up and says that the judge has failed to deal with a point. On many occasions, the judge will do precisely what the judge did in this case and make it clear that he regards that submission as unsustainable. However, even in that situation, the judge may decide to give a supplementary judgment in the interests of clarification. Such a judgment may be very brief. However, it might help prevent an unnecessary appeal with the attendant cost to the parties. Very occasionally, the judge may conclude that there is some substance in the party's point. Indeed, he may want to retire for a few moments just to consider the position. If, on reflection, he decides that a point was overlooked in the judgment, he should consider the materiality of the point, and whether it undermines the decision reached. If necessary, the judge will have to give judgment again and may reach a different, or even the opposite, conclusion (see, for example, Moon Motors Ltd v Kiuan Wou [1952] Lloyd's List Rep. 80). This does not, and should not happen, very often. But it is worth repeating that a judge is entitled to vary or reverse his order until the order is drawn. Accordingly, he is entitled to give judgment again if the circumstances require that course."

See also *Robinson v Bird (otherwise known as Robinson v Fernsby)* [2003] EWCA Civ 1820; *The Times*, January 20, 2004, where the Court of Appeal emphasised that the jurisdiction to recall, vary or alter a judgment exists up to the time it is perfected; whether the judgment had been given orally, had been handed down to the parties in draft, or had been formally handed down.

The modern practice of informing parties in advance of the likely content of a reserved judgment is described in para.37.016, above.

Re-opening of final appeals (R.52.7)

An appeal decision may be reopened and reconsidered by the court which made it if three tests are all met, namely: (1) it is necessary in order to avoid real injustice; (2) exceptional circumstances exist and it is appropriate; and (3) there is no alternative remedy. See *R. v Bow Street Metropolitan Stipendiary Magistrate Ex p. Pinochet Ugarte (No.2)* [2000] 1 A.C. 119 (concerning House of Lords decisions); *Taylor v Lawrence* [2002] 3 W.L.R. 640 (concerning Court of Appeal decisions); and *Seray-Wurie v Hackney LBC* [2003] 1.W.L.R. 257 (concerning appeal decisions made by the High Court).

43.009

In *Taylor v Lawrence* it was said that the court should exercise strong control over applications for review so as to protect the other parties who were entitled to believe the litigation was at an end save for the possibility of an appeal to a higher court.

Note that in *Re Uddin (a child)* [2005] EWCA Civ 52; *The Times*, March 31, 2005, the Court of Appeal indicated that this power can only be invoked where it is demonstrated that the integrity of the earlier litigation process, whether at trial or at the first appeal, has been critically undermined. Examples might include: fraud (where relied on to reopen a concluded appeal rather than found a fresh cause of action: see, for example, *Couwenbergh v Valkova* [2004] EWCA Civ 676; (2004) L.T.L., May 28) and bias (the eccentric case where the judge had read the wrong papers). The vice in these cases is not, or not necessarily, that the decision was factually incorrect but that it was arrived at by a corrupted process.

In *First Discount Ltd v Guinness* [2007] EWCA Civ 378, (2007) L.T.L., May 1, the Court of Appeal emphasised the importance of the third test which Arden L.J. indicated could include a remedy available against a third party. There is a useful review of the case law in *Jaffray v Society of Lloyds* [2007] EWCA Civ 586, (2007) L.T.L., June 20 (where the Court of Appeal left open the question as to whether the cases of *Flower v Lloyd (No.1)* (1877) LR 6 Ch D 297 and *Jonesco v Beard* (1930) A.C. 298 remained authority for the proposition that the jurisdiction does not extend to cases of fraud).

Permission is needed to make an application to reopen a final determination of an appeal. There is no right to an oral hearing of that application unless, exceptionally, the judge so directs. Is there a right of appeal or review from the decision of the judge on the application for permission? No, it is final. As to the procedure for making an application for permission, see PD 52 and Ch.44.

CHAPTER 44

Appeals Up To the Court of Appeal

ROUTES OF APPEAL

The routes of appeal from one judge or court to another are provided for by ss.55 to 57 of the Access to Justice Act 1999 and the Access to Justice Act 1999 (Destination of Appeals) Order 2000 (SI 2000/1071) which is summarised in para.2A of the Practice Direction Supplementing Pt 52. Note that the PD at para.2A also contains three useful tables illustrating the destination of appeals. There is also an interactive routes of appeal guide on the Court of Appeal's website (*www.hmcourts-service.gov.uk/infoabout/coa_civil/routes_app/index.htm*) Judicial guidance on this body of law is given in *Tanfern Ltd v Cameron-MacDonald (Practice Note)* [2000] 1 W.L.R. 1311 and *Clark v Perks* [2001] 1 W.L.R. 17.

44.001

The normal route of appeal is easily stated. Subject to any requirement to obtain permission to appeal (see para.44.005, below) an appeal lies to the next level of judge in the court hierarchy. Thus, in the High Court, appeals from masters, costs judges and district judges lie to a High Court Judge and appeals from High Court judges lie to the Court of Appeal. In the county court, appeals from district judges lie to the circuit judge and appeals from circuit judges lie to a High Court judge. Now consider the abnormal routes:

(1) Final decisions in multi-track cases and in specialist proceedings (see para.44.002, below).
(2) Leapfrog appeals (see para.44.003, below).
(3) Appeals from the county court acting in an appellate capacity (these so-called second appeals lie "to the Court of Appeal" and not to any other court (art.5 of SI 2000/1071) as to which see further, para.44.007).
(4) Appeals made by circuit judges against orders for committal for contempt (these appeals also lie direct to the Court of Appeal, and see further, *Hurst v Barnet LBC* [2002] EWCA Civ 1009).

Final decisions in multi-track cases and specialist proceedings

44.002　In these cases the appeal lies direct to the Court of Appeal. The simplest example is an appeal following the trial of a case allocated to the multi-track: such appeals lie to the Court of Appeal even where the trial judge was a circuit judge, district judge or master. A "final decision" is "a decision of a court that would finally determine (subject to any possible appeal or detailed assessment of costs) the entire proceedings whichever way the court decided the issues before it" (PD 52, para.2A.3). The words we have shown in italics mean that some orders which finally determine cases are nevertheless not "final decisions". For example, orders striking out the proceedings or orders giving summary judgment; these are not final decisions because, had the court reached the opposite conclusion, the proceedings would have continued. See *Scribes West Ltd v Anstalt* [2004] EWCA Civ 965; [2004] 4 All E.R. 653.

Is a decision made in the defendant's favour by a trial judge at the trial of an action in the multi-track on a submission of no case to answer (see para.37.007), when the defendant has not been put to his election, a final decision? Yes, as the claimant is appealing against the judgment entered in favour of the defendants as a consequence of the circuit judge's decision. What if the trial judge had put the defendants to their election, and they elected to call no evidence? If what was then being appealed was the judge's acceptance or rejection of the defendants' submissions at the end of a trial at which they had called no evidence, his decision would have been a final decision whichever way he decided it. See *Graham v Chorley BC* [2006] EWCA Civ 92, *The Times*, March 20, 2006.

Final decisions in specialist proceedings also go direct to the Court of Appeal. As to the meaning of "specialist proceedings"? These are proceedings under the Company Acts 1985 or 1989, see CPR Pt 49. Because specialist proceedings are included in this group, an appeal from a final decision in an arbitration application goes straight to the Court of Appeal even if it was made by a circuit judge.

Part 8 claims (See Ch.10) are not included in this group. For them the normal route of appeal (next level up) applies. This is because Pt 8 claims are not allocated to the multi-track: they are only "treated as allocated to the multi-track" (r.8.9(c)).

Leapfrog appeals

44.003　Under ss.12 and 13 of the Administration of Justice Act 1969 a "leapfrog appeal" from a High Court judge direct to House of Lords may be made if:

　　(1)　All parties consent.
　　(2)　The judge grants a certificate: this he will do only if the case involves a point of law of general public importance concerning either the construction of a statute or statutory instrument or a matter already fully considered by the Court of Appeal or the House of Lords.

(3) The House of Lords grants leave (as to which see Ch.45).

Does the refusal of the House of Lords to entertain an appeal on a particular issue from the High Court under the leapfrog procedure preclude an appellant from appealing to the Court of Appeal on that particular issue where the High Court judge had granted the appellant permission to appeal to the Court of Appeal in relation to that issue? No, held the House of Lords in *R. (on the application of Jones) v Ceredigion CC* [2007] UKHL 24, *The Times*, May 24, 2007.

Rule 52.14 permits leap frog appeals from district judges, masters and circuit judges direct to the Court of Appeal in cases in which a direction to that effect is obtained from the court appealed from or from the circuit judge or High Court judge to which such an appeal would otherwise lie. A direction for assignment to the Court of Appeal will be made only if the court considers that the case raises an important point of principle or practice or considers that there is some other compelling reason for the Court of Appeal to hear it. If such a direction is made the court will forward the appeal papers to the Court of Appeal together with a note from the judge assigning the case, stating the reasons for assignment. The court that has assigned the appeal will then inform the appellant and the respondent of the date on which the appeal papers were so forwarded.

Can a district judge, master or circuit judge who has refused permission to appeal, then make make a direction under CPR 52.14 that any appeal should be heard in the Court of Appeal? No, held the Court of Appeal in *7E Communications Ltd v Vertex Antennentechnik GMBH* [2007] EWCA Civ 140, *The Times*, March 17, 2007. Rule 52.14 does not apply to both appeals for which permission has been obtained and those for which it has not. The rule itself clearly distinguishes between an appeal and an application for permission to appeal. It is only "the appeal" that may be transferred to the Court of Appeal. The heading of the rule correctly states that it is concerned with the assignment of appeals, not applications for permission to appeal.

Note that even if an order is correctly made, subsequently, the Master of the Rolls or the Court of Appeal may direct that an appeal directed to be heard by the Court of Appeal is to be remitted to the court in which the original appeal was or would have been brought.

Rule 52.14 derives from s.57 of the Access to Justice Act 1999 which also empowers the Master of the Rolls to make an order leapfrogging to the Court of Appeal, an appeal which would otherwise be heard in the county court or High Court. The fact that the Master of the Rolls has such a power diminishes the need for a leapfrog order being made by the lower courts. In *Clark v Perks* [2001] 1 W.L.R. 17 it was said that the lower courts should use r.52.14 only if one of the criteria mentioned in the rule was satisfied and should use it sparingly. If the lower court is in any doubt whether the point is important enough to justify a transfer to the Court of Appeal, that court could always refer the matter to the Master of the Rolls for him to make the order if he thought appropriate.

Orders from which no appeal lies

44.004 Rights of appeal can be excluded by contract between the parties. In respect of decisions made in the county court the contract must be in writing signed by the parties or their legal representatives (CCA, s.79).

As a general rule no appeal will be heard which concerns merely academic points or hypothetical questions of law when there is no dispute to be resolved. Exceptions include test cases, appeals continued solely to resolve outstanding issues as to costs and appeals involving a public authority as to a question of public law (see generally *R. v Secretary of State for the Home Department Ex p. Salem* [1999] 1 A.C. 450).

Where permission to appeal is sought from an appellate court the court's decision thereon is final. No appeal lies from its grant or refusal of permission (the rule in *Lane v Esdaile* [1891] A.C. 210 which is considered in para.44.008, below).

In the High Court no appeal lies from an order granting or refusing a certificate enabling a leap frog appeal to the House of Lords (Administration of Justice Act 1969, s.12(5)) or an order refusing leave for the institution of legal proceedings by a person declared a vexatious litigant (see Ch.7).

PERMISSION TO APPEAL

44.005 Permission to appeal is now required in virtually all cases (for exceptions see below). By r.52.3(6) permission to appeal may be given only where one of 2 grounds is established. The first test for permission is whether the appeal has any real prospect of success. A fanciful prospect is insufficient. However, in very exceptional cases, permission may be given even if the appeal has no real prospect of success if the second test is met, namely that there is a compelling reason why the appeal should be heard. Usually this will be an issue which, in the public interest, should be examined by the Court of Appeal (possibly by way of a leapfrog appeal, see para.44.003 above). Examples are cases raising questions of great public interest or questions of general policy, or where authority binding on the Court of Appeal may call for reconsideration. On appeals from case management decisions there are additional factors which the court must consider even if the appeal does have some prospect of success (PD 52, para.4.5):

(a) The point sought to be raised may not be of sufficient significance to justify the costs of an appeal.
(b) The procedural consequences of an appeal (e.g. loss of the trial date) may outweigh the significance of the interim issue.
(c) It may be more convenient to determine the point at or after the trial (this factor is particularly important where the appellate court is also the trial court, e.g. interim appeals in multi-track cases from masters or district judges).

The permission granted may be limited to particular issues to be heard on the appeal or may be subject to conditions, for example, deferring the hearing of the appeal to a later date. Where appropriate (especially on interim appeals) the application for permission itself may be adjourned to a later date. Any financial condition imposed must be reasonable and not have the effect of stifling the appeal: see *Kuwait Airways Corp v Iraqi Airways Co.* [2005] EWCA Civ 943. Paragraphs 4.18 to 4.21 of PD 52 describe what should happen when a court gives a limited permission to appeal, i.e. permission on some issues only. That court will refuse permission on any remaining issues or reserve the question of permission to appeal on any remaining issues to the court hearing the appeal. If the court refuses permission to appeal the remaining issues and the appeal court also refuses permission those issues cannot be renewed at the appeal hearing. If the lower court reserves a question of appeal on the remaining issues to the court hearing the appeal, the appellant must, within the next 14 days, inform both the appeal court and the respondent, in writing, whether he intends to pursue the reserved issues.

The permission requirement in second appeals, which is more stringent, is considered further below.

In a few cases no permission to appeal is required, the intending appellant therefore having a right of appeal if he applies promptly: appeals against committal orders (note that this also includes an appeal by an appellant that a committal order is too lenient: see *Wood v Collins* [2006] EWCA Civ 743, *The Times*, June 26, 2006), a refusal to grant habeas corpus (see RSC, Ord.54), a secure accommodation order made under the Children Act 1989, s.25, or a decision made by a district judge, circuit judge or bankruptcy registrar in exercise of the bankruptcy or insolvency jurisdiction (see Ch.42 and *White Book*, vol.2, para.3E–17).

Seeking permission

Applications for permission should normally be sought orally at the hearing at which the judgment or order is given or made. If a party needs more time to make that application, the court may adjourn the hearing. If the application is refused, or if not sought, the intending appellant must include an application for permission in his appellant's notice (see para.44.010, below). But can the intending appellant apply subsequently to the lower court? Yes, if there is a good reason for the court to reconvene to hold a continuation of the original hearing in order to deal with an application for permission to appeal. The application will have to be made promptly, before the order has been drawn up and arguably within the 21 day limit: see *Multiplex Construction (UK) Ltd v Honeywell Control Systems Ltd* [2007] EWHC 236, (2007) L.T.L., March 27.

44.006

Where the lower court is asked to grant permission to appeal against its decision, PD 52 para.4.3A requires the judge's decision to record the following essential details: whether or not the judgment or order is final; whether an appeal lies from the judgment or order and, if so, to which appeal court; and if permission to appeal is not granted, the appropriate appeal court to which any further application for permission may be made.

An application for permission which is made to the appeal court will normally be considered without a hearing. If the appeal court refuses permission without a hearing, the parties will be informed and the intending appellant then has seven days in which to request a reconsideration of that decision at an oral hearing (r.52.3(4)). If still unsuccessful at that oral hearing, that is the end of the matter; no further right of appeal exists (see para.44.008). Note that by r.52.3(4A) if the Court of Appeal refuses permission to appeal without a hearing, it may at the same time, if it considers that the application is totally without merit, make an order that the person seeking permission may not request the decision to be reconsidered at a hearing. However, the court may not make such an order in family proceedings.

If the appeal court grants permission, the appeal proper begins (see para.44.009, below). The respondent does have a right to apply to the appeal court to set aside the permission, but under r.52.9 will have to show a compelling reason for doing so. What might be a compelling reason? Examples are relatively scarce but include where the court that granted permission was misled (see *Angel Airlines SA v Dean & Dean Solicitors* [2006] EWCA Civ 1505, *The Times*, November 28, 2006) or lacked jurisdiction; or some obvious and unarguably decisive statute or authority was overlooked; or the appellant had persistently breached court orders (*Taiga v Taiga* [2004] EWCA Civ 1399. Hence, in most cases, such an application is not worth making (see *Re BCCI, Morris v Bank of India* [2004] EWCA Civ 1286 and *Tradigrain SA v Intertek Testing Services (ITS) Canada Ltd* [2007] EWCA Civ 154, *The Times*, March 20, 2007).

As to judicial review appeals, see para.44.023, below.

Second appeals

44.007 Special rules govern cases in which a first appeal has already been heard in the county court or the High Court (Access to Justice Act 1999, s.55 and r.52.13). If either party wishes to bring a further appeal it will be necessary to obtain permission from the Court of Appeal. The lower courts have no jurisdiction to grant permission. The Court of Appeal will not grant permission unless the following criteria are met:

(a) The appeal would raise an important point of principle or practice (see, for example, *Voice & Script International Ltd v Alghafar* [2003] EWCA Civ 736; (2003) L.T.L., May 8); or

(b) there is some other compelling reason for the Court of Appeal to hear it (see *Uphill v BRB (Residuary) Ltd* [2005] EWCA Civ 60; *The Times*, February 8, 2005; *Vellacott v The Convergence Group Plc* [2005] EWCA Civ 290; The Times, April 25, 2005 and *Miller v Garton Shires (a firm)* [2006] EWCA Civ 1386, (2007) RTR 24).

The criteria are the same as those justifying an appeal which might have been assigned to the Court of Appeal by way of a leapfrog appeal (see para.44.003 above). Even if the criteria are met the Court of Appeal may still consider other matters such as whether it is fair to have this appeal decided at the expense of parties with very limited resources or whether, instead, the court should wait for a more suitable vehicle (see *per* Lord Hoffmann in *Piglowska v Piglowski*) [1999] 1 W.L.R. 1360, HL).

The rule in *Lane v Esdaile*

The imposition of a permission requirement on appeals is intended as a check to unnecessary or frivolous appeals. Accordingly, if the appeal court grants or refuses permission, whether conditionally or unconditionally, that decision cannot be reviewed by any higher court. This principle, previously derived from the House of Lords decision in *Lane v Esdaile* [1891] A.C. 210, now has statutory force (Access to Justice Act 1999, s.54(4)). A request for permission to appeal must be distinguished carefully from a request for an extension of time for appealing. The question whether permission to appeal is necessary goes to the jurisdiction of the appeal court; assuming such permission is necessary, the appellant's failure to obtain it is a defect whether or not the respondent takes the point (*White v Brunton* [1984] Q.B. 570; and see *Clark v Perks* [2001] 1 W.L.R. 17. The question whether an extension of time should be given does not effect the jurisdiction of the appellate court and therefore can be reviewed by it.

44.008

> "In my judgment what Lane v Esdaile decided, and all that it decided, was that where it is provided that an appeal shall lie by leave of a particular court or courts, neither the grant nor refusal of leave is an appealable decision ... The grant or refusal of an application for leave to appeal is one thing. The grant or refusal of an application to extend the time limited for taking a step in proceedings, including but not limited to giving notice of appeal, is quite another ... whilst it is true that a right of appeal may be barred either by a refusal of an extension of time, or by a refusal of leave, the routes by which this result is achieved and the underlining concepts are essentially different" (*Rickards v Rickards* [1990] Fam. 194 *per* Lord Donaldson of Lymington M.R.).

Intending appellants can therefore seek to file an appeal notice late and request the appellate court to extend the time for appealing even where the lower court refused such an extension (*Foenander v Bond Lewis & Co.* [2002] 1 W.L.R. 525, CA). In theory, unless an exception applies, if a court grants an extension of time for appealing, the prospective respondent could launch an appeal against that extension. In practice no such appeal lies to the Court of Appeal (SCA 1981, s.18(1)(b)) and, where the appellate court is a circuit judge or a High Court judge, such an appeal is likely to be doomed to failure.

THE APPELLANT'S NOTICE

Time for filing and service

44.009 In all cases the appellant (or intending appellant, if he is seeking permission from the appeal court) must file his notice at the appeal court within 21 days after the date of the decision of the lower court, or within the period directed by the lower court, if different (r.52.4). If he reasonably requires more than 21 days, he should apply to the lower court on the occasion when judgment is given. PD 52, para.5.19 indicates that the lower court should not normally direct a period exceeding 35 days. A period as long as that, and possibly longer, may be needed where the lower court judge announces his decision but reserves the reasons for his judgment or order until a later date. As we shall see, providing a suitable record of the reasons for the judgment in the lower court is one of the essential documents on the appeal (see para.44.011, below).

To appeal late an extension of time will be necessary. See r.52.6 and PD 52 para.5.2. But also note that the court will have regard to the checklist in r.3.9 (see *Sayers v Clarke-Walker (a firm)* [2002] 1 W.L.R. 3095, *Smith v Kvaerner Cementation Foundations Ltd* [2006] EWCA Civ 242, [2007] 1 W.L.R. 370 and para.33.011). If an appeal is brought out of time following a change in the law, see *Richmond upon Thames LBC v Secretary of State for Transport* [2006] EWCA Civ 193 (2006) L.T.L 2 March.

Is it open to the lower court to grant an extension of time even if the application is made to it after the expiry of 21 days? Yes, held the Court of Appeal in *Aujla v Sanghera* [2004] EWCA Civ 121; (2004) L.T.L., January 23, where Arden L.J. set out certain guidelines.

Except where the appeal court orders otherwise, a sealed copy of the appellant's notice, including any skeleton arguments relied on (see para.44.015, below) must be served on all respondents to the appeal as soon as practicable and, in any event, not later than seven days after filing. An appellant who is applying late should include an application for an extension of time in the appellant's notice (PD 52, para.5.2)

As to the time limits in judicial review appeals, see para.44.023, below.

Form and content of appellant's notice

44.010 Form N161 is the prescribed form of notice for all appeals up to the court of appeal and comprises ten sections as follows:

(1) Details of the claim or case appealing against.
(2) Details of the appeal.
(3) Legal representation.
(4) Permission to appeal.
(5) Other information.
(6) Grounds for appeal and arguments in support.

(7) Details of the order sought on the appeal.
(8) Other applications.
(9) Evidence in support.
(10) Supporting documents

Section (5) requires such details as the order or parts of the order being appealed against and any human rights claims (which should set out the information required by PD 16, para.16.1). As to section (6), the grounds of appeal must be set out clearly and specify whether a ground raises an appeal on a point of law or against a finding of fact. See PD 52 para.3.2 and *Perotti v Collyer-Bristow* [2004] EWCA Civ 639; [2004] 4 All E.R. 53. The appellant's skeleton arguments can be set out or attached or confirmation given that they will be filed within 14 days of filing the notice (see further para.44.015, below). Section (8) is optional it could include a request for an extension of time for appealing (as to which see PD 52, paras 5.2 and 5.3). It must include any request for a stay of execution pending the appeal since the appeal itself does not operate as a stay (see r.52.7 and *Moat Housing Group-South Ltd v Harris* [2004] EWCA Civ 1852, *The Times,* January 13, 2005).

What if the appellant wishes to change the basis of his appeal? The appellant should write to the court and to the other party indicating the proposed nature of the changed case which is to be advanced and seek directions as to whether the matter should be dealt with at the beginning of the hearing of the appeal or by directions being given by the court prior to the hearing of the appeal. The court should be informed of the attitude of the respondent. If the respondent objects, the court can decide whether the case is one which can be disposed of summarily because there is no merit in the new grounds. See *Shire v Secretary of State for Work and Pensions* [2003] EWCA Civ 1465; *The Times*, October 30, 2003.

Documents to accompany the appellant's notice

Practice Direction 52, paras 5.6 and 5.6A set out detailed and lengthy lists of copy notices, copy sealed orders, witness statements or affidavits in support of any application included in the notice and a bundle of additional documents in support of the appeal. In any case in which it is not possible to file all these documents , the appellant must indicate what is missing and the reasons why those documents are not currently available. Further documents must be included in the bundle where the appeal court has granted permission to appeal: see PD 52 para.6.3A.

44.011

Shorter lists of documents required are included for judicial review appeals (as to which see para.44.023, below) and for appeals relating to claims allocated to the small claims track (PD 52, para.5.8A). The small claims track list indicates what must be the minimum requirement for any appeal:

(1) A sealed copy of the order being appealed.
(2) Any order giving or refusing permission to appeal, along with a copy of the reasons for that decision.

(3) A suitable record of the reasons for judgment of the lower court, if ordered by the court.

Paragraph 5.12 gives examples of what will amount to a suitable record of the judgment: an approved transcript, a written judgment signed by the judge, or a note of the judgment (to be agreed by the respondent and approved by the judge: agreement and approval is not needed on an application for permission to appeal). Paragraph 5.12 also makes clear the duty of any advocate for the respondent in the lower court to make his or her note of the judgment promptly available free of charge to an appellant who is unrepresented if there is no approved transcript. The appellant should then submit that note to the appeal court. Where a party wishes to appeal on the ground that the lower court failed to give reasons for its decision, the lower court may be invited (by the parties or by the appeal court) to provide additional reasons (*English v Emery Reimbold and Strick Ltd* [2002] 1 W.L.R. 2409 and *Aerospace Publishing Ltd v Thames Water Utilities Ltd* [2007] EWCA Civ 3, *The Times*, January 22, 2007).

Which documents must be served on the respondent to the appeal? In all cases, he must receive a sealed copy of the appellant's notice and any skeleton argument relied on. Where permission to appeal has been given by the lower court or permission is not required, the respondent should be served with a full set of the filed documents along with the appellant's notice. However, an appellant who is applying for permission to appeal in his appellant's notice may, if he wishes, delay serving the full set of documents until after permission has been given (see para.44.012, below).

When preparing any documentation and attending at the hearing of the appeal, the appellant (and indeed the respondent) must take care not to disclose the existence of any Pt 36 offer where to do so might compromise the hearing of the appeal (r.52.12). If a breach of this rule leads to an adjournment (to enable the case to come before a differently constituted court) the court making that adjournment may make an order for costs penalising the party at fault or, if appropriate, his legal representative. See generally *Garratt v Saxby* [2004] EWCA Civ 341, [2004] 1 W.L.R. 2152.

PROCEDURE WHERE PERMISSION IS NOT REQUIRED OR IS OBTAINED

44.012 Consider first cases in which permission to appeal is given by the lower court or is not required. Once the appellant's notice is filed the appeal court will notify the parties of the date of the hearing or the period of time (the "listing window") during which the appeal is likely to be heard. In Court of Appeal cases, the notification will also state the date by which the appeal will be heard (the "hear by date"). Next consider cases in which permission to appeal is sought from the appeal court (see para.44.006, above). On the giving of permission the court will send to the parties notification of the date of hearing or listing window (and in Court of Appeal cases, the hear by date) and also a copy of the order giving permission to appeal. If he has not done so already, the appellant must, within the next seven days, serve on the respondents all the documents filed in court with the appellant's notice.

First steps by the respondent

The respondent is not required to take any step in the appeal until he has been served with the appellant's notice and, where permission to appeal is necessary, until he has been served with a copy of an order granting that permission (PD 52, para.5.22). Where an application for permission proceeds to a hearing, he will not normally be given notice of that hearing (PD 52, para.4.15). However, if he is given notice, he must also be given a copy of the appeal bundle (PD 52, para.4.16). Respondents who voluntarily make submissions upon or attend upon permission applications should not expect to be allowed their costs of doing so (PD 52, para.4.23).

44.013

If the respondent is content to rely four square on the judgment of the court below for the reasons given by that court, he is not obliged to serve a respondent's notice but may still have to provide a skeleton argument if he proposes to address arguments to the court at the hearing (see para.44.015, below).

A respondent's notice is necessary where the respondent:

(a) wishes to ask the appeal court to vary the order of the lower court in any way; or
(b) wishes to ask the appeal court to uphold the order of the lower court for reasons different from or additional to those given by the lower court.

(a) above is of course an appeal and, if the respondent requires permission to make this appeal and has not already obtained it, he must seek it in the respondent's notice.

Unless a different time was directed by the lower courts, the time for filing a respondent's notice depends upon whether the appellant needed permission to appeal and if so when and from whom he received it (see generally r.52.5). If no permission was needed or if permission was granted at the time of, or in, the decision sought to be appealed, the time limit is 14 days from the date of service of the appellant's notice. If permission was sought in the appellant's notice and was granted by the appeal court, the time limit is 14 days from the date upon which the respondent was served with a copy of the order granting permission to appeal. If permission was sought in the appellant's notice and the appeal court directs that the application for permission to appeal and the appeal itself are to be heard together, the time limit is 14 days from the date of service of notice of that direction.

In addition to filing the respondent's notice, the respondent must also serve a copy of it on the appellant and on any other respondent. Unless the appeal court orders otherwise, service must be affected as soon as practicable and in any event not later than seven days after filing.

The documents to be filed and served together with a respondent's notice are described in PD 52, para.7.10: multiple copies of the respondent's notice, two copies of any skeleton argument and a bundle of any documents the respondent wishes to rely on in addition to those filed in the appellant.

It is vital to meet the time limits laid down in the PD. The Court of Appeal will require a party who fails to do so to attend to explain the breach: see *Jeyapragash v Secretary of State for the Home Department* [2004] EWCA Civ 1260; [2005] 1 All E.R. 412.

In *Mlauzi v Secretary of State for the Home Department* [2005] EWCA Civ 128; *The Times*, February 15, 2005, the Court of Appeal stressed that it is the duty of legal representatives to comply with the time limits imposed for the lodging of documents and, in particular, those documents that should be served no later than seven days prior to the hearing as per PD 52 para.15.11A(2). In the exceptional case that a party cannot comply with that duty, the Civil Appeals Office and the other parties must be kept informed of events.

Form and content of a respondent's notice

44.014 Form N162 is the prescribed form of respondent's notice for all appeals up to the Court of Appeal and comprises ten sections as follows:

(1) Details of the claim or case.
(2) Details of the respondent.
(3) Time estimate for the appeal hearing.
(4) Details of the order(s) or part(s) of order(s) challenged.
(5) Details as to permission to file a respondent's notice.
(6) Grounds for appeal or for upholding the order.
(7) Arguments in support of the grounds.
(8) Details of the decisions which will be sought at the hearing.
(9) Other applications.
(10) Details of supporting documents.

If the respondent is seeking to rely on any issue under the Human Rights Act 1998 he must include in his respondent's notice the information required by PD 16, para.16.1 (PD 52, para.7.3A). Section (7) when completed will state that the respondent's skeleton argument is set out below or attached or will follow within 21 days of receiving the appellant's skeleton argument (see para.44.015, below). Section (9) is the ideal place in which to apply for an order for security for the costs of the appeal (see further r.25.15 which is described in Ch.26, above).

Skeleton arguments

44.015 Skeleton arguments are intended to provide a short and succinct account of the areas of controversy in the case. Form N163 is the prescribed form for use by appellant and respondents and PD 52, paras 5.10 and 5.11 give guidance as to content. We have already seen the obligations on all parties to file and serve skeleton arguments at the same time as, or soon after, filing their appellant's notice or respondent's notice as the case may be. Skeleton arguments are sought even from appellants who are not represented (PD 52, para.5.9(3)) and all respondents, including those who do not file any respondent's notice unless the appeal relates to a small claim (PD 52, paras 7.6 and 7.7A).

The obvious functions for skeleton arguments are to assist the court on any application for permission to appeal (or permission to file a respondent's notice) and on the hearing of any appeal. The practice direction requires them to be filed and served at a very early stage in the appeal. This is of value, even in cases where permission is not required or has already been obtained, because of the assistance it gives to the court office in making case management decisions and administrative arrangements as to the hearing of the appeal. The advocates in the lower court should know what the case was about and should therefore be able to formulate a brief exposition of the case listing the main arguments they wish to raise at the appeal. If the appeal is listed for hearing some months after skeleton arguments have been filed, developments in the law during those months may compel the parties to amend their skeleton arguments. No permission for amendment is required even where the skeleton argument has been included in the appellant's notice or the respondent's notice (PD 52, para.5.9(1) and 7.6).

Applications ancillary to appeals

We have already mentioned applications which are often included in appellant's notices and respondent's notices: applications for permission to appeal, for extension of time, for stays of execution and for security for the costs of an appeal. There are also several other matters upon which the parties may apply for orders or directions, for example, 44.016

(1) Directions varying any time limit set by a rule, practice direction or order. See *Southern & District Finance Plc v Turner* [2003] EWCA Civ 1574; (2003) L.T.L., November 7. Rule 52.6 excludes the parties' rights to agree such variations.

(2) Orders permitting amendments to an appellant's notice or to a respondent's notice (r.52.8).

(3) An order disposing of the appeal by consent (PD 52, paras 12.1 to 13.5): Dismissals by consent may be obtained even where terms favourable to the appellant are agreed. Orders allowing appeals by consent are more difficult to obtain.

(4) Orders striking out an appellant's notice or a respondent's notice, in whole or in part, for example, for non-compliance with a rule, practice direction or order (r.52.9). In *Bell Electric Ltd v Aweco Appliance Systems GmbH & Co. KG* [2002] EWCA Civ 1501; *The Times*, November 20, 2002, the appellant had been ordered by the

lower court to pay £135,000 in damages and costs. Although it had the means to pay this sum, it decided not to do so because of the difficulty the respondent would have in enforcing such orders overseas until the appeal was concluded. The Court of Appeal ordered a stay of the appeal unless the £135,000 was paid within the next 14 days. Also see *Contract Facilities Ltd v The Estate of Rees (Deceased)* [2003] EWCA Civ 1105; (2003) L.T.L., July 24.

(5) Order setting aside permission to appeal. This is also covered by r.52.9. Such applications are discouraged (see further para.44.005, above).

(6) An application to adjourn a permission hearing. In *Bracknell Forest BC v N*, *The Times*, November 6, 2006, the Court of Appeal stressed that there is a recognised principle that no adjournment will be granted for the convenience of counsel.

It should be remembered that video conferencing facilities are available and the court itself in *Black v Pastouna* [2005] EWCA Civ 1389, *The Independent*, December 2, 2005, directed that in matters lasting less than 30 minutes the parties should seriously consider using this facility.

Hearing of the appeal

44.017 As a general rule every appeal will be limited to a review of the decision of the lower court (see generally r.52.11). The appeal court will not normally undertake an actual rehearing of the dispute which led to the decision being appealed. To do so would merely authorise and compel the parties to re-fight their battle all over again. The general rule gives way where a practice direction makes different provision for a particular category of appeal (see, e.g. PD 52, para.9.1: certain decisions of ministers, persons or other bodies) or where the court considers that in the circumstances of an individual appeal it would be in the interest of justice to hold a re-hearing (see, e.g. *Bank of Ireland v Robertson* (2003) L.T.L., February 21, Ch.D., an appeal against an order made in the appellant's absence because an application to adjourn had been refused).

The word "review" has not been included in the glossary appended to the CPR. Its exclusion is probably wise because of the particular need for at least some flexibility in the choice by an appellate court of the procedure most apt to carry out the task. But the meaning of the word, and in particular the distinction between it and a re-hearing postulated by r.52.11, has been the subject of Court of Appeal guidance: see *El Du Pont de Nemours & Co. v ST Dupont* [2003] EWCA Civ 1368, [2006] 1 W.L.R. 2793. Another general rule laid down by r.52.11 is that, unless it orders otherwise, the appeal court will not receive oral evidence or indeed any evidence which was not before the lower court.

When might the court "otherwise order" in relation to new evidence? The pre-CPR test set out in *Ladd v Marshall* [1954] 1 W.L.R. 1489 still applies but not too rigidly under the CPR (see *Saluja v Gill* [2002] EWHC 1435 (Ch.)). The test has three limbs, namely: whether the new evidence could not have been obtained for use at the trial had reasonable diligence been deployed by the party seeking to introduce it; whether the new evidence would have been likely to have had an important influence on the outcome of the case; and whether the body of new evidence was likely to be credible. These are also echoed in the guidance notes on an appellant's notice.

> "Section (6) Grounds for Appeal . . . remember that you must not include any grounds for appealing which rely on new evidence, that is evidence which has become available since the order was made. You may not produce new evidence in your appeal without first obtaining the permission of the appeal court. (See the notes to Section 4) . . .
>
> Section (9) Evidence in support. State whether you are producing new evidence in your appeal or asking for permission to produce oral evidence at the appeal hearing. You will need to give reasons why the new evidence was not before the original court and, where oral evidence is requested, the reasons why you think it is necessary."

The satisfaction of the *Ladd v Marshall* test is a necessary but not a sufficient condition for the reception of new evidence. It does not licence an abuse of process such as conduct by which a party, deliberately and conscious of the risk involved, elects to proceed at trial without certain evidence and, moreover, resists adjournment in order that that evidence should be got in yet then, after losing the case, seeks to have access to that evidence on appeal. See *Khetani v Kanbi* [2006] EWCA Civ 1621, (2006) L.T.L., November 30.

To persuade the appeal court to allow an appeal, it is necessary to show that the decision of the lower court was wrong or unjust because of a serious procedural or other irregularity in the proceedings in the lower court (r.52.11(3)). For example, that the court decided the question of causation in a case by reference to literature narrated by a party's expert without that evidence being submitted in court (see *Breeze v Ahmad* [2005] EWCA Civ 223; (2005) L.T.L., March 8).

The burden of proof is on the appellant: the court will accept the decision previously made unless persuaded to do otherwise. The appeal court will not interfere unless the lower court erred in law, erred in fact or, on a question of discretion, has reached a conclusion which falls outside the generous ambit within which reasonable disagreement is possible. On questions of fact, deference is given to the advantages which the lower court had by actually hearing and seeing the witnesses. However, the degree of deference to be given varies with the circumstances (see generally *Assicurazioni Generali SpA v Arab Insurance Group* [2003] 1 W.L.R. 577, CA and *Manning v Stylianou* [2006] EWCA Civ 1655).

In hearing the appeal the court (unlike the parties) is not confined to the points raised in the appellant's notice or respondent's notice (r.52.11(5)). It has all the powers of the lower court (r.52.10) may draw any inference of fact which it considers justified on the evidence (r.52.11(4)) and may substitute its own decision for that of the lower court, even as to the amount of damages awarded by a jury. If the appeal court considers that the parties should re-fight their battle all over again, it may hear that battle itself or remit the matter for determination by the lower court.

It must be remembered that the Court of Appeal is an appellate court and not a court of original jurisdiction. Its power to interfere with a judge's order is derived from r.52.11(3) and in the absence of consent it does not have any power to make a different type of order from the order the judge was asked to make if the court is satisfied that the judge's approach cannot be faulted: see *King v Telegraph Group Ltd* [2004] EWCA Civ 613; *The Times*, May 21, 2004.

It is important that the time of the court is not wasted. "There is a professional obligation on those advising parties to litigation to notify the court if there is a likelihood that judicial time will be wasted in preparing for an appeal which has either been settled or is subject to negotiations which may well lead to settlement. Either way the court needs to be told, and needs to be told as soon as possible" *per* Peter Gibson L.J. in *Yell Ltd v Garton* [2004] EWCA Civ 87; *The Times*, February 26, 2004. Where serious negotiations to settle are proceeding or the case does settle, even if it is very late in the day, steps must be taken via the Royal Courts of Justice 24–hour switchboard to notify the clerks of the judges concerned. See also *Tasyurdu v Secretary of State for the Home Department* [2003] EWCA Civ 447; *The Times*, April 16, 2003.

Summary assessment of appeal costs

44.018 The procedure for the assessment of costs is described in paras 13.010 and 38.014, above. PD 52.14 lists the cases when appeal costs may be summarily assessed and warns the parties to be prepared for that (i.e. to file and serve statements of costs in advance and to make submissions thereon at the hearing).

(1) Contested directions hearings.
(2) Applications for permission to appeal at which the respondent is present.
(3) Dismissal list hearings in the Court of Appeal at which the respondent is present.
(4) Appeals from case management decisions.
(5) Appeals listed for one day or less.

As to (5), in practice such costs are not often assessed summarily. However, the statements of costs filed may enable the court to determine what sum to allow by way of a payment on account, pending detailed assessment.

If the appeal court hears an application for permission to appeal and refuses that application, it is likely to make an order for costs. The refusal of permission cannot be appealed (see para.44.008, above) but the order for costs can (*Riniker v University College London (Practice Note)* [2001] 1 W.L.R. 13.

PROCEDURE IN THE COURT OF APPEAL

Who may exercise the powers of the Court of Appeal

The Court of Appeal Civil Division is composed of the Master of the Rolls, Lords Justices of Appeal and certain other senior judges by virtue of the office they hold. Administrative support is provided by the Civil Appeals Office. Its work is conducted under the direction of the Head of the Civil Appeal Office who, when acting in a judicial capacity, is referred to as Master.

44.019

The Master has jurisdiction to deal with the majority of applications which are incidental to an appeal or as to which there is no substantial dispute between the parties except applications for bail, an injunction or, save in exceptional circumstances a stay of proceedings in a lower court. He may also make orders dismissing an appeal or application where a party has failed to comply with any rule, practice direction or court order. The Master may make decisions without a hearing. If he does so, a hearing will be held by one or more judges to reconsider that decision if any party so requests (see generally, r.52.16).

If appropriate, any application incidental to an appeal may be made direct to a single judge or may be referred to him by the Master. Unlike the Master, the single judge also has jurisdiction in respect of injunctions, stays of proceedings and applications for permission to appeal. Most applications will be considered on paper only but will be reconsidered at a hearing (by the same judge or by another judge or judges) if any party so requests. There is no appeal to the House of Lords from a decision of a single judge made at a hearing where the decision is an incidental decision (Supreme Court Act 1981, s.58(2)) or on an application for permission to appeal (see further para.44.008).

The Civil Appeals Office

Can a party file an appellant's or respondent's notice, or an application notice, by e-mail or electronically? Yes, see PD 52 paras 15.1A and B; as well as the appropriate guidelines which appear on the Court of Appeal, Civil Division website at *www.civilappeals.gov.uk*.

44.020

Immediately after the filing of notices, the parties should collaborate together in preparing a bundle of the case authorities they wish to rely on at the hearing. The appellant's advocate is duty bound to file in the Civil Appeals Office one bundle containing photocopies of the principal authorities (not normally more than ten) with the relevant passages marked. Generally speaking, this bundle should be filed at least 28 days before the date fixed for hearing. At a later stage, up to 5.30 p.m. on the working day before the hearing, either party may file a second agreed bundle or a list of authorities and texts. As to the categories of judgments that may be cited, see Practice Direction (Citation of Authorities) [2001] 1 W.L.R. 1001 which is summarised in para.36.007, above.

Documents may be taken to the Civil Appeals Office or sent there by post. They will at first undergo preliminary checks and, if they appear to be in order, will be entered in the records of the court and given a reference number. Documents which appear not to be in order will be returned to the appellant or applicant who, if aggrieved must now make an application to the Master. Because of the possibility of problems arising on the paperwork, it is unwise to delay commencement in the Court of Appeal until the last day or last days of any relevant time limit.

Applications for permission to appeal will be passed to a single judge for consideration. Of the few such applications which proceed to a hearing, each advocate at that hearing will be given a time limit of 20 minutes for oral argument unless the court otherwise orders. Courts conducting such hearings have come to be known as the "blitz courts".

Assume that the appeal notice has been filed and permission to appeal has been granted, or was granted by the lower courts or is not required. The Civil Appeals Office will send to the appellant a letter of notification which amongst other things indicates the likely hearing date and includes an Appeal Questionnaire. Within the next 14 days the appellant must complete and file the Appeal Questionnaire which, amongst other things, includes the advocate's time estimate for the hearing and confirms service of various documentation on the respondent. In some cases the Civil Appeals Office will send to each party's solicitor a letter, leaflet and response form indicating the possible benefits of alternative dispute resolution.

In most cases the letter of notification will fix a date for the hearing of the appeal. The appeal will then come on for hearing on the date fixed or on the following sitting day although there remains a possibility that, because of other changes to the listing arrangements, the date of hearing may later have to be rearranged. A major cause of rearrangement is the need to accommodate subsequent appeals which are more urgent, i.e. expedited appeals as to which see below.

Short applications to the Court of Appeal especially by parties outside of London may be dealt with by a video link facility (see above). The Civil Appeal Office will explain how the system works in appropriate cases: see *Babbings v Kirklees Metropolitan Council* [2004] EWCA Civ 1431; *The Times*, November 4, 2004.

The Civil Appeals List

44.021   The Civil Appeals List is divided into various parts the names of which are, in most cases, self explanatory:

(1) The applications list states the fixed dates for hearing of those requests for permission and ancillary applications which proceed to a hearing.

(2) The appeals list includes all cases in which permission to appeal is not required or has been obtained.

(3) The expedited list comprises appeals or applications where the court has directed an expedited hearing. A request for expedition should be

made to the Master by letter or facsimile and copied to other parties. The current practice of the court on expedited appeals is explained in *Unilever Plc v Chetaro Proprietaries Ltd (Practice Note)* [1995] 1 W.L.R. 243.

(4) The stand out list comprises appeals or applications which, for good reason, are not at present ready to proceed and therefore are not presently listed for hearing.

(5) The fixtures list comprises appeals where a hearing date has been fixed in advance.

(6) Special fixtures list comprises cases which require special listing arrangements, for example, a group of cases to be listed before the same judges, or in a particular order, or at a given location.

(7) Second fixtures list for cases which already have one fixed date. The second fixture is an earlier date upon which the appeal may be heard if other appeals listed for that day are later cancelled. This form of double booking works very well so long as information about the cancellation is received sufficiently far in advance to enable adequate notice to be given to the parties given the second fixture.

(8) The short warned list comprises cases selected by the court as being relatively short appeals which can reasonably be prepared by substitute advocates at short notice should the parties' chosen advocates not be available when the appeal is called on. Appeals assigned to the short warned list will be put "on call" from a specified date.

Hearing the appeal

In times past the court hearing the appeal consisted of an uneven number of judges not less than three. For many years two-judge courts have been empowered to hear certain types of appeal. SCA 1981, s.54(5) provides a tie-breaker in the event of an appeal being heard by an even number of judges who, in the result, are equally divided as to what the decision should be; the case must, if any party so applies, be reargued before and determined by an uneven number of judges not less than three, before any appeal is made to the House of Lords. As to the doctrine of precedent in the case of two-judge courts, see *Foster v Zott GmbH* (2000) L.T.L., May 24.

44.022

After the hearing of the appeal, the court will often adjourn for judgment to be given at a later date. The parties will be notified when the judgment is ready but, to save time, i.e. to save time attending merely to hear the judges read out their judgment, it is now the normal practice for a judgment to be handed down in writing two working days prior to the adjourned hearing date. The written judgment is still confidential at this stage and a "time embargo" will be noted upon it. This enables the parties to consider whether it is necessary to make further applications to the court, for example, for costs (i.e. the costs "here and below"); or for leave to appeal to the House of Lords (see Ch.45).

Judicial review appeals

44.023 The procedure on judicial review applications is described in para.24.001, above. Applications for permission to apply are made to a High Court judge and therefore a right of appeal, subject to a permission requirement, lies to the Court of Appeal. Rule 52.15 confirms that, if permission to appeal is refused at a hearing in the High Court, the intending appellant may apply to the Court of Appeal for permission. However, the time limit for doing so is shorter than usual (only seven days from the High Court refusal) and the documents to accompany the appellant's notice are different (see PD 52, para.15.4). More importantly, the Court of Appeal may treat the application for permission as the appeal itself and, if the applicant is successful, grant the permission to apply for judicial review instead of merely granting permission to appeal.

If the Court of Appeal refuses permission to appeal to it against the decision of the High Court refusing permission to apply for judicial review, no appeal can be made to the House of Lords (see *R. v Secretary of State for Trade and Industry, ex parte Eastaway* [2000] 1 W.L.R. 2222). But, if the Court of Appeal grants permission to appeal to it against the High Court's refusal of permission to apply for judicial review and then itself refuses permission to apply for judicial review, the House of Lords does have jurisdiction to hear an appeal against that refusal (see *R. v Hammersmith and Fulham LBC, ex parte Burkett* [2002] 1 W.L.R. 1593).

Another unusual feature of judicial review appeals is that, if the Court of Appeal gives permission to apply for judicial review, it may also, in an exceptional case, direct that the application for judicial review will be heard in the Court of Appeal rather than in the High Court. A direction such as this "will be rare, but may be appropriate where, for example, the High Court is bound by authority or for some other reason, an appeal to the Court of Appeal will be inevitable" (PD 52, para.15.3).

CHAPTER 45

Appeals to the House of Lords

INTRODUCTION

About one tenth of the cases which go to the Court of Appeal Civil Division are taken on further appeal to the House of Lords. Under the Administration of Justice (Appeals) Act 1934 the prospective appellant must obtain leave to appeal either from the Court of Appeal or from the House of Lords itself. The criteria upon which leave is granted include: (a) the general public importance of the case; (b) the likelihood of success; and (c) often the most significant, the degree of dissension the case may have previously caused, i.e. the Court of Appeal decided by a majority and/or reversed the trial judge's decision (see generally Blom-Cooper and Drewry, Final Appeal (1972), pp.125, 134; *Lonrho Ltd v Shell Petroleum Co. No.1 Ltd* [1980] 1 W.L.R. 627, HL; and *Garden Cottage Foods Ltd v Milk Marketing Board* [1984] A.C. 130). It is quite wrong to assume that, if the House refuses leave to appeal, it thereby impliedly indicates some approval of the decision sought to be appealed, *Re Wilson* [1985] A.C. 750.

45.001

Save in very exceptional circumstances, it is the function of the Court of Appeal rather than the House of Lords to supervise the administration of civil procedure: see *Callery v Gray* [2002] U.K.H.L. 28; [2002] 3 All E.R. 417 and *Birkett v James* [1978] A.C. 297.

The procedure on appeal to the House of Lords is governed by Practice Directions (HLPD) (the full text of which otherwise known as the Blue Book: 2007 edition) is at the House of Lords website (*www.publications.parliament.uk/pa/ld199697/ldinfo/ld08judg/bluebook/bluebk-1.htm*). What follows is a brief introduction to two of the main forms of petition, the petition for leave to appeal (or leave to appeal out of time) and the petition of appeal or cross-appeal. Both forms of petition are prescribed. Neither of them operates as a stay of execution of any order appealed from. A party seeking a stay should apply to the court below, not to the House of Lords (HLPD direction 43).

The title of the proceedings will be the same as the title in the court below. Save as stated below in relation to leapfrog appeals, a copy of the petition must be served on the respondents or their agents either by delivery in person or by first-class post. They must also be given notice of the intention to present the petition on or after a specified day. The original petition must then be "presented" (i.e. lodged) in the Judicial Office of the House of Lords endorsed with a certificate of service.

Respondents intending to take part in the proceedings should enter an appearance (i.e. give details of their names and addresses to the Judicial Office by post or in person) as soon as they have received service. Also, parties intending to take no part in the proceedings should so notify the Judicial Office. On a petition for leave to appeal and on a petition of appeal, fees are payable on lodging the petition, on entering appearances and at other stages (HLPD Appendix C). Solicitors outside London are not now required to appoint London agents. However, if they do not, and if this increases the costs incurred, the increased costs may be disallowed on taxation (i.e. the detailed assessment of any costs awarded) (HLPD direction 8.1).

Special provisions are made for commencement in the case of a leapfrog appeal. The petition for leave to appeal may be presented by all or any of the parties. If it is presented by some of them it need not be served on the others, although they must be given notice of the intention to present.

Next after commencement comes a short period of time in which to prepare for and complete the lodging of papers (by the appellant in the case of a petition for leave to appeal) or the lodging and exchanging of cases (by all parties in a petition of appeal or cross-appeal). Once the paperwork is complete the proceedings will move forward for determination by an Appeal Committee or an Appellate Committee, as the case may be (see further, below).

If any costs are awarded bills for taxation must be lodged with the Judicial Office within three months of the date of the relevant committee's judgment or decision (HLPD direction 22.1). All orders of the House of Lords which reverse or vary orders of a lower court must be made orders of the High Court (see further CPR, PD 40B, para.13.1). For the purposes of enforcement, other orders of the House of Lords (e.g. an order for costs) may also be made orders of the High Court.

PETITION FOR LEAVE TO APPEAL

45.002 An application for leave must first be made to the Court of Appeal (unless of course it is a leapfrog appeal). The time limit for an application to the House of Lords is one month from the date of the judgment or order being appealed, or within such extended time as the House of Lords may allow. An application for leave and for an extension of time may both be included in the same petition. The time limit for leave is automatically extended in cases in which an application for funding by the Legal Services Commission (LSC) has been made. However, in such a case, the application to the LSC must be reported to the Judicial Office before the one-month period expires and notification of the proposed petition must be given to the other parties. The time limit for the appellant to lodge the necessary papers is just one week after the lodgment of the petition.

A petition for leave to appeal (or leave to appeal out of time) is usually referred to an Appeal Committee consisting of three Lords of Appeal. In the case of a leapfrog appeal, the application for leave is always determined without a hearing. In most other cases also the application for leave to appeal will be determined without a hearing, i.e. cases where the Appeal Committee reaches a unanimous decision, whether for or against the grant of leave (a unanimous decision for the grant of leave is provisional only and the respondents will be invited to lodge written objections). A hearing will be convened in cases in which the opinions of the members of the Appeal Committee are divided, or where, for some other reason, oral argument is required. The likely time delay between lodging all necessary papers and obtaining some notification thereon is eight sitting weeks. As to applications for expedited consideration see HLPD direction 4.25. At a hearing only one agent or counsel may appear on each side and, if costs are awarded, no fees will be allowed in excess of a junior counsel's fee. As to the costs of proceedings determined without a hearing, see HLPD direction 5.1. An Appeal Committee never gives reasons for its decisions.

PETITION OF APPEAL OR CROSS-APPEAL

A party can commence an appeal or cross-appeal only if either: 45.003

(1) the Court of Appeal has granted leave and the petition is presented within three months of the decision appealed from (in the case of an appeal) or within six weeks of an appeal (in the case of a cross-appeal). In the case of an appeal there is an automatic extension of time in cases in which an application for LSC funding has been made but, in this instance, it is still necessary to give information about the case to the Judicial Office and to the respondents before the initial period expires; or
(2) the House of Lords (in determining an earlier petition, see above) has already granted leave to appeal and/or has already extended the time for appealing.

On commencing an appeal the appellant must give security for costs by payment of £25,000 into the House of Lords Security Fund Account. No interest is payable on security moneys. Security is not required from an appellant who is funded by the LSC, an appellant in a cross-appeal, or in any other case in which all the respondents agree to security for costs being waived (see generally HLPD direction 10 and Appendix L at *White Book*, vol.2, para.4A–129).

The time limit for the appellants to prepare and lodge their "Statement of Facts and Issues" and the "Appendix" and to set down the appeal is six weeks from the presentation of the appeal. House of Lords cases are, ex hypothesi, cases of general public importance which have already resulted in several previous hearings in the lower courts. It is therefore not surprising that the amount of documentation which has to be prepared and lodged within six weeks of the presentation of the petition is, on any view, formidable.

Statement of facts and issues

45.004 This is a comparatively brief document which will be read in conjunction with the Appendix (see below). It must summarise the facts and issues involved in the appeal but need not contain any account of the proceedings below or the judgments previously given. Appellants and respondents must seek to collaborate in the preparation of the statement. However, if they cannot agree any disputed material should be included in each party's case as defined below (HLPD direction 11.1).

Appendix

45.005 This should contain any extracts from documents used in evidence or in recording proceedings if they are clearly necessary for the support and understanding of the argument of the appeal. References to the contents of the Appendix must be entered in the outside margin of the statement of facts and issues. The costs of preparing the Appendix initially falls on the appellants but its contents "must be agreed between the parties" (HLPD direction 12.1).

Time estimates

45.006 Within seven days of setting down (i.e. within seven weeks of presentation of the petition) each party must notify the Judicial Office of the amount of time in hours considered necessary to present that party's case. A hearing date will then be arranged.

Appellants' and respondents' cases

45.007 After setting down and before the proposed date of hearing the parties are required to lodge their "cases", i.e. a succinct statement of the arguments to be made on their behalf (see generally, HLPD 15). The lodgement of a case carries the right to be heard by two counsel one of whom may be leading counsel.

Appellants must lodge eight copies of their case in the judicial office no later than five weeks before the proposed date of the hearing. No later than three weeks before that date, the respondents also must lodge in the Judicial Office eight copies of their case in response. Respondents can lodge separate cases if it can be shown that some conflict of interests arises between them (contrast appellants who must always combine together to lodge a single case; HLPD direction 15.8). Respondents acting as such are not entitled to lodge a case which seeks some variation of the decision of the court below. Contentions of that nature must be made the subject of a separate petition of cross-appeal. It is very important to note that the presentation of a petition of appeal does not entitle the respondents to present a cross-appeal; they, like the appellant must first obtain leave, either from the court below or from an Appeal Committee.

Parties must exchange cases but there is no obligation to do so before lodging them. Subsequently the respondent must supply copies to the appellant as to enable the appellant to prepare the 15 bound volumes each containing a miscellany of documents. Bound volumes must be lodged no later than two weeks before the proposed date of hearing. At the same time the appellant must also lodge seven bound copies of all authorities which may be needed during the hearing (see generally HLPD direction 15, 16, 17 and Appendix B).

If and when briefs to counsel are delivered the Judicial Office should be informed of the names of the advocates briefed (as to the recovery of costs of separate representation where parties have the same interest in the appeal, see *Bolton Metropolitan District Council v Secretary of State for the Environment* [1995] 1 W.L.R. 1176).

The hearing of the appeal

The hearing of the appeal usually takes place before an Appellate Committee consisting of five Lords of Appeal sitting in a committee room of the House of Lords. Any submissions as to costs should be made at the hearing of the appeal immediately the argument is concluded. Any such submission should then be repeated in writing within 14 days after the hearing (HLPD direction 19.1). In the House of Lords submissions as to costs are never postponed to the period after judgment is given as is the practice in most other courts. 45.008

As to the delivery of judgment, the speeches prepared by the members of the Appellate Committee are considered in the Chamber of the House of Lords and voted on. In theory votes are cast by the House; in practice they are cast only by the members of the Appellate Committee involved. Agents are notified in advance of the date of judgment. For each party or group of parties who have lodged a case only one junior counsel is required to attend and no more than a junior counsel's fee will be allowed on taxation.

After judgment has been given, a final order will be drawn up by the Judicial Office. Any security moneys received are returned to the appellant, subject of course to any prior claim the respondents may have if costs were awarded to them.

Bills of cost for taxation must be lodged within three months of the date of the final judgment. Applications for an extension of this period must be sought in writing before it expires. If no such application is made a bill lodged out of time will be accepted only in exceptional circumstances (see generally HLPD direction 22.1). Taxations are conducted by the Judicial Clerk, or by the senior costs judge, or, in his absence, any costs judge nominated by him. There is a right of appeal to an appellate committee, but only upon questions of principle.

As to making the order of the House of Lords an order of the High Court, see para.45.001.

INDEX

[all references are to paragraph number]

Abuse of process
  judicial review, 24.001
  striking out, 33.008
Acknowledgement of claim
  counterclaims, 18.009
  defendant's response, 6.015–6.017
Acknowledgement of service
  amendment of acknowledgment, 9.015
  documents, 8.001, 8.009, 9.013
  failure to acknowledge, 9.014, 15.001
  judicial review, 24.002, 24.003
  late filing, 15.003
  Part 8 claims, 10.003
  service on defendant, 9.013
  withdrawal of acknowledgement, 9.015
Actions
  consolidation, 7.016
  derivative claims, 7.021
  miscellaneous actions, 7.022
  representative actions
    see **Representative actions**
Addresses for service
  see also **Service**
  claim form, 8.009
  foreign companies, 8.009
  jurisdiction, within, 8.009
  last known address, 8.009, 9.006
  place of business, 8.009
  resident out of jurisdiction, 8.009
  solicitor's address, 8.009
  usual address, 8.009
Administration of estates
  claims procedure, 24.016
Administrative Court
  judicial review, 24.001
Admiralty claims
  procedure, 24.014
Admissions
  amendment, 16.009
  costs
    fixed costs, 38.010
    sanctions, 32.007
  counterclaims, 16.002, 16.003
  entire claim, 16.004
  failure to admit, 32.007
  filing, 16.003, 16.004, 16.006
  generally, 16.001
  judgment and orders
    interim payments, 25.008
    procedure, 16.002–16.004
    written admissions, 16.002
  notice to admit, 32.007, 32.008
  oral admissions, 16.002
  overriding objective, 16.001
  payments, 16.007, 16.008
  personal injury claims, 16.001
  pre-action admissions, 16.001
  response packs, 16.001, 16.003, 16.004
  specified sums, 16.004
  statement of case, 16.001
  stay of proceedings, 16.010
  unspecified sums, 16.006
  withdrawal, 16.009
  written admissions, 16.001, 16.002
Advocacy
  closing statements, 37.010
  cross-examination, 37.012
  examination in chief, 37.011
  generally, 37.008
  opening statements, 37.010
  preparation, 37.009
  presentation, 37.010, 37.013
  re-examination, 37.014
  technique, 37.008, 37.012, 37.013
Affidavits
  affirmation, 14.002
  authenticity, 14.003
  content
    details of exhibits, 14.003
    details of identity, 14.003
    ending, 14.003
    title to action, 14.003
  final version, 14.012
  inspection, 30.017
  solicitor's duties, 14.004
  swearing, 14.002
  use, 14.002

INDEX

Allocation
  allocation factors
    additional claims, 9.036
    complexity of case, 9.036
    financial value, 9.036
    nature of remedy, 9.036
    number of parties, 9.036
    value of counterclaim, 9.036
  change of track
    appeals, 9.041
    consent of parties, 9.038
    differing claims, 9.039
    key considerations, 9.038
    notice of allocation, 9.040
    re-allocation, 9.041
  court fees, 9.027
  differing claims, 9.039
  exaggerated claims
    costs, 9.035
    detection, 9.035
    generally, 9.035
    penalties, 9.035
    personal injury claims, 9.035
  fast track, 21.004
  financial value
    amounts not in dispute, 9.034
    assessment, 9.034
    contributory negligence, 9.034
    costs, 9.034
    interest claims, 9.034
  hearings
    case management powers, 9.037
    costs penalties, 9.037
    generally, 9.037
  multiple defendants, 9.027
  multi-track, 22.001
  overriding objective, 9.027
  Part 8 claims, 10.001
  possession claims, 24.005
  questionnaires
    see **Allocation questionnaires**
  small claims track
    consent, 20.007, 20.012
    directions, 20.004
    generally, 20.003
    "paper disposals", 20.006
    preliminary hearings, 20.005
  tracks
    fast track, 9.027
    multi-track, 9.027
    small claims, 9.027

Allocation questionnaires
  additional information, 9.028
  case management information, 9.028
  completion, 9.028
  costs, 9.028
  filing, 9.029, 9.037
  location of trial, 9.028
  pre-action protocols, 9.028
  proposed directions, 9.028
  service, 9.027
  settlement, 9.028
  trial estimate, 9.028

Alternative dispute resolution (ADR)
  pre-action protocols, 6.019
  preparation of evidence, 6.019
  settlement outside proceedings, 34.002

***American Cynamid* principles**
  see also **Interim injunctions**
  adequacy of damages, 27.005
  balance of convenience, 27.003, 27.005
  damages undertakings, 27.005
  economic factors, 27.005
  exceptions, 27.006, 27.011
  flexibility, 27.005
  maintaining status quo, 27.005
  prospects of success, 27.004
  receivership orders, 27.030
  serious issue to be tried, 27.004
  social factors, 27.005
  strength of case, 27.005

Antisocial behaviour
  claims procedure, 24.017

Appeals
  appellant's notice
    challenges, 44.010
    content, 44.010
    documents, 44.011
    extension of time, 44.009
    filing, 44.009
    form, 44.010
    human rights claims,
    late appeals, 44.009
    service, 44.009, 44.013
  assessment of costs, 44.018
  Court of Appeal
    see **Court of Appeal**
  cross-appeals, 45.001, 45.003
  grounds, 44.017
  grounds for exclusion
    academic points, 44.004

contractual terms, 44.004
hypothetical questions, 44.004
hearings, 44.012, 44.017
House of Lords
  see **House of Lords**
judicial review, 44.009, 44.011, 44.023
lower court's decision
  new evidence, 44.017
  procedural irregularities, 44.017
  review, 44.017
permission
  applications, 44.005, 44.006
  case management decisions, 44.005
  compelling reasons, 44.005
  conditional, 44.005
  frivolous appeals, 44.008
  grounds, 44.005
  limitations, 44.005
  not required, 44.005, 44.012
  refusal, 44.003, 44.004, 44.008, 44.018
  respondent's notice, 44.013, 44.014
  second appeals, 44.005, 44.007
  setting aside, 44.005
  unnecessary appeals, 44.008
procedure
  ancillary applications, 44.016
  date of hearing, 44.012
  hear by date, 44.012
  "listing window", 44.012
  notification, 44.012
respondents
  notice of hearing, 44.013
  respondent's notice, 44.013, 44.014
  response, 44.013
  skeleton arguments, 44.013, 44.015
routes of appeal
  abnormal routes, 44.001
  generally, 44.001
  interactive routes, 44.001
  leapfrog appeals, 44.003
  multi-track, 44.002
  specialist proceedings, 44.002
  statutory provisions, 44.001
security for costs, 26.002
small claims track, 20.014
time wasting, 44.017
Application notices
disclosure and inspection, 30.021
drafting, 14.001

interim applications, 13.002, 13.008, 14.001
interim payments, 25.008
procedure, 14.001
Arbitration
applications, 24.015
arbitration awards, 24.015, 34.002
arbitration clauses, 34.002
claim forms, 24.015
costs, 34.002
evidence, 34.002
generally, 34.001, 34.002
hearings, 34.002
privacy, 34.002
procedure, 24.015, 34.002
settlement outside proceedings, 34.001, 34.002
single arbitrator, 34.002
Attachment of earnings
application costs, 40.007
cessation of employment, 40.007
earnings, 40.006
entitlement to interest, 40.007
hearings, 40.006
normal deduction rate, 40.006
orders, 40.006
procedure, 40.006
protected earning rate, 40.006
statement of means, 40.006
statutory provisions, 40.006
Attendance
failure to attend
  claimants, 37.007
  court orders, 37.007
  defendants, 37.007
  striking out, 37.007
solicitors, 37.001
witnesses, 36.004, 37.002
witness summons, 36.003

Bankruptcy
see also **Insolvency**
bankruptcy orders
  annulment, 42.016
  discharge, 42.016
  effect, 42.015
  generally, 42.002
  pending actions, 42.015
  subsequent procedure, 42.016
bankruptcy petition
  debtor's response, 42.013

Bankruptcy—cont'd
documents, 42.012
forms, 42.012
generally, 42.011
hearings, 42.014
Land Charges Search, 42.012
presentation, 42.012
stay of execution, 42.012
Bankruptcy Restrictions Order, 42.016
creditors' meeting, 42.016
Official Receiver, 42.016
specialist topics, 42.022
statement of affairs, 42.016

Barristers
Code of Conduct, 36.011
fees
    arbitration, 2.018
    brief fees, 2.018, 36.011
    calculation, 2.018
    contractual basis, 2.018
    hourly rates, 2.018
    Legal Service Commission funding, 2.018
    non-contractual terms, 2.018
instructions
    direct instruction, 1.018, 2.018
    licensed access, 2.018
    professional client access, 2.018
    public access, 1.018, 2.018
proofs of evidence, 37.001
rights of audience, 1.018
trial briefs
    acceptance, 36.011
    brief fees, 36.011
    contents, 36.010
    delivery to counsel, 36.011
    documents, 36.010
    drafting, 36.010
    importance, 36.010
    witness statements, 36.010
witness discussions, 37.001

Benefits
attendance allowances, 4.004
damages claims
    compensation, 4.004
    special damages, 4.044
entitlement, 4.004
mobility allowances, 4.004

Brief fees
agreement, 36.011

Brussels Convention
civil jurisdiction, 11.002
enforcement of judgments, 11.002

Bundles
appeals, 44.020
contents, 36.006
core bundles, 36.007
estimates of time, 36.008
expert reports, 36.006
filing, 36.006
generally, 36.006
judicial review hearings, 24.003
original documents, 36.006
preparation, 36.006
reading lists, 36.008
skeleton arguments, 36.007

Case allocation
see **Allocation**

Case management
case management conferences, 13.007, 22.004, 22.008
case management directions, 13.007
Commercial Court, 24.012
counterclaims, 18.010
court records
    access, 1.022
    contents, 1.022
    maintenance, 1.022
court's duty, 1.006, 1.011
expert evidence, 23.005
importance, 1.011
information technology, 22.017
judicial case management, 1.006, 1.011
judicial review, 24.002, 24.003
meaning, 1.006
Part 8 claims, 10.005
parties' co-operation, 1.011
possession claims, 24.006
statements of case, 12.002
tracks
    fast track, 1.013, 21.003, 21.004
    generally, 1.011
    multi-track, 1.013, 22.002
    small claims, 1.013

Charging orders
land
    accrual of interest, 40.008
    generally, 40.008
    joint ownership, 40.009

jurisdiction, 40.009
procedure, 40.010
sales of land, 40.008
partnership property, 40.013
securities, 40.011
Charities
claims procedure, 24.016
Cheques
actions, involving, 19.009
Children
definition, 7.005
interim payments, 7.005
limitation, 5.012
litigation friends
see **Litigation friends**
parties, 7.005
service, on, 8.011
Civil Appeals Office
applications, 44.020
case bundles, 44.020
electronic filing, 44.020
letters of notification, 44.020
video links, 44.020
Civil Appeals List
appeals list, 44.021
applications list, 44.021
expedited list, 44.021
second fixtures list, 44.021
special fixtures list, 44.021
stand out list, 44.021
Civil evidence
see **Evidence**
Civil Jurisdiction and Judgments Acts (CJJA)
defendant's presence, 11.008
domicile, 11.005
jurisdiction, 11.007, 11.008
scope, 11.001, 11.002
Civil Procedure Rules (CPR)
application, 1.005
compliance, 1.015
costs, 13.009
see also **Costs**
disclosure and inspection
see **Disclosure and inspection**
guidance, 1.005
overriding objective
application, 1.006
assistance of parties, 1.011
case management, 1.006, 1.011
duty of parties, 1.006

economy, 1.008
equality of arms, 1.006, 1.009
exercise of judicial power, 1.010
fairness, 1.006, 1.011
judicial interpretation, 1.010
proportionality, 1.008
purpose, 1.006
speed, 1.008
practice directions, 1.012
primary source, 1.005
procedural code, 1.006, 1.007
purpose, 1.005
summary judgments
"no real prospects of success", 19.004, 19.006
Part 24 rules, 19.001–19.006
time limits, 1.016
Claim forms
arbitration proceedings, 24.015
Commercial Court proceedings, 24.012
Crown Proceedings, 24.018
details of claim, 9.006
drafting, 12.009
judicial review, 24.002, 24.003
nature of claim, 9.006
Part 8 claims, 10.002
particulars of claim, 9.008, 9.012
Production Centre cases, 9.021
service
address for service, 8.009
attempted service, 9.006
extensions of time, 9.006, 9.007
failure to serve
mistaken address, 9.006
notice of service, 9.007
service on agent, 8.018
specified claim, 8.008
time limits, 9.005, 9.006
unspecified claim, 8.008
statement of value, 12.010
Claims
abandoned claims, 15.016
administration of estates, 24.016
Admiralty claims, 24.014
anti-social behaviour, 24.017
arbitration procedure, 24.015
charities, 24.016
claim forms
see **Claim forms**
claim letters, 6.014

INDEX

Claims—*cont'd*
  Commercial Court proceedings, 24.012
  Crown Proceedings, 24.018
  damages
    aggravated damages, 12.014
    provisional damages, 12.015
  debt actions, 6.021
  defendant's response, 6.015–6.017
  derivative actions, 7.021
  drafting
    damages claims, 12.014, 12.015
    defamation claims, 12.017
    interest claims, 12.013
    interference with goods, 12.016
    return of goods, 12.020
  fixed date actions, 9.020
  harassment proceedings, 24.017
  intellectual property claims, 24.016
  judicial review, 24.001
  Mercantile Courts, 24.013
  patent claims, 24.016
  pre-action protocols, 6.013
  setting aside
    see **Setting aside**
  transfer of claims, 15.016
  trusts, 24.016

Claims management companies
  growth, 2.013
  insurance cover, 2.013
  litigation services, 2.013
  malpractice, 2.013
  personal injury claims, 2.013
  referrals, 2.013

Client relationship
  disputes
    see **Solicitor/client disputes**
  first interview
    client's agenda, 6.002
    client's questions, 6.007
    client's statement, 6.004
    correct parties, 6.003
    importance, 6.001
    legal advice, 6.005
    overriding objective, 6.006
    preparation, 6.001

Collision claims
  expert evidence, 23.022

Commercial Court
  case management
    case memorandum, 24.012
    conferences, 24.012
    progress monitoring, 24.012
  claim forms
    issue, 24.012
    response pack, 24.012
    service, 24.012
    statement of case, 24.012
  defence, 24.012
  disclosure, 24.012
  expert witnesses, 24.012
  procedure, 24.012

Companies
  parties, 7.007
  winding up
    see **Winding up**

Conditional fee agreements (CFAs)
  collective conditional fee agreements, 2.017
  defamation actions, 29.023
  interest payments, 29.023
  legal expenses insurance, 2.009
  regulation, 2.014, 2.015
  settlement, 6.026
  success fees
    barrister's fees, 2.016
    base fee, 2.016
    experts' fees, 2.016
    fee deferment element, 2.016, 38.023, 38.027
    interim order for costs, 2.016
    interim payments, 2.016
    "no win, no fee", 2.015
    risk element, 2.016, 38.023–38.025
    Solicitors' Code of Conduct, 2.016
  without success fees
    barrister's fees, 2.015
    consumer protection, 2.015
    experts' fees, 2.015
    insurance cover, 2.015
    interim order for costs, 2.015
    interim payments, 2.015
    liability for costs, 2.015
    "no win, no fee", 2.015
    "no win, reduced fee", 2.015
    Solicitors' Code of Conduct, 2.007, 2.015

Corporate insolvency
  see **Winding up**

Costs
  additional liability, 38.007
  appeals, 44.018

INDEX

assessment basis
  conduct of parties, 38.018
  exaggerated claims, 38.018
  indemnity, 38.016
  proportionality, 38.017
  reasonable costs, 38.016, 38.018
  standard basis, 38.016, 38.017
assessment methods
  detailed assessment, 13.011, 38.015
  fixed costs, 38.010–38.012
  fixed success fees, 38.013
  generally, 38.009
  summary assessment, 13.010, 38.014
base costs, 38.007
Bullock Orders, 38.008
contractual terms, subject to, 39.019
costs of issues, 38.008
costs only proceedings
  claim forms, 39.001
  procedure, 39.001
costs orders
  court fees, 38.002
  detailed assessment, 38.031
  discretionary nature, 38.021
  indemnity principle, 38.019
  interim hearings, 38.031
  judicial discretion, 38.008
  legal costs, 38.002
  LSC funding, 39.014
  non-parties, 39.015
  scope, 38.008
  witness payments, 38.002
definition, 38.001
detailed assessment proceedings
  see **Detailed assessment proceedings**
disclosure, 2.023
discretionary nature, 38.008, 38.021
disposal hearings, 17.005
disputes
  see **Solicitor/client disputes**
division of entitlement, 38.008
early judgment, 38.010
expenses, 38.006
fixed costs
  amounts payable, 38.010
  default judgment, 38.010
  fast track, 38.011
  generally, 38.008
  judgment on admissions, 38.010

pre-issue settlements, 38.012
road traffic accidents, 38.012
summary judgments, 38.010
foreign judgments, 40.017
funding
  non-parties, 2.022
general rule, 13.009
group litigation orders, 39.016
hearings
  interim hearings, 38.031
  procedure, 38.040
  request for hearing, 38.038
indemnity principle
  see **Indemnity principle**
insurance
  insurance market, 38.028
  premiums, 38.028–38.030
judgment and orders, 13.009
judicial discretion, 13.009
judicial review, 24.001, 24.003
legal costs, 38.003
Legal Services Commission
  see **Legal Services Commission funding**
litigants in person, 38.004
Part 36 offers
  costs advantages, 29.001, 29.016 ???
  costs penalties, 29.021
  enhanced costs, 29.023
  inconsistent provisions, 29.005
  order for costs, 29.021
  pressures, 29.004
  provision for costs, 29.016
  small claims track, 29.003
possession claims, 20.012
practice directions, 1.012
prospective costs orders, 39.018, 39.019
protective costs orders, 39.017
restrictions, 20.010, 20.011, 38.021, 38.022
road traffic accidents, 38.013
routine awards, 20.010
Sanderson Orders, 38.008
security for costs
  see **Security for costs**
small claims track, 38.021
solicitors, 38.005
  see also **Solicitor/client disputes**
success fees
  see **Success fees**

699

INDEX

Costs—*cont'd*
  unreasonable behaviour, 20.011
  unreasonable costs, 38.016, 38.018, 38.040
  wasted costs orders
    applicants, 39.002
    hearings, 39.002
    judicial powers, 39.002
    meaning, 39.002
    procedure, 39.002
    vexatious conduct, 39.002
  witness allowances, 38.006

Costs only proceedings
  claim forms, 39.001
  procedure, 39.001

Costs orders
  court fees, 38.002
  detailed assessment, 38.031
  discretionary nature, 38.021
  indemnity principle, 38.019
  interim hearings, 38.031
  judicial discretion, 38.008
  legal costs, 38.002
  LSC funding, 39.014
  non-parties, 39.015
  scope, 38.008
  witness payments, 38.002

Counterclaims
  acknowledgement of claim, 18.009
  actions
    claimants, 18.002
    co-defendants, 18.004
    non-claimants, 18.003
    non-parties, 18.005
  admissions, 16.002, 16.003
  case management, 18.010
  claims
    additional claims, 18.007
    connection with original claim, 18.007
    indemnity, 18.004
    service, 18.008
    third party, 18.006
  costs, 18.011
  Crown Proceedings, 24.018
  defences, 9.018, 9.019, 12.042, 18.002, 18.009
  drafting, 12.040
  generally, 18.002
  limitation period, 18.002
  Part 36 offers, 29.006

  particulars of claim, 18.002
  response packs, 12.041
  service, 11.014
  similar remedies, 18.007
  statement of case, 18.002
  statement of value, 18.002

County courts
  commencement of proceedings, 9.002
  financial limits, 1.002, 9.002
  jurisdictional limits, 1.002, 1.003
  money judgments, 40.002

Court fees
  exemption, 1.014
  orders for costs, 38.002
  payment stages, 1.014

Court of Appeal
  see also **Appeals**
  Civil Appeals List
    see **Civil Appeals List**
  Civil Appeals Office
    see **Civil Appeals Office**
  Civil Division, 1.004
  Criminal Division, 1.004
  hearings, 44.022
  jurisdiction, 44.017, 44.019
  procedure
    applications, 44.019
    exercise of powers, 44.019

Courts
  case management, 1.017
  court offices
    agreement, on, 9.003
    location, 9.003
    transfers, 9.003
  court records
    access, 1.022
    contents, 1.022
    maintenance, 1.022
  definition of court, 1.017
  hearings
    private hearings, 1.017
    public hearings, 1.017
  judgments and orders, 1.017
  judicial function, 1.017
  proceedings
    human rights, 1.017
    publication, 1.017
    reporting restrictions, 1.017

Criminal Injuries Compensation Authority
  applications, 6.032

INDEX

awards, 6.032
compensation scheme, 6.032
loss of earnings, 6.032
medical treatment costs, 6.032
special expenses, 6.032
Crown proceedings
additional claims, 24.018
claims forms, 24.018
claims procedure, 24.018
counterclaims, 24.018
default judgments, 24.018
documents, 24.018
enforcement action, 24.018
set-off defence, 24.018
Court offices
agreement, on, 9.003
location, 9.003
transfers, 9.003
see also **Transfer of proceedings**

Damages
adequacy of damages, 27.005
aggravated damages, 12.014
bereavement damages, 4.018, 4.020, 4.021
general damages
loss of amenities, 4.010
loss of earnings, 4.011
mental anguish, 4.009
mental impairment, 4.010
nervous shock, 4.010
pain and suffering, 4.009
interest payments
awards, 4.011, 4.019, 4.020
bereavement damages, 4.020, 4.021
calculations, 4.020
fatal accidents, 4.020
guidelines, 4.020, 4.021
loss of amenity, 4.020, 4.021
loss of earnings, 4.020
non-payment, 4.022
pain and suffering, 4.020, 4.021
special account rate, 4.020, 4.021
provisional damages
applications, 4.015
"chance" cases, 4.015
drafting, 12.015
future deterioration, 4.015
judgments and orders, 4.015
offers, 4.015
serious additional damage, 4.015

statements of case, 4.015
special damages
agreement, 4.008
contractual sick pay, 4.003
loss of earnings, 4.002
measure of damages, 4.002
medical expenses, 4.006
mitigation of loss, 4.004
non-listed benefits, 4.005
restitutio in integrum, 4.002
state benefits, 4.004
third party expenses, 4.007
structured settlements
see **Structured settlements**
undertakings, 27.002, 27.005, 27.013
Debts
debt claims, 6.021
late payment
statutory compensation, 3.006
statutory interest, 3.006, 12.013
Declarations
drafting, 12.019
judicial review, 24.001, 24.003
Declarations of incompatibility
European Convention of Human Rights, 1.024
Defamation actions
conditional fee agreements, 29.023
drafting, 12.017, 12.029
interim injunctions, 27.011
limitation periods, 5.003, 5.016
Part 36 offers, 29.019, 29.023
Default judgments
acknowledgement of service, 15.001
additional claims, 15.018
availability, 15.004
Crown Proceedings, 24.018
fixed costs, 38.010
generally, 15.001
judgment on application
application procedure, 15.009
multiple defendants, 15.010
notice to defendant, 15.009
setting aside, 15.011
judgment on request
certification of service, 15.005
delivery of goods, 15.008
multiple defendants, 15.008
payment for goods, 15.008
procedure, 15.005
specified sums, 15.006

701

Default judgments—*cont'd*
   unspecified sums, 15.007
   setting aside
      abandoned claims, 15.016
      appeals, 15.011
      conditions, 15.012, 15.015
      good reason, 15.014
      judgment on application, 15.011
      judgment wrongly entered, 15.012
      judicial discretion, 15.012–15.014
      procedure, 15.011
      prospects of success, 15.013
      transfer of claims, 15.016
   variation, 15.017
Defence case
   acknowledgment of defence, 15.001
   admissions, 16.003, 16.004, 16.006–16.008
   counterclaims, 9.018, 18.002
      see also **Counterclaims**
   default judgment, 9.017
   defence to counterclaim, 9.019
   draft defence, 9.017
   failure to serve, 9.017
   filing
      failure to file, 15.001
      generally, 9.017
      importance, 15.002
      late filing, 15.003
   reply to defence, 9.019
   service, 9.017
   summery judgment, 9.017
Defences
   abatement, 12.037
   anticipation, 12.031
   contributory negligence, 12.038
   counterclaims, 12.042
   drafting
      admissions, 12.033
      allegations, 12.033
      denials, 12.033
      non-admissions, 12.033
      statement of facts, 12.033
   Limitation Act defences, 12.036
   set-off, 12.037
   tender before claim, 12.035, 29.020
Defendants
   acknowledgement of claim, 6.015–6.017
   attendance at trial, 37.007
   co-defendants, 18.004
   default judgments, 15.009, 15.010
   motor insurance policy, 6.028
   multiple defendants, 9.027, 11.005, 15.008, 15.010
   no case to answer, 37.005
   Part 36 offers, 6.025, 29.007, 29.008
   possession claims, 24.005
   response to proceedings, 6.015–6.017
   service on defendant
      acknowledgement of service, 9.013–9.015
      admissions, 9.016
      claim forms, 9.008, 9.012
      response pack, 9.012
   summary judgments, 19.011
Detailed assessment proceedings (costs)
   see also **Costs**
   appeals, 38.044
   burden of proof, 38.040
   commencement
      notice, 38.033
      timing, 38.034
   conduct of parties, 38.040
   costs
      agreed costs certificates, 38.043
      cost of proceedings, 38.041
      costs payable, 38.045
      final costs certificates, 38.042
      default costs certificates, 38.037
   disputed points, 38.035, 38.040
   documents, 38.040
   form of bill, 38.032
   hearings, 38.038, 38.040
   interim costs certificates, 38.038, 38.039
   standard assessment basis, 38.040
   success fees, 38.036
   timing, 38.031, 38.034
   unreasonable costs, 38.040
Directions
   case management directions, 13.007
   directions on listing, 36.002
   disposal hearings, 17.005, 17.006
   expert witnesses, 23.012
   fast track, 21.004
   judge's directions, 37.004
   multi-track
      allocation, 22.009
      compliance, 22.012
      disclosure, 22.010
      expert evidence, 22.010

variation, 22.011
practice directions, 1.012, 1.015, 1.016
small claims track, 20.004
witness statements, 22.010
Disclosure and inspection
application notices, 30.021
Commercial Court proceedings, 24.012
disclosure officers, 30.008
disclosure orders, 27.019, 27.028
disclosure statements, 30.008
documents
  adverse effect, 30.003, 30.008
  control, 30.005
  failure to disclose, 30.022
  lists, 30.008, 30.009
  meaning, 30.004
  medical records, 30.008
  reliance of parties, 30.003
  single copy, 30.004
  standard disclosure documents, 30.006, 30.008
  subsequent use, 30.020
  supporting another party, 30.003, 30.008
  without prejudice communications, 30.008
duty of disclosure, 30.008, 30.009
enforcement orders
  disclosure of assets, 27.028
  disclosure of documents, 27.028
  non-compliance, 27.028
expert evidence, 23.007, 23.011
extended disclosure, 30.007
extent, 30.007, 30.008
fast track, 21.005
freezing injunctions, 27.026
generally, 30.001
harassment proceedings, 30.018
inspection
  see **Inspection**
legal professional privilege, 30.013
limited disclosure, 30.007
meaning, 30.002
medical records, 30.007
multi-track, 22.005, 22.010
non-parties, 30.023
Norwich Pharmacal Rule
  see ***Norwich Pharmacal Rule***
overriding objective, 30.007, 30.016
pre-action disclosure, 30.024

pre-action protocols, 6.017, 30.001
preparation of evidence, 6.009, 6.017
prevention orders, 30.018
privilege, 30.010
purposes
  compromise of disputes, 30.001
  cost savings, 30.001
road traffic accidents, 30.007
search orders, 27.026
self-incrimination
  criminal proceedings, 27.027
  foreign courts, 27.027
  free-standing evidence, 27.027
  incriminating documents, 27.027
  privilege against self-incrimination, 27.027
small claims track, 30.003
specific disclosure, 30.021
specific searches, 30.007
split trials, 30.016
solicitor's role, 30.005
stages, 30.016
standard disclosure
  disputed issues, 30.003
  documents, 30.003, 30.006, 30.008
  electronic documents, 30.006, 30.008
  fast track, 30.003
  multi-track, 30.003
  parties, 30.003
  proportionality, 30.006–30.008
  reasonable search, 30.006, 30.008
verification, 27.026
withholding, 30.001
Discontinuance
see also **Termination**
discontinuance by notice
  consent of parties, 35.003
  liability for costs, 35.006
  permission of court, 35.004
  service of notice, 35.002
  setting aside, 35.005
generally, 35.001
subsequent proceedings, 35.007
Disposal hearings
allocation, 17.004
contested, 17.005
costs, 17.005
directions, 17.005, 17.006
evidence, 17.005
generally, 17.001

Disposal hearings—*cont'd*
  judgment and orders
    post-allocation, 17.007
    pre-allocation, 17.003–17.006
    relevant orders, 17.002
  pre-allocation judgments
    default judgments, 17.003, 17.005
    judgments on admissions, 17.003
    striking-out decisions, 17.003
    summary judgment applications, 17.003
    unspecified sums, 17.003
  procedure, 17.005
  uncontested, 17.005
Dispute resolution
  alternative dispute resolution (ADR)
    pre-action protocols, 6.019
    preparation of evidence, 6.019
    settlement outside proceedings, 34.002
  arbitration
    see **Arbitration**
  mediation
    see **Mediation**
  settlement
    see **Settlement**
  solicitor/client disputes
    see **Solicitor/client disputes**
Documents
  court records
    access, 1.022
    contents, 1.022
    maintenance, 1.022
  disclosure
    see **Disclosure and inspection**
  inspection
    confidential documents, 30.018
    copies, 30.011
    electronic documents, 30.011
    medical records, 30.018
    physical inspection, 30.011
    privileged material, 30.019
    translations, 30.011
  multi-track, 22.005
  service
    acknowledgement of service, 8.001, 8.009, 9.013
    authorised acceptance, 8.001
    companies, 8.001
    general rule, 8.001
    solicitors, 8.001

Drafting
  claim forms, 12.009
  claims
    agreement by conduct, 12.022
    Civil Evidence Act 1968, 12.024
    consumer credit agreements, 12.023
    damages, 12.014, 12.015
    defamation, 12.017, 12.029
    interest claims, 12.013
    interference with goods, 12.016
    negligence claims, 12.006, 12.012
    oral agreement claims, 12.021
    return of goods, 12.020
    written agreement claims, 12.021
  counterclaims, 12.040
  declarations, 12.019
  defences
    admissions, 12.033
    allegations, 12.033
    counterclaims, 12.042
    denials, 12.033
    non-admissions, 12.033
    statement of facts, 12.033
  injunctions, 12.019
  particulars of claim
    breach of contract, 12.012
    claim forms, 12.011
    contents, 12.011
    necessary facts, 12.012
    negligence claims, 12.012
    preparation, 12.011
  replies, 12.042
  statement of claim
    degree of detail, 12.006
    documentary evidence, 12.007
    foreign law, 12.007
    names of witnesses, 12.007
    negligence claims, 12.006
    points of law, 12.007
    precedent material, 12.006
    sufficient facts, 12.006
    unspecified financial loss, 12.006
  statement of value, 12.010

Enforcement
  enforcement orders
    disclosure of assets, 27.028
    disclosure of documents, 27.028
    non-compliance, 27.028
  foreign judgments
    domicile, 11.005, 11.007

Brussels Convention, 11.001
EC Regulation (44/2001), 11.002
EFTA countries, 11.002
EU Member States, 11.002
Lugano Convention, 11.002
multiple defendants, 11.005
statutory provisions, 11.001
injunctions
  attendance at hearing, 41.003
  committal proceedings, 41.003
  jurisdiction, 41.003
  penal notices, 41.003
  sequestration, 41.003
  standard of proof, 41.003
  undertakings in lieu, 41.003
money judgments
  see **Money judgments**
possession claims, 41.001
return of goods, 41.002
specific performance, 41.004

European Convention on Human Rights
Convention rights, 1.023
declarations of incompatibility, 1.024
public authorities, 1.023

European Court of Justice
referrals, 24.020

Evidence
admissibility, 31.009
adverse inferences, 31.004
advice, as to, 31.025
credibility, 31.004, 31.008
cross-examination, 31.004, 31.010
documentary evidence
  admissibility, 31.020
  agreement, 31.020
  authenticity, 31.020
  availability, 31.020
  original documents, 31.020
  video evidence, 31.020
evidentiary facts
  see **Evidentiary facts**
expert evidence
  see **Expert evidence**
failure to call, 31.004
generally, 31.001
hearsay evidence
  see **Hearsay evidence**
interim hearings, 14.005
opinion evidence, 31.011
preparation of evidence
  acknowledgement of claim, 6.015

alternative dispute resolution (ADR), 6.019
claim letters, 6.014
client's statement, 6.008
debt claims, 6.021
disclosure, 6.009, 6.017
drafting, 14.005
inspection of property, 6.011
medical examinations, 6.018
official records, 6.010
police accident reports, 6.010
pre-action meetings, 6.019
pre-action protocols, 6.013
proportionate costs, 6.020
witness interviews, 6.012
proof
  burden of proof, 31.004
  evidential burden, 31.003
  legal burden, 31.002
  proofs of evidence, 37.001
  standard of proof, 31.004
real evidence, 31.021
reconstruction evidence
  cross-examination, 31.024
  material mistakes, 31.024
  recollection of events, 31.024
  weight of evidence, 31,024
relevance, 31.009
similar fact evidence, 31.023
types of evidence
  models, 31.022
  photographs, 31.022
  plans, 31.022
without prejudice communications, 6.024
witness statements, 14.002, 31.005–31.010

Evidence in chief
witnesses, 31.010

Evidentiary facts
further information
  clarification, 32.001, 32.002
  requests, 32.002, 32.003
  responses, 32.003, 32.005
requests for information
  court orders, 32.006
  "fishing expeditions", 32.004
  guidance, 32.004
  necessary matters, 32.004
  notice to admit, 32.007, 32.008
  service on request, 32.003
  timing, 32.002

705

Expert evidence
acceptance, 23.001
collision claims, 23.022
competence, 23.010
disclosure, 23.007, 23.019
fast track, 21.007
inspection, 30.017
medical experts, 6.018
medical records, 6.018
multi-track, 22.006, 22.010
need, 23.002, 23.004
obtained by each party, 23.007
opinion or fact, 23.023
oral evidence, 23.018
permission
 conditional, 23.008
 court's permission, 23.005
 refusal, 23.008
pre-action, 23.002, 23.008
preparation of evidence, 6.018
proportionality, 23.015
restrictions
 case management issues, 23.005
 costs, 23.005
 court's permission, 23.005
 evidential issues, 23.005
 reasonable requirement provision, 23.004
 single joint expert, 23.006
small claims track, 20.008
statement of truth, 23.009
witnesses
 see Expert witnesses

Expert witnesses
attendance at trial, 36.004
Commercial Court proceedings, 24.012
competence, 23.010
conflicts of interest, 23.015
directions, 23.012
duties, 23.009–23.012
expert opinions, 23.001
impartiality, 23.011, 23.015
information, 23.013
independence, 23.011, 23.015
instructions, 23.006, 23.011
legal professional privilege, 23.011
numbers, 23.014
qualifications, 23.001, 3.009
statutory provisions, 23.001

Experts
see also **Expert evidence**
Civil Procedure Rules (CPR), 23.001
discussions, between, 23.018
expert reports
 content, 23.011
 exchange, 23.016, 23.017, 23.019
 format, 23.009
 inspection, 23.021
generally, 23.001
immunity, 23.018
instructions
 cross-examination, 23.011
 disclosure, 23.011
 legal professional privilege, 23.011
 transparency, 23.011
single joint experts
 challenges, to, 23.006
 expertise, 23.006
 fast track, 23.006
 fees, 23.006
 instructions, 23.006, 23.011
 medical negligence, 23.006
 meetings, 23.006
without prejudice meetings, 23.018
witnesses
 see **Expert witnesses**
written questions, 23.020

Failure to attend
setting aside, 43.002
variation orders, 43.002
witnesses, 31.004, 31.008, 31.017, 31.018

Failure to disclose
effects, 30.022

Fast track
adjournment, 21.011
allocation
 compliance, 21.010
 cooperation of parties, 21.004, 21.009
 directions, 21.004
 disclosure, 21.005
 expert evidence, 21.007
 split trials, 21.008
 trial date, 21.008, 21.011
 witness statements, 21.006
case management, 21.004
case plans, 21.003
claims less than £15000, 9.032

disclosure and inspection, 30.003
expert evidence, 9.032, 23.014
fixed costs, 38.011
landlord and tenant cases, 21.001
length of trial, 9.032
personal injury claims, 21.001
pre-trial checklist, 21.012, 36.001
procedure at trial, 37.003, 37.004
separate trials, 9.032
speed, 21.002
types of cases, 21.001
witness statements, 31.005

Fatal accidents
bereavement damages, 4.018
concurrent tortfeasors, 4.018
damages actions, 4.018
dependants, 4.018
loss of dependency, 4.018
non-wage earning wife, 4.018
"un-replaceable services", 4.018

Fixed date actions
particulars of claim, 9.020
possession claims, 9.020, 24.005
service, 9.020

Foreign judgments
anti-suit injunctions, 11.001, 11.016
appropriate forum, 11.001
certificates of judgment, 40.017
Civil Jurisdiction and Judgments Acts (CJJA), 11.001, 11.002
enforcement of judgments
  domicile, 11.005, 11.007, 40.016
  Brussels Convention, 11.001, 11.002
  EC Regulation (44/2001), 11.002
  EFTA countries, 11.002
  EU Member States, 11.002
  Lugano Convention, 11.002
  money judgments, 40.016
  multiple defendants, 11.005
  statutory provisions, 11.001
European Judgments Convention, 40.017
forum non conveniens, 11.001, 11.004, 11.008, 11.015
freezing injunctions, 27.018
jurisdiction
  acceptance, 11.007
  challenges, 11.010
  contract claims, 11.007
  exclusive jurisdiction, 11.006
  "first seised" rule, 11.004
  jurisdictional agreements, 11.007
  special jurisdiction rules, 11.007
  tort actions, 11.007
negative declarations, 11.001, 11.017
public policy, 40.017
recognition, 40.016
registration, 40.016, 40.017
security for costs,
stay of proceedings, 11.001, 11.004, 11.008, 11.015

Foreign law
judgments and orders
  see **Foreign judgments**
limitation, 5.020

Freezing injunctions
applications, 14.002, 27.017, 27.018
arguable case, 27.017
assets
  disposal, 27.015, 27.019
  identification, 27.017, 27.026
  overseas, 27.020
  risk of dissipation, 27.017
continuing obligation, 27.019
discharge, 27.021
disclosure, 27.019, 27.026, 27.028
effect, 27.015
evidence, 27.017
foreign proceedings, 27.018
grounds, 27.016, 27.017
growth, in, 27.016
importance, 27.016
indemnity, 27.019
jurisdiction, 27.015
limitation, 27.019
Mareva injunctions, 27.015
service, 27.030
standard forms, 27.019
substantive relief, 27.017
third party rights, 27.022
variation, 27.021

Funding
see **Legal advice and funding**

Future earnings
loss of earnings, 4.011, 4.016, 4.017, 4.020

Group litigation
effect, 7.020
multiple issues, 7.020
parties, 7.020
proceedings, 7.020
publicity, 7.020

INDEX

Harassment proceedings
claims procedure, 24.017
Hearings
bankruptcy petition, 42.014
costs
  detailed assessment proceedings, 38.038, 38.040
  interim hearings, 38.031
interim applications
  allocation hearings, 13.007
  case management conferences, 13.007
  case management directions, 13.007
  face-to-face hearings, 13.007
  listing hearings, 13.007
  pre-trial reviews, 13.007
  private hearings, 13.007
  public hearings, 13.007
  telephone hearings, 13.007
  video conferences, 13.007
interim hearings
  evidence, 14.005
  hearsay evidence, 14.005, 14.010
judicial review
  bundles, 24.003
  evidence, 24.003
  preparation, 24.003
  skeleton arguments, 24.003
  undue delay, 24.003
small claims track
  date, 20.009
  litigants in person, 20.001
  procedure, 20.009
  rights of audience, 20.009
Hearsay evidence
formalities, 31.014
generally, 31.010, 31.012, 31.013
hearsay notice, 31.014
interim hearings, 14.005, 14.010
oral evidence, 31.014
weight of evidence, 31.017
witnesses
  credibility, 31.016, 31.017
  cross-examination, 31.015
  failure to attend, 31.018
  previous statements, 31.019
  video conferences, 31.018
  witness abroad, 31.017, 31.018
  witness statements, 31.014
High Court
allocation, 1.001

Chancery Division, 1.001
commencement of proceedings
  financial restrictions, 9.002
  jurisdiction, 9.002
  money claims, 9.002
  value of claim, 9.002
District registries, 1.001
Family Division, 1.001
judicial review, 24.001
jurisdiction, 1.001, 1.003
money judgments, 40.002, 40.004
powers, 1.001
practice directions, 1.012
Queen's Bench Division, 1.001
Royal Courts of Justice, 1.001
House of Lords
appeals
  costs, 45.008
  entering an appearance, 45.001
  generally, 45.001
  leapfrog appeals, 45.001
  title of proceedings, 45.001
exchange of cases, 45.007
hearings, 45.008
House of Lords Appeal Committee, 45.008
judgment, 45.008
lodgement of cases
  appellant's case, 45.007
  respondent's case, 45.007
petitions for appeal
  appendix, 45.005
  cross-appeals, 45.001, 45.003
  estimates of time, 45.006
  leave to appeal, 45.001, 45.002
  out of time, 45.001
  preparation time, 45.001
  statement of facts and issues, 45.003, 45.004
Human rights
appeals, 44.010
civil proceedings, 1.017
judicial review, 24.003
particulars of claim, 12.027
proportionality, 24.003
right to fair trial, 26.022
Human Rights Act 1998
claims, under, 12.027
declarations of incompatibility, 1.024
European Convention of Human Rights, 1.023

judicial review, 1.024
jurisdiction, 1.024
legislative interpretation, 1.023
public authorities, 1.023

Indemnity principle
see also **Costs**
conditional fee agreements (CFAs), 38.020
exceptions, 38.020
full recovery of costs, 38.020
generally, 38.019, 38.020
importance, 38.020

Information technology
benefits, 22.017
case management, 22.017

Injunctions
see also **Interim injunctions**
drafting, 12.019
enforcement procedure
  attendance at hearing, 41.003
  committal proceedings, 41.003
  jurisdiction, 41.003
  penal notices, 41.003
  sequestration, 41.003
  standard of proof, 41.003
  undertakings in lieu, 41.003
judicial review, 24.001, 24.003
service, 27.014, 27.020

Inspection
see also **Disclosure and inspection**
computer databases, 30.018
conditional inspection, 30.018
costs, 30.011
disproportionate, 30.001
documentary reference
  affidavits, 30.017
  expert evidence, 30.017
  statement of case, 30.017
  witness statements, 30.017
  witness summary, 30.017
documents
  confidential documents, 30.018
  copies, 30.011
  electronic documents, 30.011
  medical records, 30.018
  physical inspection, 30.011
  privileged material, 30.019
  translations, 30.011
failure to allow, 30.022
inadvertent, 30.019

legal professional privilege, 30.017
meaning, 30.011
objections, 30.008, 30.012, 30.017
privilege
  challenges, to, 30.015
  legal professional privilege, 30.013
  privilege against self-incrimination, 30.014
restrictions, 30.012, 30.018
supervision, 30.011
written notice, 30.011

Insolvency
administration orders, 42.003
aid to debtors, 42.003
appointment of receiver, 27.030
bankruptcy orders, 42.002, 42.015, 42.016
corporate insolvency
  see **Winding up**
enforcement of debts, 4.003
generally, 42.001
interim receivership orders, 27.030
legal advice
  commencement of proceedings, 42.010
  statutory demands, 42.010
  threat of action, 42.010
meaning, 42.002
personal insolvency
  see **Bankruptcy**
proceedings, 42.001, 42.002
statutory demands
  challenges, 42.001, 42.006, 42.007
  compliance, 42.008, 42.011, 42.012, 42.017
  failure to respond, 42.009
  legal advice, 42.010
  petitions, 42.001
  responses, 42.005
  service, 42.001, 42.004
  use, 42.001
voluntary arrangements, 42.003
winding up orders, 42.002
  see also **Winding up**

Insurance
costs
  insurance market, 38.028
  premiums, 38.028–38.030
legal expenses insurance (LEI)
  after the event (ATE), 2.009, 2.013, 38.030

Insurance—*cont'd*
   before the event (BTE), 2.008, 2.009
   benefits, 2.009
   conditional fee agreements, 2.009
   security for costs, 26.003

Intellectual property claims
   claims procedure, 24.016
   jurisdiction, 24.016

Interest
   claims
      claim partly paid, 3.007
      claim wholly paid, 3.008
      contractual interest, 3.001, 12.013
      court's discretion, 3.002
      drafting, 12.013
      interest rates, 3.001, 3.002
      late payments, 12.013
      particulars of claim, 12.013
      payable as of right, 3.001
      reduction in interest, 3.002
      specified sum, 12.013
      unspecified claims, 12.013
   compound interest, 3.002
   conditional fee agreements, 29.023
   damages
      awards, 4.011, 4.019, 4.020
      bereavement damages, 4.020, 4.021
      calculations, 4.020
      fatal accidents, 4.020
      guidelines, 4.020, 4.021
      loss of amenity, 4.020, 4.021
      loss of earnings, 4.020
      non-payment, 4.022
      pain and suffering, 4.020, 4.021
      special account rate, 4.020, 4.021
   debt actions, 3.002, 3.006, 3.008, 12.013
   default judgments, 3.002, 3.004
   delayed proceedings, 3.002
   enhanced interests, 29.023
   judgment interest
      County court, 3.009
      High Court, 3.009
      interest rates, 3.009
      right, to, 3.009
   Part 36 offers, 29.007, 29.021, 29.023
      see also **Part 36 offers**
   personal injury claims, 3.005
   simple interest, 3.002
   statement of interest, 3.003
   statutory compensation, 3.006
   statutory interest, 3.006
   success fees, 29.023

Interference with goods
   claims, 12.016

Interim applications
   application notices, 13.002, 13.008, 14.001
   applications with notice
      agreement of parties, 13.008
      filing of evidence, 13.006
      general rule, 13.006
      hearing inappropriate, 13.008
      service of notice, 13.006
   applications without notice
      consent of parties, 13.004
      court orders, 13.004, 13.005
      lack of time, 13.004
      overriding objective, 13.004
      permission of court, 13.004
      secrecy, 13.004
      urgent cases, 13.004
   documents, 13.003
   generally, 13.001, 13.002
   hearings
      allocation hearings, 13.007
      case management conferences, 13.007
      case management directions, 13.007
      face-to-face hearings, 13.007
      listing hearings, 13.007
      pre-trial reviews, 13.007
      private hearings, 13.007
      public hearings, 13.007
      telephone hearings, 13.007
      video conferences, 13.007
   interpleader proceedings, 24.004

Interim injunctions
   American Cynamid principles
      see ***American Cynamid* principles**
   applications
      applications on notice, 27.013, 27.014
      non-disclosure, 27.014
      procedure, 27.012
      without notice, 27.012
   collateral remedy, 27.001
   construction cases, 27.001
   damages undertakings, 27.002, 27.005, 27.013
   defamation claims, 27.011
   disposal of action, 27.007, 27.030

duration, 27.001
freedom of expression, 27.008
generally, 27.001
malicious falsehood, 27.011
mandatory injunctions, 27.009, 27.030
no arguable defence, 27.010
provisional remedy, 27.001
service, 27.014
striking-out, 27.029

Interim payments
applications
   application notices, 25.008
   application procedure, 25.008
   challenges, to, 25.010
   delay in assessment, 25.009
   documents, 25.008
   evidence, 25.008, 25.009
   judgment on admissions, 25.008
   medical reports, 25.008
   summary judgment, 25.008
   witness statements, 25.009
awards, 25.002
future conduct of action, 25.012
generally, 25.001
grounds
   admission of liability, 25.003
   payment needs, 25.009
   substantial sums, 25.005, 25.007
   sum to be assessed, 25.004
   use of land, 25.006
judgments and orders, 25.011
judicial discretion, 25.002, 25.009
money claims, 25.001
possession claims, 25.001
voluntary payments, 25.008

Interim possession orders
applications, 27.031
jurisdiction, 27.031
types of orders, 27.031

Interim receivership orders
American Cynamid principles, 27.030
   see also **American Cynamid principles**
appointment of receivers, 27.030

Interpleader proceedings
applicants, 24.004
generally, 24.004
interim application, 24.004
jurisdiction, 24.004
procedure, 24.004
separate action, 24.004

Interveners
joinder of parties, 7.017

Judges
judgments
   confidentiality, 37.016
   costs, 37.016
   draft judgments, 37.016
   final judgments, 37.016
   formal applications, 37.016
   reserved judgment, 37.016
   settlement discussions, 37.016
recusal, 36.012
trials
   adjournment, 37.016
   directions, 37.004
   interrogation of witnesses, 37.015
   interventions, 37.015
   judgments, 37.016
   role, 37.015

Judgments and orders
correction of judgments
   accidental slips, 43.007, 43.008
   applications, 43.007
   clarification, 43.007
   omissions, 43.007, 43.008
costs orders
   court fees, 38.002
   detailed assessment, 38.031
   discretionary nature, 38.021
   indemnity principle, 38.019
   interim hearings, 38.031
   judicial discretion, 38.008
   legal costs, 38.002
   LSC funding, 39.014
   non-parties, 39.015
   scope, 38.008
   witness payments, 38.002
court orders
   amendment, 43.008
   applications for review, 43.009
   correction, 43.007, 43.008
   two stage process, 43.008
default judgments
   see **Default judgments**
disclosure orders, 27.019, 27.028
disposal hearings
   post-allocation, 17.007
   pre-allocation, 17.003–17.006
interim receivership orders, 27.030

Judgments and orders—*cont'd*
  judgments
    confidentiality, 37.016
    correction, 43.007, 43.008
    costs, 37.016
    draft judgments, 37.016
    final judgments, 37.016
    formal applications, 37.016
    judgment on admissions, 16.002, 25.008
    reserved judgment, 37.016
    settlement discussions, 37.016
    summary judgment, 17.003, 19.014, 19.015
  registration, 1.022
  representative actions, 7.018
  setting aside
    see **Setting aside**
  striking-out decisions, 17.003
  wasted costs orders
    applicants, 39.002
    hearings, 39.002
    judicial powers, 39.002
    meaning, 39.002
    procedure, 39.002
    vexatious conduct, 39.002

Judicial case management
  conditional orders, 33.007
  control
    costs, 33.013
    evidence, 33.012
  extensions of time, 33.002
  judicial powers, 33.001
  multi-track, 33.006
  no case to answer, 33.001
  "no real prospect of success" test, 33.001, 33.008
  personal injury cases, 33.006
  preliminary issues, 33.006
  sanctions
    non-compliance, 33.011
    relief, 33.011
  split trials, 33.006
  stay of proceedings
    see **Stay of proceedings**
  striking out
    see **Striking out**

Judicial review
  abuse of process, 24.01
  appeals, 44.009, 44.011, 44.023
  case management, 24.002, 24.003
  claim forms
    acknowledgment of service, 24.002, 24.003
    contents, 24.002
    service, 24.002
  claims
    challenges, to, 24.003
    declarations, 24.001, 24.003
    definition, 24.001
    injunctions, 24.001, 24.003
    mandatory orders, 24.001
    prohibiting orders, 24.001
    quashing orders, 24.002, 24.003
    withdrawal, 24.003
  costs, 24.001, 24.003
  generally, 24.001
  hearings
    bundles, 24.003
    evidence, 24.003
    preparation, 24.003
    skeleton arguments, 24.003
    undue delay, 24.003
  human rights, 1.024, 24.003
  interpleader proceedings
    applicants, 24.004
    generally, 24.004
    interim application, 24.004
    jurisdiction, 24.004
    procedure, 24.004
    separate action, 24.004
  jurisdiction
    Administrative Court, 24.001
    High Court, 24.001
  pre-action protocol, 24.001
  procedural stages
    lodgement of claim, 24.001
    permission hearing, 24.002
    permission to proceed, 24.001–24.003
    refusal of permission, 24.003
  public law rights, 24.001
  remedy of last resort, 24.001
  speed of determination, 24.001
  time limits, 24.001

Landlord and tenant
  assured tenancies, 24.008
  fast track, 21.001
  possession claims, 24.008
  postponement of possession, 24.008
  short-hold tenancies, 24.008

statutory claims, 24.009
Latent damages claims
  limitation periods, 5.008
Leapfrog appeals
  procedure, 44.003, 45.001
Legal advice and funding
  barristers' fees
    arbitration, 2.018
    brief fees, 2.018
    calculation, 2.018
    contractual basis, 2.018
    hourly rates, 2.018
    Legal Service Commission funding, 2.018
    non-contractual terms, 2.018
  basic charging agreements (solicitors)
    amounts payable, 2.010
    contentious business, 2.010, 2.011
    hourly rates, 2.010
    justification of costs, 2.011
    non-contentious business, 2.010, 2.011
    payment, 2.012
    written agreements, 2.010, 2.011
  change of solicitors
    see also **Solicitors**
    ceasing to act, 28.001
    CLS funding, 28.001
    notice of acting, 28.001
    notice of change, 28.001
    procedure, 28.001
  claims management companies, 2.001, 2.013
  conditional fee agreements (CFAs), 2.001, 2.014, 2.015, 2.016
  insolvency proceedings
    commencing proceedings, 42.010
    statutory demands, 42.010
  Legal Aid Regulations, 2.024
  legal expenses insurance, 2.008, 2.009, 2.013
  Legal Services Commission (LSC), 2.020, 13.010, 28.001, 38.037
    see also **Legal Services Commission funding**
  litigants in person, 2.019
  Notice of Funding, 2.023, 38.007
Legal professional privilege
  clients
    communications, 30.013
    meaning, 30.013
  confidential communications, 30.013
  criminal activity, 30.013
  disclosure and inspection, 30.013, 30.017
  expert witnesses, 23.011
  foreign lawyers, 30.013
  fraudulent activity, 30.013
  justification, 30.013
  legal context, 30.013
  litigation privilege, 30.013
  scope, 30.013
  third parties, 30.013
Legal Services Commission funding
  assessment of costs
    client involvement, 39.013
    disallowed items, 39.009
    loser's bill, 39.010
    procedure, 39.008, 39.009
    reductions, 39.012
    standard basis, 39.008
    winner's bill, 39.009
  change of solicitors, 28.001
  Community Legal Service Assent Certificate, 39.009
  costs
    cost of certificates, 39.008
    costs of action, 38.037, 39.008
    costs protection, 2.021
    default cost certificate, 39.009
    final costs certificate, 39.009
    liability for costs, 2.020
  eligibility, 2.020
  enhancements, 39.011
  fixed contribution, 2.020
  funding certificates, 39.008, 39.009
  generally 2,018, 2.020, 13.010
  orders for costs
    costs to be determined, 39.014
    specified costs, 39.014
    statutory conditions, 39.014
  periodic contribution, 2.020
  personal injury claims, 2.020
  public interest, 2.020
  statutory charges, 2.020
  statutory provisions, 39.008
Limitation
  commencement of proceedings, 5.001
  extensions of time
    case examples, 5.018
    children, cases involving, 5.012
    concealment cases, 5.015

Limitation—*cont'd*
    consumer protection, 5.017
    death claims, 5.018
    debt cases, 5.014
    defamation cases, 5.016
    disability cases, 5.012
    fraud cases, 5.015
    insolvency cases, 5.013
    judicial discretion, 5.018
    patients, cases involving, 5.012
    personal injury claims, 5.018
    second actions, 5.019
  foreign law, 5.020
  limitation defence, 5.001
  limitation periods
    see **Limitation periods**
  second actions, 5.019
Limitation periods
  actions on a speciality, 5.005
  contractual actions, 5.002
  contribution claims, 5.006, 5.009
  defamation actions, 5.003
  fatal accident claims, 5.008
  indemnity claims, 5.009
  latent damage claims, 5.008
  loan contracts, 5.004
  mortgage actions, 5.009
  negligence actions, 5.008
  pending actions, 5.009
  personal injury claims, 5.007
  tort cases, 5.002
  third party proceedings, 5.009
Limited liability partnerships
  parties, 7.009
Litigants in person
  costs, 38.004
  definition, 38.004
  funding, 2.019
  rights of audience, 1.018, 1.020
  small claims track, 20.001
Litigation friends
  binding settlements, 7.005
  compromise, 7.005
  duties, 7.005
  eligibility, 7.005
  patients, 7.006
  requirement, for, 7.005
  termination of appointment, 7.005
  title to action, 7.005
Loss of earnings
  earning capacity, 4.014
  future earnings, 4.011, 4.016, 4.017, 4.020
  general damages, 4.011
  interest rates, 4.011
  life expectancy, 4.013
  marriage prospects, 4.012
  multipliers, 4.011
  Ogden Tables, 4.011
  special damages, 4.002
  structured settlements, 4.017

Measure of damages
  personal injury claims
    counsel's opinion, 4.023
    solicitor's assessment, 4.023
    sources of information, 4.023
  special damages, 4.002
Mediation
  assisted negotiation, 34.002
  compromise, 34.002
  procedure, 34.002
Medical records
  disclosure and inspection, 30.007, 30.018
Mercantile courts
  claims procedure, 24.013
Money claim online (MCOL)
  acknowledgment of service, 9.022
  claim number, 9.022
  court fees, 9.022
  date of service, 9.022
  defence, 9.022
  financial limits, 9.022
  particulars of claim, 9.022
  possession clams, 9.022
  procedure, 9.022
  response pack, 9.022
  statement of truth, 9.022
Money judgments
  attachment of earnings
    application costs, 40.007
    cessation of employment, 40.007
    earnings, 40.006
    entitlement to interest, 40.007
    hearings, 40.006
    normal deduction rate, 40.006
    orders, 40.006
    procedure, 40.006
    protected earning rate, 40.006
    statement of means, 40.006
    statutory provisions, 40.006

enforcement
  appointment of receiver, 40.012
  charging orders, 40.008, 40.011, 40.013
  County court judgments, 40.002
  foreign judgments, 40.016
  generally, 40.001
  High Court, 40.002, 40.004
  information hearings, 40.003
  judgment summons, 40.015
  legal advice, 40.019
  out of jurisdiction, 40.018
  sequestration, 40.014
  third party proceedings, 40.005
  warrant of execution, 40.004
  winding up, 40.015
  writ of *fieri facias*, 40.004
interim payments, 25.001
third party proceedings
  debt orders, 40.005
  deposit takers, 40.005
  judgment creditors, 40.005
  judgment debtors, 40.005
  hearings, 40.005
  trade debts, 40.005

Mortgages
  foreclosure, 24.006
  payment of arrears, 24.006
  possession cases
    adjournment, 24.006
    case management, 24.006
    eviction, 24.006
    evidence, 24.006
    hearings, 24.006
    jurisdiction, 24.006
    postponement of possession, 24.006
  possession orders, 24.006
  second mortgagors, 24.006

Motor insurance
  claimant's policy, 6.027
  defendant's policy, 6.028
  limitation, 6.028
  notice of action, 6.028
  small claims track, 6.027
  statutory rights, 6.028

Motor Insurers Bureau
  agreements
    uninsured drivers, 6.029, 6.030
    untraced drivers, 6.029, 6.031
  role, 6.029

Multi-track
  adjournment, 22.013
  allocation, 9.033, 22.001
  appeals, 44.002
  attendance at trial, 37.001
  case management
    case management conferences, 22.004, 22.008
    case plan, 22.002
    disclosure, 22.005, 22.010
    identification of issues, 22.003
    information technology, 22.017
    judicial case management, 33.006
    pre-trial checklist, 22.015
    Royal Courts of Justice, 22.014
  costs, 22.002
  directions
    allocation, 22.009
    compliance, 22.012
    disclosure, 22.010
    expert evidence, 22.010
    variation, 22.011
    witness statements, 22.010
  disclosure and inspection, 30.003
  documents, 22.005
  expert evidence, 22.006, 23.014
  normal track, 9.033
  Part 8 claims, 10.001
  pre-trial checklist, 36.001
  procedure, 9.033, 37.003, 37.004
  trials
    date of trial, 22.007
    judge sitting alone, 22.018
    jury trial, 22.018
    pre-trial checklist, 22.015
    pre-trial review, 22.016
  types of cases, 22.001
  witness statements, 31.005

Negligence claims
  particulars of claim, 12.012
  statement of case, 12.006

No case to answer
  defendant's election, 37.005
  evidence, 37.005
  judicial assessment, 37.005
  jury trials, 37.005

Norwich Pharmacal Rule
  see also **Disclosure and inspection**
  conditions, 30.025
  cost of disclosure, 30.025

INDEX

Norwich Pharmacal Rule—cont'd
   future actions, 30.025
   innocent third parties, 30.025
   orders, 30.025
   tort actions, 30.025
   wrongdoers, 30.025

Official Receiver
   see also **Insolvency**
   function, 42.016

Overriding objective
   see also **Civil Procedure Rules (CPR)**
   admissions, 16.001
   allocation, 9.027
   application, 1.006
   assistance of parties, 1.011
   case management, 1.006, 1.011
   disclosure and inspection, 30.007, 30.016
   duty of parties, 1.006
   economy, 1.008
   equality of arms, 1.006, 1.009
   exercise of judicial power, 1.010
   fairness, 1.006, 1.011
   judicial interpretation, 1.010
   proportionality, 1.008
   purpose, 1.006
   representative actions, 7.018
   speed, 1.008

Part 36 offers
   acceptance
      clarification, 29.012
      costs advantage, 29.004
      effect, 29.014
      generally, 29.001
      late acceptance, 29.016
      notice of acceptance, 29.013
      permission to accept, 29.013, 29.016
      prompt acceptance, 29.016
      timing, 29.013
   alteration, 29.011
   change of circumstances, 29.011
   clarification, 29.012
   clinical disputes, 6.025
   compliance, 29.010
   compromise element, 29.001
   content, 29.006
   costs
      costs advantages, 29.001, 29.016
      costs penalties, 29.021
      enhanced costs, 29.023
      inconsistent provisions, 29.005
      order for costs, 29.021
      pressures, 29.004
      provision for costs, 29.016
      small claims track, 29.003
   counterclaims, 29.006
   defence offers
      acceptance, 29.007
      future pecuniary loss, 29.007
      interest payments, 29.007
      payment of money, 29.007
      personal injury claims, 29.007, 29.008
      provisional damages claims, 29.007
      state benefit refunds, 29.008
      sub-minimum offers, 29.007
   defendant, 6.025
   effect, 29.001
   failure to beat, 29.021, 29.022, 29.024
   form, 29.006
   further consequences
      defamation actions, 29.019, 29.023
      periodical payments, 29.019
   global offer, 29.006, 29.012
   implementation
      contractual rights, 29.018
      payment of money, 29.018
      periodical payments, 29.018, 29.019
   implied offers, 29.005
   interest payments, 29.001, 29.021, 29.023
   less favourable terms, 29.011
   liability, 29.009
   non-acceptance, 29.020
   number of offers, 29.004
   offers falling outside, 29.010
   rationale, 29.001
   "relevant period", 29.006, 29.011, 29.012
   secrecy rule, 29.020
   service, 29.006
   state benefits
      allowance, for, 29.008
      gross offers, 29.008
      net offers, 29.008
      recoverable benefits, 29.008
      refunds, 29.008
   stay of proceedings, 29.015, 29.016
   sub-minimum offers, 29.004, 29.007

terms, 29.004, 29.005
timing, 29.004, 29.006
withdrawal, 29.011
without prejudice, 29.001, 29.020
Part 8 claims
  acknowledgment of service, 10.003
  allocation, 10.001
  case management, 10.005
  claim form
    addresses for service, 10.002
    completion, 10.002
    details of claim, 10.002
    issue, 10.002
    service, 10.002
    statement of truth, 10.002
  filing of evidence, 10.001, 10.004
  generally, 10.001
  mandatory procedure, 10.001
  no defence required, 10.001
  procedure at trial, 37.003
  witness statements, 10.002
Particulars of claim
  breach of trust, 12.028
  claim form, 9.008
  clinical negligence claims, 12.025
  competition infringements, 12.026
  criminal convictions, 12.024
  drafting
    breach of contract claims, 12.012
    claim forms, 12.011
    contents, 12.011
    necessary facts, 12.012
    negligence claims, 12.012
    preparation, 12.011
  failure to serve, 9.011
  fraud allegations, 12.028
  human rights claims, 12.027
  knowledge of facts, 12.028
  illegality claims, 12.028
  late service, 9.010
  misrepresentation, 12.028
  mitigation of loss, 12.028
  personal injury claims, 12.029
  possession claims, 12.029
  separate documents, 9.008
  service, 9.009
  specified proceedings, 12.039
  statement of case, 9.008
  suggested particulars, 12.045–12.049
  templates, 12.034

undue influence, 12.028
unsoundness of mind, 12.028
wilful default, 12.028
Parties
  addition, 7.013–7.015, 7.017
  beneficiaries, 7.023
  children, 7.005
  choice of parties, 7.023
  companies, 7.007
  consolidation of actions, 7.016
  deceased estates, 7.019, 7.010
  derivative actions, 7.021
  employees, 7.023
  employers, 7.023
  entitlement to remedy, 7.013
  generally, 7.001
  group litigation, 7.020
  individuals, 7.004
  insurers, 7.023
  interveners, 7.017
  limited liability partnerships, 7.009
  manufacturers, 7.023
  miscellaneous actions, 7.022
  motorists, 7.023
  multiple causes of actions, 7.012
  multiple parties, 7.012
  partnerships, 7.008
  patients, 7.006
  representative actions, 7.018
  retailers, 7.023
  substitution, 7.013–7.015
  title to action, 7.002
  trustees, 7.023
  unascertained persons, 7.019
  unborn children, 7.019
  unknown persons, 7.023
  vexatious litigants, 7.011
Partnerships
  charging orders, 40.013
  parties, 7.008
  property, 40.013
Patent claims
  claims procedure, 24.016
  jurisdiction, 24.016
Patients
  Court of Protection, 7.006
  limitation, 5.012
  litigation friends, 7.006
  meaning, 7.006
  parties, 7.006
  service, on, 8.011

Payment into court
  settlement
Personal injury claims
  admissions, 16.001
  case management, 33.006
  earning capacity, 4.013
  fast track, 21.001
  fatal accidents
    see **Fatal accidents**
  general damages
    loss of amenities, 4.010
    loss of earnings, 4.011
    mental anguish, 4.009
    mental impairment, 4.010
    nervous shock, 4.010
    pain and suffering, 4.009
  interest payments
    awards, 4.011, 4.019, 4.020
    bereavement damages, 4.020, 4.021
    calculations, 4.020
    fatal accidents, 4.020
    guidelines, 4.020, 4.021
    loss of amenity, 4.020, 4.021
    loss of earnings, 4.020
    non-payment, 4.022
    pain and suffering, 4.020, 4.021
    special account rate, 4.020, 4.021
  life expectancy, 4.013
  marriage prospects, 4.012
  measure of damages
    counsel's opinion, 4.023
    solicitor's assessment, 4.023
    sources of information, 4.023
  Ogden Tables, 4.011
  particulars of claim, 12.029
  periodical payments
    continuity, 4.016
    costs of care, 4.016
    future pecuniary loss, 4.016
    loss of earnings, 4.016
    value, 4.016
    variation, 4.016
  pre-action protocol, 6.015–6.017
  provisional damages
    applications, 4.015
    "chance" cases, 4.015
    future deterioration, 4.015
    judgments and orders, 4.015
    offers, 4.015
    serious additional damage, 4.015
    statements of case, 4.015

  special damages
    agreement, 4.008
    contractual sick pay, 4.003
    loss of earnings, 4.002
    measure of damages, 4.002
    medical expenses, 4.006
    mitigation of loss, 4.004
    non-listed benefits, 4.005
    restitutio in integrum, 4.002
    state benefits, 4.004
    third party expenses, 4.007
  statement of value, 12.010
  structured settlements
    see **Structured settlements**
Personal insolvency
  see **Bankruptcy**
Personal representatives
  probate claims, 24.010
Possession claims
  allocation, 24.005
  certificate of service, 24.005
  costs, 20.012
  date for possession, 24.005
  defendant's response, 24.005
  enforcement, 41.001
  fixed date claims, 9.020, 24.005
  hearings, 24.005
  interim payments, 25.001
  interim possession orders, 24.007
  jurisdiction, 24.005
  mortgages, 24.005, 24.006
  particulars of claim, 12.029
  procedure, 24.005
  service, 24.005
  small claims track, 20.012
  tenants, 24.008
  witness statements, 24.005
Practice directions
  compliance, 1.015
  costs, 1.012
  High Court, 1.012
  purpose, 1.012
  time limits, 1.016
Pre-action protocols
  alternative dispute resolution (ADR), 6.019
  approved protocols, 6.013
  compliance, 6.013
  debt claims, 6.021
  disclosure and inspection, 6.017, 30.001

implementation, 6.013
judicial review cases, 24.001
key elements, 6.013
personal injury protocol, 6.015–6.017
pre-action meetings, 6.019
preparation of evidence, 6.013
procedure, 6.013
Protocols Practice Direction, 6.013
purpose, 6.013
Preliminary stages
  disclosure, 6.017
  first interview, 6.001–6.007
  pre-action meetings, 6.019
  pre-action protocols, 6.013–6.017
  preparation of evidence, 6.008–6.014
Preparation for trial
  bundles
    see **Bundles**
  choice of advocate
    likely costs, 36.009
    solicitor's advice, 36.009
  directions on listing, 36.002
  organising witnesses
    attendance at trial, 36.004, 36.005
    expert witnesses, 36.004
    witness summons, 36.003
  pre-trial checklist
    completion, 36.001
    content, 36.001
    fast track, 36.001
    multi-track, 36.001
    objectives, 36.001
    return, 36.001
  pre-trial review, 36.002
  trial brief
    acceptance, 36.011
    brief fees, 36.011
    contents, 36.010
    delivery to counsel, 36.011
    documents, 36.010
    drafting, 36.010
    importance, 36.010
    witness statements, 36.010
Privilege against self-incrimination
  criminal proceedings, 27.027
  foreign courts, 27.027
  free-standing evidence, 27.027
  generally, 27.027
  incriminating documents, 27.027
Probate claims
  contentious claims, 24.010

grant of probate, 24.010
jurisdiction, 24.010
non-contentious claims, 24.010
personal representatives, 24.010
validity of will, 24.010
Proceedings
  claim form
    address for service, 8.009
    attempted service, 9.006
    extensions of time, 9.006, 9.007
    failure to serve
    mistaken address, 9.006
    notice of service, 9.007
    service on agent, 8.018
    specified claim, 8.008
    time limits, 9.005, 9.006
    unspecified claim, 8.008
  client relationship management
    see **Client relationship**
  County court, 9.002
  court office
    agreement, on, 9.003
    location, 9.003
    transfers, 9.003
  cross-examination, 37.004, 37.012
  defendant's response, 6.015–6.017
  evidence
    see **Evidence**
  examination in chief, 37.004, 37.011
  fixed date claims, 9.020
  generally, 9.001
  High Court, 9.002
  issue fee, 9.001
  judges directions, 37.004
  limitation, 5.001
  money claim online (MCOL), 9.022
  opening proceedings, 37.004
  particulars of claim
    see **Particulars of claim**
  preliminary stages
    disclosure, 6.017
    first interview, 6.001–6.007
    pre-action meetings, 6.019
    pre-action protocols,
      6.013–6.017
  preparation of evidence, 6.008–6.014
  Production Centre cases, 9.021
  proofs of evidence, 37.001
  re-examination, 37.004, 37.014
  service
    see **Service**

Proceedings—*cont'd*
  settlement
    see **Settlement**
  submissions
    opening submissions, 37.004
    oral submissions, 37.004
  time limits, 9.004
  transfer of proceedings
    see **Transfer of proceedings**
  witnesses
    see **Witnesses**
Production Centre
  default judgments, 9.021
  jurisdiction, 9.021
  multiple claim forms, 9.021
Professional conduct
  solicitors, 2.002
Provisional damages
  applications, 4.015
  "chance" cases, 4.015
  future deterioration, 4.015
  judgments and orders, 4.015
  offers, 4.015
  serious additional damage, 4.015
  statements of case, 4.015

Recognition of judgments
  foreign judgments, 40.016
Recusal
  apparent bias, 36.012
  fellow members of chambers, 36.012
  judicial impartiality, 36.012
  knowledge of witness, 36.012
Relief
  see **Injunctions; Setting aside**
Representative actions
  diverse interests, 7.018
  judgment and orders, 7.018
  overriding objective, 7.018
  same interests, 7.018
  single claim form, 7.018
Response packs
  admissions, 12.041, 16.001, 16.003, 16.004
  claim forms, 24.012
  counterclaims, 12.041
  defences, 12.041
  money claims, 9.022
  service, 9.012
Return of goods
  claims, 12.020, 41.002

Right to fair trial
  discrimination provisions, 26.002
Rights of audience
  authorised persons, 1.018, 1.019, 1.021
  barristers, 1.018
  litigants in person, 1.018, 1.020
  professional advocates, 1.018
  small claims track, 20.009
  solicitors, 1.018
Road traffic accident cases
  fixed costs, 38.013
  fixed success fees, 38.013

Search orders
  applications, 14.002, 27.024, 27.025
  discharge, 27.025
  disclosure, 27.026
  entry to premises, 27.023
  generally, 27.023
  legal advice, 27.025
  post-trial, 27.024
  pre-trial, 27.024
  publicity, 27.025
  scope, 27.024
  service, 27.025
  solicitor's duties, 27.025
  standard forms, 27.019, 27.025
  variation, 27.025
Secrecy rule
  appeals, 29.020
  effect, 29.020
  exceptions
    stay of proceedings, 29.020
    tender before claim defence, 29.020
    written agreements, 29.020
  premature disclosure, 29.020
Securities
  charging orders, 40.011
Security for costs
  appeals, 26.002
  applications
    appellants, 26.002
    claimants, 26.002
    company applications, 26.003
    defence applications, 26.004
    evidential requirements, 26.002
    joinder of parties, 26.004
    judicial discretion, 26.002
    jurisdiction, 26.003
    justifiable, 26.002
    lack of probity, 26.002

procedure, 26.003
  requirements, 26.002
  residence issues, 26.002
  right to fair trial, 26.002
  third parties, 26.002
awards
  appropriate amount, 26.003
  determination of amount, 26.003
dismissal
  no compelling reason for trial, 26.006
  no real prospect of success, 26.006
  summary dismissal, 26.006
foreign judgments, 40.017
generally, 26.001
insurance, 26.003
judgment and orders
  compliance, 26.005
  conditional orders, 26.006
  payment orders, 26.005
opposing claims, 26.002
Part 20 claims, 26.002

Self-incrimination
  see **Privilege against self-incrimination**

Service
  see also **Service out of jurisdiction**
  acknowledgement of service
    amendment of acknowledgment, 9.015
    documents, 8.001, 8.009, 9.013
    failure to acknowledge, 9.014, 15.001
    judicial review, 24.002, 24.003
    late filing, 15.003
    Part 8 claims, 10.003
    service on defendant, 9.013
    withdrawal of acknowledgement, 9.015
  addresses for service
    claim form, 8.009
    foreign companies, 8.009
    jurisdiction, within, 8.009
    last known address, 8.009, 9.006
    place of business, 8.009
    resident out of jurisdiction, 8.009
    solicitor's address, 8.009
    usual address, 8.009
  certificates of service, 8.019, 15.004, 24.005
  claim forms
    address for service, 8.009

    attempted service, 9.006
    extensions of time, 9.006, 9.007
    failure to serve
    judicial review cases, 24.002
    mistaken address, 9.006
    notice of service, 9.007
    service on agent, 8.018
    specified claim, 8.008
    time limits, 9.005, 9.006
    unspecified claim, 8.008
  deemed service
    challenges to service, 8.013
    date of service, 8.013
    generally, 8.008, 8.009
    method of service, 8.013
    transmission of document, 8.013
  dispensing with service, 8.015
  documents
    acknowledgement of service, 8.001, 8.009, 9.013
    authorised acceptance, 8.001
    claim form, 8.008
    general rule, 8.001
  injunctions, 27.014, 27.020
  methods of service
    document exchange, 8.005
    email, 8.007
    personal service, 8.002–8.004
    service by contractually agreed method, 8.016, 8.017
    service by court, 8.008
    service by fax, 8.006
    service by other electronic communications, 8.007
    service by parties, 8.008
  Part 36 offers, 29.006
  particulars of claim, 9.009–9.011
  personal service
    companies, 8.002
    partnerships, 8.002
    process servers, 8.002
    service by delivery, 8.004
  possession claims, 24.005
  postal service, 8.003, 8.008, 8.010
  recipients
    agents, 8.018
    armed forces, 8.012
    children, 8.011
    companies, 8.001, 8.010
    patients, 8.011
    solicitors, 8.001

Service—cont'd
  search orders, 27.025
  service on defendant
    acknowledgement of service,
      9.013–9.015
    admissions, 9.016
    claim form, 9.008, 9.012
    response pack, 9.012
  witness statements, 31.007
Service out of jurisdiction
  additional claims, 11.014
  challenge to jurisdiction, 11.010
  counterclaims, 11.014
  invalid service, 11.007
  methods of service, 11.012
  no proceedings pending, 11.007
  particulars of claim, 11.007
  permission to serve, 11.009
  procedure, 11.001, 11.007
  response to service, 11.013
  statement of jurisdiction, 11.007
  time limits, 11.011
  without permission, 11.007
Set-off
  counterclaim, 12.037
  defence, 12.037
  equitable, 12.037
  mutual debt, 12.037
Setting aside
  consequential issues, 43.004
  costs payable, 43.004
  default judgments
    abandoned claims, 15.016
    appeals, 15.011
    conditions, 15.012, 15.015
    good reason, 15.014
    judgment on application, 15.011
    judgment wrongly entered, 15.012
    judicial discretion, 15.012–15.014
    "no reasonable prospect of
      success", 43.002
    procedure, 15.011
    prospects of success, 15.013
    transfer of claims, 15.016
  enforcement methods, 43.004
  failure to attend trial, 43.002
  generally, 43.001
  interim applications, 43.002
  judicial powers, 43.005, 43.006
  jurisdiction, 43.004
  knowledge of proceedings, 43.002
  non-parties, 43.003
  subsidiary issues, 43.004
  supporting evidence, 43.002
Settlement
  compromise, 6.023, 6.026
  conditional fee agreements (CFAs),
    6.026
  negotiations, 6.022
  Part 36 offers, 6.025, 6.026, 29.001
    see also **Part 36 offers**
  payment into court, 29.002
  payment of costs, 6.026
  settlement outside proceedings
    see **Settlement outside proceedings**
  without prejudice communications,
    6.024
Settlement outside proceedings
  alternative dispute resolution (ADR),
    34.002
  approval of court, 34.004
  arbitration, 34.001, 34.002
  judicial powers, 34.002
  mediation, 34.001, 34.002
  negotiated settlements, 34.001
Single joint experts
  challenges, to, 23.006
  expertise, 23.006
  fast track, 23.006
  fees, 23.006
  instructions, 23.006, 23.011
  medical negligence, 23.006
  meetings, 23.006
Skeleton arguments
  case citation, 36.007
  contents, 36.007
  exchange, 36.007
  judicial review hearings, 24.003
  presentation, 36.007
  purpose, 36.007
  requirement, 36.007
  response to appeal, 44.013, 44.015
Small claims track
  allocation
    consent, 20.007, 20.012
    directions, 20.004
    generally, 20.003
    "paper disposals", 20.006
    preliminary hearings, 20.005
  appeals, 20.014
  claims less than £5000, 9.031
  costs, 38.021

INDEX

disclosure and inspection, 30.003
expert evidence, 20.008
hearings
  date, 20.009
  procedure, 20.009
  rights of audience, 20.009
landlord and tenant claims, 9.031
lay representatives, 38.021
legal representation, 38.021
litigants in person, 20.001
motor insurance, 6.027
normal track, 9.031
Part 36 offers, 29.003
personal injury claims, 9.031
possession claims, 20.012
procedure, 20.009, 37.003
solicitors
  initial advice, 20.002
  legal representation, 20.002
  preparation time, 20.002
summary judgments, 20.013
types of cases, 20.001
witness statements, 31.005

Solicitor/client disputes
applications, 39.003
award of costs
  assessment orders, 39.004
  one fifth rule, 39.004
  taxation costs, 39.004
  unpaid disbursements, 39.004
breakdown of costs, 39.003
contentious business agreements, 39.006
final costs certificate, 39.003
hearings, 39.003
indemnity basis, 39.003
non-contentious business agreements, 39.007
remuneration certificates, 39.005
procedure, 39.003
statutory provisions, 39.003

Solicitors
affidavits, 14.004
attendance at trial, 37.001
basic charging agreements
  amounts payable, 2.010
  contentious business, 2.010, 2.011
  hourly rates, 2.010
  justification of costs, 2.011
  non-contentious business, 2.010, 2.011

payment, 2.012
written agreements, 2.010, 2.011
ceasing to act
  application, 28.001
  bankruptcy, 28.001
  ceasing to practice, 28.001
  death, 28.001
  evidence, 28.001
  orders, 28.001
change of solicitors
  ceasing to act, 28.001
  CLS funding, 28.001
  notice of acting, 28.001
  notice of change, 28.001
  procedure, 28.001
clients
  advice, 20.002, 36.009
  choice of advocate, 36.009
  communications, 30.013
  disputes, 39.003
  meaning, 30.013
disclosure and inspection, 30.005
disputes
  see **Solicitor/client disputes**
in-house solicitors, 38.005
legal professional privilege, 30.013
liability for costs, 7.024
necessary authority, 7.024
proceedings, involving, 24.019
professional conduct
  basic charging agreement, 2.010
  case information, 1.005
  client relations, 2.002–2.006
  core duties, 2.002
  costs information, 2.004, 2.007, 2.009, 2.015, 2.016, 2.020
  funding information, 2.006
  insurance information, 2.009, 2.013
  law firm information, 2.003
rights of audience, 1.018
role, 7.024
search orders, 27.025
service, on, 8.001
small claims track
  initial advice, 20.002
  legal representation, 20.002
  preparation time, 20.002
statements of truth, 12.004
witness statements, 14.004

Special damages
  agreement, 4.008
  contractual sick pay, 4.003
  loss of earnings, 4.002
  measure of damages, 4.002
  medical expenses, 4.006
  mitigation of loss, 4.004
  non-listed benefits, 4.005
  restitutio in integrum, 4.002
  state benefits, 4.004
  third party expenses, 4.007
Specific performance
  enforcement, 41.004
Statements of case
  admissions, 16.001
  amendments
    after service, 12.051
    agreement to amend, 12.051
    applications, 12.054
    before service, 12.051
    consequential amendments, 12.055
    costs, 12.056
    generally, 12.043, 12.050
    human rights considerations, 12,053
    limitation period, 12.053
    mistake as to names, 12.053
    new issues, 12.051
    statement of truth, 12.057
    verification, 12.057
  contents. 12.003
  counterclaims, 18.002
  details, 12.006
  drafting
    degree of detail, 12.006
    documentary evidence, 12.007
    foreign law, 12.007
    names of witnesses, 12.007
    negligence claims, 12.006
    points of law, 12.007
    precedent material, 12.006
    sufficient facts, 12.006
    unspecified financial loss, 12.006
  formalities, 12.003
  format
    attachments, 12.005
    definitions for phrases, 12.005
    electronic format, 12.005
    headings, 12.005
    length, 12.005
    names of parties, 12.005
    numbered paragraphs, 12.005
    sequence of events, 12.005
  function, 12.002
  further statements, 12.043
  generally, 12.001
  identification of issues, 12.002
  inconsistent, 12.030
  inspection, 30.017
  meaning, 12.001
  points of law, 12.007
  precedent material, 12.006
  statement of facts, 12.006
  striking out, 33.008
  suggested documents, 12.044
Statements of truth
  expert witnesses, 23.009
  false statements, 12.004
  omission, 12.004
  Part 8 claims, 10.002
  purpose, 12.004
  signature, 12.004
  solicitor's position, 12.004
Statements of value
  challenges, 12.033
  claim forms, 12.010
  drafting, 12.010
  housing repairs, 12.010
  human rights issues, 12.010
  personal injury claims, 12.010
  prescribed forms, 12.010
Stay of proceedings
  admissions, 16.010
  foreign judgments, 11.001, 11.004, 11.008, 11.015
  generally, 33.003
  Part 36 offers, 29.015, 29.016
  payment of costs, 33.005
  pending appeal, 33.003
  pending arbitration, 33.004
  pending criminal proceedings, 33.005
  proportionality, 33.003
  secrecy rule, 29.020
  third party proceedings, 33.004
Striking out
  abuse of process, 33.008
  baseless claims, 33.008
  consequences, 33.010
  court orders, 33.001
  court's own initiative, 33.009
  failure to comply, 33.008
  "no real prospect of success", 33.008

statement of case, 33.008
vexatious proceedings, 33.008
Structured settlements
  agreements, 4.017
  "indexed terms for life", 4.017
  levels, 4.017
  loss of earnings, 4.017
  lump sum payments, 4.017
  medical expenses, 4.017
  severe injuries, 4.017
Success fees
  see also **Conditional fee agreements (CFAs)**
  assessment
    amount of fee, 38.026
    discounted success fees, 38.024, 38.026
    high value claims, 38.026
    judicial assessment, 38.025
    prospects of success, 38.024
    reasonableness, 38.023
    risk element, 38.024, 38.025
    single stage success fees, 38.024, 38.026
    solicitor's assessment, 38.024
  barrister's fees, 2.016
  base fee, 2.016
  disputed points, 38.026
  experts' fees, 2.016
  fee deferment element, 2.016, 38.023, 38.027
  fixed success fees, 38.013
  interest payments, 29.023
  interim order for costs, 2.016
  interim payments, 2.016
  "no win, no fee", 2.015
  risk element, 2.016, 38.023–38.025
  Solicitors' Code of Conduct, 2.016
  two-stage success fees, 38.026
  unenforceable, 38.023
Succession
  former partners, 24.010
  inheritance claims, 24.010
Summary judgments
  applications
    claimant, 19.010
    defendant, 19.011
    evidence, 19.013
    procedure, 19.012
  Civil Procedure Rules (Pt 24)
    effect, 19.001
    exceptions, 19.002
    no real prospects of success, 19.004, 19.006
    scope, 19.001
    summary trial, 19.005
  claims
    discrete issues, 19.001
    interim payments, 25.008
    part of claim, 19.001
    small claims track, 20.013
    whole claim, 19.001
  compelling reason for trial, 19.007
  evidence
    evidence in reply, 19.013
    evidence in response, 19.013
  fixed costs, 38.010
  generally, 19.001
  judgments and orders
    consequential orders, 19.015
    summary judgment, 19.014
  jury trial, 19.003
  "no prospects of success" test
    burden of proof, 19.006
    Civil Procedure Rules (CPR), 19.004, 19.006
  set-off, 19.008, 19.009
  summary trial, 19.005

Technology and Construction Court (TCC)
  allocation, 24.011
  case management
    conferences, 24.011
    directions, 24.011
  particulars of claim, 24.011
  procedure, 24.011
  types of cases, 24.011
Termination
  see also **Discontinuance**
  approval of court, 34.004
  consent of parties
    arbitration, 34.001, 34.002
    mediation, 34.001, 34.002
    negotiations, 34.001
  consent judgments, 34.005
  consent orders, 34.005
  settlement outside proceedings
    see **Settlement outside proceedings**
  undertakings, 34.003

Tomlin orders
  agreed terms, 34.006
  confidentiality, 34.006
  use, 34.006–34.008
Transfer of proceedings
  applications
    application of parties, 9.023
    County courts, 9.025
    High Court, 9.025
  automatic transfer, 9,023, 9.024
  court initiative, 9.023
  place of trial, 9.023
  transfer criteria, 9.025
Trial bundles
  see **Bundles**
Trials
  see also **Hearings**
  attendance
    multi-track, 37.001
    solicitors, 37.001
  cross-examination, 37.004, 37.012
  examination in chief, 37.004, 37.011
  failure to attend, 43.002
  fast track
    pre-trial checklist, 21.012
    procedure, 37.003, 37.004
    split trials, 21.008
    trial date, 21.008, 21.011
  judges
    directions, 37.004
    interrogation of witnesses, 37.015
    interventions, 37.015
    judgments, 37.016
    role, 37.015
  multi-track
    judge sitting alone, 22.018
    jury trial, 22.018
    pre-trial checklist, 22.015
    pre-trial review, 22.016
    procedure, 37.003, 37.004
  no case to answer, 37.005
  opening proceedings, 37.004
  Part 8 claims, 37.003
  preparation for trial
    directions on listing, 36.002
    organising witnesses, 36.003
    pre-trial checklist, 36.001
    pre-trial review, 36.002
  proofs of evidence, 37.001
  re-examination, 37.004, 37.014

small claims
  date of hearing, 20.009
  procedure, 20.009, 37.003
  rights of audience, 20.009
split trials, 21.008, 30.016, 33.006
submissions
  opening submissions, 37.004
  oral submissions, 37.004
trial brief
  acceptance, 36.011
  brief fees, 36.011
  contents, 36.010
  delivery to counsel, 36.011
  documents, 36.010
  drafting, 36.010
  importance, 36.010
  witness statements, 36.010
witnesses
  see **Witnesses**
Trusts
  claims procedure, 24.016

Variation orders
  failure to attend trial, 43.002
  interim applications, 43.002
  judicial powers, 43.005, 43.006
Vexatious litigants
  human rights, 7.011
  meaning, 7.011
  restraint orders, 7.011
  parties, 7.011
  penal notices, 7.011
Wasted costs orders
  applicants, 39.002
  hearings, 39.002
  judicial powers, 39.002
  meaning, 39.002
  procedure, 39.002
  vexatious conduct, 39.002

Winding-up
  creditors' petition, 42.017
  enforcement, 40.015
  grounds, 42.017
  specialist topics, 42.023
  winding up orders
    advertisements, 42.020
    effect, 42.021
    generally, 42.002
    subsequent procedures, 42.021

winding up petition
   adjournments, 42.019
   certificate of compliance, 42.019
   form of petition, 42.018
   hearings, 42.018, 42.020
   judicial discretion, 42.019
   jurisdiction, 42.018
   limitation period, 42.018
   presentation, 42.018
   service, 42.018

Witnesses
   administration of oath, 37.002
   advice, to, 37.002
   attendance, 31.004, 31.008, 31.017, 31.018, 37.002
   availability, 36.003, 36.004
   credibility, 31.016, 31.017
   cross-examination, 31.010, 31.015, 37.004, 37.012
   defence witnesses, 37.004
   discussions, 37.001
   evidence in chief, 31.010
   examination, 37.002
   forms of address, 37.002
   hearsay evidence, 31.014
   order of witnesses, 37.006
   payments, 38.002, 38.006
   previous statements, 31.019
   recusal, 36.012
   right to call, 31.010
   silence, 31.004
   video conferences, 31.018
   witness interviews, 6.012, 14.007
   witness summons, 31.008

Witness statements
   checking, 14.009
   content
      details of exhibits, 14.003
      details of identity, 14.003
      ending, 14.003
      statement of truth, 14.003
      title to action, 14.003
      witness details, 14.003
   disclosure and inspection, 30.017
   drafting, 14.005, 14.006
   evidence
      inadmissible, 31.009
      irrelevant, 31.009
   exchange, 12.002, 14.006, 14.011, 14.012, 21.006, 31.005, 31.007
   fast track, 21.006, 31.005
   final versions, 14.012, 14.013
   first-hand evidence, 14.007
   format, 12.005
   hearsay evidence, 31.014
   identification of issues, 14.007
   individual statements, 14.008
   interim payments, 25.009
   late service, 31.009
   multi-track, 22.010, 31.005
   objections, 31.009
   Part 8 claims, 10.002
   personal injury claims, 14.007
   possession claims, 24.005
   review of evidence, 14.011
   small claims track, 31.005
   solicitor's duties, 14.004
   supplemental statements, 31.006
   use, 14.002, 31.010
   witness interviews, 6.012, 14.007

Witness summons
   filing, 36.003
   issue, 36.003
   non-parties, 36.003
   separate summons, 36.003
   service, 36.003
   setting aside, 36.003